MATHEMATICS FOR THE NATURAL SCIENCES 1

MATHEMATICS FOR THE NATURAL SCIENCES 1

Selected chapters from:

Modern Engineering Mathematics
Fifth Edition
Glyn James and
David Burley, Dick Clements, Phil Dyke, John Searl, Jerry Wright

and supplementary chapters
written by Derek Arthur

Pearson

Harlow, England • London • New York • Boston • San Francisco • Toronto • Sydney • Dubai • Singapore • Hong Kong
Tokyo • Seoul • Taipei • New Dehli • Cape Town • São Paulo • Mexico City • Madrid • Amsterdam • Munich • Paris • Milan

Pearson
KAO Two
KAO Park
Harlow
Essex CM17 9NA

And associated companies throughout the world

Visit us on the World Wide Web at:
www.pearson.com/uk

Seelcted chapters from:

Modern Engineering Mathematics Fifth Edition
Glyn James, David Burley, Dick Clements, Phil Dyke, John Searl and Jerry Wright
ISBN 978-1-292-08073-4

ISBN 978-1-78726-772-5 (print)
ISBN: 978-1-78726-791-6 (eBook)

Impression: 3
Year: 2019

Printed and bound in Great Britain by Ashford Colour Press, Gosport, Hampshire.

CONTENTS

Discrete Distributions 870

Continuous Distributions 891

Statistics 906

1 Number, Algebra and Geometry

Chapter 1 Contents

1.1 Introduction

Mathematics plays an important role in our lives. It is used in everyday activities from buying food to organizing maintenance schedules for aircraft. Through applications developed in various cultural and historical contexts, mathematics has been one of the decisive factors in shaping the modern world. It continues to grow and to find new uses, particularly in engineering and technology.

Mathematics provides a powerful, concise and unambiguous way of organizing and communicating information. It is a means by which aspects of the physical universe can be explained and predicted. It is a problem-solving activity supported by a body of knowledge. Mathematics consists of facts, concepts, skills and thinking processes – aspects that are closely interrelated. It is a hierarchical subject in that new ideas and skills are developed from existing ones. This sometimes makes it a difficult subject for learners who, at every stage of their mathematical development, need to have ready recall of material learned earlier.

In the first two chapters we shall summarize the concepts and techniques that most students will already understand and we shall extend them into further developments in mathematics. There are four key areas of which students will already have considerable knowledge.

- numbers
- algebra
- geometry
- functions

These areas are vital to making progress in engineering mathematics (indeed, they will solve many important problems in engineering). Here we will aim to consolidate that knowledge, to make it more precise and to develop it. In this first chapter we will deal with the first three topics; functions are considered in Chapter 2.

1.2 Number and arithmetic

1.2.1 Number line

Mathematics has grown from primitive arithmetic and geometry into a vast body of knowledge. The most ancient mathematical skill is counting, using, in the first instance, the natural numbers and later the integers. The term **natural numbers** commonly refers to the set $\mathbb{N} = \{1, 2, 3, \dots\}$, and the term **integers** to the set $\mathbb{Z} = \{0, 1, -1, 2, -2, 3, -3, \dots\}$. The integers can be represented as equally spaced points on a line called the **number line** as shown in Figure 1.1. In a computer the integers can be stored exactly. The set of all points (not just those representing integers) on the number line represents the **real numbers** (so named to distinguish them from the complex numbers, which are

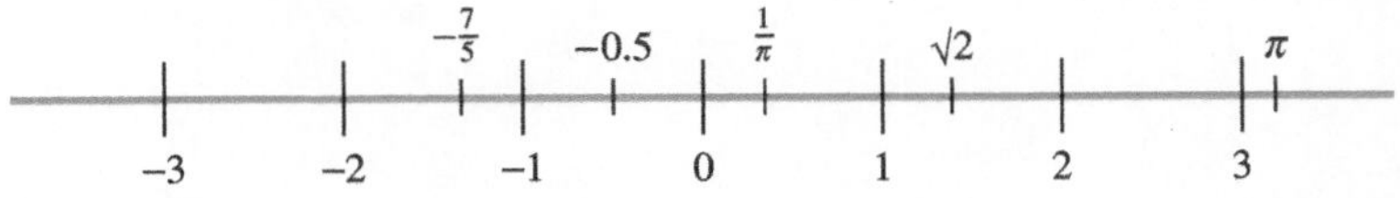

Figure 1.1
The number line.

discussed in Chapter 3). The set of real numbers is denoted by $\mathbb{R}$. The general real number is usually denoted by the letter x and we write 'x in $\mathbb{R}$', meaning x is a real number. A real number that can be written as the ratio of two integers, like $\frac{3}{2}$ or $-\frac{7}{5}$, is called a **rational number**. Other numbers, like $\sqrt{2}$ and π, that cannot be expressed in that way are called **irrational numbers**. In a computer the real numbers can be stored only to a limited number of figures. This is a basic difference between the ways in which computers treat integers and real numbers, and is the reason why the computer languages commonly used by engineers distinguish between integer values and variables on the one hand and real number values and variables on the other.

1.2.2 Representation of numbers

For everyday purposes we use a system of representation based on ten **numerals**: 0, 1, 2, 3, 4, 5, 6, 7, 8, 9. These ten symbols are sufficient to represent all numbers if a **position notation** is adopted. For whole numbers this means that, starting from the right-hand end of the number, the least significant end, the figures represent the number of units, tens, hundreds, thousands, and so on. Thus one thousand, three hundred and sixty-five is represented by 1365, and two hundred and nine is represented by 209. Notice the role of the 0 in the latter example, acting as a position keeper. The use of a decimal point makes it possible to represent fractions as well as whole numbers. This system uses ten symbols. The number system is said to be 'to base ten' and is called the **decimal** system. Other bases are possible: for example, the Babylonians used a number system to base sixty, a fact that still influences our measurement of time. In some societies a number system evolved with more than one base, a survival of which can be seen in imperial measures (inches, feet, yards, …). For some applications it is more convenient to use a base other than ten. Early electronic computers used **binary** numbers (to base two); modern computers use **hexadecimal** numbers (to base sixteen). For elementary (pen-and-paper) arithmetic a representation to base twelve would be more convenient than the usual decimal notation because twelve has more integer divisors (2, 3, 4, 6) than ten (2, 5).

In a decimal number the positions to the left of the decimal point represent units (10^0), tens (10^1), hundreds (10^2) and so on, while those to the right of the decimal point represent tenths (10^{-1}), hundredths (10^{-2}) and so on. Thus, for example

$$\begin{array}{ccccccc} 2 & 1 & 4 & \cdot & 3 & 6 \\ \downarrow & \downarrow & \downarrow & & \downarrow & \downarrow \\ 10^2 & 10^1 & 10^0 & & 10^{-1} & 10^{-2} \end{array}$$

so

$$\begin{aligned} 214.36 &= 2(10^2) + 1(10^1) + 4(10^0) + 3(\tfrac{1}{10}) + 6(\tfrac{1}{100}) \\ &= 200 + 10 + 4 + \tfrac{3}{10} + \tfrac{6}{100} \\ &= \tfrac{21436}{100} = \tfrac{5359}{25} \end{aligned}$$

In other number bases the pattern is the same: in base b the position values are b^0, b^1, b^2, … and b^{-1}, b^{-2}, … . Thus in binary (base two) the position values are units, twos, fours, eights, sixteens and so on, and halves, quarters, eighths and so on. In hexadecimal (base sixteen) the position values are units, sixteens, two hundred and fifty-sixes and so on, and sixteenths, two hundred and fifty-sixths and so on.

Example 1.1 Write (a) the binary number 1011101_2 as a decimal number and (b) the decimal number 115_{10} as a binary number.

Solution (a)
$$\begin{aligned} 1011101_2 &= 1(2^6) + 0(2^5) + 1(2^4) + 1(2^3) + 1(2^2) + 0(2^1) + 1(2^0) \\ &= 64_{10} + 0 + 16_{10} + 8_{10} + 4_{10} + 0 + 1_{10} \\ &= 93_{10} \end{aligned}$$

(b) We achieve the conversion to binary by repeated division by 2. Thus

$$\begin{array}{lll} 115 \div 2 = 57 & \text{remainder } 1 & (2^0) \\ 57 \div 2 = 28 & \text{remainder } 1 & (2^1) \\ 28 \div 2 = 14 & \text{remainder } 0 & (2^2) \\ 14 \div 2 = 7 & \text{remainder } 0 & (2^3) \\ 7 \div 2 = 3 & \text{remainder } 1 & (2^4) \\ 3 \div 2 = 1 & \text{remainder } 1 & (2^5) \\ 1 \div 2 = 0 & \text{remainder } 1 & (2^6) \end{array}$$

so that

$$115_{10} = 1110011_2$$

Example 1.2 Represent the numbers (a) two hundred and one, (b) two hundred and seventy-five, (c) five and three-quarters and (d) one-third in

(i) decimal form using the figures 0, 1, 2, 3, 4, 5, 6, 7, 8, 9;

(ii) binary form using the figures 0, 1;

(iii) duodecimal (base 12) form using the figures 0, 1, 2, 3, 4, 5, 6, 7, 8, 9, Δ, ε.

Solution (a) two hundred and one

(i) = 2 (hundreds) + 0 (tens) and 1 (units) = 201_{10}

(ii) = 1 (one hundred and twenty-eight) + 1 (sixty-four) + 1 (eight) + 1 (unit) = 11001001_2

(iii) = 1 (gross) + 4 (dozens) + 9 (units) = 149_{12}

Here the subscripts 10, 2, 12 indicate the number base.

(b) two hundred and seventy-five

(i) = 2 (hundreds) + 7 (tens) + 5 (units) = 275_{10}

(ii) = 1 (two hundred and fifty-six) + 1 (sixteen) + 1 (two) + 1 (unit) = 100010011_2

(iii) $= 1$ (gross) $+ 10$ (dozens) $+$ eleven (units) $= 1\Delta\varepsilon_{12}$
(Δ represents ten and ε represents eleven)

(c) five and three-quarters

(i) $= 5$ (units) $+ 7$ (tenths) $+ 5$ (hundredths) $= 5.75_{10}$

(ii) $= 1$ (four) $+ 1$ (unit) $+ 1$ (half) $+ 1$ (quarter) $= 101.11_2$

(iii) $= 5$ (units) $+ 9$ (twelfths) $= 5.9_{12}$

(d) one-third

(i) $= 3$ (tenths) $+ 3$ (hundredths) $+ 3$ (thousandths) $+ \ldots = 0.333\ldots_{10}$

(ii) $= 1$ (quarter) $+ 1$ (sixteenth) $+ 1$ (sixty-fourth) $+ \ldots = 0.010101\ldots_2$

(iii) $= 4$ (twelfths) $= 0.4_{12}$

1.2.3 Rules of arithmetic

The basic arithmetical operations of addition, subtraction, multiplication and division are performed subject to the **Fundamental Rules of Arithmetic**. For any three numbers a, b and c:

(a1) the commutative law of addition

$$a + b = b + a$$

(a2) the commutative law of multiplication

$$a \times b = b \times a$$

(b1) the associative law of addition

$$(a + b) + c = a + (b + c)$$

(b2) the associative law of multiplication

$$(a \times b) \times c = a \times (b \times c)$$

(c1) the distributive law of multiplication over addition and subtraction

$$(a + b) \times c = (a \times c) + (b \times c)$$

$$(a - b) \times c = (a \times c) - (b \times c)$$

(c2) the distributive law of division over addition and subtraction

$$(a + b) \div c = (a \div c) + (b \div c)$$

$$(a - b) \div c = (a \div c) - (b \div c)$$

Here the brackets indicate which operation is performed first. These operations are called **binary** operations because they associate with every two members of the set of real numbers a unique third member; for example,

$$2 + 5 = 7 \quad \text{and} \quad 3 \times 6 = 18$$

Example 1.3 Find the value of $(100 + 20 + 3) \times 456$.

Solution Using the distributive law we have

$$(100 + 20 + 3) \times 456 = 100 \times 456 + 20 \times 456 + 3 \times 456$$
$$= 45\,600 + 9120 + 1368 = 56\,088$$

Here 100×456 has been evaluated as

$$100 \times 400 + 100 \times 50 + 100 \times 6$$

and similarly 20×456 and 3×456.
This, of course, is normally set out in the traditional school arithmetic way:

$$\begin{array}{r} 456 \\ \underline{123\times} \\ 1\,368 \\ 9\,120 \\ \underline{45\,600} \\ \underline{56\,088} \end{array}$$

Example 1.4 Rewrite $(a + b) \times (c + d)$ as the sum of products.

Solution Using the distributive law we have

$$(a + b) \times (c + d) = a \times (c + d) + b \times (c + d)$$
$$= (c + d) \times a + (c + d) \times b$$
$$= c \times a + d \times a + c \times b + d \times b$$
$$= a \times c + a \times d + b \times c + b \times d$$

applying the commutative laws several times.

A further operation used with real numbers is that of **powering**. For example, $a \times a$ is written as a^2, and $a \times a \times a$ is written as a^3. In general the product of n a's where n is a positive integer is written as a^n. (Here the n is called the **index** or **exponent**.) Operations with powering also obey simple rules:

$$a^n \times a^m = a^{n+m} \qquad \textbf{(1.1a)}$$

$$a^n \div a^m = a^{n-m} \qquad \textbf{(1.1b)}$$

$$(a^n)^m = a^{nm} \qquad \textbf{(1.1c)}$$

From rule (1.1b) it follows, by setting $n = m$ and $a \neq 0$, that $a^0 = 1$. It is also convention to take $0^0 = 1$. The process of powering can be extended to include the fractional powers like $a^{1/2}$. Using rule (1.1c),

$$(a^{1/n})^n = a^{n/n} = a^1$$

and we see that

$$a^{1/n} = {}^n\sqrt{a}$$

the nth root of a. Also, we can define a^{-m} using rule (1.1b) with $n = 0$, giving

$$1 \div a^m = a^{-m}, \qquad a \neq 0$$

Thus a^{-m} is the reciprocal of a^m. In contrast with the binary operations +, ×, − and ÷, which operate on two numbers, the powering operation $(\ )^r$ operates on just one element and is consequently called a **unary** operation. Notice that the fractional power

$$a^{m/n} = ({}^n\sqrt{a})^m = {}^n\sqrt{(a^m)}$$

is the nth root of a^m. If n is an even integer, then $a^{m/n}$ is not defined when a is negative. When ${}^n\sqrt{a}$ is an irrational number then such a root is called a **surd**.

Numbers like $\sqrt{2}$ were described by the Greeks as **a-logos**, without a ratio number. An Arabic translator took the alternative meaning 'without a word' and used the arabic word for 'deaf', which subsequently became **surdus**, Latin for deaf, when translated from Arabic to Latin in the mid-twelfth century.

Example 1.5 Find the values of

(a) $27^{1/3}$ (b) $(-8)^{2/3}$ (c) $16^{-3/2}$

(d) $(-2)^{-2}$ (e) $(-1/8)^{-2/3}$ (f) $(9)^{-1/2}$

Solution

(a) $27^{1/3} = {}^3\sqrt{27} = 3$

(b) $(-8)^{2/3} = ({}^3\sqrt{(-8)})^2 = (-2)^2 = 4$

(c) $16^{-3/2} = (16^{1/2})^{-3} = (4)^{-3} = \frac{1}{4^3} = \frac{1}{64}$

(d) $(-2)^{-2} = \dfrac{1}{(-2)^2} = \frac{1}{4}$

(e) $(-1/8)^{-2/3} = [{}^3\sqrt{(-1/8)}]^{-2} = [{}^3\sqrt{(-1)}/{}^3\sqrt{(8)}]^{-2} = [-1/2]^{-2} = 4$

(f) $(9)^{-1/2} = (3)^{-1} = \frac{1}{3}$

Example 1.6 Express (a) in terms of $\sqrt{2}$ and simplify (b) to (f).

(a) $\sqrt{18} + \sqrt{32} - \sqrt{50}$ (b) $6/\sqrt{2}$ (c) $(1 - \sqrt{3})(1 + \sqrt{3})$

(d) $\dfrac{2}{1 - \sqrt{3}}$ (e) $(1 + \sqrt{6})(1 - \sqrt{6})$ (f) $\dfrac{1 - \sqrt{2}}{1 + \sqrt{6}}$

Solution (a) $\sqrt{18} = \sqrt{(2 \times 9)} = \sqrt{2} \times \sqrt{9} = 3\sqrt{2}$

$\sqrt{32} = \sqrt{(2 \times 16)} = \sqrt{2} \times \sqrt{16} = 4\sqrt{2}$

$\sqrt{50} = \sqrt{(2 \times 25)} = \sqrt{2} \times \sqrt{25} = 5\sqrt{2}$

Thus $\sqrt{18} + \sqrt{32} - \sqrt{50} = 2\sqrt{2}$.

(b) $6/\sqrt{2} = 3 \times 2/\sqrt{2}$

Since $2 = \sqrt{2} \times \sqrt{2}$, we have $6/\sqrt{2} = 3\sqrt{2}$.

(c) $(1 - \sqrt{3})(1 + \sqrt{3}) = 1 + \sqrt{3} - \sqrt{3} - 3 = -2$

(d) Using the result of part (c) $\dfrac{2}{1 - \sqrt{3}}$ can be simplified by multiplying 'top and bottom' by $1 + \sqrt{3}$ (notice the sign change in front of the $\sqrt{}$). Thus

$$\frac{2}{1 - \sqrt{3}} = \frac{2(1 + \sqrt{3})}{(1 - \sqrt{3})(1 + \sqrt{3})}$$

$$= \frac{2(1 + \sqrt{3})}{1 - 3}$$

$$= -1 - \sqrt{3}$$

(e) $(1 + \sqrt{6})(1 - \sqrt{6}) = 1 - \sqrt{6} + \sqrt{6} - 6 = -5$

(f) Using the same technique as in part (d) we have

$$\frac{1 - \sqrt{2}}{1 + \sqrt{6}} = \frac{(1 - \sqrt{2})(1 - \sqrt{6})}{(1 + \sqrt{6})(1 - \sqrt{6})}$$

$$= \frac{1 - \sqrt{2} - \sqrt{6} + \sqrt{12}}{1 - 6}$$

$$= -(1 - \sqrt{2} - \sqrt{6} + 2\sqrt{3})/5$$

This process of expressing the irrational number so that all of the surds are in the numerator is called **rationalization**.

When evaluating arithmetical expressions the following rules of precedence are observed:

- the powering operation $(\ )^r$ is performed first
- then multiplication $\times$ and/or division $\div$
- then addition $+$ and/or subtraction $-$

When two operators of equal precedence are adjacent in an expression the left-hand operation is performed first. For example

$$12 - 4 + 13 = 8 + 13 = 21$$

and

$$15 \div 3 \times 2 = 5 \times 2 = 10$$

The precedence rules are overridden by brackets; thus

$$12 - (4 + 13) = 12 - 17 = -5$$

and

$$15 \div (3 \times 2) = 15 \div 6 = 2.5$$

Example 1.7 Evaluate $7 - 5 \times 3 \div 2^2$.

Solution Following the rules of precedence, we have

$$7 - 5 \times 3 \div 2^2 = 7 - 5 \times 3 \div 4 = 7 - 15 \div 4 = 7 - 3.75 = 3.25$$

1.2.4 Exercises

1 Find the decimal equivalent of 110110.101_2.

2 Find the binary and octal (base eight) equivalents of the decimal number 16 321. Obtain a simple rule that relates these two representations of the number, and hence write down the octal equivalent of 1011100101101_2.

3 Find the binary and octal equivalents of the decimal number 30.6. Does the rule obtained in Question 2 still apply?

4 Use binary arithmetic to evaluate

(a) $100011.011_2 + 1011.001_2$

(b) $111.10011_2 \times 10.111_2$

5 Simplify the following expressions, giving the answers with positive indices and without brackets:

(a) $2^3 \times 2^{-4}$ (b) $2^3 \div 2^{-4}$ (c) $(2^3)^{-4}$

(d) $3^{1/3} \times 3^{5/3}$ (e) $(36)^{-1/2}$ (f) $16^{3/4}$

6 The expression $7 - 2 \times 3^2 + 8$ may be evaluated using the usual implicit rules of precedence. It could be rewritten as $((7 - (2 \times (3^2))) + 8)$ using brackets to make the precedence explicit. Similarly rewrite the following expressions in fully bracketed form:

(a) $21 + 4 \times 3 \div 2$

(b) $17 - 6^{2+3}$

(c) $4 \times 2^3 - 7 \div 6 \times 2$

(d) $2 \times 3 - 6 \div 4 + 3^{2-5}$

7 Express the following in the form $x + y\sqrt{2}$ with x and y rational numbers:

(a) $(7 + 5\sqrt{2})^3$ (b) $(2 + \sqrt{2})^4$

(c) $\sqrt[3]{(7 + 5\sqrt{2})}$ (d) $\sqrt{(\frac{11}{2} - 3\sqrt{2})}$

8 Show that

$$\frac{1}{a + b\sqrt{c}} = \frac{a - b\sqrt{c}}{a^2 - b^2c}$$

Hence express the following numbers in the form $x + y\sqrt{n}$ where x and y are rational numbers and n is an integer:

(a) $\dfrac{1}{7 + 5\sqrt{2}}$ (b) $\dfrac{2 + 3\sqrt{2}}{9 - 7\sqrt{2}}$

(c) $\dfrac{4 - 2\sqrt{3}}{7 - 3\sqrt{3}}$ (d) $\dfrac{2 + 4\sqrt{5}}{4 - \sqrt{5}}$

9 Find the difference between 2 and the squares of

$$\frac{1}{1}, \frac{3}{2}, \frac{7}{5}, \frac{17}{12}, \frac{41}{29}, \frac{99}{70}$$

(a) Verify that successive terms of the sequence stand in relation to each other as m/n does to $(m + 2n)/(m + n)$.

(b) Verify that if m/n is a good approximation to $\sqrt{2}$ then $(m + 2n)/(m + n)$ is a better one, and that the errors in the two cases are in opposite directions.

(c) Find the next three terms of the above sequence.

1.2.5 Inequalities

The number line (Figure 1.1) makes explicit a further property of the real numbers – that of **ordering**. This enables us to make statements like 'seven is greater than two' and 'five is less than six'. We represent this using the comparison symbols

$>$, 'greater than'
$<$, 'less than'

It also makes obvious two other comparators:

$=$, 'equals'
$\neq$, 'does not equal'

These comparators obey simple rules when used in conjunction with the arithmetical operations. For any four numbers a, b, c and d:

$$(a < b \text{ and } c < d) \quad \text{implies} \quad a + c < b + d \tag{1.2a}$$

$$(a < b \text{ and } c > d) \quad \text{implies} \quad a - c < b - d \tag{1.2b}$$

$$(a < b \text{ and } b < c) \quad \text{implies} \quad a < c \tag{1.2c}$$

$$a < b \quad \text{implies} \quad a + c < b + c \tag{1.2d}$$

$$(a < b \text{ and } c > 0) \quad \text{implies} \quad ac < bc \tag{1.2e}$$

$$(a < b \text{ and } c < 0) \quad \text{implies} \quad ac > bc \tag{1.2f}$$

$$(a < b \text{ and } ab > 0) \quad \text{implies} \quad \frac{1}{a} > \frac{1}{b} \tag{1.2g}$$

Example 1.8 Show, without using a calculator, that $\sqrt{2} + \sqrt{3} > 2(\sqrt[4]{6})$.

Solution By squaring we have that

$$(\sqrt{2} + \sqrt{3})^2 = 2 + 2\sqrt{2}\sqrt{3} + 3 = 5 + 2\sqrt{6}$$

Also

$$(2\sqrt{6})^2 = 24 < 25 = 5^2$$

implying that $5 > 2\sqrt{6}$. Thus

$$(\sqrt{2} + \sqrt{3})^2 > 2\sqrt{6} + 2\sqrt{6} = 4\sqrt{6}$$

and, since $\sqrt{2} + \sqrt{3}$ is a positive number, it follows that

$$\sqrt{2} + \sqrt{3} > \sqrt{(4\sqrt{6})} = 2(\sqrt[4]{6})$$

1.2.6 Modulus and intervals

The size of a real number x is called its modulus and is denoted by $|x|$ (or sometimes by mod (x)). Thus

$$|x| = \begin{cases} x & (x \geqslant 0) \\ -x & (x < 0) \end{cases} \tag{1.3}$$

where the comparator $\geqslant$ indicates 'greater than or equal to'. (Likewise $\leqslant$ indicates 'less than or equal to'.)

Geometrically $|x|$ is the distance of the point representing x on the number line from the point representing zero. Similarly $|x - a|$ is the distance of the point representing x on the number line from that representing a.

The set of numbers between two numbers, a and b say, defines an **open interval** on the real line. This is the set $\{x:a < x < b, x \text{ in } \mathbb{R}\}$ and is usually denoted by (a, b). Here $\{x:P\}$ denotes the set of all x that have property P.) Here the double-sided inequality means that x is greater than a and less than b; that is, the inequalities $a < x$ and $x < b$ apply simultaneously. An interval that includes the end points is called a **closed interval,** denoted by $[a, b]$, with

$$[a, b] = \{x:a \leqslant x \leqslant b, x \text{ in } \mathbb{R}\}$$

Note that the distance between two numbers a and b might either be $a - b$ or $b - a$ depending on which was the larger. An immediate consequence of this is that

$$|a - b| = |b - a|$$

since a is the same distance from b as b is from a.

Example 1.9 Find the values of x so that

$$|x - 4.3| = 5.8$$

Solution $|x - 4.3| = 5.8$ means that the distance between the real numbers x and 4.3 is 5.8 units, but does not tell us whether $x > 4.3$ or whether $x < 4.3$. The situation is illustrated in Figure 1.2, from which it is clear that the two possible values of x are -1.5 and 10.1.

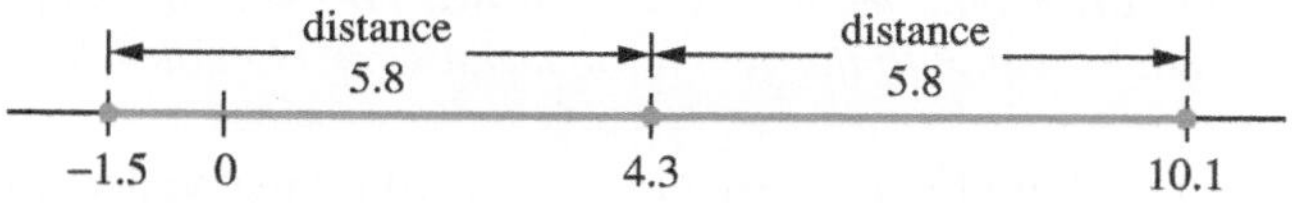

Figure 1.2 Illustration of $|x - 4.3| = 5.8$.

Example 1.10 Express the sets (a) $\{x:|x - 3| < 5, x \text{ in } \mathbb{R}\}$ and (b) $\{x:|x + 2| \leqslant 3, x \text{ in } \mathbb{R}\}$ as intervals.

Solution (a) $|x - 3| < 5$ means that the distance of the point representing x on the number line from the point representing 3 is less than 5 units, as shown in Figure 1.3(a). This implies that

$$-5 < x - 3 < 5$$

Adding 3 to each member of this inequality, using rule (1.2d), gives

$$-2 < x < 8$$

and the set of numbers satisfying this inequality is the open interval $(-2, 8)$.

(b) Similarly $|x + 2| \leqslant 3$, which may be rewritten as $|x - (-2)| \leqslant 3$, means that the distance of the point x on the number line from the point representing -2 is less than or equal to 3 units, as shown in Figure 1.3(b). This implies

$$-3 \leqslant x + 2 \leqslant 3$$

Subtracting 2 from each member of this inequality, using rule (1.2d), gives

$$-5 \leqslant x \leqslant 1$$

and the set of numbers satisfying this inequality is the closed interval [–5, 1].

It is easy (and sensible) to check these answers using spot values. For example, putting $x = -4$ in (b) gives $|-4 + 2| < 3$ correctly. Sometimes the sets $|x + 2| \leqslant 3$ and $|x + 2| < 3$ are described verbally as 'lies in the interval x equals -2 ± 3'.

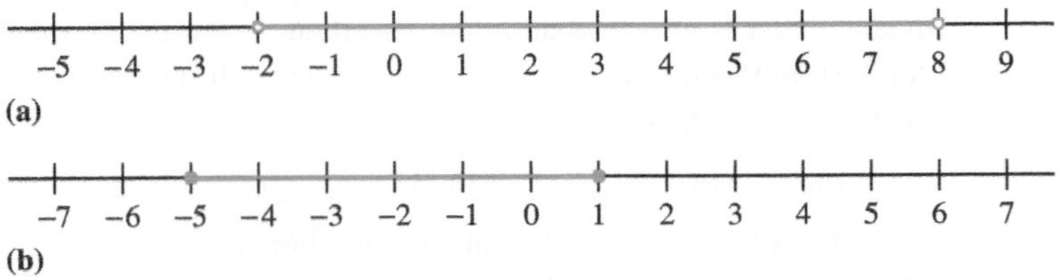

Figure 1.3
(a) The open interval (–2, 8). (b) The closed interval [–5, 1].

We note in passing the following results. For any two real numbers x and y:

$$|xy| = |x|\,|y| \qquad \textbf{(1.4a)}$$

$$|x| < a,\ a > 0, \quad \text{implies} \quad -a < x < a \qquad \textbf{(1.4b)}$$

$$|x + y| \leqslant |x| + |y|, \quad \text{known as the 'triangle inequality'} \qquad \textbf{(1.4c)}$$

$$\tfrac{1}{2}(x + y) \geqslant \sqrt{(xy)}, \quad \text{when } x \geqslant 0 \text{ and } y \geqslant 0 \qquad \textbf{(1.4d)}$$

Result (1.4d) is proved in Example 1.11 below and may be stated in words as

the arithmetic mean $\frac{1}{2}(x + y)$ of two positive numbers x and y is greater than or equal to the geometric mean $\sqrt{(xy)}$. Equality holds only when $y = x$.

Results (1.4a) to (1.4c) should be verified by the reader, who may find it helpful to try some particular values first, for example, setting $x = -2$ and $y = 3$ in (1.4c).

Example 1.11

Prove that for any two positive numbers x and y, the arithmetic–geometric inequality

$$\tfrac{1}{2}(x + y) \geqslant \sqrt{(xy)}$$

holds.

Deduce that $x + \dfrac{1}{x} \geqslant 2$ for any positive number x.

Solution The quantity xy can be interpreted as the area of a rectangle with sides x and y. The quantity $(x + y)^2$ can be interpreted as the area of a square of side $(x + y)$. Comparing areas in Figure 1.4, where the broken lines cut the square into 4 equal quarters of size A and it is assumed that $x > y$.

From Figure 1.4, we see that

$$(x + y)^2 = x^2 + y^2 + 2xy \qquad \textbf{(1.5)}$$

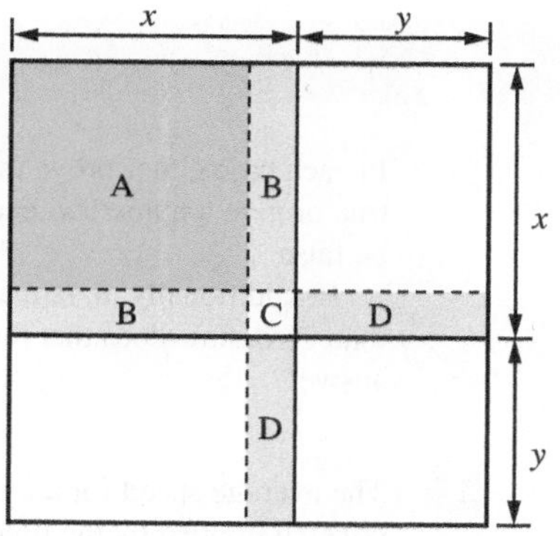

Figure 1.4
Illustration of
$x^2 + y^2 \geqslant 2xy$.

Also, from Figure 1.4, we see that

$$\left.\begin{aligned} x^2 &= A + 2B + C \\ y^2 &= A - 2D - C \end{aligned}\right\} x^2 + y^2 = 2A + 2B - 2D$$

$$xy = A - B + D$$

Since B > D, (B = D + C), it follows that

$$x^2 + y^2 > 2xy$$

In the particular case when $x = y$ then B = D = 0 and

$$x^2 + y^2 = 2xy$$

so in general

$$x^2 + y^2 \geqslant 2xy \qquad \textbf{(1.6)}$$

Combining (1.5) and (1.6) we deduce

$$(x + y)^2 \geqslant 4xy$$

and since x and y are both positive we have

$$x + y \geqslant 2\sqrt{(xy)}$$

which is equivalent to

$$\tfrac{1}{2}(x + y) \geqslant \sqrt{(xy)}$$

In the special case when $y = \dfrac{1}{x}$ we have

$$x + \frac{1}{x} \geqslant 2\sqrt{\left(x\frac{1}{x}\right)}$$

that is,

$$x + \frac{1}{x} \geqslant 2$$

1.2.7 Exercises

10 Show that $(\sqrt{5} + \sqrt{13})^2 > 34$ and determine without using a calculator the larger of $\sqrt{5} + \sqrt{13}$ and $\sqrt{3} + \sqrt{19}$.

11 Show the following sets on number lines and express them as intervals:

(a) $\{x : |x - 4| \leqslant 6\}$ (b) $\{x : |x + 3| < 2\}$

(c) $\{x : |2x - 1| \leqslant 7\}$ (d) $\{x : |\frac{1}{4}x + 3| < 3\}$

12 Show the following intervals on number lines and express them as sets in the form $\{x : |ax + b| < c\}$ or $\{x : |ax + b| \leqslant c\}$:

(a) $(1, 7)$ (b) $[-4, -2]$

(c) $(17, 26)$ (d) $[-\frac{1}{2}, \frac{3}{4}]$

13 Given that $a < b$ and $c < d$, which of the following statements are always true?

(a) $a - c < b - d$ (b) $a - d < b - c$

(c) $ac < bd$ (d) $\dfrac{1}{b} < \dfrac{1}{a}$

In each case either prove that the statement is true or give a numerical example to show it can be false.

If, additionally, a, b, c and d are all greater than zero, how does that modify your answer?

14 The average speed for a journey is the distance covered divided by the time taken.

(a) A journey is completed by travelling for the first half of the *time* at speed v_1 and the second half at speed v_2. Find the average speed v_a for the journey in terms of v_1 and v_2.

(b) A journey is completed by travelling at speed v_1 for half the *distance* and at speed v_2 for the second half. Find the average speed v_b for the journey in terms of v_1 and v_2.

Deduce that a journey completed by travelling at two different speeds for equal distances will take longer than the same journey completed at the same two speeds for equal times.

1.3 Algebra

The origins of algebra are to be found in Arabic mathematics as the name suggests, coming from the word *aljabara* meaning 'combination' or 're-uniting'. Algorithms are rules for solving problems in mathematics by standard step-by-step methods. Such methods were first described by the ninth century mathematician Abu Ja'far Mohammed ben Musa from Khwarizm, modern Khiva on the southern border of Uzbekistan. The Arabic al-Khwarizm ('from Khwarizm') was Latinized to algorithm in the late Middle Ages. Often the letter x is used to denote an unassigned (or free) variable. It is thought that this is a corruption of the script letter ꝛ abbreviating the Latin word *res*, thing. The use of unassigned variables enables us to form mathematical models of practical situations as illustrated in the following example. First we deal with a specific case and then with the general case using unassigned variables.

The idea, first introduced in the seventeenth century, of using letters to represent unspecified quantities led to the development of algebraic manipulation based on the elementary laws of arithmetic. This development greatly enhanced the problem-solving power of mathematics – so much so that it is difficult now to imagine doing mathematics without this resource.

Example 1.12 A pipe has the form of a hollow cylinder as shown in Figure 1.5. Find its mass when

(a) its length is 1.5 m, its external diameter is 205 mm, its internal diameter is 160 mm and its density is 5500 kg m^{-3};

(b) its length is l m, its external diameter is D mm, its internal diameter is d mm and its density is ρ kg m^{-3}. Notice here that the unassigned variables l, D, d, ρ are pure numbers and do not include units of measurement.

Solution (a) Standardizing the units of length, the internal and external diameters are 0.16 m and 0.205 m respectively. The area of cross-section of the pipe is

$$0.25\pi(0.205^2 - 0.160^2)\ \text{m}^2$$

(*Reminder*: The area of a circle of diameter D is $\pi D^2/4$.)

Hence the volume of the material of the pipe is

$$0.25\pi(0.205^2 - 0.160^2) \times 1.5\ \text{m}^3$$

and the mass (volume × density) of the pipe is

$$0.25 \times 5500 \times \pi(0.205^2 - 0.160^2) \times 1.5\ \text{kg}$$

Evaluating this last expression by calculator gives the mass of the pipe as 106 kg to the nearest kilogram.

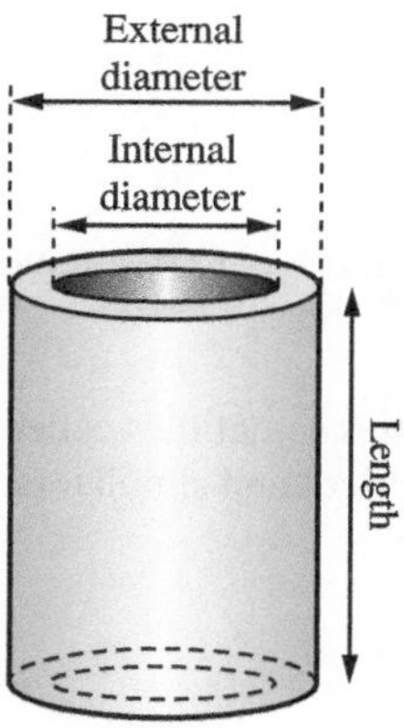

Figure 1.5
Cylindrical pipe of Example 1.12.

(b) The internal and external diameters of the pipe are $d/1000$ and $D/1000$ metres, respectively, so that the area of cross-section is

$$0.25\pi(D^2 - d^2)/1\,000\,000\ \text{m}^2$$

The volume of the pipe is

$$0.25\pi l(D^2 - d^2)/10^6\ \text{m}^3$$

Hence the mass M kg of the pipe of density ρ is given by the formulae

$$M = 0.25\pi\rho l(D^2 - d^2)/10^6 = 2.5\pi\rho l(D + d)(D - d) \times 10^{-5}$$

1.3.1 Algebraic manipulation

Algebraic manipulation made possible concise statements of well-known results, such as

$$(a + b)^2 = a^2 + 2ab + b^2 \qquad \textbf{(1.7a)}$$

Previously these results had been obtained by a combination of verbal reasoning and elementary geometry as illustrated in Figure 1.6.

Figure 1.6
Illustration of $(a + b)^2 = a^2 + 2ab + b^2$.

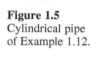

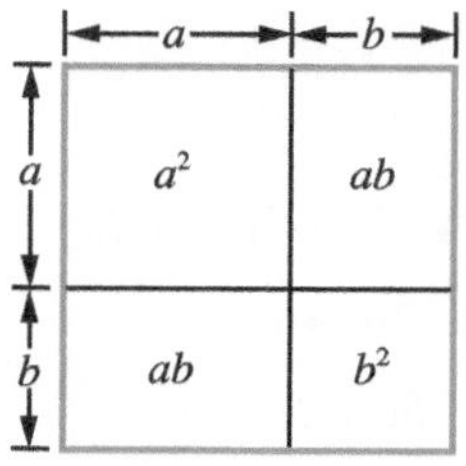

Example 1.13 Prove that

$$ab = \tfrac{1}{4}[(a+b)^2 - (a-b)^2]$$

Given $70^2 = 4900$ and $36^2 = 1296$, calculate 53×17.

Solution Since

$$(a+b)^2 = a^2 + 2ab + b^2$$

we deduce

$$(a-b)^2 = a^2 - 2ab + b^2$$

and

$$(a+b)^2 - (a-b)^2 = 4ab$$

and

$$ab = \tfrac{1}{4}[(a+b)^2 - (a-b)^2]$$

The result is illustrated geometrically in Figure 1.7. Setting $a = 53$ and $b = 17$, we have

$$53 \times 17 = \tfrac{1}{4}[70^2 - 36^2] = 901$$

This method of calculating products was used by the Babylonians and is sometimes called the 'quarter-squares' algorithm. It has been used in some analogue devices and simulators.

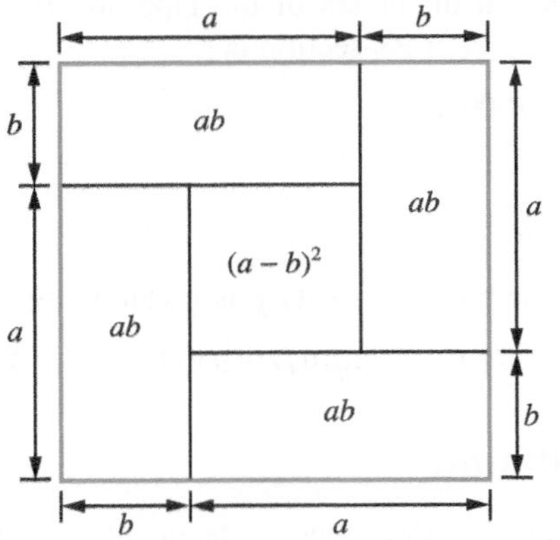

Figure 1.7 Illustration of $ab = \tfrac{1}{4}[(a+b)^2 - (a-b)^2]$.

Example 1.14 Show that

$$(a+b+c)^2 = a^2 + b^2 + c^2 + 2ab + 2bc + 2ca$$

Solution Rewriting $a+b+c$ as $(a+b)+c$ we have

$$\begin{aligned}((a+b)+c)^2 &= (a+b)^2 + 2(a+b)c + c^2 \quad \text{using (1.7a)}\\ &= a^2 + 2ab + b^2 + 2ac + 2bc + c^2\\ &= a^2 + b^2 + c^2 + 2ab + 2bc + 2ac\end{aligned}$$

Example 1.15 Verify that

$$(x+p)^2+q-p^2=x^2+2px+q$$

and deduce that

$$ax^2+bx+c=a\left(x+\frac{b}{2a}\right)^2+c-\frac{b^2}{4a}$$

Solution $(x+p)^2=x^2+2px+p^2$

so that

$$(x+p)^2+q-p^2=x^2+2px+q$$

Working in the reverse direction is more difficult

$$ax^2+bx+c=a\left(x^2+\frac{b}{a}x+\frac{c}{a}\right)$$

Comparing $x^2+\frac{b}{a}x+\frac{c}{a}$ with $x^2+2px+q$, we can identify

$$\frac{b}{a}=2p \quad \text{and} \quad \frac{c}{a}=q$$

Thus we can write

$$ax^2+bx+c=a[(x+p)^2+q-p^2]$$

where $p=\frac{b}{2a}$ and $q=\frac{c}{a}$

giving

$$ax^2+bx+c=a\left(x+\frac{b}{2a}\right)^2+a\left(\frac{c}{a}-\frac{b^2}{4a^2}\right)$$

$$=a\left(x+\frac{b}{2a}\right)^2+c-\frac{b^2}{4a}$$

This algebraic process is called 'completing the square'.

We may summarize the results so far

$$(a+b)^2=a^2+2ab+b^2 \quad \textbf{(1.7a)}$$

$$(a-b)^2=a^2-2ab+b^2 \quad \textbf{(1.7b)}$$

$$a^2-b^2=(a+b)(a-b) \quad \textbf{(1.7c)}$$

$$a^2+bx+c=a\left(x+\frac{b}{2a}\right)^2+c-\frac{b^2}{4a} \quad \textbf{(1.7d)}$$

As shown in the previous examples, the ordinary rules of arithmetic carry over to the generalized arithmetic of algebra. This is illustrated again in the following example.

Example 1.16 Express as a single fraction

(a) $\frac{1}{12} - \frac{2}{3} + \frac{3}{4}$

(b) $\frac{1}{(x+1)(x+2)} - \frac{2}{x+1} + \frac{3}{x+2}$

Solution (a) The lowest common denominator of these fractions is 12, so we may write

$$\frac{1}{12} - \frac{2}{3} + \frac{3}{4} = \frac{1-8+9}{12}$$
$$= \frac{2}{12} = \frac{1}{6}$$

(b) The lowest common multiple of the denominators of these fractions is $(x+1)(x+2)$, so we may write

$$\frac{1}{(x+1)(x+2)} - \frac{2}{x+1} + \frac{3}{x+2}$$
$$= \frac{1}{(x+1)(x+2)} - \frac{2(x+2)}{(x+1)(x+2)} + \frac{3(x+1)}{(x+1)(x+2)}$$
$$= \frac{1-2(x+2)+3(x+1)}{(x+1)(x+2)}$$
$$= \frac{1-2x-4+3x+3}{(x+1)(x+2)}$$
$$= \frac{x}{(x+1)(x+2)}$$

Example 1.17 Use the method of completing the square to manipulate the following quadratic expressions into the form of a number + (or −) the square of a term involving x.

(a) $x^2 + 3x - 7$ (b) $5 - 4x - x^2$

(c) $3x^2 - 5x + 4$ (d) $1 + 2x - 2x^2$

Solution Remember $(a+b)^2 = a^2 + 2ab + b^2$.

(a) To convert $x^2 + 3x$ into a perfect square we need to add $(\frac{3}{2})^2$. Thus we have

$$x^2 + 3x - 7 = [(x + \tfrac{3}{2})^2 - (\tfrac{3}{2})^2] - 7$$
$$= (x + \tfrac{3}{2})^2 - \tfrac{37}{4}$$

(b) $5 - 4x - x^2 = 5 - (4x + x^2)$

To convert $x^2 + 4x$ into a perfect square we need to add 2^2. Thus we have

$$x^2 + 4x = (x+2)^2 - 2^2$$

and

$$5 - 4x - x^2 = 5 - [(x + 2)^2 - 2^2] = 9 - (x + 2)^2$$

(c) First we 'take outside' the coefficient of x^2:

$$3x^2 - 5x + 4 = 3(x^2 - \tfrac{5}{3}x + \tfrac{4}{3})$$

Then we rearrange

$$x^2 - \tfrac{5}{3}x = (x - \tfrac{5}{6})^2 - \tfrac{25}{36}$$

so that $3x^2 - 5x + 4 = 3[(x - \tfrac{5}{6})^2 - \tfrac{25}{36} + \tfrac{4}{3}] = 3[(x - \tfrac{5}{6})^2 + \tfrac{23}{36}]$.

(d) Similarly

$$1 + 2x - 2x^2 = 1 - 2(x^2 - x)$$

and

$$x^2 - x = (x - \tfrac{1}{2})^2 - \tfrac{1}{4}$$

so that

$$1 + 2x - 2x^2 = 1 - 2[(x - \tfrac{1}{2})^2 - \tfrac{1}{4}] = \tfrac{3}{2} - 2(x - \tfrac{1}{2})^2$$

The reader should confirm that these results agree with identity (1.7d)

The number 45 can be factorized as $3 \times 3 \times 5$. Any product from 3, 3 and 5 is also a factor of 45. Algebraic expressions can be factorized in a similar fashion. An algebraic expression with more than one term can be factorized if each term contains common factors (either numerical or algebraic). These factors are removed by division from each term and the non-common factors remaining are grouped into brackets.

Example 1.18 Factorize $xz + 2yz - 2y - x$.

Solution There is no common factor to all four terms so we take them in pairs:

$$\begin{aligned} xz + 2yz - 2y - x &= (x + 2y)z - (2y + x) \\ &= (x + 2y)z - (x + 2y) \\ &= (x + 2y)(z - 1) \end{aligned}$$

Alternatively, we could have written

$$\begin{aligned} xz + 2yz - 2y - x &= (xz - x) + (2yz - 2y) \\ &= x(z - 1) + 2y(z - 1) \\ &= (x + 2y)(z - 1) \end{aligned}$$

to obtain the same result.

In many problems we are able to facilitate the solution by factorizing a quadratic expression $ax^2 + bx + c$ 'by-hand', using knowledge of the factors of the numerical coefficients a, b and c.

Example 1.19 Factorize the expressions

(a) $x^2 + 12x + 35$ (b) $2x^2 + 9x - 5$

Solution (a) Since

$$(x + \alpha)(x + \beta) = x^2 + (\alpha + \beta)x + \alpha\beta$$

we examine the factors of the constant term of the expression:

$$35 = 5 \times 7 = 35 \times 1$$

and notice that $5 + 7 = 12$ while $35 + 1 = 36$. So we can chose $\alpha = 5$ and $\beta = 7$ and write

$$x^2 + 12x + 35 = (x + 5)(x + 7)$$

(b) Since

$$(mx + \alpha)(nx + \beta) = mnx^2 + (n\alpha + m\beta)x + \alpha\beta$$

we examine the factors of the coefficient of x^2 and of the constant to give the coefficient of x. Here

$$2 = 2 \times 1 \text{ and } -5 = (-5) \times 1 = 5 \times (-1)$$

and we see that

$$2 \times 5 + 1 \times (-1) = 9$$

Thus we can write

$$(2x - 1)(x + 5) = 2x^2 + 9x - 5$$

It is sensible to do a 'spot-check' on the factorization by inserting a sample value of x, for example $x = 1$

$$(1)(6) = 2 + 9 - 5$$

Comment Some quadratic expressions, for example $x^2 + y^2$, do not have real factors.

The expansion of $(a + b)^2$ in (1.7a) is a special case of a general result for $(a + b)^n$ known as the binomial expansion. This is discussed again in Sections 1.3.6 and 7.7.2. Here we shall look at the cases for $n = 0, 1, \dots, 6$.

Writing these out, we have

$$(a + b)^0 = 1$$

$$(a + b)^1 = a + b$$

$$(a + b)^2 = a^2 + 2ab + b^2$$

$$(a + b)^3 = a^3 + 3a^2b + 3ab^2 + b^3$$

$$(a + b)^4 = a^4 + 4a^3b + 6a^2b^2 + 4ab^3 + b^4$$

$$(a + b)^5 = a^5 + 5a^4b + 10a^3b^2 + 10a^2b^3 + 5ab^4 + b^5$$

$$(a + b)^6 = a^6 + 6a^5b + 15a^4b^2 + 20a^3b^3 + 15a^2b^4 + 6ab^5 + b^6$$

Figure 1.8
Pascal's triangle.

$$(a+b)^0 = 1$$

$$(a+b)^1 = a+b$$

$$(a+b)^2 = a^2 + 2ab + b^2$$

$$(a+b)^3 = a^3 + 3a^2b + 3ab^2 + b^3$$

$$(a+b)^4 = a^4 + 4a^3b + 6a^2b^2 + 4ab^3 + b^4$$

$$(a+b)^5 = a^5 + 5a^4b + 10a^3b^2 + 10a^2b^3 + 5ab^4 + b^5$$

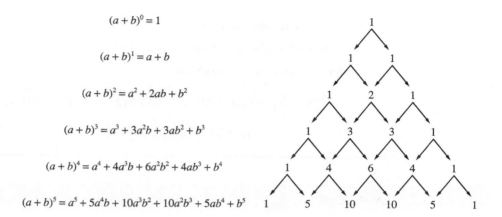

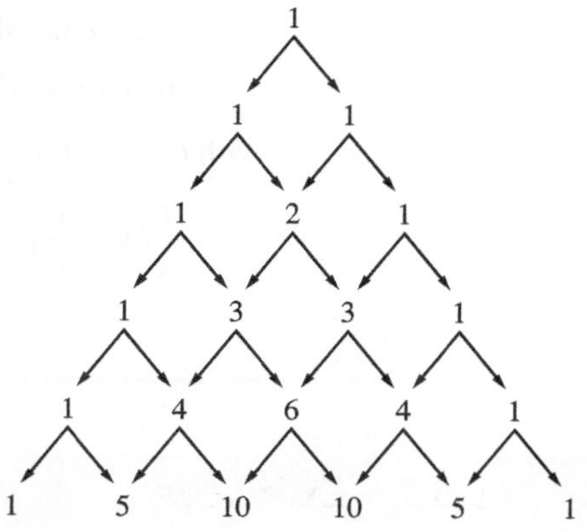

This table can be extended indefinitely. Each line can easily be obtained from the previous one. Thus, for example,

$$\begin{aligned}(a+b)^4 &= (a+b)(a+b)^3 \\ &= a(a^3 + 3a^2b + 3ab^2 + b^3) + b(a^3 + 3a^2b + 3ab^2 + b^3) \\ &= a^4 + 3a^3b + 3a^2b^2 + ab^3 + a^3b + 3a^2b^2 + 3ab^3 + b^4 \\ &= a^4 + 4a^3b + 6a^2b^2 + 4ab^3 + b^4\end{aligned}$$

The coefficients involved form a pattern of numbers called Pascal's triangle, shown in Figure 1.8. Each number in the interior of the triangle is obtained by summing the numbers to its right and left in the row above, as indicated by the arrows in Figure 1.8. This number pattern had been discovered prior to Pascal by the Chinese mathematician Chu Shih-chieh.

Example 1.20 Expand

(a) $(2x+3y)^2$ (b) $(2x-3)^3$ (c) $\left(2x - \dfrac{1}{x}\right)^4$

Solution (a) Here we use the expansion

$$(a+b)^2 = a^2 + 2ab + b^2$$

with $a = 2x$ and $b = 3y$ to obtain

$$\begin{aligned}(2x+3y)^2 &= (2x)^2 + 2(2x)(3y) + (3y)^2 \\ &= 4x^2 + 12xy + 9y^2\end{aligned}$$

(b) Here we use the expansion

$$(a+b)^3 = a^3 + 3a^2b + 3ab^2 + b^3$$

with $a = 2x$ and $b = -3$ to obtain

$$(2x-3)^3 = 8x^3 - 36x^2 + 54x - 27$$

(c) Here we use the expansion

$$(a+b)^4 = a^4 + 4a^3b + 6a^2b^2 + 4ab^3 + b^4$$

with $a = 2x$ and $b = -1/x$ to obtain

$$\left(2x - \frac{1}{x}\right)^4 = (2x)^4 + 4(2x)^3(-1/x) + 6(2x)^2(-1/x)^2 + 4(2x)(-1/x)^3 + (-1/x)^4$$

$$= 16x^4 - 32x^2 + 24 - 8/x^2 + 1/x^4$$

1.3.2 Exercises

15 Simplify the following expressions:

(a) $x^3 \times x^{-4}$ (b) $x^3 \div x^{-4}$ (c) $(x^3)^{-4}$

(d) $x^{1/3} \times x^{5/3}$ (e) $(4x^8)^{-1/2}$ (f) $\left(\frac{3}{2\sqrt{x}}\right)^{-2}$

(g) $\sqrt{x}\left(x^2 - \frac{2}{x}\right)$ (h) $\left(5x^{1/3} - \frac{1}{2x^{1/3}}\right)^2$

(i) $\frac{2x^{1/2} - x^{-1/2}}{x^{1/2}}$ (j) $\frac{(a^2b)^{1/2}}{(ab^{-2})^2}$

(k) $(4ab^2)^{-3/2}$

16 Factorize

(a) $x^2y - xy^2$

(b) $x^2yz - xy^2z + 2xyz^2$

(c) $ax - 2by - 2ay + bx$

(d) $x^2 + 3x - 10$

(e) $x^2 - \frac{1}{4}y^2$ (f) $81x^4 - y^4$

17 Simplify

(a) $\frac{x^2 - x - 12}{x^2 - 16}$ (b) $\frac{x-1}{x^2 - 2x - 3} - \frac{2}{x+1}$

(c) $\frac{1}{x^2 + 3x - 10} + \frac{1}{x^2 + 17x + 60}$

(d) $(3x + 2y)(x - 2y) + 4xy$

18 An isosceles trapezium has non-parallel sides of length 20 cm and the shorter parallel side is 30 cm, as illustrated in Figure 1.9. The perpendicular distance between the parallel sides is h cm. Show that the area of the trapezium is $h(30 + \sqrt{(400 - h^2)})\ \text{cm}^2$.

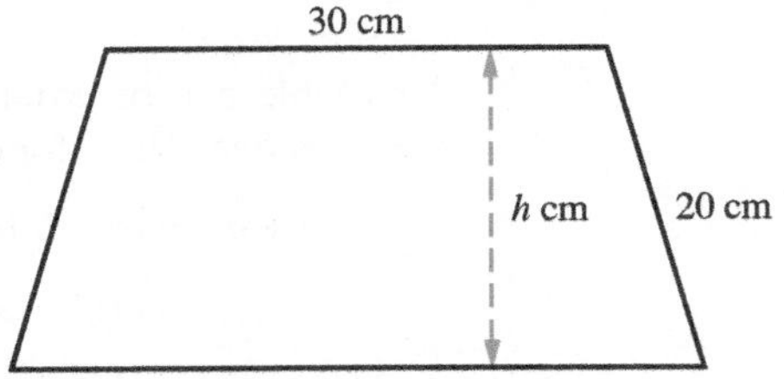

Figure 1.9

19 An open container is made from a sheet of cardboard of size 200 mm × 300 mm using a simple fold, as shown in Figure 1.10. Show that the capacity C ml of the box is given by

$$C = x(150 - x)(100 - x)/250$$

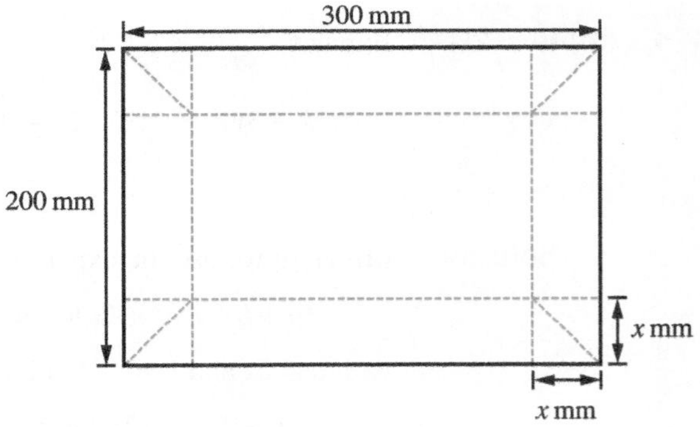

Figure 1.10 Sheet of cardboard of Question 19.

20 Rearrange the following quadratic expressions by completing the square.

(a) $x^2 + x - 12$ (b) $3 - 2x + x^2$

(c) $(x-1)^2 - (2x-3)^2$ (d) $1 + 4x - x^2$

1.3.3 Equations, inequalities and identities

It commonly occurs in the application of mathematics to practical problem-solving that the numerical value of an expression involving unassigned variables is specified and we have to find the values of the unassigned variables which yield that value. We illustrate the idea with the elementary examples that follow.

Example 1.21 A hollow cone of base diameter 100 mm and height 150 mm is held upside down and filled with a liquid. The liquid is then transferred to a hollow circular cylinder of base diameter 80 mm. To what height is the cylinder filled?

Solution The situation is illustrated in Figure 1.11. The capacity of the cone is

$$\tfrac{1}{3}(\text{base area}) \times (\text{perpendicular height})$$

Thus the volume of liquid contained in the cone is

$$\tfrac{1}{3}\pi(50^2)(150) = 125\,000\pi \text{ mm}^3$$

The volume of the liquid in the circular cylinder is

$$(\text{base area}) \times (\text{height}) = \pi(40^2)h \text{ mm}^3$$

where h mm is the height of the liquid in the cylinder. Equating these quantities (assuming no liquid is lost in the transfer) we have

$$1600\pi h = 125\,000\pi$$

This **equation** enables us to find the value of the unassigned variable h:

$$h = 1250/16 = 78.125$$

Thus the height of the liquid in the cylinder is 78mm to the nearest millimetre.

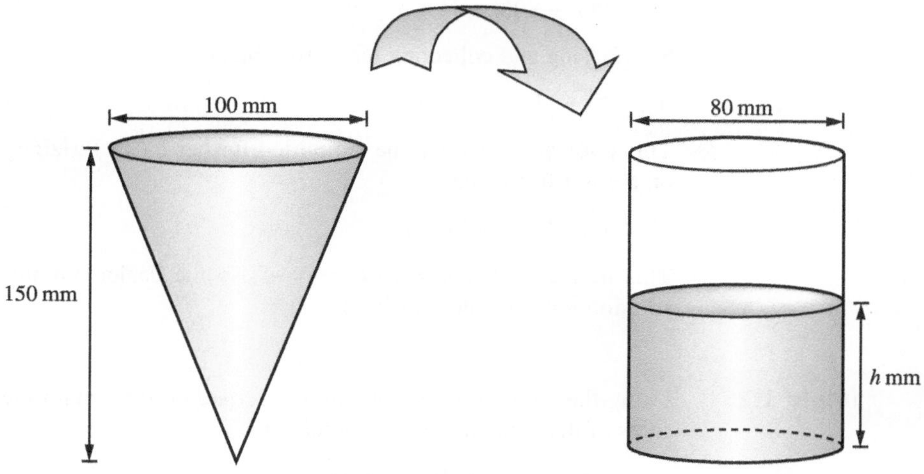

Figure 1.11 The cone and cylinder of Example 1.21.

In the previous example we made use of the formula for the volume V of a cone of base diameter D and height H. We normally shorthand this as

$$V = \tfrac{1}{12}\pi D^2 H$$

understanding that the units of measurement are compatible. This formula also tells us the height of such a cone in terms of its volume and base diameter

$$H = \frac{12V}{\pi D^2}$$

This type of rearrangement is common and is generally described as 'changing the subject of the formula'.

Example 1.22 A dealer bought a number of equally priced articles for a total cost of £120. He sold all but one of them, making a profit of £1.50 on each article with a total revenue of £135. How many articles did he buy?

Solution Let n be the number of articles bought. Then the cost of each article was £$(120/n)$. Since $(n - 1)$ articles were sold the selling price of each article was £$(135/(n - 1))$. Thus the profit per item was

$$£\left\{\frac{135}{n-1} - \frac{120}{n}\right\}$$

which we are told is equal to £1.50. Thus

$$\frac{135}{n-1} - \frac{120}{n} = 1.50$$

This implies

$$135n - 120(n - 1) = 1.50(n - 1)n$$

Dividing both sides by 1.5 gives

$$90n - 80(n - 1) = n^2 - n$$

Simplifying and collecting terms we obtain

$$n^2 - 11n - 80 = 0$$

This **equation** for n can be simplified further by factorizing the quadratic expression on the left-hand side

$$(n - 16)(n + 5) = 0$$

This implies either $n = 16$ or $n = -5$, so the dealer initially bought 16 articles (the solution $n = -5$ is not feasible).

Example 1.23 Using the method of completing the square (1.7a), obtain the formula for finding the roots of the general quadratic equation

$$ax^2 + bx + c = 0 \quad (a \neq 0)$$

Solution Dividing throughout by a gives

$$x^2 + \frac{b}{a}x + \frac{c}{a} = 0$$

Completing the square leads to

$$\left(x + \frac{b}{2a}\right)^2 + \frac{c}{a} = \left(\frac{b}{2a}\right)^2$$

giving

$$\left(x + \frac{b}{2a}\right)^2 = \frac{b^2}{4a^2} - \frac{c}{a} = \frac{b^2 - 4ac}{4a^2}$$

which on taking the square root gives

$$x + \frac{b}{2a} = +\frac{\sqrt{(b^2 - 4ac)}}{2a} \quad \text{or} \quad -\frac{\sqrt{(b^2 - 4ac)}}{2a}$$

or

$$x = \frac{-b \pm \sqrt{(b^2 - 4ac)}}{2a} \qquad \textbf{(1.8)}$$

Here the ± symbol provides a neat shorthand for the two solutions.

Comments

(a) The formula given in (1.8) makes clear the three cases: where for $b^2 > 4ac$ we have two real roots to the equation, for $b^2 < 4ac$ we have no real roots, and for $b^2 = 4ac$ we have one real root (which is repeated).

(b) The condition for equality of the roots of a quadratic equation occurs in practical applications, and we shall illustrate this in Example 2.48 after considering the trigonometric functions.

(c) The quadratic equation has many important applications. One, which is of historical significance, concerned the electrical engineer Oliver Heaviside. In 1871 the telephone cable between England and Denmark developed a fault caused by a short circuit under the sea. His task was to locate that fault. The cable had a uniform resistance per unit length. His method of solution was brilliantly simple. The situation can be represented schematically as shown in Figure 1.12.

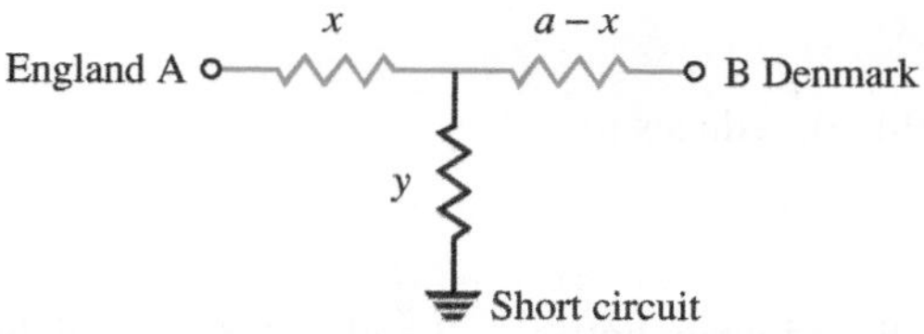

Figure 1.12
The circuit for the telephone line fault.

In the figure the total resistance of the line between A and B is a ohms and is known; x and y are unknown. If we can find x, we can locate the distance along the cable where the fault has occurred. Heaviside solved the problem by applying two tests. First he applied a battery, having voltage E, at A with the circuit open at B, and measured the resulting current I_1. Then he applied the same battery at A but with the cable earthed at B, and again measured the resulting current I_2. Using Ohm's law and the rules for combining resistances in parallel and in series, this yields the pair of equations

$$E = I_1(x + y)$$

$$E = I_2\left[x + \left(\frac{1}{y} + \frac{1}{a - x}\right)^{-1}\right]$$

Writing $b = E/I_1$ and $c = E/I_2$, we can eliminate y from these equations to obtain an equation for x:

$$x^2 - 2cx + c(a + b) - ab = 0$$

which, using (1.8), has solutions

$$x = c \pm \sqrt{[(a - c)(b - c)]}$$

From his experimental data Heaviside was able to predict accurately the location of the fault.

In some problems we have to find the values of unassigned variables such that the value of an expression involving those variables satisfies an inequality condition (that is, it is either greater than, or alternatively less than, a specified value). Solving such inequalities requires careful observance of the rules for inequalities (1.2a–1.2g) set out in Section 1.2.5.

Example 1.24 Find the values of x for which

$$\frac{1}{3 - x} < 2 \qquad \textbf{(1.9)}$$

Solution (a) When $3 - x > 0$, that is $x < 3$, we may, using (1.2e), multiply (1.9) throughout by $3 - x$ to give

$$1 < 2(3 - x)$$

which, using (1.2d, e), reduces to

$$x < \tfrac{5}{2}$$

so that (1.9) is satisfied when both $x < 3$ and $x < \tfrac{5}{2}$ are satisfied; that is, $x < \tfrac{5}{2}$.

(b) When $3 - x < 0$, that is $x > 3$, we may, using (1.2f), multiply (1.9) throughout by $3 - x$ to give

$$1 > 2(3 - x)$$

which reduces to $x > \frac{5}{2}$ so that (1.9) is also satisfied when both $x > 3$ and $x > \frac{5}{2}$; that is, $x > 3$.

Thus inequality (1.9) is satisfied by values of x in the ranges $x > 3$ and $x < \frac{5}{2}$.

Comment A common mistake made is simply to multiply (1.9) throughout by $3 - x$ to give the answer $x < \frac{5}{2}$, forgetting to consider both cases of $3 - x > 0$ and $3 - x < 0$. We shall return to consider this example from the graphical point of view in Example 2.36.

Example 1.25 Find the values of x such that

$$x^2 + 2x + 2 > 50$$

Solution Completing the square on the left-hand side of the inequality we obtain

$$(x + 1)^2 + 1 > 50$$

which gives

$$(x + 1)^2 > 49$$

Taking the square root of both sides of this inequality we deduce that

$$\text{either } (x + 1) < -7 \text{ or } (x + 1) > 7$$

Note particularly the first of these inequalities. From these we deduce that

$$x^2 + 2x + 2 > 50 \text{ for } x < -8 \text{ or } x > 6$$

The reader should check these results using spot values of x, say $x = -10$ and $x = 10$.

Example 1.26 A food manufacturer found that the sales figure for a certain item depended on its selling price. The company's market research department advised that the maximum number of items that could be sold weekly was 20 000 and that the number sold decreased by 100 for every 1p increase in its price. The total production cost consisted of a set-up cost of £200 **plus** 50p for every item manufactured. What price should the manufacturer adopt?

Solution The data supplied by the market research department suggests that if the price of the item is p pence, then the number sold would be $20\,000 - 100p$. (So the company would sell none with $p = 200$, when the price is £2.) The production cost in pounds would be 200 + 0.5 × (number sold), so that in terms of p we have the production cost £C given by

$$C = 200 + 0.5(20\,000 - 100p)$$

The revenue £R accrued by the manufacturer for the sales is (number sold) × (price), which gives

$$R = (20\,000 - 100p)p/100$$

(remember to express the amount in pounds). Thus, the profit £P is given by

$$\begin{aligned} P &= R - C \\ &= (20\,000 - 100p)p/100 - 200 - 0.5(20\,000 - 100p) \\ &= -p^2 + 250p - 10\,200 \end{aligned}$$

Completing the square we have

$$\begin{aligned} P &= 125^2 - (p - 125)^2 - 10\,200 \\ &= 5425 - (p - 125)^2 \end{aligned}$$

Since $(p - 125)^2 \geqslant 0$, we deduce that $P \leqslant 5425$ and that the maximum value of P is 5425. To achieve this weekly profit, the manufacturer should adopt the price £1.25.

It is important to distinguish between those equalities that are valid for a restricted set of values of the unassigned variable x and those that are true for all values of x. For example

$$(x - 5)(x + 7) = 0$$

is true only if $x = 5$ or $x = -7$. In contrast

$$(x - 5)(x + 7) = x^2 + 2x - 35 \qquad \textbf{(1.10)}$$

is true for all values of x. The word 'equals' here is being used in subtly different ways. In the first case '=' means 'is numerically equal to'; in the second case '=' means 'is algebraically equal to'. Sometimes we emphasize the different meaning by means of the special symbol ≡, meaning 'algebraically equal to'. (However, it is fairly common practice in engineering to use '=' in both cases.) Such equations are often called **identities**. Identities that involve an unassigned variable x as in (1.10) are valid for all values of x, and we can sometimes make use of this fact to simplify algebraic manipulations.

Example 1.27 Find the numbers A, B and C such that

$$x^2 + 2x - 35 \equiv A(x - 1)^2 + B(x - 1) + C$$

Solution Method (a): Since $x^2 + 2x - 35 \equiv A(x - 1)^2 + B(x - 1) + C$ it will be true for any value we give to x. So we choose values that make finding A, B and C easy.

Choosing $x = 0$ gives $-35 = A - B + C$
Choosing $x = 1$ gives $-32 = C$
Choosing $x = 2$ gives $-27 = A + B + C$

So we obtain $C = -32$, with $A - B = -3$ and $A + B = 5$. Hence $A = 1$ and $B = 4$ to give the identity

$$x^2 + 2x - 35 \equiv (x - 1)^2 + 4(x - 1) - 32$$

Method (b): Expanding the terms on the right-hand side, we have

$$x^2 + 2x - 35 \equiv Ax^2 + (B - 2A)x + A - B + C$$

The expressions on either side of the equals sign are algebraically equal, which means that the coefficient of x^2 on the left-hand side must equal the coefficient of x^2 on the right-hand side and so on. Thus

$$1 = A$$

$$2 = B - 2A$$

$$-35 = A - B + C$$

Hence we find $A = 1$, $B = 4$ and $C = -32$, as before.

Note: Method (a) assumes that a valid A, B and C exist.

Example 1.28 Find numbers A, B and C such that

$$\frac{x^2}{x-1} \equiv Ax + B + \frac{C}{x-1}, \qquad x \neq 1$$

Solution Expressing the right-hand side as a single term, we have

$$\frac{x^2}{x-1} \equiv \frac{(Ax + B)(x - 1) + C}{x-1}$$

which, with $x \neq 1$, is equivalent to

$$x^2 \equiv (Ax + B)(x - 1) + C$$

Choosing $x = 0$ gives $0 = -B + C$
Choosing $x = 1$ gives $1 = C$
Choosing $x = 2$ gives $4 = 2A + B + C$

Thus we obtain

$C = 1$, $B = 1$ and $A = 1$, yielding

$$\frac{x^2}{x-1} \equiv x + 1 + \frac{1}{x-1}$$

1.3.4 Exercises

21 Rearrange the following formula to make s the subject

$$m = p\sqrt{\frac{s+t}{s-t}}$$

22 Given $u = \dfrac{x^2+t}{x^2-t}$, find t in terms of u and x.

23 Solve for t

$$\frac{1}{1-t} - \frac{1}{1+t} = 1$$

24 If

$$\frac{3c^2+3xc+x^2}{3c^2+3yc+y^2} = \frac{yV_1}{xV_2}$$

find the positive value of c when

$$x = 4,\ y = 6,\ V_1 = 120,\ V_2 = 315$$

25 Solve for p the equation

$$\frac{2p+1}{p+5} + \frac{p-1}{p+1} = 2$$

26 A rectangle has a perimeter of 30 m. If its length is twice its breadth, find the length.

27 (a) A4 paper is such that a half sheet has the same shape as the whole sheet. Find the ratio of the lengths of the sides of the paper.

(b) Foolscap paper is such that cutting off a square whose sides equal the shorter side of the paper leaves a rectangle which has the same shape as the original sheet. Find the ratio of the sides of the original page.

28 Find the values of x for which

(a) $\dfrac{5}{x} < 2$ (b) $\dfrac{1}{2-x} < 1$

(c) $\dfrac{3x-2}{x-1} > 2$ (d) $\dfrac{3}{3x-2} > \dfrac{1}{x+4}$

29 Find the values of x for which

$$x^2 < 2 + |x|$$

30 Prove that

(a) $x^2 + 3x - 10 \geqslant -(\frac{7}{2})^2$

(b) $18 + 4x - x^2 \leqslant 22$

(c) $x + \dfrac{4}{x} \geqslant 4$ where $x > 0$

(*Hint*: First complete the square of the left-hand members.)

31 Find the values of A and B such that

(a) $\dfrac{1}{(x+1)(x-2)} \equiv \dfrac{A}{x+1} + \dfrac{B}{x-2}$

(b) $3x + 2 \equiv A(x-1) + B(x-2)$

(c) $\dfrac{5x+1}{\sqrt{(x^2+x+1)}} \equiv \dfrac{A(2x+1)+B}{\sqrt{(x^2+x+1)}}$

32 Find the values of A, B and C such that

$$2x^2 - 5x + 12 \equiv A(x-1)^2 + B(x-1) + C$$

1.3.5 Suffix and sigma notation

We have seen in previous sections how letters are used to denote general or unspecified values or numbers. This process has been extended in a variety of ways. In particular, the introduction of suffixes enables us to deal with problems that involve a high degree of generality or whose solutions have the flexibility to apply in a large number of situations. Consider for the moment an experiment involving measuring the temperature of an object (for example, a piece of machinery or a cooling fin in a heat exchanger) at intervals over a period of time. In giving a theoretical description of the experiment we would talk about the total period of time in general terms, say T minutes, and the time interval between measurements as h minutes, so that the total number n of time intervals would be given by T/h. Assuming that the initial and final temperatures are recorded there are $(n + 1)$ measurements. In practice we would obtain a set of experimental results, as illustrated partially in Figure 1.13.

Figure 1.13
Experimental results: temperature against lapsed time.

Lapsed time (minutes)	0	5	10	15	...	170	175	180
Temperature (°C)	97.51	96.57	93.18	91.53	...	26.43	24.91	23.57

Here we could talk about the twenty-first reading and look it up in the table. In the theoretical description we would need to talk about any one of the $(n + 1)$ temperature measurements. To facilitate this we introduce a suffix notation. We label the times at which the temperatures are recorded $t_0, t_1, t_2, \dots, t_n$, where t_0 corresponds to the time when the initial measurement is taken, t_n to the time when the final measurement is taken, and

$$t_1 = t_0 + h,\ t_2 = t_0 + 2h,\ \dots,\ t_n = t_0 + nh$$

so that $t_n = t_0 + T$. We label the corresponding temperatures by $\theta_0, \theta_1, \theta_2, \dots, \theta_n$. We can then talk about the general result θ_k as measuring the temperature at time t_k.

In the analysis of the experimental results we may also wish to manipulate the data we have obtained. For example, we might wish to work out the average value of the temperature over the time period. With the 37 specific experimental results given in Figure 1.13 it is possible to compute the average directly as

$$(97.51 + 96.57 + 93.18 + 91.53 + \dots + 23.57)/37$$

In general, however, we have

$$(\theta_0 + \theta_1 + \theta_2 + \dots + \theta_n)/(n + 1)$$

A compact way of writing this is to use the **sigma notation** for the extended summation $\theta_0 + \theta_1 + \dots + \theta_n$. We write

$$\sum_{k=0}^{n} \theta_k \qquad (\Sigma \text{ is the upper-case Greek letter sigma.})$$

to denote

$$\theta_0 + \theta_1 + \theta_2 + \dots + \theta_n$$

Thus

$$\sum_{k=0}^{3} \theta_k = \theta_0 + \theta_1 + \theta_2 + \theta_3$$

and

$$\sum_{k=5}^{10} \theta_k = \theta_5 + \theta_6 + \theta_7 + \theta_8 + \theta_9 + \theta_{10}$$

The suffix k appearing in the quantity to be summed and underneath the sigma symbol is the 'counting variable' or 'counter'. We may use any letter we please as a counter, provided that it is not being used at the same time for some other purpose. Thus

$$\sum_{i=0}^{3}\theta_i = \theta_0 + \theta_1 + \theta_2 + \theta_3 = \sum_{n=0}^{3}\theta_n = \sum_{j=0}^{3}\theta_j$$

Thus, in general, if $a_0, a_1, a_2, \ldots, a_n$ is a sequence of numbers or expressions, we write

$$\sum_{k=0}^{n}a_k = a_0 + a_1 + a_2 + \ldots + a_n$$

Example 1.29 Given $a_0 = 1$, $a_1 = 5$, $a_2 = 2$, $a_3 = 7$, $a_4 = -1$ and $b_0 = 0$, $b_1 = 2$, $b_2 = -2$, $b_3 = 11$, $b_4 = 3$, calculate

(a) $\sum_{k=0}^{4}a_k$ (b) $\sum_{i=2}^{3}a_i$ (c) $\sum_{k=1}^{3}a_kb_k$ (d) $\sum_{k=0}^{4}b_k^2$

Solution (a) $\sum_{k=0}^{4}a_k = a_0 + a_1 + a_2 + a_3 + a_4$

Substituting the given values for a_k $(k = 0, \ldots, 4)$ gives

$$\sum_{k=0}^{4}a_k = 1 + 5 + 2 + 7 + (-1) = 14$$

(b) $\sum_{i=2}^{3}a_i = a_2 + a_3 = 2 + 7 = 9$

(c) $\sum_{k=1}^{3}a_kb_k = a_1b_1 + a_2b_2 + a_3b_3 = (5 \times 2) + (2 \times (-2)) + (7 \times 11) = 83$

(d) $\sum_{k=0}^{4}b_k^2 = b_0^2 + b_1^2 + b_2^2 + b_3^2 + b_4^2 = 0 + 4 + 4 + 121 + 9 = 138$

1.3.6 Factorial notation and the binomial expansion

The special extended product of integers

$$1 \times 2 \times 3 \times \ldots \times n = n \times (n-1) \times (n-2) \times \ldots \times 1$$

has a special notation and name. It is called **factorial *n*** and is denoted by $n!$. Thus with

$$n! = n(n-1)(n-2)\ldots(1)$$

as examples

$$5! = 5 \times 4 \times 3 \times 2 \times 1 \quad \text{and} \quad 8! = 8 \times 7 \times 6 \times 5 \times 4 \times 3 \times 2 \times 1$$

Notice that $5! = 5(4!)$ so that we can write in general

$$n! = (n-1)! \times n$$

This relationship enables us to define 0!, since $1! = 1 \times 0!$ and 1! also equals 1. Thus 0! is defined by

$$0! = 1$$

Example 1.30 Evaluate

(a) 4! (b) $3! \times 2!$ (c) 6! (d) $7!/(2! \times 5!)$

Solution (a) $4! = 4 \times 3 \times 2 \times 1 = 24$

(b) $3! \times 2! = (3 \times 2 \times 1) \times (2 \times 1) = 12$

(c) $6! = 6 \times 5 \times 4 \times 3 \times 2 \times 1 = 720$

Notice that $2! \times 3! \neq (2 \times 3)!$.

(d) $$\frac{7!}{2! \times 5!} = \frac{7 \times 6 \times 5 \times 4 \times 3 \times 2 \times 1}{2 \times 1 \times 5 \times 4 \times 3 \times 2 \times 1} = \frac{7 \times 6}{2} = 21$$

Notice that we could have simplified the last item by writing

$$7! = 7 \times 6 \times (5!)$$

then

$$\frac{7!}{2! \times 5!} = \frac{7 \times 6 \times (5!)}{2! \times 5!} = \frac{7 \times 6}{2 \times 1} = 21$$

An interpretation of $n!$ is the total number of different ways it is possible to arrange n different objects in a single line. For example, the word SEAT comprises four different letters, and we can arrange the letters in $4! = 24$ different ways.

SEAT	EATS	ATSE	TSEA
SETA	EAST	ATES	TSAE
SAET	ESAT	AETS	TESA
SATE	ESTA	AEST	TEAS
STAE	ETSA	ASET	TAES
STEA	ETAS	ASTE	TASE

This is because we can choose the first letter in four different ways (S, E, A or T). Once that choice is made, we can choose the second letter in three different ways, then we can choose the third letter in two different ways. Having chosen the first three letters, the last letter is automatically fixed. For each of the four possible first choices, we have three possible choices for the second letter, giving us twelve (4×3) possible choices of the first two letters. To each of these twelve possible choices we have two possible choices of the third letter, giving us twenty-four $(4 \times 3 \times 2)$ possible choices of the first three letters. Having chosen the first three letters, there is only one possible choice of last letter. So in all we have 4! possible choices.

Example 1.31 In how many ways can the letters of the word REGAL be arranged in a line, and in how many of those do the two letters A and E appear in adjacent positions?

Solution The word REGAL has five distinct letters, so they can be arranged in a line in $5! = 120$ different ways. To find out in how many of those arrangements the A and E appear together, we consider how many arrangements can be made of RGL(AE) and RGL(EA), regarding the bracketed terms as a single symbol. There are 4! possible arrangements of both of these, so of the 120 different ways in which the letters of the word REGAL can be arranged, 48 contain the letters A and E in adjacent positions.

The introduction of the factorial notation facilitates the writing down of many complicated expressions. In particular it enables us to write down the general form of the binomial expansion discussed earlier in Section 1.3.1. There we wrote out long-hand the expansion of $(a + b)^n$ for $n = 0, 1, 2, \ldots, 6$ and noted the relationship between the coefficients of $(a + b)^n$ and those of $(a + b)^{n-1}$, shown clearly in Pascal's triangle of Figure 1.8.

If

$$(a + b)^{n-1} = c_0a^{n-1} + c_1a^{n-2}b + c_2a^{n-3}b^2 + c_3a^{n-4}b^3 + \ldots + c_{n-1}b^{n-1}$$

and

$$(a + b)^n = d_0a^n + d_1a^{n-1}b + d_2a^{n-2}b^2 + \ldots + d_{n-1}ab^{n-1} + d_nb^n$$

then, as described on p. 21 when developing Pascal's triangle,

$$c_0 = d_0 = 1, \quad d_1 = c_1 + c_0, \quad d_2 = c_2 + c_1, \quad d_3 = c_3 + c_2, \ldots$$

and in general

$$d_r = c_r + c_{r-1}$$

It is easy to verify that this relationship is satisfied by

$$d_r = \frac{n!}{r!(n-r)!}, \quad c_r = \frac{(n-1)!}{r!(n-1-r)!}, \quad c_{r-1} = \frac{(n-1)!}{(r-1)!(n-1-r+1)!}$$

and it can be shown that the coefficient of $a^{n-r}b^r$ in the expansion of $(a + b)^n$ is

$$\frac{n!}{r!(n-r)!} = \frac{n(n-1)(n-2)\ldots(n-r+1)}{r(r-1)(r-2)\ldots(1)} \quad \textbf{(1.11)}$$

This is a very important result, with many applications. Using it we can write down the general binomial expansion

$$(a + b)^n = \sum_{r=0}^{n} \frac{n!}{r!(n-r)!} a^{n-r}b^r \quad \textbf{(1.12)}$$

The coefficient $\dfrac{n!}{r!(n-r)!}$ is called the **binomial coefficient** and has the special notation

$$\binom{n}{r} = \frac{n!}{r!(n-r)!}$$

Thus we may write

$$(a+b)^n = \sum_{r=0}^{n} \binom{n}{r} a^{n-r} b^r \tag{1.13}$$

which is referred to as the general **binomial expansion**.

Example 1.32 Expand the expression $(2+x)^5$.

Solution Setting $a = 2$ and $b = x$ in the general binomial expansion we have

$$(2+x)^5 = \sum_{r=0}^{5} \binom{5}{r} 2^{5-r} x^r$$

$$= \binom{5}{0}2^5 + \binom{5}{1}2^4x + \binom{5}{2}2^3x^2 + \binom{5}{3}2^2x^3 + \binom{5}{4}2x^4 + \binom{5}{5}x^5$$

$$= (1)(2^5) + (5)(2^4)x + (10)(2^3)x^2 + (10)(2^2)x^3 + (5)(2)x^4 + 1x^5$$

since $\binom{5}{0} = \dfrac{5!}{0!5!} = 1$, $\binom{5}{1} = \dfrac{5!}{1!4!} = 5$, $\binom{5}{2} = \dfrac{5!}{2!3!} = 10$ and so on. Thus

$$(2+x)^5 = 32 + 80x + 80x^2 + 40x^3 + 10x^4 + x^5$$

1.3.7 Exercises

33 Given $a_0 = 2$, $a_1 = -1$, $a_2 = -4$, $a_3 = 5$, $a_4 = 3$ and $b_0 = 1$, $b_1 = 1$, $b_2 = 2$, $b_3 = -1$, $b_4 = 2$, calculate

(a) $\sum_{k=0}^{4} a_k$ (b) $\sum_{i=1}^{3} a_i$

(c) $\sum_{k=1}^{2} a_k b_k$ (d) $\sum_{j=0}^{4} b_j^2$

34 Evaluate

(a) 5! (b) 3!/4! (c) 7!/(3! × 4!)

(d) $\binom{5}{2}$ (e) $\binom{9}{3}$ (f) $\binom{8}{4}$

35 Using the general binomial expansion expand the following expressions:

(a) $(x-3)^4$ (b) $(x+\frac{1}{2})^3$

(c) $(2x+3)^5$ (d) $(3x+2y)^4$

1.4 Geometry

1.4.1 Coordinates

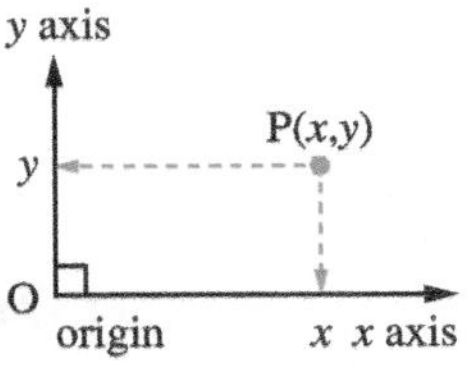

Figure 1.14
Cartesian coordinates

In addition to the introduction of algebraic manipulation another innovation made in the seventeenth century was the use of coordinates to represent the position of a point P on a plane as shown in Figure 1.14. Conventionally the point P is represented by an ordered pair of numbers contained in brackets thus: (x, y). This innovation was largely due to Descartes and consequently we often refer to (x, y) as the **cartesian coordinates** of P. This notation is the same as that for an open interval on the number line introduced in Section 1.2.6, but has an entirely separate meaning and the two should not be confused. Whether (x, y) denotes an open interval or a coordinate pair is usually clear from the context.

1.4.2 Straight lines

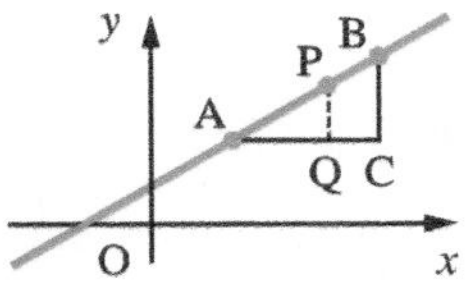

Figure 1.15
Straight line

The introduction of coordinates made possible the algebraic description of the plane curves of classical geometry and the proof of standard results by algebraic methods.

Consider, for example, the point P lying on the line AB as shown in Figure 1.15. Let P divide AB in the ratio $\lambda:1-\lambda$. Then AP/AB = λ and, by similar triangles,

$$\frac{\text{AP}}{\text{AB}} = \frac{\text{PQ}}{\text{BC}} = \frac{\text{AQ}}{\text{AC}}$$

Let A, B and P have coordinates (x_0, y_0), (x_1, y_1) and (x, y) respectively, then from the diagram

$$\text{AQ} = x - x_0,\ \text{AC} = x_1 - x_0,\ \text{PQ} = y - y_0,\ \text{BC} = y_1 - y_0$$

Thus

$$\frac{\text{PQ}}{\text{BC}} = \frac{\text{AQ}}{\text{AC}} \quad \text{implies} \quad \frac{y - y_0}{y_1 - y_0} = \frac{x - x_0}{x_1 - x_0}$$

from which we deduce, after some rearrangement,

$$y = \frac{y_1 - y_0}{x_1 - x_0}(x - x_0) + y_0 \qquad \textbf{(1.14)}$$

which represents the equation of a straight line passing through two points (x_0, y_0) and (x_1, y_1).

More simply, the equation of a straight line passing through the two points having coordinates (x_0, y_0) and (x_1, y_1) may be written as

$$y = mx + c \qquad \textbf{(1.15)}$$

where $m = \dfrac{y_1 - y_0}{x_1 - x_0}$ is the gradient (slope) of the line and $c = \dfrac{y_0x_1 - y_1x_0}{x_1 - x_0}$ is the intercept on the y axis.

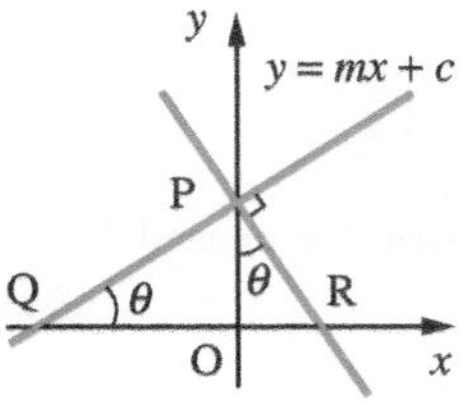

Figure 1.16
Perpendicular lines

A line perpendicular to $y = mx + c$ has gradient $-1/m$ as shown in Figure 1.16. The gradient of the line PQ is OP/QO = m. The gradient of the line PR is –OP/OR. By similar triangles POQ, POR we have OP/OR = OQ/OP = $1/m$.

Equations of the form

$$y = mx + c$$

represent straight lines on the plane and, consequently, are called **linear equations**.

Example 1.33 Find the equation of the straight line that passes through the points (1, 2) and (3, 3).

Solution Taking $(x_0, y_0) = (1, 2)$ and $(x_1, y_1) = (3, 3)$

$$\text{slope of line} = \frac{y_1 - y_0}{x_1 - x_0} = \frac{3-2}{3-1} = \frac{1}{2}$$

so from formula (1.14) the equation of the straight line is

$$y = \tfrac{1}{2}(x - 1) + 2$$

which simplifies to

$$y = \tfrac{1}{2}x + \tfrac{3}{2}$$

Example 1.34 Find the equation of the straight line passing through the point (3, 2) and parallel to the line $2y = 3x + 4$. Determine its x and y intercepts.

Solution Writing $2y = 3x + 4$ as

$$y = \tfrac{3}{2}x + 2$$

we have from (1.15) that the slope of this line is $\frac{3}{2}$. Since the required line is parallel to this line, it will also have a slope of $\frac{3}{2}$. (The slope of the line perpendicular to it is $-\frac{2}{3}$.) Thus from (1.15) it has equation

$$y = \tfrac{3}{2}x + c$$

To determine the constant c, we use the fact that the line passes through the point (3, 2), so that

$$2 = \tfrac{9}{2} + c \qquad \text{giving} \qquad c = -\tfrac{5}{2}$$

Thus the equation of the required line is

$$y = \tfrac{3}{2}x - \tfrac{5}{2} \qquad \text{or} \qquad 2y = 3x - 5$$

The y intercept is $c = -\frac{5}{2}$.

To obtain the x intercept we substitute $y = 0$, giving $x = \frac{5}{3}$, so that the x intercept is $\frac{5}{3}$.

The graph of the line is shown in Figure 1.17.

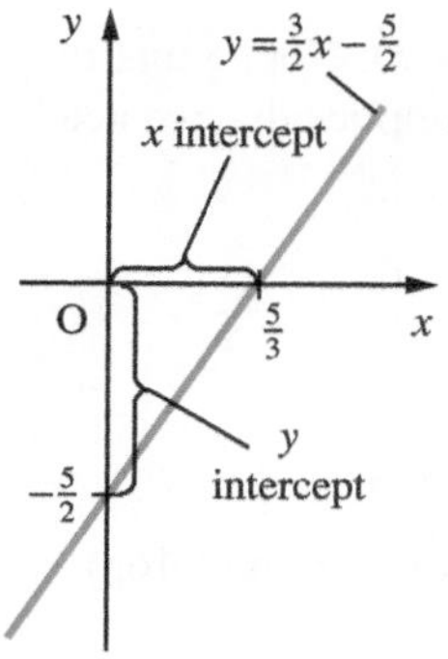

Figure 1.17 The straight line $2y = 3x - 5$.

1.4.3 Circles

A circle is the planar curve whose points are all equidistant from a fixed point called the centre of the circle. The simplest case is a circle centred at the origin with radius r, as shown in Figure 1.18(a). Applying Pythagoras' theorem to triangle OPQ we obtain

$$x^2 + y^2 = r^2$$

(Note that r is a constant.) When the centre of the circle is at the point (a, b), rather than the origin, the equation is

$$(x - a)^2 + (y - b)^2 = r^2 \qquad \textbf{(1.16a)}$$

obtained by applying Pythagoras' theorem in triangle O′PN of Figure 1.18(b). This expands to

$$x^2 + y^2 - 2ax - 2by + (a^2 + b^2 - r^2) = 0$$

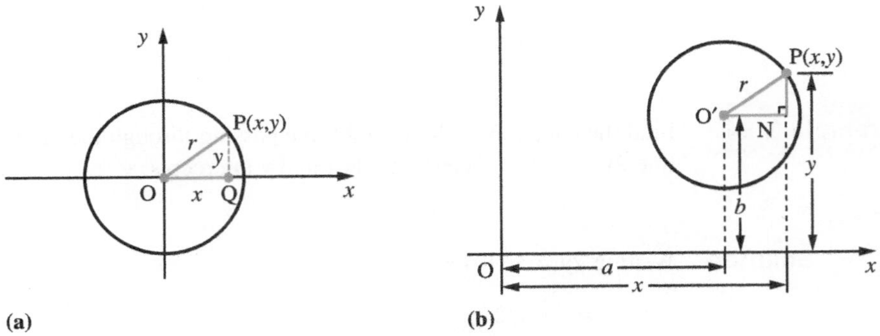

Figure 1.18
(a) A circle of centre origin, radius r. (b) A circle of centre (a, b), radius r.

Thus the general equation

$$x^2 + y^2 + 2fx + 2gy + c = 0 \qquad \textbf{(1.16b)}$$

represents a circle having centre $(-f, -g)$ and radius $\sqrt{(f^2 + g^2 - c)}$. Notice that the general circle has three constants f, g and c in its equation. This implies that we need three points to specify a circle completely.

Example 1.35 Find the equation of the circle with centre (1, 2) and radius 3.

Solution Using Pythagoras' theorem, if the point P(x, y) lies on the circle then from (1.16a)

$$(x - 1)^2 + (y - 2)^2 = 3^2$$

Thus

$$x^2 - 2x + 1 + y^2 - 4y + 4 = 9$$

giving the equation as

$$x^2 + y^2 - 2x - 4y - 4 = 0$$

Example 1.36 Find the radius and the coordinates of the centre of the circle whose equation is

$$2x^2 + 2y^2 - 3x + 5y + 2 = 0$$

Solution Dividing through by the coefficient of x^2 we obtain

$$x^2 + y^2 - \tfrac{3}{2}x + \tfrac{5}{2}y + 1 = 0$$

Now completing the square on the x terms and the y terms separately gives

$$(x - \tfrac{3}{4})^2 + (y + \tfrac{5}{4})^2 = \tfrac{9}{16} + \tfrac{25}{16} - 1 = \tfrac{18}{16}$$

Hence, from (1.16a), the circle has radius $(3\sqrt{2})/4$ and centre $(3/4, -5/4)$.

Example 1.37 Find the equation of the circle which passes through the points (0, 0), (0, 2), (4, 0).

Solution Method (a): From (1.16b) the general equation of a circle is

$$x^2 + y^2 + 2fx + 2gy + c = 0$$

Substituting the three points into this equation gives three equations for the unknowns f, g and c.

Thus substituting (0, 0) gives $c = 0$, substituting (0, 2) gives $4 + 4g + c = 0$ and substituting (4, 0) gives $16 + 8f + c = 0$. Solving these equations gives $g = -1$, $f = -2$ and $c = 0$, so the required equation is

$$x^2 + y^2 - 4x - 2y = 0$$

Method (b): From Figure 1.19 using the geometrical properties of the circle, we see that its centre lies at (2, 1) and since it passes through the origin its radius is $\sqrt{5}$. Hence, from (1.16a), its equation is

$$(x - 2)^2 + (y - 1)^2 = (\sqrt{5})^2$$

Figure 1.19 The circle of Example 1.37.

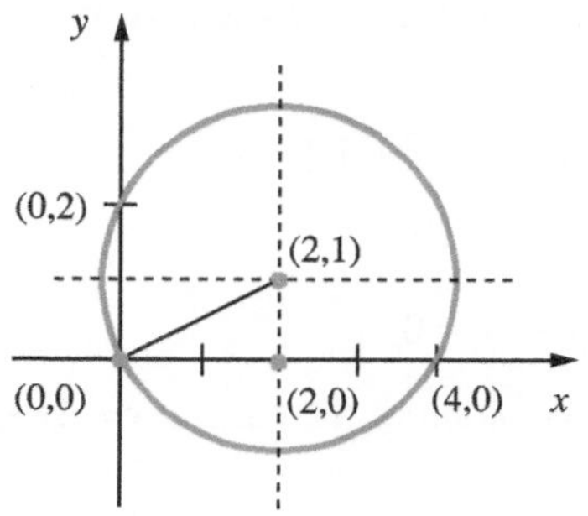

which simplifies to

$$x^2 + y^2 - 4x - 2y = 0$$

as before.

Example 1.38 Find the point of intersection of the line $y = x - 1$ with the circle $x^2 + y^2 - 4y - 1 = 0$.

Solution Substituting $y = x - 1$ into the formula for the circle gives

$$x^2 + (x - 1)^2 - 4(x - 1) - 1 = 0$$

which simplifies to

$$x^2 - 3x + 2 = 0$$

This equation may be factored to give

$$(x - 2)(x - 1) = 0$$

so that $x = 1$ and $x = 2$ are the roots. Thus the points of intersection are (1, 0) and (2, 1).

Example 1.39 Find the equation of the tangent at the point (2, 1) of the circle $x^2 + y^2 - 4y - 1 = 0$.

Solution A tangent is a line, which is the critical case between a line intersecting the circle in two distinct points and it not intersecting at all. We can describe this as the case when the line cuts the circle in two coincident points. Thus the line, which passes through (2, 1) with slope m

$$y = m(x - 2) + 1$$

is a tangent to the circle when the equation

$$x^2 + [m(x - 2) + 1]^2 - 4[m(x - 2) + 1] - 1 = 0$$

has two equal roots. Multiplying these terms out we obtain the equation

$$(m^2 + 1)x^2 - 2m(2m + 1)x + 4(m^2 + m - 1) = 0$$

The condition for this equation to have equal roots is (using comment (a) of Example 1.23)

$$4m^2(2m + 1)^2 = 4[4(m^2 + m - 1)(m^2 + 1)]$$

This simplifies to

$$m^2 - 4m + 4 = 0 \quad \text{or} \quad (m - 2)^2 = 0$$

giving the result $m = 2$ and the equation of the tangent $y = 2x - 3$.

1.4.4 Exercises

36 Find the equation of the straight line

(a) with gradient $\frac{3}{2}$ passing through the point (2, 1);

(b) with gradient −2 passing through the point (−2, 3);

(c) passing through the points (1, 2) and (3, 7);

(d) passing through the points (5, 0) and (0, 3);

(e) parallel to the line $3y - x = 5$, passing through (1, 1);

(f) perpendicular to the line $3y - x = 5$, passing through (1, 1).

37 Write down the equation of the circle with centre (1, 2) and radius 5.

38 Find the radius and the coordinates of the centre of the circle with equation

$$x^2 + y^2 + 4x - 6y = 3$$

39 Find the equation of the circle with centre (−2, 3) that passes through (1, −1).

40 Find the equation of the circle that passes through the points (1, 0), (3, 4) and (5, 0).

41 Find the equation of the tangent to the circle

$$x^2 + y^2 - 4x - 1 = 0$$

at the point (1, 2).

42 A rod, 50 cm long, moves in a plane with its ends on two perpendicular wires. Find the equation of the curve followed by its midpoint.

1.4.5 Conics

The circle is one of the conic sections (Figure 1.20) introduced around 200 BC by Apollonius, who published an extensive study of their properties in a textbook that he called *Conics*. He used this title because he visualized them as cuts made by a 'flat' or plane surface when it intersects the surface of a cone in different directions, as illustrated in Figures 1.21(a–d). Note that the conic sections degenerate into a point and straight lines at the extremities, as illustrated in Figures 1.21(e–g). Although at the time of Apollonius his work on conics appeared to be of little value in terms of applications, it has since turned out to have considerable importance. This is primarily due to the fact that the conic sections are the paths followed by projectiles, artificial satellites, moons and the Earth under the influence of gravity around planets or stars. The early Greek astronomers thought that the planets moved in circular orbits, and it was not until 1609 that the German astronomer Johannes Kepler described their paths correctly as being elliptic, with the Sun at one focus. It is quite possible for an orbit to be a curve other than an ellipse. Imagine a meteor or comet approaching the Sun from some distant region in space. The path that the body will follow depends very much on the speed at which it is moving. If the body is small compared to the Sun, say of planetary dimensions, and its speed relative to the Sun is not very high, it will never escape and will describe an *elliptic* path about it. An example is the comet observed by Edmond Halley in 1682 and now known as Halley's comet. He computed its elliptic orbit, found that it was the same comet that had been seen in 1066, 1456, 1531 and 1607, and correctly forecast its reappearance in 1758. It was most recently seen in 1986. If the speed of the body is very high, its path will be deviated by the Sun but it will not orbit forever around the Sun. Rather, it will bend around the Sun in a path in the form of a **hyperbola** and continue on its journey back to outer space. Somewhere between these two extremes there is a certain critical speed that is just too great to allow the body to

Figure 1.20
Standard equations of the four conics.

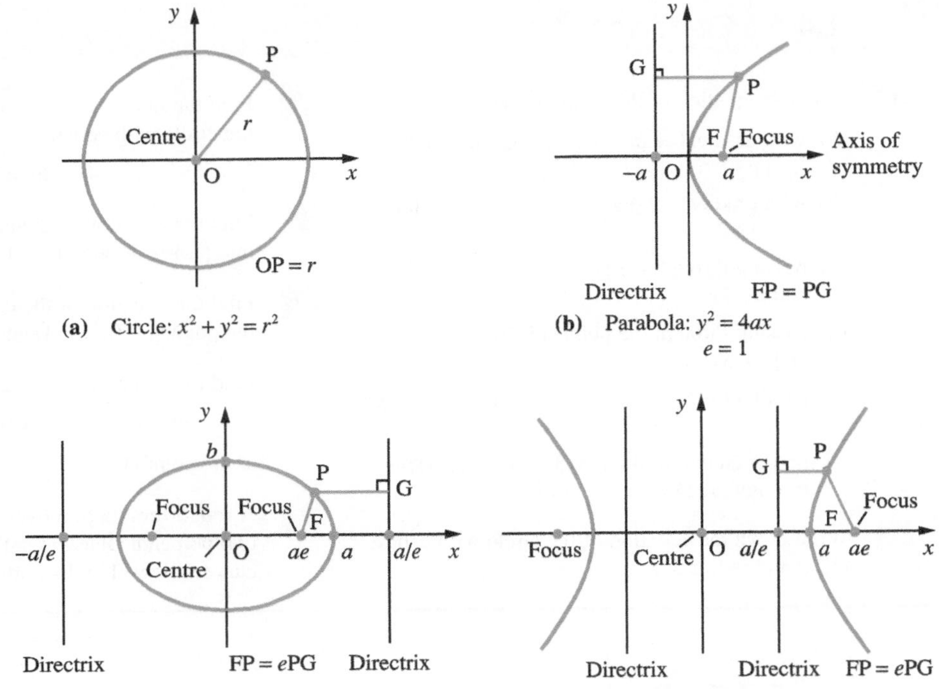

(a) Circle: $x^2 + y^2 = r^2$

(b) Parabola: $y^2 = 4ax$
$e = 1$

(c) Ellipse: $\dfrac{x^2}{a^2} + \dfrac{y^2}{b^2} = 1$
$b^2 = a^2(1 - e^2)$
and eccentricity $e < 1$

(d) Hyperbola: $\dfrac{x^2}{a^2} - \dfrac{y^2}{b^2} = 1$
$b^2 = a^2(e^2 - 1)$
and eccentricity $e > 1$

Figure 1.21

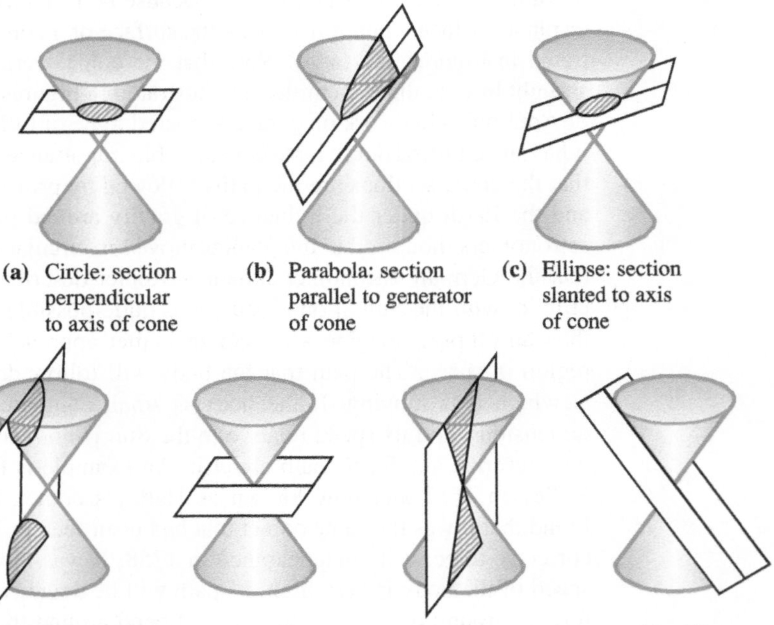

(a) Circle: section perpendicular to axis of cone

(b) Parabola: section parallel to generator of cone

(c) Ellipse: section slanted to axis of cone

(d) Hyperbola: section slanted to axis of cone

(e) Point

(f) Two intersecting lines

(g) Line

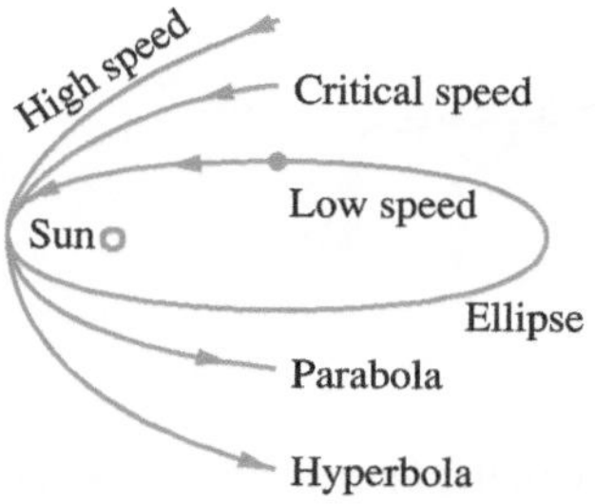

Figure 1.22 Orbital path.

orbit the Sun, but not great enough for the path to be a hyperbola. In this case the path is a **parabola**, and once again the body will bend around the Sun and continue on its journey into outer space. These possibilities are illustrated in Figure 1.22.

Examples of where conic sections appear in engineering practice include the following.

(a) A parabolic surface, obtained by rotating a parabola about its axis of symmetry, has the important property that an energy source placed at the focus will cause rays to be reflected at the surface such that after reflection they will be parallel. Reversing the process, a beam parallel to the axis impinging on the surface will be reflected onto the focus (Example 8.6). This property is involved in many engineering design projects: for example the design of a car headlamp or a radio telescope, as illustrated in Figures 1.23(a) and (b) respectively. Other examples involving a parabola are the path of a projectile (Example 2.39) and the shape of the cable on certain types of suspension bridge (Example 8.60).

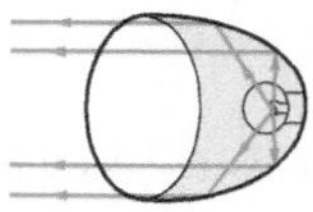

(a)

(b)

Figure 1.23
(a) Car headlamp.
(b) Radio telescope.

(b) A ray of light emitted from one focus of an elliptic mirror and reflected by the mirror will pass through the other focus, as illustrated in Figure 1.24. This property is sometimes used in designing mirror combinations for a reflecting telescope. Ellipses have been used in other engineering designs, such as aircraft wings and stereo styli. Elliptical pipes are used for foul and surface water drainage because the elliptical profile is hydraulically efficient. As described earlier, every planet orbits around the Sun in an elliptic path with the Sun at one of its foci. The planet's speed depends on its distance from the Sun; it speeds up as it nears the Sun and slows down as it moves further away. The reason for this is that for an ellipse the line drawn from the focus S (Sun) to a point P (planet) on the ellipse sweeps out areas at a constant rate as P moves around the ellipse. Thus in Figure 1.25 the planet will take the same time to travel the two different distances shown, assuming that the two shaded regions are of equal area.

(c) Consider a supersonic aircraft flying over land. As it breaks the sound barrier (that is, it travels faster than the speed of sound, which is about 750 mph ($331.4\,\mathrm{m\,s^{-1}}$)), it will create a shock wave, which we hear on the ground as a *sonic boom* – this being one of the major disadvantages of supersonic aircraft. This shock wave will trail behind

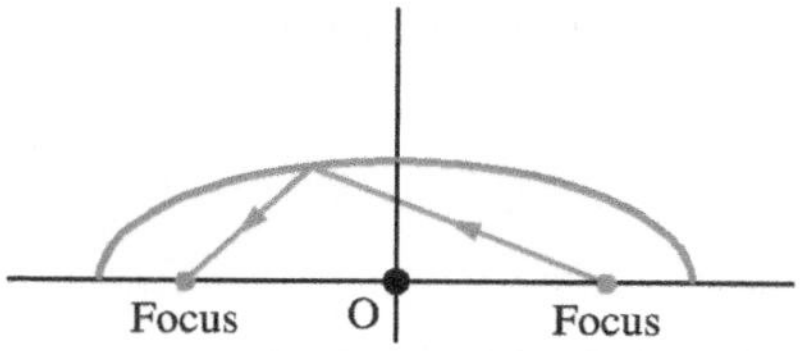

Figure 1.24 Reflection of a ray by an elliptic mirror.

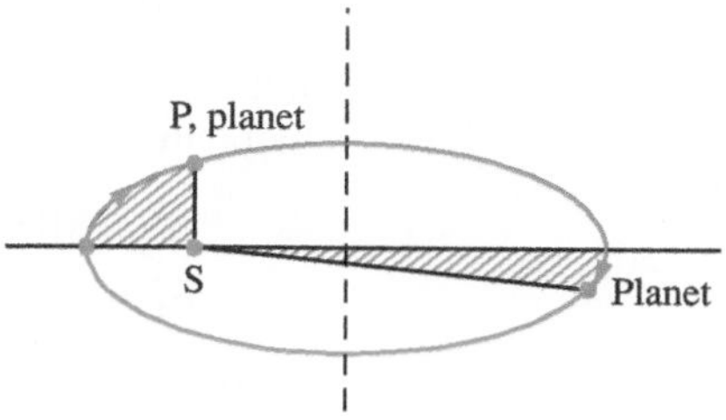

Figure 1.25 Regions of equal area.

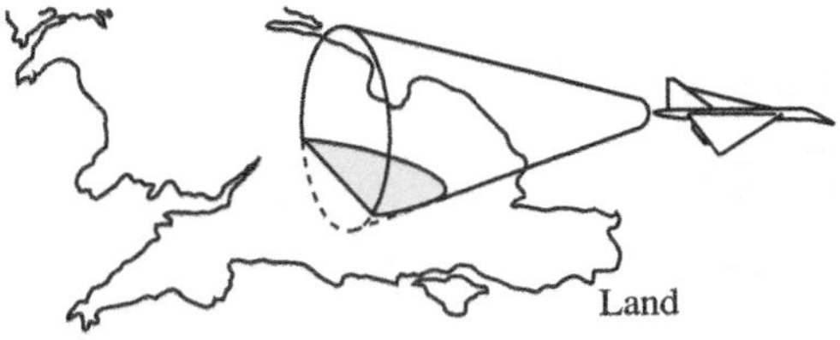

Figure 1.26
Sonic boom.

the aircraft in the form of a cone with the aircraft as vertex. This cone will intersect the ground in a *hyperbolic curve*, as illustrated in Figure 1.26. The sonic boom will hit every point on this curve at the same instant of time, so that people living on the curve will hear it simultaneously. No boom will be heard by people living outside this curve, but eventually it will be heard at every point inside it.

Figure 1.20 illustrates the conics in their standard positions, and the corresponding equations may be interpreted as the standard equations for the four curves. More generally the conic sections may be represented by the general second-order equation

$$ax^2 + by^2 + 2fx + 2gy + 2hxy + c = 0 \qquad \textbf{(1.17)}$$

Provided its graph does not degenerate into a point or straight lines, (1.17) is representative of

- a circle if $a = b \neq 0$ and $h = 0$
- a parabola if $h^2 = ab$
- an ellipse if $h^2 < ab$
- a hyperbola if $h^2 > ab$

The conics can be defined mathematically in a number of (equivalent) ways, as we will illustrate in the next examples.

Example 1.40

A point P moves in such a way that its total distance from two fixed points A and B is constant. Show that it describes an ellipse.

Solution

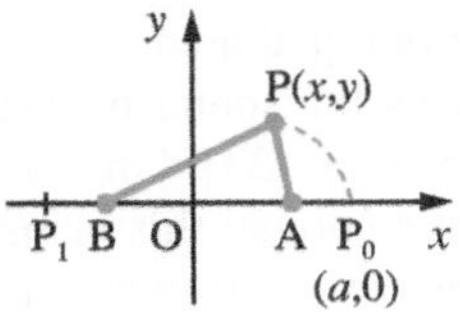

Figure 1.27
Path of Example 1.40.

The definition of the curve implies that AP + BP = constant with the origin O being the midpoint of AB. From symmetry considerations we choose x and y axes as shown in Figure 1.27. Suppose the curve crosses the x axis at P_0, then

$$AP_0 + BP_0 = AB + 2AP_0 = 2OP_0$$

so the constant in the definition is $2OP_0$ and for any point P on the curve

$$AP + BP = 2OP_0$$

Let $P = (x, y)$, $P_0 = (a, 0)$, $P_1 = (-a, 0)$, $A = (c, 0)$ and $B = (-c, 0)$. Then using Pythagoras' theorem we have

$$AP = \sqrt{[(x - c)^2 + y^2]}$$

$$BP = \sqrt{[(x + c)^2 + y^2]}$$

so that the defining equation of the curve becomes

$$\sqrt{[(x - c)^2 + y^2]} + \sqrt{[(x + c)^2 + y^2]} = 2a$$

To obtain the required equation we need to 'remove' the square root terms. This can only be done by squaring both sides of the equation. First we rewrite the equation as

$$\sqrt{[(x-c)^2+y^2]} = 2a - \sqrt{[(x+c)^2+y^2]}$$

and then square to give

$$(x-c)^2+y^2 = 4a^2 - 4a\sqrt{[(x+c)^2+y^2]} + (x+c)^2+y^2$$

Expanding the squared terms we have

$$x^2-2cx+c^2+y^2 = 4a^2 - 4a\sqrt{[(x+c)^2+y^2]} + x^2+2cx+c^2+y^2$$

Collecting together terms, we obtain

$$a\sqrt{[(x+c)^2+y^2]} = a^2+cx$$

Squaring both sides again gives

$$a^2[x^2+2cx+c^2+y^2] = a^4+2a^2cx+c^2x^2$$

which simplifies to

$$(a^2-c^2)x^2+a^2y^2 = a^2(a^2-c^2)$$

Noting that $a > c$ we write $a^2 - c^2 = b^2$, to obtain

$$b^2x^2+a^2y^2 = a^2b^2$$

which yields the standard equation of the ellipse

$$\frac{x^2}{a^2}+\frac{y^2}{b^2} = 1$$

The points A and B are the foci of the ellipse, and the property that the sum of the focal distances is a constant is known as the **string property** of the ellipse since it enables us to draw an ellipse using a piece of string.

For a hyperbola, the *difference* of the focal distances is constant.

Example 1.41

A point moves in such a way that its distance from a fixed point F is equal to its perpendicular distance from a fixed line. Show that it describes a parabola.

Solution

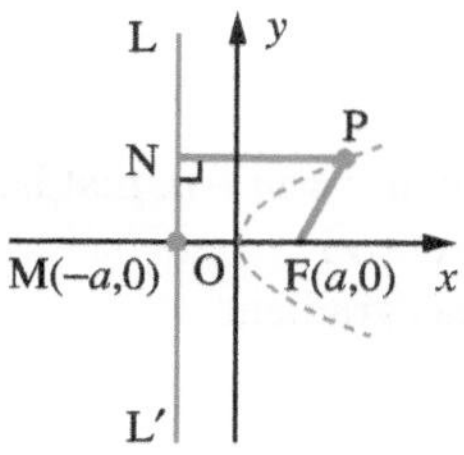

Figure 1.28
Path of point in Example 1.41.

Suppose the fixed line is LL′ shown in Figure 1.28, choosing the co-ordinate axes shown. Since PF = PN for points on the curve we deduce that the curve bisects FM, so that if F is $(a, 0)$, then M is $(-a, 0)$. Let the general point P on the curve have coordinates (x, y). Then by Pythagoras' theorem

$$PF = \sqrt{[(x-a)^2+y^2]}$$

Also $PN = x + a$, so that PN = PF implies that

$$x+a = \sqrt{[(x-a)^2+y^2]}$$

Squaring both sides gives

$$(x+a)^2 = (x-a)^2+y^2$$

which simplifies to

$$y^2 = 4ax$$

the standard equation of a parabola. The line LL′ is called the **directrix** of the parabola.

Example 1.42 (a) Find the equation of the tangent at the point (1, 1) to the parabola $y = x^2$. Show that it is parallel to the line through the points $(\frac{1}{2}, \frac{1}{4})$, $(\frac{3}{2}, \frac{9}{4})$, which also lie on the parabola.

(b) Find the equation of the tangent at the point (a, a^2) to the parabola $y = x^2$. Show that it is parallel to the line through the points $(a - h, (a - h)^2)$, $(a + h, (a + h)^2)$.

Solution (a) Consider the general line through (1, 1). It has equation $y = m(x - 1) + 1$. This cuts the parabola when

$$m(x - 1) + 1 = x^2$$

that is, when

$$x^2 - mx + m - 1 = 0$$

Factorizing this quadratic, we have

$$(x - 1)(x - m + 1) = 0$$

giving the roots $x = 1$ and $x = m - 1$

These two roots are equal when $m - 1 = 1$, that is, when $m = 2$. Hence the equation of the tangent is $y = 2x - 1$.

The line through the points $(\frac{1}{2}, \frac{1}{4})$, $(\frac{3}{2}, \frac{9}{4})$ has gradient

$$\frac{\frac{9}{4} - \frac{1}{4}}{\frac{3}{2} - \frac{1}{2}} = 2$$

so that it is parallel to the tangent at (1, 1).

(b) Consider the general line through (a, a^2). It has equation $y = m(x - a) + a^2$. This cuts the parabola $y = x^2$ when

$$m(x - a) + a^2 = x^2$$

that is, where

$$x^2 - mx + ma - a^2 = 0$$

This factorizes into

$$(x - a)(x - m + a) = 0$$

giving the roots $x = a$ and $x = m - a$. These two roots are equal when $a = m - a$, that is, when $m = 2a$. Thus the equation of the tangent at (a, a^2) is $y = 2ax - a^2$.

The line through the points $(a - h, (a - h)^2)$, $(a + h, (a + h)^2)$ has gradient

$$\frac{(a + h)^2 - (a - h)^2}{(a + h) - (a - h)} = \frac{a^2 + 2ah + h^2 - (a^2 - 2ah + h^2)}{2h}$$

$$= \frac{4ah}{2h} = 2a$$

So the symmetrically disposed chord through $(a - h, (a - h)^2)$, $(a + h, (a + h)^2)$ is parallel to the tangent at $x = a$. This result is true for all parabolas.

1.4.6 Exercises

43 Find the coordinates of the focus and the equation of the directrix of the parabola whose equation is

$$3y^2 = 8x$$

The chord which passes through the focus parallel to the directrix is called the **latus rectum** of the parabola. Show that the latus rectum of the above parabola has length 8/3.

44 For the ellipse $25x^2 + 16y^2 = 400$ find the coordinates of the foci, the eccentricity, the equations of the directrices and the lengths of the semi-major and semi-minor axes.

45 For the hyperbola $9x^2 - 16y^2 = 144$ find the coordinates of the foci and the vertices and the equations of its asymptotes.

1.5 Number and accuracy

Arithmetic that only involves integers can be performed to obtain an exact answer (that is, one without rounding errors). In general, this is not possible with real numbers, and when solving practical problems such numbers are rounded to an appropriate number of digits. In this section we shall review the methods of recording numbers, obtain estimates for the effect of rounding errors in elementary calculations and discuss the implementation of arithmetic on computers.

1.5.1 Rounding, decimal places and significant figures

The Fundamental Laws of Arithmetic are, of course, independent of the choice of representation of the numbers. Similarly, the representation of irrational numbers will always be incomplete. Because of these numbers and because some rational numbers have recurring representations (whether the representation of a particular rational number is recurring or not will of course depend on the number base used – see Example 1.2d), any arithmetical calculation will contain errors caused by truncation. In practical problems it is usually known how many figures are meaningful, and the numbers are 'rounded' accordingly. In the decimal representation, for example, the numbers are approximated by the closest decimal number with some prescribed number of figures after the decimal point. Thus, to two decimal places (dp),

$$\pi = 3.14 \quad \text{and} \quad \tfrac{5}{12} = 0.42$$

and to five decimal places

$$\pi = 3.141\,59 \quad \text{and} \quad \tfrac{5}{12} = 0.416\,67$$

Normally this is abbreviated to

$$\pi = 3.141\,59 \text{ (5dp)} \quad \text{and} \quad \tfrac{5}{12} = 0.416\,67 \text{ (5dp)}$$

Similarly

$$\sqrt{2} = 1.4142 \text{ (4dp)} \quad \text{and} \quad \tfrac{2}{3} = 0.667 \text{ (3dp)}$$

In hand computation, by convention, when shortening a number ending with a five we 'round to the even'. For example,

$$1.2345 \quad \text{and} \quad 1.2335$$

are both represented by 1.234 to three decimal places. In contrast, most calculators and computers would 'round up' in the ambiguous case, giving 1.2345 and 1.2335 as 1.235 and 1.234 respectively.

Any number occurring in practical computation will either be given an error bound or be correct to within half a unit in the least significant figure (sf). For example

$$\pi = 3.14 \pm 0.005 \quad \text{or} \quad \pi = 3.14$$

Any number given in scientific or mathematical tables observes this convention. Thus

$$g_0 = 9.806\,65$$

implies

$$g_0 = 9.806\,65 \pm 0.000\,005$$

that is,

$$9.806\,645 < g_0 < 9.806\,655$$

as illustrated in Figure 1.29.

Figure 1.29

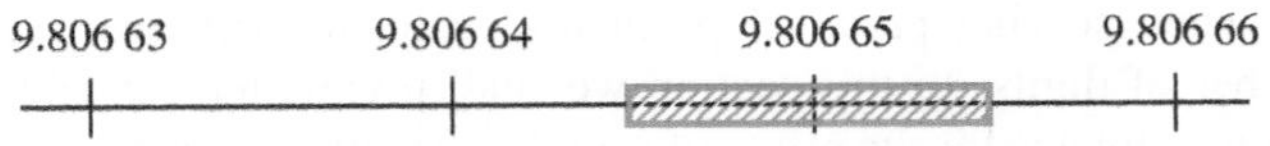

Sometimes the decimal notation may create a false impression of accuracy. When we write that the distance of the Earth from the Sun is ninety-three million miles, we mean that the distance is nearer to 93 000 000 than to 94 000 000 or to 92 000 000, not that it is nearer to 93 000 000 than to 93 000 001 or to 92 999 999. This possible misinterpretation of numerical data is avoided by either stating the number of significant figures, giving an error estimate or using scientific notation. In this example the distance d miles is given in the forms

$$d = 93\,000\,000 \text{ (2sf)}$$

or

$$d = 93\,000\,000 \pm 500\,000$$

or

$$d = 9.3 \times 10^7$$

Notice how information about accuracy is discarded by the rounding-off process. The value ninety-three million miles is actually correct to within fifty thousand miles, while the convention about rounded numbers would imply an error bound of five hundred thousand.

The number of significant figures tells us about the relative accuracy of a number when it is related to a measurement. Thus a number given to 3sf is relatively ten times more accurate than one given to 2sf. The number of decimal places, dp, merely tells us the number of digits including leading zeros after the decimal point. Thus

2.321 and 0.000 059 71

both have 4sf, while the former has 3dp and the latter 8dp.

It is not clear how many significant figures a number like 3200 has. It might be 2, 3 or 4. To avoid this ambiguity it must be written in the form 3.2×10^3 (when it is correct to 2sf) or 3.20×10^3 (3sf) or 3.200×10^3 (4sf). This is usually called **scientific notation**. It is widely used to represent numbers that are very large or very small. Essentially, a number x is written in the form

$$x = a \times 10^n$$

where $1 \leqslant |a| < 10$ and n is an integer. Thus the mass of an electron at rest is 9.11×10^{-28} g, while the velocity of light in a vacuum is $2.9978 \times 10^{10}\,\text{cm s}^{-1}$.

Example 1.43 Express the number 150.4152

(a) correct to 1, 2 and 3 dp; (b) correct to 1, 2 and 3 sf.

Solution (a)

$$\begin{aligned} 150.4152 &= 150.4 && \text{(1dp)} \\ &= 150.42 && \text{(2dp)} \\ &= 150.415 && \text{(3dp)} \end{aligned}$$

(b)

$$\begin{aligned} 150.4152 &= 1.504\,152 \times 10^2 \\ &= 2 \times 10^2 && \text{(1sf)} \\ &= 1.5 \times 10^2 && \text{(2sf)} \\ &= 1.50 \times 10^3 && \text{(3sf)} \end{aligned}$$

1.5.2 Estimating the effect of rounding errors

Numerical data obtained experimentally will often contain rounding errors due to the limited accuracy of measuring instruments. Also, because irrational numbers and some rational numbers do not have a terminating decimal representation, arithmetical operations inevitably contain errors arising from rounding off. The effect of such errors can accumulate in an arithmetical procedure and good engineering computations will include an estimate for it. This process has become more important with the widespread use of computers. When users are isolated from the computational chore, they often fail to develop a sense of the limits of accuracy of an answer. In this section we shall develop the basic ideas for such sensitivity in analyses of calculations.

Example 1.44 Compute

(a) $3.142 + 4.126$ (b) $5.164 - 2.341$ (c) 235.12×0.531

Calculate estimates for the effects of rounding errors in each answer and give the answer as a correctly rounded number.

Solution (a) $3.142 + 4.126 = 7.268$

Because of the convention about rounded numbers, 3.142 represents all the numbers a between 3.1415 and 3.1425, and 4.126 represents all the numbers b between 4.1255 and 4.1265. Thus if a and b are correctly rounded numbers, their sum $a + b$ lies between $c_1 = 7.2670$ and $c_2 = 7.2690$. Rounding c_1 and c_2 to 3dp gives $c_1 = 7.267$ and $c_2 = 7.269$. Since these disagree, we cannot give an answer to 3dp. Rounding c_1 and c_2 to 2dp gives $c_1 = 7.27$ and $c_2 = 7.27$. Since these agree, we can give the answer to 2dp; thus $a + b = 7.27$, as shown in Figure 1.30.

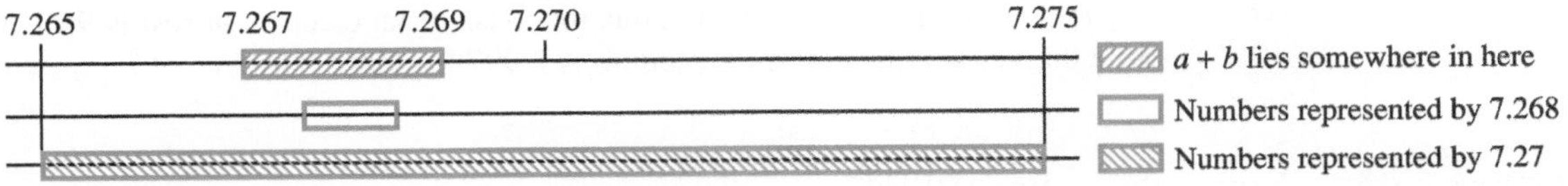

Figure 1.30

(b) $5.164 - 2.341 = 2.823$

Applying the same 'worst case' analysis to this implies that the difference lies between $5.1635 - 2.3415$ and $5.1645 - 2.3405$, that is, between 2.8220 and 2.8240. Thus the answer should be written 2.823 ± 0.001 or, as a correctly rounded number, 2.82.

(c) $235.12 \times 0.531 = 124.848\,72$

Clearly, writing an answer with so many decimal places is unjustified if we are using rounded numbers, but how many decimal places are sensible? Using the 'worst case' analysis again, we deduce that the product lies between 235.115×0.5305 and 235.125×0.5315, that is, between $c_1 = 124.728\,507\,5$ and $c_2 = 124.968\,937\,5$. Thus the answer should be written 124.85 ± 0.13. In this example, because of the place where the number occurs on the number line, c_1 and c_2 only agree when we round them to 3sf (0dp). Thus the product as a correctly rounded number is 125.

A competent computation will contain within it estimates of the effect of rounding errors. Analysing the effect of such errors for complicated expressions has to be approached systematically.

Definitions

(a) The **error** in a value is defined by

$$\text{error} = \text{approximate value} - \text{true value}$$

This is sometimes termed the dead error. Notice that the true value equals the approximate value minus the error.

(b) Similarly the **correction** is defined by

$$\text{true value} = \text{approximate value} + \text{correction}$$

so that

$$\text{correction} = -\text{error}$$

(c) The **error modulus** is the size of the error, |error|, and the **error bound** (or **absolute error bound**) is the maximum possible error modulus.

(d) The **relative error** is the ratio of the size of the error to the size of the true value:

$$\text{relative error} = \left|\frac{\text{error}}{\text{value}}\right|$$

The **relative error bound** is the maximum possible relative error.

(e) The **per cent error** (or percentage error) is 100 × relative error and the **per cent error bound** is the maximum possible per cent error.

In some contexts we think of the true value as an approximation and a remainder. In such cases the remainder is given by

$$\begin{aligned}\text{remainder} &= -\text{error}\\ &= \text{correction}\end{aligned}$$

Example 1.45

Give the absolute and relative error bounds of the following correctly rounded numbers

(a) 29.92 (b) −0.015 23 (c) 3.9×10^{10}

Solution

(a) The number 29.92 is given to 2dp, which implies that it represents a number within the domain 29.92 ± 0.005. Thus its absolute error bound is 0.005, half a unit of the least significant figure, and its relative error bound is 0.005/29.92 or 0.000 17.

(b) The absolute error bound of −0.015 23 is half a unit of the least significant figure, that is, 0.000 005. Notice that it is a positive quantity. Its relative error bound is 0.000 005/0.015 23 or 0.000 33.

(c) The absolute error bound of 3.9×10^{10} is $0.05 \times 10^{10} = 5 \times 10^8$ and its relative error bound is 0.05/3.9 or 0.013.

Usually, because we do not know the true values, we estimate the effects of error in a calculation in terms of the error bounds, the 'worst case' analysis illustrated in Example 1.44. The error bound of a value v is denoted by ε_v.

Consider, first, the sum $c = a + b$. When we add together the two rounded numbers a and b their sum will inherit a rounding error from both a and b. The true value of a lies between $a - \varepsilon_a$ and $a + \varepsilon_a$ and the true value of b lies between $b - \varepsilon_b$ and $b + \varepsilon_b$. Thus the smallest value that the true value of c can have is $a - \varepsilon_a + b - \varepsilon_b$, and its largest possible value is $a + \varepsilon_a + b + \varepsilon_b$. (Remember that ε_a and ε_b are positive.) Thus $c = a + b$ has an error bound

$$\varepsilon_c = \varepsilon_a + \varepsilon_b$$

as illustrated in Figure 1.31. A similar 'worst case' analysis shows that the difference $d = a - b$ has an error bound that is the sum of the error bounds of a and b:

$$d = a - b, \qquad \varepsilon_d = \varepsilon_a + \varepsilon_b$$

Figure 1.31

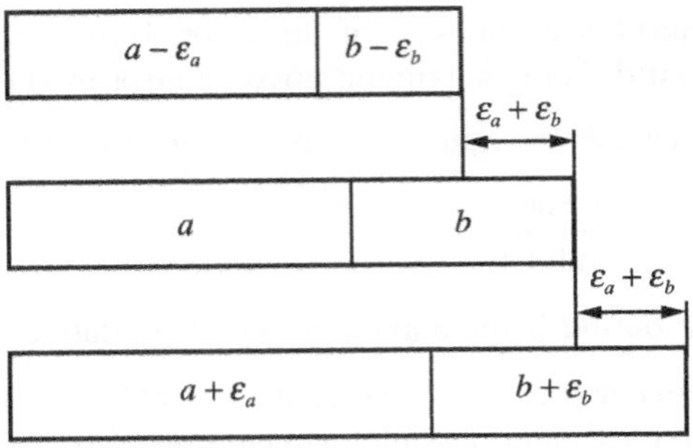

Thus for both addition and subtraction the error bound of the result is the sum of the individual error bounds.

Next consider the product $p = a \times b$, where a and b are positive numbers. The smallest possible value of p will be equal to the product of the least possible values of a and b; that is,

$$p > (a - \varepsilon_a) \times (b - \varepsilon_b)$$

Similarly

$$p < (a + \varepsilon_a) \times (b + \varepsilon_b)$$

Thus, on multiplying out the brackets, we obtain

$$ab - a\varepsilon_b - b\varepsilon_a + \varepsilon_a\varepsilon_b < p < ab + a\varepsilon_b + b\varepsilon_a + \varepsilon_a\varepsilon_b$$

Ignoring the very small term $\varepsilon_a\varepsilon_b$, we obtain an estimate for the error bound of the product:

$$\varepsilon_p = a\varepsilon_b + b\varepsilon_a, \qquad p = a \times b$$

Dividing both sides of the equation by p, we obtain

$$\frac{\varepsilon_p}{p} = \frac{\varepsilon_a}{a} + \frac{\varepsilon_b}{b}$$

Now the relative error of a is defined as the ratio of the error in a to the size of a. The above equation connects the relative error bounds for a, b and p:

$$r_p = r_a + r_b$$

Here $r_a = \varepsilon_a/|a|$ allowing for a to be negative, and so on.

A similar worst case analysis for the quotient $q = a/b$ leads to the estimate

$$r_q = r_a + r_b$$

Thus for both multiplication and division, the relative error bound of the result is the sum of the individual relative error bounds.

These elementary rules for estimating error bounds can be combined to obtain more general results. For example, consider $z = x^2$; then $r_z = 2r_x$. In general, if $z = x^y$, where x is a rounded number and y is exact, then

$$r_z = yr_x$$

Example 1.46 Evaluate 13.92×5.31 and $13.92 \div 5.31$.

Assuming that these values are correctly rounded numbers, calculate error bounds for each answer and write them as correctly rounded numbers which have the greatest possible number of significant digits.

Solution $13.92 \times 5.31 = 73.9152$; $13.92 \div 5.31 = 2.621\,468\,927$

Let $a = 13.92$ and $b = 5.31$, then $r_a = 0.000\,36$ and $r_b = 0.000\,94$, so that $a \times b$ and $a \div b$ have relative error bounds $0.000\,36 + 0.000\,94 = 0.0013$. We obtain the absolute error bound of $a \times b$ by multiplying the relative error bound by $a \times b$. Thus the absolute error bound of $a \times b$ is $0.0013 \times 73.9152 = 0.0961$. Similarly, the absolute error bound of $a \div b$ is $0.0013 \times 2.6215 = 0.0034$. Hence the values of $a \times b$ and $a \div b$ lie in the error intervals

$$73.9152 - 0.0961 < a \times b < 73.9152 + 0.0961$$

and

$$2.6215 - 0.0034 < a \div b < 2.6215 + 0.0034$$

Thus $73.8191 < a \times b < 74.0113$ and $2.6181 < a \div b < 2.6249$.

From these inequalities we can deduce the correctly rounded values of $a \times b$ and $a \div b$:

$$a \times b = 74 \quad \text{and} \quad a \div b = 2.62$$

and we see how the rounding convention discards information. In a practical context, it would probably be more helpful to write:

$$73.81 < a \times b < 74.02$$

and

$$2.618 < a \div b < 2.625$$

Example 1.47 Evaluate

$$6.721 - \frac{4.931 \times 71.28}{89.45}$$

Assuming that all the values given are correctly rounded numbers, calculate an error bound for your answer and write it as a correctly rounded number.

Solution Using a calculator, the answer obtained is

$$6.721 - \frac{4.931 \times 71.28}{89.45} = 2.791\,635\,216$$

To estimate the effect of the rounding error of the data, we first draw up a tree diagram representing the order in which the calculation is performed. Remember that +, −, ×

Figure 1.32

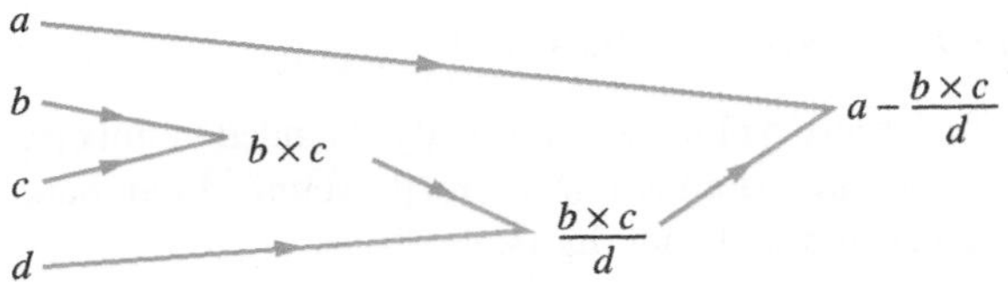

(a)

Label	*Value*	*Absolute error bound*	*Relative error bound*
b	4.931	→ 0.0005	→ $0.0005/4.931 = 0.0001$
c	71.28	→ 0.005	→ $0.005/71.28 = 0.000\,07$ +
p	351.481 68		0.000 17
d	89.45	→ 0.005	→ $0.005/89.45 = 0.000\,06$ +
q	3.929 364 784	$0.0009 = 0.000\,23 \times 3.9$	← 0.000 23
a	6.721	0.0005 +	
e	2.791 635 216	0.0014	

(b)

and ÷ are binary operations, so only one operation can be performed at each step. Here we are evaluating

$$a - \frac{b \times c}{d} = e$$

We calculate this as $b \times c = p$, then $p \div d = q$ and then $a - q = e$, as shown in Figure 1.32(a). We set this calculation out in a table as shown in Figure 1.32(b), where the arrows show the flow of the error analysis calculation. Thus the value of e lies between 2.790 235 … and 2.793 035 … , and the answer may be written as 2.7916 ± 0.0015 or as the correctly rounded number 2.79.

The calculations shown in Figure 1.32 indicate the way in which errors may accumulate in simple arithmetical calculations. The error bounds given are rarely extreme and their behaviour is 'random'. This is discussed later in Example 13.31 in the work on Statistics.

1.5.3 Exercises

46 State the numbers of decimal places and significant figures of the following correctly rounded numbers:

(a) 980.665 (b) 9.11×10^{-28}

(c) 2.9978×10^{10} (d) 2.00×10^{33}

(e) 1.759×10^{7} (f) 6.67×10^{-8}

47 In a right-angled triangle the height is measured as 1 m and the base as 2 m, both measurements being accurate to the nearest centimetre. Using Pythagoras' theorem, the hypotenuse is calculated as 2.236 07 m. Is this a sensible deduction? What other source of error will occur?

48 Determine the error bound and relative error bound for x, where

(a) $x = 35\text{ min} \pm 5\text{ s}$

(b) $x = 35\text{ min} \pm 4\%$

(c) $x = 0.58$ and x is correctly rounded to 2dp.

49 A value is calculated to be 12.9576, with a relative error bound of 0.0003. Calculate its absolute error bound and give the value as a correctly rounded number with as many significant digits as possible.

50 Using exact arithmetic, compute the values of the expressions below. Assuming that all the numbers given are correctly rounded, find absolute and relative error bounds for each term in the expressions and for your answers. Give the answers as correctly rounded numbers.

(a) $1.316 - 5.713 + 8.010$

(b) 2.51×1.01

(c) $19.61 + 21.53 - 18.67$

51 Evaluate $12.42 \times 5.675/15.63$, giving your answer as a correctly rounded number with the greatest number of significant figures.

52 Evaluate

$$a + b, \quad a - b, \quad a \times b, \quad a/b$$

for $a = 4.99$ and $b = 5.01$. Give absolute and relative error bounds for each answer.

53 Complete the table below for the computation

$$9.21 + (3.251 - 3.115)/0.112$$

and give the result as the correctly rounded answer with the greatest number of significant figures.

Label	*Value*	*Absolute error bound*	*Relative error bound*
a	3.251		
b	3.115		
$a - b$			
c	0.112		
$(a - b)/c$			
d	9.21		
$d + (a - b)/c$			

54 Evaluate $uv/(u + v)$ for $u = 1.135$ and $v = 2.332$, expressing your answer as a correctly rounded number.

55 Working to 4dp, evaluate

$$E = 1 - 1.65 + \tfrac{1}{2}(1.65)^2 - \tfrac{1}{6}(1.65)^3 + \tfrac{1}{24}(1.65)^4$$

(a) by evaluating each term and then summing,

(b) by 'nested multiplication'

$$E = 1 + 1.65(-1 + 1.65(\tfrac{1}{2} + 1.65(-\tfrac{1}{6} + \tfrac{1}{24}(1.65))))$$

Assuming that the number 1.65 is correctly rounded and that all other numbers are exact, obtain error bounds for both answers.

1.5.4 Computer arithmetic

The error estimate outlined in Example 1.44 is a 'worst case' analysis. The actual error will usually be considerably less than the error bound. For example, the maximum error in the sum of 100 numbers, each rounded to three decimal places, is 0.05. This would only occur in the unlikely event that each value has the greatest possible rounding error. In contrast, the chance of the error being as large as one-tenth of this is only about 1 in 20.

When calculations are performed on a computer the situation is modified a little by the limited space available for number storage. Arithmetic is usually performed using floating-point notation. Each number x is stored in the **normal form**

$$x = (\text{sign})b^n(a)$$

where b is the number base, usually 2 or 16, n is an integer, and the **mantissa** a is a proper fraction with a fixed number of digits such that $1/b \leqslant a < 1$. As there are a limited number of digits available to represent the mantissa, calculations will involve intermediate rounding. As a consequence, the order in which a calculation is performed may affect the outcome – in other words the Fundamental Laws of Arithmetic may no longer hold! We shall illustrate this by means of an exaggerated example for a small computer using a decimal representation whose capacity for recording numbers is limited to four figures only. In large-scale calculations in engineering such considerations are sometimes important.

Consider a computer with storage capacity for real numbers limited to four figures; each number is recorded in the form $(\pm)10^n(a)$ where the exponent n is an integer, $0.1 \leqslant a < 1$ and a has four digits. For example,

$$\pi = +10^1(0.3142)$$

$$-\tfrac{1}{3} = -10^0(0.3333)$$

$$5764 = +10^4(0.5764)$$

$$-0.000\,971\,3 = -10^{-3}(0.9713)$$

$$5\,764\,213 = +10^7(0.5764)$$

Addition is performed by first adjusting the exponent of the smaller number to that of the larger, then adding the numbers, which now have the same multiplying power of 10, and lastly truncating the number to four digits. Thus $7.182 + 0.053\,81$ becomes

$$\begin{aligned} +10^1(0.7182) + 10^{-1}(0.5381) &= 10^1(0.7182) + 10^1(0.005\,381) \\ &= 10^1(0.723\,581) \\ &= 10^1(0.7236) \end{aligned}$$

With $a = 31.68$, $b = -31.54$ and $c = 83.21$, the two calculations $(a + b) + c$ and $(a + c) + b$ yield different results on this computer:

$$(a + b) + c = 83.35, \qquad (a + c) + b = 83.34$$

Notice how the symbol '=' is being used in the examples above. Sometimes it means 'equals to 4sf'. This computerized arithmetic is usually called **floating-point arithmetic**, and the number of digits used is normally specified.

1.5.5 Exercises

56 Two possible methods of adding five numbers are

$$(((a + b) + c) + d) + e$$

and

$$(((e + d) + c) + b) + a$$

Using 4dp floating-point arithmetic, evaluate the sum

$$10^1(0.1000) + 10^1(0.1000) - 10^0(0.5000) + 10^0(0.1667) + 10^{-1}(0.4167)$$

by both methods. Explain any discrepancy in the results.

57 Find $(10^{-2}(0.3251) \times 10^{-5}(0.2011))$ and $(10^{-1}(0.2168) \div 10^2(0.3211))$ using 4-digit floating-point arithmetic.

58 Find the relative error resulting when 4-digit floating-point arithmetic is used to evaluate

$$10^4(0.1000) + 10^2(0.1234) - 10^4(0.1013)$$

1.6 Engineering applications

In this section we illustrate through two examples how some of the results developed in this chapter may be used in an engineering application.

Example 1.48

A continuous belt of length L m passes over two wheels of radii r and R m with their centres a distance l m apart, as illustrated in Figure 1.33. The belt is sufficiently tight for any sag to be negligible. Show that L is given approximately by

$$L \approx 2[l^2 - (R - r)^2]^{1/2} + \pi(R + r)$$

Find the error inherent in this approximation and obtain error bounds for L given the rounded data $R = 1.5$, $r = 0.5$ and $l = 3.5$.

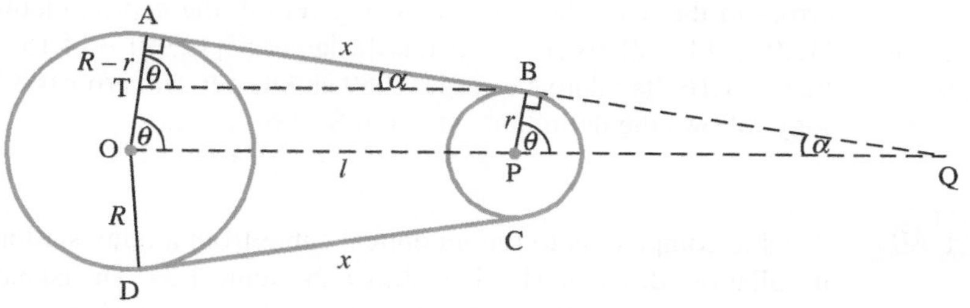

Figure 1.33 Continuous belt of Example 1.48.

Solution The length of the belt consists of the straight sections AB and CD and the wraps round the wheels $\widehat{BC}$ and $\widehat{DA}$. From Figure 1.33 it is clear that BT = OP = l and ∠OAB is a right-angle. Also, AT = AO − OT and OT = PB so that AT = $R - r$. Applying Pythagoras' theorem to the triangle TAB gives

$$AB^2 = l^2 - (R - r)^2$$

Since the length of an arc of a circle is the product of its radius and the angle (measured in radians) subtended at the centre (see 2.17), the length of wrap $\widehat{DA}$ is given by

$$(2\pi - 2\theta)R$$

where the angle is measured in radians. By geometry, $\theta = \frac{\pi}{2} - \alpha$, so that

$$\widehat{DA} = \pi R + 2R\alpha$$

Similarly, the arc $\widehat{BC} = \pi r - 2r\alpha$. Thus the total length of the belt is

$$L = 2[l^2 - (R - r)^2]^{1/2} + \pi(R + r) + 2(R - r)\alpha$$

Taking the length to be given approximately by

$$L \approx 2[l^2 - (R - r)^2]^{1/2} + \pi(R + r)$$

the error of the approximation is given by $-2(R - r)\alpha$, where the angle α is expressed in radians (remember that error = approximation − true value). The angle α is found by elementary trigonometry, since $\sin \alpha = (R - r)/l$. (Trigonometric functions will be reviewed in Section 2.6.)

For the (rounded) data given, we deduce, following the procedures of Section 1.5.2, that for $R = 1.5$, $r = 0.5$ and $l = 3.5$ we have an error interval for α of

$$\left[\sin^{-1}\left(\frac{1.45 - 0.55}{3.55}\right), \sin^{-1}\left(\frac{1.55 - 0.45}{3.45}\right)\right] = [0.256, 0.325]$$

Thus $\alpha = 0.29 \pm 0.035$, and similarly $2(R - r)\alpha = 0.572 \pm 0.111$.

Evaluating the approximation for L gives

$$2[l^2 - (R - r)^2]^{1/2} + \pi(R + r) = 12.991 \pm 0.478$$

and the corresponding value for L is

$$L = 13.563 \pm 0.589$$

Thus, allowing for both the truncation error of the approximation and for the rounding errors in the data, the value 12.991 given by the approximation has an error interval [12.974, 14.152]. Its error bound is the larger of $|12.991 - 14.152|$ and $|12.991 - 12.974|$, that is, 1.16. Its relative error is 0.089 and its per cent error is 8.9%, where the terminology follows the definitions given in Section 1.5.2.

Example 1.49

A cable company is to run an optical cable from a relay station, A, on the shore to an installation, B, on an island, as shown in Figure 1.34. The island is 6 km from the shore at its nearest point, P, and A is 9 km from P measured along the shore. It is proposed to run the cable from A along the shoreline and then underwater to the island. It costs 25% more to run the cable underwater than along the shoreline. At what point should the cable leave the shore in order to minimize the total cost?

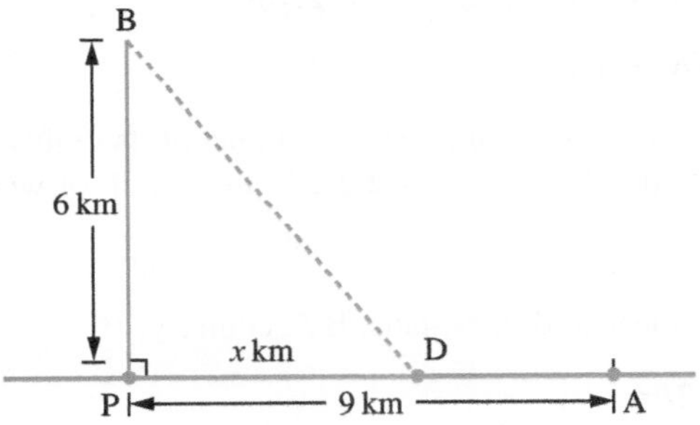

Figure 1.34 Optical cable of Example 1.49.

Solution Optimization problems frequently occur in engineering and technology and often their solution is found algebraically.

If the cable leaves the shore at D, a distance x km from P, then the underwater distance is $\sqrt{(x^2 + 36)}$ km and the overland distance is $(9 - x)$ km, assuming $0 < x < 9$. If the overland cost of laying the cable is £c per kilometre, then the total cost £C is given by

$$C(x) = [(9 - x) + 1.25\sqrt{(x^2 + 36)}]c$$

We wish to find the value of x, $0 \leqslant x \leqslant 9$, which minimizes C. To do this we first change the variable x by substituting

$$x = 3\left(t - \frac{1}{t}\right)$$

such that $x^2 + 36$ becomes a perfect square:

$$x^2 + 36 = 36 + 9(t^2 - 2 + 1/t^2)$$
$$= 9(t + 1/t)^2$$

Hence C(x) becomes

$$C(t) = [9 - 3(t - 1/t) + 3.75(t + 1/t)]c$$
$$= [9 + 0.75(t + 9/t)]c$$

Using the arithmetic–geometric inequality $x + y \geqslant 2\sqrt{(xy)}$, see (1.4d), we know that

$$t + \frac{9}{t} \geqslant 6$$

and that the equality occurs where $t = 9/t$, that is where $t = 3$.

Thus the minimum cost is achieved where $t = 3$ and $x = 3(3 - 1/3) = 8$. Hence the cable should leave the shore after laying the cable 1 km from its starting point at A.

1.7 Review exercises (1–25)

1 (a) A formula in the theory of ventilation is

$$Q = \frac{\sqrt{H}}{K}\sqrt{\frac{A^2D^2}{A^2 + D^2}}$$

Express A in terms of the other symbols.

(b) Solve the equation

$$\frac{1}{x+2} - \frac{2}{x} = \frac{3}{x-1}$$

2 Factorize the following:

(a) $ax - 2x - a + 2$

(b) $a^2 - b^2 + 2bc - c^2$

(c) $4k^2 + 4kl + l^2 - 9m^2$

(d) $p^2 - 3pq + 2q^2$

(e) $l^2 + lm + ln + mn$

3 (a) Two small pegs are 8 cm apart on the same horizontal line. An inextensible string of length 16 cm has equal masses fastened at either end and is placed symmetrically over the pegs. The middle point of the string is pulled down vertically until it is in line with the masses. How far does each mass rise?

(b) Find an 'acceptable' value of x to three decimal places if the shaded area in Figure 1.35 is 10 square units.

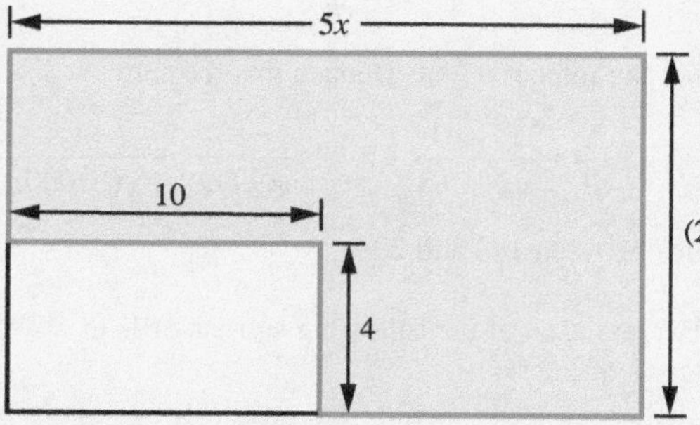

Figure 1.35 Shaded area of Question 3(b).

4 The impedance Z ohms of a circuit containing a resistance R ohms, inductance L henries and capacity C farads, when the frequency of the oscillation is n per second, is given by

$$Z = \sqrt{\left(R^2 + \left(2\pi nL - \frac{1}{2\pi nC}\right)^2\right)}$$

(a) Make L the subject of this formula.

(b) If $n = 50$, $R = 15$ and $C = 10^{-4}$ show that there are two values of L which make $Z = 20$ but only one value of L which will make $Z = 100$. Find the values of Z in each case to two decimal places.

5 Expand out (a) and (b) and rationalize (c) to (e).

(a) $(3\sqrt{2} - 2\sqrt{3})^2$

(b) $(\sqrt{5} + 7\sqrt{3})(2\sqrt{5} - 3\sqrt{3})$

(c) $\dfrac{4 + 3\sqrt{2}}{5 + \sqrt{2}}$

(d) $\dfrac{\sqrt{3} + \sqrt{2}}{2 - \sqrt{3}}$

(e) $\dfrac{1}{1 + \sqrt{2} - \sqrt{3}}$

6 Find integers m and n such that

$$\sqrt{(11 + 2\sqrt{30})} = \sqrt{m} + \sqrt{n}$$

7 Show that

$$\sqrt{(n + 1)} - \sqrt{n} = \frac{1}{\sqrt{(n + 1)} + \sqrt{n}}$$

and deduce that

$$\sqrt{(n + 1)} - \sqrt{n} < \frac{1}{2\sqrt{n}} < \sqrt{n} - \sqrt{(n - 1)}$$

for any integer $n \geqslant 1$. Deduce that the sum

$$\frac{1}{\sqrt{1}} + \frac{1}{\sqrt{2}} + \frac{1}{\sqrt{3}} + \ldots + \frac{1}{\sqrt{(9999)}} + \frac{1}{\sqrt{(10\,000)}}$$

lies between 198 and 200.

8 Express each of the following subsets of $\mathbb{R}$ in terms of intervals:

(a) $\{x : 4x^2 - 3 < 4x, x \text{ in } \mathbb{R}\}$

(b) $\{x : 1/(x + 2) > 2/(x - 1), x \text{ in } \mathbb{R}\}$

(c) $\{x : |x + 1| < 2, x \text{ in } \mathbb{R}\}$

(d) $\{x : |x + 1| < 1 + \frac{1}{2}x, x \text{ in } \mathbb{R}\}$

9 It is known that of all plane curves that enclose a given area, the circle has the least perimeter. Show that if a plane curve of perimeter L encloses an area A then $4\pi A \leqslant L^2$. Verify this inequality for a square and a semicircle.

10 The arithmetic–geometric inequality

$$\frac{x + y}{2} \geqslant \sqrt{xy}$$

implies

$$\left(\frac{x + y}{2}\right)^2 \geqslant xy$$

Use the substitution $x = \frac{1}{2}(a + b)$, $y = \frac{1}{2}(c + d)$, where a, b, c and $d > 0$, to show that

$$\left(\frac{a + b}{2}\right)\left(\frac{c + d}{2}\right) \leqslant \left(\frac{a + b + c + d}{4}\right)^2$$

and hence that

$$\left(\frac{a + b}{2}\right)^2\left(\frac{c + d}{2}\right)^2 \leqslant \left(\frac{a + b + c + d}{4}\right)^4$$

By applying the arithmetic–geometric inequality to the first two terms of this inequality, deduce that

$$abcd \leqslant \left(\frac{a + b + c + d}{4}\right)^4$$

and hence

$$\frac{a + b + c + d}{4} \geqslant \sqrt[4]{abcd}$$

11 Show that if $a < b$, $b > 0$ and $c > 0$ then

$$\frac{a}{b} < \frac{a + c}{b + c} < 1$$

Obtain a similar inequality for the case $a > b$.

12 (a) If $n = n_1 + n_2 + n_3$ show that

$$\binom{n}{n_1}\binom{n_2 + n_3}{n_2} = \frac{n!}{n_1!n_2!n_3!}$$

(This represents the number of ways in which n objects may be divided into three groups containing respectively n_1, n_2 and n_3 objects.)

(b) Expand the following expressions

(i) $\left(1 - \frac{x}{2}\right)^5$ (ii) $(3 - 2x)^6$

13 (a) Evaluate $\sum_{n=-2}^{3} [n^{n+1} + 3(-1)^n]$

(b) A square grid of dots may be divided up into a set of L-shaped groups as illustrated in Figure 1.36.

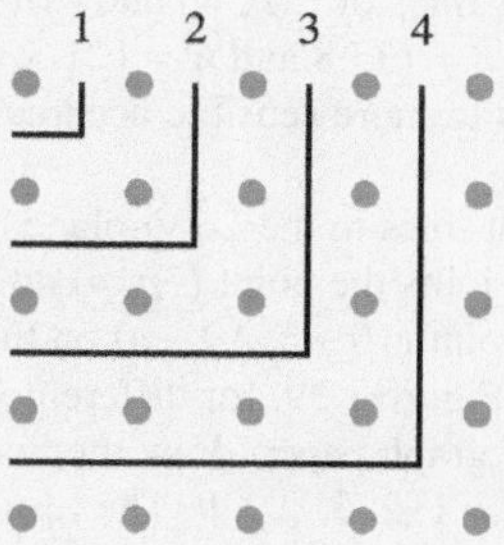

Figure 1.36

How many dots are inside the third L shape? How many extra dots are needed to extend the 3 by 3 square to one of side 4 by 4? How many dots are needed to extend an $(r - 1)$ by $(r - 1)$ square to one of size r by r? Denoting this number by P_r, use a geometric argument to obtain an expression for $\sum_{r=1}^{n} P_r$ and verify your conclusion by direct calculation in the case $n = 10$.

14 Find the equations of the straight line

(a) which passes through the points (–6, –11) and (2, 5);

(b) which passes through the point (4, –1) and has gradient $\frac{1}{3}$;

(c) which has the same intercept on the y axis as the line in (b) and is parallel to the line in (a).

15 Find the equation of the circle which touches the y axis at the point (0, 3) and passes through the point (1, 0).

16 Find the centres and radii of the following circles:

(a) $x^2 + y^2 + 2x - 4y + 1 = 0$

(b) $4x^2 - 4x + 4y^2 + 12y + 9 = 0$

(c) $9x^2 + 6x + 9y^2 - 6y = 25$

17 For each of the two parabolas

(i) $y^2 = 8x + 4y - 12$, and

(ii) $x^2 + 12y + 4x = 8$

determine

(a) the coordinates of the vertex,

(b) the coordinates of the focus,

(c) the equation of the directrix,

(d) the equation of the axis of symmetry.

Sketch each parabola.

18 Find the coordinates of the centre and foci of the ellipse with equation

$$25x^2 + 16y^2 - 100x - 256y + 724 = 0$$

What are the coordinates of its vertices and the equations of its directrices? Sketch the ellipse.

19 Find the duodecimal equivalent of the decimal number 10.386 23.

20 Show that if $y = x^{1/2}$ then the relative error bound of y is one-half that of x. Hence complete the table in Figure 1.37.

	Value	*Absolute error bound*		*Relative error bound*
a	7.01	0.005	⟶	0.0007
$\sqrt{a}$	2.6476	0.0009	⟵	0.000 35
b	52.13			
$\sqrt{b}$				
c	0.010 11			
$\sqrt{c}$				
d	5.631×10^{11}			
$\sqrt{d}$				

Correctly rounded values	$\sqrt{a}$	$\sqrt{b}$	$\sqrt{c}$	$\sqrt{d}$
	2.65			

Figure 1.37

21 Assuming that all the numbers given are correctly rounded, calculate the positive root together with its error bound of the quadratic equation

$$1.4x^2 + 5.7x - 2.3 = 0$$

Give your answer also as a correctly rounded number.

22 The quantities f, u and v are connected by

$$\frac{1}{f} = \frac{1}{u} + \frac{1}{v}$$

Find f when $u = 3.00$ and $v = 4.00$ are correctly rounded numbers. Compare the error bounds obtained for f when

(a) it is evaluated by taking the reciprocal of the sum of the reciprocals of u and v,

(b) it is evaluated using the formula

$$f = \frac{uv}{u+v}$$

23 If the number whose decimal representation is 14 732 has the representation $152\,112_b$ to base b, what is b?

24 A milk carton has capacity 2 pints (1136 ml). It is made from a rectangular waxed card using the net shown in Figure 1.38. Show that the total area A (mm^2) of card used is given by

$$A(h, w) = (2w + 145)(h + 80)$$

with $hw = 113\,600/7$. Show that

$$A(h, w) = C(h, w) + \frac{308\,400}{7}$$

where $C(h, w) = 145h + 160w$.

Use the arithmetic–geometric inequality to show that

$$C(h, w) \geqslant 2\sqrt{(160w \times 145h)}$$

with equality when $160w = 145h$. Hence show that the minimum values of $C(h, w)$ and $A(h, w)$ are achieved when $h = 133.8$ and $w = 121.3$. Give these answers to more sensible accuracy.

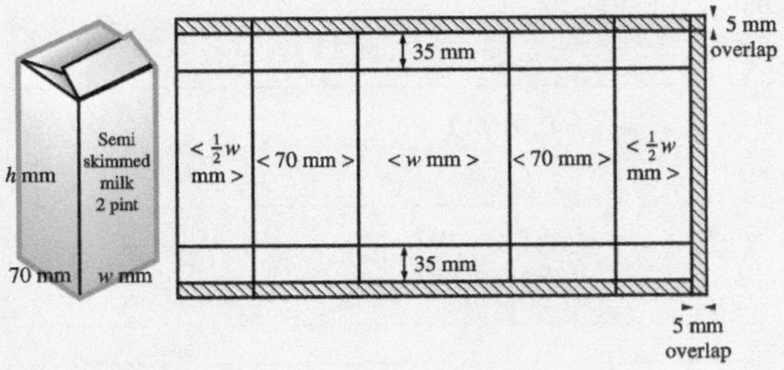

Figure 1.38 Milk carton of Question 24.

25 A family of straight lines in the (x, y)-plane is such that each line joins the point $(-p, p)$ on the line $y = -x$ to the point $(10 - p, 10 - p)$ on the line $y = x$, as shown in Figure 1.39, for different values of p. On a piece of graph paper, draw the lines corresponding to $p = 1, 2, 3, \ldots, 9$. The resulting family is seen to envelop a curve. Show that the line which joins $(-p, p)$ to $(10 - p, 10 - p)$ has equation

$$5y = 5x - px + 10p - p^2$$

Show that two lines of the family pass through the point (x_0, y_0) if $x_0^2 > 20(y_0 - 5)$, but no lines pass through (x_0, y_0) if $x_0^2 < 20(y_0 - 5)$. Deduce that the enveloping curve of the family of straight lines is

$$y = \tfrac{1}{20}x^2 + 5$$

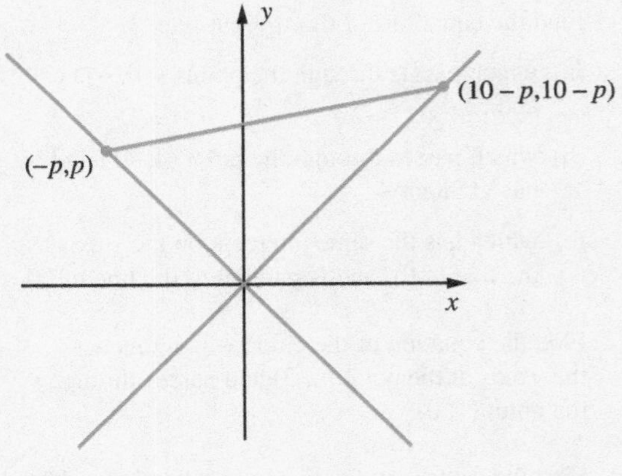

Figure 1.39

2 Functions

Chapter 2 Contents

2.1 Introduction

As we have remarked in the introductory section of Chapter 1, mathematics provides a means of solving the practical problems that occur in engineering. To do this, it uses concepts and techniques that operate on and within the concepts. In this chapter we shall describe the concept of a function – a concept that is both fundamental to mathematics and is also intuitive. We shall make the intuitive idea mathematically precise by formal definitions and is also describe why such formalism is needed for practical problem-solving.

The function concept has taken many centuries to evolve. The intuitive basis for the concept is found in the analysis of cause and effect, which underpins developments in science, technology and commerce. As with many mathematical ideas, many people use the concept in their everyday activities without being aware that they are using mathematics, and many would be surprised if they were told that they were. The abstract manner in which the developed form of the concept is expressed by mathematicians often intimidates learners but the essential idea is very simple. A consequence of the long period of development is that the way in which the concept is described often makes an idiomatic use of words. Ordinary words which in common parlance have many different shades of meaning are used in mathematics with very specific meanings.

The key idea is that of the values of two variable quantities being related. For example, the amount of tax paid depends on the selling price of an item; the deflection of a beam depends on the applied load; the cost of an article varies with the number produced, and so on. Historically, this idea has been expressed in a number of ways. The oldest gave a verbal recipe for calculating the required value. Thus, in the early Middle Ages, a very elaborate verbal recipe was given for calculating the monthly interest payments on a loan which would now be expressed very compactly by a single formula. John Napier, when he developed the logarithm function at the beginning of the seventeenth century, expressed the functional relationship in terms of two particles moving along a straight line. One particle moved with constant velocity and the other with a velocity that depended on its distance from a fixed point on the line. The relationship between the distances travelled by the particles was used to define the logarithms of numbers. This would now be described by the solution of a differential equation. The introduction of algebraic notation led to the representation of functions by algebraic rather than verbal formulae. That produced many theoretical problems. For example, a considerable controversy was caused by Fourier when he used functions that did not have the same algebraic formula for all values of the independent variable. Similarly, the existence of functions that do not have a simple algebraic representation caused considerable difficulties for mathematicians in the early nineteenth century.

2.2 Basic definitions

2.2.1 Concept of a function

The essential idea that flows through all of the developments is that of two quantities whose values are related. One of these variables, the **independent** or **free variable**,

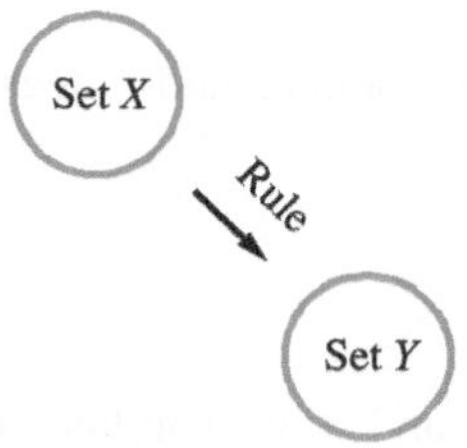

Figure 2.1 Schematic representation of a function.

may take any value in a set of values. The value it actually takes fixes uniquely the value of the second quantity, the **dependent** or **slave variable**. Thus for each value of the independent variable there is one and only one value of the dependent variable. The way in which that value is calculated will vary between functions. Sometimes it will be by means of a formula, sometimes by means of a graph and sometimes by means of a table of values. Here the words 'value' and 'quantity' cover many very different contexts, but in each case what we have is two sets of values X and Y and a rule that assigns to each value x in the set X precisely one value y from the set Y. The elements of X and Y need not be numbers, but the essential idea is that to every x in the set X there corresponds exactly one y in the set Y. Whenever this situation arises we say that there is a **function** f that maps the set X to the set Y. Such a function may be illustrated schematically as in Figure 2.1.

We represent a functional relationship symbolically in two ways: either

$$f{:}x \to y \quad (x \text{ in } X)$$

or

$$y = f(x) \quad (x \text{ in } X)$$

The first emphasizes the fact that a function f associates each element (value) x of X with exactly one element (value) y of Y: it 'maps x to y'. The second method of notation emphasizes the dependence of the elements of Y on the elements of X under the function f. In this case the value or variable appearing within the brackets is known as the **argument** of the function; we might say 'the argument x of a function $f(x)$'. In engineering it is more common to use the second notation $y = f(x)$ and to refer to this as the function $f(x)$, while modern mathematics textbooks prefer the mapping notation, on the grounds that it is less ambiguous. The set X is called the **domain** of the function and the set Y is called its **codomain**. Knowing the domain and codomain is important in computing. We need to know the type of variables, whether they are integers or reals, and their size. When $y = f(x)$, y is said to be the **image** of x under f. The set of all images $y = f(x)$, x in X, is called the **image set** or **range** of f. It is not necessary for all elements y of the codomain set Y to be images under f. We may regard x as being a variable that can be replaced by any element of the set X. The rule giving f is then completely determined if we know $f(x)$, and consequently in engineering it is common to refer to the function as being f (x) rather than f. Likewise we can regard $y = f(x)$ as being a variable. However, while x can freely take any value from the set X, the variable $y = f(x)$ depends on the particular element chosen for x. We therefore refer to x as the **free** or **independent** variable and to y as the **slave** or **dependent** variable. The function $f(x)$ is therefore specified completely by the set of ordered pairs (x, y) for all x in X. For real variables a graphical representation of the function may then be obtained by plotting a graph determined by this set of ordered pairs (x, y), with the independent variable x measured along the horizontal axis and the dependent variable y measured along the vertical axis. Obtaining a good graph by hand is not always easy but there are now available excellent graphics facilities on computers and calculators which assist in the task. Even so, some practice is required to ensure that a good choice of 'drawing window' is selected to obtain a meaningful graph.

Example 2.1 For the functions with formulae below, identify their domains, codomains and ranges and calculate values of $f(2), f(-3)$ and $f(-x)$.

(a) $f(x) = 3x^2 + 1$ (b) $f{:}x \to \sqrt{[(x+4)(3-x)]}$

Solution (a) The formula for $f(x)$ can be evaluated for all real values of x and so we can take a domain which includes all the real numbers, $\mathbb{R}$. The values obtained are also real numbers, so we may take $\mathbb{R}$ as the codomain. The range of $f(x)$ is actually less than $\mathbb{R}$ in this example because the minimum value of $y = 3x^2 + 1$ occurs at $y = 1$ where $x = 0$. Thus the range of f is the set

$$\{x{:}1 \leqslant x, x \text{ in } \mathbb{R}\} = [1, \infty)$$

Notice the convention here that the set is specified using the *dummy* variable x. We could also write $\{y{:}1 \leqslant y, y \text{ in } \mathbb{R}\}$, any letter could be used but conventionally x is used. Using the formula we find that $f(2) = 13$, $f(-3) = 28$ and $f(-x) = 3(-x)^2 + 1 = 3x^2 + 1$.

(b) The formula $f{:}x \to \sqrt{[(x+4)(3-x)]}$ only gives real values for $-4 \leqslant x \leqslant 3$, since we cannot take square roots of negative numbers. Thus the domain of f is $[-4,3]$. Within its domain the function has real values so that its codomain is $\mathbb{R}$ but its range is less than $\mathbb{R}$. The least value of f occurs at $x = -4$ and $x = 3$ when $f(-4) = f(3) = 0$. The largest value of f occurs at $x = -\frac{1}{2}$ when $f(-\frac{1}{2}) = \sqrt{(35)}/2$.

So the range of f in this example is $[0, \sqrt{(35)}/2]$. Using the formula we have $f(2) = \sqrt{6}$, $f(-3) = \sqrt{6}$, $f(-x) = \sqrt{[(4-x)(x+3)]}$.

Example 2.2 The function $y = f(x)$ is given by the minimum diameter y of a circular pipe that can contain x circular pipes of unit diameter, where $x = 1, 2, 3, 4, 5, 6, 7$. Find the domain, codomain and range of $f(x)$.

Solution This function is illustrated in Figure 2.2.

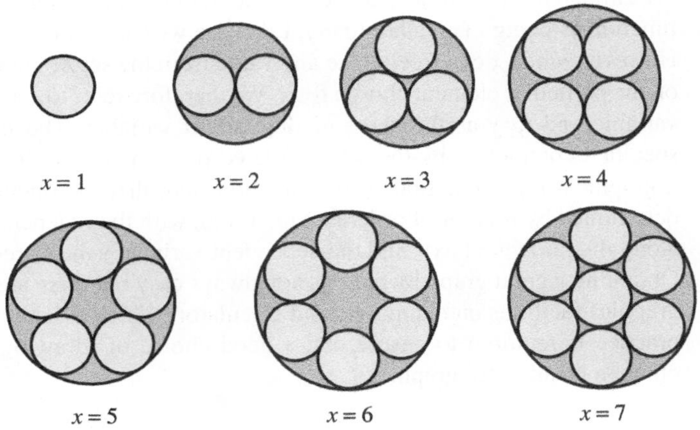

Figure 2.2 Enclosing x circular pipes in a circular pipe.

Here the domain is the set {1, 2, 3, 4, 5, 6, 7} and the codomain is $\mathbb{R}$. Calculating the range is more difficult as there is not a simple algebraic formula relating x and y. From geometry we have

$$f(1) = 1, f(2) = 2, f(3) = 1 + 2/\sqrt{3}, f(4) = 1 + \sqrt{2}, f(5) = \tfrac{1}{4}\sqrt{[2(5 - \sqrt{5})]},$$
$$f(6) = 3, f(7) = 3$$

The range of $f(x)$ is the set of these values.

Example 2.3

The relationship between the temperature T_1 measured in degrees Celsius (°C) and the corresponding temperature T_2 measured in degrees Fahrenheit (°F) is

$$T_2 = \tfrac{9}{5}T_1 + 32$$

Interpreting this as a function with T_1 as the independent variable and T_2 as the dependent variable:

(a) What are the domain and codomain of the function?

(b) What is the function rule?

(c) Plot a graph of the function.

(d) What is the image set or range of the function?

(e) Use the function to convert the following into °F:

(i) 60°C, (ii) 0°C, (iii) −50°C

Solution

(a) Since temperature can vary continuously, the domain is the set $T_1 \geqslant T_0 = -273.16$ (absolute zero). The codomain can be chosen as the set of real numbers $\mathbb{R}$.

(b) The function rule in words is

multiply by $\tfrac{9}{5}$ and then add 32

or algebraically

$$f(T_1) = \tfrac{9}{5}T_1 + 32$$

(c) Since the domain is the set $T_1 \geqslant T_0$, there must be an image for every value of T_1 on the horizontal axis which is greater than −273.16. The graph of the function is that part of the line $T_2 = \tfrac{9}{5}T_1 + 32$ for which $T_1 > -273.16$, as illustrated in Figure 2.3.

(d) Since each value of T_2 is an image of some value T_1 in its domain, it follows that the range of $f(T_1)$ is the set of real numbers greater than −459.69.

(e) The conversion may be done graphically by reading values of the graph, as illustrated by the broken lines in Figure 2.3, or algebraically using the rule

$$T_2 = \tfrac{9}{5}T_1 + 32$$

giving the values

(i) 140°F, (ii) 32°F, (iii) −58°F

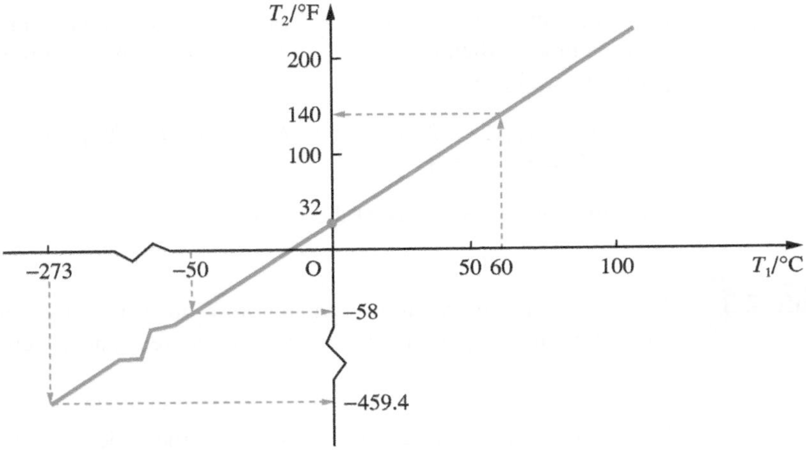

Figure 2.3
Graph of
$T_2 = f(T_1) = \frac{9}{5}T_1 + 32.$

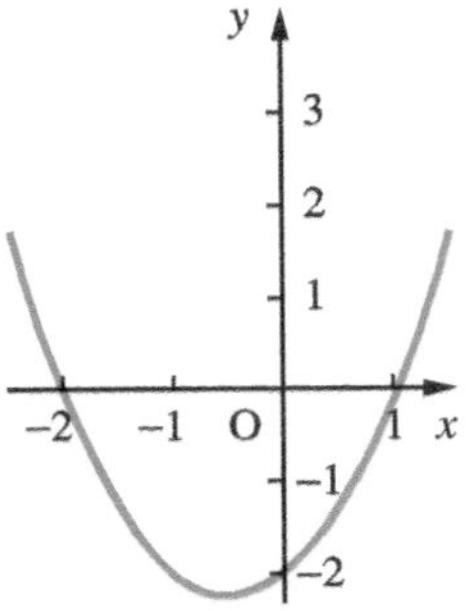

Figure 2.4
Graph of
$y = (x - 1)(x + 2).$

A value of the independent variable for which the value of a function is zero, is called a **zero** of that function. Thus the function $f(x) = (x - 1)(x + 2)$ has two zeros, $x = 1$ and $x = -2$. These correspond to where the graph of the function crosses the x axis, as shown in Figure 2.4. We can see from the diagram that, for this function, its values decrease as the values of x increase from (say) -5 up to $-\frac{1}{2}$, and then its values increase with x. We can demonstrate this algebraically by rearranging the formula for $f(x)$:

$$\begin{aligned} f(x) &= (x - 1)(x + 2) \\ &= x^2 + x - 2 \\ &= (x + \tfrac{1}{2})^2 - \tfrac{9}{4}, \end{aligned}$$

From this we can see that $f(x)$ achieves its smallest value $(-\frac{9}{4})$ where $x = -\frac{1}{2}$ and that the value of the function is greater than $-\frac{9}{4}$ both sides of $x = -\frac{1}{2}$ because $(x + \frac{1}{2})^2 \geqslant 0$. The function is said to be a **decreasing function** for $x < -\frac{1}{2}$ and an **increasing function** for $x > -\frac{1}{2}$. More formally, a function is said to be increasing on an interval (a, b) if $f(x_2) > f(x_1)$ when $x_2 > x_1$ for all x_1 and x_2 lying in (a, b). Similarly for decreasing functions, we have $f(x_2) < f(x_1)$ when $x_2 > x_1$.

The value of a function at the point where its behaviour changes from decreasing to increasing is a **minimum** (*plural* **minima**) of the function. Often this is denoted by an asterisk superscript f^* and the corresponding value of the independent variable by x^* so that $f(x^*) = f^*$. Similarly a **maximum** (*plural* **maxima**) occurs when a function changes from being increasing to being decreasing. In many cases the terms maximum and minimum refer to the local values of the function, as illustrated in Example 2.4(a). Sometimes, in practical problems, it is necessary to distinguish between the largest value the function achieves on its domain and the *local maxima* it achieves elsewhere. Similarly for *local minima*. Maxima and minima are jointly referred to as **optimal values** and as **extremal values** of the function.

The point (x^*, f^*) of the graph of $f(x)$ is often called a turning point of the graph, whether it is a maximum or a minimum. These properties will be discussed in more detail in Sections 8.2.7 and 8.5. For smooth functions as in Figure 2.5, the tangent to the graph of the function is horizontal at a turning point. This property can be used to locate maxima and minima.

Example 2.4 Draw graphs of the functions below, locating their zeros, intervals in which they are increasing, intervals in which they are decreasing and their optimal values.

(a) $y = 2x^3 + 3x^2 - 12x + 32$ (b) $y = (x - 1)^{2/3} - 1$

Solution (a) The graph of the function is shown in Figure 2.5. From the graph we can see that the function has one zero at $x = -4$. It is an increasing function on the intervals $-\infty < x < -2$ and $1 < x < \infty$ and a decreasing function on the interval $-2 < x < 1$. It achieves a maximum value of 52 at $x = -2$ and a minimum value of 25 at $x = 1$. In this example the extremal values at $x = -2$ and $x = 1$ are *local maximum* and *local minimum* values. The function is defined on the set of real numbers $\mathbb{R}$. Thus it does not have finite upper and lower values. If the domain were restricted to $[-4, 4]$, say, then the *global minimum* would be $f(-4) = 0$ and the *global maximum* would be $f(4) = 160$.

Figure 2.5
Graph of $y = 2x^3 + 3x^2 - 12x + 32$.

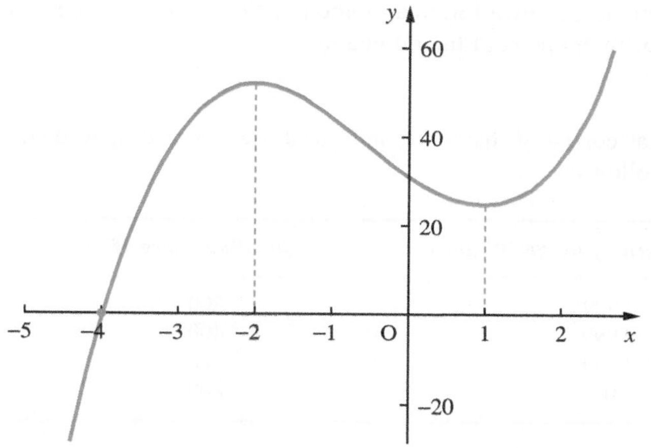

(b) The graph of the function is shown in Figure 2.6. (Note that to evaluate $(x - 1)^{2/3}$ on some calculators/computer packages it has to be expressed as $((x - 1)^2)^{1/3}$ for $x < 1$.)

Figure 2.6
Graph of $y = (x - 1)^{2/3} - 1$.

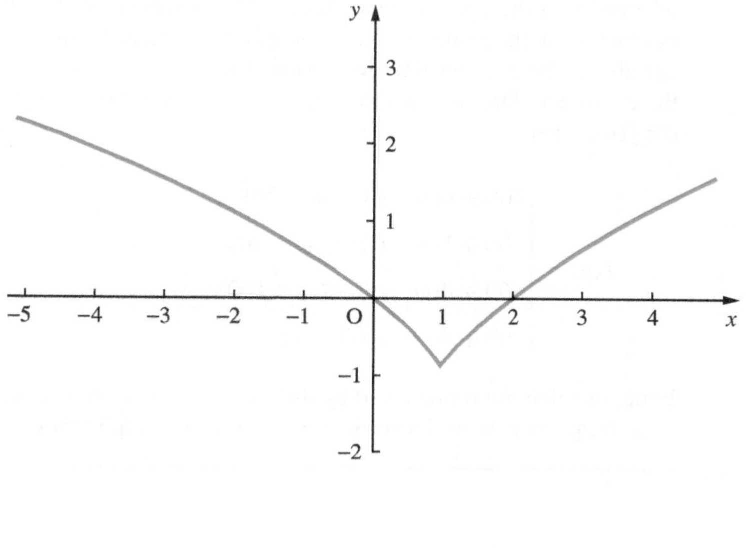

From the graph, we see that the function has two zeros, one at $x = 0$ and the other at $x = 2$. It is a decreasing function for $x < 1$ and an increasing function for $x > 1$. This is obvious algebraically since $(x - 1)^{2/3}$ is greater than or equal to zero. This example also provides an illustration of the behaviour of some algebraic functions at a maximum or minimum value. In contrast to (a) where the function changes from decreasing to increasing at $x = 1$ quite smoothly, in this case the function changes from decreasing to increasing abruptly at $x = 1$. Such a minimum value is called a **cusp**. In this example, the value at $x = 1$ is both a local minimum and a global minimum.

It is important to appreciate the difference between a function and a formula. A function is a mapping that associates one and only one member of the codomain with every member of its domain. It may be possible to express this association, as in Example 2.3, by a formula. Some functions may be represented by different formulae on different parts of their domain.

Example 2.5 A gas company charges its industrial users according to their gas usage. Their tariff is as follows:

Quarterly usage/10^3 units	*Standing charge/£*	*Charge per 10^3 units/£*
0–19.999	200	60
20–49.999	400	50
50–99.999	600	46
⩾100	800	44

What is the quarterly charge paid by a user?

Solution The charge £c paid by a user for a quarter's gas is a function, since for any number of units used there is a unique charge. The charging tariff is expressed in terms of the number u of thousands of units of gas consumed. In this situation the independent variable is the gas consumption u since that determines the charge £c which accrues to the customer. The function f: usage → cost must, however, be expressed in the form $c = f(u)$, where

$$f(u) = \begin{cases} 200 + 60u & (0 \leqslant u < 20) \\ 400 + 50u & (20 \leqslant u < 50) \\ 600 + 46u & (50 \leqslant u < 100) \\ 800 + 44u & (100 \leqslant u) \end{cases}$$

Functions that are represented by different formulae on different parts of their domains arise frequently in engineering and management applications.

The basic MATLAB package is primarily a number crunching package. It does not perform symbolic manipulations and cannot undertake algebra containing unknowns. However, such work can be undertaken by the Symbolic Math Toolbox, which incorporates many MAPLE commands to implement the algebraic work. Consequently, most of the commands in Symbolic Math Toolbox are identical to the MAPLE commands. In order to use any symbolic variables, such as x and y, in MATLAB these must be declared by entering a command, such as `syms x y;`. MAPLE does not need to construct symbols since these are assumed in the package. Another important difference is that in MAPLE assignment is performed by := rather than = and each statement must end with a semicolon '`;`'. In MATLAB inserting a semicolon at the end of a statement suppresses display on screen of the output to the command. In MAPLE output to the screen is suppressed using '`:`'. In this chapter, only MATLAB versions of any process are given since a MAPLE user can easily adapt the codes. If there are significant syntax differences these will be noted.

The MATLAB operators for the basic arithmetic operations are + for addition, - for subtraction, * for multiplication, / for division and ^ for power. The colon command `x = a:dx:b` generates an array of numbers which are the values of x between a and b in steps of dx. For example, the command

```
x = 0:0.1:1
```

generates the array

```
x = 0 0.1 0.2 0.3 0.4 0.5 0.6 0.7 0.8 0.9 1.0
```

When using the operations of multiplication, division and power on such arrays *, / and ^ are replaced respectively by `.*`, `./` and `.^` in which the 'dot' implies element by element operations. For example, if $x = [1\ 2\ 3]$ and $y = [4\ {-3}\ 5]$ are two arrays then `x.*y` denotes the array [4 −6 15] and `x.^2` denotes the array [1 4 9]. Note that to enter an array it must be enclosed within square brackets `[ ]`.

To plot the graph of $y = f(x)$, $a \leqslant x \leqslant b$, an array of x values is first produced and then a corresponding array of y values is produced. Then the command `plot(x,y)` plots a graph of y against x. Check that the sequence of commands

```
x = -5:0.1:3;
y = 2*x.^3 + 3*x.^2 - 12*x + 32;
plot(x,y)
```

plots the graph of Figure 2.5. Entering a further command

```
grid
```

draws gridlines on the existing plot. The following commands may be used for labelling the graph:

`title('text')`	prints 'text' at the top of the plot
`xlabel('text')`	labels the x-axis with 'text'
`ylabel('text')`	labels the y-axis with 'text'

Plotting the graphs of $y_1 = f(x)$ and $y_2 = g(x)$, $a \leqslant x \leqslant b$, can be achieved using the commands

```
x = [a:dx:b]'; y1 = f(x); y2 = g(x);
plot(x,y1, '-',x,y2, '- -')
```

with '-' and '- -' indicating that the graph of $y_1 = f(x)$ will appear as a 'solid line' and that of $y_2 = g(x)$ as a 'dashed line'. These commands can be extended to include more than two graphs as well as colour. To find out more, use the *help* facility in MATLAB.

Using the Symbolic Math Toolbox the `sym` command enables us to construct symbolic variables and expressions. For example

```
x = sym('x')
```

creates the variable x, that prints as x; whilst the command

```
f = sym('2*x + 3')
```

assigns the symbolic expression $2x + 3$ to the variable f. If f includes parameters then these must be declared as symbolic terms at the outset. For example, the sequence of commands

```
syms x a b
f = sym('a*x + b')
```

prints

```
f = ax + b
```

(Note the use of spacing when specifying variables under `syms`.)

The command `ezplot(y)` produces the plot of $y = f(x)$, making a reasonable choice for the range of the x axis and resulting scale of the y axis, the default domain of the x axis being $-2\pi \leqslant x \leqslant 2\pi$. The domain can be changed to $a \leqslant x \leqslant b$ using the command `ezplot(y,[a,b])`. Check that the commands

```
syms x
y = sym(2*x^3 + 3*x^2 - 12*x + 32);
ezplot(y,[-5,3])
```

reproduce the graph of Figure 2.5 and that the commands

```
syms x
y = sym(((x - 1)^2)^(1/3) - 1)
ezplot(y,[-5,3])
```

reproduce the graph of Figure 2.6. (Note that in the second case the function is expressed in the form indicated in the solution to Example 2.4(b).)

The corresponding commands in MAPLE are

```
y: = f(x);
plot(y,x = a..b);
```

2.2.2 Exercises

Check your answers using MATLAB or MAPLE whenever possible.

1 Determine the largest valid domains for the functions whose formulae are given below. Identify the corresponding codomains and ranges and evaluate $f(5), f(-4), f(-x)$.

(a) $f(x) = \sqrt{(25 - x^2)}$ (b) $f: x \to \sqrt[3]{(x + 3)}$

2 A straight horizontal road is to be constructed through rough terrain. The width of the road is to be 10 m, with the sides of the embankment sloping at 1 (vertical) in 2 (horizontal), as shown in Figure 2.7. Obtain a formula for the cross-sectional area of the road and its embankment, taken at right-angles to the road, where the rough ground lies at a depth x below the level of the proposed road. Use your formula to complete the table below, and draw a graph to represent this function.

x/m	0	1	2	3	4	5
Area/m^2	0		28			100

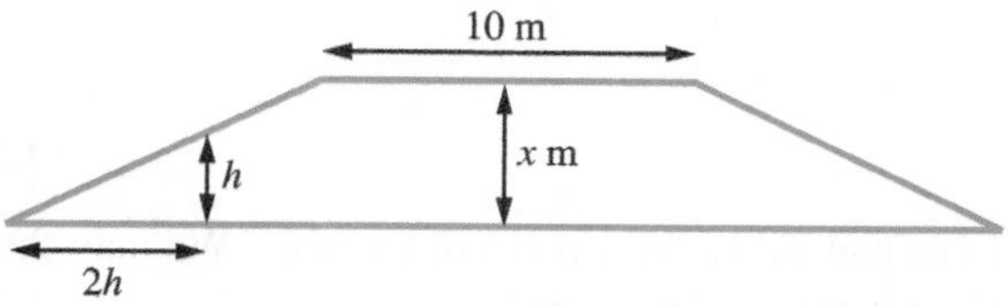

Figure 2.7

What is the value given by the formula when $x = -2$, and what is the meaning of that value?

3 A hot-water tank has the form of a circular cylinder of internal radius r, topped by a hemisphere as shown in Figure 2.8. Show that the internal surface area A is given by

$$A = 2\pi rh + 3\pi r^2$$

and the volume V enclosed is

$$V = \pi r^2 h + \tfrac{2}{3}\pi r^3$$

Find the formula relating the value of A to the value of r for tanks with capacity 0.15 m^3. Complete the table below for A in terms of r and draw a graph to represent the function.

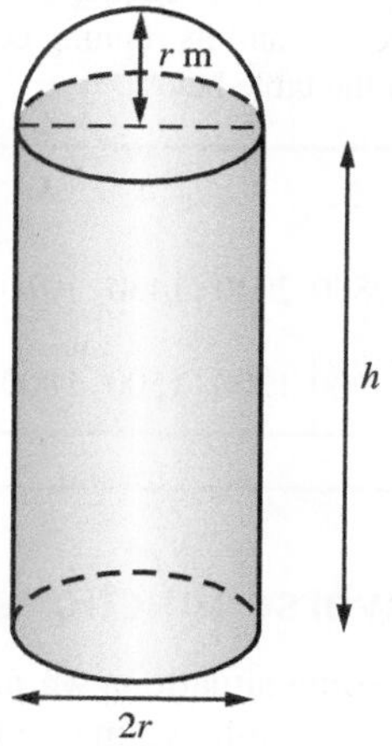

Figure 2.8

r/m	0.10	0.15	0.20	0.25	0.30	0.35	0.40
A/m^2	3.05		1.71			1.50	

The cost of the tank is proportional to the amount of metal used in its manufacture. Estimate the value of r that will minimize that cost, carefully listing the assumptions you make in your analysis. [Recall: the volume of a sphere of radius a is $4\pi a^3/3$ and its surface area is $4\pi a^2$]

4 An oil storage tank has the form of a circular cylinder with its axis horizontal, as shown in Figure 2.9. The volume of oil in the tank when the depth is h is given in the table below.

hm	0.5	1.0	1.5	2.0	2.5	3.0	3.5	4.0
V/1000l	7.3	19.7	34.4	50.3	66.1	80.9	93.9	100.5

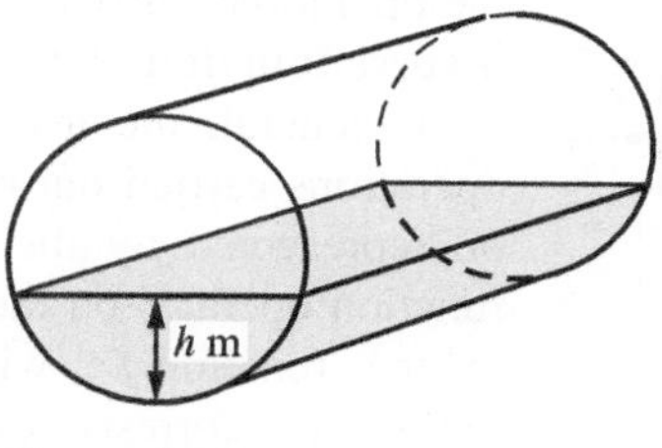

Figure 2.9

Draw a careful graph of V against h, and use it to design the graduation marks on a dipstick to be used to assess the volume of oil in the tank.

5 The initial cost of buying a car is £6000. Over the years, its value depreciates and its running costs increase, as shown in the table below.

t	1	2	3	4	5	6
Value after t years	4090	2880	2030	1430	1010	710
Running cost in year t	600	900	1200	1500	1800	2100

Draw up a table showing (a) the cumulative running cost after t years, (b) the total cost (that is, running cost plus depreciation) after t years and (c) the average cost per year over t years. Estimate the optimal time to replace the car.

6 Plot graphs of the functions below, locating their zeros, intervals in which they are increasing, intervals in which they are decreasing and their optimal values.

(a) $y = x(x - 2)$ (b) $y = 2x^3 - 3x^2 - 12x + 20$

(c) $y = x^2(x^2 - 2)$ (d) $y = 1/[x(x - 2)]$

2.2.3 Inverse functions

In some situations we may need to use the functional dependence in the reverse sense. For example we may wish to use the function

$$T_2 = f(T_1) = \tfrac{9}{5}T_1 + 32 \tag{2.1}$$

of Example 2.3, relating T_2 in °F to the corresponding T_1 in °C to convert degrees Fahrenheit to degrees Celsius. In this simple case we can rearrange the relationship (2.1) algebraically

$$T_1 = \tfrac{5}{9}(T_2 - 32)$$

giving us the function

$$T_1 = g(T_2) = \tfrac{5}{9}(T_2 - 32) \tag{2.2}$$

having T_2 as the independent variable and T_1 as the dependent variable. We may then use this to convert degrees Fahrenheit into degrees Celsius.

Looking more closely at the two functions $f(T_1)$ and $g(T_2)$ associated with (2.1) and (2.2), we have the function rule for $f(T_1)$ as

multiply by $\tfrac{9}{5}$ and then add 32

If we reverse the process, we have the rule

take away 32 and then multiply by $\tfrac{5}{9}$

which is precisely the function rule for $g(T_2)$. Thus the function $T_1 = g(T_2)$ reverses the operations carried out by the function $T_2 = f(T_1)$, and for this reason is called the **inverse function** of $T_2 = f(T_1)$.

In general, the inverse function of a function f is a function that reverses the operations carried out by f. It is denoted by f^{-1}. Writing $y = f(x)$, the function f may be represented by the block diagram of Figure 2.10(a), which indicates that the function operates on the input variable x to produce the output variable $y = f(x)$. The inverse function f^{-1} will reverse the process, and will take the value of y back to the original corresponding values of x. It can be represented by the block diagram of Figure 2.10(b).

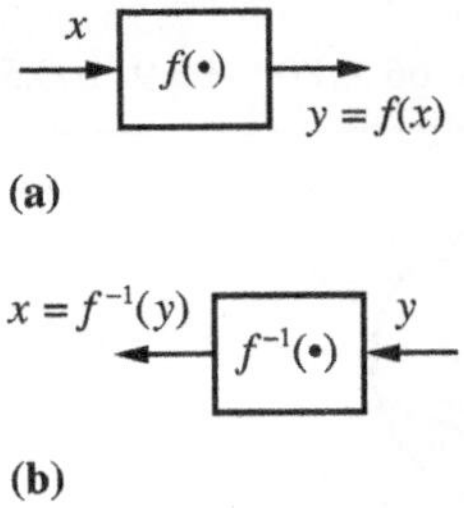

Figure 2.10 Block diagram of (a) function and (b) inverse function.

We therefore have

$$x = f^{-1}(y), \quad \text{where } y = f(x) \tag{2.3}$$

that is, the independent variable x for f acts as the dependent variable for f^{-1}, and correspondingly the dependent variable y for f becomes the independent variable for f^{-1}. At the same time the range of f becomes the domain of f^{-1} and the domain of f becomes the range of f^{-1}.

Since it is usual to denote the independent variable of a function by x and the dependent variable by y, we interchange the variables x and y in (2.3) and define the inverse function by

$$\text{if } y = f^{-1}(x) \quad \text{then } x = f(y) \tag{2.4}$$

Again in engineering it is common to denote an inverse function by $f^{-1}(x)$ rather than f^{-1}. Writing x as the independent variable for both $f(x)$ and $f^{-1}(x)$ sometimes leads to confusion, so you need to be quite clear as to what is meant by an inverse function. It is also important not to confuse $f^{-1}(x)$ with $[f(x)]^{-1}$, which means $1/f(x)$.

Finding an explicit formula for $f^{-1}(x)$ is often impossible and its values are calculated by special numerical methods. Sometimes it is possible to find the formula for $f^{-1}(x)$ by algebraic methods. We illustrate the technique in the next two examples.

Example 2.6 Obtain the inverse function of the real function $y = f(x) = \frac{1}{5}(4x - 3)$.

Solution Here the formula for the inverse function can be found algebraically. First rearranging

$$y = f(x) = \tfrac{1}{5}(4x - 3)$$

to express x in terms of y gives

$$x = f^{-1}(y) = \tfrac{1}{4}(5y + 3)$$

Interchanging the variables x and y then gives

$$y = f^{-1}(x) = \tfrac{1}{4}(5x + 3)$$

as the inverse function of

$$y = f(x) = \tfrac{1}{5}(4x - 3)$$

As a check, we have

$$f(2) = \tfrac{1}{5}(4 \times 2 - 3) = 1$$

while

$$f^{-1}(1) = \tfrac{1}{4}(5 \times 1 + 3) = 2$$

Example 2.7 Obtain the inverse function of $y = f(x) = \dfrac{x+2}{x+1}$, $x \neq -1$.

Solution We rearrange $y = \dfrac{x+2}{x+1}$ to obtain x in terms of y. (Notice that y is not defined where $x = -1$.) Thus

$$y(x+1) = x+2 \quad \text{so that} \quad x(y-1) = 2-y$$

giving $x = \dfrac{2-y}{y-1}$, $y \neq 1$ (Notice that x is not defined where $y = 1$. Putting $y = 1$ into the formula for y results in the equation $x + 1 = x + 2$ which is not possible.)

Thus $f^{-1}(x) = \dfrac{2-x}{x-1}$, $x \neq 1$

If we are given the graph of $y = f(x)$ and wish to obtain the graph of the inverse function $y = f^{-1}(x)$ then what we really need to do is interchange the roles of x and y. Thus we need to manipulate the graph of $y = f(x)$ so that the x and y axes are interchanged. This can be achieved by taking the mirror image in the line $y = x$ and relabelling the axes as illustrated in Figures 2.11(a) and (b). It is important to recognize that the graphs of $y = f(x)$ and $y = f^{-1}(x)$ are symmetrical about the line $y = x$, since this property is frequently used in mathematical arguments. Notice that the x and y axes have the same scale.

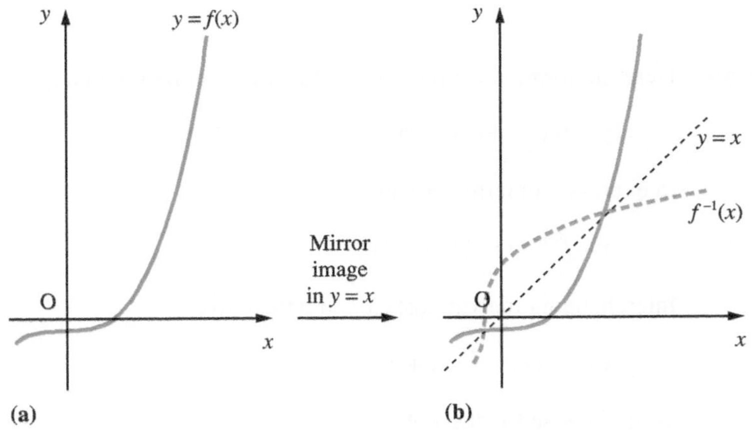

Figure 2.11 The graph of $y = f^{-1}(x)$.

Example 2.8 Obtain the graph of $f^{-1}(x)$ when (a) $f(x) = \frac{9}{5}x + 32$, (b) $f(x) = \dfrac{x+2}{x+1}$, $x \neq -1$, (c) $f(x) = x^2$.

Solution (a) This is the formula for converting the temperature measured in °C to the temperature in °F and its graph is shown by the blue line in Figure 2.12(a). Reflecting the graph in the line $y = x$ yields the graph of the inverse function $y = g(x) = \frac{5}{9}(x - 32)$ as illustrated by the black line in Figure 2.12(a).

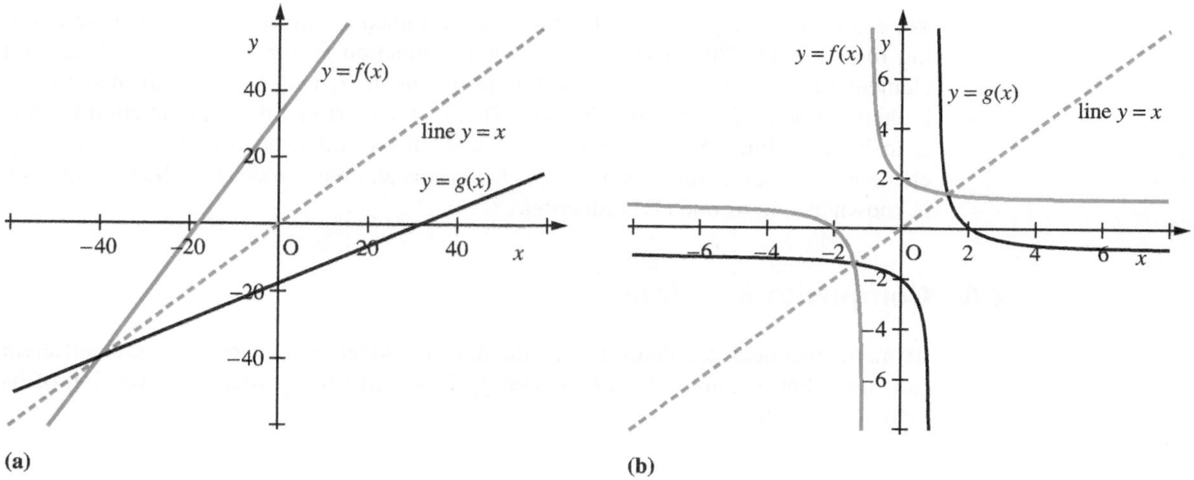

Figure 2.12 (a) Graph of $f(x) = \frac{9}{5}x + 32$ and its inverse $g(x)$, (b) Graph of $f(x) = \dfrac{x+2}{x+1}$ and its inverse $g(x)$.

(b) The graph of $y = f(x) = \dfrac{x+2}{x+1}$, $x \neq -1$ is shown in blue in Figure 2.12(b). The graph of its inverse function $y = g(x) = \dfrac{2-x}{x-1}$, $x \neq 1$ can be seen as the mirror image illustrated in black in Figure 2.12(b).

(c) The graph of $y = x^2$ is shown in Figure 2.13(a). Its mirror image in the line $y = x$ gives the graph of Figure 2.13(b). We note that this graph is not representative of a function according to our definition, since for all values of $x > 0$ there are two images – one positive and one negative – as indicated by the broken line. This follows because $y = x^2$ corresponds to $x = +\sqrt{y}$ or $x = -\sqrt{y}$. In order to avoid this ambiguity, we define the inverse function of $f(x) = x^2$ to be $f^{-1}(x) = +\sqrt{x}$, which corresponds to the upper half of the graph as illustrated in Figure 2.13(c). $\sqrt{x}$ therefore denotes a positive number (cf. calculators), so the range of $\sqrt{x}$ is $x \geqslant 0$. Thus the inverse function of $y = f(x) = x^2$ $(x \geqslant 0)$ is $y = f^{-1}(x) = \sqrt{x}$. Note that the domain of $f(x)$ had to be restricted to $x \geqslant 0$ in order that an inverse could be defined. In modern usage, the symbol $\sqrt{x}$ denotes a positive number.

Figure 2.13 Graphs of $f(x) = x^2$ and its inverse.

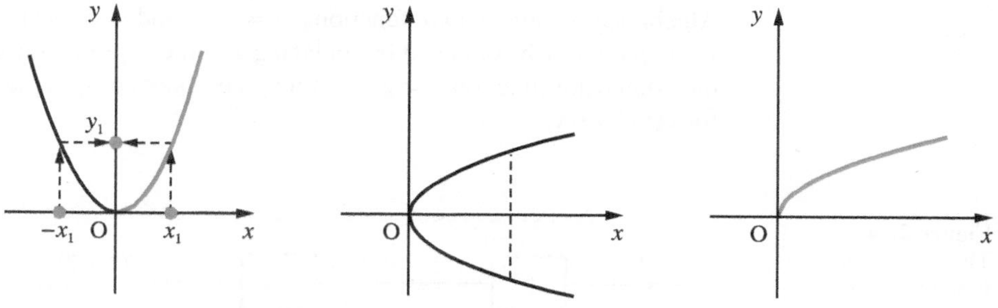

(a) $y = f(x) = x^2$ **(b)** $y^2 = x$ **(c)** $y = f^{-1}(x) = +\sqrt{x}$

We see from Example 2.8(c) that there is no immediate inverse function corresponding to $f(x) = x^2$. This arises because for the function $f(x) = x^2$ there is a codomain element that is the image of two domain elements x_1 and $-x_1$, as indicated by the broken arrowed lines in Figure 2.13(a). That is, $f(x_1) = f(-x_1) = y_1$. If a function $y = f(x)$ is to have an immediate inverse $f^{-1}(x)$, without any imposed conditions, then *every* element of its range must occur *precisely once* as an image under $f(x)$. Such a function is known as one-to-one (1:1) function.

2.2.4 Composite functions

In many practical problems the mathematical model will involve several different functions. For example, the kinetic energy T of a moving particle is a function of its velocity v, so that

$$T = f(v)$$

Also, the velocity v itself is a function of time t, so that

$$v = g(t)$$

Clearly, by eliminating v, it is possible to express the kinetic energy as a function of time according to

$$T = f(g(t))$$

A function of the form $y = f(g(x))$ is called a **function of a function** or a **composite** of the functions $f(x)$ and $g(x)$. In modern mathematical texts it is common to denote the composite function by $f \circ g$ so that

$$y = f \circ g(x) = f(g(x)) \tag{2.5}$$

We can represent the composite function (2.5) schematically by the block diagram of Figure 2.14, where $u = g(x)$ is called the intermediate variable.

It is important to recognize that the composition of functions is not in general commutative. That is, for two general functions $f(x)$ and $g(x)$

$$f(g(x)) \neq g(f(x))$$

Algebraically, given two functions $y = f(x)$ and $y = g(x)$, the composite function $y = f(g(x))$ may be obtained by replacing x in the expression for $f(x)$ by $g(x)$. Likewise, the composite function $y = g(f(x))$ may be obtained by replacing x in the expression for $g(x)$ by $f(x)$.

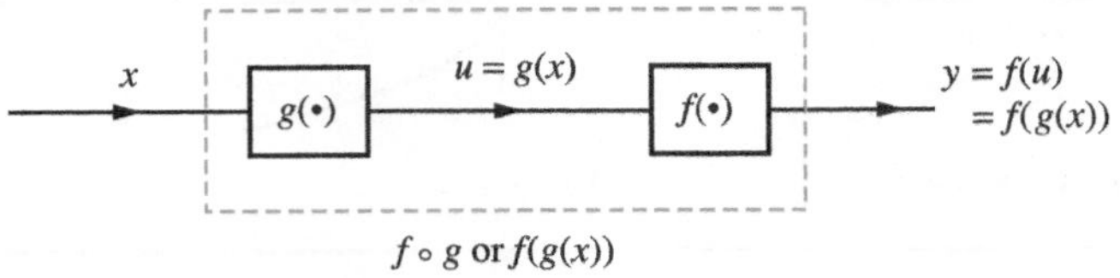

Figure 2.14 The composite function $f(g(x))$.

Example 2.9 If $y = f(x) = x^2 + 2x$ and $y = g(x) = x - 1$, obtain the composite functions $f(g(x))$ and $g(f(x))$.

Solution To obtain $f(g(x))$, replace x in the expression for $f(x)$ by $g(x)$, giving

$$y = f(g(x)) = (g(x))^2 + 2(g(x))$$

But $g(x) = x - 1$, so that

$$y = f(g(x)) = (x - 1)^2 + 2(x - 1)$$
$$= x^2 - 2x + 1 + 2x - 2$$

That is,

$$f(g(x)) = x^2 - 1$$

Similarly,

$$y = g(f(x)) = (f(x)) - 1$$
$$= (x^2 + 2x) - 1$$

That is,

$$g(f(x)) = x^2 + 2x - 1$$

Note that this example confirms the result that in general $f(g(x)) \neq g(f(x))$.

Given a function $y = f(x)$, two composite functions that occur frequently in engineering are

$$y = f(x + k) \quad \text{and} \quad y = f(x - k)$$

where k is a positive constant. As illustrated in Figures 2.15(b) and (c), the graphs of these two composite functions are readily obtained given the graph of $y = f(x)$ as in Figure 2.15(a). The graph of $y = f(x - k)$ is obtained by displacing the graph of $y = f(x)$ by k units to the right, while the graph of $y = f(x + k)$ is obtained by displacing the graph of $y = f(x)$ by k units to the left.

Viewing complicated functions as composites of simpler functions often enables us to 'get to the heart' of a practical problem, and to obtain and understand the solution. For example, recognizing that $y = x^2 + 2x - 3$ is the composite function $y = (x + 1)^2 - 4$, tells us that the function is essentially the squaring function. Its graph is a parabola with minimum point at $x = -1$, $y = -4$ (rather than at $x = 0$, $y = 0$). A similar process of

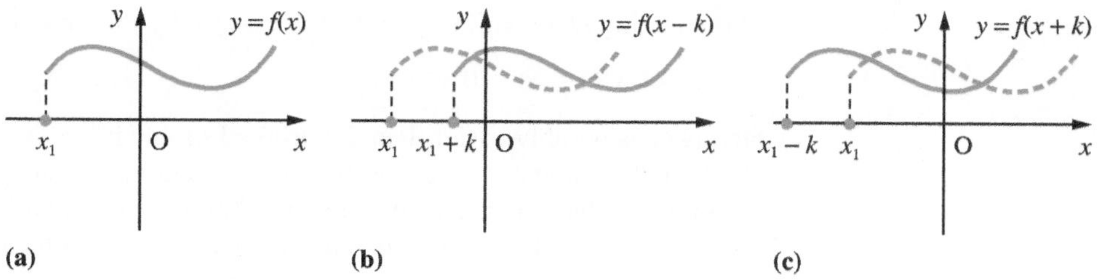

Figure 2.15 Graphs of $f(x)$, $f(x - k)$ and $f(x + k)$, with $k > 0$.

reducing a complicated problem to a simpler one occurred in the solution of the practical problem discussed in Example 1.49 on p. 58.

Example 2.10 An open conical container is made from a sector of a circle of radius 10 cm as illustrated in Figure 2.16, with sectional angle θ (radians). The capacity C cm^3 of the cone depends on θ. Find the algebraic formula for C in terms of θ and the simplest associated function that could be studied if we wish to maximize C with respect to θ.

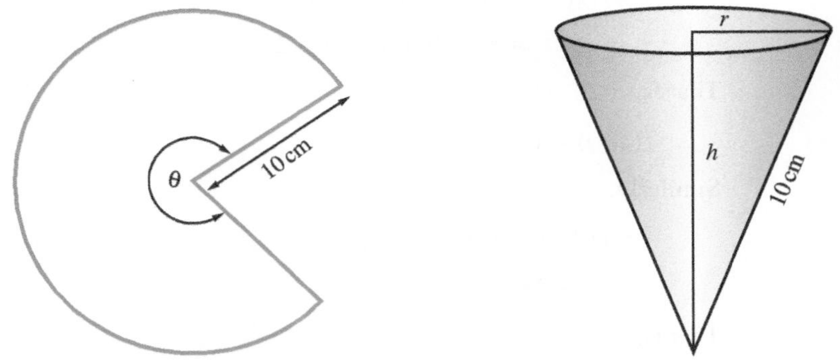

Figure 2.16 Conical container of Example 2.10.

Solution Let the cone have base radius r cm and height h cm. Then its capacity is given by $C = \frac{1}{3}\pi r^2 h$ with r and h dependent upon the sectorial angle θ (since the perimeter of the sector has to equal the circumference of the base of the cone). Thus, by Pythagoras' theorem,

$$10\theta = 2\pi r \quad \text{and} \quad h^2 = 10^2 - r^2$$

so that

$$C(\theta) = \frac{1}{3}\pi\left(\frac{10\theta}{2\pi}\right)^2\left[10^2 - \left(\frac{10\theta}{2\pi}\right)^2\right]^{1/2}$$

$$= \frac{1000}{3}\pi\left(\frac{\theta}{2\pi}\right)^2\left[1 - \left(\frac{\theta}{2\pi}\right)^2\right]^{1/2}, \quad 0 \leqslant \theta \leqslant 2\pi$$

Maximizing $C(\theta)$ with respect to θ is essentially the same problem as maximizing

$$D(x) = x(1 - x)^{1/2}, \quad 0 \leqslant x \leqslant 1$$

(where $x = (\theta/2\pi)^2$).

Maximizing $D(x)$ with respect to x is essentially the same problem as maximizing

$$E(x) = x^2(1 - x), \quad 0 \leqslant x \leqslant 1$$

which is considerably easier than the original problem.

Plotting the graph of $E(x)$ suggests that it has a minimum at $x = \frac{2}{3}$ where its value is $\frac{4}{27}$. We can prove that this is true by showing that the horizontal line $y = \frac{4}{27}$ is a tangent to the graph at $x = \frac{2}{3}$; that is, the line cuts the graph at two coincident points at $x = \frac{2}{3}$.

Setting $x^2(1-x)=\frac{4}{27}$ gives $27x^3-27x^2+4=0$ which factorizes into

$$(3x-2)^2(3x+1)=0$$

Thus the equation has a double root at $x=\frac{2}{3}$ and a single root at $x=-\frac{1}{3}$. Thus $E(x)$ has a maximum at $x=\frac{2}{3}$ and the corresponding optimal value of θ is $2\pi\sqrt{(\frac{2}{3})}$. (In Section 8.5 (see also Question 5 in Review Exercises 8.13) we shall consider theoretical methods of confirming such results.)

When we compose a function with its inverse function, we usually obtain the identity function $y=x$. Thus from Example 2.6, we have

$$f(x)=\tfrac{1}{5}(4x-3) \quad \text{and} \quad f^{-1}(x)=\tfrac{1}{4}(5x+3)$$

and

$$f(f^{-1}(x))=\tfrac{1}{5}\{4[\tfrac{1}{4}(5x+3)]-3\}=x$$

and

$$f^{-1}(f(x))=\tfrac{1}{4}\{5[\tfrac{1}{5}(4x-3)]+3\}=x$$

We need to take care with the exceptional cases that occur, like the square root function, where the inverse function is defined only after restricting the domain of the original function. Thus for $f(x)=x^2$ $(x\geqslant 0)$ and $f^{-1}(x)=\sqrt{x}$ $(x\geqslant 0)$, we obtain

$$f(f^{-1}(x))=x, \quad \text{for } x\geqslant 0 \text{ only}$$

and

$$f^{-1}(f(x))=\begin{cases} x, & \text{for } x\geqslant 0 \\ -x, & \text{for } x\leqslant 0 \end{cases}$$

2.2.5 Exercises

7 A function $f(x)$ is defined by $f(x)=\frac{1}{2}(10^x+10^{-x})$, for x in $\mathbb{R}$. Show that

(a) $2(f(x))^2=f(2x)+1$

(b) $2f(x)f(y)=f(x+y)+f(x-y)$

8 Draw separate graphs of the functions f and g where

$$f(x)=(x+1)^2 \text{ and } g(x)=x-2$$

The functions F and G are defined by

$$F(x)=f(g(x)) \text{ and } G(x)=g(f(x))$$

Find formulae for $F(x)$ and $G(x)$ and sketch their graphs. What relationships do the graphs of F and G bear to those of f and g?

9 A function f is defined by

$$f(x)=\begin{cases} 0 & (x<-1) \\ x+1 & (-1\leqslant x<0) \\ 1-x & (0\leqslant x\leqslant 1) \\ 0 & (x>1) \end{cases}$$

Sketch on separate diagrams the graphs of $f(x)$, $f(x+\frac{1}{2}), f(x+1), f(x+2), f(x-\frac{1}{2}), f(x-1)$ and $f(x-2)$.

10 Find the inverse function (if it is defined) of the following functions:

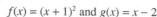

(a) $f(x) = 2x - 3$ (x in $\mathbb{R}$)

(b) $f(x) = \dfrac{2x - 3}{x + 4}$ (x in $\mathbb{R}$, $x \neq -4$)

(c) $f(x) = x^2 + 1$ (x in $\mathbb{R}$)

If $f(x)$ does not have an inverse function, suggest a suitable restriction of the domain of $f(x)$ that will allow the definition of an inverse function.

11 Show that

$$f(x) = \frac{2x - 3}{x + 4}$$

may be expressed in the form

$$f(x) = g(h(l(x)))$$

where

$$l(x) = x + 4$$

$$h(x) = 1/x$$

$$g(x) = 2 - 11x$$

Interpret this result graphically.

12 The stiffness of a rectangular beam varies directly with the cube of its height and directly with its breadth. A beam of rectangular section is to be cut from a circular log of diameter d. Show that the optimal choice of height and breadth of the beam in terms of its stiffness is related to the value of x which maximizes the function

$$E(x) = x^3(d^2 - x), \quad 0 \leqslant x \leqslant d^2$$

13 A beam is used to support a building as shown in Figure 2.17. The beam has to pass over a 3 m brick wall which is 2 m from the building. Show that the minimum length of the beam is associated with the value of x which minimizes

$$E(x) = (x + 2)^2\left(1 + \frac{9}{x^2}\right)$$

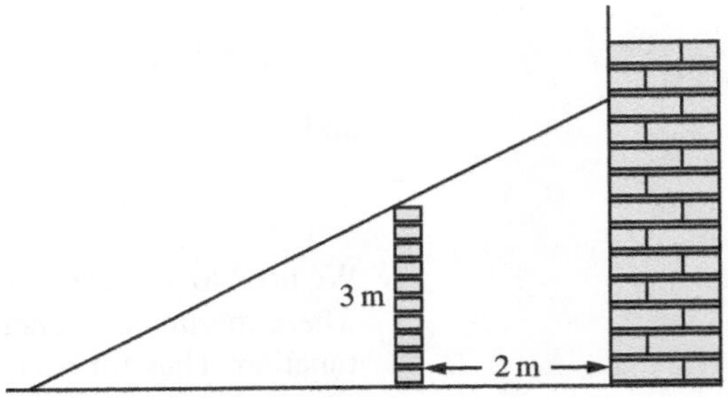

Figure 2.17 Beam of Question 13.

2.2.6 Odd, even and periodic functions

Some commonly occurring functions in engineering contexts have the special properties of oddness or evenness or periodicity. These properties are best understood from the graphs of the functions.

An **even function** is one that satisfies the functional equation

$$f(-x) = f(x)$$

Thus the value of $f(-2)$ is the same as $f(2)$, and so on. The graph of such a function is symmetrical about the y axis, as shown in Figure 2.18.

In contrast, an **odd function** has a graph which is antisymmetrical about the origin, as shown in Figure 2.19, and satisfies the equation

$$f(-x) = -f(x)$$

We notice that $f(0) = 0$ or is undefined.

Polynomial functions like $y = x^4 - x^2 - 1$, involving only even powers of x, are examples of even functions, while those like $y = x - x^5$, involving only odd powers of x, provide examples of odd functions. Of course, not all functions have the property of oddness or evenness.

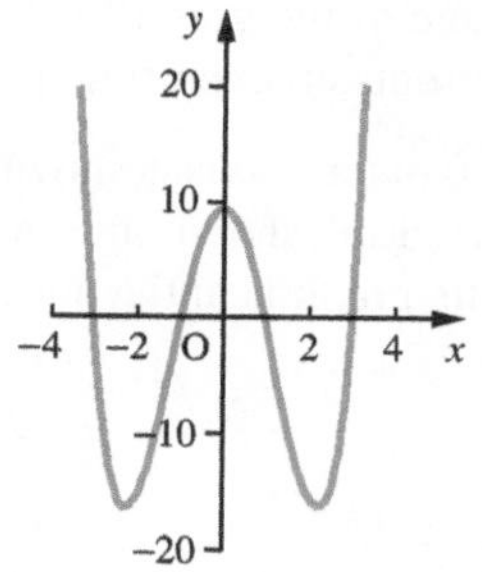

Figure 2.18 Graph of an even function.

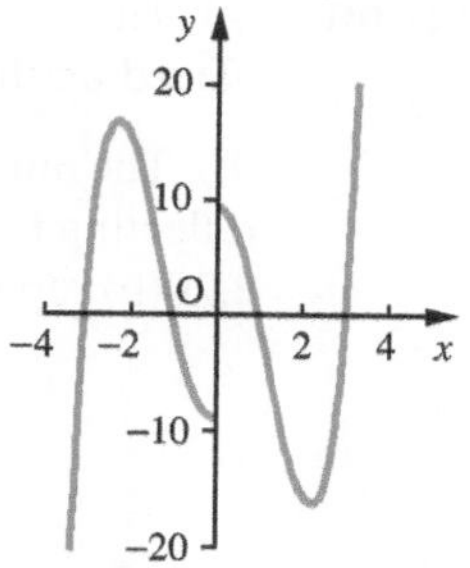

Figure 2.19 Graph of an odd function.

Example 2.11

Which of the functions $y = f(x)$ whose graphs are shown in Figure 2.20 are odd, even or neither odd nor even?

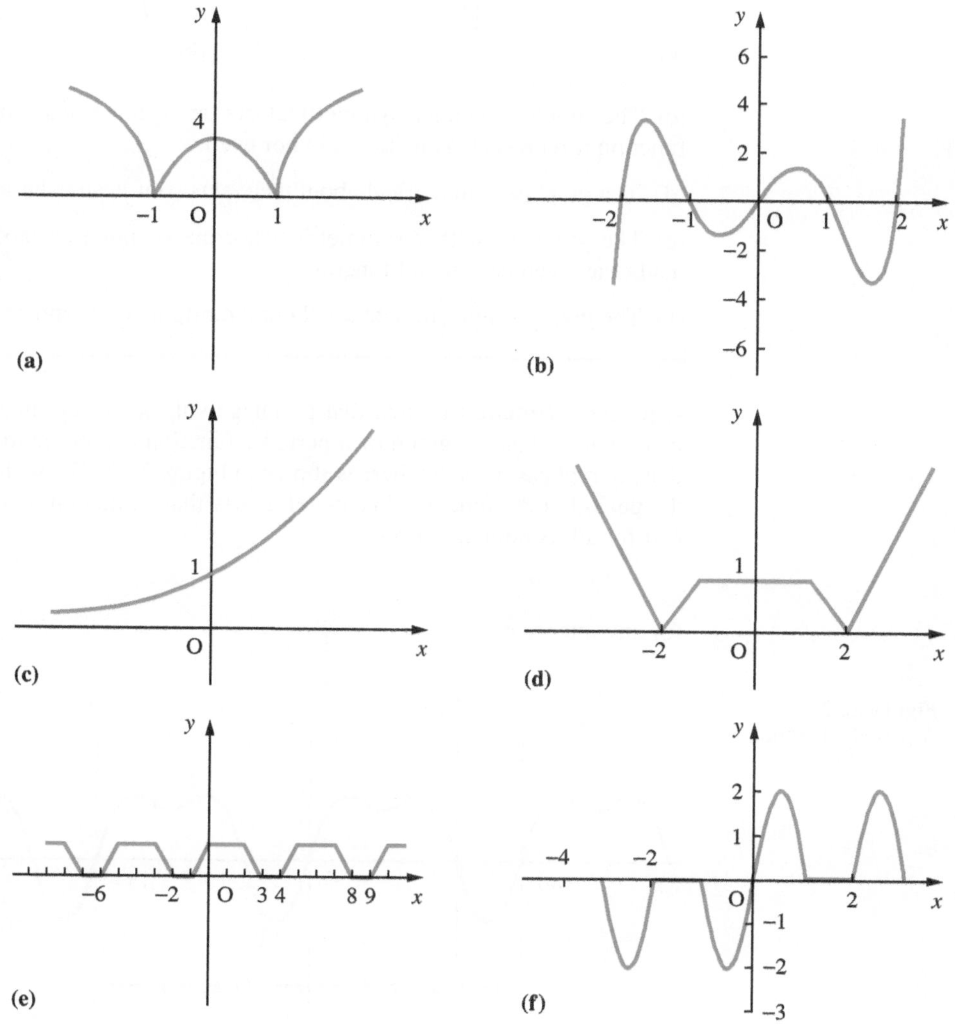

Figure 2.20 Graphs of Example 2.11.

Solution (a) The graph for $x < 0$ is the mirror image of the graph for $x > 0$ when the mirror is placed on the y axis. Thus the graph represents an even function.

(b) The mirror image of the graph for $x > 0$ in the y axis is shown in Figure 2.21(a). Now reflecting that image in the x axis gives the graph shown in Figure 2.21(b). Thus Figure 2.20(b) represents an odd function since its graph is antisymmetrical about the origin.

Figure 2.21

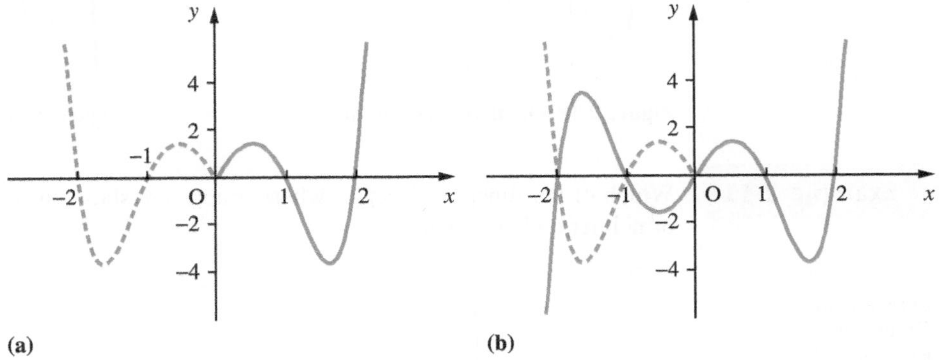

(c) The graph is neither symmetrical nor antisymmetrical about the origin, so the function it represents is neither odd nor even.

(d) The graph is symmetrical about the y axis so it is an even function.

(e) The graph is neither symmetrical nor antisymmetrical about the origin, so it is neither an even nor an odd function.

(f) The graph is antisymmetrical about the origin, so it represents an odd function.

A **periodic function** is such that its image values are repeated at regular intervals in its domain. Thus the graph of a periodic function can be divided into 'vertical strips' that are replicas of each other, as shown in Figure 2.22. The width of each strip is called the **period** of the function. We therefore say that a function $f(x)$ is periodic with period P if for all its domain values x

$$f(x + nP) = f(x)$$

for any integer n.

Figure 2.22
A periodic function of period P.

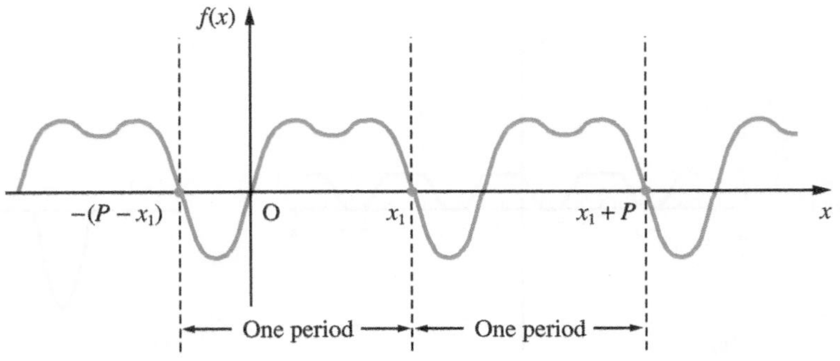

To provide a measure of the number of repetitions per unit of x, we define the **frequency** of a periodic function to be the reciprocal of its period, so that

$$\textit{frequency} = \frac{1}{\textit{period}}$$

The Greek letter ν ('nu') is usually used to denote the frequency, so that $\nu = 1/P$. The term **circular frequency** is also used in some engineering contexts. This is denoted by the Greek letter ω ('omega') and is defined by

$$\omega = 2\pi\nu = \frac{2\pi}{P}$$

It is measured in radians per unit of x, the free variable. When the meaning is clear from the context the adjective 'circular' is commonly omitted.

Example 2.12

A function $f(x)$ has the graph on [0, 1] shown in Figure 2.23. Sketch its graph on [−3, 3] given that

(a) $f(x)$ is periodic with period 1;

(b) $f(x)$ is periodic with period 2 and is even;

(c) $f(x)$ is periodic with period 2 and is odd.

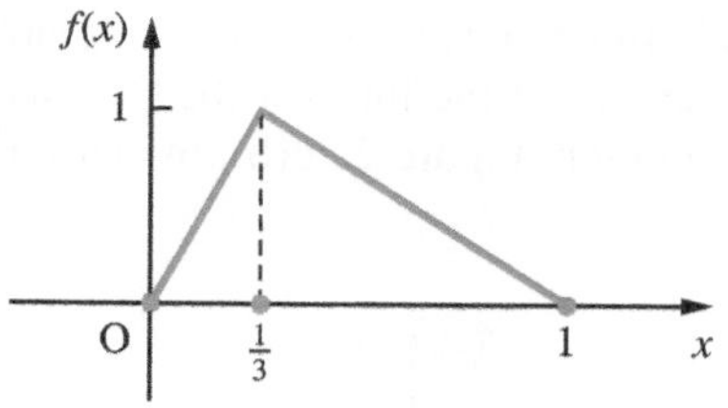

Figure 2.23
$f(x)$ of Example 2.12 defined on [0, 1].

Solution

(a) Since $f(x)$ has period 1, strips of width 1 unit are simply replicas of the graph between 0 and 1. Hence we obtain the graph shown in Figure 2.24.

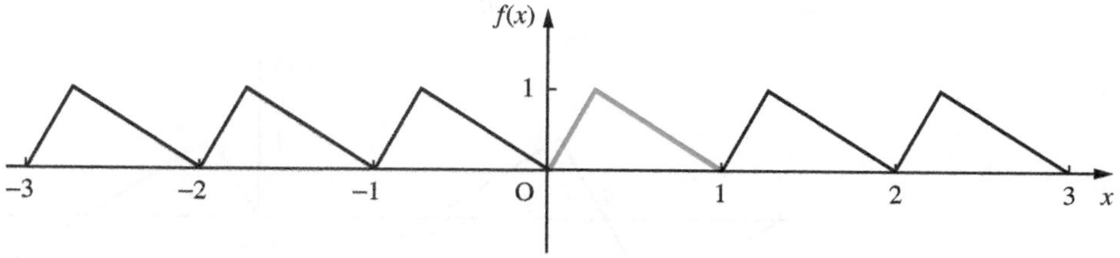

Figure 2.24
$f(x)$ having period 1.

(b) Since $f(x)$ has period 2 we need to establish the graph over a complete period before we can replicate it along the domain of $f(x)$. Since it is an even function and we

Figure 2.25
$f(x)$ periodic with period 2 and is even.

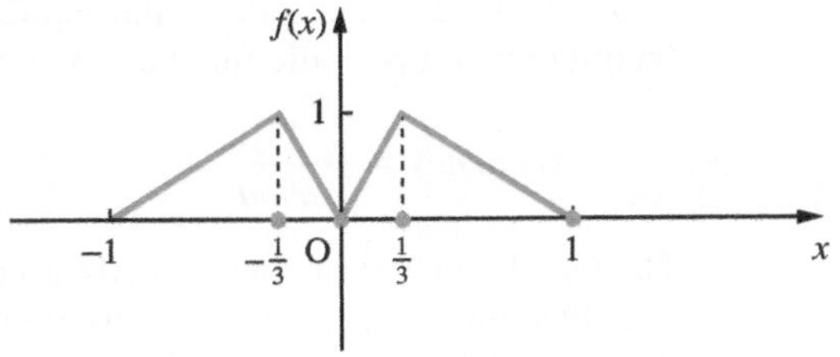

(a)

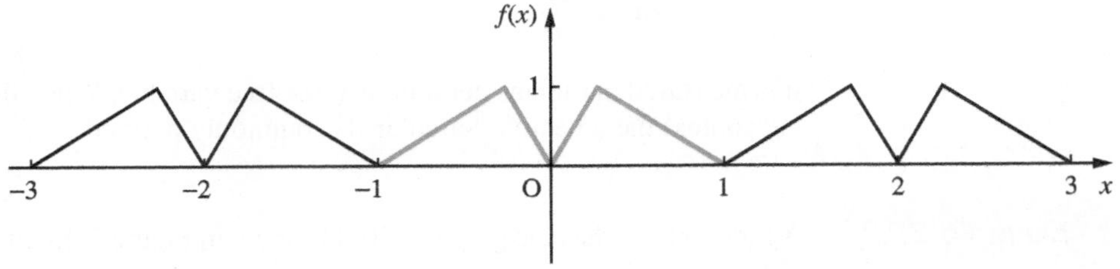

(b)

know its values between 0 and 1, we also know its values between −1 and 0. We can obtain the graph of $f(x)$ between −1 and 0 by reflecting in the y axis, as shown in Figure 2.25(a). Thus we have the graph over a complete period, from −1 to +1, and so we can replicate along the x axis, as shown in Figure 2.25(b).

(c) Similarly, if $f(x)$ is an odd function we can obtain the graph for the interval [−1, 0] using antisymmetry and the graph for the interval [0, 1]. This gives us Figure 2.26(a) and we then obtain the whole graph, Figure 2.26(b), by periodic extension.

Figure 2.26
$f(x)$ periodic with period 2 and is odd.

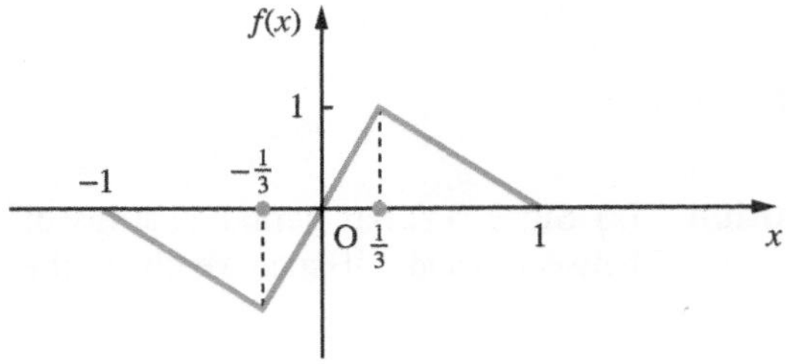

(a)

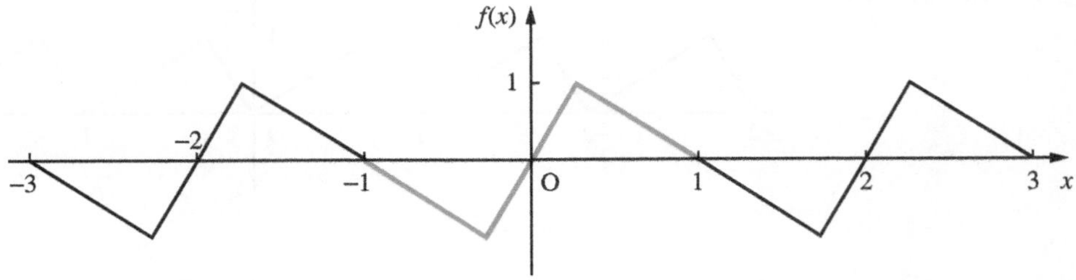

(b)

2.2.7 Exercises

14 Which of the functions $y = f(x)$ whose graphs are shown in Figure 2.27 are odd, even or neither odd nor even?

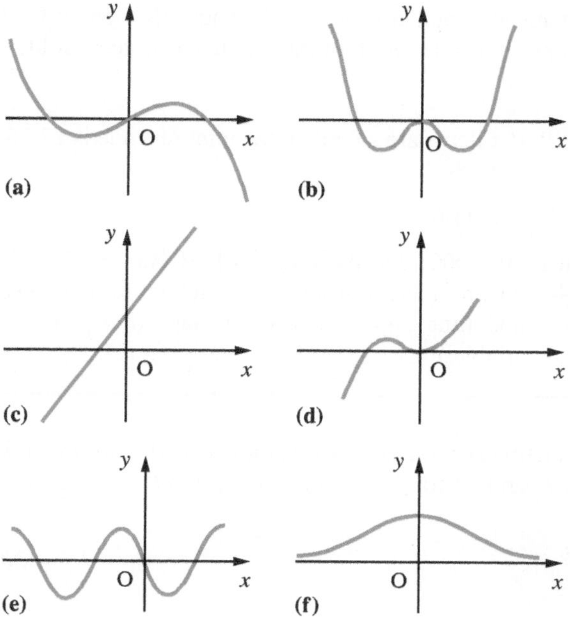

Figure 2.27 Graphs of Question 14.

15 Three different functions, $f(x)$, $g(x)$ and $h(x)$, have the same graph on [0, 2] as shown in Figure 2.28. On separate diagrams, sketch their graphs for [−4, 4] given that

(a) $f(x)$ is periodic with period 2;

(b) $g(x)$ is periodic with period 4 and is even;

(c) $h(x)$ is periodic with period 4 and is odd.

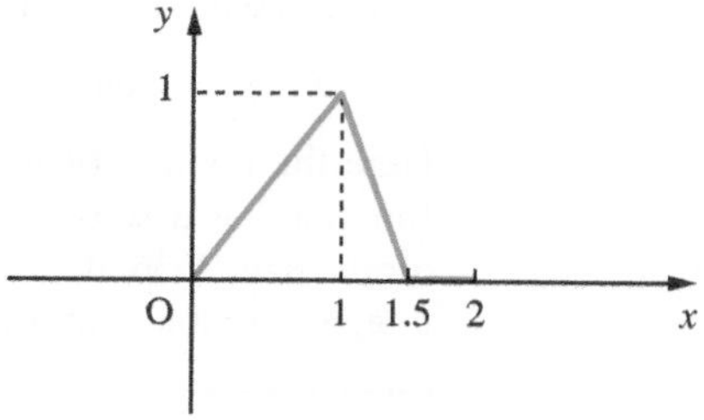

Figure 2.28 Graph of Question 15.

16 Show that

$$h(x) = \tfrac{1}{2}[f(x) - f(-x)]$$

is an odd function and that any function $f(x)$ may be written as the sum of an odd and an even function.

Illustrate this result with $f(x) = (x - 1)^3$.

2.3 Linear and quadratic functions

Among the more commonly used functions in engineering contexts are the linear and quadratic functions. This is because the mathematical models of practical problems often involve linear functions and also because more complicated functions are often well approximated locally by linear or quadratic functions. We will review the properties of these functions and in the process describe some of the contexts in which they occur.

2.3.1 Linear functions

The **linear function** is the simplest function that occurs in practical problems. It has the formula $f(x) = mx + c$ where m and c are constant numbers and x is the unassigned or independent variable as usual. The graph of $f(x)$ is the set of points (x, y) where $y = mx + c$, which is the equation of a straight line on a cartesian coordinate plot (see Section 1.4.2). Hence, the function is called the linear function. An example of a linear function is the conversion of a temperature T_1 °C to the temperature T_2 °F. Here

$$T_2 = \tfrac{9}{5}T_1 + 32$$

and $m = \frac{9}{5}$ with $c = 32$.

To determine the formula for a particular linear function the two constants m and c have to be found. This implies that we need two pieces of information to determine $f(x)$.

Example 2.13 A manufacturer produces 5000 items at a total cost of £10 000 and sells them at £2.75 each. What is the manufacturer's profit as a function of the number x of items sold?

Solution Let the manufacturer's profit be £P. If x items are sold then the total revenue is £$2.75x$, so that the amount of profit $P(x)$ is given by

$$P(x) = \text{revenue} - \text{cost} = 2.75x - 10\,000$$

Here the domain of the function is [0, 5000] and the range is [−10 000, 3750]. This function has a zero at $x = 3636\frac{4}{11}$. Thus to make a profit, the manufacturer has to sell more than 3636 items. (Note the modelling approximation in that, strictly, x is an integer variable, not a general real variable.)

If we know the values that the function $f(x)$ takes at two values, x_0 and x_1, of the independent variable x we can find the formula for $f(x)$. Let $f(x_0) = f_0$ and $f(x_1) = f_1$, then

$$f(x) = \frac{x - x_1}{x_0 - x_1} f_0 + \frac{x - x_0}{x_1 - x_0} f_1 \tag{2.6}$$

This formula is known as **Lagrange's formula**. It is obvious that the function is linear since we can arrange it as

$$f(x) = x\left[\frac{f_1 - f_0}{x_1 - x_0}\right] + \left[\frac{x_1 f_0 - x_0 f_1}{x_1 - x_0}\right]$$

The reader should verify from (2.6) that $f(x_0) = f_0$ and $f(x_1) = f_1$.

Example 2.14 Use Lagrange's formula to find the linear function $f(x)$ where $f(10) = 1241$ and $f(15) = 1556$.

Solution Taking $x_0 = 10$ and $x_1 = 15$ so that $f_0 = 1241$ and $f_1 = 1556$ we obtain

$$\begin{aligned} f(x) &= \frac{x - 15}{10 - 15}(1241) + \frac{x - 10}{15 - 10}(1556) \\ &= \frac{x}{5}(1556 - 1241) + 3(1241) - 2(1556) \\ &= \frac{x}{5}(315) + (3723 - 3112) = 63x + 611 \end{aligned}$$

The **rate of change** of a function, between two values $x = x_0$ and $x = x_1$ in its domain, is defined by the ratio of the change in the values of the function to the change in the values of x. Thus

$$\text{rate of change} = \frac{\text{change in values of } f(x)}{\text{change in values of } x} = \frac{f(x_1) - f(x_0)}{x_1 - x_0}$$

For a linear function with formula $f(x) = mx + c$ we have

$$\text{rate of change} = \frac{(mx_1 + c) - (mx_0 + c)}{x_1 - x_0}$$

$$= \frac{m(x_1 - x_0)}{x_1 - x_0} = m$$

which is a constant. If we know the rate of change m of a linear function $f(x)$ and the value f_0 at a point $x = x_0$, then we can write the formula for $f(x)$ as

$$f(x) = mx + f_0 - mx_0$$

For a linear function, the slope (gradient) of the graph is the rate of change of the function.

Example 2.15

The labour cost of producing a certain item is £21 per 10 000 items and the raw materials cost is £4 for 1000 items. Each time a new production run is begun, there is a set-up cost of £8. What is the cost, £$C(x)$, of a production run of x items?

Solution

Here the cost function has a rate of change comprising the labour cost per item (21/10 000) and the materials cost per item (4/1000). Thus the rate of change is 0.0061. We also know that if there is a production run with zero items, there is still a set-up cost of £8 so $f(0) = 8$. Thus the required function is

$$C(x) = 0.0061x + 8$$

2.3.2 Least squares fit of a linear function to experimental data

Because the linear function occurs in many mathematical models of practical problems, we often have to 'fit' linear functions to experimental data. That is, we have to find the values of m and c which yield the best overall description of the data. There are two distinct mathematical models that occur. These are given by the functions with formulae

(a) $y = ax$ and (b) $y = mx + c$

For example, the extension of an ideal spring under load may be represented by a function of type (a), while the velocity of a projectile launched vertically may be represented by a function of type (b).

From experiments we obtain a set of data points (x_k, y_k), $k = 1, 2, \dots, n$. We wish to find the value of the constant(s) of the linear function that best describes the phenomenon the data represents.

Case (a): the theoretical model has the form $y = ax$

The difference between theoretical value ax_k and the experimental value y_k at x_k is $(ax_k - y_k)$. This is the 'error' of the model at $x = x_k$. We define the value of a for which $y = ax$ best represents the data to be that value which minimizes the sum S of the squared errors:

$$S = \sum_{k=1}^{n} (ax_k - y_k)^2$$

(Hence the name 'least squares fit': the squares of the errors are chosen to avoid simple cancellation of two large errors of opposite sign.)

It is easy to find the minimizing value of a since S is essentially a quadratic expression in a. (All the x_k's and y_k's are numbers.) Rewriting, we have

$$\begin{aligned} S &= \sum_{k=1}^{n} (a^2x_k^2 - 2ax_ky_k + y_k^2) \\ &= \sum_{k=1}^{n} (a^2x_k^2) + \sum_{k=1}^{n} (-2ax_ky_k) + \sum_{k=1}^{n} y_k^2 \\ &= a^2 \sum_{k=1}^{n} x_k^2 - 2a \sum_{k=1}^{n} x_ky_k + \sum_{k=1}^{n} y_k^2 \end{aligned}$$

(Notice the 'taking out' of the common factors a^2 and $-2a$ in these sums.) Writing

$$P = \sum_{k=1}^{n} x_k^2, \quad Q = \sum_{k=1}^{n} x_ky_k \quad \text{and} \quad R = \sum_{k=1}^{n} y_k^2$$

we have

$$S = Pa^2 - 2aQ + R$$

On 'completing the square'

$$S = P\left(a - \frac{Q}{P}\right)^2 + \frac{RP - Q^2}{P}$$

and we see that the minimizing value of a is given by Q/P, when the first term is zero. Thus S is minimized when

$$a = \frac{\sum_{k=1}^{n} x_ky_k}{\sum_{k=1}^{n} x_k^2} \tag{2.7}$$

Take care not to claim too high precision in the calculated value of a.

Example 2.16 Find the value of a which provides the least squares fit to the model $y = ax$ for the data given in Figure 2.29.

Figure 2.29
Data of Example 2.16.

k	1	2	3	4	5	6
x_k	50	100	150	200	250	300
y_k	5	8	9	11	12	15

Solution From (2.7) the least squares fit is provided by

$$a = \left(\sum_{k=1}^{6} x_k y_k\right) \Big/ \left(\sum_{k=1}^{6} x_k^2\right)$$

Here

$$\sum_{k=1}^{6} x_k y_k = 250 + 800 + 1350 + 2200 + 3000 + 4500 = 12\,100$$

and

$$\sum_{k=1}^{6} x_k^2 = 50^2 + 100^2 + 150^2 + 200^2 + 250^2 + 300^2 = 227\,500$$

so that $a = 121/2275 = 0.053$.

Case (b): the theoretical model has the form $y = mx + c$

Analagous to case (a), this can be seen as minimizing the sum

$$S = \sum_{k=1}^{n} (mx_k + c - y_k)^2$$

The algebraic approach to this minimization uses completion of squares in two variables. The details are complicated but are given below. Working through the details provides useful practice and consolidation of the use of the sigma notation.

Multiplying out the terms gives

$$S = m^2 \sum_{k=1}^{n} x_k^2 - 2m \sum_{k=1}^{n} x_k y_k + 2mc \sum_{k=1}^{n} x_k - 2c \sum_{k=1}^{n} y_k + nc^2 + \sum_{k=1}^{n} y_k^2$$

Now $\sum_{k=1}^{n} x_k = n\bar{x}$ and $\sum_{k=1}^{n} y_k = n\bar{y}$, where $\bar{x}$ and $\bar{y}$ are the **mean values** of the x_k's and y_k's respectively, so S can be written

$$S = m^2 \sum_{k=1}^{n} x_k^2 - 2m \sum_{k=1}^{n} x_k y_k + 2mcn\bar{x} - 2cn\bar{y} + nc^2 + \sum_{k=1}^{n} y_k^2$$

Completing the square with terms involving n gives

$$S = n(c - \bar{y} + m\bar{x})^2 + m^2 \left\{\sum_{k=1}^{n} x_k^2 - n\bar{x}^2\right\} - 2m \left\{\sum_{k=1}^{n} x_k y_k - n\bar{x}\bar{y}\right\} + \sum_{k=1}^{n} y_k^2 - n\bar{y}^2$$

Now completing the square with the remaining terms involving m we have

$$S = n(c - \bar{y} + m\bar{x})^2 + p(m - q/p)^2 + r - q^2/p$$

where

$$p = \sum_{k=1}^{n} x_k^2 - n\bar{x}^2 \quad \text{and} \quad q = \sum_{k=1}^{n} x_k y_k - n\bar{x}\bar{y} \quad \text{and} \quad r = \sum_{k=1}^{n} y_k^2 - n\bar{y}^2$$

Thus S is minimized where

$$m = \frac{\sum_{k=1}^{n} x_k y_k - n\bar{x}\bar{y}}{\sum_{k=1}^{n} x_k^2 - n\bar{x}^2} \quad \text{and} \quad c = \bar{y} - m\bar{x} \tag{2.8}$$

To avoid loss of significance, the formula for m is usually expressed in the form

$$m = \frac{\sum_{k=1}^{n} (x_k - \bar{x})(y_k - \bar{y})}{\sum_{k=1}^{n} (x_k - \bar{x})^2} \tag{2.9}$$

We can observe that in this case the best straight line passes through the average data point $(\bar{x}, \bar{y})$, and the best straight line has the formula

$$y = mx + c$$

with $c = \bar{y} - m\bar{x}$.

Example 2.17 Find the values of m and c which provide the least squares fit to the linear model $y = mx + c$ for the data given in Figure 2.30.

Figure 2.30
Data of Example 2.17.

k	1	2	3	4	5
x_k	0	1	2	3	4
y_k	1	1	2	2	3

Solution From (2.9) the least squares fit is provided by

$$m = \frac{\sum_{k=1}^{n} (x_k - \bar{x})(y_k - \bar{y})}{\sum_{k=1}^{n} (x_k - \bar{x})^2}$$

Here $\bar{x} = \frac{1}{5}(10) = 2.0$, $\bar{y} = \frac{1}{5}(9) = 1.8$, $\sum_{k=1}^{n} (x_k - \bar{x})(y_k - \bar{y}) = 5.0$ and $\sum_{k=1}^{n} (x_k - \bar{x})^2 = 10$, so that

$$m = 0.5$$

and hence $c = 1.8 - 0.5(2) = 0.8$.

Thus the best straight line fit to the data is provided by $y = 0.5x + 0.8$.

See page 109 for MATLAB commands to reproduce the answer.

The formula for case (b) is the one most commonly given on calculators and in computer packages (where it is called **linear regression**). It is important to have a theoretical justification to fitting data to a function, otherwise it is easy to produce nonsense. For example, the data in Example 2.16 actually related to the extension of a soft spring under a load, so that it would be inappropriate to fit that data to $y = mx + c$. A non-zero value for c would imply an extension with zero load! A little care is needed when using computer packages. Some use the form $y = ax + b$ and others the form $y = a + bx$ as the basic formula.

2.3.3 Exercises

17 Obtain the formula for the linear functions $f(x)$ such that

(a) $f(0) = 3$ and $f(2) = -1$

(b) $f(-1) = 2$ and $f(3) = 4$

(c) $f(1.231) = 2.791$ and $f(2.492) = 3.112$

18 Calculate the rate of change of the linear functions given by

(a) $f(x) = 3x - 2$

(b) $f(x) = 2 - 3x$

(c) $f(-1) = 2$ and $f(3) = 4$

19 The total labour cost of producing a certain item is £43 per 100 items produced. The raw materials cost £25 per 1000 items. There is a set-up cost of £50 for each production run. Obtain the formula for the cost of a production run of x items.

The manufacturer decides to have a production run of 2000 items. What is its cost? If the items are sold at £1.20 each, write down a formula for the manufacturer's profit if x items are sold. What is the breakeven number of items sold?

20 Find the least squares fit to the linear function $y = ax$ of the data given in Figure 2.31.

k	1	2	3	4	5
x_k	10.1	10.2	10.3	10.4	10.5
y_k	3.10	3.12	3.21	3.25	3.32

Figure 2.31 Table of Question 20.

21 Find the least squares fit to the linear function $y = mx + c$ for the experimental data given in Figure 2.32.

k	1	2	3	4	5
x_k	55	60	65	70	75
y_k	107	109	114	118	123

Figure 2.32 Table of Question 21.

22 On the graph of the line $y = x$, draw the lines $y = 0$, $x = a$ and $x = b$. Show that the area enclosed by these four lines is $\frac{1}{2}(b^2 - a^2)$ (assume $b > a$).

Deduce that this area is the average value of $y = x$ on the interval $[a, b]$ multiplied by the size of that interval.

23 The velocity of an object falling under gravity is $v(t) = gt$ where t is the lapsed time from its release from rest and g is the acceleration due to gravity. Draw a graph of $v(t)$ to show that its average velocity over that time period is $\frac{1}{2}gt$ and deduce that the distance travelled is $\frac{1}{2}gt^2$.

2.3.4 The quadratic function

The general quadratic function has the form

$$f(x) = ax^2 + bx + c$$

where a, b and c are constants and $a \neq 0$. By 'completing the square' we can show that (see Example 1.15)

$$f(x) = a\left[\left(x + \frac{b}{2a}\right)^2 + \frac{4ac - b^2}{4a^2}\right] \tag{2.10}$$

which implies that the graph of $f(x)$ is either a 'cup' ($a > 0$) or a 'cap' ($a < 0$), as shown in Figure 2.33, and is a parabola.

We can see that, because the quadratic function has three constants, to determine a specific quadratic function requires three data points. The formula for the quadratic function $f(x)$ taking the values f_0, f_1, f_2 at the values x_0, x_1, x_2, of the independent variable x, may be written in Lagrange's form:

$$f(x) = \frac{(x - x_1)(x - x_2)}{(x_0 - x_1)(x_0 - x_2)}f_0 + \frac{(x - x_0)(x - x_2)}{(x_1 - x_0)(x_1 - x_2)}f_1 + \frac{(x - x_0)(x - x_1)}{(x_2 - x_0)(x_2 - x_1)}f_2 \tag{2.11}$$

The right-hand side of this formula is clearly a quadratic function. The reader should spend a few minutes verifying that inserting the values $x = x_0$, x_1 and x_2 yields $f(x_0) = f_0$, $f(x_1) = f_1$ and $f(x_2) = f_2$.

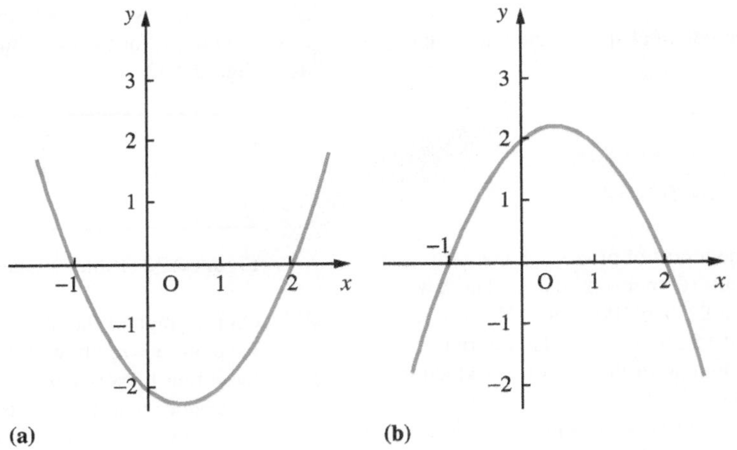

Figure 2.33
(a) $a > 0$; (b) $a < 0$.

Example 2.18 Find the formula of the quadratic function which satisfies the data points (1, 2), (2, 4) and (3, 8).

Solution Choose $x_0 = 1$, $x_1 = 2$ and $x_2 = 3$ so that $f_0 = 2$, $f_1 = 4$ and $f_2 = 8$. Then using Lagrange's formula (2.10) we have

$$f(x) = \frac{(x-2)(x-3)}{(1-2)(1-3)}(2) + \frac{(x-1)(x-3)}{(2-1)(2-3)}(4) + \frac{(x-1)(x-2)}{(3-1)(3-2)}(8)$$

$$= (x-2)(x-3) - 4(x-1)(x-3) + 4(x-1)(x-2) = x^2 - x + 2$$

Lagrange's formula is not always the best way to obtain the formula of a quadratic function. Sometimes we wish to obtain the formula as an expansion about a specific point, as illustrated in Example 2.19.

Example 2.19 Find the quadratic function in the form

$$f(x) = A(x-2)^2 + B(x-2) + C$$

which satisfies $f(1) = 2, f(2) = 4, f(3) = 8$.

Solution Setting $x = 1$, 2 and 3 into the formula for $f(x)$ we obtain

$$f(1)\colon A - B + C = 2$$

$$f(2)\colon \qquad C = 4$$

$$f(3)\colon A + B + C = 8$$

from which we quickly find $A = 1, B = 3$ and $C = 4$. Thus

$$f(x) = (x-2)^2 + 3(x-2) + 4$$

The way we express the quadratic function depends on the problem context. The form $f(x) = ax^2 + bx + c$ is convenient for values of x near $x = 0$, while the form $f(x) = A(x - x_0)^2 + B(x - x_0) + C$ is convenient for values of x near $x = x_0$. (The second form here is sometimes called the **Taylor expansion** of $f(x)$ about $x = x_0$.) This is discussed for the general function in Section 9.4, where we make use of the differential calculus to obtain the expansion.

Since we can write $f(x)$ in the form (2.10), we see that when $b^2 > 4ac$ we can factorize $f(x)$ into the product of two linear factors and $f(x)$ has two zeros given as in (1.8) by

$$x = \frac{-b \pm \sqrt{(b^2 - 4ac)}}{2a}$$

When $b^2 < 4ac$, $f(x)$ cannot be factorized and does not have a zero. In this case it is called an **irreducible quadratic function**.

Example 2.20 Complete the squares of the following quadratics and specify which are irreducible.

(a) $y = x^2 + x + 1$ (b) $y = 3x^2 - 2x - 1$

(c) $y = 4 + 3x - x^2$ (d) $y = 2x - 1 - 2x^2$

Solution (a) In this case, $a = b = c = 1$ so that $b^2 - 4ac = -3 < 0$ and we deduce that the quadratic is irreducible. Alternatively, using the method of completing the square we have

$$y = x^2 + x + 1 = (x + \tfrac{1}{2})^2 + \tfrac{3}{4} = (x + \tfrac{1}{2})^2 + (\tfrac{\sqrt{3}}{2})^2$$

Since this is a sum of squares, like $A^2 + B^2$, it cannot, unlike a difference of squares, $A^2 - B^2 = (A - B)(A + B)$, be factorized. Thus this is an irreducible quadratic function.

(b) Here $a = 3$, $b = -2$ and $c = -1$, so that $b^2 - 4ac = 16 > 0$ and we deduce that this is not an irreducible quadratic. Alternatively, completing the square we have

$$\begin{aligned} y &= 3x^2 - 2x - 1 = 3(x^2 - \tfrac{2}{3}x - \tfrac{1}{3}) \\ &= 3[(x - \tfrac{1}{3})^2 - \tfrac{4}{9}] = 3[(x - \tfrac{1}{3}) - \tfrac{2}{3}][(x - \tfrac{1}{3}) + \tfrac{2}{3}] \\ &= 3[x - 1][x + \tfrac{1}{3}] = (x - 1)(3x + 1) \end{aligned}$$

Thus this is not an irreducible quadratic function.

(c) Here $a = -1$, $b = 3$ and $c = 4$, so that $b^2 - 4ac = 25 > 0$ and we deduce that the quadratic is irreducible. Alternatively, completing the square we have

$$\begin{aligned} y &= 4 + 3x - x^2 = 4 + \tfrac{9}{4} - (x - \tfrac{3}{2})^2 \\ &= \tfrac{25}{4} - (x - \tfrac{3}{2})^2 = [\tfrac{5}{2} - (x - \tfrac{3}{2})][\tfrac{5}{2} + (x - \tfrac{3}{2})] \\ &= (4 - x)(1 + x) \end{aligned}$$

Thus y is a product of two linear factors and $4 + 3x - x^2$ is not an irreducible quadratic function.

(d) Here $a = -2$, $b = 2$ and $c = -1$, so that $b^2 - 4ac = -4 < 0$ and we deduce that the quadratic is irreducible. Alternatively we may complete the square

$$\begin{aligned} y &= 2x - 1 - 2x^2 = -1 - 2(x^2 - x) \\ &= -1 + \tfrac{1}{2} - 2(x - \tfrac{1}{2})^2 = -\tfrac{1}{2} - 2(x - \tfrac{1}{2})^2 \\ &= -2[\tfrac{1}{4} + (x - \tfrac{1}{2})^2] \end{aligned}$$

Since the term inside the square brackets is the sum of squares, we have an irreducible quadratic function.

The quadratic function

$$f(x) = ax^2 + bx + c$$

has a maximum when $a < 0$ and a minimum when $a > 0$, as illustrated earlier in Figure 2.33. The position and value of that extremal point (that is, of the maximum or the minimum) can be obtained from the completed square form (2.10) of $f(x)$. These occur where

$$x + \frac{b}{2a} = 0$$

Thus, when $a > 0$, $f(x)$ has a minimum value $(4ac - b^2)/(4a)$ where $x = -b/(2a)$. When $a < 0$, $f(x)$ has a maximum value $(4ac - b^2)/(4a)$ at $x = -b/(2a)$.

This result is important in engineering contexts when we are trying to optimize costs or profits or to produce an optimal design (see Section 2.10).

Example 2.21 Find the extremal values of the functions

(a) $y = x^2 + x + 1$ (b) $y = 3x^2 - 2x - 1$

(c) $y = 4 + 3x - x^2$ (d) $y = 2x - 1 - 2x^2$

Solution This uses the completed squares of Example 2.20.

(a) $y = x^2 + x + 1 = (x + \frac{1}{2})^2 + \frac{3}{4}$

Clearly the smallest value y can take is $\frac{3}{4}$ and this occurs when $x + \frac{1}{2} = 0$; that is, when $x = -\frac{1}{2}$.

(b) $y = 3x^2 - 2x - 1 = 3(x - \frac{1}{3})^2 - \frac{4}{3}$

Clearly the smallest value of y occurs when $x = \frac{1}{3}$ and is equal to $-\frac{4}{3}$.

(c) $y = 4 + 3x - x^2 = \frac{25}{4} - (x - \frac{3}{2})^2$

Clearly the largest value y can take is $\frac{25}{4}$ and this occurs when $x = \frac{3}{2}$.

(d) $y = 2x - 1 - 2x^2 = -\frac{1}{2} - 2(x - \frac{1}{2})^2$

Thus the maximum value of y equals $-\frac{1}{2}$ and occurs where $x = \frac{1}{2}$.

Confirm that these results conform with the theory above.

2.3.5 Exercises

24 Find the formulae of the quadratic functions $f(x)$ such that

(a) $f(1) = 3, f(2) = 7$ and $f(4) = 19$

(b) $f(-1) = 1, f(1) = -1$ and $f(4) = 2$

25 Find the numbers A, B and C such that

$$\begin{aligned} f(x) &= x^2 - 8x + 10 \\ &= A(x - 2)^2 + B(x - 2) + C \end{aligned}$$

26 Determine which of the following quadratic functions are irreducible.

(a) $f(x) = x^2 + 2x + 3$ (b) $f(x) = 4x^2 - 12x + 9$

(c) $f(x) = 6 - 4x - 3x^2$ (d) $f(x) = 3x - 1 - 5x^2$

27 Find the maximum or minimum values of the quadratic functions given in Question 26.

28 For what values of x are the values of the quadratic functions below greater than zero?

(a) $f(x) = x^2 - 6x + 8$ (b) $f(x) = 15 + x - 2x^2$

29 A car travelling at u mph has to make an emergency stop. There is an initial reaction time T_1 before the driver applies a constant braking deceleration of a mph^2. After a further time T_2 the car comes to rest. Show that $T_2 = u/a$ and that the average speed during the braking period is $u/2$. Hence show that the total stopping distance D may be expressed in the form

$$D = Au + Bu^2$$

where A and B depend on T_1 and a.

The stopping distances for a car travelling at 20 mph and 40 mph are 40 feet and 120 feet respectively. Estimate the stopping distance for a car travelling at 70 mph.

A driver sees a hazard 150 feet ahead. What is the maximum possible speed of the car at that moment if a collision is to be avoided?

2.4 Polynomial functions

A **polynomial function** has the general form

$$f(x) = a_n x^n + a_{n-1}x^{n-1} + \ldots + a_1 x + a_0, \quad x \text{ in } \mathbb{R} \tag{2.12}$$

where n is a positive integer and a_r is a real number called the coefficient of x^r, $r = 0, 1, \ldots, n$. The index n of the highest power of x occurring is called the **degree of the polynomial**. For $n = 1$ we obtain the linear function

$$f(x) = a_1 x + a_0$$

and for $n = 2$ the quadratic function

$$f(x) = a_2 x^2 + a_1 x + a_0$$

and so on.

We obtained in Sections 2.3.1 and 2.3.4 Lagrange's formulae for linear and for quadratic functions. The basic idea of the formulae can be used to obtain a formula for a polynomial of degree n which is such that $f(x_0) = f_0$, $f(x_1) = f_1$, $f(x_2) = f_2$, … , $f(x_n) = f_n$. Notice we need $(n + 1)$ values to determine a polynomial of degree n. We can write Lagrange's formula in the form.

$$f(x) = L_0(x)f_0 + L_1(x)f_1 + L_2(x)f_2 + \ldots + L_n(x)f_n$$

where $L_0(x), L_1(x), \ldots, L_n(x)$ are polynomials of degree n such that

$$L_k(x_j) = 0, \quad x_j \neq x_k \text{ (or } j \neq k)$$

$$L_k(x_k) = 1$$

This implies that L_k has the form

$$L_k(x) = \frac{(x - x_0)(x - x_1)(x - x_2)\ldots(x - x_{k-1})(x - x_{k+1})\ldots(x - x_n)}{(x_k - x_0)(x_k - x_1)(x_k - x_2)\ldots(x_k - x_{k-1})(x_k - x_{k+1})\ldots(x_k - x_n)}$$

(It is easy to verify that L_k has degree n and that $L_k(x_j) = 0$, $j \neq k$ and $L_k(x_k) = 1$.)

Example 2.22 Find the cubic function such that $f(-3) = 528$, $f(0) = 1017$, $f(2) = 1433$ and $f(5) = 2312$.

Solution Notice that we need four data points to determine a cubic function. We can write

$$f(x) = L_0(x)f_0 + L_1(x)f_1 + L_2(x)f_2 + L_3(x)f_3$$

where $x_0 = -3$, $f_0 = 528$, $x_1 = 0$, $f_1 = 1017$, $x_2 = 2$, $f_2 = 1433$, $x_3 = 5$ and $f_3 = 2312$. Thus

$$L_0(x) = \frac{(x - 0)(x - 2)(x - 5)}{(-3 - 0)(-3 - 2)(-3 - 5)} = -\tfrac{1}{120}(x^3 - 7x^2 + 10x)$$

$$L_1(x) = \frac{(x + 3)(x - 2)(x - 5)}{(0 + 3)(0 - 2)(0 - 5)} = \tfrac{1}{30}(x^3 - 4x^2 - 11x + 30)$$

$$L_2(x) = \frac{(x+3)(x-0)(x-5)}{(2+3)(2-0)(2-5)} = -\tfrac{1}{30}(x^3 - 2x^2 - 15x)$$

$$L_3(x) = \frac{(x+3)(x-0)(x-2)}{(5+3)(5-0)(5-2)} = \tfrac{1}{120}(x^3 + x^2 - 6x)$$

Notice that each of the L_k's is a cubic function, so that their sum will be a cubic function

$$\begin{aligned} f(x) &= -\tfrac{1}{120}(x^3 - 7x^2 + 10x)(528) + \tfrac{1}{30}(x^3 - 4x^2 - 11x + 30)(1017) \\ &\quad - \tfrac{1}{30}(x^3 - 2x^2 - 15x)(1433) + \tfrac{1}{120}(x^3 + x^2 - 6x)(2312) \\ &= x^3 + 10x^2 + 184x + 1017 \end{aligned}$$

2.4.1 Basic properties

Polynomials have two important mathematical properties.

Property (i)

If two polynomials are equal for all values of the independent variable then corresponding coefficients of the powers of the variable are equal. Thus if

$$f(x) = a_n x^n + a_{n-1} x^{n-1} + \ldots + a_1 x + a_0$$

$$g(x) = b_n x^n + b_{n-1} x^{n-1} + \ldots + b_1 x + b_0$$

and

$$f(x) = g(x) \quad \text{for all } x$$

then

$$a_i = b_i \quad \text{for } i = 0, 1, 2, \ldots, n$$

This property forms the basis of a technique called **equating coefficients**, which will be used in determining partial fractions in Section 2.5.

Property (ii)

Any polynomial with real coefficients can be expressed as a product of linear and irreducible quadratic factors.

Example 2.23 Find the values of A, B and C that ensure that

$$x^2 + 1 = A(x-1) + B(x+2) + C(x^2+2)$$

for all values of x.

Solution Multiplying out the right-hand side, we have

$$x^2 + 0x + 1 = Cx^2 + (A+B)x + (-A + 2B + 2C)$$

Using Property (i), we compare, or equate, the coefficients of x^2, x and x^0 in turn to give

$$C = 1$$
$$A + B = 0$$
$$-A + 2B + 2C = 1$$

which we then solve to give

$$A = \tfrac{1}{3}, \quad B = -\tfrac{1}{3}, \quad C = 1$$

Checking, we have

$$\tfrac{1}{3}(x-1) - \tfrac{1}{3}(x+2) + (x^2+2) = \tfrac{1}{3}x - \tfrac{1}{3} - \tfrac{1}{3}x - \tfrac{2}{3} + x^2 + 2 = x^2 + 1$$

2.4.2 Factorization

Although Property (ii) was known earlier, the first rigorous proof was published by Gauss in 1799. The result is an 'existence theorem'. It tells us that polynomials can be factored but does not indicate how to find the factors!

Example 2.24 Factorize the polynomials

(a) $x^3 - 3x^2 + 6x - 4$ (b) $x^4 - 16$ (c) $x^4 + 16$

Solution (a) The function $f(x) = x^3 - 3x^2 + 6x - 4$ clearly has the value zero at $x = 1$. Thus $x - 1$ must be a factor of $f(x)$. We can now divide $x^3 - 3x^2 + 6x - 4$ by $x - 1$ using algebraic division, a process akin to long division of numbers. The process may be set out as follows.

Step 1

$$x - 1)x^3 - 3x^2 + 6x - 4($$

In order to produce the term x^3, $x - 1$ must be multiplied by x^2. Do this and subtract the result from $x^3 - 3x^2 + 6x - 4$.

$$x - 1)x^3 - 3x^2 + 6x - 4(x^2$$
$$\underline{x^3 - x^2}$$
$$-2x^2 + 6x - 4$$

Step 2

Now repeat the process on the polynomial $-2x^2 + 6x - 4$. In this case, in order to eliminate the term $-2x^2$, we must multiply $x - 1$ by $-2x$.

$$x - 1)x^3 - 3x^2 + 6x - 4(x^2 - 2x$$
$$\underline{x^3 - x^2}$$
$$-2x^2 + 6x - 4$$
$$\underline{-2x^2 + 2x}$$
$$4x - 4$$

Step 3

Finally we must multiply $x - 1$ by 4 to eliminate $4x - 4$ as follows:

$$
\begin{array}{r}
x - 1)x^3 - 3x^2 + 6x - 4(x^2 - 2x + 4 \\
\underline{x^3 - x^2} \qquad\qquad\qquad \\
-2x^2 + 6x - 4 \\
\underline{-2x^2 + 2x} \qquad \\
4x - 4 \\
\underline{4x - 4}
\end{array}
$$

Thus

$$f(x) = (x - 1)(x^2 - 2x + 4)$$

The quadratic factor $x^2 - 2x + 4$ is an **irreducible factor**, as is shown by 'completing the square':

$$x^2 - 2x + 4 = (x - 1)^2 + 3$$

(b) The functions $f_1(x) = x^4$ and $f_2(x) = x^4 - 16$ have similar graphs, as shown in Figures 2.34(a) and (b). It is clear from these graphs that $f_2(x)$ has zeros at two values of x, where $x^4 = 16$; that is, at $x^2 = 4$ ($x^2 = -4$ is not allowed for real x). Thus the zeros of f_2 are at $x = 2$ and $x = -2$, and we can write

$$
\begin{aligned}
f_2(x) &= x^4 - 16 = (x^2 - 4)(x^2 + 4) \\
&= (x - 2)(x + 2)(x^2 + 4)
\end{aligned}
$$

(c) The functions $f_1(x) = x^4$ and $f_3(x) = x^4 + 16$ have similar graphs, as shown in Figures 2.34(a) and (c). It is clear from these graphs that $f_3(x)$ does not have any real zeros, so we expect it to be factored into two quadratic terms. We can write

$$x^4 + 16 = (x^2 + 4)^2 - 8x^2$$

which is a difference of squares and may be factored.

$$(x^2 + 4)^2 - 8x^2 = (x^2 + 4)^2 - (x\sqrt{8})^2 = [(x^2 + 4) - x\sqrt{8}][(x^2 + 4) + x\sqrt{8}]$$

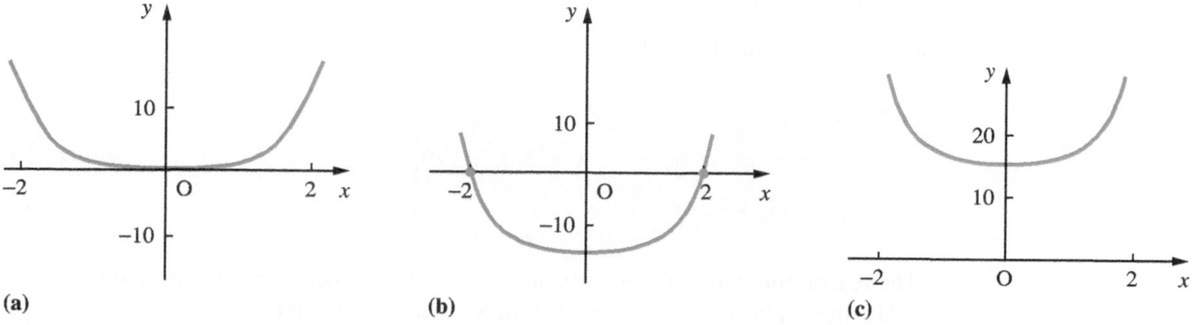

Figure 2.34 Graphs of (a) $y = f_1(x) = x^4$, (b) $y = f_2(x) = x^4 - 16$ and (c) $y = f_3(x) = x^4 + 16$.

Thus we obtain

$$f_3(x) = x^4 + 16 = (x^2 - 2x\sqrt{2} + 4)(x^2 + 2x\sqrt{2} + 4)$$

Since $x^2 \pm 2x\sqrt{2} + 4 = (x \pm \sqrt{2})^2 + 2$, we deduce that these are irreducible quadratics.

2.4.3 Nested multiplication and synthetic division

In Example 2.24(a) we found the image value of the polynomial at $x = 1$ by direct substitution. In general, however, the most efficient way to evaluate the image values of a polynomial function is to use **nested multiplication**. Consider the cubic function

$$f(x) = 4x^3 - 5x^2 + 2x + 3$$

This may be written as

$$f(x) = [(4x - 5)x + 2]x + 3$$

We evaluate this by evaluating each bracketed expression in turn, working from the innermost. Thus to find $f(6)$, the following steps are taken:

(1) Multiply 4 by x and subtract 5; in this case $4 \times 6 - 5 = 19$.
(2) Multiply the result of step 1 by x and add 2; in this case $19 \times 6 + 2 = 116$.
(3) Multiply the result of step 2 by x and add 3; in this case $116 \times 6 + 3 = 699$.

Thus $f(6) = 699$.

On a computer this is performed by means of a simple recurrence relation. To evaluate

$$f(x) = a_n x^n + a_{n-1} x^{n-1} + \ldots + a_0$$

at $x = t$, we use the formulae

$$\begin{aligned} b_{n-1} &= a_n \\ b_{n-2} &= tb_{n-1} + a_{n-1} \\ b_{n-3} &= tb_{n-2} + a_{n-2} \\ &\vdots \\ b_1 &= tb_2 + a_2 \\ b_0 &= tb_1 + a_1 \\ f(t) &= tb_0 + a_0 \end{aligned}$$

which may be summarized as

$$\left.\begin{aligned} b_{n-1} &= a_n \\ b_{n-k} &= tb_{n-k+1} + a_{n-k+1} \quad (k = 2, 3, \ldots, n) \\ f(t) &= tb_0 + a_0 \end{aligned}\right\} \quad \textbf{(2.13)}$$

(The reason for storing the intermediate values b_k will become obvious below.)

Having evaluated $f(x)$ at $x = t$, it follows that for a given t

$$f(x) - f(t) = 0$$

at $x = t$; that is, $f(x) - f(t)$ has a factor $x - t$. Thus we can write

$$f(x) - f(t) = (x - t)(c_{n-1}x^{n-1} + c_{n-2}x^{n-2} + \dots + c_1x + c_0)$$

Multiplying out the right-hand side, we have

$$f(x) - f(t) = c_{n-1}x^n + (c_{n-2} - tc_{n-1})x^{n-1} + (c_{n-3} - tc_{n-2})x^{n-2} + \dots + (c_0 - tc_1)x + (-tc_0)$$

so that we may write

$$f(x) = c_{n-1}x^n + (c_{n-2} - tc_{n-1})x^{n-1} + (c_{n-3} - tc_{n-2})x^{n-2} + \dots + (c_0 - tc_1)x + f(t) - tc_0$$

But

$$f(x) = a_nx^n + a_{n-1}x^{n-1} + a_{n-2}x^{n-2} + \dots + a_1x + a_0$$

So, using Property (i) of Section 2.4.1 and comparing coefficients of like powers of x, we have

$$\begin{aligned}
c_{n-1} &= a_n & & \\
c_{n-2} - tc_{n-1} &= a_{n-1} & \text{implying} \quad & c_{n-2} = tc_{n-1} + a_{n-1} \\
c_{n-3} - tc_{n-2} &= a_{n-2} & \text{implying} \quad & c_{n-3} = tc_{n-2} + a_{n-2} \\
&\vdots & \vdots \quad & \vdots \\
c_0 - tc_1 &= a_1 & \text{implying} \quad & c_0 = tc_1 + a_1 \\
f(t) - tc_0 &= a_0 & \text{implying} \quad & f(t) = tc_0 + a_0
\end{aligned}$$

Thus c_k satisfies exactly the same formula as b_k, so that the intermediate numbers generated by the method are the coefficients of the quotient polynomial. We can then write

$$f(x) = (b_{n-1}x^{n-1} + b_{n-2}x^{n-2} + \dots + b_1x + b_0)(x - t) + f(t) \tag{2.14}$$

or

$$\frac{f(x)}{x - t} = b_{n-1}x^{n-1} + b_{n-2}x^{n-2} + \dots + b_1x + b_0 + \frac{f(t)}{x - t}$$

Result (2.14) tells us that if the polynomial $f(x)$ given in (2.12) is divided by $x - t$ then this results in a quotient polynomial $q(x)$ given by

$$q(x) = b_{n-1}x^{n-1} + \dots + b_0$$

and a remainder $r = f(t)$ that is independent of x. Because of this property, the method of nested multiplication is sometimes called **synthetic division.**

The coefficients b_i, $i = 0, \dots, n - 1$, of the quotient polynomial and remainder term $f(t)$ may be determined using the formulae (2.13). The process may be carried out in the following tabular form:

	a_n	a_{n-1}	a_{n-2}	$\dots$	a_2	a_1	a_0
$\times t$		tb_{n-1}	tb_{n-2}	$\dots$	tb_2	tb_1	tb_0
	b_{n-1}	b_{n-2}	b_{n-3}	$\dots$	b_1	b_0	r

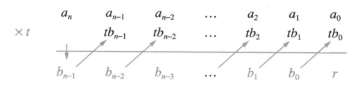

After the number below the line is calculated as the sum of the two numbers immediately above it, it is multiplied by t and placed in the next space above the line as indicated by the arrows. This procedure is repeated until all the terms are calculated.

The method of synthetic division could have been used as an alternative to algebraic division in Example 2.24.

Example 2.25 Show that $f(x) = x^3 - 3x^2 + 6x - 4$ is zero at $x = 1$, and hence factorize $f(x)$.

Solution Using the nested multiplication procedure to divide $x^3 - 3x^2 + 6x - 4$ by $x - 1$ gives the tabular form

	a_3	a_2	a_1	a_0
	1	−3	6	−4
×1	0	1	−2	4
	1	−2	4	0
	b_2	b_1	b_0	$f(1)$

Since the remainder $f(1)$ is zero, it follows that $f(x)$ is zero at $x = 1$. Thus

$$f(x) = (x^2 - 2x + 4)(x - 1)$$

and we have extracted the factor $x - 1$. We may then examine the quadratic factor $x^2 - 2x + 4$ as we did in Example 2.24(a) and show that it is an irreducible quadratic factor.

Sometimes in problem-solving we need to rearrange the formula for the polynomial function as an expansion about a point, $x = a$, other than $x = 0$. That is, we need to find the numbers $A_0, A_1, \ldots, A_n$ such that

$$\begin{aligned} f(x) &= a_n x^n + a_{n-1}x^{n-1} + \ldots + a_1 x + a_0 \\ &= A_n(x-a)^n + A_{n-1}(x-a)^{n-1} + \ldots + A_1(x-a) + A_0 \end{aligned}$$

This transformation can be achieved using the technique illustrated for the quadratic function in Example 2.19 which depends on the identity property of polynomials. It can be achieved more easily using **repeated synthetic division**, as is shown in Example 2.26.

Example 2.26 Obtain the expansion about $x = 2$ of the function $y = x^3 - 3x^2 + 6x - 4$.

Solution Using the numerical scheme as set out in Example 2.25 we have

	1	−3	6	−4
×2	0	2	−2	8
	1	−1	4	4

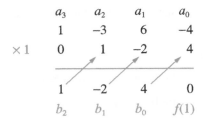

so that

$$x^3 - 3x^2 + 6x - 4 = (x - 2)(x^2 - x + 4) + 4$$

Now repeating the process with $y = x^2 - x + 4$, we have

	1	−1	4
×2	0	2	2
	1	1	6

so that

$$x^2 - x + 4 = (x - 2)(x + 1) + 6$$

and

$$x^3 - 3x^2 + 6x - 4 = (x - 2)[(x - 2)(x + 1) + 6] + 4$$

Lastly,

$$x + 1 = (x - 2) + 3$$

so that

$$\begin{aligned} y &= (x - 2)[(x - 2)^2 + 3(x - 2) + 6] + 4 \\ &= (x - 2)^3 + 3(x - 2)^2 + 6(x - 2) + 4 \end{aligned}$$

For hand computation the whole process can be set out as a single table:

	1	−3	6	−4
×2	0	2	−2	8
	1	−1	4	⋮4
×2	0	2	2	
	1	1	⋮6	
×2	0	2		
	1	⋮3		

Here, then, 1, 3, 6 and 4 provide the coefficients of $(x - 2)^3$, $(x - 2)^2$, $(x - 2)^1$ and $(x - 2)^0$ in the Taylor expansion.

2.4.4 Roots of polynomial equations

Polynomial equations occur frequently in engineering applications, from the identification of resonant frequencies when concerned with rotating machinery to the stability analysis of circuits. It is often useful to see the connections between the roots of a polynomial equation and its coefficients.

Example 2.27 Show that any real roots of the equation

$$x^3 - 3x^2 + 6x - 4 = 0$$

lie between $x = 0$ and $x = 2$.

Solution From Example 2.26 we know that

$$x^3 - 3x^2 + 6x - 4 \equiv (x-2)^3 + 3(x-2)^2 + 6(x-2) + 4$$

Now if $x > 2$, $(x-2)^3$, $(x-2)^2$ and $(x-2)$ are all positive numbers, so that for $x > 2$

$$(x-2)^3 + 3(x-2)^2 + 6(x-2) + 4 > 0$$

Thus $x^3 - 3x^2 + 6x - 4 = 0$ does not have a root that is greater than $x = 2$.

Similarly for $x < 0$, x^3 and x are both negative and $x^3 - 3x^2 + 6x - 4 < 0$ for $x < 0$. Thus $x^3 - 3x^2 + 6x - 4 = 0$ does not have a root that is less than $x = 0$. Hence all the real roots of

$$x^3 - 3x^2 + 6x - 4 = 0$$

lie between $x = 0$ and $x = 2$.

We can generalize the results of Example 2.27. Defining

$$f(x) = \sum_{k=0}^{n} A_n(x-a)^n$$

then the polynomial equation $f(x) = 0$ has no roots greater than $x = a$ if all of the A_k's have the same sign and has no roots less than $x = a$ if the A_k's alternate in sign.

The roots of a polynomial equation are related to its coefficients in more direct ways. Consider, for the moment, the quadratic equation with roots α and β. Then we can write the equation as

$$(x-\alpha)(x-\beta) = 0$$

which is equivalent to

$$x^2 - (\alpha+\beta)x + \alpha\beta = 0$$

Comparing this to the standard quadratic equation we have

$$a(x^2 - (\alpha+\beta)x + \alpha\beta) \equiv ax^2 + bx + c$$

Thus $-a(\alpha+\beta) = b$ and $a\alpha\beta = c$ so that

$$\alpha+\beta = -b/a \quad \text{and} \quad \alpha\beta = c/a$$

This gives us direct links between the sum of the roots of a quadratic equation and its coefficients and between the product of the roots and the coefficients. Similarly, we can show that if α, β and γ are the roots of the cubic equation

$$ax^3 + bx^2 + cx + d = 0$$

then

$$\alpha+\beta+\gamma = -b/a, \ \alpha\beta+\beta\gamma+\gamma\alpha = c/a, \ \alpha\beta\gamma = -d/a$$

In general, for the polynomial equation

$$a_n x^n + a_{n-1}x^{n-1} + a_{n-2}x^{n-2} + \dots + a_1 x + a_0 = 0$$

the sum of the products of the roots, k at a time, is $(-1)^k a_{n-k}/a_n$.

Example 2.28

Show that the roots, α, β of the quadratic equation

$$ax^2 + bx + c = 0$$

may be written in the form

$$\frac{-b - \sqrt{(b^2 - 4ac)}}{2a} \quad \text{and} \quad \frac{2c}{-b - \sqrt{(b^2 - 4ac)}}$$

Obtain the roots of the equation

$$1.0x^2 + 17.8x + 1.5 = 0$$

Assuming the numbers given are correctly rounded, calculate error bounds for the roots.

Solution

Using the formula for the roots of a quadratic equation we can select one root, α say, so that

$$\alpha = \frac{-b - \sqrt{(b^2 - 4ac)}}{2a}$$

Then, since $\alpha\beta = c/a$, we have

$$\beta = \frac{c}{a\alpha} = \frac{2c}{-b - \sqrt{(b^2 - 4ac)}}$$

Now consider the equation

$$1.0x^2 + 17.8x + 1.5 = 0$$

whose coefficients are correctly rounded numbers. Using the quadratic formula we obtain the roots

$$\alpha \approx -17.715\,327\,56$$

and

$$\beta \approx -0.084\,672\,44$$

Using the results of Section 1.5.2 we can estimate error bounds for these answers as shown in Figure 2.35. From that table we can see that using the form

$$\frac{-b - \sqrt{(b^2 - 4ac)}}{2a}$$

to estimate α we have an error bound of 0.943, while using

$$\frac{-b + \sqrt{(b^2 - 4ac)}}{2a}$$

Figure 2.35 Estimating error bounds for roots.

Label	*Value*	*Absolute error bound*	*Relative error bound*
a	1.0	0.05	0.05
b	17.8	0.05	0.0028
c	1.5	0.05	0.0333
b^2	316.84	1.77	0.0056
$4ac$	6.00	0.50	0.0833
$b^2 - 4ac$	310.84	2.27	0.0073
$d = \sqrt{(b^2 - 4ac)}$	17.630 66	0.065	0.0037
$-b - d$	−35.430 66	0.115	0.0032
$(-b - d)/(2a)$	−17.715 33	0.943	0.0532
$-b + d$	−0.169 34	0.115	0.6791
$(-b + d)/(2a)$	−0.084 67	0.062	0.7291
$2c/(-b - d)$	−0.084 67	0.003	0.0365

to estimate β we have an error bound of 0.062. As this latter estimate of error is almost as big as the root itself we might be inclined to regard the answer as valueless. But calculating the error bound using the form

$$\beta = \frac{2c}{-b - \sqrt{(b^2 - 4ac)}}$$

gives an estimate of 0.003. Thus we can write

$$\alpha = -17.7 \pm 5\% \text{ and } \beta = -0.085 \pm 4\%$$

The reason for the discrepancy between the two error estimates for β lies in the fact that in the traditional form of the formula we are subtracting two nearly equal numbers, and consequently the error bounds dominate.

Example 2.29 The equation $3x^3 - x^2 - 3x + 1 = 0$ has a root at $x = 1$. Obtain the other two roots.

Solution If α, β and γ are the roots of the equation then

$$\alpha + \beta + \gamma = \tfrac{1}{3}$$

$$\alpha\beta + \beta\gamma + \gamma\alpha = -\tfrac{3}{3}$$

$$\alpha\beta\gamma = -\tfrac{1}{3}$$

Setting $\alpha = 1$ simplifies these to

$$\beta + \gamma = -\tfrac{2}{3}$$

$$\beta + \gamma + \beta\gamma = -1$$

$$\beta\gamma = -\tfrac{1}{3}$$

Hence $\gamma = -1/(3\beta)$ and $3\beta^2 + 2\beta - 1 = 0$. Factorizing this equation gives

$$(3\beta - 1)(\beta + 1) = 0$$

from which we obtain the solution $x = -1$ and $x = \tfrac{1}{3}$.

The numerical method most often used for evaluating the roots of a polynomial is the Newton–Raphson procedure. This will be described in Section 9.5.8.

In MATLAB a polynomial is represented by an array of its coefficients, with the highest coefficient listed first. For example, the polynomial function

$$f(x) = x^3 - 5x^2 - 17x + 21$$

is represented by

```
f = [1 -5 -17 21]
```

The roots of the corresponding polynomial equation $f(x) = 0$ are obtained using the command `roots(f)`, so for the above example the command

```
r = roots(f)
```

returns the roots as

```
r = 7.0000
   -3.0000
    1.0000
```

which also indicate that the factors of $f(x)$ are $(x - 7)$, $(x + 3)$ and $(x - 1)$. It is noted that the output gives the roots r as a column array of numbers (and not a row array). If the roots are known and we wish to determine the corresponding polynomial $f(x)$, having unity as the coefficient of its highest power, then use is made of the command `poly(r)`. To use this command the roots r must be specified as a row array; so the commands

```
r = [7 -3 1]
f = poly(r)
```

return the answer

```
f = 1.0000 -5.0000 -17.0000 21.0000
```

indicating that the polynomial is

$$f(x) = x^3 - 5x^2 - 17x + 21$$

To determine the polynomial of degree n that passes through $n + 1$ points we use the command `polyfit(x,y,n);` which outputs the array of coefficients of a polynomial of order n that fits the pairs (x, y). If the number of points (x, y) is greater than n then the command will give the best fit in the least squares sense. Check that the commands

```
x = [-3 0 2 5]; y = [528 1017 1433 2312];
f = polyfit(x,y,3)
```

reproduce the answer of Example 2.22 and that the commands

```
x = [0 1 2 3 4]; y = [1 1 2 2 3];
polyfit(x,y,1)
```

reproduce the answer to Example 2.17.

Graphs of polynomial functions may be plotted using the commands given earlier (see p. 71). The result of multiplying two polynomials $f(x)$ and $g(x)$ is obtained using the command `conv(f,g)`, where f and g are the array specification of $f(x)$ and $g(x)$ respectively. With reference to Example 2.25 confirm that the product $f(x) = (x^2 - 2x + 4)(x - 1)$ is obtained using the commands

```
f1 = [1 -2 4]; f2 = [1 -1];
f = conv(f1, f2)
```

The division of two polynomials $f(x)$ and $g(x)$ is obtained, by the process of deconvolution, using the command

```
[Q,R] = deconv(f,g)
```

which produces two outputs Q and R, with Q being the coefficients of the quotient polynomial and R the coefficients of the remainder polynomial. Again with reference to Example 2.25 check that $x^3 - 3x^2 + 6x - 4$ divided by $x - 1$ gives a quotient $x^2 - 2x + 4$ and a remainder of zero.

Using the Symbolic Math Toolbox operations on polynomials may be undertaken in symbolic form. Some useful commands, for carrying out algebraic manipulations, are:

(a) `factor` command

If $f(x)$ is a polynomial function, expressed in symbolic form, with rational coefficients (see Section 1.2.1) then the commands

```
syms x
f = factor(f(x))
```

factorize $f(x)$ as the product of polynomials of lower degree with rational coefficients. For example, to factorize the cubic $f(x) = x^3 - 5x^2 - 17x + 21$ the commands

```
syms x
f = factor(x^3 - 5*x^2 - 17*x + 21)
```

return

```
f = (x - 1)*(x - 7)*(x + 3)
```

Using the `pretty` command

```
pretty(f)
```

returns the more readable display

```
f = (x - 1)(x - 7)(x + 3)
```

Using the `factor` command, confirm the factorization of polynomials (a) and (b) in Example 2.24.

(b) `horner` command

This command transforms a polynomial $f(x)$ expressed in symbolic form into its nested (or Horner) representation. For example the commands

```
syms x
f = horner(4*x^3 - 5*x^2 + 2*x + 3)
```

return

```
f = 3 + (2 + (-5 + 4*x)*x)*x
```

which confirms the nested representation at the outset of Section 2.4.3.

(c) `collect` command

This collects all the coefficients with the same power of x. For example, if

$$f(x) = 4x(x^2 + 2x + 1) - 5(x(x + 2) - x^3) + (x + 3)^3$$

then the commands

```
syms x
f = collect(4*x*(x^2 + 2*x + 1) - 5*(x*(x + 2) - x^3)
    + (x + 3)^3);
pretty(f)
```

return

```
f = 27 + 10x^3 + 12x^2 + 21x
```

The `collect` command may also be used to multiply two polynomials. With reference to Example 2.25 the product of the two polynomials $x^2 - 2x + 4$ and $x - 1$ is returned by the commands

```
syms x
f = collect((x - 1)*(x^2 - 2*x + 4));
pretty(f)
```

as

```
f = x^3 - 3x^2 + 6x - 4
```

(d) `simplify` command

This is a powerful general purpose command that can be used with a wide range of functions. For example, if $f(x) = (9 - x^2)/(3 + x)$ then the commands

```
syms x
f = simplify((9 - x^2)/(3 + x))
```

return

```
f = -x + 3
```

(e) `simple` command

This command seeks to find a simplification of a symbolic expression so that it has the fewest number of characters; that is, it seeks to obtain the shortest form of the expression. The command sometimes improves on the result returned by the `simplify` command. There is no corresponding command in MAPLE.

(f) `expand` command

This is another general purpose command which can be used with a wide range of functions. It distributes products over sums and differences. For example, if $f(x) = a(x + y)$ then the commands

```
syms x a y
f = expand(a*(x + y));
pretty(f)
```

return

```
f = ax + ay
```

(g) `solve` command

If $f(x)$ is a symbolic expression in the variable x (the expression may also include parameters) then the command

```
s = solve (f)
```

seeks to solve the equation $f(x) = 0$, returning the solution in a column array. To solve an equation expressed in the form $f(x) = g(x)$ use is made of the command

```
s = solve('f(x) = g(x)')
```

For example, considering the general quadratic equation $ax^2 + bx + c = 0$ the commands

```
syms x a b c
s = solve(a*x^2 + b*x + c);
pretty(s)
```

return the well-known answers (see Example 1.21)

```
[        -b + (b^2 - 4ac)^(1/2) ]
[ 1/2    ---------------------- ]
[                  a            ]

[        -b - (b^2 - 4ac)^(1/2) ]
[ 1/2    ---------------------- ]
[                  a            ]
```

2.4.5 Exercises

Check your answers using MATLAB or MAPLE whenever possible.

30 Factorize the following polynomial functions and sketch their graphs:

(a) $x^3 - 2x^2 - 11x + 12$

(b) $x^3 + 2x^2 - 5x - 6$

(c) $x^4 + x^2 - 2$

(d) $2x^4 + 5x^3 - x^2 - 6x$

(e) $2x^4 - 9x^3 + 14x^2 - 9x + 2$

(f) $x^4 + 5x^2 - 36$

31 Find the coefficients A, B, C, D and E such that

$$\begin{aligned} y &= 2x^4 - 9x^3 + 145x^2 - 9x + 2 \\ &= A(x-2)^4 + B(x-2)^3 + C(x-2)^2 \\ &\quad + D(x-2) + E \end{aligned}$$

32 Show that the zeros of

$$y = x^4 - 5x^3 + 5x^2 - 10x + 6$$

lie between $x = 0$ and $x = 5$.

33 Show that the roots α, β of the equation

$$x^2 + 4x + 1 = 0$$

satisfy the equations

$$\alpha^2 + \beta^2 = 14$$
$$\alpha^3 + \beta^3 = -52$$

Hence find the quadratic equations whose roots are

(a) α^2 and β^2 (b) α^3 and β^3

34 Use Lagrange's formula to find the formula for the cubic function that passes through the points (5.2, 6.408), (5.5, 16.125), (5.6, 19.816) and (5.8, 27.912).

35 Find a formula for the quadratic function whose graph passes through the points (1, 403), (3, 471) and (7, 679).

36 (a) Show that if the equation $ax^3 + bx + c = 0$ has a repeated root α then $3a\alpha^2 + b = 0$.

(b) A can is to be made in the form of a circular cylinder of radius r (in cm) and height h (in cm), as shown in Figure 2.36. Its capacity is to be 0.5 l. Show that the surface area A (in cm^2) of the can is

$$A = 2\pi r^2 + \frac{1000}{r}$$

Using the result of (a), deduce that A has a minimum value A^* when $6\pi r^2 - A^* = 0$. Hence find the corresponding values of r and h.

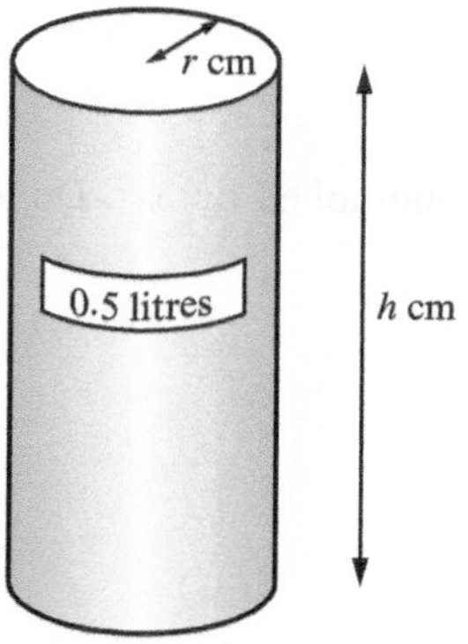

Figure 2.36

37 A box is made from a sheet of plywood, 2 m × 1 m, with the waste shown in Figure 2.37(a). Find the maximum capacity of such a box and compare it with the capacity of the box constructed without the wastage, as shown in Figure 2.37(b).

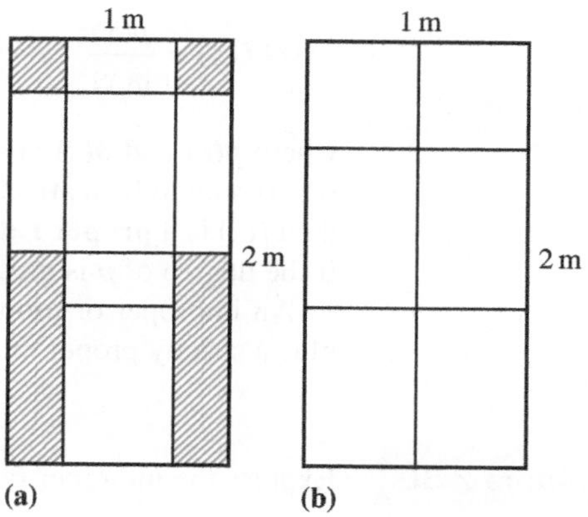

Figure 2.37

38 Two ladders, of lengths 12 m and 8 m, lean against buildings on opposite sides of an alley, as shown in Figure 2.38. Show that the heights x and y

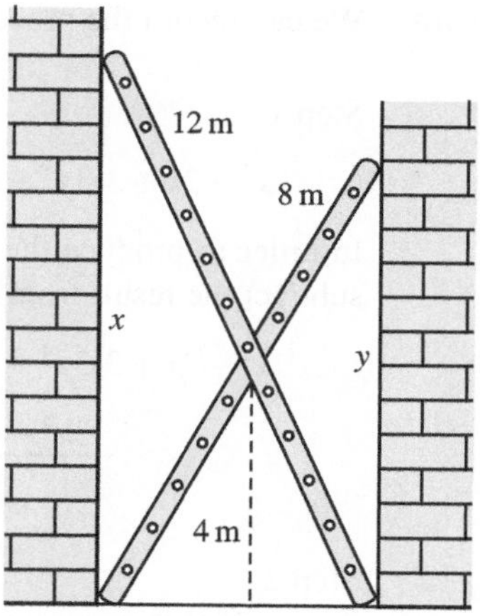

Figure 2.38

(in metres) reached by the tops of the ladders in the positions shown satisfy the equations

$$\frac{1}{x}+\frac{1}{y}=\frac{1}{4} \quad \text{and} \quad x^2-y^2=80$$

Show that x satisfies the equation

$$x^4-8x^3-80x^2+640x-1280=0$$

and that the width of the alley is given by $\sqrt{(12^2-x_0^2)}$, where x_0 is the positive root of this equation. By first tabulating the polynomial over a suitable domain and then drawing its graph, estimate the value of x_0 and the width of the alley. Check your solution of the quartic (to 2dp) using a suitable software package.

2.5 Rational functions

Rational functions have the general form

$$f(x)=\frac{p(x)}{q(x)}$$

where $p(x)$ and $q(x)$ are polynomials. If the degree of p is less than the degree of q, $f(x)$ is said to be a **strictly proper rational function.** If p and q have the same degree then $f(x)$ is a **proper rational function.** It is said to be an **improper rational function** if the degree of p is greater than the degree of q.

An improper or proper rational function can always be expressed as a polynomial plus a strictly proper rational function, for example, by algebraic division.

Example 2.30 Express the improper rational function

$$f(x)=\frac{3x^4+2x^3-5x^2+6x-7}{x^2-2x+3}$$

as the sum of a polynomial function and a strictly proper rational function.

Solution We can record the process of division in a manner similar to that of Example 2.22.

Step 1

$$x^2-2x+3)3x^4+2x^3-5x^2+6x-7($$

In order to produce the term $3x^4$, x^2-2x+3 must be multiplied by $3x^2$. Do this and subtract the result from $3x^4+2x^3-5x^2+6x-7$.

$$\begin{array}{l} x^2-2x+3)3x^4+2x^3-5x^2+6x-7(3x^2 \\ \qquad\qquad\quad \underline{3x^4-6x^3+9x^2} \\ \qquad\qquad\qquad\qquad 8x^3-14x^2+6x-7 \end{array}$$

Step 2

Now repeat the process on the polynomial $8x^3-14x^2+6x-7$. In this case, in order to eliminate the term $8x^3$ we must multiply x^2-2x+3 by $8x$.

$$
\begin{array}{r}
x^2 - 2x + 3)\overline{3x^4 + 2x^3 - 5x^2 + 6x - 7}(3x^2 + 8x \\
\underline{3x^4 - 6x^3 + 9x^2} \qquad\qquad\quad \\
8x^3 - 14x^2 + 6x - 7 \\
\underline{8x^3 - 16x^2 + 24x} \qquad \\
2x^2 - 18x - 7
\end{array}
$$

Step 3

Finally, to eliminate the $2x^2$ term, we must multiply $x^2 - 2x + 3$ by 2.

$$
\begin{array}{r}
x^2 - 2x + 3)\overline{3x^4 + 2x^3 - 5x^2 + 6x - 7}(3x^2 + 8x + 2 \\
\underline{3x^4 - 6x^3 + 9x^2} \qquad\qquad\quad \\
8x^3 - 14x^2 + 6x - 7 \\
\underline{8x^3 - 16x^2 + 24x} \qquad \\
2x^2 - 18x - 7 \\
\underline{2x^2 - 4x + 6} \\
-14x - 13
\end{array}
$$

We cannot eliminate the $-14x - 13$ terms, so we have

$$f(x) = 3x^2 + 8x + 2 - \frac{14x + 13}{x^2 - 2x + 3}$$

Any strictly proper rational function can be expressed as a sum of simpler functions whose denominators are linear or irreducible quadratic functions. For example:

$$\frac{x^2 + 1}{(1 + x)(1 - x)(2 + 2x + x^2)} = \frac{1}{1 + x} + \frac{1}{5(1 - x)} - \frac{4x + 7}{5(2 + 2x + x^2)}$$

These simpler functions are called the **partial fractions** of the rational function, and are often useful in the mathematical analysis and design of engineering systems. Notice that strictly the equality above is an identity since it is true for all values of x in the domain of the expressions. Here we are following the common practice of writing = instead of ≡ (as we did in Section 1.3.3).

The construction of the partial fraction form of a rational function is the inverse process to that of collecting together separate rational expressions into a single rational function. For example:

$$\frac{1}{1 + x} + \frac{1}{5(1 - x)} - \frac{4x + 7}{5(2 + 2x + x^2)}$$

$$= \frac{1(5)(1 - x)(2 + 2x + x^2) + (1 + x)(2 + 2x + x^2) - (1 + x)(1 - x)(4x + 7)}{5(1 + x)(1 - x)(2 + 2x + x^2)}$$

$$= \frac{5(2 - x^2 - x^3) + (2 + 4x + 3x^2 + x^3) - (1 - x^2)(4x + 7)}{5(1 - x^2)(2 + 2x + x^2)}$$

$$= \frac{5(2 - x^2 - x^3) + (2 + 4x + 3x^2 + x^3) - (7 + 4x - 7x^2 - 4x^3)}{5(2 + 2x - x^2 - 2x^3 - x^4)}$$

$$= \frac{5 + 5x^2}{5(2 + 2x - x^2 - 2x^3 - x^4)}$$

$$= \frac{1 + x^2}{2 + 2x - x^2 - 2x^3 - x^4}$$

But it is clear from this example that reversing the process (working backwards from the final expression) is not easy, and we require a different method in order to find the partial fractions of a given function. To describe the method in its full generality is easy but difficult to understand, so we will apply the method to a number of commonly occurring types of function in the next section before stating the general algorithm.

2.5.1 Partial fractions

In this section we will illustrate how proper rational functions of the form $p(x)/q(x)$ may be expressed in partial fractions.

(a) Distinct linear factors

Each distinct linear factor, of the form $(x + \alpha)$, in the denominator $q(x)$ will give rise to a partial fraction of the form $\dfrac{A}{x + \alpha}$, where A is a real constant.

Example 2.31 Express in partial fractions the rational function

$$\frac{3x}{(x - 1)(x + 2)}$$

Solution In this case we have two distinct linear factors $(x - 1)$ and $(x + 2)$ in the denominator, so the corresponding partial fractions are of the form

$$\frac{3x}{(x - 1)(x + 2)} = \frac{A}{x - 1} + \frac{B}{x + 2} = \frac{A(x + 2) + B(x - 1)}{(x - 1)(x + 2)}$$

where A and B are constants to be determined. Since both expressions are equal and their denominators are identical we must therefore make their numerators equal, yielding

$$3x = A(x + 2) + B(x - 1)$$

This identity is true for all values of x, so we can find A and B by setting first $x = 1$ and then $x = -2$. So

$$x = 1 \quad \text{gives} \quad 3 = A(3) + B(0); \qquad \text{that is} \quad A = 1$$

and

$$x = -2 \quad \text{gives} \quad -6 = A(0) + B(-3); \quad \text{that is} \quad B = 2$$

Thus

$$\frac{3x}{(x-1)(x+2)} = \frac{1}{x-1} + \frac{2}{x+2}$$

When the denominator $q(x)$ of a strictly proper rational function $\frac{p(x)}{q(x)}$ is a product of linear factors, as in Example 2.31, there is a quick way of expressing $\frac{p(x)}{q(x)}$ in partial fractions.

Considering again Example 2.31, if

$$\frac{3x}{(x-1)(x+2)} = \frac{A}{(x-1)} + \frac{B}{(x-2)}$$

then to obtain A simply **cover up** the factor $(x - 1)$ in

$$\frac{3x}{(x-1)(x+2)}$$

and evaluate what is left at $x = 1$, giving

$$A = \frac{3(1)}{(x-1)(1+2)} = 1$$

Likewise, to obtain B **cover up** the factor $(x + 2)$ in the left-hand side and evaluate what is left at $x = -2$, giving

$$B = \frac{3(-2)}{(-2-1)(x+2)} = 2$$

Thus, as before,

$$\frac{3x}{(x-1)(x+2)} = \frac{1}{x-1} + \frac{2}{x+2}$$

This method of obtaining partial fractions is called the **cover up rule.**

Example 2.32 Using the cover up rule, express in partial fractions the rational function

$$\frac{2x+1}{(x-2)(x+1)(x-3)}$$

Solution The corresponding partial fractions are of the form

$$\frac{2x+1}{(x-2)(x+1)(x-3)} = \frac{A}{(x-2)} + \frac{B}{(x+1)} + \frac{C}{(x-3)}$$

Using the cover up rule

$$A = \frac{2(2)+1}{(x-2)(2+1)(2-3)} = -\tfrac{5}{3}$$

$$B = \frac{2(-1)+1}{(-1-2)(x+1)(-1-3)} = -\tfrac{1}{12}$$

$$C = \frac{2(3)+1}{(3-2)(3+1)(x-3)} = \tfrac{7}{4}$$

so that

$$\frac{2x+1}{(x-2)(x+1)(x-3)} = -\frac{\tfrac{5}{3}}{x-2} - \frac{\tfrac{1}{12}}{x+1} + \frac{\tfrac{7}{4}}{x-3}$$

Because it is easy to make an error with this process, it is sensible to check the answers obtained. This can be done by using a 'spot' value to check that the left- and right-hand sides yield the same value. When doing this avoid using $x = 0$ or any of the special values of x that were used in finding the coefficients.

For example, taking $x = 1$ in the partial fraction expansion of Example 2.32, we have

$$\text{left-hand side} \quad = \frac{2(1)+1}{(1-2)(1+1)(1-3)} = \tfrac{3}{4}$$

$$\text{right-hand side} \quad = -\frac{\tfrac{5}{3}}{1-2} - \frac{\tfrac{1}{12}}{1+1} + \frac{\tfrac{7}{4}}{1-3} = \tfrac{3}{4}$$

giving a positive check.

(b) Repeated linear factors

Each k times repeated linear factor, of the form $(x - \alpha)^k$, in the denominator $q(x)$ will give rise to a partial fraction of the form

$$\frac{A_1}{(x-\alpha)} + \frac{A_2}{(x-\alpha)^2} + \ldots + \frac{A_k}{(x-\alpha)^k}$$

where $A_1, A_2, \ldots, A_k$ are real constants.

Example 2.33 Express as partial fractions the rational function

$$\frac{3x+1}{(x-1)^2(x+2)}$$

Solution In this case the denominator consists of the distinct linear factor $(x + 2)$ and the twice repeated linear factor $(x - 1)$. Thus, the corresponding partial fractions are of the form

$$\frac{3x+1}{(x-1)^2(x+2)} = \frac{A}{(x-1)} + \frac{B}{(x-1)^2} + \frac{C}{(x+2)}$$
$$= \frac{A(x-1)(x+2) + B(x+2) + C(x-1)^2}{(x-1)^2(x+2)}$$

which gives

$$3x + 1 = A(x-1)(x+2) + B(x+2) + C(x-1)^2$$

Setting $x = 1$ gives $4 = B(3)$ and $B = \frac{4}{3}$. Setting $x = -2$ gives $-5 = C(-3)^2$ and $C = -\frac{5}{9}$. To obtain A we can give x any other value, so taking $x = 0$ gives

$$1 = (-2)A + 2B + C$$

and substituting the values of B and C gives $A = \frac{5}{9}$. Hence

$$\frac{3x+1}{(x-1)^2(x+2)} = \frac{\frac{5}{9}}{x-1} + \frac{\frac{4}{3}}{(x-1)^2} - \frac{\frac{5}{9}}{(x+2)}$$

(c) Irreducible quadratic factors

Each distinct irreducible quadratic factor, of the form $(ax^2 + bx + c)$, in the denominator $q(x)$ will give rise to a partial fraction of the form

$$\frac{Ax+B}{ax^2+bx+c}$$

where A and B are real constants.

Example 2.34 Express as partial fractions the rational function

$$\frac{5x}{(x^2+x+1)(x-2)}$$

Solution In this case the denominator consists of the distinct linear factor $(x - 2)$ and the distinct irreducible quadratic factor $(x^2 + x + 1)$. Thus, the corresponding partial fractions are of the form

$$\frac{5x}{(x^2+x+1)(x-2)} = \frac{Ax+B}{x^2+x+1} + \frac{C}{x-2} = \frac{(Ax+B)(x-2) + C(x^2+x+1)}{(x^2+x+1)(x-2)}$$

giving

$$5x = (Ax + B)(x - 2) + C(x^2 + x + 1)$$

Setting $x = 2$ enables us to calculate C:

$$10 = (2A + B)(0) + C(7) \quad \text{and} \quad C = \tfrac{10}{7}$$

Here, however, we cannot select special values of x that give A and B immediately, because $x^2 + x + 1$ is an irreducible quadratic and cannot be factorized. Instead we make use of Property (i) of polynomials, described in Section 2.4.1, which stated that if two polynomials are equal in value for all values of x then the corresponding coefficients are equal. Applying this to

$$5x = (Ax + B)(x - 2) + C(x^2 + x + 1)$$

we see that the coefficient of x^2 on the right-hand side is $A + C$ while that on the left-hand side is zero. Thus

$$A + C = 0 \quad \text{and} \quad A = -C = -\tfrac{10}{7}$$

Similarly the coefficient of x^0 on the right-hand side is $-2B + C$ and that on the left-hand side is zero, and we obtain $-2B + C = 0$, which implies $B = \tfrac{1}{2}C = \tfrac{5}{7}$. Hence

$$\frac{5x}{(x^2 + x + 1)(x - 2)} = \frac{\tfrac{5}{7} - \tfrac{10}{7}x}{x^2 + x + 1} + \frac{\tfrac{10}{7}}{x - 2}$$

Example 2.35 Express as partial fractions the rational function

$$\frac{3x^2}{(x - 1)(x + 2)}$$

Solution In this example the numerator has the same degree as the denominator.

The first step in such examples is to divide the bottom into the top to obtain a polynomial and a strictly proper rational function. Thus

$$\frac{3x^2}{(x - 1)(x + 2)} = 3 + \frac{6 - 3x}{(x - 1)(x + 2)}$$

We then apply the partial-fraction process to the remainder, setting

$$\frac{6 - 3x}{(x - 1)(x + 2)} = \frac{A}{x - 1} + \frac{B}{x + 2}$$

$$= \frac{A(x + 2) + B(x - 1)}{(x - 1)(x + 2)}$$

giving

$$6 - 3x = A(x + 2) + B(x - 1)$$

Setting first $x = 1$ and then $x = -2$ gives $A = 1$ and $B = -4$ respectively. Thus

$$\frac{3x^2}{(x - 1)(x + 2)} = 3 + \frac{1}{x - 1} - \frac{4}{x + 2}$$

Summary of method

In general, the method for finding the partial fractions of a given function $f(x) = p(x)/q(x)$ consists of the following steps.

Step 1: If the degree of p is greater than or equal to the degree of q, divide q into p to obtain

$$f(x) = r(x) + \frac{s(x)}{q(x)}$$

where the degree of s is less than the degree of q.

Step 2: Factorize $q(x)$ fully into real linear and irreducible quadratic factors, collecting together all like factors.

Step 3: Each **linear factor** $ax + b$ in $q(x)$ will give rise to a fraction of the type

$$\frac{A}{ax + b}$$

(Here a and b are known and A is to be found.)

Each **repeated linear factor** $(ax + b)^n$ will give rise to n fractions of the type

$$\frac{A_1}{ax + b} + \frac{A_2}{(ax + b)^2} + \frac{A_3}{(ax + b)^3} + \ldots + \frac{A_n}{(ax + b)^n}$$

Each **irreducible quadratic factor** $ax^2 + bx + c$ in $q(x)$ will give rise to a fraction of the type

$$\frac{Ax + B}{ax^2 + bx + c}$$

Each **repeated irreducible quadratic factor** $(ax^2 + bx + c)^n$ will give rise to n fractions of the type

$$\frac{A_1x + B_1}{ax^2 + bx + c} + \frac{A_2x + B_2}{(ax^2 + bx + c)^2} + \ldots + \frac{A_nx + B_n}{(ax^2 + bx + c)^n}$$

Put $p(x)/q(x)$ (or $s(x)/q(x)$, if that case occurs) equal to the sum of all the fractions involved.

Step 4: Multiply both sides of the equation by $q(x)$ to obtain an identity involving polynomials, from which the multiplying constants of the linear combination may be found (because of Property (i) in Section 2.4.1).

Step 5: To find these coefficients, two strategies are used.

- *Strategy 1*: Choose special values of x that make finding the values of the unknown coefficients easy: for example, choose x equal to the roots of $q(x) = 0$ in turn and use the 'cover up' rule.
- *Strategy 2*: Compare the coefficients of like powers of x on both sides of the identity. Starting with the highest and lowest powers usually makes it easier.

Strategy 1 may leave some coefficients undetermined. In that case we complete the process using Strategy 2.

Step 6: Lastly, check the answer either by choosing a test value for x or by putting the partial fractions over a common denominator.

There is no command in MATLAB that will symbolically express rational functions in partial fractions. However use of the `maple` command in MATLAB enables us to access MAPLE commands directly. Thus, adopting the `convert` command in MAPLE a rational function $f(x)$ may be expressed in partial fraction '*pf*' form using, in MATLAB, the commands

```
syms x
pf = maple('convert',f(x),' parfrac',x);
pretty(pf)
```

For example, considering Example 2.32, the commands

```
syms x
pf = maple('convert',(2*x + 1)/((x - 2)*(x + 1)*(x - 3)),
'parfrac',x);
pretty(pf)
```

return

```
         1            1            1
-1/12 -------  + 7/4 -------  - 5/3 -------
       x + 1         x - 3          x - 2
```

confirming the answer in the example.

For practice, check the answers to Examples 2.33–2.35.

2.5.2 Exercises

Where appropriate, check your answers using MATLAB or MAPLE.

39 Express the following improper rational functions as the sum of a polynomial function and a strictly proper rational function.

(a) $f(x) = (x^2 + x + 1)/[(x + 1)(x - 1)]$

(b) $f(x) = (x^5 - x^4 - x + 1)/(x^2 + x + 1)$

40 Express as a single fraction

(a) $\dfrac{1}{x} - \dfrac{2}{x-2} + \dfrac{x-1}{x^2+1}$

(b) $\dfrac{1}{x^3 - 3x^2 + 3x - 1} - \dfrac{1}{x^3 - x^2 - x + 1}$

(c) $\dfrac{x+1}{x^2+1} + \dfrac{1}{x-1} - \dfrac{1}{(x-1)^2} + \dfrac{2}{x-2}$

41 Express as partial fractions

(a) $\dfrac{1}{(x+1)(x-2)}$ (b) $\dfrac{2x-1}{(x+1)(x-2)}$

(c) $\dfrac{x^2-2}{(x+1)(x-2)}$ (d) $\dfrac{x-1}{(x+1)(x-2)^2}$

(e) $\dfrac{1}{(x+1)(x^2+2x+2)}$ (f) $\dfrac{1}{(x+1)(x^2-4)}$

42 Express as partial fractions

(a) $\dfrac{1}{x^2 - 5x + 4}$ (b) $\dfrac{1}{x^3 - 1}$

(c) $\dfrac{3x-1}{x^3 - 3x - 2}$ (d) $\dfrac{x^2-1}{x^2 - 5x + 6}$

(e) $\dfrac{x^2 + x - 1}{(x^2+1)^2}$ (f) $\dfrac{18x^2 - 5x + 47}{(x^2+4)(x-1)(x+5)}$

2.5.3 Asymptotes

Sketching the graphs of rational functions gives rise to the concept of an asymptote. To illustrate, let us consider the graph of the function

$$y = f(x) = \frac{x}{1+x} \quad (x > 0)$$

and that of its inverse

$$y = f^{-1}(x) = \frac{x}{1-x} \quad (0 \leqslant x < 1)$$

Expressing $x/(x + 1)$ as $(x + 1 - 1)/(x + 1) = 1 - 1/(x + 1)$, we see that as x gets larger and larger $1/(x + 1)$ gets smaller and smaller, so that $x/(x + 1)$ approaches closer and closer to the value 1. This is illustrated in the graph of $y = f(x)$ shown in Figure 2.39(a). The line $y = 1$ is called a **horizontal asymptote** to the curve, and we note that the graph of $f(x)$ approaches this asymptote as $|x|$ becomes large.

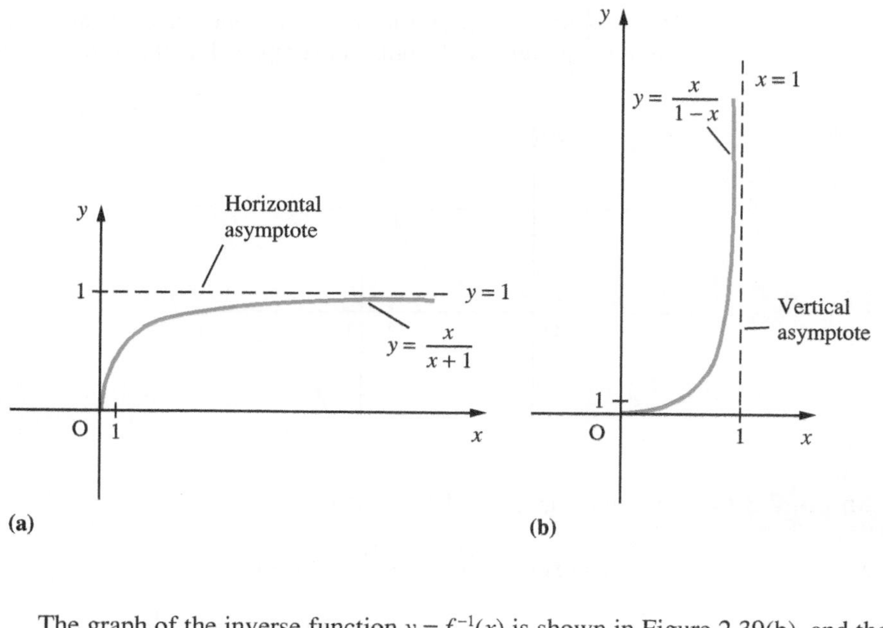

Figure 2.39 Horizontal and vertical asymptotes.

The graph of the inverse function $y = f^{-1}(x)$ is shown in Figure 2.39(b), and the line $x = 1$ is called a **vertical asymptote** to the curve.

The existence of asymptotes is a common feature of the graphs of rational functions. They feature in various engineering applications, such as in the plotting of root locus plots in control engineering. In more advanced applications of mathematics to engineering the concept of an asymptote is widely used for the purposes of making approximations. Asymptotes need not necessarily be horizontal or vertical lines; they may be sloping lines or indeed non-linear graphs, as we shall see in Example 2.37.

Example 2.36 Sketch the graph of the function

$$y = \frac{1}{3 - x} \quad (x \neq 3)$$

and find the values of x for which

$$\frac{1}{3 - x} < 2$$

Solution We can see from the formula for y that the line $x = 3$ is a vertical asymptote of the function. As x gets closer and closer to the value $x = 3$ from the left-hand side (that is, $x < 3$), y gets larger and larger and is positive. As x gets closer and closer to $x = 3$ from the right-hand side (that is, $x > 3$), y is negative and large. As x gets larger and larger, y gets smaller and smaller for both $x > 0$ and $x < 0$, so $y = 0$ is a horizontal asymptote. Thus we obtain the sketch shown in Figure 2.40. By drawing the line $y = 2$ on the sketch, we see at once that

$$\frac{1}{3 - x} < 2$$

for $x < \frac{5}{2}$ and $x > 3$. This result was obtained algebraically in Example 1.24. Generally we use a mixture of algebraic and graphical methods to solve such problems.

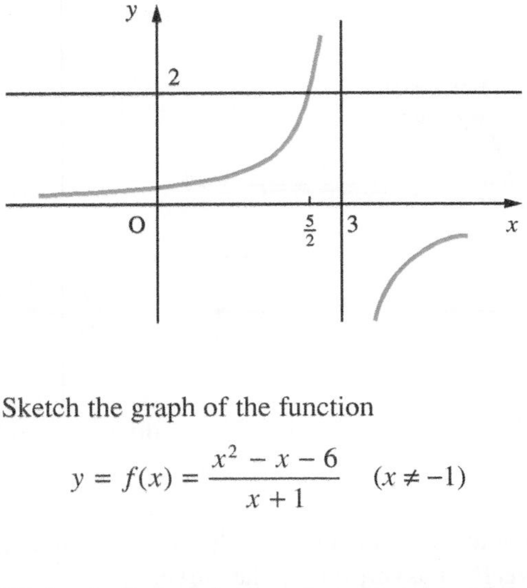

Figure 2.40

Graph of $y = \frac{1}{3 - x}$.

Example 2.37 Sketch the graph of the function

$$y = f(x) = \frac{x^2 - x - 6}{x + 1} \quad (x \neq -1)$$

Solution We begin the task by locating points at which the function is zero. Now $f(x) = 0$ implies that $x^2 - x - 6 = (x - 3)(x + 2) = 0$, from which we deduce that $x = 3$ and $x = -2$ are zeros of the function. Thus the graph $y = f(x)$ crosses the x axis at $x = -2$ and $x = 3$.

Next we locate the points at which the denominator of the rational function is zero, which in this case is $x = -1$. As x approaches such a point, the value of $f(x)$ becomes infinitely large in magnitude, and the value of the rational function is undefined at such a point. Thus the graph of $y = f(x)$ has a vertical asymptote at $x = -1$. (There is usually a vertical asymptote to the graph of the rational function $y = p(x)/q(x)$ at points where the denominator $q(x) = 0$.)

Next we consider the behaviour of the function as x gets larger and larger, that is as $x \to \infty$ or $x \to -\infty$. To do this, we first simplify the rational function by algebraic division, giving

$$y = f(x) = x - 2 - \frac{4}{x + 1}$$

As $x \to \pm\infty$, $4/(x + 1) \to 0$. Thus, for large values of x, both positive and negative, $4/(x + 1)$ becomes negligible compared with x, so that $f(x)$ tends to behave like $x - 2$. Thus the line $y = x - 2$ is also an asymptote to the graph of $y = f(x)$.

Having located the asymptotes, we then need to find how the graph approaches them. When x is large and positive the term $4/(x + 1)$ will be small but positive, so that $f(x)$ is slightly less than $x - 2$. Hence the graph approaches the asymptote from below. When x is large and negative the term $4/(x + 1)$ is small but negative, so the graph approaches the asymptote from above. To consider the behaviour of the function near $x = -1$, we examine the factorized form

$$y = f(x) = \frac{(x - 3)(x + 2)}{x + 1}$$

When x is slightly less than -1, $f(x)$ is positive. When x is slightly greater than -1, $f(x)$ is negative.

We are now in a position to sketch the graph of $y = f(x)$ as shown in Figure 2.41.

Figure 2.41
Graph of $y = \dfrac{x^2 - x - 6}{x + 1}$.

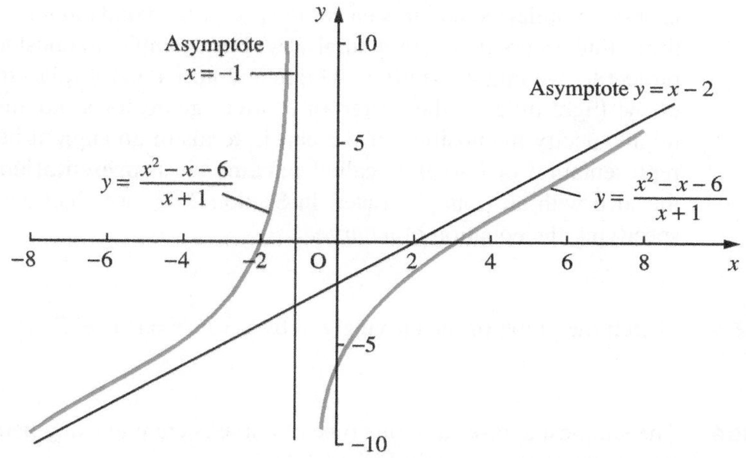

Modern computational aids have made graphing functions much easier, but to obtain graphs of a reasonably good quality some preliminary analysis is always necessary. This helps to select the correct range of values for the independent variable and for the function. For example, asking a computer package to plot the function

$$y = \frac{13x^2 - 34x + 25}{x^2 - 3x + 2}$$

Figure 2.42

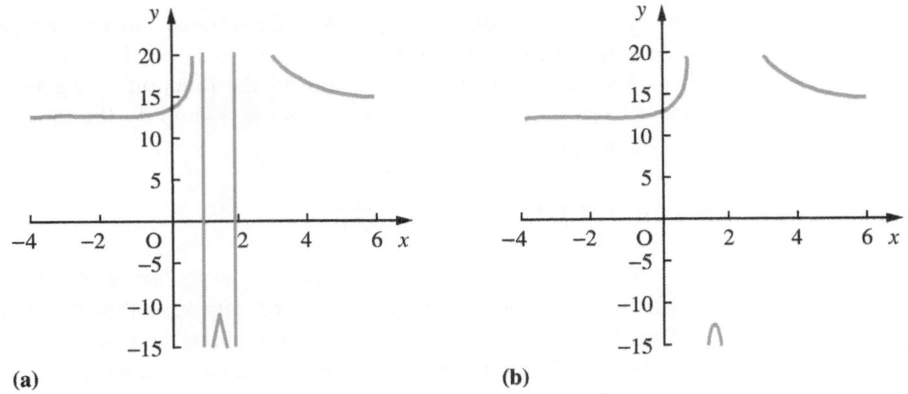

without prior analysis might result in the graph shown in Figure 2.42(a). A little analysis shows that the function is undefined at $x = 1$ and 2. Excluding these points from the range of values for x produces the more acceptable plot shown in Figure 2.42(b), although it is not clear from either plot that the graph has a horizontal asymptote $y = 13$. Clearly, much more preliminary work is needed to obtain a good quality graph of the function.

2.5.4 Parametric representation

In some practical situations the equation describing a curve in cartesian coordinates is very complicated and it is easier to specify the points in terms of a parameter. Sometimes this occurs in a very natural way. For example, in considering the trajectory of a projectile, we might specify its height and horizontal displacement separately in terms of the flight time. In the design of a safety guard for a moving part in a machine we might specify the position of the part in terms of an angle it has turned through. Such representation of curves is called **parametric representation** and we will illustrate the idea with an example. Later, in Section 2.6.6, we shall consider the polar form of specifying the equation of a curve.

Example 2.38 Sketch the graph of the curve given by $x = t^3$, $y = t^2$ ($t \in \mathbb{R}$).

Solution The simplest approach to this type of curve sketching using pencil and paper is to draw up a table of values, as in Figure 2.43.

Figure 2.43 Table of values for Example 2.38.

t	−4	−3	−2	−1	0	1	2	3	4
x	−64	−27	−8	−1	0	1	8	27	64
y	16	9	4	1	0	1	4	9	16

Clearly in this example we need to evaluate x and y at intermediate values of t to obtain a good drawing. A sketch is shown in Figure 2.44.

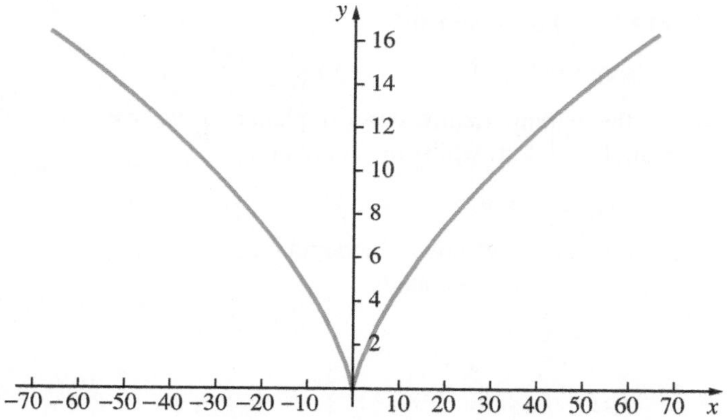

Figure 2.44 Graph of the semi-cubical parabola $x = t^3$, $y = t^2$ $(t \in \mathbb{R})$.

Example 2.39 Show that the horizontal and vertical displacements, x, y, of a projectile at time t are x and y, respectively, where $x = ut$ and $y = vt - \frac{1}{2}gt^2$ where u and v are the initial horizontal and vertical velocities and g is the acceleration due to gravity. Show that its trajectory is a parabola, that it attains a maximum height $v^2/2g$ and range $2uv/g$.

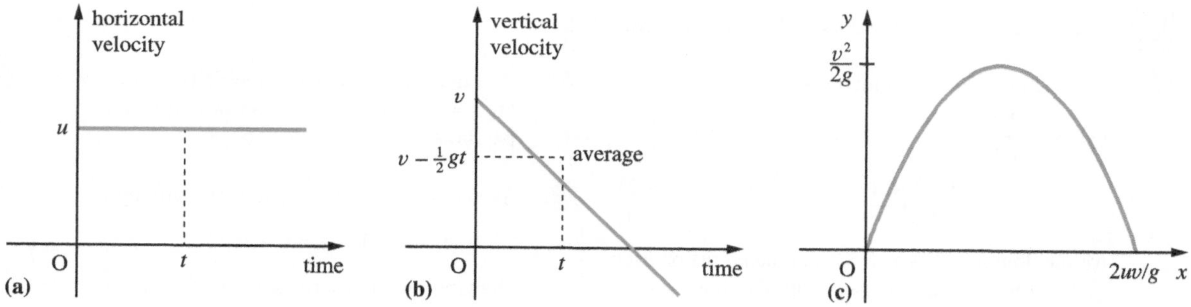

Figure 2.45 (a) Velocity – time graph (horizontal). (b) Velocity – time graph (vertical). (c) Path of a projectile.

Solution The velocity time graphs in the horizontal and vertical directions are shown in Figures 2.45(a) and (b). The horizontal displacement after time t is $x = ut$ (velocity × time), and the vertical displacement is $y = (v - \frac{1}{2}gt)t$ (average velocity × time). Thus the trajectory of the projectile is given (parametrically) by

$$x = ut,\ y = vt - \tfrac{1}{2}gt^2$$

Since $x = ut$ we may write $t = x/u$. Substituting this into the expression for y gives

$$y = \frac{vx}{u} - \frac{gx^2}{2u^2}$$

which is the equation of a parabola.

Completing the square we obtain

$$y = \frac{v^2}{2g} - \frac{g}{2u^2}\left(\frac{uv}{g} - x\right)^2$$

from which we can see that the projectile attains its maximum height, $\frac{v^2}{2g}$, at $x = uv/g$.

The range of the projectile is found by setting $y = 0$ which gives $x = \frac{2uv}{g}$. The path of the projectile is illustrated in Figure 2.45(c).

In MATLAB the command

```
ezplot(x,y)
```

plots the parametrically defined planar curve $x = x(t)$, $y = y(t)$ over the default domain $0 < t < \pi$, whilst the command

```
ezplot(x,y,[tmin,tmax])
```

plots $x = x(t)$, $y = y(t)$ over the domain $t_{min} < t < t_{max}$.

Check that the commands

```
syms x y t
x = t^3; y = t^2;
ezplot(x,y, [-4,4] )
```

return the plot of Figure 2.44.

2.5.5 Exercises

Check the graphs obtained using MATLAB or MAPLE.

43 Plot the graphs of the functions

(a) $y = \dfrac{2 + x}{1 + x}$ (b) $y = \dfrac{1}{2}\left(x + \dfrac{2}{x}\right)$

(c) $y = \dfrac{3x^4 + 12x^2 - 4}{8x^3}$ (d) $y = \dfrac{(x-1)(x-2)}{(x+1)(x-3)}$

for the domain $-3 \leqslant x \leqslant 3$. Find the points on each graph at which they intersect with the line $y = x$.

44 Sketch the graphs of the functions given below, locating their turning points and asymptotes.

(a) $y = \dfrac{x^2 - 8x + 15}{x}$ (b) $y = \dfrac{x + 1}{x - 1}$

(c) $y = \dfrac{x^2 + 5x - 14}{x + 5}$

(*Hint*: Writing (a) as

$$y = (\sqrt{x} - \sqrt{(15/x)})^2 + 2\sqrt{15} - 8$$

shows that there is a turning point at $x = \sqrt{15}$.)

45 Plot the curve whose parametric equations are $x = t(t + 4)$, $y = t + 1$. Show that it is a parabola.

46 Sketch the curve given parametrically by

$$x = t^2 - 1, \quad y = t^3 - t$$

showing that it describes a closed curve as t increases from -1 to 1.

47 Sketch the curve (the Cissoid of Diocles) given by

$$x = \frac{2t^2}{t^2 + 1}, \quad y = \frac{2t^3}{t^2 + 1}$$

Show that the cartesian form of the curve is

$$y^2 = x^3/(2 - x)$$

2.6 Circular functions

The study of circular functions has a long history. The earliest known table of a circular function dates from 425 BCE and was calculated using complicated geometrical methods by the Greek astronomer-mathematician Hipparchus. He calculated the lengths of chords subtended by angles at the centre of a circle from 0° to 60° at intervals of $\frac{1}{2}$° (see Figure 2.46(a)). His work was developed by succeeding generations of Greek

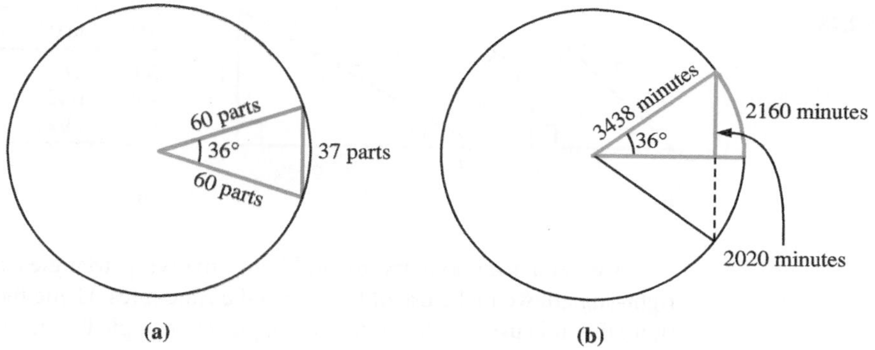

Figure 2.46
(a) Hipparchus: chords as a function of angle, expressed as parts of a radius. (b) Aryabhata: half-chords as a function of angle, expressed as parts of the arc subtended by the angle with $\pi \simeq 31\,416/10\,000$.

mathematicians culminating in the publication in the second century CE of a book by Ptolemy. His book *Syntaxis*, commonly called '*The Great Collection*', was translated first into Arabic, where it became *Al-majisti* and then into Latin, *Almagestus*.

Another contribution came from the Hindu mathematician Aryabhata (about 500 CE) who developed a radial measure related to angle measures and the function we now call the sine function (see Figure 2.46(b)). His work was first translated from Hindi into Arabic and then from Arabic into Latin. The various terms we use in studying these functions reflect this rich history of applied mathematics (360° from the Babylonians through the Greeks, degrees from the Latin *degradus*, minutes from *pars minuta*, sine from the Latin *sinus*, a mistranslation of the Hindu-Arabic *jiva*).

There are two approaches to the definition of the **circular** or **trigonometric functions** and this is reflected in their double name. One approach is static in nature and the other dynamic.

2.6.1 Trigonometric ratios

The static approach began with practical problems of surveying and gave rise to the mathematical problems of triangles and their measurement that we call trigonometry. We consider a right-angled triangle ABC, where ∠CAB is the right-angle, and define the sine, cosine and tangent functions in relation to that triangle. Thus in Figure 2.47 we have

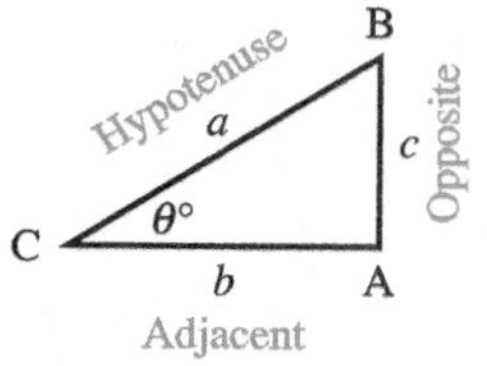

Figure 2.47

$$\text{sine}\,\theta° = \sin\theta° = \frac{c}{a} = \frac{\text{opposite}}{\text{hypotenuse}}$$

$$\text{cosine}\,\theta° = \cos\theta° = \frac{b}{a} = \frac{\text{adjacent}}{\text{hypotenuse}}$$

$$\text{tangent}\,\theta° = \tan\theta° = \frac{c}{b} = \frac{\text{opposite}}{\text{adjacent}}$$

The way in which these functions were defined led to their being called the 'trigonometrical ratios'. The context of the applications implied that the angles were measured in the sexagesimal system (degees, minutes, seconds): for example, 35°21′41″ which today is written in the decimal form 35.36°. In modern textbooks this is shown explicitly, writing, for example, sin 30°, or cos 35.36°, or tan θ°, so that the independent variable θ is a pure number. For example, by considering the triangles shown in Figure 2.48(a), we can readily write down the trigonometric ratios for 30°, 45° and 60°, as indicated in the table of Figure 2.48(b).

Figure 2.48

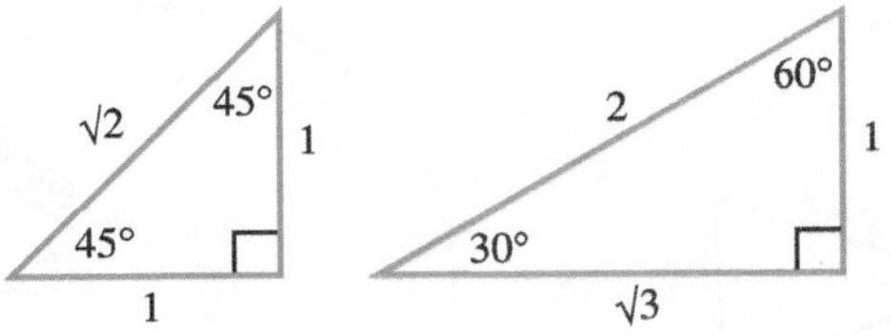

(a)

$\theta°$	$\sin\theta°$	$\cos\theta°$	$\tan\theta°$
30°	1/2	$\sqrt{3}/2$	$1/\sqrt{3}$
45°	$1/\sqrt{2}$	$1/\sqrt{2}$	1
60°	$\sqrt{3}/2$	1/2	$\sqrt{3}$

(b)

To extend trigonometry to problems involving triangles that are not necessarily right-angled, we make use of the sine and cosine rules. Using the notation of Figure 2.49 (note that it is usual to label the side opposite an angle by the corresponding lower-case letter), we have, for any triangle ABC:

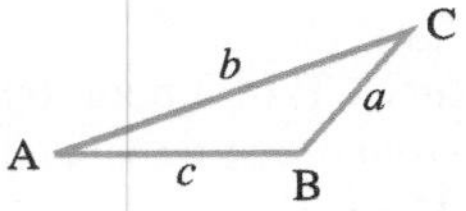

Figure 2.49

The sine rule

$$\frac{a}{\sin A} = \frac{b}{\sin B} = \frac{c}{\sin C} \tag{2.15}$$

The cosine rule

$$a^2 = b^2 + c^2 - 2bc\cos A \tag{2.16}$$

or

$$b^2 = a^2 + c^2 - 2ac\cos B$$

or

$$c^2 = a^2 + b^2 - 2ab\cos C$$

Example 2.40 Consider the surveying problem illustrated in Figure 2.50. The height of the tower is to be determined using the data measured at two points A and B, which are 20 m apart. The angles of elevation at A and B are 28°53′ and 48°51′ respectively.

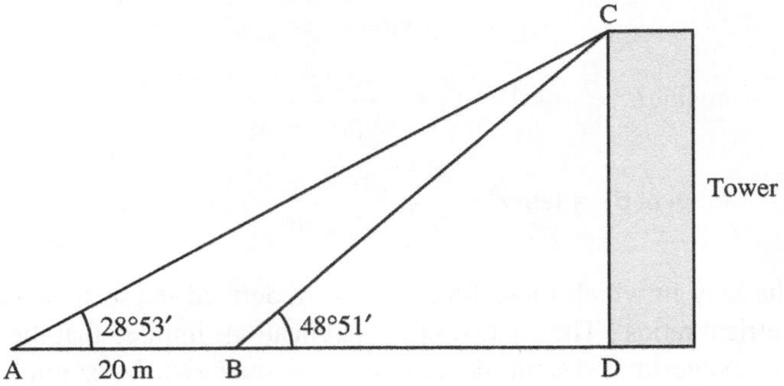

Figure 2.50 Tower of Example 2.40.

Solution By elementary geometry

$$\angle ACB = 48°51' - 28°53' = 19°58'$$

Using the sine rule, we have

$$\frac{\text{CB}}{\sin(28°53')} = \frac{\text{AB}}{\sin(19°58')}$$

so that

$$\text{CB} = 20 \sin(28°53')/\sin(19°58')$$

The height required CD is given by

$$\text{CD} = \text{CB} \sin(48°51')$$

$$= 20 \sin(28°53') \times \sin(48°51')/\sin(19°58')$$

$$= 21.3027$$

Hence the height of the tower is 21.3 m.

2.6.2 Exercises

48 In the triangles shown in Figure 2.51, calculate $\sin \theta°$, $\cos \theta°$ and $\tan \theta°$. Use a calculator to determine the value of θ in each case.

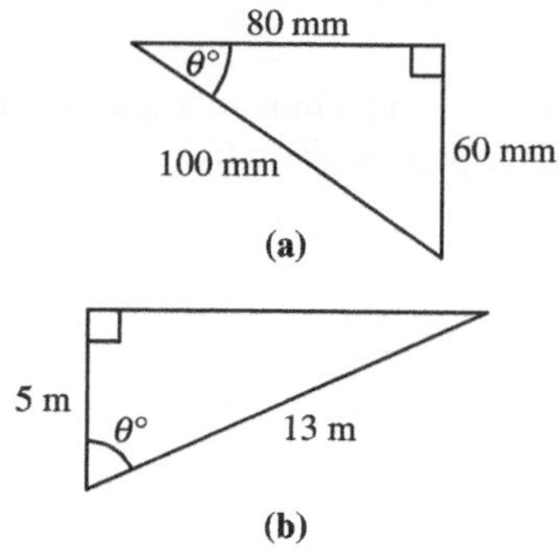

Figure 2.51

49 In the triangle ABC shown in Figure 2.52, calculate the lengths of the sides AB and BC.

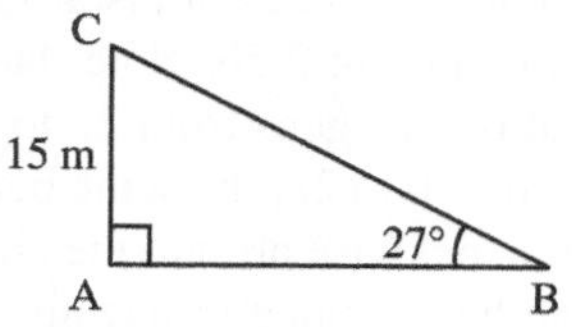

Figure 2.52

50 Calculate the value of θ where

$$\sin \theta° = \sin 10° \cos 20° + \cos 10° \sin 20°$$

51 Calculate the value of θ where

$$\cos \theta° = 2 \cos^2 30° - 1$$

52 In triangle ABC, angle A is 40°, angle B is 60° and side BC is 20 mm. Calculate the lengths of the remaining two sides.

53 In triangle ABC, the angle C is 35° and the sides AC and BC have lengths 42 mm and 73 mm respectively. Calculate the length of the third side AB.

54 The lower edge of a mural, which is 4 m high, is 2 m above an observer's eye level, as shown in Figure 2.53. Show that the optical angle $\theta°$ is given by

$$\cos \theta° = \frac{12 + d^2}{\sqrt{[(4 + d^2)(36 + d^2)]}}$$

where d m is the distance of the observer from the mural. See Review exercises Question 23.

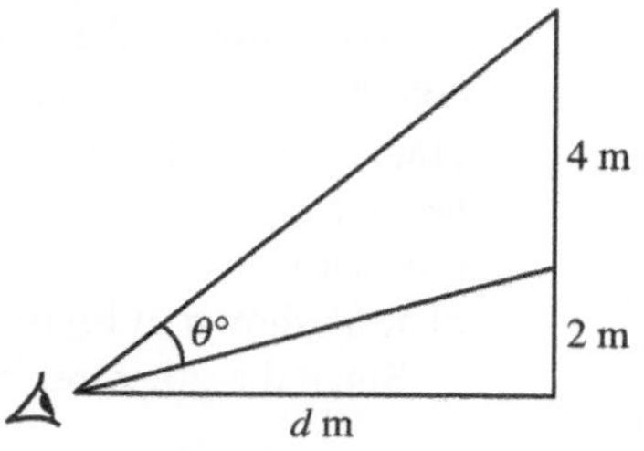

Figure 2.53 Optical angle of mural of Question 54.

2.6.3 Circular functions

The dynamic definition of the functions arises from considering the motion of a point P around a circle, as shown in Figure 2.54. Many practical mechanisms involve this mathematical model.

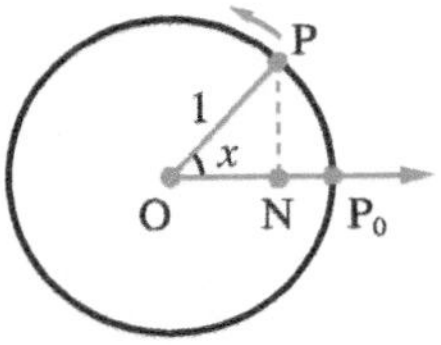

Figure 2.54

The distance OP is one unit, and the perpendicular distance NP of P from the initial position OP_0 of the rotating radius is the **sine** of the angle $\angle P_0OP$. Note that we are measuring NP positive when P is above OP_0 and negative when P is below OP_0. Similarly, the distance ON defines the **cosine** of $\angle P_0OP$ as being positive when N is to the right of O and negative when it is to the left of O.

Because we are concerned with circles and rotations in these definitions, it is natural to use circular measure so that $\angle P_0OP$, which we denote by x, is measured in radians. In this case we write simply $\sin x$ or $\cos x$, where, as before, x is a pure number. One radian is the angle that, in the notation of Figure 2.54, is subtended at the centre when the arclength P_0P is equal to the radius OP_0. Obviously therefore

$$180° = \pi \text{ radians}$$

a result we can use to convert degrees to radians and vice versa. It also follows from the definition of a radian that

(a) the length of the arc AB shown in Figure 2.55(a), of a circle of radius r, subtending an angle θ radians at the centre of the circle, is given by

$$\text{length of arc} = r\theta \tag{2.17}$$

(b) the area of the sector OAB of a circle of radius r, subtending an angle θ radians at the centre of the circle (shown shaded in Figure 2.55(b)), is given by

$$\text{area of sector} = \tfrac{1}{2}r^2\theta \tag{2.18}$$

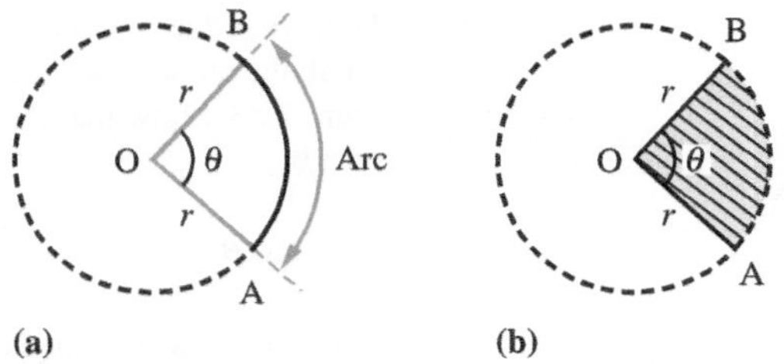

Figure 2.55
(a) Arc of a circle.
(b) Sector of a circle.

To obtain the graph of $\sin x$, we simply need to read off the values of PN as the point P moves around the circle, thus generating the graph of Figure 2.56. Note that as we continue around the circle for a second revolution (that is, as x goes from 2π to 4π) the graph produced is a replica of that produced as x goes from 0 to 2π, the same being true for subsequent intervals of 2π. By allowing P to rotate clockwise around the circle, we see that $\sin(-x) = -\sin x$, so that the graph of $\sin x$ can be extended to negative values of x, as shown in Figure 2.57.

Since the graph replicates itself for every interval of 2π,

$$\sin(x + 2\pi k) = \sin x,\ k = 0, \pm 1, \pm 2, \ldots \tag{2.19}$$

and the function $\sin x$ is said to be **periodic with period** 2π.

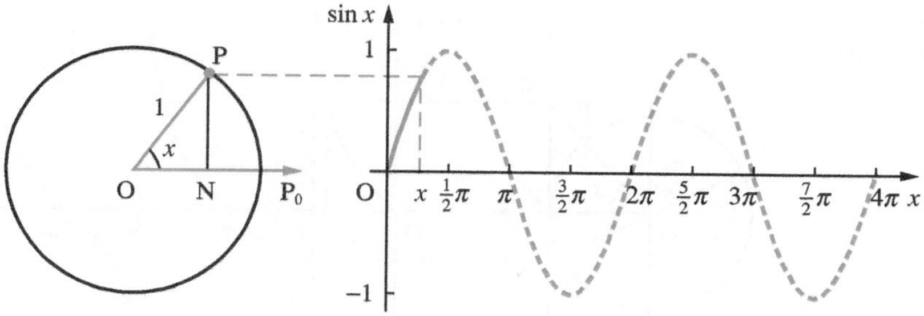

Figure 2.56
Generating the graph of sin x.

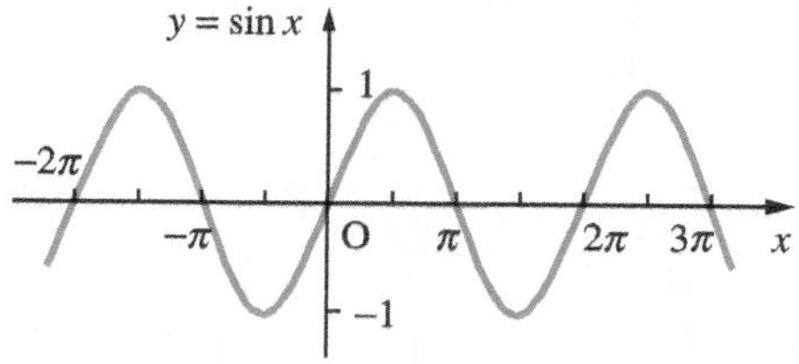

Figure 2.57
Graph of $y = \sin x$.

To obtain the graph of $y = \cos x$, we need to read off the value of ON as the point P moves around the circle. To make the plotting of the graph easier, we first rotate the circle through 90° anticlockwise and then proceed as for $y = \sin x$ to produce the graph of Figure 2.58. By allowing P to rotate clockwise around the circle, we see that $\cos(-x) = \cos x$, so that the graph can be extended to negative values of x, as shown in Figure 2.59.

Again, the function $\cos x$ is periodic with period 2π, so that

$$\cos(x + 2\pi k) = \cos x,\ k = 0, \pm 1, \pm 2, \ldots \tag{2.20}$$

Note also that the graph of $y = \sin x$ is that of $y = \cos x$ moved $\frac{1}{2}\pi$ units to the right, while that of $y = \cos x$ is the graph of $y = \sin x$ moved $\frac{1}{2}\pi$ units to the left. Thus, from Section 2.2.3,

$$\sin x = \cos(x - \tfrac{1}{2}\pi) \quad \text{or} \quad \cos x = \sin(x + \tfrac{1}{2}\pi) \tag{2.21}$$

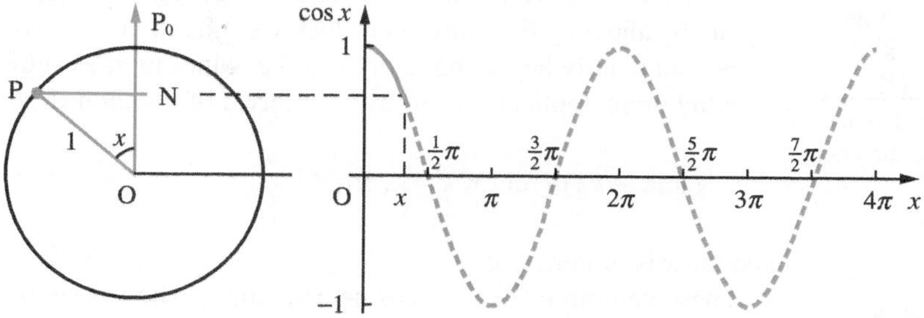

Figure 2.58
Generating the graph of cos x.

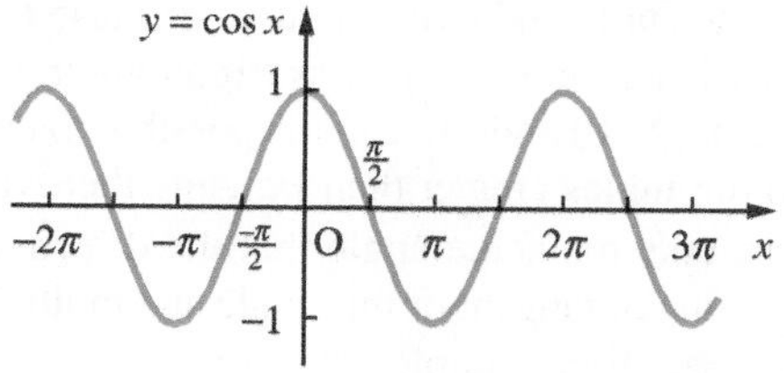

Figure 2.59
Graph of $y = \cos x$.

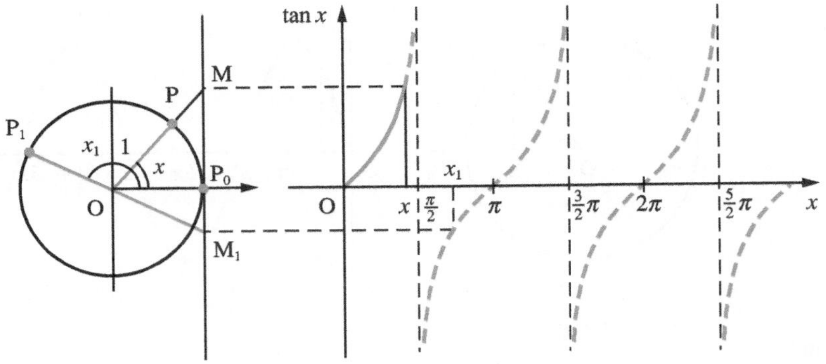

Figure 2.60
Generating the graph of $\tan x$

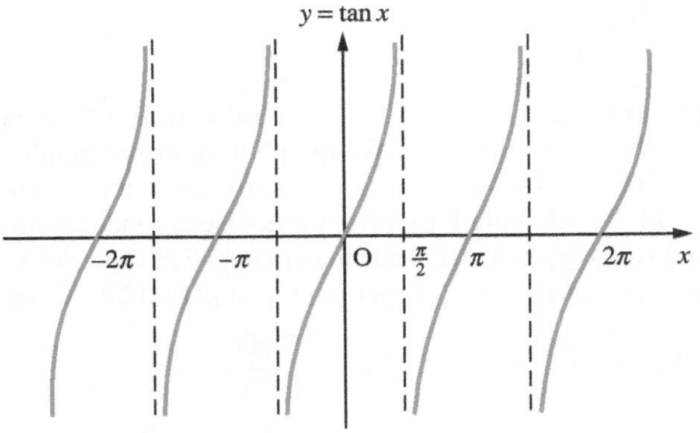

Figure 2.61
Graph of $y = \tan x$

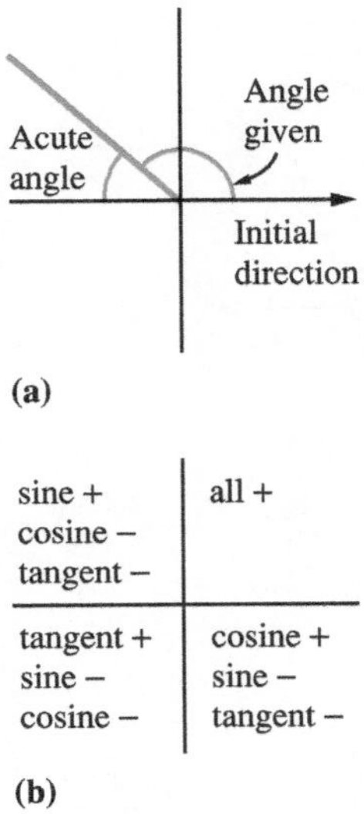

Figure 2.62

The definition of tan x is similar, and makes obvious the origin of the name 'tangent' for this function. In Figure 2.60 the rotating radius OP is extended until it cuts the tangent P_0M to the circle at the initial position P_0. The length P_0M is the **tangent** of $\angle P_0OP$. Allowing P to move around the circle, we generate the graph shown in Figure 2.60. Again, by allowing P to move in a clockwise direction, we have $\tan(-x) = -\tan x$, and the graph can readily be extended to negative values of x, as shown in Figure 2.61. In this case the graph replicates itself every interval of duration π, so that

$$\tan(x + \pi k) = \tan x, \; k = 0, \pm 1, \pm 2, \ldots \tag{2.22}$$

and tan x is of period π.

These definitions of sine, cosine and tangent show how they are associated with the properties of the circle, and consequently they are called **circular functions.** Often in an engineering context, the static and dynamic uses of these functions occur simultaneously. Consequently, we often refer to them as trigonometric functions.

Using the results (2.19), (2.20) and (2.22), it is possible to calculate the values of the trigonometric functions for angles greater than $\frac{1}{2}\pi$ using their values for angles between zero and $\frac{1}{2}\pi$. The rule is: take the acute angle that the direction makes with the initial direction, find the sine, cosine or tangent of this angle and multiply by +1 or −1 according to the scheme of Figure 2.62. For example

$$\cos(135°) = \cos(180° - 45°) = -\cos 45° = -\sqrt{\tfrac{1}{2}}$$
$$\sin(330°) = \sin(360° - 30°) = -\sin 30° = -\tfrac{1}{2}$$
$$\tan(240°) = \tan(180° + 60°) = \tan 60° = \sqrt{3}$$

As we frequently move between measuring angles in degrees and in radians, it is important to check that your calculator is in the correct mode.

If the radius OP is rotating with constant angular velocity ω (in rad s^{-1}) about O then $x = \omega t$, where t is the time (in s). The time T taken for one complete revolution is given by $\omega T = 2\pi$; that is, $T = 2\pi/\omega$. This is the **period** of the motion. In one second the radius makes $\omega/2\pi$ such revolutions. This is the **frequency**, ν. Its value is given by

$$\nu = \text{frequency} = \frac{1}{\text{period}} = \frac{\omega}{2\pi}$$

Thus, the function $y = A \sin \omega t$, which is associated with oscillatory motion in engineering, has period $2\pi/\omega$ and **amplitude** A. The term amplitude is used to indicate the maximum distance of the graph of $y = A \sin \omega t$ from the horizontal axis.

Example 2.41

Sketch using the same set of axes the graphs of the functions

(a) $y = 2 \sin t$ (b) $y = \sin t$ (c) $y = \frac{1}{2} \sin t$

and discuss.

Solution The graphs of the three functions are shown in Figure 2.63. The functions (a), (b) and (c) have amplitudes 2, 1 and $\frac{1}{2}$ respectively. We note that the effect of changing the amplitude is to alter the size of the 'humps' in the sine wave. Note that changing only the amplitude does not alter the points at which the graph crosses the x axis. All three functions have period 2π.

Figure 2.63

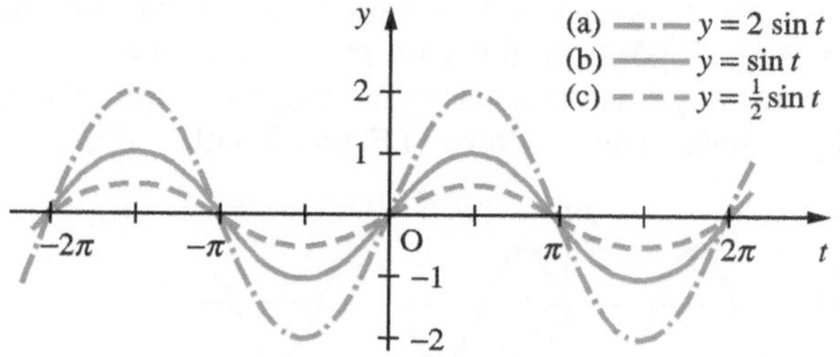

Example 2.42

Sketch using the same axes the graphs of the functions

(a) $y = \sin t$ (b) $y = \sin 2t$ (c) $y = \sin \frac{1}{2}t$

and discuss.

Solution The graphs of the three functions (a), (b) and (c) are shown in Figure 2.64. All three have amplitude 1 and periods 2π, π and 4π respectively. We note that the effect of changing the parameter ω in $\sin \omega t$ is to 'squash' or 'stretch' the basic sine wave $\sin t$. All that happens is that the basic pattern repeats itself less or more frequently; that is, the period changes.

Figure 2.64

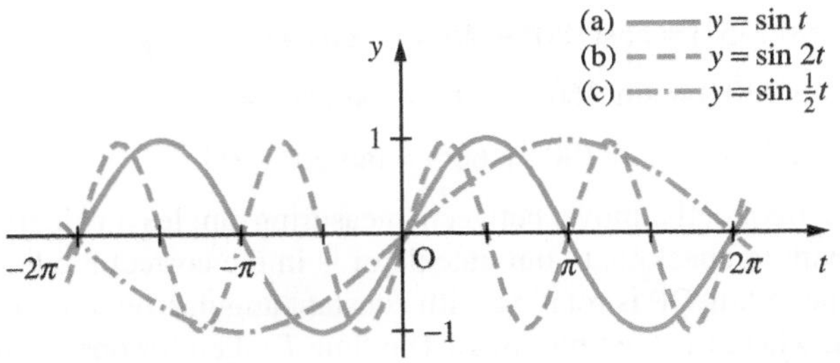

In engineering we frequently encounter the sinusoidal function

$$y = A\sin(\omega t + \alpha), \quad \omega > 0 \tag{2.23}$$

Following the discussion in Section 2.2.4, we have that the graph of this function is obtained by moving the graph of $y = A\sin\omega t$ horizontally:

$\dfrac{\alpha}{\omega}$ units to the left if α is positive

or

$\dfrac{|\alpha|}{\omega}$ units to the right if α is negative

The sine wave of (2.23) is said to 'lead' the sine wave $A\sin\omega t$ when α is positive and to 'lag' it when α is negative.

Example 2.43 Sketch the graph of $y = 3\sin(2t + \frac{1}{3}\pi)$.

Solution First we sketch the graph of $y = 3\sin 2t$, which has amplitude 3 and period π, as shown in Figure 2.65(a). In this case $\alpha = \frac{1}{3}\pi$ and $\omega = 2$, so it follows that the graph of $y = 3\sin(2t + \frac{1}{3}\pi)$ is obtained by moving the graph of $y = 3\sin 2t$ horizontally to the left by $\frac{1}{6}\pi$ units. This is shown in Figure 2.65(b).

Figure 2.65

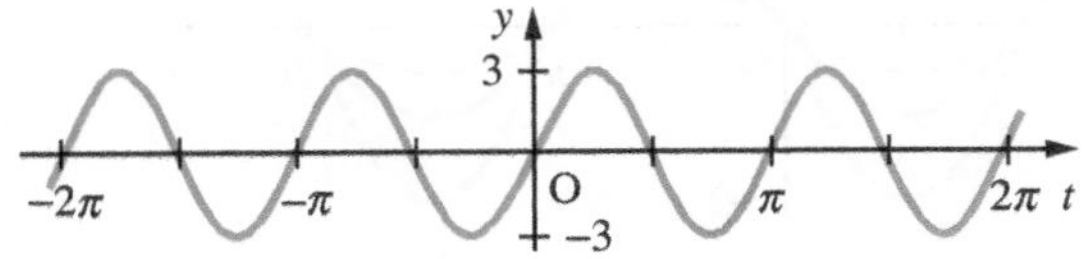

(a) $y = 3\sin 2t$

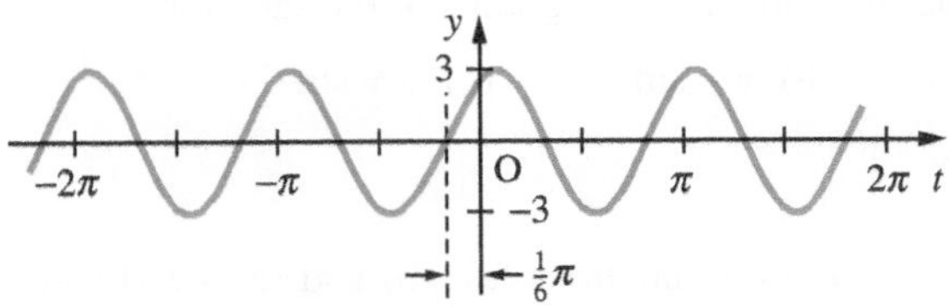

(b) $y = 3\sin(2t + \frac{1}{3}\pi)$

Example 2.44 Consider the crank and connecting rod mechanism illustrated in Figure 2.66. Determine a functional relationship between the displacement of Q and the angle through which the crank OP has turned.

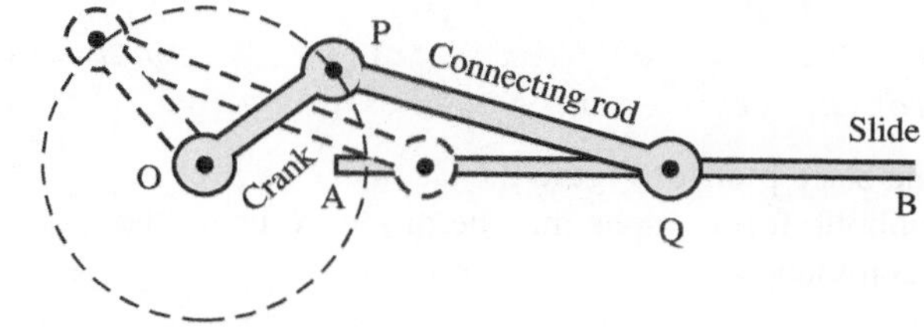

Figure 2.66 Crank and connecting rod mechanism.

Solution As the crank OP rotates about O, the other end of the connecting rod moves backwards and forwards along the slide AB. The displacement of Q from its initial position depends on the angle through which the crank OP has turned. A mathematical model for the mechanism replaces the crank and connecting rod, which have thickness as well as length, by straight lines, which have length only, and we consider the motion of the point Q as the line OP rotates about O, with PQ fixed in length and Q constrained to move on the line AB, as shown in Figure 2.67. We can specify the dependence of Q on the angle of rotation of OP by using some elementary trigonometry. Labelling the length of OP as r units, the length of PQ as l units, the length of OQ as y units and the angle $\angle$AOP as x radians, and applying the cosine formula gives

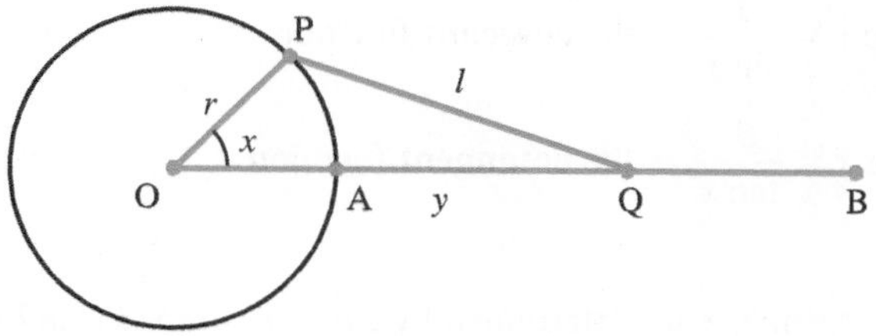

Figure 2.67 Model of crank and connecting rod.

$$l^2 = r^2 + y^2 - 2yr\cos x$$

which implies

$$\begin{aligned}(y - r\cos x)^2 &= l^2 - r^2 + r^2\cos^2 x \\ &= l^2 - r^2\sin^2 x\end{aligned}$$

and

$$y = r\cos x + \sqrt{(l^2 - r^2\sin^2 x)}$$

Thus for any angle x we can calculate the corresponding value of y. We can represent this relationship by means of a graph, as shown in Figure 2.68.

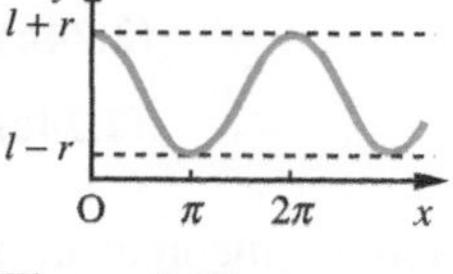

Figure 2.68

In MATLAB the circular functions are represented by `sin(x)`, `cos(x)` and `tan(x)` respectively. (Note that MATLAB uses radians in function evaluation.) Also in MATLAB `pi` (`Pi` in MAPLE) is a predefined variable representing the quantity π. As an example check that the commands

```
t = -2*pi : pi/90 : 2*pi;
y1 = sin(t); y2 = sin(2*t); y3 = sin(0.5*t);
plot(t, y1, '-',t ,y2, '- -', t, y3, '-.')
```

output the basic plots of Figure 2.64.

In symbolic form graphs may be produced using the `ezplot` command. Check that the commands

```
syms t
y = sym(3*sin(2*t + pi/3));
ezplot(y,[-2*pi,2*pi] )
grid
```

produce the plot of Figure 2.65(b).

2.6.4 Trigonometric identities

Other circular functions are defined in terms of the three basic functions sine, cosine and tangent. In particular, we have

$\sec x = \dfrac{1}{\cos x}$, the **secant** function

$\operatorname{cosec} x = \dfrac{1}{\sin x}$, the **cosecant** function

$\cot x = \dfrac{1}{\tan x}$, the **cotangent** function

In MATLAB these are determined by `sec(x)`, `csc(x)` and `cot(x)` respectively.

From the basic definitions it is possible to deduce the following trigonometric identities relating the functions.

Triangle identities

$$\cos^2 x + \sin^2 x = 1 \tag{2.24a}$$

$$1 + \tan^2 x = \sec^2 x \tag{2.24b}$$

$$1 + \cot^2 x = \operatorname{cosec}^2 x \tag{2.24c}$$

The first of these follows immediately from the use of Pythagoras' theorem in a right-angled triangle with a unit hypotenuse. Dividing (2.24a) through by $\cos^2 x$ yields identity (2.24b), and dividing through by $\sin^2 x$ yields identity (2.24c).

Compound-angle identities

$$\sin(x + y) = \sin x \cos y + \cos x \sin y \tag{2.25a}$$

$$\sin(x - y) = \sin x \cos y - \cos x \sin y \tag{2.25b}$$

$$\cos(x + y) = \cos x \cos y - \sin x \sin y \tag{2.25c}$$

$$\cos(x - y) = \cos x \cos y + \sin x \sin y \tag{2.25d}$$

$$\tan(x + y) = \frac{\tan x + \tan y}{1 - \tan x \tan y} \tag{2.25e}$$

$$\tan(x - y) = \frac{\tan x - \tan y}{1 + \tan x \tan y} \tag{2.25f}$$

Sum and product identities

$$\sin x + \sin y = 2 \sin \tfrac{1}{2}(x + y) \cos \tfrac{1}{2}(x - y) \tag{2.26a}$$

$$\sin x - \sin y = 2 \sin \tfrac{1}{2}(x - y) \cos \tfrac{1}{2}(x + y) \tag{2.26b}$$

$$\cos x + \cos y = 2 \cos \tfrac{1}{2}(x + y) \cos \tfrac{1}{2}(x - y) \tag{2.26c}$$

$$\cos x - \cos y = -2 \sin \tfrac{1}{2}(x + y) \sin \tfrac{1}{2}(x - y) \tag{2.26d}$$

From identities (2.25a), (2.25c) and (2.25e) we can obtain the double-angle formulae.

$$\sin 2x = 2 \sin x \cos x \tag{2.27a}$$

$$\cos 2x = \cos^2 x - \sin^2 x \tag{2.27b}$$

$$= 2 \cos^2 x - 1 \tag{2.27c}$$

$$= 1 - 2 \sin^2 x \tag{2.27d}$$

$$\tan 2x = \frac{2 \tan x}{1 - \tan^2 x} \tag{2.27e}$$

(Writing $x = \theta/2$ we can obtain similar identities called half-angle formulae.)

Example 2.45 Express $\cos(\pi/2 + 2x)$ in terms of $\sin x$ and $\cos x$.

Solution Using identity (2.25c) we obtain

$$\cos(\pi/2 + 2x) = \cos \pi/2 \cos 2x - \sin \pi/2 \sin 2x$$

Since $\cos \pi/2 = 0$ and $\sin \pi/2 = 1$, we can simplify to obtain

$$\cos(\pi/2 + 2x) = -\sin 2x$$

Now using the double-angle formula (2.27a), we obtain

$$\cos(\pi/2 + 2x) = -2 \sin x \cos x$$

Example 2.46 Show that

$$\sin(A + B) + \sin(A - B) = 2 \sin A \cos B$$

and deduce that

$$\sin x + \sin y = 2 \sin \tfrac{1}{2}(x + y) \cos \tfrac{1}{2}(x - y)$$

Hence sketch the graph of $y = \sin 4x + \sin 2x$.

Solution Using identities (2.25a) and (2.25b) we have

$$\sin(A + B) = \sin A \cos B + \cos A \sin B$$

$$\sin(A - B) = \sin A \cos B - \cos A \sin B$$

Adding these two identities gives

$$\sin(A + B) + \sin(A - B) = 2 \sin A \cos B$$

Now setting $A + B = x$ and $A - B = y$, we see that $A = \frac{1}{2}(x + y)$ and $B = \frac{1}{2}(x - y)$ so that

$$\sin x + \sin y = 2 \sin \tfrac{1}{2}(x + y) \cos \tfrac{1}{2}(x - y)$$

which is identity (2.26a). (The identities (2.26b–d) can be proved in the same manner.)
Applying the formula to

$$y = \sin 4x + \sin 2x$$

we obtain

$$y = 2 \sin 3x \cos x$$

The graphs of $y = \sin 3x$ and $y = \cos x$ are shown in Figures 2.69(a) and (b). The combination of these two graphs yields Figure 2.69(c). This type of combination of oscillations in practical situations leads to the phenomena of 'beats'.

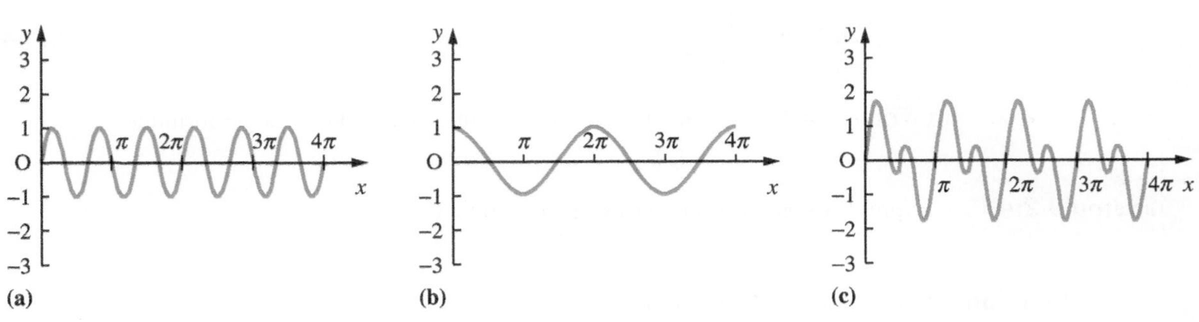

Figure 2.69 (a) $y = \sin 3x$; (b) $y = \cos x$; (c) $y = 2 \sin 3x \cos x$

The identities 2.26(a–d) are useful for turning the sum or difference of sines and cosines into a product of sines and/or cosines in many problems. But the reverse process is also useful in others! So we summarize here the expressing of products as sums or differences.

$$\sin x \cos y = \tfrac{1}{2}[\sin(x+y) + \sin(x-y)] \qquad \textbf{(2.28a)}$$

$$\cos x \sin y = \tfrac{1}{2}[\sin(x+y) - \sin(x-y)] \qquad \textbf{(2.28b)}$$

$$\cos x \cos y = \tfrac{1}{2}[\cos(x+y) + \cos(x-y)] \qquad \textbf{(2.28c)}$$

$$\sin x \sin y = -\tfrac{1}{2}[\cos(x+y) - \cos(x-y)] \qquad \textbf{(2.28d)}$$

Note the minus sign before the bracket in (2.28d). Before the invention of calculating machines, these identities were used to perform multiplications. Commonly the mathematical tables used only tabulated the functions up to 45° to save space so that all four identities were used.

Example 2.47 Solve the equation $2\cos^2 x + 3\sin x = 3$ for $0 \leqslant x \leqslant 2\pi$.

Solution First we express the equation in terms of $\sin x$ only. This can be done by eliminating $\cos^2 x$ using the identity (2.24a), giving

$$2(1 - \sin^2 x) + 3\sin x = 3$$

which reduces to

$$2\sin^2 x - 3\sin x + 1 = 0$$

This is now a quadratic equation in $\sin x$, and it is convenient to write $\lambda = \sin x$, giving

$$2\lambda^2 - 3\lambda + 1 = 0$$

Factorizing then gives $\quad (2\lambda - 1)(\lambda - 1) = 0$

leading to the two solutions $\lambda = \tfrac{1}{2}$ and $\lambda = 1$

We now return to the fact that $\lambda = \sin x$ to determine the corresponding values of x.

(i) If $\lambda = \tfrac{1}{2}$ then $\sin x = \tfrac{1}{2}$. Remembering that $\sin x$ is positive for x lying in the first and second quadrants and that $\sin \tfrac{1}{6}\pi = \tfrac{1}{2}$, we have two solutions corresponding to $\lambda = \tfrac{1}{2}$, namely $x = \tfrac{1}{6}\pi$ and $x = \tfrac{5}{6}\pi$.

(ii) If $\lambda = 1$ then $\sin x = 1$, giving the single solution $\lambda = \tfrac{1}{2}\pi$.

Thus there are three solutions to the given equation, namely

$$x = \tfrac{1}{6}\pi, \quad \tfrac{1}{2}\pi \quad \text{and} \quad \tfrac{5}{6}\pi$$

Example 2.48 The path of a projectile fired with speed V at an angle α to the horizontal is given by

$$y = x\tan\alpha - \frac{1}{2}\frac{gx^2}{V^2\cos^2\alpha}$$

(See Example 2.39 with $u = V\cos\alpha$, $v = V\sin\alpha$.)

For fixed V a family of trajectories, for various angles of projection α, is obtained, as shown in Figure 2.70. Find the condition for a point P with coordinates (X, Y) to lie beyond the reach of the projectile.

Solution Given the coordinates (X, Y), the possible angles α of launch are given by the roots of the equation

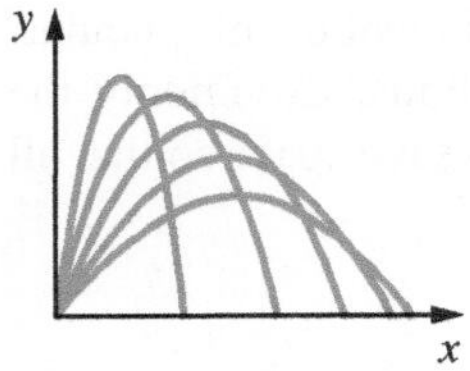

Figure 2.70 Trajectories for different launch angles.

$$Y = X \tan\alpha - \frac{1}{2}\frac{gX^2}{V^2\cos^2\alpha}$$

Using the trigonometric identity

$$1 + \tan^2\alpha = \frac{1}{\cos^2\alpha}$$

gives

$$Y = X\tan\alpha - \frac{1}{2}\frac{gX^2}{V^2}(1 + \tan^2\alpha)$$

Writing $T = \tan\alpha$, this may be rewritten as

$$(gX^2)T^2 - (2XV^2)T + (gX^2 + 2V^2Y) = 0$$

which is a quadratic equation in T. From (1.8), this equation will have two different real roots if

$$(2XV^2)^2 > 4(gX^2)(gX^2 + 2V^2Y)$$

but no real roots if

$$(2XV^2)^2 < 4(gX^2)(gX^2 + 2V^2Y)$$

Thus the point $P(X, Y)$ is 'safe' if

$$V^4 < g^2X^2 + 2gV^2Y$$

The critical case where the point (X, Y) lies on the curve

$$V^4 = g^2x^2 + 2gV^2y$$

gives us the so-called 'parabola of safety', with the safety region being that above this parabola

$$y = \frac{V^2}{2g} - \frac{gx^2}{2V^2}$$

2.6.5 Amplitude and phase

Often in engineering contexts we are concerned with vibrations of parts of a structure or machine. These vibrations are a response to a periodic external force and will usually have the same frequency as that force. Usually, also, the response will lag behind the exciting force. Mathematically this is often represented by an external force of the form $F \sin \omega t$ with a response of the form $a \sin \omega t + b \cos \omega t$, where a and b are constants dependent on F, ω and the physical characteristics of the system. To find the size of the response we need to write it in the form $A \sin(\omega t + \alpha)$, where

$$A \sin(\omega t + \alpha) = a \sin \omega t + b \cos \omega t$$

This we can always do, as is illustrated in Example 2.49.

Example 2.49 Express $y = 4 \sin 3t - 3 \cos 3t$ in the form $y = A \sin(3t + \alpha)$.

Solution To determine the appropriate values of A and α, we proceed as follows.

Using the identity (2.25a), we have

$$\begin{aligned} A \sin(3t + \alpha) &= A(\sin 3t \cos \alpha + \cos 3t \sin \alpha) \\ &= (A \cos \alpha) \sin 3t + (A \sin \alpha) \cos 3t \end{aligned}$$

Since this must equal the expression

$$4 \sin 3t - 3 \cos 3t$$

for all values of t, the respective coefficients of $\sin 3t$ and $\cos 3t$ must be the same in both expressions, so that

$$4 = A \cos \alpha \quad \textbf{(2.29)}$$

and

$$-3 = A \sin \alpha \quad \textbf{(2.30)}$$

The angle α is shown in Figure 2.71. By Pythagoras' theorem,

$$A = \sqrt{(16 + 9)} = 5$$

and clearly

$$\tan \alpha = -\tfrac{3}{4}$$

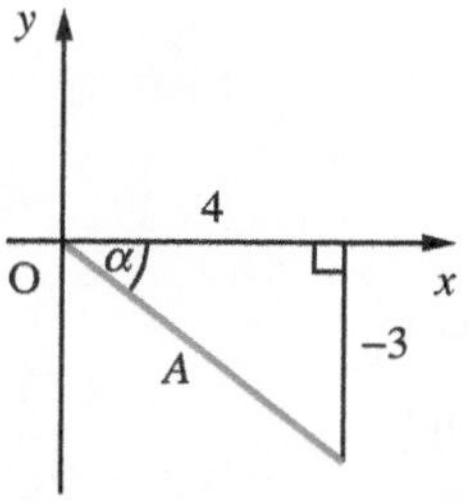

Figure 2.71
The angle α.

The value of α may now be determined using a calculator. However, care must be taken to ensure that the correct quadrant is chosen for α. Since A is taken to be positive, it follows from Figure 2.71 that α lies in the fourth quadrant. Thus, using a calculator, we have $\alpha = -0.64$ rad and

$$y = 4 \sin 3t - 3 \cos 3t = 5 \sin(3t - 0.64)$$

Using the Symbolic Math Toolbox in MATLAB, commands such as *expand*, *simplify* and *simple* may be used to manipulate trigonometric functions, and the command *solve* may be used to solve trigonometric equations (these commands have been introduced earlier). Some illustrations are:

(a) The commands

```
syms x y
expand(cos(x + y))
```

return

```
cos(x)*cos(y) - sin(x)*sin(y)
```

(b) The commands

```
syms x
simplify(cos(x)^2 + sin(x)^2)
```

return

```
1
```

(c) The commands

```
syms (x)
simplify(cos(x)^2 - sin(x)^2)
```

return

```
2*cos(x)^2-1
```

whilst the command

```
simple(cos(x)^2 - sin(x)^2)
```

returns

```
cos(2*x)
```

(d) The commands

```
syms x
s = solve('2*cos(x)^2 + 3*sin(x) = 3')
```

return

```
s = 1/2*pi
    1/6*pi
    5/6*pi
```

confirming the answer obtained in Example 2.47.

If numeric answers are required then use the command

```
double(s)
```

to obtain

```
s = 1.5708
    0.5236
    2.6180
```

2.6.6 Exercises

Check your answers using MATLAB or MAPLE whenever possible.

55 Copy and complete the table in Figure 2.72.

degrees	0	30		60			150	
radians			$\pi/4$		$\pi/2$	$2\pi/3$		π

degrees	210	225	240	270	300	315	330	
radians								2π

Figure 2.72 Conversion table: degrees to radians.

56 Sketch for $-3\pi \leqslant x \leqslant 3\pi$ the graphs of

(a) $y = \sin 2x$ (b) $y = \sin \frac{1}{2}x$

(c) $y = \sin^2 x$ (d) $y = \sin x^2$

(e) $y = \dfrac{1}{\sin x}$ $(x \neq n\pi,\ n = 0, \pm 1, \pm 2, \dots)$

(f) $y = \sin\left(\dfrac{1}{x}\right)$ $(x \neq 0)$

57 Solve the following equations for $0 \leqslant x \leqslant 2\pi$:

(a) $3 \sin^2 x + 2 \sin x - 1 = 0$

(b) $4 \cos^2 x + 5 \cos x + 1 = 0$

(c) $2 \tan^2 x - \tan x - 1 = 0$

(d) $\sin 2x = \cos x$

58 By referring to an equilateral triangle, show that $\cos \frac{1}{3}\pi = \frac{1}{2}\sqrt{3}$ and $\tan \frac{1}{6}\pi = \frac{1}{3}\sqrt{3}$, and find values for $\sin \frac{1}{3}\pi$, $\tan \frac{1}{3}\pi$, $\cos \frac{1}{6}\pi$ and $\sin \frac{1}{6}\pi$. Hence, using the double-angle formulae, find $\sin \frac{1}{12}\pi$, $\cos \frac{1}{12}\pi$ and $\tan \frac{1}{12}\pi$. Using appropriate properties from Section 2.6, calculate

(a) $\sin \frac{2}{3}\pi$ (b) $\tan \frac{7}{6}\pi$ (c) $\cos \frac{11}{6}\pi$

(d) $\sin \frac{5}{12}\pi$ (e) $\cos \frac{7}{12}\pi$ (f) $\tan \frac{11}{12}\pi$

59 Given $s = \sin \theta$, where $\frac{1}{2}\pi < \theta < \pi$, find, in terms of s,

(a) $\cos \theta$ (b) $\sin 2\theta$

(c) $\sin 3\theta$ (d) $\sin \frac{1}{2}\theta$

60 Show that

$$\frac{1 + \sin 2\theta + \cos 2\theta}{1 + \sin 2\theta - \cos 2\theta} = \cot \theta$$

61 Given $t = \tan \frac{1}{2}x$, prove that

(a) $\sin x = \dfrac{2t}{1 + t^2}$

(b) $\cos x = \dfrac{1 - t^2}{1 + t^2}$

(c) $\tan x = \dfrac{2t}{1 - t^2}$

Hence solve the equation

$$2 \sin x - \cos x = 1$$

62 In each of the following, the value of one of the six circular functions is given. Without using a calculator, find the values of the remaining five.

(a) $\sin x = \frac{1}{2}$ (b) $\cos x = -\frac{1}{2}\sqrt{3}$

(c) $\tan x = -1$ (d) $\sec x = \sqrt{2}$

(e) $\operatorname{cosec} x = -2$ (f) $\cot x = \sqrt{3}$

63 Express as a product of sines and/or cosines

(a) $\sin 3\theta + \sin \theta$ (b) $\cos \theta - \cos 2\theta$

(c) $\cos 5\theta + \cos 2\theta$ (d) $\sin \theta - \sin 2\theta$

64 Express as a sum or difference of sines or cosines

(a) $\sin 3\theta \sin \theta$ (b) $\sin 3\theta \cos \theta$

(c) $\cos 3\theta \sin \theta$ (d) $\cos 3\theta \cos \theta$

65 Express in the forms $r \cos(\theta - \alpha)$ and $r \sin(\theta - \beta)$

(a) $\sqrt{3} \sin \theta - \cos \theta$ (b) $\sin \theta - \cos \theta$

(c) $\sin \theta + \cos \theta$ (d) $2 \cos \theta + 3 \sin \theta$

66 Show that $-\frac{3}{2} \leqslant 2 \cos x + \cos 2x \leqslant 3$ for all x, and determine those values of x for which the equality holds. Plot the graph of $y = 2 \cos x + \cos 2x$ for $0 \leqslant x \leqslant 2\pi$.

2.6.7 Inverse circular (trigonometric) functions

Considering the inverse of the trigonometric functions, it follows from the definition given in (2.4) that the inverse sine function $\sin^{-1}x$ (also sometimes denoted by arcsin x) is such that

$$\text{if} \quad y = \sin^{-1}x \quad \text{then} \quad x = \sin y$$

Here x should not be interpreted as an angle – rather $\sin^{-1}x$ represents the angle whose sine is x. Applying the procedures for obtaining the graph of the inverse function given in Section 2.2.3 to the graph of $y = \sin x$ (Figure 2.55) leads to the graph shown in Figure 2.73(a). As we explained in Example 2.8, when considering the inverse of $y = x^2$, the graph of Figure 2.73(a) is not representative of a function, since for each value of x in the domain $-1 \leqslant x \leqslant 1$ there are an infinite number of image values (as indicated by the points of intersection of the broken vertical line with the graph). To overcome this problem, we restrict the range of the inverse function $\sin^{-1}x$ to $-\frac{1}{2}\pi \leqslant \sin^{-1}x \leqslant \frac{1}{2}\pi$ and define the inverse sine function by

$$\text{if } y = \sin^{-1}x \text{ then } x = \sin y, \quad \text{where } -\tfrac{1}{2}\pi \leqslant y \leqslant \tfrac{1}{2}\pi \text{ and } -1 \leqslant x \leqslant 1 \tag{2.31}$$

The corresponding graph is shown in Figure 2.73(b).

Similarly, in order to define the inverse cosine and inverse tangent functions $\cos^{-1}x$ and $\tan^{-1}x$ (also sometimes denoted by arccos x and arctan x), we have to restrict the ranges. This is done according to the following definitions.

$$\text{if } y = \cos^{-1}x \text{ then } x = \cos y, \quad \text{where } 0 \leqslant y \leqslant \pi \text{ and } -1 \leqslant x \leqslant 1 \tag{2.32}$$

$$\text{if } y = \tan^{-1}x \text{ then } x = \tan y, \quad \text{where } -\tfrac{1}{2}\pi < y < \tfrac{1}{2}\pi \text{ and } x \text{ is any real number} \tag{2.33}$$

Figure 2.73
Graph of $\sin^{-1}x$.

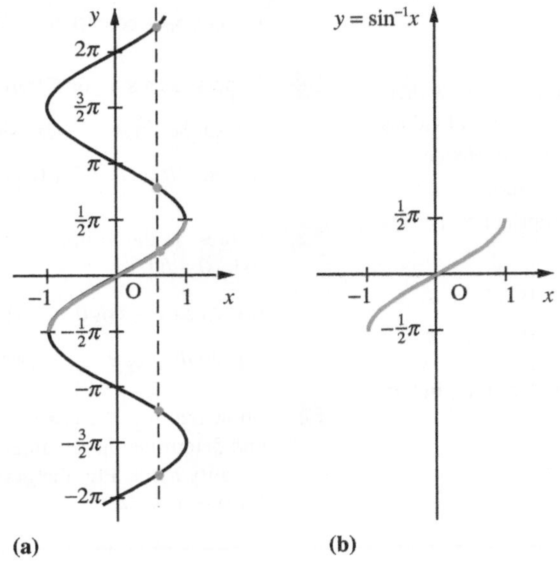

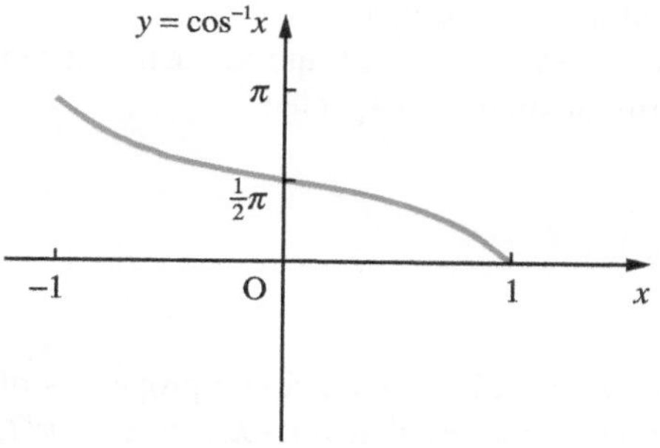

Figure 2.74 Graph of $\cos^{-1}x$.

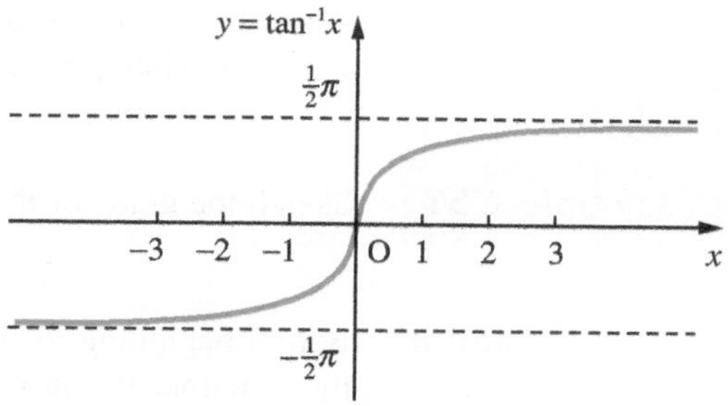

Figure 2.75 Graph of $\tan^{-1}x$.

The corresponding graphs of $y = \cos^{-1}x$ and $y = \tan^{-1}x$ are shown in Figures 2.74 and 2.75, respectively.

In some books (2.31)–(2.33) are called the *principal values* of the inverse functions. A calculator will automatically give these values.

Example 2.50 Evaluate $\sin^{-1}x$, $\cos^{-1}x$, $\tan^{-1}x$ where (a) $x = 0.35$ and (b) $x = -0.7$, expressing the answers correct to 4dp.

Solution (a) $\sin^{-1}(0.35)$ is the angle α which lies between $-\pi/2$ and $+\pi/2$ and is such that $\sin\alpha = 0.35$. Using a calculator we have

$$\sin^{-1}(0.35) = 0.3576 \text{ (4dp)} = 0.1138\pi$$

which clearly lies between $-\pi/2$ and $+\pi/2$.

$\cos^{-1}(0.35)$ is the angle β which lies between 0 and π and is such that $\cos\beta = 0.35$. Using a calculator we obtain

$$\cos^{-1}(0.35) = 1.2132 \text{ (4dp)} = 0.3862\pi$$

which lies between 0 and π.

$\tan^{-1}(0.35)$ is the angle γ which lies between $-\pi/2$ and $+\pi/2$ and is such that $\tan\gamma = 0.35$. Using a calculator we have

$$\tan^{-1}(0.35) = 0.3367 \text{ (4dp)} = 0.1072\pi$$

which lies in the correct range of values.

Notice

$$\frac{\sin^{-1}(0.35)}{\cos^{-1}(0.35)} \neq \tan^{-1}(0.35)$$

(b) $\sin^{-1}(-0.7)$ is the angle α which lies between $-\pi/2$ and $+\pi/2$ and is such that $\sin\alpha = -0.7$. Again using a calculator we obtain

$$\sin^{-1}(-0.7) = -0.7754 \text{ (4dp)}$$

which lies in the correct range of values.

$\cos^{-1}(-0.7)$ is the angle β which lies between 0 and π and is such that $\cos\beta = -0.7$.

Thus $\beta = 2.3462$, which lies in the second quadrant as expected.

$\tan^{-1}(-0.7)$ is the angle γ which lies between $-\pi/2$ and $+\pi/2$ and is such that $\tan \gamma = -0.7$. Thus $\gamma = -0.6107$, lying in the fourth quadrant, as expected.

Example 2.51 Sketch the graph of the function $y = \sin^{-1}(\sin x)$.

Solution Before beginning to sketch the graph we need to examine the algebraic properties of the function. Because of the way $\sin^{-1}$ is defined we know that for $-\pi/2 \leqslant x \leqslant \pi/2$, $\sin^{-1}(\sin x) = x$. (The function $\sin^{-1}x$ *strictly* is the inverse function of $\sin x$ with the restricted domain $-\pi/2 \leqslant x \leqslant \pi/2$.) We also know that $\sin x$ is an odd function, so that $\sin(-x) = -\sin x$. This implies that $\sin^{-1}x$ is an odd function. In fact, this is obvious from its graph (Figure 2.73(b)). Thus, $\sin^{-1}(\sin x)$ is an odd function. Lastly, since $\sin x$ is a periodic function with period 2π we conclude that $\sin^{-1}(\sin x)$ is also a periodic function of period 2π. Thus, if we can sketch the graph between 0 and π, we can obtain the graph between $-\pi$ and 0 by antisymmetry about $x = 0$ and the whole graph by periodicity elsewhere. Using Figures 2.73(a) and 2.73(b) we can obtain the graph of the function for $0 \leqslant x \leqslant \pi$, as shown in Figure 2.76 (blue). The graph between $-\pi$ and 0 is obtained by antisymmetry about the origin, as shown with the broken line in Figure 2.76, and the whole graph is obtained making use of the piece between $-\pi$ and $+\pi$ and periodicity.

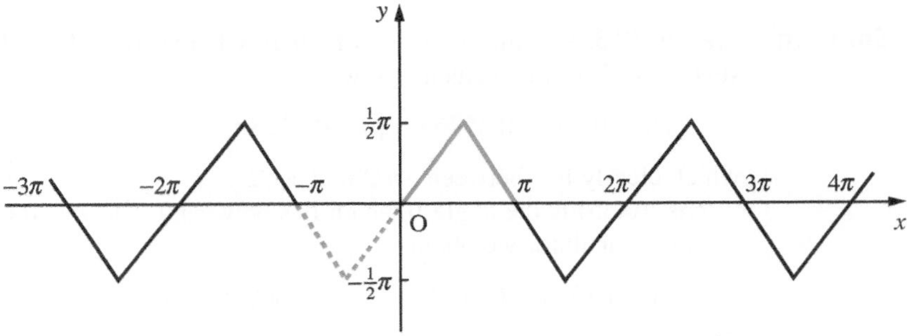

Figure 2.76 Graph of $y = \sin^{-1}(\sin x)$.

2.6.8 Polar coordinates

In some applications the position of a point P in a plane is represented by its distance r from a fixed point O and the angle θ that the line joining P to O makes with some fixed direction. The pair (r, θ) determine the point uniquely and are called the **polar coordinates** of P. If polar coordinates are chosen, sharing the same origin O as rectangular cartesian coordinates and with the angle θ measured from the direction of the Ox axis then, as can be seen from Figure 2.77, the polar coordinates (r, θ) and the cartesian coordinates (x, y) of a point are related by

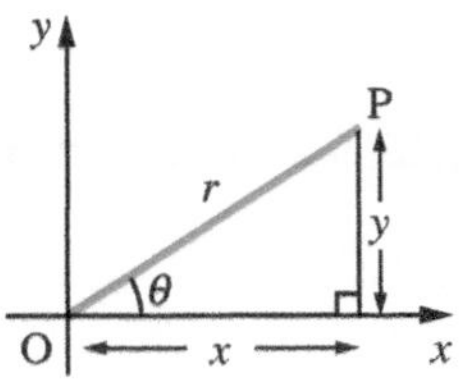

Figure 2.77

$$x = r\cos\theta, \quad y = r\sin\theta \tag{2.34}$$

and also

$$r = \sqrt{(x^2 + y^2)}, \quad \tan\theta = \frac{y}{x}$$

Note that the origin does not have a well-defined θ. Some care must be taken when evaluating θ using the above formula to ensure that it is located in the correct quadrant. The angle $\tan^{-1}(y/x)$ obtained from tables or a calculator will usually lie between $\pm\frac{1}{2}\pi$ and will give the correct value of θ if P lies in the first or fourth quadrant. If P lies in the second or third quadrant then $\theta = \tan^{-1}(y/x) + \pi$. It is sensible to use the values of $\sin\theta$ and $\cos\theta$ to check that θ lies in the correct quadrant.

Note that the angle θ is positive when measured in an anticlockwise direction and negative when measured in a clockwise direction. Many calculators have rectangular (cartesian) to polar conversion and vice versa.

Example 2.52

(a) Find the polar coordinates of the points whose cartesian coordinates are (1, 2), (−1, 3), (−1, −1), (1, −2), (1, 0), (0, 2), (0, −2).

(b) Find the cartesian coordinates of the points whose polar coordinates are $(3, \pi/4)$, $(2, -\pi/6)$, $(2, -\pi/2)$, $(5, 3\pi/4)$.

Solution

(a) Using the formula (2.34) we see that:

$$(x = 1, y = 2) \equiv (r = \sqrt{5}, \theta = \tan^{-1}(2/1) = 1.107)$$

$$(x = -1, y = 3) \equiv (r = \sqrt{10}, \theta = 1.893)$$

$$(x = -1, y = -1) \equiv (r = \sqrt{2}, \theta = 5\pi/4)$$

$$(x = 1, y = -2) \equiv (r = \sqrt{5}, \theta = -1.107)$$

$$(x = 1, y = 0) \equiv (r = 1, \theta = 0)$$

$$(x = 0, y = 2) \equiv (r = 2, \theta = \pi/2)$$

$$(x = 0, y = -2) \equiv (r = 2, \theta = -\pi/2)$$

(Here answers, where appropriate, are given to 3dp.)

(b) Using the formula (2.34) we see that

$$(r = 3, \theta = \pi/4) \equiv (x = 3/\sqrt{2}, y = 3/\sqrt{2})$$

$$(r = 2, \theta = -\pi/6) \equiv (x = \sqrt{3}, y = -1)$$

$$(r = 2, \theta = -\pi/2) \equiv (x = 0, y = -2)$$

$$(r = 5, \theta = 3\pi/4) \equiv (x = -5/\sqrt{2}, y = 5\sqrt{2})$$

To plot a curve specified using polar coordinates we first look for any features, for example, symmetry, which would reduce the amount of calculation, and then we draw up a table of values of r against values of θ. This is a tedious process and we usually use a graphics calculator or a computer package to perform the task. There are, however, different conventions in use about polar plotting. Some packages are designed to

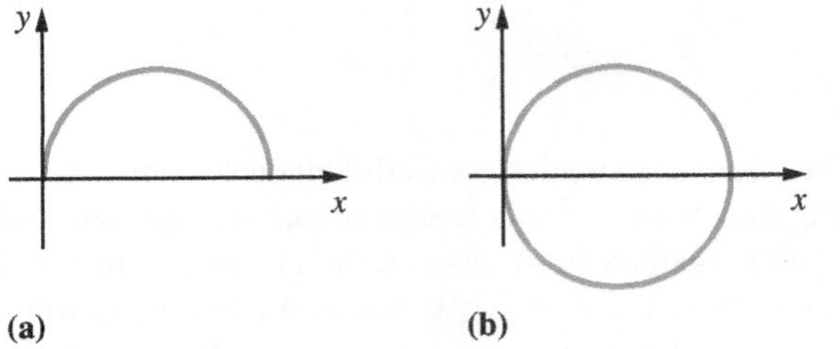

Figure 2.78
(a) $r = 2a \cos \theta$, $0 \leqslant \theta \leqslant \pi$, $r \geqslant 0$;
(b) $r = 2a \cos \theta$, $0 \leqslant \theta \leqslant \pi$, r unrestricted.

plot only points where r is positive, so that plotting $r = 2a \cos \theta$ for $0 \leqslant \theta \leqslant \pi$ would yield Figure 2.78(a) while other packages plot negative values of r, treating r as a number line, so that $r = 2a \cos \theta$ for $0 \leqslant \theta \leqslant \pi$ yields Figure 2.78(b).

Example 2.53 Express the equation of the circle

$$(x - a)^2 + y^2 = a^2$$

in polar form.

Solution Expanding the squared term, the equation of the given circle becomes

$$x^2 + y^2 - 2ax = 0$$

Using the relationships (2.34), we have

$$r^2(\cos^2\theta + \sin^2\theta) - 2ar \cos \theta = 0$$

Using the trigonometric identity (2.24a),

$$r(r - 2a \cos \theta) = 0, \quad -\pi/2 < \theta \leqslant \pi/2$$

Since $r = 0$ gives the point (0, 0), we can ignore this, and the equation of the circle becomes

$$r = 2a \cos \theta, \quad -\pi/2 < \theta \leqslant \pi/2$$

Example 2.54 Sketch the curve whose polar equation is $r = 1 + \cos \theta$.

Solution The simplest approach when sketching a curve given in polar coordinate form is to draw up a table of values as in Figure 2.79.

Figure 2.79 Table of values for $r = 1 + \cos \theta$.

θ	0	15	30	45	60	75	90	105	120	135	150	165	180
r	2	1.97	1.87	1.71	1.50	1.26	1	0.74	0.50	0.29	0.13	0.03	0

Because it is difficult to measure angles accurately it is easier to convert these values into the cartesian coordinate values using (2.34) when polar coordinate graph paper is not available. The sketch of the curve, a cardioid, is shown in Figure 2.80. Here we have made use of the symmetry of the curve about the line $\theta = 0$, that is, the line $y = 0$.

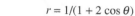

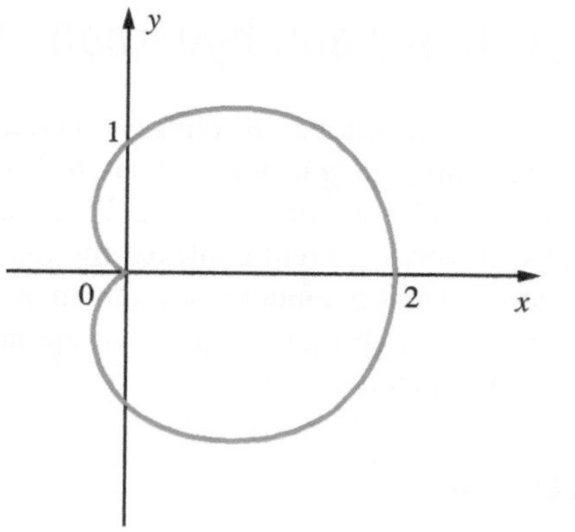

Figure 2.80 The cardioid $r = 1 + \cos\theta$.

In MATLAB the inverse circular functions $\sin^{-1}(x)$, $\cos^{-1}(x)$ and $\tan^{-1}(x)$ are denoted by `asin(x)`, `acos(x)` and `atan(x)` respectively. (In MAPLE these are denoted by `arcsin`, `arccos` and `arctan` respectively.) Using the graphical commands given on page 71, check the graphs of Figures 2.71–2.74.

Symbolically a plot of the polar curve $r = f(\theta)$ is obtained using the command `ezpolar(f)`, over the default domain $0 < \theta < 2\pi$; whilst the command `ezpolar(f,[a,b])` plots the curve over the domain $a < \theta < b$. Check that the commands

```
syms theta
r = 1 + cos(theta);
ezpolar(r)
```

plot the graph of the cardioid in Example 2.54.

2.6.9 Exercises

67 Evaluate

(a) $\sin^{-1}(0.5)$ (b) $\sin^{-1}(-0.5)$

(c) $\cos^{-1}(0.5)$ (d) $\cos^{-1}(-0.5)$

(e) $\tan^{-1}(\sqrt{3})$ (f) $\tan^{-1}(-\sqrt{3})$

68 Sketch the graph of the functions

(a) $y = \sin^{-1}(\cos x)$

(b) $y = \cos^{-1}(\sin x)$

(c) $y = \cos^{-1}(\cos x)$

(d) $y = \cos^{-1}(\cos x) - \sin^{-1}(\sin x)$

69 If $\tan^{-1}x = \alpha$ and $\tan^{-1}y = \beta$, show that

$$\tan(\alpha + \beta) = \frac{x + y}{1 - xy}$$

Deduce that

$$\tan^{-1}x + \tan^{-1}y = \tan^{-1}\left(\frac{x + y}{1 - xy}\right) + k\pi$$

where $k = -1, 0, 1$ depending on the values of x and y.

70 Sketch the curve with polar form

$$r = 1 + 2\cos\theta$$

71 Sketch the curve whose polar form is

$$r = 1/(1 + 2\cos\theta)$$

Show that its cartesian form is

$$3x^2 - 4x - y^2 + 1 = 0$$

2.7 Exponential, logarithmic and hyperbolic functions

The members of this family of functions are closely interconnected. They occur in widely varied applications, from heat transfer analysis to bridge design, from transmission line modelling to the production of chemicals. Historically the exponential and logarithmic functions arose in very different contexts, the former in the calculation of compound interest and the latter in computational mathematics, but, as often happens in mathematics, the discoveries in specialized areas of applicable mathematics have found applications widely elsewhere.

2.7.1 Exponential functions

Functions of the type $f(x) = a^x$ where a is a positive constant (and x is the independent variable as usual) are called **exponential functions.**

The graphs of the exponential functions, shown in Figure 2.81, are similar. By a simple scaling of the x axis, we can obtain the same graphs for $y = 2^x$, $y = 3^x$ and $y = 4^x$, as shown in Figure 2.82. The reason for this is that we can write $3^x = 2^{kx}$ where $k \approx 1.585$ and $4^x = 2^{2x}$. Thus all exponential functions can be expressed in terms of one exponential function. The standard exponential function that is used is $y = e^x$, where e is a special number approximately equal to

2.718 281 828 459 045 2...

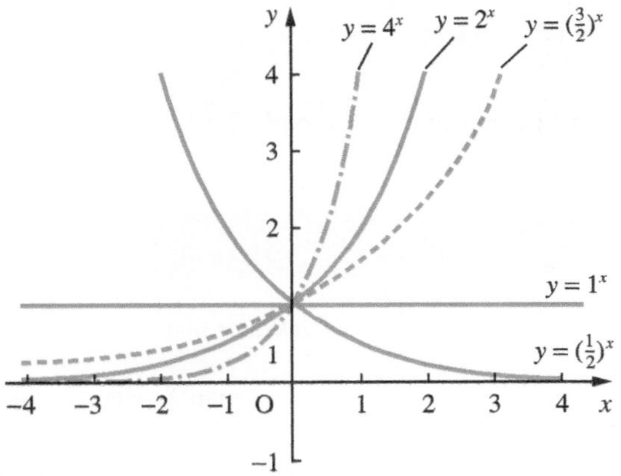

Figure 2.81
Graphs of exponential functions.

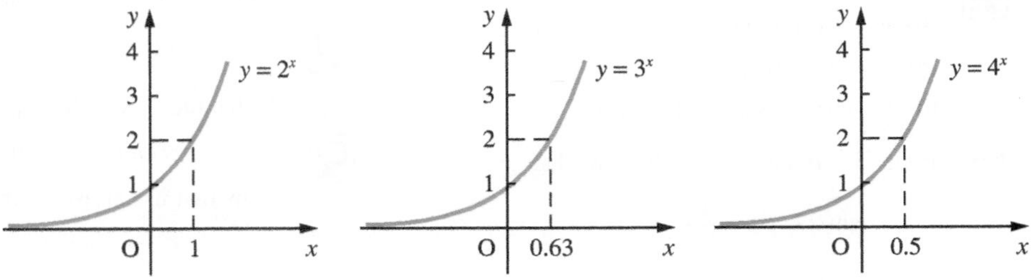

Figure 2.82
Scaled graphs of exponential functions.

Figure 2.83 The standard exponential function $y = e^x$.

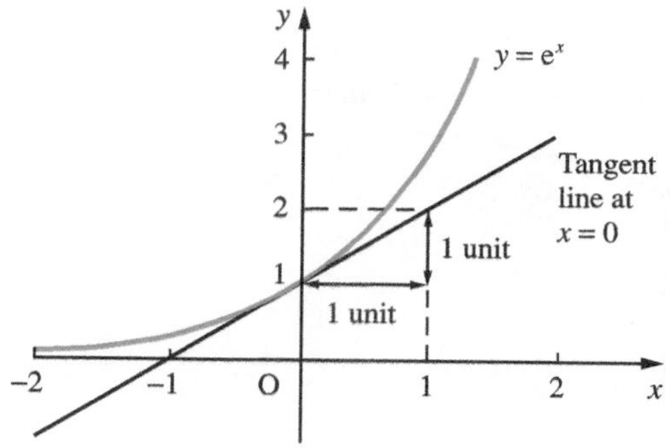

This number e is chosen because the graph of $y = e^x$ (Figure 2.83) has the property that the slope of the tangent at any point on the curve is equal to the value of the function at that point. We shall discuss this property again in Section 8.3.12.

We note that the following properties are satisfied by the exponential function:

$$e^{x_1}e^{x_2} = e^{x_1+x_2} \tag{2.35a}$$

$$e^{x+c} = e^x e^c = Ae^x, \quad \text{where } A = e^c \tag{2.35b}$$

$$\frac{e^{x_1}}{e^{x_2}} = e^{x_1-x_2} \tag{2.35c}$$

$$e^{kx} = (e^k)^x = a^x, \quad \text{where } a = e^k \tag{2.35d}$$

Often e^x is written as $\exp x$ for clarity when 'x' is a complicated expression. For example,

$$e^{(x+1)/(x+2)} = \exp\left(\frac{x+1}{x+2}\right)$$

Example 2.55

A tank is initially filled with 1000 litres of brine containing 0.25 kg of salt/litre. Fresh brine containing 0.5 kg of salt/litre flows in at a rate of 3 litres per second and a uniform mixture flows out at the same rate. The quantity $Q(t)$ kg of salt in the tank t seconds later is given by

$$Q(t) = A + Be^{-3t/1000}$$

Find the values of A and B and sketch a graph of $Q(t)$. Use the graph to estimate the time taken for $Q(t)$ to achieve the value 375.

Solution

Initially there is 1000×0.25 kg of salt in the tank, so $Q(0) = 250$. Ultimately the brine in the tank will contain 0.5 kg of salt/litre, so the terminal value of Q will be 500. The terminal value of $A + Be^{-3t/1000}$ is A, so we deduce $A = 500$. From initial data we have

$$250 = 500 + Be^0$$

and since $e^0 = 1$, $B = -250$ and

$$Q(t) = 500 - 250e^{-3t/1000}$$

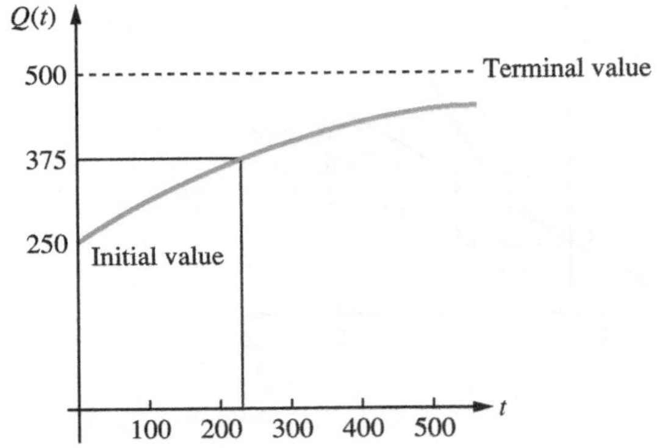

Figure 2.84
The timeline of $Q(t)$.

The graph of $Q(t)$ is shown in Figure 2.84. From the graph, an estimate for the time taken for $Q(t)$ to achieve the value 375 is 234 seconds. From the formula this gives $Q(234) = 376.1$. Investigating values near $t = 234$ using a calculator gives the more accurate time of 231 seconds.

Example 2.56 The temperature T of a body cooling in an environment, whose unknown ambient temperature is α, is given by

$$T(t) = \alpha + (T_0 - \alpha)e^{-kt}$$

where T_0 is the initial temperature of the body and k is a physical constant. To determine the value of α, the temperature of the body is recorded at two times, t_1 and t_2, where $t_2 = 2t_1$ and $T(t_1) = T_1$, $T(t_2) = T_2$. Show that

$$\alpha = \frac{T_0T_2 - T_1^2}{T_2 - 2T_1 + T_0}$$

Solution From the formula for $T(t)$ we have

$$T_1 - \alpha = (T_0 - \alpha)e^{-kt_1}$$

and

$$T_2 - \alpha = (T_0 - \alpha)e^{-2kt_1}$$

Squaring the first of these two equations and then dividing by the second gives

$$\frac{(T_1 - \alpha)^2}{T_2 - \alpha} = \frac{(T_0 - \alpha)^2e^{-2kt_1}}{(T_0 - \alpha)e^{-2kt_1}}$$

This simplifies to

$$(T_1 - \alpha)^2 = (T_2 - \alpha)(T_0 - \alpha)$$

Multiplying out both sides, we obtain

$$T_1^2 - 2\alpha T_1 + \alpha^2 = T_0T_2 - (T_0 + T_2)\alpha + \alpha^2$$

which gives

$$(T_0 - 2T_1 + T_2)\alpha = T_0T_2 - T_1^2$$

Hence the result.

2.7.2 Logarithmic functions

From the graph of $y = e^x$, given in Figure 2.83, it is clear that it is a one-to-one function, so that its inverse function is defined. This inverse is called the **natural logarithm** function and is written as

$$y = \ln x$$

(In some textbooks it is written as $\log_e x$, while in many pure mathematics books it is written simply as $\log x$.) Using the procedures given in Section 2.2.3, its graph can be drawn as in Figure 2.85. From the definition we have

$$\text{if } y = e^x \quad \text{then} \quad x = \ln y \qquad \textbf{(2.36)}$$

which implies that

$$\ln e^x = x, \quad e^{\ln y} = y$$

In the same way as there are many exponential functions (2^x, 3^x, 4^x, ...), there are also many logarithmic functions. In general,

$$y = a^x \quad \text{gives} \quad x = \log_a y \qquad \textbf{(2.37)}$$

which can be expressed verbally as 'x equals log to base a of y'. (Note that $\log_{10} x$ is often written, except in advanced mathematics books, simply as $\log x$.) Recalling that $a^x = e^{kx}$ for some constant k, we see now that $a^x = (e^k)^x$, so that $a = e^k$ and $k = \ln a$.

From the definition of $\log_a x$ it follows that

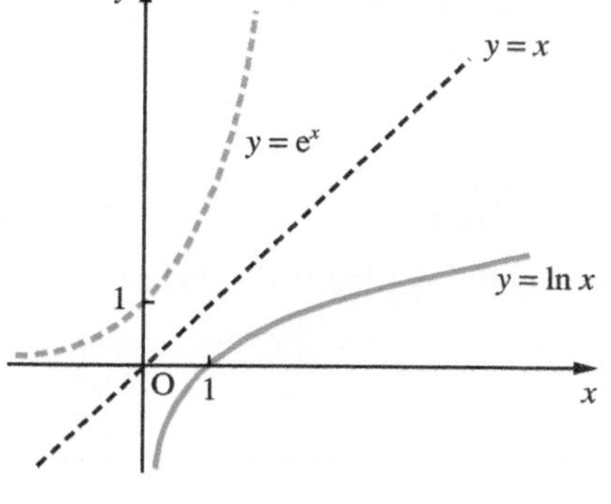

Figure 2.85
Graph of $y = \ln x$.

$$\log_a(x_1x_2) = \log_a x_1 + \log_a x_2 \tag{2.38a}$$

$$\log_a\left(\frac{x_1}{x_2}\right) = \log_a x_1 - \log_a x_2 \tag{2.38b}$$

$$\log_a x^n = n \log_a x \tag{2.38c}$$

$$x = a^{\log_a x} \tag{2.38d}$$

$$y^x = a^{x \log_a y} \tag{2.38e}$$

$$\log_a x = \frac{\log_b x}{\log_b a} \tag{2.38f}$$

Example 2.57

(a) Evaluate $\log_2 32$.

(b) Simplify $\frac{1}{3}\log_2 8 - \log_2 \frac{2}{7}$.

(c) Expand $\ln\left(\frac{\sqrt{(10x)}}{y^2}\right)$.

(d) Use the change of base formula (2.36*f*) to evaluate $\frac{\log_{10} 32}{\log_{10} 2}$.

(e) Evaluate $\frac{\log_3 x}{\log_9 x}$.

Solution

(a) Since $32 = 2^5$, $\log_2 32 = \log_2 2^5 = 5\log_2 2 = 5$, since $\log_2 2 = 1$.

(b) $\frac{1}{3}\log_2 8 - \log_2 \frac{2}{7} = \log_2 8^{1/3} - \log_2 \frac{2}{7}$

$= \log_2 2 - [\log_2 2 - \log_2 7] = \log_2 7$

(c) $\ln\left(\frac{\sqrt{(10x)}}{y^2}\right) = \ln(\sqrt{(10x)}) - \ln(y^2) = \frac{1}{2}\ln(10x) - 2\ln y$

$= \frac{1}{2}\ln(10) + \frac{1}{2}\ln x - 2\ln y$

(d) $\log_{10} 32 = \log_2 32 \log_{10} 2$, hence

$$\frac{\log_{10} 32}{\log_{10} 2} = \log_2 32 = \log_2 2^5 = 5\log_2 2 = 5$$

(e) $\log_9 x = \log_3 x \log_9 3$, so that

$$\frac{\log_3 x}{\log_9 x} = \frac{\log_3 x}{\log_3 x \log_9 3} = \frac{1}{\log_9 3}$$

But $3 = 9^{1/2}$ so that $\log_9 3 = \log_9 9^{1/2} = \frac{1}{2}\log_9 9 = \frac{1}{2}$, hence

$$\frac{\log_3 x}{\log_9 x} = 2$$

Despite the fact that these functions occur widely in engineering analysis, they first occurred in computational mathematics. Property (2.38a) transforms the problem of multiplying two numbers to that of adding their logarithms. The widespread use of scientific calculators has now made the computational application of logarithms largely irrelevant. They are, however, still used in the analysis of experimental data.

In MATLAB the exponential and logarithmic functions are represented by

exponential: `exp(x)`
natural logarithm ln: `log(x)`
logarithm to base 10: `log10(x)`

(MAPLE uses `ln(x)` and `log10(x)` for the last two, respectively, and uses `log(x)` for work with a general base.)

2.7.3 Exercises

Check your answers using MATLAB or MAPLE whenever possible.

72 Simplify

(a) $(e^2)^3 + e^2 \times e^3 + (e^3)^2$ (b) e^{7x}/e^{3x}

(c) $(e^3)^2$ (d) $\exp(3^2)$ (e) $\sqrt{(e^x)}$

73 Sketch the graphs of $y = e^{-2x}$ and $y = e^{-x^2}$ on the same axes. Note that $(e^{-x})^2 \neq e^{-x^2}$.

74 Find the following logarithms *without* using a calculator:

(a) $\log_2 8$ (b) $\log_2 \frac{1}{4}$

(c) $\log_2 \frac{1}{\sqrt{2}}$ (d) $\log_3 81$

(e) $\log_9 3$ (f) $\log_4 0.5$

75 Express in terms of $\ln x$ and $\ln y$

(a) $\ln(x^2y)$ (b) $\ln\sqrt{(xy)}$ (c) $\ln(x^5/y^2)$

76 Express as a single logarithm

(a) $\ln 14 - \ln 21 + \ln 6$

(b) $4 \ln 2 - \frac{1}{2}\ln 25$

(c) $1.5 \ln 9 - 2 \ln 6$

(d) $2 \ln(2/3) - \ln(8/9)$

77 Simplify (a) $\exp\left\{\frac{1}{2}\ln\left[\frac{1-x}{1+x}\right]\right\}$ (b) $e^{2\ln x}$

78 Sketch carefully the graphs of the functions

(a) $y = 2^x$, $y = \log_2 x$ (on the same axes)

(b) $y = e^x$, $y = \ln x$ (on the same axes)

(c) $y = 10^x$, $y = \log x$ (on the same axes)

79 Sketch the graph of $y = e^{-x} - e^{-2x}$. Prove that the maximum of y is $\frac{1}{4}$ and find the corresponding value of x. Find the two values of x corresponding to $y = \frac{1}{40}$.

80 Express $\ln y$ as simply as possible when

$$y = \frac{(x^2+1)^{3/2}}{(x^4+1)^{1/3}(x^4+4)^{1/5}}$$

2.7.4 Hyperbolic functions

In applications, certain combinations of exponential functions recur many times and these combinations are given special names. For example, the mathematical model for the steady state heat transfer in a straight bar leads to an expression for the temperature $T(x)$ at a point distance x from one end, given by

$$T(x) = \frac{T_0(e^{m(l-x)} - e^{-m(l-x)}) + T_1(e^{mx} - e^{-mx})}{e^{ml} - e^{-ml}}$$

where l is the total length of the bar, T_0 and T_1 are the temperatures at the ends and m is a physical constant. To simplify such expressions a family of functions, called the **hyperbolic** functions, is defined as follows:

$\cosh x = \frac{1}{2}(e^x + e^{-x})$, the **hyperbolic cosine**

$\sinh x = \frac{1}{2}(e^x - e^{-x})$, the **hyperbolic sine**

$\tanh x = \dfrac{\sinh x}{\cosh x}$, the **hyperbolic tangent**

The abbreviation cosh comes from the original Latin name cosinus hyperbolicus; similarly sinh and tanh.

Thus, the expression for $T(x)$ becomes

$$T(x) = \frac{T_0 \sinh m(l - x) + T_1 \sinh mx}{\sinh ml}$$

The reason for the names of these functions is geometric. They bear the same relationship to the hyperbola as the circular functions do to the circle, as shown in Figure 2.86.

Following the pattern of the circular or trigonometric functions, other hyperbolic functions are defined as follows:

$\operatorname{sech} x = \dfrac{1}{\cosh x}$, the **hyperbolic secant**

$\operatorname{cosech} x = \dfrac{1}{\sinh x}$ $(x \neq 0)$, the **hyperbolic cosecant**

$\coth x = \dfrac{1}{\tanh x}$ $(x \neq 0)$, the **hyperbolic cotangent**

The graphs of sinh x, cosh x and tanh x are shown in Figure 2.87, where the black broken lines indicate asymptotes.

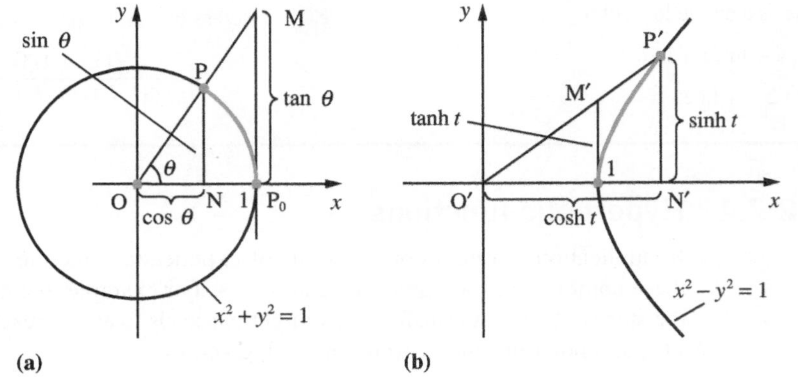

Figure 2.86
The analogy between circular and hyperbolic functions. The circle has parametric equations $x = \cos\theta$, $y = \sin\theta$. The hyperbola has parametric equations $x = \cosh t$, $y = \sinh t$.

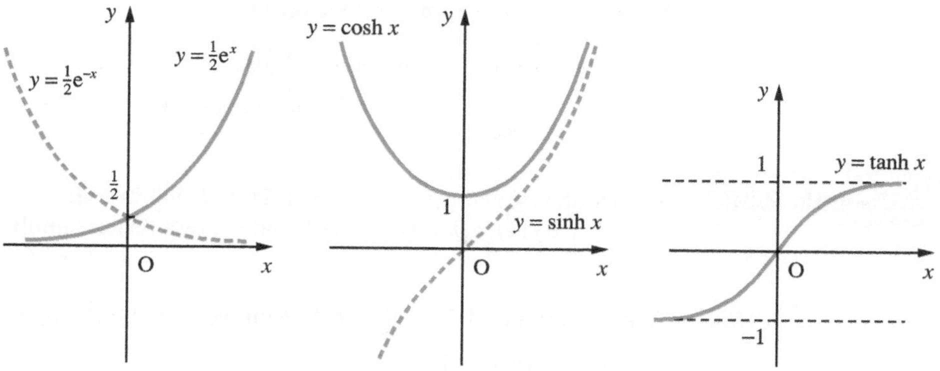

Figure 2.87 Graphs of the hyperbolic functions.

The hyperbolic functions satisfy identities analogous to those satisfied by the circular functions. From their definitions we have

$$\left.\begin{aligned}\cosh x &= \tfrac{1}{2}(e^{x} + e^{-x})\\ \sinh x &= \tfrac{1}{2}(e^{x} - e^{-x})\end{aligned}\right\} \qquad \textbf{(2.39)}$$

from which we deduce

$$\cosh x + \sinh x = e^{x}$$

$$\cosh x - \sinh x = e^{-x}$$

and

$$(\cosh x + \sinh x)(\cosh x - \sinh x) = e^{x}e^{-x}$$

that is,

$$\cosh^2 x - \sinh^2 x = 1 \qquad \textbf{(2.40)}$$

Similarly, we can show that

$$\sinh(x \pm y) = \sinh x \cosh y \pm \cosh x \sinh y \qquad \textbf{(2.41a)}$$

$$\cosh(x \pm y) = \cosh x \cosh y \pm \sinh x \sinh y \qquad \textbf{(2.41b)}$$

$$\tanh(x \pm y) = \frac{\tanh x \pm \tanh y}{1 \pm \tanh x \tanh y} \qquad \textbf{(2.41c)}$$

To prove the first two of these results, it is easier to begin with the expressions on the right-hand sides and replace each hyperbolic function by its exponential form. The third result follows immediately from the previous two by dividing them. Thus

$$\begin{aligned}\sinh x \cosh y &= \tfrac{1}{4}(e^{x} - e^{-x})(e^{y} + e^{-y})\\ &= \tfrac{1}{4}(e^{x+y} + e^{x-y} - e^{-x+y} - e^{-x-y})\end{aligned}$$

and interchanging x and y we have

$$\cosh x \sinh y = \tfrac{1}{4}(e^{x+y} + e^{y-x} - e^{-y+x} - e^{-x-y})$$

Adding these two expressions we obtain

$$\sinh x \cosh y + \cosh x \sinh y = \tfrac{1}{2}(e^{x+y} - e^{-x-y})$$
$$= \sinh(x + y)$$

Example 2.58 A function is given by $f(x) = A \cosh 2x + B \sinh 2x$, where A and B are constants and $f(0) = 5$ and $f(1) = 0$. Find A and B and express $f(x)$ as simply as possible.

Solution Given $f(x) = A \cosh 2x + B \sinh 2x$ with the conditions $f(0) = 5, f(1) = 0$, we see that

$$A(1) + B(0) = 5$$

and

$$A \cosh 2 + B \sinh 2 = 0$$

Hence we have $A = 5$ and $B = -5 \cosh 2/\sinh 2$. Substituting into the formula for $f(x)$ we obtain

$$f(x) = 5\cosh 2x - 5\cosh 2 \sinh 2x/\sinh 2$$
$$= \frac{5\sinh 2 \cosh 2x - 5\cosh 2 \sinh 2x}{\sinh 2}$$
$$= \frac{5\sinh(2 - 2x)}{\sinh 2}, \quad \text{using (2.41a)}$$
$$= \frac{5\sinh 2(1 - x)}{\sinh 2}$$

Example 2.59 Solve the equation

$$5 \cosh x + 3 \sinh x = 4$$

Solution The first step in solving problems of this type is to express the hyperbolic functions in terms of exponential functions. Thus we obtain

$$\tfrac{5}{2}(e^{x} + e^{-x}) + \tfrac{3}{2}(e^{x} - e^{-x}) = 4$$

On rearranging, this gives

$$4e^{x} - 4 + e^{-x} = 0$$

or

$$4e^{2x} - 4e^{x} + 1 = 0$$

which may be written as

$$(2e^{x} - 1)^2 = 0$$

from which we deduce

$$e^{x} = \tfrac{1}{2} \text{ (twice)}$$

and hence

$$x = -\ln 2$$

is a repeated root of the equation.

Osborn's rule

In general, to obtain the formula for hyperbolic functions from the analogous identity for the circular functions, we replace each circular function by the corresponding hyperbolic function and change the sign of every product or implied product of two sines. This result is called **Osborn's rule**. Its justification will be discussed in Section 3.2.9.

Example 2.60 Verify the identity

$$\tanh 2x = \frac{2\tanh x}{1+\tanh^2 x}$$

using the definition of $\tanh x$. Confirm that it obeys Osborn's rule.

Solution From the definition

$$\tanh 2x = \frac{e^{2x} - e^{-2x}}{e^{2x} + e^{-2x}}$$

and

$$1 + \tanh^2 x = 1 + \frac{(e^x - e^{-x})^2}{(e^x + e^{-x})^2} = \frac{(e^x + e^{-x})^2 + (e^x - e^{-x})^2}{(e^x + e^{-x})^2}$$

$$= \frac{2(e^{2x} + e^{-2x})}{(e^x + e^{-x})^2}$$

Thus

$$\frac{2\tanh x}{1+\tanh^2 x} = \frac{2(e^x - e^{-x})/(e^x + e^{-x})}{2(e^{2x} + e^{-2x})/(e^x + e^{-x})^2} = \frac{(e^x - e^{-x})(e^x + e^{-x})}{e^{2x} + e^{-2x}}$$

$$= \frac{e^{2x} - e^{-2x}}{e^{2x} + e^{-2x}} = \tanh 2x \text{ as required}$$

The formula for $\tan 2\theta$ from (2.27e) is

$$\tan 2\theta = \frac{2\tan\theta}{1-\tan^2\theta}$$

We see that this has an implied product of two sines ($\tan^2\theta$), so that in terms of hyperbolic functions we have, using Osborn's rule,

$$\tanh 2x = \frac{2\tanh x}{1+\tanh^2 x}$$

which confirms the proof above.

2.7.5 Inverse hyperbolic functions

The inverse hyperbolic functions, illustrated in Figure 2.88, are defined in a completely natural way:

$$y = \sinh^{-1}x \quad (x \text{ in } \mathbb{R})$$
$$y = \cosh^{-1}x \quad (x \geqslant 1, y \geqslant 0)$$
$$y = \tanh^{-1}x \quad (-1 < x < 1)$$

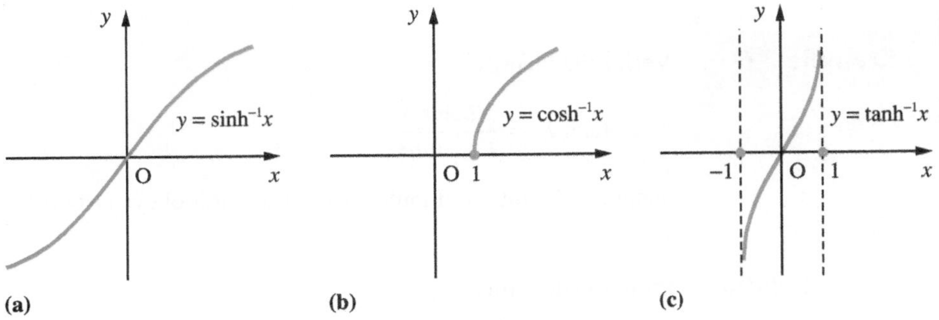

Figure 2.88
Graphs of the inverse hyperbolic functions.

(These are also sometimes denoted as arsinh x, arcosh x and artanh x – *not* arcsinh x, etc.) Note the restriction on the range of the inverse hyperbolic cosine to meet the condition that exactly one value of y be obtained. These functions, not surprisingly, can be expressed in terms of logarithms.

For example,

$$y = \sinh^{-1}x \quad \text{implies} \quad x = \sinh y = \tfrac{1}{2}(e^{y} - e^{-y})$$

Thus

$$(e^{y})^2 - 2x(e^{y}) - 1 = 0$$

and

$$e^{y} = x \pm \sqrt{(x^2 + 1)}$$

Since $e^{y} > 0$, we can discount the negative root, and we have, on taking logarithms,

$$y = \sinh^{-1}x = \ln[x + \sqrt{(x^2 + 1)}] \quad \textbf{(2.42)}$$

Similarly,

$$\cosh^{-1}x = \ln[x + \sqrt{(x^2 - 1)}] \quad (x \geqslant 1) \quad \textbf{(2.43)}$$

and

$$\tanh^{-1}x = \tfrac{1}{2}\ln\left(\frac{1 + x}{1 - x}\right) \quad (-1 < x < 1) \quad \textbf{(2.44)}$$

Example 2.61 Evaluate (to 4sf)

(a) $\sinh^{-1}(0.5)$ (b) $\cosh^{-1}(3)$ (c) $\tanh^{-1}(-2/5)$

using the logarithmic forms of these functions. Check your answers directly using a calculator.

Solution (a) Using formula (2.42), we have

$$\begin{aligned}\sinh^{-1}(0.5) &= \ln[0.5 + \sqrt{(0.25 + 1)}]\\ &= \ln(0.5 + 1.118\,034)\\ &= \ln(1.618\,034)\\ &= 0.4812\end{aligned}$$

(b) Using formula (2.43), we have

$$\cosh^{-1}(3) = \ln(3 + \sqrt{8}) = 1.7627$$

(c) Using formula (2.44), we have

$$\begin{aligned}\tanh^{-1}(-2/5) &= \frac{1}{2}\ln\left(\frac{1 - \frac{2}{5}}{1 + \frac{2}{5}}\right)\\ &= \frac{1}{2}\ln\left(\frac{5 - 2}{5 + 2}\right)\\ &= \frac{1}{2}\ln\frac{3}{7} = -0.4236\end{aligned}$$

In MATLAB, notation associated with the hyperbolic functions is

hyperbolic cosine:	`cosh(x)`
hyperbolic sine:	`sinh(x)`
hyperbolic tangent:	`tanh(x)`
inverse hyperbolic cosine:	`acosh(x)`
inverse hyperbolic sine:	`asinh(x)`
inverse hyperbolic tangent:	`atanh(x)`

with the last three denoted by *arccosh(x)*, *arcsinh(x)* and *arctanh(x)*, respectively, in MAPLE.

As an example, the commands

```
syms x
s = solve('5*cosh(x) + 3*sinh(x) = 4')
```

return

```
s = -log(2)
    -log(2)
```

confirming the answer in Example 2.60. (Note that it produces *-log(2)* twice because it is a repeated root. MAPLE only produces it once.)

2.7.6 Exercises

81 In each of the following exercises a value of one of the six hyperbolic functions of x is given. Find the remaining five.

(a) $\cosh x = \frac{5}{4}$ (b) $\sinh x = \frac{8}{15}$

(c) $\tanh x = -\frac{7}{25}$ (d) $\operatorname{sech} x = \frac{5}{13}$

(e) $\operatorname{cosech} x = -\frac{3}{4}$ (f) $\coth x = \frac{13}{12}$

82 Use Osborn's rule to write down formulae corresponding to

(a) $\tan 3x = \dfrac{(3 - \tan^2 x)\tan x}{1 - 3\tan^2 x}$

(b) $\cos(x + y) = \cos x \cos y - \sin x \sin y$

(c) $\cosh 2x = 1 + 2\sinh^2 x$

(d) $\sin x - \sin y = 2 \sin \frac{1}{2}(x - y) \cos \frac{1}{2}(x + y)$

83 Prove that

(a) $\cosh^{-1} x = \ln[x + \sqrt{(x^2 - 1)}] \quad (x \geqslant 1)$

(b) $\tanh^{-1} x = \frac{1}{2} \ln\left(\dfrac{1 + x}{1 - x}\right) \quad (|x| < 1)$

84 Find to 4dp

(a) $\sinh^{-1} 0.8$

(b) $\cosh^{-1} 2$

(c) $\tanh^{-1}(-0.5)$

85 The speed V of waves in shallow water is given by

$$V^2 = 1.8L \tanh \frac{6.3d}{L}$$

where d is the depth and L the wavelength. If $d = 30$ and $L = 270$, calculate the value of V.

86 The formula

$$\lambda = \frac{\alpha t}{2} \frac{\sinh \alpha t + \sin \alpha t}{\cosh \alpha t - \cos \alpha t}$$

gives the increase in resistance of strip conductors due to eddy currents at power frequencies. Calculate λ when $\alpha = 1.075$ and $t = 1$.

87 The functions

$$f_1(x) = \frac{1}{1 + e^{-x}}, \quad f_2(x) = \tfrac{1}{2} \tanh \tfrac{1}{2}x$$

are two different forms of activating functions representing the output of a neuron in a typical neural network. Sketch the graphs of $f_1(x)$ and $f_2(x)$ and show that $f_1(x) - f_2(x) = \frac{1}{2}$.

88 The potential difference E (in V) between a telegraph line and earth is given by

$$E = A \cosh\left(x\sqrt{\frac{r}{R}}\right) + B \sinh\left(x\sqrt{\frac{r}{R}}\right)$$

where A and B are constants, x is the distance in km from the transmitting end, r is the resistance per km of the conductor and R is the insulation resistance per km. Find the values of A and B when the length of the line is 400 km, $r = 8\,\Omega$, $R = 3.2 \times 10^7\,\Omega$ and the voltages at the transmitting and receiving ends are 250 and 200 V respectively.

2.8 Irrational functions

The circular and exponential functions are examples of **transcendental functions**. They cannot be expressed as rational functions, that is, as the quotient of two polynomials. Other irrational functions occur in engineering, and they may be classified either as algebraic or as transcendental functions. For example

$$y = \frac{\sqrt{(x + 1)} - 1}{\sqrt{(x + 1)} + 1} \quad (x \geqslant -1)$$

is an algebraic irrational function. Here y is a root of the algebraic equation

$$xy^2 - 2(2 + x)y + x = 0$$

which has polynomial coefficients in x.

On the other hand, $y = |x|$, although it satisfies $y^2 = x^2$, is not a root of that equation (whose roots are $y = x$ and $y = -x$). The modulus function $|x|$ is an example of a non-algebraic irrational function.

2.8.1 Algebraic functions

In general we have an algebraic function $y = f(x)$ defined when y is the root of a polynomial equation of the form

$$a_n(x)y^n + a_{n-1}(x)y^{n-1} + \ldots + a_1(x)y + a_0(x) = 0$$

Note that here all the coefficients $a_0 \ldots a_n$ may be polynomial functions of the independent variable x. For example, consider

$$y^2 - 2xy - 8x = 0$$

This defines, for $x \geqslant 0$, two algebraic functions with formulae

$$y = x + \sqrt{(x^2 + 8x)} \quad \text{and} \quad y = x - \sqrt{(x^2 + 8x)}$$

One of these corresponds to $y^2 - 2xy - 8x = 0$ with $y \geqslant 0$ and the other to $y^2 - 2xy - 8x = 0$ with $y \leqslant 0$. So, when we specify a function implicitly by means of an equation we often need some extra information to define it uniquely. Often, too, we cannot obtain an explicit algebraic formula for y in terms of x and we have to evaluate the function at each point of its domain by solving the polynomial equation for y numerically.

Care has to be exercised when using algebraic functions in a larger computation in case special values of parameters produce sudden changes in value, as illustrated in Example 2.62.

Example 2.62

Sketch the graphs of the function

$$y = \sqrt{(a + bx^2 + cx^3)}/(d - x)$$

for the domain $-3 < x < 3$, where

(a) $a = 18, b = 1, c = -1$ and $d = 6$

(b) $a = 0, b = 1, c = -1$ and $d = 0$

Solution

(a) $y = \sqrt{(18 + x^2 - x^3)}/(6 - x)$

We can see that the term inside the square root is positive only when $18 + x^2 - x^3 > 0$. Since we can factorize this as $(18 + x^2 - x^3) = (3 - x)(x^2 + 2x + 6)$, we deduce that y is not defined for $x > 3$. Also, for large negative values of x it behaves like $\sqrt{(-x)}$. A sketch of the graph is shown in Figure 2.89.

(b) $y = -\sqrt{(x^2 - x^3)}/x$

Here we can see that the function is defined for $x \leqslant 1, x \neq 0$. Near $x = 0$, since we can write $x = \sqrt{x^2}$ for $x > 0$ and $x = -\sqrt{x^2}$ for $x < 0$, we see that

$$y = -\sqrt{(1 - x)} \quad \text{for } x > 0$$

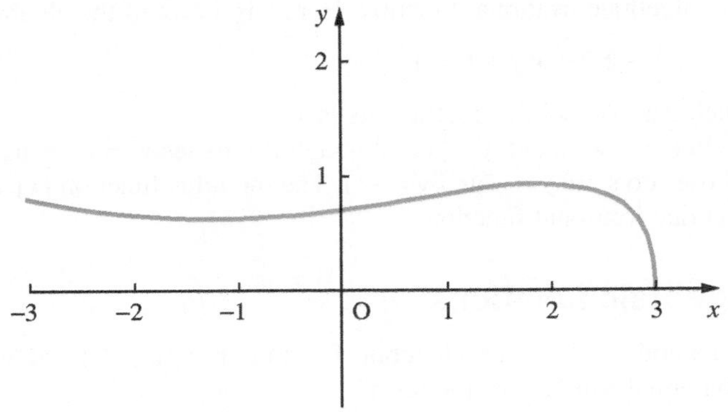

Figure 2.89
Graph of $y = \sqrt{(18 + x^2 - x^3)/(6 - x)}$.

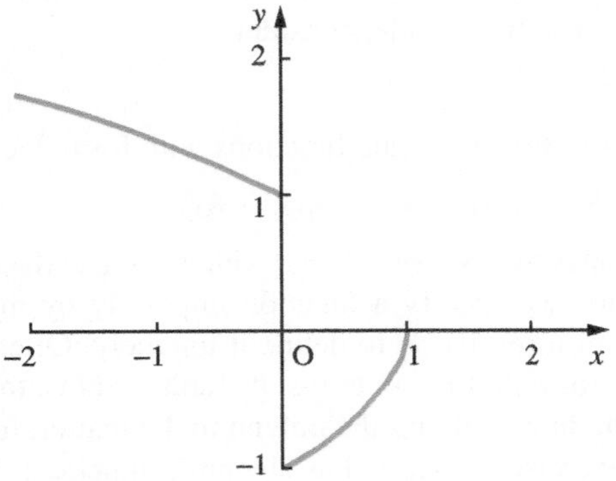

Figure 2.90
Graph of $y = -\sqrt{(x^2 - x^3)/x}$.

and

$$y = \sqrt{(1 - x)} \quad \text{for } x < 0$$

At $x = 0$ the function is not defined. The graph of the function is shown in Figure 2.90.

2.8.2 Implicit functions

We have seen in Section 2.8.1 that some algebraic functions are defined implicitly because we cannot obtain an algebraic formula for them. This applies to a wider class of functions where we have an equation relating the dependent and independent variables, but where finding the value of y corresponding to a given value of x requires a numerical solution of the equation. Generally we have an equation connecting x and y, such as

$$f(x, y) = 0$$

Sometimes we are able to draw a curve which represents the relationship (using algebraic methods), but more commonly we have to calculate for each value of x the corresponding value of y. Most computer graphics packages have an implicit function option which will perform the task efficiently.

Example 2.63 The velocity v and the displacement x of a mass attached to a non-linear spring satisfy the equation

$$v^2 = -4x^2 + x^4 + A$$

where A depends on the initial velocity v_0 and displacement x_0 of the mass. Sketch the graph of v against x where

(a) $x_0 = 1,\ v_0 = 0$

(b) $x_0 = 3,\ v_0 = 0$

and interpret your graph.

Solution (a) With $x_0 = 1$, $v_0 = 0$ we have $A = 3$ and

$$v^2 = x^4 - 4x^2 + 3 = (x^2 - 3)(x^2 - 1)$$

To sketch the graph by hand it is easiest first to sketch the graph of v^2 against x, as shown in Figure 2.91(a). Taking the 'square root' of the graph is only possible for $v^2 \geqslant 0$, but we also know we want that part of the graph which has the initial point (x_0, v_0) on it. So we obtain the closed loop shown in Figure 2.91(b). The arrows on the closed curve indicate the variation of v with x as time increases. Where the velocity v is positive, the displacement x increases. Where the velocity is negative, the displacement decreases. The closed curve indicates that this motion repeats after completing one circuit of the curve, that is, there is a periodic motion.

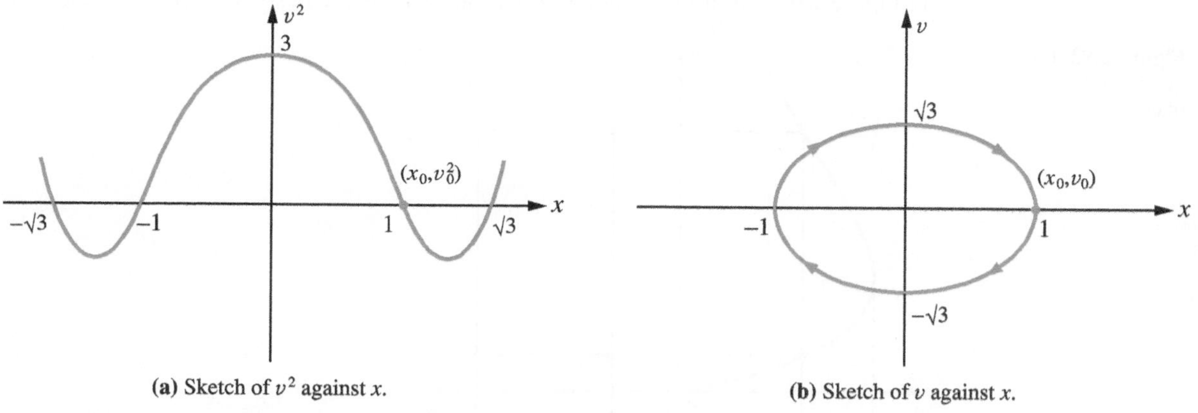

v^2
3
(x_0, v_0^2)
x
$-\sqrt{3}$
-1
1
$\sqrt{3}$
(a) Sketch of v^2 against x.
v
$\sqrt{3}$
(x_0, v_0)
x
-1
1
$-\sqrt{3}$
(b) Sketch of v against x.

Figure 2.91 Graphs for Example 2.63(a).

(b) With $x_0 = 3$, $v_0 = 0$ we have $A = -45$ and

$$v^2 = x^4 - 4x^2 - 45 = (x^2 - 9)(x^2 + 5)$$

Using the same technique as in part (a), we see that when the mass is released from rest at $x = 3$, its displacement increases without a bound and the motion is not periodic. The corresponding graphs are shown in Figures 2.92(a) and (b).

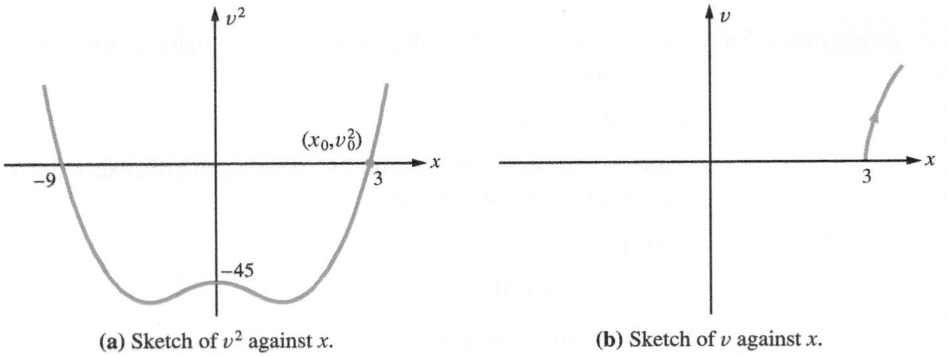

Figure 2.92 Graphs for Example 2.63(b).

Example 2.64 The concentrations of two substances in a chemical process are related by the equation

$$xye^{2-y} = 2e^{x-1}, \quad 0 < x < 3, 0 < y < 3$$

Investigate this relationship graphically and discover whether it defines a function.

Solution Separating the variables in the equation, we have

$$ye^{-y} = 2e^{-3}e^{x}/x$$

Substituting $u = e^{x}/x$ and $v = ye^{-y}$ reduces this equation to

$$v = 2e^{-3}u$$

so on the u–v plane the relationship is represented by a straight line. Putting the first quadrants of the four planes x–y, v–y, u–x, u–v together we obtain the diagram shown in Figure 2.93. From that diagram it is clear that the smallest value of u that occurs is

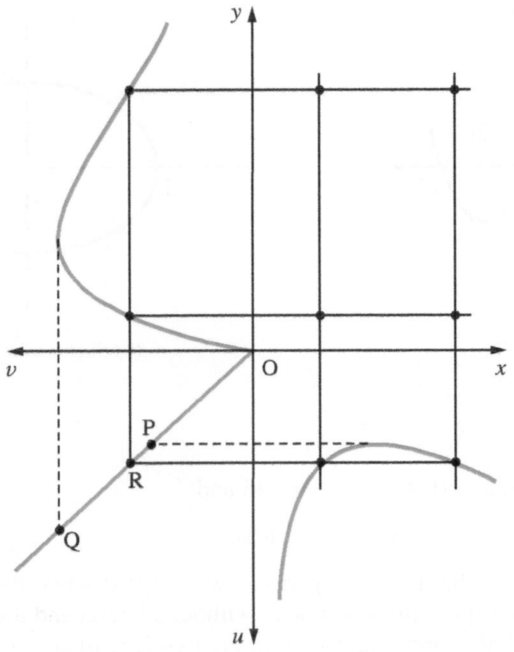

Figure 2.93 First quadrant of four planes.

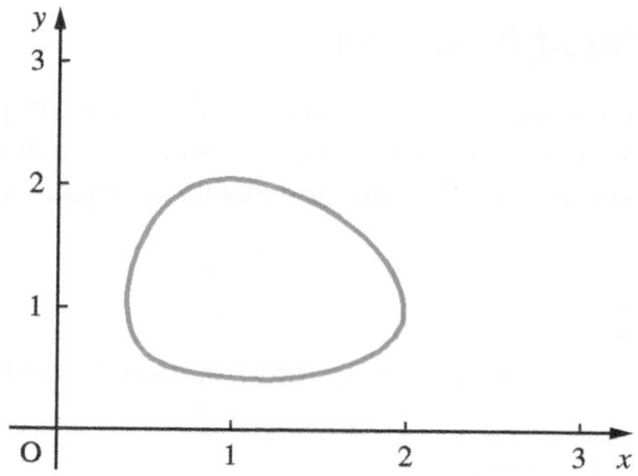

Figure 2.94 Closed form solution for Example 2.90.

at P and the largest value of v that occurs is at Q, so all the solutions of the equation lie between P and Q. Any point R which lies between P and Q on the line corresponds to two values of y and two values of x. So each point R corresponds to four points of the x–y plane. By considering all the points between P and Q we obtain the closed curve shown in Figure 2.94. We can see from that diagram that the equation does not define a function, since one value of x can give rise to two values of y. It is, of course, possible to specify the range of y and obtain, in this case, two functions, one for $y \geqslant 1$ and the other for $y \leqslant 1$.

This graphical method of studying the problem was first used in the study of predator–prey relations in fish stocks by Volterra. It is sometimes called Volterra's method. In that context the closed curve solution indicated the periodic nature of the fish stocks.

In MATLAB, using the Symbolic Math Toolbox, commands for plotting the graph of an implicitly defined function $f = f(x, y) = 0$ are

`ezplot(f)` plots $f(x, y) = 0$ over the default domain $-2\pi < x < 2\pi$, $-2\pi < y < 2\pi$
`ezplot(f, [xmin, xmax ,ymin ,ymax])` plots $f(x, y) = 0$ over $x_{min} < x < x_{max}$, $y_{min} < y < y_{max}$
`ezplot(f,[min,max])` plots $f(x, y) = 0$ over $\min < x < \max$ and $\min < y < \max$

If f is a function of the two variables u and v (rather than x and y) then the domain end points u_{min}, u_{max}, v_{min} and v_{max} are sorted alphabetically.

Check that the commands

```
syms x y
ezplot(x*y*exp(2 - y) - 2*exp(x - 1),[0,3])
```

return the plot of Figure 2.94 and that the commands

```
syms x y
ezplot(y^2 - 2*y*cos(x) - 24, [0,3*pi])
```

return a plot similar to Figure 2.68.

2.8.3 Piecewise defined functions

Such functions often occur in the mathematical models of practical problems. For example, friction always opposes the motion of an object, so that the force F is $-R$ when the velocity v is positive and $+R$ when the velocity is negative. To represent the force, we can write

$$F = -R\ \mathrm{sgn}(v)$$

where sgn is the abbreviation for the **signum function** defined by

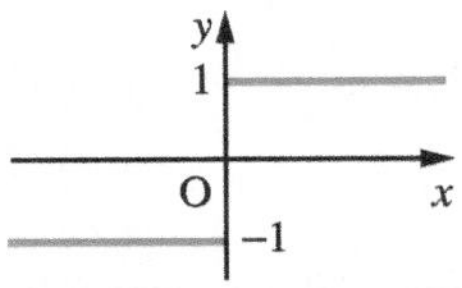

Figure 2.95
$y = \mathrm{sgn}\ x$.

$$\mathrm{sgn}(x) = \begin{cases} +1 & (x > 0) \\ -1 & (x < 0) \\ 0 & (x = 0) \end{cases}$$

and shown in Figure 2.95. The signum function is used in modelling relays.

The **Heaviside unit step function** is often used in modelling physical systems. It is defined by

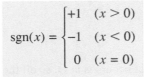

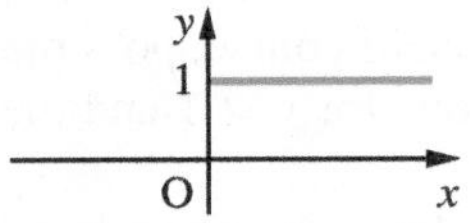

Figure 2.96
$y = H(x)$.

$$H(x) = \begin{cases} 0 & (x < 0) \\ 1 & (x \geqslant 0) \end{cases} \tag{2.45}$$

and its graph is shown in Figure 2.96.

Three other useful functions of this type are the **floor function** $\lfloor x \rfloor$, the **ceiling function** $\lceil x \rceil$ and the **fractional-part function** FRACPT (x). (In older textbooks $\lfloor x \rfloor$ is denoted by $[x]$ and is sometimes called the **integer-part function**.) These are defined by

$$\lfloor x \rfloor = \text{greatest integer not greater than } x \tag{2.46}$$

$$\lceil x \rceil = \text{least integer not less than } x \tag{2.47}$$

and

$$\mathrm{FRACPT}(x) = x - \lfloor x \rfloor \tag{2.48}$$

These definitions need to be interpreted with care. Notice, for example, that

$$\lfloor 3.43 \rfloor = 3$$

while

$$\lfloor -3.43 \rfloor = -4$$

Similarly,

$$\mathrm{FRACPT}(3.43) = 0.43 \quad \text{and} \quad \mathrm{FRACPT}(-3.43) = 0.57$$

The graphs of these functions are shown in Figure 2.97.

Figure 2.97
The graphs of the 'floor', 'ceiling' and 'fractional-part' functions.

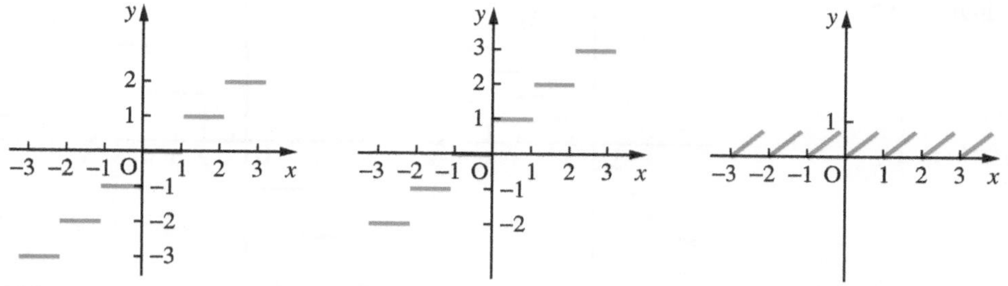

(a) $y = \lfloor x \rfloor$ **(b)** $y = \lceil x \rceil$ **(c)** $y = \text{FRACPT}(x)$

Care must be exercised when using the integer-part and fractional-part functions. Some calculators and computer implementations are different from the above definitions.

Example 2.65

Sketch the graphs of the functions with formula $y = f(x)$, where $f(x)$ is

(a) $H(x-1) - H(x-2)$ (b) $\lfloor x \rfloor - 2\lfloor \frac{1}{2}x \rfloor$

Solution (a) From the definition (2.45) of the Heaviside unit function $H(x)$ as

$$H(x) = \begin{cases} 0 & (x < 0) \\ 1 & (x \geqslant 0) \end{cases}$$

the effect of composing it with the linear function $f(x) = x - 1$ is to shift its graph one unit to the right, as shown in Figure 2.98(a). Similarly, $H(x-2)$ has the same graph as $H(x)$, but shifted two units to the right (Figure 2.98(b)). Combining the graphs in Figures 2.98(a) and (b), we can find the graph of their difference, $H(x-1) - H(x-2)$, as illustrated in Figure 2.98(c). Analytically, we can write this as

Figure 2.98

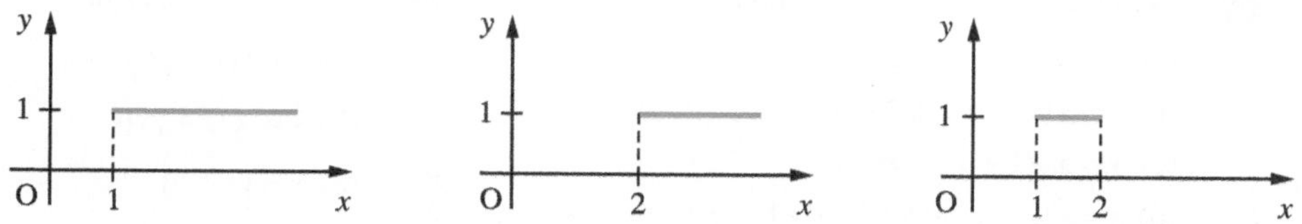

(a) $y = H(x-1)$ **(b)** $y = H(x-2)$ **(c)** $y = H(x-1) - H(x-2)$

$$H(x-1) - H(x-2) = \begin{cases} 0 & (x < 1) \\ 1 & (1 \leqslant x < 2) \\ 0 & (x \geqslant 2) \end{cases}$$

(b) The graphs of $\lfloor x \rfloor$ and $2\lfloor \frac{1}{2}x \rfloor$ are shown in Figure 2.99. Combining these, we can find the graph of their difference, which is also shown in the figure.

Figure 2.99

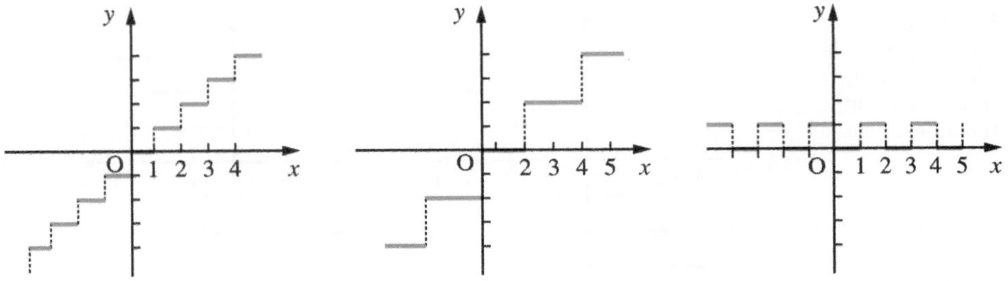

(a) $y = \lfloor x \rfloor$ **(b)** $y = 2\lfloor \frac{1}{2}x \rfloor$ **(c)** $y = \lfloor x \rfloor - 2\lfloor \frac{1}{2}x \rfloor$

In MATLAB the Heaviside step, floor and ceiling functions are denoted by `Heaviside(x)`, `floor(x)` and `ceil(x)` respectively. The FRACPT function may then be denoted by `x-floor(x)`. For example, taking $x = -3.43$ then

```
floor(-3.43)                   returns the answer -4
ceil(-3.43)                    returns the answer -3
FRACPT = -3.43 - floor(-3.43)  returns the answer 0.5700
```

In symbolic form using Symbolic Math Toolbox we have

```
x = sym(-3.43);
floor(x)                returns -4
ceil(x)                 returns -3
FRACPT = x - floor(x)   returns 57/100
```

Similar commands are available in MAPLE.

2.8.4 Exercises

Check your answers using MATLAB or MAPLE whenever possible.

89 Sketch the graphs of the functions

(a) $y = \sqrt{(x^2)}$

(b) $y = \sqrt{(x^2 + x^3)}, x \geqslant -1$

(c) $y = x\sqrt{(1 + x)}, x \geqslant -1$

(d) $y = \sqrt{(1 + x)} + \sqrt{(1 - x)}, -1 \leqslant x \leqslant 1$

90 Sketch the curves represented by

(a) $y^2 = x(x^2 - 1)$

(b) $y^2 = (x - 1)(x - 3)/x^2$

91 Sketch the curves represented by the following equations, locating their turning points and asymptotes:

(a) $x^3 + y^3 = 6x^2$ (b) $y^2 = \dfrac{x^2}{x - 1}$

92 Sketch the graphs of

(a) $y = |x|$

(b) $y = \frac{1}{2}(x + |x|)$

(c) $y = |x + 1|$

(d) $y = |x| + |x + 1| - 2|x + 2| + 3$

(e) $|x + y| = 1$

93 Sketch the graph of the functions $f(x)$ with formulae

(a) $f(x) = \dfrac{ax}{l}H(x)$

(b) $f(x) = \dfrac{ax}{l}[H(x) - H(x - l)]$

(c) $f(x) = \frac{ax}{l}H(x) - \frac{a}{l}(x - l)H(x - l)$

(d) $f(x) = \frac{ax}{l}H(x) - \frac{2a}{l}(x - l)H(x - l)$

94 Show that the function $g(x) = [H(x - a) - H(x - b)]f(x)$, $a < b$, may alternatively be expressed as

$$g(x) = \begin{cases} 0 & (x < a) \\ f(x) & (a \leqslant x < b) \\ 0 & (x \geqslant b) \end{cases}$$

In other words, $g(x)$ is a function that is identical to the function $f(x)$ in the interval $[a, b]$ and zero elsewhere. Hence express as simply as possible in terms of Heaviside functions the function defined by

$$f(x) = \begin{cases} 0 & (x < 0) \\ \dfrac{ax}{l} & (0 \leqslant x \leqslant l) \\ \dfrac{a(2l - x)}{l} & (l \leqslant x \leqslant 2l) \\ 0 & (x \geqslant 2l) \end{cases}$$

95 Sketch the graph of the function

$$y = \begin{cases} x & (x \leqslant 0) \\ 0 & (0 < x \leqslant 1) \\ 1 - x & (1 < x) \end{cases}$$

Express the formula for y in terms of Heaviside functions.

96 The function INT(x) is defined as the 'nearest integer to x, with rounding up in the ambiguous case'. Sketch the graph of this function and express it in terms of $\lfloor x \rfloor$.

97 Sketch the graphs of the functions

(a) $y = \lfloor x \rfloor - \lfloor x - \frac{1}{2} \rfloor$

(b) $y = |\text{FRACPT}(x) - \frac{1}{2}|$

98 It is a familiar observation that spoked wheels do not always appear to be rotating at the correct speed when seen on films. Show that if a wheel has s spokes and is rotating at n revolutions per second, and the camera operates at f frames per second, then the image of the wheel appears to rotate at N revolutions per second, where

$$N = \frac{f}{s}\left[\text{FRACPT}\left(\frac{sn}{f} - \frac{1}{2}\right) - \frac{1}{2}\right]$$

Hence explain the illusion.

2.9 Numerical evaluation of functions

The introduction of calculators has greatly eased the burden of the numerical evaluation of functions. Often, however, the functions encountered in solving practical problems are not standard ones, and we have to devise methods of representing them numerically. The simplest method is to use a graph, a second method is to draw up a table of values of the function, and the third method is to give an analytical approximation to the function in terms of simpler functions. To illustrate this, consider the function e^{-x}. We can represent this by a graph, as shown in Figure 2.100.

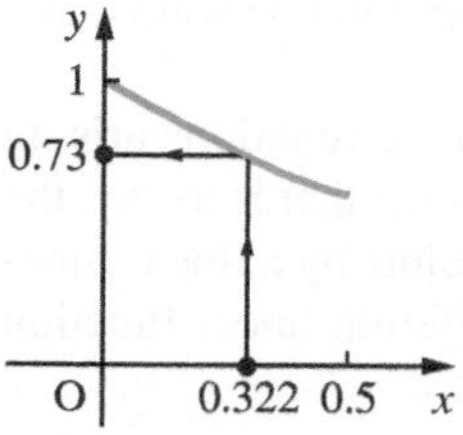

Figure 2.100
The graph of $y = e^{-x}$ for $0 \leqslant x \leqslant 0.5$.

To evaluate the function for a given value of x, we read the corresponding value of y from the graph. For example, $x = 0.322$ gives $y = 0.73$ or thereabouts. Alternatively, we can tabulate the function, as shown in Figure 2.101. Note that the notation $x = 0.00(0.05)0.50$ means for x from 0.00 to 0.50 in steps of 0.05.

Figure 2.101
Table of e^{-x} values for $x = 0.00(0.05)0.50$.

x	0.00	0.05	0.10	0.15	0.20	0.25	0.30	0.35	0.40	0.45	0.50
e^{-x}	1.0000	0.9512	0.9048	0.8607	0.8187	0.7788	0.7408	0.7047	0.6703	0.6376	0.6065

To evaluate the function for a given value of x, we interpolate linearly within the table of values, to obtain the value of y. For example, $x = 0.322$ gives

$$y \approx 0.7408 + \frac{0.322 - 0.30}{0.35 - 0.30}(0.7047 - 0.7408)$$

$$= 0.7408 + (0.44)(-0.0361) = 0.7480 - 0.015\,884$$

$$= 0.7249$$

Another way of representing the function is to use the approximation

$$e^{-x} \approx \frac{x^2 - 6x + 12}{x^2 + 6x + 12}$$

which will be obtained in Section 7.11, Example 7.38. Setting $x = 0.322$ gives

$$y \approx \frac{(0.322 - 6)0.322 + 12}{(0.322 + 6)0.322 + 12} = \frac{10.171\,684}{14.035\,684}$$

$$= 0.724\,70\ldots$$

The question remains as to how accurate these representations of the function are. The graphical method of representation has within it an implicit error bound. When we read the graph, we make a judgement about the number of significant digits in the answer. In the other two methods it is more difficult to assess the error – but it is also more important, since it is easy to write down more digits than can be justified. Are the answers correct to one decimal place or two, or how many? We shall discuss the accuracy of the tabular representation now and defer the algebraic approximation case until Section 7.11.

2.9.1 Tabulated functions and interpolation

To estimate the error involved in evaluating a function from a table of values as above, we need to look more closely at the process involved. Essentially the process assumes that the function behaves like a straight line between tabular points, as illustrated in Figure 2.102. Consequently it is called **linear interpolation**. The error involved depends on how closely a linear function approximates the function between tabular points, and this in turn depends on how close the tabular points are.

If the distance h between tabular points is sufficiently small, most functions arising from applications of mathematics behave locally like linear functions; that is to say, the error involved in approximating to the function between tabular points by a linear function is less than a rounding error. (Note that we have to use a different linear function

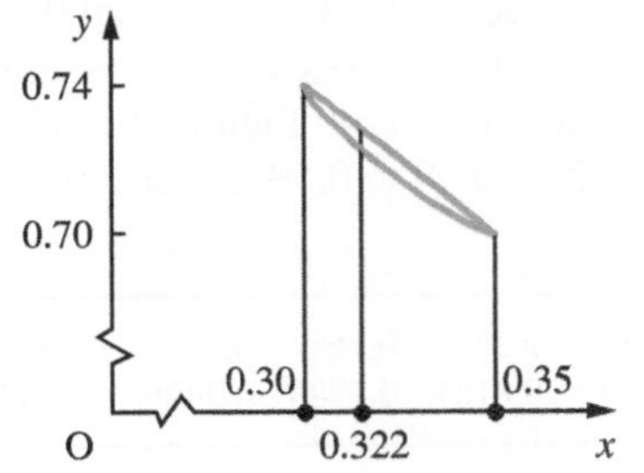

Figure 2.102 Linear interpolation for e^{-x} $(0.30 < x < 0.35)$.

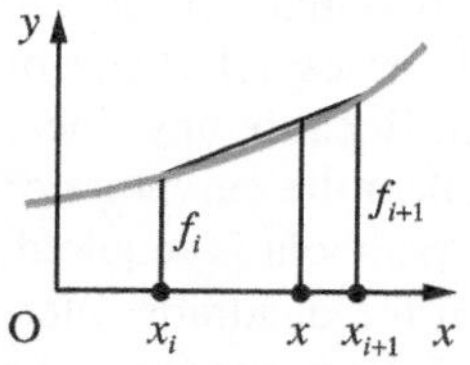

Figure 2.103

between each consecutive pair of values of the function. We have a **piecewise-linear approximation.**) This, however, is a qualitative description of the process, and we need a quantitative description. In general, consider the function $f(x)$ with values $f_i = f(x_i)$ where $x_i = x_0 + ih$, $i = 0, 1, 2, \dots, n$. To calculate the value $f(x)$ at a non-tabular point, where $x = x_i + \theta h$ and $0 < \theta < 1$, using linear interpolation, we have

$$f(x) \approx f_i + \frac{x - x_i}{x_{i+1} - x_i}(f_{i+1} - f_i) \tag{2.49}$$

as shown in Figure 2.103.

The formula (2.49) may be written in a number of different ways, but it always gives the same numerical result. The form used will depend on the computational context. Thus we may write

$$f(x) \approx f_i + \theta(f_{i+1} - f_i), \quad \text{where } \theta = \frac{x - x_i}{x_{i+1} - x_i} \text{ and } 0 < \theta < 1 \tag{2.50}$$

or

$$f(x) \approx \frac{x - x_{i+1}}{x_i - x_{i+1}} f_i + \frac{x - x_i}{x_{i+1} - x_i} f_{i+1} \quad \text{(Lagrange's form)} \tag{2.51}$$

The difference $f_{i+1} - f_i$ between successive values in the table is often denoted by Δf_i, so that (2.49) may be rewritten as

$$f(x) \approx f_i + \theta \Delta f_i$$

Example 2.66

Use linear interpolation and the data of Figure 2.101 to estimate the value of

(a) e^{-x} where $x = 0.235$ (b) x where $e^{-x} = 0.7107$

Solution

(a) From the table of values in Figure 2.101 we see that $x = 0.235$ lies between the tabular points $x = 0.20$ and $x = 0.25$. Applying the formula (2.49) with $x_i = 0.20$, $x_{i+1} = 0.25$, $f_i = 0.8187$ and $f_{i+1} = 0.7788$ we have

$$f(0.235) \approx 0.8187 + \frac{0.235 - 0.20}{0.25 - 0.20}(0.7788 - 0.8187) = 0.7868$$

(b) From the table of values we see that $e^{-x} = 0.7107$ occurs between $x = 0.30$ and $x = 0.35$. Thus the value of x is given, using formula (2.49), by the equation

$$0.7107 \approx 0.7408 + \frac{x - 0.30}{0.35 - 0.30}(0.7047 - 0.7408)$$

Hence

$$x \approx \frac{0.7107 - 0.7408}{0.7047 - 0.7408}(0.35 - 0.30) + 0.30 = 0.3417$$

The difficulty with both the estimates obtained in Example 2.66 is that we do not know how accurate the answers are. Are they correct to 4dp or 3dp or less? The size of the error in the answer depends on the curvature of the function. Because any linear interpolation formula is, by definition, a straight line it cannot reflect the curvature of the function it is trying to model. In order to model curvature a parabola is required, that is a quadratic interpolating function. The difference between the quadratic interpolation formula and the linear formula will give us a measure of the accuracy of the linear formula. We have

$$\text{function value} = \text{linear interpolation value} + C_1$$

and

$$\text{function value} = \text{quadratic interpolation value} + C_2$$

where ideally C_2 is very much smaller than C_1. Subtracting these equations we see that

$$C_1 \approx \text{quadratic interpolation value} - \text{linear interpolation value}$$

Now to determine a quadratic function we require three points. Using formula (2.11) obtained earlier, we see that the quadratic function which passes through (x_i, f_i), (x_{i+1}, f_{i+1}) and (x_{i+2}, f_{i+2}) may be expressed as

$$p(x) = \frac{(x - x_{i+1})(x - x_{i+2})f_i}{(x_i - x_{i+1})(x_i - x_{i+2})} + \frac{(x - x_i)(x - x_{i+2})f_{i+1}}{(x_{i+1} - x_i)(x_{i+1} - x_{i+2})} + \frac{(x - x_i)(x - x_{i+1})f_{i+2}}{(x_{i+2} - x_i)(x_{i+2} - x_{i+1})}$$

We can simplify $p(x)$, when the data points are equally spaced, by remembering that $x_{i+2} = x_i + 2h$, $x_{i+1} = x_i + h$ and $x = x_i + \theta h$, with $0 \leqslant \theta \leqslant 1$, giving

$$p(x) = \frac{(\theta - 1)(\theta - 2)}{2} f_i - \frac{\theta(\theta - 2)}{1} f_{i+1} + \frac{\theta(\theta - 1)}{2} f_{i+2}$$

This formula looks intimidatingly unlike that for linear interpolation, but, after some rearrangement, we have

$$\begin{aligned} p(x) &= [f_i + \theta(f_{i+1} - f_i)] + \tfrac{1}{2}\theta(\theta - 1)(f_{i+2} - 2f_{i+1} + f_i) \\ &= [f_i + \theta\Delta f_i] + \tfrac{1}{2}\theta(\theta - 1)(\Delta f_{i+1} - \Delta f_i) \end{aligned}$$

where $0 < \theta < 1$. Here the term in square brackets is the linear interpolation approximation to $f(x)$, so that

$$\tfrac{1}{2}\theta(\theta - 1)(\Delta f_{i+1} - \Delta f_i)$$

is the quadratic correction for that approximation (remember: the correction is added to eliminate the error). Note that this involves the difference of two successive differences, so we may write it as $\frac{1}{2}\theta(\theta - 1)\Delta^2 f_i$, where $\Delta^2 f_i = \Delta(\Delta f_i) = \Delta f_{i+1} - \Delta f_i$.

Error in linear interpolation

We can use this to estimate the error in linear interpolation for a function. If

$$f(x) \approx f_i + \theta\Delta f_i + \tfrac{1}{2}\theta(\theta - 1)\Delta^2 f_i$$

in the interval $[x_i, x_{i+1}]$ then the error in using the linear interpolation

$$f(x) \approx f_i + \theta\Delta f_i$$

will be approximately $\frac{1}{2}\theta(\theta - 1)\Delta^2 f_i$, and an estimate of the error bound of the linear approximation is given by

$$\max_{0 \leq \theta \leq 1} [|\tfrac{1}{2}\theta(\theta - 1)\Delta^2 f_i|]$$

Now $\theta(\theta - 1) = (\theta - \frac{1}{2})^2 - \frac{1}{4}$, so that $\max\limits_{0 \leq \theta \leq 1} |\theta(\theta - 1)| = \frac{1}{4}$, and our estimate of the error bound is

$$\tfrac{1}{8}|\Delta^2 f_i|$$

For accurate linear interpolation we require this error bound to be less than a rounding error. That is, it must be less than $\frac{1}{2}$ unit in the least significant figure. This implies

$$\tfrac{1}{8}|\Delta^2 f_i| < \tfrac{1}{2} \text{ unit of least significant figure}$$

giving the condition

$$|\Delta^2 f_i| < 4 \text{ units of the least significant figure}$$

for linear interpolation to yield answers as accurate as those in the original table.

Thus, from the table of values of the function e^{-x} shown in Figure 2.101 we can construct the table shown in Figure 2.104. The final row shows the estimate of the maximum error incurred in linear interpolation within each interval $[x_i, x_{i+1}]$. In order to complete the table with error estimates for the intervals [0.00, 0.05] and [0.45, 0.50], we need values of e^{-x} for $x = -0.05$ and 0.55. From the information we have in Figure 2.103 we can say that the largest error likely in using linear interpolation from this table of 11 values of e^{-x} is approximately 3 units in the fourth decimal place. Values obtained could therefore safely be quoted to 3dp.

i	0	1	2	3	4	5	6	7	8	9	10
x_i	0.00	0.05	0.10	0.15	0.20	0.25	0.30	0.35	0.40	0.45	0.50
e^{-x_i}	1.0000	0.9512	0.9048	0.8607	0.8187	0.7788	0.7408	0.7047	0.6703	0.6376	0.6065
$\frac{1}{8}\|\Delta^2 f_i\|$		0.000 29	0.000 28	0.000 26	0.000 25	0.000 24	0.000 23	0.000 21	0.000 20		

Figure 2.104 Table of values of e^{-x}, with error estimates for linear interpolation.

Critical tables

An ordinary table of values uses equally spaced values of the independent variable and tabulates the corresponding values of the dependent variable (the function values).

A **critical table** gives the function values at equal intervals, usually a unit of the last decimal place, and then tabulates the limits between which the independent variable gives each value. Thus, for example, $\cos x° = 0.999$ for $1.82 \leqslant x < 3.14$ and $\cos x° = 0.998$ for $3.14 \leqslant x < 4.06$ and so on. Thus we obtain the table of values shown in Figure 2.105. If a value of the independent variable falls between two tabular values, the value of the dependent variable is that printed between these values. Thus $\cos 2.62° = 0.999$. The advantages of critical tables are that they do not require interpolation, they always give answers that are accurate to within half a unit of the last decimal place and they require less space.

Figure 2.105
A critical table for $\cos x°$.

x	0.00		1.82		3.14		4.06		4.80		5.44
$\cos x°$		1.000		0.999		0.998		0.997		0.996	

2.9.2 Exercises

99 Tabulate the function $f(x) = \sin x$ for $x = 0.0(0.2)1.6$. From this table estimate, by linear interpolation, the value of sin 1.23. Construct a table equivalent to Figure 2.102, and so estimate the error in your value of sin 1.23. Use a pocket calculator to obtain a value of sin 1.23 and compare this with your estimates.

100 Tabulate the function $f(x) = x^3$ for $x = 4.8(0.1)5.6$. Construct a table equivalent to Figure 2.102, and hence estimate the largest error that would be incurred in using linear interpolation in your table of values over the range [5.0, 5.4]. Construct a similar table for $x = 4.8(0.2)5.6$ (that is, for linear interpolation with twice the tabulation interval) and estimate the largest error that would be incurred by linear interpolation from this table in the range [5.0, 5.4]. What do you think the maximum error in interpolating in a similar table formed for $x = 4.8(0.05)5.6$ might be? What tabulation interval do you think would be needed to allow linear interpolation accurate to 3dp?

101 The function $f(x)$ is tabulated at unequal intervals as follows:

x	15	18	20
$f(x)$	0.2316	0.3464	0.4864

Use linear interpolation to estimate $f(17)$, $f(16.34)$ and $f^{-1}(0.3)$.

102 Assess the accuracy of the answers obtained in Question 96 using quadratic interpolation (Lagrange's formula, (2.11)).

103 Show that Lagrange's interpolation formula for cubic interpolation (see Section 2.4) is

$$f(x) = \frac{(x - x_1)(x - x_2)(x - x_3)}{(x_0 - x_1)(x_0 - x_2)(x_0 - x_3)} f_0 + \frac{(x - x_0)(x - x_2)(x - x_3)}{(x_1 - x_0)(x_1 - x_2)(x_1 - x_3)} f_1 + \frac{(x - x_0)(x - x_1)(x - x_3)}{(x_2 - x_0)(x_2 - x_1)(x_2 - x_3)} f_2 + \frac{(x - x_0)(x - x_1)(x - x_2)}{(x_3 - x_0)(x_3 - x_1)(x_3 - x_2)} f_3$$

Use this formula to find a cubic polynomial that fits the function f given in the following table:

x	−1	0	1	8
$f(x)$	−1	0	1	2

Draw the graph of the cubic for $-1 < x < 8$ and compare it with the graph of $y = x^{1/3}$.

104 Construct a critical table for

$$y = \sqrt[3]{x}$$

for $y = 14.50(0.01)14.55$.

2.10 Engineering application: a design problem

Mathematics plays an important role in engineering design. We shall illustrate how some of the elementary ideas described in this chapter are used to produce optimal designs. Consider the open container shown in Figure 2.106. The base and long sides are constructed from material of thickness t cm and the short sides from material of thickness $3t$ cm. The internal dimensions of the container are l cm × b cm × h cm. The design problem is to produce a container of a given capacity that uses the least amount of material. (Mass production of such items implies that small savings on individual items produce large savings in the bulk product.) First we obtain an expression for the volume A of material used in the manufacture of the container.

Figure 2.106

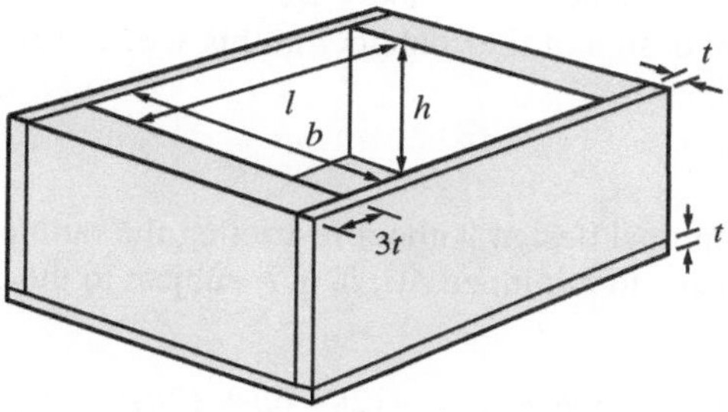

The capacity C of the box is $C(l, b, h) = lbh$. Then

$$\begin{aligned} A(l, b, h, t) &= C(l + 6t, b + 2t, h + t) - C(l, b, h) \\ &= (l + 6t)(b + 2t)(h + t) - lbh \\ &= (lb + 6bh + 2hl)t + (2l + 6b + 12h)t^2 + 12t^3 \qquad (2.52) \end{aligned}$$

For a specific design the thickness t of the material and the capacity K of the container would be specified, so, since $lbh = K$, we can define one of the variables l, b and h in terms of the other two. For example $l = K/bh$.

For various reasons, for example, ease of handling, marketing display and so on, the manufacturer may impose other constraints on the design. We shall illustrate this by first considering a special case, and then look at the more general case.

Special case

Let us seek the optimal design of a container whose breadth b is four times its height h and whose capacity is 10 000 cm^3, using material of thickness 0.4 cm and 1.2 cm (so that $t = 0.4$). The function $f(h)$ that we wish to minimize is given by $A(l, b, h, t)$, where $t = 0.4$, $b = 4h$ and $lbh = 10\,000$ (so that $l = 2500/h^2$). Substituting these values in (2.52) gives, after some rearrangement,

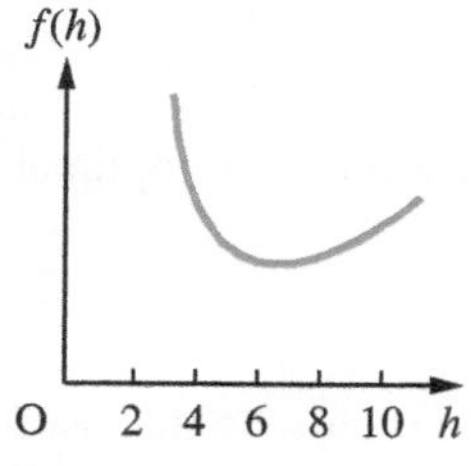

Figure 2.107

$$f(h) = 9.6h^2 + 5.76h + 0.768 + 6000/h + 800/h^2$$

The graph of this function is shown in Figure 2.107. The graph has a minimum point *near* $h = 7$. We can obtain a better estimate for the optimal choice for h by approximating $f(h)$ locally by a quadratic function. Evaluating f at $h = 6$, 7 and 8 gives

$$f(6) = 1403.2, f(7) = 1385.0, f(8) = 1423.7$$

This shows clearly that the minimum value occurs between $h = 6$ and $h = 8$.

We approximate to $f(h)$ using a local quadratic approximation of the form

$$f(h) \simeq A(h-7)^2 + B(h-7) + C$$

Setting $h = 7$ gives $\quad C = 1385.0$
Setting $h = 6$ gives $\quad A - B + C = 1403.2$
Setting $h = 8$ gives $\quad A + B + C = 1423.7$

Hence $C = 1385.0$, $A = 28.45$ and $B = 10.25$. The minimum of the approximating quadratic function occurs where $h - 7 = -B/(2A)$, that is, at $h = 7 - 0.18 = 6.82$. Thus the optimal choice for h is approximately 6.82 giving a value for $f(h)$ at that point of 1383.5.

The corresponding values for b and l are $b = 27.3$ and $l = 53.7$. Thus we have obtained an optimal design of the container in this special case.

General case

Here we seek the optimal design without restricting the ratio of b to h. For a container of capacity K, we have to minimize $A(l, b, h, t)$ subject to the constraint $C(l, b, h) = K$. Here

$$A(l, b, h, t) = (lb + 6bh + 2hl)t + (2l + 6b + 12h)t^2 + 12t^3$$

and

$$C(l, b, h) = lbh$$

These functions have certain algebraic symmetries that enable us to solve the problem algebraically. Consider the formula for A and set $x = 2h$ and $y = l/3$, then

$$\begin{aligned} A(l, b, h, t) &= 3(by + bx + xy)t + 6(y + b + x)t^2 + 12t^3 \\ &= A^*(y, b, x, t) \end{aligned}$$

and

$$C(l, b, h) = 3bxy/2$$

From this we can conclude that if $A^*(y, b, x, t)$ has a minimum value at (y_0, b_0, x_0) for a given value of t, then it has the same value at (x_0, b_0, y_0), (x_0, y_0, b_0), (y_0, x_0, b_0), (b_0, y_0, x_0) and (b_0, x_0, y_0). Assuming that the function has a unique minimum point, we conclude that these six points are the same, that is $b_0 = y_0 = x_0$. Thus we deduce that the minimum occurs where $l = 6h$ and $b = 2h$. Since the capacity is fixed, we have $lbh = K$, which implies that $12h^3 = K$.

Thus the optimal choice for h in the general case is $(\frac{1}{12}K)^{1/3}$.

Returning to the special case where $K = 10\,000$ and $t = 0.4$, we obtain an optimal design when

$$h = 9.41, \quad b = 18.82, \quad l = 56.46$$

using 1330.1 cm^3 of material. Note that the amount of material used is close to that used in the special case where $b = 4h$. This indicates that the design is not sensitive to small errors made during its construction.

2.11 Engineering application: an optimization problem

A company owns two mines: mine X produces 1 ton of high grade ore, 3 tons of medium grade ore and 5 tons of low grade ore each day while mine Y produces 2 tons of each grade ore each day. The company needs 80 tons of high, 160 tons of medium and 200 tons of low grade ore. It costs £2000 a day to operate each mine. How many days should each mine be operated to minimize the cost?

We can summarize the information using a table:

Mine	X	Y	*Requirements*
Grade			
High	1	2	80
Medium	3	2	160
Low	5	2	200
Cost/day	2000	2000	

Running X for x days and Y for y days to meet the requirements gives the inequalities

$$x + 2y \geqslant 80$$

$$3x + 2y \geqslant 160$$

$$5x + 2y \geqslant 200$$

with the associated cost $C = 2000x + 2000y$. Also we know that $x \geqslant 0$ and $y \geqslant 0$.

The set of feasible solutions is shown tinted in Figure 2.108. The feasible costs are also shown in the diagram. They are represented by lines parallel to $x + y = C/2000$. The minimum cost is given by the cost line closest to the origin. This is the line that passes through the point A(40, 20).

Thus the company should operate mine X for 40 days and mine Y for 20 days to minimize the cost. This is an example of optimization using linear programming.

Figure 2.108 Set of feasible solutions.

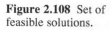

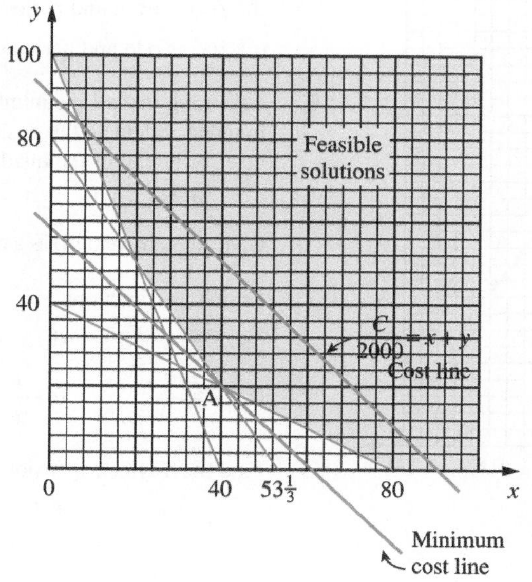

2.12 Review exercises (1–23)

Check your answers using MATLAB or MAPLE whenever possible.

1 The functions f and g are defined by

$$f(x) = x^2 - 4 \quad (x \text{ in } [-20, 20])$$

$$g(x) = x^{1/2} \quad (x \text{ in } [0, 200])$$

Let $h(x)$ and $k(x)$ be the compositions $f \circ g(x)$ and $g \circ f(x)$ respectively. Determine $h(x)$ and $k(x)$. Is the composite function $k(x)$ defined for all x in the domain of $f(x)$? If not, then for what part of the domain of $f(x)$ is $k(x)$ defined?

2 The perimeter of an ellipse depends on the lengths of its major and minor axes, and is given by

$$\text{perimeter} = 2 \times (\text{major axis}) \times E(m)$$

where

$$m = \frac{(\text{major axis})^2 - (\text{minor axis})^2}{(\text{major axis})^2}$$

and E is the function whose graph is given in Figure 2.109.

(a) Calculate the perimeter of the ellipse whose axes are of length 10 cm and 6 cm.

(b) A fairing is to be made from sheet metal bent into the shape of an ellipse of major axis 55 cm and minor axis 13 cm, and is to be of length 2 m. Estimate the area of sheet metal required.

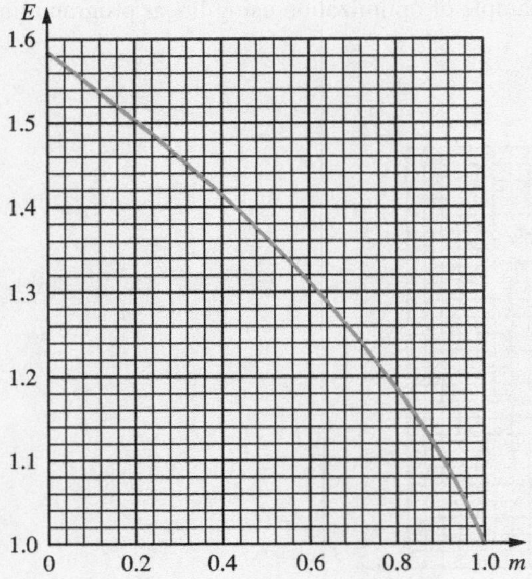

Figure 2.109

3 The sales volume of a product depends on its price as follows:

Price/£	1.00	1.05	1.10	1.15	1.20	1.25	1.30
Sales/000	8	7	6	5	4	3	2

The cost of production is £1 per unit. Draw up a table showing the sales revenue, the cost and the profits for each selling price, and deduce the selling price to be adopted.

4 A function f is defined by

$$f = \begin{cases} x + 1 & (x < -1) \\ 0 & (-1 \leqslant x \leqslant 1) \\ x - 1 & (x > 1) \end{cases}$$

Draw the graphs of $f(x)$, $f(x - 2)$ and $f(2x)$. The function $g(x)$ is defined as $f(x + 2) - f(2x - 1)$. Draw a graph of $g(x)$.

5 The function $f(x)$ has formula $y = x^2$ for $0 \leqslant x < 1$. Sketch the graphs of $f(x)$ for $-4 < x < 4$ when

(a) $f(x)$ is periodic with period 1;

(b) $f(x)$ is even and periodic with period 2;

(c) $f(x)$ is odd and periodic with period 2.

6 Assuming that all the numbers given are correctly rounded, calculate the positive root together with its error bound of the quadratic equation

$$1.4x^2 + 5.7x - 2.3 = 0$$

Give your answer also as a correctly rounded number.

7 Sketch the functions

(a) $x^2 - 4x + 7$ (b) $x^3 - 2x^2 + 4x - 3$

(c) $\dfrac{x + 4}{x^2 - 1}$ (d) $\dfrac{x^2 - 2x + 3}{x^2 + 2x - 3}$

8 Find the Taylor expansion of

$$x^4 + 3x^3 - x^2 + 2x - 1 \text{ about } x = 1$$

9 Find the partial fractions of

(a) $\dfrac{x+2}{(x-1)(x-4)}$ (b) $\dfrac{x^2+4}{(x+1)(x-3)}$

(c) $\dfrac{x^2-2x+3}{(x+2)^2(x-1)}$ (d) $\dfrac{x(2x-1)}{(x^2-x+1)(x+3)}$

10 Express as products of sines and/or cosines

(a) $\sin 2\theta - \sin\theta$ (b) $\cos 2\theta + \cos 3\theta$

(c) $\sin 4\theta - \sin 7\theta$

11 Express in the form $r\sin(\theta-\alpha)$

(a) $4\sin\theta - 2\cos\theta$ (b) $\sin\theta + 8\cos\theta$

(c) $\sqrt{3}\sin\theta + \cos\theta$

12 (a) From the definition of the hyperbolic sine function prove

$$\sinh 3x = 3\sinh x + 4\sinh^3 x$$

(b) Sketch the graph of $y = x^3 + x$ carefully, and show that for each value of y there is exactly one value of x. Setting $z = \frac{1}{2}x\sqrt{3}$, show that

$$4z^3 + 3z = \frac{3\sqrt{3}}{2}y$$

and using (a), deduce that

$$x = \frac{2}{\sqrt{3}}\sinh\left[\frac{1}{3}\sinh^{-1}\left(\frac{3\sqrt{3}}{2}y\right)\right]$$

13 The parts produced by three machines along a factory aisle (shown in Figure 2.110 as the x axis) are to be taken to a nearby bench for assembly before they undergo further processing. Each assembly takes one part from each machine. There is a fixed cost per metre for moving any of the parts. Show that if x represents the position of the assembly bench the cost $C(x)$ of moving the parts for each assembled item is given by

$$C(x) \propto d(x)$$

where $d(x) = |x+3| + |x-2| + |x-4|$.

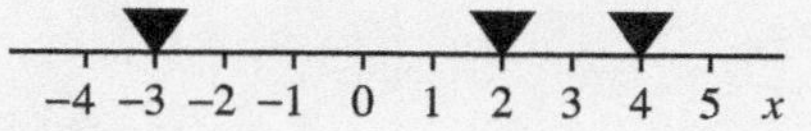

Figure 2.110

Draw the graph of $d(x)$ and find the optimal position of the bench.

14 Sketch the graphs of the functions

(a) $\lfloor \frac{1}{2}x \rfloor - \frac{3}{2}\lfloor \frac{1}{3}x \rfloor$

(b) $xH(x) - (x-1)H(x-1) + (x-2)H(x-2)$

15 Draw up a table of values of the function $f(x) = x^2 e^{-x}$ for $x = -0.1(0.1)1.1$. Determine the maximum error incurred in linearly interpolating for the function $f(x)$ in this table, and hence estimate the value of $f(0.83)$, giving your estimate to an appropriate number of decimal places.

16 By setting $t = \tan\frac{1}{2}x$, find the maximum value of $(\sin x)/(2-\cos x)$.

17 (a) Show that a root x_0 of the equation

$$x^4 - px^3 + q = 0$$

is a repeated root if and only if

$$4x_0 - 3p = 0$$

(b) The stiffness of a rectangular beam varies with the cube of its height h and directly with its breadth b. Find the section of the beam that can be cut from a circular log of diameter D that has the maximum stiffness.

18 Starting at the point $(x_0, y_0) = (1, 0)$, a sequence of right-angled triangles is constructed as shown in Figure 2.111. Show that the coordinates of the vertices satisfy the recurrence relations

$$x_i = x_{i-1} - w_i y_{i-1}$$

$$y_i = w_i x_{i-1} + y_{i-1}$$

where $w_i = \tan\alpha_i^\circ$, $x_0 = 1$ and $y_0 = 0$.

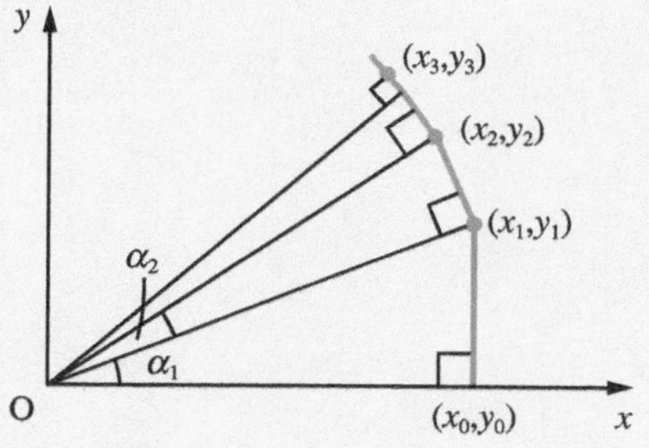

Figure 2.111

Any angle $0° < \theta° < 360°$ can be expressed in the form

$$\theta = \sum_{i=0}^{\infty} n_i \phi_i$$

where $\tan \phi_i° = 10^{-i}$ and n_i is a non-negative integer. Express $\theta = 56.5$ in this form and, using the recurrence relations above, calculate $\sin \theta°$ and $\cos \theta°$ to 5dp. (This method of calculating the trigonometric functions is used in some calculators.)

19 A mechanism consists of the linkage of three rods AB, BC and CD, as shown in Figure 2.112, where AB = CD (= a, say), BC = AD = $a\sqrt{2}$, and M is the midpoint. The rods are freely jointed at B and C, and are free to rotate about A and D. Using polar coordinates with their pole O at the midpoint of AD and initial line OD, show that the curve described by M as CD rotates about D

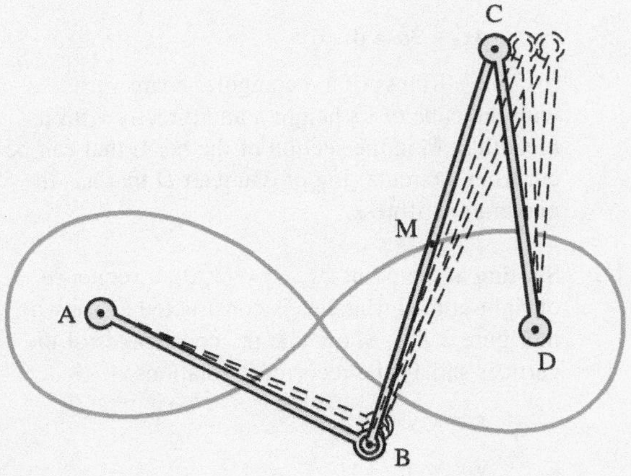

Figure 2.112

is $r^2 = a^2 \cos 2\theta$. Draw a careful graph of this curve, the 'lemniscate' of Bernoulli.

Show that

(a) the cartesian coordinates of M satisfy

$$(x^2 + y^2)^2 = a^2(x^2 - y^2)$$

(b) $AM \times DM = \frac{1}{2}a^2$.

20 Show that the equation

$$r = p/\sin(\theta - \alpha)$$

represents a straight line which cuts the x axis at the angle α and whose perpendicular distance from the origin is p.

21 Use the result of Question 20 to find the polar coordinate representation of the line which passes through the points (1, 2) and (3, 3).

22 Show that the equation

$$r = ep/(1 + e\cos\theta)$$

where e and p are constants, represents an ellipse where $0 < e < 1$, a parabola where $e = 1$ and a hyperbola where $e > 1$, the origin of the coordinate system being at a focus of the conic concerned.

23 Continuing Question 54 of Exercises 2.6.2, show that

$$\cot\theta = \frac{12 + d^2}{4d}$$

and by applying the arithmetic-geometric inequality to

$$\frac{3}{d} + \frac{d}{4}$$

deduce that $\theta°$ achieves its maximum value where $d = 2\sqrt{3}$.

3 Complex Numbers

Chapter 3 Contents

3.1 Introduction

Complex numbers first arose in the solution of cubic equations in the sixteenth century using a method known as Cardano's solution. This gives the solution of the equation

$$x^3 + qx + r = 0$$

as

$$x = {}^3\sqrt{[-\tfrac{1}{2}r + \sqrt{(\tfrac{1}{4}r^2 + \tfrac{1}{27}q^3)}]} + {}^3\sqrt{[-\tfrac{1}{2}r - \sqrt{(\tfrac{1}{4}r^2 + \tfrac{1}{27}q^3)}]}$$

which may be verified by direct substitution. This solution gave difficulties when it unexpectedly involved square roots of negative numbers. For example, the equation

$$x^3 - 15x - 4 = 0$$

was known to have three roots. An obvious one is $x = 4$, but the corresponding root obtained using the formula was

$$x = {}^3\sqrt{[2 + \sqrt{(-121)}]} + {}^3\sqrt{[2 - \sqrt{(-121)}]}$$

Writing in 1572, Bombelli showed that

$$2 + \sqrt{(-121)} = [2 + \sqrt{(-1)}]^3$$

and

$$2 - \sqrt{(-121)} = [2 - \sqrt{(-1)}]^3$$

and so

$$x = [2 + \sqrt{(-1)}] + [2 - \sqrt{(-1)}] = 4$$

as expected. Since

$$\sqrt{(-x)} = \sqrt{(-1)}\sqrt{x}$$

where x is a positive number, the square roots of negative numbers can be represented as a number multiplied by $\sqrt{(-1)}$. Thus $\sqrt{(-121)} = 11\sqrt{(-1)}$, $\sqrt{(-4900)} = 70\sqrt{(-1)}$ and so on. Because the introduction of the special number $\sqrt{(-1)}$ simplified calculations, it quickly gained acceptance by mathematicians. Denoting $\sqrt{(-1)}$ by the letter j, we obtain the general number z where

$$z = x + \mathrm{j}y$$

Here x and y are ordinary **real numbers** and obey the Fundamental Rules of Arithmetic. (Most mathematics and physics texts use the letter i instead of j. However, we shall follow the standard engineering practice and use j.) The number z is called a **complex number**. The ordinary processes of arithmetic still apply, but become a little more complicated. As well as simplifying the process of obtaining roots as above, the introduction of $\mathrm{j} = \sqrt{(-1)}$ simplified the theory of equations, so that, for example, the quadratic equation

$$ax^2 + bx + c = 0$$

always has two roots

$$x = \frac{-b \pm \sqrt{(b^2 - 4ac)}}{2a}$$

These roots are real numbers when $b^2 \geqslant 4ac$ and complex numbers when $b^2 < 4ac$. Thus, any irreducible quadratic (see Section 2.3.4) may be factorized into two complex factors. Thus $x^2 + 2x + 5 = (x + 1 + j2)(x + 1 - j2)$. It then follows from property (ii) of the polynomial functions, given in Section 2.4.1, that any polynomial equation of degree n having real coefficients has exactly n roots which may be real or complex. This is a result known as the **Fundamental Theorem of Algebra**, which is also valid for polynomial equations having complex coefficients. Thus

$$x^7 - 7x^5 - 6x^4 + 4x^3 - 28x - 24 = 0$$

is an equation of degree seven and has the seven roots

$$x = -1, -2, -3, -1 - j, -1 + j, 1 - j, 1 + j$$

As has often been the case, what began as a mathematical curiosity has turned out to be of considerable practical importance, and complex numbers are invaluable in many aspects of engineering analysis. An elementary, but important, application is discussed later in this chapter.

3.2 Properties

To specify a complex number z, we use two real numbers, x and y, and write

$$z = x + jy$$

where $j = \sqrt{(-1)}$, and x is called the **real part** of z and y its **imaginary part**. This is often abbreviated to

$$z = x + jy, \quad \text{where } x = \text{Re}(z) \text{ and } y = \text{Im}(z)$$

Note that the imaginary part of z does *not* include the j. For example, if $z = 3 - j2$ then $\text{Re}(z) = 3$ and $\text{Im}(z) = -2$. If $x = 0$, the complex number is said to be **purely imaginary** and if $y = 0$ it is said to be **purely real**.

3.2.1 The Argand diagram

Geometrically, complex numbers can be represented as points on a plane similar to the way in which real numbers are represented by points on a straight line (see Section 1.2.1). The number $z = x + jy$ is represented by the point P with coordinates (x, y), as shown in Figure 3.1. Such a diagram is called an **Argand diagram**, after one of its inventors. The x axis is called the **real axis** and the y axis is called the **imaginary axis**.

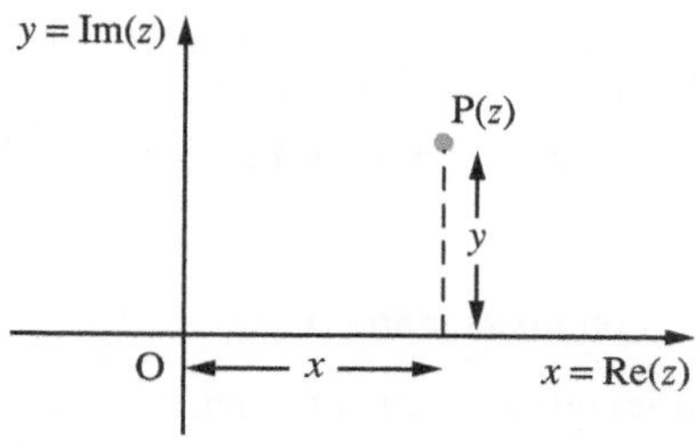

Figure 3.1 The Argand diagram: $z = x + jy$.

Example 3.1 Represent on an Argand diagram the complex numbers

(a) $3 + j2$ (b) $-5 + j3$ (c) $8 - j5$ (d) $-2 - j3$

Solution (a) The number $3 + j2$ is represented by the point A(3, 2)

(b) The number $-5 + j3$ is represented by the point B(−5, 3)

(c) The number $8 - j5$ is represented by the point C(8, −5)

(d) The number $-2 - j3$ is represented by the point D(−2, −3)

as shown in Figure 3.2.

Figure 3.2

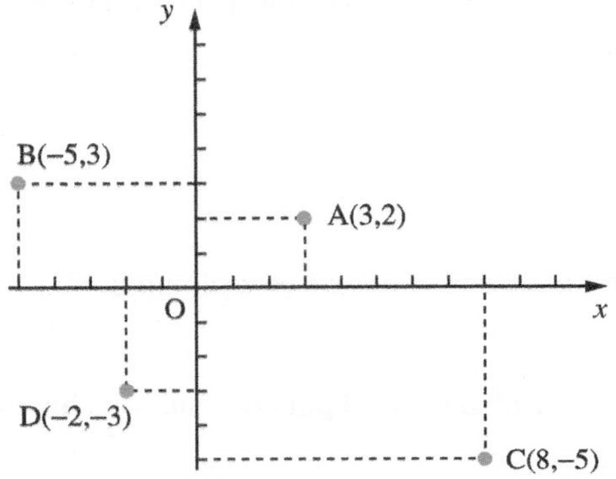

3.2.2 The arithmetic of complex numbers

(i) Equality

If two complex numbers $z_1 = x_1 + jy_1$ and $z_2 = x_2 + jy_2$ are equal then they are represented by the same point on the Argand diagram and it clearly follows that

$$x_1 = x_2 \quad \text{and} \quad y_1 = y_2$$

That is, when two complex numbers are equal we can equate their respective real and imaginary parts.

Example 3.2 If the two complex numbers

$$z_1 = (3a + 2) + j(3b - 1) \quad \text{and} \quad z_2 = (b + 1) - j(a + 2 - b)$$

are equal

(a) find the values of the real numbers a and b;

(b) write down the real and imaginary parts of z_1 and z_2.

Solution (a) Since $z_1 = z_2$ we can equate their respective real and imaginary parts, giving

$$(3a + 2) = (b + 1) \qquad \text{or} \quad 3a - b = -1$$

and

$$(3b - 1) = -(a + 2 - b) \quad \text{or} \quad a + 2b = -1$$

Solving for a and b then gives

$$a = -\tfrac{3}{7}, \quad b = -\tfrac{2}{7}$$

(b)
$$\left.\begin{aligned} \mathrm{Re}(z_1) &= 3a + 2 = \tfrac{5}{7} \\ \mathrm{Re}(z_2) &= b + 1 = \tfrac{5}{7} \end{aligned}\right\} \quad \text{thus} \quad \mathrm{Re}(z_1) = \mathrm{Re}(z_2) = \tfrac{5}{7}$$

$$\left.\begin{aligned} \mathrm{Im}(z_1) &= 3b - 1 = -\tfrac{13}{7} \\ \mathrm{Im}(z_2) &= -(a + 2 - b) = -\tfrac{13}{7} \end{aligned}\right\} \quad \text{thus} \quad \mathrm{Im}(z_1) = \mathrm{Im}(z_2) = -\tfrac{13}{7}$$

(ii) Addition and subtraction

To add or subtract two complex numbers, we simply perform the operations on their corresponding real and imaginary parts. In general, if $z_1 = x_1 + \mathrm{j}y_1$ and $z_2 = x_2 + \mathrm{j}y_2$ then

$$z_1 + z_2 = (x_1 + x_2) + \mathrm{j}(y_1 + y_2)$$

and

$$z_1 - z_2 = (x_1 - x_2) + \mathrm{j}(y_1 - y_2)$$

In Section 4.2.5 we shall interpret complex numbers geometrically as two-dimensional vectors and illustrate how the rules for the addition of vectors can be used to represent addition of complex numbers in the Argand diagram.

Example 3.3 If $z_1 = 3 + \mathrm{j}2$ and $z_2 = 5 - \mathrm{j}3$ determine

(a) $z_1 + z_2$ (b) $z_1 - z_2$

Solution (a) Adding the corresponding real and imaginary parts gives

$$z_1 + z_2 = (3 + 5) + \mathrm{j}(2 - 3) = 8 - \mathrm{j}1$$

(b) Subtracting the corresponding real and imaginary parts gives

$$z_1 - z_2 = (3 - 5) + \mathrm{j}(2 - (-3)) = -2 + \mathrm{j}5$$

(iii) Multiplication

When multiplying two complex numbers the normal rules for multiplying out brackets hold. Thus, in general, if $z_1 = x_1 + \mathrm{j}y_1$ and $z_2 = x_2 + \mathrm{j}y_2$ then

$$z_1z_2 = (x_1 + jy_1)(x_2 + jy_2)$$
$$= x_1x_2 + jy_1x_2 + jx_1y_2 + j^2y_1y_2$$

Making use of the fact that $j^2 = -1$ then gives

$$z_1z_2 = x_1x_2 - y_1y_2 + j(x_1y_2 + x_2y_1)$$

Example 3.4 If $z_1 = 3 + j2$ and $z_2 = 5 + j3$ determine z_1z_2.

Solution

$$z_1z_2 = (3 + j2)(5 + j3) = 15 + j10 + j9 + j^2 6$$
$$= 15 - 6 + j(10 + 9), \text{ using the fact that } j^2 = -1$$
$$= 9 + j19$$

(iv) Division

The division of two complex numbers is less straightforward. If $z_1 = x_1 + jy_1$ and $z_2 = x_2 + jy_2$, then we use the following technique to obtain the quotient. We multiply 'top and bottom' by $x_2 - jy_2$, giving

$$\frac{z_1}{z_2} = \frac{x_1 + jy_1}{x_2 + jy_2} = \frac{(x_1 + jy_1)(x_2 - jy_2)}{(x_2 + jy_2)(x_2 - jy_2)}$$

Multiplying out 'top and bottom', we obtain

$$\frac{z_1}{z_2} = \frac{(x_1x_2 + y_1y_2) + j(x_2y_1 - x_1y_2)}{x_2^2 + y_2^2}$$

giving

$$\frac{z_1}{z_2} = \frac{(x_1x_2 + y_1y_2)}{x_2^2 + y_2^2} + j\frac{(x_2y_1 - x_1y_2)}{x_2^2 + y_2^2}$$

The number $x - jy$ is called the **complex conjugate** of $z = x + jy$ and is denoted by z^*. (Sometimes the complex conjugate is denoted with an overbar as $\bar{z}$.) Note that the complex conjugate z^* is obtained by changing the sign of the imaginary part of z.

Example 3.5 If $z_1 = 3 + j2$ and $z_2 = 5 + j3$ determine $\frac{z_1}{z_2}$.

Solution

$$\frac{z_1}{z_2} = \frac{3 + j2}{5 + j3}$$

Multiplying 'top and bottom' by the conjugate $5 - j3$ of the denominator gives

$$\frac{z_1}{z_2} = \frac{(3 + j2)(5 - j3)}{(5 + j3)(5 - j3)}$$

Multiplying out 'top and bottom' we obtain

$$\frac{3+\mathrm{j}2}{5+\mathrm{j}3}=\frac{(15+6)+\mathrm{j}(10-9)}{(25+9)+\mathrm{j}(15-15)}=\frac{21+\mathrm{j}}{34}=\tfrac{21}{34}+\mathrm{j}\tfrac{1}{34}$$

Example 3.6 Find the real and imaginary parts of the complex number $z + 1/z$ for $z = (2 + \mathrm{j})/(1 - \mathrm{j})$.

Solution

$$z=\frac{2+\mathrm{j}}{1-\mathrm{j}}=\frac{(2+\mathrm{j})(1+\mathrm{j})}{(1-\mathrm{j})(1+\mathrm{j})}=\frac{1+\mathrm{j}3}{2}=\tfrac{1}{2}+\mathrm{j}\tfrac{3}{2}$$

then

$$z^{-1}=\frac{2}{1+\mathrm{j}3}=\frac{2(1-\mathrm{j}3)}{(1+\mathrm{j}3)(1-\mathrm{j}3)}=\frac{2-\mathrm{j}6}{10}=\tfrac{1}{5}-\mathrm{j}\tfrac{3}{5}$$

so that

$$z+\frac{1}{z}=(\tfrac{1}{2}+\mathrm{j}\tfrac{3}{2})+(\tfrac{1}{5}-\mathrm{j}\tfrac{3}{5})=(\tfrac{1}{2}+\tfrac{1}{5})+\mathrm{j}(\tfrac{3}{2}-\tfrac{3}{5})=\tfrac{7}{10}+\mathrm{j}\tfrac{9}{10}$$

giving

$$\mathrm{Re}\left(z+\frac{1}{z}\right)=\tfrac{7}{10}\quad\text{and}\quad\mathrm{Im}\left(z+\frac{1}{z}\right)=\tfrac{9}{10}$$

3.2.3 Complex conjugate

As we have seen above, the complex conjugate of $z = x + \mathrm{j}y$ is $z^* = x - \mathrm{j}y$. In the Argand diagram z^* is the mirror image of z in the real or x axis. The following important results are readily deduced.

$$\begin{aligned}&z+z^*=2x=2\,\mathrm{Re}(z)\\&z-z^*=2\mathrm{j}y=2\mathrm{j}\,\mathrm{Im}(z)\\&zz^*=(x+\mathrm{j}y)(x-\mathrm{j}y)=x^2+y^2\\&(z_1z_2)^*=z_1^*z_2^*\end{aligned}\qquad(3.1)$$

with the next to last result indicating that the product of a complex number and its complex conjugate is a real number.

The zeros of an irreducible quadratic function, which has real coefficients, are complex conjugates of each other.

Example 3.7 Express the zeros of $f(x) = x^2 - 6x + 13$ as complex numbers.

Solution The zeros of $f(x)$ are the roots of the equation

$$x^2 - 6x + 13 = 0$$

Using the quadratic formula (1.8) we obtain

$$x = \frac{6 \pm \sqrt{(36 - 52)}}{2} = \frac{6 \pm \sqrt{(-16)}}{2}$$

$$= \frac{6 \pm 4\sqrt{(-1)}}{2} = 3 \pm \mathrm{j}2$$

So the two zeros form a conjugate pair.

Example 3.8 Find all the roots of the quartic equation

$$x^4 + 4x^2 + 16 = 0$$

Solution Rewriting the equation we can achieve a difference of squares which makes possible a first factorization

$$x^4 + 8x^2 + 16 - 4x^2 = (x^2 + 4)^2 - 4x^2$$

$$= [(x^2 + 4) - 2x][(x^2 + 4) + 2x]$$

Now $x^2 - 2x + 4 = (x - 1)^2 + 3$ and $x^2 + 2x + 4 = (x + 1)^2 + 3$, so we obtain the equations

$$x - 1 = \pm \mathrm{j}\sqrt{3} \quad \text{and} \quad x + 1 = \pm \mathrm{j}\sqrt{3}$$

and the four roots of the quartic equation are

$$x = 1 + \mathrm{j}\sqrt{3},\ 1 - \mathrm{j}\sqrt{3},\ -1 + \mathrm{j}\sqrt{3},\ -1 - \mathrm{j}\sqrt{3}$$

These roots form two conjugate pairs.

Example 3.9 For the complex numbers $z_1 = 5 + \mathrm{j}3$ and $z_2 = 3 - \mathrm{j}2$ verify the identity

$$(z_1 z_2)^* = z_1^* z_2^*$$

Solution

$$z_1 z_2 = (5 + \mathrm{j}3)(3 - \mathrm{j}2) = 15 + 6 + \mathrm{j}(9 - 10) = 21 - \mathrm{j}$$

$$(z_1 z_2)^* = 21 + \mathrm{j}$$

$$z_1^* z_2^* = (5 - \mathrm{j}3)(3 + \mathrm{j}2) = 15 + 6 + \mathrm{j}(10 - 9) = 21 + \mathrm{j}$$

Thus $(z_1 z_2)^* = z_1^* z_2^*$.

3.2.4 Modulus and argument

As indicated in the Argand diagram of Figure 3.3, the point P is specified uniquely if we know the length of the line OP and the angle it makes with the positive x direction. The length of OP is a measure of the size of z and is called the **modulus** of z, which is usually denoted by mod z or $|z|$. The angle between the positive real axis and OP is called the **argument** of z and is denoted by arg z. Since the polar coordinates (r, θ) and $(r, \theta + 2\pi)$ represent the same point, a convention is used to determine the argument

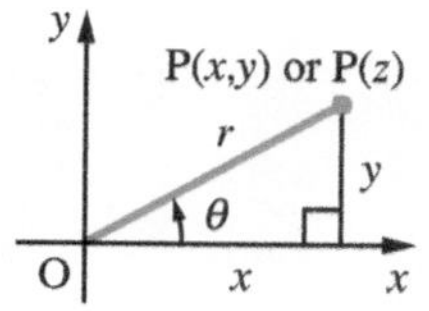

Figure 3.3 Modulus (r) and argument (θ) of the complex number $z = x + jy$.

of z uniquely, restricting its range so that $-\pi < \arg z \leqslant \pi$. (In some textbooks this is referred to as the 'principal value' of the argument.) The argument of the complex number $0 + j0$ is not defined.

Thus from Figure 3.3, $|z|$ and $\arg z$ are given by

$$\left.\begin{aligned}|z| &= r = \sqrt{(x^2 + y^2)}\\ \arg z &= \theta \quad \text{where } \tan\theta = y/x,\ z \neq 0\end{aligned}\right\} \tag{3.2}$$

Note that from equations (3.1)

$$zz^* = x^2 + y^2 = |z|^2$$

There are two common mistakes to avoid when calculating $|z|$ and $\arg z$ using (3.2). First note that the modulus of z is the square root of the sum of squares of x and y, *not* of x and jy. The j part of the number has been accounted for in the representation of the Argand diagram. The second common mistake is to place θ in the wrong quadrant. To avoid this, it is advisable when evaluating $\arg z$ to draw a sketch of the Argand diagram showing the location of the number.

Example 3.10 Determine the modulus and argument of

(a) $3 + j2$ (b) $1 - j$ (c) $-1 + j$ (d) $-\sqrt{6} - j\sqrt{2}$

Solution Note that the sketches of the Argand diagrams locating the positions of the complex numbers are given in Figure 3.4(a–d).

(a) $|3 + j2| = \sqrt{(3^2 + 2^2)} = \sqrt{(9 + 4)} = \sqrt{13} = 3.606$

$$\arg(3 + j2) = \tan^{-1}\left(\frac{2}{3}\right) = 0.588$$

(b) $|1 - j| = \sqrt{[1^2 + (-1)^2]} = \sqrt{2} = 1.414$

$$\arg(1 - j) = -\tan^{-1}\left(\frac{1}{1}\right) = -\tfrac{1}{4}\pi$$

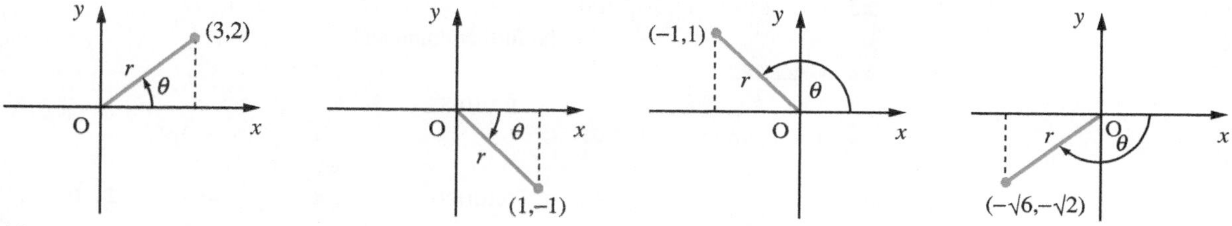

Figure 3.4

(c) $|-1+j| = \sqrt{[(-1)^2 + 1^2]} = \sqrt{2} = 1.414$

$$\arg(-1+j) = \pi - \tan^{-1}\left(\frac{1}{1}\right) = \pi - \tfrac{1}{4}\pi = \tfrac{3}{4}\pi$$

(d) $|-\sqrt{6} - j\sqrt{2}| = \sqrt{(6+2)} = \sqrt{8} = 2.828$

$$\arg(-\sqrt{6} - j\sqrt{2}) = -(\pi - \tan^{-1}\tfrac{\sqrt{2}}{\sqrt{6}}) = -(\pi - \tan^{-1}\sqrt{\tfrac{1}{3}}) = -(\pi - \tfrac{1}{6}\pi) = -\tfrac{5}{6}\pi$$

MATLAB handles complex numbers automatically. Either *i* or *j* can be used to denote the imaginary part, but in any output to a command, MATLAB will always use *i*. Consequently, to avoid confusion *i* will be used throughout when using MATLAB, so, for example, the complex number $z = 4 + j3$ will be entered as:

```
z = 4 + 3i
```

Note that the *i* is located after the number 3 and there is no need to insert the multiplication sign * between the 3 and the *i* (if it is located before then * must be included). However, in some cases it is necessary to insert *; for example, the complex number $z = -\frac{1}{2} + j\frac{1}{2}$ must be entered as

```
z = -1/2 + (1/2)*i
```

MAPLE is similar to MATLAB in dealing with complex numbers, except it uses *I* and * is always required.

The complex conjugate z^* of a complex number z is obtained using the command *conj*; for example, to obtain the conjugate of $z = 4 + j3$ enter the commands

MATLAB		MAPLE
`z = 4 + 3i;`		`z:= 4 + 3*I;`
`zbar = conj(z)`		`zbar:= conjugate(z);`
	which return	
`zbar = 4 - 3i`		`zbar = 4 - 3I`

The arithmetical operations of addition, subtraction, multiplication and division are carried out by the standard operators +, −, *, and / respectively. For example, if $z_1 = 4 + j3$ and $z_2 = -3 + j2$ then $z_3 = z_1 + z_2$ and $z_4 = z_1/z_2$ are determined as follows:

MATLAB		MAPLE
`z1 = 4 + 3i;`		`z1:= 4 + 3*I;`
`z2 = -3 + 2i;`		`z2:= -3 + 2*I;`
`z3 = z1 + z2`		`z3:= z1 + z2;`
	return	
`z3 = 1.0000 + 5.0000i`		`z3 = 1 + 5I`
	and the further command	
`z4 = z1/z2`		`z4:= z1/z2;`
	returns	
`z4 = -0.4615 - 1.3077i`		`z4:=` $-\frac{6}{13} - \frac{17}{13}I$
		`evalf(%);`
	returns	`z4 = -0.4615 - 1.3077I`

Note that MAPLE produces exact arithmetic; the command *evalf* is used to produce the numerical answer. Exact arithmetic may be undertaken in MATLAB using the Symbolic Math Toolbox with the command *double* used to obtain numerical results. For example the commands

```
syms z1 z2 z4
z1 = sym(4 + 3i); z2 = sym(3 + 2i); z4 = z1/z2
```

return

$$z4 = -\frac{6}{13} - \frac{17}{13}*i$$

and

```
double(z4)
```

returns

```
z4 = -0.4615 - 1.3077i
```

The real and imaginary parts of a complex number are determined using the commands *real* and *imag* respectively. Considering Example 3.6 the MATLAB commands

```
z = (2 + i)/(1 - i); z1 = z + 1/z;
real(z1)
```

return the answer *0.7000* and the further command

```
imag(z1)
```

returns the answer *0.9000*, thus confirming the answers obtained in the given solution. MAPLE uses *Re* and *Im*.

To represent complex numbers as points on an Argand diagram check that the following commands reaffirm the solution given in Example 3.1:

```
z1 = 3 + 2i; x = real(z1); y = imag(z1);
plot(x,y,'*')
xlabel('x = Re(z)')
ylabel('y = Im(z)')
hold on
plot([-6,9],[0,0], 'k')
plot([0,0],[-6,4], 'k')
z2 = -5 + 3i; x = real(z2); y = imag(z2);
plot(x,y, '*')
z3 = 8 - 5i; x = real(z3); y = imag(z3);
plot(x,y, '*')
z4 = -2 - 3i; x = real(z4); y = imag(z4);
plot(x,y, '*')
```

To label the points add the additional commands

```
text(3.2,2 'A(3,2)')
text(-5,3.3, 'B(-5,3)')
text(8.2,-5, 'C(8,-5)')
text(-2,-3.3, 'D(-2,3)')
plot(x,y,'*')
hold off
```

[Note: (1) The `'*'` in the plot commands means that the point will be printed as an asterisk; alternatives include `'.'`, 'x' and `'+'`.
(2) The *hold on* command holds the current axes for subsequent plots.
(3) The two plot commands following the *hold on* command draw the x and y axes with the entry *k* indicating that the lines are drawn in black (alternatives include *b* for blue, *r* for red and *g* for green).]

Symbolically the MATLAB commands

```
syms x y real
z = x + i*y
```

create symbolic variables x and y that have the additional property that they are real. Then z is a complex variable and can be manipulated as such. For example

`conj(z)` returns `x - i*y` and `expand(z*conj(z))` returns `x^2 + y^2`

The modulus and argument (measured in radians) of a complex number z can be calculated directly using the commands *abs* and *angle* respectively (*abs* and *argument* in MAPLE). For example, considering Example 3.10(a) the commands

```
z = 3 + 2i;
modz = abs(z)
```

return

```
modz = 3.6056
```

and the additional command

```
argz = angle(z)
```

returns

```
argz = 0.5880
```

confirming the answers obtained in the given solution. Using these commands check the answers to Examples 3.10(b)–(d).

3.2.5 Exercises

Check your answers using MATLAB or MAPLE whenever possible.

1 Show in an Argand diagram the points representing the following complex numbers:

(a) $1 + j$ (b) $\sqrt{3} - j$

(c) $-3 + j4$ (d) $1 - j\sqrt{3}$

(e) $-1 + j\sqrt{3}$ (f) $-1 - j\sqrt{3}$

2 Find $z_1 + z_2$, $z_1 - z_2$, $2z_1$, $-3z_2$, $5z_1 - 2z_2$, $2z_1 + z_2$ where z_1 and z_2 are the complex numbers $z_1 = 1 + j2$, $z_2 = 3 - j$.

3 Obtain the roots of the equations below using complex numbers where necessary:

(a) $x^2 + 6x + 13 = 0$

(b) $x^2 - x + 2 = 0$

(c) $4x^2 + 4x + 5 = 0$

(d) $x^3 + 2x - 3 = 0$

(e) $x^4 - x^2 - 6 = 0$

4 Express in the form $x + jy$:

(a) $(6 - j3)(2 + j4)$ (b) $(7 + j)(2 - j3)$

(c) $(-1 + j)(-2 + j3)$ (d) $(-3 + j2)(4 + j7)$

5 Express in the form $x + jy$:

(a) $(4 - j6)/(1 + j)$ (b) $(5 + j3)/(3 - j2)$

(c) $(1 - j)/(4 + j3)$ (d) $(-4 - j3)/(2 - j)$

6 Express in the form $x + jy$ where x and y are real numbers:

(a) $(5 + j3)(2 - j) - (3 + j)$ (b) $(1 - j2)^2$

(c) $\dfrac{5 - j8}{3 - j4}$ (d) $\dfrac{1 - j}{1 + j}$

(e) $\frac{1}{2}(1 + j)^2$ (f) $(3 - j2)^2$

(g) $\dfrac{1}{5 - j3} - \dfrac{1}{5 + j3}$ (h) $\dfrac{1}{2} - \dfrac{3 - j4}{5 - j8}$

7 What is the complex conjugate of

(a) $2 + j7$ (b) $-3 - j$ (c) $-j6$ (d) $\frac{2}{3} - j\frac{2}{3}$

8 Find the roots of the equations

(a) $x^2 + 2x + 2 = 0$ (b) $x^3 + 8 = 0$

9 Find z such that

$$zz^* + 3(z - z^*) = 13 + j12$$

10 With $z = 2 - j3$, find

(a) jz (b) z^* (c) $1/z$ (d) $(z^*)^*$

11 Find the modulus and argument of each of the complex numbers given in Question 1.

12 Find the complex numbers w, z which satisfy the simultaneous equations

$$4z + 3w = 23$$

$$z + jw = 6 + j8$$

13 For $z = x + jy$ (x and y real) satisfying

$$\frac{2z}{1 + j} - \frac{2z}{j} = \frac{5}{2 + j}$$

find x and y.

14 Given $z = 2 - j2$ is a root of

$$2z^3 - 9z^2 + 20z - 8 = 0$$

find the remaining roots of the equation.

15 Find the real and imaginary parts of z when

$$\frac{1}{z} = \frac{2}{2 + j3} + \frac{1}{3 - j2}$$

16 Find $z = z_1 + z_2z_3/(z_2 + z_3)$ when $z_1 = 2 + j3$, $z_2 = 3 + j4$ and $z_3 = -5 + j12$.

17 Find the values of the real numbers x and y which satisfy the equation

$$\frac{2 + x - jy}{3x + jy} = 1 + j2$$

18 Find z_3 in the form $x + jy$, where x and y are real numbers, given that

$$\frac{1}{z_3} = \frac{1}{z_1} + \frac{1}{z_1z_2}$$

where $z_1 = 3 - j4$ and $z_2 = 5 + j2$.

3.2.6 Polar form of a complex number

Figure 3.3 on page 193 shows that the relationships between (x, y) and (r, θ) are

$$x = r\cos\theta \quad \text{and} \quad y = r\sin\theta$$

Hence the complex number $z = x + jy$ can be expressed in the form

$$z = r\cos\theta + jr\sin\theta = r(\cos\theta + j\sin\theta) \tag{3.3}$$

This is called the **polar form** of the complex number. In engineering it is frequently written as $r \angle \theta$, so that

$$z = r \angle \theta = r(\cos\theta + j\sin\theta)$$

Example 3.11 Express the following complex numbers in polar form.

(a) $12 + j5$ (b) $-3 + j4$ (c) $-4 - j3$

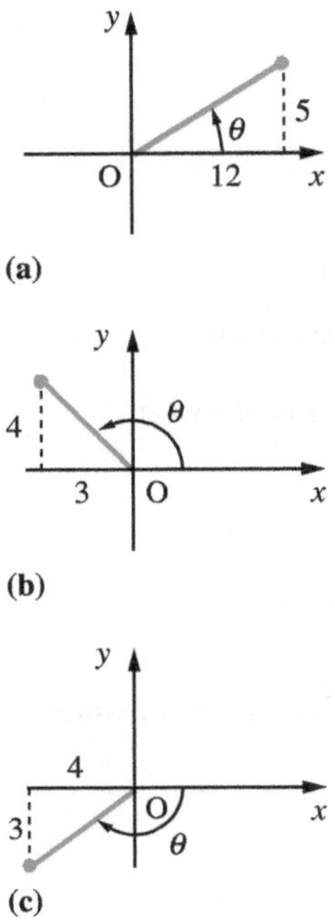

Figure 3.5

Solution (a) A sketch of the Argand diagram locating the position of $12 + j5$ is given in Figure 3.5(a). Thus

$$|12 + j5| = \sqrt{(144 + 25)} = 13$$

$$\arg(12 + j5) = \tan^{-1}\tfrac{5}{12} = 0.395$$

Thus in polar form

$$12 + j5 = 13[\cos(0.395) + j\sin(0.395)]$$

(b) A sketch of the Argand diagram locating the position of $-3 + j4$ is given in Figure 3.5(b). Thus

$$|-3 + j4| = \sqrt{(9 + 16)} = 5$$

$$\arg(-3 + j4) = \pi - \tan^{-1}\tfrac{4}{3} = \pi - 0.9273$$

$$= 2.214$$

Thus in polar form

$$-3 + j4 = 5[\cos(2.214) + j\sin(2.214)]$$

(c) A sketch of the Argand diagram locating the position of $-4 - j3$ is given in Figure 3.5(c). Thus

$$|-4 - j3| = \sqrt{(16 + 9)} = 5$$

$$\arg(-4 - j3) = -(\pi - \tan^{-1}\tfrac{3}{4}) = -(\pi - 0.643)$$

$$= -2.498$$

Thus in polar form

$$-4 - j3 = 5[\cos(-2.498) + j\sin(-2.498)]$$

$$= 5[\cos(2.498) - j\sin(2.498)]$$

using the results $\cos(-t) = \cos t$ and $\sin(-t) = -\sin t$.

Note: Rectangular to polar conversion can be done using a calculator and students are encouraged to check the answers in this way.

Multiplication in polar form

Let

$$z_1 = r_1(\cos\theta_1 + j\sin\theta_1) \quad \text{and} \quad z_2 = r_2(\cos\theta_2 + j\sin\theta_2)$$

then

$$z_1z_2 = r_1r_2(\cos\theta_1 + j\sin\theta_1)(\cos\theta_2 + j\sin\theta_2)$$

$$= r_1r_2[(\cos\theta_1\cos\theta_2 - \sin\theta_1\sin\theta_2) + j(\sin\theta_1\cos\theta_2 + \cos\theta_1\sin\theta_2)]$$

which, on using the trigonometric identities (2.24a, c), gives

$$z_1z_2 = r_1r_2[\cos(\theta_1 + \theta_2) + \mathrm{j}\sin(\theta_1 + \theta_2)] \tag{3.4}$$

Hence

$$|z_1z_2| = r_1r_2 = |z_1||z_2| \tag{3.5a}$$

and

$$\arg(z_1z_2) = \theta_1 + \theta_2 = \arg z_1 + \arg z_2 \tag{3.5b}$$

When using these results, care must be taken to ensure that $-\pi < \arg(z_1z_2) \leqslant \pi$.

Example 3.12

If $z_1 = -12 + \mathrm{j}5$ and $z_2 = -4 + \mathrm{j}3$, determine, using (3.5a) and (3.5b), $|z_1z_2|$ and $\arg(z_1z_2)$.

Solution

$$|z_1| = \sqrt{(144 + 25)} = \sqrt{(169)} = 13$$

$$\arg(z_1) = \pi - \tan^{-1}\tfrac{5}{12} = \pi - 0.395 = 2.747$$

$$|z_2| = \sqrt{(16 + 9)} = 5$$

$$\arg(z_2) = \pi - \tan^{-1}\tfrac{3}{4} = 2.498$$

Thus from (3.4) and (3.5)

$$|z_1z_2| = |z_1||z_2| = (13)(5) = 65$$

$$\arg(z_1z_2) = \arg z_1 + \arg z_2 = 2.747 + 2.498$$

$$= 5.245 \text{ (or } 300.51^\circ)$$

However, this does not express $\arg(z_1z_2)$ within the defined range $-\pi < \arg \leqslant \pi$. Thus

$$\arg(z_1z_2) = -2\pi + 5.245 = -1.038$$

Geometrical representation of multiplication by j

Since

$$z = r(\cos\theta + \mathrm{j}\sin\theta) \quad \text{and} \quad \mathrm{j} = 1(\cos\tfrac{1}{2}\pi + \mathrm{j}\sin\tfrac{1}{2}\pi)$$

it follows from (3.4) that

$$\mathrm{j}z = r[\cos(\theta + \tfrac{1}{2}\pi) + \mathrm{j}\sin(\theta + \tfrac{1}{2}\pi)]$$

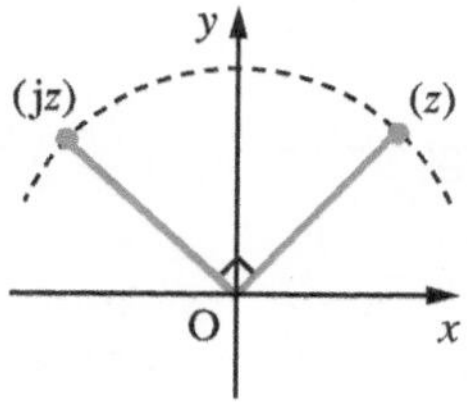

Figure 3.6 Relationship between z and jz.

Thus the effect of multiplying a complex number by j is to leave the modulus unaltered but to increase the argument by $\tfrac{1}{2}\pi$, as indicated in Figure 3.6. This property is of importance in the application of complex numbers to the theory of alternating current.

Division in polar form

Now

$$\frac{1}{\cos\theta + \mathrm{j}\sin\theta} = \frac{1}{\cos\theta + \mathrm{j}\sin\theta}\,\frac{\cos\theta - \mathrm{j}\sin\theta}{\cos\theta - \mathrm{j}\sin\theta}$$

$$= \frac{\cos\theta - \mathrm{j}\sin\theta}{\cos^2\theta + \sin^2\theta}$$

$$= \cos\theta - \mathrm{j}\sin\theta, \quad \text{since} \quad \cos^2\theta + \sin^2\theta = 1$$

Thus if

$$z_1 = r_1(\cos\theta_1 + \mathrm{j}\sin\theta_1) \quad \text{and} \quad z_2 = r_2(\cos\theta_2 + \mathrm{j}\sin\theta_2)$$

then

$$\frac{z_1}{z_2} = \frac{r_1(\cos\theta_1 + \mathrm{j}\sin\theta_1)}{r_2(\cos\theta_2 + \mathrm{j}\sin\theta_2)}$$

$$= \frac{r_1}{r_2}(\cos\theta_1 + \mathrm{j}\sin\theta_1)(\cos\theta_2 - \mathrm{j}\sin\theta_2) \quad \text{(from above)}$$

$$= \frac{r_1}{r_2}[(\cos\theta_1\cos\theta_2 + \sin\theta_1\sin\theta_2) + \mathrm{j}(\sin\theta_1\cos\theta_2 - \cos\theta_1\sin\theta_2)]$$

or

$$\frac{z_1}{z_2} = \frac{r_1}{r_2}[\cos(\theta_1 - \theta_2) + \mathrm{j}\sin(\theta_1 - \theta_2)] \tag{3.6}$$

using the trigonometric identities (2.25b, d). Hence

$$\left|\frac{z_1}{z_2}\right| = \frac{r_1}{r_2} = \frac{|z_1|}{|z_2|} \tag{3.7}$$

and

$$\arg\left(\frac{z_1}{z_2}\right) = \theta_1 - \theta_2 = \arg z_1 - \arg z_2 \tag{3.8}$$

Again some adjustment may be necessary to ensure that $-\pi < \arg(z_1/z_2) \leqslant \pi$.

Example 3.13 For the following pairs of complex numbers obtain z_1/z_2 and z_2/z_1.

(a) $z_1 = 4(\cos\pi/2 + \mathrm{j}\sin\pi/2), \quad z_2 = 9(\cos\pi/3 + \mathrm{j}\sin\pi/3)$

(b) $z_1 = \cos 3\pi/4 + \mathrm{j}\sin 3\pi/4, \quad z_2 = 2(\cos\pi/8 + \mathrm{j}\sin\pi/8)$

Solution (a) $|z_1| = 4, \quad \arg z_1 = \pi/2; \quad |z_2| = 9, \quad \arg z_2 = \pi/3$

From (3.7)

$$\left|\frac{z_1}{z_2}\right| = \frac{4}{9} \quad \text{and} \quad \left|\frac{z_2}{z_1}\right| = \frac{9}{4}$$

From (3.8)

$$\arg\left(\frac{z_1}{z_2}\right) = \frac{\pi}{2} - \frac{\pi}{3} = \frac{\pi}{6} \quad \text{and} \quad \arg\left(\frac{z_2}{z_1}\right) = \frac{\pi}{3} - \frac{\pi}{2} = -\frac{\pi}{6}$$

Thus $\dfrac{z_1}{z_2} = \dfrac{4}{9}\left(\cos\dfrac{\pi}{6} + \mathrm{j}\sin\dfrac{\pi}{6}\right)$

and $\dfrac{z_2}{z_1} = \dfrac{9}{4}\left(\cos\dfrac{\pi}{6} - \mathrm{j}\sin\dfrac{\pi}{6}\right)$

(b) $|z_1| = 1, \quad \arg z_1 = 3\pi/4; \quad |z_2| = 2, \quad \arg z_2 = \pi/8$

From (3.7)

$$\left|\frac{z_1}{z_2}\right| = \frac{1}{2} \quad \text{and} \quad \left|\frac{z_2}{z_1}\right| = 2$$

From (3.8)

$$\arg\left(\frac{z_1}{z_2}\right) = \frac{3\pi}{4} - \frac{\pi}{8} = \frac{5\pi}{8} \quad \text{and} \quad \arg\left(\frac{z_2}{z_1}\right) = \frac{\pi}{8} - \frac{3\pi}{4} = -\frac{5\pi}{8}$$

Thus $\dfrac{z_1}{z_2} = \dfrac{1}{2}\left(\cos\dfrac{5\pi}{8} + \mathrm{j}\sin\dfrac{5\pi}{8}\right)$

and $\dfrac{z_2}{z_1} = 2\left(\cos\dfrac{5\pi}{8} - \mathrm{j}\sin\dfrac{5\pi}{8}\right)$

Example 3.14 Find the modulus and argument of

$$z = \frac{(1 + \mathrm{j}2)^2(4 - \mathrm{j}3)^3}{(3 + \mathrm{j}4)^4(2 - \mathrm{j})^3}$$

Solution

$$|z| = \frac{|1 + \mathrm{j}2|^2|4 - \mathrm{j}3|^3}{|3 + \mathrm{j}4|^4|2 - \mathrm{j}|^3}$$

$$= \frac{[\sqrt{(1 + 4)}]^2[\sqrt{(16 + 9)}]^3}{[\sqrt{(9 + 16)}]^4[\sqrt{(4 + 1)}]^3} = \frac{1}{25}\sqrt{5}$$

$$\arg z = 2\arg(1 + \mathrm{j}2) + 3\arg(4 - \mathrm{j}3) - 4\arg(3 + \mathrm{j}4) - 3\arg(2 - \mathrm{j})$$

$$= 2(1.107) + 3(-0.643) - 4(0.927) - 3(-0.461) = -2.035$$

3.2.7 Euler's formula

In Section 2.7.3 we obtained the result

$$e^x = \cosh x + \sinh x$$

which links the exponential and hyperbolic functions. A similar, but more important, formula links the exponential and circular functions. It is

$$e^{j\theta} = \cos\theta + j\sin\theta \qquad \textbf{(3.9)}$$

This formula is known as **Euler's formula**. The justification for this definition depends on the following facts.

We know from the properties of the exponential function that

$$e^{j\theta_1}e^{j\theta_2} = e^{j(\theta_1+\theta_2)}$$

When expressed in terms of Euler's formula this becomes

$$(\cos\theta_1 + j\sin\theta_1)(\cos\theta_2 + j\sin\theta_2) = \cos(\theta_1 + \theta_2) + j\sin(\theta_1 + \theta_2)$$

which is just (3.4) with $r_1 = r_2 = 1$.

Similarly

$$\frac{e^{j\theta_1}}{e^{j\theta_2}} = e^{j(\theta_1-\theta_2)}$$

becomes

$$\frac{\cos\theta_1 + j\sin\theta_1}{\cos\theta_2 + j\sin\theta_2} = \cos(\theta_1 - \theta_2) + j\sin(\theta_1 - \theta_2)$$

which is just (3.6) with $r_1 = r_2 = 1$.

Euler's formula enables us to write down the polar form of the complex number z very concisely:

$$z = r(\cos\theta + j\sin\theta) = re^{j\theta} = r\angle\theta \qquad \textbf{(3.10)}$$

This is known as the **exponential form** of the complex number z.

Example 3.15 Express the following complex numbers in exponential form:

(a) $2 + j3$ (b) $-2 + j$

Solution (a) A sketch of the Argand diagram showing the position of $2 + j3$ is given in Figure 3.7(a).

$$|2 + j3| = \sqrt{(2^2 + 3^2)} = \sqrt{13}$$

$$\arg(2 + j3) = \tan^{-1}(3/2) = 0.9828$$

Thus $2 + j3 = \sqrt{13}e^{j0.9828}$

(b) A sketch of the Argand diagram showing the position of $-2 + j$ is given in Figure 3.7(b).

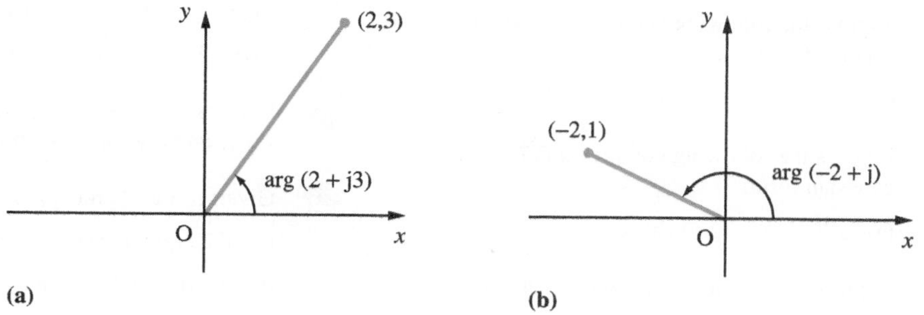

Figure 3.7
Argand diagrams for Example 3.15.

$$|-2 + j| = \sqrt{5}$$

$$\arg(-2 + j) = \pi - \tan^{-1}(1/2) = 2.6779$$

Thus $-2 + j = \sqrt{5}e^{j2.6779}$

Example 3.16 Express in cartesian form the complex number $e^{2+j\pi/3}$.

Solution $e^{2+j\pi/3} = e^2e^{j\pi/3} = e^2(\cos \pi/3 + j \sin \pi/3)$

Now $e^2 = 7.3891$, $\cos \pi/3 = 0.5$ and $\sin \pi/3 = 0.8660$, so that

$$e^{2+j\pi/3} = 3.6945 + j6.3991$$

Having determined the modulus `r` and argument `theta` of a complex number, its polar form is given in MATLAB by

```
r*(cos(theta) + i*sin(theta))
```

and its exponential form by

```
r*exp(i*theta)
```

3.2.8 Exercises

Check your answers using MATLAB or MAPLE whenever possible.

19 If $z_1 = 1 + j$ and $z_2 = \sqrt{3} + j$, determine $|z_1z_2|$, $|z_1/z_2|$, $\arg(z_1z_2)$ and $\arg(z_1/z_2)$.

20 For the following pairs of numbers obtain z_1z_2, z_1/z_2, and z_2/z_1:

(a) $z_1 = 2\left[\cos\left(\frac{3\pi}{4}\right) + j\sin\left(\frac{3\pi}{4}\right)\right]$

$z_2 = 8\left[\cos\left(\frac{\pi}{6}\right) + j\sin\left(\frac{\pi}{6}\right)\right]$

(b) $z_1 = 3\left[\cos\left(\frac{\pi}{3}\right) + j\sin\left(\frac{\pi}{3}\right)\right]$

$z_2 = 5\left[\cos\left(\frac{5\pi}{6}\right) + j\sin\left(\frac{5\pi}{6}\right)\right]$

21 Obtain the modulus and argument of z where

$$z = \frac{(2 + j)^3(-3 + j4)^2}{(12 - j5)^4(1 - j)^4}$$

and write z in the form $x + jy$.

22 Express the following complex numbers in exponential form:

(a) $3 + j4$ (b) $-1 + j\sqrt{3}$

23 Express the following complex numbers in cartesian form:

(a) $e^{3+j\frac{\pi}{4}}$ (b) $e^{-1+j\frac{\pi}{3}}$

24 Express in polar form the complex numbers

(a) j (b) 1

(c) -1 (d) $1 - j$

(e) $\sqrt{3} - j\sqrt{3}$ (f) $-2 + j$

(g) $-3 - j2$ (h) $7 - j5$

(i) $(2 - j)(2 + j)$ (j) $(-2 + j7)^2$

25 Express $z = (2 - j)(3 + j2)/(3 - j4)$ in the form $x + jy$ and also in polar form.

26 Given $z_1 = e^{j\pi/4}$ and $z_2 = e^{-j\pi/3}$, find

(a) the arguments of $z_1z_2^2$ and z_1^3/z_2

(b) the real and imaginary parts of $z_1^2 + jz_2$

27 Given $z_1 = 2e^{j\pi/3}$ and $z_2 = 4e^{-2j\pi/3}$, find the modulus and argument of

(a) $z_1^3z_2^2$ (b) $z_1^2z_2^4$ (c) z_1^2/z_2^3

3.2.9 Relationship between circular and hyperbolic functions

Euler's formula provides the theoretical link between circular and hyperbolic functions. Since

$$e^{j\theta} = \cos\theta + j\sin\theta \quad \text{and} \quad e^{-j\theta} = \cos\theta - j\sin\theta$$

we deduce that

$$\cos\theta = \frac{e^{j\theta} + e^{-j\theta}}{2} \tag{3.11a}$$

and

$$\sin\theta = \frac{e^{j\theta} - e^{-j\theta}}{2j} \tag{3.11b}$$

In Section 2.7 we defined the hyperbolic functions by

$$\cosh x = \frac{e^{x} + e^{-x}}{2} \tag{3.12a}$$

and

$$\sinh x = \frac{e^{x} - e^{-x}}{2} \tag{3.12b}$$

Comparing (3.12a, b) with (3.11a, b), we have

$$\cosh jx = \frac{e^{jx} + e^{-jx}}{2} = \cos x \tag{3.13a}$$

$$\sinh jx = \frac{e^{jx} - e^{-jx}}{2} = j\sin x \tag{3.13b}$$

so that

$$\tanh jx = j \tan x \tag{3.13c}$$

Also,

$$\cos jx = \frac{e^{j^2x} + e^{-j^2x}}{2} = \frac{e^{-x} + e^{x}}{2} = \cosh x \tag{3.14a}$$

$$\sin jx = \frac{e^{j^2x} - e^{-j^2x}}{2j} = \frac{e^{-x} - e^{x}}{2j} = j\sinh x \tag{3.14b}$$

so that

$$\tan jx = j \tanh x \tag{3.14c}$$

These relationships provide the justification for Osborn's rule used in Section 2.7.4 for obtaining hyperbolic function identities from those satisfied by circular functions, since whenever a product of two sines occurs, j^2 will also occur.

Using these results we can evaluate functions such as $\sin z$, $\cos z$, $\tan z$, $\sinh z$, $\cosh z$ and $\tanh z$. For example, to evaluate

$$\cos z = \cos(x + jy)$$

we use the identity

$$\cos(A + B) = \cos A \cos B - \sin A \sin B$$

and obtain

$$\cos z = \cos x \cos jy - \sin x \sin jy$$

Using results (3.14a, b), this gives

$$\cos z = \cos x \cosh y - j \sin x \sinh y$$

Example 3.17

Find the values of

(a) $\sin[\frac{1}{4}\pi(1 + j)]$ (b) $\sinh(3 + j4)$

(c) $\tan(\frac{\pi}{4} - j3)$ (d) z such that $\cos z = 2$

(e) z such that $\tanh z = 2$

Solution

(a) We may use the identity

$$\sin(A + B) = \sin A \cos B + \cos A \sin B$$

and obtain

$$\sin(\tfrac{1}{4}\pi + j\tfrac{1}{4}\pi) = \sin \tfrac{1}{4}\pi \cos j\tfrac{1}{4}\pi + \cos \tfrac{1}{4}\pi \sin j\tfrac{1}{4}\pi$$

Here $\sin \frac{1}{4}\pi$ and $\cos \frac{1}{4}\pi$ are evaluated as usual $(= \sqrt{\frac{1}{2}})$, while we make use of results (3.14a, b) to obtain

$$\cos j\tfrac{1}{4}\pi = \cosh \tfrac{1}{4}\pi \text{ and } \sin j\tfrac{1}{4}\pi = j \sinh \tfrac{1}{4}\pi$$

giving

$$\sin[\tfrac{1}{4}\pi(1+\mathrm{j})] = \sin\tfrac{1}{4}\pi\cosh\tfrac{1}{4}\pi + \mathrm{j}\cos\tfrac{1}{4}\pi\sinh\tfrac{1}{4}\pi$$
$$= (0.7071)(1.3246) + \mathrm{j}(0.7071)(0.8687)$$
$$= 0.9366 + \mathrm{j}0.6142$$

(b) Using the identity

$$\sinh(A+B) = \sinh A\cosh B + \cosh A\sinh B$$

we obtain

$$\sinh(3+\mathrm{j}4) = \sinh 3\cosh \mathrm{j}4 + \cosh 3\sinh \mathrm{j}4$$

which, on using results (3.13a, b), gives

$$\sinh(3+\mathrm{j}4) = \sinh 3\cos 4 + \mathrm{j}\cosh 3\sin 4$$
$$= (10.0179)(-0.6536) + \mathrm{j}(10.0677)(-0.7568)$$
$$= -6.548 - \mathrm{j}7.619$$

(c) Using the identity

$$\tan(A-B) = \frac{\tan A - \tan B}{1+\tan A\tan B}$$

we obtain

$$\tan(\tfrac{1}{4}\pi - \mathrm{j}3) = \frac{\tan\tfrac{1}{4}\pi - \tan \mathrm{j}3}{1+\tan\tfrac{1}{4}\pi\tan \mathrm{j}3}$$

which, on using result (3.14c) and $\tan\frac{1}{4}\pi = 1$, gives

$$\tan(\tfrac{1}{4}\pi - \mathrm{j}3) = \frac{1-\mathrm{j}\tanh 3}{1+\mathrm{j}\tanh 3} = \frac{(1-\mathrm{j}\tanh 3)^2}{1+\tanh^2 3}$$
$$= \frac{1-\tanh^2 3}{1+\tanh^2 3} - \mathrm{j}\frac{2\tanh 3}{1+\tanh^2 3}$$
$$= \frac{1}{\cosh^2 3+\sinh^2 3} - \mathrm{j}\frac{2\sinh 3\cosh 3}{\cosh^2 3+\sinh^2 3}$$
$$= \frac{1}{\cosh 6} + \mathrm{j}\frac{\sinh 6}{\cosh 6} = 0.005 - \mathrm{j}1.000$$

(d) Writing $z = x + \mathrm{j}y$, we have

$$2 = \cos(x+\mathrm{j}y)$$

Expanding the right-hand side gives

$$2 = \cos x\cos \mathrm{j}y - \sin x\sin \mathrm{j}y$$
$$= \cos x\cosh y - \sin x\,(\mathrm{j}\sinh y)$$
$$2 = \cos x\cosh y - \mathrm{j}\sin x\sinh y$$

Equating real and imaginary parts of each side of this equation gives

$$2 = \cos x \cosh y$$

and

$$0 = \sin x \sinh y$$

The latter equation implies either $\sin x = 0$ or $y = 0$. If $y = 0$ then the first equation implies $2 = \cos x$, so clearly that is not a solution since x is a real number . The alternative, $\sin x = 0$, implies $x = 0, \pm\pi, \pm 2\pi, \pm 3\pi, \ldots$, and hence

$$2 = \cos(\pm n\pi) \cosh y, \quad n = 0, 1, 2, \ldots$$

This gives

$$\begin{aligned} 2 &= \cos n\pi \cosh y \\ &= (-1)^n \cosh y \end{aligned}$$

But $\cosh y \geqslant 1$, so n must be an even number. Thus the values of z such that $\cos z = 2$ are

$$\begin{aligned} z &= \pm 2n\pi \pm \mathrm{j} \cosh^{-1} 2, \; n = 0, 1, 2, \ldots \\ &= \pm 2n\pi \pm \mathrm{j}(1.3170) \end{aligned}$$

(e) Writing $z = x + \mathrm{j}y$ we obtain

$$\tanh(x + \mathrm{j}y) = 2$$

which implies

$$\sinh(x + \mathrm{j}y) = 2 \cosh(x + \mathrm{j}y)$$

Expanding both sides we have

$$\sinh x \cosh \mathrm{j}y + \cosh x \sinh \mathrm{j}y = 2 \cosh x \cosh \mathrm{j}y + 2 \sinh x \sinh \mathrm{j}y$$

or

$$\sinh x \cos y + \mathrm{j} \cosh x \sin y = 2 \cosh x \cos y + 2\mathrm{j} \sinh x \sin y$$

Equating real and imaginary parts we obtain

$$\sinh x \cos y = 2 \cosh x \cos y$$

$$\cosh x \sin y = 2 \sinh x \sin y.$$

Since $\sinh x \neq 2 \cosh x$ for real values of x, $\cos y = 0$ so that

$$y = (2n + 1)\pi/2 \text{ for } n = 0, \pm 1, \pm 2, \ldots$$

This implies that $\sin y \neq 0$, so that $\tanh z = \frac{1}{2}$. Thus

$$\begin{aligned} z &= \tanh^{-1}\tfrac{1}{2} + \mathrm{j}\tfrac{2n+1}{2}\pi, \; n = 0, \pm 1, \pm 2, \ldots \\ &= \tfrac{1}{2}\ln 3 + \mathrm{j}\tfrac{2n+1}{2}\pi, \quad n = 0, \pm 1, \pm 2, \ldots \end{aligned}$$

using the identity 2.44.

3.2.10 Logarithm of a complex number

Consider the equation

$$z = e^w$$

Writing $z = x + jy$ and $w = u + jv$, we have

$$x + jy = e^{u+jv} = e^u e^{jv}$$

$$= e^u(\cos v + j \sin v), \quad \text{by Euler's formula}$$

Equating real and imaginary parts,

$$x = e^u \cos v \quad \text{and} \quad y = e^u \sin v$$

Squaring both these equations and adding gives

$$x^2 + y^2 = e^{2u}(\cos^2 v + \sin^2 v) = e^{2u}$$

so that

$$u = \tfrac{1}{2} \ln(x^2 + y^2) = \ln |z|$$

Dividing the two equations,

$$\tan v = \frac{y}{x}$$

From this and $x = e^u \cos v$

$$v = \arg z + 2n\pi, \quad n = 0, \pm 1, \pm 2, \ldots$$

Hence

$$v = \ln |z| + j \arg z + j2n\pi, \quad n = 0, \pm 1, \pm 2, \ldots$$

We select just one of these solutions to define for us the logarithm of the complex number z, writing

$$\ln z = \ln |z| + j \arg z \qquad \textbf{(3.15)}$$

This is sometimes called its **principal value**.

Example 3.18 Evaluate $\ln(-3 + j4)$ in the form $x + jy$.

Solution

$$|-3 + j4| = \sqrt{(9 + 16)} = 5$$

$$\arg(-3 + j4) = \pi - \tan^{-1} \tfrac{4}{3} = 2.214$$

Thus from (3.15)

$$\ln(-3 + j4) = \ln 5 + j2.214 = 1.609 + j2.214$$

In MATLAB functions of a complex variable can be evaluated as easily as functions of a real variable. For example, in relation to Example 3.17 (a) and (b), entering

`sin((pi/4)*(1 + i))` returns the answer `0.9366 + 0.6142i`

whilst entering

`sinh(3 + 4i)` returns the answer `-6.5481 - 7.6192i`

confirming the answers obtained in the given solution. Similarly, considering Example 3.18, entering

`log(-3 + 4i)` returns the answer `1.6094 + 2.2143i`

confirming the answer obtained in the solution. In MAPLE, functions of a complex variable must be evaluated using *evalc*. The result is exact and the numerical values require *evalf*; for example

```
evalc(sin((Pi/4)*(1 + I)));
```

returns

$\frac{1}{2}\sqrt{2}\cosh(\frac{1}{4}\pi) + \frac{1}{2}\sqrt{2}\,I\sinh(\frac{1}{4}\pi)$

and `evalf(%);` returns `0.9366 + 0.6142I.`

3.2.11 Exercises

Check your answers using MATLAB or MAPLE whenever possible.

28 Using the exponential forms of $\cos\theta$ and $\sin\theta$ given in (3.11a, b), prove the following trigonometric identities:

(a) $\sin(\alpha+\beta) = \sin\alpha\cos\beta + \cos\alpha\sin\beta$

(b) $\sin^3\theta = \frac{3}{4}\sin\theta - \frac{1}{4}\sin 3\theta$

29 Express in the form $x + jy$

(a) $\sin(\frac{5}{6}\pi + j)$ (b) $\cos(j\frac{3}{4})$

(c) $\sinh[\frac{\pi}{3}(1 + j)]$ (d) $\cosh(j\frac{\pi}{4})$

30 Solve $z = x + jy$ when

(a) $\sin z = 2$ (b) $\cos z = j\frac{3}{4}$

(c) $\sin z = 3$ (d) $\cosh z = -2$

31 Show that

(a) $\ln(5 + j12) = \ln 13 + j1.176$

(b) $\ln(-\frac{1}{2} - j\frac{1}{2}\sqrt{3}) = -j\frac{2\pi}{3}$

32 Writing $\tanh(u + jv) = x + jy$, with x, y, u and v real, determine x and y in terms of u and v. Hence evaluate $\tanh(2 + j\frac{1}{4}\pi)$ in the form $x + jy$.

33 In a certain cable of length l the current I_0 at the sending end when it is raised to a potential V_0 and the other end is earthed is given by

$$I_0 = \frac{V_0}{Z_0}\tanh Pl$$

Calculate the value of I_0 when $V_0 = 100$, $Z_0 = 500 + j400$, $l = 10$ and $P = 0.1 + j0.15$.

3.3 Powers of complex numbers

In earlier sections we have discussed the extensions of ordinary arithmetic, including $+, -, \times, \div$, to complex numbers. We now extend the arithmetical operations to include the operation of powers.

3.3.1 De Moivre's theorem

From (3.10) a complex number z may be expressed in terms of its modulus r and argument θ in the exponential form

$$z = re^{j\theta}$$

Using the rules of indices and the property (2.33a) of the exponential function, we have, for any n,

$$z^n = r^n(e^{j\theta})^n = r^n e^{j(n\theta)}$$

so that

$$z^n = r^n(\cos n\theta + j \sin n\theta) \qquad \textbf{(3.16)}$$

This result is known as **de Moivre's theorem**.

Example 3.19 Express $1 - j$ in the form $r(\cos\theta + j\sin\theta)$ and hence evaluate $(1 - j)^{12}$.

Solution From Example 3.7(b)

$$|1 - j| = \sqrt{2} \quad \text{and} \quad \arg(1 - j) = -\tfrac{1}{4}\pi$$

so that

$$\begin{aligned} 1 - j &= \sqrt{2}[\cos(-\tfrac{1}{4}\pi) + j\sin(-\tfrac{1}{4}\pi)] \\ &= \sqrt{2}(\cos\tfrac{1}{4}\pi - j\sin\tfrac{1}{4}\pi) \end{aligned}$$

Then

$$(1 - j)^{12} = (\sqrt{2})^{12}(\cos\tfrac{1}{4}\pi - j\sin\tfrac{1}{4}\pi)^{12}$$

which, on using de Moivre's theorem (3.16), gives

$$\begin{aligned} (1 - j)^{12} &= 2^6[\cos(12 \times \tfrac{1}{4}\pi) - j\sin(12 \times \tfrac{1}{4}\pi)] \\ &= 2^6(\cos 3\pi - j\sin 3\pi) \\ &= 2^6(-1 - j0) \\ &= -64 \end{aligned}$$

Most commonly, we use de Moivre's theorem to find the roots of complex numbers like $\sqrt{z}$ and $\sqrt[3]{z}$. More generally, we want to find $z^{1/n}$, the nth root, where n is a natural number. Setting $w = z^{1/n}$, we see that $z = w^n$, and by (3.16),

$$w^n = R^n(\cos n\phi + \mathrm{j}\sin n\phi), \quad \text{where } |w| = R \text{ and } \arg w = \phi$$

$$z = r(\cos\theta + \mathrm{j}\sin\theta), \quad \text{where } |z| = r \text{ and } \arg z = \theta$$

Comparing real and imaginary parts in the equality $z = w^n$, we deduce that

$$r\cos\theta = R^n\cos n\phi$$

and

$$r\sin\theta = R^n\sin n\phi$$

Squaring and adding these two equations gives $r^2 = R^{2n}$; that is, $R = r^{1/n}$. Substituting this value into the equations gives

$$\cos\theta = \cos n\phi$$

and

$$\sin\theta = \sin n\phi$$

This pair of simultaneous equations has an infinite number of solutions because of the 2π-periodicity of the sine and cosine functions. Thus

$$n\phi = \theta + 2\pi k, \quad \text{where } k \text{ is an integer}$$

and

$$\phi = \frac{\theta}{n} + \frac{2\pi k}{n}, \quad \text{where } k = 0, 1, -1, 2, -2, 3, -3, \ldots$$

Substituting these values for R and ϕ into the formula for w gives

$$z^{1/n} = r^{1/n}\left[\cos\left(\frac{\theta}{n} + \frac{2\pi k}{n}\right) + \mathrm{j}\sin\left(\frac{\theta}{n} + \frac{2\pi k}{n}\right)\right] \quad \mathbf{(3.17)}$$

where k is an integer. This expression yields exactly n different roots, corresponding to $k = 0, 1, 2, \ldots, n - 1$. The value for $k = n$ is the same as that for $k = 0$, the value for $k = n + 1$ is the same as that for $k = 1$, and so on. The n values of $z^{1/n}$ are equally spaced around a circle of radius $r^{1/n}$ whose centre is the origin of the Argand diagram. Also, the arguments increase in arithmetic progression, so that joining the roots on the circle creates a regular polygon inscribed in the latter.

Equation (3.17) may be written alternatively in the exponential form

$$z^{1/n} = r^{1/n}\mathrm{e}^{\mathrm{j}(\theta/n + 2\pi k/n)}, \quad k = 0, 1, 2, \ldots, n - 1 \quad \mathbf{(3.18)}$$

Example 3.20

Given $z = -\frac{1}{2} + \mathrm{j}\frac{1}{2}$, evaluate

(a) $z^{1/2}$ (b) $z^{1/3}$

and display the roots on an Argand diagram.

Solution

We first express z in polar form.

Since $r = |z| = \sqrt{(\frac{1}{4} + \frac{1}{4})} = 2^{-1/2}$, and $\theta = \arg(z) = \pi - \tan^{-1}1 = \frac{3}{4}\pi$, we have

$$z = 2^{-1/2}(\cos\tfrac{3}{4}\pi + \mathrm{j}\sin\tfrac{3}{4}\pi)$$

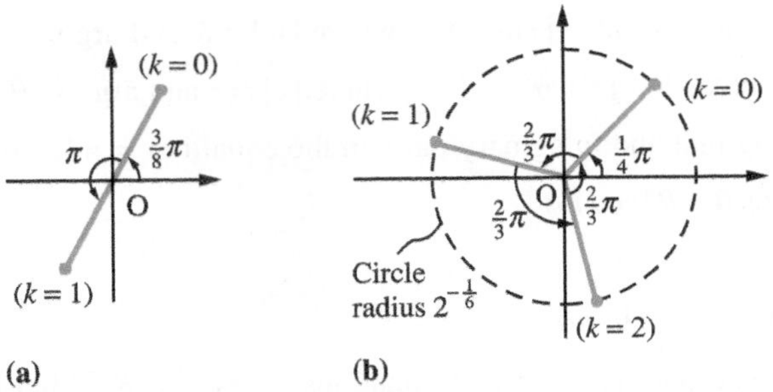

Figure 3.8 Roots on an Argand diagram for Example 3.20.

(a) From (3.17)

$$z^{1/2} = r^{1/2}\left[\cos\left(\frac{\theta}{2} + \frac{2\pi k}{2}\right) + \mathrm{j}\sin\left(\frac{\theta}{2} + \frac{2\pi k}{2}\right)\right], \quad k = 0, 1$$

$$= 2^{-1/4}[\cos(\tfrac{3}{8}\pi + \pi k) + \mathrm{j}\sin(\tfrac{3}{8}\pi + \pi k)], \quad k = 0, 1$$

Thus we have two square roots:

$$z^{1/2} = 2^{-1/4}(\cos \tfrac{3}{8}\pi + \mathrm{j}\sin \tfrac{3}{8}\pi) \quad (\text{for } k = 0)$$

and

$$z^{1/2} = 2^{-1/4}(\cos \tfrac{11}{8}\pi + \mathrm{j}\sin \tfrac{11}{8}\pi) \quad (\text{for } k = 1)$$

as shown in Figure 3.8(a). These can be evaluated numerically, giving respectively (to 4dp) $z = 0.3218 + \mathrm{j}0.7769$ and $z = -0.3218 - \mathrm{j}0.7769$.

(b) From (3.17)

$$z^{1/3} = r^{1/3}\left[\cos\left(\frac{\theta}{3} + \frac{2\pi k}{3}\right) + \mathrm{j}\sin\left(\frac{\theta}{3} + \frac{2\pi k}{3}\right)\right], \quad k = 0, 1, 2$$

$$= 2^{-1/6}[\cos(\tfrac{1}{4}\pi + \tfrac{2}{3}\pi k) + \mathrm{j}\sin(\tfrac{1}{4}\pi + \tfrac{2}{3}\pi k)], \quad k = 0, 1, 2$$

Thus we obtain three cube roots:

$$z^{1/3} = 2^{-1/6}(\cos \tfrac{1}{4}\pi + \mathrm{j}\sin \tfrac{1}{4}\pi) \quad (\text{for } k = 0)$$

$$z^{1/3} = 2^{-1/6}(\cos \tfrac{11}{12}\pi + \mathrm{j}\sin \tfrac{11}{12}\pi) \quad (\text{for } k = 1)$$

and

$$z^{1/3} = 2^{-1/6}(\cos \tfrac{19}{12}\pi + \mathrm{j}\sin \tfrac{19}{12}\pi) \quad (\text{for } k = 2)$$

as shown in Figure 3.8(b). Note that the three roots are equally spaced around a circle of radius $2^{-1/6}$ with centre at the origin.

Formula (3.17) can easily be extended to deal with the general rational power z^p of z. Let $p = \dfrac{m}{n}$, where n is a natural number and m is an integer, then

$$
\begin{aligned}
z^p &= (z^{1/n})^m \\
&= \left\{ r^{1/n}\left[\cos\left(\frac{\theta}{n} + \frac{2\pi k}{n}\right) + \mathrm{j}\sin\left(\frac{\theta}{n} + \frac{2\pi k}{n}\right)\right]\right\}^m, \quad k = 0, 1, 2, \dots, (n-1) \\
&= r^{m/n}\left[\cos\left(\frac{m\theta}{n} + \frac{2\pi km}{n}\right) + \mathrm{j}\sin\left(\frac{m\theta}{n} + \frac{2\pi km}{n}\right)\right] \\
&= r^p[\cos(p\theta + 2\pi kp) + \mathrm{j}\sin(p\theta + 2\pi kp)], \quad k = 0, 1, 2, \dots, (n-1)
\end{aligned}
$$

Example 3.21 Evaluate $(-\frac{1}{2} + \mathrm{j}\frac{1}{2})^{-2/3}$ and display the roots on an Argand diagram.

Solution From Example 3.17, we can write

$$-\tfrac{1}{2} + \mathrm{j}\tfrac{1}{2} = 2^{-1/2}(\cos\tfrac{3}{4}\pi + \mathrm{j}\sin\tfrac{3}{4}\pi)$$

giving

$$
\begin{aligned}
z^{-2/3} &= r^{-2/3}\left[\cos\left(-\frac{2\theta}{3} - \frac{4\pi k}{3}\right) + \mathrm{j}\sin\left(-\frac{2\theta}{3} - \frac{4\pi k}{3}\right)\right], \quad k = 0, 1, 2 \\
&= 2^{1/3}[\cos(-\tfrac{1}{2}\pi - \tfrac{4}{3}\pi k) + \mathrm{j}\sin(-\tfrac{1}{2}\pi - \tfrac{4}{3}\pi k)], \quad k = 0, 1, 2
\end{aligned}
$$

Thus we obtain three values:

$$z^{-2/3} = 2^{1/3}[\cos(-\tfrac{1}{2}\pi) + \mathrm{j}\sin(-\tfrac{1}{2}\pi)] \quad (\text{for } k = 0)$$

$$z^{-2/3} = 2^{1/3}(\cos\tfrac{1}{6}\pi + \mathrm{j}\sin\tfrac{1}{6}\pi) \quad (\text{for } k = 1)$$

and

$$z^{-2/3} = 2^{1/3}(\cos\tfrac{5}{6}\pi + \mathrm{j}\sin\tfrac{5}{6}\pi) \quad (\text{for } k = 2)$$

as shown in Figure 3.9.

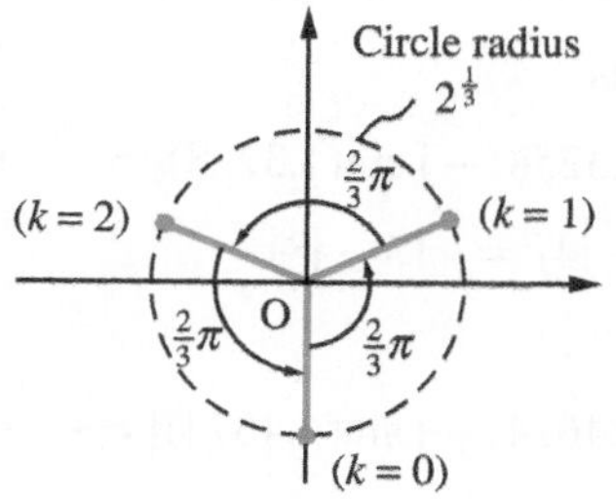

Figure 3.9 Roots on an Argand diagram for Example 3.2.1.

Example 3.22 Solve the quadratic equation

$$z^2 + (2\mathrm{j} - 3)z + (5 - \mathrm{j}) = 0$$

Solution Using formula (1.5)

$$z = \frac{-(2\mathrm{j} - 3) \pm \sqrt{[(2\mathrm{j} - 3)^2 - 4(5 - \mathrm{j})]}}{2}$$

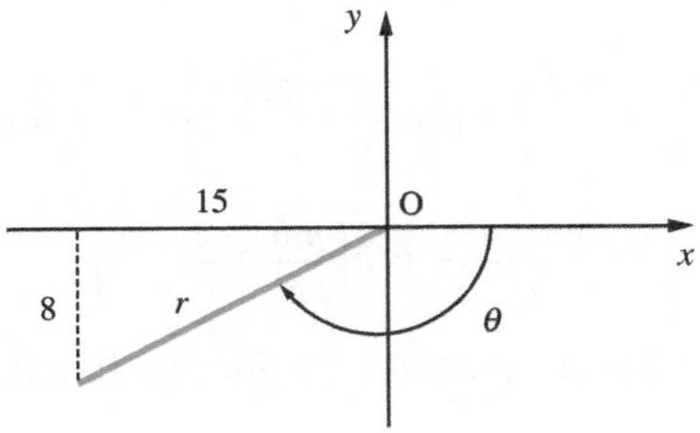

Figure 3.10
The complex number $-15 - j8$.

that is,

$$z = \frac{-(2j - 3) \pm \sqrt{(-15 - j8)}}{2} \quad \textbf{(3.19)}$$

Now we need to determine $(-15 - j8)^{1/2}$ so first we express it in polar form. Since

$$|-15 - j8| = \sqrt{[(15)^2 + (8)^2]} = 17$$

and from Figure 3.10

$$\arg(-15 - j8) = -(\pi - \tan^{-1}\tfrac{8}{15})$$
$$= -2.6516$$

we have

$$-15 - j8 = 17[\cos(2.6516) - j\sin(2.6516)]$$

From (3.17)

$$(-15 - j8)^{1/2} = (17)^{1/2}\left[\cos\left(\frac{2.6516}{2} + \frac{2\pi k}{2}\right) - j\sin\left(\frac{2.6516}{2} + \frac{2\pi k}{2}\right)\right]$$
$$= (17)^{1/2}[\cos(1.3258 + \pi k) - j\sin(1.3258 + \pi k)], \quad k = 0, 1$$

Thus we have the two square roots

$$(-15 - j8)^{1/2} = (17)^{1/2}[\cos(1.3258) - j\sin(1.3258)] = 1 - j4 \quad (\text{for } k = 0)$$

(the reader should verify that $(1 - j4)^2 = -15 - j8$)

and

$$(-15 - j8)^{1/2} = (17)^{1/2}[\cos(4.4674) - j\sin(4.4674)] = -1 + j4 \quad (\text{for } k = 1)$$

Substituting back in (3.19) gives the roots of the quadratic as

$$z = 2 - j3 \quad \text{and} \quad 1 + j$$

3.3.2 Powers of trigonometric functions and multiple angles

Euler's formula may be used to express $\sin^n\theta$ and $\cos^n\theta$ in terms of sines and cosines of multiple angles. If $z = \cos\theta + j\sin\theta$ then

$$z^n = \cos n\theta + j\sin n\theta$$

and

$$z^{-n} = \cos n\theta - \mathrm{j}\sin n\theta$$

so that

$$z^n + z^{-n} = 2\cos n\theta \tag{3.20a}$$

$$z^n - z^{-n} = 2\mathrm{j}\sin n\theta \tag{3.20b}$$

Using these results, $\cos^n\theta$ and $\sin^n\theta$ can be expressed in terms of sines and cosines of multiple angles, as illustrated in Example 3.23.

Example 3.23

Expand in terms of sines and cosines of multiple angles

(a) $\cos^5\theta$ (b) $\sin^6\theta$

Solution

(a) Using (3.20a) with $n = 1$,

$$(2\cos\theta)^5 = \left(z + \frac{1}{z}\right)^5 = z^5 + 5z^3 + 10z + \frac{10}{z} + \frac{5}{z^3} + \frac{1}{z^5}$$

so that

$$32\cos^5\theta = \left(z^5 + \frac{1}{z^5}\right) + 5\left(z^3 + \frac{1}{z^3}\right) + 10\left(z + \frac{1}{z}\right)$$

which, on using (3.20a) with $n = 5$, 3 and 1, gives

$$\cos^5\theta = \tfrac{1}{32}(2\cos 5\theta + 10\cos 3\theta + 20\cos\theta) = \tfrac{1}{16}(\cos 5\theta + 5\cos 3\theta + 10\cos\theta)$$

(b) Using (3.20b) with $n = 1$,

$$(2\mathrm{j}\sin\theta)^6 = \left(z - \frac{1}{z}\right)^6 = z^6 - 6z^4 + 15z^2 - 20 + \frac{15}{z^2} - \frac{6}{z^4} + \frac{1}{z^6}$$

which, on noting that $\mathrm{j}^6 = -1$, gives

$$-64\sin^6\theta = \left(z^6 + \frac{1}{z^6}\right) - 6\left(z^4 + \frac{1}{z^4}\right) + 15\left(z^2 + \frac{1}{z^2}\right) - 20$$

Using (3.20a) with $n = 6$, 4 and 2 then gives

$$\sin^6\theta = -\tfrac{1}{64}(2\cos 6\theta - 12\cos 4\theta + 30\cos 2\theta - 20)$$

$$= \tfrac{1}{32}(10 - 15\cos 2\theta + 6\cos 4\theta - \cos 6\theta)$$

Conversely, de Moivre's theorem may be used to expand $\cos n\theta$ and $\sin n\theta$, where n is a positive integer, as polynomials in $\cos\theta$ and $\sin\theta$. From the theorem

$$\cos n\theta + \mathrm{j}\sin n\theta = (\cos\theta + \mathrm{j}\sin\theta)^n$$

we obtain, writing $s = \sin\theta$ and $c = \cos\theta$ for convenience,

$$\cos n\theta + \mathrm{j}\sin n\theta = (c + \mathrm{j}s)^n = c^n + \mathrm{j}nc^{n-1}s + \mathrm{j}^2\frac{n(n-1)}{2!}c^{n-2}s^2 + \ldots + \mathrm{j}^n s^n$$

Equating real and imaginary parts yields

$$\cos n\theta = c^n - \frac{n(n-1)}{2!}c^{n-2}s^2 + \frac{n(n-1)(n-2)(n-3)}{4!}c^{n-4}s^4 + \dots$$

and

$$\sin n\theta = nc^{n-1}s - \frac{n(n-1)(n-2)}{3!}c^{n-3}s^3 + \dots$$

Using the trigonometric identity $\cos^2\theta = 1 - \sin^2\theta$ (so that $c^2 = 1 - s^2$), we see that

(a) $\cos n\theta$ can be expanded in terms of $(\cos\theta)^n$ for any n or in terms of $(\sin\theta)^n$ if n is even;

(b) $\sin n\theta$ can be expanded in terms of $(\sin\theta)^n$ if n is odd.

Example 3.24 Expand $\cos 4\theta$ as a polynomial in $\cos\theta$.

Solution By de Moivre's theorem,

$$\begin{aligned}(\cos 4\theta + \text{j}\sin 4\theta) &= (\cos\theta + \text{j}\sin\theta)^4 = (c + \text{j}s)^4 \\ &= c^4 + \text{j}4c^3s + \text{j}^2 6c^2s^2 + \text{j}^3 4cs^3 + \text{j}^4 s^4 \\ &= c^4 + \text{j}4c^3s - 6c^2s^2 - \text{j}4cs^3 + s^4\end{aligned}$$

Equating real parts,

$$\cos 4\theta = c^4 - 6c^2s^2 + s^4$$

which on using $s^2 = 1 - c^2$ gives

$$\cos 4\theta = c^4 - 6c^2(1 - c^2) + (1 - c^2)^2 = 8c^4 - 8c^2 + 1$$

Thus

$$\cos 4\theta = 8\cos^4\theta - 8\cos^2\theta + 1$$

Note that by equating imaginary parts we could have obtained a polynomial expansion for $\sin 4\theta$.

In MATLAB, raising to a power is obtained using the standard operator ^. For example, considering Example 3.19, entering

`(1 - i)^12` returns the answer `-64`

as determined in the given solution. Considering Example 3.20(a), entering the commands

```
z = -1/2 + (1/2)*i; z1 = z^1/2
```

returns

```
z1 = 0.3218 + 0.7769i
```

which is the root corresponding to $k = 0$. From knowledge that the two roots are equally spaced around a circle the second root may be easily written down.

In Example 3.22 the solution may be obtained symbolically using the `solve` command. Entering

```
syms z
solve(z^2 + (2*i - 3)*z + (5 - i))
```

returns the answer

```
2 - 3*i
1 + i
```

which checks with the answer given in the solution.

Expanding in terms of sines and cosines of multiple angles may be undertaken symbolically using the `expand` command. For example, considering Example 3.24 the commands

```
syms theta
expand(cos(4*theta))
```

return the answer

```
8*cos(theta)^4 - 8*cos(theta)^2 + 1
```

which checks with the answer obtained in the given solution.

With the usual small modifications, MAPLE uses the same instructions.

3.3.3 Exercises

Check your answer using MATLAB or MAPLE whenever possible.

34 Use de Moivre's theorem to calculate the third and fourth powers of the complex numbers

(a) $1 + \mathrm{j}$ (b) $\sqrt{3} - \mathrm{j}$ (c) $-3 + \mathrm{j}4$

(d) $1 - \mathrm{j}\sqrt{3}$ (e) $-1 + \mathrm{j}\sqrt{3}$ (f) $-1 - \mathrm{j}\sqrt{3}$

(The moduli and arguments of these numbers were found in Exercises 3.2.5, Question 11.)

35 Expand in terms of multiple angles

(a) $\cos^4\theta$ (b) $\sin^3\theta$

36 Use the method of Section 3.3.2 to prove the following results:

(a) $\sin 3\theta = 3\cos^2\theta \sin\theta - \sin^3\theta$

(b) $\cos 8\theta = 128\cos^8\theta - 256\cos^6\theta + 160\cos^4\theta - 32\cos^2\theta + 1$

(c) $\tan 5\theta = \dfrac{5\tan\theta - 10\tan^3\theta + \tan^5\theta}{1 - 10\tan^2\theta + 5\tan^4\theta}$

37 Find the three values of $(8 + \mathrm{j}8)^{1/3}$ and show them on an Argand diagram.

38 Find the following complex numbers in their polar forms:

(a) $(\sqrt{3} - \mathrm{j})^{1/4}$ (b) $(\mathrm{j}8)^{1/3}$

(c) $(3 - \mathrm{j}3)^{-2/3}$ (d) $(-1)^{1/4}$

(e) $(2 + \mathrm{j}2)^{4/3}$ (f) $(5 - \mathrm{j}3)^{-1/2}$

39 Obtain the four solutions of the equation

$$z^4 = 3 - \mathrm{j}4$$

giving your answers to three decimal places.

40 Solve the quadratic equation

$$z^2 - (3 + \mathrm{j}5)z + \mathrm{j}8 - 5 = 0$$

41 Find the values of $z^{1/3}$, where $z = \cos 2\pi + \mathrm{j}\sin 2\pi$. Generalize this to an expression for $1^{1/n}$. Hence solve the equations

(a) $\left[\dfrac{z-2}{z+2}\right]^5 = 1$ (*Hint*: First show that there are only 4 roots)

(b) $(z - 3)^6 - z^6 = 0$

3.4 Loci in the complex plane

A **locus** (plural **loci**) is the set of points that have a specified property. For example, a circle is the locus of the points in a plane that are a fixed distance, its radius, from a fixed point, its centre. The property may be specified in words or algebraically. Loci occur frequently in engineering contexts, from the design of safety guards around moving machinery to the design of aircraft wing sections. The Argand diagram representation of complex numbers as points on a plane often makes it possible to represent complicated loci very concisely in terms of a complex variable, and this simplifies the engineering analysis. This occurs in a wide range of engineering problems, from the water percolation through dams to the design of microelectronic devices.

3.4.1 Straight lines

There are many ways in which straight lines may be represented using complex numbers. We will illustrate these with a number of examples.

Example 3.25

Describe the locus of z given by

(a) $\text{Re}(z) = 4$ (b) $\arg(z - 1 - j) = \pi/4$

(c) $\left|\frac{z - j2}{z - 1}\right| = 1$ (d) $\text{Im}((1 - j2)z) = 3$

Solution

(a) Here $z = 4 + jy$ for any real y, so that the locus is the vertical straight line with equation $x = 4$ illustrated in Figure 3.11(a).

(b) Here $z = 1 + j + r(\cos \pi/4 + j \sin \pi/4)$ for any positive (> 0) real number r, so that the locus is a half-line making an angle $\pi/4$ with the positive x direction with the end point (1, 1) *excluded* (since arg 0 is not defined). Algebraically we can write it as $y = x$, $x > 1$, and it is illustrated in Figure 3.11(b).

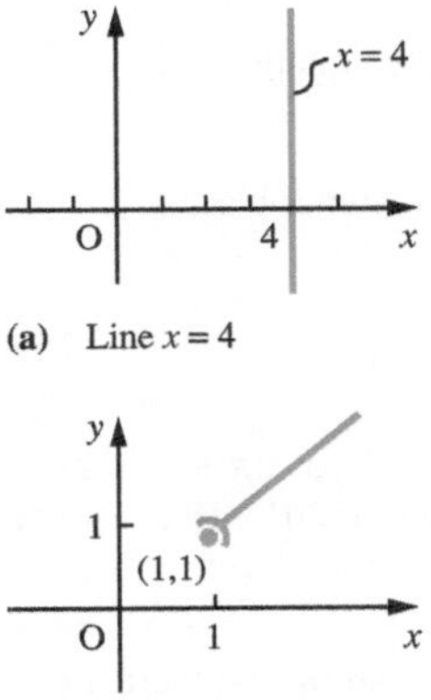

(a) Line $x = 4$

(b) Half-line $y = x, x > 1$

Figure 3.11

(c) The equation, in this case, may be written

$$|z - j2| = |z - 1|$$

Recalling the definition of modulus, we can rewrite this as

$$\sqrt{[x^2 + (y - 2)^2]} = \sqrt{[(x - 1)^2 + y^2]}$$

Squaring both sides and multiplying out, we obtain

$$x^2 + y^2 - 4y + 4 = x^2 - 2x + 1 + y^2$$

which simplifies to

$$y = \tfrac{1}{2}x + \tfrac{3}{4}$$

the equation of a straight line.

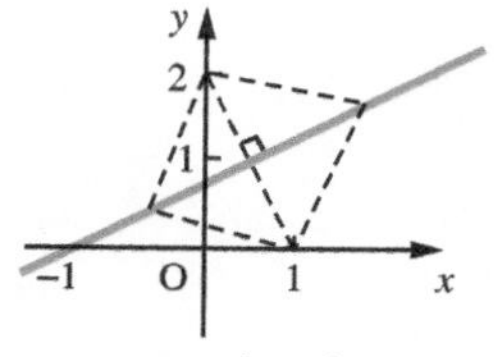

(c) Line $y = \frac{1}{2}x + \frac{3}{4}$

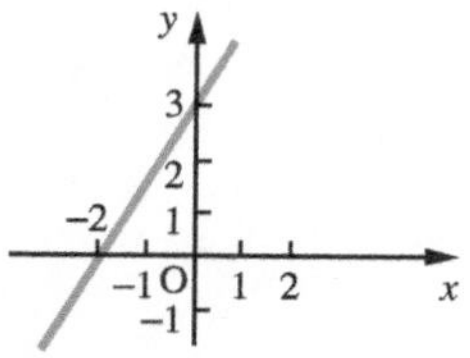

(d) Line $y = 2x + 3$

Figure 3.11 *continued*

Alternatively, we can interpret $|z - j2|$ as the distance on the Argand diagram from the point $0 + j2$ to the point z, and $|z - 1|$ as the distance from the point $1 + j0$ to the point z, so that

$$|z - j2| = |z - 1|$$

is the locus of points that are equidistant from the two fixed points (0, 2) and (1, 0), as shown in Figure 3.11(c).

(d) Writing $z = x + jy$,

$$(1 - j2)z = (1 - j2)(x + jy) = x + 2y + j(y - 2x)$$

so that $\text{Im}((1 - j2)z) = 3$, implies $y - 2x = 3$.

Thus $\text{Im}((1 - j2)z) = 3$ describes the straight line

$$y = 2x + 3$$

illustrated in Figure 3.11(d).

3.4.2 Circles

The simplest representation of a circle on the Argand diagram makes use of the fact that $|z - z_1|$ is the distance between the point $z = x + jy$ and the point $z_1 = a + jb$ on the diagram. Thus a circle of radius R and centre (a, b), illustrated in Figure 3.12, may be written

$$|z - z_1| = R$$

We can also write this as $z - z_1 = Re^{jt}$, where t is a parameter such that

$$-\pi < t \leqslant \pi$$

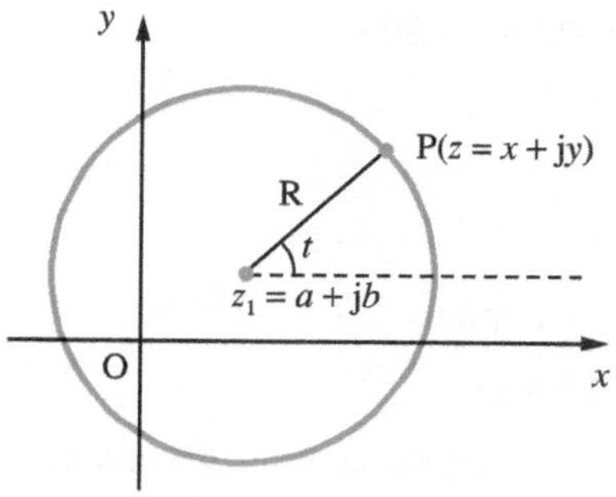

Figure 3.12
The circle $|z - z_1| = R$.

Example 3.26 Find the cartesian equation of the circle

$$|z - (2 + j3)| = 2$$

Solution Now,

$$z - (2 + j3) = (x - 2) + j(y - 3)$$

so that

$$|z - (2 + j3)| = \sqrt{[(x - 2)^2 + (y - 3)^2]}$$

and hence on the circle

$$|z - (2 + j3)| = 2$$

we have

$$\sqrt{[(x - 2)^2 + (y - 3)^2]} = 2$$

which implies

$$(x - 2)^2 + (y - 3)^2 = 4$$

indicating that the circle has centre (2, 3) and radius 2.

This may be written in the standard form

$$x^2 + y^2 - 4x - 6y + 9 = 0$$

This is not the only method of representing a circle, as is shown in the following two examples.

Example 3.27 Find the cartesian equation of the curve whose equation on the Argand diagram is

$$\left|\frac{z - j}{z - 1 - j2}\right| = \sqrt{2}$$

Solution By expressing it in the form $|z - j| = \sqrt{2}|z - (1 + j2)|$ we can interpret this equation as 'the distance between z and j is $\sqrt{2}$ times the distance between z and $(1 + j2)$', so this is different from Example 3.25(d).

Putting $z = x + jy$ into the equation gives

$$|x + j(y - 1)| = \sqrt{2}|(x - 1) + j(y - 2)|$$

Thus

$$\sqrt{[x^2 + (y - 1)^2]} = \sqrt{2}\sqrt{[(x - 1)^2 + (y - 2)^2]}$$

which, on squaring both sides, implies

$$x^2 + (y - 1)^2 = 2[(x - 1)^2 + (y - 2)^2]$$

Multiplying out the brackets and collecting terms we obtain

$$x^2 + y^2 - 4x - 6y + 9 = 0 \quad \text{or} \quad (x - 2)^2 + (y - 3)^2 = 4$$

which, from (1.14), is the equation of the circle of centre (2, 3), and radius 2.

This is a special case of a general result. If z_1 and z_2 are fixed complex numbers and k is a positive real number, then the locus of z which satisfies $\left|\frac{z - z_1}{z - z_2}\right| = k$ is a circle, known as the circle of Apollonius, *unless* $k = 1$. When $k = 1$, the locus is a straight line, as we saw in Example 3.25(d).

Example 3.28 Find the locus of z in the Argand diagram such that

$$\text{Re}[(z - \text{j})/(z + 1)] = 0$$

Solution Setting $z = x + \text{j}y$, as usual, we obtain

$$\frac{z - \text{j}}{z + 1} = \frac{x + \text{j}(y - 1)}{(x + 1) + \text{j}y} = \frac{[x + \text{j}(y - 1)][(x + 1) - \text{j}y]}{(x + 1)^2 + y^2}$$

Hence $\text{Re}[(z - \text{j})/(z + 1)] = 0$ implies $x(x + 1) + y(y - 1) = 0$.

Rearranging this, we have

$$x^2 + y^2 + x - y = 0$$

and

$$(x + \tfrac{1}{2})^2 + (y - \tfrac{1}{2})^2 = \tfrac{1}{2}$$

Hence the locus of z on the Argand diagram is a circle of centre $(-\frac{1}{2}, \frac{1}{2})$ and radius $\sqrt{2}/2$.

3.4.3 More general loci

In general we approach the problem of finding the locus of z on the Argand diagram using a mixture of elementary pure geometry and algebraic manipulation of expressions involving $z = x + \text{j}y$. We illustrate this in Example 3.29.

Example 3.29 Find the cartesian equation of the locus of z given by

$$|z + 1| + |z - 1| = 4$$

Solution The defining equation here may be interpreted as the sum of the distances of the point z from the points 1 and -1 is a constant ($= 4$). By elementary considerations (Figure 3.13) we can see that the locus passes through $(2, 0)$, $(0, \sqrt{3})$, $(-2, 0)$ and $(0, -\sqrt{3})$. Results from classical geometry would identify the locus as an ellipse with foci at $(1, 0)$ and $(-1, 0)$, using the 'string property' (see Example 1.40). Using algebraic methods, however, we set $z = x + \text{j}y$ into the equation, giving

$$\sqrt{[(x + 1)^2 + y^2]} + \sqrt{[(x - 1)^2 + y^2]} = 4$$

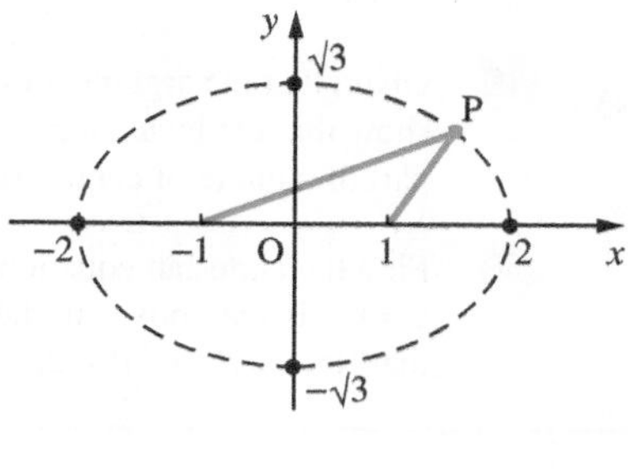

Figure 3.13 The ellipse of Example 3.29.

Rewriting this equation as

$$\sqrt{[(x+1)^2 + y^2]} = 4 - \sqrt{[(x-1)^2 + y^2]}$$

and squaring both sides gives

$$(x+1)^2 + y^2 = 16 - 8\sqrt{[(x-1)^2 + y^2]} + (x-1)^2 + y^2$$

This simplifies to give

$$4 - x = 2\sqrt{[(x-1)^2 + y^2]}$$

so that squaring both sides again gives

$$16 - 8x + x^2 = 4[x^2 - 2x + 1 + y^2]$$

which reduces to

$$\frac{x^2}{4} + \frac{y^2}{3} = 1$$

in the standard form of an ellipse.

3.4.4 Exercises

42 Let $z = 8 + \mathrm{j}$ and $w = 4 + \mathrm{j}4$. Calculate the distance on the Argand diagram from z to w and from z to $-w$.

43 Describe the locus of z when

(a) $\operatorname{Re} z = 5$ (b) $|z - 1| = 3$

(c) $\left|\dfrac{z-1}{z+1}\right| = 3$ (d) $\arg(z - 2) = \pi/4$

44 The circle $x^2 + y^2 + 4x = 0$ and the straight line $y = 3x + 2$ are taken to lie on the Argand diagram. Describe the circle and the straight line in terms of z.

45 Identify and sketch the loci on the complex plane given by

(a) $\operatorname{Re}\left(\dfrac{z+\mathrm{j}}{z-\mathrm{j}}\right) = 1$ (b) $\operatorname{Re}\left(\dfrac{z+\mathrm{j}}{z-\mathrm{j}}\right) = 2$

(c) $\left|\dfrac{z+\mathrm{j}}{z-\mathrm{j}}\right| = 3$ (d) $\tan\arg\left(\dfrac{z+\mathrm{j}}{z-\mathrm{j}}\right) = \sqrt{3}$

(e) $\operatorname{Im}(z^2) = 2$ (f) $|z + \mathrm{j}| + |z - 1| = 2$

(g) $|z + \mathrm{j}| - |z - 1| = \frac{1}{2}$ (h) $\arg(z + \mathrm{j}2) = \frac{1}{4}\pi$

(i) $\arg(2z - 3) = -\frac{2}{3}\pi$ (j) $|z - \mathrm{j}2| = 1$

46 Express as simply as possible the following loci in terms of a complex variable:

(a) $y = 3x - 2$ (b) $x^2 + y^2 + 4x = 0$

(c) $x^2 + y^2 + 2x - 4y - 4 = 0$ (d) $x^2 - y^2 = 1$

47 Find the locus of the point z in the Argand diagram which satisfies the equation

(a) $|z - 1| = 2$ (b) $|2z - 1| = 3$

(c) $|z - 2 - \mathrm{j}3| = 4$ (d) $\arg(z) = 0$

(e) $|z - 4| = 3|z + 1|$ (f) $\arg\left(\dfrac{z-1}{z-\mathrm{j}}\right) = \frac{1}{2}\pi$

48 Find the cartesian equation of the circle given by

$$\left|\frac{z+\mathrm{j}}{z-1}\right| = \sqrt{2}$$

and give two other representations of the circle in terms of z.

49 Given that the argument of $(z - 1)/(z + 1)$ is $\frac{1}{4}\pi$, show that the locus of z in the Argand diagram is part of a circle of centre (0, 1) and radius $\sqrt{2}$.

50 Find the cartesian equation of the locus of the point $z = x + \mathrm{j}y$ that moves in the Argand diagram such that $|(z + 1)/(z - 2)| = 2$.

3.5 Functions of a complex variable

In Section 2.2.1 the basic idea of a function was described. Essentially it involves two sets X and Y and a rule that assigns to every element x in the set X precisely one element y in the set Y. In Chapter 2 we were concerned with real functions so that x and y were real numbers. When the independent variable is a complex number $z = x + jy$ then, in general, a function $f(z)$ of z will have values which are complex numbers. Conventionally $w = u + jv$ is used to denote the dependent variable of a function of a complex variable, thus

$$w = u + jv = f(z) \quad \text{where} \quad z = x + jy$$

Example 3.30

Express u and v in terms of x and y where $w = u + jv$, $z = x + jy$, $w = f(z)$ and

(a) $f(z) = z^2$ (b) $f(z) = \dfrac{z - j}{z + 1}$, $z \neq -1$

Solution

(a) When $w = z^2$, we have $u + jv = (x + jy)^2$. This may be rewritten as

$$u + jv = x^2 - y^2 + j2xy$$

so that comparing real and imaginary parts on either side of this equation we have

$$u = x^2 - y^2 \quad \text{and} \quad v = 2xy$$

(b) When $w = \dfrac{z - j}{z + 1}$, we have

$$u + jv = \frac{x + j(y - 1)}{(x + 1) + jy} = \frac{[x + j(y - 1)][(x + 1) - jy]}{(x + 1)^2 + y^2}$$

Hence comparing real and imaginary parts we have

$$u = \frac{x(x + 1) + y(y - 1)}{(x + 1)^2 + y^2} \quad \text{and} \quad v = \frac{(x + 1)(y - 1) - xy}{(x + 1)^2 + y^2}$$

These may be written as

$$u = \frac{x^2 + y^2 + x - y}{x^2 + y^2 + 2x + 1} \quad \text{and} \quad v = \frac{y - x - 1}{x^2 + y^2 + 2x + 1}$$

The graphical representation of functions of a complex variable requires two planes, one for the independent variable $z = x + jy$ and another for the dependent variable $w = u + jv$. Thus the function $w = f(z)$ can be regarded as a ***mapping*** of points on the z plane to points on the w plane. Under such a mapping a region A on the z plane is ***transformed*** into the region A' on the w plane.

Example 3.31

Find the image on the w plane of the strip between $x = 1$ and $x = 2$ on the z plane under the mapping defined by

$$w = \frac{z + 2}{z}$$

Solution The easiest approach to this problem is firstly to find x in terms of u and v. So solving $w = \dfrac{z+2}{z}$ for z we have

$$z = \frac{2}{w-1}$$

and

$$x + jy = \frac{2}{(u-1) + jv} = \frac{2[(u-1) - jv]}{(u-1)^2 + v^2}$$

Equating real parts then gives

$$x = \frac{2(u-1)}{(u-1)^2 + v^2}$$

The line $x = 1$ maps into

$$1 = \frac{2u - 2}{u^2 - 2u + 1 + v^2}$$

which simplifies to give the circle on the w plane

$$(u-2)^2 + v^2 = 1$$

The line $x = 2$ maps into

$$2 = \frac{2u - 2}{u^2 - 2u + 1 + v^2}$$

which simplifies to give the circle on the w plane

$$(u - \tfrac{3}{2})^2 + v^2 = \tfrac{1}{4}$$

Thus the strip between $x = 1$ and $x = 2$ maps into that portion of the w plane between these two circles, as illustrated in Figure 3.14. The point $z = \frac{3}{2}$ maps to $w = \frac{7}{3}$ confirming that the shaded areas correspond.

As will be shown in the companion text *Advanced Modern Engineering Mathematics*, these properties are used to solve steady state potential problems in two dimensions.

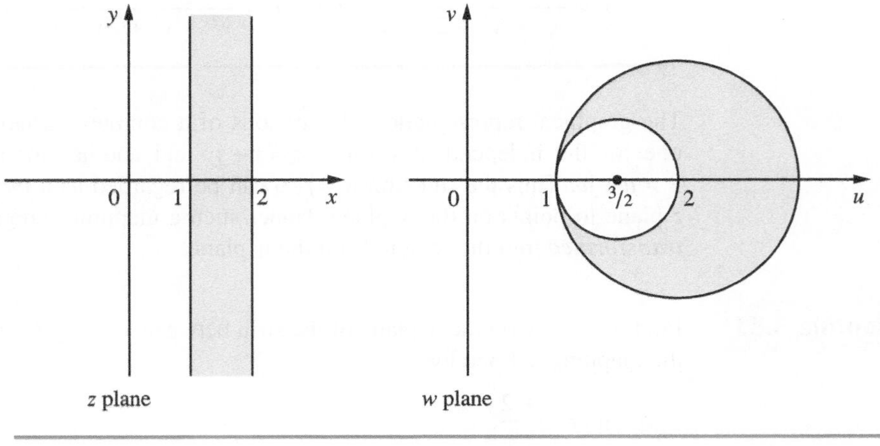

Figure 3.14 Transformation of the strip $1 < \text{Re}\, z < 2$ onto the w plane.

3.5.1 Exercises

51 Find u and v in terms of x and y where $w = f(z)$, $z = x + jy$, $w = u + jv$ and

(a) $f(z) = (1 - j)z$ (b) $f(z) = (z - 1)^2$

(c) $f(z) = z + \frac{1}{z}$

52 Find the values of the complex numbers a and b such that the function $w = az + b$ maps the point $z = 1 + j$ to $w = j$ and the point $z = -1$ to the point $w = 1 + j$.

53 Show that the line $y = 1$ on the z plane is transformed into the line $u = 1$ on the w plane by the function $w = (z + j)/(z - j)$.

54 Show that the function $w = (jz - 1)/(z - 1)$ maps the line $y = x$ on the z plane onto the circle

$$(u - 1)^2 + (v - 1)^2 = 1$$

on the w plane.

55 Show that the line $x = 1$ on the z plane is transformed into the circle

$$u^2 + v^2 - u = 0$$

on the w plane by the function

$$w = (z - 1)/(z + 1).$$

56 By writing $z = x + jy$ and $w = u + jv$, show that the line $y = \frac{\pi}{4}$ on the z plane is transformed into the line $v = u$ on the w plane by the function

$$w = e^z$$

Find the image of the line $x = 0$ under the same function.

3.6 Engineering application: alternating currents in electrical networks

When an alternating current $i = I \sin \omega t$ (ω is a constant and t is the time) flows in a circuit the corresponding voltage depends on ω and on the resistance, capacitance and inductance of the circuit. (Note that the frequency of the current is $\omega/2\pi$.) For simplicity we shall separate these three elements and consider their effects individually.

For a resistor of resistance R the corresponding voltage is $v = IR \sin \omega t$. This voltage is 'in phase' with the current. It is zero at the same times as i and achieves its maxima at the same times as i, as shown in Figure 3.15. For a capacitor of capacitance C the corresponding voltage is $v = (I/\omega C) \sin(\omega t - \frac{1}{2}\pi)$, as shown in Figure 3.16. Here the voltage 'lags' behind the current by a phase of $\frac{1}{2}\pi$. For an inductor of inductance

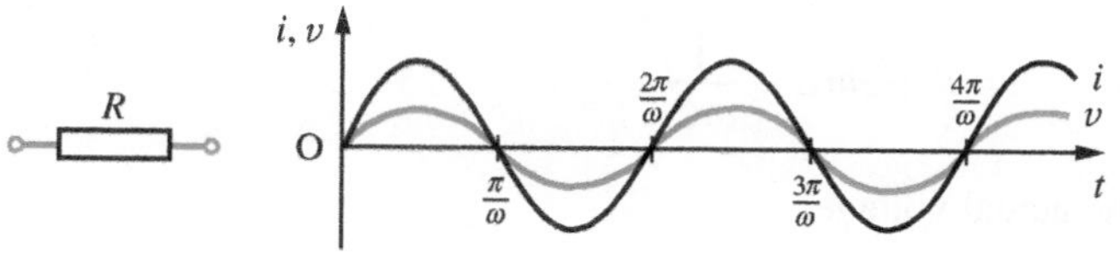

Figure 3.15 A resistor of resistance R.

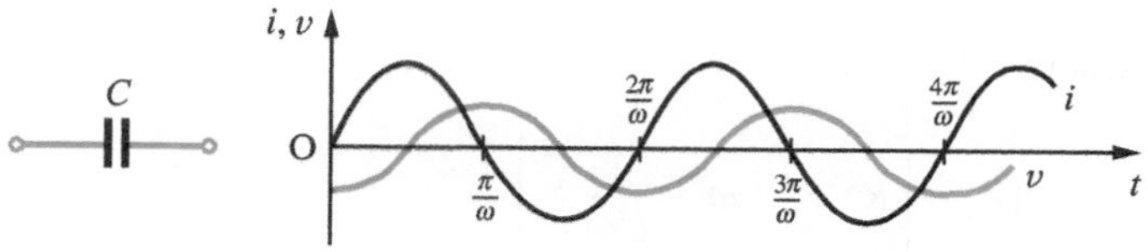

Figure 3.16 A capacitor of capacitance C.

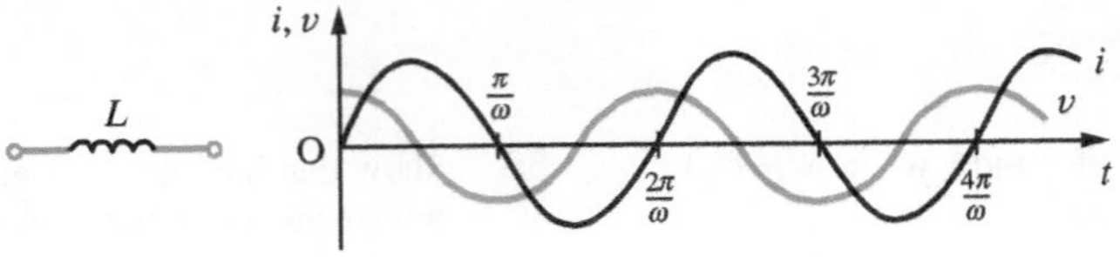

Figure 3.17 An inductor of inductance L.

L the corresponding voltage is $v = \omega LI \sin(\omega t + \frac{1}{2}\pi)$, as shown in Figure 3.17. Here the voltage 'leads' the current by a phase of $\frac{1}{2}\pi$.

Combining these results to find v in the case of a general network is easily done using the properties of complex numbers. Remembering that $\sin\theta = \mathrm{Im}(e^{j\theta})$, we can summarize the results as

$$v = \begin{cases} \mathrm{Im}(IRe^{j\omega t}) & \text{for a resistor} \\ \mathrm{Im}\left(\dfrac{I}{\omega C} e^{j(\omega t - \pi/2)}\right) & \text{for a capacitor} \\ \mathrm{Im}(\omega LIe^{j(\omega t + \pi/2)}) & \text{for an inductor} \end{cases}$$

Now $e^{j\pi/2} = \cos\frac{1}{2}\pi + j\sin\frac{1}{2}\pi = j$ and $e^{-j\pi/2} = -j$, so we may rewrite these as

$$v = \mathrm{Im}(IZe^{j\omega t})$$

where

$$Z = \begin{cases} R & \text{for a resistor} \\ -\dfrac{j}{\omega C} & \text{for a capacitor} \\ j\omega L & \text{for an inductor} \end{cases}$$

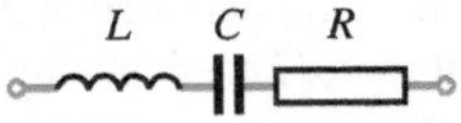

Figure 3.18 A linear LCR circuit.

Z is called the **complex impedance** of the element, and $V = IZ$ is the **complex voltage**.

For the general LCR circuit shown in Figure 3.18 the complex voltage V is the algebraic sum of the complex voltages of the individual elements; that is,

$$V = IR + j\omega LI - \frac{jI}{\omega C} = IZ$$

where

$$Z = R + j\omega L - \frac{j}{\omega C}$$

The actual voltage

$$v = \mathrm{Im}(Ve^{j\omega t}) = I|Z|\sin(\omega t + \phi)$$

where

$$|Z| = \left[R^2 + \left(L\omega - \frac{1}{C\omega}\right)^2\right]^{1/2}$$

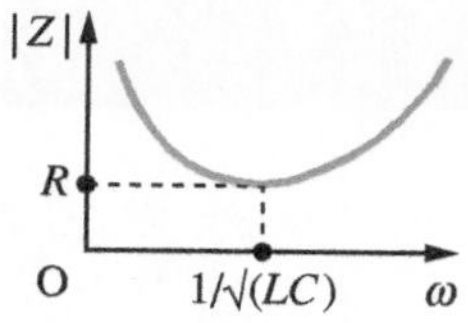

Figure 3.19
The impedance of an LCR circuit.

is the **impedance** of the circuit and

$$\phi = \tan^{-1}\left(\frac{L\omega - 1/C\omega}{R}\right)$$

is the **phase**. The impedance $|Z|$ clearly varies with ω, and the graph of this dependence is shown in Figure 3.19. The minimum value occurs when $L\omega = 1/C\omega$; that is, when $\omega = 1/\sqrt{(LC)}$. This implies that the circuit 'blocks' currents with low and high frequencies, and 'passes' currents with frequencies near $1/(2\pi\sqrt{(LC)})$.

Example 3.32 Calculate the complex impedance of the element shown in Figure 3.20 when an alternating current of frequency 100 Hz flows.

Solution The complex impedance is the sum of the individual impedances. Thus

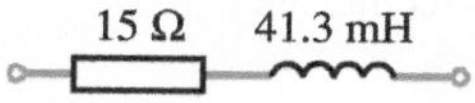

Figure 3.20
The element of Example 3.32.

$$Z = R + j\omega L$$

Here $R = 15\,\Omega$, $\omega = 2\pi \times 100\,\text{rad s}^{-1}$ and $L = 41.3 \times 10^{-3}\,\text{H}$, so that

$$Z = 15 + j25.9$$

and $|Z| = 30\,\Omega$ and $\phi = \frac{1}{3}\pi$.

3.6.1 Exercises

57 Calculate the complex impedance for the circuit shown in Figure 3.21 when an alternating current of frequency 50 Hz flows.

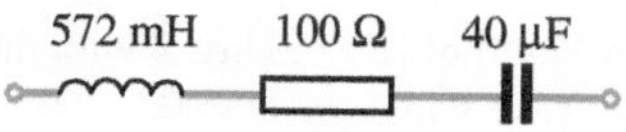

Figure 3.21

58 The complex impedance of two circuit elements in series as shown in Figure 3.22(a) is the sum of the complex impedances of the individual elements, and the reciprocal of the impedance of two elements in parallel is the sum of the reciprocals of the individual impendances, as shown in Figure 3.22(b). Use these results to calculate the complex impedance of the network shown in Figure 3.23, where $Z_1 = 1 + j\,\Omega$, $Z_2 = 5 - j5\,\Omega$ and $Z_3 = 1 + j2\,\Omega$.

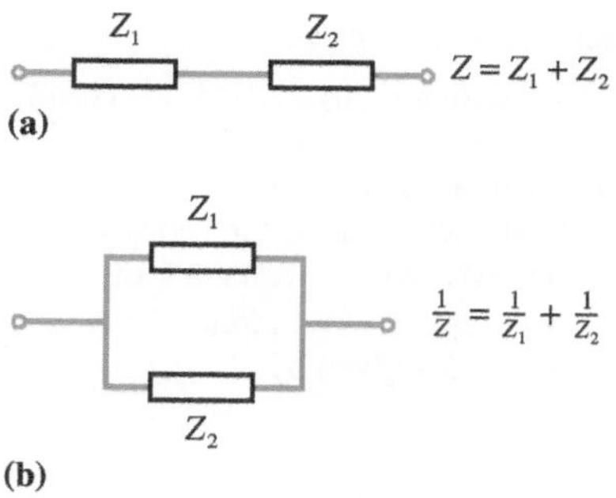

Figure 3.22

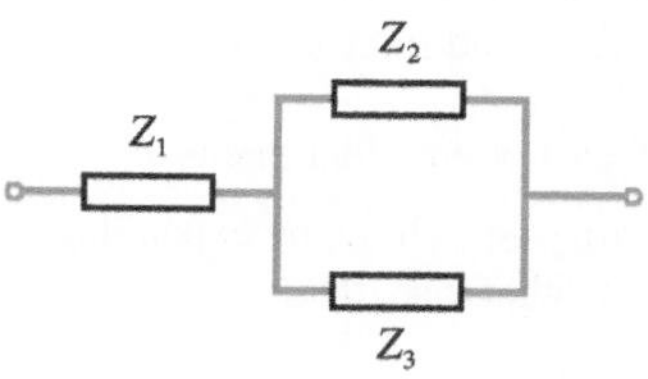

Figure 3.23

3.7 Review exercises (1–34)

Check your answers using MATLAB or MAPLE whenever possible.

1 Let $z = 4 + j3$ and $w = 2 - j$. Calculate

(a) $3z$ (b) w^* (c) zw

(d) z^2 (e) $|z|$ (f) w/z

(g) $z - \dfrac{1}{w}$ (h) $\arg z$ (i) $z^{\frac{3}{2}}$

2 For x and y real solve the equation

$$\frac{jy}{jx + 1} - \frac{3y + j4}{3x + y} = 0$$

3 Given $z = (2 + j)/(1 - j)$, find the real and imaginary parts of $z + z^{-1}$.

4 (a) Find the loci in the Argand diagram corresponding to the equation

$$|z - 1| = 2|z - j|$$

(b) If the point $z = x + jy$ describes the circle $|z - 1| = 1$, show that the real part of $1/(z - 2)$ is constant.

5 Writing $\ln[(x + jy + a)/(x + jy - a)] = u + jv$, show that

(a) $x^2 + y^2 - 2ax \coth u + a^2 = 0$

(b) $x = a \sinh u/(\cosh u - \cos v)$

(c) $|x + jy|^2 = a^2(\cosh u + \cos v)/(\cosh u - \cos v)$

6 A circuit consists of a resistance R_1 and an inductance L in parallel connected in series with a second resistance R_2. When a voltage V of frequency $\omega/2\pi$ is applied to the circuit the complex impedance Z is given by

$$\frac{1}{Z - R_2} = \frac{1}{R_1} + \frac{1}{j\omega L}$$

Show that if R_1 varies from zero to infinity the locus of Z on the Argand diagram is part of a circle and find its centre and radius.

7 (a) Express $\cos 6\theta$ as a polynomial in $\cos\theta$.

(b) Given $z = \cos\theta + j\sin\theta$ show, by expanding $(z + 1/z)^5(z - 1/z)^5$ or otherwise, that

$$\sin^5\theta\cos^5\theta = \frac{1}{2^9}(\sin 10\theta - 5\sin 6\theta + 10\sin 2\theta)$$

8 Show that the solutions of

$$z^4 - 3z^2 + 1 = 0$$

are given by

$$z = 2\cos 36°, 2\cos 72°, 2\cos 216°, 2\cos 252°$$

Hence show that

(a) $\cos 36° = \frac{1}{4}(\sqrt{5} + 1)$

(b) $\cos 72° = \frac{1}{4}(\sqrt{5} - 1)$

9 Prove that if $p(z)$ is a polynomial in z with real coefficients then $[p(z)]^* = p(z^*)$. Deduce that the roots of a polynomial equation with real coefficients occur in complex-conjugate pairs.

10 Show that

(a) $\sin^4\theta = \frac{1}{8}[\cos 4\theta - 4\cos 2\theta + 3]$

(b) $\sin^5\theta = \frac{1}{16}[\sin 5\theta - 5\sin 3\theta + 10\sin\theta]$

(c) $\cos^6\theta = \frac{1}{32}[\cos 6\theta + 6\cos 4\theta + 15\cos 2\theta + 10]$

(d) $\cos^2\theta\sin^3\theta = \frac{1}{16}[2\sin\theta + \sin 3\theta - \sin 5\theta]$

11 Prove that the statements

(a) $|z + 1| > |z - 1|$ (b) $\text{Re}(z) > 0$

are equivalent.

12 For a certain network the impedance Z is given by

$$Z = \frac{1 + j\omega}{1 + j\omega - \omega^2}$$

Sketch the variation of $|Z|$ and $\arg Z$ with the frequency ω. (Take values of $\omega \geqslant 0$.)

13 The characteristic impedance Z_0 and the propagation constant C of a transmission line are given by

$$Z_0 = \sqrt{(Z/Y)} \text{ and } C = \sqrt{(ZY)}$$

where Z is the series impedance and Y the admittance of the line, and $\text{Re}(Z_0) > 0$ and $\text{Re}(C) > 0$. Find Z_0 and C when $Z = 0.5 + j0.3\,\Omega$ and $Y = (1 - j250) \times 10^{-8}\,\Omega$.

14 The input impedance Z of a particular network is related to the terminating impedance z by the equation

$$Z = \frac{(1 + j)z - 2 + j4}{z + 1 + j}$$

Find Z when $z = 0$, 1 and j Ω and sketch the variation of $|Z|$ and arg Z as z moves along the positive real axis from the origin.

15 Find the modulus and argument of

$$\frac{(3 + j4)^4(12 - j5)^2}{(3 - j4)^2(12 + j5)^3}$$

16 Express in the form $a + jb$, with a and b expressed to 2dp

(a) $\sin(0.2 + j0.48)$ (b) $\cosh^{-1}(j2)$

(c) $\cosh(3.8 - j5.2)$ (d) $\ln(2 + j)$

(e) $\cos(\frac{1}{4}\pi - j)$

17 Using complex numbers, show that

$$\sin^7\theta = \tfrac{1}{64}(35 \sin\theta - 21 \sin 3\theta + 7 \sin 5\theta - \sin 7\theta)$$

18 Two impedances Z_1 and Z_0 are related by the equation

$$Z_1 = Z_0 \tanh(\alpha l + j\beta l)$$

where α, β and l are real. If αl is so small that we may take $\sinh \alpha l = \alpha l$, $\cosh \alpha l = 1$ and $(\alpha l)^2$ as negligible, show that

$$Z_1 = Z_0[\alpha l \sec^2\beta l + j \tan \beta l]$$

19 In a transmission line the voltage reflection equation is given by

$$Ke^{j\theta} = \frac{Z - Z_0}{Z + Z_0}$$

where K is a real constant, $Z = R + jX$ and $Z_0 = R_0 + jX_0$. Obtain an expression for θ, the phase angle, in terms of R_0, R, X_0 and X. Hence show that if Z_0 is purely resistive (that is, real) then

$$\theta = \tan^{-1}\left[\frac{2R_0X}{R^2 + X^2 - R_0^2}\right]$$

assuming $R_0^2 < R^2 + X^2$.

20 The voltage in a cable is given by the expression

$$\cosh nx + \frac{Z_0}{Z_r} \sinh nx$$

Calculate its value in the form $a + jb$, giving a and b correct to 2dp, when

$nx = 0.40 + j0.93$

$Z_0 = 15 - j20$ $\quad$ $Z_r = 3 + j4$

21 Express $Z = \cosh(0.5 + j\frac{1}{4}\pi)$ in the forms

(a) $x + jy$ (b) $re^{j\theta}$

The current in a cable is equal to the real part of the expression $e^{j0.7}/Z$. Calculate the current, giving your answer correct to 3dp.

22 Show that if the propagation constant of a cable is given by

$$X + jY = \sqrt{[(R + j\omega L)(G + j\omega C)]}$$

where R, G, ω, L and C are real, then the value of X^2 is given by

$$X^2 = \tfrac{1}{2}[RG - \omega^2LC + \sqrt{\{(R^2 + \omega^2L^2) \times (G^2 + \omega^2C^2)\}}]$$

23 Given $Z = (1 + j)/(3 - j4)$ obtain

(a) Z (b) $\sqrt{Z}$ (c) e^Z

(d) $\ln Z$ (e) $\sin Z$

in the form $a + jb$, a, b real, giving a and b correct to 2dp.

24 Find, in exponential form, the four values of

$$\left[\frac{7 + j24}{25}\right]^{1/4}$$

Denoting any one of these by p, show that the other three are given by j^np ($n = 1, 2, 3$).

25 Determine the six roots of the complex number $-1 + j\sqrt{3}$, in the form $re^{j\theta}$ where $-\pi < \theta \leq \pi$, and show that three of these are also solutions of the equation

$$\sqrt{2}Z^3 + 1 + j\sqrt{3} = 0$$

26 Find the real part of

$$\frac{(R + j\omega L)/j\omega C}{j\omega L + R + 1/j\omega C}$$

and deduce that if R^2 is negligible compared with $(\omega L)^2$ and $(LC\omega^2)^2$ is negligible compared with unity then the real part is approximately $R(1 + 2LC\omega^2)$.

27 Show that if ω is a complex cube root of unity, then $\omega^2 + \omega + 1 = 0$. Deduce that

$$(x + y + z)(x + \omega y + \omega^2 z)(x + \omega^2 y + \omega z) = x^3 + y^3 + z^3 - 3xyz$$

Hence show that the three roots of

$$x^3 + (-3yz)x + (y^3 + z^3) = 0$$

are

$$x = -(y + z), -(\omega y + \omega^2 z), -(\omega^2 y + \omega z)$$

Use this result to obtain Cardano's solution to the cubic equation

$$x^3 + qx + r = 0$$

in the form

$$-(u + v)$$

where $u^3 = \frac{1}{2}r + \sqrt{[\frac{1}{4}r^2 + \frac{1}{27}q^3]}$

and $v^3 = \frac{1}{2}r - \sqrt{[\frac{1}{4}r^2 + \frac{1}{27}q^3]}$

Express the remaining two roots in terms of u, v and ω and find the condition that all three roots are real.

28 ABCD is a square, lettered anticlockwise, on an Argand diagram. If the points A, B represent $3 + j2$, $-1 + j4$ respectively, show that C lies on the real axis, and find the number represented by D and the length of AB.

29 If $z_1 = 3 + j2$ and $z_2 = 1 + j$, and O, P, Q, R represent the numbers 0, z_1, z_1z_2, z_1/z_2 on the Argand diagram, show that RP is parallel to OQ and is half its length.

30 Show that as z describes the circle $z = be^{j\theta}$, $u + jv = z + a^2/z$ describes an ellipse ($a \neq b$). What is the image locus when $a = b$?

31 Show that the function

$$w = \frac{4}{z}$$

where $z = x + jy$ and $w = u + jv$, maps the line $3x + 4y = 1$ in the z plane onto a circle in the w plane and determine its radius and centre.

32 Show that the function

$$w = (1 + j)z + 1$$

where $z = x + jy$ and $w = u + jv$, maps the line $y = 2x - 1$ in the z plane onto a line in the w plane and determine its equation.

33 Show that the function

$$w = \frac{z - 1}{z + 1}$$

where $z = x + jy$ and $w = u + jv$, maps the circle $|z| = 3$ on the z plane onto a circle in the w plane.

Find the centre and radius of this circle in the w plane and indicate, by means of shading on a sketch, the region in the w plane that corresponds to the interior of the circle $|z| = 3$ in the z plane.

34 Show that as θ varies the point $z = a(h + \cos\theta) + ja(k + \sin\theta)$ describes a circle. The Joukowski transformation $u + jv = z + l^2/z$ is applied to this circle to produce an aerofoil shape in the u–v plane. Show that the coordinates of the aerofoil can be written in the form

$$\frac{u}{a} = (h + \cos\theta) \times \left\{1 + \frac{l^2}{a^2(1 + h^2 + k^2 + 2h\cos\theta + 2k\sin\theta)}\right\}$$

$$\frac{v}{a} = (k + \sin\theta) \times \left\{1 - \frac{l^2}{a^2(1 + h^2 + k^2 + 2h\cos\theta + 2k\sin\theta)}\right\}$$

Taking the case $a = 1$ and $l^2 = 8$, trace the aerofoil where

(a) $h = k = 0$, and show that it is an ellipse;

(b) $h = 0.04$, $k = 0$ and show that it is a symmetrical aerofoil with a blunt leading and trailing edge;

(c) $h = 0$, $k = 0.1$ and show that it is a symmetrical aerofoil (about v axis) with camber;

(d) $h = 0.04$, $k = 0.1$ and show that it is a non-symmetrical aerofoil with camber and rounded leading and trailing edges.

4 Vector Algebra

Chapter 4 Contents

4.1 Introduction

Much of the work of engineers and scientists involves forces. Ensuring the structural integrity of a building or a bridge involves knowing the forces acting on the system and designing the structural members to withstand them. Many have seen the dramatic pictures of the Tacoma bridge disaster (see also Section 10.10.3), when the forces acting on the bridge were not predicted accurately. To analyse such a system requires the use of Newton's laws in a situation where vector notation is essential. Similarly, in a reciprocating engine, periodic forces act, and Newton's laws are used to design a crankshaft that will reduce the side forces to zero, thereby minimizing wear on the moving parts. Forces are three-dimensional quantities and provide one of the commonest examples of vectors. Associated with these forces are accelerations and velocities, which can also be represented by vectors. The use of formal mathematical notation and rules becomes progressively more important as problems become complicated and, in particular, in three-dimensional situations. Forces, velocities and accelerations all satisfy rules of addition that identify them as vectors. In this chapter we shall construct an algebraic theory for the manipulation of vectors and see how it can be applied to some simple practical problems.

The ideas behind vectors as formal quantities developed mainly during the nineteenth century, and they became a well-established tool in the twentieth century. Vectors provide a convenient and compact way of dealing with multi-dimensional situations without the problem of writing down every bit of information. They allow the principles of the subject to be developed without being obscured by complicated notation.

It is inconceivable that modern scientists and engineers could work successfully without computers. Since such machines cannot think like an engineer or scientist, they have to be told in a totally precise and formal way what to do. For instance, a robot arm needs to be given instructions on how to position itself to perform a spot weld. Three-dimensional vectors prove to be the perfect way to tell the computer how to specify the position of the workpiece of the robot arm and a set of rules then tells the robot how to move to its working position.

Computers have put a great power at the disposal of the engineer; problems that proved to be impossible fifty years ago are now routine. With the aid of numerical algorithms, equations can often be solved very quickly. The stressing of a large structure or an aircraft wing, the lubrication of shafts and bearings, the flow of sewage in pipes and the flow past the fuselage of an aircraft are all examples of systems that were well understood in principle but could not be analysed until the necessary computer power became available. Algorithms are usually written in terms of vectors and matrices (see Chapter 5), since these form a natural setting for the numerical solution of engineering problems and are also ideal for the computer. It is vital that the manipulation of vectors be understood before embarking on more complex mathematical structures used in engineering computations.

Perhaps the most powerful influence of computers is in their graphical capabilities, which have proved invaluable in displaying the static and dynamic behaviour of systems. We accept this tool without thinking how it works. A simple example shows the complexity. How do we display a box with an open top with 'hidden' lines when we look at it from a given angle? The problem is a complicated three-dimensional one that must be analysed instantly by a computer. Vectors allow us to define lines that can be projected onto the screen, and intersections can then be computed so that the 'hidden' portion can be eliminated. Extending the analysis to a less regular shape is a formidable vector problem. Work of this type is the basis of CAD/CAM systems, which now assist engineers in all stages of the manufacturing process, from design to production of a finished product. Such systems typically allow engineers to manipulate the product geometry during initial design, to produce working drawings, to generate toolpaths in the production process and generally to automate a host of previously tedious and time-consuming tasks.

The general development of the theory of vectors is closely associated with coordinate geometry, so we shall introduce a few ideas in the next section that will be used later in the chapter. The comments largely concern the two- and three-dimensional cases, but we shall mention higher-dimensional extensions where they are relevant to later work, such as on the theory of matrices. While in two and three dimensions we can appeal to geometrical intuition, it is necessary to work in a much more formal way in higher dimensions, as with many other areas of mathematics.

4.2 Basic definitions and results

4.2.1 Cartesian coordinates

Setting up rectangular cartesian axes Oxyz or O$x_1x_2x_3$, we define the position of a point by **coordinates** or **components** (x, y, z) or (x_1, x_2, x_3), as indicated in Figure 4.1(a). The indicial notation is particularly important when we consider vectors in many dimensions $(x_1, x_2, \dots, x_n)$. The axes Ox, Oy, Oz, in that order, are assumed to be right-handed in the sense of Figure 4.1(b), so that a rotation of a right-handed screw from Ox to Oy advances it along Oz, a rotation from Oy to Oz advances it along Ox and a rotation from Oz to Ox advances it along Oy. This is an accepted convention, and it will be seen to be particularly important in Section 4.2.10 when we deal with the vector product.

The length of OP in Figure 4.1(a) is obtained from Pythagoras' theorem as

$$r = (x^2 + y^2 + z^2)^{1/2}$$

The angle $\alpha = \angle$POA in the right-angled triangle OAP is the angle that OP makes with the positive x direction, as in Figure 4.2. We can see that

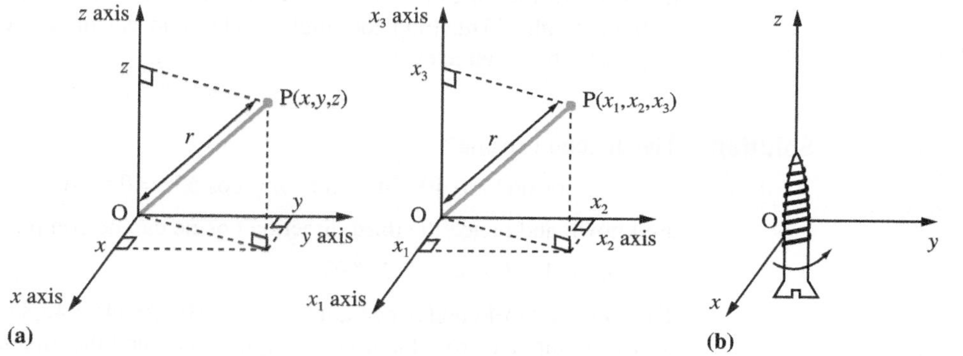

Figure 4.1
(a) Right-handed coordinate axes.
(b) Right-hand rule.

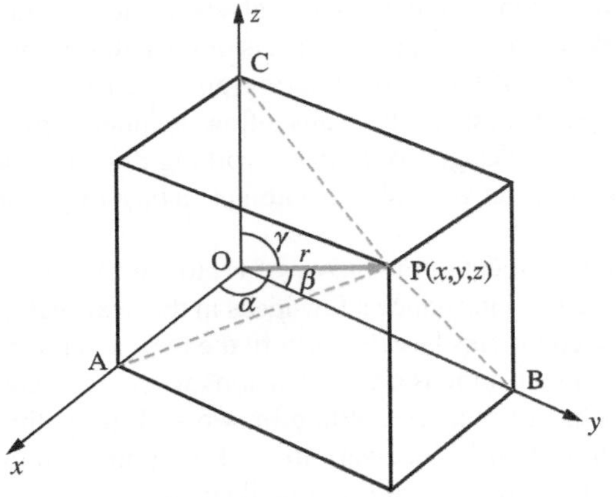

Figure 4.2 Direction cosines of OP, $l = \cos\alpha$, $m = \cos\beta$, $n = \cos\gamma$.

$$l = \cos\alpha = \frac{x}{r}$$

Likewise, β and γ are the angles that OP makes with y and z directions respectively, so

$$m = \cos\beta = \frac{y}{r}, \quad n = \cos\gamma = \frac{z}{r}$$

The triad (l, m, n) are called the **direction cosines** of the line OP. Note that

$$l^2 + m^2 + n^2 = \frac{x^2}{r^2} + \frac{y^2}{r^2} + \frac{z^2}{r^2} = \frac{x^2 + y^2 + z^2}{r^2} = 1$$

Example 4.1 If P has coordinates (2, −1, 3), find the length OP and the direction cosines of OP.

Solution $OP^2 = (2)^2 + (-1)^2 + (3)^2 = 4 + 1 + 9$, so that $OP = \sqrt{14}$

The direction cosines are

$$l = 2\sqrt{\tfrac{1}{14}}, \quad m = -\sqrt{\tfrac{1}{14}}, \quad n = 3\sqrt{\tfrac{1}{14}}$$

Example 4.2 A surveyor sets up his theodolite on horizontal ground, at a point O, and observes the top of a church spire, as illustrated in Figure 4.3. Relative to axes Oxyz, with Oz vertical, the surveyor measures the angles $\angle$TOx = 66° and $\angle$TOz = 57°. The church is known to have height 35 m. Find the angle $\angle$TOy and calculate the coordinates of T with respect to the given axes.

Solution The direction cosines

$$l = \cos 66° = 0.406\,74 \quad \text{and} \quad n = \cos 57° = 0.544\,64$$

are known and hence the third direction cosine can be computed as

$$m^2 = 1 - l^2 - n^2 = 0.537\,93$$

Thus, $m = 0.733\,44$ and hence $\angle TOy = \cos^{-1}(0.733\,44) = 42.82°$. The length OT = r can now be computed from the known height, 35 m, and the direction cosine n, as

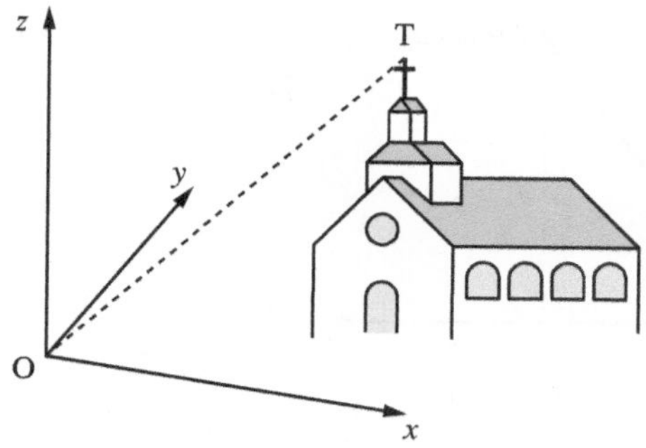

Figure 4.3 Representation of the axes and church spire in Example 4.2.

$$\cos 57° = 35/r, \quad \text{so} \quad r = 64.26\,\text{m}$$

The remaining coordinates are obtained from

$$x/r = \cos 66° \quad \text{and} \quad y/r = \cos 42.82°$$

giving $x = r\cos 66° = 26.14$ and $y = r\cos 42.82° = 47.13$

Hence the coordinates of T are (26.14, 47.13, 35).

4.2.2 Scalars and vectors

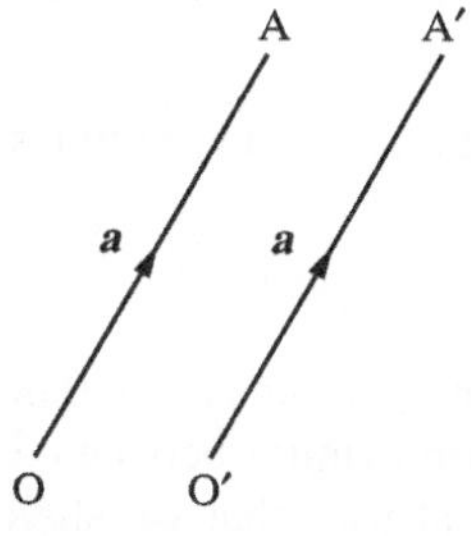

Figure 4.4 Line segments representing a vector ***a***.

Quantities like distance or temperature are represented by real numbers in appropriate units, for instance 5 m or 10°C. Such quantities are called **scalars** – they obey the usual rules of real numbers and they have no direction associated with them. However, **vectors** have both a magnitude and a direction associated with them; these include force, velocity and magnetic field. To qualify as vectors, the quantities must have more than just magnitude and direction – they must also satisfy some particular rules of combination. Angular displacement in three dimensions gives an example of a quantity which has a direction and magnitude but which does not add by the addition rules of vectors, so angular displacements are *not* vectors.

We represent a vector geometrically by a line segment whose length represents the vector's magnitude in some appropriate units and whose direction represents the vector's direction, with the arrowhead indicating the sense of the vector, as shown in Figure 4.4. According to this definition, the starting point of the vector is irrelevant. In Figure 4.4, the two line segments OA and O′A′ represent the same vector because their lengths are the same, their directions are the same and the sense of the arrows is the same. Thus each of these vectors is equivalent to the vector through the origin, with A given by its coordinates (a_1, a_2, a_3), as in Figure 4.5. We can therefore represent a vector in a three-dimensional space by an ordered set of three numbers or a 3-tuple. We shall see how this representation is used in Section 4.2.5.

We shall now introduce some of the basic notation and definitions for vectors. The vector of Figure 4.5 is handwritten or typewritten as $\underset{\sim}{a}$, $\underline{a}$, $\overrightarrow{OA}$. On the printed page, bold-face type $\boldsymbol{a}$ is used. Using the coordinate definition, the vector could equally be written as (a_1, a_2, a_3). (Note: There are several possible coordinate notations; the traditional one is (a_1, a_2, a_3), but in Section 5.2.1 of Chapter 5 on matrices we shall use an alternative standard notation.)

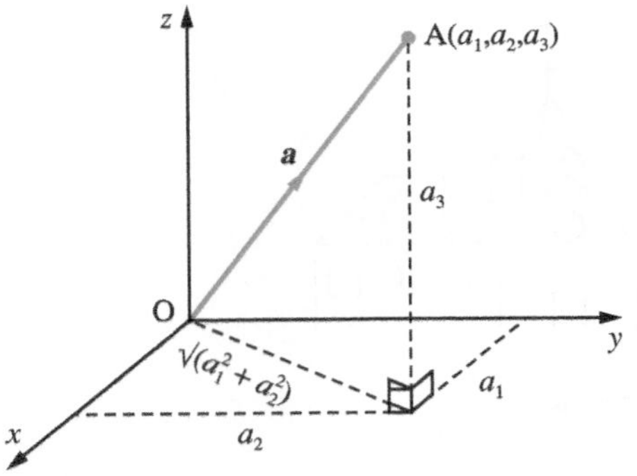

Figure 4.5
Representation of the vector ***a*** by the line segment OA.

Some basic properties of vectors are:

(a) Equality

As we considered earlier, two vectors ***a*** and ***b*** are equal if and only if they have the same modulus and the same direction and sense. We write this in the usual way

$$\boldsymbol{a} = \boldsymbol{b}$$

We shall see in Section 4.2.5 that in component form, two vectors $\boldsymbol{a} = (a_1, a_2, a_3)$ and $\boldsymbol{b} = (b_1, b_2, b_3)$ are **equal** if and only if the components are equal, that is

$$a_1 = b_1, \quad a_2 = b_2, \quad a_3 = b_3$$

(b) Multiplication by a scalar

If λ is a scalar and the vectors are related by $\boldsymbol{a} = \lambda \boldsymbol{b}$ then

- if $\lambda > 0$, ***a*** is a vector in the same direction as ***b*** with magnitude λ times the magnitude of ***b***;
- if $\lambda < 0$, ***a*** is a vector in the opposite direction to ***b*** with magnitude $|\lambda|$ times the magnitude of ***b***.

(c) Parallel vectors

The vectors ***a*** and ***b*** in (*b*) are said to be **parallel** or **antiparallel** according as $\lambda > 0$ or $\lambda < 0$ respectively. (Note that we do not insert any multiplication symbol between λ and ***b*** since the common symbols $\cdot$ and $\times$ are reserved for special uses that we shall discuss later.)

(d) Modulus

The **modulus** or **length** or **magnitude** of a vector ***a*** is written as $|\boldsymbol{a}|$ or $|\overrightarrow{\mathrm{OA}}|$ or a if there is no ambiguity. A vector with modulus one is called a **unit vector** and is written $\hat{\boldsymbol{a}}$, with the hat (ˆ) indicating a unit vector. Clearly

$$\boldsymbol{a} = |\boldsymbol{a}|\hat{\boldsymbol{a}} \quad \text{or} \quad \hat{\boldsymbol{a}} = \frac{\boldsymbol{a}}{|\boldsymbol{a}|}$$

(e) Zero vector

The **zero** or **null vector** has zero modulus; it is written as **0** or often just as 0 when there is no ambiguity whether it is a vector or not.

Example 4.3 A cyclist travels at a steady 16 km/h on the four legs of his journey. From his origin, O, he travels for one hour in a NE direction to the point A; he then travels due E for half an hour to point B. He then cycles in a NW direction until he reaches the point C, which is due N of his starting point. He returns due S to the starting point. Indicate the path of the cyclist using vectors and calculate the modulus of the vectors along BC and CO.

Solution The four vectors are shown in Figure 4.6. If $\hat{\imath}$ and $\hat{\jmath}$ are the unit vectors along the two axes then by property (*b*)

$$\overrightarrow{AB} = 8\hat{\imath} \quad \text{and} \quad \overrightarrow{CO} = -L\hat{\jmath}$$

where L is still to be determined. By trigonometry

$$DB = 8 + 16 \sin 45^\circ = 8 + 8\sqrt{2}$$

and hence the modulus of the vector $\overrightarrow{BC}$ is

$$|BC| = \frac{DB}{\cos 45^\circ} = 8\sqrt{2} + 16$$

The modulus L of the vector $\overrightarrow{CO}$ is

$$L = |\overrightarrow{CO}| = CD + DO = (8 + 8\sqrt{2}) + 16 \cos 45^\circ = 8 + 16\sqrt{2}$$

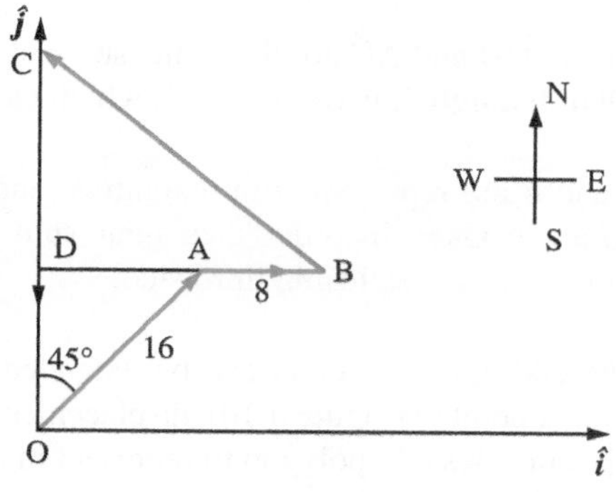

Figure 4.6 Cyclist's path in Example 4.3.

4.2.3 Addition of vectors

Having introduced vectors and their basic properties, it is natural to ask if vectors can be combined. The simplest form of vector combination is addition and it is the definition of addition that finally identifies a vector. Consider the following situation. The helmsman of a small motor boat steers his vessel due east (E) at 4 knots for one hour. The path taken by the boat could be represented by the line OA, or $\boldsymbol{a}$, in Figure 4.7. Unfortunately there is also a tidal stream, $\boldsymbol{b}$, running north-north-east (NNE) at $2\frac{1}{2}$ knots. Where will the boat actually be at the end of one hour?

If we imagine the vessel to be steaming E for one hour through still water, and then lying still in the water and drifting with the tidal stream for one hour, we can see that it will travel from O to A in the first hour and from A to C in the second hour. If, on the

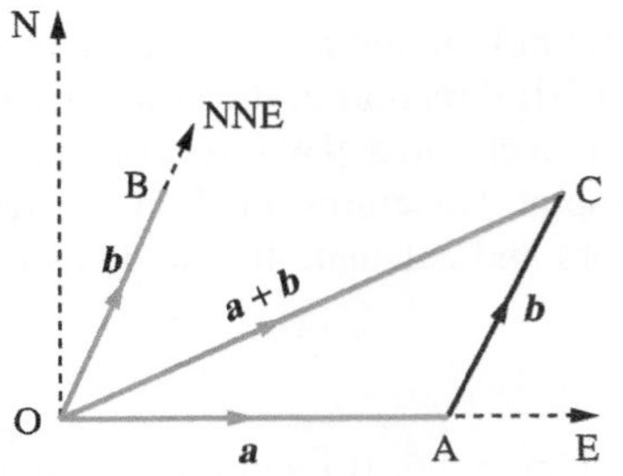

Figure 4.7 Addition of two vectors.

other hand, the vessel steams due E through water that is simultaneously moving NNE with the tidal stream then the result will be to arrive at C after one hour. The net velocity of the boat is represented by the line OC. Putting this another way, the result of subjecting the boat to a velocity $\overrightarrow{OA}$ and a velocity $\overrightarrow{AC}$ simultaneously is the same as the result of subjecting it to a velocity $\overrightarrow{OC}$. Thus the velocity $\overrightarrow{OC} = \boldsymbol{a} + \boldsymbol{b}$ is the sum of the velocity $\overrightarrow{OA} = \boldsymbol{a}$ and the velocity $\overrightarrow{AC} = \boldsymbol{b}$.

This leads us to the **parallelogram rule** for vector addition illustrated in Figure 4.8 and stated as follows:

> The sum, or resultant, of two vectors $\boldsymbol{a}$ and $\boldsymbol{b}$ is found by forming a parallelogram with $\boldsymbol{a}$ and $\boldsymbol{b}$ as two adjacent sides. The sum $\boldsymbol{a} + \boldsymbol{b}$ is the vector represented by the diagonal of the parallelogram.

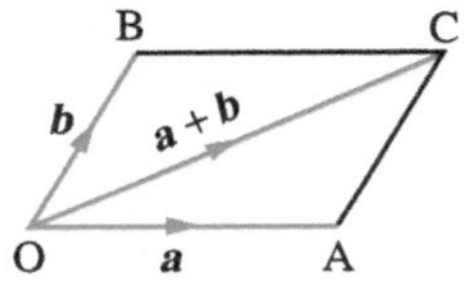

Figure 4.8 Parallelogram rule for addition of vectors.

In Figure 4.8 the vectors $\overrightarrow{OB}$ and $\overrightarrow{AC}$ are the same, so we can rewrite the parallelogram rule as an equivalent **triangle law** (Figure 4.9), which can be stated as follows:

> If two vectors $\boldsymbol{a}$ and $\boldsymbol{b}$ are represented in magnitude and direction by the two sides of a triangle taken in order then their sum is represented in magnitude and direction by the closing third side.

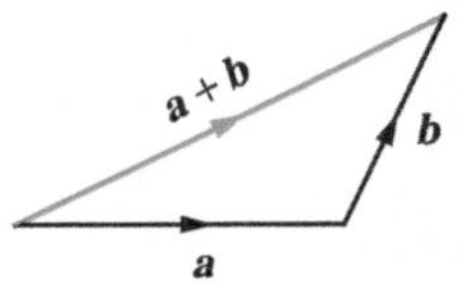

Figure 4.9 Triangle law for addition of vectors.

The triangle law for the addition of vectors can be extended to the addition of any number of vectors. If from a point O (Figure 4.10), displacements $\overrightarrow{OA}$, $\overrightarrow{AB}$, $\overrightarrow{BC}$, … , $\overrightarrow{LK}$ are drawn along the adjacent sides of a polygon to represent in magnitude and direction the vectors $\boldsymbol{a}, \boldsymbol{b}, \boldsymbol{c}, \ldots, \boldsymbol{k}$ respectively then the sum

$$\boldsymbol{r} = \boldsymbol{a} + \boldsymbol{b} + \boldsymbol{c} + \ldots + \boldsymbol{k}$$

of these vectors is represented in magnitude and direction by the closing side OK of the polygon, the sense of the sum vector being represented by the arrow in Figure 4.10. This is referred to as the **polygon law** for the addition of vectors.

We now need to look at the usual rules of algebra for scalar quantities to check whether or not they are satisfied for vectors.

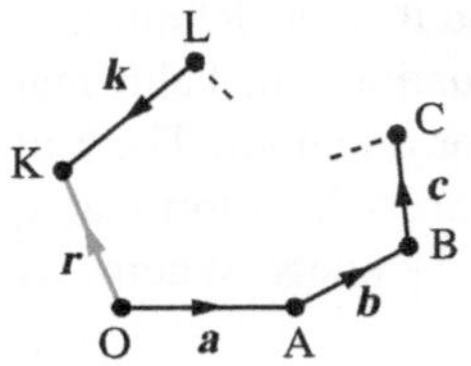

Figure 4.10 Polygon law for addition of vectors.

(a) Commutative law

$$\boldsymbol{a} + \boldsymbol{b} = \boldsymbol{b} + \boldsymbol{a}$$

This result is obvious from the geometrical definition, and says that order does not matter.

(b) Associative law

$$(\boldsymbol{a} + \boldsymbol{b}) + \boldsymbol{c} = \boldsymbol{a} + (\boldsymbol{b} + \boldsymbol{c})$$

Geometrically, the result can be deduced using the triangle and polygon laws, as shown in Figure 4.11. We see that brackets do not matter and can be omitted.

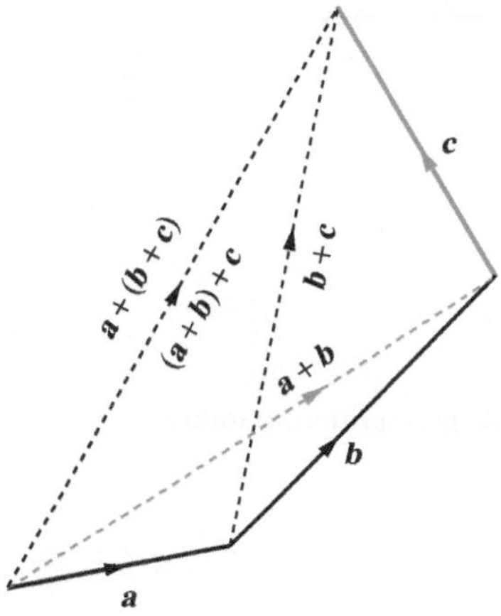

Figure 4.11 Deduction of the associative law.

(c) Distributive law

$$\lambda(\boldsymbol{a} + \boldsymbol{b}) = \lambda\boldsymbol{a} + \lambda\boldsymbol{b}$$

The result follows from similar triangles. In Figure 4.12 the side O′B′ is just λ times OB in length and in the same direction, so $\overrightarrow{\mathrm{O'B'}} = \lambda(\boldsymbol{a} + \boldsymbol{b})$. The triangle law therefore gives the required result since $\overrightarrow{\mathrm{O'B'}} = \overrightarrow{\mathrm{O'A'}} + \overrightarrow{\mathrm{A'B'}} = \lambda\boldsymbol{a} + \lambda\boldsymbol{b}$. This result just says that we can multiply brackets out by the usual laws of algebra.

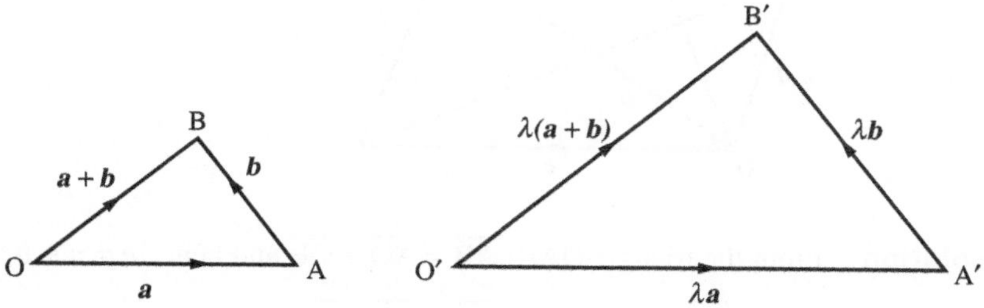

Figure 4.12 Similar triangles for the proof of the distributive law.

(d) Subtraction

We define subtraction in the obvious way:

$$\boldsymbol{a} - \boldsymbol{b} = \boldsymbol{a} + (-\boldsymbol{b})$$

This is illustrated geometrically in Figure 4.13. Applying the triangle rule to triangle OAB gives

$$\begin{aligned}\overrightarrow{\mathrm{BA}} &= \overrightarrow{\mathrm{BO}} + \overrightarrow{\mathrm{OA}} = \overrightarrow{\mathrm{OA}} + \overrightarrow{\mathrm{BO}} \\ &= \overrightarrow{\mathrm{OA}} - \overrightarrow{\mathrm{OB}} \quad \text{since} \quad \overrightarrow{\mathrm{BO}} = -\overrightarrow{\mathrm{OB}}\end{aligned}$$

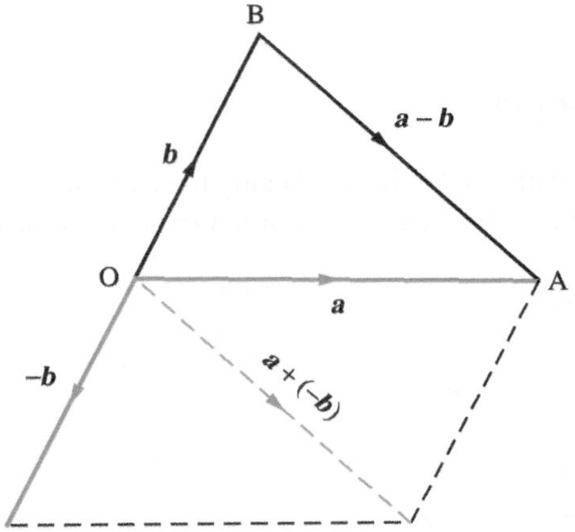

Figure 4.13
Subtraction of vectors.

from which the important result is obtained, namely

$$\overrightarrow{BA} = \overrightarrow{OA} - \overrightarrow{OB}$$

Example 4.4

From Figure 4.14, evaluate

$\boldsymbol{g}$ in terms of $\boldsymbol{a}$ and $\boldsymbol{b}$, $\boldsymbol{f}$ in terms of $\boldsymbol{b}$ and $\boldsymbol{c}$

$\boldsymbol{e}$ in terms of $\boldsymbol{c}$ and $\boldsymbol{d}$, $\boldsymbol{e}$ in terms of $\boldsymbol{f}$, $\boldsymbol{g}$ and $\boldsymbol{h}$

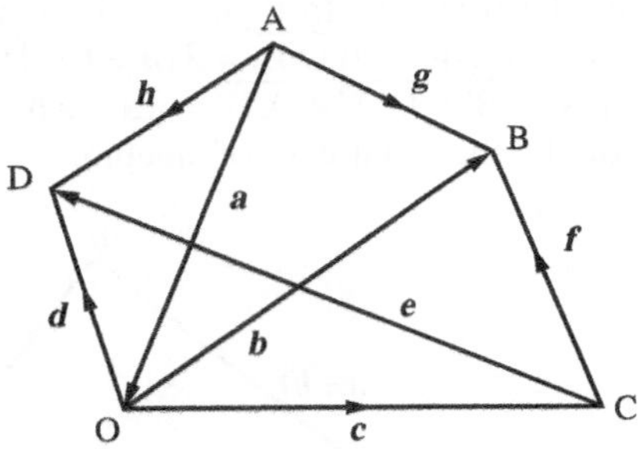

Figure 4.14
Figure of Example 4.4.

Solution

From the triangle OAB: $\overrightarrow{AB} = \overrightarrow{AO} + \overrightarrow{OB}$ and hence $\boldsymbol{g} = \boldsymbol{a} + \boldsymbol{b}$

From the triangle OBC: $\overrightarrow{CB} = \overrightarrow{OB} - \overrightarrow{OC}$ and hence $\boldsymbol{f} = \boldsymbol{b} - \boldsymbol{c}$

From the triangle OCD: $\overrightarrow{CD} = \overrightarrow{OD} - \overrightarrow{OC}$ and hence $\boldsymbol{e} = \boldsymbol{d} - \boldsymbol{c}$

From the quadrilateral CBAD the polygon rule gives

$\overrightarrow{CD} + \overrightarrow{DA} + \overrightarrow{AB} + \overrightarrow{BC} = 0$ and hence $\boldsymbol{e} + (-\boldsymbol{h}) + \boldsymbol{g} + (-\boldsymbol{f}) = \boldsymbol{0}$ so $\boldsymbol{e} = \boldsymbol{f} - \boldsymbol{g} + \boldsymbol{h}$

Example 4.5

A quadrilateral OACB is defined in terms of the vectors $\overrightarrow{OA} = \boldsymbol{a}$, $\overrightarrow{OB} = \boldsymbol{b}$ and $\overrightarrow{OC} = \boldsymbol{b} + \frac{1}{2}\boldsymbol{a}$. Calculate the vector representing the other two sides $\overrightarrow{BC}$ and $\overrightarrow{CA}$.

Solution Now as in rule (d)

$$\overrightarrow{BC} = \overrightarrow{BO} + \overrightarrow{OC} = -\overrightarrow{OB} + \overrightarrow{OC}$$

so

$$\overrightarrow{BC} = \overrightarrow{OC} - \overrightarrow{OB} = (\boldsymbol{b} + \tfrac{1}{2}\boldsymbol{a}) - \boldsymbol{b} = \tfrac{1}{2}\boldsymbol{a}$$

and similarly $\overrightarrow{CA} = \overrightarrow{OA} - \overrightarrow{OC} = \boldsymbol{a} - (\boldsymbol{b} + \tfrac{1}{2}\boldsymbol{a}) = \tfrac{1}{2}\boldsymbol{a} - \boldsymbol{b}$

Example 4.6 A force $\boldsymbol{F}$ has magnitude 2 N and a second force $\boldsymbol{F}'$ has magnitude 1 N and is inclined at an angle of 60° to $\boldsymbol{F}$, as illustrated in Figure 4.15. Find the magnitude of the resultant force $\boldsymbol{R}$ and the angle it makes to the force $\boldsymbol{F}$.

Solution (i) Now, from Figure 4.15 we have $\boldsymbol{R} = \boldsymbol{F} + \boldsymbol{F}'$, so we require the length OC and the angle CON.

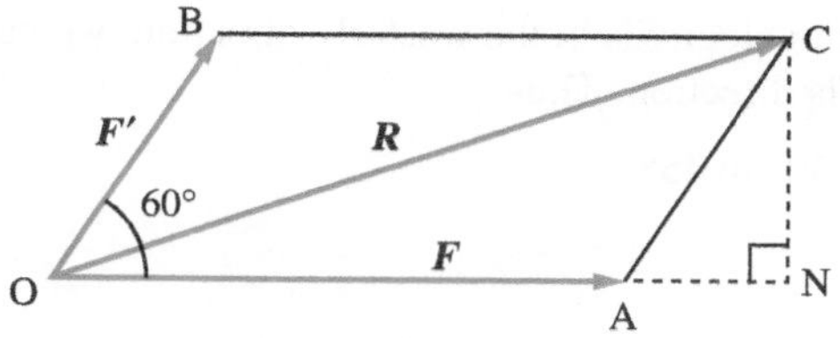

Figure 4.15
Figure of Example 4.6.

(ii) We first need to calculate CN and AN using trigonometry. Noting that $|\boldsymbol{F}'| = \text{OB} = \text{AC} = 1$ we see that

$$\text{CN} = \text{AC} \sin 60° = \tfrac{\sqrt{3}}{2} \quad \text{and} \quad \text{AN} = \text{AC} \cos 60° = \tfrac{1}{2}$$

(iii) Noting that $|\boldsymbol{F}| = \text{OA} = 2$ then $\text{ON} = \text{OA} + \text{AN} = \tfrac{5}{2}$. Thus using Pythagoras' theorem

$$\text{OC}^2 = \text{ON}^2 + \text{CN}^2 = \left(\tfrac{\sqrt{3}}{2}\right)^2 + \left(\tfrac{5}{2}\right)^2 = 7$$

and hence the resultant has magnitude $\sqrt{7}$.

(iv) The angle CON is determined from $\tan \text{CON} = \dfrac{\text{CN}}{\text{ON}} = \tfrac{\sqrt{3}}{5}$ giving angle CON = 19.1°.

Example 4.7 An aeroplane is flying at 400 knots in a strong NW wind of 50 knots. The pilot wishes to fly due west. In which direction should the pilot fly the plane to achieve this end, and what will be his actual speed over the ground?

Solution The resultant velocity of the plane is the vector sum of 50 knots from the NW direction and 400 knots in a direction $\alpha°$ north of west. In appropriate units the situation is shown in Figure 4.16(a). The vector $\overrightarrow{OA}$ represents the wind velocity and $\overrightarrow{OB}$ represents the aeroplane velocity. The resultant velocity is $\overrightarrow{OP}$, which is required to be due W. We wish to determine the angle α (giving the direction of flight) and magnitude of the resultant velocity (giving the ground speed).

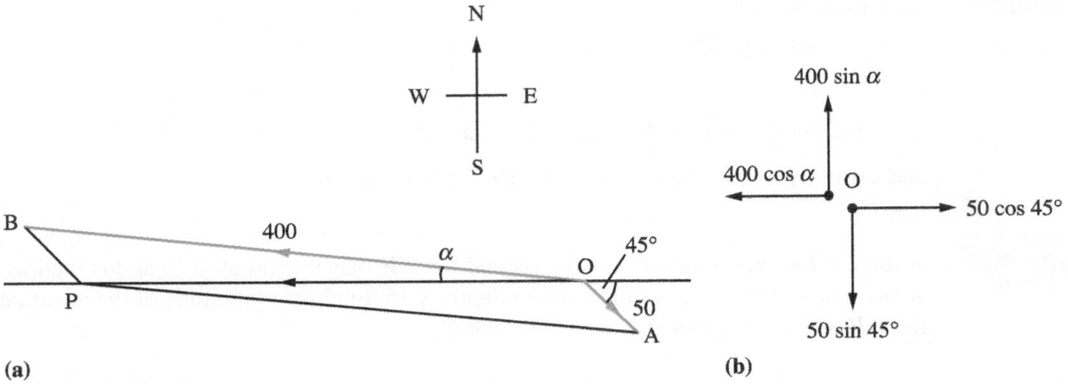

Figure 4.16 (a) The track of the aeroplane in Example 4.7. (b) Resolving the velocity into components.

Resolving the velocity into components as illustrated in Figure 4.16(b) and recognizing that the resultant velocity is in the westerly direction, we have no resultant velocity perpendicular to this direction. Thus

$$400 \sin \alpha° = 50 \sin 45°$$

so that

$$\alpha = 5.07°$$

The resultant speed due west is

$$400 \cos \alpha° - 50 \cos 45° = 363 \text{ knots}$$

Example 4.8

If ABCD is any quadrilateral, show that $\overrightarrow{AD} + \overrightarrow{BC} = 2\overrightarrow{EF}$, where E and F are the midpoints of AB and DC respectively, and that

$$\overrightarrow{AB} + \overrightarrow{AD} + \overrightarrow{CB} + \overrightarrow{CD} = 4\overrightarrow{XY}$$

where X and Y are the midpoints of the diagonals AC and BD respectively.

Solution Applying the polygon law for the addition of vectors to Figure 4.17,

$$\overrightarrow{EF} = \overrightarrow{EA} + \overrightarrow{AD} + \overrightarrow{DF}$$

and

$$\overrightarrow{EF} = \overrightarrow{EB} + \overrightarrow{BC} + \overrightarrow{CF}$$

Adding these two then gives

$$2\overrightarrow{EF} = \overrightarrow{EA} + \overrightarrow{AD} + \overrightarrow{DF} + \overrightarrow{EB} + \overrightarrow{BC} + \overrightarrow{CF}$$

$$= \overrightarrow{AD} + \overrightarrow{BC} + (\tfrac{1}{2}\overrightarrow{BA} + \tfrac{1}{2}\overrightarrow{CD} - \tfrac{1}{2}\overrightarrow{BA} - \tfrac{1}{2}\overrightarrow{CD})$$

since E and F are the midpoints of AB and CD respectively. Thus

$$2\overrightarrow{EF} = \overrightarrow{AD} + \overrightarrow{BC}$$

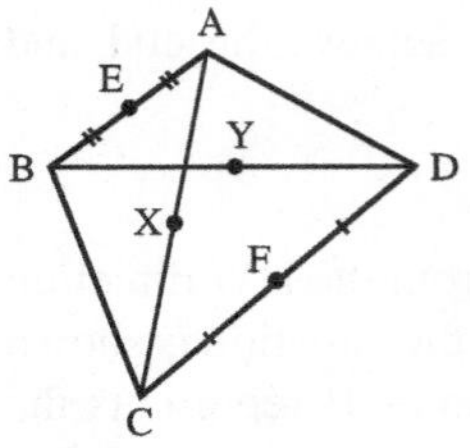

Figure 4.17 Quadrilateral of Example 4.8.

Also, by the polygon law for addition of vectors,

$$\overrightarrow{XY} = \overrightarrow{XA} + \overrightarrow{AB} + \overrightarrow{BY}$$

and

$$\overrightarrow{XY} = \overrightarrow{XC} + \overrightarrow{CB} + \overrightarrow{BY}$$

Adding and multiplying by two gives

$$\begin{aligned}4\overrightarrow{XY} &= 2\overrightarrow{XA} + 2\overrightarrow{AB} + 2\overrightarrow{BY} + 2\overrightarrow{XC} + 2\overrightarrow{CB} + 2\overrightarrow{BY} \\ &= 2\overrightarrow{AB} + 2\overrightarrow{CB} + 4\overrightarrow{BY} \qquad (\text{since } \overrightarrow{XA} = -\overrightarrow{XC}) \\ &= 2\overrightarrow{AB} + 2\overrightarrow{CB} + 2\overrightarrow{BD} \qquad (\text{since } \overrightarrow{BD} = 2\overrightarrow{BY}) \\ &= \overrightarrow{AB} + \overrightarrow{CB} + (\overrightarrow{AB} + \overrightarrow{BD}) + (\overrightarrow{CB} + \overrightarrow{BD})\end{aligned}$$

so that

$$4\overrightarrow{XY} = \overrightarrow{AB} + \overrightarrow{CB} + \overrightarrow{AD} + \overrightarrow{CD}$$

4.2.4 Exercises

1 Given two non-parallel vectors $\boldsymbol{a}$ and $\boldsymbol{b}$, indicate on a diagram the vectors $\boldsymbol{a}+\boldsymbol{b}$, $\frac{1}{2}\boldsymbol{a}+\boldsymbol{b}$, $\boldsymbol{b}-\frac{1}{2}\boldsymbol{a}$, $\frac{3}{2}\boldsymbol{a}-\boldsymbol{b}$.

2 An aeroplane flies 100 km in a NE direction, then 120 km in a ESE direction and finally S for a further 50 km. Sketch the vectors representing this flight path. What is the distance from start to finish and also the length of the flight path?

3 (a) Given two non-parallel vectors $\boldsymbol{a}$ and $\boldsymbol{b}$, show on a diagram that any other vector $\boldsymbol{r}$ can be written as $\boldsymbol{r} = \alpha\boldsymbol{a} + \beta\boldsymbol{b}$ with constants α and β.

(b) Given three non-coplanar, non-parallel vectors $\boldsymbol{a}$, $\boldsymbol{b}$ and $\boldsymbol{c}$, show on a diagram that any other vector $\boldsymbol{r}$ can be written as $\boldsymbol{r} = \alpha\boldsymbol{a} + \beta\boldsymbol{b} + \gamma\boldsymbol{c}$ with constants α, β and γ.

4 The vector $\overrightarrow{OP}$ makes an angle of 60° with the positive x axis and 45° with the positive y axis. Find the possible angles that the vector can make with the z axis.

5 The vectors $\overrightarrow{OA} = \boldsymbol{a}$ and $\overrightarrow{OB} = \boldsymbol{b}$ are given. Find the vector $\overrightarrow{OC}$ representing the point C on AB that divides AB in the ratio AC:CB = 1:2.

6 (a) For two vectors $\boldsymbol{a} = \overrightarrow{OA}$ and $\boldsymbol{b} = \overrightarrow{OB}$ show that the midpoint of AB has the vector $\frac{1}{2}(\boldsymbol{a}+\boldsymbol{b})$.

(b) The midpoints of the sides of the quadrilateral ABCD are PQRS. Show that PQRS forms a parallelogram.

7 A regular hexagon OACDEB has adjacent sides $\overrightarrow{OA} = \boldsymbol{a}$ and $\overrightarrow{OB} = \boldsymbol{b}$. Find the vectors $\overrightarrow{OC}$, $\overrightarrow{OD}$, $\overrightarrow{OE}$ representing the other three corners in terms of $\boldsymbol{a}$ and $\boldsymbol{b}$.

8 A bird flies N at a speed of 20 m/s but the wind is simutaneously carrying it E at 5 m/s. Find the actual speed of the bird and the angle it deviates from N.

9 A cyclist travelling east at 8 kilometres per hour finds that the wind appears to blow directly from the north. On doubling his speed it appears to blow from the north-east. Find the actual velocity of the wind.

10 A weight of 100 N is suspended by two wires from a horizontal beam, as in Figure 4.18. Find the tension in the wires.

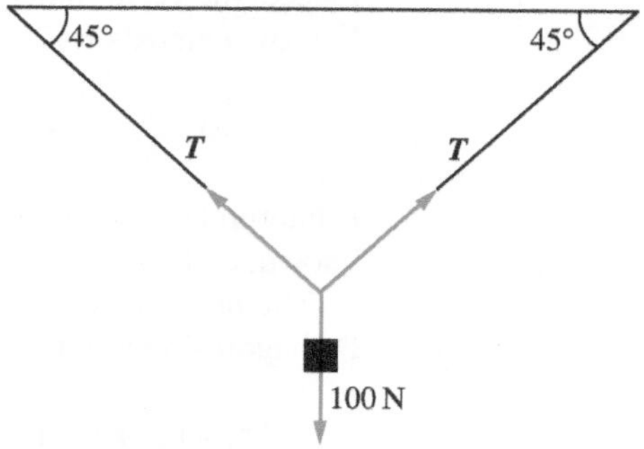

Figure 4.18 Suspended weight in Exercise 10

4.2.5 Cartesian components and basic properties

In Section 4.2.2 we saw that vectors could be written as an ordered set of three numbers or 3-tuple. We shall now explore the properties of these ordered triples and how they relate to the geometrical definitions used in previous sections.

In Figure 4.19, we denote mutually perpendicular unit vectors in the three coordinate directions by $\boldsymbol{i}$, $\boldsymbol{j}$ and $\boldsymbol{k}$. (Sometimes the alternative notation $\hat{\boldsymbol{e}}_1$, $\hat{\boldsymbol{e}}_2$ and $\hat{\boldsymbol{e}}_3$ is used.) The notation $\boldsymbol{i}$, $\boldsymbol{j}$, $\boldsymbol{k}$ is so standard that the 'hats' indicating unit vectors are usually omitted.

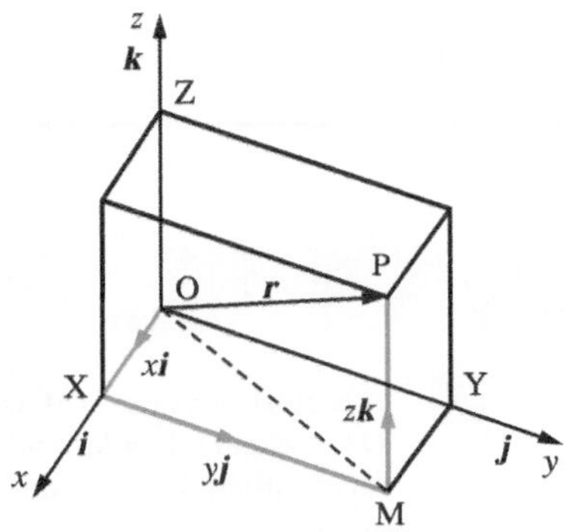

Figure 4.19
The component form of a vector.

Applying the triangle law to the triangle OXM, we have

$$\overrightarrow{OM} = \overrightarrow{OX} + \overrightarrow{XM} = x\boldsymbol{i} + y\boldsymbol{j}$$

Applying the triangle law to the triangle OMP then yields

$$\overrightarrow{OP} = \overrightarrow{OM} + \overrightarrow{MP} = x\boldsymbol{i} + y\boldsymbol{j} + z\boldsymbol{k} \tag{4.1}$$

The analysis applies to any point, so we can write any vector $\boldsymbol{r}$ in terms of its **components** x, y, z with respect to the unit vectors $\boldsymbol{i}, \boldsymbol{j}, \boldsymbol{k}$ as

$$\boldsymbol{r} = x\boldsymbol{i} + y\boldsymbol{j} + z\boldsymbol{k}$$

Indeed, the vector notation $\boldsymbol{r} = (x, y, z)$ should be intepreted as the vector given in (4.1). In some contexts it is more convenient to use a suffix notation for the coordinates, and

$$(x_1, x_2, x_3) = x_1\hat{\boldsymbol{e}}_1 + x_2\hat{\boldsymbol{e}}_2 + x_3\hat{\boldsymbol{e}}_3$$

is interpreted in exactly the same way. It is assumed that the three basic unit vectors are known, and all vectors in coordinate form are referred to them.

The **modulus** of a vector is just the length OP, so from Figure 4.19 we have, using Pythagoras' theorem,

$$|\boldsymbol{r}| = (x^2 + y^2 + z^2)^{1/2}$$

The basic properties of vectors follow easily from the component definition in (4.1).

(a) Equality

Two vectors $\boldsymbol{a} = (a_1, a_2, a_3)$ and $\boldsymbol{b} = (b_1, b_2, b_3)$ are **equal** if and only if the three components are equal, that is

$$a_1 = b_1, \quad a_2 = b_2, \quad a_3 = b_3$$

(b) Zero vector

The zero vector has zero components, so

$$\mathbf{0} = (0, 0, 0)$$

(c) Addition

The addition rule is expressed very simply in terms of vector components:

$$\boldsymbol{a} + \boldsymbol{b} = (a_1 + b_1, a_2 + b_2, a_3 + b_3)$$

The equivalence of this definition with the geometrical definition for addition using the parallelogram rule can be deduced from Figure 4.20. We know that $\overrightarrow{OB} = \overrightarrow{AC}$, since they are equivalent displacements, and hence their x components are the same, so that we have OL = MN. Thus if we take the x component of $\boldsymbol{a} + \boldsymbol{b}$

$$(\boldsymbol{a} + \boldsymbol{b})_1 = \text{ON} = \text{OM} + \text{MN} = \text{OM} + \text{OL} = a_1 + b_1$$

the y and z components can be considered in a similar manner, giving $(\boldsymbol{a} + \boldsymbol{b})_2 = a_2 + b_2$ and $(\boldsymbol{a} + \boldsymbol{b})_3 = a_3 + b_3$.

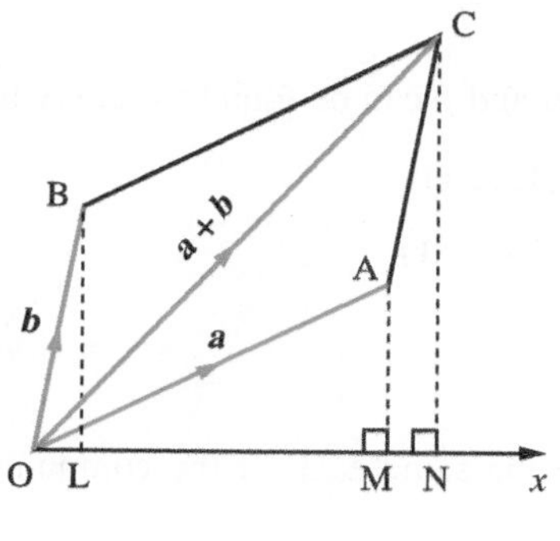

Figure 4.20
Parallelogram rule, x component.

(d) Multiplication by a scalar

If λ is a scalar and the vectors are related by $\boldsymbol{a} = \lambda \boldsymbol{b}$ then the components satisfy

$$a_1 = \lambda b_1, \quad a_2 = \lambda b_2, \quad a_3 = \lambda b_3$$

which follows from the similar triangles of Figure 4.12.

(e) Distributive law

The distributive law in components is simply a restatement of the distributive law for the addition of numbers:

$$\begin{aligned}\lambda(\mathbf{a}+\mathbf{b}) &= \lambda(a_1+b_1, a_2+b_2, a_3+b_3)\\ &= (\lambda(a_1+b_1), \lambda(a_2+b_2), \lambda(a_3+b_3))\\ &= (\lambda a_1+\lambda b_1, \lambda a_2+\lambda b_2, \lambda a_3+\lambda b_3)\\ &= (\lambda a_1, \lambda a_2, \lambda a_3)+(\lambda b_1, \lambda b_2, \lambda b_3)\\ &= \lambda\mathbf{a}+\lambda\mathbf{b}\end{aligned}$$

(f) Subtraction

Subtraction is again straightforward and the components are just subtracted from each other:

$$\mathbf{a}-\mathbf{b} = (a_1-b_1, a_2-b_2, a_3-b_3)$$

The component form of vectors allows problems to be solved algebraically and results can be interpreted either as algebraic ideas or in a geometrical manner. Both these interpretations can be very useful in applications of vectors to engineering.

In MATLAB a vector is inserted as an array within square brackets, so, for example, a vector $\mathbf{a} = (1, 2, 3)$ is inserted as `a = [1 2 3]` or `a = [1,2,3]`, where in the latter commas have been used instead of spaces. It is inserted as `a:= array([1,2,3]);` in MAPLE, where it is usually necessary to invoke the *linalg* package first. The operations of addition, subtraction and multiplication by a scalar are represented by `+`, `-` and `*` respectively, but to evaluate the operations numerically requires the instruction *evalm*. The magnitude or length of a vector **a** appears in MATLAB as `norm(a)` and in MAPLE as `norm(a,2)`.

Example 4.9 Determine whether constants α and β can be found to satisfy the vector equations

(a) $(2, 1, 0) = \alpha(-2, 0, 2) + \beta(1, 1, 1)$

(b) $(-3, 1, 2) = \alpha(-2, 0, 2) + \beta(1, 1, 1)$

and interpret the results.

Solution (a) For the two vectors to be the same each of the components must be equal, and hence

$$\begin{aligned}2 &= -2\alpha+\beta\\ 1 &= \beta\\ 0 &= 2\alpha+\beta\end{aligned}$$

Thus the second equation gives $\beta = 1$ and both of the other two equations give the same value of α, namely $\alpha = -\frac{1}{2}$, so the equations can be satisfied.

(b) A similar argument gives

$$\begin{aligned}-3 &= -2\alpha+\beta\\ 1 &= \beta\\ 2 &= 2\alpha+\beta\end{aligned}$$

Again, the second equation gives $\beta = 1$ but the first equation leads to $\alpha = 2$ and the third to $\alpha = \frac{1}{2}$. The equations are now not consistent and no appropriate α and β can be found.

In case (a) the three vectors lie in a plane, and any vector in a plane, including the one given, can be written as the vector sum of the two vectors (–2, 0, 2) and (1, 1, 1) with appropriate multipliers. In case (b), however, the vector (–3, 1, 2) does not lie in the plane of the two vectors (–2, 0, 2) and (1, 1, 1) and can, therefore, never be written as the vector sum of the two vectors (–2, 0, 2) and (1, 1, 1) with appropriate multipliers.

Example 4.10 Given the vectors $\boldsymbol{a} = (1, 1, 1)$, $\boldsymbol{b} = (-1, 2, 3)$ and $\boldsymbol{c} = (0, 3, 4)$, find

(a) $\boldsymbol{a} + \boldsymbol{b}$ (b) $2\boldsymbol{a} - \boldsymbol{b}$ (c) $\boldsymbol{a} + \boldsymbol{b} - \boldsymbol{c}$

(d) the unit vector in the direction of $\boldsymbol{c}$

Solution (a) $\boldsymbol{a} + \boldsymbol{b} = (1 - 1, 1 + 2, 1 + 3) = (0, 3, 4)$

(b) $2\boldsymbol{a} - \boldsymbol{b} = (2 \times 1 - (-1), 2 \times 1 - 2, 2 \times 1 - 3) = (3, 0, -1)$

(c) $\boldsymbol{a} + \boldsymbol{b} - \boldsymbol{c} = (1 - 1 + 0, 1 + 2 - 3, 1 + 3 - 4) = (0, 0, 0) = \boldsymbol{0}$

(d) $|\boldsymbol{c}| = (3^2 + 4^2)^{1/2} = 5$, so

$$\hat{\boldsymbol{c}} = \frac{\boldsymbol{c}}{5} = (0, \tfrac{3}{5}, \tfrac{4}{5})$$

Example 4.11 Given $\boldsymbol{a} = (2, -3, 1) = 2\boldsymbol{i} - 3\boldsymbol{j} + \boldsymbol{k}$, $\boldsymbol{b} = (1, 5, -2) = \boldsymbol{i} + 5\boldsymbol{j} - 2\boldsymbol{k}$ and $\boldsymbol{c} = (3, -4, 3) = 3\boldsymbol{i} - 4\boldsymbol{j} + 3\boldsymbol{k}$

(a) find the vector $\boldsymbol{d} = \boldsymbol{a} - 2\boldsymbol{b} + 3\boldsymbol{c}$;

(b) find the magnitude of $\boldsymbol{d}$ and write down a unit vector in the direction of $\boldsymbol{d}$;

(c) what are the direction cosines of $\boldsymbol{d}$?

Solution (a)

$$\begin{aligned} \boldsymbol{d} &= \boldsymbol{a} - 2\boldsymbol{b} + 3\boldsymbol{c} \\ &= (2\boldsymbol{i} - 3\boldsymbol{j} + \boldsymbol{k}) - 2(\boldsymbol{i} + 5\boldsymbol{j} - 2\boldsymbol{k}) + 3(3\boldsymbol{i} - 4\boldsymbol{j} + 3\boldsymbol{k}) \\ &= (2\boldsymbol{i} - 3\boldsymbol{j} + \boldsymbol{k}) - (2\boldsymbol{i} + 10\boldsymbol{j} - 4\boldsymbol{k}) + (9\boldsymbol{i} - 12\boldsymbol{j} + 9\boldsymbol{k}) \\ &= (2 - 2 + 9)\boldsymbol{i} + (-3 - 10 - 12)\boldsymbol{j} + (1 + 4 + 9)\boldsymbol{k} \end{aligned}$$

that is, $\boldsymbol{d} = 9\boldsymbol{i} - 25\boldsymbol{j} + 14\boldsymbol{k}$.

(b) The magnitude of $\boldsymbol{d}$ is $d = \sqrt{[9^2 + (-25)^2 + 14^2]} = \sqrt{902}$
A unit vector in the direction of $\boldsymbol{d}$ is $\hat{\boldsymbol{d}}$, where

$$\hat{\boldsymbol{d}} = \frac{\boldsymbol{d}}{d} = \frac{9}{\sqrt{902}}\boldsymbol{i} - \frac{25}{\sqrt{902}}\boldsymbol{j} + \frac{14}{\sqrt{902}}\boldsymbol{k}$$

(c) The direction cosines of $\boldsymbol{d}$ are $9/\sqrt{902}$, $-25/\sqrt{902}$ and $14/\sqrt{902}$.

Check that in MATLAB the commands

```
a = [2 -3 1]; b = [1 5 -2]; c = [3 -4 3];
d = a - 2*b + 3*c
```

return the answer given in (a) and that the further command

```
norm(d)
```

gives the magnitude of $\boldsymbol{d}$ as 30.0333. Here MATLAB gives the numeric answer; to obtain the answer in the exact form then the calculation in MATLAB must be done symbolically using the Symbolic Math Toolbox. To do this the vector $\boldsymbol{d}$ must first be expressed in symbolic form using the `sym` command. Since the command `norm` does not appear to be available directly in the Toolbox, use can be made of the `maple` command to access the command in MAPLE. Check that the commands

```
d = sym(d);
maple('norm',d,2)
```

return the answer `902^(1/2)` given in (b).

Example 4.12

A molecule XY_3 has a tetrahedral form; the position vector of the X atom is $(2\sqrt{3}+\sqrt{2}, 0, -2+\sqrt{6})$ and those of the three Y atoms are

$$\overrightarrow{OY} = (\sqrt{3}, -2, -1), \quad \overrightarrow{OY'} = (\sqrt{3}, 2, -1), \quad \overrightarrow{OY''} = (\sqrt{2}, 0, \sqrt{6})$$

(a) Show that all of the bond lengths are equal.

(b) Show that $\overrightarrow{XY} + \overrightarrow{YY'} + \overrightarrow{Y'Y''} + \overrightarrow{Y''X} = \mathbf{0}$

Solution

(a) $\overrightarrow{XY} = \overrightarrow{OY} - \overrightarrow{OX} = (-\sqrt{3}-\sqrt{2}, -2, 1-\sqrt{6})$ and the bond length is

$$|\overrightarrow{XY}| = [(-\sqrt{3}-\sqrt{2})^2 + (-2)^2 + (1-\sqrt{6})^2]^{1/2} = 4$$

$\overrightarrow{YY'} = \overrightarrow{OY'} - \overrightarrow{OY} = (0, 4, 0)$ and clearly the bond length is again 4.

The other four bonds $\overrightarrow{XY'}$, $\overrightarrow{XY''}$, $\overrightarrow{Y'Y''}$, $\overrightarrow{Y''Y}$ are treated in exactly the same way, and each gives a bond length of 4.

(b) Now $\overrightarrow{Y'Y''} = \overrightarrow{OY''} - \overrightarrow{OY'} = (\sqrt{2}-\sqrt{3}, -2, \sqrt{6}+1)$ and $\overrightarrow{Y''X} = \overrightarrow{OX} - \overrightarrow{OY''} = (2\sqrt{3}, 0, -2)$, so adding the four vectors gives

$$\overrightarrow{XY} + \overrightarrow{YY'} + \overrightarrow{Y'Y''} + \overrightarrow{Y''X}$$
$$= (-\sqrt{3}-\sqrt{2}, -2, 1-\sqrt{6}) + (0, 4, 0) + (\sqrt{2}-\sqrt{3}, -2, \sqrt{6}+1) + (2\sqrt{3}, 0, -2)$$
$$= \mathbf{0}$$

and is just a verification of the polygon law.

Example 4.13

Three forces, with units of newtons,

$$\boldsymbol{F}_1 = (1, 1, 1)$$

F_2 has magnitude 6 and acts in the direction (1, 2, −2)

F_3 has magnitude 10 and acts in the direction (3, −4, 0)

act on a particle. Find the resultant force that acts on the particle. What additional force must be imposed on the particle to reduce the resultant force to zero?

Solution The first force is given in the usual vector form. The second two are given in an equally acceptable way but it is necessary to convert the information to the normal vector form so that the resultant can be found by vector addition. First the unit vector in the given direction of F_2 is required:

$$|(1, 2, -2)| = (1 + 2^2 + (-2)^2)^{1/2} = 3$$

and hence the unit vector in this direction is $\frac{1}{3}(1, 2, -2)$. Since F_2 is in the direction of this unit vector and has magnitude 6 it can be written $F_2 = 6(\frac{1}{3}, \frac{2}{3}, -\frac{2}{3}) = (2, 4, -4)$

Similarly for F_3, the unit vector is $\frac{1}{5}(3, -4, 0)$ and hence $F_3 = (6, -8, 0)$. The resultant force is obtained by vector addition.

$$F = F_1 + F_2 + F_3 = (1, 1, 1) + (2, 4, -4) + (6, -8, 0) = (9, -3, -3)$$

Clearly to make the resultant force zero, the additional force (−9, 3, 3) must be imposed on the particle.

Example 4.14 Two geostationary satellites have known positions $(0, 0, h)$ and $(0, A, H)$ relative to a fixed set of axes on the earth's surface (which is assumed flat, with the x and y axes lying on the surface and the z axis vertical). Radar signals measure the distance of a ship from the satellites. Find the position of the ship relative to the given axes.

Solution Figure 4.21 illustrates the situation described, with R $(a, b, 0)$ describing the position of the ship and P and Q the positions of the satellites.

The radar signals measure PR and QR which are denoted by p and q respectively. The vectors

$$\overrightarrow{PR} = \overrightarrow{OR} - \overrightarrow{OP} = (a, b, 0) - (0, 0, h) = (a, b, -h)$$

$$\overrightarrow{QR} = \overrightarrow{OR} - \overrightarrow{OQ} = (a, b, 0) - (0, A, H) = (a, b - A, -H)$$

Figure 4.21

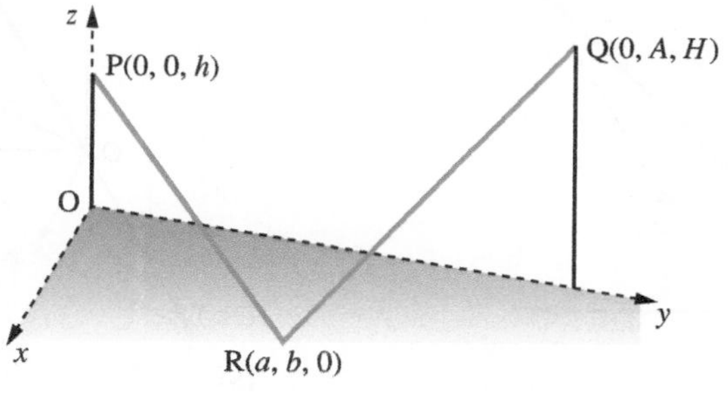

are calculated by the triangle law. The lengths of the two vectors are

$$p^2 = |\overrightarrow{PR}|^2 = a^2 + b^2 + h^2 \quad \text{and} \quad q^2 = |\overrightarrow{QR}|^2 = a^2 + (b - A)^2 + H^2$$

Subtracting gives

$$p^2 - q^2 = A(2b - A) + h^2 - H^2$$

and hence

$$b = (p^2 - q^2 - h^2 + H^2 + A^2)/2A$$

Having calculated b then a can be calculated from

$$a = \pm\sqrt{(p^2 - b^2 - h^2)}$$

Note the ambiguity in sign; clearly it will need to be known on which side of the y axis the ship is lying.

Comment In practice the axes will need to be transformed to standard latitude and longitude and the curvature of the earth will need to be taken into consideration.

4.2.6 Complex numbers as vectors

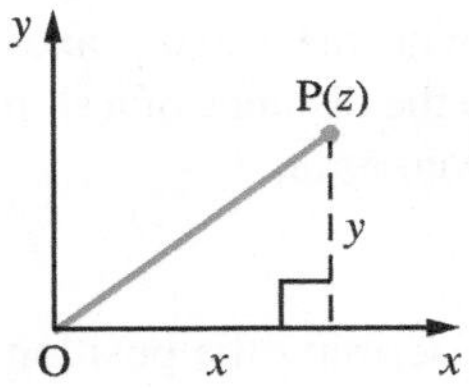

Figure 4.22 Argand diagram representation of $z = x + jy$.

We saw in Section 3.2.1, that a complex number $z = x + jy$ can be represented geometrically by the point P in the Argand diagram, as illustrated in Figure 4.22. We could equally well represent the point P by the vector $\overrightarrow{OP}$. Hence we can express the complex number z as a two-dimensional vector

$$z = \overrightarrow{OP}$$

With this interpretation of a complex number we can use the parallelogram rule to represent the addition and subtraction of complex numbers geometrically, as illustrated in Figures 4.23(a, b).

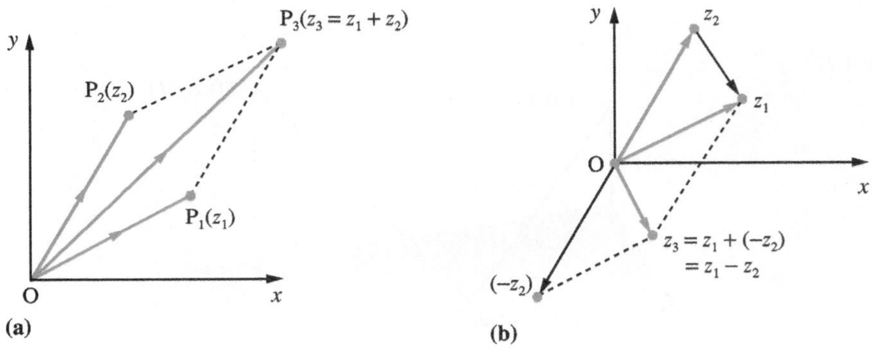

Figure 4.23 (a) Addition of complex numbers. (b) Subtraction of complex numbers.

Example 4.15

A square is formed in the first and second quadrant with OP as one side of the square and $\overrightarrow{OP} = (1, 2)$. Find the coordinates of the other two vertices of the square.

Solution

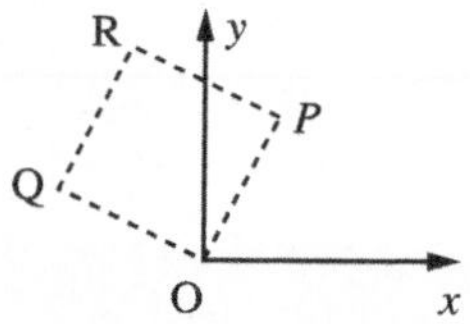

Figure 4.24 Square of Example 4.15.

The situation is illustrated in Figure 4.24. Using the complex form $\overrightarrow{OP} = 1 + 2j$ the side OQ is obtained by rotating OP through $\pi/2$ radians, then

$$\overrightarrow{OQ} = j(1 + 2j) = -2 + j$$

The fourth point R is found by observing that $\overrightarrow{OR}$ is the vector sum of $\overrightarrow{OP}$ and $\overrightarrow{OQ}$, and hence

$$\overrightarrow{OR} = \overrightarrow{OP} + \overrightarrow{OQ} = -1 + j3$$

The four coordinates are therefore

$$(0, 0), (1, 2), (-2, 1) \text{ and } (-1, 3)$$

Example 4.16

M is the centre of a square with vertices A, B, C and D taken anticlockwise in that order. If, in the Argand diagram, M and A are represented by the complex numbers $-2 + j$ and $1 + j5$ respectively, find the complex numbers represented by the vertices B, C and D.

Solution

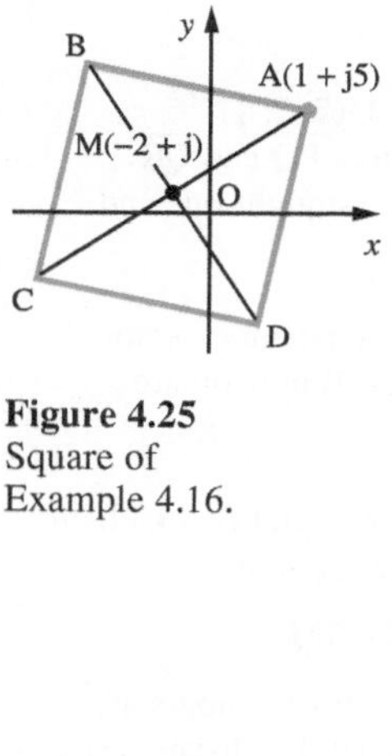

Figure 4.25 Square of Example 4.16.

Applying the triangle law for addition of vectors of Figure 4.25 gives

$$\begin{aligned}\overrightarrow{MA} &= \overrightarrow{MO} + \overrightarrow{OA}\\ &= \overrightarrow{OA} - \overrightarrow{OM}\\ &\equiv (1 + j5) - (-2 + j)\\ &= 3 + j4\end{aligned}$$

Since ABCD is a square,

$$MA = MB = MC = MD$$

$$\angle AMB = \angle BMC = \angle CMD = \angle DMA = \tfrac{1}{2}\pi$$

Remembering that multiplying a complex number by j rotates it through $\frac{1}{2}\pi$ radians in an anticlockwise direction, we have

$$\overrightarrow{MB} = j\overrightarrow{MA} \equiv j(3 + j4) = -4 + j3$$

giving

$$\overrightarrow{OB} = \overrightarrow{OM} + \overrightarrow{MB} \equiv (-2 + j) + (-4 + j3) = -6 + j4$$

Likewise

$$\overrightarrow{MC} = j\overrightarrow{MB} \equiv j(-4 + j3) = -3 - j4$$

giving

$$\overrightarrow{OC} = \overrightarrow{OM} + \overrightarrow{MC} \equiv -5 - j3$$

and

$$\overrightarrow{MD} = \mathrm{j}\overrightarrow{MC} \equiv \mathrm{j}(-3 - \mathrm{j}4) = 4 - \mathrm{j}3$$

giving

$$\overrightarrow{OD} = \overrightarrow{OM} + \overrightarrow{MD} \equiv 2 - \mathrm{j}2$$

Thus the vertices B, C and D are represented by the complex numbers $-6 + \mathrm{j}4$, $-5 - \mathrm{j}3$ and $2 - \mathrm{j}2$ respectively.

4.2.7 Exercises

Check your answers using MATLAB or MAPLE whenever possible.

11 Given $\boldsymbol{a} = (1, 1, 0)$, $\boldsymbol{b} = (2, 2, 1)$ and $\boldsymbol{c} = (0, 1, 1)$, evaluate

(a) $\boldsymbol{a} + \boldsymbol{b}$ (b) $\boldsymbol{a} + \frac{1}{2}\boldsymbol{b} + 2\boldsymbol{c}$ (c) $\boldsymbol{b} - 2\boldsymbol{a}$

(d) $|\boldsymbol{a}|$ (e) $|\boldsymbol{b}|$ (f) $|\boldsymbol{a} - \boldsymbol{b}|$

(g) $\hat{\boldsymbol{a}}$ (h) $\hat{\boldsymbol{b}}$

12 If the position vectors of the points P and Q are $\boldsymbol{i} + 3\boldsymbol{j} - 7\boldsymbol{k}$ and $5\boldsymbol{i} - 2\boldsymbol{j} + 4\boldsymbol{k}$ respectively, find $\overrightarrow{PQ}$ and determine its length and direction cosines.

13 A particle P is acted upon by forces (measured in newtons) $\boldsymbol{F}_1 = 3\boldsymbol{i} - 2\boldsymbol{j} + 5\boldsymbol{k}$, $\boldsymbol{F}_2 = -\boldsymbol{i} + 7\boldsymbol{j} - 3\boldsymbol{k}$, $\boldsymbol{F}_3 = 5\boldsymbol{i} - \boldsymbol{j} + 4\boldsymbol{k}$ and $\boldsymbol{F}_4 = -2\boldsymbol{j} + 3\boldsymbol{k}$. Determine the magnitude and direction of the resultant force acting on P.

14 If $\boldsymbol{a} = 3\boldsymbol{i} - 2\boldsymbol{j} + \boldsymbol{k}$, $\boldsymbol{b} = -2\boldsymbol{i} + 5\boldsymbol{j} + 4\boldsymbol{k}$, $\boldsymbol{c} = -4\boldsymbol{i} + \boldsymbol{j} - 2\boldsymbol{k}$ and $\boldsymbol{d} = 2\boldsymbol{i} - \boldsymbol{j} + 4\boldsymbol{k}$, determine α, β and γ such that

$$\boldsymbol{d} = \alpha\boldsymbol{a} + \beta\boldsymbol{b} + \gamma\boldsymbol{c}$$

15 Prove that the vectors $2\boldsymbol{i} - 4\boldsymbol{j} - \boldsymbol{k}$, $3\boldsymbol{i} + 2\boldsymbol{j} - 2\boldsymbol{k}$ and $5\boldsymbol{i} - 2\boldsymbol{j} - 3\boldsymbol{k}$ can form the sides of a triangle. Find the lengths of each side of the triangle and show that it is right-angled.

16 Find the components of the vector $\boldsymbol{a}$ of magnitude 2 units which makes angles 60°, 60° and 135° with axes Ox, Oy, Oz respectively.

17 The points A, B and C have coordinates (1, 2, 2), (7, 2, 1) and (2, 4, 1) relative to rectangular coordinate axes. Find:

(a) the vectors $\overrightarrow{AB}$ and $\overrightarrow{AC}$

(b) $|\overrightarrow{AB} - 3\overrightarrow{AC}|$

(c) the unit vector in the direction of $\overrightarrow{AB} - 3\overrightarrow{AC}$

(d) the lengths of the vectors $\overrightarrow{AB}$ and $\overrightarrow{AC}$

(e) the vector $\overrightarrow{AM}$ where M is the midpoint of BC.

18 In the xy plane $\overrightarrow{AB} = (1, -2)$ and B is the point with coordinates (2, 2). Find the coordinates of the point A. The point C has coordinates (3, 2); find D so that $\overrightarrow{AB} = \overrightarrow{CD}$.

19 Given the points P(1, −3, 4), Q(2, 2, 1) and R(3, 7, −2), find the vectors $\overrightarrow{PQ}$ and $\overrightarrow{QR}$. Show that P, Q and R lie on a straight line and find the ratio PQ:QR.

20 Relative to a landing stage, the position vectors in kilometres of two boats A and B at noon are

$$3\boldsymbol{i} + \boldsymbol{j} \quad \text{and} \quad \boldsymbol{i} - 2\boldsymbol{j}$$

respectively. The velocities of A and B, which are constant and in kilometres per hour, are

$$10\boldsymbol{i} + 24\boldsymbol{j} \quad \text{and} \quad 24\boldsymbol{i} + 32\boldsymbol{j}$$

Find the distance between the boats t hours after noon and find the time at which this distance is a minimum.

21 If the complex numbers z_1, z_2 and z_3 are represented on the Argand diagram by the points P_1, P_2 and P_3 respectively and

$$\overrightarrow{OP_2} = 2\mathrm{j}\overrightarrow{OP_1} \quad \text{and} \quad \overrightarrow{OP_3} = \tfrac{2}{5}\mathrm{j}\overrightarrow{P_2P_1}$$

prove that P_3 is the foot of the perpendicular from O onto the line P_1P_2.

22 ABCD is a square, lettered anticlockwise, on an Argand diagram, with A representing 3 + j2 and B representing −1 + j4. Show that C lies on the real axis and find the complex number represented by D and the length of AB.

23 A triangle has vertices A, B, C represented by 1 + j, 2 − j and −1 respectively. Find the point that is equidistant from A, B and C.

24 Given the triangle OAB, where O is the origin, and denoting the midpoints of the opposite sides as O′, A′ and B′, show vectorially that the lines OO′, AA′ and BB′ meet at a point. (Note that this is the result that the medians of a triangle meet at the centroid.)

25 Three weights W_1, W_2 and W_3 hang in equilibrium on the pulley system shown in Figure 4.26. The pulleys are considered to be smooth and the forces add by the rules of vector addition. Calculate θ and ϕ, the angles the ropes make with the horizontal.

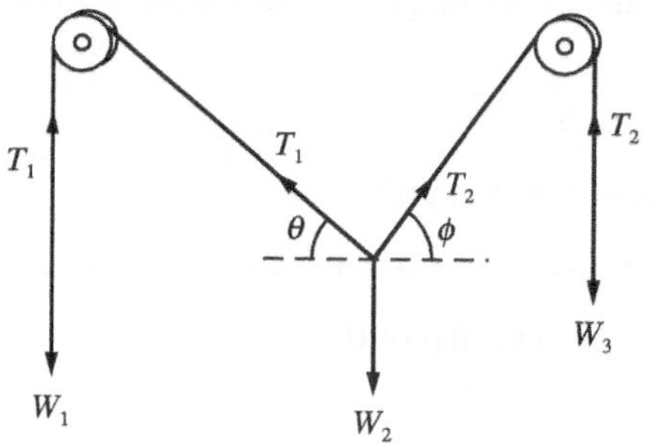

Figure 4.26 Pulley system in Question 25.

26 A telegraph pole OP has three wires connected to it at P. The other ends of the wires are connected to houses at A, B and C. Axes are set up as shown in Figure 4.27. The points relative to these axes, with distances in metres, are $\overrightarrow{OP} = 8\boldsymbol{k}$, $\overrightarrow{OA} = 20\boldsymbol{j} + 6\boldsymbol{k}$, $\overrightarrow{OB} = -\boldsymbol{i} - 18\boldsymbol{j} + 10\boldsymbol{k}$ and $\overrightarrow{OC} = -22\boldsymbol{i} + 3\boldsymbol{j} + 7\boldsymbol{k}$. The tension in each wire is 900 N. Find the total force acting at P. A tie cable at an angle of 45° is connected to P and fixed in the ground. Where should the ground fixing be placed, and what is the tension required to ensure a zero horizontal resultant force at P?

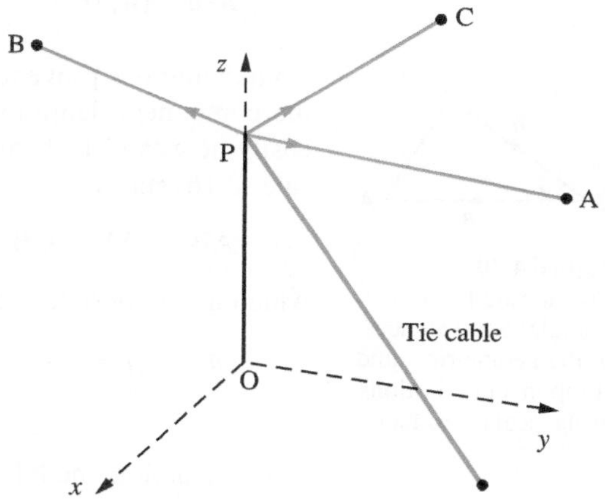

Figure 4.27 The telegraph pole of Question 26.

4.2.8 The scalar product

A natural idea in mathematics, explored in Chapter 1, is not only to add quantities but also to multiply them together. The concept of multiplication of vectors translates into a useful tool for many engineering applications, with two different products of vectors – the 'scalar' and 'vector' products – turning out to be particularly important.

The determination of a component of a vector is a basic procedure in analysing many physical problems. For the vector $\boldsymbol{a}$ shown in Figure 4.28 the component of $\boldsymbol{a}$ in the direction of OP is just ON = $|\boldsymbol{a}|\cos\theta$. The component is relevant in the physical context of work done by a force. Suppose the point of application, O, of a constant force $\boldsymbol{F}$ is moved along the vector $\boldsymbol{a}$ from O to the point A, as in Figure 4.29. The component of $\boldsymbol{F}$ in the $\boldsymbol{a}$ direction is $|\boldsymbol{F}|\cos\theta$, and O is moved a distance $|\boldsymbol{a}|$. The work done is defined as the product of the distance moved by the point of application and the component of the force in this direction. It is thus given by

$$\text{work done} = |\boldsymbol{F}|\,|\boldsymbol{a}|\cos\theta$$

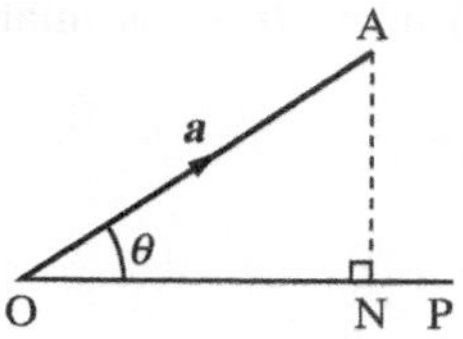

Figure 4.28 The component of $\boldsymbol{a}$ in the direction OP is ON = $|\boldsymbol{a}|\cos\theta$.

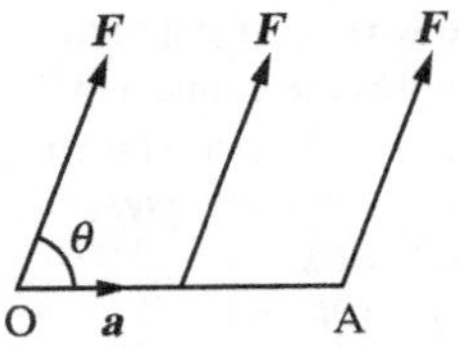

Figure 4.29
The work done by a constant force $\boldsymbol{F}$ with point of application moved from O to A is $|\boldsymbol{F}||\boldsymbol{a}|\cos\theta$.

The definition of the scalar product in geometrical terms takes the form of this expression for the work done by a force. Again there is an equivalent component definition, and both are now presented.

Definition

The **scalar** (or **dot** or **inner**) **product** of two vectors $\boldsymbol{a} = (a_1, a_2, a_3)$ and $\boldsymbol{b} = (b_1, b_2, b_3)$ is defined as follows:

In components

$$\boldsymbol{a}\cdot\boldsymbol{b} = a_1b_1 + a_2b_2 + a_3b_3 \qquad \textbf{(4.2a)}$$

Geometrically

$\boldsymbol{a}\cdot\boldsymbol{b} = |\boldsymbol{a}|\,|\boldsymbol{b}|\cos\theta$, where θ $(0 \leqslant \theta \leqslant \pi)$ is the angle between the two vectors

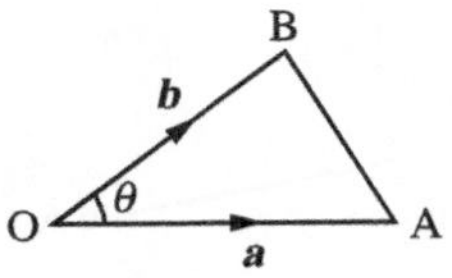

Figure 4.30
Cosine rule for a triangle; equivalence of the geometrical and component definitions of the scalar product.

Both definitions prove to be useful in different contexts, but to establish the basic rules the component definition is the simpler. The equivalence of the two definitions can easily be established from the cosine rule for a triangle. Using Figure 4.30 the cosine rule (2.16) states

$$\mathrm{AB}^2 = \mathrm{OA}^2 + \mathrm{OB}^2 - 2(\mathrm{OA})(\mathrm{OB})\cos\theta$$

which in appropriate vector or component notation gives

$$(a_1 - b_1)^2 + (a_2 - b_2)^2 + (a_3 - b_3)^2 = (a_1^2 + a_2^2 + a_3^2) + (b_1^2 + b_2^2 + b_3^2) - 2|\boldsymbol{a}|\,|\boldsymbol{b}|\cos\theta$$

Thus expanding the left-hand side gives

$$\begin{aligned} &a_1^2 - 2a_1b_1 + b_1^2 + a_2^2 - 2a_2b_2 + b_2^2 + a_3^2 - 2a_3b_3 + b_3^2 \\ &= a_1^2 + b_1^2 + a_2^2 + b_2^2 + a_3^2 + b_3^2 - 2|\boldsymbol{a}|\,|\boldsymbol{b}|\cos\theta \end{aligned}$$

and hence

$$\boldsymbol{a}\cdot\boldsymbol{b} = a_1b_1 + a_2b_2 + a_3b_3 = |\boldsymbol{a}|\,|\boldsymbol{b}|\cos\theta \qquad \textbf{(4.2b)}$$

Two important points to note are: (i) the scalar product of two vectors gives a **number**. (ii) the scalar product is only defined as the product of two vectors and *not* between any other two quantities. For this reason, the presence of the dot (·) in $\boldsymbol{a}\cdot\boldsymbol{b}$ is essential between the two vectors.

Basic rules and properties

The basic rules are now very straightforward to establish.

(a) Commutative law

$$\boldsymbol{a}\cdot\boldsymbol{b} = \boldsymbol{b}\cdot\boldsymbol{a}$$

This rule follows immediately from the component definition (4.2a), since interchanging a_i and b_i does not make any difference to the products. The rule says that 'order does not matter'.

(b) Associative law

The idea of associativity involves the product of three vectors. Since $\boldsymbol{a}\cdot\boldsymbol{b}$ is a scalar, it cannot be dotted with a third vector, so the idea of associativity is not applicable here and $\boldsymbol{a}\cdot\boldsymbol{b}\cdot\boldsymbol{c}$ is not defined.

(c) Distributive law for products with a scalar λ

$$\boldsymbol{a}\cdot(\lambda\boldsymbol{b}) = (\lambda\boldsymbol{a})\cdot\boldsymbol{b} = \lambda(\boldsymbol{a}\cdot\boldsymbol{b})$$

These results follow directly from the component definition (4.2a). The implication is that scalars can be multiplied out in the normal manner.

(d) Distributive law over addition

$$\boldsymbol{a}\cdot(\boldsymbol{b}+\boldsymbol{c}) = \boldsymbol{a}\cdot\boldsymbol{b} + \boldsymbol{a}\cdot\boldsymbol{c}$$

The proof is straightforward, since

$$\begin{aligned}\boldsymbol{a}\cdot(\boldsymbol{b}+\boldsymbol{c}) &= a_1(b_1+c_1) + a_2(b_2+c_2) + a_3(b_3+c_3)\\ &= (a_1b_1 + a_2b_2 + a_3b_3) + (a_1c_1 + a_2c_2 + a_3c_3)\\ &= \boldsymbol{a}\cdot\boldsymbol{b} + \boldsymbol{a}\cdot\boldsymbol{c}\end{aligned}$$

Thus the normal rules of algebra apply, and brackets can be multiplied out in the usual way.

(e) Powers of a

One simple point to note is that

$$\boldsymbol{a}\cdot\boldsymbol{a} = a_1^2 + a_2^2 + a_3^2 = |\boldsymbol{a}|\,|\boldsymbol{a}|\cos 0 = |\boldsymbol{a}|^2$$

in agreement with Section 4.2.5. This expression is written $\boldsymbol{a}^2 = \boldsymbol{a}\cdot\boldsymbol{a}$ and, where there is no ambiguity, $\boldsymbol{a}^2 = a^2$ is also used. No other powers of vectors can be constructed, since, as in (*b*) above, scalar products of more than two vectors do not exist. For the standard unit vectors, $\boldsymbol{i}, \boldsymbol{j}$ and $\boldsymbol{k}$,

$$\boldsymbol{i}^2 = \boldsymbol{i}\cdot\boldsymbol{i} = 1, \quad \boldsymbol{j}^2 = \boldsymbol{j}\cdot\boldsymbol{j} = 1, \quad \boldsymbol{k}^2 = \boldsymbol{k}\cdot\boldsymbol{k} = 1 \qquad \textbf{(4.3)}$$

(f) Perpendicular vectors

It is clear from (4.2b) that if $\boldsymbol{a}$ and $\boldsymbol{b}$ are perpendicular (orthogonal) then $\cos\theta = \cos\frac{1}{2}\pi = 0$, and hence $\boldsymbol{a}\cdot\boldsymbol{b} = 0$, or in component notation

$$\boldsymbol{a}\cdot\boldsymbol{b} = a_1b_1 + a_2b_2 + a_3b_3 = 0$$

However, the other way round, $\boldsymbol{a} \cdot \boldsymbol{b} = 0$, *does not* imply that $\boldsymbol{a}$ and $\boldsymbol{b}$ are perpendicular. There are three possibilities:

$$\text{either } \boldsymbol{a} = 0 \quad \text{or} \quad \boldsymbol{b} = 0 \quad \text{or} \quad \theta = \tfrac{1}{2}\pi$$

It is only when the first two possibilities have been dismissed that perpendicularity can be deduced.

The commonest mistake is to deduce from

$$\boldsymbol{a} \cdot \boldsymbol{b} = \boldsymbol{a} \cdot \boldsymbol{c}$$

that $\boldsymbol{b} = \boldsymbol{c}$. This is only one of three possible solutions – the other two being $\boldsymbol{a} = 0$ and $\boldsymbol{a}$ perpendicular to $\boldsymbol{b} - \boldsymbol{c}$. The rule to follow is that *you can't cancel vectors in the same way as scalars.*

Since the unit vectors $\boldsymbol{i}, \boldsymbol{j}$ and $\boldsymbol{k}$ are mutually perpendicular,

$$\boldsymbol{i} \cdot \boldsymbol{j} = \boldsymbol{j} \cdot \boldsymbol{k} = \boldsymbol{k} \cdot \boldsymbol{i} = 0 \tag{4.4}$$

Using the distributive law over addition, we obtain using (4.3) and (4.4)

$$\begin{aligned}(a_1, a_2, a_3) \cdot (b_1, b_2, b_3) &= (a_1\boldsymbol{i} + a_2\boldsymbol{j} + a_3\boldsymbol{k}) \cdot (b_1\boldsymbol{i} + b_2\boldsymbol{j} + b_3\boldsymbol{k}) \\ &= a_1b_1\boldsymbol{i} \cdot \boldsymbol{i} + a_1b_2\boldsymbol{i} \cdot \boldsymbol{j} + a_1b_3\boldsymbol{i} \cdot \boldsymbol{k} + a_2b_1\boldsymbol{j} \cdot \boldsymbol{i} + a_2b_2\boldsymbol{j} \cdot \boldsymbol{j} \\ &\quad + a_2b_3\boldsymbol{j} \cdot \boldsymbol{k} + a_3b_1\boldsymbol{k} \cdot \boldsymbol{i} + a_3b_2\boldsymbol{k} \cdot \boldsymbol{j} + a_3b_3\boldsymbol{k} \cdot \boldsymbol{k} \\ &= a_1b_1 + a_2b_2 + a_3b_3\end{aligned}$$

which is consistent with the component definition of a scalar product.

Perpendicularity is a very important idea, which is used a great deal in both mathematics and engineering. Pressure acts on a surface in a direction perpendicular to the surface, so that the force per unit area is given by $p\hat{\boldsymbol{n}}$, where p is the pressure and $\hat{\boldsymbol{n}}$ is the unit normal. To perform many calculations, we must be able to find a vector that is perpendicular to another vector. We shall also see that many matrix methods rely on being able to construct a set of mutually orthogonal vectors. Such constructions are not only of theoretical interest, but form the basis of many practical numerical methods used in engineering. The whole of the study of Fourier series, which is central to much of signal processing and is heavily used by electrical engineers, is based on constructing functions that are orthogonal.

In MATLAB the scalar product of two vectors $\boldsymbol{a}$ and $\boldsymbol{b}$ is given by the command `dot(a,b)`. In MAPLE it is given by `innerprod(a,b)`.

Example 4.17 Given the vectors $\boldsymbol{a} = (1, -1, 2)$, $\boldsymbol{b} = (-2, 0, 2)$ and $\boldsymbol{c} = (3, 2, 1)$, evaluate

(a) $\boldsymbol{a} \cdot \boldsymbol{c}$ (b) $\boldsymbol{b} \cdot \boldsymbol{c}$ (c) $(\boldsymbol{a} + \boldsymbol{b}) \cdot \boldsymbol{c}$

(d) $\boldsymbol{a} \cdot (2\boldsymbol{b} + 3\boldsymbol{c})$ (e) $(\boldsymbol{a} \cdot \boldsymbol{b})\boldsymbol{c}$

Solution (a) $\boldsymbol{a}\cdot\boldsymbol{c} = (1 \times 3) + (-1 \times 2) + (2 \times 1) = 3$

(b) $\boldsymbol{b}\cdot\boldsymbol{c} = (-2 \times 3) + (0 \times 2) + (2 \times 1) = -4$

(c) $(\boldsymbol{a} + \boldsymbol{b}) = (1, -1, 2) + (-2, 0, 2) = (-1, -1, 4)$ so that

$$(\boldsymbol{a} + \boldsymbol{b})\cdot\boldsymbol{c} = (-1, -1, 4)\cdot(3, 2, 1) = -3 - 2 + 4 = -1$$

(note that $(\boldsymbol{a} + \boldsymbol{b})\cdot\boldsymbol{c} = \boldsymbol{a}\cdot\boldsymbol{c} + \boldsymbol{b}\cdot\boldsymbol{c}$)

(d) $\boldsymbol{a}\cdot(2\boldsymbol{b} + 3\boldsymbol{c}) = (1, -1, 2)\cdot[(-4, 0, 4) + (9, 6, 3)]$

$$= (1, -1, 2)\cdot(5, 6, 7) = (5 - 6 + 14) = 13$$

(note that $2(\boldsymbol{a}\cdot\boldsymbol{b}) + 3(\boldsymbol{a}\cdot\boldsymbol{c}) = 4 + 9 = 13$)

(e) $(\boldsymbol{a}\cdot\boldsymbol{b})\boldsymbol{c} = [(1, -1, 2)\cdot(-2, 0, 2)](3, 2, 1) = [-2 + 0 + 4](3, 2, 1)$

$$= 2(3, 2, 1) = (6, 4, 2)$$

(note that $\boldsymbol{a}\cdot\boldsymbol{b}$ is a scalar, so $(\boldsymbol{a}\cdot\boldsymbol{b})\boldsymbol{c}$ is a vector parallel or antiparallel to $\boldsymbol{c}$)

Check that in MATLAB the commands

```
a = [1 -1 2]; b = [-2 0 2]; c = [3 2 1];
dot(a,c), dot(b,c), dot(a + b,c), dot(a,2*b + 3*c),
dot(a,b)*c
```

return the answers given in this example.

Example 4.18 Find the angle between the vectors $\boldsymbol{a} = (1, 2, 3)$ and $\boldsymbol{b} = (2, 0, 4)$.

Solution By definition

$$\boldsymbol{a}\cdot\boldsymbol{b} = |\boldsymbol{a}|\,|\boldsymbol{b}|\cos\theta = a_1b_1 + a_2b_2 + a_3b_3$$

We have in the right-hand side

$$(1, 2, 3)\cdot(2, 0, 4) = 2 + 0 + 12 = 14$$

Also

$$|(1, 2, 3)| = \sqrt{(1^2 + 2^2 + 3^2)} = \sqrt{14}$$

and

$$|(2, 0, 4)| = \sqrt{(2^2 + 0^2 + 4^2)} = \sqrt{20}$$

Thus, from the definition of the scalar product,

$$14 = \sqrt{(14)}\sqrt{(20)}\cos\theta$$

giving

$$\theta = \cos^{-1}\sqrt{\tfrac{7}{10}}$$

Example 4.19 Given $\boldsymbol{a} = (1, 0, 1)$ and $\boldsymbol{b} = (0, 1, 0)$, show that $\boldsymbol{a} \cdot \boldsymbol{b} = 0$, and interpret this result.

Solution

$$\boldsymbol{a} \cdot \boldsymbol{b} = (1, 0, 1) \cdot (0, 1, 0) = 0$$

Since $|\boldsymbol{a}| \neq 0$ and $|\boldsymbol{b}| \neq 0$, the two vectors are perpendicular. We can see this result geometrically, since $\boldsymbol{a}$ lies in the x–z plane and $\boldsymbol{b}$ is parallel to the y axis.

Example 4.20 The three vectors

$$\boldsymbol{a} = (1, 1, 1), \quad \boldsymbol{b} = (3, 2, -3) \quad \text{and} \quad \boldsymbol{c} = (-1, 4, -1)$$

are given. Show that $\boldsymbol{a} \cdot \boldsymbol{b} = \boldsymbol{a} \cdot \boldsymbol{c}$ and interpret the result.

Solution Now $\boldsymbol{a} \cdot \boldsymbol{b} = 1 \times 3 + 1 \times 2 - 1 \times 3 = 2$

and $\boldsymbol{a} \cdot \boldsymbol{c} = 1 \times (-1) + 1 \times 4 + 1 \times (-1) = 2$

so the two scalar products are clearly equal. Certainly $\boldsymbol{b} \neq \boldsymbol{c}$ since they are given to be unequal and $\boldsymbol{a}$ is non-zero, so the conclusion from

$$\boldsymbol{a} \cdot (\boldsymbol{b} - \boldsymbol{c}) = 0$$

is that the vectors $\boldsymbol{a}$ and $(\boldsymbol{b} - \boldsymbol{c}) = (4, -2, -2)$ are perpendicular.

Example 4.21 In a triangle ABC show that the perpendiculars from the vertices to the opposite sides intersect in a point.

Solution Let the perpendiculars AD and BE meet in O, as indicated in Figure 4.31, and choose O to be the origin. Define $\overrightarrow{OA} = \boldsymbol{a}$, $\overrightarrow{OB} = \boldsymbol{b}$ and $\overrightarrow{OC} = \boldsymbol{c}$. Then

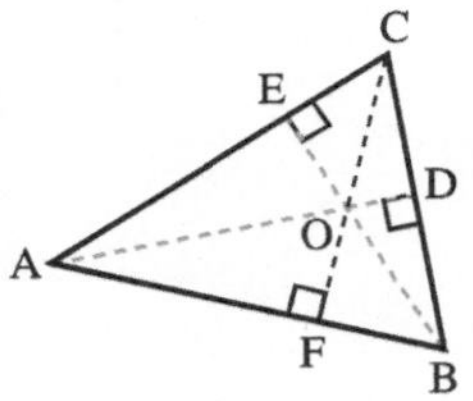

Figure 4.31
The altitudes of a triangle meet in a point (Example 4.21).

AD perpendicular to BC implies $\boldsymbol{a} \cdot (\boldsymbol{b} - \boldsymbol{c}) = 0$

BE perpendicular to AC implies $\boldsymbol{b} \cdot (\boldsymbol{c} - \boldsymbol{a}) = 0$

Hence, adding,

$$\boldsymbol{a} \cdot \boldsymbol{b} - \boldsymbol{a} \cdot \boldsymbol{c} + \boldsymbol{b} \cdot \boldsymbol{c} - \boldsymbol{b} \cdot \boldsymbol{a} = 0$$

so

$$\boldsymbol{b} \cdot \boldsymbol{c} - \boldsymbol{a} \cdot \boldsymbol{c} = \boldsymbol{c} \cdot (\boldsymbol{b} - \boldsymbol{a}) = 0$$

This statement implies that $\boldsymbol{b} - \boldsymbol{a}$ is perpendicular to $\boldsymbol{c}$ or AB is perpendicular to CF, as required. The case $\boldsymbol{b} - \boldsymbol{a} = 0$ is dismissed, since then the triangle would collapse. The case $\boldsymbol{c} = 0$ implies that C is at O; the triangle is then right-angled and the result is trivial.

Example 4.22 Find the work done by the force $\boldsymbol{F} = (3, -2, 5)$ in moving a particle from a point P to a point Q having position vectors $(1, 4, -1)$ and $(-2, 3, 1)$ respectively.

Solution Applying the triangle law to Figure 4.32, we have the displacement of the particle given by

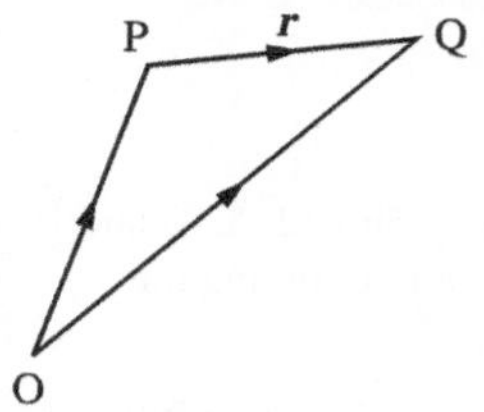

Figure 4.32 Triangle law for Example 4.22.

$$r = \overrightarrow{PQ} = \overrightarrow{PO} + \overrightarrow{OQ} = \overrightarrow{OQ} - \overrightarrow{OP}$$
$$= (-2, 3, 1) - (1, 4, -1) = (-3, -1, 2)$$

Then the work done by the force F is

$$F \cdot r = (3, -2, 5) \cdot (-3, -1, 2) = -9 + 2 + 10$$
$$= 3 \text{ units}$$

The **component** of a vector in a given direction was discussed at the start of this section, and, as indicated in Figure 4.28, the component of F in the a direction is $|F|\cos\theta$. Taking $\hat{a}$ to be the unit vector in the a direction,

$$F \cdot \hat{a} = |F|\,|\hat{a}|\cos\theta = |F|\cos\theta$$
$$= \text{the component of } F \text{ in the } a \text{ direction}$$

Example 4.23 Find the component of the vector $F = (2, -1, 3)$ in

(a) the i direction

(b) the direction $(\frac{1}{3}, \frac{2}{3}, \frac{2}{3})$

(c) the direction $(4, 2, -1)$

Solution (a) The direction i is represented by the vector $(1, 0, 0)$, so the component of F in the i direction is

$$F \cdot (1, 0, 0) = (2, -1, 3) \cdot (1, 0, 0) = 2$$

(note how this result just picks out the x component and agrees with the usual idea of a component).

(b) Since $\sqrt{(\frac{1}{9} + \frac{4}{9} + \frac{4}{9})} = 1$, the vector $(\frac{1}{3}, \frac{2}{3}, \frac{2}{3})$ is a unit vector. Thus the component of F in the direction $(\frac{1}{3}, \frac{2}{3}, \frac{2}{3})$ is

$$F \cdot (\tfrac{1}{3}, \tfrac{2}{3}, \tfrac{2}{3}) = \tfrac{2}{3} - \tfrac{2}{3} + 2 = 2$$

(c) Since $\sqrt{(16 + 4 + 1)} \neq 1$, the vector $(4, 2, -1)$ is not a unit vector. Therefore we must first compute its magnitude as

$$\sqrt{(4^2 + 2^2 + 1^2)} = \sqrt{21}$$

indicating that a unit vector in the direction of $(4, 2, -1)$ is $(4, 2, -1)/\sqrt{21}$. Thus the component of F in the direction of $(4, 2, -1)$ is

$$F \cdot (4, 2, -1)/\sqrt{21} = 3/\sqrt{21}$$

4.2.9 Exercises

Where appropiate check your answers using MATLAB or MAPLE.

27 Given that $\boldsymbol{u} = (4, 0, -2)$, $\boldsymbol{v} = (3, 1, -1)$, $\boldsymbol{w} = (2, 1, 6)$ and $\boldsymbol{s} = (1, 4, 1)$, evaluate

(a) $\boldsymbol{u}\cdot\boldsymbol{v}$ (b) $\boldsymbol{v}\cdot\boldsymbol{s}$

(c) $\hat{\boldsymbol{w}}$ (d) $(\boldsymbol{v}\cdot\boldsymbol{s})\hat{\boldsymbol{u}}$

(e) $(\boldsymbol{u}\cdot\boldsymbol{w})(\boldsymbol{v}\cdot\boldsymbol{s})$ (f) $(\boldsymbol{u}\cdot\boldsymbol{i})\boldsymbol{v} + (\boldsymbol{w}\cdot\boldsymbol{s})\boldsymbol{k}$

28 Given $\boldsymbol{u}$, $\boldsymbol{v}$, $\boldsymbol{w}$ and $\boldsymbol{s}$ as for Question 27, find

(a) the angle between $\boldsymbol{u}$ and $\boldsymbol{w}$;

(b) the angle between $\boldsymbol{v}$ and $\boldsymbol{s}$;

(c) the value of λ for which the vectors $\boldsymbol{u} + \lambda\boldsymbol{k}$ and $\boldsymbol{v} - \lambda\boldsymbol{i}$ are perpendicular;

(d) the value of μ for which the vectors $\boldsymbol{w} + \mu\boldsymbol{i}$ and $\boldsymbol{s} - \mu\boldsymbol{i}$ are perpendicular.

29 Given the vectors $\boldsymbol{u} = (1, 0, 0)$, $\boldsymbol{v} = (1, 1, 0)$, $\boldsymbol{w} = (1, 1, 1)$ and $\boldsymbol{s} = (2, 1, 2)$, find α, β, γ that satisfy $\boldsymbol{s} = \alpha\boldsymbol{u} + \beta\boldsymbol{v} + \gamma\boldsymbol{w}$. If $\boldsymbol{u}' = (1, -1, 0)$, $\boldsymbol{v}' = (0, 1, -1)$ and $\boldsymbol{w}' = (0, 0, 1)$ show that

$$\boldsymbol{s} = (\boldsymbol{s}\cdot\boldsymbol{u})\boldsymbol{u}' + (\boldsymbol{s}\cdot\boldsymbol{v})\boldsymbol{v}' + (\boldsymbol{s}\cdot\boldsymbol{w})\boldsymbol{w}'$$

30 Given $|\boldsymbol{a}| = 3$, $|\boldsymbol{b}| = 2$ and $\boldsymbol{a}\cdot\boldsymbol{b} = 5$ find $|\boldsymbol{a} + 2\boldsymbol{b}|$ and $|3\boldsymbol{a} - \boldsymbol{b}|$. Find the angle between the vectors $\boldsymbol{a} + 2\boldsymbol{b}$ and $3\boldsymbol{a} - \boldsymbol{b}$.

31 Find the work done by the force $\boldsymbol{F} = (-2, -1, 3)$ in moving a particle from the point P to the point Q having position vectors $(-1, 2, 3)$ and $(1, -3, 4)$ respectively.

32 Find the resolved part in the direction of the vector $(3, 2, 1)$ of a force of 5 units acting in the direction of the vector $(2, -3, 1)$.

33 Find the value of t that makes the angle between the two vectors $\boldsymbol{a} = (3, 1, 0)$ and $\boldsymbol{b} = (t, 0, 1)$ equal to 45°.

34 For any four points A, B, C and D in space, prove that

$$(\overrightarrow{DA}\cdot\overrightarrow{BC}) + (\overrightarrow{DB}\cdot\overrightarrow{CA}) + (\overrightarrow{DC}\cdot\overrightarrow{AB}) = 0$$

35 If $(\mathbf{c} - \frac{1}{2}\mathbf{a})\cdot\mathbf{a} = (\mathbf{c} - \frac{1}{2}\mathbf{b})\cdot\mathbf{b} = 0$, prove that the vector $\mathbf{c} - \frac{1}{2}(\mathbf{a} + \mathbf{b})$ is perpendicular to $\mathbf{a} - \mathbf{b}$.

36 Prove that the line joining the points $(2, 3, 4)$ and $(1, 2, 3)$ is perpendicular to the line joining the points $(1, 0, 2)$ and $(2, 3, -2)$.

37 Show that the diagonals of a rhombus intersect at right-angles. If one diagonal is twice the length of the other, show that the diagonals have length $2a/\sqrt{5}$ and $4a/\sqrt{5}$, where a is the length of the side of the rhombus.

38 Find the equation of a circular cylinder with the origin on the axis of the cylinder, the unit vector $\boldsymbol{a}$ along the axis and radius R.

39 A cube has corners with coordinates $(0, 0, 0)$, $(1, 0, 0)$, $(0, 1, 0)$, $(1, 1, 0)$, $(0, 0, 1)$, $(1, 0, 1)$, $(0, 1, 1)$ and $(1, 1, 1)$. Find the vectors representing the diagonals of the cube and hence find the length of the diagonals and the angle between the diagonals.

40 A lifeboat hangs from a davit, as shown in Figure 4.33, with the x direction, the vertical part of the davit and the arm of the davit being mutually perpendicular. The rope is fastened to the deck at a distance X from the davit. It is known that the maximum force in the x direction that the davit can withstand is 200 N. If the weight supported is 500 N and the pulley system is a single loop so that the tension is 250 N, then determine the maximum value that X can take.

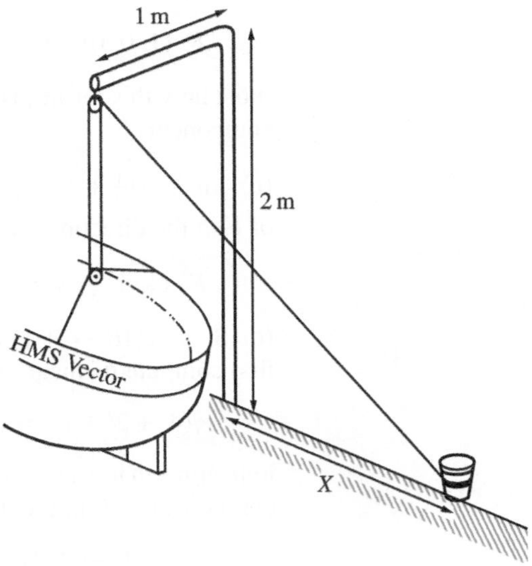

Figure 4.33 Davit in Question 40.

4.2.10 The vector product

The **vector** or **cross product** was developed during the nineteenth century, its main practical use being to define the moment of a force in three dimensions. It is generally only in three dimensions that the vector product is used. The adaptation for two-dimensional vectors is of restricted scope, since for two-dimensional problems, where all vectors are confined to a plane, the direction of the vector product is always perpendicular to that plane.

Definition

Given two vectors $\boldsymbol{a}$ and $\boldsymbol{b}$, we define the vector product geometrically as

$$\boldsymbol{a} \times \boldsymbol{b} = |\boldsymbol{a}|\,|\boldsymbol{b}| \sin\theta\, \hat{\boldsymbol{n}} \tag{4.5}$$

where θ is the angle between $\boldsymbol{a}$ and $\boldsymbol{b}$ $(0 \leqslant \theta \leqslant \pi)$, and $\hat{\boldsymbol{n}}$ is the unit vector perpendicular to both $\boldsymbol{a}$ and $\boldsymbol{b}$ such that $\boldsymbol{a}, \boldsymbol{b}, \hat{\boldsymbol{n}}$ form a right-handed set – see Figure 4.34 and the definition at the beginning of Section 4.2.1.

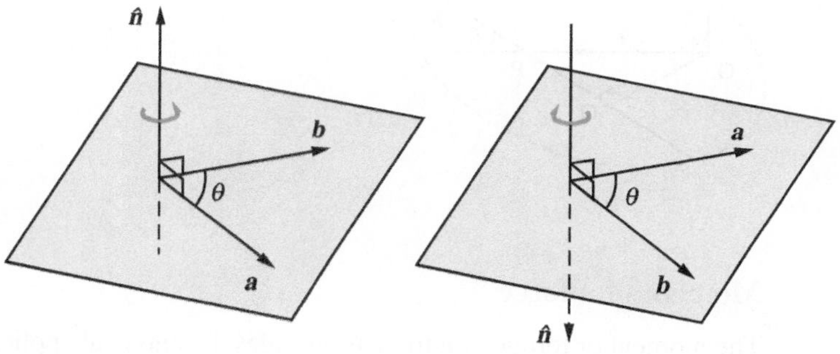

Figure 4.34
Vector product $\boldsymbol{a} \times \boldsymbol{b}$, right-hand rule.

It is important to recognize that the vector product of two vectors is itself a vector. The alternative notation $\boldsymbol{a} \wedge \boldsymbol{b}$ is also sometimes used to denote the vector product, but this is less common since the similar wedge symbol $\wedge$ is also used for other purposes (see e.g. Section 6.4.2).

There are wide-ranging applications of the vector product.

Motion of a charged particle in a magnetic field

- If a charged particle has velocity $\boldsymbol{v}$ and moves in a magnetic field $\boldsymbol{H}$ then the particle experiences a force perpendicular to both $\boldsymbol{v}$ and $\boldsymbol{H}$, which is proportional to $\boldsymbol{v} \times \boldsymbol{H}$. It is this force that is used to direct the beam in a television tube.
- Similarly a wire moving with velocity $\boldsymbol{v}$ in a magnetic field $\boldsymbol{H}$ produces a current proportional to $\boldsymbol{v} \times \boldsymbol{H}$ (see Figure 4.35), thus converting mechanical energy into electric current, and provides the principle of the **dynamo**.
- For an **electric motor** the idea depends on the observation that an electric current $\boldsymbol{C}$ in a wire that lies in a magnetic field $\boldsymbol{H}$ produces a mechanical force proportional to $\boldsymbol{C} \times \boldsymbol{H}$; again see Figure 4.35. Thus electrical energy is converted to a mechanical force.

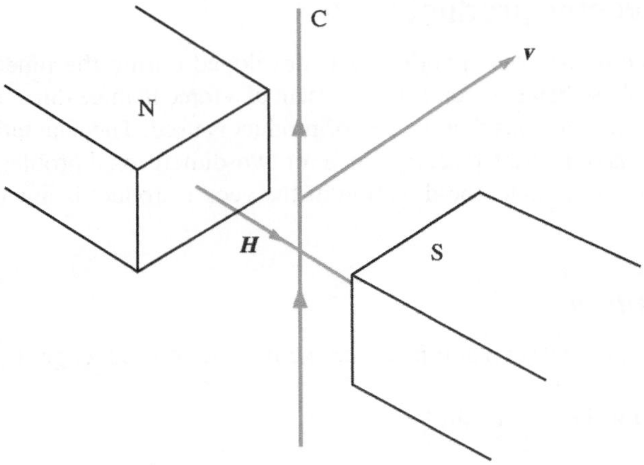

Figure 4.35
In a magnetic field $\boldsymbol{H}$, (i) motion of the wire in the $\boldsymbol{v}$ direction creates a current in the $\boldsymbol{H} \times \boldsymbol{v}$ (dynamo), (ii) a current $\boldsymbol{C}$ causes motion $\boldsymbol{v}$ in the $\boldsymbol{C} \times \boldsymbol{H}$ direction (electric motor).

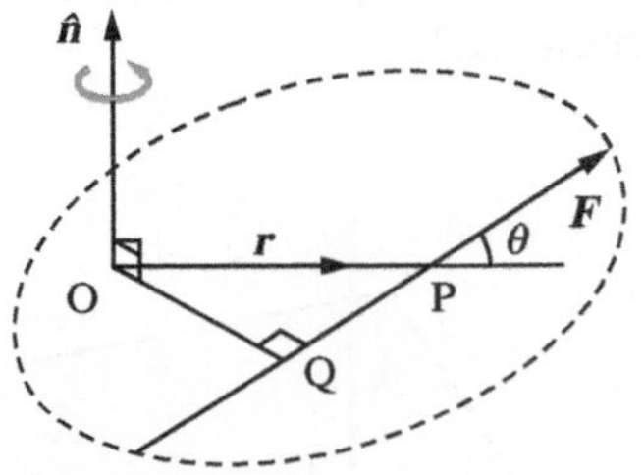

Figure 4.36
Moment of a force.

Moment of a force

The moment or torque of a force $\boldsymbol{F}$ provides the classical application of the vector product in a mechanical context. Although moments are easy to define in two dimensions, the extension to three dimensions is not so easy. In vector notation, however, if the force passes through the point P and $\overrightarrow{OP} = \boldsymbol{r}$, as illustrated in Figure 4.36, then the moment $\boldsymbol{M}$ of the force about O is simply defined as

$$\boldsymbol{M} = \boldsymbol{r} \times \boldsymbol{F} = |\boldsymbol{r}||\boldsymbol{F}|\sin\theta\,\hat{\boldsymbol{n}} = \mathrm{OQ}|\boldsymbol{F}|\,\hat{\boldsymbol{n}} \qquad \textbf{(4.6)}$$

This is a vector in the direction of the normal $\hat{\boldsymbol{n}}$, and moments add by the usual parallelogram law.

Angular velocity of a rigid body

A further application of the vector product relates to rotating bodies. Consider a rigid body rotating with angular speed ω (in rad s^{-1}) about a fixed axis LM that passes through a fixed point O, as illustrated in Figure 4.37. A point P of the rigid body having position vector $\boldsymbol{r}$ relative to O will move in a circular path whose plane is perpendicular to OM and whose centre N is on OM. If NQ is a fixed direction and the angle QNP is equal to χ then

$$\text{the magnitude of angular velocity } = \frac{d\chi}{dt} = \omega$$

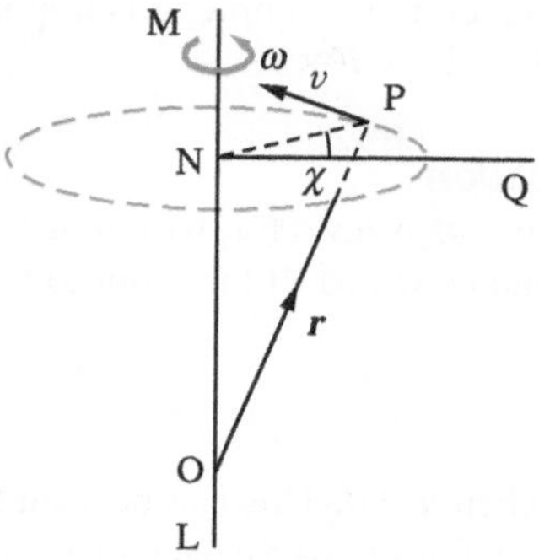

Figure 4.37 Angular velocity of a rigid body.

(Note that we have used here the idea of a derivative.) The velocity $\boldsymbol{v}$ of P will be in the direction of the tangent shown and will have magnitude

$$v = \text{NP}\frac{\mathrm{d}\chi}{\mathrm{d}t} = \text{NP}\omega$$

If we define $\boldsymbol{\omega}$ to be a vector of magnitude ω and having direction along the axis of rotation, in the sense in which the rotation would drive a right-handed screw, then

$$\boldsymbol{v} = \boldsymbol{\omega} \times \boldsymbol{r} \qquad (4.7)$$

correctly defines the velocity of P in both magnitude and direction. This vector $\boldsymbol{\omega}$ is called the **angular velocity** of the rigid body.

Area of parallelogram and a triangle

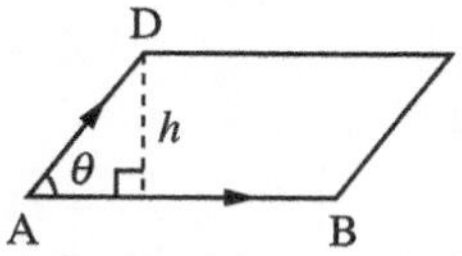

Figure 4.38 Representation of a parallelogram.

Geometrically we have from Figure 4.38 that the area of a parallelogram ABCD is given by

$$\text{area} = h|\overrightarrow{\text{AB}}| = |\overrightarrow{\text{AD}}|\sin\theta|\overrightarrow{\text{AB}}| = |\overrightarrow{\text{AD}} \times \overrightarrow{\text{AB}}|$$

Note also that the area of the triangle ABD is $\frac{1}{2}|\overrightarrow{\text{AD}} \times \overrightarrow{\text{AB}}|$, which corresponds to the result

$$\text{area of triangle ABD} = \tfrac{1}{2}(\text{AD})(\text{AB})\sin\theta$$

We now examine the properties of vector products in order to determine whether or not the usual laws of algebra apply.

Basic properties

(a) Anti-commutative law

$$\boldsymbol{a} \times \boldsymbol{b} = -(\boldsymbol{b} \times \boldsymbol{a})$$

This follows directly from the right-handedness of the set in the geometrical definition (4.5), since $\hat{\boldsymbol{n}}$ changes direction when the order of multiplication is reversed. Thus the vector product does not commute, but rather anti-commutes, unlike the multiplication of scalars or the scalar product of two vectors. Therefore the order of multiplication matters when using the vector product. For example, it is important that the moment of a force is calculated as $\boldsymbol{M} = \boldsymbol{r} \times \boldsymbol{F}$ and *not* $\boldsymbol{F} \times \boldsymbol{r}$.

(b) Non-associative multiplication

Since the vector product of two vectors is a vector, we can take the vector product with a third vector, and associativity can be tested. It turns out to *fail in general*, and

$$\boldsymbol{a} \times (\boldsymbol{b} \times \boldsymbol{c}) \neq (\boldsymbol{a} \times \boldsymbol{b}) \times \boldsymbol{c}$$

except in special cases, such as when $\boldsymbol{a} = 0$. This can be seen to be the case from geometrical considerations using the definition (4.5). The vector $\boldsymbol{b} \times \boldsymbol{c}$ is perpendicular to both $\boldsymbol{b}$ and $\boldsymbol{c}$, and is thus perpendicular to the plane containing $\boldsymbol{b}$ and $\boldsymbol{c}$. Also, by definition, $\boldsymbol{a} \times (\boldsymbol{b} \times \boldsymbol{c})$ is perpendicular to $\boldsymbol{b} \times \boldsymbol{c}$, and is therefore in the plane of $\boldsymbol{b}$ and $\boldsymbol{c}$. Similarly, $(\boldsymbol{a} \times \boldsymbol{b}) \times \boldsymbol{c}$ is in the plane of $\boldsymbol{a}$ and $\boldsymbol{b}$. Hence, in general, $\boldsymbol{a} \times (\boldsymbol{b} \times \boldsymbol{c})$ and $(\boldsymbol{a} \times \boldsymbol{b}) \times \boldsymbol{c}$ are different vectors.

Since the associative law does not hold in general, we never write $\boldsymbol{a} \times \boldsymbol{b} \times \boldsymbol{c}$, since it is ambiguous. Care must be taken to maintain the correct order and thus brackets must be inserted when more than two vectors are involved in a vector product.

(c) Distributive law over multiplication by a scalar

The definition (4.5) shows trivially that

$$\boldsymbol{a} \times (\lambda \boldsymbol{b}) = \lambda(\boldsymbol{a} \times \boldsymbol{b}) = (\lambda \boldsymbol{a}) \times \boldsymbol{b}$$

and the usual algebraic rule applies.

(d) Distributive law over addition

$$\boldsymbol{a} \times (\boldsymbol{b} + \boldsymbol{c}) = (\boldsymbol{a} \times \boldsymbol{b}) + (\boldsymbol{a} \times \boldsymbol{c})$$

This law holds for the vector product. It can be proved geometrically using the definition (4.5). The proof, however, is rather protracted and is omitted here.

(e) Parallel vectors

It is obvious from the definition (4.5) that if $\boldsymbol{a}$ and $\boldsymbol{b}$ are parallel or antiparallel then $\theta = 0$ or π, so that $\boldsymbol{a} \times \boldsymbol{b} = 0$, and this includes the case $\boldsymbol{a} \times \boldsymbol{a} = 0$. We note, however, that if $\boldsymbol{a} \times \boldsymbol{b} = 0$ then we have three possible cases: either $\boldsymbol{a} = 0$ or $\boldsymbol{b} = 0$ or $\boldsymbol{a}$ and $\boldsymbol{b}$ are parallel. As with the scalar product, if we have $\boldsymbol{a} \times \boldsymbol{b} = \boldsymbol{a} \times \boldsymbol{c}$ then we cannot deduce that $\boldsymbol{b} = \boldsymbol{c}$. We first have to show that $\boldsymbol{a} \neq 0$ and that $\boldsymbol{a}$ is not parallel to $\boldsymbol{b} - \boldsymbol{c}$.

(f) Cartesian form

From the definition (4.5), it clearly follows that the three unit vectors, $\boldsymbol{i}, \boldsymbol{j}$ and $\boldsymbol{k}$ parallel to the coordinate axes satisfy

$$\begin{aligned} &\boldsymbol{i} \times \boldsymbol{i} = \boldsymbol{j} \times \boldsymbol{j} = \boldsymbol{k} \times \boldsymbol{k} = 0 \\ &\boldsymbol{i} \times \boldsymbol{j} = \boldsymbol{k}, \quad \boldsymbol{j} \times \boldsymbol{k} = \boldsymbol{i}, \quad \boldsymbol{k} \times \boldsymbol{i} = \boldsymbol{j} \end{aligned} \tag{4.8}$$

Note the cyclic order of these latter equations. Using these results, we can obtain the cartesian or component form of the vector product. Taking

$$\boldsymbol{a} = (a_1, a_2, a_3) = a_1\boldsymbol{i} + a_2\boldsymbol{j} + a_3\boldsymbol{k}$$

and

$$\boldsymbol{b} = (b_1, b_2, b_3) = b_1\boldsymbol{i} + b_2\boldsymbol{j} + b_3\boldsymbol{k}$$

then, using rules (c), (d) and (a),

$$\begin{aligned}\boldsymbol{a} \times \boldsymbol{b} &= (a_1\boldsymbol{i} + a_2\boldsymbol{j} + a_3\boldsymbol{k}) \times (b_1\boldsymbol{i} + b_2\boldsymbol{j} + b_3\boldsymbol{k})\\ &= a_1b_1(\boldsymbol{i} \times \boldsymbol{i}) + a_1b_2(\boldsymbol{i} \times \boldsymbol{j}) + a_1b_3(\boldsymbol{i} \times \boldsymbol{k}) + a_2b_1(\boldsymbol{j} \times \boldsymbol{i}) + a_2b_2(\boldsymbol{j} \times \boldsymbol{j})\\ &\quad + a_2b_3(\boldsymbol{j} \times \boldsymbol{k}) + a_3b_1(\boldsymbol{k} \times \boldsymbol{i}) + a_3b_2(\boldsymbol{k} \times \boldsymbol{j}) + a_3b_3(\boldsymbol{k} \times \boldsymbol{k})\\ &= a_1b_2\boldsymbol{k} + a_1b_3(-\boldsymbol{j}) + a_2b_1(-\boldsymbol{k}) + a_2b_3\boldsymbol{i} + a_3b_1\boldsymbol{j} + a_3b_2(-\boldsymbol{i})\end{aligned}$$

so that

$$\boldsymbol{a} \times \boldsymbol{b} = (a_2b_3 - a_3b_2)\boldsymbol{i} + (a_3b_1 - a_1b_3)\boldsymbol{j} + (a_1b_2 - a_2b_1)\boldsymbol{k} \tag{4.9}$$

The cartesian form (4.9) can be more easily remembered in its determinant form (actually an accepted misuse of the determinant form)

$$\begin{aligned}\boldsymbol{a} \times \boldsymbol{b} &= \begin{vmatrix} \boldsymbol{i} & \boldsymbol{j} & \boldsymbol{k} \\ a_1 & a_2 & a_3 \\ b_1 & b_2 & b_3 \end{vmatrix} = \boldsymbol{i}\begin{vmatrix} a_2 & a_3 \\ b_2 & b_3 \end{vmatrix} - \boldsymbol{j}\begin{vmatrix} a_1 & a_3 \\ b_1 & b_3 \end{vmatrix} + \boldsymbol{k}\begin{vmatrix} a_1 & a_2 \\ b_1 & b_2 \end{vmatrix}\\ &= (a_2b_3 - b_2a_3)\boldsymbol{i} - (a_1b_3 - b_1a_3)\boldsymbol{j} + (a_1b_2 - b_1a_2)\boldsymbol{k}\end{aligned} \tag{4.10}$$

This notation is so convenient that we use it here before formally introducing determinants in the next chapter.

An alternative way to work out the cross product, which is easy to memorize, is to write the vectors (a, b, c) and (A, B, C) twice and read off the components by taking the products as indicated in Figure 4.39.

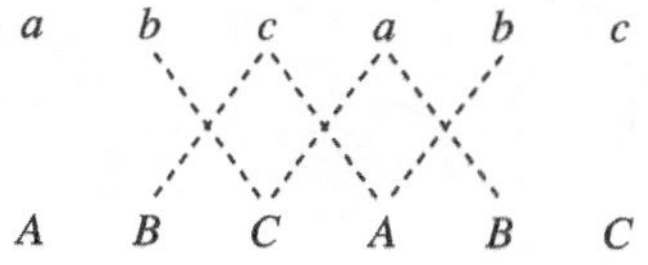

Figure 4.39 Gives the three components as $bC - cB$, $cA - aC$, $aB - bA$.

In MATLAB the vector product of two vectors $\boldsymbol{a}$ and $\boldsymbol{b}$ is given by the command `cross(a,b)`. In MAPLE it is given by `crossprod(a,b)`.

Example 4.24 Given the vectors $\boldsymbol{a} = (2, 1, 0)$, $\boldsymbol{b} = (2, -1, 1)$ and $\boldsymbol{c} = (0, 1, 1)$, evaluate

(a) $\boldsymbol{a} \times \boldsymbol{b}$ (b) $(\boldsymbol{a} \times \boldsymbol{b}) \times \boldsymbol{c}$ (c) $(\boldsymbol{a} \cdot \boldsymbol{c})\boldsymbol{b} - (\boldsymbol{b} \cdot \boldsymbol{c})\boldsymbol{a}$

(d) $\boldsymbol{b} \times \boldsymbol{c}$ (e) $\boldsymbol{a} \times (\boldsymbol{b} \times \boldsymbol{c})$ (f) $(\boldsymbol{a} \cdot \boldsymbol{c})\boldsymbol{b} - (\boldsymbol{a} \cdot \boldsymbol{b})\boldsymbol{c}$

Solution

(a) $\mathbf{a} \times \mathbf{b} = \begin{vmatrix} \mathbf{i} & \mathbf{j} & \mathbf{k} \\ 2 & 1 & 0 \\ 2 & -1 & 1 \end{vmatrix} = \mathbf{i}\begin{vmatrix} 1 & 0 \\ -1 & 1 \end{vmatrix} - \mathbf{j}\begin{vmatrix} 2 & 0 \\ 2 & 1 \end{vmatrix} + \mathbf{k}\begin{vmatrix} 2 & 1 \\ 2 & -1 \end{vmatrix} = (1, -2, -4)$

(b) $(\mathbf{a} \times \mathbf{b}) \times \mathbf{c} = \begin{vmatrix} \mathbf{i} & \mathbf{j} & \mathbf{k} \\ 1 & -2 & -4 \\ 0 & 1 & 1 \end{vmatrix} = \mathbf{i}\begin{vmatrix} -2 & -4 \\ 1 & 1 \end{vmatrix} - \mathbf{j}\begin{vmatrix} 1 & -4 \\ 0 & 1 \end{vmatrix} + \mathbf{k}\begin{vmatrix} 1 & -2 \\ 0 & 1 \end{vmatrix} = (2, -1, 1)$

(c) $\mathbf{a} \cdot \mathbf{c} = (2, 1, 0) \cdot (0, 1, 1) = 1$, $\mathbf{b} \cdot \mathbf{c} = (2, -1, 1) \cdot (0, 1, 1) = 0$ and hence $(\mathbf{a}\cdot\mathbf{c})\mathbf{b} - (\mathbf{b}\cdot\mathbf{c})\mathbf{a} = 1\mathbf{b} - 0\mathbf{a} = (2, -1, 1)$

(Note that (b) and (c) give the same result.)

(d) $\mathbf{b} \times \mathbf{c} = \begin{vmatrix} \mathbf{i} & \mathbf{j} & \mathbf{k} \\ 2 & -1 & 1 \\ 0 & 1 & 1 \end{vmatrix} = \mathbf{i}\begin{vmatrix} -1 & 1 \\ 1 & 1 \end{vmatrix} - \mathbf{j}\begin{vmatrix} 2 & 1 \\ 0 & 1 \end{vmatrix} + \mathbf{k}\begin{vmatrix} 2 & -1 \\ 0 & 1 \end{vmatrix} = (-2, -2, 2)$

(e) $\mathbf{a} \times (\mathbf{b} \times \mathbf{c}) = \begin{vmatrix} \mathbf{i} & \mathbf{j} & \mathbf{k} \\ 2 & 1 & 0 \\ -2 & -2 & 2 \end{vmatrix} = \mathbf{i}\begin{vmatrix} 1 & 0 \\ -2 & 2 \end{vmatrix} - \mathbf{j}\begin{vmatrix} 2 & 0 \\ -2 & 2 \end{vmatrix} + \mathbf{k}\begin{vmatrix} 2 & 1 \\ -2 & -2 \end{vmatrix} = (2, -4, -2)$

(Note that (b) and (e) do not give the same result and the cross product is *not* associative.)

(f) $\mathbf{a} \cdot \mathbf{c} = (2, 1, 0) \cdot (0, 1, 1) = 1$, $\mathbf{a} \cdot \mathbf{b} = (2, 1, 0) \cdot (2, -1, 1) = 3$ and hence $(\mathbf{a}\cdot\mathbf{c})\mathbf{b} - (\mathbf{a}\cdot\mathbf{b})\mathbf{c} = 1\mathbf{b} - 3\mathbf{c} = (2, -4, -2)$

(Note that (e) and (f) give the same result.)

Check that in MATLAB the commands

```
a = [2 1 0]; b = [2 -1 1]; c = [0 1 1];
cross(a,b)
cross(cross(a,b),c)
```

return the answers to (a) and (b).

Example 4.25 Find a unit vector perpendicular to the plane of the vectors $\mathbf{a} = (2, -3, 1)$ and $\mathbf{b} = (1, 2, -4)$.

Solution A vector perpendicular to the plane of the two vectors is the vector product

$$\mathbf{a} \times \mathbf{b} = \begin{vmatrix} \mathbf{i} & \mathbf{j} & \mathbf{k} \\ 2 & -3 & 1 \\ 1 & 2 & -4 \end{vmatrix} = (10, 9, 7)$$

whose modulus is

$$|\boldsymbol{a} \times \boldsymbol{b}| = \sqrt{(100 + 81 + 49)} = \sqrt{230}$$

Hence a unit vector perpendicular to the plane of $\boldsymbol{a}$ and $\boldsymbol{b}$ is $(10/\sqrt{230}, 9/\sqrt{230}, 7/\sqrt{230})$.

Example 4.26 Find the area of the triangle having vertices at P(1, 3, 2), Q(−2, 1, 3) and R(3, −2, −1).

Solution We have seen in Figure 4.38 that the area of the parallelogram formed with sides PQ and PR is $|\overrightarrow{PQ} \times \overrightarrow{PR}|$, so the area of the triangle PQR is $\frac{1}{2}|\overrightarrow{PQ} \times \overrightarrow{PR}|$. Now

$$\overrightarrow{PQ} = (-2 - 1, 1 - 3, 3 - 2) = (-3, -2, 1)$$

and

$$\overrightarrow{PR} = (3 - 1, -2 - 3, -1 - 2) = (2, -5, -3)$$

so that

$$\overrightarrow{PQ} \times \overrightarrow{PR} = \begin{vmatrix} \boldsymbol{i} & \boldsymbol{j} & \boldsymbol{k} \\ -3 & -2 & 1 \\ 2 & -5 & -3 \end{vmatrix} = (11, -7, 19)$$

Hence the area of the triangle PQR is

$$\tfrac{1}{2}|\overrightarrow{PQ} \times \overrightarrow{PR}| = \tfrac{1}{2}\sqrt{(121 + 49 + 361)} = \tfrac{1}{2}\sqrt{531} \approx 11.52 \text{ square units.}$$

Example 4.27 Four vectors are constructed corresponding to the four faces of a tetrahedron. The magnitude of a vector is equal to the area of the corresponding face and its direction is the outward perpendicular to the face, as shown in Figure 4.40. Show that the sum of the four vectors is zero.

Solution In Figure 4.40(a) let $\overrightarrow{AB} = \boldsymbol{b}$, $\overrightarrow{AC} = \boldsymbol{c}$ and $\overrightarrow{AD} = \boldsymbol{d}$. The outward perpendicular to triangle ABD is parallel to

$$\boldsymbol{n} = \overrightarrow{AD} \times \overrightarrow{AB} = \boldsymbol{d} \times \boldsymbol{b}$$

Figure 4.40
(a) Tetrahedron for Example 4.27;
(b) triangle from (a).

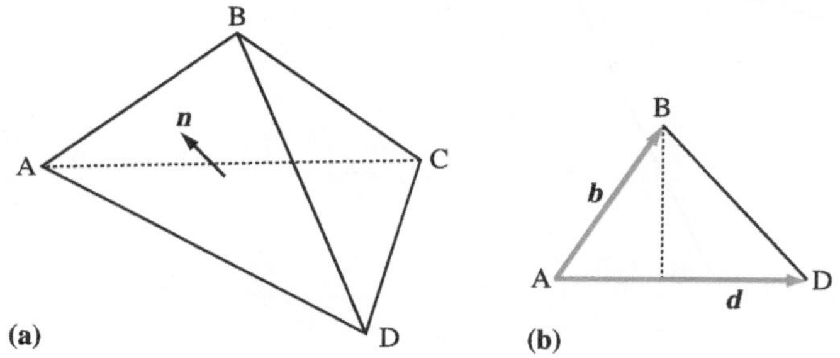

and the unit vector in the outward normal direction is

$$\hat{\boldsymbol{n}} = \frac{\boldsymbol{d} \times \boldsymbol{b}}{|\boldsymbol{d} \times \boldsymbol{b}|}$$

From Figure 4.40(b) the area of triangle ABD follows from the definition of cross product as

$$\text{area} = \tfrac{1}{2}\text{AD}(\text{AB} \sin \theta) = \tfrac{1}{2}|\boldsymbol{d} \times \boldsymbol{b}|$$

so the vector we require is

$$\boldsymbol{v}_1 = \text{area} \times \hat{\boldsymbol{n}} = \tfrac{1}{2}\boldsymbol{d} \times \boldsymbol{b}$$

In a similar manner for triangles ACB and ADC the vectors are

$$\boldsymbol{v}_2 = \tfrac{1}{2}\boldsymbol{b} \times \boldsymbol{c} \quad \text{and} \quad \boldsymbol{v}_3 = \tfrac{1}{2}\boldsymbol{c} \times \boldsymbol{d}$$

For the fourth face BCD the appropriate vector is

$$\boldsymbol{v}_4 = \tfrac{1}{2}\overrightarrow{\text{BD}} \times \overrightarrow{\text{BC}} = \tfrac{1}{2}(\boldsymbol{d} - \boldsymbol{b}) \times (\boldsymbol{c} - \boldsymbol{b}) = \tfrac{1}{2}(\boldsymbol{d} \times \boldsymbol{c} - \boldsymbol{d} \times \boldsymbol{b} - \boldsymbol{b} \times \boldsymbol{c})$$

Adding the four vectors $\boldsymbol{v}_1$, $\boldsymbol{v}_2$, $\boldsymbol{v}_3$ and $\boldsymbol{v}_4$ together gives the zero vector.

Example 4.28

A force of 4 units acts through the point P(2, 3, –5) in the direction of the vector (4, 5, –2). Find its moment about the point A(1, 2, –3). See Figure 4.41.

What are the moments of the force about axes through A parallel to the coordinate axes?

Solution

To express the force in vector form we first need the unit vector in the direction of the force.

$$\frac{4\boldsymbol{i} + 5\boldsymbol{j} - 2\boldsymbol{k}}{\sqrt{(16 + 25 + 4)}} = \frac{1}{\sqrt{45}}(4, 5, -2)$$

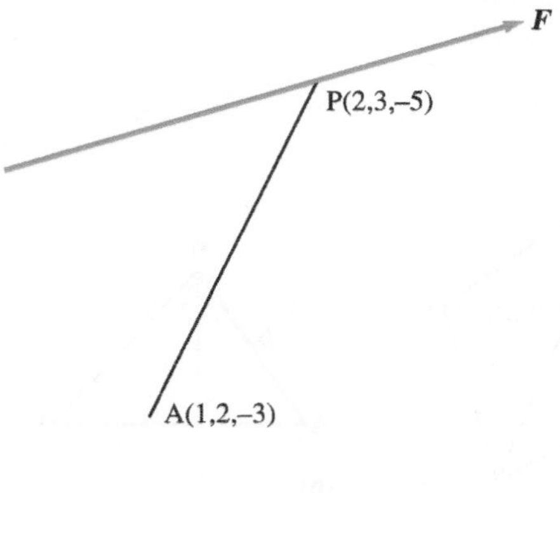

Figure 4.41
Moment of the force $\boldsymbol{F}$ about the point A in Example 4.28.

Since the force $\boldsymbol{F}$ has a magnitude of 4 units

$$\boldsymbol{F} = \frac{4}{\sqrt{45}}(4, 5, -2)$$

The position vector of P relative to A is

$$\overrightarrow{AP} = (1, 1, -2)$$

Thus from (4.6) the moment $\boldsymbol{M}$ of the force about A is

$$\boldsymbol{M} = \overrightarrow{AP} \times \boldsymbol{F} = \frac{4}{\sqrt{45}}\begin{vmatrix} \boldsymbol{i} & \boldsymbol{j} & \boldsymbol{k} \\ 1 & 1 & -2 \\ 4 & 5 & -2 \end{vmatrix}$$

$$= (32/\sqrt{45}, -24/\sqrt{45}, 4/\sqrt{45})$$

The moments about axes through A parallel to the coordinate axes are $32/\sqrt{45}$, $-24/\sqrt{45}$ and $4/\sqrt{45}$.

Example 4.29

A rigid body is rotating with an angular velocity of 5 rad s^{-1} about an axis in the direction of the vector (1, 3, −2) and passing through the point A(2, 3, −1). Find the linear velocity of the point P(−2, 3, 1) of the body.

Solution

A unit vector in the direction of the axis of rotation is $\frac{1}{\sqrt{14}}(1, 3, -2)$. Thus the angular velocity vector of the rigid body is

$$\boldsymbol{\omega} = (5/\sqrt{14})(1, 3, -2)$$

The position vector of P relative to A is

$$\overrightarrow{AP} = (-2 - 2, 3 - 3, 1 + 1) = (-4, 0, 2)$$

Thus from (4.7) the linear velocity of P is

$$\boldsymbol{v} = \boldsymbol{\omega} \times \overrightarrow{AP} = \frac{5}{\sqrt{14}}\begin{vmatrix} \boldsymbol{i} & \boldsymbol{j} & \boldsymbol{k} \\ 1 & 3 & -2 \\ -4 & 0 & 2 \end{vmatrix}$$

$$= (30/\sqrt{14}, 30/\sqrt{14}, 60/\sqrt{14})$$

Example 4.30

A trapdoor is raised and lowered by a rope attached to one of its corners. The rope is pulled via a pulley fixed to a point A, 50 cm above the hinge, as shown in Figure 4.42. If the trapdoor is uniform and of weight 20 N, what is the tension required to lift the door?

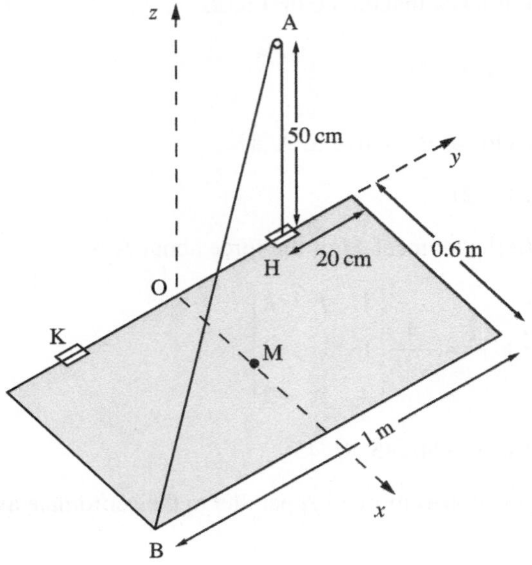

Figure 4.42 Trapdoor in Example 4.30.

Solution From the data given we can calculate various vectors immediately.

$$\overrightarrow{OA} = (0, 30, 50), \quad \overrightarrow{OB} = (60, -50, 0), \quad \overrightarrow{OH} = (0, 30, 0)$$

If M is the midpoint of the trapdoor then

$$\overrightarrow{OM} = (30, 0, 0)$$

The forces acting are the tension $\boldsymbol{T}$ in the rope along BA, the weight $\boldsymbol{W}$ through M in the $-z$ direction and reactions $\boldsymbol{R}$ and $\boldsymbol{S}$ at the hinges. Now

$$\overrightarrow{AB} = \overrightarrow{OB} - \overrightarrow{OA} = (60, -80, -50)$$

so that $|\overrightarrow{AB}| = 112$, and hence

$$\boldsymbol{T} = -T(60, -80, -50)/112$$

Taking moments about the hinge H, we first note that there is no moment of the reaction at H. For the remaining forces

$$\begin{aligned}\boldsymbol{M}_{\mathrm{H}} &= \overrightarrow{HM} \times \boldsymbol{W} + \overrightarrow{HB} \times \boldsymbol{T} + \overrightarrow{HK} \times \boldsymbol{R} \\ &= (30, -30, 0) \times (0, 0, -20) + (60, -80, 0) \times (60, -80, -50)(-T/112) + \overrightarrow{HK} \times \boldsymbol{R} \\ &= (600, 600, 0) + T(-35.8, -26.8, 0) + \overrightarrow{HK} \times \boldsymbol{R}\end{aligned}$$

Since we require the moment about the y axis, we take the scalar product of $\boldsymbol{M}_{\mathrm{H}}$ and $\boldsymbol{j}$. The vector $\overrightarrow{HK}$ is along $\boldsymbol{j}$, so $\boldsymbol{j} \cdot (\overrightarrow{HK} \times \boldsymbol{R})$ must be zero. Thus the $\boldsymbol{j}$ component of $\boldsymbol{M}_{\mathrm{H}}$ must be zero as the trapdoor just opens; that is,

$$0 = 600 - 26.8T$$

so

$$T = 22.4 \text{ N}$$

4.2.11 Exercises

Check your answers using MATLAB or MAPLE whenever possible.

41 Given $\boldsymbol{p} = (1, 1, 1)$, $\boldsymbol{q} = (0, -1, 2)$ and $\boldsymbol{r} = (2, 2, 1)$, evaluate

(a) $\boldsymbol{p} \times \boldsymbol{q}$ (b) $\boldsymbol{p} \times \boldsymbol{r}$

(c) $\boldsymbol{r} \times \boldsymbol{q}$ (d) $(\boldsymbol{p} \times \boldsymbol{r}) \cdot \boldsymbol{q}$

(e) $\boldsymbol{q} \cdot (\boldsymbol{r} \times \boldsymbol{p})$ (f) $(\boldsymbol{p} \times \boldsymbol{r}) \times \boldsymbol{q}$

42 The vectors $\boldsymbol{a} = (1, -1, 2)$, $\boldsymbol{b} = (0, 1, 3)$, $\boldsymbol{c} = (-2, 2, -4)$ are given.

(a) Evaluate $\boldsymbol{a} \times \boldsymbol{b}$ and $\boldsymbol{b} \times \boldsymbol{c}$

(b) Write down the vectors $\boldsymbol{b} \times \boldsymbol{a}$ and $\boldsymbol{c} \times \boldsymbol{b}$

(c) Show that $\boldsymbol{c} \times \boldsymbol{a} = 0$ and explain this result.

43 Evaluate $2\boldsymbol{j} \times (3\boldsymbol{i} - 4\boldsymbol{k})$ and $(\boldsymbol{i} + 2\boldsymbol{j}) \times \boldsymbol{k}$.

44 Given the vectors $\boldsymbol{a} = (-3, -1, -2)$ and $\boldsymbol{b} = (2, 3, 1)$, find $|\boldsymbol{a} \times \boldsymbol{b}|$ and $(\boldsymbol{a} + 2\boldsymbol{b}) \times (2\boldsymbol{a} - \boldsymbol{b})$.

45 Let $\boldsymbol{a} = (1, 2, 3)$, $\boldsymbol{b} = (2, 1, 4)$ and $\boldsymbol{c} = (1, -1, 2)$. Calculate $(\boldsymbol{a} \times \boldsymbol{b}) \times \boldsymbol{c}$ and $\boldsymbol{a} \times (\boldsymbol{b} \times \boldsymbol{c})$ and verify that these two vectors are not equal.

46 Show that the area of the triangle ABC in Figure 4.43 is $\frac{1}{2}|\overrightarrow{AB} \times \overrightarrow{AC}|$. Show that

$$\overrightarrow{AB} \times \overrightarrow{AC} = \overrightarrow{BC} \times \overrightarrow{BA} = \overrightarrow{CA} \times \overrightarrow{CB}$$

and hence deduce the sine rule

$$\frac{\sin A}{a} = \frac{\sin B}{b} = \frac{\sin C}{c}$$

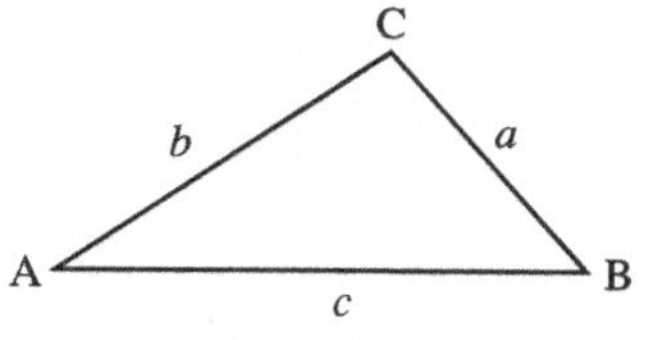

Figure 4.43 Sine rule: Section 2.6.1.

47 Prove that

$$(\boldsymbol{a} - \boldsymbol{b}) \times (\boldsymbol{a} + \boldsymbol{b}) = 2(\boldsymbol{a} \times \boldsymbol{b})$$

and interpret geometrically.

48 The points A, B and C have coordinates (1, −1, 2), (9, 0, 8) and (5, 0, 5) relative to rectangular cartesian axes. Find

(a) the vectors $\overrightarrow{AB}$ and $\overrightarrow{AC}$;

(b) a unit vector perpendicular to the triangle ABC;

(c) the area of the triangle ABC.

49 Use the definitions of the scalar and vector products to show that

$$|\boldsymbol{a} \cdot \boldsymbol{b}|^2 + |\boldsymbol{a} \times \boldsymbol{b}|^2 = a^2 b^2$$

50 If $\boldsymbol{a}$, $\boldsymbol{b}$ and $\boldsymbol{c}$ are three vectors such that $\boldsymbol{a} + \boldsymbol{b} + \boldsymbol{c} = 0$, prove that

$$\boldsymbol{a} \times \boldsymbol{b} = \boldsymbol{b} \times \boldsymbol{c} = \boldsymbol{c} \times \boldsymbol{a}$$

and interpret geometrically.

51 A rigid body is rotating with angular velocity $6\,\text{rad s}^{-1}$ about an axis in the direction of the vector (3, −2, 1) and passing through the point A(3, −2, 5). Find the linear velocity of the point P(3, −2, 1) on the body.

52 A force of 4 units acts through the point P(4, −1, 2) in the direction of the vector (2, −1, 4). Find its moment about the point A(3, −1, 4).

53 The moment of a force $\boldsymbol{F}$ acting at a point P about a point O is defined to be a vector $\boldsymbol{M}$ perpendicular to the plane containing $\boldsymbol{F}$ and the point O such that $|\boldsymbol{M}| = p|\boldsymbol{F}|$, where p is the perpendicular distance from O to the line of action of $\boldsymbol{r}$. Figure 4.44 illustrates such a force $\boldsymbol{F}$. Show that the perpendicular distance from O to the line of action

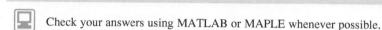

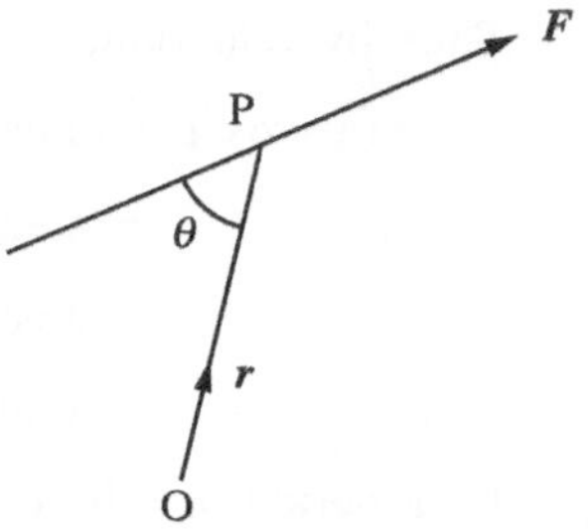

Figure 4.44 Moment of force $\boldsymbol{F}$ about O.

of $\boldsymbol{F}$ is $|\boldsymbol{r}|\sin\theta$, where $\boldsymbol{r}$ is the position vector of P. Hence deduce that $\boldsymbol{M} = \boldsymbol{r} \times \boldsymbol{F}$. Show that the moment of $\boldsymbol{F}$ about O is the same for any point P on the line of action of $\boldsymbol{F}$.

Forces (1, 0, 0), (1, 2, 0) and (1, 2, 3) act through the points (1, 1, 1), (0, 1, 1) and (0, 0, 1) respectively:

(a) Find the moment of each force about the origin.

(b) Find the moment of each force about the point (1, 1, 1).

(c) Find the total moment of the three forces about the point (1, 1, 1).

54 Find a unit vector perpendicular to the plane of the two vectors (2, −1, 1) and (3, 4, −1). What is the sine of the angle between these two vectors?

55 Prove that the shortest distance of a point P from the line through the points A and B is

$$\frac{|\overrightarrow{AP} \times \overrightarrow{AB}|}{|\overrightarrow{AB}|}$$

A satellite is stationary at P(2, 5, 4) and a warning signal is activated if any object comes within a distance of 3 units. Determine whether a rocket moving in a straight line passing through A(1, 5, 2) and B(3, −1, 5) activates the warning signal.

56 The position vector $\boldsymbol{r}$, with respect to a given origin O, of a charged particle of mass m and charge e at time t is given by

$$\boldsymbol{r} = \left(\frac{Et}{B} + a\sin(\omega t)\right)\boldsymbol{i} + a\cos(\omega t)\boldsymbol{j} + ct\boldsymbol{k}$$

where E, B, a and ω are constants. The corresponding velocity and acceleration are

$$\boldsymbol{v} = \left(\frac{E}{B} + a\omega\cos(\omega t)\right)\boldsymbol{i} - a\omega\sin(\omega t)\boldsymbol{j} + c\boldsymbol{k}$$

$$\boldsymbol{f} = -a\omega^2\sin(\omega t)\boldsymbol{i} - a\omega^2\cos(\omega t)\boldsymbol{j}$$

For the case when $\boldsymbol{B} = B\boldsymbol{k}$, show that the equation of motion

$$m\boldsymbol{f} = e(E\boldsymbol{j} + \boldsymbol{v} \times \boldsymbol{B})$$

is satisfied provided ω is chosen suitably.

4.2.12 Triple products

In Example 4.24, products of several vectors were computed: the product $(\boldsymbol{a} \times \boldsymbol{b})\cdot\boldsymbol{c}$ is called the **triple scalar product** and the product $(\boldsymbol{a} \times \boldsymbol{b}) \times \boldsymbol{c}$ is called the **triple vector product**.

Triple scalar product

The triple scalar product is of interest because of its geometrical interpretation. Looking at Figure 4.45, we see that

$$\begin{aligned}\boldsymbol{a} \times \boldsymbol{b} &= |\boldsymbol{a}|\,|\boldsymbol{b}|\sin\theta\boldsymbol{k}\\ &= (\text{area of the parallelogram OACB})\boldsymbol{k}\end{aligned}$$

Thus, by definition,

$$\begin{aligned}(\boldsymbol{a} \times \boldsymbol{b})\cdot\boldsymbol{c} &= (\text{area of OACB})\boldsymbol{k}\cdot\boldsymbol{c}\\ &= (\text{area of OACB})|\boldsymbol{k}|\,|\boldsymbol{c}|\cos\phi\\ &= (\text{area of OACB})h \quad (\text{where } h \text{ is the height of the parallelepiped})\\ &= \text{volume of the parallelepiped}\end{aligned}$$

Considering $(\boldsymbol{a} \times \boldsymbol{b})\cdot\boldsymbol{c}$ to be the volume of the parallelepiped mounted on $\boldsymbol{a}$, $\boldsymbol{b}$, $\boldsymbol{c}$ has several useful consequences.

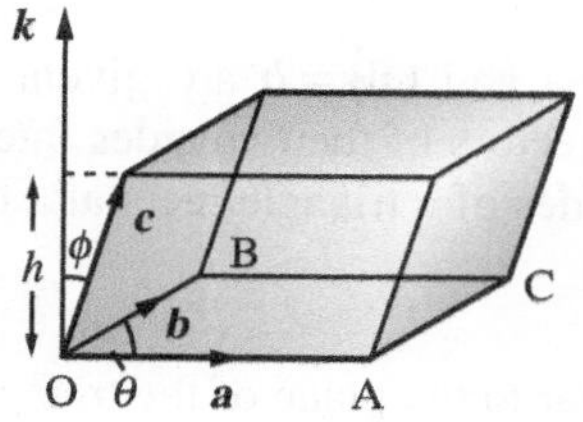

Figure 4.45
Triple scalar product as the volume of a parallelepiped.

(a) If two of the vectors $\boldsymbol{a}$, $\boldsymbol{b}$ and $\boldsymbol{c}$ are parallel then $(\boldsymbol{a} \times \boldsymbol{b}) \cdot \boldsymbol{c} = 0$. This follows immediately since the parallelepiped collapses to a plane and has zero volume. In particular,

$$(\boldsymbol{a} \times \boldsymbol{b}) \cdot \boldsymbol{a} = 0 \quad \text{and} \quad (\boldsymbol{a} \times \boldsymbol{b}) \cdot \boldsymbol{b} = 0$$

(b) If the three vectors are coplanar then $(\boldsymbol{a} \times \boldsymbol{b}) \cdot \boldsymbol{c} = 0$. The same reasoning as in (a) gives this result.

(c) If $(\boldsymbol{a} \times \boldsymbol{b}) \cdot \boldsymbol{c} = 0$ then either $\boldsymbol{a} = 0$ or $\boldsymbol{b} = 0$ or $\boldsymbol{c} = 0$ or two of the vectors are parallel or the three vectors are coplanar.

(d) In the triple scalar product the dot $\cdot$ and the cross $\times$ can be interchanged:

$$(\boldsymbol{a} \times \boldsymbol{b}) \cdot \boldsymbol{c} = \boldsymbol{a} \cdot (\boldsymbol{b} \times \boldsymbol{c})$$

since it is easily checked that they measure the same volume mounted on $\boldsymbol{a}$, $\boldsymbol{b}$, $\boldsymbol{c}$. If we retain the same cyclic order of the three vectors then we obtain

$$\boldsymbol{a} \cdot (\boldsymbol{b} \times \boldsymbol{c}) = \boldsymbol{b} \cdot (\boldsymbol{c} \times \boldsymbol{a}) = \boldsymbol{c} \cdot (\boldsymbol{a} \times \boldsymbol{b}) \tag{4.11}$$

(e) In cartesian form the scalar triple product can be written as the determinant

$$\boldsymbol{a} \cdot (\boldsymbol{b} \times \boldsymbol{c}) = \begin{vmatrix} a_1 & a_2 & a_3 \\ b_1 & b_2 & b_3 \\ c_1 & c_2 & c_3 \end{vmatrix} \tag{4.12}$$
$$= a_1b_2c_3 - a_1b_3c_2 - a_2b_1c_3 + a_2b_3c_1 + a_3b_1c_2 - a_3b_2c_1$$

Example 4.31 Find λ so that $\boldsymbol{a} = (2, -1, 1)$, $\boldsymbol{b} = (1, 2, -3)$ and $\boldsymbol{c} = (3, \lambda, 5)$ are coplanar.

Solution None of these vectors are zero or parallel, so by property (b) the three vectors are coplanar if $(\boldsymbol{a} \times \boldsymbol{b}) \cdot \boldsymbol{c} = 0$. Now

$$\boldsymbol{a} \times \boldsymbol{b} = (1, 7, 5)$$

so

$$(\boldsymbol{a} \times \boldsymbol{b}) \cdot \boldsymbol{c} = 3 + 7\lambda + 25$$

This will be zero, and the three vectors coplanar, when $\lambda = -4$.

Example 4.32 In a triangle OAB the sides $\overrightarrow{OA} = \boldsymbol{a}$ and $\overrightarrow{OB} = \boldsymbol{b}$ are given. Find the point P, with $\boldsymbol{c} = \overrightarrow{OP}$, where the perpendicular bisectors of the two sides intersect. Hence prove that the perpendicular bisectors of the sides of a triangle meet at a point.

Solution Let $\hat{\boldsymbol{k}}$ be the unit vector perpendicular to the plane of the triangle; the situation is illustrated in Figure 4.46.

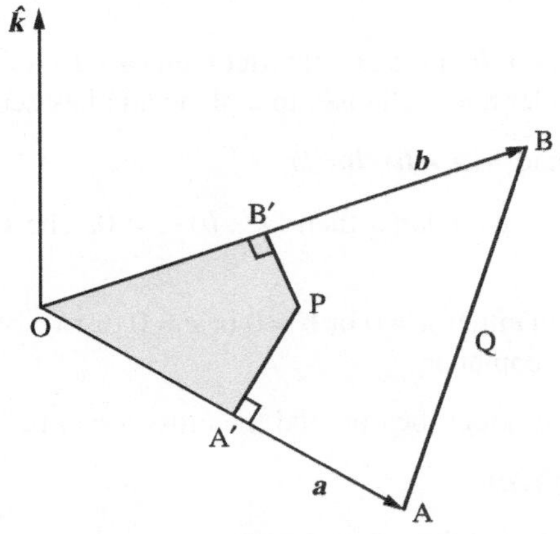

Figure 4.46 Perpendicular bisectors in Example 4.32.

Now

$$\overrightarrow{OP} = \overrightarrow{OA'} + \overrightarrow{A'P} = \tfrac{1}{2}\boldsymbol{a} + \alpha\hat{\boldsymbol{k}} \times \boldsymbol{a}$$

for some α, since the vector $\hat{\boldsymbol{k}} \times \boldsymbol{a}$ is in the direction perpendicular to $\boldsymbol{a}$. Similarly

$$\overrightarrow{OP} = \overrightarrow{OB'} + \overrightarrow{B'P} = \tfrac{1}{2}\boldsymbol{b} + \beta\hat{\boldsymbol{k}} \times \boldsymbol{b}$$

Subtracting these two equations

$$\tfrac{1}{2}\boldsymbol{a} + \alpha\hat{\boldsymbol{k}} \times \boldsymbol{a} = \tfrac{1}{2}\boldsymbol{b} + \beta\hat{\boldsymbol{k}} \times \boldsymbol{b}$$

Take the dot product of this equation with $\boldsymbol{b}$, which eliminates the final term, since $\boldsymbol{b} \cdot (\hat{\boldsymbol{k}} \times \boldsymbol{b}) = 0$, and gives

$$\tfrac{1}{2}\boldsymbol{b} \cdot (\boldsymbol{b} - \boldsymbol{a}) = \alpha\boldsymbol{b} \cdot (\hat{\boldsymbol{k}} \times \boldsymbol{a})$$

Hence α has been computed in terms of the known data, so assuming $\boldsymbol{b} \cdot (\hat{\boldsymbol{k}} \times \boldsymbol{a}) \neq 0$

$$\overrightarrow{OP} = \tfrac{1}{2}\boldsymbol{a} + \frac{\tfrac{1}{2}\boldsymbol{b} \cdot (\boldsymbol{b} - \boldsymbol{a})}{\boldsymbol{b} \cdot (\hat{\boldsymbol{k}} \times \boldsymbol{a})}\hat{\boldsymbol{k}} \times \boldsymbol{a}$$

We now need to check that PQ is perpendicular to AB:

$$\overrightarrow{AB} = \overrightarrow{OB} - \overrightarrow{OA} = \boldsymbol{b} - \boldsymbol{a}$$

and

$$\overrightarrow{PQ} = \overrightarrow{OQ} - \overrightarrow{OP} = \tfrac{1}{2}(\boldsymbol{a} + \boldsymbol{b}) - \tfrac{1}{2}\boldsymbol{a} - \frac{\tfrac{1}{2}\boldsymbol{b} \cdot (\boldsymbol{b} - \boldsymbol{a})}{\boldsymbol{b} \cdot (\hat{\boldsymbol{k}} \times \boldsymbol{a})}\hat{\boldsymbol{k}} \times \boldsymbol{a}$$

Now take the dot product of these two vectors

$$\left[\tfrac{1}{2}\boldsymbol{b} - \frac{\tfrac{1}{2}\boldsymbol{b}\cdot(\boldsymbol{b}-\boldsymbol{a})}{\boldsymbol{b}\cdot(\hat{\boldsymbol{k}}\times\boldsymbol{a})}\hat{\boldsymbol{k}}\times\boldsymbol{a}\right]\cdot(\boldsymbol{b}-\boldsymbol{a}) = \tfrac{1}{2}\boldsymbol{b}\cdot(\boldsymbol{b}-\boldsymbol{a}) - \frac{\tfrac{1}{2}\boldsymbol{b}\cdot(\boldsymbol{b}-\boldsymbol{a})}{\boldsymbol{b}\cdot(\hat{\boldsymbol{k}}\times\boldsymbol{a})}\boldsymbol{b}\cdot(\hat{\boldsymbol{k}}\times\boldsymbol{a}) = 0$$

Since neither $\overrightarrow{\mathrm{PQ}}$ nor $\overrightarrow{\mathrm{AB}}$ is zero, the two vectors must therefore be perpendicular. Hence the three perpendicular bisectors of the sides of a triangle meet at a point.

Example 4.33 Three non-zero, non-parallel and non-coplanar vectors $\boldsymbol{a}$, $\boldsymbol{b}$ and $\boldsymbol{c}$ are given. Three further vectors are written in terms of $\boldsymbol{a}$, $\boldsymbol{b}$ and $\boldsymbol{c}$ as

$$\boldsymbol{A} = \alpha\boldsymbol{a} + \beta\boldsymbol{b} + \gamma\boldsymbol{c}$$

$$\boldsymbol{B} = \alpha'\boldsymbol{a} + \beta'\boldsymbol{b} + \gamma'\boldsymbol{c}$$

$$\boldsymbol{C} = \alpha''\boldsymbol{a} + \beta''\boldsymbol{b} + \gamma''\boldsymbol{c}$$

Find how the triple scalar product $\boldsymbol{A}\cdot(\boldsymbol{B}\times\boldsymbol{C})$ is related to $\boldsymbol{a}\cdot(\boldsymbol{b}\times\boldsymbol{c})$.

Solution To find the result we use the facts that (i) the vector product of identical vectors is zero and (ii) the triple scalar product is zero if two of the vectors in the product are the same. Now

$$\begin{aligned}\boldsymbol{A}\cdot(\boldsymbol{B}\times\boldsymbol{C}) &= (\alpha\mathbf{a}+\beta\mathbf{b}+\gamma\mathbf{c})\cdot[(\alpha'\mathbf{a}+\beta'\mathbf{b}+\gamma'\mathbf{c})\times(\alpha''\mathbf{a}+\beta''\mathbf{b}+\gamma''\mathbf{c})]\\
&= (\alpha\mathbf{a}+\beta\mathbf{b}+\gamma\mathbf{c})\cdot[\alpha'\beta''\mathbf{a}\times\mathbf{b}+\alpha'\gamma''\mathbf{a}\times\mathbf{c}+\beta'\alpha''\mathbf{b}\times\mathbf{a}\\
&\qquad +\beta'\gamma''\mathbf{b}\times\mathbf{c}+\gamma'\alpha''\mathbf{c}\times\mathbf{a}+\gamma'\beta''\mathbf{c}\times\mathbf{b}]\\
&= (\alpha\mathbf{a}+\beta\mathbf{b}+\gamma\mathbf{c})\cdot[(\alpha'\beta''-\beta'\alpha'')\mathbf{a}\times\mathbf{b}+(\beta'\gamma''-\gamma'\beta'')\mathbf{b}\times\mathbf{c}\\
&\qquad +(\gamma'\alpha''-\alpha'\gamma'')\mathbf{c}\times\mathbf{a}]\\
&= \gamma(\alpha'\beta''-\beta'\alpha'')\mathbf{c}\cdot\mathbf{a}\times\mathbf{b}+\alpha(\beta'\gamma''-\gamma'\beta'')\mathbf{a}\cdot\mathbf{b}\times\mathbf{c}\\
&\qquad +\beta(\gamma'\alpha''-\alpha'\gamma'')\mathbf{b}\cdot\mathbf{c}\times\mathbf{a}\\
&= (\mathbf{a}\cdot\mathbf{b}\times\mathbf{c})[\alpha(\beta'\gamma''-\gamma'\beta'')+\beta(\gamma'\alpha''-\alpha'\gamma'')+\gamma(\alpha'\beta''-\beta'\alpha'')]\end{aligned}$$

The result can be written most conveniently in determinant form (see Section 5.3 of the next chapter) as

$$\boldsymbol{A}\cdot(\boldsymbol{B}\times\boldsymbol{C}) = \begin{vmatrix}\alpha & \beta & \gamma\\ \alpha' & \beta' & \gamma'\\ \alpha'' & \beta'' & \gamma''\end{vmatrix}(\mathbf{a}\cdot\mathbf{b}\times\mathbf{c})$$

Triple vector product

For the triple vector product we shall show in general that

$$(\mathbf{a}\times\boldsymbol{b})\times\mathbf{c} = (\mathbf{a}\cdot\mathbf{c})\boldsymbol{b} - (\boldsymbol{b}\cdot\boldsymbol{c})\mathbf{a} \qquad \textbf{(4.13)}$$

as suggested in Example 4.24. We have from (4.9)

$$\mathbf{a} \times \mathbf{b} = (a_2b_3 - a_3b_2, a_3b_1 - a_1b_3, a_1b_2 - a_2b_1)$$

and hence

$$\begin{aligned}(\mathbf{a} \times \mathbf{b}) \times \mathbf{c} = ((a_3b_1 - a_1b_3)c_3 - (a_1b_2 - a_2b_1)c_2,\\ (a_1b_2 - a_2b_1)c_1 - (a_2b_3 - a_3b_2)c_3,\\ (a_2b_3 - a_3b_2)c_2 - (a_3b_1 - a_1b_3)c_1)\end{aligned}$$

The first component of this vector is

$$\begin{aligned}a_3c_3b_1 - b_3c_3a_1 - b_2c_2a_1 + a_2c_2b_1 &= (a_1c_1 + a_2c_2 + a_3c_3)b_1 - (b_1c_1 + b_2c_2 + b_3c_3)a_1\\ &= (\mathbf{a}\cdot\mathbf{c})b_1 - (\mathbf{b}\cdot\mathbf{c})a_1\end{aligned}$$

Treating the second and third components similarly, we find

$$\begin{aligned}(\mathbf{a} \times \mathbf{b}) \times \mathbf{c} &= ((\mathbf{a}\cdot\mathbf{c})b_1 - (\mathbf{b}\cdot\mathbf{c})a_1, (\mathbf{a}\cdot\mathbf{c})b_2 - (\mathbf{b}\cdot\mathbf{c})a_2, (\mathbf{a}\cdot\mathbf{c})b_3 - (\mathbf{b}\cdot\mathbf{c})a_3)\\ &= (\mathbf{a}\cdot\mathbf{c})\mathbf{b} - (\mathbf{b}\cdot\mathbf{c})\mathbf{a}\end{aligned}$$

In a similar way we can show that

$$\mathbf{a} \times (\mathbf{b} \times \mathbf{c}) = (\mathbf{a}\cdot\mathbf{c})\mathbf{b} - (\mathbf{a}\cdot\mathbf{b})\mathbf{c} \qquad \textbf{(4.14)}$$

We can now see why the associativity of the vector product does not hold in general. The vector in (4.13) is in the plane of **b** and **a**, while the vector in (4.14) is in the plane of **b** and **c**; hence they are not in the same planes in general, as we inferred geometrically in Section 4.2.10. Consequently, in general

$$\mathbf{a} \times (\mathbf{b} \times \mathbf{c}) \neq (\mathbf{a} \times \mathbf{b}) \times \mathbf{c}$$

so use of brackets is essential.

Example 4.34 If **a** = (3, −2, 1), **b** = (−1, 3, 4) and **c** = (2, 1, −3), confirm that

$$\mathbf{a} \times (\mathbf{b} \times \mathbf{c}) = (\mathbf{a}\cdot\mathbf{c})\mathbf{b} - (\mathbf{a}\cdot\mathbf{b})\mathbf{c}$$

Solution

$$\mathbf{b} \times \mathbf{c} = \begin{vmatrix} \mathbf{i} & \mathbf{j} & \mathbf{k} \\ -1 & 3 & 4 \\ 2 & 1 & -3 \end{vmatrix} = (-13, 5, -7)$$

$$\mathbf{a} \times (\mathbf{b} \times \mathbf{c}) = \begin{vmatrix} \mathbf{i} & \mathbf{j} & \mathbf{k} \\ 3 & -2 & 1 \\ -13 & 5 & -7 \end{vmatrix} = (9, 8, -11)$$

$$\begin{aligned}(\boldsymbol{a}\cdot\boldsymbol{c})\boldsymbol{b}-(\boldsymbol{a}\cdot\boldsymbol{b})\boldsymbol{c} &= [(3)(2)+(-2)(1)+(1)(-3)](-1, 3, 4)\\ &\quad -[(3)(-1)+(-2)(3)+(1)(4)](2, 1, -3)\\ &= (-1, 3, 4)+5(2, 1, -3)\\ &= (9, 8, -11)\end{aligned}$$

thus confirming the result

$$\boldsymbol{a}\times(\boldsymbol{b}\times\boldsymbol{c}) = (\boldsymbol{a}\cdot\boldsymbol{c})\boldsymbol{b}-(\boldsymbol{a}\cdot\boldsymbol{b})\boldsymbol{c}$$

Example 4.35

Verify that $\boldsymbol{a}\times(\boldsymbol{b}\times\boldsymbol{c}) \neq (\boldsymbol{a}\times\boldsymbol{b})\times\boldsymbol{c}$ for the three vectors $\boldsymbol{a}=(1, 0, 0)$, $\boldsymbol{b}=(-1, 2, 0)$ and $\boldsymbol{c}=(1, 1, 1)$.

Solution

Evaluate the cross products in turn:

$$\boldsymbol{b}\times\boldsymbol{c} = (-1, 2, 0)\times(1, 1, 1) = (2, 1, -3)$$

and therefore

$$\boldsymbol{a}\times(\boldsymbol{b}\times\boldsymbol{c}) = (1, 0, 0)\times(2, 1, -3) = (0, 3, 1)$$

Similarly for the right-hand side:

$$\boldsymbol{a}\times\boldsymbol{b} = (1, 0, 0)\times(-1, 2, 0) = (0, 0, 2)$$

and hence

$$(\boldsymbol{a}\times\boldsymbol{b})\times\boldsymbol{c} = (0, 0, 2)\times(1, 1, 1) = (-2, 2, 0)$$

Clearly for these three vectors $\boldsymbol{a}\times(\boldsymbol{b}\times\boldsymbol{c}) \neq (\boldsymbol{a}\times\boldsymbol{b})\times\boldsymbol{c}$.

Example 4.36

The vectors $\boldsymbol{a}$, $\boldsymbol{b}$ and $\boldsymbol{c}$ and the scalar p satisfy the equations

$$\boldsymbol{a}\cdot\boldsymbol{b} = p \quad \text{and} \quad \boldsymbol{a}\times\boldsymbol{b} = \boldsymbol{c}$$

and $\boldsymbol{a}$ is not parallel to $\boldsymbol{b}$. Solve for $\boldsymbol{a}$ in terms of the other quantities and give a geometrical interpretation of the result.

Solution

First evaluate the cross product of the second equation with $\boldsymbol{b}$

$$\boldsymbol{b}\times(\boldsymbol{a}\times\boldsymbol{b}) = \boldsymbol{b}\times\boldsymbol{c}$$

gives

$$(\boldsymbol{b}\cdot\boldsymbol{b})\boldsymbol{a}-(\boldsymbol{b}\cdot\boldsymbol{a})\boldsymbol{b} = \boldsymbol{b}\times\boldsymbol{c}$$

and hence, using $\boldsymbol{a}\cdot\boldsymbol{b} = p$, and collecting the terms

$$\boldsymbol{a} = \frac{p\boldsymbol{b}+\boldsymbol{b}\times\boldsymbol{c}}{|\boldsymbol{b}|^2}$$

Since $\boldsymbol{b}\times\boldsymbol{c}$ is in the plane of $\boldsymbol{a}$ and $\boldsymbol{b}$, any vector in the plane can be written as a linear combination of $\boldsymbol{b}$ and $\boldsymbol{b}\times\boldsymbol{c}$. The expression for $\boldsymbol{a}$ gives the values of the coefficients in the linear combination.

4.2.13 Exercises

Check your answers using MATLAB or MAPLE whenever possible.

57 Find the volume of the parallelepiped whose edges are represented by the vectors (2, −3, 4), (1, 3, −1), (3, −1, 2).

58 Prove that the vectors (3, 2, −1), (5, −7, 3) and (11, −3, 1) are coplanar.

59 Find the constant λ such that the three vectors (3, 2, −1), (1, −1, 3) and (2, −3, λ) are coplanar.

60 Prove that the four points having position vectors (2, 1, 0), (2, −2, −2), (7, −3, −1) and (13, 3, 5) are coplanar.

61 Given $\boldsymbol{p} = (1, 4, 1)$, $\boldsymbol{q} = (2, 1, -1)$ and $\boldsymbol{r} = (1, -3, 2)$, find

(a) a unit vector perpendicular to the plane containing $\boldsymbol{p}$ and $\boldsymbol{q}$;

(b) a unit vector in the plane containing $\boldsymbol{p} \times \boldsymbol{q}$ and $\boldsymbol{p} \times \boldsymbol{r}$ that has zero x component.

62 Show that if $\boldsymbol{a}$ is any vector and $\hat{\boldsymbol{u}}$ any unit vector then

$$\boldsymbol{a} = (\boldsymbol{a} \cdot \hat{\boldsymbol{u}})\hat{\boldsymbol{u}} + \hat{\boldsymbol{u}} \times (\boldsymbol{a} \times \hat{\boldsymbol{u}})$$

and draw a diagram to illustrate this relation geometrically.

The vector (3, −2, 6) is resolved into two vectors along and perpendicular to the line whose direction cosines are proportional to (1, 1, 1). Find these vectors.

63 Three vectors $\boldsymbol{u}, \boldsymbol{v}, \boldsymbol{w}$ are expressed in terms of the three vectors $\boldsymbol{l}, \boldsymbol{m}, \boldsymbol{n}$ in the form

$$\boldsymbol{u} = u_1\boldsymbol{l} + u_2\boldsymbol{m} + u_3\boldsymbol{n}$$

$$\boldsymbol{v} = v_1\boldsymbol{l} + v_2\boldsymbol{m} + v_3\boldsymbol{n}$$

$$\boldsymbol{w} = w_1\boldsymbol{l} + w_2\boldsymbol{m} + w_3\boldsymbol{n}$$

Show that

$$\boldsymbol{u} \cdot (\boldsymbol{v} \times \boldsymbol{w}) = \lambda \boldsymbol{l} \cdot (\boldsymbol{m} \times \boldsymbol{n})$$

and evaluate λ.

64 Forces $\boldsymbol{F}_1, \boldsymbol{F}_2, \ldots, \boldsymbol{F}_n$ act at the points $\boldsymbol{r}_1, \boldsymbol{r}_2, \ldots, \boldsymbol{r}_n$ respectively. The total force and the total moment about the origin O are

$$\boldsymbol{F} = \sum \boldsymbol{F}_i \quad \text{and} \quad \boldsymbol{G} = \sum \boldsymbol{r}_i \times \boldsymbol{F}_i$$

Show that for any other origin O′ the moment is given by

$$\boldsymbol{G}' = \boldsymbol{G} + \overrightarrow{O'O} \times \boldsymbol{F}$$

If O′ lies on the line

$$\overrightarrow{OO'} = \boldsymbol{r} = \alpha(\boldsymbol{F} \times \boldsymbol{G}) + t\boldsymbol{F}$$

find the constant α that ensures that $\boldsymbol{G}'$ is parallel to $\boldsymbol{F}$. This line is called the central axis of the system of forces.

65 Extended exercise on products of four vectors.

(a) Use (4.11) to show

$$(\boldsymbol{a} \times \boldsymbol{b}) \cdot (\boldsymbol{c} \times \boldsymbol{d}) = [(\boldsymbol{a} \times \boldsymbol{b}) \times \boldsymbol{c}] \cdot \boldsymbol{d}$$

and use (4.13) to simplify the expression on the right-hand side.

(b) Use (4.13) to show that

$$(\boldsymbol{a} \times \boldsymbol{b}) \times (\boldsymbol{a} \times \boldsymbol{c}) = [\boldsymbol{a} \cdot (\boldsymbol{a} \times \boldsymbol{c})]\boldsymbol{b} - [\boldsymbol{b} \cdot (\boldsymbol{a} \times \boldsymbol{c})]\boldsymbol{a}$$

and show that the right-hand side can be simplified to

$$[(\boldsymbol{a} \times \boldsymbol{b}) \cdot \boldsymbol{c}]\boldsymbol{a}$$

(c) Use (4.14) to show that

$$\boldsymbol{a} \times [\boldsymbol{b} \times (\boldsymbol{a} \times \boldsymbol{c})] = \boldsymbol{a} \times [(\boldsymbol{b} \cdot \boldsymbol{c})\boldsymbol{a} - (\boldsymbol{b} \cdot \boldsymbol{a})\boldsymbol{c}]$$

and simplify the right-hand side further. Note that the product is different from the result in (b), verifying that the position of the brackets matters in cross products.

(d) Use the result in (a) to show that

$$(\boldsymbol{l} \times \boldsymbol{m}) \cdot (\boldsymbol{l} \times \boldsymbol{n}) = l^2(\boldsymbol{m} \cdot \boldsymbol{n}) - (\boldsymbol{l} \cdot \boldsymbol{m})(\boldsymbol{l} \cdot \boldsymbol{n})$$

Take $\boldsymbol{l}$, $\boldsymbol{m}$ and $\boldsymbol{n}$ to be unit vectors along the sides of a regular tetrahedron. Deduce that the angle between two faces of the tetrahedron is $\cos^{-1}\frac{1}{3}$.

4.3 The vector treatment of the geometry of lines and planes

4.3.1 Vector equation of a line

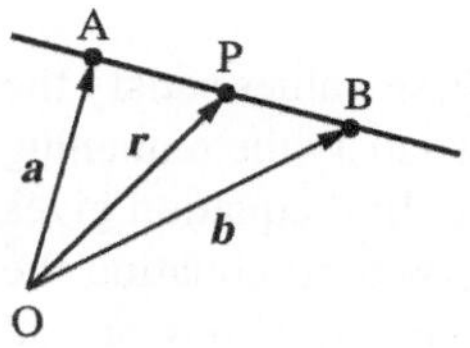

Figure 4.47
Line AB in terms of $\boldsymbol{r} = \overrightarrow{OP}$.

Take an arbitrary origin O and let $\overrightarrow{OA} = \boldsymbol{a}$, $\overrightarrow{OB} = \boldsymbol{b}$ and $\overrightarrow{OP} = \boldsymbol{r}$, as in Figure 4.47. If P is any point on the line then

$$\overrightarrow{OP} = \overrightarrow{OA} + \overrightarrow{AP}, \quad \text{by the triangle law}$$

giving

$$\boldsymbol{r} = \boldsymbol{a} + t\overrightarrow{AB} \qquad (\text{since } \overrightarrow{AP} \text{ is a multiple of } \overrightarrow{AB})$$

$$= \boldsymbol{a} + t(\boldsymbol{b} - \boldsymbol{a}) \qquad (\text{since } \boldsymbol{a} + \overrightarrow{AB} = \boldsymbol{b})$$

Thus the equation of the line is

$$\boldsymbol{r} = (1 - t)\boldsymbol{a} + t\boldsymbol{b} \tag{4.15}$$

As t varies from $-\infty$ to $+\infty$, the point P sweeps along the line, with $t = 0$ corresponding to point A and $t = 1$ to point B.

Since $\overrightarrow{OP} = \overrightarrow{OA} + \overrightarrow{AP} = \overrightarrow{OA} + t\overrightarrow{AB}$, we have $\boldsymbol{r} = \boldsymbol{a} + t(\boldsymbol{b} - \boldsymbol{a})$. If we write $\boldsymbol{c} = \boldsymbol{b} - \boldsymbol{a}$ then we have an alternative intepretation of a line through A in the direction $\boldsymbol{c}$:

$$\boldsymbol{r} = \boldsymbol{a} + t\boldsymbol{c} \tag{4.16}$$

The cartesian or component form of this equation is

$$\frac{x - a_1}{c_1} = \frac{y - a_2}{c_2} = \frac{z - a_3}{c_3} (= t) \tag{4.17}$$

where $\boldsymbol{a} = (a_1, a_2, a_3)$ and $\boldsymbol{c} = (c_1, c_2, c_3)$. Alternatively the cartesian equation of (4.15) may be written in the form

$$\frac{x - a_1}{b_1 - a_1} = \frac{y - a_2}{b_2 - a_2} = \frac{z - a_3}{b_3 - a_3} (= t)$$

where $\boldsymbol{a} = (a_1, a_2, a_3)$ and $\boldsymbol{b} = (b_1, b_2, b_3)$ are two points on the line. If any of the denominators is zero, then both forms of the equation of a line are interpreted as the corresponding numerator is zero.

Example 4.37

Find the equation of the lines L_1 through the points (0, 1, 0) and (1, 3, −1) and L_2 through (1, 1, 1) and (−1, −1, 1). Do the two lines intersect and, if so, at what point?

Solution From (4.15) L_1 has the equation

$$\boldsymbol{r} = (0, 1 - t, 0) + (t, 3t, -t) = (t, 1 + 2t, -t)$$

and L_2 has the equation

$$\boldsymbol{r} = (1 - s, 1 - s, 1 - s) + (-s, -s, s) = (1 - 2s, 1 - 2s, 1)$$

Note that the cartesian equation of L_2 reduces to $x = y$; $z = 1$. The two lines intersect if it is possible to find s and t such that

$$t = 1 - 2s, \quad 1 + 2t = 1 - 2s, \quad -t = 1$$

Solving two of these equations will give the values of s and t. If these values satisfy the remaining equation then the lines intersect; however, if they do not satisfy the remaining equation then the lines do not intersect. In this particular case, the third equation gives $t = -1$ and the first equation $s = 1$. Putting these values into the second equation the left-hand side equals -1 and the right-hand side equals -1, so the equations are all satisfied and therefore the lines intersect. Substituting back into either equation, the point of intersection is $(-1, -1, 1)$.

Example 4.38 The position vectors of the points A and B are

$$(1, 4, 6) \quad \text{and} \quad (3, 5, 7)$$

Find the vector equation of the line AB and find the points where the line intersects the coordinate planes.

Solution The line has equation

$$\boldsymbol{r} = (1, 4, 6) + t(2, 1, 1)$$

or in components

$$x = 1 + 2t$$

$$y = 4 + t$$

$$z = 6 + t$$

Thus the line meets the y–z plane when $x = 0$ and hence $t = -\frac{1}{2}$ and the point of intersection with the plane is $(0, \frac{7}{2}, \frac{11}{2})$.

The line meets the z–x plane when $y = 0$ and hence $t = -4$ and the point of intersection with the plane is $(-7, 0, 2)$.

The line meets the x–y plane when $z = 0$ and hence $t = -6$ and the point of intersection with the plane is $(-11, -2, 0)$.

Example 4.39 The line L_1 passes through the points with position vectors

$$(5, 1, 7) \quad \text{and} \quad (6, 0, 8)$$

and the line L_2 passes through the points with position vectors

$$(3, 1, 3) \quad \text{and} \quad (-1, 3, \alpha)$$

Find the value of α for which the two lines L_1 and L_2 intersect.

Solution Using the vector form:

From (4.15) the equations of the two lines can be written in vector form as

$$L_1: \quad \mathbf{r} = (5, 1, 7) + t(1, -1, 1)$$

$$L_2: \quad \mathbf{r} = (3, 1, 3) + s(-4, 2, \alpha - 3)$$

These two lines intersect if t, s and α can be chosen so that the two vectors are equal, that is, they have the same components. Thus

$$5 + t = 3 - 4s$$

$$1 - t = 1 + 2s$$

$$7 + t = 3 + s(\alpha - 3)$$

The first two of these equations are simultaneous equations for t and s. Solving gives $t = 2$ and $s = -1$. Putting these values into the third equation

$$9 = 3 - (\alpha - 3) \Rightarrow \alpha = -3$$

and it can be checked that the point of intersection is $(7, -1, 9)$.

Using the cartesian form:

Equation (4.17) gives the equations of the lines as

$$L_1: \quad \frac{x-5}{6-5} = \frac{y-1}{0-1} = \frac{z-7}{8-7}$$

$$L_2: \quad \frac{x-3}{-1-3} = \frac{y-1}{3-1} = \frac{z-3}{\alpha-3}$$

The two equations for x and y are

$$x - 5 = 1 - y$$

$$\tfrac{1}{4}(3 - x) = \tfrac{1}{2}(y - 1)$$

and are solved to give $x = 7$ and $y = -1$. Putting in these values, the equations for z and α become

$$z - 7 = 2$$

$$\frac{z-3}{\alpha-3} = -1$$

which give $z = 9$ and $\alpha = -3$.

Example 4.40 A tracking station observes an aeroplane at two successive times to be

$$(-500, 0, 1000) \quad \text{and} \quad (400, 400, 1050)$$

relative to axes x in an easterly direction, y in a northerly direction and z vertically upwards, with distances in metres. Find the equation of the path of the aeroplane. Control advises the aeroplane to change course from its present position to level flight at the current height and turn east through an angle of 90°; what is the equation of the new path?

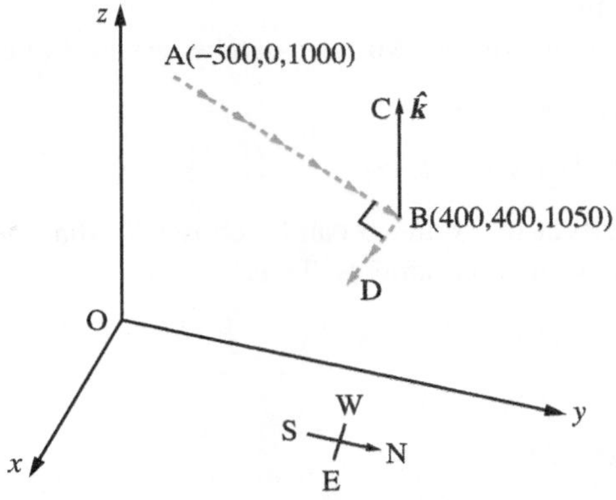

Figure 4.48
Path of aeroplane in Example 4.40.

Solution The situation is illustrated in Figure 4.48. The equation of the path of the aeroplane is

$$\boldsymbol{r} = (-500, 0, 1000) + t(900, 400, 50)$$

The new path starts at the point (400, 400, 1050). The vector $\overrightarrow{AB} \times \hat{\boldsymbol{k}}$ is a vector in the direction $\overrightarrow{BD}$ which is perpendicular to $\hat{\boldsymbol{k}}$, and is therefore horizontal, and at 90° to AB in the easterly direction. Thus we have a 90° turn to horizontal flight. Since

$$(900, 400, 0) \times \boldsymbol{k} = (400, -900, 0)$$

the new path is

$$\boldsymbol{r} = (400, 400, 1050) + s(400, -900, 0)$$

Equating the components

$$x = 400 + 400s$$

$$y = 400 - 900s$$

$$z = 1050$$

In cartesian coordinates the equations are

$$9x + 4y = 5200$$

$$z = 1050$$

Example 4.41 It is necessary to drill to an underground pipeline in order to undertake repairs, so it is decided to aim for the nearest point from the measuring point. Relative to axes x, y in the horizontal ground and with z vertically downwards, remote measuring instruments locate two points on the pipeline at

$$(20, 20, 30) \quad \text{and} \quad (0, 15, 32)$$

with distances in metres. Find the nearest point on the pipeline from the origin O.

Solution The situation is illustrated in Figure 4.49. The direction of the pipeline is

$$\boldsymbol{d} = (0, 15, 32) - (20, 20, 30) = (-20, -5, 2).$$

Thus any point on the pipeline will have position vector

$$\boldsymbol{r} = (20, 20, 30) + t(-20, -5, 2)$$

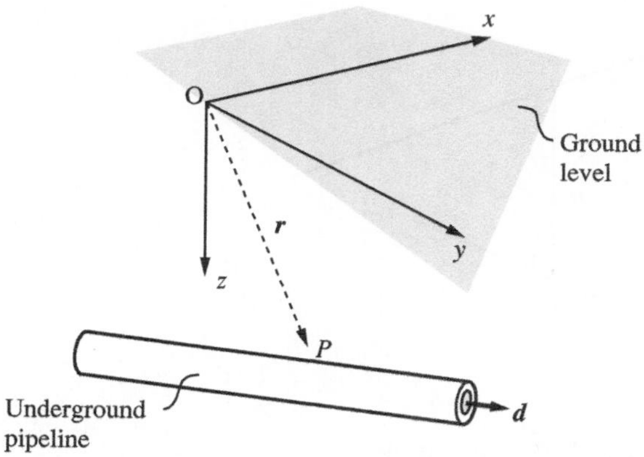

Figure 4.49 Pipeline of Example 4.41

for some t. Note that this is just the equation of the line given in (4.15). At the shortest distance from O to the pipeline the vector $\boldsymbol{r} = \overrightarrow{OP}$ is perpendicular to $\boldsymbol{d}$, so $\boldsymbol{r} \cdot \boldsymbol{d} = 0$ gives the required condition to evaluate t. Thus

$$(-20, -5, 2) \cdot [(20, 20, 30) + t(-20, -5, 2)] = 0$$

and hence $-440 + 429t = 0$. Putting this value back into $\boldsymbol{r}$ gives

$$\boldsymbol{r} = (-0.51, 14.87, 32.05)$$

Note that the value of t is close to 1, so the optimum point is not far from the second of the points located.

Example 4.42

Find the shortest distance between the two skew lines

$$\frac{x}{3} = \frac{y-9}{-1} = \frac{z-2}{1} \quad \text{and} \quad \frac{x+6}{-3} = \frac{y+5}{2} = \frac{z-10}{4}$$

Also determine the equation of the common perpendicular. (Note that two lines are said to be skew if they do not intersect and are not parallel.)

Solution In vector form the equations of the lines are

$$\boldsymbol{r} = (0, 9, 2) + t(3, -1, 1)$$

and

$$\boldsymbol{r} = (-6, -5, 10) + s(-3, 2, 4)$$

The shortest distance between the two lines will be their common perpendicular; see Figure 4.50. Let P_1 and P_2 be the end points of the common perpendicular, having position vectors $\boldsymbol{r}_1$ and $\boldsymbol{r}_2$ respectively, where

$$\boldsymbol{r}_1 = (0, 9, 2) + t_1(3, -1, 1)$$

and

$$\boldsymbol{r}_2 = (-6, -5, 10) + t_2(-3, 2, 4)$$

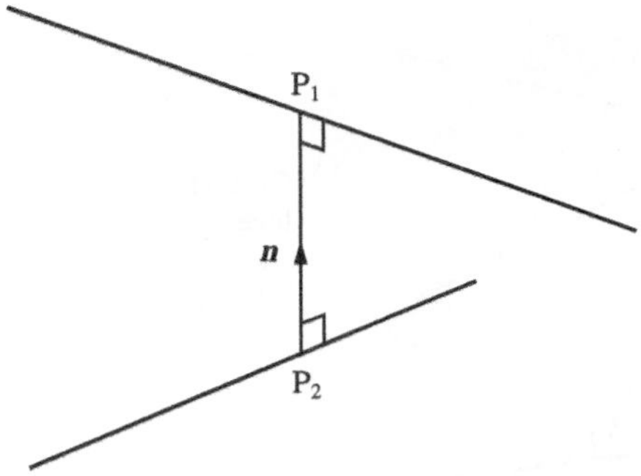

Figure 4.50
Skew lines in Example 4.42.

Then the vector $\overrightarrow{P_2P_1}$ is given by

$$\overrightarrow{P_2P_1} = \boldsymbol{r}_1 - \boldsymbol{r}_2 = (6, 14, -8) + t_1(3, -1, 1) - t_2(-3, 2, 4) \qquad \textbf{(4.18)}$$

Since (3, −1, 1) and (−3, 2, 4) are vectors in the direction of each of the lines, it follows that a vector $\boldsymbol{n}$ perpendicular to both lines is

$$\boldsymbol{n} = (-3, 2, 4) \times (3, -1, 1) = (6, 15, -3)$$

So a unit vector perpendicular to both lines is

$$\hat{\boldsymbol{n}} = (6, 15, -3)/\sqrt{270} = (2, 5, -1)/\sqrt{30}$$

Thus we can also express $\overrightarrow{P_2P_1}$ as

$$\overrightarrow{P_2P_1} = d\hat{\boldsymbol{n}}$$

where d is the shortest distance between the two lines.

Equating the two expressions for $\overrightarrow{P_2P_1}$ gives

$$(6, 14, -8) + t_1(3, -1, 1) - t_2(-3, 2, 4) = (2, 5, -1)d/\sqrt{30}$$

Taking the scalar product throughout with the vector (2, 5, −1) gives

$$(6, 14, -8)\cdot(2, 5, -1) + t_1(3, -1, 1)\cdot(2, 5, -1) - t_2(-3, 2, 4)\cdot(2, 5, -1)$$
$$= (2, 5, -1)\cdot(2, 5, -1)d/\sqrt{30}$$

which reduces to

$$90 + 0t_1 + 0t_2 = 30d/\sqrt{30}$$

giving the shortest distance between the two lines as

$$d = 3\sqrt{30}$$

To obtain the equation of the common perpendicular, we need to find the coordinates of either P_1 or P_2 – and to achieve this we need to find the value of either t_1 or t_2. We therefore take the scalar product of (4.18) with (3, −1, 1) and (−3, 2, 4) in turn, giving respectively

$$11t_1 + 7t_2 = 4$$

and

$$-7t_1 - 29t_2 = 22$$

which on solving simultaneously give $t_1 = 1$ and $t_2 = -1$. Hence the coordinates of the end points P_1 and P_2 of the common perpendicular are

$$r_1 = (0, 9, 2) + 1(3, -1, 1) = (3, 8, 3)$$

and

$$r_2 = (-6, -5, 10) - 1(-3, 2, 4) = (-3, -7, 6)$$

From (4.16) the equation of the common perpendicular is

$$r = (3, 8, 3) + s(2, 5, -1)$$

or in cartesian form

$$\frac{x-3}{2} = \frac{y-8}{5} = \frac{z-3}{-1} = s$$

MAPLE contains a geometry package which takes a bit of time to master but which can solve many coordinate geometry problems. For the current problem the code is given: note that printing has been largely suppressed, but replace ':' by ';' at the end of statements for more information.

```
with (geom3d):
point (A, [0, 9, 2]): v:= [3, -1, 1]: line
(L1, [A, v]): detail (L1);
point (B, [-6, -5, 10]): w:= [-3, 2, 4]: line
(L2, [B, w]): detail (L2);
distance (L1, L2);                    (gives result 3√30 in the text)
z:= Equation (L1, t): y:= Equation (L2, s):
with (linalg):
m:= innerprod (z - y, v): n:= innerprod (z - y, w):
solve ({m, n}, {s, t});               (gives solution t = 1 and s = -1)
point (P, eval (z, t = 1)): point (Q, eval (y, s = -1)):
line (L3, [P, Q]): detail (L3);       (gives the required equation of
                                       the common perpendicular)
```

Note that the package may give parameters different from the hand computation calculation, but they still represent the same line – for instance in the final result of Example 4.42, s was replaced by $-3t$ in the version of MAPLE used.

Example 4.43 A box with an open top and unit side length is observed from the direction (a, b, c), as in Figure 4.51. Determine the part of OC that is visible.

Solution The line or ray through Q$(0, 0, \alpha)$ parallel to the line of sight has the equation

$$r = (0, 0, \alpha) + t(a, b, c)$$

where $0 \leqslant \alpha \leqslant 1$ to ensure that Q lies between O and C. The line RS passes through R(1, 0, 1) and is in the direction (0, 1, 0), so from (4.16) it has the equation

$$r = (1, 0, 1) + s(0, 1, 0)$$

The ray that intersects RS must therefore satisfy

$$ta = 1, \quad tb = s, \quad \alpha = 1 - \frac{c}{a}$$

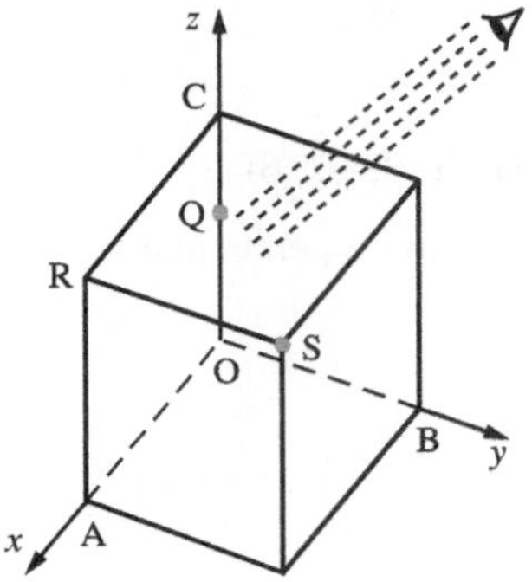

Figure 4.51
Looking for hidden lines in Example 4.43.

Note that if $c = 0$ then we are looking parallel to the open top and can only see the point C. If $c < 0$ then we are looking up at the box; since $\alpha > 1$, we cannot see any of side OC, so the line is hidden. If, however, $c > a$ then the solution gives α to be negative, so that all of the side OC is visible. For $0 < c < a$ the parameter α lies between 0 and 1, and only part of the line is visible. A similar analysis needs to be performed for the other sides of the open top. Other edges of the box also need to be analysed to check whether or not they are visible to the ray.

4.3.2 Exercises

66 If A and B have position vectors (1, 2, 3) and (4, 5, 6) respectively, find

(a) the direction vector of the line through A and B;

(b) the vector equation of the line through A and B;

(c) the cartesian equation of the line.

67 Find the vector equation of the line through the point A with position vector $\overrightarrow{OA} = (2, 1, 1)$ in the direction $\boldsymbol{d} = (1, 0, 1)$. Does this line pass through any of the points (1, 1, 0), (1, 1, 1), (3, 1, 3), $(\frac{1}{2}, 1, -\frac{1}{2})$? Find the vector equation of the line through the point A and perpendicular to the plane of $\overrightarrow{OA}$ and $\boldsymbol{d}$.

68 Show that the line joining (2, 3, 4) to (1, 2, 3) is perpendicular to the line joining (1, 0, 2) to (2, 3, −2).

69 Prove that the lines $\boldsymbol{r} = (1, 2, -1) + t(2, 2, 1)$ and $\boldsymbol{r} = (-1, -2, 3) + s(4, 6, -3)$ intersect, and find the coordinates of their point of intersection. Also find the acute angle between the lines.

70 P is a point on a straight line with position vector $\boldsymbol{r} = \boldsymbol{a} + t\boldsymbol{b}$. Show that

$$r^2 = a^2 + 2\boldsymbol{a}\cdot\boldsymbol{b}t + b^2t^2$$

By completing the square, show that r^2 is a minimum for the point P for which $t = -\boldsymbol{a}\cdot\boldsymbol{b}/b^2$. Show that at this point $\overrightarrow{OP}$ is perpendicular to the line $\boldsymbol{r} = \boldsymbol{a} + t\boldsymbol{b}$. (This proves the well-known result that the shortest distance from a point to a line is the length of the perpendicular from that point to the line.)

71 Find the vector equation of the line through the points with position vectors $\boldsymbol{a} = (2, 0, -1)$ and $\boldsymbol{b} = (1, 2, 3)$. Write down the equivalent cartesian coordinate form. Does this line intersect the line through the points $\boldsymbol{c} = (0, 0, 1)$ and $\boldsymbol{d} = (1, 0, 1)$?

72 Find the shortest distance between the two lines

$$\boldsymbol{r} = (4, -2, 3) + t(2, 1, -1)$$

and

$$\boldsymbol{r} = (-7, -2, 1) + s(3, 2, 1)$$

4.3.3 Vector equation of a plane

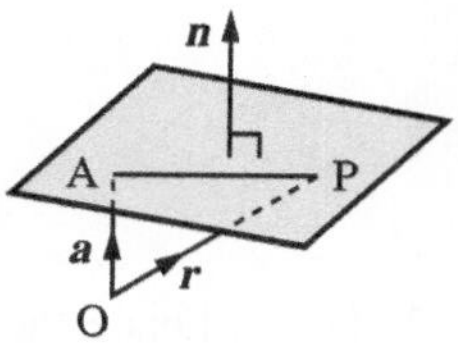

Figure 4.52
Equation of a plane; $\boldsymbol{n}$ is perpendicular to the plane.

To obtain the equation of a plane, we use the result that the line joining any two points in the plane is perpendicular to the normal to the plane, as illustrated in Figure 4.52. The vector $\boldsymbol{n}$ is perpendicular to the plane, $\boldsymbol{a}$ is the position vector of a given point A in the plane and $\boldsymbol{r}$ is the position vector of any point P on the plane. The vector $\overrightarrow{AP} = \boldsymbol{r} - \boldsymbol{a}$ is perpendicular to $\boldsymbol{n}$, and hence

$$(\boldsymbol{r} - \boldsymbol{a}) \cdot \boldsymbol{n} = 0$$

so that

$$\boldsymbol{r} \cdot \boldsymbol{n} = \boldsymbol{a} \cdot \boldsymbol{n} \quad \text{or} \quad \boldsymbol{r} \cdot \boldsymbol{n} = p \tag{4.19}$$

is the general form for the **equation of a plane** with normal $\boldsymbol{n}$. In the particular case when $\boldsymbol{n}$ is a unit vector, p in (4.19) represents the perpendicular distance from the origin to the plane. In cartesian form we take $\boldsymbol{n} = (\alpha, \beta, \gamma)$, and the equation becomes

$$\alpha x + \beta y + \gamma z = p \tag{4.20}$$

which is just a linear relation between the variables x, y and z.

Example 4.44 Find the equation of the plane through the three points

$$\boldsymbol{a} = (1, 1, 1), \quad \boldsymbol{b} = (0, 1, 2) \quad \text{and} \quad \boldsymbol{c} = (-1, 1, -1)$$

Solution The vectors $\boldsymbol{a} - \boldsymbol{b} = (1, 0, -1)$ and $\boldsymbol{a} - \boldsymbol{c} = (2, 0, 2)$ will lie in the plane. The normal $\boldsymbol{n}$ to the plane can thus be constructed as $(\boldsymbol{a} - \boldsymbol{b}) \times (\boldsymbol{a} - \boldsymbol{c})$, giving

$$\boldsymbol{n} = (1, 0, -1) \times (2, 0, 2) = (0, -4, 0)$$

Thus from (4.19) the equation of the plane is given by

$$\boldsymbol{r} \cdot \boldsymbol{n} = \boldsymbol{a} \cdot \boldsymbol{n}$$

or

$$\boldsymbol{r} \cdot (0, -4, 0) = (1, 1, 1) \cdot (0, -4, 0)$$

giving

$$\boldsymbol{r} \cdot (0, -4, 0) = -4$$

In cartesian form

$$(x, y, z) \cdot (0, -4, 0) = -4$$

or simply $y = 1$.

Example 4.45 A metal has a simple cubic lattice structure so that the atoms lie on the lattice points given by

$$\boldsymbol{r} = a(l, m, n)$$

where a is the lattice spacing and l, m, n are integers. The metallurgist needs to identify the points that lie on two lattice planes

$$LP_1 \text{ through } a(0, 0, 0), \quad a(1, 1, 0) \quad \text{and} \quad a(0, 1, 2)$$
$$LP_2 \text{ through } a(0, 0, 2), \quad a(1, 1, 0) \quad \text{and} \quad a(0, 1, 0)$$

Solution The direction perpendicular to LP_1 is $(1, 1, 0) \times (0, 1, 2) = (2, -2, 1)$ and hence the equation of LP_1 is

$$\boldsymbol{r}\cdot(2, -2, 1) = 0 \quad \text{or in cartesian form} \quad 2x - 2y + z = 0 \tag{4.21}$$

The direction perpendicular to LP_2 is $(1, 1, -2) \times (0, 1, -2) = (0, 2, 1)$ and hence the equation of LP_2 is

$$\boldsymbol{r}\cdot(0, 2, 1) = 2 \quad \text{or in cartesian form} \quad 2y + z = 2 \tag{4.22}$$

Points that lie on both lattice planes must satisfy both (4.21) and (4.22). It is easiest to solve these equations in their cartesian form. The coordinates must be integers, so take $y = m$, then z can easily be calculated from (4.22) as

$$z = 2 - 2m$$

and then x is computed from (4.21) to be $x = 2m - 1$.

Hence the required points all lie on a line and take the form

$$\boldsymbol{r} = a(2m - 1, m, 2 - 2m)$$

where m is an integer.

Example 4.46 Find the point where the plane

$$\boldsymbol{r}\cdot(1, 1, 2) = 3$$

meets the line

$$\boldsymbol{r} = (2, 1, 1) + \lambda(0, 1, 2)$$

Solution At the point of intersection, $\boldsymbol{r}$ must satisfy both equations, so

$$[(2, 1, 1) + \lambda(0, 1, 2)]\cdot(1, 1, 2) = 3$$

or

$$5 + 5\lambda = 3$$

so

$$\lambda = -\tfrac{2}{5}$$

Substituting back into the equation of the line gives the point of intersection as

$$\boldsymbol{r} = (2, \tfrac{3}{5}, \tfrac{1}{5})$$

Example 4.47 Find the equation of the line of intersection of the two planes $x + y + z = 5$ and $4x + y + 2z = 15$.

Solution In vector form the equations of the two planes are

$$\boldsymbol{r}\cdot(1, 1, 1) = 5$$

and

$$\boldsymbol{r}\cdot(4, 1, 2) = 15$$

The required line lies in both planes, and is therefore perpendicular to the vectors (1, 1, 1) and (4, 1, 2), which are normal to the individual planes. Hence a vector $\boldsymbol{c}$ in the direction of the line is

$$\boldsymbol{c} = (1, 1, 1) \times (4, 1, 2) = (1, 2, -3)$$

To find the equation of the line, it remains only to find the coordinates of any point on the line. To do this, we are required to find the coordinates of a point satisfying the equation of the two planes. Taking $x = 0$, the corresponding values of y and z are given by

$$y + z = 5 \quad \text{and} \quad y + 2z = 15$$

that is, $y = -5$ and $z = 10$. Hence it can be checked that the point (0, −5, 10) lies in both planes and is therefore a point on the line. From (4.16) the equation of the line is

$$\boldsymbol{r} = (0, -5, 10) + t(1, 2, -3)$$

or in cartesian form

$$\frac{x}{1} = \frac{y+5}{2} = \frac{z-10}{-3} = t$$

The MAPLE instructions to solve this example are

```
with (geom3d):
plane (P1, x + y + z = 5, [x, y, z]): plane (P2, 4*x
+ y + 2*z = 15, [x, y, z]): intersection (L, P1, P2):
detail (L);
```

Example 4.48 Find the perpendicular distance from the point P(2, −3, 4) to the plane $x + 2y + 2z = 13$.

Solution In vector form the equation of the plane is

$$\boldsymbol{r}\cdot(1, 2, 2) = 13$$

and a vector perpendicular to the plane is

$$\boldsymbol{n} = (1, 2, 2)$$

Thus from (4.16) the equation of a line perpendicular to the plane and passing through P(2, −3, 4) is

$$\boldsymbol{r} = (2, -3, 4) + t(1, 2, 2)$$

This will meet the plane when

$$\boldsymbol{r}\cdot(1, 2, 2) = (2, -3, 4)\cdot(1, 2, 2) + t(1, 2, 2)\cdot(1, 2, 2) = 13$$

giving

$$4 + 9t = 13$$

so that

$$t = 1$$

Thus the line meets the plane at N having position vector

$$\boldsymbol{r} = (2, -3, 4) + 1(1, 2, 2) = (3, -1, 6)$$

Hence the perpendicular distance is

$$\text{PN} = \sqrt{[(3-2)^2 + (-1+3)^2 + (6-4)^2]} = 3$$

4.3.4 Exercises

Many of the exercises can be checked using the geom3d package in MAPLE.

73 Find the vector equation of the plane that passes through the points (1, 2, 3), (2, 4, 5) and (4, 5, 6). What is its cartesian equation?

74 Find the equation of the plane with perpendicular $\boldsymbol{n} = (1, -1, 1)$ that passes through the point with position vector (2, 3, 3). Show that the line with equation $\boldsymbol{r} = (-1, -1, 2) + \boldsymbol{t}(2, 0, -2)$ lies in this plane.

75 Find the vector equation of the plane that contains the line $\boldsymbol{r} = \boldsymbol{a} + \lambda \boldsymbol{b}$ and passes through the point with position vector $\boldsymbol{c}$.

76 The line of intersection of two planes $\boldsymbol{r}\cdot\boldsymbol{n}_1 = p_1$ and $\boldsymbol{r}\cdot\boldsymbol{n}_2 = p_2$ lies in both planes. It is therefore perpendicular to both $\boldsymbol{n}_1$ and $\boldsymbol{n}_2$. Give an expression for this direction, and so show that the equation of the line of intersection may be written as $\boldsymbol{r} = \boldsymbol{r}_0 + t(\boldsymbol{n}_1 \times \boldsymbol{n}_2)$, where $\boldsymbol{r}_0$ is any vector satisfying $\boldsymbol{r}_0\cdot\boldsymbol{n}_1 = p_1$ and $\boldsymbol{r}_0\cdot\boldsymbol{n}_2 = p_2$. Hence find the line of intersection of the planes $\boldsymbol{r}\cdot(1, 1, 1) = 5$ and $\boldsymbol{r}\cdot(4, 1, 2) = 15$.

77 Find the equation of the line through the point (1, 2, 4) and in the direction of the vector (1, 1, 2). Find where this line meets the plane $x + 3y - 4z = 5$.

78 Find the acute angle between the planes $2x + y - 2z = 5$ and $3x - 6y - 2z = 7$.

79 Given that $\boldsymbol{a} = (3, 1, 2)$ and $\boldsymbol{b} = (1, -2, -4)$ are the position vectors of the points P and Q respectively, find

(a) the equation of the plane passing through Q and perpendicular to PQ;

(b) the distance from the point (−1, 1, 1) to the plane obtained in (a).

80 Find the equation of the line joining (1, −1, 3) to (3, 3, −1). Show that it is perpendicular to the plane $2x + 4y - 4z = 5$, and find the angle that the line makes with the plane $12x - 15y + 16z = 10$.

81 Find the equation of the plane through the line

$$\boldsymbol{r} = (1, -3, 4) + t(2, 1, 1)$$

and parallel to the line

$$\boldsymbol{r} = s(1, 2, 3)$$

82 Find the equation of the line through $P(-1, 0, 1)$ that cuts the line $\boldsymbol{r} = (3, 2, 1) + t(1, 2, 2)$ at right-angles at Q. Also find the length PQ and the equation of the plane containing the two lines.

83 Show that the equation of the plane through the points P_1, P_2 and P_3 with position vectors $\boldsymbol{r}_1$, $\boldsymbol{r}_2$ and $\boldsymbol{r}_3$ respectively takes the form

$$\boldsymbol{r}\cdot[(\boldsymbol{r}_1\times\boldsymbol{r}_2) + (\boldsymbol{r}_2\times\boldsymbol{r}_3) + (\boldsymbol{r}_3\times\boldsymbol{r}_1)] = \boldsymbol{r}_1\cdot(\boldsymbol{r}_2\times\boldsymbol{r}_3)$$

4.4 Engineering application: spin-dryer suspension

Vectors are at their most powerful when dealing with complicated three-dimensional situations. Geometrical and physical intuition are often difficult to use, and it becomes necessary to work quite formally to analyse such situations. For example, the front suspension of a motor car has two struts supported by a spring-and-damper system and subject to a variety of forces and torques from both the car and the wheels. To analyse the stresses and the vibrations in the various components of the structure is non-trivial, even in a two-dimensional version; the true three-dimensional problem provides a testing exercise for even the most experienced automobile engineer. In the present text a much simpler situation is analysed to illustrate the use of vectors.

4.4.1 Point-particle model

As with the car suspension, many machines are mounted on springs to isolate vibrations. A typical example is a spin-dryer, which consists of a drum connected to the casing by heavy springs. Oscillations can be very severe when spinning at high speed, and it is essential to know what forces are transmitted to the casing and hence to the mounts. Before the dynamical situation can be analysed, it is necessary to compute the restoring forces on the drum when it is displaced from its equilibrium position. This is a static problem that is best studied using vectors.

We model the spin-dryer as a heavy point particle connected to the eight corners of the casing by springs (Figure 4.53). The drum has weight W and the casing is taken to be a cube of side $2L$. The springs are all equal, having spring constant k and natural

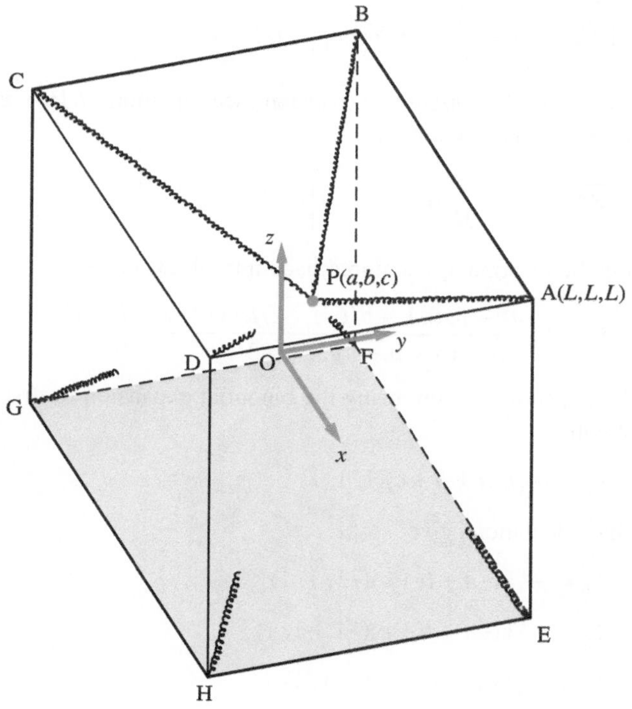

Figure 4.53 The particle P is attached by equal springs to the eight corners of the cube.

length $L\sqrt{3}$. Thus when the drum is at the midpoint of the cube the springs are neither compressed nor extended.

The particle is displaced from its central position by a small amount (a, b, c), where the natural coordinates illustrated in Figure 4.53 are used; the origin is at the centre of the cube and the axes are parallel to the sides. What is required is the total force acting on the particle arising from the weight and the springs. Clearly, this information is needed before any dynamical calculations can be performed. It will be assumed that the displacements are sufficiently small that squares $(a/L)^2$, $(b/L)^2$, $(c/L)^2$ and higher powers are neglected.

Consider a typical spring PA. The tension in the spring is assumed to obey Hooke's law: that the force is along PA and has magnitude proportional to extension. $\overrightarrow{PA}/|\overrightarrow{PA}|$ is the unit vector in the direction along PA, and $|\overrightarrow{PA}| - L\sqrt{3}$ is the extension of the spring over its natural length $L\sqrt{3}$, so in vector form the tension can be written as

$$\boldsymbol{T}_A = k\frac{\overrightarrow{PA}}{|\overrightarrow{PA}|}(|\overrightarrow{PA}| - L\sqrt{3}) \tag{4.23}$$

where k is the proportionality constant.

Now

$$\overrightarrow{PA} = \overrightarrow{OA} - \overrightarrow{OP} = (L - a, L - b, L - c)$$

so calculating the modulus squared gives

$$\begin{aligned}|\overrightarrow{PA}|^2 &= (L - a)^2 + (L - b)^2 + (L - c)^2\\ &= 3L^2 - 2L(a + b + c) + \text{quadratic terms}\end{aligned}$$

Thus

$$|\overrightarrow{PA}| = \left[1 - \frac{2}{3L}(a + b + c)\right]^{1/2} L\sqrt{3}$$

and, on using the binomial expansion (see equation (7.16)) and neglecting quadratic and higher terms, we obtain

$$|\overrightarrow{PA}| = \left[1 - \frac{1}{3L}(a + b + c)\right]L\sqrt{3}$$

Putting the information acquired back into (4.23) gives

$$\boldsymbol{T}_A = kL\frac{(1 - a/L, 1 - b/L, 1 - c/L)}{[1 - (a + b + c)/3L]L\sqrt{3}}\,\frac{(-1)(a + b + c)L\sqrt{3}}{3L}$$

and by expanding again, using the binomial expansion to first order in a/L and so on, we obtain

$$\boldsymbol{T}_A = -\tfrac{1}{3}k(a + b + c)(1, 1, 1)$$

Similar calculations give

$$\boldsymbol{T}_B = -\tfrac{1}{3}k(-a + b + c)(-1, 1, 1)$$

$$\boldsymbol{T}_C = -\tfrac{1}{3}k(-a - b + c)(-1, -1, 1)$$

$$\boldsymbol{T}_D = -\tfrac{1}{3}k(a - b + c)(1, -1, 1)$$

$$\boldsymbol{T}_E = -\tfrac{1}{3}k(a + b - c)(1, 1, -1)$$

$$\boldsymbol{T}_F = -\tfrac{1}{3}k(-a + b - c)(-1, 1, -1)$$

$$\boldsymbol{T}_G = -\tfrac{1}{3}k(-a - b - c)(-1, -1, -1)$$

$$\boldsymbol{T}_H = -\tfrac{1}{3}k(a - b - c)(1, -1, -1)$$

The total spring force is therefore obtained by adding these eight tensions together:

$$\boldsymbol{T} = -\tfrac{8}{3}k(a, b, c)$$

The restoring force is therefore towards the centre of the cube, as expected, in the direction PO and with magnitude $\frac{8}{3}k$ times the length of PO.

When the weight is included, the total force is

$$\boldsymbol{F} = (-\tfrac{8}{3}ka, -\tfrac{8}{3}kb, -\tfrac{8}{3}kc - W)$$

If the drum just hangs in equilibrium then $\boldsymbol{F} = 0$, and hence

$$a = b = 0 \quad \text{and} \quad c = -\frac{3W}{8k}$$

Typical values are $W = 400\,\text{N}$ and $k = 10\,000\,\text{N m}^{-1}$, and hence

$$c = -3 \times 400/8 \times 10\,000 = -0.015\,\text{m}$$

so that the centre of the drum hangs 1.5 cm below the midpoint of the centre of the casing.

It is clear that the model used in this section is an idealized one, but it is helpful in describing how to calculate spring forces in complicated three-dimensional static situations. It also gives an idea of the size of the forces involved and the deflections. The next major step is to put these forces into the equations of motion of the drum; this, however, requires a good knowledge of calculus – and, in particular, of differential equations – so it is not appropriate at this point. You may wish to consider this problem after studying the relevant chapters later in this book. A more advanced model must include the fact that the drum is of finite size.

4.5 Engineering application: cable-stayed bridge

One of the standard methods of supporting bridges is with cables. Readers will no doubt be familiar with suspension bridges such as the Golden Gate in the USA, the Humber bridge in the UK and the Tsing Ma bridge in Hong Kong with their spectacular form. Cable-stayed bridges are similar in that they have towers and cables that support a roadway but they are not usually on such a grand scale as suspension bridges. They are often used when the foundations can only support a single tower at one end of the roadway. They are commonly seen on bridges over motorways and footbridges over steep narrow valleys.

In any of the situations described it is essential that information is available on the tension in the wire supports and the forces on the towers. The geometry is fully three-dimensional and quite complicated. Vectors provide a logical and efficient way of dealing with the situation.

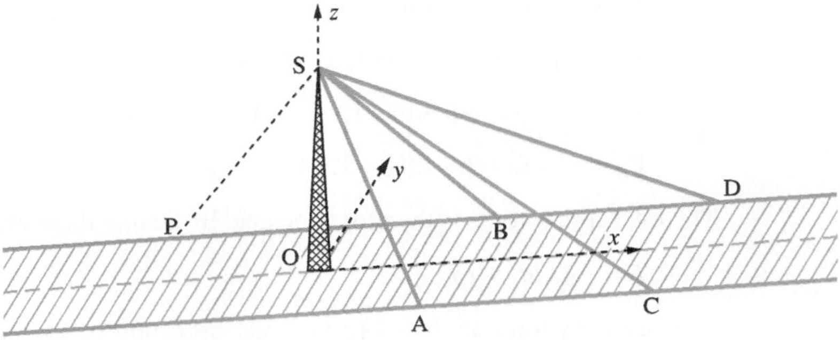

Figure 4.54
Model of a stayed bridge.

4.5.1 A simple stayed bridge

There are many configurations that stayed bridges can take; they can have one or more towers and a variety of arrangements of stays. In Figure 4.54 a simple example of a cable-stayed footbridge is illustrated. It is constructed with a central vertical pillar with four ties attached by wires to the sides of the pathway.

Relative to the axes, with the z axis vertical, the various points are given, in metres, as A(5, −2, 0.5), B(10, 2, 1), C(15, −2, 1.5), D(20, 2, 1) and S(0, 0, 10). Assuming the weight is evenly distributed, there is an equivalent weight of 2 KN at each of the four points A, B, C and D. An estimate is required of the tensions in the wires and the force at the tie point S.

The vectors along the ties can easily be evaluated:

$$\overrightarrow{\mathrm{AS}} = (-5, 2, 9.5), \quad \overrightarrow{\mathrm{BS}} = (-10, -2, 9)$$
$$\overrightarrow{\mathrm{CS}} = (-15, 2, 8.5), \quad \overrightarrow{\mathrm{DS}} = (-20, -2, 9)$$

The tension at S in the tie AS can be written $\boldsymbol{T}_{\mathrm{A}} = t_{\mathrm{A}}\overrightarrow{\mathrm{SA}}$. Assuming the whole system is in equilibrium, the vertical components at A must be equal

$$\boldsymbol{T}_{\mathrm{A}} \cdot \boldsymbol{k} = 2 \quad \text{and hence} \quad t_{\mathrm{A}} = \frac{2}{9.5}$$

and the four tensions can be computed similarly.

$$\boldsymbol{T}_{\mathrm{A}} = \tfrac{2}{9.5}(5, -2, -9.5) = (1.052, -0.421, -2) \quad \text{and} \quad |\boldsymbol{T}_{\mathrm{A}}| = 2.299\ kN$$
$$\boldsymbol{T}_{\mathrm{B}} = \tfrac{2}{9}(10, 2, -9) = (2.222, 0.444, -2) \quad \text{and} \quad |\boldsymbol{T}_{\mathrm{B}}| = 3.022\ kN$$
$$\boldsymbol{T}_{\mathrm{C}} = \tfrac{2}{8.5}(15, -2, -8.5) = (3.529, -0.471, -2) \quad \text{and} \quad |\boldsymbol{T}_{\mathrm{C}}| = 4.084\ kN$$
$$\boldsymbol{T}_{\mathrm{D}} = \tfrac{2}{9}(20, 2, -9) = (4.444, 0.444, -2) \quad \text{and} \quad |\boldsymbol{T}_{\mathrm{D}}| = 4.894\ kN$$

The total force acting at the tie point S is

$$\boldsymbol{T} = \boldsymbol{T}_{\mathrm{A}} + \boldsymbol{T}_{\mathrm{B}} + \boldsymbol{T}_{\mathrm{C}} + \boldsymbol{T}_{\mathrm{D}} = (11.25, -0.004, -8)$$

Thus with straightforward addition of vectors we have been able to compute the tensions and the total force on the tower.

The question now is how to compensate for the total force on the tower and to try to ensure that it is subject to zero force or a force as small as possible. Suppose that it is decided to have just a single compensating tie wire attached to S and to one side on the pathway at P. It is assumed that on this side of the footbridge the pathway is flat and lies in the x–y plane. Where should we position the attachment of the compensating wire so that it produces zero horizontal force at S?

Let the attachment point P on the side of the footbridge be $(-a, 2, 0)$ so that the tension in the compensating cable is

$$\boldsymbol{T}_\text{P} = t_\text{P}\overrightarrow{\text{SP}} = t_\text{P}(-a, 2, -10)$$

We require the y component of $(\boldsymbol{T} + \boldsymbol{T}_\text{P})$ to be zero so that

$$2t_\text{P} - 0.004 = 0 \quad \text{and hence} \quad t_\text{P} = 0.002$$

which in turn gives for the x component

$$at_\text{P} = 11.248 \quad \text{and hence} \quad a = 5624 \text{ metres!}$$

Clearly the answer is ridiculous and either more than one compensating cable must be used or the y component can be neglected completely since the force in this direction is only 4 N.

As a second attempt we specify the attachment wire at P(−5, 2, 0). Requiring the x component of $\boldsymbol{T} + \boldsymbol{T}_\text{P}$ to be zero we see that

$$\boldsymbol{T} + \boldsymbol{T}_\text{P} = \boldsymbol{T} + t_\text{P}\overrightarrow{\text{SP}} = (11.25, -0.004, -8) + t_\text{P}(-5, 2, -10)$$

gives $t_\text{P} = 2.25$. Hence the total force at S is (0, 4.5, −30.5). Although the force in the x direction has been reduced to zero, an unacceptable side force on the tower in the y direction has been introduced.

In a further effort, we introduce two equal compensating wires connected to the points P(−5, −2, 0) and P′(−5, 2, 0). The total force at S is now

$$\begin{aligned}\boldsymbol{T} + \boldsymbol{T}_\text{P} + \boldsymbol{T}_{\text{P}'} &= \boldsymbol{T} + t_\text{P}\overrightarrow{\text{SP}} + t_\text{P}\overrightarrow{\text{SP}'}\\ &= (11.25, -0.004, -8) + t_\text{P}(-5, 2, -10) + t_\text{P}(-5, -2, -10)\end{aligned}$$

Now choosing $t_\text{P} = 1.125$ gives a total force (0, −0.004, −30.5). We now have a satisfactory resolution of the problem with the only significant force being in the downwards direction.

The different forms of stayed-bridge construction will require a similar analysis to obtain an estimate of the forces involved. The example given should be viewed as illustrative.

4.6 Review exercises (1–22)

Check your answers using MATLAB or MAPLE whenever possible.

1 Given that $\boldsymbol{a} = 3\boldsymbol{i} - \boldsymbol{j} - 4\boldsymbol{k}$, $\boldsymbol{b} = -2\boldsymbol{i} + 4\boldsymbol{j} - 3\boldsymbol{k}$ and $\boldsymbol{c} = \boldsymbol{i} + 2\boldsymbol{j} - \boldsymbol{k}$, find

(a) the magnitude of the vector $\boldsymbol{a} + \boldsymbol{b} + \boldsymbol{c}$;

(b) a unit vector parallel to $3\boldsymbol{a} - 2\boldsymbol{b} + 4\boldsymbol{c}$;

(c) the angles between the vectors $\boldsymbol{a}$ and $\boldsymbol{b}$ and between $\boldsymbol{b}$ and $\boldsymbol{c}$;

(d) the position vector of the centre of mass of particles of masses 1, 2 and 3 placed at points A, B and C with position vectors $\boldsymbol{a}$, $\boldsymbol{b}$ and $\boldsymbol{c}$ respectively.

2 If the vertices X, Y and Z of a triangle have position vectors

$$\boldsymbol{x} = (2, 2, 6), \quad \boldsymbol{y} = (4, 6, 4) \quad \text{and} \quad \boldsymbol{z} = (4, 1, 7)$$

relative to the origin O, find

(a) the midpoint of the side XY of the triangle;

(b) the area of the triangle;

(c) the volume of the tetrahedron OXYZ.

3 The vertices of a tetrahedron are the points

$$\text{W}(2, 1, 3), \quad \text{X}(3, 3, 3), \quad \text{Y}(4, 2, 4) \quad \text{and} \quad \text{Z}(3, 3, 5)$$

Determine

(a) the vectors $\overrightarrow{\text{WX}}$ and $\overrightarrow{\text{WY}}$;

(b) the area of the face WXZ;

(c) the volume of the tetrahedron WXZY;

(d) the angles between the faces WXY and WYZ.

4 Given $\boldsymbol{a} = (-1, -3, -1)$, $\boldsymbol{b} = (q, 1, 1)$ and $\boldsymbol{c} = (1, 1, q)$ determine the values of q for which

(a) $\boldsymbol{a}$ is perpendicular to $\boldsymbol{b}$

(b) $\boldsymbol{a} \times (\boldsymbol{b} \times \boldsymbol{c}) = 0$

5 Given the vectors $\boldsymbol{a} = (2, 1, 2)$ and $\boldsymbol{b} = (-3, 0, 4)$, evaluate the unit vectors $\hat{\boldsymbol{a}}$ and $\hat{\boldsymbol{b}}$. Use these unit vectors to find a vector that bisects the angle between $\boldsymbol{a}$ and $\boldsymbol{b}$.

6 A triangle, ABC, is inscribed in a circle, centre O, with AOC as a diameter of the circle. Take $\overrightarrow{OA} = \boldsymbol{a}$ and $OB = \boldsymbol{b}$. By evaluating $\overrightarrow{AB} \cdot \overrightarrow{CB}$ show that angle ABC is a right angle.

7 According to the inverse square law, the force on a particle of mass m_1 at the point P_1 due to a particle of mass m_2 at the point P_2 is given by

$$\gamma \frac{m_1 m_2}{r^2} \hat{\boldsymbol{r}} \quad \text{where } \boldsymbol{r} = \overrightarrow{P_1 P_2}$$

Particles of mass $3m$, $3m$, m are fixed at the points A(1, 0, 1), B(0, 1, 2) and C(2, 1, 2) respectively. Show that the force on the particle at A due to the presence of B and C is

$$\frac{2\gamma m^2}{\sqrt{3}}(-1, 2, 2)$$

8 Show that the vector $\boldsymbol{a}$ which satisfies the vector equation

$$\boldsymbol{a} \times (\boldsymbol{i} + 2\boldsymbol{j}) = -2\boldsymbol{i} + \boldsymbol{j} + \boldsymbol{k}$$

must take the form $\boldsymbol{a} = (\alpha, 2\alpha - 1, 1)$. If in addition the vector $\boldsymbol{a}$ makes an angle $\cos^{-1}(\frac{1}{3})$ with the vector $(\boldsymbol{i} - \boldsymbol{j} + \boldsymbol{k})$ show that there are now two such vectors that satisfy both conditions.

9 The electric field at a point having position vector $\boldsymbol{r}$, due to a charge e at $\boldsymbol{R}$, is $e(\boldsymbol{r} - \boldsymbol{R})/|\boldsymbol{r} - \boldsymbol{R}|^3$. Find the electric field $\boldsymbol{E}$ at the point P(2, 1, 1) given that there is a charge e at each of the points (1, 0, 0), (0, 1, 0) and (0, 0, 1).

10 Given that $\overrightarrow{OP} = (3, 1, 2)$ and $\overrightarrow{OQ} = (1, -2, -4)$ are the position vectors of the points P and Q respectively, find

(a) the equation of the plane passing through Q and perpendicular to PQ;

(b) the perpendicular distance from the point (−1, 1, 1) to the plane.

11 (a) Determine the equation of the plane that passes through the points (1, 2, −2), (−1, 1, −9) and (2, −2, −12). Find the perpendicular distance from the origin to this plane.

(b) Calculate the area of the triangle whose vertices are at the points (1, 1, 0), (1, 0, 1) and (0, 1, 1).

12 Find the point P on the line L through the points

A(5, 1, 7) and B(6, 0, 8)

and the point Q on the line M through the points

C(3, 1, 3) and D(−1, 3, 3)

such that the line through P and Q is perpendicular to both lines L and M. Verify that P and Q are at a distance $\sqrt{6}$ apart, and find the point where the line through P and Q intersects the coordinate plane Oxy.

13 The angular momentum vector $\boldsymbol{H}$ of a particle of mass m is defined by

$$\boldsymbol{H} = \boldsymbol{r} \times (m\boldsymbol{v})$$

where $\boldsymbol{v} = \boldsymbol{\omega} \times \boldsymbol{r}$.

Using the result

$$\boldsymbol{a} \times (\boldsymbol{b} \times \boldsymbol{c}) = (\boldsymbol{a} \cdot \boldsymbol{c})\boldsymbol{b} - (\boldsymbol{a} \cdot \boldsymbol{b})\boldsymbol{c}$$

show that if $\boldsymbol{r}$ is perpendicular to $\boldsymbol{\omega}$ then $\boldsymbol{H} = mr^2\boldsymbol{\omega}$.

Given that $m = 100$, $\boldsymbol{r} = 0.1(\boldsymbol{i} + \boldsymbol{j} + \boldsymbol{k})$ and $\boldsymbol{\omega} = 5\boldsymbol{i} + 5\boldsymbol{j} - 10\boldsymbol{k}$ calculate

(a) $(\boldsymbol{r} \cdot \boldsymbol{\omega})$ (b) $\boldsymbol{H}$

14 A particle of mass m, charge e and moving with velocity $\boldsymbol{v}$ in a magnetic field of strength $\boldsymbol{H}$ is known to have acceleration

$$\frac{e}{mc}(\boldsymbol{v} \times \boldsymbol{H})$$

where c is the speed of light. Show that the component of acceleration parallel to $\boldsymbol{H}$ is zero.

15 A force $\boldsymbol{F}$ is of magnitude 14 N and acts at the point A(3, 2, 4) in the direction of the vector $-2\boldsymbol{i} + 6\boldsymbol{j} + 3\boldsymbol{k}$. Find the moment of the force about the point B(1, 5, −2). Find also the angle between $\boldsymbol{F}$ and $\overrightarrow{AB}$.

16 Points A, B, C have coordinates (1, 2, 1), (−1, 1, 3) and (−2, −2, −2) respectively.

Calculate the vector product $\overrightarrow{AB} \times \overrightarrow{AC}$, the angle BAC and a unit vector perpendicular to the plane containing A, B and C. Hence obtain

(a) the equation of the plane ABC;

(b) the equation of a second plane, parallel to ABC, and containing the point D(1, 1, 1);

(c) the shortest distance between the point D and the plane containing A, B and C.

17 A plane Π passes through the three non-collinear points A, B and C having position vectors $\mathbf{a}$, $\mathbf{b}$ and $\mathbf{c}$ respectively. Show that the parametric vector equation of the plane Π is

$$\mathbf{r} = \mathbf{a} + \lambda(\mathbf{b} - \mathbf{a}) + \mu(\mathbf{c} - \mathbf{a})$$

The plane Π passes through the points (−3, 0, 1), (5, −8, −7) and (2, 1, −2) and the plane Θ passes through the points (3, −1, 1), (1, −2, 1) and (2, −1, 2). Find the parametric vector equation of Π and the normal vector equation of Θ, and hence show that their line of intersection is

$$\mathbf{r} = (1, -4, -3) + t(5, 1, -3)$$

where t is a scalar variable.

18 Two skew lines L_1, L_2 have respective equations

$$\frac{x+3}{4} = \frac{y-3}{-1} = \frac{z-2}{1} \quad \text{and}$$

$$\frac{x-1}{2} = \frac{y-5}{1} = \frac{z+3}{2}$$

Obtain the equation of a plane through L_1 parallel to L_2 and show that the shortest distance between the lines is 6.

19 The three vectors $\mathbf{a} = (1, 0, 0)$, $\mathbf{b} = (1, 1, 0)$ and $\mathbf{c} = (1, 1, 1)$ are given. Evaluate

(a) $\mathbf{a} \times \mathbf{b}$, $\mathbf{b} \times \mathbf{c}$, $\mathbf{c} \times \mathbf{a}$

(b) $\mathbf{a} \cdot (\mathbf{b} \times \mathbf{c})$

For the vector $\mathbf{d} = (2, -1, 2)$ calculate

(c) the parameters α, β, γ in the expression

$$\mathbf{d} = \alpha\mathbf{a} + \beta\mathbf{b} + \gamma\mathbf{c}$$

(d) the parameters p, q, r in the expression

$$\mathbf{d} = p\mathbf{a} \times \mathbf{b} + q\mathbf{b} \times \mathbf{c} + r\mathbf{c} \times \mathbf{a}$$

and show that

$$p = \frac{\mathbf{c} \cdot \mathbf{d}}{\mathbf{a} \cdot (\mathbf{b} \times \mathbf{c})}, \quad q = \frac{\mathbf{a} \cdot \mathbf{d}}{\mathbf{a} \cdot (\mathbf{b} \times \mathbf{c})} \quad \text{and}$$

$$r = \frac{\mathbf{b} \cdot \mathbf{d}}{\mathbf{a} \cdot (\mathbf{b} \times \mathbf{c})}$$

20 Given the line with parametric equation

$$\mathbf{r} = \mathbf{a} + \lambda\mathbf{d}$$

show that the perpendicular distance p from the origin to this line can take either of the forms

$$\text{(i) } p = \frac{|\mathbf{a} \times \mathbf{d}|}{|\mathbf{d}|} \quad \text{(ii) } p = \left|\mathbf{a} - \frac{\mathbf{a} \cdot \mathbf{d}}{\mathbf{d} \cdot \mathbf{d}}\mathbf{d}\right|$$

Find the parametric equation of the straight line through the points

A(1, 0, 2) and B(2, 3, 0)

and determine

(a) the length of the perpendicular from the origin to the line;

(b) the point at which the line intersects the y–z plane;

(c) the coordinates of the foot of the perpendicular to the line from the point (1, 1, 1).

21 Given the three non-coplanar vectors $\mathbf{a}$, $\mathbf{b}$, $\mathbf{c}$, and defining $v = \mathbf{a} \cdot \mathbf{b} \times \mathbf{c}$, three further vectors are defined as

$$\mathbf{a}' = \mathbf{b} \times \mathbf{c}/v \quad \mathbf{b}' = \mathbf{c} \times \mathbf{a}/v \quad \mathbf{c}' = \mathbf{a} \times \mathbf{b}/v$$

Show that

$$\mathbf{a} = \mathbf{b}' \times \mathbf{c}'/v' \quad \mathbf{b} = \mathbf{c}' \times \mathbf{a}'/v' \quad \mathbf{c} = \mathbf{a}' \times \mathbf{b}'/v'$$

where

$$v' = \mathbf{a}' \cdot \mathbf{b}' \times \mathbf{c}'$$

Deduce that

$$\mathbf{a} \cdot \mathbf{a}' = \mathbf{b} \cdot \mathbf{b}' = \mathbf{c} \cdot \mathbf{c}' = 1$$

$$\mathbf{a} \cdot \mathbf{b}' = \mathbf{a} \cdot \mathbf{c}' = \mathbf{b} \cdot \mathbf{a}' = \mathbf{b} \cdot \mathbf{c}' = \mathbf{c} \cdot \mathbf{a}' = \mathbf{c} \cdot \mathbf{b}' = 0$$

If a vector is written in terms of $\mathbf{a}$, $\mathbf{b}$, $\mathbf{c}$ as

$$\mathbf{r} = \alpha\mathbf{a} + \beta\mathbf{b} + \gamma\mathbf{c}$$

evaluate α, β, γ in terms of $\mathbf{a}'$, $\mathbf{b}'$ and $\mathbf{c}'$.

Note: These sets of vectors are called **reciprocal sets** and are widely used in crystallography and materials science.

22 An unbalanced machine can be approximated by two masses, 2 kg and 1.5 kg, placed at the ends A and B respectively of light rods OA and OB of lengths 0.7 m and 1.1 m. The point O lies on the axis of rotation and OAB forms a plane perpendicular to this axis; OA and OB are at right-angles. The machine rotates about the axis with an angular velocity ω, which gives a centrifugal force $mr\omega^2$ for a mass m and rod length r. Find the unbalanced force at the axis. To balance the machine a mass of 1 kg is placed at the end of a light rod OC so that C is coplanar with OAB. Determine the position of C.

5 Matrix Algebra

Chapter 5	Contents	

5.1 Introduction

The solution of simultaneous equations is part of elementary algebra. Many engineering problems can be formulated in terms of simultaneous equations, but in most practical situations the number of equations is extremely large and traditional methods of solution are not feasible. Even the question of whether solutions exist is not easy to answer. Setting the equations up in matrix form provides a systematic way of answering this question and also suggests practical methods of solution. Over the past 150 years or so, a large number of matrix techniques have been developed, and many have been applied to the solution of engineering and scientific problems. The advent of quantum mechanics and the matrix representation developed by Heisenberg did much to stimulate their popularity, since scientists and engineers were then able to appreciate the convenience and economy of matrix formulations.

In many problems the relationships between vector quantities can be represented by matrices. We saw in Chapter 4 that vectors in three dimensions are represented by three numbers (x_1, x_2, x_3) with respect to some coordinate system. If the coordinate system is changed, the representation of the vector changes to another triple (x_1', x_2', x_3'), related to the original through a matrix. In this three-dimensional case the matrix is a 3×3 array of numbers. Such matrices satisfy various addition and multiplication properties, which we shall develop in this chapter, and indeed it is change of axes that provides the most natural way of introducing the matrix product.

In the previous chapter we noted that forces provide an excellent example of vectors and that they have wide use in engineering. When we are dealing with a continuous medium – for instance when we try to specify the forces in a beam or an aircraft wing or the forces due to the flow of a fluid – we have to extend our ideas and define the **stress** at a point. This can be represented by a 3×3 matrix, and matrix algebra is therefore required for a better understanding of the mathematical manipulations involved.

Perhaps the major impact on engineering applications came with the advent of computers since these are ideally set up to deal with vectors and arrays (matrices), and matrix formulations of problems are therefore already in a form highly suitable for computation. Indeed, all of the widely used aspects of matrices are incorporated into most computer packages, either just for calculation or for the algebraic manipulation of matrices. Packages that are currently popular with students include MATLAB, which is highly suitable for numerical computation, and either, MAPLE or the Symbolic Math Toolbox in MATLAB, for algebraic manipulation. These packages are used throughout this chapter.

Many physical problems can be modelled using differential equations, and such models form the basis of much modern science and technology. Most of these equations cannot be solved analytically because of their complexity, and it is necessary to revert to numerical solution. This almost always involves convenient vector and matrix formulations. For instance, a popular method of analysing structures is in terms of finite elements. Finite-element packages have been developed over the past 50 years or so to deal with problems having 10^5 or more variables. A major part of such packages involves setting up the data in matrix form and then solving the resulting matrix equations. They are now used to design large buildings, to stress aircraft, to determine the flow through a turbine, to study waveguides and in many other situations of great interest to engineers and scientists.

In most of the previous comments, matrices are used to simplify the notation in problems that require the solution of sets of linear equations. It is in this context that engineers and scientists usually encounter matrices. The chapter will therefore focus largely on matrix properties and methods that relate to the solution of such linear equations.

5.2 Basic concepts, definitions and properties

Some examples will be used to introduce the basic concepts of matrices which will then be formally defined and developed. In particular, they will illustrate the matrix product, which is the most interesting property in the theory since it enables complicated sets of equations to be written in a convenient and compact way.

Intersection of planes

The first example is one from geometry. In Section 4.3.3, we saw that the equation of a plane can be written in the form

$$\alpha x + \beta y + \gamma z = p$$

where α, β, γ and p are constants. The four planes

$$\left.\begin{aligned} 4x + 2y + z &= 7 \\ 2x + y - z &= 5 \\ x + 2y + 2z &= 3 \\ 3x - 2y - z &= 0 \end{aligned}\right\} \tag{5.1}$$

meet in a single point. What are the coordinates of that point? Obviously they are those values of x, y and z that satisfy all four of (5.1) simultaneously.

Equations (5.1) provide an example of a mathematical problem that arises in a wide range of engineering problems: the simultaneous solution of a set of linear equations, as mentioned in the introduction. The general form of a linear equation is the sum of a set of variables, each multiplied only by a numerical factor, set equal to a constant. No variable is raised to any power or multiplied by any other variable. In this case we have four linear equations in three variables x, y and z. We shall see that there is a large body of mathematical theory concerning the solution of such equations.

As is common in mathematics, one of the first stages in solving the problem is to introduce a better notation to represent the problem. In this case we introduce the idea of an array of numbers called a **matrix**. We write

$$\boldsymbol{A} = \begin{bmatrix} 4 & 2 & 1 \\ 2 & 1 & -1 \\ 1 & 2 & 2 \\ 3 & -2 & -1 \end{bmatrix}$$

and call $\boldsymbol{A}$ a 4×3 (read as '4 by 3') matrix; that is, a matrix with four rows and three columns. We also introduce an alternative notation for a vector, writing

$$X = \begin{bmatrix} x \\ y \\ z \end{bmatrix} \quad \text{and} \quad b = \begin{bmatrix} 7 \\ 5 \\ 3 \\ 0 \end{bmatrix}$$

We call these column vectors; they are 3 × 1 and 4 × 1 matrices respectively. Equations (5.1) can then be expressed in the form

$$AX = b$$

where the product of the matrix A and the vector X is understood to produce the left-hand sides of (5.1).

Change of axes

In many problems it is convenient to change rectangular axes Oxy coordinates to a new O$x'y'$ coordinate system by rotating the Oxy system anticlockwise about the origin O through an angle θ, as illustrated in Figure 5.1. We then seek the relation between the coordinates (x, y) of a point P in the Oxy system and the coordinates (x', y') of P in the O$x'y'$ system. Trigonometry gives

$$x = r\cos\phi, \quad y = r\sin\phi$$

and

$$x' = r\cos(\phi - \theta), \quad y' = r\sin(\phi - \theta)$$

Expanding the trigonometrical expressions gives

$$x' = r\cos\phi\cos\theta + r\sin\phi\sin\theta = x\cos\theta + y\sin\theta \tag{5.2}$$

$$y' = r\sin\phi\cos\theta - r\cos\phi\sin\theta = y\cos\theta - x\sin\theta$$

If we take

$$B = \begin{bmatrix} \cos\theta & \sin\theta \\ -\sin\theta & \cos\theta \end{bmatrix}, \quad X = \begin{bmatrix} x \\ y \end{bmatrix}, \quad X' = \begin{bmatrix} x' \\ y' \end{bmatrix}$$

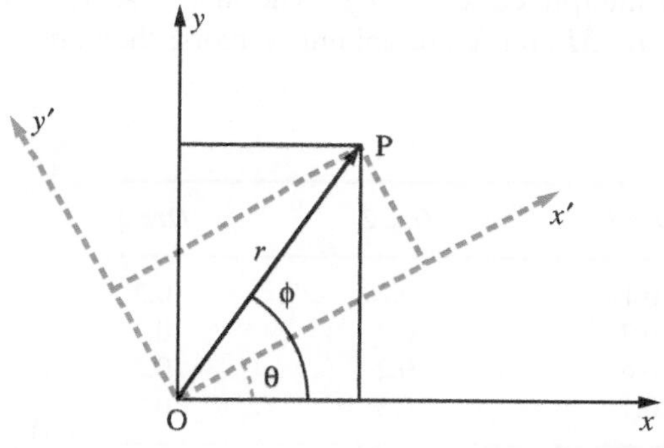

Figure 5.1
Change of axes from Oxy to O$x'y'$.

then (5.2) can be written in standard matrix notation as

$$\boldsymbol{X}' = \boldsymbol{B}\boldsymbol{X}$$

We see that a change of axes can be written in a natural manner in matrix form, with $\boldsymbol{B}$ containing all the information about the transformation.

'Ore' problem

A more physical problem concerns the mixing of ores. Three ores are known to contain fractions of Pb, Fe, Cu and Mn as indicated in Figure 5.2. If we mix the ores so that there are x_1 kg of ore 1, x_2 kg of ore 2 and x_3 kg of ore 3 then we can compute the amount of each element as

$$\left.\begin{aligned} \text{amount of Pb} &= A_{\text{Pb}} = 0.1x_1 + 0.2x_2 + 0.3x_3 \\ \text{amount of Fe} &= A_{\text{Fe}} = 0.2x_1 + 0.3x_2 + 0.3x_3 \\ \text{amount of Cu} &= A_{\text{Cu}} = 0.6x_1 + 0.2x_2 + 0.2x_3 \\ \text{amount of Mn} &= A_{\text{Mn}} = 0.1x_1 + 0.3x_2 + 0.2x_3 \end{aligned}\right\} \tag{5.3}$$

We can rewrite the array in Figure 5.2 as a matrix

$$\boldsymbol{A} = \begin{bmatrix} 0.1 & 0.2 & 0.3 \\ 0.2 & 0.3 & 0.3 \\ 0.6 & 0.2 & 0.2 \\ 0.1 & 0.3 & 0.2 \end{bmatrix}$$

and if we define the vectors

$$\boldsymbol{M} = \begin{bmatrix} A_{\text{Pb}} \\ A_{\text{Fe}} \\ A_{\text{Cu}} \\ A_{\text{Mn}} \end{bmatrix} \quad \text{and} \quad \boldsymbol{X} = \begin{bmatrix} x_1 \\ x_2 \\ x_3 \end{bmatrix}$$

then the equations can be written in matrix form

$$\boldsymbol{M} = \boldsymbol{A}\boldsymbol{X}$$

with the product interpreted as in (5.3). The matrix $\boldsymbol{A}$ has 4 rows and 3 columns, so it is a 4×3 matrix. $\boldsymbol{M}$ and $\boldsymbol{X}$ are column vectors; they are 4×1 and 3×1 matrices respectively.

Figure 5.2
Table of fractions in each kilogram of ore.

	Ore 1	*Ore 2*	*Ore 3*
Pb	0.1	0.2	0.3
Fe	0.2	0.3	0.3
Cu	0.6	0.2	0.2
Mn	0.1	0.3	0.2

In each of these examples arrays A and B and vectors $\boldsymbol{X}$ and $\boldsymbol{X}'$ appear in a natural way, and the method of multiplication of the arrays and vectors is consistent. We build on this idea to define matrices generally.

5.2.1 Definitions

An array of real numbers

$$\mathsf{A} = \begin{bmatrix} a_{11} & a_{12} & a_{13} & \dots & a_{1n} \\ a_{21} & a_{22} & a_{23} & \dots & a_{2n} \\ \vdots & \vdots & \vdots & & \vdots \\ a_{m1} & a_{m2} & a_{m3} & \dots & a_{mn} \end{bmatrix} \tag{5.4}$$

is called a **matrix** of order $m \times n$, with m rows and n columns. The entry a_{ij} denotes the **element** in the ith row and jth column. The element can be real or complex (but in this chapter we deal mainly with real matrices). If $m = n$ then the array is square, and A is then called a **square matrix** of order n. If the matrix has one column or one row

$$\boldsymbol{b} = \begin{bmatrix} b_1 \\ b_2 \\ \vdots \\ b_m \end{bmatrix} \quad \text{or} \quad \boldsymbol{c} = [c_1 \quad c_2 \quad \dots \quad c_n] \tag{5.5}$$

then it is called a **column vector** or a **row vector** respectively. The row vector was used in Section 4.2.2 as the basic definition of a vector, but in matrix theory a vector is normally taken to be a column vector unless otherwise stated. This slight inconsistency in the notation between vector theory and matrix theory can be inconvenient, but it is so standard in the literature that we must accept it. We have to get used to vectors appearing in several different notations. It is also a common convention to use upper-case letters to represent matrices and lower-case ones for vectors. We shall adopt this convention in this chapter with one exception: the vectors

$$\begin{bmatrix} x \\ y \\ z \end{bmatrix} \quad \text{and} \quad \begin{bmatrix} x \\ y \end{bmatrix}$$

will be denoted by $\boldsymbol{X}$. (Vectors and matrices are further distinguished here by the use of a 'serif' bold face for the former (e.g. $\boldsymbol{b}$) and a 'sans serif' bold face for the latter (e.g. A).) As an example of the notation used, consider the matrix A and the vector $\boldsymbol{b}$

$$\mathsf{A} = \begin{bmatrix} 0 & -1 & 2 \\ 3 & 0 & 1 \end{bmatrix} \quad \text{and} \quad \boldsymbol{b} = \begin{bmatrix} 0.15 \\ 1.11 \\ -3.01 \end{bmatrix}$$

The matrix A is a 2×3 matrix with elements $a_{11} = 0$, $a_{12} = -1$, $a_{13} = 2$, $a_{21} = 3$ and so on. The vector $\boldsymbol{b}$ is a column vector with elements $b_1 = 0.15$, $b_2 = 1.11$ and $b_3 = -3.01$.

In a square matrix of order n the diagonal containing the elements $a_{11}, a_{22}, \dots, a_{nn}$ is called the **principal**, **main** or **leading** diagonal. The sum of the elements of the leading diagonal is called the **trace** of the square matrix $\boldsymbol{A}$, that is

$$\text{trace}\,\boldsymbol{A} = a_{11} + a_{22} + \dots + a_{nn} = \sum_{i=1}^{n} a_{ii}$$

A **diagonal matrix** is a square matrix that has its only non-zero elements along the leading diagonal. (It may have zeros on the leading diagonal also.)

$$\begin{bmatrix} a_{11} & 0 & 0 & \dots & 0 \\ 0 & a_{22} & 0 & \dots & 0 \\ 0 & 0 & a_{33} & \dots & 0 \\ \vdots & \vdots & \vdots & & \vdots \\ 0 & 0 & 0 & \dots & a_{nn} \end{bmatrix}$$

An important special case of a diagonal matrix is the **unit matrix** or **identity matrix** $\boldsymbol{I}$, for which $a_{11} = a_{22} = \dots = a_{nn} = 1$.

$$\boldsymbol{I} = \begin{bmatrix} 1 & 0 & 0 & \dots & 0 \\ 0 & 1 & 0 & \dots & 0 \\ 0 & 0 & 1 & \dots & 0 \\ \vdots & \vdots & \vdots & & \vdots \\ 0 & 0 & 0 & \dots & 1 \end{bmatrix}$$

The unit matrix can be written conveniently in terms of the Kronecker delta. This is defined as

$$\delta_{ij} = \begin{cases} 1 & \text{if} \quad i = j \\ 0 & \text{if} \quad i \neq j \end{cases}$$

The unit matrix thus has elements δ_{ij}. The notation $\boldsymbol{I}_n$ is sometimes used to denote the $n \times n$ unit matrix where its size is important or not clear.

The **zero** or **null matrix** is the matrix with every element zero, and is written as either 0 or $\mathbf{0}$. Sometimes a zero matrix of order $m \times n$ is written $\mathbf{O}_{m\times n}$.

The **transposed matrix** $\boldsymbol{A}^{\mathrm{T}}$ of (5.4) is the matrix with elements $b_{ij} = a_{ji}$ and is written in full as the $n \times m$ matrix

$$\boldsymbol{A}^{\mathrm{T}} = \begin{bmatrix} a_{11} & a_{21} & a_{31} & \dots & a_{m1} \\ a_{12} & a_{22} & a_{32} & \dots & a_{m2} \\ \vdots & \vdots & \vdots & & \vdots \\ a_{1n} & a_{2n} & a_{3n} & \dots & a_{mn} \end{bmatrix}$$

This is just the matrix in (5.4) with rows and columns interchanged. We may note from (5.5) that

$$\boldsymbol{b}^{\mathrm{T}} = [b_1 \quad b_2 \quad \dots \quad b_m] \quad \text{and} \quad \boldsymbol{c}^{\mathrm{T}} = \begin{bmatrix} c_1 \\ c_2 \\ \vdots \\ c_n \end{bmatrix}$$

so that a column vector is transposed to a row vector and vice versa.

If a square matrix is such that $\boldsymbol{A}^{\mathrm{T}} = \boldsymbol{A}$ then $a_{ij} = a_{ji}$, and the elements are therefore symmetric about the diagonal. Such a matrix is called a **symmetric matrix**; symmetric matrices play important roles in many computations. If $\boldsymbol{A}^{\mathrm{T}} = -\boldsymbol{A}$, so that $a_{ij} = -a_{ji}$, the matrix is called **skew-symmetric** or **antisymmetric**. Obviously the diagonal elements of a skew-symmetric matrix satisfy $a_{ii} = -a_{ii}$ and so must all be zero.

A few examples will illustrate these definitions:

$$\boldsymbol{A} = \begin{bmatrix} 2 & 3 \\ 1 & 2 \\ 4 & 5 \end{bmatrix} \text{ is a } 3 \times 2 \text{ matrix}$$

$$\boldsymbol{A}^{\mathrm{T}} = \begin{bmatrix} 2 & 1 & 4 \\ 3 & 2 & 5 \end{bmatrix} \text{ is a } 2 \times 3 \text{ matrix}$$

$$\boldsymbol{B} = \begin{bmatrix} 1 & 2 & 3 \\ 2 & 3 & 4 \\ 3 & 4 & 5 \end{bmatrix} \text{ is a symmetric } 3 \times 3 \text{ matrix}$$

$$\text{trace } \boldsymbol{B} = 1 + 3 + 5 = 9$$

$$\boldsymbol{C} = \begin{bmatrix} 0 & 7 & -1 \\ -7 & 0 & 4 \\ 1 & -4 & 0 \end{bmatrix} \quad \text{and} \quad \boldsymbol{C}^{\mathrm{T}} = \begin{bmatrix} 0 & -7 & 1 \\ 7 & 0 & -4 \\ -1 & 4 & 0 \end{bmatrix} \text{ are skew-symmetric } 3 \times 3 \text{ matrices}$$

$$\boldsymbol{D} = \begin{bmatrix} 2 & 0 & 0 \\ 0 & 3 & 0 \\ 0 & 0 & 4 \end{bmatrix} \text{ is a } 3 \times 3 \text{ diagonal matrix}$$

$$\text{trace } \boldsymbol{D} = 2 + 3 + 4 = 9$$

$$\boldsymbol{I} = \begin{bmatrix} 1 & 0 & 0 & 0 \\ 0 & 1 & 0 & 0 \\ 0 & 0 & 1 & 0 \\ 0 & 0 & 0 & 1 \end{bmatrix} \text{ is the } 4 \times 4 \text{ unit matrix (sometimes written } \boldsymbol{I}_4\text{)}$$

5.2.2 Basic operations of matrices

(a) Equality

Two matrices $\boldsymbol{A}$ and $\boldsymbol{B}$ are said to be **equal** if and only if all their elements are the same, $a_{ij} = b_{ij}$ for $1 \leqslant i \leqslant m$, $1 \leqslant j \leqslant n$, and this equality is written as

$$\boldsymbol{A} = \boldsymbol{B}$$

Note that this requires the two matrices to be of the same order $m \times n$.

(b) Addition and subtraction

Addition of matrices is straightforward; we can only add an $m \times n$ matrix to another $m \times n$ matrix, and an element of the sum is the sum of the corresponding elements. If $\boldsymbol{A}$ has elements a_{ij} and $\boldsymbol{B}$ has elements b_{ij} then $\boldsymbol{A} + \boldsymbol{B}$ has elements $a_{ij} + b_{ij}$.

$$\begin{bmatrix} a_{11} & a_{12} & a_{13} & \cdots \\ a_{21} & a_{22} & a_{23} & \cdots \\ \vdots & \vdots & \vdots & \end{bmatrix} + \begin{bmatrix} b_{11} & b_{12} & b_{13} & \cdots \\ b_{21} & b_{22} & b_{23} & \cdots \\ \vdots & \vdots & \vdots & \end{bmatrix}$$

$$= \begin{bmatrix} a_{11} + b_{11} & a_{12} + b_{12} & a_{13} + b_{13} & \cdots \\ a_{21} + b_{21} & a_{22} + b_{22} & a_{23} + b_{23} & \cdots \\ \vdots & \vdots & \vdots & \end{bmatrix}$$

Similarly for subtraction, $\boldsymbol{A} - \boldsymbol{B}$ has elements $a_{ij} - b_{ij}$.

(c) Multiplication by a scalar

The matrix $\lambda\boldsymbol{A}$ has elements λa_{ij}; that is, we just multiply each element by the scalar λ

$$\lambda \begin{bmatrix} a_{11} & a_{12} & a_{13} & \cdots \\ a_{21} & a_{22} & a_{23} & \cdots \\ \vdots & \vdots & \vdots & \end{bmatrix} = \begin{bmatrix} \lambda a_{11} & \lambda a_{12} & \lambda a_{13} & \cdots \\ \lambda a_{21} & \lambda a_{22} & \lambda a_{23} & \cdots \\ \vdots & \vdots & \vdots & \end{bmatrix}$$

(d) Properties of the transpose

From the definition, the transpose of a matrix is such that

$$(\boldsymbol{A} + \boldsymbol{B})^{\mathrm{T}} = \boldsymbol{A}^{\mathrm{T}} + \boldsymbol{B}^{\mathrm{T}}$$

Similarly, we observe that

$$(\boldsymbol{A}^{\mathrm{T}})^{\mathrm{T}} = \boldsymbol{A}$$

so that transposing twice gives back the original matrix.

We may note as a special case of this result that for a square matrix $\boldsymbol{A}$

$$(\boldsymbol{A}^{\mathrm{T}} + \boldsymbol{A})^{\mathrm{T}} = (\boldsymbol{A}^{\mathrm{T}})^{\mathrm{T}} + \boldsymbol{A}^{\mathrm{T}} = \boldsymbol{A} + \boldsymbol{A}^{\mathrm{T}}$$

and hence $\boldsymbol{A}^{\mathrm{T}} + \boldsymbol{A}$ must be a symmetric matrix. This proves to be a very useful result, which we shall see used in several places. Similarly, $\boldsymbol{A} - \boldsymbol{A}^{\mathrm{T}}$ is a skew-symmetric matrix, so that any square matrix $\boldsymbol{A}$ may be expressed as the sum of a symmetric and a skew-symmetric matrix:

$$\boldsymbol{A} = \tfrac{1}{2}(\boldsymbol{A} + \boldsymbol{A}^{\mathrm{T}}) + \tfrac{1}{2}(\boldsymbol{A} - \boldsymbol{A}^{\mathrm{T}})$$

(e) Basic rules of addition

Because the usual rules of arithmetic are followed in the definitions of the sum of matrices and of multiplication by scalars, the

commutative law $\boldsymbol{A} + \boldsymbol{B} = \boldsymbol{B} + \boldsymbol{A}$

associative law $(\boldsymbol{A} + \boldsymbol{B}) + \boldsymbol{C} = \boldsymbol{A} + (\boldsymbol{B} + \boldsymbol{C})$

and

distributive law $\lambda(\boldsymbol{A} + \boldsymbol{B}) = \lambda\boldsymbol{A} + \lambda\boldsymbol{B}$

all hold for matrices.

Example 5.1 Let

$$\boldsymbol{A} = \begin{bmatrix} 1 & 2 & 1 \\ 1 & 1 & 2 \\ 1 & 1 & 1 \end{bmatrix}, \quad \boldsymbol{B} = \begin{bmatrix} 2 & 1 \\ 1 & 0 \\ 1 & 1 \end{bmatrix}, \quad \boldsymbol{C} = \begin{bmatrix} 0 & 1 & 1 \\ 0 & 0 & 1 \\ 1 & 0 & 0 \end{bmatrix}$$

Find, where possible, (a) $\boldsymbol{A} + \boldsymbol{B}$, (b) $\boldsymbol{A} + \boldsymbol{C}$, (c) $\boldsymbol{C} - \boldsymbol{A}$, (d) $3\boldsymbol{A}$, (e) $4\boldsymbol{B}$, (f) $\boldsymbol{C} + \boldsymbol{B}$, (g) $3\boldsymbol{A} + 2\boldsymbol{C}$, (h) $\boldsymbol{A}^{\mathrm{T}} + \boldsymbol{A}$ and (i) $\boldsymbol{A} + \boldsymbol{C}^{\mathrm{T}} + \boldsymbol{B}^{\mathrm{T}}$.

Solution (a) $\boldsymbol{A} + \boldsymbol{B}$ is not possible, since $\boldsymbol{A}$ is 3×3 and $\boldsymbol{B}$ is 3×2.

(b) $$\boldsymbol{A} + \boldsymbol{C} = \begin{bmatrix} 1+0 & 2+1 & 1+1 \\ 1+0 & 1+0 & 2+1 \\ 1+1 & 1+0 & 1+0 \end{bmatrix} = \begin{bmatrix} 1 & 3 & 2 \\ 1 & 1 & 3 \\ 2 & 1 & 1 \end{bmatrix}$$

(c) $$\boldsymbol{C} - \boldsymbol{A} = \begin{bmatrix} 0-1 & 1-2 & 1-1 \\ 0-1 & 0-1 & 1-2 \\ 1-1 & 0-1 & 0-1 \end{bmatrix} = \begin{bmatrix} -1 & -1 & 0 \\ -1 & -1 & -1 \\ 0 & -1 & -1 \end{bmatrix}$$

(d) $3\mathbf{A} = \begin{bmatrix} 3 & 6 & 3 \\ 3 & 3 & 6 \\ 3 & 3 & 3 \end{bmatrix}$

(e) $4\mathbf{B} = \begin{bmatrix} 8 & 4 \\ 4 & 0 \\ 4 & 4 \end{bmatrix}$

(f) $\mathbf{C} + \mathbf{B}$ is not possible, since $\mathbf{C}$ and $\mathbf{B}$ are not of the same order.

(g) $3\mathbf{A} + 2\mathbf{C} = \begin{bmatrix} 3 & 6 & 3 \\ 3 & 3 & 6 \\ 3 & 3 & 3 \end{bmatrix} + \begin{bmatrix} 0 & 2 & 2 \\ 0 & 0 & 2 \\ 2 & 0 & 0 \end{bmatrix} = \begin{bmatrix} 3 & 8 & 5 \\ 3 & 3 & 8 \\ 5 & 3 & 3 \end{bmatrix}$

(h) $\mathbf{A}^{\mathrm{T}} + \mathbf{A} = \begin{bmatrix} 1 & 1 & 1 \\ 2 & 1 & 1 \\ 1 & 2 & 1 \end{bmatrix} + \begin{bmatrix} 1 & 2 & 1 \\ 1 & 1 & 2 \\ 1 & 1 & 1 \end{bmatrix} = \begin{bmatrix} 2 & 3 & 2 \\ 3 & 2 & 3 \\ 2 & 3 & 2 \end{bmatrix}$

(Note that this matrix is symmetric.)

(i) $\mathbf{A} + \mathbf{C}^{\mathrm{T}} + \mathbf{B}^{\mathrm{T}}$ is not possible, since $\mathbf{B}^{\mathrm{T}}$ is not of the same order as $\mathbf{A}$ and $\mathbf{C}^{\mathrm{T}}$.

Example 5.2 A local roadside cafe serves beefburgers, eggs, chips and beans in four combination meals:

Slimmers	–	150 g chips	100 g beans	1 burger
Normal	1 egg	250 g chips	150 g beans	1 burger
Jumbo	2 eggs	350 g chips	200 g beans	2 burgers
Veggie	1 egg	200 g chips	150 g beans	–

A party orders 1 slimmer, 4 normal, 2 jumbo and 2 veggie meals. What is the total amount of materials that the kitchen staff need to cook? One of the customers sees the size of a jumbo meal and changes his order to a normal meal. How much less material will the kitchen staff need?

Solution The meals written in matrix form are

$$\mathbf{s} = \begin{bmatrix} 0 \\ 150 \\ 100 \\ 1 \end{bmatrix}, \quad \mathbf{n} = \begin{bmatrix} 1 \\ 250 \\ 150 \\ 1 \end{bmatrix}, \quad \mathbf{j} = \begin{bmatrix} 2 \\ 350 \\ 200 \\ 2 \end{bmatrix}, \quad \mathbf{v} = \begin{bmatrix} 1 \\ 200 \\ 150 \\ 0 \end{bmatrix}$$

and hence the kitchen requirements are

$$s + 4n + 2j + 2v = \begin{bmatrix} 10 \\ 2250 \\ 1400 \\ 9 \end{bmatrix}$$

The change in requirements is

$$j - n = \begin{bmatrix} 2 \\ 350 \\ 200 \\ 2 \end{bmatrix} - \begin{bmatrix} 1 \\ 250 \\ 150 \\ 1 \end{bmatrix} = \begin{bmatrix} 1 \\ 100 \\ 50 \\ 1 \end{bmatrix}$$

less materials needed.

Although this may appear to be a rather trivial example, the basic problem is identical to any production process that requires a supply of parts.

Example 5.3 (a) Show that the only solution to the vector equation

$$\alpha \begin{bmatrix} 1 \\ 1 \\ 1 \end{bmatrix} + \beta \begin{bmatrix} 0 \\ 1 \\ 1 \end{bmatrix} + \gamma \begin{bmatrix} 0 \\ 0 \\ 1 \end{bmatrix} = 0$$

is $\alpha = \beta = \gamma = 0$.

(b) Find a non-zero solution for α, β, γ, δ to the vector equation

$$\alpha \begin{bmatrix} 1 \\ 1 \\ 0 \\ 0 \end{bmatrix} + \beta \begin{bmatrix} 1 \\ 2 \\ 1 \\ 0 \end{bmatrix} + \gamma \begin{bmatrix} 0 \\ 0 \\ 1 \\ 1 \end{bmatrix} + \delta \begin{bmatrix} 0 \\ 1 \\ 0 \\ -1 \end{bmatrix} = 0$$

Solution (a) Rewrite as

$$\alpha \begin{bmatrix} 1 \\ 1 \\ 1 \end{bmatrix} + \beta \begin{bmatrix} 0 \\ 1 \\ 1 \end{bmatrix} + \gamma \begin{bmatrix} 0 \\ 0 \\ 1 \end{bmatrix} = \begin{bmatrix} \alpha \\ \alpha + \beta \\ \alpha + \beta + \gamma \end{bmatrix} = 0$$

Hence $\alpha = 0$, $\alpha + \beta = 0$ and $\alpha + \beta + \gamma = 0$, equations which only have the solution $\alpha = \beta = \gamma = 0$.

(b) Adding the four row entries, which are all zero, gives the equations

$$\alpha + \beta = 0$$

$$\alpha + 2\beta + \delta = 0$$

$$\beta + \gamma = 0$$

$$\gamma - \delta = 0$$

The first equation gives $\beta = -\alpha$, the third gives $\gamma = -\beta = \alpha$ and the fourth $\delta = \gamma = \alpha$. Substituting, the second equation is satisfied identically. Thus for any t the solution $\alpha = t$, $\beta = -t$, $\gamma = t$, $\delta = t$ satisfies all the equations.

The important concept of **linear dependence/independence** is illustrated in Example 5.3. It will be used later in the chapter and particularly in Section 5.7.4 in the discussion of the number of eigenvectors associated with a repeated eigenvalue. The vectors $\mathbf{a}_1, \mathbf{a}_2, \ldots, \mathbf{a}_n$ form a **linearly independent** set if the *only* solution to the equation

$$\alpha_1 \mathbf{a}_1 + \alpha_2 \mathbf{a}_2 + \ldots + \alpha_n \mathbf{a}_n = 0$$

is $\alpha_1 = \alpha_2 = \ldots = \alpha_n = 0$. Otherwise the set is said to be **linearly dependent**. Note that in Example 5.3 the vectors in (a) are linearly independent and those in (b) are linearly dependent.

All the basic matrix operations may be implemented in MATLAB and MAPLE using simple commands.

MATLAB

A matrix is entered as an array, with row elements separated by a space (or a comma) and each row of elements separated by a semicolon. Thus, for example

```
A = [1 2 3; 4 0 5; 7 6 2]
```

gives A as

```
A =
      1  2  3
      4  0  5
      7  6  2
```

The transpose of a matrix is written `A'`, with an apostrophe.

```
A' =
       1  4  7
       2  0  6
       3  5  2
```

and *`trace`*`(A)` produces the obvious answer = 3.

Having specified two matrices $\boldsymbol{A}$ and $\boldsymbol{B}$ the usual operations are written

```
C = A + B, C = A - B
```

and multiplication with a scalar as

```
C = 2*A + 3*B
```

MAPLE

There are several ways of setting up arrays in MAPLE; the simplest is to use the linear algebra package

```
with (linalg):
array([list of elements]);
```

Thus, for example

```
A:=array([[1,2,3],[4,0,5],
[7,6,2]]);
```

produces

```
        1  2  3
    A = 4  0  5
        7  6  2
```

The transpose and trace are obtained from

`transpose(A);` and `trace(A);`

Having specified two matrices $\boldsymbol{A}$ and $\boldsymbol{B}$ the usual operations are written

`C := evalm (A + B);` and
`C := evalm (A - B);`

because MAPLE is a symbolic package. The *evaluation* of the multiplication of a matrix by a scalar requires the command

```
C:= evalm(2*A + 3*B);
```

5.2.3 Exercises

Check your answers using MATLAB or MAPLE whenever possible.

1 Given the matrices

$$\boldsymbol{a} = \begin{bmatrix} 1 \\ 2 \\ 0 \end{bmatrix}, \quad \boldsymbol{b} = [0 \quad 1 \quad 1],$$

$$\boldsymbol{C} = \begin{bmatrix} 3 & 2 & 1 \\ 1 & 2 & -1 \end{bmatrix}, \quad \boldsymbol{D} = \begin{bmatrix} 5 & 6 \\ 7 & 8 \\ 9 & 10 \end{bmatrix}$$

evaluate, where possible, (a) $\boldsymbol{a} + \boldsymbol{b}$, (b) $\boldsymbol{b}^{\mathrm{T}} + \boldsymbol{a}$, (c) $\boldsymbol{b} + \boldsymbol{C}^{\mathrm{T}}$, (d) $\boldsymbol{C} + \boldsymbol{D}$, (e) $\boldsymbol{D}^{\mathrm{T}} + \boldsymbol{C}$.

2 Given the matrices

$$\boldsymbol{A} = \begin{bmatrix} 1 & 0 & 1 \\ 2 & 2 & 0 \\ 0 & 1 & 2 \end{bmatrix} \quad \text{and} \quad \boldsymbol{B} = \begin{bmatrix} -1 & 1 & 0 \\ 1 & 0 & -1 \\ 0 & -1 & 1 \end{bmatrix}$$

evaluate $\boldsymbol{C}$ in the three cases.

(a) $\boldsymbol{C} = \boldsymbol{A} + \boldsymbol{B}$ (b) $2\boldsymbol{A} + 3\boldsymbol{C} = 4\boldsymbol{B}$

(c) $\boldsymbol{A} - \boldsymbol{C} = \boldsymbol{B} + \boldsymbol{C}$

3 Solve for the matrix $\boldsymbol{X}$

$$\boldsymbol{X} - 2\begin{bmatrix} 3 & 2 & -1 \\ 7 & 2 & 6 \end{bmatrix} = \begin{bmatrix} -2 & 3 & 1 \\ 4 & 6 & 2 \end{bmatrix}$$

4 If

$$\boldsymbol{A} = \begin{bmatrix} 1 & 2 & -3 \\ 5 & 0 & 2 \\ 1 & -1 & 1 \end{bmatrix}, \quad \boldsymbol{B} = \begin{bmatrix} 3 & -1 & 2 \\ 4 & 2 & 5 \\ 2 & 0 & 5 \end{bmatrix}$$

$$\text{and} \quad \boldsymbol{C} = \begin{bmatrix} 4 & 0 & -2 \\ 5 & 3 & 1 \\ 2 & 5 & 4 \end{bmatrix}$$

(a) show that

$$\operatorname{trace}(\boldsymbol{A} + \boldsymbol{B}) = \operatorname{trace} \boldsymbol{A} + \operatorname{trace} \boldsymbol{B};$$

(b) find $\boldsymbol{D}$ so that $\boldsymbol{A} + \boldsymbol{D} = \boldsymbol{C}$;

(c) verify the associative law

$$(\boldsymbol{A} + \boldsymbol{B}) + \boldsymbol{C} = \boldsymbol{A} + (\boldsymbol{B} + \boldsymbol{C}).$$

5 Find the values of x, y, z and t from the equation

$$\begin{bmatrix} x & y - x + t \\ t - z & z - 1 \end{bmatrix} = \begin{bmatrix} 1 & 2 \\ 0 & 1 \end{bmatrix}$$

6 Find the values of α, β, γ that satisfy

$$\alpha\begin{bmatrix} 1 \\ 0 \\ 0 \end{bmatrix} + \beta\begin{bmatrix} 1 \\ -1 \\ 0 \end{bmatrix} + \gamma\begin{bmatrix} 0 \\ 1 \\ -1 \end{bmatrix} = \begin{bmatrix} 0 \\ 3 \\ -2 \end{bmatrix}$$

7 (a) Show that the vectors $\begin{bmatrix} 1 \\ 0 \\ 0 \end{bmatrix}, \begin{bmatrix} 1 \\ -1 \\ 0 \end{bmatrix}, \begin{bmatrix} 0 \\ 1 \\ -1 \end{bmatrix}$ are linearly independent.

(b) Show that the vectors $\begin{bmatrix} 1 \\ 0 \\ 0 \end{bmatrix}, \begin{bmatrix} 1 \\ -1 \\ 0 \end{bmatrix}, \begin{bmatrix} 0 \\ 1 \\ -1 \end{bmatrix}, \begin{bmatrix} 0 \\ 3 \\ -2 \end{bmatrix}$ are linearly dependent.

8 Show that, for any vector $\begin{bmatrix} p \\ q \\ r \end{bmatrix}$, constants α, β, γ can always be found so that

$$\begin{bmatrix} p \\ q \\ r \end{bmatrix} = \alpha\begin{bmatrix} 1 \\ 1 \\ 0 \end{bmatrix} + \beta\begin{bmatrix} 1 \\ 0 \\ 1 \end{bmatrix} + \gamma\begin{bmatrix} 0 \\ 1 \\ 1 \end{bmatrix}$$

Note: Exercises 7(b) and 8 are special cases of a general result that given three 3×1 linearly independent vectors $\mathbf{a}$, $\mathbf{b}$, $\mathbf{c}$ then *any* 3×1 vector can be written $\alpha\mathbf{a} + \beta\mathbf{b} + \gamma\mathbf{c}$).

9 Given the matrix

$$\boldsymbol{A} = \lambda\begin{bmatrix} 1 & 0 \\ 0 & 1 \end{bmatrix} + \mu\begin{bmatrix} 1 & 1 \\ 0 & 1 \end{bmatrix} + \nu\begin{bmatrix} 0 & 0 \\ 0 & 1 \end{bmatrix}$$

(a) find the value of λ, μ, ν so that $\boldsymbol{A} = \begin{bmatrix} 0 & -1 \\ 0 & 3 \end{bmatrix}$;

(b) show that no solution is possible if

$$\boldsymbol{A} = \begin{bmatrix} 1 & -1 \\ 1 & 0 \end{bmatrix}.$$

10 Market researchers are testing customers' preferences for five products. There are four researchers who are allocated to different groups: researcher R_1 deals with men under 40, R_2 deals with men over 40, R_3 deals with women under 40 and R_4 deals with women over 40. They return their findings as a vector giving the number of customers with first preference for a particular product.

Product	R_1	R_2	R_3	R_4
a	23	32	28	39
b	34	22	33	21
c	18	21	22	17
d	9	15	10	12
e	16	10	7	11

Find the average over the whole sample. The company decides that their main target is older women, so they weight the returns in the ratio 1 : 1 : 2 : 3; find the weighted average.

11 A builder's yard organizes its stock in the form of a vector

Bricks – type A
Bricks – type B
Bricks – type C
Bags of cement
Tons of sand

The current stock, $\boldsymbol{S}$, and the minimum stock, $\boldsymbol{M}$, required to avoid running out of materials, are given as

$$\boldsymbol{S} = \begin{bmatrix} 45\,750 \\ 23\,600 \\ 17\,170 \\ 462 \\ 27 \end{bmatrix} \quad \text{and} \quad \boldsymbol{M} = \begin{bmatrix} 5000 \\ 4000 \\ 3500 \\ 100 \\ 10 \end{bmatrix}$$

The firm has five lorries which take materials from stock for deliveries; Lorry1 makes three deliveries in the day with the same load each time; Lorry2 makes two deliveries in the day with the same load each time; the other lorries make one delivery. The loads are

$$\boldsymbol{L}_1 = \begin{bmatrix} 5500 \\ 0 \\ 3800 \\ 75 \\ 3 \end{bmatrix} \quad \boldsymbol{L}_2 = \begin{bmatrix} 2500 \\ 1500 \\ 0 \\ 40 \\ 2 \end{bmatrix} \quad \boldsymbol{L}_3 = \begin{bmatrix} 7500 \\ 2000 \\ 1500 \\ 0 \\ 3 \end{bmatrix}$$

$$\boldsymbol{L}_4 = \begin{bmatrix} 0 \\ 4000 \\ 2500 \\ 20 \\ 2 \end{bmatrix} \quad \boldsymbol{L}_5 = \begin{bmatrix} 2000 \\ 0 \\ 1500 \\ 15 \\ 0 \end{bmatrix}$$

How much material has gone from stock, what is the current stock position and has any element gone below the minimum?

5.2.4 Matrix multiplication

The most important property of matrices as far as their practical applications are concerned is the multiplication of one matrix by another. We saw informally in Section 5.2 how multiplication arose and how to define multiplication of a matrix and a vector. The idea can be extended further by looking again at change of axes. We consider three coordinate systems in a plane, denoted by Ox_1x_2, Oy_1y_2, Oz_1z_2 and related by the linear transformations, illustrated as mappings $\boldsymbol{A}$ and $\boldsymbol{B}$ in Figure 5.3.

$$z_1 = a_{11}y_1 + a_{12}y_2, \quad y_1 = b_{11}x_1 + b_{12}x_2$$
$$z_2 = a_{21}y_1 + a_{22}y_2, \quad y_2 = b_{21}x_1 + b_{22}x_2$$

We then seek the composite transformation that expresses z_1, z_2 in terms of x_1, x_2. This we can do by straight substitution:

$$z_1 = (a_{11}b_{11} + a_{12}b_{21})x_1 + (a_{11}b_{12} + a_{12}b_{22})x_2$$
$$z_2 = (a_{21}b_{11} + a_{22}b_{21})x_1 + (a_{21}b_{12} + a_{22}b_{22})x_2$$

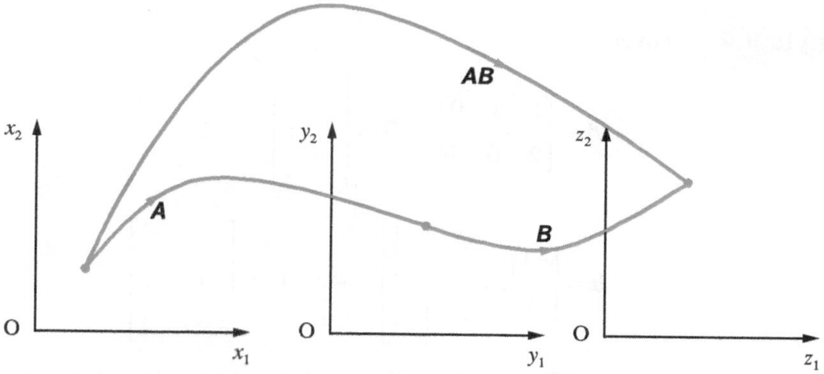

Figure 5.3
Linear transformation, $\boldsymbol{A}$, from Ox_1x_2 to Oy_1y_2 and linear transformation, $\boldsymbol{B}$, from Oy_1y_2 to Oz_1z_2 and the composite, $\boldsymbol{AB}$, from Ox_1x_2 to Oz_1z_2.

Illustration

$z_1 = y_1 + 3y_2$
$z_2 = 2y_1 - y_2$

$y_1 = -x_1 + 2x_2$
$y_2 = 2x_1 - x_2$

Substitute to get

$z_1 = 5x_1 - x_2$
$z_2 = -4x_1 + 5x_2$

In matrix form

$$\boldsymbol{A} = \begin{bmatrix} 1 & 3 \\ 2 & -1 \end{bmatrix}$$

$$\boldsymbol{B} = \begin{bmatrix} -1 & 2 \\ 2 & -1 \end{bmatrix}$$

$$\boldsymbol{AB} = \begin{bmatrix} 5 & -1 \\ -4 & 5 \end{bmatrix}$$

If we write the first two transformations as

$$\boldsymbol{A} = \begin{bmatrix} a_{11} & a_{12} \\ a_{21} & a_{22} \end{bmatrix} \quad \text{and} \quad \boldsymbol{B} = \begin{bmatrix} b_{11} & b_{12} \\ b_{21} & b_{22} \end{bmatrix}$$

then the composite transformation is written

$$\boldsymbol{AB} = \begin{bmatrix} a_{11}b_{11} + a_{12}b_{21} & a_{11}b_{12} + a_{12}b_{22} \\ a_{21}b_{11} + a_{22}b_{21} & a_{21}b_{12} + a_{22}b_{22} \end{bmatrix}$$

and this is precisely how we define the matrix product.

Definition

If $\boldsymbol{A}$ is an $m \times p$ matrix with elements a_{ij} and $\boldsymbol{B}$ a $p \times n$ matrix with elements b_{ij} then we define the **product** $\boldsymbol{C} = \boldsymbol{AB}$ as the $m \times n$ matrix with components

$$c_{ij} = \sum_{k=1}^{p} a_{ik} b_{kj} \quad \text{for } i = 1, \ldots, m \quad \text{and} \quad j = 1, \ldots, n$$

In pictorial form, the ith row of $\boldsymbol{A}$ is multiplied term by term with the jth column of $\boldsymbol{B}$ and the products are added to form the ijth component of $\boldsymbol{C}$. This is commonly referred to as the 'row-by-column' method of multiplication. Clearly, in order for multiplication to be possible, $\boldsymbol{A}$ must have p columns and $\boldsymbol{B}$ must have p rows otherwise the product $\boldsymbol{AB}$ is not defined.

$$i \rightarrow \overset{\substack{j \\ \downarrow}}{\begin{bmatrix} & \vdots & \\ \cdots & c_{ij} & \cdots \\ & \vdots & \end{bmatrix}} = i \rightarrow \begin{bmatrix} & & & \\ a_{i1} & a_{i2} & \cdots & a_{ip} \\ & & & \end{bmatrix} \overset{\substack{j \\ \downarrow}}{\begin{bmatrix} b_{1j} \\ b_{2j} \\ \vdots \\ b_{pj} \end{bmatrix}}$$

Example 5.4 Given

$$\boldsymbol{A}=\begin{bmatrix}1 & 1 & 0\\ 2 & 0 & 1\end{bmatrix},\quad \boldsymbol{B}=\begin{bmatrix}2 & 0\\ 0 & 1\\ 1 & 3\end{bmatrix},$$

$$\boldsymbol{b}=\begin{bmatrix}-1\\ 2\end{bmatrix},\quad \boldsymbol{c}=\begin{bmatrix}1\\ 1\\ -1\end{bmatrix}\quad\text{and}\quad \boldsymbol{C}=\begin{bmatrix}1 & -2\\ -1 & 2\\ -2 & 4\end{bmatrix}$$

find (a) $\boldsymbol{AB}$, (b) $\boldsymbol{BA}$, (c) $\boldsymbol{Bb}$, (d) $\boldsymbol{A}^{\mathrm{T}}\boldsymbol{b}$, (e) $\boldsymbol{c}^{\mathrm{T}}(\boldsymbol{A}^{\mathrm{T}}\boldsymbol{b})$ and (f) $\boldsymbol{AC}$.

Solution

(a) $$\boldsymbol{AB}=\begin{bmatrix}1 & 1 & 0\\ 2 & 0 & 1\end{bmatrix}\begin{bmatrix}2 & 0\\ 0 & 1\\ 1 & 3\end{bmatrix}=\begin{bmatrix}\text{row}\,1\times\text{col}\,1 & \text{row}\,1\times\text{col}\,2\\ \text{row}\,2\times\text{col}\,1 & \text{row}\,2\times\text{col}\,2\end{bmatrix}$$

$$=\begin{bmatrix}(1)(2)+(1)(0)+(0)(1) & (1)(0)+(1)(1)+(0)(3)\\ (2)(2)+(0)(0)+(1)(1) & (2)(0)+(0)(1)+(1)(3)\end{bmatrix}=\begin{bmatrix}2 & 1\\ 5 & 3\end{bmatrix}$$

(b) $$\boldsymbol{BA}=\begin{bmatrix}2 & 0\\ 0 & 1\\ 1 & 3\end{bmatrix}\begin{bmatrix}1 & 1 & 0\\ 2 & 0 & 1\end{bmatrix}=\begin{bmatrix}2+0 & 2+0 & 0+0\\ 0+2 & 0+0 & 0+1\\ 1+6 & 1+0 & 0+3\end{bmatrix}=\begin{bmatrix}2 & 2 & 0\\ 2 & 0 & 1\\ 7 & 1 & 3\end{bmatrix}$$

(Note that $\boldsymbol{BA}$ is not equal to $\boldsymbol{AB}$.)

(c) $$\boldsymbol{Bb}=\begin{bmatrix}2 & 0\\ 0 & 1\\ 1 & 3\end{bmatrix}\begin{bmatrix}-1\\ 2\end{bmatrix}=\begin{bmatrix}-2\\ 2\\ 5\end{bmatrix}$$

(d) $$\boldsymbol{A}^{\mathrm{T}}\boldsymbol{b}=\begin{bmatrix}1 & 2\\ 1 & 0\\ 0 & 1\end{bmatrix}\begin{bmatrix}-1\\ 2\end{bmatrix}=\begin{bmatrix}3\\ -1\\ 2\end{bmatrix}$$

(e) $$\boldsymbol{c}^{\mathrm{T}}(\boldsymbol{A}^{\mathrm{T}}\boldsymbol{b})=\begin{bmatrix}1 & 1 & -1\end{bmatrix}\begin{bmatrix}3\\ -1\\ 2\end{bmatrix}=[0]=0$$

(Note that this matrix is the zero 1×1 matrix, which can just be written 0.)

(f) $$\boldsymbol{AC}=\begin{bmatrix}1 & 1 & 0\\ 2 & 0 & 1\end{bmatrix}\begin{bmatrix}1 & -2\\ -1 & 2\\ -2 & 4\end{bmatrix}=\begin{bmatrix}0 & 0\\ 0 & 0\end{bmatrix}=0$$

(Note that the product $\boldsymbol{AC}$ is zero even though neither $\boldsymbol{A}$ nor $\boldsymbol{C}$ is zero.)

Example 5.5 If

$$A = \begin{bmatrix} 1 & 2 & 0 \\ 1 & 1 & 0 \\ 2 & 1 & 1 \end{bmatrix} \quad \text{and} \quad X = \begin{bmatrix} x \\ y \\ z \end{bmatrix}$$

evaluate (a) X^TX, (b) AX, (c) $X^T(AX)$ and (d) $\frac{1}{2}X^T[(A^T + A)X]$.

Solution

(a) $$X^TX = [x \quad y \quad z]\begin{bmatrix} x \\ y \\ z \end{bmatrix} = x^2 + y^2 + z^2$$

(b) $$AX = \begin{bmatrix} 1 & 2 & 0 \\ 1 & 1 & 0 \\ 2 & 1 & 1 \end{bmatrix}\begin{bmatrix} x \\ y \\ z \end{bmatrix} = \begin{bmatrix} x + 2y \\ x + y \\ 2x + y + z \end{bmatrix}$$

(c) $$X^T(AX) = [x \quad y \quad z]\begin{bmatrix} x + 2y \\ x + y \\ 2x + y + z \end{bmatrix} = (x^2 + 2xy) + (yx + y^2) + (2xz + yz + z^2)$$

$$= x^2 + y^2 + z^2 + 3xy + 2xz + yz$$

(d) $$\tfrac{1}{2}(A^T + A) = \begin{bmatrix} 1 & \frac{3}{2} & 1 \\ \frac{3}{2} & 1 & \frac{1}{2} \\ 1 & \frac{1}{2} & 1 \end{bmatrix}$$

and

$$\tfrac{1}{2}(A^T + A)X = \begin{bmatrix} 1 & \frac{3}{2} & 1 \\ \frac{3}{2} & 1 & \frac{1}{2} \\ 1 & \frac{1}{2} & 1 \end{bmatrix}\begin{bmatrix} x \\ y \\ z \end{bmatrix} = \begin{bmatrix} x + \frac{3}{2}y + z \\ \frac{3}{2}x + y + \frac{1}{2}z \\ x + \frac{1}{2}y + z \end{bmatrix}$$

Therefore

$$\tfrac{1}{2}X^T[(A^T + A)X] = [x \quad y \quad z]\begin{bmatrix} x + \frac{3}{2}y + z \\ \frac{3}{2}x + y + \frac{1}{2}z \\ x + \frac{1}{2}y + z \end{bmatrix}$$

$$= x^2 + y^2 + z^2 + 3xy + 2xz + yz$$

(Note that this is the same as the result of part (c).)

There are several points to note from the preceding examples. One-by-one matrices are just numbers, so the square brackets become redundant and are usually omitted. The expression $\boldsymbol{X}^{\mathrm{T}}\boldsymbol{X}$ just gives the square of the length of the vector $\boldsymbol{X}$ in the usual sense, namely $\boldsymbol{X}^{\mathrm{T}}\boldsymbol{X} = x^2 + y^2 + z^2$. Similarly,

$$\boldsymbol{X}^{\mathrm{T}}\boldsymbol{X}' = [x \quad y \quad z]\begin{bmatrix} x' \\ y' \\ z' \end{bmatrix} = xx' + yy' + zz'$$

which is the usual **scalar** or **inner product**, here written in matrix form. The expression $\boldsymbol{AX}$ gives a column vector with linear expressions as its elements. Using Example 5.5(b), we can rewrite the linear equations

$$\begin{aligned} x + 2y \quad &= 3 \\ x + y \quad &= 4 \\ 2x + y + z &= 5 \end{aligned}$$

as

$$\begin{bmatrix} 1 & 2 & 0 \\ 1 & 1 & 0 \\ 2 & 1 & 1 \end{bmatrix}\begin{bmatrix} x \\ y \\ z \end{bmatrix} = \begin{bmatrix} 3 \\ 4 \\ 5 \end{bmatrix}$$

which may be written in the standard matrix form for linear equations as

$$\boldsymbol{AX} = \boldsymbol{b}$$

It is also important to realize that if $\boldsymbol{AB} = 0$ it does not follow that either $\boldsymbol{A}$ or $\boldsymbol{B}$ is zero. In Example 5.4(f) we saw that the product $\boldsymbol{AC} = 0$, but neither $\boldsymbol{A}$ nor $\boldsymbol{C}$ is the zero matrix.

Matrix multiplication is an important part of computer packages and is easily implemented.

MATLAB

If $\boldsymbol{A}$ and $\boldsymbol{B}$ have been defined and have the correct dimensions then

```
A * B  and  A^2
```

have the usual meaning of matrix multiplication and squaring.

For matrices involving algebraic quantities, or when exact arithmetic is desirable, use of the Symbolic Math Toolbox is required; in which case the matrices $\boldsymbol{A}$ and $\boldsymbol{B}$ must be expressed in symbolic form using the *sym* command, that is

```
A = sym(A); B = sym(B)
```

MAPLE

If $\boldsymbol{A}$ and $\boldsymbol{B}$ have been defined and have the correct dimensions then it is best first to invoke the linalg package

```
with(linalg):
multiply(A,B);
evalm(A &* B);
```

both produce the product of the two matrices.

```
evalm(A&^2);
```

squares the matrix $\boldsymbol{A}$.

Because MAPLE is a symbolic package all variables are assumed to be symbols and there is no need to declare them to be so.

5.2.5 Exercises

Most of these exercises can be checked using MATLAB. For non-numerical exercises use either MAPLE or the Symbolic Math Toolbox of MATLAB.

12 Given the matrices

$$\boldsymbol{A} = \begin{bmatrix} 1 & 1 & 1 \\ 1 & 1 & 1 \end{bmatrix}, \quad \boldsymbol{B} = \begin{bmatrix} 1 & 1 & 0 \\ 1 & 1 & 0 \\ 0 & 0 & -1 \end{bmatrix}$$

and

$$\boldsymbol{C} = \begin{bmatrix} 0 & 2 \\ 1 & 1 \\ -1 & -1 \end{bmatrix}$$

evaluate $\boldsymbol{AB}$, $\boldsymbol{AC}$, $\boldsymbol{BC}$, $\boldsymbol{CA}$ and $\boldsymbol{BA}^{\mathrm{T}}$. Which if any of these are diagonal, unit or symmetric?

13 The matrices

$$\boldsymbol{A} = \begin{bmatrix} 1 & 2 & 1 \\ 3 & 0 & 2 \end{bmatrix}, \quad \boldsymbol{B} = \begin{bmatrix} 4 & 1 & 3 \\ 0 & 2 & 1 \end{bmatrix}$$

and

$$\boldsymbol{C} = \begin{bmatrix} 1 & 2 \\ 3 & 1 \\ 2 & 3 \end{bmatrix}$$

are given.

(a) Which of the following make sense: $\boldsymbol{AB}$, $\boldsymbol{AC}$, $\boldsymbol{BC}$, $\boldsymbol{AB}^{\mathrm{T}}$, $\boldsymbol{AC}^{\mathrm{T}}$ and $\boldsymbol{BC}^{\mathrm{T}}$?

(b) Evaluate those products that do exist.

(c) Evaluate $(\boldsymbol{A}^{\mathrm{T}}\boldsymbol{B})\boldsymbol{C}$ and $\boldsymbol{A}^{\mathrm{T}}(\boldsymbol{BC})$ and show that they are equal.

14 (a) Represent each of the linear transformations

$$\begin{aligned} y_1 &= x_1 + 2x_2 \\ y_2 &= x_1 - x_2 \end{aligned} \quad \text{and} \quad \begin{aligned} z_1 &= 2y_2 \\ z_2 &= y_1 + y_2 \end{aligned}$$

in matrix form and find the composite transformation that expresses z_1, z_2 in terms of x_1, x_2

(b) Represent each of the linear transformations

$$\begin{aligned} y_1 &= x_1 + 2x_2 \\ y_2 &= x_2 + x_3 \\ y_3 &= 3x_1 + x_3 \end{aligned} \quad \text{and} \quad \begin{aligned} z_1 &= y_1 \\ z_2 &= y_1 - y_2 \\ z_3 &= y_1 + 2y_2 + 3y_3 \end{aligned}$$

in matrix form and find the composite transformation that expresses z_1, z_2, z_3 in terms of x_1, x_2, x_3.

15 Given

$$\boldsymbol{A} = \begin{bmatrix} 3 & 2 \\ 5 & 4 \end{bmatrix} \quad \text{and} \quad \boldsymbol{B} = \begin{bmatrix} 4 & -2 \\ -5 & 3 \end{bmatrix}$$

evaluate $\boldsymbol{AB}$ and $\boldsymbol{BA}$ and hence show that these two matrices commute. Solve the equation

$$\boldsymbol{AX} = \begin{bmatrix} 1 \\ 0 \end{bmatrix}$$

for the vector $\boldsymbol{X}$ by multplying both sides by $\boldsymbol{B}$.

16 Show that for any x the matrix

$$\boldsymbol{A} = \begin{bmatrix} \cos(2x) & \sin(2x) \\ \sin(2x) & -\cos(2x) \end{bmatrix}$$

satisfies the relation $\boldsymbol{A}^2 = \boldsymbol{I}$.

17 If

$$\boldsymbol{A} = \begin{bmatrix} a & b \\ -b & a \end{bmatrix} \quad \text{and} \quad \boldsymbol{B} = \begin{bmatrix} c & d \\ -d & c \end{bmatrix}$$

show that the product $\boldsymbol{AB}$ has exactly the same form.

18 Given

$$\boldsymbol{A} = \begin{bmatrix} 1 & 2 & 3 \\ 3 & 4 & 5 \\ 5 & 6 & 7 \end{bmatrix}, \quad \boldsymbol{X} = \begin{bmatrix} x \\ y \\ z \end{bmatrix} \quad \text{and} \quad \boldsymbol{b} = \begin{bmatrix} 2 \\ 3 \\ 4 \end{bmatrix}$$

evaluate $\boldsymbol{X}^{\mathrm{T}}\boldsymbol{X}$ and $\boldsymbol{X}^{\mathrm{T}}\boldsymbol{AX}$ and write out the equations given by $\boldsymbol{AX} = \boldsymbol{b}$.

5.2.6 Properties of matrix multiplication

We now consider the basic properties of matrix multiplication. These may be proved using the definition of matrix multiplication and this is left as an exercise for the reader.

(a) Commutative law

Matrices *do not commute in general*, although they may do in special cases. In Example 5.4 we saw that $\boldsymbol{AB} \neq \boldsymbol{BA}$, and a further example illustrates the same result:

$$\boldsymbol{A} = \begin{bmatrix} 1 & 0 \\ 0 & 0 \end{bmatrix}, \quad \boldsymbol{B} = \begin{bmatrix} 1 & 2 \\ 1 & 0 \end{bmatrix}$$

$$\boldsymbol{AB} = \begin{bmatrix} 1 & 2 \\ 0 & 0 \end{bmatrix}, \quad \boldsymbol{BA} = \begin{bmatrix} 1 & 0 \\ 1 & 0 \end{bmatrix}$$

so again $\boldsymbol{AB} \neq \boldsymbol{BA}$. The products do not necessarily have the same size, as shown in Example 5.4(a and b), where $\boldsymbol{AB}$ is a 2×2 matrix while $\boldsymbol{BA}$ is 3×3. In fact, even if $\boldsymbol{AB}$ exists, it does not follow that $\boldsymbol{BA}$ does. Take, for example, the matrices $\boldsymbol{a} = [1 \quad 1 \quad 1]$ and $\boldsymbol{B} = \begin{bmatrix} 1 & 2 \\ 2 & 1 \\ 1 & 1 \end{bmatrix}$. The product $\boldsymbol{aB} = [4 \quad 4]$ is well defined but $\boldsymbol{Ba}$ cannot be computed since a 3×2 matrix cannot be multiplied on the right by a 1×3 matrix. Thus order matters, and we need to distinguish between $\boldsymbol{AB}$ and $\boldsymbol{BA}$. To do this, we talk of **pre-multiplication** of $\boldsymbol{B}$ by $\boldsymbol{A}$ to form $\boldsymbol{AB}$, and **post-multiplication** of $\boldsymbol{B}$ by $\boldsymbol{A}$ to form $\boldsymbol{BA}$.

(b) Associative law

It follows from the definition of the matrix product and a careful use of double summations that

$$\boldsymbol{A}(\boldsymbol{BC}) = (\boldsymbol{AB})\boldsymbol{C}$$

where $\boldsymbol{A}$ is $m \times p$, $\boldsymbol{B}$ is $p \times q$ and $\boldsymbol{C}$ is $q \times n$.

Matrix multiplication is associative and we can therefore omit the brackets.

(c) Distributive law over multiplication by a scalar

$$(\lambda\boldsymbol{A})\boldsymbol{B} = \boldsymbol{A}(\lambda\boldsymbol{B}) = \lambda\boldsymbol{AB} \text{ holds}$$

(d) Distributive law over addition

$$(\boldsymbol{A} + \boldsymbol{B})\boldsymbol{C} = \boldsymbol{AC} + \boldsymbol{BC} \quad \text{and} \quad \boldsymbol{A}(\boldsymbol{B} + \boldsymbol{C}) = \boldsymbol{AB} + \boldsymbol{AC}$$

so we can multiply out brackets in the usual way, but making sure that the order of the products is maintained.

(e) Multiplication by unit matrices

If $\boldsymbol{A}$ is an $m \times n$ matrix and if $\boldsymbol{I}_m$ and $\boldsymbol{I}_n$ are the unit matrices of orders m and n then

$$\boldsymbol{I}_m\boldsymbol{A} = \boldsymbol{A}\boldsymbol{I}_n = \boldsymbol{A}$$

Thus pre- or post-multiplication by the appropriate unit matrix leaves $\boldsymbol{A}$ unchanged.

(f) Transpose of a product

$$(\boldsymbol{AB})^{\mathrm{T}} = \boldsymbol{B}^{\mathrm{T}}\boldsymbol{A}^{\mathrm{T}}$$

where $\boldsymbol{A}$ is an $m \times p$ matrix and $\boldsymbol{B}$ a $p \times n$ matrix. The proof follows from the definition of matrix transpose and matrix multiplication but requires careful treatment of summation signs. Thus the transpose of the product of matrices is the product of the transposed matrices in the reverse order.

Example 5.6 Given the matrices

$$\boldsymbol{A} = \begin{bmatrix} 1 & 2 & 2 \\ 0 & 1 & 1 \\ 1 & 0 & 1 \end{bmatrix}, \quad \boldsymbol{B} = \begin{bmatrix} 1 & -2 & 0 \\ 1 & -1 & -1 \\ -1 & 2 & 1 \end{bmatrix}, \quad \boldsymbol{X} = \begin{bmatrix} x \\ y \\ z \end{bmatrix} \quad \text{and} \quad \boldsymbol{c} = \begin{bmatrix} 1 \\ 0 \\ 1 \end{bmatrix}$$

(a) find (i) $\boldsymbol{AB}$, (ii) $(\boldsymbol{AB})^{\mathrm{T}}$ and (iii) $\boldsymbol{B}^{\mathrm{T}}\boldsymbol{A}^{\mathrm{T}}$;

(b) pre-multiply each side of the equation $\boldsymbol{BX} = \boldsymbol{c}$ by $\boldsymbol{A}$.

Solution (a) It would be a useful exercise to check these products using MATLAB or MAPLE.

(i) $\boldsymbol{AB} = \begin{bmatrix} 1 & 2 & 2 \\ 0 & 1 & 1 \\ 1 & 0 & 1 \end{bmatrix}\begin{bmatrix} 1 & -2 & 0 \\ 1 & -1 & -1 \\ -1 & 2 & 1 \end{bmatrix} = \begin{bmatrix} 1 & 0 & 0 \\ 0 & 1 & 0 \\ 0 & 0 & 1 \end{bmatrix} = \boldsymbol{I}$

The MATLAB commands

```
A = [1 2 2; 0 1 1; 1 0 1];
B = [1 -2 0; 1 -1 -1; -1 2 1]; A*B
```

produce the correct unit matrix.

(ii) $(\boldsymbol{AB})^{\mathrm{T}} = \begin{bmatrix} 1 & 0 & 0 \\ 0 & 1 & 0 \\ 0 & 0 & 1 \end{bmatrix} = \boldsymbol{I}$

(iii) $\boldsymbol{B}^{\mathrm{T}}\boldsymbol{A}^{\mathrm{T}} = \begin{bmatrix} 1 & 1 & -1 \\ -2 & -1 & 2 \\ 0 & -1 & 1 \end{bmatrix}\begin{bmatrix} 1 & 0 & 1 \\ 2 & 1 & 0 \\ 2 & 1 & 1 \end{bmatrix} = \begin{bmatrix} 1 & 0 & 0 \\ 0 & 1 & 0 \\ 0 & 0 & 1 \end{bmatrix} = \boldsymbol{I}$

(b) The equation $\boldsymbol{BX} = \boldsymbol{c}$ can be rewritten as

$$\begin{bmatrix} 1 & -2 & 0 \\ 1 & -1 & -1 \\ -1 & 2 & 1 \end{bmatrix}\begin{bmatrix} x \\ y \\ z \end{bmatrix} = \begin{bmatrix} 1 \\ 0 \\ 1 \end{bmatrix} \quad \text{or} \quad \begin{aligned} x - 2y \quad &= 1 \\ x - y - z &= 0 \\ -x + 2y + z &= 1 \end{aligned}$$

If we now pre-multiply the equation by $\boldsymbol{A}$ we obtain

$$\boldsymbol{ABX} = \boldsymbol{Ac}$$

and since $\boldsymbol{AB} = \boldsymbol{I}$, we obtain

$$\boldsymbol{IX} = \begin{bmatrix} 1 & 2 & 2 \\ 0 & 1 & 1 \\ 1 & 0 & 1 \end{bmatrix}\begin{bmatrix} 1 \\ 0 \\ 1 \end{bmatrix} = \begin{bmatrix} 3 \\ 1 \\ 2 \end{bmatrix} \quad \text{or} \quad \begin{bmatrix} x \\ y \\ z \end{bmatrix} = \begin{bmatrix} 3 \\ 1 \\ 2 \end{bmatrix}$$

and we see that we have a solution to our set of linear equations.

In MATLAB the solution $\boldsymbol{X}$ to the set of linear equations $\boldsymbol{BX} = \boldsymbol{c}$ is determined by the command `B\c`. Check that the commands

```
B = [1 -2 0; 1 -1 -1; -1 2 1];
c = [1;0;1];
B\c
```

return the given answer.

Example 5.7

Given the three matrices

$$\boldsymbol{A} = \begin{bmatrix} 1 & -1 & 1 \\ -2 & 0 & 3 \\ 0 & 1 & -2 \end{bmatrix}, \quad \boldsymbol{B} = \begin{bmatrix} 0 & 0 & 1 \\ 0 & 2 & 3 \\ 1 & 2 & 3 \end{bmatrix} \quad \text{and} \quad \boldsymbol{C} = \begin{bmatrix} 2 & 3 \\ -1 & 2 \\ -3 & 1 \end{bmatrix}$$

verify the associative law and the distributive law over addition.

Solution

Now $\boldsymbol{BC} = \begin{bmatrix} 0 & 0 & 1 \\ 0 & 2 & 3 \\ 1 & 2 & 3 \end{bmatrix}\begin{bmatrix} 2 & 3 \\ -1 & 2 \\ -3 & 1 \end{bmatrix} = \begin{bmatrix} -3 & 1 \\ -11 & 7 \\ -9 & 10 \end{bmatrix}$ and

$$\boldsymbol{A}(\boldsymbol{BC}) = \begin{bmatrix} 1 & -1 & 1 \\ -2 & 0 & 3 \\ 0 & 1 & -2 \end{bmatrix}\begin{bmatrix} -3 & 1 \\ -11 & 7 \\ -9 & 10 \end{bmatrix} = \begin{bmatrix} -1 & 4 \\ -21 & 28 \\ 7 & -13 \end{bmatrix}$$

Likewise $\boldsymbol{AB} = \begin{bmatrix} 1 & -1 & 1 \\ -2 & 0 & 3 \\ 0 & 1 & -2 \end{bmatrix}\begin{bmatrix} 0 & 0 & 1 \\ 0 & 2 & 3 \\ 1 & 2 & 3 \end{bmatrix} = \begin{bmatrix} 1 & 0 & 1 \\ 3 & 6 & 7 \\ -2 & -2 & -3 \end{bmatrix}$ and

$$(\boldsymbol{AB})\boldsymbol{C} = \begin{bmatrix} 1 & 0 & 1 \\ 3 & 6 & 7 \\ -2 & -2 & -3 \end{bmatrix}\begin{bmatrix} 2 & 3 \\ -1 & 2 \\ -3 & 1 \end{bmatrix} = \begin{bmatrix} -1 & 4 \\ -21 & 28 \\ 7 & -13 \end{bmatrix}$$

Thus the associative law is satisfied for these three matrices. For the distributive law we need to evaluate

$$(\boldsymbol{A} + \boldsymbol{B})\boldsymbol{C} = \begin{bmatrix} 1 & -1 & 2 \\ -2 & 2 & 6 \\ 1 & 3 & 1 \end{bmatrix}\begin{bmatrix} 2 & 3 \\ -1 & 2 \\ -3 & 1 \end{bmatrix} = \begin{bmatrix} -3 & 3 \\ -24 & 4 \\ -4 & 10 \end{bmatrix}$$

and

$$\boldsymbol{AC} + \boldsymbol{BC} = \begin{bmatrix} 1 & -1 & 1 \\ -2 & 0 & 3 \\ 0 & 1 & -2 \end{bmatrix}\begin{bmatrix} 2 & 3 \\ -1 & 2 \\ -3 & 1 \end{bmatrix} + \begin{bmatrix} 0 & 0 & 1 \\ 0 & 2 & 3 \\ 1 & 2 & 3 \end{bmatrix}\begin{bmatrix} 2 & 3 \\ -1 & 2 \\ -3 & 1 \end{bmatrix}$$

$$= \begin{bmatrix} 0 & 2 \\ -13 & -3 \\ 5 & 0 \end{bmatrix} + \begin{bmatrix} -3 & 1 \\ -11 & 7 \\ -9 & 10 \end{bmatrix} = \begin{bmatrix} -3 & 3 \\ -24 & 4 \\ -4 & 10 \end{bmatrix}$$

The two matrices are equal, so the distributive law is verified for the three given matrices.

Example 5.8 Show that the transformation

$$\begin{bmatrix} x' \\ y' \end{bmatrix} = \begin{bmatrix} \cos\theta & \sin\theta \\ -\sin\theta & \cos\theta \end{bmatrix}\begin{bmatrix} x \\ y \end{bmatrix}$$

with $\theta = 60°$, maps the square with corners $\begin{bmatrix} 1 \\ 1 \end{bmatrix}, \begin{bmatrix} 1 \\ 2 \end{bmatrix}, \begin{bmatrix} 2 \\ 2 \end{bmatrix}$ and $\begin{bmatrix} 2 \\ 1 \end{bmatrix}$ onto a square.

Solution Substituting the given vectors in turn for $\begin{bmatrix} x \\ y \end{bmatrix}$ into the equation

$$\begin{bmatrix} x' \\ y' \end{bmatrix} = \begin{bmatrix} 0.5 & 0.8660 \\ -0.8660 & 0.5 \end{bmatrix}\begin{bmatrix} x \\ y \end{bmatrix}$$

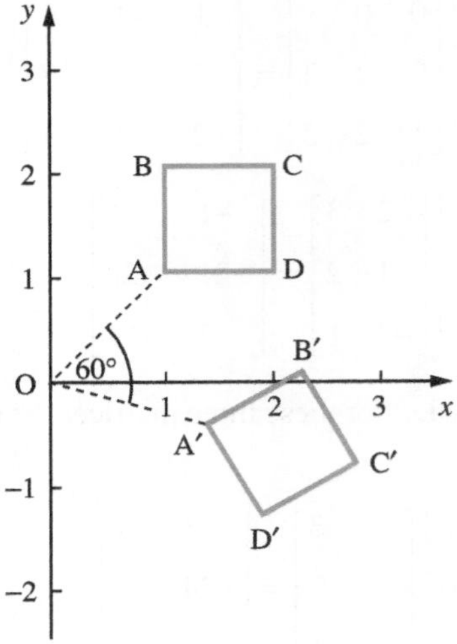

Figure 5.4
Transformation of a square in Example 5.8.

we find the following vectors for $\begin{bmatrix} x' \\ y' \end{bmatrix}$

$$\begin{bmatrix} 1.366 \\ -0.366 \end{bmatrix}, \quad \begin{bmatrix} 2.232 \\ 0.134 \end{bmatrix}, \quad \begin{bmatrix} 2.732 \\ -0.732 \end{bmatrix} \quad \text{and} \quad \begin{bmatrix} 1.866 \\ -1.232 \end{bmatrix}$$

Plotting these points on the plane, as in Figure 5.4, we see that the square has been rotated through an angle of 60° about the origin. It is left as an exercise for the reader to verify the result.

This type of analysis forms the basis of manipulation of diagrams on a computer screen, and is used in many CAD/CAM situations.

Example 5.9

In quantum mechanics the components of the spin of an electron can be repesented by the Pauli matrices

$$\boldsymbol{A} = \begin{bmatrix} 0 & 1 \\ 1 & 0 \end{bmatrix}, \quad \boldsymbol{B} = \begin{bmatrix} 0 & -\mathrm{j} \\ \mathrm{j} & 0 \end{bmatrix}, \quad \boldsymbol{C} = \begin{bmatrix} 1 & 0 \\ 0 & -1 \end{bmatrix}$$

Show that

(a) the matrices anticommute:

$$\boldsymbol{AB} + \boldsymbol{BA} = 0, \quad \boldsymbol{BC} + \boldsymbol{CB} = 0, \quad \boldsymbol{CA} + \boldsymbol{AC} = 0$$

(b) $\boldsymbol{AB} - \boldsymbol{BA} = 2\mathrm{j}\boldsymbol{C}, \quad \boldsymbol{BC} - \boldsymbol{CB} = 2\mathrm{j}\boldsymbol{A}, \quad \boldsymbol{CA} - \boldsymbol{AC} = 2\mathrm{j}\boldsymbol{B}$

(c) $\boldsymbol{AB} = \mathrm{j}\boldsymbol{C}, \quad \boldsymbol{BC} = \mathrm{j}\boldsymbol{A}, \quad \boldsymbol{CA} = \mathrm{j}\boldsymbol{B}$

Solution (a) $\boldsymbol{AB} = \begin{bmatrix} 0 & 1 \\ 1 & 0 \end{bmatrix}\begin{bmatrix} 0 & -j \\ j & 0 \end{bmatrix} = \begin{bmatrix} j & 0 \\ 0 & -j \end{bmatrix}$ and $\boldsymbol{BA} = \begin{bmatrix} 0 & -j \\ j & 0 \end{bmatrix}\begin{bmatrix} 0 & 1 \\ 1 & 0 \end{bmatrix} = \begin{bmatrix} -j & 0 \\ 0 & j \end{bmatrix}$

so

$$\boldsymbol{AB} + \boldsymbol{BA} = 0$$

and the other two results follow similarly.

(b) From part (a)

$$\boldsymbol{AB} - \boldsymbol{BA} = \begin{bmatrix} j & 0 \\ 0 & -j \end{bmatrix} - \begin{bmatrix} -j & 0 \\ 0 & j \end{bmatrix} = \begin{bmatrix} 2j & 0 \\ 0 & -2j \end{bmatrix} = 2j\boldsymbol{C}$$

and again the other two results follow similarly.

(c) These results can be obtained directly from part (a) since $\boldsymbol{AB}$ has already been calculated, similarly for $\boldsymbol{BC}$ and $\boldsymbol{CA}$.

Note: This example illustrates the use of matrices that have complex elements. Pauli discovered that the matrices $\boldsymbol{A}$, $\boldsymbol{B}$ and $\boldsymbol{C}$ have the properties (a), (b) and (c) required of the components of the spin of an electron.

Example 5.10 A rectangular site is to be levelled, and the amount of earth that needs to be removed must be determined. A survey of the site at a regular mesh of points 10 m apart is made. The heights in metres above the level required are given in the following table.

0	0.31	0.40	0.45	0.51	0.60
0.12	0.33	0.51	0.58	0.66	0.75
0.19	0.38	0.60	0.69	0.78	0.86
0.25	0.46	0.68	0.77	0.89	0.97

It is known that the approximate volume of a cell of side x and with corner heights of a, b, c and d is

$$V = \tfrac{1}{4}x^2(a + b + c + d)$$

Write the total approximate volume in matrix form and hence estimate the volume to be removed.

Solution Note that for the first row of cells the volume is

$$\begin{aligned} 25(\ 0 \quad &+ 0.31 \quad +0.31 + 0.40 \quad +0.40 + 0.45 \quad +0.45 + 0.51 \quad +0.51 + 0.60 \\ &+0.12 + 0.33 \quad +0.33 + 0.51 \quad +0.51 + 0.58 \quad +0.58 + 0.66 \quad +0.66 + 0.75) \end{aligned}$$

$$\begin{aligned} &= 25[0 + 2(0.31 + 0.40 + 0.45 + 0.51) + 0.60] \\ &\quad + 25[0.12 + 2(0.33 + 0.51 + 0.58 + 0.66) + 0.75] \end{aligned}$$

The second and third rows of cells are dealt with in a similar manner, so that, when we compute the total volume, we need to multiply the corner values by 1, the other side values by 2 and the centre values by 4. In matrix form this multiplication can be performed as

$$
\begin{bmatrix} 1 & 2 & 2 & 1 \end{bmatrix}
\begin{bmatrix} 0 & 0.31 & 0.40 & 0.45 & 0.51 & 0.60 \\ 0.12 & 0.33 & 0.51 & 0.58 & 0.66 & 0.75 \\ 0.19 & 0.38 & 0.60 & 0.69 & 0.78 & 0.86 \\ 0.25 & 0.46 & 0.68 & 0.77 & 0.86 & 0.97 \end{bmatrix}
\begin{bmatrix} 1 \\ 2 \\ 2 \\ 2 \\ 2 \\ 1 \end{bmatrix}
$$

This can be checked by multiplying the matrices out. The checking can be done on one of the symbolic manipulation packages, such as MAPLE or the Symbolic Math Toolbox of MATLAB, by putting in general symbols for the matrix and verifying that, after the matrix multiplications, the elements are multiplied by the stated factors. Performing the calculation and multiplying by the 25 gives the total volume as $816.5\,m^3$.

A similar analysis can be applied to other situations – all that is needed is measured heights and a matrix multiplication routine on a computer to deal with the large amount of data that would be required. For other mesh shapes, or even irregular meshes, the method is similar, but the multiplying vectors will need careful calculation.

Example 5.11 A contractor makes two products P_1 and P_2. The four components required to make the products are subcontracted out and each of the components is made up from three ingredients A, B and C as follows:

Component	*Units of A*	*Units of B*	*Units of C*	*Make-up cost and profit for subcontractor*
1 requires	5	4	3	10
2 requires	2	1	1	7
3 requires	0	1	3	5
4 requires	3	4	1	2

The cost per unit of the ingredients A, B and C are a, b and c respectively. The contractor makes the product P_1 with 2 of component 1, 3 of component 2 and 4 of component 4, and the make-up cost is 15; product P_2 requires 1 of component 1, 1 of component 2, 1 of component 3 and 2 of component 4, and the make-up cost is 12. Find the cost to the contractor for P_1 and P_2. What is the change in costs if a increases to $(a + 1)$? It is found that the 5 units of A required for component 1 can be reduced to 4. What is the effect on the costs?

Solution The information presented can be written naturally in matrix form. Let C_1, C_2, C_3 and C_4 be the cost the subcontractor charges the contractor for the four components, then the cost C_1 is computed as $C_1 = 5a + 4b + 3c + 10$. This expression is the first row of the matrix equation

$$\begin{bmatrix} C_1 \\ C_2 \\ C_3 \\ C_4 \end{bmatrix} = \begin{bmatrix} 5 & 4 & 3 \\ 2 & 1 & 1 \\ 0 & 1 & 3 \\ 3 & 4 & 1 \end{bmatrix} \begin{bmatrix} a \\ b \\ c \end{bmatrix} + \begin{bmatrix} 10 \\ 7 \\ 5 \\ 2 \end{bmatrix}$$

and the other three costs follow in a similar manner. Now let p_1, p_2 be the costs of producing the final products. The costs are constructed in exactly the same way as

$$\begin{bmatrix} p_1 \\ p_2 \end{bmatrix} = \begin{bmatrix} 2 & 3 & 0 & 4 \\ 1 & 1 & 1 & 2 \end{bmatrix} \begin{bmatrix} C_1 \\ C_2 \\ C_3 \\ C_4 \end{bmatrix} + \begin{bmatrix} 15 \\ 12 \end{bmatrix}$$

Substituting gives

$$\begin{bmatrix} p_1 \\ p_2 \end{bmatrix} = \begin{bmatrix} 2 & 3 & 0 & 4 \\ 1 & 1 & 1 & 2 \end{bmatrix} \begin{bmatrix} 5 & 4 & 3 \\ 2 & 1 & 1 \\ 0 & 1 & 3 \\ 3 & 4 & 1 \end{bmatrix} \begin{bmatrix} a \\ b \\ c \end{bmatrix} + \begin{bmatrix} 2 & 3 & 0 & 4 \\ 1 & 1 & 1 & 2 \end{bmatrix} \begin{bmatrix} 10 \\ 7 \\ 5 \\ 2 \end{bmatrix} + \begin{bmatrix} 15 \\ 12 \end{bmatrix}$$

or

$$\begin{bmatrix} p_1 \\ p_2 \end{bmatrix} = \begin{bmatrix} 28 & 27 & 13 \\ 13 & 14 & 9 \end{bmatrix} \begin{bmatrix} a \\ b \\ c \end{bmatrix} + \begin{bmatrix} 64 \\ 38 \end{bmatrix}$$

Thus a simple matrix formulation gives a convenient way of coding the data. If a is increased to $(a + 1)$ then multiplying out shows that p_1 increases by 28 and p_2 by 13. If the 5 in the first matrix is reduced to 4 then the costs will be

$$\begin{bmatrix} p_1 \\ p_2 \end{bmatrix} = \begin{bmatrix} 26 & 27 & 13 \\ 12 & 14 & 9 \end{bmatrix} \begin{bmatrix} a \\ b \\ c \end{bmatrix} + \begin{bmatrix} 64 \\ 38 \end{bmatrix}$$

so p_1 is reduced by $2a$ and p_2 by a.

A similar approach can be used in more complicated, realistic situations. Storing and processing the information is convenient, particularly in conjunction with a computer package or spreadsheet.

Example 5.12 (a) Given the matrix $\boldsymbol{A} = \begin{bmatrix} \frac{3}{2} & -1 \\ 1 & -1 \end{bmatrix}$ verify that

$$\mathbf{A}\begin{bmatrix}2\\1\end{bmatrix}=\begin{bmatrix}2\\1\end{bmatrix} \text{ and } \mathbf{A}\begin{bmatrix}1\\2\end{bmatrix}=\left(-\tfrac{1}{2}\right)\begin{bmatrix}1\\2\end{bmatrix}$$

and show that $2\mathbf{A}^2 = \mathbf{A} + \mathbf{I}$.

(b) By repeated application of this result show also that for any integer n

$$\mathbf{A}^n = \alpha\mathbf{A} + \beta\mathbf{I}$$

for some α, β.

Solution (a) The first two results follow by applying matrix multiplication; the importance of such results will be seen in Section 5.7 on eigenvalues. The next result follows since

$$\mathbf{A}^2 = \begin{bmatrix}\frac{3}{2} & -1\\ 1 & -1\end{bmatrix}\begin{bmatrix}\frac{3}{2} & -1\\ 1 & -1\end{bmatrix} = \begin{bmatrix}\frac{5}{4} & -\frac{1}{2}\\ \frac{1}{2} & 0\end{bmatrix} \quad \text{and} \quad \mathbf{A}+\mathbf{I} = \begin{bmatrix}\frac{5}{2} & -1\\ 1 & 0\end{bmatrix}$$

and hence $2\mathbf{A}^2 = \mathbf{A} + \mathbf{I}$.

(b) To show the final result, note that multiplying by $2\mathbf{A}$ gives

$$4\mathbf{A}^3 = 2\mathbf{A}^2 + 2\mathbf{A} = (\mathbf{A} + \mathbf{I}) + 2\mathbf{A} = 3\mathbf{A} + \mathbf{I}$$

and repeating the process, multiplying by $2\mathbf{A}$

$$8\mathbf{A}^4 = 6\mathbf{A}^2 + 2\mathbf{A} = 3(\mathbf{A} + \mathbf{I}) + 2\mathbf{A} = 5\mathbf{A} + 3\mathbf{I}$$

The process of multiplying by $2\mathbf{A}$ and replacing $2\mathbf{A}^2$ by $(\mathbf{A} + \mathbf{I})$ can be applied repeatedly to give the final result.

Example 5.13 Find the values of x that make the matrix $\mathbf{Z}^5$ a diagonal matrix, where

$$\mathbf{Z} = \begin{bmatrix}x & 0 & 0\\ 0 & x & 1\\ 0 & -1 & 0\end{bmatrix}$$

Solution Although this problem can be done by hand it is tedious and a MAPLE solution is given.

```
with (linalg):
Z:= array ([[x, 0, 0], [0, x, 1], [0, -1, 0]]):
Z5:= simplify (multiply (Z, Z, Z, Z, Z));
```

$$Z5 := \begin{bmatrix}x^5 & 0 & 0\\ 0 & 3x - 4x^3 + x^5 & 1 - 3x^2 + x^4\\ 0 & -1 + 3x^2 - x^4 & 2x - x^3\end{bmatrix}$$

```
evalf (solve ({Z5 [2, 3] = 0}, {x}));
{x = 1.618}, {x =-0.618}, {x = 0.618}, {x =-1.618}
```

Using MATLAB's Symbolic Math Toolbox the commands

```
syms x
Z = syms([x 0 0; 0 x 1; 0 -1 0]);
Z5 = Z^5; simplify(Z5);
pretty(ans)
```

produce the same matrix as above. The additional commands

```
solve(1 - 3*x^2 + x^4); double(ans)
```

produce the same values of x.

5.2.7 Exercises

Check the answers to the exercises using MATLAB or MAPLE whenever possible.

19 Given the matrices

$$\boldsymbol{A} = \begin{bmatrix} 1 & 0 & 1 \\ 2 & 1 & 2 \end{bmatrix}, \quad \boldsymbol{B} = \begin{bmatrix} 0 & 1 \\ 1 & 0 \\ 0 & 1 \end{bmatrix},$$

$$\boldsymbol{C} = \begin{bmatrix} 2 & 1 \\ -1 & 2 \end{bmatrix}$$

evaluate where possible

$$\boldsymbol{AB}, \boldsymbol{BA}, \boldsymbol{BC}, \boldsymbol{CB}, \boldsymbol{CA}, \boldsymbol{AC}$$

20 For the matrices

$$\boldsymbol{A} = \begin{bmatrix} 1 & 1 \\ 0 & 1 \end{bmatrix} \quad \text{and} \quad \boldsymbol{B} = \begin{bmatrix} 0 & 1 \\ 1 & 0 \end{bmatrix}$$

(a) evaluate $(\boldsymbol{A} + \boldsymbol{B})^2$ and $\boldsymbol{A}^2 + 2\boldsymbol{AB} + \boldsymbol{B}^2$

(b) evaluate $(\boldsymbol{A} + \boldsymbol{B})(\boldsymbol{A} - \boldsymbol{B})$ and $\boldsymbol{A}^2 - \boldsymbol{B}^2$

Repeat the calculations with the matrices

$$\boldsymbol{A} = \begin{bmatrix} 1 & 2 \\ 5 & 2 \end{bmatrix} \quad \text{and} \quad \boldsymbol{B} = \begin{bmatrix} 2 & -2 \\ -5 & 1 \end{bmatrix}$$

and explain the differences between the results for the two sets.

21 Show that for a square matrix $(\boldsymbol{A}^2)^{\mathrm{T}} = (\boldsymbol{A}^{\mathrm{T}})^2$.

22 Show that $\boldsymbol{AA}^{\mathrm{T}}$ is a symmetric matrix.

23 Find all the 2×2 matrices that commute (that is $\boldsymbol{AB} = \boldsymbol{BA}$) with $\begin{bmatrix} 1 & -1 \\ 0 & 2 \end{bmatrix}$.

24 A matrix with m rows and n columns is said to be of type $m \times n$. Give simple examples of matrices $\boldsymbol{A}$ and $\boldsymbol{B}$ to illustrate the following situations:

(a) $\boldsymbol{AB}$ is defined but $\boldsymbol{BA}$ is not;

(b) $\boldsymbol{AB}$ and $\boldsymbol{BA}$ are both defined but have different type;

(c) $\boldsymbol{AB}$ and $\boldsymbol{BA}$ are both defined and have the same type but are unequal.

25 Given

$$\boldsymbol{A} = \begin{bmatrix} 1 & 3 & 2 \\ 2 & -1 & 0 \\ 1 & 4 & 1 \end{bmatrix}$$

determine a symmetric matrix $\boldsymbol{C}$ and a skew-symmetric matrix $\boldsymbol{D}$ such that

$$\boldsymbol{A} = \boldsymbol{C} + \boldsymbol{D}$$

26 Given the matrices

$$\boldsymbol{a} = [3 \quad 2 \quad -1], \quad \boldsymbol{b} = \begin{bmatrix} 11 \\ 0 \\ 2 \end{bmatrix} \quad \text{and}$$

$$\boldsymbol{C} = \begin{bmatrix} 4 & 1 & 1 \\ -1 & 7 & -3 \\ -1 & 3 & 5 \end{bmatrix}$$

determine the elements of $\boldsymbol{G}$ where

$$(ab)\boldsymbol{I} + \boldsymbol{C}^2 = \boldsymbol{C}^T + \boldsymbol{G}$$

and $\boldsymbol{I}$ is the unit matrix.

27 A firm allocates staff into four categories: welders, fitters, designers and administrators. It is estimated that for their three main products the time spent, in hours, on each item is given in the following matrix.

	Boiler	Water tank	Holding frame
Welder	2	0.75	1.25
Fitter	1.4	0.5	1.75
Designer	0.3	0.1	0.1
Admin	0.1	0.25	0.3

The wages, pension contributions and overheads, in £ per hour, are known to be

	Welder	Fitter	Designer	Administrator
Wages	12	8	20	10
Pension	1	0.5	2	1
O/heads	0	0	1	3

Write the problem in matrix form and use matrix products to find the total cost of producing 10 boilers, 25 water tanks and 35 frames.

28 Given

$$\boldsymbol{A} = \begin{bmatrix} 1 & 1 & 1 \\ 2 & 1 & 2 \\ -2 & 1 & -1 \end{bmatrix}$$

evaluate $\boldsymbol{A}^2$ and $\boldsymbol{A}^3$. Verify that

$$\boldsymbol{A}^3 - \boldsymbol{A}^2 - 3\boldsymbol{A} + \boldsymbol{I} = 0$$

29 Given

$$\boldsymbol{A} = \begin{bmatrix} 5 & -2 & 0 \\ -2 & 6 & 2 \\ 0 & 2 & 7 \end{bmatrix} \quad \text{and} \quad \boldsymbol{X} = \begin{bmatrix} x_1 \\ x_2 \\ x_3 \end{bmatrix}$$

show that

$$\boldsymbol{X}^T\boldsymbol{A}\boldsymbol{X} = 27 \qquad \textbf{(5.6)}$$

implies that

$$5x_1^2 + 6x_2^2 + 7x_3^2 - 4x_1x_2 + 4x_2x_3 = 27$$

Under the transformation

$$\boldsymbol{X} = \boldsymbol{B}\boldsymbol{Y}$$

show that (5.6) becomes

$$\boldsymbol{Y}^T(\boldsymbol{B}^T\boldsymbol{A}\boldsymbol{B})\boldsymbol{Y} = 27$$

If

$$\boldsymbol{B} = \begin{bmatrix} 2 & 2 & -1 \\ 2 & -1 & 2 \\ -1 & 2 & 2 \end{bmatrix} \quad \text{and} \quad \boldsymbol{Y} = \begin{bmatrix} y_1 \\ y_2 \\ y_3 \end{bmatrix}$$

evaluate $\boldsymbol{B}^T\boldsymbol{A}\boldsymbol{B}$, and hence show that

$$y_1^2 + 2y_2^2 + 3y_3^2 = 1$$

30 A well-known problem concerns a mythical country that has three cities, A, B and C, with a total population of 2400. At the end of each year it is decreed that all people must move to another city, half to one and half to the other. If a, b and c are the populations in the cities A, B and C respectively, show that in the next year the populations are given by

$$\begin{bmatrix} a' \\ b' \\ c' \end{bmatrix} = \begin{bmatrix} 0 & \frac{1}{2} & \frac{1}{2} \\ \frac{1}{2} & 0 & \frac{1}{2} \\ \frac{1}{2} & \frac{1}{2} & 0 \end{bmatrix} \begin{bmatrix} a \\ b \\ c \end{bmatrix}$$

Supposing that the three cities have initial populations of 600, 800 and 1000, what are the populations after 10 years and after a very long time (a package such as MATLAB is ideal for the calculations)? (Note that this example is a version of a **Markov chain** problem. Markov chains have applications in many areas of science and engineering.)

31 Find values of h, k, l and m so that $\boldsymbol{A} \neq 0$, $\boldsymbol{B} \neq 0$, $\boldsymbol{A}^2 = \boldsymbol{A}$, $\boldsymbol{B}^2 = \boldsymbol{B}$ and $\boldsymbol{AB} = 0$, where

$$\boldsymbol{A} = h\begin{bmatrix} 1 & 1 & 1 \\ 1 & 1 & 1 \\ 1 & 1 & 1 \end{bmatrix} \quad \text{and}$$

$$\boldsymbol{B} = \begin{bmatrix} k & -l & -l \\ -l & m & m \\ -l & m & m \end{bmatrix}$$

32 A computer screen has dimensions 20 cm × 30 cm. Axes are set up at the centre of the screen, as illustrated in Figure 5.5. A box containing an arrow has dimensions 2 cm × 2 cm and is situated with its centre at the point (−16, 10). It is first to be rotated through 45° in an anticlockwise direction. Find this transformation in the form

$$\begin{bmatrix} x' + 16 \\ y' - 10 \end{bmatrix} = \boldsymbol{A}\begin{bmatrix} x + 16 \\ y - 10 \end{bmatrix}$$

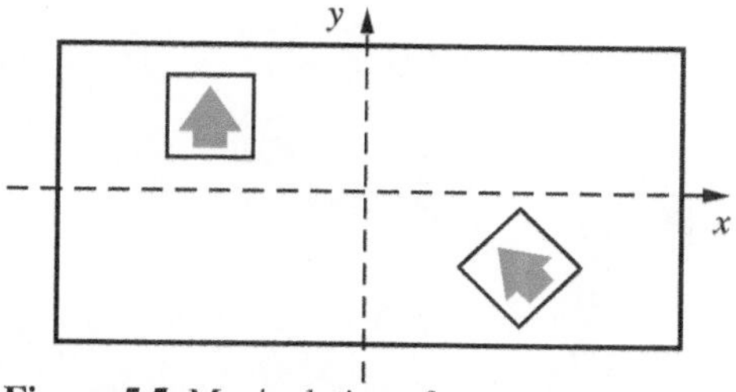

Figure 5.5 Manipulation of a computer screen in Question 32.

The rotated box is now moved to a new position with its centre at (16, −10). Find the overall transformation in the form

$$\begin{bmatrix} x'' \\ y'' \end{bmatrix} = \begin{bmatrix} a \\ b \end{bmatrix} + \mathbf{B}\begin{bmatrix} x \\ y \end{bmatrix}$$

33 Given the matrix

$$\mathbf{A} = \begin{bmatrix} 0 & 1 & 0 & 0 & 0 & 0 & 0 & 0 \\ 0 & 0 & 0 & 1 & 0 & 0 & 0 & 0 \\ 0 & 0 & 1 & 0 & 0 & 0 & 0 & 0 \\ 1 & 0 & 0 & 0 & 0 & 0 & 0 & 0 \\ 0 & 0 & 0 & 0 & 0 & 0 & 0 & 1 \\ 0 & 0 & 0 & 0 & 1 & 0 & 0 & 0 \\ 0 & 0 & 0 & 0 & 0 & 0 & 1 & 0 \\ 0 & 0 & 0 & 0 & 0 & 1 & 0 & 0 \end{bmatrix}$$

it is known that $\mathbf{A}^n = \mathbf{I}$, the unit matrix, for some integer n; find this value.

5.3 Determinants

The idea of a determinant is closely related to that of a square matrix and is crucial to the solution of linear equations. We shall deal here mainly with 2 × 2 and 3 × 3 determinants.

Given the square matrices

$$\mathbf{A} = \begin{bmatrix} a_{11} & a_{12} \\ a_{21} & a_{22} \end{bmatrix} \quad \text{and} \quad \mathbf{B} = \begin{bmatrix} a_{11} & a_{12} & a_{13} \\ a_{21} & a_{22} & a_{23} \\ a_{31} & a_{32} & a_{33} \end{bmatrix}$$

the **determinant** of $\mathbf{A}$, denoted by det $\mathbf{A}$ or $|\mathbf{A}|$, is given by

$$|\mathbf{A}| = a_{11}a_{22} - a_{12}a_{21} \tag{5.7}$$

For the 3 × 3 matrix $\mathbf{B}$

$$|\mathbf{B}| = a_{11}\begin{vmatrix} a_{22} & a_{23} \\ a_{32} & a_{33} \end{vmatrix} - a_{12}\begin{vmatrix} a_{21} & a_{23} \\ a_{31} & a_{33} \end{vmatrix} + a_{13}\begin{vmatrix} a_{21} & a_{22} \\ a_{31} & a_{32} \end{vmatrix} \tag{5.8}$$

This is known as the expansion of the determinant along the first row.

The determinant of a 1 × 1 matrix, $\mathbf{A} = [a]$, having a single entry a is simply its entry. Thus

$$|\mathbf{A}| = a$$

It is important that this be distinguished from mod a which is also written as $|a|$.

Example 5.14 Evaluate the third-order determinant

$$\begin{vmatrix} 1 & 2 & 4 \\ -1 & 0 & 3 \\ 3 & 1 & -2 \end{vmatrix}$$

Solution Expanding along the first row as in (5.8), we have

$$\begin{vmatrix} 1 & 2 & 4 \\ -1 & 0 & 3 \\ 3 & 1 & -2 \end{vmatrix} = 1\begin{vmatrix} 0 & 3 \\ 1 & -2 \end{vmatrix} - 2\begin{vmatrix} -1 & 3 \\ 3 & -2 \end{vmatrix} + 4\begin{vmatrix} -1 & 0 \\ 3 & 1 \end{vmatrix}$$

$$\begin{aligned} &= 1[(0)(-2) - (1)(3)] - 2[(-1)(-2) - (3)(3)] \\ &\quad + 4[(-1)(1) - (3)(0)] \quad \text{(using (5.7))} \\ &= 1(-3) - 2(-7) + 4(-1) \\ &= 7 \end{aligned}$$

If we take a determinant and delete row i and column j then the determinant remaining is called the **minor** M_{ij}. In general we can take *any* row (or column) and evaluate an $n \times n$ determinant $|\boldsymbol{A}|$ as

$$|\boldsymbol{A}| = \sum_{j=1}^{n} (-1)^{i+j} a_{ij} M_{ij} \tag{5.9}$$

The fact that the determinant is the same for *any* i requires detailed proof. The determinant in (5.8) is just the expansion (5.9) with $i = 1$ and $n = 3$ and gives the expansion by the first row.

The sign associated with a minor is given in the array

$$\begin{vmatrix} + & - & + & - & + & \cdots \\ - & + & - & + & - & \cdots \\ + & - & + & - & + & \cdots \\ \vdots & \vdots & \vdots & \vdots & \vdots & \end{vmatrix}$$

A minor multiplied by the appropriate sign is called the **cofactor** A_{ij} of the element, so

$$A_{ij} = (-1)^{i+j} M_{ij}$$

and thus

$$|\boldsymbol{A}| = \sum_{j} a_{ij} A_{ij}$$

Example 5.15 Evaluate the minors and cofactors of the determinant

$$|\mathbf{A}| = \begin{vmatrix} 3 & 4 & 5 \\ 6 & -4 & 2 \\ 2 & -1 & 1 \end{vmatrix}$$

associated with the first row, and hence evaluate the determinant.

Solution

$$\begin{vmatrix} 3 & 4 & 5 \\ 6 & -4 & 2 \\ 2 & -1 & 1 \end{vmatrix} \rightarrow \begin{vmatrix} -4 & 2 \\ -1 & 1 \end{vmatrix} = -4 - (-2) = -2$$

Element a_{11} has minor $M_{11} = -2$ and cofactor $A_{11} = -2$.

$$\begin{vmatrix} 3 & 4 & 5 \\ 6 & -4 & 2 \\ 2 & -1 & 1 \end{vmatrix} \rightarrow \begin{vmatrix} 6 & 2 \\ 2 & 1 \end{vmatrix} = 2$$

Element a_{12} has minor $M_{12} = 2$ and cofactor $A_{12} = -2$.

$$\begin{vmatrix} 3 & 4 & 5 \\ 6 & -4 & 2 \\ 2 & -1 & 1 \end{vmatrix} \rightarrow \begin{vmatrix} 6 & -4 \\ 2 & -1 \end{vmatrix} = 2$$

Element a_{13} has minor $M_{13} = 2$ and cofactor $A_{13} = 2$. Thus the determinant is

$$|\mathbf{A}| = 3 \times (-2) + 4 \times (-2) + 5 \times 2 = -4$$

It may be checked that the same result is obtained by expanding along any row (or column), care being taken to incorporate the correct signs.

The properties of determinants are not always obvious, and are often quite difficult to prove in full generality. The commonly useful row operations are as follows.

(a) Two rows (or columns) equal

$$|\mathbf{A}| = \begin{vmatrix} a_{11} & a_{12} & a_{13} \\ a_{21} & a_{22} & a_{23} \\ a_{21} & a_{22} & a_{23} \end{vmatrix} = a_{11}\begin{vmatrix} a_{22} & a_{23} \\ a_{22} & a_{23} \end{vmatrix} - a_{12}\begin{vmatrix} a_{21} & a_{23} \\ a_{21} & a_{23} \end{vmatrix} + a_{13}\begin{vmatrix} a_{21} & a_{22} \\ a_{21} & a_{22} \end{vmatrix} = 0$$

Thus if two rows (or columns) are the same, the determinant is zero.

(b) Multiple of a row by a scalar

$$|\boldsymbol{B}| = \begin{vmatrix} \lambda a_{11} & \lambda a_{12} & \lambda a_{13} \\ a_{21} & a_{22} & a_{23} \\ a_{31} & a_{32} & a_{33} \end{vmatrix} = \lambda|\boldsymbol{A}|$$

The proof of this result follows from the definition. A consequence of (a) and (b) is that if any row (or column) is a multiple of another row (or column) then the determinant is zero.

(c) Interchange of two rows (or columns)

Consider $|\boldsymbol{A}|$ and $|\boldsymbol{B}|$ in which rows 1 and 2 are interchanged

$$|\boldsymbol{A}| = \begin{vmatrix} a_{11} & a_{12} & a_{13} \\ a_{21} & a_{22} & a_{23} \\ a_{31} & a_{32} & a_{33} \end{vmatrix} \quad \text{and} \quad |\boldsymbol{B}| = \begin{vmatrix} a_{21} & a_{22} & a_{23} \\ a_{11} & a_{12} & a_{13} \\ a_{31} & a_{32} & a_{33} \end{vmatrix}$$

Expanding $|\boldsymbol{A}|$ by the first row,

$$|\boldsymbol{A}| = a_{11}\begin{vmatrix} a_{22} & a_{23} \\ a_{32} & a_{33} \end{vmatrix} - a_{12}\begin{vmatrix} a_{21} & a_{23} \\ a_{31} & a_{33} \end{vmatrix} + a_{13}\begin{vmatrix} a_{21} & a_{22} \\ a_{31} & a_{32} \end{vmatrix}$$

and $|\boldsymbol{B}|$ by the second row

$$|\boldsymbol{B}| = -a_{11}\begin{vmatrix} a_{22} & a_{23} \\ a_{32} & a_{33} \end{vmatrix} + a_{12}\begin{vmatrix} a_{21} & a_{23} \\ a_{31} & a_{33} \end{vmatrix} - a_{13}\begin{vmatrix} a_{21} & a_{22} \\ a_{31} & a_{32} \end{vmatrix}$$

Thus

$$|\boldsymbol{A}| = -|\boldsymbol{B}|$$

so that interchanging two rows changes the sign of the determinant. Entirely similar results apply when changing two columns.

(d) Addition rule

Expanding by the first row:

$$\begin{vmatrix} a_{11}+b_{11} & a_{12}+b_{12} & a_{13}+b_{13} \\ a_{21} & a_{22} & a_{23} \\ a_{31} & a_{32} & a_{33} \end{vmatrix}$$

$$= (a_{11}+b_{11})A_{11} + (a_{12}+b_{12})A_{12} + (a_{13}+b_{13})A_{13}$$

$$= (a_{11}A_{11} + a_{12}A_{12} + a_{13}A_{13}) + (b_{11}A_{11} + b_{12}A_{12} + b_{13}A_{13})$$

$$= \begin{vmatrix} a_{11} & a_{12} & a_{13} \\ a_{21} & a_{22} & a_{23} \\ a_{31} & a_{32} & a_{33} \end{vmatrix} + \begin{vmatrix} b_{11} & b_{12} & b_{13} \\ a_{21} & a_{22} & a_{23} \\ a_{31} & a_{32} & a_{33} \end{vmatrix}$$

It should be noted that $|\boldsymbol{A}+\boldsymbol{B}|$ is *not* equal to $|\boldsymbol{A}|+|\boldsymbol{B}|$ in *general*.

(e) Adding multiples of rows (or columns)

Consider

$$|\boldsymbol{A}| = \begin{vmatrix} a_{11} & a_{12} & a_{13} \\ a_{21} & a_{22} & a_{23} \\ a_{31} & a_{32} & a_{33} \end{vmatrix}$$

Then

$$|\boldsymbol{B}| = \begin{vmatrix} a_{11} + \lambda a_{21} & a_{12} + \lambda a_{22} & a_{13} + \lambda a_{23} \\ a_{21} & a_{22} & a_{23} \\ a_{31} & a_{32} & a_{33} \end{vmatrix}$$

$$= \begin{vmatrix} a_{11} & a_{12} & a_{13} \\ a_{21} & a_{22} & a_{23} \\ a_{31} & a_{32} & a_{33} \end{vmatrix} + \lambda \begin{vmatrix} a_{21} & a_{22} & a_{23} \\ a_{21} & a_{22} & a_{23} \\ a_{31} & a_{32} & a_{33} \end{vmatrix} \quad \text{(using (d) and then (b))}$$

$$= |\boldsymbol{A}| \quad \text{(since, by (a), the second determinant is zero)}$$

This means that adding multiples of rows (or columns) together makes no difference to the determinant.

(f) Transpose

$$|\boldsymbol{A}^{\mathrm{T}}| = |\boldsymbol{A}|$$

This just states that expanding by the first row or the first column gives the same result.

(g) Product

$$|\boldsymbol{AB}| = |\boldsymbol{A}||\boldsymbol{B}|$$

This result is difficult to prove generally, but it can be verified rather tediously for the 2 × 2 or 3 × 3 cases. For the 2 × 2 case

$$|\boldsymbol{A}||\boldsymbol{B}| = (a_{11}a_{22} - a_{12}a_{21})(b_{11}b_{22} - b_{12}b_{21})$$

$$= a_{11}a_{22}b_{11}b_{22} - a_{11}a_{22}b_{12}b_{21} - a_{12}a_{21}b_{11}b_{22} + a_{12}a_{21}b_{12}b_{21}$$

and

$$|\boldsymbol{AB}| = \begin{vmatrix} a_{11}b_{11} + a_{12}b_{21} & a_{11}b_{12} + a_{12}b_{22} \\ a_{21}b_{11} + a_{22}b_{21} & a_{21}b_{12} + a_{22}b_{22} \end{vmatrix}$$

$$= (a_{11}b_{11} + a_{12}b_{21})(a_{21}b_{12} + a_{22}b_{22}) - (a_{11}b_{12} + a_{12}b_{22})(a_{21}b_{11} + a_{22}b_{21})$$

$$= a_{11}a_{22}b_{11}b_{22} - a_{11}a_{22}b_{12}b_{21} - a_{12}a_{21}b_{11}b_{22} + a_{12}a_{21}b_{12}b_{21}$$

Example 5.16 Evaluate the 3×3 determinants

$$\text{(a)} \begin{vmatrix} 1 & 0 & 1 \\ 0 & 1 & 2 \\ 1 & 1 & 0 \end{vmatrix}, \quad \text{(b)} \begin{vmatrix} 1 & 0 & 1 \\ 1 & 1 & 0 \\ 0 & 1 & 2 \end{vmatrix}, \quad \text{(c)} \begin{vmatrix} 1 & 1 & 0 \\ 0 & 1 & 1 \\ 1 & 0 & 2 \end{vmatrix}, \quad \text{(d)} \begin{vmatrix} 1 & 0 & 1 \\ 0 & 2 & 4 \\ 3 & 3 & 0 \end{vmatrix}$$

Solution (a) Expand by the first row:

$$\begin{vmatrix} 1 & 0 & 1 \\ 0 & 1 & 2 \\ 1 & 1 & 0 \end{vmatrix} = 1\begin{vmatrix} 1 & 2 \\ 1 & 0 \end{vmatrix} - 0\begin{vmatrix} 0 & 2 \\ 1 & 0 \end{vmatrix} + 1\begin{vmatrix} 0 & 1 \\ 1 & 1 \end{vmatrix} = -2 - 0 - 1 = -3$$

(b) Expand by the first column:

$$\begin{vmatrix} 1 & 0 & 1 \\ 1 & 1 & 0 \\ 0 & 1 & 2 \end{vmatrix} = 1\begin{vmatrix} 1 & 0 \\ 1 & 2 \end{vmatrix} - 1\begin{vmatrix} 0 & 1 \\ 1 & 2 \end{vmatrix} + 0\begin{vmatrix} 0 & 1 \\ 1 & 0 \end{vmatrix} = 2 + 1 + 0 = 3$$

Note that (a) and (b) are the same determinant, but with two rows interchanged. The result confirms property (c) just stated above.

(c) Expand by the third row:

$$\begin{vmatrix} 1 & 1 & 0 \\ 0 & 1 & 1 \\ 1 & 0 & 2 \end{vmatrix} = 1\begin{vmatrix} 1 & 0 \\ 1 & 1 \end{vmatrix} - 0\begin{vmatrix} 1 & 0 \\ 0 & 1 \end{vmatrix} + 2\begin{vmatrix} 1 & 1 \\ 0 & 1 \end{vmatrix} = 1 - 0 + 2 = 3$$

Note that the matrix associated with the determinant in (c) is just the transpose of the matrix associated with the determinant in (b).

$$\text{(d)} \quad \begin{vmatrix} 1 & 0 & 1 \\ 0 & 2 & 4 \\ 3 & 3 & 0 \end{vmatrix} = 2\begin{vmatrix} 1 & 0 & 1 \\ 0 & 1 & 2 \\ 3 & 3 & 0 \end{vmatrix} = 6\begin{vmatrix} 1 & 0 & 1 \\ 0 & 1 & 2 \\ 1 & 1 & 0 \end{vmatrix} = -18$$

Note that we have used the multiple of a row rule on two occasions; the final determinant is the same as (a).

In MATLAB and MAPLE the determinant of a matrix $\boldsymbol{A}$ is given by the command `det(A)`. Considering Example 5.16(d) the MATLAB commands

```
A = [1 0 1; 0 2 4; 3 3 0];
det(A)
```

return the answer `-18`.

Example 5.17 Given the matrices

$$\boldsymbol{A} = \begin{bmatrix} 1 & 2 & 3 \\ 2 & 3 & 4 \\ 4 & 5 & 6 \end{bmatrix} \quad \text{and} \quad \boldsymbol{B} = \begin{bmatrix} 1 & 0 & 1 \\ 1 & 1 & 1 \\ 1 & 2 & 3 \end{bmatrix}$$

evaluate (a) $|\boldsymbol{A}|$, (b) $|\boldsymbol{B}|$ and (c) $|\boldsymbol{AB}|$.

Solution

(a) $$|\boldsymbol{A}| = 1\begin{vmatrix} 3 & 4 \\ 5 & 6 \end{vmatrix} - 2\begin{vmatrix} 2 & 4 \\ 4 & 6 \end{vmatrix} + 3\begin{vmatrix} 2 & 3 \\ 4 & 5 \end{vmatrix}$$

$$= 1 \times (-2) - 2 \times (-4) + 3 \times (-2) = 0$$

(b) $$|\boldsymbol{B}| = \begin{vmatrix} 1 & 0 & 1 \\ 1 & 1 & 1 \\ 1 & 2 & 3 \end{vmatrix}$$

$$= \begin{vmatrix} 1 & 0 & 0 \\ 1 & 1 & 0 \\ 1 & 2 & 2 \end{vmatrix} \quad \text{(subtracting column 1 from column 3)}$$

$$= 1\begin{vmatrix} 1 & 0 \\ 2 & 2 \end{vmatrix} = 2 \quad \text{(expanding by first row)}$$

(c) $$|\boldsymbol{AB}| = \begin{vmatrix} 6 & 8 & 12 \\ 9 & 11 & 17 \\ 15 & 17 & 27 \end{vmatrix}$$

$$= 6[(11)(27) - (17)(17)] - 8[(9)(27) - (17)(15)] + 12[(9)(17) - (11)(15)]$$

$$= 48 + 96 - 144 = 0$$

We can use properties (a)–(e) to reduce the amount of computation involved in evaluating a determinant. We introduce as many zeros as possible into a row or column, and then expand along that row or column.

Example 5.18 Evaluate

$$D = \begin{vmatrix} 1 & 1 & 1 & 1 \\ 1 & 1+a & 1 & 1 \\ 1 & 1 & 1+b & 1 \\ 1 & 1 & 1 & 1+c \end{vmatrix}$$

Solution

$$D = \begin{vmatrix} 1 & 0 & 0 & 0 \\ 1 & a & 0 & 0 \\ 1 & 0 & b & 0 \\ 1 & 0 & 0 & c \end{vmatrix} \quad \text{(by subtracting col. 1 from col. 2, col. 3 and col. 4)}$$

$$= 1\begin{vmatrix} a & 0 & 0 \\ 0 & b & 0 \\ 0 & 0 & c \end{vmatrix} \quad \text{(by expanding by the top row)}$$

$$= a\begin{vmatrix} b & 0 \\ 0 & c \end{vmatrix} = abc$$

A solution using MAPLE is given by the commands

```
with (linalg):
E:= array ([[1, 1, 1, 1], [1, 1+a, 1, 1],
[1, 1, 1+b, 1], [1, 1, 1, 1+c]]):
det(E);
```

Using MATLAB's Symbolic Math Toolbox the commands

```
syms a b c
E = sym([1 1 1 1; 1 1+a 1 1; 1 1 1+b 1; 1 1 1 1+c]);
det(E);
pretty(ans)
```

return the answer `abc`.

A point that should be carefully noted concerns large determinants; they are extremely difficult and time-consuming to evaluate (using the basic definition (5.9) for an $n \times n$ determinant involves $n!(n-1)$ multiplications). This is a problem even with computers – which in fact use alternative methods. If at all possible, evaluation of large determinants should be avoided. They do, however, play a central role in matrix theory.

The cofactors $A_{11}, A_{12}, \ldots$ defined earlier have the property that

$$|\mathbf{A}| = a_{11}A_{11} + a_{12}A_{12} + a_{13}A_{13}$$

Consider the expression $a_{21}A_{11} + a_{22}A_{12} + a_{23}A_{13}$. In determinant form we have

$$a_{21}A_{11} + a_{22}A_{12} + a_{23}A_{13} = \begin{vmatrix} a_{21} & a_{22} & a_{23} \\ a_{21} & a_{22} & a_{23} \\ a_{31} & a_{32} & a_{33} \end{vmatrix} = 0$$

since two rows are identical. Similarly,

$$a_{31}A_{11} + a_{32}A_{12} + a_{33}A_{13} = 0$$

In general it can be shown that

$$\sum_k a_{ik}A_{jk} = \begin{cases} |\mathbf{A}| & \text{if } i = j \\ 0 & \text{if } i \neq j \end{cases} \tag{5.10}$$

and, expanding by columns that,

$$\sum_k a_{ki}A_{kj} = \begin{cases} |\mathbf{A}| & \text{if } i = j \\ 0 & \text{if } i \neq j \end{cases} \tag{5.11}$$

A numerical example illustrates these points.

Example 5.19 Illustrate the use of cofactors in the expansion of determinants on the matrix

$$\mathbf{A} = \begin{bmatrix} 1 & 2 & 3 \\ 6 & 5 & 4 \\ 7 & 8 & 1 \end{bmatrix}$$

Solution The cofactors are evaluated as

$$A_{11} = \begin{vmatrix} 5 & 4 \\ 8 & 1 \end{vmatrix} = -27, \quad A_{12} = -\begin{vmatrix} 6 & 4 \\ 7 & 1 \end{vmatrix} = 22, \quad A_{13} = \begin{vmatrix} 6 & 5 \\ 7 & 8 \end{vmatrix} = 13$$

and continuing in the same way

$$A_{21} = 22, A_{22} = -20, A_{23} = 6, A_{31} = -7, A_{32} = 14 \text{ and } A_{33} = -7$$

A selection of the evaluations in (5.10), that is expansion by rows, is

$$a_{11}A_{11} + a_{12}A_{12} + a_{13}A_{13} = 1 \times (-27) + 2 \times 22 + 3 \times 13 = 56$$

$$a_{21}A_{11} + a_{22}A_{12} + a_{23}A_{13} = 6 \times (-27) + 5 \times 22 + 4 \times 13 = 0$$

$$a_{31}A_{21} + a_{32}A_{22} + a_{33}A_{23} = 7 \times 22 + 8 \times (-20) + 1 \times 6 = 0$$

and in (5.11), that is expansion by columns, is

$$a_{11}A_{12} + a_{21}A_{22} + a_{31}A_{32} = 1 \times 22 + 6 \times (-20) + 7 \times 14 = 0$$

$$a_{12}A_{12} + a_{22}A_{22} + a_{32}A_{32} = 2 \times 22 + 5 \times (-20) + 8 \times 14 = 56$$

$$a_{13}A_{11} + a_{23}A_{21} + a_{33}A_{31} = 3 \times (-27) + 4 \times 22 + 1 \times (-7) = 0$$

The other expansions in (5.10) and (5.11) can be verified in this example. It may be noted that the determinant of the matrix is 56.

A matrix with particularly interesting properties is the **adjoint** or **adjugate matrix**, which is defined as the transpose of the matrix of cofactors; that is,

$$\text{adj}\,\boldsymbol{A} = \begin{bmatrix} A_{11} & A_{12} & A_{13} \\ A_{21} & A_{22} & A_{23} \\ A_{31} & A_{32} & A_{33} \end{bmatrix}^{\mathrm{T}} \tag{5.12}$$

If we now calculate $\boldsymbol{A}$ (adj $\boldsymbol{A}$), we have

$$[\boldsymbol{A}\,(\text{adj}\,\boldsymbol{A})]_{ij} = \sum_k a_{ik}(\text{adj}\,\boldsymbol{A})_{kj} = \sum_k a_{ik}A_{jk}$$

$$= \begin{cases} |\boldsymbol{A}| & \text{if } i = j \quad \text{(from (5.10))} \\ 0 & \text{if } i \neq j \end{cases}$$

So

$$\boldsymbol{A}(\text{adj}\,\boldsymbol{A}) = \begin{bmatrix} |\boldsymbol{A}| & 0 & 0 \\ 0 & |\boldsymbol{A}| & 0 \\ 0 & 0 & |\boldsymbol{A}| \end{bmatrix} = |\boldsymbol{A}|\boldsymbol{I} \tag{5.13}$$

and we have thus discovered a matrix that when multiplied by $\boldsymbol{A}$ gives a scalar times the unit matrix.

If $\boldsymbol{A}$ is a square matrix of order n then, taking determinants on both sides of (5.13),

$$|\boldsymbol{A}|\,|\text{adj}\,\boldsymbol{A}| = |\boldsymbol{A}(\text{adj}\,\boldsymbol{A})| = ||\boldsymbol{A}|\boldsymbol{I}_n| = |\boldsymbol{A}|^n$$

If $|\boldsymbol{A}| \neq 0$, it follows that

$$|\text{adj}\,\boldsymbol{A}| = |\boldsymbol{A}|^{n-1} \tag{5.14}$$

a result known as **Cauchy's theorem**.

It is also the case that

$$\text{adj}(\boldsymbol{AB}) = (\text{adj}\,\boldsymbol{B})(\text{adj}\,\boldsymbol{A}) \tag{5.15}$$

so in taking the adjoint of a product the order is reversed.

An important piece of notation that has significant implications for the solution of sets of linear equations concerns whether or not a matrix has zero determinant. A square matrix $\boldsymbol{A}$ is called **non-singular** if $|\boldsymbol{A}| \neq 0$ and **singular** if $|\boldsymbol{A}| = 0$.

Example 5.20 Derive the adjoint of the 2 × 2 matrices

$$\boldsymbol{A} = \begin{bmatrix} 1 & 3 \\ 2 & 8 \end{bmatrix} \quad \text{and} \quad \boldsymbol{B} = \begin{bmatrix} -1 & 2 \\ -3 & -4 \end{bmatrix}$$

and verify the results in (5.13), (5.14) and (5.15).

Solution The cofactors are very easy to evaluate in the 2 × 2 case: for the matrix $\boldsymbol{A}$

$$A_{11} = 8, A_{12} = -2, A_{21} = -3 \quad \text{and} \quad A_{22} = 1$$

and for the matrix $\boldsymbol{B}$

$$B_{11} = -4, B_{12} = 3, B_{21} = -2 \quad \text{and} \quad B_{22} = -1$$

The adjoint or adjugate matrices can be written down immediately as

$$\text{adj}\,\boldsymbol{A} = \begin{bmatrix} 8 & -3 \\ -2 & 1 \end{bmatrix} \quad \text{and} \quad \text{adj}\,\boldsymbol{B} = \begin{bmatrix} -4 & -2 \\ 3 & -1 \end{bmatrix}$$

Now (5.13) gives

$$\boldsymbol{A}(\text{adj}\,\boldsymbol{A}) = \begin{bmatrix} 1 & 3 \\ 2 & 8 \end{bmatrix}\begin{bmatrix} 8 & -3 \\ -2 & 1 \end{bmatrix} = \begin{bmatrix} 2 & 0 \\ 0 & 2 \end{bmatrix} = 2\boldsymbol{I}$$

$$\boldsymbol{B}(\text{adj}\,\boldsymbol{B}) = \begin{bmatrix} -1 & 2 \\ -3 & -4 \end{bmatrix}\begin{bmatrix} -4 & -2 \\ 3 & -1 \end{bmatrix} = \begin{bmatrix} 10 & 0 \\ 0 & 10 \end{bmatrix} = 10\boldsymbol{I}$$

so the property is satisfied and the determinants are 2 and 10 respectively. For (5.14) we have $n = 2$, so

$$|\text{adj}\,\boldsymbol{A}| = \begin{vmatrix} 8 & -3 \\ -2 & 1 \end{vmatrix} = 2 \quad \text{and} \quad |\text{adj}\,\boldsymbol{B}| = \begin{vmatrix} -4 & -2 \\ 3 & -1 \end{vmatrix} = 10$$

as required.

Evaluating the matrices in (5.15)

$$\text{adj}(\boldsymbol{AB}) = \text{adj}\begin{bmatrix} -10 & -10 \\ -26 & -28 \end{bmatrix} = \begin{bmatrix} -28 & 10 \\ 26 & -10 \end{bmatrix}$$

and

$$\text{adj}\,\boldsymbol{B}\;\text{adj}\,\boldsymbol{A} = \begin{bmatrix} -4 & -2 \\ 3 & -1 \end{bmatrix}\begin{bmatrix} 8 & -3 \\ -2 & 1 \end{bmatrix} = \begin{bmatrix} -28 & 10 \\ 26 & -10 \end{bmatrix}$$

and the statement is clearly verified. It is left as an exercise to show that the product of the matrices the other way round, adj $\boldsymbol{A}$ adj $\boldsymbol{B}$, gives a totally different matrix.

Example 5.21 Given

$$\boldsymbol{A} = \begin{bmatrix} 1 & 1 & 2 \\ 2 & 0 & 1 \\ 3 & 1 & 1 \end{bmatrix}$$

determine adj $\boldsymbol{A}$ and show that $\boldsymbol{A}(\text{adj}\,\boldsymbol{A}) = (\text{adj}\,\boldsymbol{A})\boldsymbol{A} = |\boldsymbol{A}|\boldsymbol{I}$.

Solution The matrix of cofactors is

$$\begin{bmatrix} \begin{vmatrix} 0 & 1 \\ 1 & 1 \end{vmatrix} & -\begin{vmatrix} 2 & 1 \\ 3 & 1 \end{vmatrix} & \begin{vmatrix} 2 & 0 \\ 3 & 1 \end{vmatrix} \\ -\begin{vmatrix} 1 & 2 \\ 1 & 1 \end{vmatrix} & \begin{vmatrix} 1 & 2 \\ 3 & 1 \end{vmatrix} & -\begin{vmatrix} 1 & 1 \\ 3 & 1 \end{vmatrix} \\ \begin{vmatrix} 1 & 2 \\ 0 & 1 \end{vmatrix} & -\begin{vmatrix} 1 & 2 \\ 2 & 1 \end{vmatrix} & \begin{vmatrix} 1 & 1 \\ 2 & 0 \end{vmatrix} \end{bmatrix} = \begin{bmatrix} -1 & 1 & 2 \\ 1 & -5 & 2 \\ 1 & 3 & -2 \end{bmatrix}$$

so, from (5.12)

$$\text{adj}\, \boldsymbol{A} = \begin{bmatrix} -1 & 1 & 2 \\ 1 & -5 & 2 \\ 1 & 3 & -2 \end{bmatrix}^{\mathrm{T}} = \begin{bmatrix} -1 & 1 & 1 \\ 1 & -5 & 3 \\ 2 & 2 & -2 \end{bmatrix}$$

$$\boldsymbol{A}(\text{adj}\, \boldsymbol{A}) = \begin{bmatrix} 1 & 1 & 2 \\ 2 & 0 & 1 \\ 3 & 1 & 1 \end{bmatrix} \begin{bmatrix} -1 & 1 & 1 \\ 1 & -5 & 3 \\ 2 & 2 & -2 \end{bmatrix} = \begin{bmatrix} 4 & 0 & 0 \\ 0 & 4 & 0 \\ 0 & 0 & 4 \end{bmatrix}$$

$$(\text{adj}\, \boldsymbol{A})\boldsymbol{A} = \begin{bmatrix} -1 & 1 & 1 \\ 1 & -5 & 3 \\ 2 & 2 & -2 \end{bmatrix} \begin{bmatrix} 1 & 1 & 2 \\ 2 & 0 & 1 \\ 3 & 1 & 1 \end{bmatrix} = \begin{bmatrix} 4 & 0 & 0 \\ 0 & 4 & 0 \\ 0 & 0 & 4 \end{bmatrix}$$

Since $|\boldsymbol{A}| = 4$ the last result then follows.

In MAPLE the adjoint of a matrix $\boldsymbol{A}$ is determined by the command *adj*(A). There appears to be no equivalent command in either MATLAB or its Symbolic Math Toolbox. However, the *maple* command in the Toolbox may be used to access the command in MAPLE, having first expressed the matrix $\boldsymbol{A}$ in symbolic form using the *sym* command. Consequently in MATLAB's Symbolic Math Toolbox the adjoint is determined by the commands

```
A = sym(A);
adjA = maple('adj', A)
```

Check that in MATLAB the commands

```
A = [1 1 2; 2 0 1; 3 1 1];
A = sym(A);
adjA = maple('adj',A)
```

return the first answer in Example 5.21.

5.3.1 Exercises

Check your answers using MATLAB or MAPLE whenever possible.

34 Find all the minors and cofactors of the determinant

$$\begin{vmatrix} 1 & 2 & 3 \\ 1 & 0 & 1 \\ 1 & 1 & 1 \end{vmatrix}$$

Hence evaluate the determinant.

35 Evaluate the determinants of the following matrices:

(a) $\begin{bmatrix} 1 & 7 \\ 4 & 9 \end{bmatrix}$ (b) $\begin{bmatrix} 1 & 4 & 3 \\ 2 & -4 & 1 \\ 3 & 2 & -6 \end{bmatrix}$

(c) $\begin{bmatrix} 2 & -1 & 3 \\ 4 & 2 & 9 \\ 1 & 3 & -4 \end{bmatrix}$ (d) $\begin{bmatrix} 1 & 0 & 1 \\ 0 & 1 & 0 \\ 1 & 0 & 2 \end{bmatrix}$

(e) $\begin{bmatrix} 1 & -1 & 0 \\ 1 & 1 & 1 \\ 0 & 1 & -1 \end{bmatrix}$

36 Given the matrix

$$\boldsymbol{A} = \begin{bmatrix} 1 & 0 & -1 \\ 1 & 0 & 1 \\ 2 & 2 & 2 \end{bmatrix}$$

determine $|\boldsymbol{A}|$, $|\boldsymbol{AA}^{\mathrm{T}}|$, $|\boldsymbol{A}^2|$ and $|\boldsymbol{A}+\boldsymbol{A}|$.

37 Find a series of row manipulations that takes

$$\begin{vmatrix} 1 & 0 & 1 \\ 2 & 1 & 0 \\ 0 & 1 & 1 \end{vmatrix} \text{ to } -\begin{vmatrix} 2 & 1 & 0 \\ 0 & -\tfrac{1}{2} & 1 \\ 0 & 0 & 3 \end{vmatrix}$$ and hence evaluate the determinant.

38 Determine adj $\boldsymbol{A}$ when

$$\boldsymbol{A} = \begin{bmatrix} a & b \\ c & d \end{bmatrix}$$

39 Determine adj $\boldsymbol{A}$ when

$$\boldsymbol{A} = \begin{bmatrix} 2 & 1 & 1 \\ 3 & 2 & 2 \\ 1 & 1 & 2 \end{bmatrix}$$

Check that $\boldsymbol{A}(\text{adj}\,\boldsymbol{A}) = (\text{adj}\,\boldsymbol{A})\boldsymbol{A} = |\boldsymbol{A}|\boldsymbol{I}$.

40 For the matrix

$$\boldsymbol{A} = \begin{bmatrix} 2 & 0 \\ 3 & 1 \end{bmatrix}$$

evaluate $|\boldsymbol{A}|$, adj($\boldsymbol{A}$), $\boldsymbol{B} = \dfrac{\text{adj}(\boldsymbol{A})}{|\boldsymbol{A}|}$ and $\boldsymbol{AB}$.

41 Show that the matrix

$$\boldsymbol{B} = \begin{bmatrix} 1 & 0 & 2 \\ 3 & 4 & 0 \\ 6 & -2 & 1 \end{bmatrix}$$

is non-singular and verify Cauchy's theorem, namely $|\text{adj}\,\boldsymbol{B}| = |\boldsymbol{B}|^2$.

42 If $|\boldsymbol{A}| = 0$ deduce that $|\boldsymbol{A}^n| = 0$ for any integer n.

43 Given

$$\boldsymbol{A} = \begin{bmatrix} 2 & -1 & 0 \\ -4 & 3 & -1 \\ 1 & -1 & 1 \end{bmatrix} \text{ and}$$

$$\boldsymbol{B} = \begin{bmatrix} 1 & 0 & 2 \\ 3 & 4 & 0 \\ 6 & -2 & 1 \end{bmatrix}$$

verify that adj($\boldsymbol{AB}$) = (adj $\boldsymbol{B}$)(adj $\boldsymbol{A}$).

44 Find the values of λ that make the following determinants zero:

(a) $\begin{vmatrix} 2-\lambda & 7 \\ 4 & 6-\lambda \end{vmatrix}$

(b) $\begin{vmatrix} 1 & 3-\lambda & 4 \\ 4-\lambda & 2 & -1 \\ 1 & \lambda-6 & 2 \end{vmatrix}$

(c) $\begin{vmatrix} 0 & 2-\lambda & 0 \\ 2-\lambda & 4 & 1 \\ 2 & -3 & \lambda-4 \end{vmatrix}$

45 Evaluate the determinants of the square matrices

(a) $\begin{bmatrix} 0.42 & 0.31 & -0.16 \\ 0.17 & -0.22 & 0.63 \\ 0.89 & 0.93 & 0.41 \end{bmatrix}$

(b) $\begin{bmatrix} 5 & 4 & 1 & 1 \\ 4 & 5 & 1 & 1 \\ 1 & 1 & 4 & 2 \\ 1 & 1 & 2 & 4 \end{bmatrix}$

46 Show that the area of a triangle with vertices (x_1, y_1), (x_2, y_2) and (x_3, y_3) is given by the absolute value of

$$\frac{1}{2}\begin{vmatrix} 1 & x_1 & y_1 \\ 1 & x_2 & y_2 \\ 1 & x_3 & y_3 \end{vmatrix}$$

Refer to Question 46 in Exercises (4.2.11) and the definition of the vector product in Section 4.2.10.

47 Show that $x + x^2 - 2x^3$ is a factor of the determinant D where

$$D = \begin{vmatrix} 0 & x & 2 & x^2 \\ -x & 0 & 1 & x^3 \\ -2 & -1 & 0 & 1 \\ -x^2 & -x^3 & -1 & 0 \end{vmatrix}$$

and hence express D as a product of linear factors.

48 Show that

$$\begin{vmatrix} x & a & b \\ x^2 & a^2 & b^2 \\ a+b & x+b & x+a \end{vmatrix}$$

$$= (b-a)(x-a)(x-b)(x+a+b)$$

Such an exercise can be solved in two lines of code of a symbolic manipulation package such as MAPLE or MATLAB's Symbolic Math Toolbox.

49 Verify that if $\boldsymbol{A}$ is a symmetric matrix then so is adj $\boldsymbol{A}$.

50 If $\boldsymbol{A}$ is a skew-symmetric $n \times n$ matrix, verify that adj $\boldsymbol{A}$ is symmetric or skew-symmetric according to whether n is odd or even.

5.4 The inverse matrix

In Section 5.3 we constructed adj $\boldsymbol{A}$ and saw that it had interesting properties in relation to the unit matrix. We also saw, in Example 5.6, that we had a method of solving linear equations if we could construct $\boldsymbol{B}$ such that $\boldsymbol{AB} = \boldsymbol{I}$. These ideas can be brought together to provide a comprehensive theory of the solution of linear equations, which we will consider in Section 5.5.

Given a square matrix $\boldsymbol{A}$, if we can construct a matrix $\boldsymbol{B}$ such that

$$\boldsymbol{BA} = \boldsymbol{AB} = \boldsymbol{I}$$

then **we call $\boldsymbol{B}$ the inverse of $\boldsymbol{A}$ and write it as $\boldsymbol{A}^{-1}$**. From (5.13)

$$\boldsymbol{A}(\text{adj } \boldsymbol{A}) = |\boldsymbol{A}|\boldsymbol{I}$$

so that we have gone a long way to constructing the inverse. We have two cases:

- If $\boldsymbol{A}$ is non-singular then $|\boldsymbol{A}| \neq 0$ and

$$\boldsymbol{A}^{-1} = \frac{\text{adj}\,\boldsymbol{A}}{|\boldsymbol{A}|}$$

- If $\boldsymbol{A}$ is singular then $|\boldsymbol{A}| = 0$ and it can be shown that the inverse $\boldsymbol{A}^{-1}$ does not exist.

If the inverse exists then it is unique. Suppose for a given $\boldsymbol{A}$ we have two inverses $\boldsymbol{B}$ and $\boldsymbol{C}$. Then

$$\boldsymbol{AB} = \boldsymbol{BA} = \boldsymbol{I}, \quad \boldsymbol{AC} = \boldsymbol{CA} = \boldsymbol{I}$$

and therefore

$$\boldsymbol{AB} = \boldsymbol{AC}$$

Pre-multiplying by $\boldsymbol{C}$, we have

$$\boldsymbol{C}(\boldsymbol{AB}) = \boldsymbol{C}(\boldsymbol{AC})$$

But matrix multiplication is associative, so we can write this as

$$(\boldsymbol{CA})\boldsymbol{B} = (\boldsymbol{CA})\boldsymbol{C}$$

Hence

$$\boldsymbol{IB} = \boldsymbol{IC} \quad (\text{since } \boldsymbol{CA} = \boldsymbol{I})$$

and so

$$\boldsymbol{B} = \boldsymbol{C}$$

The inverse is therefore unique.

It should be noted that if both $\boldsymbol{A}$ and $\boldsymbol{B}$ are square matrices then $\boldsymbol{AB} = \boldsymbol{I}$ if and only if $\boldsymbol{BA} = \boldsymbol{I}$.

Example 5.22

Find $\boldsymbol{A}^{-1}$ and $\boldsymbol{B}^{-1}$ for the matrices

$$\text{(a) } \boldsymbol{A} = \begin{bmatrix} 1 & 2 \\ 2 & 3 \end{bmatrix} \quad \text{and} \quad \text{(b) } \boldsymbol{B} = \begin{bmatrix} 5 & 2 & 4 \\ 3 & -1 & 2 \\ 1 & 4 & -3 \end{bmatrix}$$

Solution

$$\text{(a) adj}\,\boldsymbol{A} = \begin{bmatrix} 3 & -2 \\ -2 & 1 \end{bmatrix}^{\mathrm{T}} = \begin{bmatrix} 3 & -2 \\ -2 & 1 \end{bmatrix} \quad \text{and} \quad |\boldsymbol{A}| = -1$$

so that

$$\boldsymbol{A}^{-1} = \frac{\text{adj}\,\boldsymbol{A}}{|\boldsymbol{A}|} = \begin{bmatrix} -3 & 2 \\ 2 & -1 \end{bmatrix}$$

$$\text{(b)}\ \operatorname{adj}\boldsymbol{B} = \begin{bmatrix} -5 & 11 & 13 \\ 22 & -19 & -18 \\ 8 & 2 & -11 \end{bmatrix}^{\mathrm{T}} = \begin{bmatrix} -5 & 22 & 8 \\ 11 & -19 & 2 \\ 13 & -18 & -11 \end{bmatrix} \quad \text{and} \quad |\boldsymbol{B}| = 49$$

so that

$$\boldsymbol{B}^{-1} = \frac{1}{49}\begin{bmatrix} -5 & 22 & 8 \\ 11 & -19 & 2 \\ 13 & -18 & -11 \end{bmatrix}$$

In both cases it can be checked that $\boldsymbol{AA}^{-1} = \boldsymbol{I}$ and $\boldsymbol{BB}^{-1} = \boldsymbol{I}$.

Finding the inverse of a 2×2 matrix is very easy, since for

$$\boldsymbol{A} = \begin{bmatrix} a & b \\ c & d \end{bmatrix}$$

$$\boldsymbol{A}^{-1} = \frac{1}{ad - bc}\begin{bmatrix} d & -b \\ -c & a \end{bmatrix} \quad \text{(provided that } ad - bc \neq 0\text{)}$$

Unfortunately there is no simple extension of this result to higher-order matrices. On the other hand, in most practical situations the inverse itself is rarely required – it is the solution of the corresponding linear equations that is important. To understand the power and applicability of the various methods of solution of linear equations, the role of the inverse is essential. The consideration of the adjoint matrix provides a theoretical framework for this study, but as a practical method for finding the inverse of a matrix it is virtually useless, since, as we saw earlier, it is so time-consuming to compute determinants.

To find the inverse of a product of two matrices, the order is reversed:

$$(\boldsymbol{AB})^{-1} = \boldsymbol{B}^{-1}\boldsymbol{A}^{-1} \tag{5.16}$$

(provided that $\boldsymbol{A}$ and $\boldsymbol{B}$ are invertible). To prove this, let $\boldsymbol{C} = \boldsymbol{B}^{-1}\boldsymbol{A}^{-1}$. Then

$$\boldsymbol{C}(\boldsymbol{AB}) = (\boldsymbol{B}^{-1}\boldsymbol{A}^{-1})(\boldsymbol{AB}) = \boldsymbol{B}^{-1}(\boldsymbol{A}^{-1}\boldsymbol{A})\boldsymbol{B} = \boldsymbol{B}^{-1}\boldsymbol{IB} = \boldsymbol{B}^{-1}\boldsymbol{B} = \boldsymbol{I}$$

and thus

$$\boldsymbol{C} = \boldsymbol{B}^{-1}\boldsymbol{A}^{-1} = (\boldsymbol{AB})^{-1}$$

Since matrices do not commute in general $\boldsymbol{A}^{-1}\boldsymbol{B}^{-1} \neq \boldsymbol{B}^{-1}\boldsymbol{A}^{-1}$.

In MATLAB the inverse of a matrix $\boldsymbol{A}$ is determined by the command `inv(A)`; first expressing $\boldsymbol{A}$ in symbolic form using the `sym` command if the Symbolic Math Toolbox is used. In MAPLE the corresponding command is `inverse(A)`.

Example 5.23 Given

$$A = \begin{bmatrix} 1 & 2 \\ 2 & 1 \end{bmatrix} \quad \text{and} \quad B = \begin{bmatrix} 0 & 1 \\ 1 & 1 \end{bmatrix}$$

evaluate $(AB)^{-1}$, $A^{-1}B^{-1}$, $B^{-1}A^{-1}$ and show that $(AB)^{-1} = B^{-1}A^{-1}$.

Solution

$$A^{-1} = \begin{bmatrix} -\frac{1}{3} & \frac{2}{3} \\ \frac{2}{3} & -\frac{1}{3} \end{bmatrix}, \quad B^{-1} = \begin{bmatrix} -1 & 1 \\ 1 & 0 \end{bmatrix}$$

$$AB = \begin{bmatrix} 2 & 3 \\ 1 & 3 \end{bmatrix}, \quad (AB)^{-1} = \begin{bmatrix} 1 & -1 \\ -\frac{1}{3} & \frac{2}{3} \end{bmatrix}$$

$$A^{-1}B^{-1} = \begin{bmatrix} -\frac{1}{3} & \frac{2}{3} \\ \frac{2}{3} & -\frac{1}{3} \end{bmatrix}\begin{bmatrix} -1 & 1 \\ 1 & 0 \end{bmatrix} = \begin{bmatrix} 1 & -\frac{1}{3} \\ -1 & \frac{2}{3} \end{bmatrix}$$

$$B^{-1}A^{-1} = \begin{bmatrix} -1 & 1 \\ 1 & 0 \end{bmatrix}\begin{bmatrix} -\frac{1}{3} & \frac{2}{3} \\ \frac{2}{3} & -\frac{1}{3} \end{bmatrix} = \begin{bmatrix} 1 & -1 \\ -\frac{1}{3} & \frac{2}{3} \end{bmatrix} = (AB)^{-1}$$

Example 5.24 Given the two matrices

$$A = \begin{bmatrix} 0 & -\frac{3}{5} & 0 \\ \frac{5}{3} & 0 & -\frac{5}{3} \\ 0 & 6 & -6 \end{bmatrix} \quad \text{and} \quad T = \begin{bmatrix} 0.6 & 0.3 & 0.1 \\ 1 & 1 & 0.5 \\ 1.2 & 1.5 & 1 \end{bmatrix}$$

show that the matrix $T^{-1}AT$ is diagonal.

Solution The inverse is best computed using MATLAB or a similar package. It may be verified by direct multiplication that

$$T^{-1} = \frac{1}{6}\begin{bmatrix} 25 & -15 & 5 \\ -40 & 48 & -20 \\ 30 & -54 & 30 \end{bmatrix}$$

The further multiplications give

$$\frac{1}{6}\begin{bmatrix} 25 & -15 & 5 \\ -40 & 48 & -20 \\ 30 & -54 & 30 \end{bmatrix}\begin{bmatrix} 0 & -\frac{3}{5} & 0 \\ \frac{5}{3} & 0 & -\frac{5}{3} \\ 0 & 6 & -6 \end{bmatrix}\begin{bmatrix} 0.6 & 0.3 & 0.1 \\ 1 & 1 & 0.5 \\ 1.2 & 1.5 & 1 \end{bmatrix} = \begin{bmatrix} -1 & 0 & 0 \\ 0 & -2 & 0 \\ 0 & 0 & -3 \end{bmatrix}$$

This technique is an important one mathematically (see the companion text *Advanced Modern Engineering Mathematics*) since it provides a method of uncoupling a system of coupled equations. Practically it is the process used to reduce a physical system to principal axes; in elasticity it provides the principal stresses in a body.

Check that in MATLAB the commands

```
T = [0.6 0.3 0.1; 1 1 0.5; 1.2 1.5 1];
inv(T)
```

return the inverse $\boldsymbol{T}^{-1}$ in the numeric form

$$\begin{bmatrix} 4.1667 & -2.5000 & 0.8333 \\ -6.6667 & 8.0000 & -3.3333 \\ 5.0000 & -9.0000 & 5.0000 \end{bmatrix}$$

Check also that, using the Symbolic Math Toolbox, the exact form given in the solution is obtained using the commands

```
T = [0.6 0.3 0.1; 1 1 0.5; 1.2 1.5 1];
T = sym(T);
inv(T)
```

5.4.1 Exercises

Check your answers to the exercises using MATLAB.

51 Determine whether the following matrices are singular or non-singular *and* find the inverse of the non-singular matrices.

(a) $\begin{bmatrix} 1 & 2 \\ 2 & 1 \end{bmatrix}$ (b) $\begin{bmatrix} 1 & 2 & 3 \\ 2 & 2 & 1 \\ 5 & 6 & 5 \end{bmatrix}$

(c) $\begin{bmatrix} 1 & 0 & 0 & 1 \\ 0 & 1 & 0 & 1 \\ 0 & 0 & 1 & 1 \\ 0 & 0 & 0 & 1 \end{bmatrix}$ (d) $\begin{bmatrix} 1 & 0 & 1 \\ 0 & 1 & 0 \\ 1 & 0 & 1 \end{bmatrix}$

52 Find the inverses of the matrices

(a) $\begin{bmatrix} 1 & 1 & 1 \\ 0 & 1 & 0 \\ 0 & 0 & 1 \end{bmatrix}$ (b) $\begin{bmatrix} 1 & 0 & 0 & 0 \\ 0 & 2 & 0 & 0 \\ 0 & 0 & 3 & 0 \\ 0 & 0 & 0 & 4 \end{bmatrix}$

(c) $\begin{bmatrix} 1 & \text{j} \\ -\text{j} & 2 \end{bmatrix}$ (d) $\begin{bmatrix} 1 & 2 & 3 \\ 0 & 1 & 2 \\ 2 & 3 & 1 \end{bmatrix}$

53 Verify that

$$\boldsymbol{A} = \begin{bmatrix} 0 & 1 & -3 \\ 2 & 1 & 0 \\ 1 & -2 & 1 \end{bmatrix}$$

has an inverse

$$\boldsymbol{A}^{-1} = \frac{1}{13}\begin{bmatrix} 1 & 5 & 3 \\ -2 & 3 & -6 \\ -5 & 1 & -2 \end{bmatrix}$$

and hence solve the equation

$$\boldsymbol{ACA} = \begin{bmatrix} 2 & 1 & 1 \\ 0 & 2 & 3 \\ 2 & 1 & 0 \end{bmatrix}$$

54 (a) If a square matrix $\boldsymbol{A}$ satisfies $\boldsymbol{A}^2 = \boldsymbol{A}$ and has an inverse, show that $\boldsymbol{A}$ is the unit matrix.

(b) Show that $\boldsymbol{A} = \begin{bmatrix} 1 & 0 \\ 0 & 0 \end{bmatrix}$ satisfies $\boldsymbol{A}^2 = \boldsymbol{A}$.

Note: Matrices that satisfy $\boldsymbol{A}^2 = \boldsymbol{A}$ are called idempotent.

55 If

$$\boldsymbol{A} = \begin{bmatrix} 1 & 0 & 0 \\ 1 & 1 & 0 \\ 0 & 2 & 1 \end{bmatrix}, \quad \boldsymbol{B} = \begin{bmatrix} 1 & 4 & -1 \\ 0 & 2 & 1 \\ 0 & 0 & 2 \end{bmatrix}$$

$$\text{and} \quad \boldsymbol{C} = \begin{bmatrix} 1 & 4 & -1 \\ 1 & 6 & 0 \\ 0 & 4 & 4 \end{bmatrix}$$

show that $\boldsymbol{AB} = \boldsymbol{C}$. Find the inverse of $\boldsymbol{A}$ and $\boldsymbol{B}$ and hence of $\boldsymbol{C}$.

Note: This is an example of a powerful method called **LU** decomposition.

56 Given the matrix

$$\boldsymbol{A} = \begin{bmatrix} 1 & 1 & 0 \\ 0 & 1 & 2 \\ 1 & 2 & 3 \end{bmatrix}$$

and the elementary matrices

$$\boldsymbol{E}_1 = \begin{bmatrix} 1 & 0 & 0 \\ 0 & 1 & 0 \\ -1 & 0 & 1 \end{bmatrix} \quad \boldsymbol{E}_2 = \begin{bmatrix} 1 & 0 & 0 \\ 0 & 1 & 0 \\ 0 & -1 & 1 \end{bmatrix}$$

$$\boldsymbol{E}_3 = \begin{bmatrix} 1 & 0 & 0 \\ 0 & 1 & -2 \\ 0 & 0 & 1 \end{bmatrix} \quad \boldsymbol{E}_4 = \begin{bmatrix} 1 & -1 & 0 \\ 0 & 1 & 0 \\ 0 & 0 & 1 \end{bmatrix}$$

evaluate $\boldsymbol{E}_1\boldsymbol{A}$, $\boldsymbol{E}_2\boldsymbol{E}_1\boldsymbol{A}$, $\boldsymbol{E}_3\boldsymbol{E}_2\boldsymbol{E}_1\boldsymbol{A}$ and $\boldsymbol{E}_4\boldsymbol{E}_3\boldsymbol{E}_2\boldsymbol{E}_1\boldsymbol{A}$ and hence find the inverse of $\boldsymbol{A}$.

Note: The elementary matrices manipulate the rows of the matrix $\boldsymbol{A}$.

57 For the matrix

$$\boldsymbol{A} = \begin{bmatrix} 1 & 2 & 2 \\ 2 & 1 & 2 \\ 2 & 2 & 1 \end{bmatrix}$$

show that $\boldsymbol{A}^2 - 4\boldsymbol{A} - 5\boldsymbol{I} = 0$ and hence that $\boldsymbol{A}^{-1} = \frac{1}{5}(\boldsymbol{A} - 4\boldsymbol{I})$. Calculate $\boldsymbol{A}^{-1}$ from this result. Further show that the inverse of $\boldsymbol{A}^2$ is given by $\frac{1}{25}(21\boldsymbol{I} - 4\boldsymbol{A})$ and evaluate.

58 Given

$$\boldsymbol{A} = \begin{bmatrix} 1 & 0 & 2 \\ 6 & 4 & 0 \\ 6 & -2 & 1 \end{bmatrix} \quad \text{and} \quad \boldsymbol{B} = \begin{bmatrix} 5 & 2 & 4 \\ 3 & -1 & 2 \\ 1 & 4 & -3 \end{bmatrix}$$

find $\boldsymbol{A}^{-1}$ and $\boldsymbol{B}^{-1}$. Verify that $(\boldsymbol{AB})^{-1} = \boldsymbol{B}^{-1}\boldsymbol{A}^{-1}$.

59 Given the matrices

$$\boldsymbol{A} = \begin{bmatrix} 1 & 0 & 0 & 0 \\ 0 & 0 & 1 & 0 \\ 0 & 1 & 0 & 0 \\ 0 & 0 & 0 & 1 \end{bmatrix} \quad \text{and} \quad \boldsymbol{B} = \begin{bmatrix} 1 & 0 & 0 & 0 \\ 0 & 0 & 1 & 0 \\ 0 & 0 & 0 & 1 \\ 0 & 1 & 0 & 0 \end{bmatrix}$$

show that $\boldsymbol{A}^2 = \boldsymbol{I}$ and $\boldsymbol{B}^3 = \boldsymbol{I}$, and hence find $\boldsymbol{A}^{-1}$, $\boldsymbol{B}^{-1}$ and $(\boldsymbol{AB})^{-1}$.

Note: The matrices $\boldsymbol{A}$ and $\boldsymbol{B}$ in this exercise are examples of **permutation matrices**. For instance, $\boldsymbol{A}$ gives

$$\boldsymbol{A}\begin{bmatrix} x_1 \\ x_2 \\ x_3 \\ x_4 \end{bmatrix} = \begin{bmatrix} x_1 \\ x_3 \\ x_2 \\ x_4 \end{bmatrix}$$

and the suffices are just permuted; $\boldsymbol{B}$ has similar properties.

5.5 Linear equations

Although matrices are of great importance in themselves, their practical importance lies in the solution of sets of linear equations. Such sets of equations occur in a wide range of scientific and engineering problems. In the first part of this section we shall consider whether or not a solution exists, and then in Sections 5.5.2 and 5.5.4 we shall look at practical methods of solution.

We now make some definitive statements about the solution of the system of simultaneous linear equations.

$$\left.\begin{aligned} a_{11}x_1 + a_{12}x_2 + \ldots + a_{1n}x_n &= b_1 \\ a_{21}x_1 + a_{22}x_2 + \ldots + a_{2n}x_n &= b_2 \\ \vdots \qquad\qquad & \vdots \\ a_{n1}x_1 + a_{n2}x_2 + \ldots + a_{nn}x_n &= b_n \end{aligned}\right\} \tag{5.17}$$

or, in matrix notation,

$$\begin{bmatrix} a_{11} & a_{12} & \ldots & a_{1n} \\ a_{21} & a_{22} & \ldots & a_{2n} \\ \vdots & & & \\ a_{n1} & a_{n2} & \ldots & a_{nn} \end{bmatrix} \begin{bmatrix} x_1 \\ x_2 \\ \vdots \\ x_n \end{bmatrix} = \begin{bmatrix} b_1 \\ b_2 \\ \vdots \\ b_n \end{bmatrix}$$

that is,

$$\boldsymbol{AX} = \boldsymbol{b} \tag{5.18}$$

where $\boldsymbol{A}$ is the matrix of coefficients and $\boldsymbol{X}$ the vector of unknowns. If $\boldsymbol{b} = 0$ the equations are called **homogeneous**, while if $\boldsymbol{b} \neq 0$ they are called **nonhomogeneous** (or **inhomogeneous**). There are several cases to consider.

Case (a) $b \neq 0$ and $|A| \neq 0$

We know that $\boldsymbol{A}^{-1}$ exists, and hence

$$\boldsymbol{A}^{-1}\boldsymbol{AX} = \boldsymbol{A}^{-1}\boldsymbol{b}$$

so that

$$\boldsymbol{X} = \boldsymbol{A}^{-1}\boldsymbol{b} \tag{5.19}$$

and we have a unique solution to (5.17) and (5.18).

Case (b) $b = 0$ and $|A| \neq 0$

Again $\boldsymbol{A}^{-1}$ exists, and the homogeneous equations

$$\boldsymbol{AX} = 0$$

give

$$A^{-1}AX = A^{-1}0 \quad \text{or} \quad X = 0$$

We therefore only have the **trivial solution** $X = 0$.

Case (c) $b \neq 0$ and $|A| = 0$

The inverse matrix does not exist, and this is perhaps the most complicated case. We have two possibilities: either we have no solution or we have infinitely many solutions. A simple example will illustrate the situation. The equations

$$\left.\begin{aligned} 3x + 2y &= 2 \\ 3x + 2y &= 6 \end{aligned}\right\}, \quad \text{or} \quad \begin{bmatrix} 3 & 2 \\ 3 & 2 \end{bmatrix}\begin{bmatrix} x \\ y \end{bmatrix} = \begin{bmatrix} 2 \\ 6 \end{bmatrix}$$

are clearly inconsistent, and no solution exists. However, in the case of

$$\left.\begin{aligned} 3x + 2y &= 2 \\ 6x + 4y &= 4 \end{aligned}\right\}, \quad \text{or} \quad \begin{bmatrix} 3 & 2 \\ 6 & 4 \end{bmatrix}\begin{bmatrix} x \\ y \end{bmatrix} = \begin{bmatrix} 2 \\ 4 \end{bmatrix}$$

where one equation is a multiple of the other, we have infinitely many solutions: $x = \lambda$, $y = 1 - \frac{3}{2}\lambda$ is a solution for any value of λ.

The same behaviour is observed for problems involving more than two variables, but the situation is then much more difficult to analyse. The problem of determining whether or not a set of equations has a solution will be discussed in Section 5.6.

Case (d) $b = 0$ and $|A| = 0$

As in case (c), we have infinitely many solutions. For instance, the case of two equations takes the form

$$\begin{aligned} px + qy &= 0 \\ \alpha px + \alpha qy &= 0 \end{aligned}$$

so that $|A| = 0$ and we find a solution $x = \lambda$, $y = -p\lambda/q$ if $q \neq 0$. If $q = 0$ then $x = 0$, $y = \lambda$ is a solution.

This case is one of the most important, since we can deduce the important general result that *the equation*

$$AX = 0$$

has a non-trivial solution if and only if $|A| = 0$.

Again the general result will be discussed further in Section 5.6 which looks at the rank of a matrix.

Example 5.25

Write the five sets of equations in matrix form and decide whether they have or do not have a solution.

(a) $\begin{aligned} 2x + y &= 5 \\ x - 2y &= -5 \end{aligned}$ (b) $\begin{aligned} 2x + y &= 0 \\ x - 2y &= 0 \end{aligned}$ (c) $\begin{aligned} -3x + 6y &= 15 \\ x - 2y &= -5 \end{aligned}$

(d) $\begin{aligned} -3x + 6y &= 10 \\ x - 2y &= -5 \end{aligned}$ (e) $\begin{aligned} -3x + 6y &= 0 \\ x - 2y &= 0 \end{aligned}$

Solution (a) In matrix form the equations are $\begin{bmatrix} 2 & 1 \\ 1 & -2 \end{bmatrix}\begin{bmatrix} x \\ y \end{bmatrix} = \begin{bmatrix} 5 \\ -5 \end{bmatrix}$. The determinant of the matrix has the value −5 and the right-hand side is non-zero, so the problem is of the type **Case (a)** and hence has a unique solution, namely $x = 1$, $y = 3$.

(b) In matrix form the equations are $\begin{bmatrix} 2 & 1 \\ 1 & -2 \end{bmatrix}\begin{bmatrix} x \\ y \end{bmatrix} = \begin{bmatrix} 0 \\ 0 \end{bmatrix}$. The determinant of the matrix has the value −5 and the right-hand side is now zero, so the problem is of the type **Case (b)** and hence only has the trivial solution, namely $x = 0$, $y = 0$.

(c) In matrix form the equations are $\begin{bmatrix} -3 & 6 \\ 1 & -2 \end{bmatrix}\begin{bmatrix} x \\ y \end{bmatrix} = \begin{bmatrix} 15 \\ -5 \end{bmatrix}$. The determinant of the matrix matrix is now zero and the right-hand side is non-zero, so the problem is of the type **Case (c)** and hence the solution is not so easy. Essentially the first equation is just (−3) times the second equation, so a solution can be computed. A bit of rearrangement soon gives $x = 2t - 5$, $y = t$ for any t, and thus there are infinitely many solutions to this set of equations.

(d) In matrix form the equations are $\begin{bmatrix} -3 & 6 \\ 1 & -2 \end{bmatrix}\begin{bmatrix} x \\ y \end{bmatrix} = \begin{bmatrix} 10 \\ -5 \end{bmatrix}$. The determinant of the matrix is zero again and the right-hand side is non-zero, so the problem is once more of the type **Case (c)** and hence the solution is not so easy. The left-hand side of the first equation is (−3) times the second equation but the right-hand side is only (−2) times the second equation, so the equations are inconsistent and there is no solution to this set of equations.

(e) In matrix form the equations are $\begin{bmatrix} -3 & 6 \\ 1 & -2 \end{bmatrix}\begin{bmatrix} x \\ y \end{bmatrix} = \begin{bmatrix} 0 \\ 0 \end{bmatrix}$. The determinant of the matrix is zero again and the right-hand side is also zero, so the problem is of the type **Case (d)** and hence a non-trivial solution can be found. It can be seen that $x = 2s$ and $y = s$ gives the solution for any s.

Example 5.26 Find a solution of

$$\begin{aligned} x + y + z &= 6 \\ x + 2y + 3z &= 14 \\ x + 4y + 9z &= 36 \end{aligned}$$

Solution Expressing the equations in matrix form $\boldsymbol{AX} = \boldsymbol{b}$

$$\begin{bmatrix} 1 & 1 & 1 \\ 1 & 2 & 3 \\ 1 & 4 & 9 \end{bmatrix}\begin{bmatrix} x \\ y \\ z \end{bmatrix} = \begin{bmatrix} 6 \\ 14 \\ 36 \end{bmatrix}$$

we have

$$|\boldsymbol{A}| = \begin{vmatrix} 1 & 1 & 1 \\ 1 & 2 & 3 \\ 1 & 4 & 9 \end{vmatrix} = \begin{vmatrix} 1 & 0 & 0 \\ 1 & 1 & 2 \\ 1 & 3 & 8 \end{vmatrix} = 2 \neq 0 \quad \text{(subtracting column 1 from columns 2 and 3)}$$

so that a solution does exist and is unique. The inverse of $\boldsymbol{A}$ can be computed as

$$\boldsymbol{A}^{-1} = \begin{bmatrix} 3 & -\frac{5}{2} & \frac{1}{2} \\ -3 & 4 & -1 \\ 1 & -\frac{3}{2} & \frac{1}{2} \end{bmatrix}$$

and hence, from (5.19),

$$\boldsymbol{X} = \begin{bmatrix} x \\ y \\ z \end{bmatrix} = \boldsymbol{A}^{-1} \begin{bmatrix} 6 \\ 14 \\ 36 \end{bmatrix} = \begin{bmatrix} 1 \\ 2 \\ 3 \end{bmatrix}$$

so the solution is $x = 1$, $y = 2$ and $z = 3$.

Example 5.27

Find the values of k for which the equations

$$x + 5y + 3z = 0$$
$$5x + y - kz = 0$$
$$x + 2y + kz = 0$$

have a non-trivial solution.

Solution The matrix of coefficients is

$$\boldsymbol{A} = \begin{bmatrix} 1 & 5 & 3 \\ 5 & 1 & -k \\ 1 & 2 & k \end{bmatrix}$$

For a non-zero solution, $|\boldsymbol{A}| = 0$. Hence

$$0 = |\boldsymbol{A}| = \begin{vmatrix} 1 & 5 & 3 \\ 5 & 1 & -k \\ 1 & 2 & k \end{vmatrix} = 27 - 27k$$

Thus the equations have a non-trivial solution if $k = 1$; if $k \neq 1$, the only solution is $x = y = z = 0$. For $k = 1$ a simple calculation gives $x = \lambda$, $y = -2\lambda$ and $z = 3\lambda$ for any λ.

Example 5.28

Find the values of λ and the corresponding column vector $\boldsymbol{X}$ such that

$$(\boldsymbol{A} - \lambda \boldsymbol{I})\boldsymbol{X} = 0$$

has a non-trivial solution, given

$$\boldsymbol{A} = \begin{bmatrix} 3 & 1 \\ -2 & 0 \end{bmatrix}$$

Solution We require

$$0 = |\boldsymbol{A} - \lambda \boldsymbol{I}| = \begin{vmatrix} 3-\lambda & 1 \\ -2 & -\lambda \end{vmatrix}$$

$$= -3\lambda + \lambda^2 + 2 = (\lambda - 2)(\lambda - 1)$$

Non-trivial solutions occur only if $\lambda = 1$ or 2.

If $\lambda = 1$,

$$\begin{bmatrix} 2 & 1 \\ -2 & -1 \end{bmatrix}\begin{bmatrix} x \\ y \end{bmatrix} = 0, \quad \text{so } \boldsymbol{X} = \begin{bmatrix} x \\ y \end{bmatrix} = \alpha \begin{bmatrix} 1 \\ -2 \end{bmatrix} \quad \text{for any } \alpha$$

If $\lambda = 2$,

$$\begin{bmatrix} 1 & 1 \\ -2 & -2 \end{bmatrix}\begin{bmatrix} x \\ y \end{bmatrix} = 0, \quad \text{so } \boldsymbol{X} = \begin{bmatrix} x \\ y \end{bmatrix} = \beta \begin{bmatrix} 1 \\ -1 \end{bmatrix} \quad \text{for any } \beta$$

(*Note*: The problem described here is an important one. The λ and $\boldsymbol{X}$ are called **eigenvalues** and **eigenvectors**, which are introduced in Section 5.7.)

It is possible to write down the solution of a set of equations explicitly in terms of the cofactors of a matrix. However, as a method for computing the solution, this is extremely inefficient; a set of ten equations, for example, will require 4×10^8 multiplications – which takes a long time even on modern computers. The method is of great theoretical interest though. Consider the set of equations

$$\left.\begin{aligned} a_{11}x_1 + a_{12}x_2 + a_{13}x_3 &= b_1 \\ a_{21}x_1 + a_{22}x_2 + a_{23}x_3 &= b_2 \\ a_{31}x_1 + a_{32}x_2 + a_{33}x_3 &= b_3 \end{aligned}\right\} \tag{5.20}$$

Denoting the matrix of coefficients by $\boldsymbol{A}$ and recalling the definitions of the cofactors in Section 5.3, we multiply the equations by A_{11}, A_{21} and A_{31} respectively and add to give

$$\begin{aligned} (a_{11}A_{11} + a_{21}A_{21} + a_{31}A_{31})x_1 + (a_{12}A_{11} + a_{22}A_{21} + a_{32}A_{31})x_2 \\ + (a_{13}A_{11} + a_{23}A_{21} + a_{33}A_{31})x_3 \\ = b_1A_{11} + b_2A_{21} + b_3A_{31} \end{aligned}$$

Using (5.11), we obtain

$$|\boldsymbol{A}|x_1 + 0x_2 + 0x_3 = b_1A_{11} + b_2A_{21} + b_3A_{31}$$

The right-hand side can be written as a determinant, so

$$|\boldsymbol{A}|x_1 = \begin{vmatrix} b_1 & a_{12} & a_{13} \\ b_2 & a_{22} & a_{23} \\ b_3 & a_{32} & a_{33} \end{vmatrix}$$

The other x_i follow similarly, and we derive **Cramer's rule** that a solution of (5.20) is

$$x_1 = |\boldsymbol{A}|^{-1}\begin{vmatrix} b_1 & a_{12} & a_{13} \\ b_2 & a_{22} & a_{23} \\ b_3 & a_{32} & a_{33} \end{vmatrix},$$

$$x_2 = |\boldsymbol{A}|^{-1}\begin{vmatrix} a_{11} & b_1 & a_{13} \\ a_{21} & b_2 & a_{23} \\ a_{31} & b_3 & a_{33} \end{vmatrix},$$

$$x_3 = |\boldsymbol{A}|^{-1}\begin{vmatrix} a_{11} & a_{12} & b_1 \\ a_{21} & a_{22} & b_2 \\ a_{31} & a_{32} & b_3 \end{vmatrix}$$

provided $|\boldsymbol{A}| \neq 0$. Again it should be stressed that this rule should not be used as a computational method because of the large effort required to evaluate determinants.

Example 5.29

A function $u(x, y)$ is known to take values u_1, u_2 and u_3 at the points (x_1, y_1), (x_2, y_2) and (x_3, y_3) respectively. Find the linear interpolating function

$$u = a + bx + cy$$

within the triangle having its vertices at these three points.

Solution

To fit the data to the linear interpolating function

$$\begin{aligned} u_1 &= a + bx_1 + cy_1 \\ u_2 &= a + bx_2 + cy_2 \\ u_3 &= a + bx_3 + cy_3 \end{aligned} \quad \text{or in matrix form} \quad \begin{bmatrix} u_1 \\ u_2 \\ u_3 \end{bmatrix} = \begin{bmatrix} 1 & x_1 & y_1 \\ 1 & x_2 & y_2 \\ 1 & x_3 & y_3 \end{bmatrix}\begin{bmatrix} a \\ b \\ c \end{bmatrix}$$

The values of a, b and c can be obtained from Cramer's rule as

$$a = \begin{vmatrix} u_1 & x_1 & y_1 \\ u_2 & x_2 & y_2 \\ u_3 & x_3 & y_3 \end{vmatrix}/\det(\boldsymbol{A}), \quad b = \begin{vmatrix} 1 & u_1 & y_1 \\ 1 & u_2 & y_2 \\ 1 & u_3 & y_3 \end{vmatrix}/\det(\boldsymbol{A}) \quad \text{and}$$

$$c = \begin{vmatrix} 1 & x_1 & u_1 \\ 1 & x_2 & u_2 \\ 1 & x_3 & u_3 \end{vmatrix} / \det(\boldsymbol{A})$$

where $\boldsymbol{A}$ is the matrix of coefficients. The interpolation formula is now known. In finite-element analysis the evaluation of interpolation functions, such as the one described, is of great importance. Finite elements are central to many large-scale calculations in all branches of engineering.

Example 5.30 Solve the matrix equation $\boldsymbol{AX} = \boldsymbol{c}$ where

$$\boldsymbol{A} = \begin{bmatrix} 4 & 1 & 0 & 0 & 0 & 0 & 0 & 0 & 0 & 0 \\ 1 & 4 & 1 & 0 & 0 & 0 & 0 & 0 & 0 & 0 \\ 1 & 0 & 4 & 1 & 0 & 0 & 0 & 0 & 0 & 0 \\ 1 & 0 & 0 & 4 & 1 & 0 & 0 & 0 & 0 & 0 \\ 1 & 0 & 0 & 0 & 4 & 1 & 0 & 0 & 0 & 0 \\ 1 & 0 & 0 & 0 & 0 & 4 & 1 & 0 & 0 & 0 \\ 1 & 0 & 0 & 0 & 0 & 0 & 4 & 1 & 0 & 0 \\ 1 & 0 & 0 & 0 & 0 & 0 & 0 & 4 & 1 & 0 \\ 1 & 0 & 0 & 0 & 0 & 0 & 0 & 0 & 4 & 1 \\ 1 & 0 & 0 & 0 & 0 & 0 & 0 & 0 & 0 & 4 \end{bmatrix} \quad \text{and} \quad \boldsymbol{c} = \begin{bmatrix} 1 \\ 2 \\ 3 \\ 4 \\ 5 \\ 5 \\ 4 \\ 3 \\ 2 \\ 1 \end{bmatrix}$$

Solution The solution of such a problem is beyond the scope of hand computation; Cramer's rule, evaluation of the adjoint and direct evaluation of the inverse are all impracticable. Even the more practical methods in the next sections struggle with this size of problem if hand computation is tried. A computer package must be used. In MATLAB the relevant instructions are given.

```
b = zeros (10, 10);
for i = 1 : 9, b (i, i) = 4; b (i, i + 1) = 1; b (i + 1, 1)
= 1; end
b (10, 10) = 4;
c = [1; 2; 3; 4; 5; 5; 4; 3; 2; 1];
b\c
```

gives the solution

```
0.1685  0.3258  0.5282  0.7188  0.9563  1.0063  0.8063
0.6064  0.4059  0.2079
```

5.5.1 Exercises

Check your answers using MATLAB or MAPLE whenever possible.

60 Solve the matrix equation $\boldsymbol{AX} = \boldsymbol{b}$ for the vector $\boldsymbol{X}$ in the following:

(a) $\boldsymbol{A} = \begin{bmatrix} 2 & 3 \\ 5 & -2 \end{bmatrix} \quad \boldsymbol{b} = \begin{bmatrix} 8 \\ 1 \end{bmatrix}$

(b) $\boldsymbol{A} = \begin{bmatrix} 1 & 0 & 0 \\ 2 & -1 & 0 \\ 2 & 2 & 2 \end{bmatrix} \quad \boldsymbol{b} = \begin{bmatrix} 1 \\ 6 \\ -6 \end{bmatrix}$

(c) $\boldsymbol{A} = \begin{bmatrix} 2 & 1 \\ 0 & 1 \end{bmatrix}\begin{bmatrix} 1 & 0 \\ 3 & 1 \end{bmatrix} \quad \boldsymbol{b} = -\begin{bmatrix} 3 \\ 1 \end{bmatrix}$

(d) $\boldsymbol{A} = \begin{bmatrix} 1 & 0 & 0 & 0 \\ 0 & 3 & 1 & 0 \\ 0 & 1 & 2 & 0 \\ 0 & 0 & 0 & 1 \end{bmatrix} \quad \boldsymbol{b} = \begin{bmatrix} 4 \\ 11 \\ 7 \\ 1 \end{bmatrix}$

61 If

$$\boldsymbol{A} = \begin{bmatrix} \cos\alpha & -\sin\alpha \\ \sin\alpha & \cos\alpha \end{bmatrix}$$

show that

$$\boldsymbol{A}^{-1} = \begin{bmatrix} \cos\alpha & \sin\alpha \\ -\sin\alpha & \cos\alpha \end{bmatrix}$$

and hence solve for the vector $\boldsymbol{X}$ in the equation

$$\begin{bmatrix} \cos\frac{\pi}{8} & -\sin\frac{\pi}{8} \\ \sin\frac{\pi}{8} & \cos\frac{\pi}{8} \end{bmatrix}\boldsymbol{X} = \begin{bmatrix} \cos\frac{\pi}{4} \\ \sin\frac{\pi}{4} \end{bmatrix}$$

62 Solve the complex matrix equation

$$\begin{bmatrix} 1 & \mathrm{j} & 0 \\ 0 & 1 & 0 \\ \mathrm{j} & 0 & \mathrm{j} \end{bmatrix}\boldsymbol{X} = \begin{bmatrix} 0 \\ 1 \\ 0 \end{bmatrix}$$

63 Find the inverse of the matrix

$$\boldsymbol{A} = \begin{bmatrix} -1 & 2 & 1 \\ 0 & 1 & -2 \\ 1 & 4 & -1 \end{bmatrix}$$

and hence solve the equations

$$\begin{aligned} -x + 2y + z &= 2 \\ y - 2z &= -3 \\ x + 4y - z &= 4 \end{aligned}$$

64 Show that there are two values of α for which the equations

$$\begin{aligned} \alpha x - 3y + (1 + \alpha)z &= 0 \\ 2x + y - \alpha z &= 0 \\ (\alpha + 2)x - 2y + \alpha z &= 0 \end{aligned}$$

have non-trivial solutions. Find the solutions corresponding to these two values of α.

65 If

$$\boldsymbol{A} = \begin{bmatrix} -3 & 1 & -1 \\ 1 & -5 & 1 \\ -1 & 1 & -3 \end{bmatrix}$$

find the values of λ for which the equation $\boldsymbol{AX} = \lambda\boldsymbol{X}$ has non-trivial solutions.

66 Given the matrix

$$\boldsymbol{A} = \begin{bmatrix} 1 & a & -1 \\ a & -2 & 2 \\ -1 & 1 & a \end{bmatrix}$$

(a) solve $|\boldsymbol{A}| = 0$ for real a,

(b) if $a = 2$, find $\boldsymbol{A}^{-1}$ and hence solve

$$\boldsymbol{A}\begin{bmatrix} x \\ y \\ z \end{bmatrix} = \begin{bmatrix} 1 \\ 0 \\ 2 \end{bmatrix}$$

(c) if $a = 0$, find the general solution of

$$\mathbf{A}\begin{bmatrix} x \\ y \\ z \end{bmatrix} = \begin{bmatrix} 0 \\ 0 \\ 0 \end{bmatrix}$$

(d) if $a = 1$, show that

$$\mathbf{A}\begin{bmatrix} x \\ y \\ z \end{bmatrix} = 2\begin{bmatrix} x \\ y \\ z \end{bmatrix}$$

can be solved for non-zero x, y and z.

67 Use MATLAB or a similar package to find the inverse of the matrix

$$\begin{bmatrix} 6 & 2 & 1 & 0 & 0 & 0 \\ 2 & 6 & 2 & 1 & 0 & 0 \\ 1 & 2 & 6 & 2 & 1 & 0 \\ 0 & 1 & 2 & 6 & 2 & 1 \\ 0 & 0 & 1 & 2 & 6 & 2 \\ 0 & 0 & 0 & 1 & 2 & 6 \end{bmatrix}$$

and hence solve the matrix equation

$$\mathbf{AX} = \mathbf{c}$$

where $\mathbf{c}^{\mathrm{T}} = [1\ 0\ 0\ 0\ 0\ 1]$.

68 In finite-element calculations the bilinear function

$$u(x, y) = a + bx + cy + dxy$$

is commonly used for interpolation over a quadrilateral and data is always stored in matrix form. If the function fits the data $u(0, 0) = u_1$, $u(p, 0) = u_2$, $u(0, q) = u_3$ and $u(p, q) = u_4$ at the four corners of a rectangle, use matrices to find the coefficients a, b, c and d.

69 In an industrial process, water flows through three tanks in succession, as illustrated in Figure 5.6.

The tanks have unit cross-section and have heads of water x, y and z respectively. The rate of inflow into the first tank is u, the flowrate in the tube connecting tanks 1 and 2 is $6(x - y)$, the flowrate in the tube connecting tanks 2 and 3 is $5(y - z)$ and the rate of outflow from tank 3 is $4.5z$.

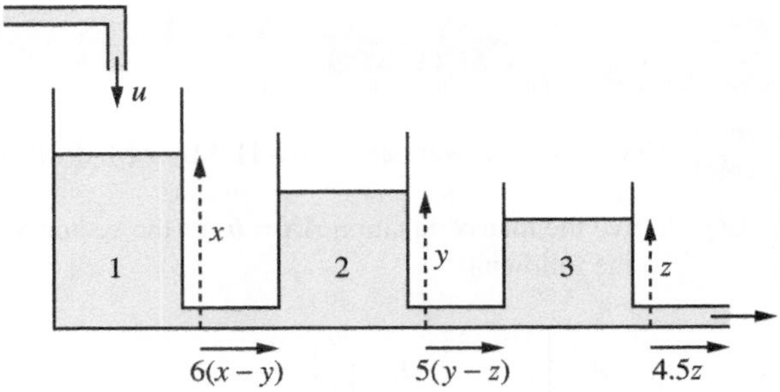

Figure 5.6 Flow through three tanks in Question 69.

Show that the equations of the system in the steady flow situation are

$$u = 6x - 6y$$
$$0 = 6x - 11y + 5z$$
$$0 = 5y - 9.5z$$

and hence find x, y and z.

70 A function is known to fit closely to the approximate function

$$f(z) = \frac{az + b}{cz + 1}$$

It is fitted to the three points ($z = 0, f = 1$), ($z = 0.5$, $f = 1.128$) and ($z = 1.3, f = 1.971$). Show that the parameters satisfy

$$\begin{bmatrix} 1 \\ 1.128 \\ 1.971 \end{bmatrix} = \begin{bmatrix} 0 & 1 & 0 \\ 0.5 & 1 & -0.5640 \\ 1.3 & 1 & -2.562 \end{bmatrix}\begin{bmatrix} a \\ b \\ c \end{bmatrix}$$

Find a, b and c and hence the approximating function (use of MATLAB is recommended). Check the value $f(1) = 1.543$. (Note that the values were chosen from tables of cosh z.)

The method described here is a simple example of a powerful approximation method.

71 A cantilever beam bends under a uniform load w per unit length and is subject to an axial force P at its free end. For small deflections a numerical approximation to the shape of the beam is given by the set of equations

$$\begin{aligned} -vy_1 + y_2 \qquad\qquad &= -u \\ y_1 - vy_2 + y_3 \qquad &= -4u \\ y_2 - vy_3 + y_4 &= -9u \\ 2y_3 - vy_4 &= -16u \end{aligned}$$

The deflections are indicated on Figure 5.7. The parameter v is defined as

$$v = 2 + \frac{PL^2}{16EI}$$

where EI is the flexural rigidity and L is the length of the beam. The parameter $u = wL^4/32EI$.

Use either Cramer's rule or the adjoint matrix to solve the equations when $v = 3$ and $u = 1$.

Note the immense effort required to solve this very simple problem using these methods. In later sections much more efficient methods will be described. A computer package such as MATLAB should be used to check the results.

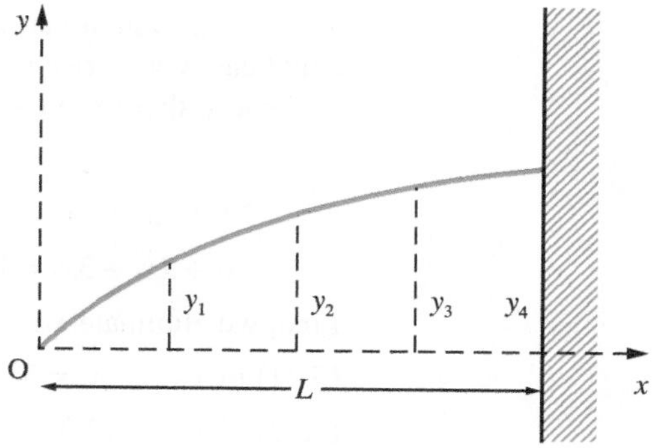

Figure 5.7 Cantilever beam in Question 71.

5.5.2 The solution of linear equations: elimination methods

The idea behind elimination techniques can be seen by considering the solution of two simultaneous equations

$$x + 2y = 4$$
$$2x + y = 5$$

Subtract 2 × (equation 1) from (equation 2) to give

$$x + 2y = 4$$
$$-3y = -3$$

Divide the second equation by −3

$$x + 2y = 4$$
$$y = 1$$

From the second of these equations $y = 1$ and substituting into the first equation gives $x = 2$.

This example illustrates the basic technique for the solution of a set of linear equations by Gaussian elimination, which is very straightforward in principle. However, it needs considerable care to ensure that the calculations are carried out efficiently. Given n linear equations in the variables $x_1, x_2, \ldots, x_n$, we solve in a series of steps:

(1) We solve the first equation for x_1 in terms of $x_2, \ldots, x_n$, and eliminate x_1 from the remaining equations.
(2) We then solve the second equation of the remaining set for x_2 in terms of $x_3, \ldots, x_n$ and eliminate x_2 from the remaining equations.
(3) We repeat the process in turn on $x_3, x_4, \ldots$ until we arrive at a final equation for x_n, which we can then solve.
(4) We substitute back to get in turn $x_{n-1}, x_{n-2}, \ldots, x_1$.

For a small number of variables, say two, three or four, the method is easy to apply and efficiency is not of the highest priority. In most science and engineering problems we are normally dealing with a large number of variables – a simple stability analysis of a vibrating system can lead to seven or eight variables, and a plate-bending problem could easily give rise to several hundred variables.

As a further example of the basic technique, we solve

$$x_1 + x_2 = 3 \quad \textbf{(5.21)}$$

$$2x_1 + x_2 + x_3 = 7 \quad \textbf{(5.22)}$$

$$x_1 + 2x_2 + 3x_3 = 14 \quad \textbf{(5.23)}$$

First, we eliminate x_1:

(5.21) gives $x_1 = 3 - x_2$ **(5.21′)**

(5.22) gives $2(3 - x_2) + x_2 + x_3 = 7, \quad \text{or} \quad -x_2 + x_3 = 1$ **(5.22′)**

(5.23) gives $(3 - x_2) + 2x_2 + 3x_3 = 14, \quad \text{or} \quad x_2 + 3x_3 = 11$ **(5.23′)**

Secondly we eliminate x_2:

(5.22′) gives $x_2 = x_3 - 1$ **(5.22″)**

(5.23′) gives $(x_3 - 1) + 3x_3 = 11, \quad \text{or} \quad 4x_3 = 12$ **(5.23″)**

Equation (5.23″) gives $x_3 = 3$; we put this into (5.22″) to obtain $x_2 = 2$; we then put this into (5.21′) to obtain $x_1 = 1$. Thus the values $x_1 = 1$, $x_2 = 2$ and $x_3 = 3$ give a solution to the original problem.

Equations (5.21)–(5.23) in matrix form become

$$\begin{bmatrix} 1 & 1 & 0 \\ 2 & 1 & 1 \\ 1 & 2 & 3 \end{bmatrix} \begin{bmatrix} x_1 \\ x_2 \\ x_3 \end{bmatrix} = \begin{bmatrix} 3 \\ 7 \\ 14 \end{bmatrix}$$

The elimination procedure has reduced the equations to (5.21), (5.22′) and (5.23″), which in matrix form become

$$\begin{bmatrix} 1 & 1 & 0 \\ 0 & -1 & 1 \\ 0 & 0 & 4 \end{bmatrix} \begin{bmatrix} x_1 \\ x_2 \\ x_3 \end{bmatrix} = \begin{bmatrix} 3 \\ 1 \\ 12 \end{bmatrix}$$

Essentially the elimination has brought the equations to **upper-triangular** form (that is, a form in which the matrix of coefficients has zeros in every position below the diagonal), which are then very easy to solve.

Elimination procedures rely on the manipulation of equations or, equivalently, the rows of the matrix equation. There are various **elementary row operations** used which do not alter the solution of the equations:

(a) multiply a row by a constant;
(b) interchange any two rows;
(c) add or subtract one row from another.

To illustrate these, we take the matrix equation

$$\begin{bmatrix} 1 & 1 & 0 \\ 2 & 1 & 1 \\ -1 & 2 & 3 \end{bmatrix} \begin{bmatrix} x_1 \\ x_2 \\ x_3 \end{bmatrix} = \begin{bmatrix} 3 \\ 7 \\ 12 \end{bmatrix}$$

which has the solution $x_1 = 1$, $x_2 = 2$, $x_3 = 3$.

Multiplying the first row by 2 (a row operation of type (a)) yields

$$\begin{bmatrix} 2 & 2 & 0 \\ 2 & 1 & 1 \\ -1 & 2 & 3 \end{bmatrix} \begin{bmatrix} x_1 \\ x_2 \\ x_3 \end{bmatrix} = \begin{bmatrix} 6 \\ 7 \\ 12 \end{bmatrix}$$

Interchanging rows 1 and 3 (a row operation of type (b)) yields

$$\begin{bmatrix} -1 & 2 & 3 \\ 2 & 1 & 1 \\ 1 & 1 & 0 \end{bmatrix} \begin{bmatrix} x_1 \\ x_2 \\ x_3 \end{bmatrix} = \begin{bmatrix} 12 \\ 7 \\ 3 \end{bmatrix}$$

Subtracting row 1 from row 2 (a row operation of type (c)) yields

$$\begin{bmatrix} 1 & 1 & 0 \\ 1 & 0 & 1 \\ -1 & 2 & 3 \end{bmatrix} \begin{bmatrix} x_1 \\ x_2 \\ x_3 \end{bmatrix} = \begin{bmatrix} 3 \\ 4 \\ 12 \end{bmatrix}$$

In each case we see that the solution of the modified equations is still $x_1 = 1$, $x_2 = 2$, $x_3 = 3$.

Elimination procedures use repeated applications of (a), (b) and (c) in some systematic manner until the equations are processed into a required form such as the upper-triangular equations

$$\begin{bmatrix} a_{11} & a_{12} & a_{13} & \dots & a_{1n} \\ 0 & a_{22} & a_{23} & \dots & a_{2n} \\ 0 & 0 & a_{33} & \dots & a_{3n} \\ \vdots & \vdots & \vdots & & \vdots \\ 0 & 0 & 0 & \dots & a_{nn} \end{bmatrix} \begin{bmatrix} x_1 \\ x_2 \\ x_3 \\ \vdots \\ x_n \end{bmatrix} = \begin{bmatrix} b_1 \\ b_2 \\ b_3 \\ \vdots \\ b_n \end{bmatrix} \tag{5.24}$$

The solution of the equations in upper-triangular form can be written as

$$x_n = b_n/a_{nn}$$

$$x_{n-1} = (b_{n-1} - a_{n-1,n}x_n)/a_{n-1,n-1}$$

$$x_{n-2} = (b_{n-2} - a_{n-2,n}x_n - a_{n-2,n-1}x_{n-1})/a_{n-2,n-2}$$

$$\vdots$$

$$x_1 = (b_1 - a_{1n}x_n - a_{1,n-1}x_{n-1} - \dots - a_{12}x_2)/a_{11}$$

A MATLAB function procedure implementing these equations is shown in Figure 5.8. The elementary row operations and the elimination technique are illustrated in Example 5.31.

Figure 5.8
Procedure to solve the upper-triangular system (5.24).

```
function x = uppertrisolve(A,b,n)
% uppertrisolve solves A*x=b where A is an nxn upper
triangular matrix with
%nonzero diagonal elements, b is an n vector
%Note the use of the 'colon' notation
%Note that if semicolons are replaced by commas intermediate
results are
%displayed
z=zeros(n,1);
z(n) = b(n)/A(n,n);
for i=n-1:-1:1
  z(i) = (b(i) -A(i,i+1:n)*z(i+1:n))/A(i,i);
end
x=z;
end
```

Example 5.31 Use elementary row operations and elimination to solve the set of linear equations

$$x + 2y + 3z = 10$$
$$-x + y + z = 0$$
$$y - z = 1$$

Solution In matrix form the equations are $\begin{bmatrix} 1 & 2 & 3 \\ -1 & 1 & 1 \\ 0 & 1 & -1 \end{bmatrix}\begin{bmatrix} x \\ y \\ z \end{bmatrix} = \begin{bmatrix} 10 \\ 0 \\ 1 \end{bmatrix}$

Add row 1 to row 2: $\begin{bmatrix} 1 & 2 & 3 \\ 0 & 3 & 4 \\ 0 & 1 & -1 \end{bmatrix}\begin{bmatrix} x \\ y \\ z \end{bmatrix} = \begin{bmatrix} 10 \\ 10 \\ 1 \end{bmatrix}$

Divide row 2 by 3: $\begin{bmatrix} 1 & 2 & 3 \\ 0 & 1 & \frac{4}{3} \\ 0 & 1 & -1 \end{bmatrix}\begin{bmatrix} x \\ y \\ z \end{bmatrix} = \begin{bmatrix} 10 \\ \frac{10}{3} \\ 1 \end{bmatrix}$

Subtract row 2 from row 3: $\begin{bmatrix} 1 & 2 & 3 \\ 0 & 1 & \frac{4}{3} \\ 0 & 0 & -\frac{7}{3} \end{bmatrix}\begin{bmatrix} x \\ y \\ z \end{bmatrix} = \begin{bmatrix} 10 \\ \frac{10}{3} \\ -\frac{7}{3} \end{bmatrix}$

Divide row 3 by $(-\frac{7}{3})$: $\begin{bmatrix} 1 & 2 & 3 \\ 0 & 1 & \frac{4}{3} \\ 0 & 0 & 1 \end{bmatrix}\begin{bmatrix} x \\ y \\ z \end{bmatrix} = \begin{bmatrix} 10 \\ \frac{10}{3} \\ 1 \end{bmatrix}$

The equations are now in a standard upper-triangular form for the application of the back substitution procedure described formally in Figure 5.8.

From the third row $z = 1$

From the second row $y = \frac{10}{3} - \frac{4}{3}z = 2$

From the first row $x = 10 - 2y - 3z = 3$

It remains to undertake the operations in the example in a routine and logical manner to make the method into one of the most powerful techniques, called **elimination methods**, available for the solution of sets of linear equations. The method is available on all computer packages. Such packages are excellent at undertaking the rather tedious arithmetic and some will even illustrate the computational detail also. They are well worth mastering. However, writing and checking your own procedures, implementing the MATLAB code in Figure 5.8 for instance, is a powerful learning tool and gives great understanding of the method, the difficulties and errors involved in a method.

Tridiagonal or Thomas algorithm

Because of the ease of solution of upper-triangular systems, many methods use the general strategy of reducing the equations to this form. As an example of this strategy, we shall look at a **tridiagonal system**, which takes the form

$$\begin{bmatrix} a_1 & b_1 & 0 & 0 & 0 & 0 & \dots & 0 \\ c_2 & a_2 & b_2 & 0 & 0 & 0 & \dots & 0 \\ 0 & c_3 & a_3 & b_3 & 0 & 0 & \dots & 0 \\ 0 & 0 & c_4 & a_4 & b_4 & 0 & \dots & 0 \\ & & & & & & & \vdots \\ \vdots & & & & & & & 0 \\ 0 & & \dots & & 0 & c_{n-1} & a_{n-1} & b_{n-1} \\ 0 & & \dots & & 0 & 0 & c_n & a_n \end{bmatrix} \begin{bmatrix} x_1 \\ x_2 \\ \\ \vdots \\ \\ \\ x_{n-1} \\ x_n \end{bmatrix} = \begin{bmatrix} d_1 \\ d_2 \\ \\ \vdots \\ \\ \\ d_{n-1} \\ d_n \end{bmatrix} \tag{5.25}$$

or

$$\begin{aligned} a_1x_1 + b_1x_2 \qquad\qquad\qquad &= d_1 \\ c_2x_1 + a_2x_2 + b_2x_3 \qquad &= d_2 \\ c_3x_2 + a_3x_3 + b_3x_4 &= d_3 \\ \ddots \qquad \ddots \qquad &\ \ \vdots \\ c_nx_{n-1} + a_nx_n &= d_n \end{aligned}$$

First we eliminate x_1:

$$\begin{aligned} x_1 + b_1'x_2 \qquad\qquad &= d_1' \\ a_2'x_2 + b_2x_3 \qquad &= d_2' \\ c_3x_2 + a_3x_3 + b_3x_4 &= d_3 \end{aligned}$$

and so on

Figure 5.9
Tridiagonal or Thomas algorithm for the solution of (5.25).

```
function x = tridiag(a,b,c,d,n)
%Solves a tridiagonal system
% a=diag(1 to n), b=upper diag(1 to n-1), c=lower diag(2 to
n), d=RHS, %all vectors of dimension n ; note c(1) and b(n)
are not used
% elimination stage
for i=1:n-1,
b(i)=b(i)/a(i);d(i)=d(i)/a(i);a(i)=1;
a(i+1)=a(i+1)-c(i+1)*b(i);d(i+1)=d(i+1)-
c(i+1)*d(i);c(i+1)=0;
end
% back substitution
x=zeros(n,1);
d(n)=d(n)/a(n);a(n)=1;
x(n)=d(n);
for j=n-1:-1:1,x(j)=d(j)-b(j)*x(j+1);end
%[a,b,c,d] %remove comment at the beginning of the line to
see final a,b,c,d
end
```

where

$$b_1' = \frac{b_1}{a_1}, \quad d_1' = \frac{d_1}{a_1}, \quad a_2' = a_2 - c_2 b_1' \quad \text{and} \quad d_2' = d_2 - c_2 d_1'$$

Next we eliminate x_2:

$$\begin{aligned}
x_1 + b_1' x_2 \qquad\qquad\qquad &= d_1' \\
x_2 + b_2'' x_3 \qquad\qquad &= d_2'' \\
a_3'' x_3 + b_3 x_4 \qquad &= d_3'' \\
c_4 x_3 + a_4 x_4 + b_4 x_5 &= d_4 \\
\text{and so on} \qquad &
\end{aligned}$$

where

$$b_2'' = \frac{b_2}{a_2'}, \quad d_2'' = \frac{d_2'}{a_2'}, \quad a_3'' = a_3 - c_3 b_2'' \quad \text{and} \quad d_3'' = d_3 - c_3 d_2''$$

We can proceed to eliminate all the variables down to the nth. We have then converted the problem to an upper-triangular form, which can be solved by the procedure in Figure 5.8. A MATLAB function to solve (5.25) called the **tridiagonal or Thomas algorithm** is shown in Figure 5.9. The algorithm is written so that each primed value, when it is computed, replaces the previous value. Similarly the double-primed values replace the primed values. This is called **overwriting**, and reduces the storage required to implement the algorithm on a computer. It should be noted, however, that the algorithm is written for clarity and not minimum storage or maximum efficiency. The algorithm is very widely used; it is exceptionally fast and requires very little storage. Again writing your own code based on Figure 5.9 can greatly enhance the understanding of the method.

Example 5.32 Use the tridiagonal procedure to solve

$$\begin{bmatrix} 2 & 1 & 0 & 0 \\ 1 & 2 & 1 & 0 \\ 0 & 1 & 2 & 1 \\ 0 & 0 & 1 & 2 \end{bmatrix} \begin{bmatrix} x \\ y \\ z \\ t \end{bmatrix} = \begin{bmatrix} 1 \\ 1 \\ 1 \\ -2 \end{bmatrix}$$

Solution The sequence of matrices is given by

$$\begin{bmatrix}1 & \frac{1}{2} & 0 & 0\\ 0 & \frac{3}{2} & 1 & 0\\ 0 & 1 & 2 & 1\\ 0 & 0 & 1 & 2\end{bmatrix}\begin{bmatrix}x\\ y\\ z\\ t\end{bmatrix}=\begin{bmatrix}\frac{1}{2}\\ \frac{1}{2}\\ 1\\ -2\end{bmatrix},\quad \begin{bmatrix}1 & \frac{1}{2} & 0 & 0\\ 0 & 1 & \frac{2}{3} & 0\\ 0 & 0 & \frac{4}{3} & 1\\ 0 & 0 & 1 & 2\end{bmatrix}\begin{bmatrix}x\\ y\\ z\\ t\end{bmatrix}=\begin{bmatrix}\frac{1}{2}\\ \frac{1}{3}\\ \frac{2}{3}\\ -2\end{bmatrix}$$

$$\begin{bmatrix}1 & \frac{1}{2} & 0 & 0\\ 0 & 1 & \frac{2}{3} & 0\\ 0 & 0 & 1 & \frac{3}{4}\\ 0 & 0 & 0 & \frac{5}{4}\end{bmatrix}\begin{bmatrix}x\\ y\\ z\\ t\end{bmatrix}=\begin{bmatrix}\frac{1}{2}\\ \frac{1}{3}\\ \frac{1}{2}\\ -\frac{5}{2}\end{bmatrix}$$

The elimination stage is now complete, and we substitute back to give

$$t=-2,\ z=\tfrac{1}{2}-\tfrac{3}{4}t=2,\ y=\tfrac{1}{3}-\tfrac{2}{3}z=-1 \quad \text{and} \quad x=\tfrac{1}{2}-\tfrac{1}{2}y=1$$

so that the complete solution is $x=1$, $y=-1$, $z=2$, $t=-2$.

Although the Thomas algorithm is efficient, the procedure in Figure 5.9 is not fool-proof, as illustrated by the simple example

$$\begin{bmatrix}-1 & 1 & 0\\ 1 & -1 & 1\\ 0 & 1 & -1\end{bmatrix}\begin{bmatrix}x\\ y\\ z\end{bmatrix}=\begin{bmatrix}-1\\ 2\\ 1\end{bmatrix}$$

After the first step we have

$$\begin{bmatrix}1 & -1 & 0\\ 0 & 0 & 1\\ 0 & 1 & -1\end{bmatrix}\begin{bmatrix}x\\ y\\ z\end{bmatrix}=\begin{bmatrix}1\\ 1\\ 1\end{bmatrix}$$

The next step divides by the diagonal element a_{22}. Since this element is zero, the method crashes to a halt. There is a perfectly good solution, however, since simply interchanging the last two rows,

$$\begin{bmatrix}1 & -1 & 0\\ 0 & 1 & -1\\ 0 & 0 & 1\end{bmatrix}\begin{bmatrix}x\\ y\\ z\end{bmatrix}=\begin{bmatrix}1\\ 1\\ 1\end{bmatrix}$$

gives an upper-triangular matrix with the obvious solution $z=1$, $y=2$, $x=3$. It is clear that checks must be put into the algorithm to prevent such failures.

Gaussian elimination

Since most matrix equations are not tridiagonal, we should like to extend the idea to a general matrix

$$\begin{bmatrix} a_{11} & a_{12} & a_{13} & \dots & a_{1n} \\ a_{21} & a_{22} & a_{23} & \dots & a_{2n} \\ \vdots & \vdots & \vdots & & \vdots \\ a_{n1} & a_{n2} & a_{n3} & \dots & a_{nn} \end{bmatrix} \begin{bmatrix} x_1 \\ x_2 \\ \vdots \\ x_n \end{bmatrix} = \begin{bmatrix} b_1 \\ b_2 \\ \vdots \\ b_n \end{bmatrix} \quad (5.26)$$

The result of doing this is a method known as **Gaussian elimination**. It is a little more involved than the Thomas algorithm. First we eliminate x_1:

$$\begin{bmatrix} 1 & a'_{12} & a'_{13} & \dots & a'_{1n} \\ 0 & a'_{22} & a'_{23} & \dots & a'_{2n} \\ 0 & a'_{32} & a'_{33} & \dots & a'_{3n} \\ \vdots & \vdots & \vdots & & \vdots \\ 0 & a'_{n2} & a'_{n3} & \dots & a'_{nn} \end{bmatrix} \begin{bmatrix} x_1 \\ x_2 \\ \\ \vdots \\ x_n \end{bmatrix} = \begin{bmatrix} b'_1 \\ b'_2 \\ \\ \vdots \\ b'_n \end{bmatrix}$$

where

$$a'_{12} = \frac{a_{12}}{a_{11}}, \quad a'_{13} = \frac{a_{13}}{a_{11}}, \quad \dots, \quad a'_{1n} = \frac{a_{1n}}{a_{11}}, \quad b'_1 = \frac{b_1}{a_{11}}$$

$$a'_{22} = a_{22} - a_{21}a'_{12}, \quad a'_{23} = a_{23} - a_{21}a'_{13}, \quad \dots, \quad b'_2 = b_2 - a_{21}b'_1$$

$$a'_{32} = a_{32} - a_{31}a'_{12}, \quad a'_{33} = a_{33} - a_{31}a'_{13}, \quad \dots, \quad b'_3 = b_3 - a_{31}b'_1$$

and so on.

Generally these can be written as

$$a'_{1j} = \frac{a_{1j}}{a_{11}}, \quad j = 1, \dots, n \quad b'_1 = \frac{b_1}{a_{11}}$$

$$\left.\begin{aligned} a'_{ij} &= a_{ij} - a_{i1}a'_{ij} \\ b'_i &= b_i - a_{i1}b'_1 \end{aligned}\right\}, \quad i = 2, \dots, n \quad \text{and} \quad j = 2, \dots, n$$

We now operate in an identical manner on the $(n - 1) \times (n - 1)$ submatrix, formed by ignoring row 1 and column 1, and repeat the process until the equations are of upper-triangular form. At the general step in the algorithm the equations will take the form

$$\begin{bmatrix} 1 & * & * & * & & & \dots & * \\ 0 & 1 & * & * & & & \dots & * \\ 0 & 0 & 1 & * & & & \dots & * \\ 0 & 0 & & \ddots & & & & \vdots \\ \vdots & \vdots & & \ddots & & & & \\ 0 & \dots & & 0 & 1 & * & \dots & * \\ 0 & \dots & & & 0 & a_{ii} & \dots & a_{in} \\ \vdots & & & & 0 & \vdots & \ddots & \vdots \\ & & & & \vdots & & & \\ 0 & \dots & & & 0 & a_{ni} & \dots & a_{nn} \end{bmatrix} \begin{bmatrix} x_1 \\ x_2 \\ \\ \\ \vdots \\ \\ \\ \\ \\ x_n \end{bmatrix} = \begin{bmatrix} * \\ * \\ \\ \\ \vdots \\ \\ \\ \\ \\ * \end{bmatrix} \quad (5.27)$$

Figure 5.10
Elimination procedure for (5.26).

```
function A= elim(m,n,a)
% elim implements Gaussian elimination for a mxn matrix a
% If a(k,k)=0 at any time the method will fail
% remove semicolons at the ends of lines 8,9 and 12 to print
all steps
  for k=1:m-1
      if k<n
      a(k,:)=a(k,:)/a(k,k);
      a(k+1:m,k:n)=a(k+1:m,k:n)-a(k+1:m,k)*a(k,k:n);
        end
    end
A=a;
end
```

Again overwriting avoids the need for introducing primed symbols; the algorithm is shown in Figure 5.10.

The procedure is written for a general $m \times n$ matrix. To solve the matrix equation $\boldsymbol{AX} = \boldsymbol{b}$, where $\boldsymbol{A}$ is a non-singular square $n \times n$ matrix, append $\boldsymbol{b}$ to $\boldsymbol{A}$ and then use the function files *elim* and *uppertrisolve*

```
B = [A,b]
C = elim (n,n+1, B)
z = uppertrisolve (C(:,[1:n]), C(:,n+1),n)
```

Although packages give the solution very efficiently, for instance $\boldsymbol{X} = \boldsymbol{A}\backslash\boldsymbol{b}$, the MATLAB procedures in Figures 5.9 and 5.10, together with these few lines of code, provide an opportunity to look at the intermediate results which can greatly enhance the understanding of the method.

This algorithm, sharing the merits of the Thomas algorithm, is very widely used by engineers to solve linear equations.

Example 5.33 Using elimination and back substitution, solve the equations

$$\begin{bmatrix} 2 & 3 & 4 \\ 1 & 2 & 3 \\ 1 & 4 & 5 \end{bmatrix}\begin{bmatrix} x \\ y \\ z \end{bmatrix} = \begin{bmatrix} 1 \\ 1 \\ 2 \end{bmatrix}$$

Solution From the method in Figure 5.10 the steps are

Divide first row by 2: $\begin{bmatrix} 1 & \frac{3}{2} & 2 \\ 1 & 2 & 3 \\ 1 & 4 & 5 \end{bmatrix}\begin{bmatrix} x \\ y \\ z \end{bmatrix} = \begin{bmatrix} \frac{1}{2} \\ 1 \\ 2 \end{bmatrix}$

Subtract row 1 from row 2 and row 3: $\begin{bmatrix} 1 & \frac{3}{2} & 2 \\ 0 & \frac{1}{2} & 1 \\ 0 & \frac{5}{2} & 3 \end{bmatrix}\begin{bmatrix} x \\ y \\ z \end{bmatrix} = \begin{bmatrix} \frac{1}{2} \\ \frac{1}{2} \\ \frac{3}{2} \end{bmatrix}$

Divide second row by $\frac{1}{2}$: $\begin{bmatrix} 1 & \frac{3}{2} & 2 \\ 0 & 1 & 2 \\ 0 & \frac{5}{2} & 3 \end{bmatrix}\begin{bmatrix} x \\ y \\ z \end{bmatrix} = \begin{bmatrix} \frac{1}{2} \\ 1 \\ \frac{3}{2} \end{bmatrix}$

Subtract $\frac{5}{2}$ × (row 2) from row 3: $\begin{bmatrix} 1 & \frac{3}{2} & 2 \\ 0 & 1 & 2 \\ 0 & 0 & -2 \end{bmatrix}\begin{bmatrix} x \\ y \\ z \end{bmatrix} = \begin{bmatrix} \frac{1}{2} \\ 1 \\ -1 \end{bmatrix}$

Divide row 3 by (−2): $\begin{bmatrix} 1 & \frac{3}{2} & 2 \\ 0 & 1 & 2 \\ 0 & 0 & 1 \end{bmatrix}\begin{bmatrix} x \\ y \\ z \end{bmatrix} = \begin{bmatrix} \frac{1}{2} \\ 1 \\ \frac{1}{2} \end{bmatrix}$

The elimination procedure is now complete and the back substitution (from Figure 5.8) is applied to the upper-triangular matrix.

From the third row $z = \frac{1}{2}$

From the second row $y = 1 - 2z = 0$

From the first row $x = \frac{1}{2} - \frac{3}{2}y - 2z = -\frac{1}{2}$

so the solution is $x = -\frac{1}{2}$, $y = 0$, $z = \frac{1}{2}$.

Example 5.34 Solve

$$\begin{bmatrix} 1 & 2 & 3 & 1 \\ 2 & 1 & 1 & 1 \\ 1 & 2 & 1 & 0 \\ 0 & 1 & 1 & 2 \end{bmatrix}\begin{bmatrix} x \\ y \\ z \\ t \end{bmatrix} = \begin{bmatrix} 5 \\ 3 \\ 4 \\ 0 \end{bmatrix}$$

Solution The elimination sequence is

$$\begin{bmatrix} 1 & 2 & 3 & 1 \\ 0 & -3 & -5 & -1 \\ 0 & 0 & -2 & -1 \\ 0 & 1 & 1 & 2 \end{bmatrix}\begin{bmatrix} x \\ y \\ z \\ t \end{bmatrix} = \begin{bmatrix} 5 \\ -7 \\ -1 \\ 0 \end{bmatrix}, \quad \begin{bmatrix} 1 & 2 & 3 & 1 \\ 0 & 1 & \frac{5}{3} & \frac{1}{3} \\ 0 & 0 & -2 & -1 \\ 0 & 0 & -\frac{2}{3} & \frac{5}{3} \end{bmatrix}\begin{bmatrix} x \\ y \\ z \\ t \end{bmatrix} = \begin{bmatrix} 5 \\ \frac{7}{3} \\ -1 \\ -\frac{7}{3} \end{bmatrix}$$

$$\begin{bmatrix} 1 & 2 & 3 & 1 \\ 0 & 1 & \frac{5}{3} & \frac{1}{3} \\ 0 & 0 & 1 & \frac{1}{2} \\ 0 & 0 & 0 & 2 \end{bmatrix}\begin{bmatrix} x \\ y \\ z \\ t \end{bmatrix} = \begin{bmatrix} 5 \\ \frac{7}{3} \\ \frac{1}{2} \\ -2 \end{bmatrix}$$

and application of the upper-triangular procedure gives $t = -1$, $z = 1$, $y = 1$ and $x = 1$.

It is clear again that if, in the algorithm shown in Figure 5.10, A(i, i) is zero at any time, the method will fail. It is, in fact, also found to be beneficial to the stability of the method to have A(i, i) as large as possible. Thus in (5.27) it is usual to perform a 'partial pivoting' so that the largest value in the column, $\max_{i \leq p \leq n} |A(p, i)|$, is chosen and the equations are swapped around to make this element the pivot. In Figure 5.11 partial pivoting is included in the `elim` procedure:

Figure 5.11
Elimination procedure for (5.26) with partial pivoting

```
function A= elimpp(m,n,a )
% elimpp implements Gaussian elimination
% with partial pivoting for an mxn matrix a
% remove semicolons at the ends of lines 8,11,12 and 13
% to print all
for k=1:m-1
  if k<n
   M=max(abs(a(k:m,k)));
   if M>0  %ensures pivot is non-zero
          kk=k;while abs(a(kk,k))<M,kk=kk+1;end
          a([k,kk],:)=a([kk,k],:);    % row swap
          a(k,:)=a(k,:)/a(k,k);
          a(k+1:m,k:n)=a(k+1:m,k:n)-
          a(k+1:m,k)*a(k,k:n);
     end
   end
A=a;
end
```

In practical computer implementations of the algorithm the elements of the rows would not be swapped explicitly. Instead, a pointer system would be used to implement a technique known as **indirect addressing**, which allows much faster computations. The interested reader is referred to texts on computer programming techniques for a full explanation of this method.

In a hand-computation version of this elimination procedure there are methods that maintain running checks and minimize the amount of writing. In this book the emphasis is on a computer implementation, and the hand computations are provided to illustrate the principle of the method. It is a powerful learning technique to write your own programs, but the practising professional engineer will normally use procedures from a computer software library, where these are available.

In MATLAB the instruction `[L, U] = lu(A)` provides in $\boldsymbol{U}$ the eliminated matrix. The method used in MATLAB always uses partial pivoting. The instruction `A\b` will give the solution for a square matrix in one step. The MAPLE package can deal with any size matrix, so the right-hand side of the matrix equation should be appended to $\boldsymbol{A}$ and hence included in the elimination, and the instruction `gausselim(A);` provides the elimination. The instruction `gaussjord(A);` uses a much more subtle elimination process – see any advanced textbook on numerical linear algebra – and gives the solution in the most convenient form. The instruction `backsub(B)` is also available for the back substitution. The instruction `linsolve(A,b);` gives the solution in one step.

Example 5.35 Solve the matrix equation

$$\begin{bmatrix} 1 & 2 & 3 & 1 \\ 2 & 1 & 1 & 1 \\ 1 & 3 & 1 & 0 \\ 0 & 1 & 1 & 2 \end{bmatrix} \begin{bmatrix} x \\ y \\ z \\ t \end{bmatrix} = \begin{bmatrix} 4 \\ 3 \\ 2 \\ 1 \end{bmatrix}$$

by Gaussian elimination with partial pivoting.

Solution The sequence is as follows. We first interchange rows 1 and 2 and eliminate:

$$\begin{bmatrix} 2 & 1 & 1 & 1 \\ 1 & 2 & 3 & 1 \\ 1 & 3 & 1 & 0 \\ 0 & 1 & 1 & 2 \end{bmatrix}\begin{bmatrix} x \\ y \\ z \\ t \end{bmatrix} = \begin{bmatrix} 3 \\ 4 \\ 2 \\ 1 \end{bmatrix} \rightarrow \begin{bmatrix} 1 & \frac{1}{2} & \frac{1}{2} & \frac{1}{2} \\ 0 & \frac{3}{2} & \frac{5}{2} & \frac{1}{2} \\ 0 & \frac{5}{2} & \frac{1}{2} & -\frac{1}{2} \\ 0 & 1 & 1 & 2 \end{bmatrix}\begin{bmatrix} x \\ y \\ z \\ t \end{bmatrix} = \begin{bmatrix} \frac{3}{2} \\ \frac{5}{2} \\ \frac{1}{2} \\ 1 \end{bmatrix}$$

We then interchange rows 2 and 3 and eliminate:

$$\begin{bmatrix} 1 & \frac{1}{2} & \frac{1}{2} & \frac{1}{2} \\ 0 & \frac{5}{2} & \frac{1}{2} & -\frac{1}{2} \\ 0 & \frac{3}{2} & \frac{5}{2} & \frac{1}{2} \\ 0 & 1 & 1 & 2 \end{bmatrix}\begin{bmatrix} x \\ y \\ z \\ t \end{bmatrix} = \begin{bmatrix} \frac{3}{2} \\ \frac{1}{2} \\ \frac{5}{2} \\ 1 \end{bmatrix} \rightarrow \begin{bmatrix} 1 & \frac{1}{2} & \frac{1}{2} & \frac{1}{2} \\ 0 & 1 & \frac{1}{5} & -\frac{1}{5} \\ 0 & 0 & \frac{11}{5} & \frac{4}{5} \\ 0 & 0 & \frac{4}{5} & \frac{11}{5} \end{bmatrix}\begin{bmatrix} x \\ y \\ z \\ t \end{bmatrix} = \begin{bmatrix} \frac{3}{2} \\ \frac{1}{5} \\ \frac{11}{5} \\ \frac{4}{5} \end{bmatrix}$$

There is no need to interchange rows at this stage, and the elimination proceeds immediately:

$$\begin{bmatrix} 1 & \frac{1}{2} & \frac{1}{2} & \frac{1}{2} \\ 0 & 1 & \frac{1}{5} & -\frac{1}{5} \\ 0 & 0 & 1 & \frac{4}{11} \\ 0 & 0 & 0 & \frac{21}{11} \end{bmatrix}\begin{bmatrix} x \\ y \\ z \\ t \end{bmatrix} = \begin{bmatrix} \frac{3}{2} \\ \frac{1}{5} \\ 1 \\ 0 \end{bmatrix}$$

Back substitution now gives $t = 0$, $z = 1$, $y = 0$ and $x = 1$.

Ill-conditioning

Elimination methods are not without their difficulties, and the following example will highlight some of them.

Example 5.36 Solve, by elimination, the equations

(a) $\begin{bmatrix} 2 & 1 \\ 1 & 0.5001 \end{bmatrix}\begin{bmatrix} x \\ y \end{bmatrix} = \begin{bmatrix} 0.3 \\ 0.6 \end{bmatrix}$ (b) $\begin{bmatrix} 2 & 1 \\ 1 & 0.4999 \end{bmatrix}\begin{bmatrix} x \\ y \end{bmatrix} = \begin{bmatrix} 0.3 \\ 0.6 \end{bmatrix}$

Solution Keeping the calculations parallel,

(a) $\begin{bmatrix} 1 & 0.5 \\ 1 & 0.5001 \end{bmatrix}\begin{bmatrix} x \\ y \end{bmatrix} = \begin{bmatrix} 0.15 \\ 0.6 \end{bmatrix}$ (b) $\begin{bmatrix} 1 & 0.5 \\ 1 & 0.4999 \end{bmatrix}\begin{bmatrix} x \\ y \end{bmatrix} = \begin{bmatrix} 0.15 \\ 0.6 \end{bmatrix}$

$\begin{bmatrix} 1 & 0.5 \\ 0 & 0.0001 \end{bmatrix}\begin{bmatrix} x \\ y \end{bmatrix} = \begin{bmatrix} 0.15 \\ 0.45 \end{bmatrix}$ $\begin{bmatrix} 1 & 0.5 \\ 0 & -0.0001 \end{bmatrix}\begin{bmatrix} x \\ y \end{bmatrix} = \begin{bmatrix} 0.15 \\ 0.45 \end{bmatrix}$

with solution

$y = 4500, \quad x = -2249.85$

with solution

$y = -4500, \quad x = 2250.15$

In Example 5.36 simple equations that have only marginally different coefficients have wildly different solutions. This situation is likely to cause problems, so it must be analysed carefully. To do so in full detail is not appropriate here, but the problem is clearly connected with taking differences of numbers that are almost equal: $0.5001 - 0.5 = 0.0001$.

Systems of equations that exhibit such awkward behaviour are called **ill-conditioned.** It is not straightforward to identify ill-conditioning in matrices involving many variables, but an example will illustrate the difficulties in the two-variable case. Suppose we solve

$$2x + \quad y = 0.3$$

$$x - \alpha y = 0$$

where $\alpha = 1 \pm 0.05$ has some error in its value. We easily obtain $x = 0.3\alpha/(1 + 2\alpha)$ and $y = 0.3/(1 + 2\alpha)$, and putting in the range of α values we get $0.0983 \leqslant x \leqslant 0.1016$ and $0.0968 \leqslant y \leqslant 0.1034$. Thus an error of ±5% in the value of α produces an error of ±2% in x and an error of ±3% in y.

If we now try to solve

$$2x + \quad y = 0.3$$

$$x + \alpha y = 0.3$$

where $\alpha = 0.4 \pm 0.05$, then we get the solution $x = 0.3(1 - \alpha)/(1 - 2\alpha)$, $y = -0.3/(1 - 2\alpha)$. Putting in the range of α values now gives $0.65 \leqslant x \leqslant 1.65$ and $-3 \leqslant y \leqslant -1$, and an error of ±12% in the value of α produces errors in x and y of up to 100%.

Figure 5.12 illustrates these equations geometrically. We see that a small change in the slope of the line $x - \alpha y = 0$ makes only a small difference in the solution. However, changing the slope of the line $x + \alpha y = 0.3$ makes a large difference, because the lines are nearly parallel. Identifying such behaviour for higher-dimensional problems is not at all easy. Sets of equations of this kind do occur in engineering contexts, so the difficulties outlined here should be appreciated. In each of the ill-conditioned cases we have studied, the determinant of the system is 'small':

$$\begin{vmatrix} 2 & 1 \\ 1 & 0.5001 \end{vmatrix} = 0.0002,$$

$$\begin{vmatrix} 2 & 1 \\ 1 & 0.4999 \end{vmatrix} = -0.0002$$

$$\begin{vmatrix} 2 & 1 \\ 1 & 0.4 \pm 0.05 \end{vmatrix} = -0.2 \pm 0.1$$

Thus the equations are 'nearly singular' – and this is one means of identifying the problem. However, the reader should refer to a more advanced book on numerical analysis to see how to identify and deal with ill-conditioning in the general case.

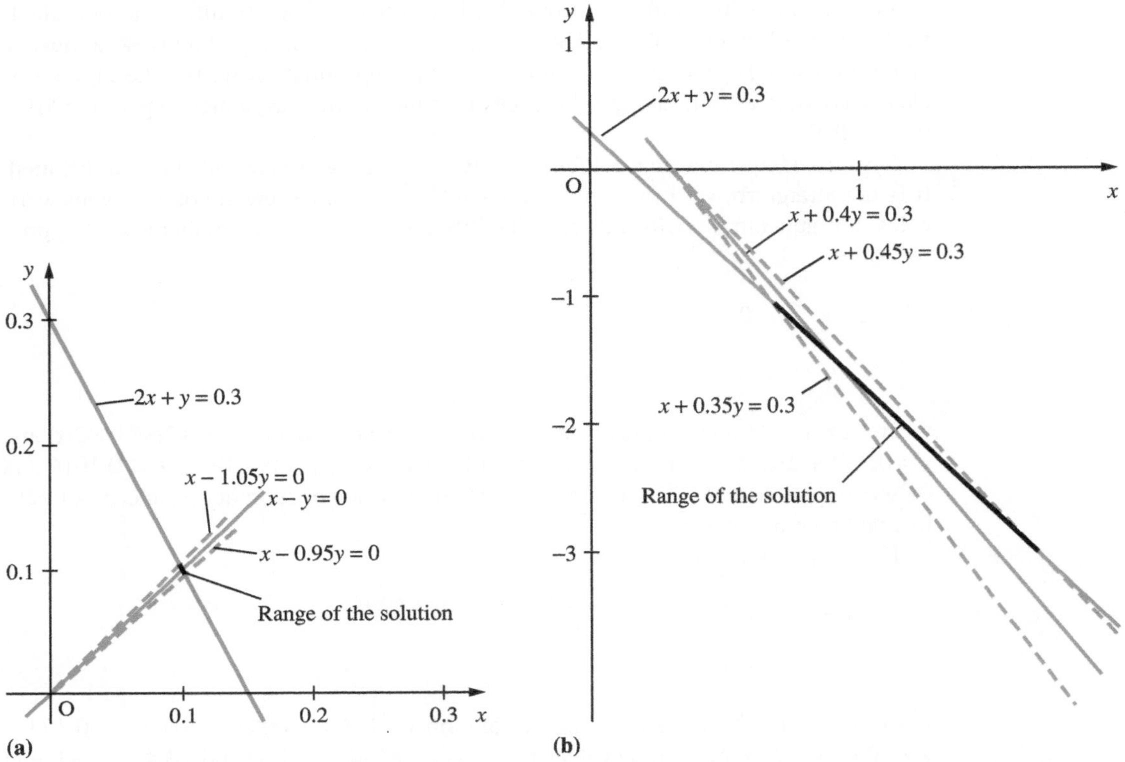

Figure 5.12 Solution of (a) $2x + y = 0.3$, $x - \alpha y = 0$ with $\alpha = 1 \pm 0.05$; and (b) $2x + y = 0.3$, $x + \alpha y = 0.3$ with $\alpha = 0.4 \pm 0.05$. The heavy black lines indicate the ranges of the solutions.

5.5.3 Exercises

Most of these exercises will require MATLAB or MAPLE for their solution. To appreciate the elimination method, hand computation should be tried on the first few exercises.

72 Use elimination with or without partial pivoting, to solve the equations

(a) $\begin{bmatrix} 1 & 3 & 2 \\ 2 & 1 & 4 \\ 3 & -1 & 5 \end{bmatrix} \begin{bmatrix} x \\ y \\ z \end{bmatrix} = \begin{bmatrix} 1 \\ 2 \\ 1 \end{bmatrix}$

(b) $\begin{bmatrix} 0 & 1 & 1 \\ 3 & -1 & 1 \\ 1 & 1 & -3 \end{bmatrix} \begin{bmatrix} x \\ y \\ z \end{bmatrix} = \begin{bmatrix} 6 \\ -7 \\ -13 \end{bmatrix}$

(c) $\begin{bmatrix} 1 & 2 & 4 \\ -6 & 2 & 10 \\ 2 & 8 & 7 \end{bmatrix} \begin{bmatrix} x \\ y \\ z \end{bmatrix} = \begin{bmatrix} 0 \\ 1 \\ 0 \end{bmatrix}$

73 Solve the equations

$$\begin{aligned} 4x - y &= 2 \\ -x + 4y - z &= 5 \\ -y + 4z - t &= 3 \\ -z + 4t &= 10 \end{aligned}$$

using the tridiagonal algorithm.

74 Solve the equations

$$\begin{aligned} 4x - y - t &= -4 \\ -x + 4y - z &= 1 \\ -y + 4z - t &= 4 \\ -x - z + 4t &= 10 \end{aligned}$$

using Gaussian elimination.

75 Solve, using Gaussian elimination with partial pivoting, the following equations:

(a) $$\begin{bmatrix} 1.17 & 2.64 & 7.41 \\ 3.37 & 1.22 & 9.64 \\ 4.10 & 2.89 & 3.37 \end{bmatrix} \begin{bmatrix} x \\ y \\ z \end{bmatrix} = \begin{bmatrix} 1.27 \\ 3.91 \\ 4.63 \end{bmatrix}$$

(b) $$\begin{bmatrix} 3.21 & 4.18 & -2.31 \\ -4.17 & 3.63 & 4.20 \\ 1.88 & -8.14 & 0.01 \end{bmatrix} \begin{bmatrix} x \\ y \\ z \end{bmatrix} = \begin{bmatrix} 3.27 \\ -1.21 \\ 4.88 \end{bmatrix}$$

(c) $$\begin{bmatrix} 1 & 7 & 2 & -1 \\ 11 & 4 & -3 & 9 \\ 7 & 6 & 4 & -2 \\ 5 & 8 & -5 & 3 \end{bmatrix} \begin{bmatrix} x \\ y \\ z \\ t \end{bmatrix} = \begin{bmatrix} 12 \\ -12 \\ 7 \\ -7 \end{bmatrix}$$

76 The two almost identical matrix equations are given

$$\begin{bmatrix} 0.11 & 0.19 & 0.10 \\ 0.49 & -0.31 & 0.21 \\ 1.55 & -0.70 & 0.70 \end{bmatrix} \begin{bmatrix} x \\ y \\ z \end{bmatrix} = \begin{bmatrix} 1 \\ 1 \\ 1 \end{bmatrix} \quad \text{and}$$

$$\begin{bmatrix} 0.11 & 0.19 & 0.10 \\ 0.49 & -0.31 & 0.21 \\ 1.55 & -0.70 & 0.71 \end{bmatrix} \begin{bmatrix} x \\ y \\ z \end{bmatrix} = \begin{bmatrix} 1 \\ 1 \\ 1 \end{bmatrix}$$

Use MATLAB or MAPLE to show that the solutions are wildly different. Evaluate the determinants of the two 3×3 matrices.

77 Show that a tridiagonal matrix can be written in the form

$$\begin{bmatrix} a_1 & b_1 & & & \mathbf{0} \\ c_2 & a_2 & b_2 & & \\ & c_3 & a_3 & b_3 & \\ & \ddots & & \ddots & \ddots \\ \mathbf{0} & c_{n-1} & & a_{n-1} & b_{n-1} \\ & & & c_n & a_n \end{bmatrix}$$

$$= \begin{bmatrix} l_{11} & & & \mathbf{0} \\ l_{21} & l_{22} & & \\ & l_{32} & l_{33} & \\ & \ddots & \ddots & \\ \mathbf{0} & & l_{n,n-1} & l_{nn} \end{bmatrix}$$

$$\times \begin{bmatrix} 1 & u_{12} & & & \mathbf{0} \\ & 1 & u_{23} & & \\ & & 1 & u_{34} & \\ & & \ddots & \ddots & \\ & & & 1 & u_{n-1,n} \\ \mathbf{0} & & & & 1 \end{bmatrix}$$

A matrix that has zeros in every position below the diagonal is called an **upper-triangular matrix** and one with zeros everywhere above the diagonal is called a **lower-triangular matrix**. A matrix that only has non-zero elements in certain diagonal lines is called a **banded matrix**. In this case we have shown that a tridiagonal matrix can be written as the product of a lower-triangular banded matrix and an upper-triangular banded matrix.

78 A wire is loaded with equal weights W at nine uniformly spaced points, as illustrated in Figure 5.13. The wire is sufficiently taut that the tension T may be considered to be constant. The end points are at the same level, so that $u_0 = u_{10} = 0$ and the system is symmetrical about its midpoint. The equations to determine the displacements u_i are

$$W = (T/d)(2u_1 - u_2)$$
$$W = (T/d)(-u_1 + 2u_2 - u_3)$$
$$W = (T/d)(-u_2 + 2u_3 - u_4)$$
$$W = (T/d)(-u_3 + 2u_4 - u_5)$$
$$W = (T/d)(- 2u_4 + 2u_5)$$

Taking $Wd/T = l$, calculate u_i/l for $i = 1, \dots, 5$.

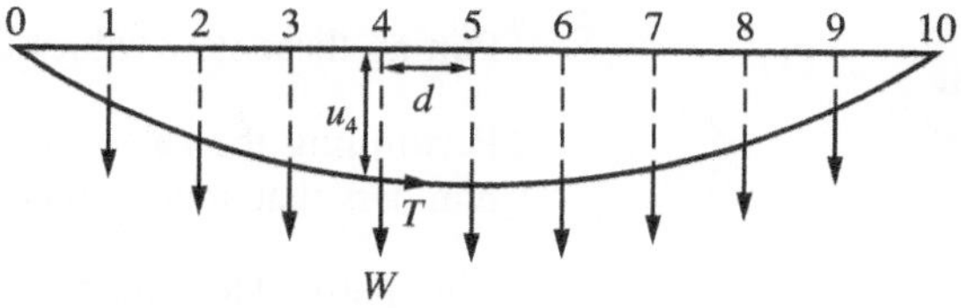

Figure 5.13 Loaded wire.

5.5.4 The solution of linear equations: iterative methods

An alternative and very popular way of solving linear equations is by iteration. This has the attraction of being easy to program. In practice, the availability of efficient procedures in computer libraries means that elimination methods are usually preferred for small problems. However, when the number of variables gets large, say several hundred, elimination methods struggle because the matrices can contain 10^6 or more elements. Problems of such size commonly occur in those scientific and engineering computations that require numerical solution on a mesh. Typically, in a turbine flow, we have a three-dimensional fluid flow problem that would need to be solved for three velocities and pressure on a $30 \times 30 \times 30$ mesh. The problem would require the solution of a $27\,000 \times 27\,000$ matrix equation. The saving feature of such problems is that it is very common for almost all the entries in the matrix to be zero. Matrices in which the large majority of elements are zero are called **sparse matrices**. Unless there is special structure to the equations, elimination will quickly destroy the sparseness. On the other hand, iterative methods only have to deal with the non-zero terms, so there is considerable computational saving. As usual, there is a price to pay:

(a) it is not always easy to decide when the method has converged;
(b) if the method takes a very large number of iterations to converge, any savings are quickly consumed.

A simple example will illustrate the way the method proceeds; in this example exact fractions will be used.

To solve the equations

$$4x + y = 2$$

$$x + 4y = -7$$

we first rearrange them as

$$x = \tfrac{1}{4}(2 - y)$$

$$y = \tfrac{1}{4}(-7 - x)$$

and start with $x = 0$, $y = 0$.

Putting these values into the right-hand side gives $x = \frac{1}{2}$, $y = -\frac{7}{4}$

Putting these new values into the right-hand side gives $x = \frac{15}{16}$, $y = -\frac{15}{8}$

Putting these new values into the right-hand side gives $x = \frac{31}{32}$, $y = -\frac{127}{64}$

Putting these new values into the right-hand side gives $x = \frac{255}{256}$, $y = -\frac{255}{128}$

Putting these new values into the right-hand side gives $x = \frac{511}{512}$, $y = -\frac{2047}{1024}$

Performing the same procedure repeatedly, normally called **iteration**, gives a set of numbers that appear to be tending to the solution $x = 1$, $y = -2$.

This particular example shows the strength of the method but we are not always so fortunate, as illustrated in the next example.

Consider the tridiagonal equations in Example 5.32:

$$\begin{aligned} 2x + y \quad\quad\quad &= 1 \\ x + 2y + z \quad\quad &= 1 \\ y + 2z + t &= 1 \\ z + 2t &= -2 \end{aligned}$$

We can rearrange these as

$$\begin{aligned} x &= \tfrac{1}{2}(1 - y) \\ y &= \tfrac{1}{2}(1 - x - z) \\ z &= \tfrac{1}{2}(1 - y - t) \\ t &= \tfrac{1}{2}(-2 - z) \end{aligned} \quad \text{or} \quad \begin{bmatrix} x \\ y \\ z \\ t \end{bmatrix} = \frac{1}{2}\begin{bmatrix} 0 & -1 & 0 & 0 \\ -1 & 0 & -1 & 0 \\ 0 & -1 & 0 & -1 \\ 0 & 0 & -1 & 0 \end{bmatrix}\begin{bmatrix} x \\ y \\ z \\ t \end{bmatrix} + \frac{1}{2}\begin{bmatrix} 1 \\ 1 \\ 1 \\ -2 \end{bmatrix} \quad \textbf{(5.28)}$$

Suppose we start with $x = y = z = t = 0$. We substitute these into the right-hand side and evaluate the new x, y, z and t; we then substitute the new values back in and repeat the process. Such iteration gives the results shown in Figure 5.14. This shows values going depressingly slowly to the solution 1, −1, 2, −2: even after 20 iterations the values are 0.9381, −0.9767, 1.9727, −1.9856. The method just described is called the **Jacobi method**, and can be written, using superscripts as iteration counters, in the form

$$\begin{aligned} x^{(r+1)} &= \tfrac{1}{2}(1 - y^{(r)}) \\ y^{(r+1)} &= \tfrac{1}{2}(1 - x^{(r)} - z^{(r)}) \\ z^{(r+1)} &= \tfrac{1}{2}(1 - y^{(r)} - t^{(r)}) \\ t^{(r+1)} &= \tfrac{1}{2}(-2 - z^{(r)}) \end{aligned}$$

An obvious step is to use the new values as soon as they are available. In the two-variable example the same equations

$$\begin{aligned} x &= \tfrac{1}{4}(2 - y) \\ y &= \tfrac{1}{4}(-7 - x) \end{aligned}$$

Iteration	*0*	*1*	*2*	*3*	*4*	*5*	*6*	*7*	*8*	*9*	*10*
x	0	0.5	0.25	0.5	0.5	0.6562	0.6719	0.7734	0.7852	0.8516	0.8594
y	0	0.5	0	0	−0.3125	−0.3437	−0.5469	−0.5703	−0.7031	−0.7187	−0.8057
z	0	0.5	0.75	1.1250	1.1875	1.4375	1.4687	1.6328	1.6523	1.7598	1.7725
t	0	−1	−1.25	−1.3750	−1.5625	−1.5937	−1.7187	−1.7344	−1.8164	−1.8262	−1.8799

Figure 5.14 Iterative solution of (5.28) using Jacobi iteration.

Iteration	*0*	*1*	*2*	*3*	*4*	*5*	*6*	*7*	*8*	*9*	*10*
x	0	0.5	0.375	0.4375	0.6172	0.7480	0.8350	0.8920	0.9293	0.9537	0.9697
y	0	0.25	0.125	−0.2344	−0.4961	−0.6699	−0.7839	−0.8586	−0.9074	−0.9394	−0.9603
z	0	0.375	1.0312	1.3750	1.5918	1.7329	1.8252	1.8856	1.9251	1.9510	1.9679
t	0	−1.1875	−1.5156	−1.6875	−1.7959	−1.8665	−1.9126	−1.9426	−1.9626	−1.9755	−1.9840

Figure 5.15 Iterative solution of (5.28) using Gauss–Seidel iteration.

are used and the same starting point $x = 0$, $y = 0$ is used. The iteration proceeds slightly differently:

Put the values 0, 0 in the first equation $\Rightarrow x = \frac{1}{2}$

Put the values $\frac{1}{2}$, 0 in the second equation $\Rightarrow y = -\frac{15}{8}$

Put the values $\frac{1}{2}$, $-\frac{15}{8}$ in the first equation $\Rightarrow x = \frac{31}{32}$

Put the values $\frac{31}{32}$, $-\frac{15}{8}$ in the second equation $\Rightarrow y = -\frac{255}{128}$

Put the values $\frac{31}{32}$, $-\frac{255}{128}$ in the first equation $\Rightarrow x = \frac{511}{512}$

and continue in the same way. It can be seen that already the convergence is very much faster.

In the second example we use the new values of x, y, z and t as soon as they are calculated: the method is called **Gauss–Seidel iteration.** This can be written as

$$
\begin{aligned}
x^{(r+1)} &= \tfrac{1}{2}(1 - y^{(r)}) \\
y^{(r+1)} &= \tfrac{1}{2}(1 - x^{(r+1)} - z^{(r)}) \\
z^{(r+1)} &= \tfrac{1}{2}(1 - y^{(r+1)} - t^{(r)}) \\
t^{(r+1)} &= \tfrac{1}{2}(-2 - z^{(r+1)})
\end{aligned}
$$

The calculation now yields the results shown in Figure 5.15. We see that, after the ten iterations quoted, the solution obtained by Gauss–Seidel iteration is within 4% of the actual solution whereas that obtained by Jacobi iteration still has an error of about 20%. The Gauss–Seidel method is both faster and more convenient for computer implementation. Within 20 iterations the Gauss–Seidel solution is accurate to three decimal places.

Although the two iteration methods have been described in terms of a particular example, the method is quite general. To solve

$$\boldsymbol{AX} = \boldsymbol{b}$$

we rewrite

$$\boldsymbol{A} = \boldsymbol{D} + \boldsymbol{L} + \boldsymbol{U}$$

where $\boldsymbol{D}$ is diagonal, $\boldsymbol{L}$ only has non-zero elements below the diagonal and $\boldsymbol{U}$ only has non-zero elements above the diagonal, so that

$$A = \begin{bmatrix} a_{11} & & & & \\ & a_{22} & & 0 & \\ & & a_{33} & & \\ & 0 & & \ddots & \\ & & & & a_{nn} \end{bmatrix} + \begin{bmatrix} 0 & & & & & \\ a_{21} & 0 & & & 0 & \\ a_{31} & a_{32} & 0 & & & \\ \vdots & \vdots & & & \ddots & \\ a_{n1} & a_{n2} & \dots & & a_{n,n-1} & 0 \end{bmatrix}$$

$$+ \begin{bmatrix} 0 & a_{12} & a_{13} & \dots & a_{1n} \\ & 0 & a_{23} & \dots & a_{2n} \\ & & & \ddots & \vdots \\ & & 0 & 0 & a_{n-1,n} \\ & & & & 0 \end{bmatrix}$$

The Jacobi method is written in this notation as

$$\boldsymbol{DX}^{(r+1)} = -(\boldsymbol{L} + \boldsymbol{U})\boldsymbol{X}^{(r)} + \boldsymbol{b}$$

and the Gauss–Seidel method as

$$\boldsymbol{DX}^{(r+1)} = -\boldsymbol{LX}^{(r+1)} - \boldsymbol{UX}^{(r)} + \boldsymbol{b}$$

(Remember that $\boldsymbol{X}^{(r)}$ denotes the rth iteration of $\boldsymbol{X}$, not $\boldsymbol{X}$ raised to the power r.)

By changing the method slightly, we have been able to speed up the method, so it is natural to ask if it can be speeded up even further. A popular method for doing this is **successive over-relaxation (SOR)**. This anticipates what the x_i values might be and overshoots the values obtained by Gauss–Seidel iteration. The new value of each component of the vector $\boldsymbol{X}^{(r+1)}$ is taken to be

$$wx_i^{(r+1)} + (1 - w)x_i^{(r)} \qquad \textbf{(5.29)}$$

which is the weighted average of the previous value and the new value given by Gauss–Seidel iteration. In the two-variable example the weighted average rearranges the equations as

$$x = w[\tfrac{1}{4}(2 - y)] + (1 - w)x = x + w[\tfrac{1}{4}(2 - y - 4x)]$$

$$y = w[\tfrac{1}{4}(-7 - x)] + (1 - w)y = y + w[\tfrac{1}{4}(-7 - x - 4y)]$$

The convergence for this example is so rapid that the enhanced convergence of SOR is hardly worth the effort; an optimum value of $w = 1.05$ reduces the convergence, to six significant figures, from seven to six iterations. However, for most problems the improved convergence is significant. Note that $w = 1$ gives the Gauss–Seidel method.

If we repeat the calculation for (5.28) including (5.29) with $w = 1.2$, we obtain the results shown in Figure 5.16, together with a comparison of the other two methods. It may be noted that the iterations converge even faster than the two previous methods, with a solution accurate to about 0.1% after ten steps. The optimum value of w is of

Jacobi	Gauss–Seidel	SOR with $w = 1.2$

`X=[0.5;0.5;0.5;0.5]; Xold=X;`
`XX=X;`
`for i=1:20`
`  X(1)=(1-Xold(2))/2;`
`  X(2)=(1-Xold(1)-Xold(3))/2;`
`  X(3)=(1-Xold(2)-Xold(4))/2;`
`  X(4)=(-2-Xold(3))/2;`
`  Xold=X;XX=[XX,X];`
`end`
	`X=[0.5;0.5;0.5;0.5];`
	`Xold=X; XX=X;`
	`for i=1:20`
	`  X(1)=(1-Xold(2))/2;`
	`  X(2)=(1-X(1)-Xold(3))/2;`
	`  X(3)=(1-X(2)-Xold(4))/2;`
	`  X(4)=(-2-X(3))/2;`
	`  Xold=X;XX=[XX,X];`
	`end`
		`X=[0.5;0.5;0.5;0.5]; Xold=X;`
		`XX=X; w=1.2;`
		`for i=1:20`
		`  X(1)=(1-w)*Xold(1)+w*(1-`
		`  Xold(2))/2;`
		`  X(2)=(1-w)*Xold(2)+w*(1-X(1)-`
		`  Xold(3))/2;`
		`  X(3)=(1-w)*Xold(3)+w*(1-X(2)-`
		`  Xold(4))/2;`
		`  X(4)=(1-w)*Xold(4)+w*(-2-`
		`  X(3))/2;`
		`  Xold=X;XX=[XX,X];`
		`end`

After 20 iterations $X = \begin{matrix} 0.9883 \\ -0.9682 \\ 1.9811 \\ -1.9804 \end{matrix}$	After 20 iterations $X = \begin{matrix} 0.9995 \\ -0.9994 \\ 1.9995 \\ -1.9998 \end{matrix}$	After 20 iterations $X = \begin{matrix} 1.0000 \\ -1.0000 \\ 2.0000 \\ -2.0000 \end{matrix}$

Figure 5.16 Algorithm to implement Jacobi, Gauss–Seidel and SOR iterations for (5.28) starting at $\boldsymbol{X}^{\mathrm{T}} = [0.5, 0.5, 0.5, 0.5]$

SOR factor w	0.2	0.4	0.6	0.8	1.0	1.2	1.4	1.6	1.8
Iterations required for convergence	>50	>50	47	34	26	21	17	29	>50

Figure 5.17 Variation of rate of convergence with SOR factor w.

great interest, and specialist books on numerical analysis give details of how this can be computed (for example, *Applied Linear Algebra*, Peter Olver and Cheri Shakiban (2005), Pearson). Usually the best approach is a heuristic one – experiment with w to find a value that gives the fastest convergence. For 'one-off' problems this is hardly worth the effort so long as convergence is achieved, but in many scientific and engineering problems the same calculation may be done many hundreds of times, so the optimum value of w can reduce calculation time by half or more. For the current problem the number of iterations required to give four-decimal-place accuracy is shown in Figure 5.17.

It can be shown that outside the region $0 < w < 2$ the method will diverge but that inside it may or may not converge. The case $w < 1$ is called **under-relaxation** and $w > 1$ is called **over-relaxation**. In straightforward problems, w in the range 1.2–1.8 usually gives the most rapid convergence, and this is normally the region to explore as a first guess. In the problem studied, a value of $w = 1.4$ gives just about the fastest convergence, requiring only about two-thirds of the iterations required for the Gauss–Seidel method. In some physical problems, however, under-relaxation is required in order to avoid too rapid variation from iteration to iteration.

Great care must be taken with iterative methods, and convergence for some equations can be particularly difficult. Considerable experience is needed in looking at sets of equations to decide whether or not convergence can be expected, and often – even for the experienced mathematician – the answer is 'try it and see'. A rearrangement of equations can greatly affect the convergence of iterative methods. For instance, in the 2×2 example, if the equations are interchanged

$$\begin{aligned} x + 4y &= -7 \\ 4x + y &= 2 \end{aligned} \quad \text{and the Jacobi iteration is written} \quad \begin{aligned} x^{(r+1)} &= -7 - 4y^{(r)} \\ y^{(r+1)} &= 2 - x^{(r)} \end{aligned}$$

the iteration diverges wildly even from a starting value $x = 1.1$, $y = -2.1$, which is close to the exact solution. One simple test that will guarantee convergence is to test whether the matrix is **diagonally dominant**. This means that the magnitude of a diagonal element is larger than or equal to the sum of the magnitudes of the off-diagonal elements in that row, or $|a_{ii}| \geqslant \sum_{\substack{j=1 \\ i \neq j}}^{n} |a_{ij}|$ for each i. If the system is not diagonally dominant, the iteration method may or may not converge.

A detailed analysis of the convergence of iterative methods is not possible without a study of eigenvalues, and can be found in specialist numerical analysis books.

Iterative methods described in this section are fairly easy to program and an implementation in MATLAB, or similar package, is highly suitable, as in Figure 5.16.

5.5.5 Exercises

Note: All of these exercises are best solved using a computer matrix package such as MATLAB.

79 Solve the equations in Question 73 (Exercises 5.5.3) using Jacobi iteration starting from the estimate $X = [1 \quad 1 \quad 1 \quad 1]^T$. How accurate is the solution obtained after five iterations?

80 Solve the equations in Question 74 (Exercises 5.5.3) using Gauss–Seidel iteration, starting from the estimate $X = [1 \quad 0 \quad 0 \quad 0]^T$. How accurate is the solution obtained after three iterations?

81 Write a computer program in MATLAB or similar package to obtain the solution, by SOR, to the equations in Question 75 (Exercises 5.5.3). Determine the optimum SOR factor for each equation.

82 Use a SOR program to solve the equations

$$\begin{aligned} x - 0.7y &= -4 \\ -0.7x + y - 0.7z &= 34 \\ -0.7y + z &= -44 \end{aligned}$$

so that successive iterations differ by no more than 1 in the fourth decimal place. Find a SOR factor that produces this convergence in less than 50 iterations.

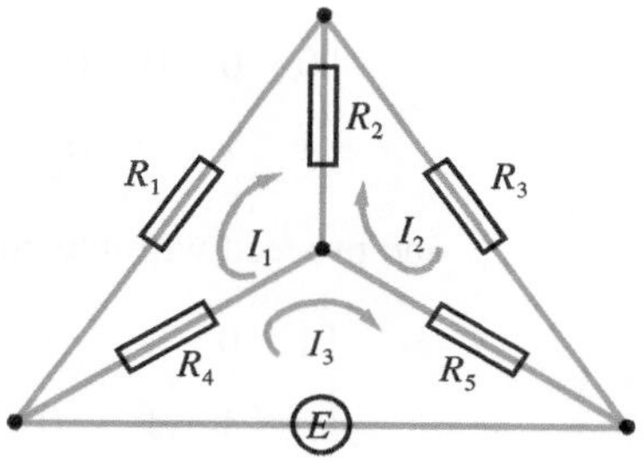

Figure 5.18 Circuit for Question 83.

83 Show that the circuit in Figure 5.18 has equations

$$\begin{bmatrix} R_1 + R_2 + R_4 & -R_2 & -R_4 \\ -R_2 & R_3 + R_5 + R_2 & -R_5 \\ -R_4 & -R_5 & R_4 + R_5 \end{bmatrix} \begin{bmatrix} I_1 \\ I_2 \\ I_3 \end{bmatrix} = \begin{bmatrix} 0 \\ 0 \\ E \end{bmatrix}$$

Take $R_1 = 1$, $R_2 = 2$, $R_3 = 2$, $R_4 = 2$ and $R_5 = 3$ (all in Ω) and $E = 1.5$ V. Show that the equations are diagonally dominant, and hence solve the equations by an iterative method.

84 Solve the 10×10 matrix equation in Example 5.30 using an iterative method starting from $X = [1 \quad 1 \quad 1 \quad 1 \quad 1 \quad 1 \quad 1 \quad 1 \quad 1 \quad 1]^T$. Verify that a solution to four-figure accuracy can be obtained in less than ten iterations.

5.6 Rank

The solution of sets of linear equations has been considered in Section 5.5. Provided the determinant of a matrix is non-zero, we can obtain explicit solutions in terms of the inverse matrix. However, when we looked at cases with zero determinant the results were much less clear. The idea of the **rank** of a matrix helps to make these results more precise. Unfortunately, rank is not an easy concept, and it is usually difficult to compute. We shall take an informal approach that is not fully general but is sufficient to deal with the cases (c) and (d) of Section 5.5. The method we shall use is to take the Gaussian elimination procedure described in Figure 5.11 (Section 5.5.2) and examine the consequences for a zero-determinant situation.

If we start with the equations

$$\begin{bmatrix} 1 & 0 & 1 & 1 & 0 & 0 \\ 0 & 1 & 1 & 0 & 1 & 2 \\ 1 & 1 & 2 & 1 & 1 & 2 \\ 1 & 0 & 1 & 0 & 1 & 3 \\ 0 & 0 & 0 & 0 & 1 & 3 \\ 1 & 1 & 2 & 0 & 2 & 5 \end{bmatrix} \begin{bmatrix} x_1 \\ x_2 \\ . \\ . \\ . \\ x_6 \end{bmatrix} = \begin{bmatrix} 1 \\ 1 \\ 2 \\ 0 \\ 0 \\ 1 \end{bmatrix} \tag{5.30}$$

and proceed with the elimination, the first and second steps are quite normal:

$$\begin{bmatrix} 1 & 0 & 1 & 1 & 0 & 0 \\ 0 & 1 & 1 & 0 & 1 & 2 \\ 0 & 1 & 1 & 0 & 1 & 2 \\ 0 & 0 & 0 & -1 & 1 & 3 \\ 0 & 0 & 0 & 0 & 1 & 3 \\ 0 & 1 & 1 & -1 & 2 & 5 \end{bmatrix} \begin{bmatrix} x_1 \\ x_2 \\ . \\ . \\ . \\ x_6 \end{bmatrix} = \begin{bmatrix} 1 \\ 1 \\ 1 \\ -1 \\ 0 \\ 0 \end{bmatrix}, \quad \begin{bmatrix} 1 & 0 & 1 & 1 & 0 & 0 \\ 0 & 1 & 1 & 0 & 1 & 2 \\ 0 & 0 & 0 & 0 & 0 & 0 \\ 0 & 0 & 0 & -1 & 1 & 3 \\ 0 & 0 & 0 & 0 & 1 & 3 \\ 0 & 0 & 0 & -1 & 1 & 3 \end{bmatrix} \begin{bmatrix} x_1 \\ x_2 \\ . \\ . \\ . \\ x_6 \end{bmatrix} = \begin{bmatrix} 1 \\ 1 \\ 0 \\ -1 \\ 0 \\ -1 \end{bmatrix}$$

The next step in the elimination procedure looks for a non-zero entry in the third column on or below the diagonal element. All the entries are zero – so the procedure, as it stands, fails. To overcome the problem, we just proceed to the next column and repeat the normal sequence of operations. We interchange the third and fourth rows and perform the elimination on column 4. Finally we interchange rows 4 and 5 to give

$$\begin{bmatrix} 1 & 0 & 1 & 1 & 0 & 0 \\ 0 & 1 & 1 & 0 & 1 & 2 \\ 0 & 0 & 0 & 1 & -1 & -3 \\ 0 & 0 & 0 & 0 & 1 & 3 \\ 0 & 0 & 0 & 0 & 0 & 0 \\ 0 & 0 & 0 & 0 & 0 & 0 \end{bmatrix} \begin{bmatrix} x_1 \\ x_2 \\ . \\ . \\ . \\ x_6 \end{bmatrix} = \begin{bmatrix} 1 \\ 1 \\ 1 \\ 0 \\ 0 \\ 0 \end{bmatrix} \tag{5.31}$$

To perform the back substitution we put $x_6 = \mu$. Then

$$\begin{array}{lll} \text{row 4} & \text{gives} & x_5 = -3x_6 = -3\mu \\ \text{row 3} & \text{gives} & x_4 = 1 + x_5 + 3x_6 = 1 \\ \text{put} & & x_3 = \lambda \\ \text{row 2} & \text{gives} & x_2 = 1 - x_3 - x_5 - 2x_6 = 1 - \lambda + \mu \\ \text{row 1} & \text{gives} & x_1 = 1 - x_3 - x_4 = -\lambda \end{array}$$

Thus our solution is

$$x_1 = -\lambda, \quad x_2 = 1 - \lambda + \mu, \quad x_3 = \lambda, \quad x_4 = 1, \quad x_5 = -3\mu, \quad x_6 = \mu$$

The equations have been reduced to **echelon form**, and it is clear that the same process can be followed for any matrix.

In general we use the elementary row operations, introduced in Section 5.5.2, to manipulate the equation or matrix to **echelon form**:

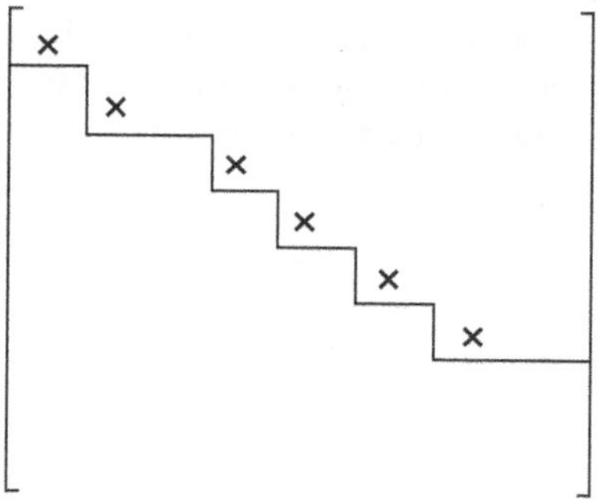

Below the line all the entries are zero, and the leading element, marked ×, in each row above the line is non-zero. The row operations do not change the solution to the set of equations corresponding to the matrix.

When this procedure is applied to a non-singular matrix, the method reduces to that shown in Figure 5.10, the final matrix has non-zero diagonal elements, and back substitution gives a unique solution. When the determinant is zero, as in (5.30), the elimination gives a matrix with some zeros in the diagonal and some zero rows, as in (5.31). The number of non-zero rows in the echelon form is called the **rank** of the matrix, rank $\boldsymbol{A}$; in the case of the matrix in (5.30) and that derived from it by row manipulation (5.31), we have rank $\boldsymbol{A} = 4$.

Example 5.37 Find the rank of the matrices

$$\text{(a)} \begin{bmatrix} 1 & 1 & -1 \\ 2 & -1 & 2 \\ 0 & -3 & 4 \end{bmatrix} \quad \text{(b)} \begin{bmatrix} 1 & -1 & 1 \\ -2 & 2 & -2 \\ -1 & 1 & -1 \end{bmatrix} \quad \text{(c)} \begin{bmatrix} 1 & 0 & 0 \\ 0 & 1 & 1 \\ 2 & 0 & 1 \end{bmatrix}$$

Solution Using the usual elimination method gives in each case

(a) $$\begin{bmatrix} 1 & 1 & -1 \\ 2 & -1 & 2 \\ 0 & -3 & 4 \end{bmatrix} \to \begin{bmatrix} 1 & 1 & -1 \\ 0 & -3 & 4 \\ 0 & -3 & 4 \end{bmatrix} \to \begin{bmatrix} 1 & 1 & -1 \\ 0 & -3 & 4 \\ 0 & 0 & 0 \end{bmatrix} \Rightarrow \text{rank } 2$$

(b) $$\begin{bmatrix} 1 & -1 & 1 \\ -2 & 2 & -2 \\ -1 & 1 & -1 \end{bmatrix} \to \begin{bmatrix} 1 & -1 & 1 \\ 0 & 0 & 0 \\ 0 & 0 & 0 \end{bmatrix} \Rightarrow \text{rank } 1$$

(c) $$\begin{bmatrix} 1 & 0 & 0 \\ 0 & 1 & 1 \\ 2 & 0 & 1 \end{bmatrix} \to \begin{bmatrix} 1 & 0 & 0 \\ 0 & 1 & 1 \\ 0 & 0 & 1 \end{bmatrix} \Rightarrow \text{rank } 3$$

The more common definition of rank is given by the order of the largest square submatrix with non-zero determinant. A square submatrix is formed by deleting rows and columns to form a square matrix. In (5.30) the 6×6 determinant is zero and all the 5×5 submatrices have zero determinant; however, if we delete columns 3 and 6 and rows 3 and 4, we obtain

$$\begin{bmatrix} 1 & 0 & 1 & 0 \\ 0 & 1 & 0 & 1 \\ 0 & 0 & 0 & 1 \\ 1 & 1 & 0 & 2 \end{bmatrix}$$

which has determinant equal to one, hence confirming that the matrix is of rank 4. To show equivalence of the two definitions is not straightforward and is omitted here. To determine the rank of a matrix, it is very much easier to look at the echelon form.

If we find any of the rows of the echelon matrix to be zero then, for consistency, the corresponding right-hand sides of the matrix equation must also be zero. The elementary row operations reduce the equation to echelon form, so that the equations take the form

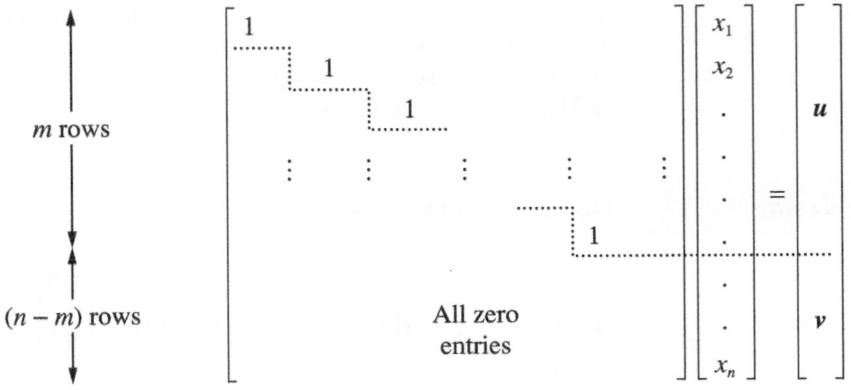

where $\boldsymbol{u}$ is a vector with m elements and $\boldsymbol{v}$ is a vector with $(n - m)$ elements. Note that each of the m non-zero rows will have a leading non-zero entry of 1 but this entry will not necessarily be on a diagonal, as illustrated for example in (5.31). Three statements follow from this reduction.

(i) The matrix has rank $(\boldsymbol{A}) = m$.
(ii) If $\boldsymbol{x} \neq 0$ then the equations are inconsistent.
(iii) If $\boldsymbol{v} = 0$ then the equations are consistent and have a solution. In addition the solution has $(n - m)$ free parameters.

For rows $1, 2, \ldots, m$ the leading term 1 occurs in columns $c_1, c_2, \ldots, c_m$ and hence the variables $x_{c_1}, x_{c_2}, \ldots, x_{c_m}$ can be calculated in terms of the RHS and the other $(n - m)$ variables, which can be specified arbitrarily. Thus the solution has $(n - m)$ free parameters and establishes result (iii).

Writing the equations as

$$\boldsymbol{AX} = \boldsymbol{b} \tag{5.32}$$

we define the **augmented matrix** $(\boldsymbol{A} : \boldsymbol{b})$ as the matrix $\boldsymbol{A}$ with the $\boldsymbol{b}$ column added to it. When reduced to echelon form the matrix and the augmented matrix take the form

$\boldsymbol{A} =$

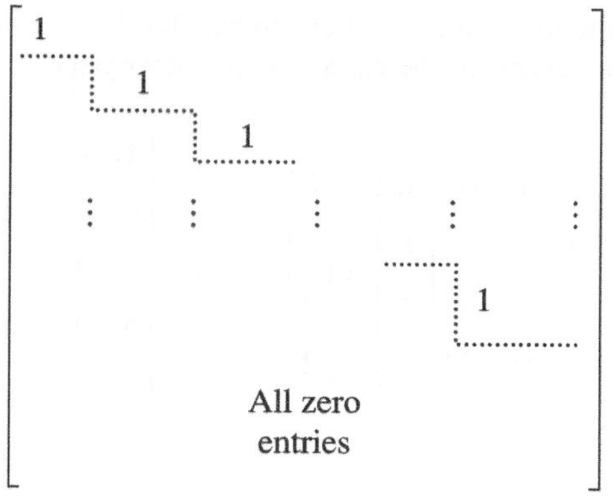

and $(\boldsymbol{A} : \boldsymbol{b}) =$

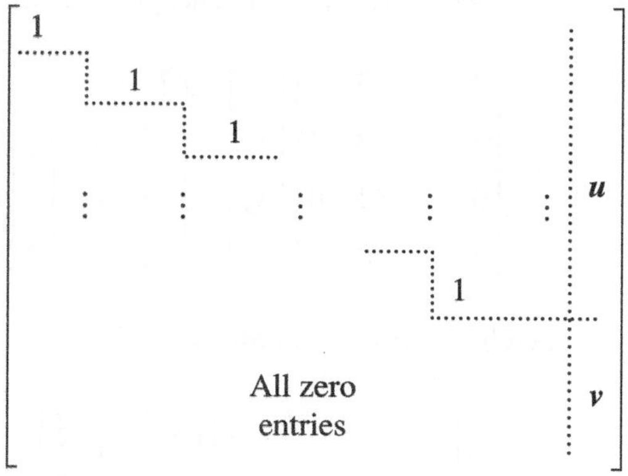

and the solution of the equations can be written in terms of *rank*. It is easy to see from the echelon form that $\boldsymbol{A}$ and $(\boldsymbol{A} : \boldsymbol{b})$ must have the same rank to ensure consistency. The original equations must have the same property, so we can state the results (c) and (d) of Section 5.5 more clearly in terms of rank.

If $\boldsymbol{A}$ and the augmented matrix $(\boldsymbol{A}:\boldsymbol{b})$ have different rank then we have no solution to the equations (5.32). If the two matrices have the same rank then a solution exists, and furthermore the solution will contain a number of free parameters equal to $n - \text{rank}\,\boldsymbol{A}$.

The calculation of rank is not easy, so, while the result is rigorous, it is not simple to apply. Reducing equations to echelon form tells us immediately the rank of the associated matrix, and gives a constructive method of solution. There is a large amount of arithmetic in the reduction, but if the solution is required then this is inevitable anyway. The numerical calculation of rank does not normally entail reduction to echelon form; rather more advanced methods such as singular value decomposition are used.

The instruction `rank(A)` evaluates the rank of an $m \times n$ matrix $\boldsymbol{A}$ in both MATLAB and MAPLE.

Example 5.38

Reduce the following equations to echelon form, calculate the rank of the matrices and find the solutions of the equations (if they exist):

(a) $$\begin{bmatrix} 0 & 1 & 1 & 0 \\ 1 & 0 & 3 & 2 \\ 2 & 1 & 5 & 4 \\ 1 & -2 & 0 & 2 \end{bmatrix} \begin{bmatrix} x_1 \\ x_2 \\ x_3 \\ x_4 \end{bmatrix} = \begin{bmatrix} 1 \\ 3 \\ 7 \\ 2 \end{bmatrix}$$

(b) $$\begin{bmatrix} 1 & 0 & -1 & 1 & -1 \\ 0 & 1 & 1 & -1 & 1 \\ 1 & 1 & 0 & 0 & 0 \\ 2 & 3 & 1 & -1 & 1 \\ 2 & 2 & 0 & 0 & 0 \end{bmatrix} \begin{bmatrix} x_1 \\ x_2 \\ x_3 \\ x_4 \\ x_5 \end{bmatrix} = \begin{bmatrix} 0 \\ 1 \\ 1 \\ 3 \\ 2 \end{bmatrix}$$

Solution (a) Rows 1 and 3 are interchanged, and the elimination then proceeds as follows:

$$\begin{bmatrix} 2 & 1 & 5 & 4 \\ 1 & 0 & 3 & 2 \\ 0 & 1 & 1 & 0 \\ 1 & -2 & 0 & 2 \end{bmatrix} \begin{bmatrix} x_1 \\ x_2 \\ x_3 \\ x_4 \end{bmatrix} = \begin{bmatrix} 7 \\ 3 \\ 1 \\ 2 \end{bmatrix} \rightarrow \begin{bmatrix} 1 & \frac{1}{2} & \frac{5}{2} & 2 \\ 0 & -\frac{1}{2} & \frac{1}{2} & 0 \\ 0 & 1 & 1 & 0 \\ 0 & -\frac{5}{2} & -\frac{5}{2} & 0 \end{bmatrix} \begin{bmatrix} x_1 \\ x_2 \\ x_3 \\ x_4 \end{bmatrix} = \begin{bmatrix} \frac{7}{2} \\ -\frac{1}{2} \\ 1 \\ -\frac{3}{2} \end{bmatrix}$$

Interchange row 2 and row 4:

$$\rightarrow \begin{bmatrix} 1 & \frac{1}{2} & \frac{5}{2} & 2 \\ 0 & -\frac{5}{2} & -\frac{5}{2} & 0 \\ 0 & 1 & 1 & 0 \\ 0 & -\frac{1}{2} & \frac{1}{2} & 0 \end{bmatrix} \begin{bmatrix} x_1 \\ x_2 \\ x_3 \\ x_4 \end{bmatrix} = \begin{bmatrix} \frac{7}{2} \\ -\frac{3}{2} \\ 1 \\ -\frac{1}{2} \end{bmatrix}$$

Eliminate elements in column 2:

$$\begin{bmatrix} 1 & \frac{1}{2} & \frac{5}{2} & 2 \\ 0 & 1 & 1 & 0 \\ 0 & 0 & 0 & 0 \\ 0 & 0 & 1 & 0 \end{bmatrix} \begin{bmatrix} x_1 \\ x_2 \\ x_3 \\ x_4 \end{bmatrix} = \begin{bmatrix} \frac{7}{2} \\ \frac{3}{5} \\ \frac{2}{5} \\ -\frac{1}{5} \end{bmatrix}$$

Interchange row 3 and row 4:

$$\begin{bmatrix} 1 & \frac{1}{2} & \frac{5}{2} & 2 \\ 0 & 1 & 1 & 0 \\ 0 & 0 & 1 & 0 \\ 0 & 0 & 0 & 0 \end{bmatrix} \begin{bmatrix} x_1 \\ x_2 \\ x_3 \\ x_4 \end{bmatrix} = \begin{bmatrix} \frac{7}{2} \\ \frac{3}{5} \\ -\frac{1}{5} \\ \frac{2}{5} \end{bmatrix}$$

The rank of the matrix is 3 while that of the augmented matrix ($\boldsymbol{A} : \boldsymbol{b}$) is 4, so the equations represented by the matrix equation (a) are not consistent. Note that the last row cannot be satisfied and hence the equations have no solution.

(b) Interchanging the first and last rows, making the pivot 1 and performing the first elimination, we obtain

$$\begin{bmatrix} 1 & 1 & 0 & 0 & 0 \\ 0 & 1 & 1 & -1 & 1 \\ 0 & 0 & 0 & 0 & 0 \\ 0 & 1 & 1 & -1 & 1 \\ 0 & -1 & -1 & 1 & -1 \end{bmatrix} \begin{bmatrix} x_1 \\ \cdot \\ \cdot \\ \cdot \\ x_5 \end{bmatrix} = \begin{bmatrix} 1 \\ 1 \\ 0 \\ 1 \\ -1 \end{bmatrix} \rightarrow \begin{bmatrix} 1 & 1 & 0 & 0 & 0 \\ 0 & 1 & 1 & -1 & 1 \\ 0 & 0 & 0 & 0 & 0 \\ 0 & 0 & 0 & 0 & 0 \\ 0 & 0 & 0 & 0 & 0 \end{bmatrix} \begin{bmatrix} x_1 \\ \cdot \\ \cdot \\ \cdot \\ x_5 \end{bmatrix} = \begin{bmatrix} 1 \\ 1 \\ 0 \\ 0 \\ 0 \end{bmatrix}$$

The matrix and the augmented matrix both have rank 2, so the equations are consistent and we can compute the solution:

$$x_1 = 1 - \lambda, \quad x_2 = \lambda, \quad x_3 = 1 - \lambda + \mu - v, \quad x_4 = \mu, \quad x_5 = v$$

As expected, the solution contains three free parameters, since the order of the equation is 5 and the rank is 2.

In most practical problems that reduce to the solution of linear equations, it is usual that there are n independent variables to be computed from n equations. This is not always the case and the resulting matrix form is *not* square. A geometrical example of four equations and three unknowns was described in equation (5.1). The idea of a determinant is only sensible if matrices are square, so the simple results about the solution of the equations cannot be used. However, the ideas of elementary row operations, reduction to echelon form and rank still hold and the existence or non-existence of solutions can be written in terms of these concepts. Some examples will illustrate the possible situations that can occur.

Underspecified sets of equations

Here there are more variables than equations.

Case (a)

Solve $\begin{bmatrix} 1 & 1 & 1 \\ 1 & 2 & 3 \end{bmatrix}\begin{bmatrix} x \\ y \\ z \end{bmatrix} = \begin{bmatrix} 1 \\ 2 \end{bmatrix}$

Subtract row 1 from row 2: $\begin{bmatrix} 1 & 1 & 1 \\ 0 & 1 & 2 \end{bmatrix}\begin{bmatrix} x \\ y \\ z \end{bmatrix} = \begin{bmatrix} 1 \\ 1 \end{bmatrix}$

The elimination is now complete and the back substitution starts:

Put $z = t$

From row 2 $\quad y = 1 - 2t$

From row 1 $\quad x = 1 - y - z = t$

so the full solution is

$$x = t, \quad y = 1 - 2t, \quad z = t$$

for any t. Note that rank ($\boldsymbol{A}$) = rank ($\boldsymbol{A} : \boldsymbol{b}$) = 2 and $n = 3$ so the solution has one free parameter.

Case (b)

Solve $\begin{bmatrix} 1 & 1 & 1 \\ 2 & 2 & 2 \end{bmatrix}\begin{bmatrix} x \\ y \\ z \end{bmatrix} = \begin{bmatrix} 1 \\ 1 \end{bmatrix}$

Subtract 2 × (row 1) from row 2: $\begin{bmatrix} 1 & 1 & 1 \\ 0 & 0 & 0 \end{bmatrix}\begin{bmatrix} x \\ y \\ z \end{bmatrix} = \begin{bmatrix} 1 \\ -1 \end{bmatrix}$

and it is clear that rank ($\boldsymbol{A}$) = 1 and rank ($\boldsymbol{A} : \boldsymbol{b}$) = 2 so there is no solution. Obviously the last row is inconsistent. Although this example may be seen to be almost trivial since the equations are obviously inconsistent [$x + y + z = 1$ and $2(x + y + z) = 1$], in larger systems the situation is hardly ever obvious.

Overspecified sets of equations

Here there are more equations than variables.

Case (c)

Solve $\begin{bmatrix} 1 & 1 \\ 1 & 2 \\ 1 & 3 \end{bmatrix} \begin{bmatrix} x \\ y \end{bmatrix} = \begin{bmatrix} -1 \\ 0 \\ 1 \end{bmatrix}$

Subtract row 1 from rows 2 and 3: $\begin{bmatrix} 1 & 1 \\ 0 & 1 \\ 0 & 2 \end{bmatrix} \begin{bmatrix} x \\ y \end{bmatrix} = \begin{bmatrix} -1 \\ 1 \\ 2 \end{bmatrix}$

Subtract 2 × (row 2) from row 3: $\begin{bmatrix} 1 & 1 \\ 0 & 1 \\ 0 & 0 \end{bmatrix} \begin{bmatrix} x \\ y \end{bmatrix} = \begin{bmatrix} -1 \\ 1 \\ 0 \end{bmatrix}$

It can be observed that rank ($\boldsymbol{A}$) = rank ($\boldsymbol{A} : \boldsymbol{b}$) = 2 and that the equations are consistent since the last row contains all zeros. Since $n = 2$ a unique solution is obtained as $x = -2$ and $y = 1$ using back substitution.

However, for overspecified equations the more common situation is that no solution is possible.

Case (d)

Solve $\begin{bmatrix} 1 & 1 \\ 1 & 2 \\ 1 & 3 \end{bmatrix} \begin{bmatrix} x \\ y \end{bmatrix} = \begin{bmatrix} 0 \\ 1 \\ -2 \end{bmatrix}$

Subtract row 1 from rows 2 and 3: $\begin{bmatrix} 1 & 1 \\ 0 & 1 \\ 0 & 2 \end{bmatrix} \begin{bmatrix} x \\ y \end{bmatrix} = \begin{bmatrix} 0 \\ 1 \\ -2 \end{bmatrix}$

Subtract 2 × (row 2) from row 3: $\begin{bmatrix} 1 & 1 \\ 0 & 1 \\ 0 & 0 \end{bmatrix} \begin{bmatrix} x \\ y \end{bmatrix} = \begin{bmatrix} 0 \\ 1 \\ -4 \end{bmatrix}$

The equations are now clearly inconsistent since the last row says 0 = −4 and rank ($\boldsymbol{A}$) = 2, rank ($\boldsymbol{A} : \boldsymbol{b}$) = 3 confirms this observation.

The existence or non-existence of solutions can be deduced from the echelon form and hence the idea of rank, and we can understand the solution of matrix equations involving non-square matrices. If $\boldsymbol{A}$ is a $p \times q$ matrix and $\boldsymbol{b}$ a $p \times 1$ *column vector, the matrix equation* $\boldsymbol{AX} = \boldsymbol{b}$ represents p linear equations in q variables. The rank of a matrix, being the number of non-zero rows in the echelon form of the matrix, cannot exceed p. On the other hand, the row reduction process will produce an echelon form with at most q non-zero rows. Hence the rank of a $p \times q$ matrix cannot exceed the smaller of p and q. Figure 5.19 summarizes the results.

		rank($\boldsymbol{A}$: $\boldsymbol{b}$) > rank($\boldsymbol{A}$)	rank($\boldsymbol{A}$: $\boldsymbol{b}$) = rank($\boldsymbol{A}$)	
			$r = q -$ rank($\boldsymbol{A}$) > 0	$q =$ rank($\boldsymbol{A}$)
$p < q$	$[A][\boldsymbol{X}] = [\boldsymbol{b}]$	No solution for $\boldsymbol{X}$	Solution for $\boldsymbol{X}$ with r free parameters	Not possible since rank($\boldsymbol{A}$) $\leq p < q$
			$\boldsymbol{b} = 0$, a solution $\boldsymbol{X} \neq 0$ exists	
$p > q$	$[A][\boldsymbol{X}] = [\boldsymbol{b}]$	No solution for $\boldsymbol{X}$	Solution for $\boldsymbol{X}$ with r free parameters	Unique solution for $\boldsymbol{X}$
			$\boldsymbol{b} = 0$, a solution $\boldsymbol{X} \neq 0$ exists	$\boldsymbol{b} = 0$, only solution is $\boldsymbol{X} = 0$
$p = q$	$[A][\boldsymbol{X}] = [\boldsymbol{b}]$	No solution for $\boldsymbol{X}$	Solution for $\boldsymbol{X}$ with r free parameters	Unique solution for $\boldsymbol{X}$
			det($\boldsymbol{A}$) = 0	det($\boldsymbol{A}$) $\neq 0$
			$\boldsymbol{b} = 0$, a solution $\boldsymbol{X} \neq 0$ exists	$\boldsymbol{b} = 0$, only solution is $\boldsymbol{X} = 0$

Figure 5.19 Summary of the existence of solutions of the matrix equation $\boldsymbol{AX} = \boldsymbol{b}$ where $\boldsymbol{A}$ is $p \times q$ matrix

Notes:

(i) In Section 5.5 the existence of solutions for p equations in p unknowns was stated in Cases (a) to (d). These results are clarified in the table. In particular, it establishes the very important result that $\boldsymbol{AX} = 0$ has a non-trivial solution if and only if det($\boldsymbol{A}$) = 0.

(ii) The MAPLE instruction `linsolve(A,b)` produces a null reply if no solution exists and gives a solution with the r free parameters when appropriate. MATLAB requires the use of `pinv` and `null` instructions to obtain the full r free parameter solution; there is no single instruction for the task.

(iii) An alternative view of linear dependence/independence can be extracted from the table for the case $\boldsymbol{b} = 0$. Recall from Section 5.2.2 and Example 5.3 that the vectors $\boldsymbol{a}_1, \boldsymbol{a}_2, \ldots, \boldsymbol{a}_q$ of order $p \times 1$ are linearly dependent/independent if the equation

$$\alpha_1\boldsymbol{a}_1 + \alpha_2\boldsymbol{a}_2 + \ldots + \alpha_q\boldsymbol{a}_q = 0$$

has a non-zero/zero solution for $\alpha_1, \alpha_2, \ldots, \alpha_q$. Write the vectors as the columns of a $p \times q$ matrix and the coefficients as a $q \times 1$ column vector

$$\boldsymbol{A} = [\boldsymbol{a}_1, \boldsymbol{a}_2, \ldots, \boldsymbol{a}_q] \text{ and } \boldsymbol{X}^{\mathrm{T}} = [\alpha_1, \alpha_2, \ldots, \alpha_q]$$

We are therefore looking for a solution of the matrix equation

$$\boldsymbol{AX} = 0$$

Since rank($\boldsymbol{A}$: 0) = rank($\boldsymbol{A}$), reading from the last two columns of the table:

(a) if $r = q -$ rank($\boldsymbol{A}$) > 0 then $\boldsymbol{X} \neq 0$ exists, so the vectors are linearly dependent;
(b) if $r = q -$ rank($\boldsymbol{A}$) $= 0$ with $p > q$ then $\boldsymbol{X} = 0$ is the only solution and the vectors are linearly independent.

(iv) From (iii) (a) any $(p + 1)$ vectors of order $p \times 1$ are linearly dependent.

(v) For the square matrix case, p vectors of order $p \times 1$ placed in the columns of $\boldsymbol{A}$, linear dependence/independence is determined by det($\boldsymbol{A}$) = 0/det($\boldsymbol{A}$) $\neq 0$.

Example 5.39 Determine whether the following sets of vectors are linearly dependent or independent

(a) $\begin{bmatrix}1\\2\\3\end{bmatrix}, \begin{bmatrix}2\\3\\1\end{bmatrix}$ (b) $\begin{bmatrix}1\\2\\3\end{bmatrix}, \begin{bmatrix}2\\3\\1\end{bmatrix}, \begin{bmatrix}3\\5\\4\end{bmatrix}$ (c) $\begin{bmatrix}1\\2\\3\end{bmatrix}, \begin{bmatrix}2\\3\\4\end{bmatrix}, \begin{bmatrix}0\\0\\1\end{bmatrix}$ (d) $\begin{bmatrix}1\\2\\3\end{bmatrix}, \begin{bmatrix}2\\3\\4\end{bmatrix}, \begin{bmatrix}0\\0\\1\end{bmatrix}, \begin{bmatrix}0\\2\\1\end{bmatrix}$

Solution (a) $\alpha\begin{bmatrix}1\\2\\3\end{bmatrix} + \beta\begin{bmatrix}2\\3\\1\end{bmatrix} = 0$ only has the solution $\alpha = \beta = 0$. Alternatively, the matrix of vectors $\boldsymbol{A} = \begin{bmatrix}1 & 2\\2 & 3\\3 & 1\end{bmatrix}$ has the number of columns $q = 2$ and rank = 2 so $[q - \text{rank}(\boldsymbol{A})] = 0$ and the vectors are linearly independent.

(b) $\begin{bmatrix}1\\2\\3\end{bmatrix} + \begin{bmatrix}2\\3\\1\end{bmatrix} = \begin{bmatrix}3\\5\\4\end{bmatrix}$ so the vectors are linearly dependent. Alternatively, in the matrix of vectors $\boldsymbol{B} = \begin{bmatrix}1 & 2 & 3\\2 & 3 & 5\\3 & 1 & 4\end{bmatrix}$ we have col 3 = col 1 + col 2, so has zero determinant and rank = 2. The vectors are linearly dependent since $[q - \text{rank}(\boldsymbol{B})] = 1$.

(c) The matrix $\boldsymbol{C} = \begin{bmatrix}1 & 2 & 0\\2 & 3 & 0\\3 & 1 & 1\end{bmatrix}$ has non-zero determinant, so the vectors are linearly independent.

(d) The matrix $\boldsymbol{D} = \begin{bmatrix}1 & 2 & 0 & 0\\2 & 3 & 0 & 2\\3 & 4 & 1 & 1\end{bmatrix}$ has rank = 3 since the last three columns have a determinant of –4. There are four columns, so $[q - \text{rank}(\boldsymbol{C})] = 1$; the vectors are linearly dependent, in agreement with note (iii)(a). It may be checked that $\begin{bmatrix}0\\2\\1\end{bmatrix} = 4\begin{bmatrix}1\\2\\3\end{bmatrix} - 2\begin{bmatrix}2\\3\\4\end{bmatrix} - 3\begin{bmatrix}0\\0\\1\end{bmatrix}$.

5.6.1 Exercises

Check your answers using MATLAB or MAPLE whenever possible.

85 Find the rank of $\boldsymbol{A}$ and of the augmented matrix $(\boldsymbol{A} : \boldsymbol{b})$. Solve $\boldsymbol{AX} = \boldsymbol{b}$ where possible and check that there are $(n - \text{rank}(\boldsymbol{A}))$ free parameters.

(a) $\boldsymbol{A} = \begin{bmatrix} 1 & 2 \\ 2 & 1 \end{bmatrix}$ $\quad \boldsymbol{b} = \begin{bmatrix} 0 \\ 1 \end{bmatrix}$

(b) $\boldsymbol{A} = \begin{bmatrix} 1 & 0 \\ 0 & 0 \end{bmatrix}$ $\quad \boldsymbol{b} = \begin{bmatrix} 0 \\ 1 \end{bmatrix}$

(c) $\boldsymbol{A} = \begin{bmatrix} 1 & 0 & 0 \\ 0 & 1 & 1 \\ 0 & 1 & 1 \end{bmatrix}$ $\quad \boldsymbol{b} = \begin{bmatrix} 1 \\ 0 \\ 0 \end{bmatrix}$

(d) $\boldsymbol{A} = \begin{bmatrix} 1 & 0 & 1 \\ 0 & 1 & 0 \end{bmatrix}$ $\quad \boldsymbol{b} = \begin{bmatrix} 2 \\ 1 \end{bmatrix}$

(e) $\boldsymbol{A} = \begin{bmatrix} 1 & 0 \\ 0 & 1 \\ 1 & 0 \end{bmatrix}$ $\quad \boldsymbol{b} = \begin{bmatrix} 1 \\ 0 \\ 0 \end{bmatrix}$

(f) $\boldsymbol{A} = \begin{bmatrix} 0 & 0 & 0 & 1 \\ 0 & 0 & 2 & 0 \\ 0 & 3 & 0 & 0 \\ 4 & 0 & 0 & 0 \end{bmatrix}$ $\quad \boldsymbol{b} = \begin{bmatrix} 1 \\ 0 \\ 1 \\ 0 \end{bmatrix}$

86 Find the rank of the coefficient matrix and of the augmented matrix in the matrix equation

$$\begin{bmatrix} 1 & 1-\alpha \\ \alpha & -2 \end{bmatrix}\begin{bmatrix} x \\ y \end{bmatrix} = \begin{bmatrix} \alpha^2 \\ \alpha \end{bmatrix}$$

For each value of α, find, where possible, the solution of the equation.

87 Find the rank of the matrices

(a) $\begin{bmatrix} 2 & 1 & 1 & 1 \\ 4 & 2 & 2 & 3 \\ 0 & 0 & 0 & 1 \\ -2 & -1 & -1 & 0 \end{bmatrix}$, (b) $\begin{bmatrix} 1 & 1 & 1 & 1 \\ 2 & 1 & 2 & 1 \\ 0 & 1 & 0 & 1 \\ 1 & 0 & 1 & 1 \end{bmatrix}$

88 Reduce the matrices in the following equations to echelon form, determine their ranks and solve the equations, if a solution exists:

(a) $\begin{bmatrix} 1 & 2 & 3 \\ 3 & 2 & 1 \\ 1 & 1 & 1 \end{bmatrix}\begin{bmatrix} x \\ y \\ z \end{bmatrix} = \begin{bmatrix} 8 \\ 4 \\ 3 \end{bmatrix}$

(b) $\begin{bmatrix} 1 & 2 & -1 & 1 \\ 1 & 1 & 0 & 0 \\ 0 & 1 & -1 & 1 \\ 1 & 0 & 1 & -1 \end{bmatrix}\begin{bmatrix} x \\ y \\ z \\ t \end{bmatrix} = \begin{bmatrix} 0 \\ 1 \\ -1 \\ 1 \end{bmatrix}$

89 By obtaining the order of the largest square submatrix with non-zero determinant, determine the rank of the matrix

$$\boldsymbol{A} = \begin{bmatrix} 1 & 1 & 0 & 1 \\ 1 & 0 & 0 & 1 \\ 0 & 1 & 0 & 0 \\ 1 & 1 & 1 & 1 \end{bmatrix}$$

Reduce the matrix to echelon form and confirm your result. Check the rank of the augmented matrix $(\boldsymbol{A} : \boldsymbol{b})$, where $\boldsymbol{b}^T = [-1 \quad 0 \quad -1 \quad 0]$. Does the equation $\boldsymbol{AX} = \boldsymbol{b}$ have a solution?

90 Solve, where possible, the following matrix equations:

(a) $\begin{bmatrix} 1 & 3 & 4 \\ -1 & 3 & 4 \end{bmatrix}\begin{bmatrix} x \\ y \\ z \end{bmatrix} = \begin{bmatrix} 1 \\ 3 \end{bmatrix}$

(b) $\begin{bmatrix} 2 & 1 \\ 4 & 6 \\ 3 & 5 \end{bmatrix}\begin{bmatrix} x \\ y \end{bmatrix} = \begin{bmatrix} 1 \\ 4 \\ -2 \end{bmatrix}$

(c) $\begin{bmatrix} 1 & 4 & 7 & -3 \\ -2 & 3 & -6 & 1 \\ 0 & 11 & 8 & -5 \end{bmatrix}\begin{bmatrix} x \\ y \\ z \\ t \end{bmatrix} = \begin{bmatrix} 1 \\ 3 \\ 5 \end{bmatrix}$

(d) $\begin{bmatrix} 2 & 1 & 4 \\ 3 & 2 & 9 \\ 4 & 1 & 3 \\ 3 & 3 & 3 \end{bmatrix} \begin{bmatrix} x \\ y \\ z \end{bmatrix} = \begin{bmatrix} 1 \\ 4 \\ -2 \\ -3 \end{bmatrix}$

91 In a fluid flow problem there are five natural parameters. These have dimensions in terms of length L, mass M and time T as follows:

$$\text{velocity} = V = \mathrm{LT}^{-1}, \quad \text{density} = \rho = \mathrm{ML}^{-3}$$

$$\text{distance} = D = \mathrm{L}, \quad \text{gravity} = g = \mathrm{LT}^{-2}$$

and

$$\text{viscosity} = \mu = \mathrm{ML}^{-1}\mathrm{T}^{-1}$$

To determine how many non-dimensional parameters can be constructed, seek values of p, q, r, s and t so that

$$V^p \rho^q D^r g^s \mu^t$$

is dimensionless. Write the equations for p, q, r, s and t in matrix form and show that the resulting 3×5 matrix has rank 3. Thus there are two parameters that can be chosen independently. By choosing these appropriately, show that they correspond to the Reynolds number $Re = V\rho D/\mu$ and the Froude number $Fr = Dg/V^2$.

92 Four points in a three-dimensional space have coordinates (x_i, y_i, z_i) for $i = 1, \ldots, 4$. From the rank of the matrix

$$\begin{bmatrix} x_1 & y_1 & z_1 & 1 \\ x_2 & y_2 & z_2 & 1 \\ x_3 & y_3 & z_3 & 1 \\ x_4 & y_4 & z_4 & 1 \end{bmatrix}$$

determine whether the points lie on a plane or a line or whether there are other possibilities.

93 A popular method of numerical integration involves Gaussian integration; it is used in finite-element calculations which are well used in most of engineering. As a simple example, the numerical integral over the interval $-1 \leqslant x \leqslant 1$ is written

$$\int_{-1}^{1} f(x)\mathrm{d}x = C_1 f(x_1) + C_2 f(x_2)$$

and the formula is made exact for the four functions $f = 1, f = x, f = x^2$ and $f = x^3$, so it must be accurate for all cubics. This leads to the four equations

$$C_1 + C_2 = 2$$

$$C_1 x_1 + C_2 x_2 = 0$$

$$C_1 x_1^2 + C_2 x_2^2 = \tfrac{2}{3}$$

$$C_1 x_1^3 + C_2 x_2^3 = 0$$

Use Gaussian elimination to reduce the equations and hence deduce that the equations are only consistent if x_1 and x_2 are chosen at the 'Gauss' points $\pm\frac{1}{\sqrt{3}}$.

5.7 The eigenvalue problem

A problem that leads to a concept of crucial importance in many branches of mathematics and its applications is that of seeking non-trivial solutions $\boldsymbol{X} \neq 0$ to the matrix equation

$$\boldsymbol{AX} = \lambda \boldsymbol{X}$$

This is referred to as the eigenvalue problem; values of the scalar λ for which non-trivial solutions exist are called **eigenvalues** and the corresponding solutions $\boldsymbol{X} \neq 0$ are called the **eigenvectors**. We saw an example of eigenvalues in Example 5.28. Such problems arise naturally in many branches of engineering. For example, in vibrations the eigenvalues and eigenvectors describe the frequency and mode of vibration respectively, while in mechanics they represent principal stresses and the principal axes of stress in bodies subjected to external forces. Eigenvalues also play an important role in the stability analysis of dynamical systems and are central to the evaluation of energy levels in quantum mechanics.

5.7.1 The characteristic equation

The set of simultaneous equations

$$\boldsymbol{A}X = \lambda X \tag{5.33}$$

where $\boldsymbol{A}$ is an $n \times n$ matrix and $X = [x_1 \quad x_2 \quad \dots \quad x_n]^T$ is an $n \times 1$ column vector can be written in the form

$$(\lambda \boldsymbol{I} - \boldsymbol{A})X = 0 \tag{5.34}$$

where $\boldsymbol{I}$ is the identity matrix. The matrix equation (5.34) represents simply a set of homogeneous equations, and we know that a non-trivial solution exists if

$$c(\lambda) = |\lambda \boldsymbol{I} - \boldsymbol{A}| = 0 \tag{5.35}$$

Here $c(\lambda)$ is the expansion of the determinant and is a polynomial of degree n in λ, called the **characteristic polynomial** of $\boldsymbol{A}$. Thus

$$c(\lambda) = \lambda^n + c_{n-1}\lambda^{n-1} + c_{n-2}\lambda^{n-2} + \dots + c_1\lambda + c_0$$

and the equation $c(\lambda) = 0$ is called the **characteristic equation** of $\boldsymbol{A}$. We note that this equation can be obtained just as well by evaluating $|\boldsymbol{A} - \lambda \boldsymbol{I}| = 0$; however, the form (5.35) is preferred for the definition of the characteristic equation since the coefficient of λ^n is then always +1.

In many areas of engineering, particularly in those involving vibration or the control of processes, the determination of those values of λ for which (5.34) has a non-trivial solution (that is, a solution for which $X \neq 0$) is of vital importance. These values of λ are precisely the values that satisfy the characteristic equation and are called the eigenvalues of $\boldsymbol{A}$.

Example 5.40 Find the characteristic equation and the eigenvalues of the matrix

$$\boldsymbol{A} = \begin{bmatrix} -2 & 1 \\ 1 & -2 \end{bmatrix}$$

Solution Equation (5.35) gives

$$0 = |\lambda \boldsymbol{I} - \boldsymbol{A}| = \begin{vmatrix} \lambda + 2 & -1 \\ -1 & \lambda + 2 \end{vmatrix} = (\lambda + 2)^2 - 1$$

so the characteristic equation is

$$\lambda^2 + 4\lambda + 3 = 0$$

The roots of this equation, namely $\lambda = -1$ and -3, give the eigenvalues.

Example 5.41 Find the characteristic equation for the matrix

$$A = \begin{bmatrix} 1 & 1 & -2 \\ -1 & 2 & 1 \\ 0 & 1 & -1 \end{bmatrix}$$

Solution By (5.35), the characteristic equation for $\boldsymbol{A}$ is the cubic equation

$$c(\lambda) = \begin{vmatrix} \lambda - 1 & -1 & 2 \\ 1 & \lambda - 2 & -1 \\ 0 & -1 & \lambda + 1 \end{vmatrix} = 0$$

Expanding the determinant along the first column gives

$$c(\lambda) = (\lambda - 1)\begin{vmatrix} \lambda - 2 & -1 \\ -1 & \lambda + 1 \end{vmatrix} - \begin{vmatrix} -1 & 2 \\ -1 & \lambda + 1 \end{vmatrix}$$

$$= (\lambda - 1)[(\lambda - 2)(\lambda + 1) - 1] - [2 - (\lambda + 1)]$$

Thus

$$c(\lambda) = \lambda^3 - 2\lambda^2 - \lambda + 2 = 0$$

is the required characteristic equation.

For matrices of large order, determining the characteristic polynomial by direct expansion of $|\lambda \boldsymbol{I} - \boldsymbol{A}|$ is unsatisfactory in view of the large number of terms involved in the determinant expansion, but alternative procedures are available.

5.7.2 Eigenvalues and eigenvectors

The roots of the characteristic equation (5.35) are called the eigenvalues of the matrix $\boldsymbol{A}$ (the terms latent roots, proper roots and characteristic roots are also sometimes used). By the Fundamental Theorem of Algebra, a polynomial equation of degree n has exactly n roots, so that the matrix $\boldsymbol{A}$ has exactly n eigenvalues λ_i, $i = 1, 2, \dots, n$. These eigenvalues may be real or complex, and not necessarily distinct. Corresponding to each eigenvalue λ_i, there is a non-zero solution $\boldsymbol{X} = \boldsymbol{e}_i$ of (5.34); $\boldsymbol{e}_i$ is called the eigenvector of $\boldsymbol{A}$ corresponding to the eigenvalue λ_i. (Again the terms latent vector, proper vector and characteristic vector are sometimes seen, but are generally obsolete.) We note that if $\boldsymbol{X} = \boldsymbol{e}_i$ satisfies (5.34) then any scalar multiple $\beta_i \boldsymbol{e}_i$ of $\boldsymbol{e}_i$ also satisfies (5.34), so that the eigenvector $\boldsymbol{e}_i$ may only be determined to within a scalar multiple.

Example 5.42 Verify that $\begin{bmatrix} 1 \\ 1 \end{bmatrix}$ and $\begin{bmatrix} 1 \\ -1 \end{bmatrix}$ are eigenvectors of the matrix

$$A = \begin{bmatrix} -2 & 1 \\ 1 & -2 \end{bmatrix}$$

Solution The matrix is the same as the one given in Example 5.40, so we would expect that these eigenvectors correspond to the eigenvalues −1 and −3. To verify the fact we must check that equation (5.33) is satisfied. Now for the first column vector

$$\begin{bmatrix} -2 & 1 \\ 1 & -2 \end{bmatrix}\begin{bmatrix} 1 \\ 1 \end{bmatrix} = \begin{bmatrix} -1 \\ -1 \end{bmatrix} = -1\begin{bmatrix} 1 \\ 1 \end{bmatrix}$$

so $\begin{bmatrix} 1 \\ 1 \end{bmatrix}$ is an eigenvector corresponding to the eigenvector −1.

For the second column vector

$$\begin{bmatrix} -2 & 1 \\ 1 & -2 \end{bmatrix}\begin{bmatrix} 1 \\ -1 \end{bmatrix} = \begin{bmatrix} -3 \\ 3 \end{bmatrix} = -3\begin{bmatrix} 1 \\ -1 \end{bmatrix}$$

so $\begin{bmatrix} 1 \\ -1 \end{bmatrix}$ is an eigenvector corresponding to the eigenvector −3.

Example 5.43 Find the eigenvalues and eigenvectors of the matrix $\boldsymbol{A} = \begin{bmatrix} 0 & -1 \\ 1 & 0 \end{bmatrix}$.

Solution To find the eigenvalues use equation (5.35)

$$0 = |\lambda \boldsymbol{I} - \boldsymbol{A}| = \begin{vmatrix} \lambda & 1 \\ -1 & \lambda \end{vmatrix} = \lambda^2 + 1$$

This characteristic equation has two roots $\lambda = +\mathrm{j}$ and $-\mathrm{j}$, which are the eigenvalues, in this case complex. Note that in general eigenvalues are complex, although in most of the remaining examples in this section they have been constructed to be real.

To obtain the eigenvectors use equation (5.34).

For the eigenvalue $\lambda = \mathrm{j}$ then (5.34) gives

$$(\lambda \boldsymbol{I} - \boldsymbol{A})\begin{bmatrix} a \\ b \end{bmatrix} = \begin{bmatrix} \mathrm{j} & 1 \\ -1 & \mathrm{j} \end{bmatrix}\begin{bmatrix} a \\ b \end{bmatrix} = 0$$

or in expanded form

$$\begin{aligned} \mathrm{j}a + b &= 0 \\ -a + \mathrm{j}b &= 0 \end{aligned} \quad \text{with solution } a = \mathrm{j} \text{ and } b = 1$$

and hence the eigenvector corresponding to $\lambda = \mathrm{j}$ is $\begin{bmatrix} \mathrm{j} \\ 1 \end{bmatrix}$.

For the eigenvalue $\lambda = -\mathrm{j}$ then (5.34) gives

$$(\lambda I - A)\begin{bmatrix} c \\ d \end{bmatrix} = \begin{bmatrix} -j & 1 \\ -1 & -j \end{bmatrix}\begin{bmatrix} c \\ d \end{bmatrix} = 0$$

or in expanded form

$$\begin{aligned} -jc + d &= 0 \\ -c - jd &= 0 \end{aligned} \quad \text{with solution } c = 1 \text{ and } d = j$$

and hence the eigenvector corresponding to $\lambda = -j$ is $\begin{bmatrix} 1 \\ j \end{bmatrix}$.

Example 5.44 Determine the eigenvalues and eigenvectors for the matrix $\boldsymbol{A}$ of Example 5.41.

Solution

$$\boldsymbol{A} = \begin{bmatrix} 1 & 1 & -2 \\ -1 & 2 & 1 \\ 0 & 1 & -1 \end{bmatrix}$$

The eigenvalues λ_i of $\boldsymbol{A}$ satisfy the characteristic equation $c(\lambda) = 0$, and this has been obtained in Example 5.41 as the cubic

$$\lambda^3 - 2\lambda^2 - \lambda + 2 = 0$$

which can be solved to obtain the eigenvalues λ_1, λ_2 and λ_3.

Alternatively, it may be possible, using the determinant form $|\boldsymbol{A} - \lambda \boldsymbol{I}|$, to carry out suitable row and/or column operations to factorize the determinant.

In this case

$$|\boldsymbol{A} - \lambda \boldsymbol{I}| = \begin{vmatrix} 1-\lambda & 1 & -2 \\ -1 & 2-\lambda & 1 \\ 0 & 1 & -1-\lambda \end{vmatrix}$$

and adding column 1 to column 3 gives

$$\begin{vmatrix} 1-\lambda & 1 & -1-\lambda \\ -1 & 2-\lambda & 0 \\ 0 & 1 & -1-\lambda \end{vmatrix} = -(1+\lambda)\begin{vmatrix} 1-\lambda & 1 & 1 \\ -1 & 2-\lambda & 0 \\ 0 & 1 & 1 \end{vmatrix}$$

Subtracting row 3 from row 1 gives

$$-(1+\lambda)\begin{vmatrix} 1-\lambda & 0 & 0 \\ -1 & 2-\lambda & 0 \\ 0 & 1 & 1 \end{vmatrix} = -(1+\lambda)(1-\lambda)(2-\lambda)$$

Setting $|\boldsymbol{A} - \lambda \boldsymbol{I}| = 0$ gives the eigenvalues as $\lambda_1 = 2$, $\lambda_2 = 1$ and $\lambda_3 = -1$. The order in which they are written is arbitrary, but for consistency we shall adopt the convention of taking $\lambda_1, \lambda_2, \ldots, \lambda_n$ in decreasing order.

Having obtained the eigenvalues λ_i $(i = 1, 2, 3)$, the corresponding eigenvectors $\boldsymbol{e}_i$ are obtained by solving the appropriate homogeneous equations

$$(\boldsymbol{A} - \lambda_i \boldsymbol{I})\boldsymbol{e}_i = 0 \qquad \textbf{(5.36)}$$

When $i = 1$, $\lambda_1 = 2$ and (5.36) is

$$\begin{bmatrix} -1 & 1 & -2 \\ -1 & 0 & 1 \\ 0 & 1 & -3 \end{bmatrix} \begin{bmatrix} e_{11} \\ e_{12} \\ e_{13} \end{bmatrix} \equiv 0$$

that is,

$$-e_{11} + \ e_{12} - 2e_{13} = 0$$

$$-e_{11} + 0e_{12} + \ e_{13} = 0$$

$$0e_{11} + \ e_{12} - 3e_{13} = 0$$

leading to the solution

$$\frac{e_{11}}{-1} = \frac{-e_{12}}{3} = \frac{e_{13}}{-1} = \beta_1$$

where β_1 is an arbitrary non-zero scalar. Thus the eigenvector $\boldsymbol{e}_1$ corresponding to the eigenvalue $\lambda_1 = 2$ is

$$\boldsymbol{e}_1 = \beta_1[1 \quad 3 \quad 1]^{\mathrm{T}}$$

As a check, we can compute

$$\boldsymbol{A}\boldsymbol{e}_1 = \beta_1 \begin{bmatrix} 1 & 1 & -2 \\ -1 & 2 & 1 \\ 0 & 1 & -1 \end{bmatrix} \begin{bmatrix} 1 \\ 3 \\ 1 \end{bmatrix} = \beta_1 \begin{bmatrix} 2 \\ 6 \\ 2 \end{bmatrix} = 2\beta_1 \begin{bmatrix} 1 \\ 3 \\ 1 \end{bmatrix} = \lambda_1 \boldsymbol{e}_1$$

and thus conclude that our calculation was correct.

When $i = 2$, $\lambda_2 = 1$ and we have to solve

$$\begin{bmatrix} 0 & 1 & -2 \\ -1 & 1 & 1 \\ 0 & 1 & -2 \end{bmatrix} \begin{bmatrix} e_{21} \\ e_{22} \\ e_{23} \end{bmatrix} = 0$$

that is,

$$0e_{21} + e_{22} - 2e_{23} = 0$$

$$-e_{21} + e_{22} + \ \ e_{23} = 0$$

$$0e_{21} + e_{22} - 2e_{23} = 0$$

leading to the solution

$$\frac{e_{21}}{-3} = \frac{-e_{22}}{2} = \frac{e_{23}}{-1} = \beta_2$$

where β_2 is an arbitrary scalar. Thus the eigenvector $\boldsymbol{e}_2$ corresponding to the eigenvalue $\lambda_2 = 1$ is

$$\boldsymbol{e}_2 = \beta_2[3 \quad 2 \quad 1]^{\mathrm{T}}$$

Again a check could be made by computing $\boldsymbol{Ae}_2$.

Finally, when $i = 3$, $\lambda_3 = -1$ and we obtain from (5.36)

$$\begin{bmatrix} 2 & 1 & -2 \\ -1 & 3 & 1 \\ 0 & 1 & 0 \end{bmatrix} \begin{bmatrix} e_{31} \\ e_{32} \\ e_{33} \end{bmatrix} = 0$$

that is,

$$2e_{31} + \ \ e_{32} - 2e_{33} = 0$$

$$-e_{31} + 3e_{32} + \ \ e_{33} = 0$$

$$0e_{31} + \ \ e_{32} + 0e_{33} = 0$$

and hence

$$\frac{e_{31}}{-1} = \frac{e_{32}}{0} = \frac{e_{33}}{-1} = \beta_3$$

Here again β_3 is an arbitrary scalar, and the eigenvector $\boldsymbol{e}_3$ corresponding to the eigenvalue λ_3 is

$$\boldsymbol{e}_3 = \beta_3[1 \quad 0 \quad 1]^{\mathrm{T}}$$

The calculation can be checked as before. Thus we have found that the eigenvalues of the matrix $\boldsymbol{A}$ are 2, 1 and −1, with corresponding eigenvectors

$$\beta_1[1 \quad 3 \quad 1]^{\mathrm{T}}, \quad \beta_2[3 \quad 2 \quad 1]^{\mathrm{T}} \quad \text{and} \quad \beta_3[1 \quad 0 \quad 1]^{\mathrm{T}}$$

respectively.

Since in Example 5.44 the β_i, $i = 1, 2, 3$, are arbitrary, it follows that there are an infinite number of eigenvectors, scalar multiples of each other, corresponding to each eigenvalue. Sometimes it is convenient to scale the eigenvectors according to some convention. A convention frequently adopted is to **normalize** the eigenvectors so that they are uniquely determined up to a scale factor of ±1. The normalized form of an eigenvector $\boldsymbol{e} = [e_1 \quad e_2 \quad \dots \quad e_n]^T$ is denoted by $\hat{\boldsymbol{e}}$ and is given by

$$\hat{\boldsymbol{e}} = \frac{\boldsymbol{e}}{|\boldsymbol{e}|}$$

where

$$|\boldsymbol{e}| = \sqrt{(e_1^2 + e_2^2 + \dots + e_n^2)}$$

For example, for the matrix $\boldsymbol{A}$ of Example 5.44, the normalized forms of the eigenvectors are

$$\hat{\boldsymbol{e}}_1 = [1/\sqrt{11} \quad 3/\sqrt{11} \quad 1/\sqrt{11}]^T, \quad \hat{\boldsymbol{e}}_2 = [3/\sqrt{14} \quad 2/\sqrt{14} \quad 1/\sqrt{14}]^T$$

and

$$\hat{\boldsymbol{e}}_3 = [1/\sqrt{2} \quad 0 \quad 1/\sqrt{2}]^T$$

However, throughout the text, unless otherwise stated, the eigenvectors will always be presented in their 'simplest' form, so that for the matrix of Example 5.44 we take $\beta_1 = \beta_2 = \beta_3 = 1$ and write

$$\boldsymbol{e}_1 = [1 \quad 3 \quad 1]^T, \quad \boldsymbol{e}_2 = [3 \quad 2 \quad 1]^T \quad \text{and} \quad \boldsymbol{e}_3 = [1 \quad 0 \quad 1]^T$$

It may be noted that the three eigenvalues in Example 5.44 are linearly independent since putting the eigenvalues into matrix form gives

$$\det\begin{bmatrix} 1 & 3 & 1 \\ 3 & 2 & 0 \\ 1 & 1 & 1 \end{bmatrix} = -6 \neq 0.$$

From Section 5.6, Figure 5.19, this is enough to establish linearly independence. There is a general result, which can be proved by contradiction arguments

> that if an $n \times n$ matrix has n distinct eigenvalues then the corresponding eigenvectors are linearly independent.

The result has considerable theoretical and practical interest, but the main development of the idea is left to the companion volume *Advanced Modern Engineering Mathematics*. An example will illustrate one aspect of the ideas which is widely used in the theory of iterative methods similar to those in Section 5.5.4.

Example 5.45 Write the Fibonacci series 1, 1, 2, 3, 5, 8, . . . where the next term is the sum of the previous two, in matrix form and compute the general term.

Solution Let F_k be the kth Fibonacci number, then it can be checked that

$$\begin{bmatrix} F_{k+1} \\ F_k \end{bmatrix} = \begin{bmatrix} 1 & 1 \\ 1 & 0 \end{bmatrix}\begin{bmatrix} F_k \\ F_{k-1} \end{bmatrix} \text{with } F_1 = F_2 = 1$$

is the matrix relation that generates these numbers. The eigenvalues and eigenvectors of the matrix, $\boldsymbol{A}$, are calculated as

$$\tfrac{1}{2}+\tfrac{\sqrt{5}}{2} \text{ with eigenvector } \boldsymbol{X} = \begin{bmatrix} \frac{1}{2}+\frac{\sqrt{5}}{2} \\ 1 \end{bmatrix} \text{ and}$$

$$\tfrac{1}{2}-\tfrac{\sqrt{5}}{2} \text{ with eigenvector } \boldsymbol{Y} = \begin{bmatrix} \frac{1}{2}-\frac{\sqrt{5}}{2} \\ 1 \end{bmatrix}$$

The matrix formulation can be applied repeatedly:

$$\begin{bmatrix} F_{k+1} \\ F_k \end{bmatrix} = \boldsymbol{A}\begin{bmatrix} F_k \\ F_{k-1} \end{bmatrix} = \boldsymbol{A}^2\begin{bmatrix} F_{k-1} \\ F_{k-2} \end{bmatrix} = \boldsymbol{A}^3\begin{bmatrix} F_{k-2} \\ F_{k-3} \end{bmatrix} = \ldots = \boldsymbol{A}^{k-1}\begin{bmatrix} F_2 \\ F_1 \end{bmatrix}$$

Since the eigenvalues are distinct, the eigenvectors are linearly independent, so *any* vector can be written as $a\boldsymbol{X} + b\boldsymbol{Y}$ for some constants a, b and in particular

$$\begin{bmatrix} F_2 \\ F_1 \end{bmatrix} = \begin{bmatrix} 1 \\ 1 \end{bmatrix} = \tfrac{1}{\sqrt{5}}(\tfrac{1}{2}+\tfrac{\sqrt{5}}{2})\boldsymbol{X} - \tfrac{1}{\sqrt{5}}(\tfrac{1}{2}-\tfrac{\sqrt{5}}{2})\boldsymbol{Y}$$

Since $\boldsymbol{A}^{k-1}\boldsymbol{X} = (\tfrac{1}{2}+\tfrac{\sqrt{5}}{2})^{k-1}\boldsymbol{X}$ and $\boldsymbol{A}^{k-1}\boldsymbol{Y} = (\tfrac{1}{2}-\tfrac{\sqrt{5}}{2})^{k-1}\boldsymbol{Y}$

$$\begin{bmatrix} F_{k+1} \\ F_k \end{bmatrix} = \boldsymbol{A}^{k-1}\begin{bmatrix} 1 \\ 1 \end{bmatrix} = \tfrac{1}{\sqrt{5}}(\tfrac{1}{2}+\tfrac{\sqrt{5}}{2})^k\boldsymbol{X} - \tfrac{1}{\sqrt{5}}(\tfrac{1}{2}-\tfrac{\sqrt{5}}{2})\boldsymbol{Y}$$

We can then deduce from the second row that

$$F_k = \tfrac{1}{\sqrt{5}}(\tfrac{1}{2}+\tfrac{\sqrt{5}}{2})^k - \tfrac{1}{\sqrt{5}}(\tfrac{1}{2}-\tfrac{\sqrt{5}}{2})^k$$

and this formula generates the Fibonacci numbers.

Example 5.46 Find the eigenvalues and eigenvectors of

$$\boldsymbol{A} = \begin{bmatrix} \cos\theta & -\sin\theta \\ \sin\theta & \cos\theta \end{bmatrix}$$

Solution Now

$$|\lambda \boldsymbol{I} - \boldsymbol{A}| = \begin{vmatrix} \lambda - \cos\theta & \sin\theta \\ -\sin\theta & \lambda - \cos\theta \end{vmatrix}$$

$$= \lambda^2 - 2\lambda\cos\theta + \cos^2\theta + \sin^2\theta = \lambda^2 - 2\lambda\cos\theta + 1$$

So the eigenvalues are the roots of

$$\lambda^2 - 2\lambda\cos\theta + 1 = 0$$

that is,

$$\lambda = \cos\theta \pm \mathrm{j}\sin\theta$$

Solving for the eigenvectors as in Example 5.43, we obtain

$$\boldsymbol{e}_1 = [1 \quad -\mathrm{j}]^{\mathrm{T}} \quad \text{and} \quad \boldsymbol{e}_2 = [1 \quad \mathrm{j}]^{\mathrm{T}}$$

In Examples 5.43 and 5.46 we see that eigenvalues can be complex numbers, and that the eigenvectors may have complex components. This situation arises when the characteristic equation has complex (conjugate) roots.

For an $n \times n$ matrix $\boldsymbol{A}$ the MATLAB command `p=poly(A)` generates an $n+1$ element row vector whose elements are the coefficients of the characteristic polynomial of $\boldsymbol{A}$, the coefficients being ordered in descending powers. The eigenvalues of $\boldsymbol{A}$ are the roots of the polynomial and are generated using the command `roots(p)`. The command

```
[M,S]=eig(A)
```

generates the normalized eigenvectors of $\boldsymbol{A}$ as the columns of the matrix $\boldsymbol{M}$ and its corresponding eigenvalues as the diagonal elements of the diagonal matrix $\boldsymbol{S}$ ($\boldsymbol{M}$ and $\boldsymbol{S}$ are called respectively the modal and spectral matrices of $\boldsymbol{A}$). In the absence of the left-hand arguments, the command `eig(A)` by itself simply generates the eigenvalues of $\boldsymbol{A}$.

For the matrix $\boldsymbol{A}$ of Example 5.44 the commands

```
A=[1 1 -2; -1 2 1; 0 1 -1];
[M,S]=eig(A)
```

generate the output

```
  0.3015   -0.8018   0.7071        2.0000  0          0
M=0.9045   -0.5345   0.0000     S=0        1.0000   0
  0.3015   -0.2673   0.7071        0        0         -1.0000
```

These concur with our calculated answers, with $\beta_1 = 0.3015$, $\beta_2 = -0.2673$ and $\beta_3 = 0.7071$.

Using the Symbolic Math Toolbox in MATLAB the matrix $\boldsymbol{A}$ may be converted from numeric into symbolic form using the command `A=sym(A)`. Then its symbolic eigenvalues and eigenvectors are generated using the sequence of commands

```
A=[1 1 -2; -1 2 1; 0 1 -1];
A=sym(A);
[M, S]=eig(A)
```

as

```
M=[3, 1, 1]     S=[1, 0, 0]
  [2, 3, 0]       [0, 2, 0]
  [1, 1, 1]       [0, 0, -1]
```

In MAPLE `eigenvectors(A);` produces the corresponding results using the linalg package.

5.7.3 Exercises

Check your answers using MATLAB or MAPLE.

94 Obtain the characteristic polynomials of the matrices

(a) $\begin{bmatrix} 2 & -1 \\ -1 & 2 \end{bmatrix}$ (b) $\begin{bmatrix} 2 & 1 \\ 1 & 1 \end{bmatrix}$

(c) $\begin{bmatrix} 1 & 2 & 3 \\ 0 & 2 & 3 \\ 0 & 0 & 3 \end{bmatrix}$ (d) $\begin{bmatrix} 1 & 2 & 0 \\ 0 & 2 & 2 \\ 0 & 1 & 3 \end{bmatrix}$

(e) $\begin{bmatrix} 3 & 2 & 1 \\ 4 & 5 & -1 \\ 2 & 3 & 4 \end{bmatrix}$ (f) $\begin{bmatrix} 2 & 1 \\ -1 & a \end{bmatrix}$

and hence evaluate the eigenvalues of the matrices.

95 Find the eigenvalues and corresponding eigenvectors of the matrices

(a) $\begin{bmatrix} 1 & 1 \\ 1 & 1 \end{bmatrix}$ (b) $\begin{bmatrix} 1 & 2 \\ 3 & 2 \end{bmatrix}$

(c) $\begin{bmatrix} 1 & 0 & -4 \\ 0 & 5 & 4 \\ -4 & 4 & 3 \end{bmatrix}$ (d) $\begin{bmatrix} 1 & 1 & 2 \\ 0 & 2 & 2 \\ -1 & 1 & 3 \end{bmatrix}$

(e) $\begin{bmatrix} 5 & 0 & 6 \\ 0 & 11 & 6 \\ 6 & 6 & -2 \end{bmatrix}$ (f) $\begin{bmatrix} 1 & -1 & 0 \\ 1 & 2 & 1 \\ -2 & 1 & -1 \end{bmatrix}$

(g) $\begin{bmatrix} 4 & 1 & 1 \\ 2 & 5 & 4 \\ -1 & -1 & 0 \end{bmatrix}$ (h) $\begin{bmatrix} 1 & -4 & -2 \\ 0 & 3 & 1 \\ 1 & 2 & 4 \end{bmatrix}$

5.7.4 Repeated eigenvalues

In the examples considered so far the eigenvalues λ_i $(i = 1, 2, \dots)$ of the matrix $\boldsymbol{A}$ have been distinct, and in such cases the corresponding eigenvectors are linearly independent. The matrix $\boldsymbol{A}$ is then said to have a full set of independent eigenvectors. It is clear that the roots of the characteristic equation $c(\lambda)$ may not all be distinct; and when $c(\lambda)$ has $p \leqslant n$ distinct roots, $c(\lambda)$ may be factorized as

$$c(\lambda) = (\lambda - \lambda_1)^{m_1}(\lambda - \lambda_2)^{m_2} \dots (\lambda - \lambda_p)^{m_p}$$

indicating that the root $\lambda = \lambda_i$, $i = 1, 2, \dots, p$, is a root of order m_i, where the integer m_i is called the **algebraic multiplicity** of the eigenvalue λ_i. Clearly $m_1 + m_2 + \dots + m_p = n$. When a matrix $\boldsymbol{A}$ has repeated eigenvalues, the question arises as to whether it is possible to obtain a full set of independent eigenvectors for $\boldsymbol{A}$. We first consider some examples to illustrate the situation.

Example 5.47 Determine the eigenvalues and corresponding eigenvectors of the matrices

(a) $\boldsymbol{A} = \begin{bmatrix} 1 & 0 \\ 0 & 1 \end{bmatrix}$ (b) $\boldsymbol{B} = \begin{bmatrix} 1 & 1 \\ 0 & 1 \end{bmatrix}$

Solution (a) The eigenvalues of $\boldsymbol{A}$ are obtained from

$$0 = |\lambda \boldsymbol{I} - \boldsymbol{A}| = \begin{vmatrix} \lambda - 1 & 0 \\ 0 & \lambda - 1 \end{vmatrix} = (\lambda - 1)^2$$

giving the value 1 repeated twice.

The eigenvectors we calculate from

$$0 = (\boldsymbol{I} - \boldsymbol{A})\begin{bmatrix} a \\ b \end{bmatrix} = \begin{bmatrix} 0 & 0 \\ 0 & 0 \end{bmatrix}\begin{bmatrix} a \\ b \end{bmatrix}$$

which is clearly satisfied by any values of a and b. Thus taking

$$\begin{bmatrix} a \\ b \end{bmatrix} = a\begin{bmatrix} 1 \\ 0 \end{bmatrix} + b\begin{bmatrix} 0 \\ 1 \end{bmatrix}$$

it can be seen that there are two independent eigenvectors $\begin{bmatrix} 1 \\ 0 \end{bmatrix}$ and $\begin{bmatrix} 0 \\ 1 \end{bmatrix}$. Any linear combination of the two vectors is also an eigenvector. Geometrically this corresponds to the fact that the unit matrix maps *every* vector onto itself.

(b) The eigenvalues of $\boldsymbol{B}$ are obtained from

$$0 = |\lambda \boldsymbol{I} - \boldsymbol{B}| = \begin{vmatrix} \lambda - 1 & -1 \\ 0 & \lambda - 1 \end{vmatrix} = (\lambda - 1)^2$$

giving the value 1 repeated twice.

The eigenvectors we calculate from

$$0 = (\boldsymbol{I} - \boldsymbol{B})\begin{bmatrix} c \\ d \end{bmatrix} = \begin{bmatrix} 0 & -1 \\ 0 & 0 \end{bmatrix}\begin{bmatrix} c \\ d \end{bmatrix} = \begin{bmatrix} -d \\ 0 \end{bmatrix}$$

Thus $d = 0$ and there is *only one* eigenvector $\begin{bmatrix} 1 \\ 0 \end{bmatrix}$ and, of course, any multiple of this vector.

We note from Example 5.47 that the evaluation of eigenvectors leads to a much more complicated situation when there are multiple eigenvalues. In contrast to the case of distinct eigenvalues, where it is known that the corresponding eigenvectors are linearly independent, for repeated eigenvalues it is not even clear how many linearly independent eigenvectors are associated with a multiple eigenvalue λ. The idea of rank (introduced in Section 5.6) of the matrix $(\lambda \boldsymbol{I} - \boldsymbol{A})$ is the key to the clarification.

A second problem occurs when there are several linearly independent eigenvectors associated with a multiple eigenvalue, as in Example 5.47(a). For instance, suppose the eigenvalue λ has two such eigenvectors $\boldsymbol{X}$ and $\boldsymbol{Y}$ so that

$$\boldsymbol{AX} = \lambda \boldsymbol{X} \quad \text{and} \quad \boldsymbol{AY} = \lambda \boldsymbol{Y}$$

then adding with multiples α, β

$$A(\alpha X + \beta Y) = \lambda(\alpha X + \beta Y)$$

We see that $(\alpha X + \beta Y)$ is also an eigenvector for *any* α, β. This can cause confusion since a method or computer package can throw up two eigenvectors which are different from the ones expected but that are equally valid and belong to the set $(\alpha X + \beta Y)$ for some α, β. In Example 5.47(a) the calculated eigenvectors are $\begin{bmatrix} 1 \\ 0 \end{bmatrix}$ and $\begin{bmatrix} 0 \\ 1 \end{bmatrix}$ but equally well eigenvectors $\begin{bmatrix} 1 \\ 1 \end{bmatrix}$ and $\begin{bmatrix} 1 \\ -1 \end{bmatrix}$ could have been chosen. The vectors belong to the same set, with $\alpha = \beta = 1$ in the first case and $\alpha = -\beta = 1$ in the second case. This situation should be noted carefully when undertaking exercises involving a multiple eigenvalue.

The following two 3×3 examples illustrate similar points.

Example 5.48 Determine the eigenvalues and corresponding eigenvectors of the matrix

$$A = \begin{bmatrix} 3 & -3 & 2 \\ -1 & 5 & -2 \\ -1 & 3 & 0 \end{bmatrix}$$

Solution We find the eigenvalues from

$$\begin{vmatrix} 3-\lambda & -3 & 2 \\ -1 & 5-\lambda & -2 \\ -1 & 3 & -\lambda \end{vmatrix} = 0$$

as $\lambda_1 = 4$, $\lambda_2 = \lambda_3 = 2$.

The eigenvectors are obtained from

$$(A - \lambda I)e_i = 0 \tag{5.37}$$

and when $\lambda = \lambda_1 = 4$, we obtain from (5.37)

$$e_1 = [1 \quad -1 \quad -1]^{\mathrm{T}}$$

When $\lambda = \lambda_2 = \lambda_3 = 2$, (5.37) becomes

$$\begin{bmatrix} 1 & -3 & 2 \\ -1 & 3 & -2 \\ -1 & 3 & -2 \end{bmatrix}\begin{bmatrix} e_{21} \\ e_{22} \\ e_{23} \end{bmatrix} = 0$$

The matrix has rank = 1, so $[q - \text{rank}(A - 2I)] = 3 - 1 = 2$ and we expect two free parameters so two linearly independent eigenvectors. They are obtained explicitly from the single equation

$$e_{21} - 3e_{22} + 2e_{23} = 0 \qquad \mathbf{(5.38)}$$

Clearly we are free to choose any two of the components e_{21}, e_{22} or e_{23} at will, with the remaining one determined by (5.38). Suppose we set $e_{22} = \alpha$ and $e_{23} = \beta$; then (5.38) means that $e_{21} = 3\alpha - 2\beta$, and thus

$$\begin{aligned} \boldsymbol{e}_2 &= [3\alpha - 2\beta \quad \alpha \quad \beta]^{\mathrm{T}} \\ &= \alpha\begin{bmatrix}3\\1\\0\end{bmatrix} + \beta\begin{bmatrix}-2\\0\\1\end{bmatrix} \end{aligned} \qquad \mathbf{(5.39)}$$

Now $\lambda = 2$ is an eigenvalue of multiplicity 2, and we seek, if possible, two independent eigenvectors defined by (5.39). Setting $\alpha = 1$ and $\beta = 0$ yields

$$\boldsymbol{e}_2 = [3 \quad 1 \quad 0]^{\mathrm{T}}$$

and setting $\alpha = 0$ and $\beta = 1$ gives a second vector

$$\boldsymbol{e}_3 = [-2 \quad 0 \quad 1]^{\mathrm{T}}$$

These two vectors are independent and of the form defined by (5.39), but many other choices are possible. However, any other choices of the form (5.39) will be linear combinations of $\boldsymbol{e}_2$ and $\boldsymbol{e}_3$ as chosen above. For example, $\boldsymbol{e} = [1 \quad 1 \quad 1]^{\mathrm{T}}$ satisfies (5.38), but $\boldsymbol{e} = \boldsymbol{e}_2 + \boldsymbol{e}_3$.

In this example, although there was a repeated eigenvalue of algebraic multiplicity 2, it was possible to construct two independent eigenvectors corresponding to this eigenvalue. Thus the matrix $\boldsymbol{A}$ has three and only three independent eigenvectors.

The MATLAB commands for Example 5.48

```
A=[3 -3 2; -1 5 -2; -1 3 0];
[M, S]=eig(A)
```

generate

```
    0.5774  -0.5774  -0.7513         4.0000  0        0
M=-0.5774  -0.5774   0.1735     S=0       2.0000   0
   -0.5774  -0.5774   0.6361        0       0        2.0000
```

Clearly the first column of $\boldsymbol{M}$ (corresponding to the eighenvalue $\lambda_1 = 4$) is a scalar multiple of $\mathbf{e}_1$. The second and third columns of $\boldsymbol{M}$ (corresponding to the repeated eigenvalue $\lambda_2 = \lambda_3 = 2$) are not scalar multiples of $\mathbf{e}_2$ and $\mathbf{e}_3$. However, both satisfy (5.37) and are equally acceptable as a pair of linearly independent eigenvectors corresponding to the repeated eigenvalue. It is left as an exercise to show that both are linear combinations of $\mathbf{e}_2$ and $\mathbf{e}_3$.

Check that in symbolic form the commands

```
A=sym(A);
[M, S]=eig(A)
```

generate

```
M=[-1, 3, -2]        S=[4, 0, 0]
  [1, 1, 0]            [0, 2, 0]
  [1, 0, 1]            [0, 0, 2]
```

In the linalg package of MAPLE, `eigenvectors(A);` produces the corresponding results.

Example 5.49 Determine the eigenvalues and corresponding eigenvectors of the matrix

$$\boldsymbol{A} = \begin{bmatrix} 1 & 2 & 2 \\ 0 & 2 & 1 \\ -1 & 2 & 2 \end{bmatrix}$$

Solution Solving $|\boldsymbol{A} - \lambda \boldsymbol{I}| = 0$ gives the eigenvalues as $\lambda_1 = \lambda_2 = 2$, $\lambda_3 = 1$. The eigenvector corresponding to the non-repeated or simple eigenvalue $\lambda_3 = 1$ is easily found as

$$\boldsymbol{e}_3 = [1 \quad 1 \quad -1]^{\mathrm{T}}$$

When $\lambda = \lambda_1 = \lambda_2 = 2$, the corresponding eigenvector is given by

$$(\boldsymbol{A} - 2\boldsymbol{I})\boldsymbol{e}_1 = 0$$

The matrix $(\boldsymbol{A} - 2\boldsymbol{I}) = \begin{bmatrix} -1 & 2 & 2 \\ 0 & 0 & 1 \\ -1 & 2 & 0 \end{bmatrix}$ has rank = 2, so $[q - \text{rank}(\boldsymbol{A})] = 1$ and we expect to have one free parameter and hence only one independent eigenvector. Writing out in full we look for solutions of

$$-e_{11} + 2e_{12} + 2e_{13} = 0 \qquad \textbf{(i)}$$

$$e_{13} = 0 \qquad \textbf{(ii)}$$

$$-e_{11} + 2e_{12} \qquad = 0 \qquad \textbf{(iii)}$$

From (ii) we have $e_{13} = 0$, and from both (i) and (iii) it follows that $e_{11} = 2e_{12}$. We deduce that there is only one independent eigenvector corresponding to the repeated eigenvalue $\lambda = 2$, namely

$$\boldsymbol{e}_1 = [2 \quad 1 \quad 0]^{\mathrm{T}}$$

and in this case the matrix $\boldsymbol{A}$ does not possess a full set of independent eigenvectors.

We see from Examples 5.47–5.49 that if an $n \times n$ matrix $\boldsymbol{A}$ has repeated eigenvalues then a full set of n independent eigenvectors may or may not exist.

The complications introduced are seen to be resolved by determining the rank of the matrix $(\boldsymbol{A} - \lambda_i \boldsymbol{I})$ for each of the repeated eigenvalues. This is not a simple resolution; further details and a systematic development of the ideas can be found in the companion volume *Advanced Modern Engineering Mathematics*.

5.7.5 Exercises

Check your answers using MATLAB or MAPLE whenever possible.

96 Find the eigenvalues and eigenvectors of the matrices

$$\begin{bmatrix} 3 & 0 \\ 0 & 3 \end{bmatrix}, \begin{bmatrix} 2 & 0 \\ 1 & 2 \end{bmatrix}, \begin{bmatrix} 3 & \frac{1}{4} \\ -1 & 2 \end{bmatrix}, \begin{bmatrix} \frac{1}{2} & \frac{1}{4} \\ -1 & -\frac{1}{2} \end{bmatrix}$$

97 Show that the matrix

$$\boldsymbol{A} = \begin{bmatrix} -2 & 2 & -3 \\ 2 & 1 & -6 \\ -1 & -2 & 0 \end{bmatrix}$$

has eigenvalues 5, −3, −3. Find the corresponding eigenvectors. For the repeated eigenvalue, show that it has two linearly independent eigenvectors and that any vector of the general form

$$\alpha \begin{bmatrix} -2 \\ 1 \\ 0 \end{bmatrix} + \beta \begin{bmatrix} 3 \\ 0 \\ 1 \end{bmatrix}$$

is also an eigenvector.

98 Obtain the eigenvalues and corresponding eigenvectors of the matrices

(a) $\begin{bmatrix} 2 & 2 & 1 \\ 1 & 3 & 1 \\ 1 & 2 & 2 \end{bmatrix}$ (b) $\begin{bmatrix} 0 & -2 & -2 \\ -1 & 1 & 2 \\ -1 & -1 & 2 \end{bmatrix}$

(c) $\begin{bmatrix} 4 & 6 & 6 \\ 1 & 3 & 2 \\ -1 & -5 & -2 \end{bmatrix}$ (d) $\begin{bmatrix} 7 & -2 & -4 \\ 3 & 0 & -2 \\ 6 & -2 & -3 \end{bmatrix}$

99 Given that $\lambda = 1$ is a three-times repeated eigenvalue of the matrix

$$\boldsymbol{A} = \begin{bmatrix} -3 & -7 & -5 \\ 2 & 4 & 3 \\ 1 & 2 & 2 \end{bmatrix}$$

determine how many independent eigenvectors correspond to this value of λ. Determine a corresponding set of independent eigenvectors.

100 Given that $\lambda = 1$ is a twice-repeated eigenvalue of the matrix

$$\boldsymbol{A} = \begin{bmatrix} 2 & 1 & -1 \\ -1 & 0 & 1 \\ -1 & -1 & 2 \end{bmatrix}$$

determine a set of independent eigenvectors.

101 Find all the eigenvalues and eigenvectors of the matrix

$$\begin{bmatrix} 1 & 0 & 0 & 2 \\ 0 & 2 & 0 & 0 \\ 0 & 0 & 2 & 0 \\ 2 & 0 & 0 & 1 \end{bmatrix}$$

5.7.6 Some useful properties of eigenvalues

The following basic properties of the eigenvalues $\lambda_1, \lambda_2, \ldots, \lambda_n$ of an $n \times n$ matrix $\boldsymbol{A}$ are sometimes useful. The results are readily proved from either the definition of eigenvalues as the values of λ satisfying (5.33), or by comparison of corresponding characteristic polynomials (5.35). Consequently, the proofs are left to Exercise 102.

Property 1

The sum of the eigenvalues of $\mathbf{A}$ is

$$\sum_{i=1}^{n} \lambda_i = \text{trace}\,\mathbf{A} = \sum_{i=1}^{n} a_{ii}$$

Property 2

The product of the eigenvalues of $\mathbf{A}$ is

$$\prod_{i=1}^{n} \lambda_i = \det \mathbf{A}$$

where $\det \mathbf{A}$ denotes the determinant of the matrix $\mathbf{A}$.

Property 3

The eigenvalues of the inverse matrix $\mathbf{A}^{-1}$, provided it exists, are

$$\frac{1}{\lambda_1},\quad \frac{1}{\lambda_2},\quad \dots,\quad \frac{1}{\lambda_n}$$

Property 4

The eigenvalues of the transposed matrix $\mathbf{A}^{\mathrm{T}}$ are

$$\lambda_1,\quad \lambda_2,\quad \dots,\quad \lambda_n$$

as for the matrix $\mathbf{A}$.

Property 5

If k is a scalar then the eigenvalues of $k\mathbf{A}$ are

$$k\lambda_1,\quad k\lambda_2,\quad \dots,\quad k\lambda_n$$

Property 6

If k is a scalar and $\mathbf{I}$ the $n \times n$ identity (unit) matrix then the eigenvalues of $\mathbf{A} \pm k\mathbf{I}$ are respectively

$$\lambda_1 \pm k,\quad \lambda_2 \pm k,\quad \dots,\quad \lambda_n \pm k$$

Property 7

If k is a positive integer then the eigenvalues of $\boldsymbol{A}^k$ are

$$\lambda_1^k, \quad \lambda_2^k, \quad \ldots, \quad \lambda_n^k$$

Property 8

As a consequence of Properties 5 and 7, any polynomial in $\boldsymbol{A}$

$$\boldsymbol{A}^m + \alpha_{m-1}\boldsymbol{A}^{m-1} + \ldots + \alpha_1\boldsymbol{A} + \alpha_0\boldsymbol{I}$$

has eigenvalues

$$\lambda_i^m + \alpha_{m-1}\lambda_i^{m-1} + \ldots + \alpha_1\lambda_i + \alpha_0 \qquad \text{for} \qquad i = 1, 2, \ldots, n$$

5.7.7 Symmetric matrices

A square matrix $\boldsymbol{A}$ is said to be **symmetric** if $\boldsymbol{A}^{\mathrm{T}} = \boldsymbol{A}$. Such matrices form an important class and arise in a variety of practical situations. Such symmetry imposes a powerful structure to the eigenvalues and eigenvectors which is summarized in the statements:

(i) The eigenvalues of a real symmetric matrix are real.
(ii) For an $n \times n$ real symmetric matrix it is always possible to find n independent eigenvectors $\boldsymbol{e}_1, \boldsymbol{e}_2, \ldots, \boldsymbol{e}_n$ that are mutually orthogonal so that $\boldsymbol{e}_i^{\mathrm{T}}\boldsymbol{e}_j = 0$ for $i \neq j$.

If the orthogonal eigenvectors of a symmetric matrix are normalized as

$$\hat{\boldsymbol{e}}_1, \hat{\boldsymbol{e}}_2, \ldots, \hat{\boldsymbol{e}}_n$$

then the **inner (scalar) product** is

$$\hat{\boldsymbol{e}}_i^{\mathrm{T}}\hat{\boldsymbol{e}}_j = \delta_{ij} \quad (i, j = 1, 2, \ldots, n)$$

where δ_{ij} is the Kronecker delta defined in Section 5.2.1.

The set of normalized eigenvectors of a symmetric matrix therefore form an orthonormal set (that is, they form a mutually orthogonal normalized set of vectors).

In general, eigenvalues and eigenvectors are complex, so (i) gives a considerable simplification and it can be proved as follows:

Proof of statement (i)

Let $\boldsymbol{AX} = \lambda\boldsymbol{X}$
Take the complex conjugate $\boldsymbol{A}^*\boldsymbol{X}^* = \lambda^*\boldsymbol{X}^*$; since $\boldsymbol{A}$ is real then $\boldsymbol{AX}^* = \lambda^*\boldsymbol{X}^*$
Take the transpose $\boldsymbol{X}^{\mathrm{T}}\boldsymbol{A}^{\mathrm{T}} = \lambda\boldsymbol{X}^{\mathrm{T}}$; since $\boldsymbol{A}$ is symmetric then $\boldsymbol{X}^{\mathrm{T}}\boldsymbol{A} = \lambda\boldsymbol{X}^{\mathrm{T}}$
Pre-multiply the complex conjugate eigenvalue equation by $\boldsymbol{X}^{\mathrm{T}}$ to give

$$\boldsymbol{X}^{\mathrm{T}}\boldsymbol{AX}^* = \lambda^*\boldsymbol{X}^{\mathrm{T}}\boldsymbol{X}^* \rightarrow \lambda\boldsymbol{X}^{\mathrm{T}}\boldsymbol{X}^* = \lambda^*\boldsymbol{X}^{\mathrm{T}}\boldsymbol{X}^* \quad \text{since} \quad \boldsymbol{X}^{\mathrm{T}}\boldsymbol{A} = \lambda\boldsymbol{X}^{\mathrm{T}}$$

Because $\boldsymbol{X}^{\mathrm{T}}\boldsymbol{X}^* \neq 0$ we deduce that $\lambda = \lambda^*$ and the eigenvalue is therefore real.

Proof of statement (ii) when all the eigenvalues are distinct

We first show that the eigenvectors are orthogonal and then that they are linearly independent. Two distinct eigenvalues satisfy

$$\boldsymbol{AX}_i = \lambda_i \boldsymbol{X}_i \quad \text{and} \quad \boldsymbol{AX}_j = \lambda_j \boldsymbol{X}_j \quad \text{with} \quad \lambda_i \neq \lambda_j$$

Multiply the first equation by $\boldsymbol{X}_j^{\mathrm{T}}$ to give

$$\boldsymbol{X}_j^{\mathrm{T}}\boldsymbol{AX}_i = \lambda_i \boldsymbol{X}_j^{\mathrm{T}}\boldsymbol{X}_i \tag{5.40}$$

Multiply the second equation by $\boldsymbol{X}_i^{\mathrm{T}}$ to give

$$\boldsymbol{X}_i^{\mathrm{T}}\boldsymbol{AX}_j = \lambda_j \boldsymbol{X}_i^{\mathrm{T}}\boldsymbol{X}_j \quad \text{with transpose} \quad (\boldsymbol{X}_i^{\mathrm{T}}\boldsymbol{AX}_j)^T = \lambda_j(\boldsymbol{X}_i^{\mathrm{T}}\boldsymbol{X}_j)^{\mathrm{T}}$$

and hence using the symmetry of $\boldsymbol{A}$

$$\boldsymbol{X}_j^{\mathrm{T}}\boldsymbol{AX}_i = \lambda_j \boldsymbol{X}_j^{\mathrm{T}}\boldsymbol{X}_i \tag{5.41}$$

Now subtract (5.41) from (5.40), then

$$(\lambda_i - \lambda_j)\, \boldsymbol{X}_j^{\mathrm{T}}\boldsymbol{X}_i = 0$$

Since the eigenvalues are distinct we have $\boldsymbol{X}_j^{\mathrm{T}}\boldsymbol{X}_i = 0$ and the corresponding vectors are orthogonal.

To test linear independence, consider solutions of

$$\alpha_1\boldsymbol{X}_1 + \alpha_2\boldsymbol{X}_2 + \ldots + \alpha_n\boldsymbol{X}_n = 0$$

Multiply by $\boldsymbol{X}_i^{\mathrm{T}}$. From the othogonality of the eigenvectors, when *all* the eigenvlaues are distinct, the only term to survive is

$$\alpha_i\boldsymbol{X}_i^{\mathrm{T}}\boldsymbol{X}_i = 0$$

and since the eigenvectors are not zero the conclusion is $\alpha_i = 0$ for all i. Hence the eigenvectors are linearly independent.

The second statement (ii) is much more difficult to prove for repeated eigenvalues and is left to the companion volume *Advanced Modern Engineering Mathematics*.

The results (i) and (ii) are well used in both theory and in computational practice since they make it clear that only real values need to be sought and any vector can be written as the combination of the linearly independent eigenvalues. Considerable effort goes into transforming a problem to symmetric matrix form. Review Exercise 22 gives an illustration of spectral decomposition. Singular Value Decomposition, Jacobi and Householder methods all rely on (i) and (ii).

Example 5.50 Obtain the eigenvalues and corresponding orthogonal eigenvectors of the symmetric matrix

$$\boldsymbol{A} = \begin{bmatrix} 2 & 2 & 0 \\ 2 & 5 & 0 \\ 0 & 0 & 3 \end{bmatrix}$$

and show that the normalized eigenvectors form an orthonormal set.

Solution The eigenvalues of $\boldsymbol{A}$ are $\lambda_1 = 6$, $\lambda_2 = 3$ and $\lambda_3 = 1$, with corresponding eigenvectors

$$\boldsymbol{e}_1 = [1 \quad 2 \quad 0]^{\mathrm{T}}, \quad \boldsymbol{e}_2 = [0 \quad 0 \quad 1]^{\mathrm{T}}, \quad \boldsymbol{e}_3 = [-2 \quad 1 \quad 0]^{\mathrm{T}}$$

which in normalized form are

$$\hat{\boldsymbol{e}}_1 = [1 \quad 2 \quad 0]^{\mathrm{T}}/\sqrt{5}, \quad \hat{\boldsymbol{e}}_2 = [0 \quad 0 \quad 1]^{\mathrm{T}}, \quad \hat{\boldsymbol{e}}_3 = [-2 \quad 1 \quad 0]^{\mathrm{T}}/\sqrt{5}$$

Evaluating the inner products, we see that, for example,

$$\hat{\boldsymbol{e}}_1^{\mathrm{T}}\hat{\boldsymbol{e}}_1 = \tfrac{1}{5} + \tfrac{4}{5} + 0 = 1, \quad \hat{\boldsymbol{e}}_1^{\mathrm{T}}\hat{\boldsymbol{e}}_3 = -\tfrac{2}{5} + \tfrac{2}{5} + 0 = 0$$

and that

$$\hat{\boldsymbol{e}}_i^{\mathrm{T}}\hat{\boldsymbol{e}}_j = \delta_{ij} \quad (i, j = 1, 2, 3)$$

confirming that the eigenvectors form an orthonormal set.

Example 5.51 considers the case of a repeated eigenvalue and gives a hint of the Gram–Schmidt process for making a set of linearly independent vectors into an orthogonal set.

Example 5.51 Show that the matrix

$$\boldsymbol{A} = \begin{bmatrix} 1 & 1 & 1 \\ 1 & 1 & 1 \\ 1 & 1 & 1 \end{bmatrix}$$

has eigenvalues 3, 0, 0 and construct three mutually orthogonal eigenvectors.

Solution The characteristic equation is

$$\mathbf{0} = \begin{bmatrix} 1-\lambda & 1 & 1 \\ 1 & 1-\lambda & 1 \\ 1 & 1 & 1-\lambda \end{bmatrix} = -\lambda^2(\lambda - 3)$$

so has roots 3, 0, 0. For the eigenvalue 3, check that $[1 \quad 1 \quad 1]^{\mathrm{T}}$ is a solution of

$$\begin{bmatrix} -2 & 1 & 1 \\ 1 & -2 & 1 \\ 1 & 1 & -2 \end{bmatrix}\begin{bmatrix} x \\ y \\ z \end{bmatrix} = 0$$

For the eigenvalue 0, look for solutions of

$$\begin{bmatrix} 1 & 1 & 1 \\ 1 & 1 & 1 \\ 1 & 1 & 1 \end{bmatrix}\begin{bmatrix} x \\ y \\ z \end{bmatrix} = 0$$

The matrix has rank = 1, so we have $[q - \mathrm{rank}(\boldsymbol{A} - 0\boldsymbol{I})] = 2$ and expect two linearly independent eigenvectors. It may be checked that $[-1 \quad 0 \quad 1]^{\mathrm{T}}$ and $[-1 \quad 1 \quad 0]^{\mathrm{T}}$ are two linearly independent eigenvectors corresponding to the zero eigenvalue.

Thus three *real* eigenvalues have been found, as required by the general result (i), and three linearly independent eigenvectors have been constructed, as required by the general result (ii). The eigenvectors, however, are *not* mutually orthogonal. The eigenvector $[1 \quad 1 \quad 1]^T$ is orthogonal to $[-1 \quad 0 \quad 1]^T$ and $[-1 \quad 1 \quad 0]^T$, but the last two eigenvectors are not orthogonal to each other. However, we know that any vector

$$a\begin{bmatrix}-1\\0\\1\end{bmatrix} + b\begin{bmatrix}-1\\1\\0\end{bmatrix}$$

is also an eigenvector. Choosing $a = 1$ and $b = -2$ gives $[1 \quad -2 \quad 1]^T$ which is orthogonal to both $[1 \quad 1 \quad 1]^T$ and $[-1 \quad 0 \quad 1]^T$. Thus three normalized mutually orthogonal eigenvectors are

$$\frac{1}{\sqrt{3}}\begin{bmatrix}1\\1\\1\end{bmatrix}, \frac{1}{\sqrt{2}}\begin{bmatrix}-1\\0\\1\end{bmatrix}, \frac{1}{\sqrt{6}}\begin{bmatrix}1\\-2\\1\end{bmatrix}$$

5.7.8 Exercises

Check your answers using MATLAB or MAPLE whenever possible.

102 Verify Properties 1–8 of Section 5.7.6.

103 Given that the eigenvalues of the matrix

$$\boldsymbol{A} = \begin{bmatrix}4 & 1 & 1\\2 & 5 & 4\\-1 & -1 & 0\end{bmatrix}$$

are 5, 3 and 1:

(a) confirm Properties 1–4 of Section 5.7.6;

(b) taking $k = 2$, confirm Properties 5–8 of Section 5.7.6.

104 Determine the eigenvalues and corresponding eigenvectors of the symmetric matrix

$$\boldsymbol{A} = \begin{bmatrix}-3 & -3 & -3\\-3 & 1 & -1\\-3 & -1 & 1\end{bmatrix}$$

and verify that the eigenvectors are mutually orthogonal.

105 The 3×3 symmetric matrix $\boldsymbol{A}$ has eigenvalues 6, 3 and 2. The eigenvectors corresponding to the eigenvalues 6 and 3 are $[1 \quad 1 \quad 2]^T$ and $[1 \quad 1 \quad -1]^T$ respectively. Find an eigenvector corresponding to the eigenvalue 2.

106 Verify that the matrix

$$\boldsymbol{A} = \begin{bmatrix}-\frac{3}{20} & \frac{1}{5}\\ \frac{1}{5} & \frac{3}{20}\end{bmatrix}$$

has eigenvalues $\pm\frac{1}{4}$ and corresponding eigenvectors $\boldsymbol{X} = \begin{bmatrix}2\\-1\end{bmatrix}$ and $\boldsymbol{Y} = \begin{bmatrix}1\\2\end{bmatrix}$. What are the eigenvalues of $\boldsymbol{A}^n$? Show that any vector $\boldsymbol{Z} = \begin{bmatrix}a\\b\end{bmatrix}$ can be written as $\boldsymbol{Z} = \alpha\boldsymbol{X} + \beta\boldsymbol{Y}$ and hence deduce that $\boldsymbol{A}^n\boldsymbol{Z} \to \boldsymbol{0}$ as $n \to \infty$.

5.8 Engineering application: spring systems

The vibration of many mechanical systems can be modelled very satisfactorily by spring and damper systems. The shock absorbers and springs of a motor car give one of the simplest practical examples. On a more fundamental level, the vibration of the atoms or molecules of a solid can be modelled by a lattice containing atoms or molecules that interact with each other through spring forces. The model gives a detailed understanding of the structure of the solid and the strength of interactions and has practical applications in such areas as the study of impurities or 'doped' materials in semiconductor physics.

The motion of these systems demands the use of Newton's equations, which in turn require the calculus. In this case study we shall not consider vibrations but shall restrict our attention to the static situation. This is the first step in the solution of vibrational systems. Even here, we shall see that matrices and vectors allow a systematic approach to the more complicated situation.

5.8.1 A two-particle system

We start with the very simple situation illustrated in Figure 5.20. Two masses are connected by springs of stiffnesses k_1, k_2 and k_3 and of natural lengths l_1, l_2 and l_3 that are fixed to the walls at A and B, with distance AB = L. It is required to calculate the equilibrium values of x_1 and x_2. We use Hooke's law – that force is proportional to extension – to calculate the tension:

$$T_1 = k_1(x_1 - l_1)$$
$$T_2 = k_2(x_2 - x_1 - l_2)$$
$$T_3 = k_3(L - x_2 - l_3)$$

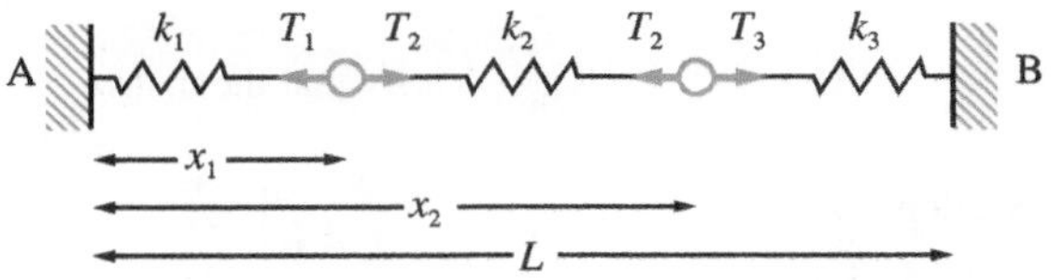

Figure 5.20
Two-particle system.

Since the forces are in equilibrium,

$$k_1(x_1 - l_1) = k_2(x_2 - x_1 - l_2)$$
$$k_2(x_2 - x_1 - l_2) = k_3(L - x_2 - l_3)$$

We have two simultaneous equations in the two unknowns, which can be written in matrix form as

$$\begin{bmatrix} k_1 + k_2 & -k_2 \\ -k_2 & k_2 + k_3 \end{bmatrix} \begin{bmatrix} x_1 \\ x_2 \end{bmatrix} = \begin{bmatrix} k_1 l_1 - k_2 l_2 \\ k_2 l_2 - k_3 l_3 + k_3 L \end{bmatrix}$$

It is easy to invert 2 × 2 matrices, so we can compute the solution as

$$\begin{bmatrix} x_1 \\ x_2 \end{bmatrix} = \frac{1}{(k_1 + k_2)(k_2 + k_3) - k_2^2} \begin{bmatrix} k_2 + k_3 & k_2 \\ k_2 & k_1 + k_2 \end{bmatrix} \begin{bmatrix} k_1 l_1 - k_2 l_2 \\ k_2 l_2 - k_3 l_3 + k_3 L \end{bmatrix}$$

If we take the simplest situation when $k_1 = k_2 = k_3$ and $l_1 = l_2 = l_3$ then we obtain the obvious solution $x_1 = \frac{1}{3}L$, $x_2 = \frac{2}{3}L$.

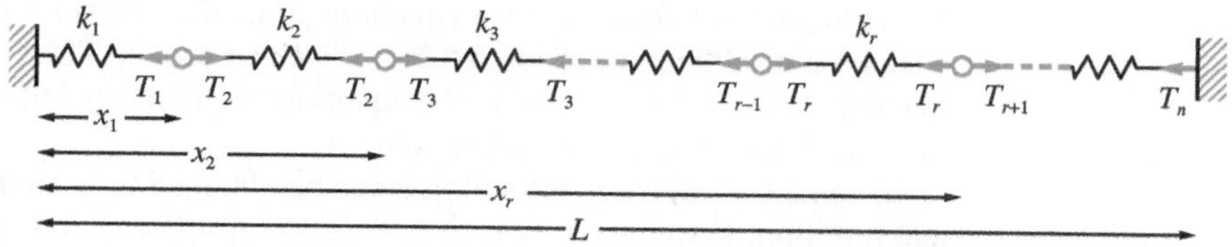

Figure 5.21
n-particle system.

5.8.2 An *n*-particle system

In the simplest situation, described in Section 5.8.1, matrix notation is convenient but not really necessary. If we try to extend the problem to many particles and many springs then such notation simplifies the statement of the problem considerably. Consider the problem illustrated in Figure 5.21. From Hooke's law

$$\begin{aligned}
T_1 &= k_1(x_1 - l_1)\\
T_2 &= k_2(x_2 - x_1 - l_2)\\
T_3 &= k_3(x_3 - x_2 - l_3)\\
&\vdots\\
T_r &= k_r(x_r - x_{r-1} - l_r)\\
&\vdots\\
T_n &= k_n(L - x_{n-1} - l_n)
\end{aligned}$$

The equilibrium equations for each 'unit' are

$$\begin{aligned}
k_1(x_1 - l_1) &= k_2(x_2 - x_1 - l_2)\\
k_2(x_2 - x_1 - l_2) &= k_3(x_3 - x_2 - l_3)\\
&\vdots\\
k_r(x_r - x_{r-1} - l_r) &= k_{r+1}(x_{r+1} - x_r - l_{r+1})\\
&\vdots\\
k_{n-1}(x_{n-1} - x_{n-2} - l_{n-1}) &= k_n(L - x_{n-1} - l_n)
\end{aligned}$$

In matrix form, these become

$$\begin{bmatrix}
k_1 + k_2 & -k_2 & & & & & \\
-k_2 & k_2 + k_3 & -k_3 & & & 0 & \\
 & -k_3 & k_3 + k_4 & -k_4 & & & \\
 & \ddots & \ddots & & \ddots & & \\
 & 0 & & -k_{n-2} & k_{n-2} + k_{n-1} & -k_{n-1} & \\
 & & & & -k_{n-1} & k_{n-1} + k_n &
\end{bmatrix}
\begin{bmatrix} x_1 \\ x_2 \\ \\ \vdots \\ \\ x_{n-1} \end{bmatrix}
= \begin{bmatrix}
k_1 l_1 - k_2 l_2 \\
k_2 l_2 - k_3 l_3 \\
\\
\vdots \\
\\
k_{n-2} l_{n-2} - k_{n-1} l_{n-1} \\
k_{n-1} l_{n-1} - k_n l_n + k_n L
\end{bmatrix}$$

We recognize the form of these equations immediately, since they constitute a tridiagonal system studied in Section 5.5.2, and we can use the Thomas algorithm (Figure 5.9) to solve them. Thus, by writing the equations in matrix form, we are immediately able to identify an efficient method of solution.

In some special cases the solution can be obtained by a mixture of insight and physical intuition. If we take $k_1 = k_2 = \ldots = k_n$ and $l_1 = l_2 = \ldots = l_n$ and the couplings are all the same then the equations become

$$\begin{bmatrix} 2 & -1 & & & & & \\ -1 & 2 & -1 & & & \mathbf{0} & \\ & -1 & 2 & -1 & & & \\ & & -1 & 2 & & & \\ & & \ddots & \ddots & \ddots & & \\ & \mathbf{0} & & -1 & 2 & -1 & \\ & & & & -1 & 2 \end{bmatrix} \begin{bmatrix} x_1 \\ x_2 \\ \vdots \\ \\ x_{n-1} \end{bmatrix} = \begin{bmatrix} 0 \\ 0 \\ \vdots \\ 0 \\ L \end{bmatrix}$$

We should expect all the spacings to be uniform, so we seek a solution $x_1 = \alpha$, $x_2 = 2\alpha$, $x_3 = 3\alpha, \ldots$. The first $n - 2$ equations are satisfied identically, as expected, and the final equation in matrix formulation gives $[-(n-2) + 2(n-1)]\alpha = L$. Thus $\alpha = L/n$, and our intuitive solution is justified.

In a second special case where a simple solution is possible, we assume one of the couplings to be a 'rogue'. We take $k_1 = k_2 = \ldots = k_{r-1} = k_{r+1} = \ldots = k_n = k$, $k_r = k'$ and $l_1 = l_2 = \ldots = l_n = l$. If we divide all the equations in the matrix by k and write $\lambda = k'/k$ then the matrix takes the form

$$\begin{bmatrix} 2 & -1 & & & & & & & \\ -1 & 2 & -1 & & & \mathbf{0} & & & \\ & -1 & 2 & -1 & & & & & \\ & \ddots & \ddots & \ddots & & & & & \\ & & -1 & 2 & -1 & & & & \\ & & & -1 & 1+\lambda & -\lambda & & & \\ & & & & -\lambda & 1+\lambda & -1 & & \\ & & & & & -1 & 2 & -1 & \\ & & & & & \ddots & \ddots & \ddots & \\ & \mathbf{0} & & & & & & & -1 \\ & & & & & & & -1 & 2 \end{bmatrix} \begin{bmatrix} x_1 \\ x_2 \\ \vdots \\ \\ x_{r-1} \\ x_r \\ \vdots \\ \\ x_{n-1} \end{bmatrix} = \begin{bmatrix} 0 \\ 0 \\ \\ 0 \\ l(1-\lambda) \\ l(\lambda-1) \\ \\ 0 \\ \vdots \\ L \end{bmatrix}$$

A reasonable assumption is that the spacings between 'good' links are all the same. Thus we try a solution of the form

$$x_1 = a, \quad x_2 = 2a, \quad \ldots, \quad x_{r-1} = (r-1)a, \quad x_r = b$$

$$x_{r+1} = b + a, \quad x_{r+2} = b + 2a, \quad \ldots, \quad x_{n-1} = b + (n-1-r)a$$

It can be checked that the matrix equation is satisfied except for the $(r-1)$th, rth and $(n-1)$th rows. These give respectively

$$-\lambda b + a(-\lambda + 1 + \lambda r) = l(1 - \lambda)$$

$$\lambda b + a(\lambda - 1 - \lambda r) = l(\lambda - 1)$$

and

$$b + a(n - r) = L$$

The first two of these are identical, so we have two equations in the two unknowns, a and b, to solve. We obtain

$$a = \frac{L - l(1 - \lambda^{-1})}{n - (1 - \lambda^{-1})}, \quad b = \frac{rL - (1 - \lambda^{-1})[L - (n - r)l]}{n - (1 - \lambda^{-1})}$$

We note that if $\lambda = 1$ then the solution reduces to the previous one, as expected.

The solution just obtained gives the deformation due to a single rogue coupling. Although this problem is of limited interest, its two- and three-dimensional extensions are of great interest in the theory of crystal lattices. It is possible to determine the deformation due to a single impurity, to compute the effect of two or more impurities and how close they have to be to interact with each other. These are problems with considerable application in materials science.

5.9 Engineering application: steady heat transfer through composite materials

5.9.1 Introduction

In many practical situations heat is transferred through several layers of different materials. Perhaps the simplest example is a double glazing unit, which comprises a layer of glass, a layer of air and another layer of glass. The thermal properties and the thicknesses of the individual layers are known but what is required is the overall thermal properties of the composite unit. How do the overall properties depend on the components? Which parameters are the most important? How sensitive is the overall heat transfer to changes in each of the components?

A second example looks at the thickness of a furnace wall. A furnace wall will comprise three layers: refractory bricks for heat resistance, insulating bricks for heat insulation and steel casing for mechanical protection. Such a furnace is enormously expensive to construct, so it is important that the thickness of the wall is minimized subject to acceptable heat losses, working within the serviceable temperatures and known thickness constraints. The basic problem is again to construct a model that will give some idea how heat is transferred through such a composite material.

The basic properties of heat conduction will be discussed, and it will then be seen that matrices give a natural method of solving the theoretical equations of composite layers.

5.9.2 Heat conduction

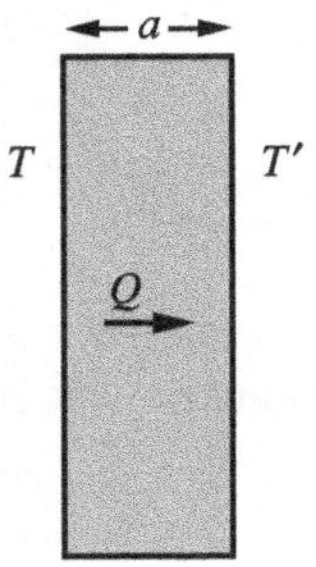

Figure 5.22 Heat transfer through layers.

In its full generality heat conduction forms a part of partial differential equations (see Chapter 9 of *Advanced Modern Engineering Mathematics* 3rd edition). However, for current purposes a simplified one-dimensional version is sufficient. The theory is based on the well-established **Fourier law**:

> Heat transferred per unit area is proportional to the temperature gradient.

Provided a layer is not too thick and the thermal properties do not vary, then the temperature varies linearly across the solid. If Q is the amount of heat transferred per unit area from left, at temperature T, to right, at temperature T', as shown in Figure 5.22, then this law can be written mathematically as

$$Q = -k\frac{T' - T}{a}$$

where k is the proportionality constant, called the thermal conductivity, a is the thickness of the layer and the minus sign is to ensure that heat is transferred from hot to cold.

For the conduction *through* an interface between two solids with good contact, as in the situation of the furnace wall, it is assumed that

(i) the temperatures at each side of the interface are equal;
(ii) the heat transferred out of the left side is equal to the heat transferred into the right side.

With the Fourier law and these interface conditions the multilayer situation can be analysed satisfactorily, provided, of course, the heat flow remains one-dimensional and steady.

5.9.3 The three-layer situation

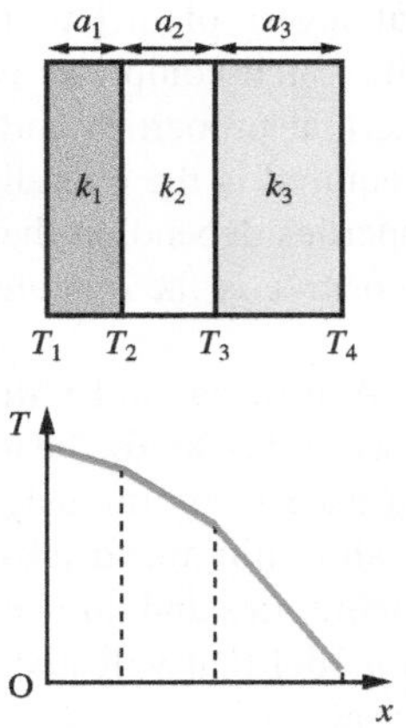

Figure 5.23 Temperature distribution across three layers.

Let the three layers have thicknesses a_1, a_2 and a_3 and thermal conductivities k_1, k_2 and k_3, as illustrated in Figure 5.23. At the interfaces the temperatures are taken to be T_1, T_2, T_3 and T_4. The simplest problem to study is to fix the temperatures T_1 and T_4 at the edges and determine how the temperatures T_2 and T_3 depend on the known parameters.

From the specification of the problem the temperatures at the interfaces are specified, so it only remains to satisfy the heat transfer condition across the interface.

At the first interface

$$\frac{k_1}{a_1}(T_2 - T_1) = \frac{k_2}{a_2}(T_3 - T_2)$$

and at the second interface

$$\frac{k_2}{a_2}(T_3 - T_2) = \frac{k_3}{a_3}(T_4 - T_3)$$

It turns out to be convenient to let $u_1 = \dfrac{a_1}{k_1}$, $u_2 = \dfrac{a_2}{k_2}$ and so on. The equations then become

$$u_2(T_2 - T_1) = u_1(T_3 - T_2)$$
$$u_3(T_3 - T_2) = u_2(T_4 - T_3)$$

or in matrix form

$$\begin{bmatrix} (u_1 + u_2) & -u_1 \\ -u_3 & (u_2 + u_3) \end{bmatrix} \begin{bmatrix} T_2 \\ T_3 \end{bmatrix} = u_2 \begin{bmatrix} T_1 \\ T_4 \end{bmatrix}$$

The determinant of the matrix is easily calculated as $u_2(u_1 + u_2 + u_3)$, which is non-zero, so a solution can be computed as

$$\begin{bmatrix} T_2 \\ T_3 \end{bmatrix} = \frac{1}{(u_1 + u_2 + u_3)} \begin{bmatrix} (u_2 + u_3) & u_1 \\ u_3 & (u_1 + u_2) \end{bmatrix} \begin{bmatrix} T_1 \\ T_4 \end{bmatrix}$$

Thus the temperatures T_2 and T_3 are now known, and any required properties can be deduced.

For the furnace problem described in Section 5.9.1 the following data is known:

$T_1 = 1650$ K and $T_4 = 300$ K

and

	Maximum working temperature (K)	*Thermal conductivity at 100 K ($W\,m^{-1}K^{-1}$)*	*Thermal conductivity at 2000 K ($W\,m^{-1}K^{-1}$)*
Refractory brick	1700	3.1	6.2
Insulating brick	1400	1.6	3.1
Steel	–	45.2	45.2

It may be noted that the thermal conductivity depends on the temperature but in these calculations it is assumed constant (a more sophisticated analysis is required to take these variations into account). Average values $k_1 = 5$, $k_2 = 2.5$ and $k_3 = 45.2$ are chosen. The required temperatures are evaluated as

$$T_2 = \frac{(0.4a_2 + 0.022a_3)1650 + (0.2a_1)300}{0.2a_1 + 0.4a_2 + 0.022a_3}$$

$$T_3 = \frac{(0.022a_3)1650 + (0.2a_1 + 0.4a_2)300}{0.2a_1 + 0.4a_2 + 0.022a_3}$$

A typical question that would be asked is how to minimize the thickness (or perhaps the cost) subject to appropriate constraints. For instance find

$\min(a_1 + a_2 + a_3)$

subject to

$\frac{k_3}{a_3}(300 - T_3) < 50000$ (allowable heat loss at the right-hand boundary)

$T_2 < 1400$ (below the maximum working temperature)

$a_1 > 0.1$ (must have a minimum refractory thickness)

The problem is beyond the scope of the present book, but it illustrates the type of question that can be answered.

A more straightforward question is to evaluate the effective conductivity of the composite. It may be noted that in the general case, the heat flow is

$$Q = -\frac{1}{u_1}(T_2 - T_1) \quad \text{which on substitution gives } Q = -\frac{T_4 - T_1}{u_1 + u_2 + u_3}$$

so the effective conductivity over the whole region is

$$k = \frac{a_1 + a_2 + a_3}{u_1 + u_2 + u_3} \quad \text{or} \quad \frac{a_1 + a_2 + a_3}{k} = \frac{a_1}{k_1} + \frac{a_2}{k_2} + \frac{a_3}{k_3}$$

5.9.4 Many-layer situation

Although matrix theory was used to solve the three-layer problem, it was unnecessary since the mathematics reduced to the solution of a pair of simultaneous equations. However, for the many-layer system it is important to approach the problem in a logical and systematic manner, and matrix theory proves to be the ideal mathematical method to use.

Consider the successive interfaces in turn and construct the heat flow equation for each of them (Figure 5.24).

$$\frac{k_1}{a_1}(T_2 - T_1) = \frac{k_2}{a_2}(T_3 - T_2)$$

$$\frac{k_2}{a_2}(T_3 - T_2) = \frac{k_3}{a_3}(T_4 - T_3)$$

$$\vdots$$

$$\frac{k_{n-1}}{a_{n-1}}(T_n - T_{n-1}) = \frac{k_n}{a_n}(T_{n+1} - T_n)$$

As in the three-layer case, it is convenient to define $u_1 = \frac{a_1}{k_1}$, $u_2 = \frac{a_2}{k_2}$ and so on. The equations then become

$$u_2(T_2 - T_1) = u_1(T_3 - T_2)$$

$$u_3(T_3 - T_2) = u_2(T_4 - T_3)$$

$$u_4(T_4 - T_3) = u_3(T_5 - T_4)$$

$$\vdots$$

$$u_n(T_n - T_{n-1}) = u_{n-1}(T_{n+1} - T_n)$$

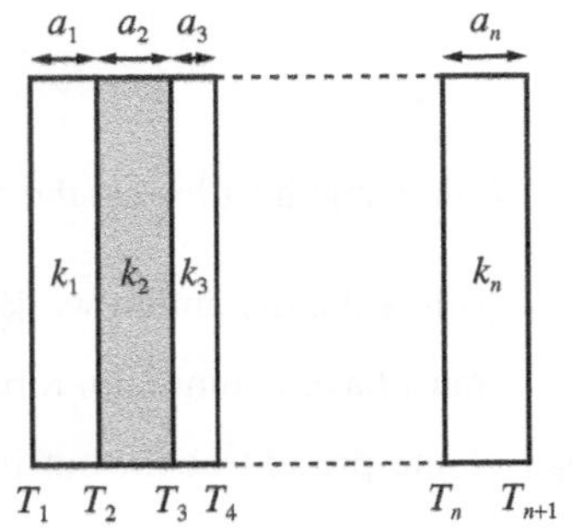

Figure 5.24
n-layered problem.

or in matrix form

$$\begin{bmatrix} (u_1+u_2) & -u_1 & 0 & . & . & . & . & 0 \\ -u_3 & (u_2+u_3) & -u_2 & 0 & . & . & . & 0 \\ 0 & -u_4 & (u_3+u_4) & -u_3 & 0 & . & . & 0 \\ . & . & . & . & . & . & . & . \\ . & . & . & . & . & . & . & . \\ . & . & . & . & . & . & . & . \\ 0 & 0 & 0 & . & . & 0 & -u_n & (u_{n-1}+u_n) \end{bmatrix} \begin{bmatrix} T_2 \\ . \\ . \\ . \\ . \\ T_n \end{bmatrix}$$

$$= \begin{bmatrix} u_2T_1 \\ 0 \\ 0 \\ . \\ . \\ 0 \\ u_{n-1}T_{n+1} \end{bmatrix}$$

The matrix equation is of tridiagonal form, hence we know that there is an efficient algorithm for solution. An explicit solution, as in the three-layer case, is not so easy and requires a lot of effort. However, it is a comparatively easy exercise to prove that the effective conductivity (k) of the whole composite is obtained from the equivalent formula

$$\frac{\Sigma a_i}{k} = \frac{a_1}{k_1} + \frac{a_2}{k_2} + \ldots + \frac{a_n}{k_n}$$

5.10 Review exercises (1–26)

Check your answers using MATLAB or MAPLE whenever possible.

1 Given

$$P = \begin{bmatrix} 2 & 4 & 1 \\ 0 & 2 & 1 \\ 0 & 0 & 4 \end{bmatrix} \quad Q = \begin{bmatrix} 6 & 2 & -1 \\ 0 & 2 & -2 \\ 0 & 0 & 4 \end{bmatrix}$$

and

$$R = \begin{bmatrix} 2 & 7 & -6 \\ 0 & 0 & 2 \\ 0 & 0 & 1 \end{bmatrix}$$

(a) calculate $\boldsymbol{RQ}$ and $\boldsymbol{Q}^{\mathrm{T}}\boldsymbol{R}^{\mathrm{T}}$;

(b) calculate $\boldsymbol{Q} + \boldsymbol{R}$, $\boldsymbol{PQ}$ and $\boldsymbol{PR}$, and hence verify that in this particular case

$$\boldsymbol{P}(\boldsymbol{Q} + \boldsymbol{R}) = \boldsymbol{PQ} + \boldsymbol{PR}$$

2 Let

$$\boldsymbol{A} = \begin{bmatrix} -1 & 2 \\ 4 & 1 \end{bmatrix} \quad \text{and} \quad \boldsymbol{B} = \begin{bmatrix} 1 & 1 \\ \lambda & \mu \end{bmatrix}$$

where $\lambda \neq \mu$. Find all pairs of values λ, μ such that $\boldsymbol{B}^{-1}\boldsymbol{AB}$ is a diagonal matrix.

3 At a point in an elastic continuum the matrix representation of the infinitesimal strain tensor referred to axes $Ox_1x_2x_3$ is

$$\boldsymbol{E} = \begin{bmatrix} 1 & -3 & \sqrt{2} \\ -3 & 1 & -\sqrt{2} \\ \sqrt{2} & -\sqrt{2} & 4 \end{bmatrix}$$

If $\boldsymbol{i}, \boldsymbol{j}$ and $\boldsymbol{k}$ are unit vectors in the direction of the $Ox_1x_2x_3$ coordinate axes, determine the normal strain in the direction of

$$\boldsymbol{n} = \tfrac{1}{2}(\boldsymbol{i} - \boldsymbol{j} + \sqrt{2}\boldsymbol{k})$$

and the shear strain between the directions $\boldsymbol{n}$ and

$$\boldsymbol{m} = \tfrac{1}{2}(-\boldsymbol{i} + \boldsymbol{j} + \sqrt{2}\boldsymbol{k})$$

Note: Using matrix notation, the normal strain is $\boldsymbol{En}$, and the shear strain between two directions is $\boldsymbol{m}^{\mathrm{T}}\boldsymbol{En}$.

4 Express the determinant

$$\begin{vmatrix} \alpha & \beta & \gamma \\ \beta\gamma & \gamma\alpha & \alpha\beta \\ -\alpha+\beta+\gamma & \alpha-\beta+\gamma & \alpha+\beta-\gamma \end{vmatrix}$$

as a product of linear factors.

5 Determine the values of θ for which the system of equations

$$x + y + z = 1$$

$$x + 2y + 4z = \theta$$

$$x + 4y + 10z = \theta^2$$

possesses a solution, and for each such value find all solutions.

6 Given

$$\boldsymbol{A} = \begin{bmatrix} 1 & 1 & 1 \\ 2 & 1 & 2 \\ -2 & 1 & -1 \end{bmatrix}$$

evaluate $\boldsymbol{A}^2$ and $\boldsymbol{A}^3$. Verify that

$$\boldsymbol{A}^3 - \boldsymbol{A}^2 - 3\boldsymbol{A} + \boldsymbol{I} = 0$$

where $\boldsymbol{I}$ is the unit matrix of order 3. Using this result, or otherwise, find the inverse $\boldsymbol{A}^{-1}$ of $\boldsymbol{A}$, and hence solve the equations

$$x + y + z = 3$$

$$2x + y + 2z = 7$$

$$-2x + y - z = 6$$

7 (a) If $\boldsymbol{P} = \dfrac{1}{3}\begin{bmatrix} 2 & 1 & 2 \\ -2 & 2 & 1 \\ -1 & -2 & 2 \end{bmatrix}$ write down the transpose matrix $\boldsymbol{P}^{\mathrm{T}}$. Calculate $\boldsymbol{PP}^{\mathrm{T}}$ and hence show that $\boldsymbol{P}^{\mathrm{T}} = \boldsymbol{P}^{-1}$. What does this mean about the solution of the matrix equation $\boldsymbol{Px} = \boldsymbol{b}$?

(b) The matrix $\boldsymbol{F} = \begin{bmatrix} I_x & I_{xy} & Q_x \\ I_{xy} & I_y & Q_y \\ Q_x & Q_y & A \end{bmatrix}$ occurs in the structural analysis of an arch. If

$$\boldsymbol{B} = \begin{bmatrix} 1 & 0 & -Q_x/A \\ 0 & 1 & -Q_y/A \\ 0 & 0 & 1 \end{bmatrix}$$

find $\boldsymbol{E} = \boldsymbol{BFB}^{\mathrm{T}}$ and show that it is a symmetric matrix.

8 (a) If the matrix $\boldsymbol{A} = \begin{bmatrix} 1 & 0 & 0 \\ 1 & -1 & 0 \\ 1 & -2 & 1 \end{bmatrix}$ show that $\boldsymbol{A}^2 = \boldsymbol{I}$ and derive the elements of a square matrix $\boldsymbol{B}$ which satisfies

$$\boldsymbol{BA} = \begin{bmatrix} 1 & 4 & 3 \\ 0 & 2 & 1 \\ -1 & 0 & 0 \end{bmatrix}$$

(b) Find suitable values for k in order that the following system of linear simultaneous equations are consistent:

$$6x + (k - 6)y = 3$$

$$2x + y = 5$$

$$(2k + 1)x + 6y = 1$$

9 Express the system of linear equations

$$3x - y + 4z = 13$$
$$5x + y - 3z = 5$$
$$x - y + z = 3$$

in the form $\boldsymbol{AX} = \boldsymbol{b}$, where $\boldsymbol{A}$ is a 3×3 matrix and $\boldsymbol{X}$, $\boldsymbol{b}$ are appropriate column matrices.

(a) Find adj $\boldsymbol{A}$, $|\boldsymbol{A}|$ and $\boldsymbol{A}^{-1}$ and hence solve the system of equations.

(b) Find a matrix $\boldsymbol{Y}$ which satisfies the equation

$$\boldsymbol{AYA}^{-1} = 22\boldsymbol{A}^{-1} + 2\boldsymbol{A}$$

(c) Find a matrix $\boldsymbol{Z}$ which satisfies the equation

$$\boldsymbol{AZ} = 44\boldsymbol{I}_3 - \boldsymbol{A} + \boldsymbol{AA}^{\mathrm{T}}$$

where $\boldsymbol{I}_3$ is the 3×3 identity matrix.

10 (a) Using the method of Gaussian elimination, find the solution of the equation

$$\begin{bmatrix} 1 & 2 & 4 & 8 \\ 2 & 7 & 13 & 25 \\ -1 & 1 & 5 & 9 \\ 2 & 1 & 11 & 24 \end{bmatrix} \begin{bmatrix} x_1 \\ x_2 \\ x_3 \\ x_4 \end{bmatrix} = \begin{bmatrix} 19 \\ 57 \\ 16 \\ 52 \end{bmatrix}$$

Hence evaluate the determinant of the matrix in the equation.

(b) Solve by the method of Gaussian elimination

$$\begin{bmatrix} 1 & 1 & -1 & 1 \\ 2 & 3 & -3 & 3 \\ -1 & 1 & 0 & 0 \\ 2 & 3 & -1 & 2 \end{bmatrix} \begin{bmatrix} x_1 \\ x_2 \\ x_3 \\ x_4 \end{bmatrix} = \begin{bmatrix} 4 \\ 11 \\ 1 \\ 13 \end{bmatrix}$$

with partial pivoting.

11 Rearrange the equations

$$x_1 - x_2 + 3x_3 = 8$$
$$4x_1 + x_2 - x_3 = 3$$
$$x_1 + 2x_2 + x_3 = 8$$

so that they are diagonally dominant to ensure convergence of the Gauss–Seidel method. Write a MATLAB program to obtain the solution of these equations using this method, starting from (0, 0, 0). Compare your solution with that from a program when the equations are not rearranged. Use SOR, with $\omega = 1.3$, to solve the equations. Is there any improvement?

12 Find the rank of the matrix

$$\begin{bmatrix} 0 & c & b & a \\ -c & 0 & a & b \\ -b & -a & 0 & c \\ -a & -b & -c & 0 \end{bmatrix}$$

where $b \neq 0$ and $a^2 + c^2 = b^2$.

13 For a given set of discrete data points (x_i, f_i) $(i = 0, 1, 2, \dots, n)$, show that the coefficients a_k $(k = 0, 1, \dots, n)$ fitted to the polynomial

$$y(x) = \sum_{k=0}^{n} a_k x^k$$

are given by the solution of the equations written in the matrix form as

$$\boldsymbol{Aa} = \boldsymbol{f}$$

where

$$\boldsymbol{A} = \begin{bmatrix} 1 & x_0 & x_0^2 & \dots & x_0^n \\ 1 & x_1 & x_1^2 & \dots & x_1^n \\ \vdots & \vdots & \vdots & & \vdots \\ 1 & x_n & x_n^2 & \dots & x_n^n \end{bmatrix}$$

$$\boldsymbol{a} = [a_0 \ \ a_1 \ \ \dots \ \ a_n]^{\mathrm{T}}$$
$$\boldsymbol{f} = [f_0 \ \ f_1 \ \ \dots \ \ f_n]^{\mathrm{T}}$$

(See Question 103 in Exercises 2.9.2 for the Lagrange interpolation solution of these equations for the case $n = 3$.)

The following data is taken from the tables of the Airy function $f(x) = \mathrm{Ai}(-x)$:

x	1	1.5	2.3	3.0	3.9
$f(x)$	0.535 56	0.464 26	0.026 70	−0.378 81	−0.147 42

Estimate from the polynomial approximation the values of $f(2.0)$ and $f(3.5)$.

14 Data is fitted to a cubic

$$f = ax^3 + bx^2 + cx + d$$

with the slope of the curve given by

$$f' = 3ax^2 + 2bx + c$$

If $f_1 = f(x_1), f_2 = f(x_2), f'_1 = f'(x_1)$ and $f'_2 = f'(x_2)$, show that fitting the data gives the matrix equation for a, b, c and d as

$$\begin{bmatrix} f_1 \\ f_2 \\ f'_1 \\ f'_2 \end{bmatrix} = \begin{bmatrix} x_1^3 & x_1^2 & x_1 & 1 \\ x_2^3 & x_2^2 & x_2 & 1 \\ 3x_1^2 & 2x_1 & 1 & 0 \\ 3x_2^2 & 2x_2 & 1 & 0 \end{bmatrix} \begin{bmatrix} a \\ b \\ c \\ d \end{bmatrix}$$

Use Gaussian elimination to evaluate a, b, c and d. For the case

x	f	f'
0.4	0.327 54	0.511 73
0.8	0.404 90	−0.054 14

evaluate a, b, c and d. Plot the cubic and estimate the maximum value of f in the region $0 < x < 1$. Note that this exercise forms the basis of one of the standard methods for finding the maximum of a function $f(x)$ numerically.

15 The transformation $\mathbf{y} = \mathbf{AX}$ where

$$\mathbf{A} = \frac{1}{9}\begin{bmatrix} 8 & -1 & -4 \\ 4 & 4 & 7 \\ 1 & -8 & 4 \end{bmatrix}$$

$$\mathbf{y} = \begin{bmatrix} y_1 \\ y_2 \\ y_3 \end{bmatrix} \quad \text{and} \quad \mathbf{X} = \begin{bmatrix} x_1 \\ x_2 \\ x_3 \end{bmatrix}$$

takes a point with coordinates (x_1, x_2, x_3) into a point with coordinates (y_1, y_2, y_3). Show that the coordinates of the points that transform into themselves satisfy the matrix equation $\mathbf{BX} = 0$, where $\mathbf{B} = \mathbf{A} - \mathbf{I}$, with $\mathbf{I}$ the identity matrix. Find the rank of $\mathbf{B}$ and hence deduce that for points which transform into themselves

$$[x_1 \quad x_2 \quad x_3] = \alpha[-3 \quad -1 \quad 1]$$

where α is a parameter.

Find $\mathbf{AA}^{\mathrm{T}}$. What is the inverse of $\mathbf{A}$?

If $y_1 = 3$, $y_2 = -1$ and $y_3 = 2$, determine the values of x_1, x_2 and x_3 under this transformation.

16 (a) If

$$\mathbf{A} = \begin{bmatrix} 1 & 0 & 1 & 0 \\ 2 & 1 & 2 & 1 \\ 1 & -2 & 2 & -2 \\ 2 & 0 & 3 & 1 \end{bmatrix}$$

verify that

$$\mathbf{A}^{-1} = \begin{bmatrix} 6 & -2 & -1 & 0 \\ -5 & 3 & 1 & -1 \\ -5 & 2 & 1 & 0 \\ 3 & -2 & -1 & 1 \end{bmatrix}$$

(b) Use the inverse matrix given in (a) to solve the system of linear equations $\mathbf{AX} = \mathbf{b}$ in which

$$\mathbf{b}^{\mathrm{T}} = [5 \quad -5 \quad -4 \quad 4]$$

17 When a body is deformed in a certain manner, the particle at point $\mathbf{X}$ moves to $\mathbf{AX}$, where

$$\mathbf{X} = \begin{bmatrix} x \\ y \\ z \end{bmatrix} \quad \text{and} \quad \mathbf{A} = \begin{bmatrix} 1 & -2 & 0 \\ -2 & 3 & 0 \\ 0 & 0 & 2 \end{bmatrix}$$

(a) Where would the point $\begin{bmatrix} 2 \\ 1 \\ 1 \end{bmatrix}$ move to?

(b) Find the point from which the particle would move to the point $\begin{bmatrix} 2 \\ 1 \\ 1 \end{bmatrix}$.

18 Find the eigenvalues and the normalized eigenvectors of the matrices

(a) $\begin{bmatrix} 4 & 1 & 1 \\ 2 & 1 & -1 \\ -2 & 2 & 4 \end{bmatrix}$ (b) $\begin{bmatrix} 1 & -1 & 2 \\ -2 & 0 & 5 \\ 6 & -3 & 6 \end{bmatrix}$

(c) $\begin{bmatrix} 5 & -2 & 0 \\ -2 & 6 & 2 \\ 0 & 2 & 7 \end{bmatrix} = \boldsymbol{C}$

In (c) write the normalized eigenvectors as the columns of the matrix $\boldsymbol{U}$ and show that $\boldsymbol{U}^{\mathrm{T}}\boldsymbol{CU}$ is a diagonal matrix with the eigenvalues in the diagonal.

19 The vector $[1 \quad 0 \quad 1]^{\mathrm{T}}$ is an eigenvector of the symmetric matrix

$$\begin{bmatrix} 6 & -1 & 3 \\ -1 & 7 & \alpha \\ 3 & \alpha & \beta \end{bmatrix}$$

Find the values of α and β and find the corresponding eigenvalue.

20 Show that the matrix $\begin{bmatrix} -1 & 0 & 2 \\ 0 & 1 & 0 \\ 2 & 0 & -1 \end{bmatrix}$ has eigenvalues 1, 1 and −3. Find the corresponding eigenvectors. Is there a full set of three independent eigenvectors?

21 A colony of insects is observed at regular intervals and comprises four age groups containing n_1, n_2, n_3, n_4 insects in the groups. At the end of an interval, of the n_1 in group 1 some have died and $(1 - \beta_1)n_1$ become the new group 2. Similarly $(1 - \beta_2)n_2$ of group 2 become the new group 3 and $(1 - \beta_3)n_3$ of group 3 become the new group 4. All group 4 die out at the end of the interval. Groups 2, 3 and 4 produce $\alpha_2 n_2$, $\alpha_3 n_3$ and $\alpha_4 n_4$ infant insects that enter group 1. Show that the changes from one interval to the next can be written

$$\begin{bmatrix} n_1 \\ n_2 \\ n_3 \\ n_4 \end{bmatrix}_{\text{new}} = \begin{bmatrix} 0 & \alpha_2 & \alpha_3 & \alpha_4 \\ 1-\beta_1 & 0 & 0 & 0 \\ 0 & 1-\beta_2 & 0 & 0 \\ 0 & 0 & 1-\beta_3 & 0 \end{bmatrix} \begin{bmatrix} n_1 \\ n_2 \\ n_3 \\ n_4 \end{bmatrix}_{\text{old}}$$

Take $\alpha_3 = 0.5$, $\alpha_4 = 0.25$, $\beta_1 = 0.2$, $\beta_2 = 0.25$ and $\beta_3 = 0.5$. Try the values $\alpha_2 = 0.77$, 0.78, 0.79 and check whether the population grows or dies out over many intervals starting from an initial population $\begin{bmatrix} 100 \\ 90 \\ 50 \\ 30 \end{bmatrix}$.

Find the eigenvalues in the three cases and check the magnitudes of the eigenvalues. Is there any connection between survival and eigenvalues?

Realistic populations can be modelled using this approach; the matrices are called Leslie matrices.

22 (a) Find the eigenvalues λ_1, λ_2 and the normalized eigenvectors $\boldsymbol{X}_1$, $\boldsymbol{X}_2$ of the matrix $\boldsymbol{A} = \begin{bmatrix} 2 & 1 \\ 1 & 2 \end{bmatrix}$. Check that

$$\boldsymbol{A} = \lambda_1 \boldsymbol{X}_1 \boldsymbol{X}_1^{\mathrm{T}} + \lambda_2 \boldsymbol{X}_2 \boldsymbol{X}_2^{\mathrm{T}}$$

(b) Use MATLAB or MAPLE to repeat a similar calculation for the three eigenvalues and normalized eigenvectors of

$$\boldsymbol{B} = \begin{bmatrix} -1 & 1 & 0 \\ 1 & 0 & 1 \\ 0 & 1 & -2 \end{bmatrix}$$

Note: The process described in this question calculates the spectral decomposition of a symmetric matrix.

23 In Section 5.7.7 it was stated that a symmetric matrix $\boldsymbol{A}$ has real eigenvalues $\lambda_1, \lambda_2, \ldots, \lambda_n$ (written in descending order) and corresponding orthonormal eigenvectors $\mathbf{e}_1, \mathbf{e}_2, \ldots, \mathbf{e}_n$, that is $\mathbf{e}_i^{\mathrm{T}}\mathbf{e}_j = \delta_{ij}$. In consequence any vector can be written as

$$\boldsymbol{X} = c_1\mathbf{e}_1 + c_2\mathbf{e}_2 + \ldots + c_n\mathbf{e}_n$$

Deduce that

$$\frac{\boldsymbol{X}^{\mathrm{T}}\boldsymbol{AX}}{\boldsymbol{X}^{\mathrm{T}}\boldsymbol{X}} \leqslant \lambda_1 \qquad \textbf{(5.40)}$$

so that a lower bound of the largest eigenvalue has been found. The left-hand side of (5.40) is called the Rayleigh quotient.

It is known that the matrix $\begin{bmatrix} 0 & 1 & 0 & 0 \\ 1 & 0 & 1 & 0 \\ 0 & 1 & 0 & 1 \\ 0 & 0 & 1 & 0 \end{bmatrix}$ has a largest eigenvalue of $\frac{1}{2}(1 + \sqrt{5})$. Check that the result (5.40) holds for any vector of your choice.

24 A rotation of a set of rectangular cartesian axes $\Phi(Ox_1x_2x_3)$ to a set $\Phi'(Ox_1'x_2'x_3')$ is described by the matrix $\boldsymbol{L} = (l_{ij})$ $(i, j = 1, 2, 3)$, where l_{ij} is the cosine of the angle between Ox_i' and Ox_j. Show that $\boldsymbol{L}$ is such that

$$\boldsymbol{L}\boldsymbol{L}^{T} = \boldsymbol{I}$$

and that the coordinates of a point in space referred to the two sets of axes are related by

$$\boldsymbol{X}' = \boldsymbol{L}\boldsymbol{X}$$

where $\boldsymbol{X}' = [x_1' \quad x_2' \quad x_3']^T$ and $\boldsymbol{X} = [x_1 \quad x_2 \quad x_3]^T$. Prove that

$$x_1'^2 + x_2'^2 + x_3'^2 = x_1^2 + x_2^2 + x_3^2$$

Describe the relationship between the axes Φ and Φ', given that

$$\boldsymbol{L} = \begin{bmatrix} \frac{1}{2} & 0 & \frac{1}{2}\sqrt{3} \\ 0 & 1 & 0 \\ -\frac{1}{2}\sqrt{3} & 0 & \frac{1}{2} \end{bmatrix}$$

The axes Φ' are now rotated through 45° about Ox_3' in the sense from Ox_1' to Ox_2' to form a new set Φ''. Show that the angle θ between the line OP and the axis Ox_1'', where P is the point with coordinates $(1, 2, -1)$ referred to the original system Φ, is

$$\theta = \cos^{-1}\left(\frac{5\sqrt{3} - 3}{12}\right)$$

25 A car is at rest on horizontal ground, as shown in Figure 5.25. The weight W acts through the centre of gravity, and the springs have stiffness constants k_1 and k_2 and natural lengths a_1 and a_2. Show that the height z and the angle θ (assumed too small) satisfy the matrix equation

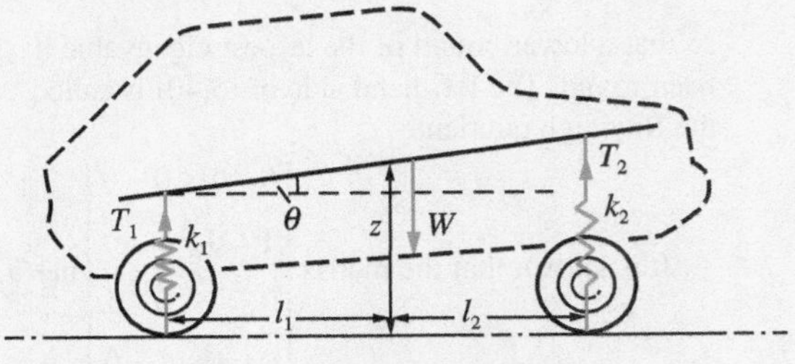

Figure 5.25 Car at rest on horizontal ground.

$$\begin{bmatrix} -W + a_1k_1 + a_2k_2 \\ l_1k_1a_1 - l_2k_2a_2 \end{bmatrix} = \begin{bmatrix} k_1 + k_2 & -l_1k_1 + l_2k_2 \\ l_1k_1 - l_2k_2 & -l_1^2k_1 - l_2^2k_2 \end{bmatrix} \begin{bmatrix} z \\ \theta \end{bmatrix}$$

Obtain reasonable values for the various parameters to ensure that $\theta = 0$.

26 In the circuit in Figure 5.26(a) show that the equations can be written

$$\begin{bmatrix} E_1 \\ I_1 \end{bmatrix} = \begin{bmatrix} 1 & Z_1 \\ 0 & 1 \end{bmatrix} \begin{bmatrix} E_2 \\ I_2 \end{bmatrix}$$

and that in Figure 5.26(b) they take the form

$$\begin{bmatrix} E_1 \\ I_1 \end{bmatrix} = \begin{bmatrix} 1 & 0 \\ 1/Z_2 & 1 \end{bmatrix} \begin{bmatrix} E_2 \\ I_2 \end{bmatrix}$$

Dividing the circuit in Figure 5.26(c) into blocks, with the output from one block inputting to the next block, analyse the relation between I_1, E_1 and I_2, E_2.

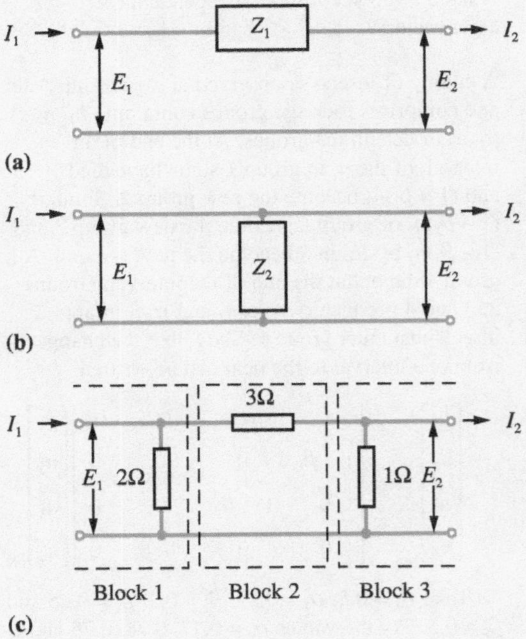

Figure 5.26

6 Sequences, Series and Limits

Chapter 6 Contents

6.1 Introduction

In the analysis of practical problems, certain mathematical ideas and techniques appear in many different contexts. One such idea is the concept of a sequence. Sequences occur in management activities such as the determination of programmes for the maintenance of hardware or production schedules for bulk products. They also arise in investment plans and financial control. They are intrinsic to computing activities, since the most important feature of computers is their ability to perform sequences of instructions quickly and accurately. Sequences are of great importance in the numerical methods that are essential for modern design and the development of new products. As well as illustrating these basic applications, we shall show how these simple ideas lead to the idea of a limit, which is a prerequisite for a proper understanding of the calculus and numerical methods. Without that understanding, it is not possible to form mathematical models of real problems, to solve them or to interpret their solutions adequately. At the same time, we shall illustrate some of the elementary properties of the standard functions described in Chapter 2 and how they link together, and we shall look forward to further applications in more advanced engineering applications, in particular to the work on Z transforms contained in the companion text *Advanced Modern Engineering Mathematics*.

6.2 Sequences and series

6.2.1 Notation

Consider a function f whose domain is the set of whole numbers $\{0, 1, 2, 3, \dots\}$. The set of values of the function $\{f(0), f(1), f(2), f(3), \dots\}$ is called a **sequence**. Usually we denote the values using a subscript, so that $f(0) = f_0, f(1) = f_1, f(2) = f_2$, and so on. Often we list the elements of a sequence in order, on the assumption that the first in the list is f_0, the second is f_1 and so on. For example, we may write

'Consider the sequence 1, 1, 2, 3, 5, 8, 13, 21, 34, …'

implying $f_0 = 1, f_5 = 8, f_8 = 34$ and so on. In this example the continuation dots … are used to imply that the sequence does not end. Such a sequence is called an **infinite** sequence to distinguish it from **finite** or **terminating** sequences. The finite sequence $\{f_0, f_1, \dots, f_n\}$ is often denoted by $\{f_k\}_{k=0}^{n}$ and the infinite sequence by $\{f_k\}_{k=0}^{\infty}$. When the context makes the meaning clear, the notation is further abbreviated to $\{f_k\}$. Here the letter k is used as the 'counting' variable. It is a **dummy variable** in the sense that we could replace it by any other letter and not change the result. Often n and r are used as dummy variables.

Example 6.1

A bank pays interest at a fixed rate of 8.5% per year, compounded annually. A customer deposits the fixed sum of £1000 into an account at the beginning of each year. How much is in the account at the beginning of each of the first four years?

Solution Let £x_n denote the amount in the account at the beginning of the $(n + 1)$th year. Then

Amount at beginning of first year	$x_0 = 1000$
Amount at beginning of 2nd year	$x_1 = 1000(1 + \frac{8.5}{100}) + 1000 = 2085$
Amount at beginning of 3rd year	$x_2 = 2085(1 + 0.085) + 1000 = 3262.22$
Amount at beginning of 4th year	$x_3 = 3262.22(1.085) + 1000 = 4539.51$

We can see that in general

$$x_n = 1.085x_{n-1} + 1000$$

This is a **recurrence relation**, which gives the value of each element of the sequence in terms of the value of the previous element.

Example 6.2 Consider, again, the ducting of a number of cables of the same diameter d (Example 2.2). The diameter D_n of the smallest duct with circular cross-section depends on the number n of cables to be enclosed, as shown in Figure 6.1:

$$D_0 = 0, \quad D_1 = d, \quad D_2 = 2d, \quad D_3 = (1 + 2/\sqrt{3})d, \quad D_4 = (1 + \sqrt{2})d$$

$$D_5 = \tfrac{1}{4}\sqrt{[2(5 - \sqrt{5})]}d, \quad D_6 = 3d, \quad D_7 = 3d, \ldots$$

Thus the duct diameters form a sequence of values $\{D_1, D_2, D_3, \ldots\} = \{D_n\}_{n=1}^{\infty}$.

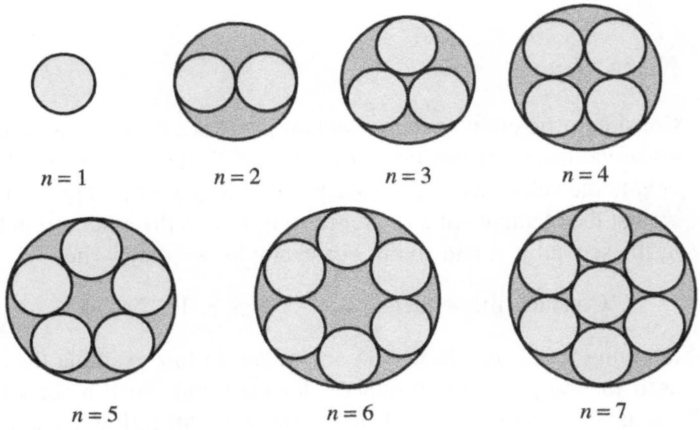

Figure 6.1 Enclosing a number of cables in a circular duct.

Example 6.3 A computer simulation of the crank and connecting rod mechanism considered in Example 2.44 evaluates the position of the end Q of the connecting rod at equal intervals of the angle $x°$. Given that the displacement y of Q satisfies

$$y = r\cos x° + \sqrt{(l^2 - r^2\sin^2 x°)}$$

find the sequence of values of y where $r = 5$, $l = 10$ and the interval between successive values of $x°$ is 1°.

Solution In this example the independent variable x is restricted to the sequence of values $\{0, 1, 2, \ldots, 360\}$. The corresponding sequence of values of y can be calculated from the formula

$$\begin{aligned} y_k &= 5\cos k° + \sqrt{(100 - 25\sin^2 k°)} \\ &= 5[\cos k° + \sqrt{(4 - \sin^2 k°)}] \\ &= 5[\cos k° + \sqrt{(3 + \cos^2 k°)}] \end{aligned}$$

Thus

$$\{y_k\}_{k=0}^{360} = \{15, 14.999, 14.995, 14.990, \ldots, 14.999, 15\}$$

This example is considered again in Section 12.5.

Notice how in Example 6.3 we did not list every element of the sequence. Instead, we relied on the formula for y_k to supply the value of a particular element in the sequence. In Example 6.1 we could use the recurrence relation to determine the elements of the sequence. In Example 6.2, however, there is no formula or recurrence relation that enables us to work out the elements of the sequence. These three examples are representative of the general situation.

A **series** is an extended sum of terms. For example, a very simple series is the sum

$$1 + 2 + 3 + 4 + 5 + 6 + 7 + 8 + 9 + 10 + 11$$

When we look for a general formula for summing such series, we effectively turn it into a sequence, writing, for example, the sum to eleven terms as S_{11} and the sum to n terms as S_n, where

$$S_n = 1 + 2 + 3 + \ldots + n = \sum_{k=1}^{n} k$$

Series often occur in the mathematical analysis of practical problems and we give some important examples later in this chapter.

6.2.2 Graphical representation of sequences

Sequences, as remarked earlier, are functions whose domains are the whole numbers. We can display their properties using a conventional graph with the independent variable (now an integer n) represented as points along the positive x axis. This will show the behaviour of the sequence for low values of n but will not display the whole behaviour adequately. An alternative approach displays the terms of the sequence against the values of $1/n$. This enables us to see the whole sequence but in a rather 'telescoped' manner. When the terms of a sequence are generated by a recurrence relation a third method, known as a **cobweb diagram**, is available to us. We will illustrate these three methods in the examples below.

Example 6.4 Calculate the sequence $\left\{1 + \frac{(-1)^n}{n}\right\}_{n=1}^{10}$ and illustrate the answer graphically.

Solution By means of a calculator we can obtain the terms of the sequence explicitly (to 2dp) as

$$\{0, 1.50, 0.67, 1.25, 0.80, 1.17, 0.86, 1.12, 0.89, 1.10\}$$

The graph of this function is strictly speaking the set of points

$$\{(1, 0), (2, 1.5), (3, 0.67), \ldots, (10, 1.1)\}$$

These can be displayed on a graph as isolated points but it is more helpful to the reader to join the points by straight line segments, as shown in Figure 6.2. The figure tells us that the values of the sequence oscillate about the value 1, getting closer to it as n increases.

Example 6.5 Calculate the sequence $\{n^{1/n}\}_{n=4}^{10}$ and show the points $\{(1/n, n^{1/n})\}_{n=4}^{10}$ on a graph.

Solution Using a calculator we obtain (to 2dp)

$$\{n^{1/n}\}_{n=4}^{10} = \{1.41, 1.38, 1.35, 1.32, 1.30, 1.28, 1.26\}$$

and the set of points is

$$\{(1/n, n^{1/n})\}_{n=4}^{10} = \{(0.25, 1.41), (0.2, 1.38), \ldots, (0.1, 1.26)\}$$

In Figure 6.3 these points are displayed with a smooth curve drawn through them. The graph suggests that as n increases (i.e. $1/n$ decreases), $n^{1/n}$ approaches the value 1.

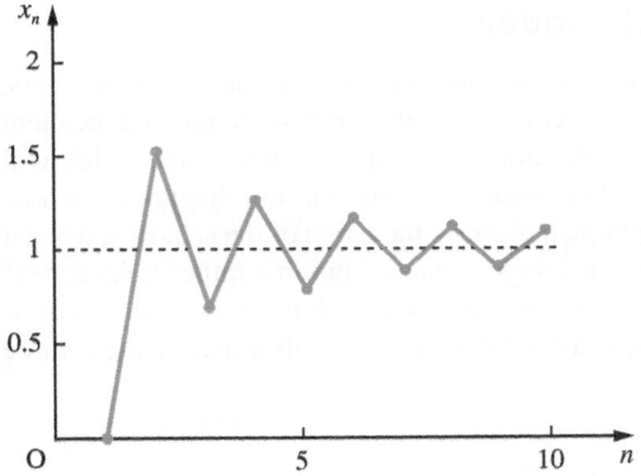

Figure 6.2 Graph of the sequence defined by $x_n = 1 + (-1)^n/n$.

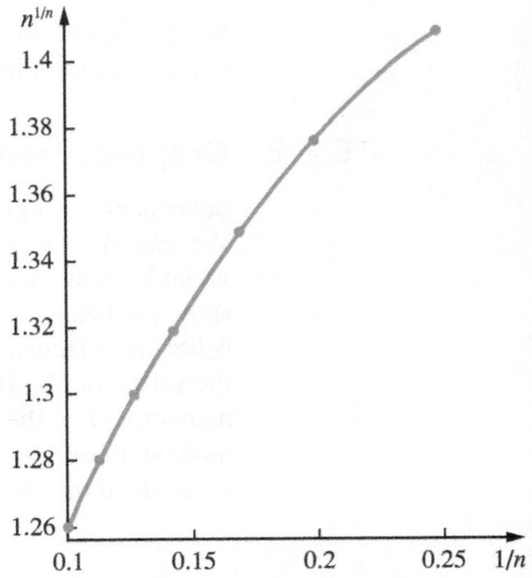

Figure 6.3 Graph of the points $\{(\frac{1}{n}, n^{1/n})\}_{n=4}^{10}$.

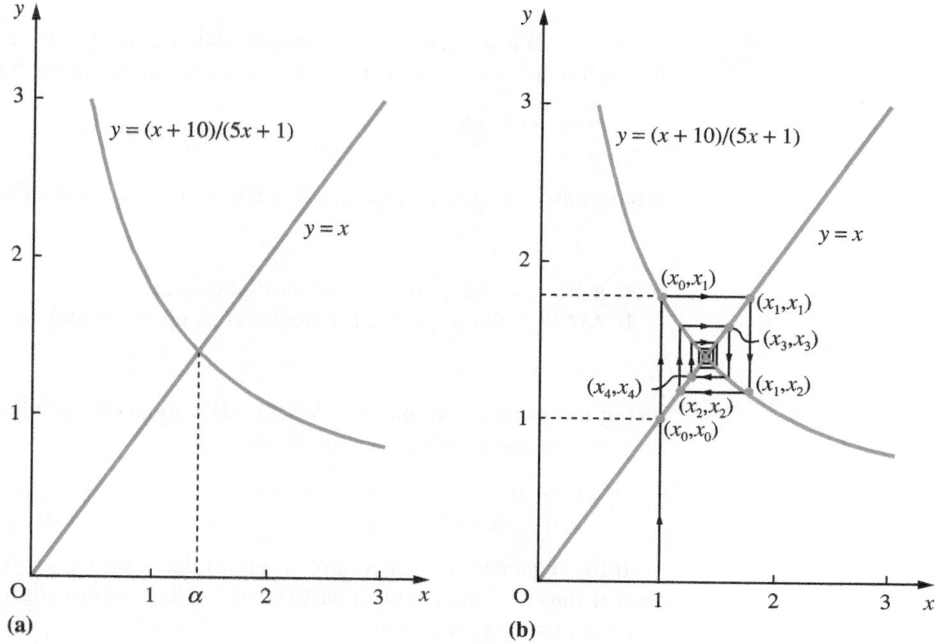

Figure 6.4 (a) Graphs of $y = (x + 10)/(5x + 1)$ and $y = x$. (b) Construction of the sequence defined by $x_{n+1} = (x_n + 10)/(5x_n + 1)$, $x_0 = 1$.

Example 6.6 Calculate the sequence $\{x_n\}_{n=0}^{6}$ where $x_0 = 1$ and $x_{n+1} = \dfrac{x_n + 10}{5x_n + 1}$.

Solution Using a calculator we obtain (to 2dp) the values of the sequence

$$\{x_n\}_{n=0}^{6} = \{1, 1.83, 1.16, 1.64, 1.27, 1.54, 1.33\}$$

We can display this sequence very effectively using a **cobweb diagram**. To construct this we first draw the graphs of $y = (x + 10)/(5x + 1)$ and $y = x$, as shown in Figure 6.4(a). Then we construct the points of the sequence by starting at $x = x_0 = 1$. Drawing a vertical line through $x = 1$, we cut $y = x$ at x_0 and $y = (x + 10)/(5x + 1)$ at $y = x_1$. Now drawing the horizontal line through (x_0, x_1) we find it cuts $y = x$ at x_1. Next we draw the vertical line through (x_1, x_1) to locate x_2 and so on, as shown in Figure 6.4(b). We can see from this diagram that as n increases, x_n approaches the point of intersection of the two graphs, that is, the value α where

$$\alpha = \frac{\alpha + 10}{5\alpha + 1} \quad (\alpha > 0)$$

This gives $\alpha = \sqrt{2}$. The value α is termed the **fixed point** of the iteration. Setting $x_n = \alpha$ returns the value $x_{n+1} = \alpha$.

As we have seen, three different methods can be used for representing sequences graphically. The choice of method will depend on the problem context.

In MATLAB a sequence $\{f_n\}_{n=a}^{n=b}$ may be calculated by setting up an array of values for both n and $y=f_n$. Considering the sequence of Example 6.4, the commands

```
n = 1:1:10;
y = 1 + ((-1).^n)./n
```

produce an array for the calculated values of the sequence. The additional command

```
plot(n,y '*')
```

plots a graph of the points shown in Figure 6.2.

In MAPLE the sequence is calculated using the command

```
evalf(seq(1 + (-1)^n/n, n = 1..10));
```

Using the `maple` command in MATLAB's Symbolic Math Toolbox the sequence may be calculated using the commands

```
syms n
maple('evalf(seq(1 + (-1)^n/n,n = 1..10))')
```

If the sequence is given as a recurrence relationship $x_{n+1}=f(x_n)$, as in Example 6.6, then it may be calculated in MATLAB by first expressing f as an `inline` object and then using a simple `for-end` loop. Thus for the sequence of Example 6.6 the commands

```
f = inline('(x + 10)/(5*x + 1)')
x = 1; y(1) = x;
for n = 1:6
y(n + 1) = f(x); x = y(n + 1);
end
double(y)
```

return the answer:

```
1.0000 1.8333 1.1639 1.2669 1.5361 1.3290
```

and the additional command

```
plot(y '-')
```

plots a graph of the sequence.

6.2.3 Exercises

1 Write down x_1, x_2 and x_3 for the sequences defined by

(a) $x_n = \dfrac{n^2}{n+2}$

(b) $x_{n+1} = x_n + 4$, $x_0 = 2$

(c) $x_{n+1} = \dfrac{-x_n}{4}$, $x_0 = 256$

2 On the basis of the evidence of the first four terms give a recurrence relation for the sequence

$$\{5, 15/8, 45/64, 135/512, \ldots\}$$

3 A sequence is defined by $x_n = pn + q$ where p and q are constants. If $x_2 = 7$ and $x_8 = -11$, find p and q and write down

(a) the first four terms of the sequence;

(b) the defining recurrence relation for the sequence.

4 Triangular numbers (T_n) are defined by the number of dots that occur when arranged in equilateral triangles, as shown in Figure 6.5. Show that $T_n = \frac{1}{2}n(n+1)$ for every positive integer n.

Figure 6.5 Triangular numbers.

5 A detergent manufacturer wishes to forecast their future sales. Their market research department assesses that their 'Number One' brand has 20% of the potential market at present. They also estimate that 15% of those who bought 'Number One' in a given month will buy a different detergent in the following month and that 35% of those who bought a rival brand will buy 'Number One' in the next month. Show that their share P_n% of the market in the nth month satisfies the recurrence relation

$$P_{n+1} = 35 + 0.5P_n, \quad \text{with } P_0 = 20$$

Find the values of P_n for $n = 1, 2, 3$ and 4 and illustrate them on an appropriate diagram.

6 (a) If $x_r = r(r-1)(2r-5)$, calculate $\sum_{r=0}^{4} x_r$

(b) If $x_r = r^{r+1} + 3(-1)^r$, calculate $\sum_{r=1}^{5} x_r$

(c) If $x_r = r^2 - 3r + 1$, calculate $\sum_{r=2}^{6} x_r$

7 A precipitate at the bottom of a beaker of capacity V always retains about it a volume v of liquid. What percentage of the original solution remains about it after it has been washed n times by filling the beaker with distilled water and emptying it?

8 A certain process in statistics involves the following steps S_i ($i = 1, 2, \dots, 6$):

S_1: Selecting a number from the set $T = \{x_1, x_2, \dots, x_n\}$

S_2: Subtracting 10 from it

S_3: Squaring the result

S_4: Repeating steps S_1–S_3 with the remaining numbers in T

S_5: Adding the results obtained at stage S_3 of each run through

S_6: Dividing the result of S_5 by n

Express the final outcome algebraically using Σ notation.

9 Newton's recurrence formula for determining the root of a certain equation is

$$x_{n+1} = \frac{x_n^2 - 1}{2x_n - 3}$$

Taking $x_0 = 3$ as your initial approximation, obtain the root correct to 4sf.

By setting $x_{n+1} = x_n = \alpha$ show that the fixed points of the iteration are given by the equation $\alpha^2 - 3\alpha + 1 = 0$.

10 Calculate the terms of the sequence

$$\left\{\frac{n^4}{n^4 + n^3 + 1}\right\}_{n=0}^{5}$$

and show them on graphs similar to Figures 6.2 and 6.3.

11 Calculate the sequence $\{x_n\}_{n=0}^{6}$ where

$$x_{n+1} = \frac{x_n + 2}{x_n + 1}, \quad x_0 = 1$$

Show the sequence using a cobweb diagram similar to Figure 6.4.

12 A steel ball-bearing drops onto a smooth hard surface from a height h. The time to the first impact is $T = \sqrt{(2h/g)}$ where g is the acceleration due to gravity. The times between successive bounces are $2eT, 2e^2T, 2e^3T, \dots$, where e is the coefficient of restitution between the ball and the surface ($0 < e < 1$). Find the total time taken up to the fifth bounce. If $T = 1$ and $e = 0.1$, show in a diagram the times taken up to the first, second, third, fourth and fifth bounces and estimate how long the total motion lasts.

13 Consider the following puzzle: how many single, loose, smooth 30 cm bricks are necessary to form a single leaning pile with no part of the bottom brick under the top brick? Begin by considering

a pile of 2 bricks. The top brick cannot project further than 15 cm without collapse. Then consider a pile of 3 bricks. Show that the top one cannot project further than 15 cm beyond the second one and that the second one cannot project further than 7.5 cm beyond the bottom brick (so that the maximum total lean is $(\frac{1}{2}+\frac{1}{4})$ 30 cm). Show that the maximum total lean for a pile of 4 bricks is $(\frac{1}{2}+\frac{1}{4}+\frac{1}{6})$ 30 cm and deduce that for a pile of n bricks it is $(\frac{1}{2}+\frac{1}{4}+\frac{1}{6}+\ldots+\frac{1}{2n+2})$ 30 cm. Hence solve the puzzle.

6.3 Finite sequences and series

In this section we consider some finite sequences and series that are frequently used in engineering.

6.3.1 Arithmetical sequences and series

An **arithmetical sequence** is one in which the difference between successive terms is a constant number. Thus, for example, {2, 5, 8, 11, 14} and {2, 0, −2, −4, −6, −8, −10} define arithmetical sequences. In general an arithmetical sequence has the form $\{a+kd\}_{k=0}^{n-1}$ where a is the first term, d is the common difference and n is the number of terms in the sequence. Thus, in the first example above, $a = 2$, $d = 3$ and $n = 5$, and in the second example, $a = 2$, $d = -2$ and $n = 7$. (The old name for such sequences was **arithmetical progressions**.) The sum of the terms of an arithmetical sequence is an **arithmetical series**. The general arithmetical series is

$$S_n = a + (a+d) + (a+2d) + \ldots + [a+(n-1)d] = \sum_{k=0}^{n-1}(a+kd) \qquad \textbf{(6.1)}$$

To obtain an expression for the sum of the n terms in this series, write the series in the reverse order,

$$S_n = \quad a \quad + \quad (a+d) \quad + \quad (a+2d) \quad + \ldots + [a+(n-1)d]$$

$$S_n = [a+(n-1)d] + [a+(n-2)d] + [a+(n-3)d] + \ldots + \quad a$$

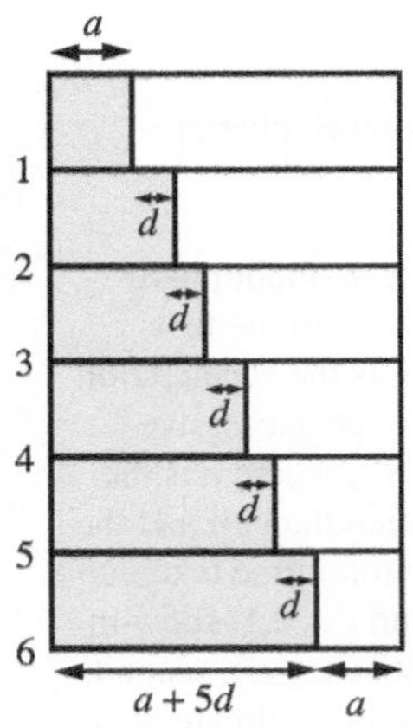

Figure 6.6

$$S_6 = \sum_{k=0}^{5}(a+kd)$$
$$= \tfrac{1}{2} \times 6 \times (2a+5d).$$

Summing the two series then gives

$$2S_n = [2a+(n-1)d] + [2a+(n-1)d] + [2a+(n-1)d] + \ldots + [2a+(n-1)d]$$

giving the sum S_n of the first n terms of an arithmetical series as

$$S_n = \tfrac{1}{2}n[2a+(n-1)d] = \tfrac{1}{2}n(\text{first term} + \text{last term}) \qquad \textbf{(6.2)}$$

The result is illustrated geometrically for $n = 6$ in Figure 6.6, where the breadth of each rectangle is unity and the area under each shaded step is equal to a term of the series.

In particular, when $a = 1$ and $d = 1$,

$$S_n = 1 + 2 + \ldots + n = \sum_{k=1}^{n} k = \tfrac{1}{2}n(n+1) \qquad \textbf{(6.3)}$$

Example 6.7 How many terms of the arithmetical series 11, 15, 19, etc. will give a sum of 341?

Solution In this particular case the first term $a = 11$ and the common difference $d = 4$. We need to find the number of terms n such that the sum S_n is 341. Using the result in (6.2)

$$S_n = 341 = \tfrac{1}{2}n[2(11) + (n-1)(4)]$$

leading to

$$4n^2 + 18n - 682 = 0$$

or

$$(4n + 62)(n - 11) = 0$$

giving

$$n = 11 \quad \text{or} \quad n = -\tfrac{31}{2}$$

Since $n = -\frac{31}{2}$ is not a whole number, the number of terms required is $n = 11$.

Example 6.8 A contractor agrees to sink a well 40 metres deep at a cost of £30 for the first metre, £35 for the second metre and increasing by £5 for each subsequent metre.

(a) What is the total cost of sinking the well?

(b) What is the cost of drilling the last metre?

Solution (a) The total cost constitutes an arithmetical series whose terms are the cost per metre. Thus, taking $a = 30$, $d = 5$ and $n = 40$ in (6.2) gives the total cost

$$S_n = £\tfrac{40}{2}[2(30) + (40 - 1)5] = £5100$$

(b) The cost of drilling the last metre is given by the 40th term of the series. Since the nth term is $a + (n - 1)d$, the cost of drilling the last metre $= 30 + (40 - 1)5 = £225$.

6.3.2 Geometric sequences and series

A **geometric sequence** is one in which the ratio of successive terms is a constant number. Thus, for example, $\{2, 4, 8, 16, 32\}$ and $\{2, -1, \frac{1}{2}, -\frac{1}{4}, \frac{1}{8}, -\frac{1}{16}, \frac{1}{32}\}$ define geometric sequences. In general a geometric sequence has the form $\{ar^k\}_{k=0}^{n-1}$ where a is the first term, r is the common ratio and n is the number of terms in the sequence. Thus, in the first example above, $a = 2$, $r = 2$, $n = 5$ and, in the second example, $a = 2$, $r = -\frac{1}{2}$ and $n = 7$. (The old name for such sequences was **geometric progressions**.) The sum of the terms of a geometric sequence is called a **geometric series**. The general geometric series has the form

$$S_n = a + ar + ar^2 + ar^3 + \ldots + ar^{n-1}$$

To obtain the sum S_n of the first n terms of the series we multiply S_n by the common ratio r, to obtain

$$rS_n = ar + ar^2 + \ldots + ar^{n-1} + ar^n$$

Subtracting this from S_n then gives

$$S_n - rS_n = a - ar^n$$

so that

$$(1 - r)S_n = a(1 - r^n)$$

Thus for $r \neq 1$, the sum of the first n terms is

$$S_n = \sum_{k=0}^{n-1} ar^k = \frac{a(1 - r^n)}{1 - r} \tag{6.4}$$

Clearly, for the particular case of $r = 1$ the sum is $S_n = an$.

The geometric series is very important. It has many applications in practical problems as well as within mathematics.

Example 6.9 In its publicity material an insurance company guarantees that, for a fixed annual premium payable at the beginning of each year for a period of 25 years, the return will be at least equivalent to the premiums paid, together with 3% per annum compound interest. For an annual premium of £250 what is the guaranteed sum at the end of 25 years?

Solution The first-year premium earns interest for 25 years and thus guarantees

$$£250(1 + 0.03)^{25}$$

The second-year premium earns interest for 24 years and thus guarantees

$$£250(1 + 0.03)^{24}$$

$$\vdots$$

The final-year premium earns interest for 1 year and thus guarantees

$$£250(1 + 0.03)$$

Thus, the total sum guaranteed is

$$£250[(1.03) + (1.03)^2 + \ldots + (1.03)^{25}]$$

The term inside the square brackets is a geometric series. Thus, taking $a = 1.03$, $r = 1.03$ and $n = 25$ in (6.4) gives

$$\text{Guaranteed sum} = £250\left[1.03\frac{(1.03^{25} - 1)}{(1.03 - 1)}\right] \approx £9388.$$

6.3.3 Other finite series

In addition to the arithmetical and geometric series, there are other finite series that occur in engineering applications for which an expression can be obtained for the sum of the first n terms. We shall illustrate this in Examples 6.10 and 6.11.

Example 6.10 Consider the sum-of-squares series

$$S_n = 1^2 + 2^2 + 3^2 + \ldots + n^2 = \sum_{k=1}^{n} k^2$$

Obtain an expression for the sum of this series.

Solution There are various methods for finding the sum. A method that can be generalized makes use of the identity

$$(k + 1)^3 - k^3 = 3k^2 + 3k + 1$$

Thus

$$\sum_{k=1}^{n} [(k + 1)^3 - k^3] = \sum_{k=1}^{n} (3k^2 + 3k + 1)$$

The left-hand side equals

$$2^3 - 1^3 + 3^3 - 2^3 + 4^3 - 3^3 + \ldots + (n + 1)^3 - n^3 = (n + 1)^3 - 1$$

The right-hand side equals

$$3\sum_{k=1}^{n} k^2 + 3\sum_{k=1}^{n} k + \sum_{k=1}^{n} 1$$

Now

$$\sum_{k=1}^{n} k = \tfrac{1}{2}n(n + 1) \text{ from (6.3)} \quad \text{and} \quad \sum_{k=1}^{n} 1 = n$$

so that

$$(n + 1)^3 - 1 = 3\sum_{k=1}^{n} k^2 + \frac{3n}{2}(n + 1) + n$$

whence

$$\sum_{k=1}^{n} k^2 = \tfrac{1}{6}n(n + 1)(2n + 1) \qquad \textbf{(6.5)}$$

This method can be generalized to obtain the sum of other similar series. For example, to find the sum of cubes series $\sum_{k=1}^{n} k^3$, we would consider $(k + 1)^4 - k^4$ and so on.

Example 6.11 Obtain the sum of the series

$$S_n = \frac{1}{1\cdot 2} + \frac{1}{2\cdot 3} + \frac{1}{3\cdot 4} + \ldots + \frac{1}{n(n+1)} = \sum_{k=1}^{n} \frac{1}{k(k+1)}$$

Solution The technique for summing this series is to express the general term in its partial fractions:

$$\frac{1}{k(k+1)} = \frac{1}{k} - \frac{1}{k+1}$$

Then

$$S_n = \sum_{k=1}^{n} \frac{1}{k} - \sum_{k=1}^{n} \frac{1}{k+1}$$

$$= \left(1 + \frac{1}{2} + \frac{1}{3} + \ldots + \frac{1}{n}\right) - \left(\frac{1}{2} + \frac{1}{3} + \ldots + \frac{1}{n} + \frac{1}{n+1}\right)$$

$$= 1 - \frac{1}{n+1}$$

giving

$$S_n = \frac{n}{n+1}$$

There are many other similar series that can be summed by expressing the general term in its partial fractions. Some examples are given in Exercises 6.3.4.

Example 6.12 Obtain the sum of the series

$$S_n = 1 + 2r + 3r^2 + 4r^3 + \ldots + nr^{n-1} = \sum_{k=1}^{n} kr^{k-1} \qquad r \neq 1$$

Solution The technique for summing this *arithmetico-geometric* series is similar to that for summing geometric series. We multiply S_n *by* r and then subtract the result from S_n. Thus

$$rS_n = r + 2r^2 + 3r^3 + \ldots + nr^n$$

and

$$(1-r)S_n = 1 + r + r^2 + r^3 + \ldots r^{n-1} - nr^n$$

The first n terms on the right-hand side of this equation form a geometric series, and using result (6.4) we can write

$$(1-r)S_n = \frac{1-r^n}{1-r} - nr^n$$

Hence

$$S_n = \frac{1 - r^n - nr^n(1 - r)}{(1 - r)^2} = \frac{1 - (n + 1)r^n + nr^{n+1}}{(1 - r)^2} \tag{6.6}$$

Where $r = 1$, $S_n = \frac{1}{2}n(n + 1)$ of course. This method can be generalized to obtain the sum of other similar series, for example

$$\sum_{k=1}^{n} (2k + 1)r^{k-1} \quad \text{and} \quad \sum_{k=1}^{n} k^2 r^{k-1}$$

Example 6.13 Sum the series

$$S_n = 1 + \cos\theta + \cos 2\theta + \ldots + \cos(n - 1)\theta$$

Solution The easiest way of summing this series is to recall Euler's formula (Section 3.2.7)

$$e^{j\theta} = \cos\theta + j\sin\theta$$

Then we can write

$$S_n = Re\{1 + e^{j\theta} + e^{j2\theta} + e^{j3\theta} + \ldots + e^{j(n-1)\theta}\}$$

The series inside the brackets is a geometric series with common ratio $e^{j\theta}$ and using result (6.4) we obtain

$$S_n = Re\left\{\frac{1 - e^{jn\theta}}{1 - e^{j\theta}}\right\}$$

Rearranging the expression inside the brackets we have

$$S_n = Re\left\{\frac{e^{j(n-\frac{1}{2})\theta} - e^{-j\frac{1}{2}\theta}}{e^{j\frac{1}{2}\theta} - e^{-j\frac{1}{2}\theta}}\right\}$$

$$= Re\left\{\frac{\cos(n - \frac{1}{2})\theta + j\sin(n - \frac{1}{2})\theta - \cos\frac{1}{2}\theta + j\sin\frac{1}{2}\theta}{2j\sin\frac{1}{2}\theta}\right\}$$

$$= \frac{1}{2}\left\{\frac{\sin(n - \frac{1}{2})\theta}{\sin\frac{1}{2}\theta} + 1\right\}$$

The same method can be used to show that $\sum_{k=1}^{n} \sin k\theta = \sin(n + 1)\theta\sin(n\theta)/\sin\frac{1}{2}\theta$.

Symbolic summation may be achieved in MATLAB using the *symsum* command. The MAPLE command is similar with minor syntax differences. For example, to sum of the series in Example 6.10 we have

MATLAB

```
syms x k n
s = symsum(k^2,1,n);
s = factor(s);
pretty(ans)
```

MAPLE

```
sum('k^2','k' = 1..n):
factor(%);
```

returns

```
s = 1/6n(n + 1)(2n + 1)
```

Similarly, considering Example 6.11

```
syms x k n
s = symsum(1/(k*(k + 1)),1,n);
s = simplify(s)
```

```
sum('1/(k*(k + 1))',
'k' = 1..n);
```

returns

```
s = n/(n + 1)
```

```
    1
- ----- + 1
  n + 1
```

Note: When using MAPLE it is recommended and often necessary (see MAPLE help) that both f and k be enclosed in single quotes to prevent premature evaluation (for example, k may have a previous value). Thus the common format is `sum('f', 'k' = m..n)`.

6.3.4 Exercises

14 (a) Find the fifth and tenth terms of the arithmetical sequence whose first and second terms are 4 and 7.
(b) The first and sixth terms of a geometric sequence are 5 and 160 respectively. Find the intermediate terms.

15 An individual starts a business and loses £150k in the first year, £120k in the second year and £90k in the third year. If the improvement continues at the same rate, find the individual's total profit or loss at the end of 20 years.
After how many years would the losses be just balanced by the gains?

16 Show that

$$\frac{1}{1+\sqrt{x}},\quad \frac{1}{1-x},\quad \frac{1}{1-\sqrt{x}}$$

are in arithmetical progression and find the nth term of the sequence of which these are the first three terms.

17 The area of a circle of radius 1 is a transcendental number (that is, a number that cannot be obtained by the process of solving algebraic equations) denoted by the Greek letter π. To calculate its value, we may use a limiting process in which π is the limit of a sequence of known numbers. The method used by Archimedes was to inscribe in the circle a sequence of regular polygons. As the number of sides increased, so the polygon 'filled' the circle. Show, by use of the trigonometric identity $\cos 2\theta = 1 - 2\sin^2\theta$, that the area a_n of an inscribed regular polygon of n sides satisfies the equation

$$2\left(\frac{a_{2n}}{n}\right)^2 = 1 - \sqrt{\left[1-\left(\frac{2a_n}{n}\right)^2\right]} \quad (n \geqslant 4)$$

Show that $a_4 = 2$ and use the recurrence relation to find a_{64}.

18 A **harmonic sequence** is a sequence with the property that every three consecutive terms (a, b and c, say) of the sequence satisfy

$$\frac{a}{c} = \frac{a-b}{b-c}$$

Prove that the reciprocals of the terms of a harmonic sequence form an arithmetical progression. Hence find the intermediate terms of a harmonic sequence of 8 terms whose first and last terms are $\frac{2}{3}$ and $\frac{2}{17}$ respectively.

19 The price of houses increases at 10% per year. Show that the price P_n in the nth year satisfies the recurrence relation

$$P_{n+1} = 1.1P_n$$

A house is currently priced at £80 000. What was its price two years ago? What will be its price in five years' time? After how many years will its price be double what it is now?

20 Evaluate each of the following sums:

(a) $1 + 2 + 3 + \ldots + 152 + 153$

(b) $1^2 + 2^2 + 3^2 + \ldots + 152^2 + 153^2$

(c) $\frac{1}{2} + \frac{1}{4} + \frac{1}{8} + \ldots + (\frac{1}{2})^{152} + (\frac{1}{2})^{153}$

(d) $2 + 6 + 18 + \ldots + 2(3)^{152} + 2(3)^{153}$

(e) $1 \cdot 2 + 2 \cdot 3 + 3 \cdot 4 + \ldots + 152 \cdot 153 + 153 \cdot 154$

(f) $\frac{1}{1 \cdot 2} + \frac{1}{2 \cdot 3} + \frac{1}{3 \cdot 4} + \ldots + \frac{1}{152 \cdot 153} + \frac{1}{153 \cdot 154}$

21 A certain bacterium propagates itself by subdividing, creating four additional bacteria, each identical to the parent bacterium. If the bacteria subdivide in this manner n times, then, assuming that none of the bacteria die, the number of bacteria present after each subdivision is given by the sequence $\{B_k\}_{k=0}^{n}$, where

$$B_k = \frac{4^{k+1} - 1}{3}$$

Three such bacteria subdivide n times and none of the bacteria die. The total number of bacteria is then 1 048 575. How many times did the bacteria divide?

22 By considering the sum

$$\sum_{k=1}^{n} [(k + 1)^4 - k^4]$$

show that

$$\sum_{k=1}^{n} k^3 = [\tfrac{1}{2}n(n + 1)]^2$$

23 The repayment instalment of a fixed rate, fixed period loan may be calculated by summing the *present values* of each instalment. This sum must equal the amount borrowed. The present value of an instalment £x paid after k years where $r\%$ is the rate of interest is

$$£\frac{x}{(1 + r/100)^k}$$

Thus £1000 borrowed over n years at $r\%$ satisfies the equation

$$1000 = \frac{x}{1 + r/100} + \frac{x}{(1 + r/100)^2} + \ldots + \frac{x}{(1 + r/100)^n}$$

Find x in terms of r and n and compute its value when $r = 10$ and $n = 20$.

24 Consider the series

$$S_n = \frac{1}{2} + \frac{2}{4} + \frac{3}{8} + \ldots + \frac{n}{2^n}$$

Show that

$$\tfrac{1}{2}S_n = \frac{1}{4} + \frac{2}{8} + \frac{3}{16} + \ldots + \frac{n}{2^{n+1}}$$

and hence that

$$S_n - \tfrac{1}{2}S_n = \frac{1}{2} + \frac{1}{4} + \frac{1}{8} + \frac{1}{16} + \ldots + \frac{1}{2^n} + \frac{n}{2^{n+1}}$$

Hence sum the series.

25 Consider the general arithmetico-geometric series

$$S_n = a + (a + d)r + (a + 2d)r^2 + \ldots + [a + (n - 1)d]r^{n-1}$$

Show that

$$(1 - r)S_n = a + dr + dr^2 + \ldots + dr^{n-1} - [a + (n - 1)d]r^n$$

and find a simple expression for S_n.

6.4 Recurrence relations

We saw in Example 6.1 that sometimes the elements of a sequence satisfy a recurrence relation such that the value of an element x_n of a sequence $\{x_k\}$ can be expressed in terms of the values of earlier elements of the sequence. In general we may have a formula of the form

$$x_n = f(x_{n-1}, x_{n-2}, \dots, x_1, x_0)$$

In this section we are going to consider two commonly occurring types of recurrence relation. These will provide sufficient background to make possible the solution of more difficult problems.

6.4.1 First-order linear recurrence relations with constant coefficients

These relations have the general form

$$x_{n+1} = ax_n + b_n, \quad n = 0, 1, 2, \dots$$

where a is constant and b_n is a known sequence. The simplest case that occurs is when $b_n = 0$, when the relation reduces to

$$x_{n+1} = ax_n \tag{6.7}$$

This is called a **homogeneous relation** and every solution is a geometric sequence of the form

$$x_n = Aa^n \tag{6.8}$$

This is called the **general solution** of (6.7) since A is a constant which may be given any value. To determine the value of A we require more information about the sequence. For example, if we know the value of x_0 (say C) then $C = Aa^0$, which gives the value of A.

A slightly more difficult example is

$$x_{n+1} = ax_n + b \tag{6.9}$$

where b is a constant as well as a.

If the first term of the sequence is $x_0 = C$, as before, then

$$x_1 = aC + b$$

$$x_2 = ax_1 + b = a(aC + b) + b = Ca^2 + b(1 + a)$$

$$x_3 = ax_2 + b = a[Ca^2 + b(1 + a)] + b = Ca^3 + b(1 + a + a^2)$$

and so on.

In general, we obtain

$$x_n = Ca^n + \left(\frac{1 - a^n}{1 - a}\right)b, \quad a \neq 1$$

Rearranging, we can express this as

$$x_n = Aa^n + \frac{b}{1 - a}, \quad a \neq 1 \tag{6.10}$$

where $A = C - b/(1 - a)$. After the next example we will see that this solution (and that of more general problems) can be obtained more quickly by an alternative method.

Notice that Aa^n is the general solution of the homogeneous relation (6.7) and that $x_n = b/(1 - a)$, for all n, satisfies the full recurrence relation $x_{n+1} = ax_n + b$, so that it is a **particular solution** of the relation.

Example 6.14 Calculate the fixed annual payments £B required to amortize a debt of £D over N years, when the rate of interest is fixed at $100i\%$.

Solution Let £d_n denote the debt after n years. Then, following the same argument as in Example 6.1, $d_0 = D$ and

$$d_{n+1} = (1 + i)d_n - B$$

This is similar to the recurrence relation (6.9) but with $a = (1 + i)$ an $b = -B$. Hence, using (6.10) we can write the general solution as

$$d_n = A(1 + i)^n - \frac{B}{1 - (1 + i)} = A(1 + i)^n + B/i$$

In addition, we know that $d_0 = D$ so that $D = A + B/i$ and thus the particular solution is given by

$$d_n = (D - B/i)(1 + i)^n + B/i$$

We require the value of B so that the debt is zero after N years, that is $d_N = 0$. Thus

$$0 = (D - B/i)(1 + i)^N + B/i$$

Solving this equation for B gives

$$B = \frac{iD(1 + i)^N}{(1 + i)^N - 1} = iD/[1 - (1 + i)^{-N}]$$

as the required payment.

In summary, we have that the general solution to the first-order recurrence relation

$$x_{n+1} = ax_n + b$$

can be expressed as the sum of the **general solution** of the reduced relation

$$x_{n+1} = ax_n$$

and a **particular solution** of the full relation (6.9).

This is true for linear recurrence relations in general, that is, recurrence relations of the form

$$x_{n+1} = a_n x_n + a_{n-1}x_{n-1} + \ldots + a_1 x_1 + a_0$$

where the coefficients a_k are independent of the x_k but may depend on n. The property is easy to show in full generality but the same proof holds for the simplest case (6.9) above.

Suppose we can identify one particular solution p_n of (6.9) so that

$$p_{n+1} = ap_n + b$$

Now we seek a function q_n which complements p_n in such a way that

$$x_n = p_n + q_n$$

is the general solution of (6.9). Substituting x_n into this relation gives

$$p_{n+1} + q_{n+1} = ap_n + aq_n + b$$

Since $p_{n+1} = ap_n + b$, this implies that

$$q_{n+1} = aq_n$$

From (6.8), the general solution of this relation is

$$q_n = Aa^n$$

where A is a constant. Thus the general solution of (6.9) is

$$x_n = p_n + Aa^n$$

Because q_n complements p_n to form the general solution, it is usually called the **complementary solution**. As we have seen, with first-order recurrence relations, we can always find the complementary solution. Thus we are left with the task of finding the particular solution p_n. The method for finding p_n depends on the term b, as we illustrate in Example 6.15.

Indeed, the property of the general solution being the sum of a particular solution and a complementary solution applies to all linear systems, both continuous and discrete. We will meet it again in Chapter 9 when considering the general solution of linear ordinary differential equations.

Example 6.15 Find the general solutions of the recurrence relations

(a) $x_{n+1} = 3x_n + 4$ (b) $x_{n+1} = x_n + 4$

(c) $x_{n+1} = \alpha x_n + C\beta^n$ (d) $x_{n+1} = \alpha x_n + C\alpha^n$ (α, β, C given constants)

Solution (a) First we try to find any function of n which will satisfy the relation. Since it contains the constant term 4, it is common sense to see if a constant K can be found which satisfies the relation. (Then all terms will be constants.) Setting $x_n = K$ implies $x_{n+1} = K$ and we have

$$K = 3K + 4$$

which gives $K = -2$. Thus, in this case, we can choose $p_n = -2$. Next we find the complementary solution q_n, which is the general solution of

$$x_{n+1} = 3x_n$$

From (6.8) we can see that $q_n = A3^n$ where A is a constant. Thus the general solution of (a) is

$$x_n = -2 + A3^n$$

(b) The basic steps are the same for this relation. We first find a particular solution p_n of the relation. Then we find the complementary solution q_n, so that $x_n = p_n + q_n$ is the general solution. In this case trying $x_n = K$ leads nowhere, since we obtain the inconsistent equation $K = K + 4$. Trying something a little more complicated than just a constant, we set $x_n = Kn$ and $x_{n+1} = K(n + 1)$ and we have

$$K(n + 1) = Kn + 4$$

which yields $K = 4$ and $p_n = 4n$. The general solution of $x_{n+1} = x_n$ is $q_n = A1^n$, so that the general solution of (b) is

$$x_n = 4n + A$$

(c) Since the recurrence relation has the term $C\beta^n$, it is natural to expect a solution of the form $K\beta^n$, where K is a constant, to satisfy the relation. Setting $x_n = K\beta^n$ gives

$$K\beta^{n+1} = \alpha K\beta^n + C\beta^n$$

Dividing through by β^n gives $K\beta = \alpha K + C$, from which we deduce $K = C/(\beta - \alpha)$ provided that $\beta \neq \alpha$. Thus we deduce the particular solution

$$p_n = C\beta^n/(\beta - \alpha)$$

The complementary solution q_n is the general solution of

$$x_{n+1} = \alpha x_n$$

which, using (6.7), is $q_n = A\alpha^n$. Hence the general solution of (c) is

$$x_n = C\beta^n/(\beta - \alpha) + A\alpha^n$$

(d) This is the special case of (c) where $\beta = \alpha$. If we set $p_n = K\alpha^n$, we obtain the equation $K\alpha^{n+1} = K\alpha^{n+1} + C\alpha^n$, which can only be true if $C = 0$. (We see then that p_n is the solution of $x_{n+1} = \alpha x_n$, that is, it is the complementary solution.) As in case (b), we instead seek a solution of the form $p_n = Kn\alpha^n$, so that $p_{n+1} = K(n + 1)\alpha^{n+1}$ and

$$K(n + 1)\alpha^{n+1} = \alpha Kn\alpha^n + C\alpha^n$$

This last equation gives $K = C/\alpha$. Hence the general solution of (d) is

$$x_n = Cn\alpha^{n-1} + A\alpha^n$$

where A is an arbitrary constant.

6.4.2 Exercises

Return to check your answers to Questions 26 and 28 using MATLAB or MAPLE on completion of Section 6.4.3.

26 Find the general solutions of the recurrence relations

(a) $x_{n+1} = 2x_n - 3$ (b) $x_{n+1} = 3x_n + 10n$

(c) $x_{n+1} = -x_n + (\frac{1}{2})^n$ (d) $x_{n+1} = 2x_n + 3 \times 2^n$

27 If a debt is amortized by equal annual payments of amount B, and if interest is charged at rate i per annum, then the debt after n years, d_n, satisfies $d_{n+1} = (1 + i)d_n - B$, where $d_0 = D$, the initial debt. Show that $d_n = D(1 + i)^n + B\dfrac{1 - (1 + i)^n}{i}$

and deduce that to clear the debt on the Nth payment we must take $B = \dfrac{Di}{1 - (1 + i)^{-N}}$.

If £10 000 is borrowed at an interest rate of

0.12 (= 12%) per annum, calculate (to the nearest £) the appropriate annual payment which will amortize the debt at the end of 10 years.

For this annual payment calculate the amount of the debt d_n for $n = 1, 2, \ldots, 10$ (use the recurrence rather than its solution, and record your answers to the nearest £) and calculate the first differences for this sequence. Comment briefly on the behaviour of the first differences.

28 Find the general solution of the linear recurrence relation

$$(n+1)^2 x_{n+1} - n^2 x_n = 1, \quad \text{for } n \geqslant 1$$

(*Hint*: The coefficients are not constants. Use the substitution $z_n = n^2 x_n$ to find a constant coefficient equation for z_n. Find the general solution for z_n and hence for x_n.)

6.4.3 Second-order linear recurrence relations with constant coefficients

Example 6.16 Evaluate the expression $E(n) = 3x_{n+2} + 5x_{n+1} - 2x_n$ where x_n is defined for $n \geqslant 0$ by

(a) $x_n = 3^n$ (b) $x_n = 3^{-n}$ (c) $x_n = 3(2^{-n})$ (d) $x_n = (-2)^n$.

Solution (a) $E(n) = 3 \times 3^{n+2} + 5 \times 3^{n+1} - 2 \times 3^n$

$$= (27 + 15 - 2)3^n$$

$$= 40 \times 3^n$$

(b) $E(n) = 3 \times 3^{-n-2} + 5 \times 3^{-n-1} - 2 \times 3^{-n}$

$$= (3 \times 3^{-2} + 5 \times 3^{-1} - 2)3^{-n}$$

$$= \left(\frac{1}{3} + \frac{5}{3} - 2\right)3^{-n} = 0$$

(c) $E(n) = 3 \times 3 \times 2^{-n-2} + 5 \times 3 \times 2^{-n-1} - 2 \times 3 \times 2^{-n}$

$$= 3\left(\frac{3}{4} + \frac{5}{2} - 2\right)2^{-n}$$

$$= \frac{15}{4} \times 2^{-n} = 15 \times 2^{-n-2}$$

(d) $E(n) = 3(-2)^{n+2} + 5(-2)^{n+1} - 2(-2)^n$

$$= (3 \times 4 - 5 \times 2 - 2)(-2)^n$$

$$= 0$$

Hence $x_n = (-2)^n$ and $x_n = (\frac{1}{3})^n$ both satisfy the recurrence relation

$$3x_{n+2} + 5x_{n+1} - 2x_n = 0$$

Example 6.17 (a) Show by direct sustitution into the recurrence relation

$$x_{n+2} - x_{n+1} - 6x_n = 0$$

that $x_n = 3^n$ and $x_n = (-2)^n$ are two solutions.

(b) Further verify that $x_n = A(-2)^n + B3^n$, where A and B are constants, is also a solution.

Solution (a) Where $x_n = 3^n$

$$x_{n+2} - x_{n+1} - 6x_n = 3^{n+2} - 3^{n+1} - 6x3^n$$
$$= (3^2 - 3 - 6)3^n = 0$$

Where $x_n = (-2)^n$

$$x_{n+2} - x_{n+1} - 6x_n = (-2)^{n+2} - (-2)^{n+1} - 6(-2)^n = (4 + 2 - 6)(-2)^n = 0$$

Hence $x_n = 3^n$ and $x_n = (-2)^n$ are solutions of the recurrence relation.

(b) Setting $x_n = A(-2)^n + B(3^n)$ gives

$$A(-2)^{n+2} + B3^{n+2} - A(-2)^{n+1} - B3^{n+1} - 6A(-2)^n - 6B(3)^n$$
$$= A[(-2)^{n+2} - (-2)^{n+1} - 6(-2)^n] + B[3^{n+2} - 3^{n+1} - 6(3^n)]$$
$$= A.0 + B.0 = 0$$

So $x_n = A(-2)^n + B3^n$ is a solution of the recurrence relation also.

A second-order linear recurrence with constant coefficients has the form

$$x_{n+2} = ax_{n+1} + bx_n + c_n \quad \textbf{(6.11)}$$

If $c_n = 0$ for all n, then the relation is said to be **homogeneous**. As before, the solution of (6.11) can be expressed in the form

$$x_n = p_n + q_n$$

where p_n is any solution which satisfies (6.11), while q_n is the general solution of the associated homogeneous recurrence relation

$$x_{n+2} = ax_{n+1} + bx_n \quad \textbf{(6.12)}$$

Let α and β be the two roots of the algebraic equation

$$\lambda^2 = a\lambda + b$$

so that $\alpha^{n+2} = a\alpha^{n+1} + b\alpha^n$ and $\beta^{n+2} = a\beta^{n+1} + b\beta^n$, which imply that $y_n = \alpha^n$ and $y_n = \beta^n$ are particular solutions of (6.12). Since $(\lambda - \alpha)(\lambda - \beta) = 0$ implies $\lambda^2 = (\alpha + \beta)\lambda - \alpha\beta$ we may rewrite (6.12) as

$$x_{n+2} = (\alpha + \beta)x_{n+1} - \alpha\beta x_n$$

Rearranging the relation, we have

$$x_{n+2} - \alpha x_{n+1} = \beta(x_{n+1} - \alpha x_n)$$

Substituting $t_n = x_{n+1} - \alpha x_n$, this becomes

$$t_{n+1} = \beta t_n$$

with general solution, from (6.8), $t_n = C\beta^n$ where C is any constant.

Thus

$$x_{n+1} - \alpha x_n = C\beta^n$$

which, using the results of Example 6.15(c) and (d), has the general solution

$$x_n = \begin{cases} C\beta^n/(\beta - \alpha) + A\alpha^n, & \alpha \neq \beta \\ Cn\alpha^{n-1} + A\alpha^n, & \alpha = \beta \end{cases}$$

Since C is any constant, we can rewrite this in the neater form

$$x_n = \begin{cases} A\alpha^n + B\beta^n, & \alpha \neq \beta \\ A\alpha^n + Bn\alpha^n, & \alpha = \beta \end{cases} \qquad \textbf{(6.13)}$$

where A and B are arbitrary constants. Thus (6.13) gives the general solution of (6.12) where α and β are the roots of the equation

$$\lambda^2 = a\lambda + b$$

This is called the **characteristic equation** of the recurrence relation; the Greek letter *lambda* λ is used as the unknown instead of x to avoid confusion.

Example 6.18 Find the solution of the Fibonacci recurrence relation

$$x_{n+2} = x_{n+1} + x_n$$

given $x_0 = 1$, $x_1 = 1$.

Solution The characteristic equation of the recurrence relation is

$$\lambda^2 = \lambda + 1$$

which has roots $\lambda_1 = (1 + \sqrt{5})/2$ and $\lambda_2 = (1 - \sqrt{5})/2$.

Hence its general solution is

$$x_n = A\left(\frac{1+\sqrt{5}}{2}\right)^n + B\left(\frac{1-\sqrt{5}}{2}\right)^n$$

Since $x_0 = 1$, we deduce $1 = A + B$

Since $x_1 = 1$, we deduce $1 = A\left(\frac{1+\sqrt{5}}{2}\right) + B\left(\frac{1-\sqrt{5}}{2}\right)$

Solving these simultaneous equations gives

$$A = (1 + \sqrt{5})/(2\sqrt{5}) \text{ and } B = -(1 - \sqrt{5})/(2\sqrt{5})$$

and hence

$$x_n = \frac{1}{\sqrt{5}}\left[\left(\frac{1+\sqrt{5}}{2}\right)^{n+1} - \left(\frac{1-\sqrt{5}}{2}\right)^{n+1}\right]$$

defining the Fibonacci sequence explicitly.

We have seen that we can always find the complementary solution q_n of the recurrence relation (6.11)

$$x_{n+2} = ax_{n+1} + bx_n + c_n$$

The general solution of this relation is the sum of a particular solution p_n of the relation and its complementary solution q_n. The problem, then, is how to find one solution p_n. Here we will use methods based on experience and trial and error.

Example 6.19 Find all the solutions of

(a) $x_{n+2} = \frac{7}{2}x_{n+1} - \frac{3}{2}x_n + 12$, where $x_0 = x_1 = 1$ (b) $x_{n+2} = \frac{7}{2}x_{n+1} - \frac{3}{2}x_n + 12n$

(c) $x_{n+2} = \frac{7}{2}x_{n+1} - \frac{3}{2}x_n + 3(2^n)$

Solution (a) First we find the general solution of the associated homogeneous relation $x_{n+2} = \frac{7}{2}x_{n+1} - \frac{3}{2}x_n$ which has characteristic equation $\lambda^2 = \frac{7}{2}\lambda - \frac{3}{2}$ with roots $\lambda = 3$ and $\lambda = \frac{1}{2}$. Thus, the complementary solution is

$$x_n = A3^n + B(\tfrac{1}{2})^n$$

Next we find a particular solution of

$$x_{n+2} = \tfrac{7}{2}x_{n+1} - \tfrac{3}{2}x_n + 12$$

We try the simplest possible function $x_n = K$ (for all n). Then, if this is a solution, we have

$$K = \tfrac{7}{2}K - \tfrac{3}{2}K + 12$$

giving $K = -12$.

Thus $p_n = -12$ and the general solution is

$$x_n = -12 + A3^n + B(\tfrac{1}{2})^n$$

Applying the initial data $x_0 = 1$, $x_1 = 1$ gives two equations for the arbitrary constants A and B

$$A + B - 12 = 1$$

$$3A + \tfrac{1}{2}B - 12 = 1$$

from which we deduce $A = 13/5$ and $B = 52/5$. Thus the particular solution which fits the initial data is

$$x_n = \tfrac{13}{5}\,3^n + \tfrac{52}{5}\,\tfrac{1}{2^n} - 12$$

(b) This has the same complementary solution as (a), so we have only to find a particular solution. We try the function $x_n = Kn + L$, where K and L are constants. Substituting into the recurrence relation gives

$$K(n + 2) + L \equiv \tfrac{7}{2}[K(n + 1) + L] - \tfrac{3}{2}[Kn + L] + 12n$$

Thus

$$Kn + 2K + L \equiv 2Kn + \tfrac{7}{2}K + 2L + 12n$$

Comparing coefficients of n gives

$$K = 2K + 12$$

so that $K = -12$.

Comparing the terms independent of n gives

$$2K + L \equiv \tfrac{7}{2}K + 2L$$

so that $L = -\tfrac{3}{2}K = 18$, and the general solution required is

$$x_n = -12n + 18 + A3^n + B(\tfrac{1}{2})^n$$

(c) This has the same complementary function as (a) so we only need to find a particular solution. To find this we try $x_n = K2^n$, giving

$$K(2^{n+2}) = \tfrac{7}{2}K(2^{n+1}) - \tfrac{3}{2}K(2^n) + 3(2^n)$$

so that

$$(4 - 7 + \tfrac{3}{2})K(2^n) = 3(2^n)$$

Hence $K = -2$ and the general solution required is

$$x_n = -2(2^n) + A3^n + B/2^n$$

Difference equations can be solved directly in MAPLE using the `rsolve` command. For example, considering Example 6.19(a) the general solution is given by the command

```
rsolve({x(n + 2) - 7/2*x(n + 1) + 3/2*x(n) = 12},x(n));
```

as

$$-(\tfrac{1}{5}x(0) - \tfrac{2}{5}x(1))3^n - \tfrac{1}{2}(-\tfrac{12}{5}x(0) + \tfrac{4}{5}x(1))(\tfrac{1}{2})^n + \tfrac{12}{5}(3)^n$$
$$+ (\tfrac{48}{5})(\tfrac{1}{2})^n - 12$$

which is equivalent to the given solution, with $A = (-1/5x(0) - 2/5x(1) + 12/5)$ and $B = (6/5x(0) + 2/5x(1) - 48/5)$. Given initial conditions $x(0) = 1$ *and* $x(1) = 1$, then these are incorporated directly in the command

```
rsolve({x(n + 2) - 7/2*x(n + 1) + 3/2*x(n)
= 12,x(0) = 1,x(1) = 1},x(n));
```

to give the particular solution

$$\tfrac{13}{5}3^n + \tfrac{52}{5}(\tfrac{1}{2})^n - 12$$

In MATLAB's Symbolic Math Toolbox there is no equivalent command, so we make use of the `maple` command to access the MAPLE kernel. Check that the command

```
maple('rsolve({x(n + 2) - 7/2*x(n + 1) + 3/2*x(n)
= 12,x(0) = 1,x(1) = 1},x(n))')
```

returns the same answer as above.

As further examples we consider Examples 6.15(a) and 6.18. For 6.15(a) the commands

```
syms x n
maple('rsolve({x(n + 1) - 3*x(n) = 4, x(n))')
```

return

```
ans = x(0)*3^n - 2 + 2*3^n
```

This corresponds to the answer given in the solution with $A = (x(0) + 2)$.

For 6.18 the commands

```
syms x n
maple('rsolve({x(n + 2) - x(n + 1) - x(n)
= 0,x(0) = 1,x(1) = 1, x(n))')
```

return

```
ans = (1/10*5^(1/2) + 1/2)*(1/2 + 1/2*5^(1/2))^n
+ (1/2 - 1/10*5^(1/2))*(1/2 - 1/2*5^(1/2))^n
```

Simple rearrangement gives

$$\frac{1}{\sqrt{5}}\left(\frac{1}{2}+\frac{\sqrt{5}}{2}\right)\left(\frac{1}{2}+\frac{\sqrt{5}}{2}\right)^n+\frac{1}{\sqrt{5}}\left(\frac{\sqrt{5}}{2}-\frac{1}{2}\right)\left(\frac{1}{2}-\frac{\sqrt{5}}{2}\right)^n$$

which reduces to the answer given in the solution.

When the roots of the characteristic equation are complex numbers, the general solution of the homogeneous recurrence relation has a different form, as illustrated in Example 6.20.

Example 6.20

Show that the general solution of the recurrence relation

$$x_{n+2} = 6x_{n+1} - 25x_n$$

may be expressed in the form

$$x_n = 5^n(A\cos n\theta + B\sin n\theta)$$

where θ is such that $\sin\theta = \frac{4}{5}$ and $\cos\theta = \frac{3}{5}$.

Solution

The characteristic equation

$$\lambda^2 = 6\lambda - 25$$

has the (complex) roots $\lambda = 3 + j4$ and $\lambda = 3 - j4$, so that we can write the general solution in the form

$$x_n = A(3 + j4)^n + B(3 - j4)^n$$

Now writing the complex numbers in polar form we have

$$x_n = A(re^{j\theta})^n + B(re^{-j\theta})^n$$

where $r^2 = 3^2 + 4^2$ and $\tan\theta = \frac{4}{3}$ with $0 < \theta < \pi/2$ (or $\cos\theta = \frac{3}{5}$, $\sin\theta = \frac{4}{5}$). This can be simplified to give

$$x_n = A(5^n e^{jn\theta}) + B(5^n e^{-jn\theta}) = A5^n(\cos n\theta + j\sin n\theta) + B5^n(\cos n\theta - j\sin n\theta)$$
$$= (A + B)5^n \cos n\theta + j(A - B)5^n \sin n\theta$$

Here A and B are arbitrary complex constants, so their sum and difference are also arbitrary constants and we can write

$$x_n = P5^n \cos n\theta + Q5^n \sin n\theta$$

giving the form required. (Since P and Q are constants we can replace them by A and B if we wish.)

Example 6.21 Find the solution of the recurrence relation

$$x_{n+2} + 2x_n = 0$$

which satisfies $x_0 = 1$, $x_1 = 2$.

Solution Here the characteristic equation is

$$\lambda^2 + 2 = 0$$

and has roots $\pm j\sqrt{2}$, so that we can write the general solution in the form

$$x_n = A(j\sqrt{2})^n + B(-j\sqrt{2})^n$$

Since $e^{j\pi/2} = \cos\frac{\pi}{2} + j\sin\frac{\pi}{2} = j$, we can rewrite the solution as

$$x_n = A(\sqrt{2})^n e^{jn\pi/2} + B(\sqrt{2})^n e^{-jn\pi/2}$$
$$= A2^{n/2}\left(\cos\frac{n\pi}{2} + j\sin\frac{n\pi}{2}\right) + B2^{n/2}\left(\cos\frac{n\pi}{2} - j\sin\frac{n\pi}{2}\right)$$
$$= (A + B)2^{n/2}\cos\frac{n\pi}{2} + j(A - B)2^{n/2}\sin\frac{n\pi}{2}$$
$$= P2^{n/2}\cos\frac{n\pi}{2} + Q2^{n/2}\sin\frac{n\pi}{2}$$

We can find the values of P and Q by applying the initial data $x_0 = 1$, $x_1 = 2$, giving

$$P = 1 \text{ and } 2^{1/2}Q = 2$$

Hence the required solution is

$$x_n = 2^{n/2}\cos\frac{n\pi}{2} + 2^{(n+1)/2}\sin\frac{n\pi}{2}$$

If complex roots are involved then using the command `evalc` alongside `rsolve` attempts to express complex exponentials in terms of trigonometric functions, leading in most cases to simplified answers. Considering Example 6.21 the MATLAB commands

```
syms x n
maple('evalc(rsolve({x(n + 2) + 2*x(n) = 0,x(0)
= 1,x(1) = 2}, x(n)))')
```

return the answer

```
2^(1/2*n)*cos(1/2*n*pi) + 2^(1/2*n)*sin(1/2*n*pi)*2^(1/2)
```

which reduces to

$$2^{n/2}\cos(n\pi/2) + 2^{(n+1)/2}\sin(n\pi/2)$$

Check that for the equation of Example 6.20 the MATLAB commands

```
syms x n
maple('evalc(rsolve({x(n + 2) - 6*x(n + 1) + 25*x(n)
= 0}, x(n)))')
```

subject to noting that $\exp(n*\log 5) = 5^n$, $\operatorname{atan}(4/3) = \theta$ and the collection of terms, produce the answer

$$x(0)5^n\cos(n\theta) + (1/4x(1) - 3/4x(0))5^n\sin(n\theta))$$

which is of the required form.

The general result corresponding to that obtained in Example 6.18 is that if the roots of the characteristic equation can be written in the form

$$\lambda = u \pm jv$$

where u, v are real numbers, then the general solution of the homogeneous recurrence relation is

$$x_n = r^n(A\cos n\theta + B\sin n\theta)$$

where $r = \sqrt{(u^2 + v^2)}$, $\cos\theta = u/r$, $\sin\theta = v/r$ and A and B are arbitrary constants.

Recurrence relations are sometimes called **difference equations**. This name is used since we can rearrange the relations in terms of the differences of unknown sequence x_n. Thus

$$x_{n+1} = ax_n + b$$

can be rearranged as

$$\Delta x_n = (a - 1)x_n + b$$

where $\Delta x_n = x_{n+1} - x_n$.

Similarly, after some algebraic manipulation, we may write

$$x_{n+2} = ax_{n+1} + bx_n + c$$

as

$$\Delta^2 x_n = (a-2)\Delta x_n + (a+b-1)x_n + c$$

where

$$\Delta^2 x_n = \Delta x_{n+1} - \Delta x_n = x_{n+2} - 2x_{n+1} + x_n$$

The method for solving second-order linear recurrence relations with constant coefficients is summarized in Figure 6.7.

Figure 6.7 Summary: second-order linear recurrence relation with constant coefficients.

Homogeneous case:

$$x_{n+2} = ax_{n+1} + bx_n \qquad (1)$$

(i) Solve the characteristic equation.
(ii) Write down the general solution for x_n from the table:

Roots of characteristic equation	***General solution (A and B are arbitrary constants)***
Real α, β and $\alpha \neq \beta$	$A\alpha^n + B\beta^n$
Real α, β and $\alpha = \beta$	$(A + Bn)\alpha^n$
Non-real α, $\beta = u \pm jv$	$(u^2 + v^2)^{n/2}(A\cos n\theta + B\sin n\theta)$ where $\cos\theta = u/(u^2+v^2)^{1/2}$, $\sin\theta = v/(u^2+v^2)^{1/2}$

Nonhomogeneous case:

$$x_{n+2} = ax_{n+1} + bx_n + c_n \text{ where } c_n \text{ is a known sequence.} \qquad (2)$$

(i) Find the general solution of the associated homogeneous problem (1).
(ii) Find a particular solution of (2).
(iii) The general solution of (2) is the sum of (i) and (ii).

To find a particular solution to (2) substitute a likely form of particular solution into (2). If the correct form has been chosen then comparing coefficients will be enough to determine the values of the constants in the trial solution. Here are some suitable forms of particular solutions:

c_n	7	$3n+5$	$2n^2+3n+8$	$3\cos(7n) + 5\sin(7n)$	6^n	$n5^n$
p_n	C	$Cn+D$	Cn^2+Dn+E	$C\cos(7n) + D\sin(7n)$	$C6^n$	$5^n(C+Dn)$

In solving problems, note that the top line of the table involves any *known* constants (these will be different from problem to problem), while the bottom line involves *unknown* constants, C, D, E, which must be determined by substituting the trial form into the nonhomogeneous relation.

An exceptional case arises when the suggested form for p_n already is present in the general solution of the associated homogeneous problem. If this happens, just multiply the suggested form by n (and if that does not work, by n repeatedly until it does).

6.4.4 Exercises

Check your answers using MATLAB or MAPLE whenever possible.

29 Evaluate the expression $2x_{n+2} - 7x_{n+1} + 3x_n$ when x_n is defined for all $n \geqslant 0$ by

(a) $x_n = 3^n$ (b) $x_n = 2^n$

(c) $x_n = 2^{-n}$ (d) $x_n = 3(-2)^n$

Which of (a) to (d) are solutions of the following recurrence relation?

$$2x_{n+2} - 7x_{n+1} + 3x_n = 0$$

30 Show, by substituting them into the recurrence relation, that $x_n = 2^n$ and $x_n = (-1)^n$ are two solutions of $x_{n+2} - x_{n+1} - 2x_n = 0$. Verify similarly that $x_n = A(2^n) + B(-1)^n$ is also a solution of the recurrence relation for all constants A and B.

31 Obtain the general solutions of

(a) $Y_{n+2} - 7Y_{n+1} + 10Y_n = 0$

(b) $u_{n+2} - u_{n+1} - 6u_n = 0$

(c) $25T_{n+2} = -T_n$

(d) $p_{n+2} - 5p_{n+1} = 5(p_{n+1} - 5p_n)$

(e) $2E_{n+2} = E_{n+1} + E_n$

32 Solve the nonhomogeneous problems (use parts of Question 31)

(a) $Y_{n+2} - 7Y_{n+1} + 10Y_n = 1, \quad Y_0 = 5/4, \quad Y_1 = 2$

(b) $2E_{n+2} - E_{n+1} - E_n = 1, \quad E_0 = 2, \quad E_1 = 0$

(c) $u_{n+2} - u_{n+1} - 6u_n = n$ (general solution only)

33 Show that the characteristic equation for the recurrence relation $x_{n+2} - 2ax_{n+1} + a^2x_n = 0$, where a is a non-zero constant, has two equal roots $\lambda = a$.

(a) Verify (by substituting into the relation) that $x_n = (A + Bn)a^n$ is a solution for all constants A and B.

(b) Find the particular solution which satisfies $x_0 = 1$, $x_1 = 0$. (Your answer will involve a, of course.)

(c) Find the particular solution for which $x_0 = 3$, $x_{10} = 20$.

34 Let x be a constant such that $|x| < 1$. Find the solution of

$$T_{n+2} - 2xT_{n+1} + T_n = 0, \quad T_0 = 1, \quad T_1 = x$$

Find T_2, T_3 and T_4 also directly by recursion and deduce that $\cos(2\cos^{-1}x) = 2x^2 - 1$ and express $\cos(3\cos^{-1}x)$ and $\cos(4\cos^{-1}x)$ as polynomials in x.

35 A topic from information theory: imagine an information transmission system that uses an alphabet consisting of just two symbols 'dot' and 'dash', say. Messages are transmitted by first encoding them into a string of these symbols, and no other symbols (e.g. blank spaces) are allowed. Each symbol requires some length of time for its transmission. Therefore, for a fixed total time duration only a finite number of different message strings is possible. Let N_t denote the number of different message strings possible in t time units.

(a) Suppose that dot and dash each require one time unit for transmission. What is the value of N_1? Why is $N_{t+1} = 2N_t$ for all $t \geqslant 1$? Write down a simple formula for N_t for $t \geqslant 1$.

(b) Suppose instead that dot requires one unit of time for transmission while dash requires two units. What are the values of N_1 and N_2? Justify the relation $N_{t+2} = N_{t+1} + N_t$ for $t \geqslant 1$. Hence write down a formula for N_t in terms of t.

(*Hint*: The general solution of Fibonacci recurrence is given in Example 6.18.)

6.5 Limit of a sequence

In Section 6.2.1 the idea of a sequence and the associated notation were described. We shall now develop the concept of a limit of a sequence and then discuss the properties of sequences that have limits (termed convergent sequences) and methods for evaluating those limits algebraically and numerically.

6.5.1 Convergent sequences

In Example 6.6, we obtained the following sequence of approximations (working to 2dp) for $\sqrt{2}$:

$$x_0 = 1, \quad x_1 = 1.83, \quad x_2 = 1.16, \quad x_3 = 1.64$$

Continuing with the process, we obtain

$$x_{22} = 1.41, \quad x_{23} = 1.41$$

and

$$x_n = 1.41 \quad \text{for } n \geqslant 22$$

The terms x_{22} and x_{23} of the sequence are indistinguishable to two decimal places; in other words, their difference is less than a rounding error. This situation is shown clearly in Figure 6.4(b). This phenomenon occurs with many sequences, and we say that the sequence **tends to a limit** or **has a limiting value** or **converges** or **is convergent**. While it is clear in the above example what we mean by saying that the sequence converges to $\sqrt{2}$, we need a precise definition for all the cases that may occur.

In general, a sequence $\{a_k\}_{k=0}^{\infty}$ has the limiting value a as n becomes large if, given a small positive number ε (no matter how small), a_n differs from a by less than ε for all sufficiently large n. More concisely,

> $a_n \to a$ as $n \to \infty$ if, given any $\varepsilon > 0$, there is a number N such that $|a_n - a| < \varepsilon$ for all $n > N$

Here the $\to$ stands for 'tends to the value' or 'converges to the limit'. An alternative notation for $a_n \to a$ as $n \to \infty$ is

$$\lim_{n\to\infty} a_n = a$$

Diagrammatically, this means that the terms of the sequence lie between $y = a - \varepsilon$ and $y = a + \varepsilon$ for $n > N$, as shown in Figure 6.8.

Note that the limit of a sequence need not actually be an element of the sequence. For example $\{n^{-1}\}_{n=1}^{\infty}$ has limit 0, but 0 does not occur in the sequence.

Returning to the square-root example discussed above, we have

$$x_n \to \sqrt{2} \quad \text{as} \quad n \to \infty$$

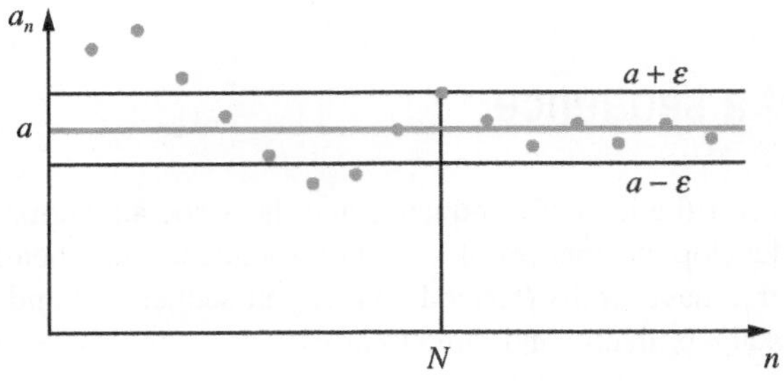

Figure 6.8 Convergence of $\{a_n\}$ to limit a.

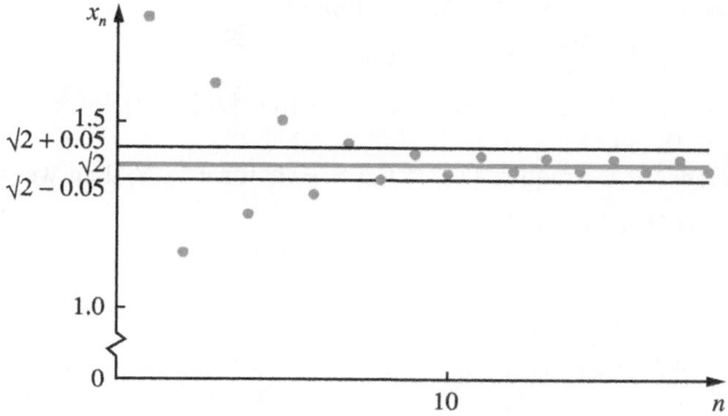

Figure 6.9
Convergence of $\{x_n\}$ to $\sqrt{2}$.

It is clear from the terms of the sequence that for an error bound of 0.05 we need $n > 8$ (see Figure 6.9). Thus $\sqrt{2} = 1.4$ (to 1dp). However, to prove convergence in the formal sense, we have to be able to say how many terms we need to take in order to obtain a specified level of precision. Suppose we need an answer correct to 10dp, or 100dp, or whatever; we must be able to give the corresponding value of N in the definition of convergence. Finding an expression for N is not often easy.

We shall illustrate the type of methods used by finding an expression for N for a classical method for calculating $\sqrt{2}$. This uses the iteration

$$x_{n+1} = \frac{2 + x_n}{1 + x_n} \quad \text{with } x_0 = 1$$

This produces the rational approximations

$$\left\{1, \frac{3}{2}, \frac{7}{5}, \frac{17}{12}, \frac{41}{29}, \frac{99}{70}, \dots\right\}$$

The last given approximation has an error of less than 0.0001. Suppose we require an approximation which is correct to p decimal places, then we need to find an N such that

$$|x_n - \sqrt{2}| < 0.5 \times 10^{-p}$$

for $n > N$. Writing $\varepsilon_n = x_n - \sqrt{2}$ so that $x_0 = \sqrt{2} + \varepsilon_0$, $x_1 = \sqrt{2} + \varepsilon_1$, … , $x_{n+1} = \sqrt{2} + \varepsilon_{n+1}$ (and so on) we have

$$\sqrt{2} + \varepsilon_{n+1} = \frac{2 + \sqrt{2} + \varepsilon_n}{1 + \sqrt{2} + \varepsilon_n}$$

Multiplying across, we have

$$(\sqrt{2} + \varepsilon_{n+1})(1 + \sqrt{2} + \varepsilon_n) = 2 + \sqrt{2} + \varepsilon_n$$

which gives

$$\sqrt{2} + 2 + \sqrt{2}\varepsilon_n + (1 + \sqrt{2})\varepsilon_{n+1} + \varepsilon_{n+1}\varepsilon_n = 2 + \sqrt{2} + \varepsilon_n$$

Simplifying further we have

$$(1 + \sqrt{2} + \varepsilon_n)\varepsilon_{n+1} = -\varepsilon_n(\sqrt{2} - 1)$$

Thus, since $x_n = \sqrt{2} + \varepsilon_n$

$$|\varepsilon_{n+1}| = \frac{(\sqrt{2} - 1)|\varepsilon_n|}{1 + x_n}$$

Since $x_n \geqslant 1$ and $\sqrt{2} < 1.5$, this implies

$$|\varepsilon_{n+1}| < \tfrac{0.5}{2}|\varepsilon_n| < 0.25|\varepsilon_n|$$

Since $x_0 = 1$ we have $|\varepsilon_0| < \frac{1}{2}$, so that $|\varepsilon_1| < 0.25(\frac{1}{2})$, $|\varepsilon_2| < 0.25^2(\frac{1}{2})$, ... and $|\varepsilon_n| < 0.25^n(\frac{1}{2})$.

Hence if we require $|\varepsilon_n| < 0.5 \times 10^{-p}$, for $n > N$, then we may find m such that

$$0.25^m(\tfrac{1}{2}) < 0.5 \times 10^{-p}$$

or

$$\frac{1}{4^m} < \frac{1}{10^p}$$

which implies $4^m > 10^p$.

Taking logarithms to base 10, this gives

$$m > p/\log 4$$

Then choose N to be the greatest integer not greater than m, that is, $N = \lfloor p/\log 4 \rfloor$. Thus, to guarantee 10dp, we need to evaluate at most $\lfloor 10/\log 4 \rfloor = 16$ iterations, which you may verify on your calculator.

6.5.2 Properties of convergent sequences

As we have seen in the $\sqrt{2}$ example, it is usually difficult and tedious to prove the convergence of a sequence from first principles. Normally we are able to compute the limit of a sequence from simpler sequences by means of very simple rules based on the properties of convergent sequences. These are:

(a) Every convergent sequence is bounded; that is, if $\{a_n\}_{n=0}^{\infty}$ is convergent then there is a positive number M such that $|a_n| < M$ for all n.

(b) If $\{a_n\}$ has limit a, and $\{b_n\}$ has limit b, then
- (i) $\{a_n + b_n\}$ has limit $a + b$
- (ii) $\{a_n - b_n\}$ has limit $a - b$
- (iii) $\{a_n b_n\}$ has limit ab
- (iv) $\{a_n/b_n\}$ has limit a/b, for $b_n \neq 0$, $b \neq 0$.

We illustrate the technique in Example 6.22.

Example 6.22 Find the limits of the sequence $\{x_n\}_{n=0}^{\infty}$ defined by

(a) $x_n = \dfrac{n}{n+1}$ (b) $x_n = \dfrac{2n^2 + 3n + 1}{5n^2 + 6n + 2}$

Solution (a) With $x_n = n/(n+1)$, we generate the sequence $\{0, \frac{1}{2}, \frac{2}{3}, \frac{3}{4}, \frac{4}{5}, \ldots\}$. From these values it seems clear that $x_n \to 1$ as $n \to \infty$. This can be proved by rewriting x_n as

$$x_n = 1 - \frac{1}{n+1}$$

and we make $1/(n+1)$ as small as we please by taking n sufficiently large.

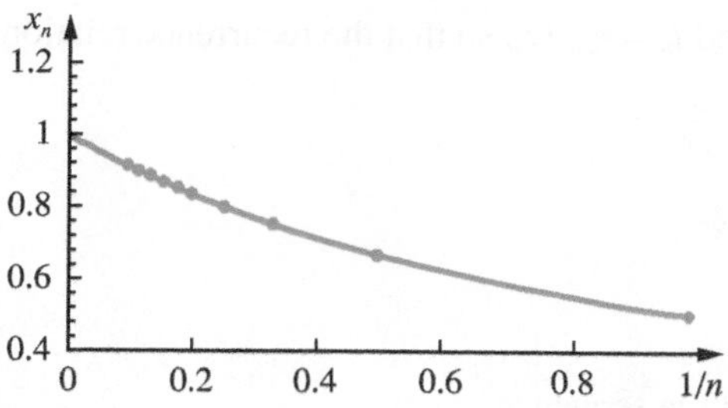

Figure 6.10 Sequence $x_n = n/(n + 1)$ plotted against $1/n$.

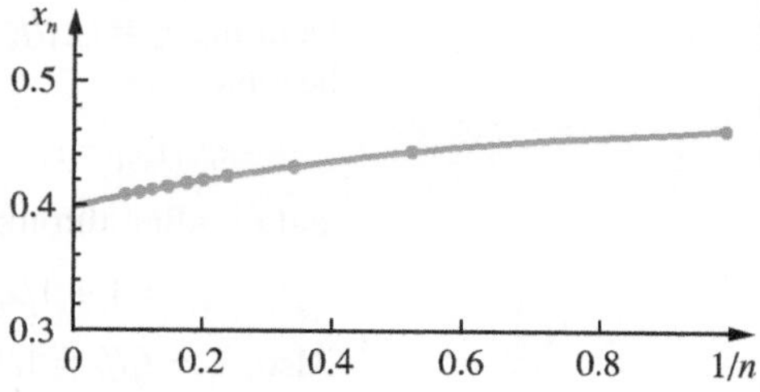

Figure 6.11 Sequence $x_n = \dfrac{2n^2 + 3n + 1}{5n^2 + 6n + 2}$ plotted against $1/n$.

Alternatively, we write

$$x_n = \frac{1}{1 + 1/n}$$

Now $1/n \to 0$ as $n \to \infty$. Hence, by the property (b)(i), $1 + 1/n \to 1$ and so, by the property (b)(iv),

$$\frac{1}{1 + 1/n} \to 1 \quad \text{as } n \to \infty$$

as illustrated in Figure 6.10.

(b) For

$$x_n = \frac{2n^2 + 3n + 1}{5n^2 + 6n + 2}$$

the easiest approach is to divide both numerator and denominator by the highest power of n occurring and use the fact that $1/n \to 0$ as $n \to \infty$. Thus

$$x_n = \frac{2 + 3/n + 1/n^2}{5 + 6/n + 2/n^2}$$

The limits of numerator and denominator are 2 and 5 (using the property (b)(i) repeatedly), and so $x_n \to \frac{2}{5}$ as $n \to \infty$ (using (b)(iv)). This is shown clearly in Figure 6.11.

Example 6.23 Show that the ratio x_n of successive terms of the Fibonacci sequence satisfies the recurrence relation

$$x_{n+1} = 1 + 1/x_n, \quad x_0 = 1$$

Calculate the first few terms of this sequence and find the value of its limit.

Solution The Fibonacci sequence was defined in Example 6.18 as

$$f_{n+2} = f_{n+1} + f_n \quad \text{with} \quad f_0 = f_1 = 1$$

Defining $x_n = f_{n+1}/f_n$ gives $f_{n+2} = x_{n+1} \times f_{n+1}$ and $f_n = f_{n+1}/x_n$, so that the recurrence relation becomes

$$x_{n+1}f_{n+1} = f_{n+1} + f_{n+1}/x_n$$

and dividing through by f_{n+1} we have

$$x_{n+1} = 1 + 1/x_n$$

Also, $x_0 = f_1/f_0 = 1/1 = 1$.

Using the recurrence relation, we obtain the sequence

$$\{1, 2, 1.5, 1.6667, 1.6, 1.625, 1.6154, 1.6190, \dots\}$$

The numerical results suggest a limiting value near 1.62. Indeed, the oscillatory nature of the sequence suggests $1.6154 < x_n < 1.6190$ for $n > 8$, which implies a limit value $x = 1.62$ correct to 2dp.

In this case we can check this conclusion, for if $x_n \to x$ as $n \to \infty$ then $x_{n+1} \to x$ also, and so the recurrence relation yields

$$x = 1 + \frac{1}{x}, \quad \text{with } x > 0$$

Thus $x^2 - x - 1 = 0$, which implies $x = \frac{1}{2}(1 + \sqrt{5})$ or $x = \frac{1}{2}(1 - \sqrt{5})$. Since the sequence has positive values only, it is clear that the appropriate root is $x = \frac{1}{2}(1 + \sqrt{5}) = 1.62$ (to 2dp).

This limiting value is called the **golden number** and is often denoted by the Greek letter tau τ. A rectangle the ratio of whose sides is the golden number is said to be the most pleasing aesthetically, and this has often been adopted by architects as a basis of design.

6.5.3 Computation of limits

The examples considered so far tend to create the impression that all sequences converge, but this is not so. An important sequence that illustrates this is the geometric sequence

$$a_n = r^n, \quad r \text{ constant}$$

For this sequence we have

$$\lim_{n\to\infty} a_n = \begin{cases} 0 & (-1 < r < 1) \\ 1 & (r = 1) \end{cases}$$

If $r > 1$, the sequence increases without bound as $n \to \infty$, and we say it **diverges**. If $r = -1$, the sequence takes the values -1 and 1 alternately, and there is no limiting value. If $r < -1$, the sequence is unbounded and the terms alternate in sign.

Often in computational applications of sequences the limit of the sequence is not known, so that it is not possible to apply the formal definition to determine the number of terms N we need to take in order to obtain a specified level of precision. If we do not know the limit a, to which a sequence $\{a_n\}$ converges, then we cannot measure $|a_n - a|$. In the computational context, when we apply a recurrence relation to find a solution to a problem, we say that the sequence $\{a_n\}$ has converged to its limit when all subsequent terms yield the same value of the approximation required. In other words, we say that the sequence of finite terms is convergent if, for any n and $m > N$,

$$|a_n - a_m| < \varepsilon$$

where the bound ε is specified. Thus a sequence tends to a limit if all the terms of the sequence for $n > N$ are restricted to an interval that can be made arbitrarily small by choosing N sufficiently large. This is called **Cauchy's test for convergence**.

In many practical problems we need to find a numerical estimate for the limit of a sequence. A graphical method for this is to sketch the graph defined by the points $\{(1/n, a_n) : n = 1, 2, 3, \dots\}$ and then extrapolate from it, since $1/n \to 0$ as $n \to \infty$. If greater precision is required than can be obtained in this way, an effective numerical procedure is a form of repeated linear extrapolation due to Aitken. We illustrate the procedure in Example 6.24.

Example 6.24 Examine the convergence of the sequence $\{a_n\}_{n=1}^{\infty}$, $a_n = (1 + 1/n)^n$.

Solution It can be shown that $\lim_{n\to\infty} a_n = \mathrm{e}$, but convergence is rather slow. In fact,

$$a_1 = 2,\quad a_2 = 2.2500,\quad a_3 = 2.3704,\quad a_4 = 2.4414,\quad \dots$$
$$a_8 = 2.5658,\quad \dots,\quad a_{16} = 2.6379,\quad \dots,\quad a_{32} = 2.6770,\quad \dots$$
$$a_{64} = 2.6973,\quad \dots,\quad \text{and}\quad \mathrm{e} = 2.7183 \text{ to 4dp}$$

Now consider the two terms corresponding to $n = 16$ and $n = 32$ and set $x_n = 1/n$. Then

$$n = 16 \quad \text{gives} \quad x_{16} = 0.0625 \quad \text{and} \quad a_{16} = 2.6379$$
$$n = 32 \quad \text{gives} \quad x_{32} = 0.031\,25 \quad \text{and} \quad a_{32} = 2.6770$$

We wish to find the value corresponding to $x = 0$. To estimate this, we may use linear extrapolation, as shown in Figure 6.12. This gives

$$b_{16,32} = \frac{x_{16}a_{32} - x_{32}a_{16}}{x_{16} - x_{32}} = 2.7161$$

Note that $b_{16,32}$ is a better estimate for e than either a_{16} or a_{32}.

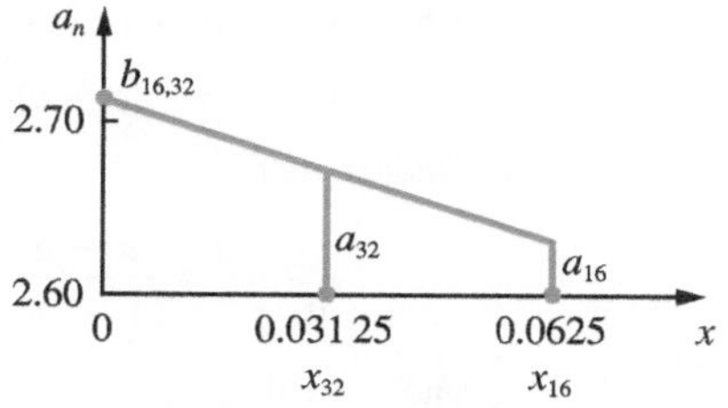

Figure 6.12 Linear extrapolation for the limit of a sequence.

In MATLAB's Symbolic Math Toolbox the limit as $n \to \infty$ of the sequence defined by $x_n = f(n)$ is determined by the commands

```
syms n
limit(f_n, n, inf)
```

the corresponding command in MAPLE being

```
limit(f_n, n = infinity);
```

As illustrative examples, consider Examples 6.22(a) and 6.24:

MATLAB		MAPLE
`syms n`		
`limit(n/(n + 1), n,inf)`		`limit(n/(n + 1), n = infinity);`
	returns `ans 1`	
`limit((1 + 1/n)^n, n, inf)`		`limit((1 + 1/n)^n, n = infinity);`
	returns	
`exp(1)`		`e`

6.5.4 Exercises

Check your answers using MATLAB or MAPLE whenever possible.

36 Calculate the first six terms of each of the following sequences $\{a_n\}$ and draw a graph of a_n versus $1/n$. (Some care is needed in choosing the scale of the y axis.) What is the behaviour of a_n as $n \to \infty$?

(a) $a_n = \dfrac{n}{n^2+1} \quad (n \geqslant 1)$

(b) $a_n = \dfrac{3n^2+2n+1}{6n^2+5n+2} \quad (n \geqslant 1)$

(c) $a_n = (2n)^{1/n} \quad (n \geqslant 1)$

(d) $a_n = \left(1+\dfrac{1}{2n}\right)^n \quad (n \geqslant 1)$

(e) $a_n = \sqrt{(1+a_{n-1})}, \quad a_1 = 1 \quad (n \geqslant 2)$

(f) $a_n = \dfrac{n}{2}\sin\dfrac{2\pi}{n} \quad (n \geqslant 1)$

Note: Part (f) is the area of a regular polygon of n sides inscribed in a circle of unit radius.

37 Calculate the first six terms of each of the following sequences $\{a_n\}$ and draw a graph of a_n against n. What is the behaviour of a_n as $n \to \infty$?

(a) $a_n = \dfrac{n^2+1}{n+1} \quad (n \geqslant 0)$

(b) $a_n = (\sin \tfrac{1}{2}n\pi)^n \quad (n \geqslant 1)$

(c) $a_n = 3/a_{n-1}, \quad a_0 = 1 \quad (n \geqslant 1)$

38 Find the least value of N such that when $n \geqslant N$,

(a) $n^2 + 2n > 100$ (b) $\dfrac{n^2}{2^n} < \dfrac{1}{1000}$

(c) $\dfrac{1}{n} - \dfrac{(-1)^n}{n^2} < 0.000\,001$

(d) $\sqrt{(n+1)} - \sqrt{n} < \frac{1}{10}$

(e) $\dfrac{n^2+2}{n^2-1} - 1 < 0.01$

39 What is the long-term share of the detergent market achieved by the brand 'Number One', described in Question 5 (Exercises 6.2.3)?

40 A **linearly convergent** sequence has the property that

$$a_n - a = \lambda(a_{n-1} - a) \quad \text{for all } n$$

where λ is a constant and $a = \lim_{n\to\infty} a_n$. Show that

$$a_{n+1} - a = \lambda(a_n - a)$$

Deduce that

$$\frac{a_{n+1}-a}{a_n - a} = \frac{a_n - a}{a_{n-1}-a}$$

and show that

$$a = a_{n-1} - \frac{(a_n - a_{n-1})^2}{a_{n+1} - 2a_n + a_{n-1}}$$

This is known as **Aitken's estimate** for the limit of a sequence.

Compute the first four terms of the sequence

$$a_0 = 2, \quad a_{n+1} = \tfrac{1}{5}(3 + 4a_n^2 - a_n^3) \quad (n \geqslant 0)$$

and estimate the limit of the sequence.

6.6 Infinite series

Infinite series occur in a large variety of practical problems, from estimating the long-term effects of pollution to the stability analysis of the motions of machinery parts. They also occur in the development of computer algorithms for the numerical solution of practical problems. In this section we will consider the underlying ideas. Care has to be exercised when dealing with infinite series, since it is easy to generate fallacious results. For example, consider the infinite series

$$S = 1 - 2 + 4 - 8 + 16 - 32 + \dots$$

Then we can write

$$2S = 2 - 4 + 8 - 16 + 32 - 64 + \dots$$

and adding these two results, we obtain

$$3S = 1 \quad \text{or} \quad S = \tfrac{1}{3}$$

which is clearly wrong. Such blunders, however, are not always so glaringly obvious, so we have to develop simple methods for determining whether an infinite series sums to a finite value and for obtaining or estimating that value.

6.6.1 Convergence of infinite series

As we discussed in Section 6.2.1, series and sequences are closely connected. When the sum S_n of a series of n terms tends to a limit as $n \to \infty$, the series is **convergent**. When we can express S_n in a simple form, it is usually easy to establish whether or not the series converges. To find the sum of an infinite series, the sequence of partial sums $\{S_n\}$ is taken to the limit.

Example 6.25 Examine the following series for convergence:

(a) $1 + 3 + 5 + 7 + 9 + \dots + (2k + 1) + \dots$

(b) $1^2 + 2^2 + 3^2 + 4^2 + 5^2 + \dots + k^2 + \dots$

(c) $1 + \dfrac{1}{2} + \dfrac{1}{4} + \dfrac{1}{8} + \dfrac{1}{16} + \dots + \dfrac{1}{2^k} + \dots$

(d) $\dfrac{1}{1\cdot 2} + \dfrac{1}{2\cdot 3} + \dfrac{1}{3\cdot 4} + \dfrac{1}{4\cdot 5} + \dots + \dfrac{1}{(k+1)(k+2)} + \dots$

Solution (a) This is an arithmetic series, so we can write its finite sum as a simple formula

$$S_n = \sum_{k=0}^{n-1}(2k + 1) = 1 + 3 + 5 + \dots + (2n - 1) = n^2 \quad (n \text{ terms})$$

It is clear from this that $S_n \to \infty$ as $n \to \infty$ and the series does not converge to a limit. It is a **divergent** series.

(b) As we saw in Example 6.10

$$S_n = 1^2 + 2^2 + 3^2 + \dots + n^2 = \tfrac{1}{6}n(n+1)(2n+1) \quad (n \text{ terms})$$

As n becomes large, so does S_n, and $S_n \to \infty$ as $n \to \infty$. Hence the series is divergent.

(c) $S_n = 1 + \tfrac{1}{2} + \tfrac{1}{4} + \dots + \dfrac{1}{2^{n-1}}$ (n terms)

This is a geometric series with common ratio $\tfrac{1}{2}$. Using the formula (6.4) with $a = 1$ and $r = \tfrac{1}{2}$ gives

$$S_n = \frac{1 - \dfrac{1}{2^n}}{1 - \dfrac{1}{2}} = 2\left(1 - \frac{1}{2^n}\right)$$

As $n \to \infty$, $\dfrac{1}{2^n} \to 0$, so that $S_n \to 2$. Hence the series converges to the sum 2.

(d) We showed in Example 6.11 that

$$S_n = \frac{1}{1\cdot 2} + \frac{1}{2\cdot 3} + \dots + \frac{1}{n(n+1)} = 1 - \frac{1}{n+1}$$

As $n \to \infty$, $1/(n+1) \to 0$, so that $S_n \to 1$. Hence the series converges to the sum 1.

Among the elementary series, the geometric series is the most important.

$$S_n = a + ar + ar^2 + \dots + ar^{n-1} \quad (n \text{ terms})$$

$$= \frac{a(1-r^n)}{1-r}$$

$$= \frac{a}{1-r} - \frac{ar^n}{1-r}$$

Since $r^n \to 0$ as $n \to \infty$ when $|r| < 1$, we conclude that $S_n \to a/(1-r)$ where $|r| < 1$ and the series is convergent. Where $|r| \geqslant 1$, the series is divergent. These results are used in many applications and the sum of the infinite series is

$$S = a + ar + ar^2 + ar^3 + \dots = \frac{a}{1-r}, \quad |r| < 1 \tag{6.14}$$

Similarly

$$S_n = a + 2ar + 3ar^2 + \dots + nar^{n-1}$$

$$= \frac{a}{(1-r)^2} - (n+1)ar^n + anr^{n-1}$$

$$\to \frac{a}{(1-r)^2} \quad \text{as } n \to \infty$$

Summation may be carried out in MATLAB using the *symsum* command. For Example 6.25(a) the sum of the first n terms is determined by the commands

```
syms k n
sn = symsum(2*k + 1,0,n)
```

as

```
sn = n^2
```

which tends to infinity as $n \to \infty$, so it is a divergent series.

For Example 6.25(d) the sum to infinity is determined by the commands

```
syms k
sinf = symsum(1/((k + 1)*(k + 2)),0,inf)
```

as `sn = 1`, so it is a convergent series.

6.6.2 Tests for convergence of positive series

The convergence or divergence of the series discussed in Example 6.25 was established by considering the behaviour of the partial sum S_n as $n \to \infty$. In many cases, however, it is not possible to express S_n in a closed form. When this occurs, the convergence or divergence of the series is established by means of a test. Two tests are commonly used.

(a) Comparison test

Suppose we have a series, $\sum_{k=0}^{\infty} c_k$, of positive terms ($c_k \geqslant 0$, all k) which is known to be convergent. If we have another series, $\sum_{k=0}^{\infty} u_k$, of positive terms such that $u_k \leqslant c_k$ for all k then $\sum_{k=0}^{\infty} u_k$ is convergent also.

Also, if $\sum_{k=0}^{\infty} c_k$ diverges and $u_k \geqslant c_k \geqslant 0$ for all k, then $\sum_{k=0}^{\infty} u_k$ also diverges.

Example 6.26 Examine for convergence the series

(a) $1 + \frac{1}{1!} + \frac{1}{2!} + \frac{1}{3!} + \frac{1}{4!} + \ldots + \frac{1}{n!} + \ldots$ (the **factorial series**)

(b) $1 + \frac{1}{2} + \frac{1}{3} + \frac{1}{4} + \ldots + \frac{1}{n} + \ldots$ (the **harmonic series**)

Solution (a) We can establish the convergence of the series (a) by considering its partial sum

$$A_n = 1 + \frac{1}{1!} + \frac{1}{2!} + \frac{1}{3!} + \frac{1}{4!} + \ldots + \frac{1}{n!}$$

Each term of this series is less than or equal to the corresponding term of the series

$$C_n = 1 + 1 + 1 + \frac{1}{2} + \frac{1}{2^2} + \frac{1}{2^3} + \ldots + \frac{1}{2^{n-1}}$$

This geometric series may be summed to give

$$C_n = 3 - \frac{1}{2^{n-1}}$$

Thus

$$A_n < 3 - \frac{1}{2^{n-1}}$$

which implies that, since all the terms of the series are positive numbers, A_n tends to a limit less than 3 as $n \to \infty$. Thus the series is convergent.

(b) The divergence of the series (b) is similarly established.

$$1 + \tfrac{1}{2} + \tfrac{1}{3} + \tfrac{1}{4} + \tfrac{1}{5} + \tfrac{1}{6} + \tfrac{1}{7} + \tfrac{1}{8} + \tfrac{1}{9} + \ldots$$

Collecting together successive groups of two, four, eight, … terms, we have

$$1 + \tfrac{1}{2} + (\tfrac{1}{3} + \tfrac{1}{4}) + (\tfrac{1}{5} + \tfrac{1}{6} + \tfrac{1}{7} + \tfrac{1}{8}) + (\tfrac{1}{9} + \ldots + \tfrac{1}{16}) + (\tfrac{1}{17} + \ldots$$

which may be compared with the series

(c) $$1 + \tfrac{1}{2} + (\tfrac{1}{4} + \tfrac{1}{4}) + (\tfrac{1}{8} + \tfrac{1}{8} + \tfrac{1}{8} + \tfrac{1}{8}) + (\tfrac{1}{16} + \ldots + \tfrac{1}{16}) + (\tfrac{1}{32} + \ldots$$

Each term of the rearranged (b) is greater than or at least equal to the corresponding term of the series (c), and so the 'sum' of the series (b) is greater than the 'sum' of the series (c), which is

$$1 + \tfrac{1}{2} + \tfrac{1}{2} + \tfrac{1}{2} + \tfrac{1}{2} + \ldots$$

on summing the terms in brackets and which is clearly divergent.

Note that the harmonic series is divergent despite the fact that its nth term tends to zero as $n \to \infty$.

The harmonic series is the borderline case for divergence/convergence of the series

$$S(r) = \sum_{k=1}^{\infty} \frac{1}{k^r}$$

For $r > 1$, this series converges; for $r \leqslant 1$, it diverges as shown in the table below, where the values have been calculated using the `symsum` command (followed by the `double` command) in MATLAB's Symbolic Math Toolbox

r	1	1.01	1.05	1.10	1.20	1.50	2
$S(r)$	∞	100.58	20.58	10.58	5.59	2.61	1.64

(b) d'Alembert's ratio test

Suppose we have a series of positive terms, $\sum_{k=0}^{\infty} u_k$, and also $\lim_{n\to\infty} \frac{u_{n+1}}{u_n} = l$ exists. Then the series is convergent if $l < 1$ and divergent if $l > 1$. If $l = 1$, we are not able to decide, using this test, whether the series converges or diverges.

The proof of this result is straightforward. Assume that $\lim_{n\to\infty} \frac{u_{n+1}}{u_n} = l < 1$ and choose r to be any number between l and 1. Then since the values of u_{n+1}/u_n, when n is sufficiently large, differ from l by as little as we please, we have

$$\frac{u_{n+1}}{u_n} < r$$

for $n \geqslant N$. Thus

$$u_{N+1} < ru_N, \quad u_{N+2} < r^2u_N, \ldots$$

Thus, from and after the term u_N of the series, the terms do not exceed those of the convergent geometric series

$$u_N(1 + r + r^2 + r^3 + \ldots)$$

Hence $\Sigma_{k=0}^{\infty} u_k$ converges.

It is left as an exercise for the reader to show that the series diverges when $l > 1$.

Example 6.27 Use d'Alembert's test to determine whether the following series are convergent.

(a) $\displaystyle\sum_{k=0}^{\infty} \frac{2^k}{k!}$ (b) $\displaystyle\sum_{k=0}^{\infty} \frac{2^k}{(k+1)^2}$

Solution (a) Let $u_k = \dfrac{2^k}{k!}$, then

$$\frac{u_{n+1}}{u_n} = \frac{2^{n+1}}{(n+1)!}\bigg/\frac{2^n}{n!} = \frac{2}{n+1}$$

which tends to zero as $n \to \infty$. Thus $l = 0$ and the series is convergent.

(b) Here

$$l = \lim_{n\to\infty}\left[\frac{2^{n+1}}{(n+2)^2}\bigg/\frac{2^n}{(n+1)^2}\right] = 2$$

so that the series diverges.

A necessary condition for convergence of all series is that the terms of the series must tend to zero as $n \to \infty$. Thus a simple test for divergence is

if $u_n \to u \neq 0$ as $n \to \infty$, then $\Sigma_{k=0}^{\infty} u_k$ is divergent

Notice, however, that $u_n \to 0$ as $n \to \infty$ does not guarantee that $\Sigma_{k=0}^{\infty} u_k$ is convergent. To prove that, we need more information. (Recall, for example, the harmonic series $1 + \frac{1}{2} + \frac{1}{3} + \frac{1}{4} + \ldots$, of Example 6.26, which is divergent.)

Example 6.28 Show that the series $\frac{1}{2}+\frac{2}{3}+\frac{3}{4}+\ldots$ is divergent.

Solution Here $u_k = \dfrac{k}{k+1}$, so that d'Alembert's ratio test does not give a conclusion (since $l = 1$). However, we note that $u_n = 1 - \dfrac{1}{n+1}$, so that $u_n \to 1$ as $n \to \infty$, from which we conclude that $\sum_{k=1}^{\infty} u_k$ diverges.

6.6.3 The absolute convergence of general series

In practical problems, we are concerned with series which may have both positive and negative terms. **Absolutely convergent** series are a special case of such series. Consider the general series

$$S = \sum_{k=0}^{\infty} u_k$$

which may have both positive and negative terms u_k. If the associated series

$$T = \sum_{k=0}^{\infty} |u_k|$$

is convergent then S is convergent and is said to be **absolutely convergent**. If it is impossible to obtain a value for the limit of the partial sum T_n, we must use some other test to determine the convergence (or divergence) of T. A simple test for absolute convergence of a series $\sum_{k=1}^{\infty} u_k$ is a natural extension of d'Alembert's ratio test.

If $\lim_{n\to\infty}\left|\dfrac{u_{n+1}}{u_n}\right| < 1$ then $\sum_{k=0}^{\infty} u_k$ is absolutely convergent

If $\lim_{n\to\infty}\left|\dfrac{u_{n+1}}{u_n}\right| > 1$ then $\sum_{k=0}^{\infty} u_k$ is divergent

If $\lim_{n\to\infty}\left|\dfrac{u_{n+1}}{u_n}\right| = 1$ then no conclusion is possible

Absolutely convergent series have the following useful properties:

(a) the insertion of brackets into the series does not alter its sum;

(b) the rearrangment of the series does not alter its sum;

(c) the product of two absolutely convergent series $A = \sum a_n$ and $B = \sum b_n$ is an absolutely convergent series C, where

$$C = a_1b_1 + (a_2b_1 + a_1b_2) + (a_3b_1 + a_2b_2 + a_1b_3) + (a_4b_1 + a_3b_2 + a_2b_3 + a_1b_4) + \ldots$$

There are convergent series that are not absolutely convergent; that is $\sum_{k=1}^{\infty} u_k$ converges but $\sum_{k=0}^{\infty} |u_k|$ diverges. The most common series of this type are alternating series. Here the u_k alternate in sign. If, in addition, the terms decrease in size and tend to zero,

$$|u_n| < |u_{n-1}| \quad \text{for all } n, \quad \text{with } u_n \to 0 \quad \text{as} \quad n \to \infty$$

then the series converges. Thus

$$\sum_{k=1}^{\infty} (-1)^{k+1} \frac{1}{k} = 1 - \tfrac{1}{2} + \tfrac{1}{3} - \tfrac{1}{4} + \tfrac{1}{5} - \tfrac{1}{6} + \ldots$$

which we write as

$$\sum_{k=1}^{\infty} (-1)^{k+1} \frac{1}{k} = 1 + (-\tfrac{1}{2}) + (\tfrac{1}{3}) + (-\tfrac{1}{4}) + (\tfrac{1}{5}) + (-\tfrac{1}{6}) + \ldots$$

converges. Its sum is ln 2, as we shall show in Section 6.7. The associated series of positive terms, $\sum_{k=1}^{\infty}(1/k)$, diverges of course (see Example 6.26b).

6.6.4 Exercises

41 Decide which of the following geometric series are convergent.

(a) $2 + \dfrac{2}{3} + \dfrac{2}{9} + \dfrac{2}{27} + \ldots + \dfrac{2}{3^k} + \ldots$

(b) $4 - 2 + 1 - \dfrac{1}{2} + \ldots + \dfrac{(-1)^k 4}{2^k} + \ldots$

(c) $10 + 11 + \frac{121}{10} + \frac{1331}{100} + \ldots + 10(\frac{11}{10})^k + \ldots$

(d) $1 - \frac{5}{4} + \frac{25}{16} - \frac{125}{64} + \ldots + (\frac{-5}{4})^k + \ldots$

42 Show that if

$$T_n = a + 2ar + 3ar^2 + 4ar^3 + \ldots + nar^{n-1}$$

then $(1 - r)T_n = a + ar + ar^2 + \ldots + ar^{n-1} - nar^n$

Deduce that

$$T_n = \frac{a(1 - r^n)}{(1 - r)^2} - \frac{nar^n}{1 - r}$$

Show that if $|r| < 1$, then $T_n \to a/(1 - r)^2$ as $n \to \infty$. Hence sum the infinite series

$$1 + \frac{2}{3} + \frac{1}{3} + \frac{4}{27} + \frac{5}{81} + \ldots + \frac{k}{3^{k-1}} + \ldots$$

43 For each of the following series find the sum of the first N terms, and, by letting $N \to \infty$, show that the infinite series converges and state its sum.

(a) $\frac{2}{1\cdot 3} + \frac{2}{3\cdot 5} + \frac{2}{5\cdot 7} + \ldots$

(b) $\frac{1}{1} + \frac{2}{2} + \frac{3}{2^2} + \frac{4}{2^3} + \frac{5}{2^4} + \ldots$

(c) $\frac{1}{1\cdot 2\cdot 3} + \frac{1}{2\cdot 3\cdot 4} + \frac{1}{3\cdot 4\cdot 5} + \ldots$

44 Which of the following series are convergent?

(a) $\displaystyle\sum_{k=1}^{\infty} (-1)^k$ (b) $-\frac{2}{3} + \frac{3}{4} - \frac{4}{5} + \ldots$

(c) $\displaystyle\sum_{k=0}^{\infty} \frac{1}{3^k + 1}$

45 By comparison with the series $\sum_{k=2}^{\infty}[1/k(k-1)]$ and $\sum_{k=2}^{\infty}[1/k(k+1)]$, show that $S = \sum_{k=2}^{\infty}(1/k^2)$ is convergent and $\frac{1}{2} < S < 1$.
(In fact, $\sum_{k=1}^{\infty}(1/k^2) = S + 1 = \frac{1}{6}\pi^2$.)

46 Show that $0.\dot{5}\dot{7}$ (that is, 0.575 757 ...) may be expressed as $57 \times 10^{-2} + 57 \times 10^{-4} + \ldots$, and so $0.\dot{5}\dot{7} = 57\sum_{r=1}^{\infty}100^{-r}$. Hence express $0.\dot{5}\dot{7}$ as a rational number. Use a similar method to express as rational numbers

(a) $0.\dot{4}1\dot{3}$ (b) 0.101 010 ...

(c) 0.999 999 ... (d) 17.231 723 172 3 ...

47 Consider the series $\sum_{r=1}^{\infty}k^{-p}$. By means of the inequalities ($p > 0$)

$$\frac{1}{2^p} + \frac{1}{3^p} < \frac{2}{2^p}$$

$$\frac{1}{4^p} + \frac{1}{5^p} + \frac{1}{6^p} + \frac{1}{7^p} < \frac{4}{4^p}$$

$$\frac{1}{8^p} + \frac{1}{9^p} + \frac{1}{10^p} + \frac{1}{11^p} + \frac{1}{12^p} + \frac{1}{13^p} + \frac{1}{14^p} + \frac{1}{15^p} < \frac{8}{8^p}$$

and so on, deduce that the series is convergent for $p > 1$. Show that it is divergent for $p \leqslant 1$.

48 Two attempts to evaluate the sum $\sum_{k=1}^{\infty} k^{-4}$ are made on a computer working to 8 digits. The first evaluates the sum

$$1 + \frac{1}{2^4} + \frac{1}{3^4} + \frac{1}{4^4} + \ldots + \frac{1}{72^4}$$

from the left; the second evaluates it from the right. The first method yields the result 1.082 320 2, the second 1.082 322 1. Which is the better approximation and why?

49 Show that

$$\sum_{k=1}^{2n} \frac{(-1)^{k+1}}{k^4} = \sum_{k=1}^{2n} \frac{1}{k^4} - \tfrac{1}{8}\sum_{k=1}^{n} \frac{1}{k^4}$$

and deduce that

$$\sum_{k=1}^{\infty} \frac{(-1)^{k+1}}{k^4} = \tfrac{7}{8}\sum_{k=1}^{\infty} \frac{1}{k^4}$$

Deduce that the modulus of error in the estimate for the sum $\sum_{k=1}^{\infty} k^{-4}$ obtained by computing $\frac{8}{7}\sum_{k=1}^{N}(-1)^k k^{-4}$ is less than $\frac{8}{7}(N+1)^{-4}$.

6.7 Power series

Power series frequently occur in the solution of practical problems, as we shall see in Sections 9.4.2, 9.8 and elsewhere. Often they are used to determine the sensitivity of systems to small changes in design parameters, to examine whether such systems are stable when small variations occur (as they always will in real life). The basic mathematics involved in power series is a natural extension of the series considered earlier.

A series of the type

$$a_0 + a_1x + a_2x^2 + a_3x^3 + \ldots + a_nx^n + \ldots$$

where the a_0, a_1, a_2, … are independent of x is called a **power series**.

6.7.1 Convergence of power series

Power series will, in general, converge for certain values of x and diverge elsewhere. Applying d'Alembert's ratio test to the above series, we see that it is absolutely convergent when

$$\lim_{n\to\infty} \left| \frac{a_{n+1}x^{n+1}}{a_nx^n} \right| < 1$$

Thus the series converges if

$$|x| \lim_{n\to\infty} \left| \frac{a_{n+1}}{a_n} \right| < 1$$

that is, if

$$|x| < \lim_{n\to\infty} \left| \frac{a_n}{a_{n+1}} \right|$$

Denoting $\lim_{n\to\infty} |a_n/a_{n+1}|$ by r, we see that the series is absolutely convergent for $-r < x < r$ and divergent for $x < -r$ and $x > r$. The limit r is called the **radius of convergence** of the series. The behaviour at $x = \pm r$ has to be determined by other methods.

The various cases that occur are shown in Example 6.29.

Example 6.29 Find the radius of convergences of the series

$$\text{(a)} \sum_{n=1}^{\infty} \frac{x^n}{n} \qquad \text{(b)} \sum_{n=1}^{\infty} n^n x^n$$

Solution (a) Here $a_n = 1/n$, so that $|a_n/a_{n+1}| = (n + 1)/n$ and $r = 1$. Thus the domain of absolute convergence of the series is $-1 < x < 1$. The series diverges for $|x| > 1$ and for $x = 1$. At $x = -1$ the series is

$$-1 + \tfrac{1}{2} - \tfrac{1}{3} + \tfrac{1}{4} + \ldots$$

which is convergent to $\ln \tfrac{1}{2}$ (see Section 6.6.3 and formula (6.18) below). Thus the series

$$\sum_{n=1}^{\infty} \frac{x^n}{n} = x + \tfrac{1}{2}x^2 + \tfrac{1}{3}x^3 + \tfrac{1}{4}x^4 + \ldots$$

is convergent for $-1 \leqslant x < 1$.

(b) Here $a_n = n^n$ and

$$\left|\frac{a_n}{a_{n+1}}\right| = \frac{n^n}{(n+1)^{n+1}} = \left(\frac{n}{n+1}\right)^n \frac{1}{n+1}$$

Now

$$\left(\frac{n}{n+1}\right)^n = \frac{1}{(1+1/n)^n} \to \mathrm{e}^{-1} \quad \text{as } n \to \infty \text{ (see Example 6.24)}$$

and

$$\frac{1}{n+1} \to 0 \quad \text{as } n \to \infty$$

so that $a_n/a_{n+1} \to 0$ as $n \to \infty$. Thus the series converges only at $x = 0$, and diverges elsewhere.

6.7.2 Special power series

Power series may be added, multiplied and divided within their common domains of convergence (provided the denominator is non-zero within this common domain) to give power series that are convergent, and these properties are often exploited to express a given power series in terms of standard series and to obtain power series expansions of complicated functions.

Four elementary power series that are of widespread use are

(a) The geometric series

$$\frac{1}{1+x} = 1 - x + x^2 - x^3 + \ldots + (-1)^n x^n + \ldots \quad (-1 < x < 1) \qquad \textbf{(6.15)}$$

(b) The binomial series

$$(1+x)^r = 1 + \binom{r}{1}x + \binom{r}{2}x^2 + \binom{r}{3}x^3 + \ldots + \binom{r}{n}x^n + \ldots \quad (-1 < x < 1) \qquad \textbf{(6.16)}$$

where

$$\binom{r}{n} = \frac{r(r-1)\ldots(r-n+1)}{1\cdot 2\cdot 3\cdot \ldots \cdot n}$$

is the binomial coefficient.

In series (6.16) r is any real number. When r is a positive integer, N say, the series terminates at the term x^N and we have the binomial expansion discussed in Chapter 1. When r is not a positive integer, the series does not terminate.

We can see that setting $r = -1$ gives

$$(1+x)^{-1} = \frac{1}{1+x} = 1 + \frac{(-1)}{1}x + \frac{(-1)(-2)}{1\cdot 2}x^2 + \frac{(-1)(-2)(-3)}{1\cdot 2\cdot 3}x^3 + \ldots$$

which simplifies to the geometric series

$$\frac{1}{1+x} = 1 - x + x^2 - x^3 + \ldots$$

So the geometric series may be thought of as a special case of the binomial series.

Comment (The series is often written as $(1+x)^{-1} = 1 - x + x^2 - x^3 + O(x^4)$, where $O(x^4)$ means terms involving powers of x greater than or equal to 4.)

Similarly,

$$(1+x)^{-2} = 1 + \frac{(-2)}{1}x + \frac{(-2)(-3)}{1\cdot 2}x^2 + \frac{(-2)(-3)(-4)}{1\cdot 2\cdot 3}x^3 + \ldots$$

which simplifies to the arithmetical-geometric series

$$\frac{1}{(1+x)^2} = 1 - 2x + 3x^2 - 4x^3 + \ldots$$

(Compare Exercises 6.6.4, Question 42.)

(c) The exponential series

$$e^x = 1 + \frac{x}{1!} + \frac{x^2}{2!} + \frac{x^3}{3!} + \ldots + \frac{x^n}{n!} + \ldots \quad (\text{all } x) \qquad \textbf{(6.17)}$$

We saw in Example 6.22 that the number e is defined by

$$e = \lim_{n\to\infty}\left(1 + \frac{1}{n}\right)^n$$

Similarly, the function e^x is defined by

$$e^x = \lim_{n\to\infty}\left(1 + \frac{x}{n}\right)^n$$

(or, equivalently, by $\lim_{n\to\infty}(1 + \frac{1}{n})^{nx}$).

Using the binomial expansion, we have

$$e^x = \lim_{n\to\infty}\left\{1 + \frac{n}{1}\left(\frac{x}{n}\right) + \frac{n(n-1)}{1\cdot 2}\left(\frac{x}{n}\right)^2 + \frac{n(n-1)(n-2)}{1\cdot 2\cdot 3}\left(\frac{x}{n}\right)^3 + \ldots\right\}$$

$$= \lim_{n\to\infty}\left\{1 + \frac{1}{1}x + \frac{(1-\frac{1}{n})}{1\cdot 2}x^2 + \frac{(1-\frac{1}{n})(1-\frac{2}{n})}{1\cdot 2\cdot 3}x^3 + \ldots\right\}$$

$$= 1 + \frac{x}{1!} + \frac{x^2}{2!} + \frac{x^3}{3!} + \ldots$$

So we see the connection between the binomial and exponential series.

(d) The logarithmic series

$$\ln(1 + x) = x - \frac{x^2}{2} + \frac{x^3}{3} - \frac{x^4}{4} + \ldots + (-1)^n\frac{x^{n+1}}{n+1} + \ldots \quad (-1 < x \leqslant 1) \qquad \textbf{(6.18)}$$

The logarithmic function is the inverse function of the exponential function, so that

$$y = \ln(1 + x)$$

implies $1 + x = e^y = \lim_{n\to\infty}\left(1 + \frac{y}{n}\right)^n$.

Unscrambling the limit to solve for y gives

$$y = \lim_{n\to\infty}\{n[(1 + x)^{1/n} - 1]\}$$

Using the binomial expansion again gives

$$y = \lim_{n\to\infty}\left\{n\left[\frac{\frac{1}{n}}{1}x + \frac{\frac{1}{n}(\frac{1}{n}-1)}{1\cdot 2}x^2 + \frac{\frac{1}{n}(\frac{1}{n}-1)(\frac{1}{n}-2)}{1\cdot 2\cdot 3}x^3 + \ldots\right]\right\}$$

$$= x - \frac{x^2}{2} + \frac{x^3}{3} - \frac{x^4}{4} + \ldots$$

Thus we see the connection between the binomial and logarithmic series. Note that taking $x = 1$ in series (6.18) we have the result

$$\sum_{k=1}^{\infty} \frac{1}{k}(-1)^{k+1} = \ln 2$$

used in Section 6.6.3.

A summary of the standard series introduced together with some other useful series deduced from them is given in Figure 6.13. Note that, using the series expansions for e^x, $\sin x$ and $\cos x$ given in the figure, we can demonstrate the validity of Euler's formula

$$e^{jx} = \cos x + j \sin x$$

introduced in equation (3.9). The radius of convergence of all these series may be determined using d'Alembert's test.

Figure 6.13 Table of some useful series.

$$\frac{1}{1+x} = 1 - x + x^2 - x^3 + \ldots + (-1)^n x^n + \ldots \quad (-1 < x < 1)$$

$$\frac{1}{1-x} = 1 + x + x^2 + x^3 + \ldots + x^n + \ldots \quad (-1 < x < 1)$$

$$(1+x)^r = 1 + \binom{r}{1}x + \binom{r}{2}x^2 + \binom{r}{3}x^3 + \ldots + \binom{r}{n}x^n + \ldots \quad (-1 < x < 1)$$

$$\ln(1+x) = x - \frac{x^2}{2} + \frac{x^3}{3} - \frac{x^4}{4} + \ldots + (-1)^n \frac{x^{n+1}}{n+1} + \ldots \quad (-1 < x \leqslant 1)$$

$$-\ln(1-x) = x + \frac{x^2}{2} + \frac{x^3}{3} + \frac{x^4}{4} + \ldots + \frac{x^{n+1}}{n+1} + \ldots \quad (-1 \leqslant x < 1)$$

$$\ln\frac{1+x}{1-x} = 2\left(x + \frac{x^3}{3} + \frac{x^5}{5} + \ldots + \frac{x^{2n+1}}{2n+1} \ldots\right) \quad (-1 < x < 1)$$

$$e^x = 1 + \frac{x}{1!} + \frac{x^2}{2!} + \frac{x^3}{3!} + \ldots + \frac{x^n}{n!} + \ldots \quad \text{(all } x)$$

$$e^{-x} = 1 - \frac{x}{1!} + \frac{x^2}{2!} - \frac{x^3}{3!} + \frac{x^4}{4!} + \ldots + (-1)^n \frac{x^n}{n!} + \ldots \quad \text{(all } x)$$

$$\cosh x = 1 + \frac{x^2}{2!} + \frac{x^4}{4!} + \frac{x^6}{6!} + \ldots + \frac{x^{2n}}{(2n)!} + \ldots \quad \text{(all } x)$$

$$\sinh x = x + \frac{x^3}{3!} + \frac{x^5}{5!} + \frac{x^7}{7!} + \ldots + \frac{x^{2n+1}}{(2n+1)!} + \ldots \quad \text{(all } x)$$

$$\cos x = 1 - \frac{x^2}{2!} + \frac{x^4}{4!} - \frac{x^6}{6!} + \ldots + (-1)^n \frac{x^{2n}}{(2n)!} + \ldots \quad \text{(all } x)$$

$$\sin x = x - \frac{x^3}{3!} + \frac{x^5}{5!} - \frac{x^7}{7!} + \ldots + (-1)^n \frac{x^{2n+1}}{(2n+1)!} + \ldots \quad \text{(all } x)$$

(*Note*: In the last two series x is an angle measured in radians.)

Example 6.30 Obtain the power series expansions of

(a) $\dfrac{1}{\sqrt{(1-x^2)}}$ (b) $\dfrac{1}{(1-x)(1+3x)}$ (c) $\dfrac{\ln(1+x)}{1+x}$

Solution (a) Using the binomial series (6.16) with $n = -\frac{1}{2}$ gives

$$\frac{1}{\sqrt{(1+x)}} = (1+x)^{-1/2}$$

$$= 1 + \frac{(-\frac{1}{2})}{1!}x + \frac{(-\frac{1}{2})(-\frac{3}{2})}{2!}x^2 + \frac{(-\frac{1}{2})(-\frac{3}{2})(-\frac{5}{2})}{3!}x^3 + \dots \quad (-1 < x < 1)$$

Now replacing x with $-x^2$ gives the required result

$$\frac{1}{\sqrt{(1-x^2)}} = 1 + \frac{(\frac{1}{2})}{1!}x^2 + \frac{(\frac{1}{2})(\frac{3}{2})}{2!}x^4 + \frac{(\frac{1}{2})(\frac{3}{2})(\frac{5}{2})}{3!}x^6 + \dots \quad (-1 < x < 1)$$

$$= 1 + \frac{1}{2}x^2 + \frac{1\cdot 3}{2\cdot 4}x^4 + \frac{1\cdot 3\cdot 5}{2\cdot 4\cdot 6}x^6 + \dots \quad (-1 < x < 1)$$

(b) Expressed in partial fractions

$$\frac{1}{(1-x)(1+3x)} = \frac{\frac{1}{4}}{1-x} + \frac{\frac{3}{4}}{1+3x}$$

From the table of Figure 6.13

$$\frac{1}{1-x} = 1 + x + x^2 + x^3 + \dots + x^n + \dots \quad (-1 < x < 1)$$

and replacing x by $3x$ in (6.15) gives

$$\frac{1}{1+3x} = 1 - (3x) + (3x)^2 - (3x)^3 + \dots + (-1)^n(3x)^n + \dots \quad (-\tfrac{1}{3} < x < \tfrac{1}{3})$$

Thus

$$\frac{1}{(1-x)(1+3x)}$$

$$= \tfrac{1}{4}[1 + x + x^2 + x^3 + \dots] + \tfrac{3}{4}[1 - 3x + 9x^2 - 27x^3 + \dots] \quad (-\tfrac{1}{3} < x < \tfrac{1}{3})$$

$$= 1 - 2x + 7x^2 - 20x^3 + \dots + \tfrac{1}{4}(1 + (-1)^n 3^{n+1})x^n + \dots \quad (-\tfrac{1}{3} < x < \tfrac{1}{3})$$

(c) Using the series for $\ln(1 + x)$ and $(1 + x)^{-1}$ from (6.18) and (6.15),

$$\frac{\ln(1+x)}{1+x} = (x - \tfrac{1}{2}x^2 + \tfrac{1}{3}x^3 - \tfrac{1}{4}x^4 + \dots)(1 - x + x^2 - x^3 + \dots)$$

$$= x - (1 + \tfrac{1}{2})x^2 + (1 + \tfrac{1}{2} + \tfrac{1}{3})x^3 - (1 + \tfrac{1}{2} + \tfrac{1}{3} + \tfrac{1}{4})x^4 + \dots$$

$$(-1 < x < 1)$$

There is no separate command for power series expansion in either MATLAB or MAPLE. However, in MAPLE the command `series` is more general and can cope with many situations; it does not tell us how the series is constructed but may be used for checking answers. As illustrations, for Example 6.30(a) the command

```
series(1/sqrt(1 - x^2), x = 0);
```

returns the answer

$$1 + \frac{1}{2}x^2 + \frac{3}{8}x^4 + \frac{5}{16}x^6 + O(x^8)$$

and for Example 6.30(c) the command

```
series(ln(1 + x)/(1 + x), x = 0);
```

returns the answer

$$x - \frac{3}{2}x^2 + \frac{11}{6}x^3 - \frac{25}{12}x^4 + \frac{137}{60}x^5 + O(x^6)$$

Making use of the `maple` command the `series` command may be used in MATLAB's Symbolic Math Toolbox. Check that the commands

```
syms x
maple('series((1/sqrt(1 - x^2), x = 0))')
```

return the same answer for Example 6.30(a).

Power series are examples of Maclaurin series dealt with later in Section 9.4.2. They can be obtained using the `taylor` command `taylor(f,n)`. For example, the first five terms of the series expansion for Example 6.30(b) are determined by the commands

```
syms x
f = 1/((1 - x)*(1 + 3*x));
taylor(f,5);
pretty(ans)
```

as

$$1 - 2x + 7x^2 - 20x^3 + 61x^4$$

In MAPLE the commands

```
series(1/((1 - x)*(1 + 3*x)), x = 0); and
taylor(1/((1 - x)*(1 + 3*x)), x = 0);
```

produce the answer

$$1 - 2x + 7x^2 - 20x^3 + 61x^4 - 182x^5 + O(x^6)$$

The inverse process of expressing the sum of a power series in terms of the elementary functions is often difficult or impossible, but when it can be achieved it usually results in dramatic simplification of a practical problem.

Example 6.31 Sum the series

(a) $1^2 + 2^2x + 3^2x^2 + 4^2x^3 + 5^2x^4 + \dots$ (b) $1 + \dfrac{x}{2!} + \dfrac{x^2}{4!} + \dfrac{x^3}{6!} + \dfrac{x^4}{8!} + \dots$

Solution (a) Set

$$S = 1^2 + 2^2x + 3^2x^2 + 4^2x^3 + 5^2x^4 + \dots + (n+1)^2x^n + \dots$$

Then

$$xS = 1^2x + 2^2x^2 + 3^2x^3 + 4^2x^4 + \dots + n^2x^n + \dots$$

and subtracting this from S gives

$$\begin{aligned}(1-x)S &= 1^2 + (2^2 - 1^2)x + (3^2 - 2^2)x^2 + (4^2 - 3^2)x^3 + \dots + [(n+1)^2 - n^2]x^n + \dots \\ &= 1 + 3x + 5x^2 + 7x^3 + \dots + (2n+1)x^n + \dots \\ &= (1 + x + x^2 + x^3 + \dots + x^n \dots) + 2(x + 2x^2 + 3x^3 + \dots + nx^n + \dots) \\ &= (1 + x + x^2 + x^3 + \dots + x^n + \dots) + 2x(1 + 2x + 3x^2 + 4x^3 + \dots \\ &\quad + nx^{n-1} + \dots)\end{aligned}$$

The first bracket is a geometric series of ratio x and sums to $\dfrac{1}{1-x}$, $|x| < 1$.

The second bracket is an arithmetico-geometric series of ratio x and sums to $\dfrac{1}{(1-x)^2}$, $|x| < 1$ (see Exercises 6.6.4, question 42). Thus

$$(1-x)S = \frac{1}{1-x} + \frac{2x}{(1-x)^2} = \frac{1+x}{(1-x)^2}$$

and

$$S = \frac{1+x}{(1-x)^2} \quad (-1 < x < 1)$$

(b) Summing this series relies on recognizing its similarity to the series for the hyperbolic cosine:

$$\cosh x = 1 + \frac{x^2}{2!} + \frac{x^4}{4!} + \frac{x^6}{6!} + \dots \quad (-\infty < x < \infty)$$

Replacing x by $\sqrt{x}$ gives

$$\cosh \sqrt{x} = 1 + \frac{x}{2!} + \frac{x^2}{4!} + \frac{x^3}{6!} + \dots \quad (-\infty < x < \infty)$$

and thus the series is summed.

Example 6.32 Sum the series

$$\text{(a)}\ S(\lambda) = \sum_{r=0}^{\infty} r\frac{\lambda^r e^{-\lambda}}{r!} \qquad (b)\ T(\lambda) = \sum_{0}^{\infty} r^2 \frac{\lambda^r e^{-\lambda}}{r!}$$

and show that

$$T(\lambda) - [S(\lambda)]^2 = \lambda$$

Solution (a) By re-writing $S(\lambda)$ in the form

$$S(\lambda) = \lambda \sum_{r=1}^{\infty} \frac{\lambda^{r-1}}{(r-1)!} e^{-\lambda}$$

and setting $n = r - 1$ we have

$$S(\lambda) = \lambda \sum_{n=0}^{\infty} \frac{\lambda^n}{n!} e^{-\lambda} = \lambda e^{-\lambda} \sum_{n=0}^{\infty} \frac{\lambda^n}{n!}$$

$$= \lambda e^{-\lambda} e^{\lambda}, \text{ using the result 6.7.2 (c)}$$

$$= \lambda$$

(b) Similarly $T(\lambda) = \sum_{r=0}^{\infty} \frac{r(r-1)+r}{r!} \lambda^r e^{-\lambda}$

$$= \sum_{r=0}^{\infty} \left[\frac{1}{(r-2)!} + \frac{1}{(r-1)!} \right] \lambda^r e^{-\lambda}$$

$$= \lambda^2 \sum_{r=2}^{\infty} \frac{\lambda^{r-2}}{(r-2)!} e^{-\lambda} + \lambda \sum_{r=1}^{\infty} \frac{\lambda^{r-1}}{(r-1)!} e^{-\lambda}$$

$$= \lambda^2 e^{\lambda} e^{-\lambda} + \lambda e^{-\lambda} e^{\lambda}$$

$$= \lambda^2 + \lambda$$

Hence

$$T(\lambda) - S(\lambda)^2 = \lambda$$

These results show that mean and variance of Poisson probability distribution both equal λ (see Section 13.5.2).

Series may be summed in MATLAB using the `symsum` command. For Example (6.31) the series sums are

```
syms x k
Sa = symsum(k*x^(k - 1),k,1,inf)
```

giving

```
Sa = 1/(x - 1)^2
Sb = symsum(x^(k - 1)/'factorial(2*(k - 1))',k,1,inf)
```

giving

```
Sb = cosh(x^(1/2))
```

Commands in MAPLE are the same except for minor syntax differences; use can be made of `(2*(k - 1))!` So the command

```
sum('x^(k - 1)/(2*(k - 1))!', 'k' = 1..infinity);
```

returns the answer `cosh(√x)`.

6.7.3 Exercises

Check your answers using MATLAB or MAPLE whenever possible.

50 For what values of x are the following series convergent?

(a) $\sum_{n=1}^{\infty} (2n - 1)x^n$

(b) $\sum_{n=0}^{\infty} (-1)^n \dfrac{x^{2n}}{(2n + 1)!}$

(c) $\sum_{n=1}^{\infty} \dfrac{x^n}{n(n + 1)}$

(d) $\sum_{n=1}^{\infty} \dfrac{n^2}{1 + n^2} x^n$

51 From known series deduce the following:

(a) $\dfrac{1}{1 + x^2} = 1 - x^2 + x^4 - x^6 + \dots$

(b) $\frac{1}{2} \ln \dfrac{1 + x}{1 - x} = x + \frac{1}{3}x^3 + \frac{1}{5}x^5 + \frac{1}{7}x^7 + \dots$

(c) $\dfrac{1}{(1 + x)^2} = 1 - 2x + 3x^2 - 4x^3 + 5x^4 - \dots$

(d) $\sqrt{(1 - x)} = 1 - \frac{1}{2}x - \frac{1}{8}x^2 + \frac{1}{16}x^3 - \frac{5}{128}x^4 - \dots$

(e) $\dfrac{1}{(1 - 2x)(2 + x)} = \frac{1}{2} + \frac{3}{4}x + \frac{13}{8}x^2 + \frac{51}{16}x^3 + \dots$

(f) $\dfrac{1}{(1 - x)(1 + x^2)} = 1 + x + x^4 + x^5 + \dots$

In each case give the general term and the radius of convergence.

52 Calculate the binomial coefficients

(a) $\dbinom{5}{2}$ (b) $\dbinom{-2}{3}$

(c) $\dbinom{1/2}{3}$ (d) $\dbinom{-1/2}{4}$

53 From known series deduce the following (the general term is not required):

(a) $\tan x = x + \frac{1}{3}x^3 + \frac{2}{15}x^5 + \dots$

(b) $\cos^2 x = 1 - \dfrac{2x^2}{2!} + \dfrac{2^3x^4}{4!} - \dfrac{2^5x^6}{6!} + \dots$

(c) $e^x \cos x = 1 + x - \dfrac{2x^3}{3!} - \dfrac{2^2x^4}{4!} - \dfrac{2^2x^5}{5!} + \dots$

(d) $\ln(1 + \sin x) = x - \frac{1}{2}x^2 + \frac{1}{6}x^3 + \frac{1}{12}x^4 + \dots$

54 Show that

$$\frac{1}{1 - x} = 1 + x + x^2 + \dots + x^{n-1} + \frac{x^n}{1 - x} \quad (x \neq 1)$$

Hence derive a polynomial approximation to $(1 - x)^{-1}$ with an error that, in modulus, is less than 0.5×10^{-4} for $0 \leq x \leq 0.25$.

Using nested multiplication, calculate from your approximation the reciprocal of 0.84 to 4dp, and compare your answer with the value given by your calculator. How many multiplications are needed in this case?

55 Find the sums of the following power series:

(a) $\sum_{k=0}^{\infty}(-1)^k 2^k x^{2k}$

(b) $1 + \frac{1}{2}x + \frac{1\cdot 3}{2\cdot 4}x^2 + \frac{1\cdot 3\cdot 5}{2\cdot 4\cdot 6}x^3 + \frac{1\cdot 3\cdot 5\cdot 7}{2\cdot 4\cdot 6\cdot 8}x^4 + \dots$

(c) $\sum_{k=1}^{\infty}\frac{x^k}{k(k+1)}$

(d) $\frac{1}{2}x^2 + \frac{2}{3}x^3 + \frac{3}{4}x^4 + \frac{4}{5}x^5 + \dots$

56 A regular polygon of n sides is inscribed in a circle of unit diameter. Show that its perimeter p_n is given by

$$p_n = n\sin\frac{\pi}{n}$$

Using the series expansion for sine, prove that

$$\pi = p_n + \frac{\pi^3}{3!}\frac{1}{n^2} - \frac{\pi^5}{5!}\frac{1}{n^4} + \dots$$

and deduce that

$$\pi = \frac{1}{3}(4p_{2n} - p_n) + \frac{1}{4}\frac{\pi^5}{5!}\frac{1}{n^4} + \dots$$

Given $p_{12} = 3.1058$ and $p_{24} = 3.1326$, use this result to obtain a better estimate of π.

6.8 Functions of a real variable

So far in this chapter we have concentrated on sequences and series. The terms of a sequence may be seen as defining a function whose domain is a subset of integers, such as N. We now turn to the fundamental properties that are essential to mathematical modelling and problem-solving, but we shall also be developing some basic mathematics that is necessary for later chapters.

6.8.1 Limit of a function of a real variable

The notion of limit can be extended in a natural way to include functions of a real variable:

> A function $f(x)$ is said to approach a limit l as x approaches the value a if, given any small positive quantity ε, it is possible to find a positive number δ such that $|f(x) - l| < \varepsilon$ for all x satisfying $0 < |x - a| < \delta$.

Less formally, this means that we can make the value of $f(x)$ as close as we please to l by taking x sufficiently close to a. Note that, using the formal definition, there is no need to evaluate $f(a)$; indeed, $f(a)$ may or may not equal l. The limiting value of f as $x \to a$ depends only on nearby values!

Example 6.33 Using a calculator, examine the values of $f(x)$ near $x = 0$ where

$$f(x) = \frac{x}{1 - \sqrt{(1+x)}}, \quad x \neq 0$$

What is the value of $\lim_{x\to 0} f(x)$?

Solution Note that $f(x)$ is not defined where $x = 0$. At nearby values of x we can calculate $f(x)$, and some values are shown in Figure 6.14.

Figure 6.14
Values of $f(x)$ to 6dp.

x	−0.1	−0.01	−0.001	0.001	0.01	0.1
$f(x)$	−1.948 683	−1.994 987	−1.999 500	−2.000 500	−2.004 988	−2.048 809

It seems that as x gets close to the value of 0, $f(x)$ gets close to the value of −2. Indeed, it can be proved that for $0 < |x| < 2\varepsilon - \varepsilon^2$, $|f(x) + 2| < \varepsilon$, so that

$$\lim_{x \to 0} f(x) = -2.$$

Comment Notice that this is a rather artificial example to illustrate the idea and theory. In this case we can rewrite the formula for $f(x)$ to give

$$f(x) = \frac{x(1 + \sqrt{(1 + x)})}{(1 - \sqrt{(1 + x)})(1 + \sqrt{(1 + x)})}$$

which gives

$$f(x) = \frac{x(1 + \sqrt{(1 + x)})}{1 - (1 + x)} = -(1 + \sqrt{(1 + x)})$$

It is clear from this that $f(x) \to -2$ as $x \to 0$.

The elementary rules for limits (listed in Section 6.5.2) carry over from those of sequences, and these enable us to evaluate many limits by reduction to standard cases. Some common standard limits are

(i) $\lim_{x \to a} \dfrac{x^r - a^r}{x - a} = ra^{r-1}$, where r is a real number

(ii) $\lim_{x \to 0} \dfrac{\sin x}{x} = 1$, where x is in radians

(iii) $\lim_{h \to 0} (1 + xh)^{1/h} = e^x$

These results can be deduced from the results of Section 6.7.2. For instance, consider $x^r - a^r$. Since $x \to a$, set $x = a + h$. Then as $x \to a$, $h \to 0$. We have

$$x^r - a^r = a^r\left(1 + \frac{h}{a}\right)^r - a^r \quad (a \neq 0)$$

Expanding $(1 + h/a)^r$ by the binomial series (6.16), we have

$$x^r - a^r = \frac{r}{1!}ha^{r-1} + \frac{r(r-1)}{2!}h^2a^{r-2} + \frac{r(r-1)(r-2)}{3!}h^3a^{r-3} + \ldots$$

But $x - a = h$, so

$$\frac{x^r - a^r}{x - a} = ra^{r-1} + \frac{r(r-1)}{2!}ha^{r-2} + \ldots$$

and letting $h \to 0$ yields the result (i)

$$\lim_{x\to a}\frac{x^r - a^r}{x - a} = ra^{r-1}$$

(When $a = 0$, the result is obtained trivially.)

The result (ii) is obtained even more simply. The series expansion

$$\sin x = x - \frac{x^3}{3!} + \frac{x^5}{5!} - \ldots$$

gives

$$\lim_{x\to 0}\frac{\sin x}{x} = 1$$

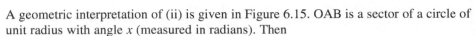

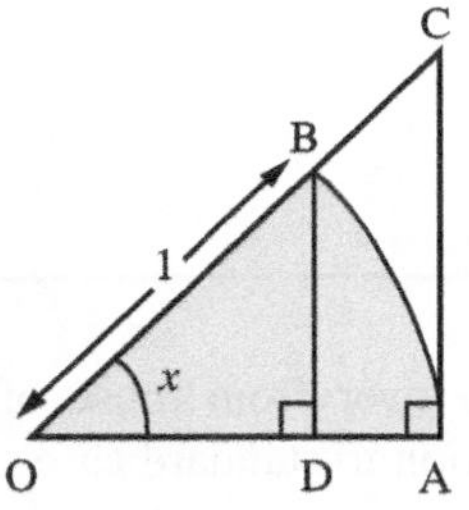

Figure 6.15 Geometric interpretation of $\lim_{x\to 0}\frac{\sin x}{x} = 1$.

A geometric interpretation of (ii) is given in Figure 6.15. OAB is a sector of a circle of unit radius with angle x (measured in radians). Then

the area of ΔOBD < area of sector OBA < area of ΔOCA

Algebraically, we have

$$\tfrac{1}{2}\sin x\cos x < \tfrac{1}{2}x < \tfrac{1}{2}\tan x$$

Considering $x > 0$, we may write this as

$$1 < \frac{\sin x}{x} < \frac{1}{\cos x}$$

As $x \to 0$, $\cos x \to 1$, so that $\frac{\sin x}{x} \to 1$ also.

The result (iii) is obtained from a binomial series:

$$(1 + xh)^{1/h} = 1 + \frac{1}{1!}\frac{1}{h}xh + \frac{1}{2!}\frac{1}{h}\left(\frac{1}{h} - 1\right)(xh)^2 + \frac{1}{3!}\frac{1}{h}\left(\frac{1}{h} - 1\right)\left(\frac{1}{h} - 2\right)(xh)^3 + \ldots$$

$$= 1 + \frac{x}{1!} + \frac{x^2(1-h)}{2!} + \frac{x^3(1-h)(1-2h)}{3!} + \ldots$$

and, as $h \to 0$,

$$(1 + xh)^{1/h} \to 1 + \frac{x}{1!} + \frac{x^2}{2!} + \frac{x^3}{3!} + \ldots = \mathrm{e}^x$$

Example 6.34 Evaluate the following limits:

(a) $\lim_{x\to 0} \dfrac{\sqrt{(1+x^2)}-1}{x^2}$ (b) $\lim_{x\to 0} \dfrac{1-\cos x}{x^2}$

Solution (a) Method 1: Expand $\sqrt{(1+x^2)}$ by the binomial series (6.16), giving

$$\sqrt{(1+x^2)} = (1+x^2)^{1/2} = 1 + \tfrac{1}{2}x^2 - \tfrac{1}{8}x^4 + \dots$$

so that

$$\frac{\sqrt{(1+x^2)}-1}{x^2} = \frac{\tfrac{1}{2}x^2 - \tfrac{1}{8}x^4 + \dots}{x^2} = \tfrac{1}{2} - \tfrac{1}{8}x^2 + \dots$$

Thus

$$\lim_{x\to 0} \frac{\sqrt{(1+x^2)}-1}{x^2} = \tfrac{1}{2}$$

Method 2: Multiply numerator and denominator by $\sqrt{(1+x^2)}+1$, giving

$$\frac{[\sqrt{(1+x^2)}-1][\sqrt{(1+x^2)}+1]}{x^2[\sqrt{(1+x^2)}+1]} = \frac{(1+x^2)-1}{x^2[\sqrt{(1+x^2)}+1]} = \frac{1}{\sqrt{(1+x^2)}+1}$$

Now let $x \to 0$, to obtain

$$\lim_{x\to 0} \frac{\sqrt{(1+x^2)}-1}{x^2} = \tfrac{1}{2}$$

(b) Method 1: Replace $\cos x$ by its power series expansion (see Figure 6.13),

$$\cos x = 1 - \frac{x^2}{2!} + \frac{x^4}{4!} - \frac{x^6}{6!} - \dots$$

giving

$$\frac{1-\cos x}{x^2} = \frac{x^2/2! - x^4/4! + x^6/6! - \dots}{x^2} = \frac{1}{2!} - \frac{x^2}{4!} + \frac{x^4}{6!} - \dots$$

Thus

$$\lim_{x\to 0} \frac{1-\cos x}{x^2} = \tfrac{1}{2}$$

Method 2: Using the half-angle formula for $\cos x$ (see 2.7d), we have

$$1 - \cos x = 2\sin^2 \tfrac{1}{2}x$$

so

$$\frac{1-\cos x}{x^2} = \frac{2\sin^2 \tfrac{1}{2}x}{x^2} = 2\left(\frac{\sin \tfrac{1}{2}x}{x}\right)^2 = \frac{1}{2}\left(\frac{\sin\varphi}{\varphi}\right)^2 \quad \text{where } \varphi = \tfrac{1}{2}x$$

On letting $x \to 0$, we have $\varphi \to 0$ and $(\sin\varphi)/\varphi \to 1$, so that

$$\frac{1-\cos x}{x^2} \to \tfrac{1}{2}$$

Example 6.35

The volume of a sphere of radius a is $4\pi a^3/3$. Show that the volume of material used in constructing a hollow sphere of interior radius a and exterior radius $a+t$ is

$$V = 4\pi(3a^2t + 3at^2 + t^3)/3$$

Deduce that the surface area of the sphere of radius a is $S = 4\pi a^2$ and show that it is equal to the area of the curved surface of the enclosing cylinder.

Solution

$$V = \frac{4\pi}{3}[(a+t)^3 - a^3] = \frac{4\pi}{3}[a^3 + 3a^2t + 3at^2 + t^3 - a^3]$$

$$= \frac{4\pi}{3}(3a^2t + 3at^2 + t^3)$$

The volume V is approximately the surface area S of the interior sphere times the thickness t. That is

$$V = St + O(t^2)$$

Hence

$$S = V/t + O(t) = \frac{4\pi}{3}(3a^2 + 3at + t^2) + O(t)$$

Now proceeding to the limit as $t \to 0$, gives

$$S = 4\pi a^2$$

The radius of the enclosing cylinder is a and its height is $2a$ so that its curved surface area is

$$(2\pi a) \times (2a) = 4\pi a^2$$

as shown in Figure 6.16.

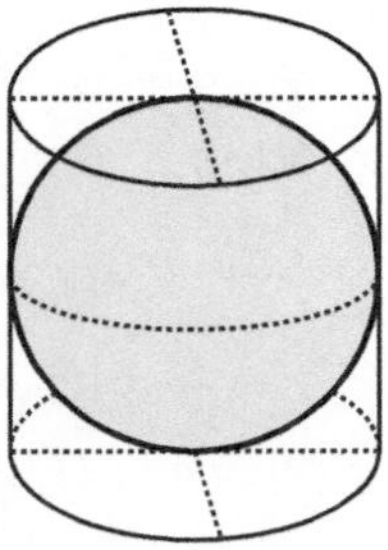

Figure 6.16 Enclosing cylinder in Example 6.35.

6.8.2 One-sided limits

In some applications we have to use one-sided limits, for example

$$\lim_{x\to 0+} \sqrt{x} = 0 \quad \text{(as } x \text{ tends to zero 'from above')}$$

In this example, $\lim_{x\to 0-} \sqrt{x}$ (as x tends to zero 'from below') does not exist, since no negative numbers are in the domain of $\sqrt{x}$. When we write

$$\lim_{x \to a} f(x) = l$$

we mean that

$$\lim_{x \to a-} f(x) = \lim_{x \to a+} f(x) = l$$

Example 6.36 Sketch the graph of the function $f(x)$ where

$$f(x) = \frac{\sqrt{(x^2 - x^3)}}{x}, \quad x \neq 0 \text{ and } x < 1$$

and show that $\lim_{x \to 0} f(x)$ does not exist.

Solution Notice that the function is not defined for $x = 0$. A sketch of the function is given for $-1 \leqslant x \leqslant 1$, $x \neq 0$ in Figure 6.17. From that diagram we see that $f(x) \to -1$ as $x \to 0$ from below and $f(x) \to +1$ as $x \to 0$ from above. Since the existence of a limit requires the same value whether we approach from above or below we deduce that $\lim_{x \to 0} f(x)$ does not exist.

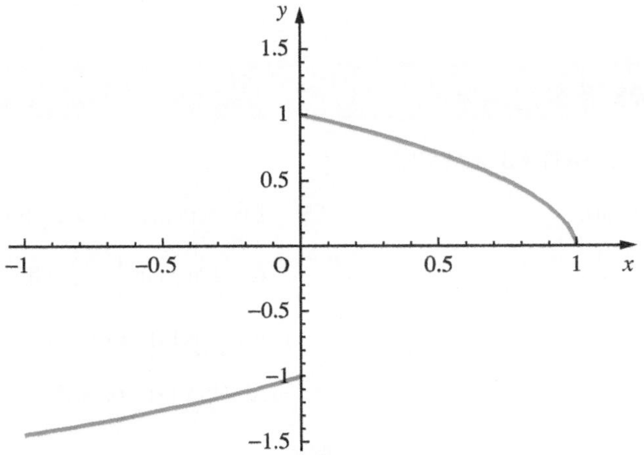

Figure 6.17 Graph of $y = \frac{\sqrt{(x^2 - x^3)}}{x}$.

Symbolically in MATLAB, limits are determined using the following commands:

$\lim_{x \to a} f(x)$ by `limit(f,x,a)` or `limit(f,a)`

$\lim_{x \to a^-} f(a)$ by `limit(f,x,a, 'left')`

and

$\lim_{x \to a^+} f(a)$ by `limit(f,x,a, 'right')`

MAPLE deals with the problem in the same way but with minor differences in syntax.

The limits of Example 6.34 may be evaluated as follows:

MATLAB

```
syms x
limit((sqrt(1 + x^2) -
1)/x^2,x,0)
```

MAPLE

```
limit((sqrt(1 + x^2) -
1)/x^2,x = 0);
```

giving *ans* = 1/2

MATLAB

```
limit((1 - cos(x))/
x^2,x,0)
```

MAPLE

```
limit((1 - cos(x))/
x^2,x = 0);
```

giving *ans* = 1/2

For Example 6.36 the left and right limits are determined as follows:

MATLAB

```
syms x
limit((x^2 - x^3)^(1/2)/
x,x,0, 'left')
```

MAPLE

```
limit((x^2 - x^3)^(1/2)/
x,x = 0, left);
```

giving *ans* = -1

MATLAB

```
limit((x^2 - x^3)^(1/2)/
x,x,0,'right')
```

MAPLE

```
limit((x^2 - x^3)^(1/2)/
x,x = 0, right)
```

giving *ans* = 1

Note: The command `sqrt` could also be used to represent the square root term.

6.8.3 Exercises

Check your answers using MATLAB or MAPLE.

57 Evaluate the following limits:

(a) $\lim_{x\to 0} \dfrac{\sqrt{(1+x)} - \sqrt{(1-x)}}{3x}$

(b) $\lim_{x\to 0} \dfrac{\cos x \sin x - x}{x^3}$

(c) $\lim_{x\to 0} \dfrac{\sin^{-1} 2x}{x}$

(d) $\lim_{x\to \pi/2} (\sec x - \tan x)$

58 Show that

$$\lim_{x\to\infty} f(x) = \lim_{y\to 0+} f\left(\frac{1}{y}\right)$$

Hence find

(a) $\lim_{x\to\infty} \dfrac{3x^2 - x - 2}{x^2 - 1}$

(b) $\lim_{x\to\infty} x(\sqrt{(1+x^2)} - x)$

59 Evaluate the following limits:

(a) $\lim_{x\to 0-} \tanh \dfrac{1}{x}$ (b) $\lim_{x\to 0+} \tanh \dfrac{1}{x}$

(c) $\lim_{x\to n-} \lfloor x \rfloor \quad (n \in \mathbb{Z})$

(d) $\lim_{x\to n+} \lfloor x \rfloor \quad (n \in \mathbb{Z})$

60 Draw (carefully) graphs of

(a) xe^{-x} (b) x^2e^{-x} (c) x^3e^{-x}

for $0 \leqslant x \leqslant 5$. Use the series expansion of e^x to prove that $x^n e^{-x} \to 0$ as $x \to \infty$ for all $n \in \mathbb{Z}$.

61 Use a calculator to evaluate the function $f(x) = x^x$ for $x = 1, 0.1, 0.01, \ldots, 0.000\,000\,001$. What do these calculations suggest about $\lim_{x\to 0+} f(x)$? Since $x^x = e^{x \ln x}$, the value of this limit is related to $\lim_{x\to 0+} (x \ln x)$. By setting $x = e^{-y}$ and using the results of Question 60, prove that $x^x \to 1$ as $x \to 0+$.

6.9 Continuity of functions of a real variable

In Chapter 2 we examined the properties of elementary functions. Often these were described by means of graphs. A property that is clear from the graphical representation of a function is that of **continuity**. Consider the two functions whose graphs are shown in Figure 6.18. For the function $f(x)$ we can draw the whole curve without lifting the pencil from the paper, but this is not possible for the function $g(x)$. The function $f(x)$ is said to be **continuous everywhere**, while $g(x)$ has a **discontinuity** at $x = 0$. In Section 2.8.3, we described several functions that are used to model practical problems and that have points of discontinuity similar to the function $g(x)$. The most important of these is Heaviside's unit function

$$H(x) = \begin{cases} 0 & (x < 0) \\ 1 & (x \geqslant 0) \end{cases}$$

which has a discontinuity at $x = 0$.

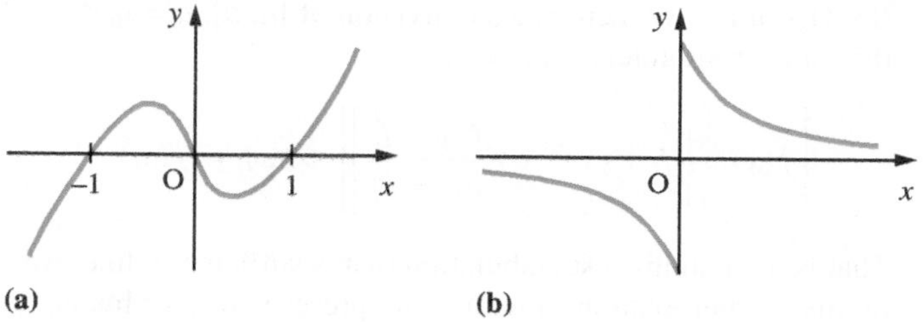

Figure 6.18 Graphs of the functions (a) $f(x) = x(x^2 - 1)$ and (b) $g(x) = \tan^{-1}(1/x)$, $x \neq 0$.

The formal mathematical definition of continuity for a function $f(x)$ defined in the neighbourhood of a point $x = x_0$ and at the point itself is that

$$f(x) \to f(x_0) \quad \text{as } x \to x_0$$

A function with this property is said to be **continuous at** $x = x_0$.

Continuous functions have some very special properties, which we shall now list.

6.9.1 Properties of continuous functions

If $f(x)$ is continuous in the interval $[a, b]$ then it has the following properties.

(a) $f(x)$ is a bounded function: there are numbers m and M such that

$$m < f(x) < M \quad \text{for all } x \in [a, b]$$

Any numbers satisfying this relation are called a **lower bound** and an **upper bound** respectively.

(b) $f(x)$ has a largest and a least value on $[a, b]$. The least value of $f(x)$ on $[a, b]$ is called the **minimum** of $f(x)$ on $[a, b]$, the largest value is the **maximum** of $f(x)$ on $[a, b]$ and the difference between the two is called the **oscillation** of $f(x)$ on $[a, b]$. This is illustrated in Figure 6.19.

(c) $f(x)$ takes every value between its least and its largest value somewhere between $x = a$ and $x = b$. This property is known as the **intermediate value theorem**.

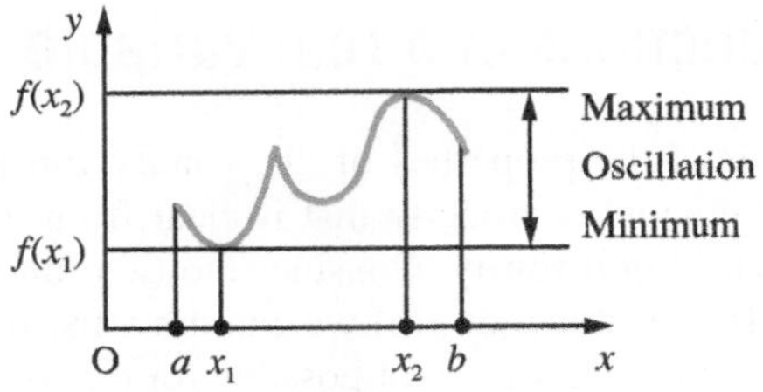

Figure 6.19
The oscillation of a function.

(d) If $a \leqslant x_1 \leqslant x_2 \leqslant x_3 \leqslant \ldots \leqslant x_n < b$, there is an $X \in [a, b]$ such that

$$f(X) = \frac{f(x_1) + f(x_2) + \ldots + f(x_n)}{n}$$

This property is known as the **average value theorem**.

(e) Given $\varepsilon > 0$, the interval $[a, b]$ can be divided into a number of intervals in each of which the oscillation of the function is less than ε.

(f) Given $\varepsilon > 0$, there is a subdivision of $[a, b]$, $a = x_0 < x_1 < x_2 < \ldots < x_n = b$, such that in each subinterval (x_i, x_{i+1})

$$\left| f(x) - \left[f_i + (x - x_i)\frac{f_{i+1} - f_i}{x_{i+1} - x_i} \right] \right| < \varepsilon, \; f_i = f(x_i)$$

That is, by making a subtabulation that is sufficiently fine, we can represent $f(x)$ locally by linear interpolation to within any prescribed error bound.

(g) Given $\varepsilon > 0$, $f(x)$ can be approximated on the interval $[a, b]$ by a polynomial of suitable degree such that

$$|f(x) - p_n(x)| < \varepsilon \quad \text{for } x \in [a, b]$$

This is known as the **Weierstrass theorem**. Note, however, that the theorem does not tell us how to obtain $p_n(x)$.

The properties of limits listed in Section 6.5.2 enable us to determine the continuity of functions formed by combining continuous functions. Thus if $f(x)$ and $g(x)$ are continuous functions then so are the functions

(a) $af(x)$, where a is a constant
(b) $f(x) + g(x)$
(c) $f(x)g(x)$
(d) $f(x)/g(x)$, except where $g(x) = 0$

Also the composite function $f(g(x))$ is continuous at x_0 if $g(x)$ is continuous at x_0 and $f(x)$ is continuous at $x = g(x_0)$.

Some of the properties of continuous functions are illustrated in Example 6.37 and in Exercises 6.9.4.

Example 6.37

Show that $f(x) = 2x/(1 + x^2)$ for $x \in \mathbb{R}$ is continuous on its whole domain. Find its maximum and minimum values and show that it attains every value between these extrema.

Figure 6.20
Graph of $2x/(1+x^2)$.

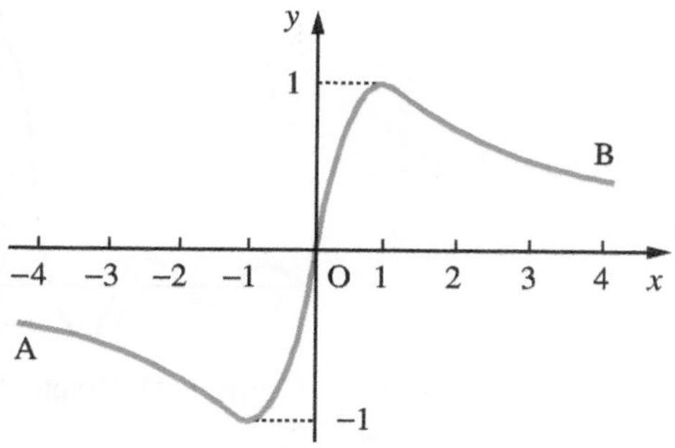

Solution The graph of the function is shown in Figure 6.20, from which we can see that the part shown is a continuous curve. That is to say, we can put a pencil at point A at the left-hand end of the graph and trace along the whole length of the curve to reach the point B at the right-hand end without lifting the pencil from the page. We can prove this more formally as follows. Select any point x_0 of the domain of the function. Then we have to show that $|f(x)-f(x_0)|$ can be made as small as we please by taking x sufficiently close to x_0. Now

$$\frac{2x}{1+x^2}-\frac{2x_0}{1+x_0^2}=\frac{2x(1+x_0^2)-2x_0(1+x^2)}{(1+x^2)(1+x_0^2)}=\frac{2(1-xx_0)(x-x_0)}{(1+x^2)(1+x_0^2)}$$

$$\to 0 \quad \text{as } x \to x_0$$

This implies that $f(x)$ is continuous at x_0, and since x_0 is any point of the domain, it follows that $f(x)$ is continuous for all x.

Then to show that the function takes a given value y we have to solve the equation $y=f(x)$ for x in terms of y. So that in this example

$$y=\frac{2x}{1+x^2} \quad \text{gives} \quad yx^2-2x+y=0$$

where we are now solving the equation for x in terms of y. Hence we obtain

$$x=\frac{1\pm\sqrt{(1-y^2)}}{y}, \qquad y\neq 0 \text{ and } -1\leqslant y\leqslant 1$$

This gives two values of x for each $y \in (-1, 1)$, $y \neq 0$. Clearly $y = 0$ is also attained for $x = 0$. The maximum and minimum values for y are 1 and −1 respectively, and the corresponding values of x are 1 and −1. Thus $f(x)$ is a continuous function on its domain, and it attains its maximum and minimum values and every value in between.

6.9.2 Continuous and discontinuous functions

The technique used to show that $f(x)$ is a continuous function in Example 6.37 can be used to show that polynomials, rational functions (except where the denominator is zero) and many transcendental functions are continuous on their domains. We frequently make use of the properties of continuous functions unconsciously in problem-solving! For example, in solving equations we trap the root between two points x_1 and x_2 where $f(x_1) < 0$ and $f(x_2) > 0$ and conclude that the root we seek lies between x_1 and x_2. The

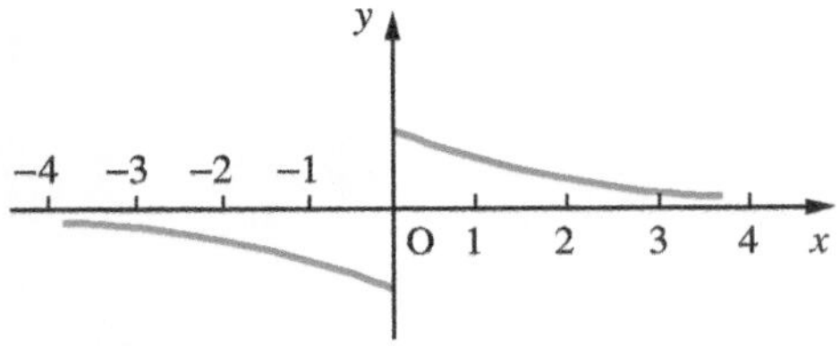

Figure 6.21 Graph of $\tan^{-1}(1/x)$, $x \neq 0$.

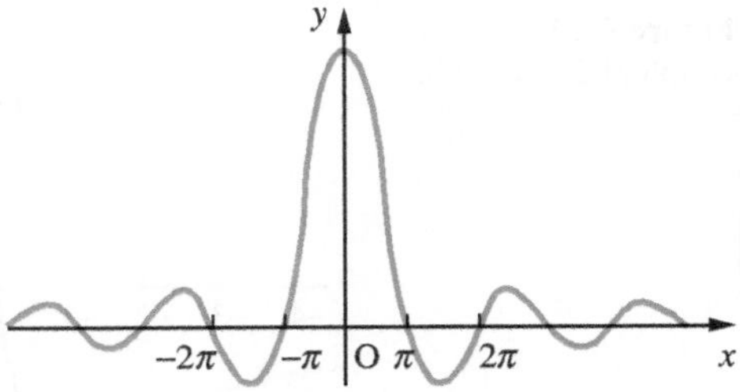

Figure 6.22 Graph of sinc $x = (\sin x)/x$.

need for continuity here is shown by the graph of $y = \tan^{-1}(1/x)$ (Figure 6.21). There is no value of x corresponding to $y = 0$, despite the facts that $\tan^{-1}(1/0.01)$ is positive and $\tan^{-1}[1/(-0.01)]$ is negative.

Similarly, when locating the maximum or minimum value of a function $y = f(x)$, in many practical situations we would be content with a solution that yields a value close to the true optimum value, and property (e) above tells us we can make that value as close as we please. Sometimes we use the continuity idea to fill in 'gaps' in function definitions. A simple example of this is $f(x) = (\sin x)/x$ for $x \neq 0$. This function is defined everywhere except at $x = 0$. We can extend it to include $x = 0$ by insisting that it be continuous at $x = 0$. Since $(\sin x)/x \to 1$ as $x \to 0$, defining $f(x)$ as

$$f(x) = \begin{cases} \dfrac{\sin x}{x} & (x \neq 0) \\ 1 & (x = 0) \end{cases} \tag{6.19}$$

yields a function with no 'gaps' in its domain. The function $f(x)$ in (6.19) is known as the **sinc function**; that is,

$$\text{sinc}\, x = \begin{cases} \dfrac{\sin x}{x} & (x \neq 0) \\ 1 & (x = 0) \end{cases}$$

and its graph is drawn in Figure 6.22. This function has important applications in engineering, particularly in digital signal analysis. See the chapter on Fourier transforms in the companion text *Advanced Modern Engineering Mathematics*.

Of course it is not always possible to fill in 'gaps' in function definitions. The function

$$g(x) = \frac{x}{\sin x} \quad (x \neq n\pi,\ n = 0, \pm 1, \pm 2, \ldots)$$

can have its domain extended to include the points $x = n\pi$, but it will always have a discontinuity at those points (except perhaps $x = 0$). Thus

$$f(x) = \begin{cases} \dfrac{x}{\sin x} & (x \neq n\pi,\ n = 0, \pm 1, \pm 2, \ldots) \\ 1 & (x = 0) \\ 0 & (x = n\pi,\ n = \pm 1, \pm 2, \ldots) \end{cases}$$

yields a function that is defined everywhere but is discontinuous at an infinite set of points.

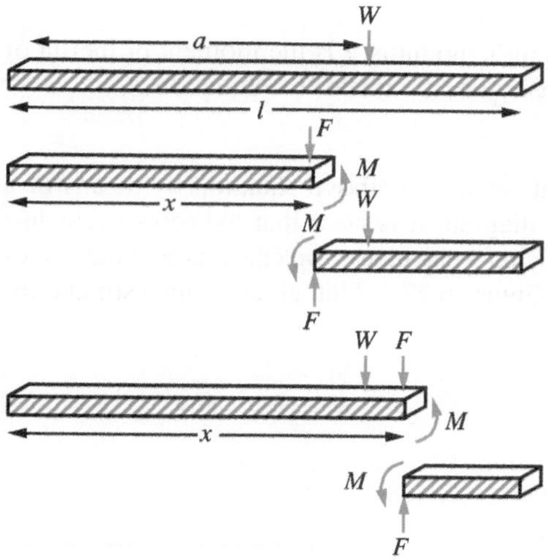

Figure 6.23 A beam, hinged at both ends, carrying a point load.

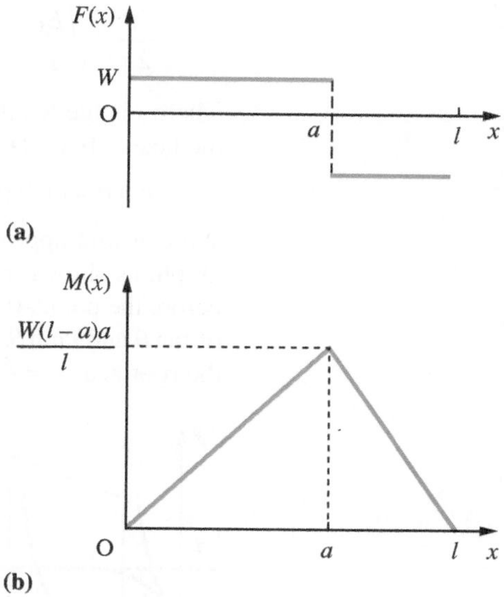

Figure 6.24 (a) The shear force and (b) the bending moment for a freely hinged beam.

In the analysis of practical problems we frequently use functions that have different formulae on different parts of their domain. For example, consider a beam of length l that is freely hinged at both ends and carries a concentrated load W at $x = a$, as shown in Figure 6.23. Then the shear force F is given by

$$F(x) = \begin{cases} W - Wa/l & (0 < x < a) \\ -Wa/l & (a \leqslant x < l) \end{cases}$$

and is sketched in Figure 6.24(a).

The bending moment M is

$$M(x) = \begin{cases} W(l - a)x/l & (0 < x \leqslant a) \\ W(l - x)a/l & (a \leqslant x < l) \end{cases}$$

and is sketched in Figure 6.24(b). (The terms 'shear force' and 'bending moment' are discussed in the next chapter.)

Notice here that F has a finite discontinuity at $x = a$ while M is continuous there.

6.9.3 Numerical location of zeros

Many practical engineering problems may involve the determination of the points at which a function takes a specific value (often zero) or the points at which it takes its maximum or minimum values. There are many different numerical procedures for solving such problems and we shall illustrate the technique by considering its application to the analysis of structural vibration.

Figure 6.25 A beam built in at one end and simply supported at the other.

This is a very common problem in engineering. To avoid resonance effects, it is necessary to calculate the natural frequencies of vibration of a structure. For a beam built in at one end and simply supported at the other, as shown in Figure 6.25, the natural frequencies are given by

$$\frac{\theta^2}{2\pi l^2}\sqrt{\frac{EI}{\rho}}$$

where l is the length of the beam, E is Young's modulus, I is the moment of inertia of the beam about its neutral axis, ρ is its density and θ satisfies the equation

$$\tan\theta = \tanh\theta$$

We can find approximate values for θ that satisfy the above equation by means of a graph, as shown in Figure 6.26. From the diagram it is clear that the roots occur just before the points $\theta = 0, \frac{5}{4}\pi, \frac{9}{4}\pi, \frac{13}{4}\pi, \ldots$. Using a calculator, we can compare the values of $\tan\theta$ and $\tanh\theta$, to produce the table of Figure 6.27, which gives us the estimate for the root near $\theta = \frac{5}{4}\pi$ as 3.925 ± 0.005.

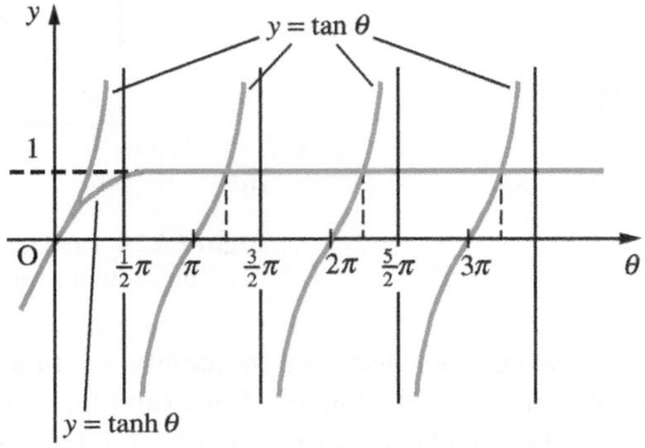

Figure 6.26 The roots of the equation $\tan\theta = \tanh\theta$.

θ	$\tan\theta$	$\tanh\theta$
3.90	0.9474	0.9992
3.91	0.9666	0.9992
3.92	0.9861	0.9992
3.93	1.0060	0.9992

Figure 6.27 Table of values.

If we require a more precise answer than this provides, we can resort to a finer subtabulation. In some problems this can be very tedious and time-consuming. A better strategy is to use an **interval-halving** or **bisection method**. We know that the root lies between $\theta_1 = 3.92$ and $\theta_2 = 3.93$. We work out the value of the functions at the midpoint of this interval, $\theta_3 = 3.925$, and determine whether the root lies between θ_1 and θ_3 or between θ_3 and θ_2. The process is then repeated on the subinterval that contains the root, and so on until sufficient precision is obtained.

The process is set out in tabular form in Figure 6.28. Note the renaming of the end points of the root-bracketing interval at each step, so that the interval under scrutiny is always denoted by $[\theta_1, \theta_2]$. After five applications we have $\theta = 3.926\,72 \pm (0.005/2^5)$.

Figure 6.28 Solution of $\tan\theta - \tanh\theta = 0$ by the bisection method.

θ_1	$f(\theta_1)$	θ_2	$f(\theta_2)$	θ_m	$f(\theta_m)$
3.92	−0.013 098	3.93	0.006 808	3.925	−0.003 195
3.925	−0.003 195	3.93	0.006 808	3.927 5	0.001 794
3.925	−0.003 195	3.927 5	0.001 794	3.926 25	−0.000 703
3.926 25	−0.000 703	3.927 5	0.001 794	3.926 875	0.000 545
3.926 25	−0.000 703	3.926 875	0.000 545	3.926 562 5	−0.000 079

A refinement of the bisection method is the **method of false position** (also known as ***regula falsa***). To solve the equation $f(x) = 0$, given x_1 and x_2 such that $f(x_1) > 0$ and $f(x_2) < 0$ and $f(x)$ is continuous in (x_1, x_2), the bisection method takes the point

Figure 6.29 Solution of $\tan\theta - \tanh\theta = 0$ by *regula falsa*.

θ_1	$f(\theta_1)$	θ_2	$f(\theta_2)$	$\dfrac{\theta_1 f(\theta_2) - \theta_2 f(\theta_1)}{f(\theta_2) - f(\theta_1)}$	$f\left(\dfrac{\theta_1 f(\theta_2) - \theta_2 f(\theta_1)}{f(\theta_2) - f(\theta_1)}\right)$
3.92	−0.013 098	3.93	0.006 808	3.926 580	−0.000 045
3.926 580	−0.000 045	3.93	0.006 808	3.926 602	−0.000 000

$\frac{1}{2}(x_1 + x_2)$ as the next estimate of the root. The method of false position uses linear interpolation to derive the next estimate of the root. The straight line joining the points $(x_1, f(x_1))$ and $(x_2, f(x_2))$ is given by

$$\frac{y - f(x_1)}{f(x_2) - f(x_1)} = \frac{x - x_1}{x_2 - x_1}$$

This line cuts the x axis where

$$x = \frac{x_1 f(x_2) - x_2 f(x_1)}{f(x_2) - f(x_1)}$$

so this is the new estimate of the root. This method usually converges more rapidly than the bisection method. The computation of the root of $\tan\theta - \tanh\theta = 0$ in the interval (3.92, 3.93) is shown in Figure 6.29. Notice how, as a result of the first step, the estimate of the root is $\theta = 3.926\,580$ and $f(3.926\,580) = 0.000\,045$. The root is now bracketed in the interval (3.926 580, 3.93), and the method is repeated. In two steps we have an estimate of the root giving a value of $f(\theta) < 10^{-6}$. This obviously converges much faster than the bisection method.

Both the bisection method and the method of false position are **bracketing methods** – the root is known to lie in an interval of steadily decreasing size. As such, they are guaranteed to converge to a solution. An alternative method of solution for an equation $f(x) = 0$ is to devise a scheme producing a convergent sequence whose limit is the root of the equation. Such **fixed point iteration methods** are based on a relation of the form $x_{n+1} = g(x_n)$. If $\lim_{n\to\infty} x_n = \alpha$, say, then evidently $\alpha = g(\alpha)$. The simplest way to devise an iterative scheme for the solution of an equation $f(x) = 0$ is to find some rearrangement of the equation in the form $x = g(x)$. Then, if the scheme $x_{n+1} = g(x_n)$ converges, the limit will be a root of $f(x) = 0$.

We can arrange the equation $\tan\theta = \tanh\theta$ in the form

$$\theta = \tan^{-1}(\tanh\theta) + k\pi \quad (k = 0, \pm1, \pm2, \dots)$$

If we take $k = 1$ and $\theta_0 = \frac{5}{4}\pi$ we obtain, using the iteration scheme,

$$\theta_n = \tan^{-1}(\tanh\theta_{n-1}) + \pi$$

the sequence

$$\theta_0 = 3.926\,991, \quad \theta_1 = 3.926\,603, \quad \theta_2 = 3.926\,602, \quad \theta_3 = 3.926\,602$$

and the root is $\theta = 3.926\,602$ to 6dp. (Taking other values of k will, of course, give schemes that converge to other roots of $\tan\theta = \tanh\theta$.)

The disadvantage of such iterative schemes is that not all of them converge. We shall return to this topic in Section 9.3.2.

6.9.4 Exercises

Check your answers using MATLAB or MAPLE whenever possible.

62 Draw sketches and discuss the continuity of

(a) $\dfrac{|x|}{x}$ (b) $\dfrac{x-1}{2-x}$

(c) $\tanh\dfrac{1}{x}$ (d) $\lfloor 1-x^2 \rfloor$

63 Find upper and lower bounds obtained by

(a) $2x^2 - 4x + 7 \quad (0 \leqslant x \leqslant 2)$

(b) $-x^2 + 4x - 1 \quad (0 \leqslant x \leqslant 3)$

in the appropriate domains. Draw sketches to illustrate your answers.

64 Use the intermediate value theorem to show that the equation

$$x^3 + 10x^2 + 8x - 50 = 0$$

has roots between 1 and 2, between −4 and −3 and between −9 and −8. Find the root between 1 and 2 to 2dp using the bisection method.

65 Show that the equation $3^x = 3x$ has a root in the interval (0.7, 0.9). Use the intermediate value theorem and the method of *regula falsa* to find this root to 3dp.

66 Show that the equation

$$x^3 - 3x + 1 = 0$$

has three roots α, β and γ, where $\alpha < -1$, $0 < \beta < 1$ and $\gamma > 1$. For which of these is the iterative scheme

$$x_{n+1} = \tfrac{1}{3}(x_n^3 + 1)$$

convergent? Calculate the roots to 3dp.

67 The cubic equation $x^3 + 2x - 2 = 0$ can be written as

(a) $x = 1 - \tfrac{1}{2}x^3$ (b) $x = \dfrac{2}{2+x^2}$

(c) $x = (2-2x)^{1/3}$

Determine which of the corresponding iteration processes converges most rapidly to find the real root of the equation. Hence calculate the root to 3dp.

68 Show that the iteration

$$x_{n+1} = \frac{1}{3}\left(2x_n + \frac{a}{x_n^2}\right)$$

converges to the limit $a^{1/3}$. Use the formula with $a = 157$ and $x_0 = 5$ to compare x_1 and x_2.

Show that the error ε_n in the nth iterate is given by $\varepsilon_{n+1} \approx \varepsilon_n^2/x_{n-1}$, where $x_n = a^{1/3} + \varepsilon_n$. Hence estimate the error in x_1 obtained above.

69 The periods of natural vibrations of a cantilever are given by

$$\frac{2\pi l^2}{\theta^2}\sqrt{\frac{\rho}{EI}}$$

where l, E, I and ρ are physical constants dependent on the shape and material of the cantilever and θ is a root of the equation

$$\cosh\theta\cos\theta = -1$$

Examine this equation graphically. Estimate its lowest root α_0 and obtain an approximation for the kth root α_k. Compare the two iterations:

$$\theta_{n+1} = \cosh^{-1}(-\sec\theta_n)$$

and

$$\theta_{n+1} = \cos^{-1}(-\operatorname{sech}\theta_n)$$

Which should be used to find an improved approximation to x_0?

6.10 Engineering application: insulator chain

The voltage V_k at the kth pin of the insulator chain shown in Figure 6.30 satisfies the recurrence relation

$$V_{k+2} - \left(2 + \frac{C_2}{C_1}\right)V_{k+1} + V_k = 0$$

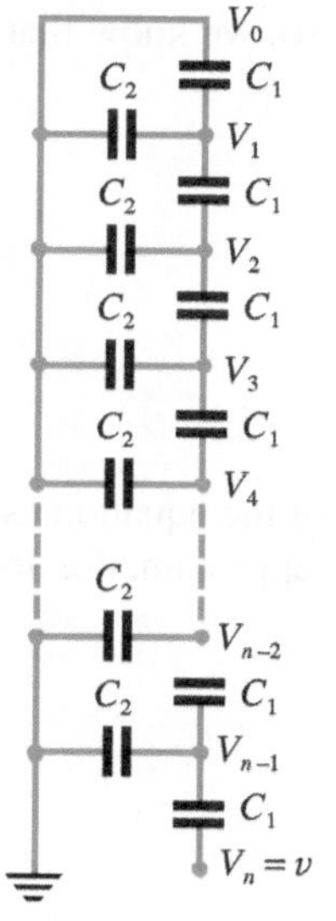

Figure 6.30

with $V_0 = 0$ and $V_n = v$, the amplitude of the voltage applied at the head of the chain. The characteristic equation for this recurrence relation is

$$\lambda^2 - \left(2 + \frac{C_2}{C_1}\right)\lambda + 1 = 0$$

which has real roots

$$\lambda_{1,2} = 1 + \frac{C_2}{2C_1} \pm \sqrt{\left[\frac{C_2}{C_1}\left(1 + \frac{C_2}{4C_1}\right)\right]}$$

Thus, the general solution is

$$V_k = A\lambda_1^k + B\lambda_2^k$$

Applying the condition $V_0 = 0$ gives

$$A + B = 0$$

Applying the condition $V_n = v$ gives

$$A\lambda_1^n + B\lambda_2^n = v$$

Hence $B = -A$ and $A = v/(\lambda_1^n - \lambda_2^n)$ and

$$V_k = \frac{v(\lambda_1^k - \lambda_2^k)}{\lambda_1^n - \lambda_2^n}$$

In a typical insulator chain $C_2/C_1 = 0.1$ and $n = 10$. It is left to the reader to calculate V_k/v for $k = 1, 2, \ldots, 9$.

6.11 Engineering application: approximating functions and Padé approximants

In Section 2.9.1 we introduced linear and quadratic interpolation as a means of obtaining estimates of the values of functions in between known values. Often in engineering applications it is of considerable importance to obtain good approximations to functions. In this section we shall show how what we have learned about power series representation can be used to produce a type of approximate representation of a function widely used by engineers, for example, when approximating exponentials by rational functions in modelling time delays in control systems. The approach is attributed to Padé and is based on the matching of series expansion.

Example 6.38 Obtain an approximation to the function e^{-x} in the form

$$e^{-x} \approx \frac{a + bx + cx^2}{A + Bx + Cx^2}$$

and find an estimate for the error.

Solution Assuming an exact match at $x = 0$, we deduce at once that $a = A$. Also, we know that $1/e^x = e^{-x}$, and assuming a similar relation for the approximation

$$\frac{A - Bx + Cx^2}{a - bx + cx^2} \equiv \frac{a + bx + cx^2}{A + Bx + Cx^2}$$

This holds if we choose $A = a$ (as above), $B = -b$ and $C = c$, giving

$$e^{-x} \approx \frac{A - Bx + Cx^2}{A + Bx + Cx^2}$$

We can see from this that it would be possible to express both sides of the equation as power series in x (at least in a restricted domain). We can rewrite the approximation to make it exact:

$$(A + Bx + Cx^2)e^{-x} = (A - Bx + Cx^2) + px^3 + qx^4 + rx^5 + \dots$$

where p, q, … are to be found.

Replacing e^{-x} by its power series representation, we have

$$(A + Bx + Cx^2)(1 - x + \tfrac{1}{2}x^2 - \tfrac{1}{6}x^3 + \tfrac{1}{24}x^4 - \tfrac{1}{120}x^5 + \dots)$$
$$= A - Bx + Cx^2 + px^3 + qx^4 + rx^5 + \dots$$

Multiplying out the left-hand side and collecting terms, we obtain

$$A + (B - A)x + (\tfrac{1}{2}A - B + C)x^2 + (-\tfrac{1}{6}A + \tfrac{1}{2}B - C)x^3$$
$$+ (\tfrac{1}{24}A - \tfrac{1}{6}B + \tfrac{1}{2}C)x^4 + (-\tfrac{1}{120}A + \tfrac{1}{24}B - \tfrac{1}{6}C)x^5 + \dots$$
$$= A - Bx + Cx^2 + px^3 + qx^4 + rx^5 + \dots$$

Comparing the coefficients of like powers of x on either side of this equation gives

$$A = A$$
$$B - A = -B$$
$$\tfrac{1}{2}A - B + C = C$$
$$-\tfrac{1}{6}A + \tfrac{1}{2}B - C = p$$
$$\tfrac{1}{24}A - \tfrac{1}{6}B + \tfrac{1}{2}C = q$$
$$-\tfrac{1}{120}A + \tfrac{1}{24}B - \tfrac{1}{6}C = r$$

and so on.

We see from this that there is not a unique solution for A, B and C, but that we may choose them (or some of them) arbitrarily. Taking $A = 1$ gives $B = \frac{1}{2}$ and $\frac{1}{12} - C = p$. Setting $p = 0$ will make the error term smaller near $x = 0$, so we adopt that choice, giving $C = \frac{1}{12}$. This gives $q = 0$ and $r = -\frac{1}{720}$. Thus

$$(1 + \tfrac{1}{2}x + \tfrac{1}{12}x^2)e^{-x} = (1 - \tfrac{1}{2}x + \tfrac{1}{12}x^2) - \tfrac{1}{720}x^5 + \dots$$

so that

$$e^{-x} = \frac{1 - \frac{1}{2}x + \frac{1}{12}x^2}{1 + \frac{1}{2}x + \frac{1}{12}x^2} - \frac{\frac{1}{720}x^5 + \dots}{1 + \frac{1}{2}x + \frac{1}{12}x^2}$$
$$= \frac{12 - 6x + x^2}{12 + 6x + x^2} - \tfrac{1}{720}x^5 + \dots$$

The principal term of the error, $-\frac{1}{720}x^5$, enables us to decide the domain of usefulness of the approximation. For example, if we require an approximation correct to 4dp, we need $\frac{1}{720}x^5$ to be less then $\frac{1}{2} \times 10^{-4}$. Thus the approximation

$$e^{-x} \approx \frac{12 - 6x + x^2}{12 + 6x - x^2}$$

yields answers correct to 4dp for $|x| < 0.51$.

This particular approximation is used by control engineers to enable them to apply linear systems techniques to the analysis and design of systems characterizing a time delay in their dynamics. Since the degree of both the numerator and denominator is 2, this is referred to as the (2, 2) Padé approximant.

As an extended exercise, the reader should obtain the following (1, 1) and (3, 3) Padé approximants:

$$e^{-x} \approx \frac{2 - x}{2 + x} \quad \text{and} \quad e^{-x} \approx \frac{120 - 60x + 12x^2 - x^3}{120 + 60x + 12x^2 + x^3}$$

6.12 Review exercises (1–25)

Check your answers using MATLAB or MAPLE whenever possible.

1 There are two methods of assessing the value of a wasting asset. The first assumes that it decreases each year by a fixed amount; the second assumes that it depreciates by a fixed percentage.

A piece of equipment costs £1000 and has a 'lifespan' of six years after which its scrap value is £100. Estimate the value of the equipment by both methods for the intervening years.

2 A machine that costs £1000 has a working life of three years, after which it is valueless and has to be replaced. It saves the owner £500 per year while it is in use. Show that the true total saving £S to the owner over the three years is

$$S = 500\left[\frac{1}{1 + r/100} + \frac{1}{(1 + r/100)^2} + \frac{1}{(1 + r/100)^3}\right] - 1000$$

where r% is the current rate of interest. Estimate S for $r = 5$, 10, 15 and 20. When does the machine truly save the owner money?

3 An economic model for the supply $S(P)$ and demand $D(P)$ of a product at a market price of P is given by

$$D(P) = 2 - P$$

$$S(P) = \tfrac{1}{2} + \tfrac{1}{2}P$$

and

$$D(P_{t+1}) = S(P_t)$$

(so that supply lags behind demand by one time unit). Show that

$$P_{t+1} - 1 = -\tfrac{1}{2}(P_t - 1)$$

and deduce that

$$P_t = 1 + (-\tfrac{1}{2})^t(P_0 - 1)$$

Find the particular solution of the recurrence relation corresponding to $P_0 = 0.8$ and sketch it in a cobweb diagram. What is the steady-state price of the product?

4 Show that

$$\sum_{k=1}^{n} \frac{1}{T_k} = \frac{T_{n-1} + T_n}{T_n}$$

where T_k is the kth triangular number. (See Question 4 in Exercises 6.2.3.)

5 Find the general solutions of the following linear recurrence relations:

(a) $f_{n+2} - 5f_{n+1} + 6f_n = 0$ (b) $f_{n+2} - 4f_{n+1} + 4f_n = 0$

(c) $f_{n+2} - 5f_{n+1} + 6f_n = 4^n$ (d) $f_{n+2} - 5f_{n+1} + 6f_n = 3^n$

6 Suppose that consumer spending in period t, C_t, is related to personal income two periods earlier, I_{t-2}, by

$$C_t = 0.875I_{t-2} - 0.2C_{t-1} \quad (t \geqslant 2)$$

Deduce that if personal income increases by a factor 1.05 each period, that is

$$I_{t+1} = 1.05I_t$$

then $I_t = 1.05^t I_0$ and hence

$$C_t = (C_1 - 0.7I_0)(-0.2)^{t-1} + 0.7I_0(1.05)^{t-1}$$

Describe the behaviour of C_t in the long run.

7 An economist believes that the price P_t of a seasonal commodity in period t satisfies the recurrence relation

$$P_{t+2} = 2(P_{t+1} - P_t) + C \quad (t \geqslant 0)$$

where C is a positive constant.

Show that

$$P_t = A(1 + \mathrm{j})^t + B(1 - \mathrm{j})^t + C$$

where A and B are complex conjugate constants. Noting that $1 \pm \mathrm{j} = \sqrt{2}(\cos\frac{\pi}{4} \pm \mathrm{j}\sin\frac{\pi}{4})$, explain why the economist is mistaken.

8 The cobweb model applied to agricultural commodities assumes that current supply depends on prices in the previous season. If P_t denotes market price in any period and Q_{St}, Q_{Dt} supply and demand in that period, then

$$Q_{Dt} = 180 - 0.75P_t$$

$$Q_{St} = -30 + 0.3P_{t-1} \quad \text{where } P_0 = 220$$

Find the market price and comment on its form.

9 Solve for National Income, Y_t, the set of recurrence relations

$$Y_t = 1 + C_t + I_t$$

$$C_t = \tfrac{1}{2}Y_{t-1}$$

$$I_t = 2(C_t - C_{t-1})$$

Comment on your solution.

10 A sequence is defined by

$$a_k = 1 + \frac{1}{2} + \frac{1}{3} + \ldots + \frac{1}{k} - \ln k \quad (k = 1, 2, \ldots)$$

Given $a_{10} = 0.626\,383$, $a_{16} = 0.608\,140$ and $a_{20} = 0.602\,009$ estimate $\gamma = \lim_{n\to\infty} a_n$, using repeated linear extrapolation. (γ is known as **Euler's constant.**)

11 Discuss the convergence of

(a) $\dfrac{2}{1^2} + \dfrac{3}{2^2} + \dfrac{4}{3^2} + \dfrac{5}{4^2} + \ldots$

(b) $\displaystyle\sum_{k=1}^{\infty} \frac{k^p}{k!}$ (all p)

(c) $\frac{1}{11} - \frac{2}{13} + \frac{3}{15} - \frac{4}{17} + \ldots$

(d) $1 - \frac{1}{3} + \frac{1}{5} - \frac{1}{7} + \ldots$

12 Express the following recurring decimal numbers in the form p/q where p and q are integers:

(a) $1.231\,231\,23\ldots$ (b) $0.429\,429\,429\ldots$

(c) $0.101\,101\,101\ldots$ (d) $0.517\,251\,72\ldots$

13 Determine which of the following series are convergent:

(a) $\displaystyle\sum_{n=0}^{\infty} \frac{1}{n^2 + 1}$ (b) $\displaystyle\sum_{n=1}^{\infty} \frac{n + 2}{n^2}$

(c) $\displaystyle\sum_{n=1}^{\infty} \frac{n - 1}{2n^5 - 1}$ (d) $\displaystyle\sum_{n=1}^{\infty} \frac{n - 1}{n^2 + n - 3}$

14 A rational function $f(x)$ has the following power series representation for $-1 < x < 1$:

$$f(x) = 1^2x + 2^2x^2 + 3^2x^3 + 4^2x^4 + \ldots$$

Find a closed-form expression for $f(x)$.

15 Find the values of a and b such that

$$\tan x = \frac{ax}{1 + bx^2} + cx^5 + O(x^7)$$

giving the value of c. (The series for $\tan x$ is given in Question 53(a) in Exercises 6.7.3.)

For what values of x will the approximation

$$\tan x = \frac{ax}{1 + bx^2}$$

be valid to 4dp? Use the approximation to calculate tan 0.29 and tan 0.295, and compare your answers with the values given by your calculator. Comment on your results.

[Here $O(x^7)$ mean terms involving powers of x greater than or equal to 7.]

16 The function $f(x) = \sinh^{-1}x$ has the power series expansion

$$\sinh^{-1}x = x - \frac{1}{2}\frac{x^3}{3} + \frac{1\cdot 3}{2\cdot 4}\frac{x^5}{5} - \frac{1\cdot 3\cdot 5}{2\cdot 4\cdot 6}\frac{x^7}{7} + \ldots$$

Obtain polynomial approximations for $\sinh^{-1}x$ for $-0.5 < x < 0.5$ such that the truncation error is less than (a) 0.005 and (b) 0.000 05.

17 A chord of a circle is half a mile long and supports an arc whose length is 1 foot longer (1 mile = 5280 feet). Show that the angle θ subtended by the arc at the centre of the circle satisfies

$$\sin\tfrac{1}{2}\theta = \frac{1320}{2641}\theta$$

Use the series expansion for sine to obtain an approximate solution of this equation, and estimate the maximum height of the arc above its chord.

18 A machine is purchased for £3600. The annual running cost of the machine is initially £1800, but rises annually by 10%. After x years its secondhand value is £$3600\mathrm{e}^{-0.35x}$. Show that the average annual cost £C (including depreciation) after x years is given by

$$C = \frac{3600(1 - \mathrm{e}^{-0.35x})}{x} + 90(19 + x)$$

Show graphically that the machine should be replaced after about 4 years, and use an iterative method to refine this estimate.

19 Consider the sequence ϕ_n defined by

$$\phi_n = \frac{1}{2}\left[\left(1+\frac{1}{n}\right)^n + \left(1-\frac{1}{n}\right)^{-n}\right]$$

Show that $\phi_n \to \mathrm{e}$ as $n \to \infty$. Using the power series expansions of $\ln(1 + x)$ and e^x, show that

$$\left(1+\frac{1}{n}\right)^n = \exp\left[n\ln\left(1+\frac{1}{n}\right)\right]$$

$$= \mathrm{e}\left(1 - \frac{1}{2n} + \frac{11}{24n^2} - \frac{7}{16n^3} + \ldots\right)$$

and deduce that

$$\phi_n = \mathrm{e}\left(1 + \frac{11}{24n^2} + \ldots\right)$$

Evaluate ϕ_{64} and ϕ_{128} (without using the y^x key of your calculator), and use extrapolation to estimate the value of e.

20 A beam of weight W per unit length is simply supported at the same level at $(N + 1)$ equidistant points, the extreme supports being at the ends of the beam. The bending moment M_k at the kth support satisfies the recurrence relation

$$M_{k+2} + 4M_{k+1} + M_k = \tfrac{1}{2}Wa^2$$

where a is the distance between the supports and $M_0 = 0$ and $M_N = 0$. (This is a consequence of Clapeyron's theorem of three moments.) Show that if the sequences $\{A_k\}_{k=0}^{N}$ and $\{B_k\}_{k=0}^{N}$ are calculated by the recurrences

$$A_0 = A_1 = 0$$

$$A_{k+2} + 4A_{k+1} + A_k = 1 \quad (k = 0, 1, \ldots, N-2)$$

and

$$B_0 = 0, \quad B_1 = 1$$

$$B_{k+2} + 4B_{k+1} + B_k = 0 \quad (k = 0, 1, \ldots, N-2)$$

then the solution of the bending-moment problem is given by

$$M_k = \tfrac{1}{2}Wa^2A_k + M_1B_k \quad (k = 0, \ldots, N)$$

with $\tfrac{1}{2}Wa^2A_N + M_1B_N = 0$ determining the value of M_1.

Perform the calculation for the case where $N = 8$, $a = 1$ and $W = 25$.

21 A complex voltage E is applied to the ladder network of Figure 6.31. Show that the (complex) mesh currents I_k satisfy the equations

$$\tfrac{1}{2}L\omega\mathrm{j}I_0 - \frac{\mathrm{j}}{C\omega}(I_0 - I_1) = E$$

$$L\omega\mathrm{j}I_k - \frac{\mathrm{j}}{C\omega}(I_k - I_{k+1}) + \frac{\mathrm{j}}{C\omega}(I_{k-1} - I_k) = 0$$

$$(k = 1, \ldots, N-1) \quad \textbf{(6.20)}$$

$$\tfrac{1}{2}L\omega\mathrm{j}I_n + \frac{\mathrm{j}}{C\omega}(I_{n-1} - I_n) = 0$$

(See Section 3.6 for the application of complex numbers to alternating circuits.)

Show that $I_k = A(\mathrm{e}^{\theta})^k = A\mathrm{e}^{k\theta}$ satisfies (6.20) provided that $\cosh\theta = 1 - \tfrac{1}{2}LC\omega^2$. Note that this equation yields two values for θ, so that in general I_k may be written as

$$I_k = A\mathrm{e}^{k\theta} + B\mathrm{e}^{-k\theta}$$

where A and B are independent of k. Using the special equations for I_0 and I_n, obtain the values of A and B and prove that

$$I_k = \mathrm{j}EC\omega\frac{\cosh(n-k)\theta}{\sinh\theta\sinh n\theta}$$

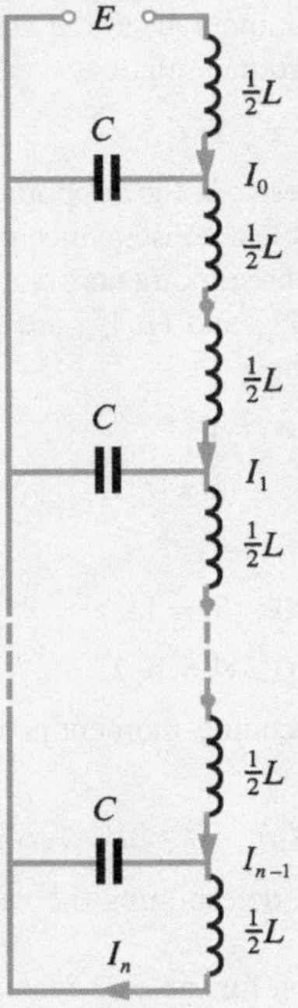

Figure 6.31

22 A lightweight beam of length l is clamped horizontally at both ends. It carries a concentrated load W at a distance a from one end ($x = 0$). The shear force F and bending moment M at the point x on the beam are given by

$$F = \begin{cases} \dfrac{W(l-a)^2(l+2a)}{l^3} & (0 < x < a) \\ \dfrac{-Wa^2(3l-2a)}{l^3} & (a < x < l) \end{cases}$$

and

$$M = \begin{cases} \dfrac{W(l-a)^2[al - x(l+2a)]}{l^3} & (0 < x < a) \\ \dfrac{Wa^2[al - 2l^2 + x(3l-2a)]}{l^3} & (a < x < l) \end{cases}$$

Draw the graphs of these functions. Use Heaviside functions to obtain single formulae for M and F.

23 (a) Show that

$$\sin 4\theta = 4\sin\theta\,(1 - 2\sin^2\theta)\sqrt{(1-\sin^2\theta)},$$
$$-\pi/2 < \theta < \pi/2$$

and explain why there is a restriction on the domain of θ.

(b) Use the binomial expansion to show that

$$\sqrt{(1-\sin^2\theta)} = 1 - \tfrac{1}{2}\sin^2\theta - \tfrac{1}{8}\sin^4\theta - \tfrac{1}{16}\sin^6\theta + A\sin^8\theta + \dots\ \dots$$

giving the value of A.

(c) Show that $\sin 4\theta$ can be expressed in the form

$$\sin 4\theta = 4\sin\theta - 10\sin^3\theta + \tfrac{7}{2}\sin^5\theta + \tfrac{3}{4}\sin^7\theta + \dots$$

24 The series

$$\sum_{k=0}^{\infty} \frac{1}{(2k+1)^2} = 1 + \frac{1}{3^2} + \frac{1}{5^2} + \frac{1}{7^2} + \dots$$

sums to the value $\pi^2/8$. Lagrange's formula for linear interpolation is

$$f(x) \simeq \frac{(x-x_0)f_1 - (x-x_1)f_0}{x_1 - x_0}$$

By setting $x = 1/n$ and $f(x) = S_n$ where

$$S_n = 1 + \frac{1}{3^2} + \frac{1}{5^2} + \dots + \frac{1}{(2n-1)^2},$$

show that

$$S_\infty \simeq \frac{qS_q - pS_p}{q - p}$$

where p and q are integers. Choosing $p = 5$ and $q = 10$, estimate the value of $\pi^2/8$.

25 The expression $\dfrac{x}{1+ax^2}$ is to be used as an approximation to $\frac{1}{2}\ln[(1+x)/(1-x)]$ on $-1 < x < 1$, by choosing a suitable value for the constant a. Show that

$$\frac{x}{1+ax^2} - \tfrac{1}{2}\ln\left(\frac{1+x}{1-x}\right) = -(\tfrac{1}{3} + a)x^3 - (\tfrac{1}{5} - a^2)x^5 - (\tfrac{1}{7} + a^3)x^7 + \dots$$

for $|x| < R$ giving the value of R. The error in this approximation is dominated by the first term in this expansion. Obtain the value of a which makes this term equal zero and compute the corresponding value of the coefficient of x^5.

Draw on the same diagram the graphs of

$$y = \tfrac{1}{2}\ln\left(\frac{1+x}{1-x}\right), \quad y = x + \tfrac{1}{3}x^3$$

$$\text{and}\quad y = \frac{3x}{3-x^2} \quad \text{for } 0 \le x \le 1$$

7 Differentiation and Integration

Chapter 7 Contents

7.1 Introduction

Many of the practical situations that engineers have to analyse involve quantities that are varying. Whether it is the temperature of a coolant, the voltage on a transmission line or the torque on a turbine blade, the mathematical tools for performing such analyses are the same. One of the most successful of these is **calculus**, which involves two fundamental operations: differentiation and integration. Historically, integration was discovered first, and indeed some of the ideas and results date back over 2000 years to when the Greeks developed the **method of exhaustion** to evaluate the area of a region bounded on one side by a curve – a method used by Archimedes (287–212 BC) to obtain the exact formula for the area of a circle. Differentiation was discovered very much later, during the seventeenth century, in relation to the problem of determining the tangent at an arbitrary point on a curve. Its characteristic features were probably first used by Fermat in 1638 to find the maximum and minimum points of some special functions. He noticed that tangents must be horizontal at some points, and developed a method for finding them by slightly changing the variable in a single algebraic equation and then letting the change 'disappear'. The connection between the two processes of determining the area under a curve and obtaining a tangent at a point on a curve was first realized in 1663 by Barrow, who was Newton's professor at the University of Cambridge. However, it was Newton (1642–1727) and Leibniz (1646–1716), working independently, who fully recognized the implications of this relationship. This led them to develop the calculus as a way of dealing with change and motion. Exploitation of their work resulted in an era of tremendous mathematical activity, much of which was motivated by the desire to solve applied problems, particularly by Newton, whose accomplishments were immense and included the formulation of the laws of gravitation. The calculus was put on a firmer mathematical basis in the nineteenth century by Cauchy and Riemann. It remains today one of the most powerful mathematical tools used by engineers. In this chapter and the next we shall review its basic ideas and techniques, refreshing some prior knowledge of the reader and extending it, and show their application both in the formulation of mathematical models of practical problems and in their solution.

In recent years we have seen significant developments in symbolic algebra packages, such as MAPLE and the Symbolic Math Toolbox in MATLAB, which are capable of performing algebraic manipulation, including the calculation of derivatives and integrals. To the inexperienced, this development may appear to eliminate the need for engineers to be able to carry out even basic operations in calculus by hand. This, however, is far from the truth. If engineers are to apply the powerful techniques associated with the calculus to the design and analysis of industrial problems then it is essential that they have a sound grounding of differentiation and integration. First, this allows effective formulation, comprehension and analysis of mathematical models. Secondly, it provides the basis for understanding symbolic algebra packages, particularly when specific forms of results are desired. In order to acquire this understanding it is necessary to have a certain degree of fluency in the manipulation of associated basic techniques. It is the objective of this chapter and the next to provide the minimum requirements for this. At the same time, students should be given the opportunity to develop their skills in the use of a symbolic algebra package and, whenever appropriate, be encouraged to check their answers to the exercises using such a package.

7.2 Differentiation

Here we shall introduce the concept of differentiation and illustrate its role in some problem-solving and modelling situations.

7.2.1 Rates of change

Consider an object moving along a straight line with constant velocity u (in $\mathrm{m\,s^{-1}}$). The distance s (in metres) travelled by the object in time t (in seconds) is given by the formula $s = ut$. The distance–time graph of this motion is the straight line shown in Figure 7.1. Note that the velocity u is the rate of change of distance with respect to time, and that on the distance–time graph it is the gradient (slope) of the straight line representing the relationship between the distance travelled and the time elapsed. This, of course, is a special case where the velocity is constant and the distance travelled is a linear function of time. Even when the velocity varies with time, however, it is still given by the gradient of the distance–time graph, although it then varies from point to point along the curve.

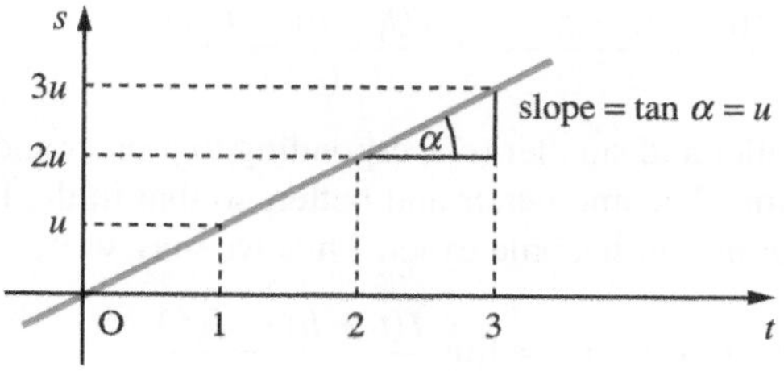

Figure 7.1 Distance–time graph for constant velocity u.

Consider the distance–time graph shown in Figure 7.2(a). Suppose we wish to find the velocity at the time $t = t_1$. The velocity at $t = t_1$ is given by the gradient of the graph at $t = t_1$. To find that we can enlarge that piece of the graph near $t = t_1$, as shown in Figure 7.2(b) and (c). We recall that continuous functions have the property that locally they may be approximated by linear functions (see Section 7.9.1, property f). We see that as we increase the magnification, that is, zooming closer, the graph takes on the

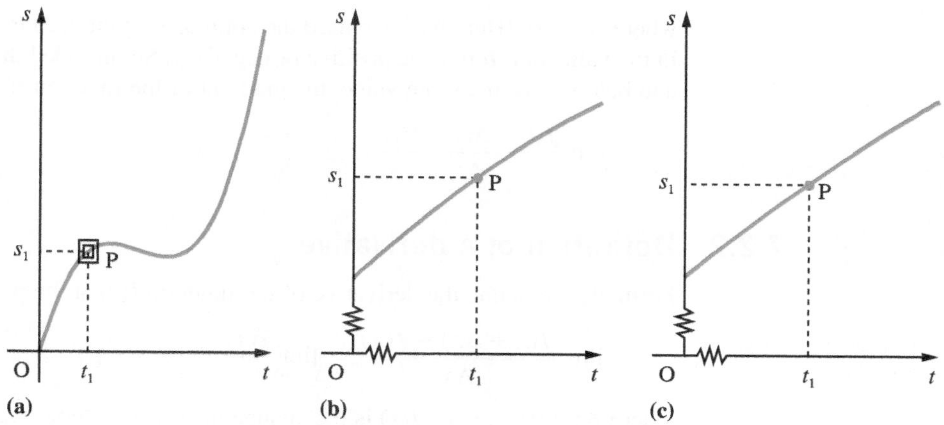

Figure 7.2 (a) Distance–time graph, (b) enlargement of outer rectangle surrounding (t_1, s_1) and (c) enlargement of inner rectangle surrounding (t_1, s_1).

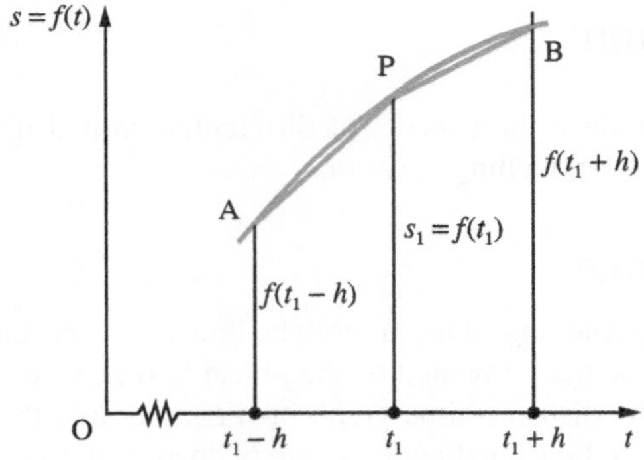

Figure 7.3
Section of the distance–time graph.

appearance of a straight line through the point $P(t_1, s_1)$. The gradient of that straight line (in the limit) gives us the gradient of the graph at P. Consider that section of the graph contained in the rectangle whose sides parallel to the s axis are $t = t_1 + h$ and $t = t_1 - h$ where h is a positive (small) number, as shown in Figure 7.3. If we denote the function relating distance and time by $f(t)$, then $s_1 = f(t_1)$ and we can approximate the gradient of the function $f(t)$ at the point P by the gradients of either of the chords AP or BP. Thus

$$\text{gradient} \simeq \frac{f(t_1 + h) - f(t_1)}{h} \simeq \frac{f(t_1 - h) - f(t_1)}{(-h)}$$

As h becomes smaller and smaller (corresponding to greater and greater magnifications) these approximations become better and better, so that in the limit ($h \to 0$) they cease being approximations and become exact. Thus we may write

$$(\text{gradient of } f(t) \text{ at } t = t_1) = \lim_{h\to 0} \frac{f(t_1 + h) - f(t_1)}{h}$$

$$= \lim_{h\to 0} \frac{f(t_1 - h) - f(t_1)}{(-h)}$$

Here we specified $h > 0$, which means that the former limit is the limit from above and the latter is the limit from below of the expression

$$\frac{f(t_1 + \Delta t) - f(t)}{\Delta t}$$

where $\Delta t \to 0$. (Here we have used the composite symbol Δt to indicate a small change in the value of t. It may be positive or negative.) So provided that the limits from above and below have the same value, the gradient of the function $f(t)$ is defined at $t = t_1$ by

$$\lim_{\Delta t\to 0} \frac{f(t_1 + \Delta t) - f(t)}{\Delta t}$$

7.2.2 Definition of a derivative

Formally we define the derivative of the function $f(x)$ at the point x to be

$$\lim_{\Delta x\to 0} \frac{f(x + \Delta x) - f(x)}{\Delta x} = \lim_{\Delta x\to 0} \frac{\Delta f}{\Delta x}$$

where $\Delta f = f(x + \Delta x) - f(x)$ is the change in $f(x)$ corresponding to the change Δx in x.

Two notations are used for the derivative. One uses a composite symbol, $\frac{\mathrm{d}f}{\mathrm{d}x}$, and the other uses a prime, $f'(x)$, so that

$$\frac{\mathrm{d}f}{\mathrm{d}x} = f'(x) = \lim_{\Delta x \to 0} \frac{\Delta f}{\Delta x} = \lim_{\Delta x \to 0} \frac{f(x + \Delta x) - f(x)}{\Delta x} \tag{7.1}$$

In terms of the function $y = f(x)$, we write $\Delta y = \Delta f$ and $y + \Delta y = y(x + \Delta x)$ and

$$\frac{\mathrm{d}y}{\mathrm{d}x} = \lim_{\Delta x \to 0} \frac{\Delta y}{\Delta x} \tag{7.2}$$

Example 7.1 Using the definition of a derivative given in (7.1), find $f'(x)$ when $f(x)$ is

(a) x^2 (b) $\frac{1}{x}$ (c) $mx + c$ (m, c constants)

Solution (a) With $f(x) = x^2$, $f(x + \Delta x) = (x + \Delta x)^2 = x^2 + 2x\Delta x + (\Delta x)^2$

so that $\frac{\Delta f}{\Delta x} = \frac{f(x + \Delta x) - f(x)}{\Delta x} = \frac{2x\Delta x + (\Delta x)^2}{\Delta x} = 2x + \Delta x$

Thus, from (7.1), the derivative of $f(x)$ is

$$\frac{\mathrm{d}f}{\mathrm{d}x} = f'(x) = \lim_{\Delta x \to 0} \frac{\Delta f}{\Delta x} = \lim_{\Delta x \to 0} (2x + \Delta x) = 2x$$

so that $\frac{\mathrm{d}}{\mathrm{d}x}(x^2) = 2x$

(b) With $f(x) = \frac{1}{x}$, $f(x + \Delta x) = \frac{1}{x + \Delta x}$

so that $\frac{\Delta f}{\Delta x} = \frac{f(x + \Delta x) - f(x)}{\Delta x} = \left[\frac{\frac{1}{x + \Delta x} - \frac{1}{x}}{\Delta x}\right] = \left[\frac{x - x - \Delta x}{\Delta x(x + \Delta x)x}\right]$

$$= \left[\frac{-1}{x^2 + x\Delta x}\right]$$

Thus, from (7.1), the derivative of $f(x)$ is

$$\frac{\mathrm{d}f}{\mathrm{d}x} = \lim_{\Delta x \to 0} \frac{\Delta f}{\Delta x} = \lim_{\Delta x \to 0} \left[\frac{-1}{x^2 + x\Delta x}\right] = -\frac{1}{x^2}$$

so that $\frac{\mathrm{d}}{\mathrm{d}x}(x^{-1}) = -1x^{-2}$

(c) With $f(x) = mx + c$, $f(x + \Delta x) = m(x + \Delta x) + c$

so that $\dfrac{\Delta f}{\Delta x} = \dfrac{f(x + \Delta x) - f(x)}{\Delta x} = \dfrac{m\Delta x}{\Delta x} = m$

Thus, from (7.1), the derivative of $f(x)$ is

$$\frac{df}{dx} = \lim_{\Delta x \to 0} \frac{\Delta f}{\Delta x} = m$$

so the gradient of the function $f(x) = mx + c$ is the same as that of the straight line $y = mx + c$, as we would expect.

7.2.3 Interpretation as the slope of a tangent

The definition is illustrated graphically in Figure 7.4, where Δx denotes a small incremental change in the independent variable x and Δf is the corresponding incremental change in $f(x)$. P and Q are the points on the graph with coordinates $(x, f(x))$, $(x + \Delta x, f(x + \Delta x))$ respectively. The slope of the line segment PQ is

$$\frac{\Delta f}{\Delta x} = \frac{f(x + \Delta x) - f(x)}{\Delta x}$$

In the limit as Δx tends to zero the point Q approaches P, and the line segment becomes the tangent to the curve at P, whose slope is given by the derivative

$$\frac{df}{dx} = \lim_{\Delta x \to 0} \frac{\Delta f}{\Delta x}$$

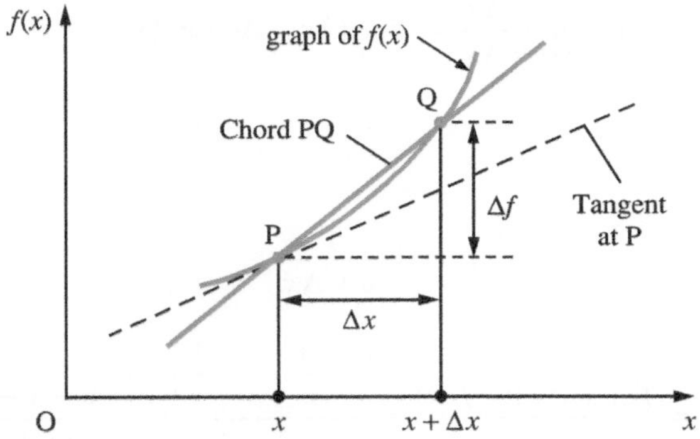

Figure 7.4 Illustration of derivative as slope of a tangent.

Summary

If $y = f(x)$ then the derivative of $f(x)$ is defined by

$$\frac{dy}{dx} = \frac{df}{dx} = f'(x) = \lim_{\Delta x \to 0} \frac{\Delta y}{\Delta x} = \lim_{\Delta x \to 0} \frac{\Delta f}{\Delta x} = \lim_{\Delta x \to 0} \frac{f(x + \Delta x) - f(x)}{\Delta x}$$

The derivative may be interpreted as

(a) the rate of change of the function $y = f(x)$ with respect to x, or

(b) the slope of the tangent at the point (x, y) on the graph of $y = f(x)$.

Example 7.2 Consider the function $f(x) = 25x - 5x^2$. Find

(a) the derivative of $f(x)$ from first principles;

(b) the rate of change of $f(x)$ at $x = 1$;

(c) the equation of the tangent to the graph of $f(x)$ at the point (1, 20);

(d) the equation of the normal to the graph of $f(x)$ at the point (1, 20).

Solution (a) $f(x) = 25x - 5x^2$

$$f(x + \Delta x) = 25(x + \Delta x) - 5(x + \Delta x)^2 = 25x + 25\Delta x - 5x^2 - 10x\,\Delta x - 5(\Delta x)^2$$

so that

$$\frac{\Delta f}{\Delta x} = \frac{f(x + \Delta x) - f(x)}{\Delta x} = \frac{25\Delta x - 10x\,\Delta x - 5(\Delta x)^2}{\Delta x} = 25 - 10x - 5\Delta x$$

Thus the derivative of $f(x)$ is

$$\frac{\mathrm{d}f}{\mathrm{d}x} = f'(x) = \lim_{\Delta x \to 0} \frac{\Delta f}{\Delta x} = \lim_{\Delta x \to 0} (25 - 10x - 5\Delta x) = 25 - 10x$$

(b) The rate of change of $f(x)$ at $x = 1$ is $f'(1) = 15$.

(c) The slope of the tangent to the graph of $f(x)$ at (1, 20) is $f'(1) = 15$. Remembering from equation (1.14) that the equation of a line passing through a point (x_1, y_1) and having slope m is

$$y - y_1 = m(x - x_1)$$

we have the equation of the tangent to the graph of $y = f(x)$ at (1, 20) is

$$y - 20 = 15(x - 1)$$

or

$$y = 15x + 5$$

(d) The slope n of the normal to the graph is given by the relation $mn = -1$, where m is the slope of the tangent. This is illustrated in Figure 7.5. Thus in this example the slope of the normal at (1, 20) is $-1/15$ and hence the equation of the normal at (1, 20) is

$$y - 20 = -\frac{1}{15}(x - 1)$$

or

$$y = \frac{1}{15}(301 - x)$$

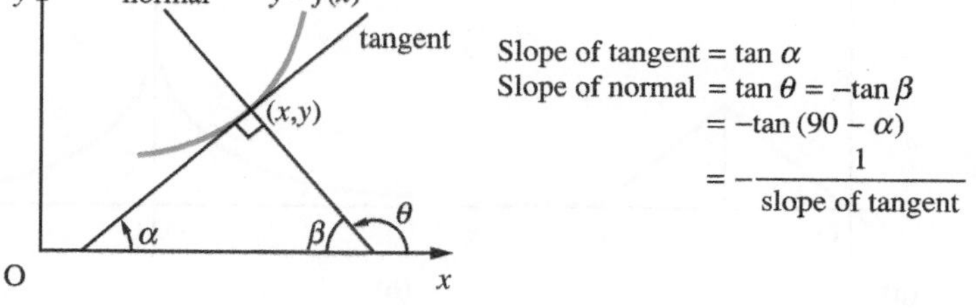

Figure 7.5 Relationship between slopes of the tangent and normal to a plane curve.

7.2.4 Differentiable functions

The formal definition of the derivative of $f(x)$ implies that the limits from below and above are equal. In some cases this does not happen. For example, the function $f(x) = \sqrt{(1 + \sin x)}$ is such that its two limits are

$$\lim_{\Delta x \to 0-} \frac{f(3\pi/2 + \Delta x) - f(3\pi/2)}{\Delta x} = \frac{-1}{\sqrt{2}}$$

$$\lim_{\Delta x \to 0+} \frac{f(3\pi/2 + \Delta x) - f(3\pi/2)}{\Delta x} = \frac{1}{\sqrt{2}}$$

Clearly the derivative of the function is not defined at $x = 3\pi/2$ (the two limits above are sometimes referred to as 'left-hand' and 'right-hand' derivatives, respectively).

The graph of $y = \sqrt{(1 + \sin x)}$ is shown in Figure 7.6, and it is clear that at $x = 3\pi/2$ a unique tangent cannot be drawn to the graph of the function. This is not surprising since from the interpretation of the derivative as the slope of the tangent, it follows that for a function $f(x)$ to be **differentiable** at $x = a$, the graph of $f(x)$ must have a unique, non-vertical well-defined tangent at $x = a$. Otherwise the limit

$$\lim_{\Delta x \to 0} \frac{f(a + \Delta x) - f(a)}{\Delta x}$$

does not exist. We say that a function $f(x)$ is differentiable if it is differentiable at all points in its domain. For practical purposes it is sufficient to interpret a differentiable function as one having a smooth continuous graph with no sharp corners. Engineers frequently refer to such functions as being 'well behaved'. Clearly the function having the graph shown in Figure 7.7(a) is differentiable at all points except $x = x_1$ and $x = x_2$, since a unique tangent cannot be drawn at these points. Similarly, the function having the graph shown in Figure 7.7(b) is differentiable at all points except at $x = 0$.

Figure 7.6
The graph of $y = \sqrt{(1 + \sin x)}$.

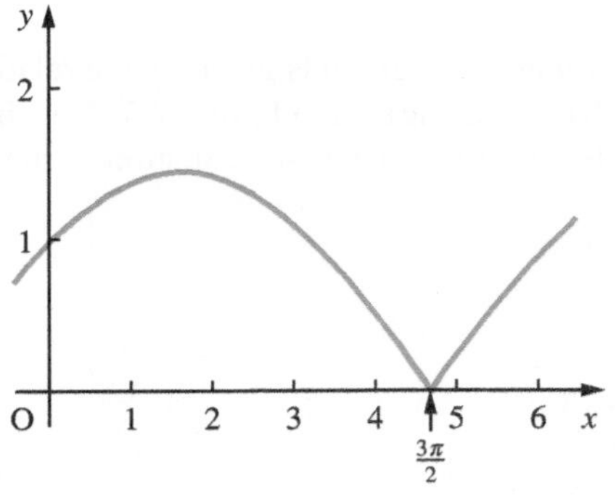

Figure 7.7

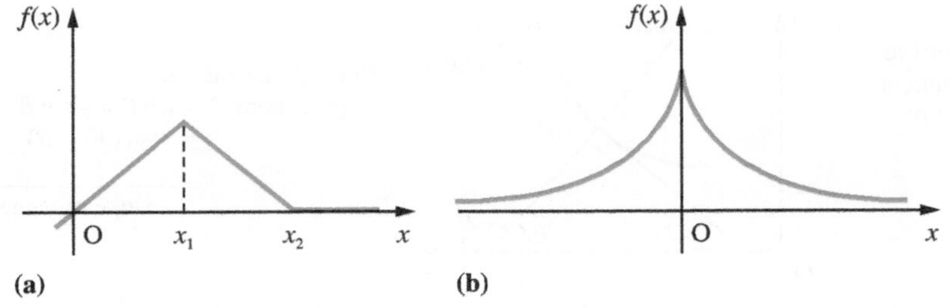

7.2.5 Speed, velocity and acceleration

Considering the motion of the object in Section 7.2.1 enables us to distinguish between the terms **speed** and **velocity**. In everyday usage we talk of speed rather than velocity, and always regard it as being positive or zero. As we saw in Chapter 4, velocity is a vector quantity and has a direction associated with it, while speed is a scalar quantity, being the magnitude or modulus of the velocity. When s and v are measured horizontally, the object will have a positive velocity when travelling to the right and a negative velocity when travelling to the left. Throughout its motion, the speed of the particle will be positive or zero. Likewise, **acceleration** a, being the rate of change of velocity with respect to time, is a vector quantity and is determined by

$$a(t) = \frac{dv}{dt}$$

Example 7.3

A particle is thrown vertically upwards into the air. Its height s (in m) above the ground after time t (in seconds) is given by

$$s = 25t - 5t^2$$

(a) What height does the particle reach?

(b) What is its velocity when it returns to hit the ground?

(c) What is its acceleration?

Solution

Since velocity v is rate of change of distance s with time t we have

$$v = \frac{ds}{dt}$$

In this particular example

$$s(t) = 25t - 5t^2 \qquad \textbf{(7.3)}$$

so, from Example 7.2,

$$v(t) = \frac{ds}{dt} = 25 - 10t \qquad \textbf{(7.4)}$$

(a) When the particle reaches its maximum height, it will be momentarily at rest, so that its velocity will be momentarily zero. From (7.4) this will occur when $t = 25/10 = 2.5$. Then, from (7.3), the height reached at this instant is

$$s(2.5) = 25 \times \tfrac{5}{2} - 5 \times (\tfrac{5}{2})^2 = \tfrac{125}{4}$$

That is, the maximum height reached by the particle is 31.25 m.

(b) First we need to find the time at which the particle will return to hit the ground. This will occur when the height s is again zero, which from (7.3) is when $t = 5$. Then, from (7.4), the velocity of the particle when it hits the ground is

$$v(5) = -25$$

That is, when it returns to hit the ground, the particle will be travelling at 25 m s^{-1}, with the negative sign indicating that it is travelling downwards, since s and v are measured upwards.

(c) The acceleration, a, is the rate of change of velocity with respect to time. Thus, from (7.4)

$$a(t) = \frac{dv}{dt} = -10$$

that is, $a \approx -g = -9.806\,65$ (m s^{-2}), the acceleration due to gravity.

The MATLAB Symbolic Math Toolbox and MAPLE provide commands to do the basic operations of calculus and many of these will be introduced in this chapter. If $y = f(x)$ then we denote dy/dx by dy or df (we could use any name such as, for example, dyd$x$ or dybyd$x$). Denoting Δx by h the derivative of $f(x)$, as given in (7.1), is determined by the commands

MATLAB

```
syms h x
df = limit((f(x + h) -
f(x))/h,h,0)
```

MAPLE

```
f:= x -> f(x);
df:= limit((f(x + h) -
f(x))/h,h = 0);
```

For example, if $f(x) = 25x - 5x^2$ then its derivative df is determined by the MATLAB commands

```
syms h x
df = limit(((25*(x + h) - 5*(x + h)^2) -
(25*x - 5*x^2))/h,h,0)
```

as

```
df = 25 - 10*x
```

which checks with the answer obtained in the solution to Example 7.2(a).

7.2.6 Exercises

Check your answers using MATLAB or MAPLE whenever possible.

1 Using the definition of a derivative given in (7.1), find $f'(x)$ when $f(x)$ is

(a) a constant K (b) x (c) $x^2 - 2$

(d) x^3 (e) $\sqrt{x}$ (f) $1/(1 + x)$

2 Consider the function $f(x) = 2x^2 - 5x - 12$. Find

(a) the derivative of $f(x)$ from first principles;

(b) the rate of change of $f(x)$ at $x = 1$;

(c) the points at which the line through (1, −15) with slope m cuts the graph of $f(x)$;

(d) the value of m such that the points of intersection found in (c) are coincident;

(e) the equation of the tangent to the graph of $f(x)$ at the point (1, −15).

3 Consider the function $f(x) = 2x^3 - 3x^2 + x + 3$. Find

(a) the derivative of $f(x)$ from first principles;

(b) the rate of change of $f(x)$ at $x = 1$;

(c) the points at which the line through (1, 3) with slope m cuts the graph of $f(x)$;

(d) the values of m such that two of the points of intersection found in (c) are coincident;

(e) the equations of the tangents to the graph of $f(x)$ at $x = 1$ and $x = \frac{1}{4}$.

4 Show from first principles that the derivative of

$$f(x) = ax^2 + bx + c$$

is

$$f'(x) = 2ax + b$$

Hence confirm the result of Section 2.3.4 (page 96) and using the calculus method verify the results of Example 2.21 (page 97).

5 Show that if $f(x) = ax^3 + bx^2 + cx + d$, then

$$f(x + \Delta x) = ax^3 + bx^2 + cx + d + (3ax^2 + 2bx + c)\Delta x + (3ax + b)(\Delta x)^2 + a(\Delta x)^3$$

Deduce that

$$f'(x) = 3ax^2 + 2bx + c.$$

6 The displacement–time graph for a vehicle is given by

$$s(t) = \begin{cases} t, & 0 \leqslant t \leqslant 1 \\ t^2 - t + 1, & 1 \leqslant t \leqslant 2 \\ 3t - 3, & 2 \leqslant t \leqslant 3 \\ 9 - t, & 3 \leqslant t \leqslant 9 \end{cases}$$

Obtain the formula for the velocity–time graph.

7 Consider the function $f(x) = \sqrt{(1 + \sin x)}$. Show that $f(3\pi/2 \pm h) = \sqrt{2} \sin \frac{1}{2}h$ $(h > 0)$ and deduce that $f'(x)$ does not exist at $x = 3\pi/2$.

7.2.7 Mathematical modelling using derivatives

We have seen that the gradient of a tangent to the graph $y = f(x)$ can be expressed as a derivative, but derivatives have much wider application than just this. Any quantity that can be expressed as a limit of the form (7.1) can be represented by a derivative, and such quantities arise in many practical situations. Because gradients of tangents to graphs can be expressed as derivatives, it follows that we can always interpret a derivative geometrically as the slope of a tangent to a graph. In Example 7.3 we saw that the particle reached its maximum height 31.25 m when $t = 2.5$ s. This maximum height occurred when $v = \mathrm{d}s/\mathrm{d}t = 0$. This implies that the tangent to the graph of **distance** against **time** was horizontal. In general at a maximum or minimum of a function, its derivative is zero and its tangent horizontal (as discussed in Section 2.2.1). This is discussed fully later, in Section 7.5.

Example 7.4 Suppose that a tank initially contains 80 litres of pure water. At a given instant (taken to be $t = 0$) a salt solution containing 0.25 kg of salt per litre flows into the tank at a rate of 8 litres min^{-1}. The liquid in the tank is kept homogeneous by constant stirring. Also, at time $t = 0$ liquid is allowed to flow out from the tank at a rate of 12 litres min^{-1}. Show that the amount of salt $x(t)$ (in kg) in the tank at time t (min) $\geqslant 0$ is determined by the mathematical model

$$\frac{\mathrm{d}x(t)}{\mathrm{d}t} + \frac{3x(t)}{20 - t} = 2 \quad (t < 20)$$

Solution The situation is illustrated in Figure 7.8. Since $x(t)$ denotes the amount of salt in the tank at time $t \geqslant 0$, the rate of increase of the amount of salt in the tank is $\mathrm{d}x/\mathrm{d}t$, and is given by

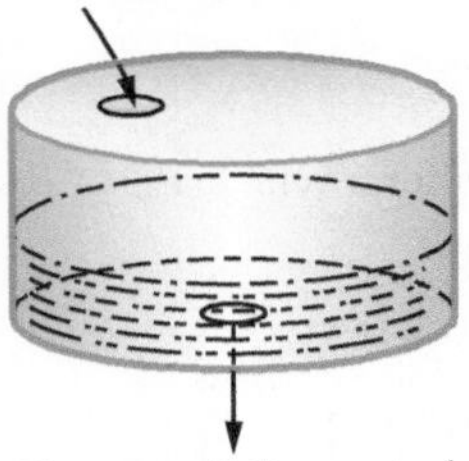

Figure 7.8
Water tank of Example 7.4.

$$\frac{dx}{dt} = \text{rate of inflow of salt} - \text{rate of outflow of salt} \qquad \textbf{(7.5)}$$

The rate of inflow of salt is $(0.25\,\text{kg litre}^{-1})\,(8\,\text{litres min}^{-1}) = 2\,\text{kg min}^{-1}$.

The rate of outflow of salt is $c \times (\text{rate of outflow of liquid}) = c \times 12\,\text{litres min}^{-1}$

$$= 12c \quad (\text{in kg min}^{-1})$$

where $c(t)$ is the concentration of salt in the tank (in kg litre^{-1}). The concentration at time t is given by

$$c(t) = \frac{\text{amount of salt in the tank at time } t}{\text{volume of liquid in the tank at time } t}$$

After time t (in min) $8t$ litres have entered the tank and $12t$ litres have left. Also, at $t = 0$ there were 80 litres in the tank. Therefore the volume V of liquid in the tank at time t is given by

$$V(t) = 80 - (12t - 8t) = (80 - 4t)$$

(Note that $V(t) \geqslant 0$ only if $t \leqslant 20$ min; after this time the liquid will flow out as quickly as it flows in and none will accumulate in the tank.) Thus the concentration $c(t)$ is given by

$$c(t) = \frac{x(t)}{V(t)} = \frac{x(t)}{80 - 4t}$$

so that

$$\text{rate of outflow of salt} = 12 \times \frac{x(t)}{80 - 4t} = \frac{3x(t)}{20 - t}$$

Substituting back into (7.5) gives the rate of increase as

$$\frac{dx}{dt} = 2 - \frac{3x}{20 - t}$$

or

$$\frac{dx(t)}{dt} + \frac{3x(t)}{20 - t} = 2$$

This equation involving the derivative of $x(t)$ is called a *differential equation*, and in Question 9 of Review Exercises 10.13 we shall show how it can be solved to give the quantity $x(t)$ of salt in the tank at time t.

Example 7.5 In a suspension bridge a roadway, of length $2l$, is suspended by vertical hangers from cables carried by towers at the ends of the span, as illustrated in Figure 7.9(a). The lowest points of the cables are a distance h below the top of the supporting towers. Find an equation which represents the line shape of the cables.

Solution To solve this problem we have to make some simplifying assumptions. We assume that the roadway is massive compared to the cables, so that the weight W of the roadway is the dominant factor in determining the shape of the cables. Secondly, we assume

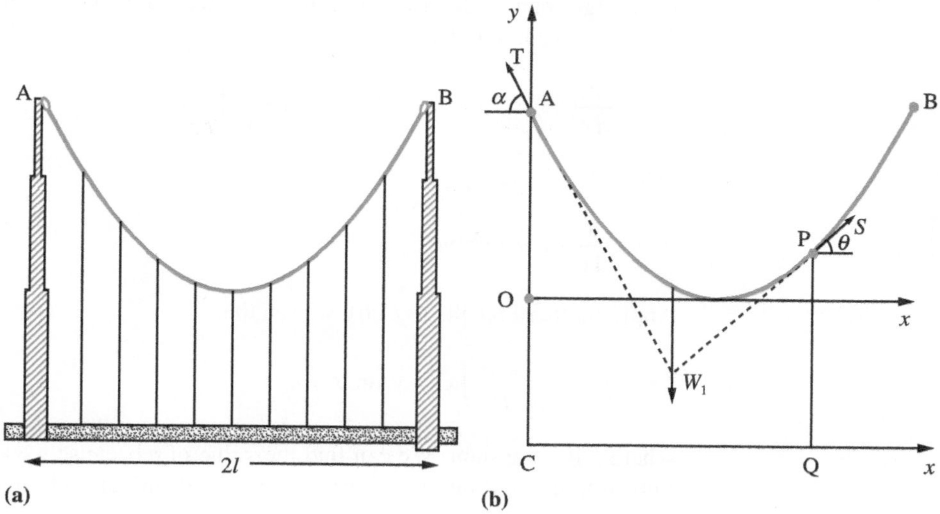

Figure 7.9
(a) Schematic diagram for a suspension bridge. (b) Forces acting on the cable between A and B.

that the weight of the roadway is uniformly distributed along its length, and if the hangers are equally spaced they can be adjusted in length so that they carry equal vertical loads.

We solve this problem using elementary statics because at each point P(x, y) on the cable the forces are in equilibrium. Figure 7.9(b) shows the forces acting on the part of the cable between A and P. These are the weight W_1 of the roadway between C and Q ($W_1 = Wx/2l$, where x = CQ), the tension T in the cable acting at the angle α at A and the tension S in the cable acting at the angle θ at P.

Resolving forces horizontally, we have $T\cos\alpha = S\cos\theta$

Resolving forces vertically, we have $T\sin\alpha + S\sin\theta = \dfrac{Wx}{2l}$

Eliminating S between these equations gives $T\sin\alpha + T\cos\alpha\tan\theta = \dfrac{Wx}{2l}$

Also, we know that the total weight W of the roadway is supported by the tensions at A and B, so that $2T\sin\alpha = W$. Hence, substituting, we obtain

$$\frac{W}{2\sin\alpha}\sin\alpha + \frac{W}{2\sin\alpha}\cos\alpha\tan\theta = \frac{Wx}{2l}$$

giving

$$\tan\theta = x\frac{\tan\alpha}{l} - \tan\alpha$$

Now $\tan\theta$ is the slope of the curve at P (the tensions act along the direction of the tangent at each point of the curve), so that

$$\frac{dy}{dx} = x\frac{\tan\alpha}{l} - \tan\alpha \tag{7.6}$$

using the coordinate system shown in Figure 7.9(b). This is another example of a differential equation. To solve this equation we have to find the function whose derivative is the right-hand side of (7.6). In this case we can make use of the results of Example 7.1, since we know that

$$\frac{\mathrm{d}}{\mathrm{d}x}(x^2) = 2x \quad \text{(which implies } \frac{\mathrm{d}}{\mathrm{d}x}(\tfrac{1}{2}x^2) = x\text{)}$$

and

$$\frac{\mathrm{d}}{\mathrm{d}x}(mx + c) = m$$

Applying these results to (7.6), we see that

$$y = \tfrac{1}{2}\left(\frac{\tan\alpha}{l}\right)x^2 - x\tan\alpha + c \qquad \textbf{(7.7)}$$

where c is a constant. We can find the value of c because we know that $y = h$ at $x = 0$. Substituting $x = 0$ into (7.7), we see that $c = h$, and the solution becomes

$$y = \tfrac{1}{2}\left(\frac{\tan\alpha}{l}\right)x^2 - x\tan\alpha + h \qquad \textbf{(7.8)}$$

But we also know that $y = 0$ where $x = l$. This enables us to find the value of $\tan\alpha$. Substituting $x = l$ into (7.8), we have

$$0 = \tfrac{1}{2}l\tan\alpha - l\tan\alpha + h$$

which implies $\tan\alpha = 2h/l$. Thus the shape of the supporting cable is given by

$$\begin{aligned} y &= \frac{hx^2}{l^2} - \frac{2hx}{l} + h \\ &= h(x - l)^2/l^2 \end{aligned}$$

indicating that the points of attachment of the hangers to the cable lie on a parabolic curve.

Example 7.6 A radio telescope has the shape of a paraboloid of revolution (see Figure 1.23). Show that all the radio waves arriving in a direction parallel to its axis of symmetry are reflected to pass through the same point on that axis of symmetry.

Solution The diagram in Figure 7.10 shows a section of the paraboloid through its axis of symmetry. We choose the coordinate system such that the equation of the parabola shown is $y = x^2$. Let AP represent the path of a radio signal travelling parallel to the y axis. At P it is reflected to pass through the point B on the y axis. The laws of reflection state that $\angle$APN = $\angle$BPN, where PN is the normal to the curve at P. Now given the coordinates (a, a^2) of the point P we have to find the coordinates $(0, b)$ of the point B. From the diagram we can see that if $\angle$PTQ = θ, then $\angle$PQT = $\pi/2 - \theta$, which implies that $\angle$ONP = θ. Since AP is parallel to NB, we see that $\angle$APN = θ and hence $\angle$BPN = θ. This implies that $\angle$PBN = $\pi - 2\theta$. With all of these angles known we can calculate the coordinates of B. From the diagram

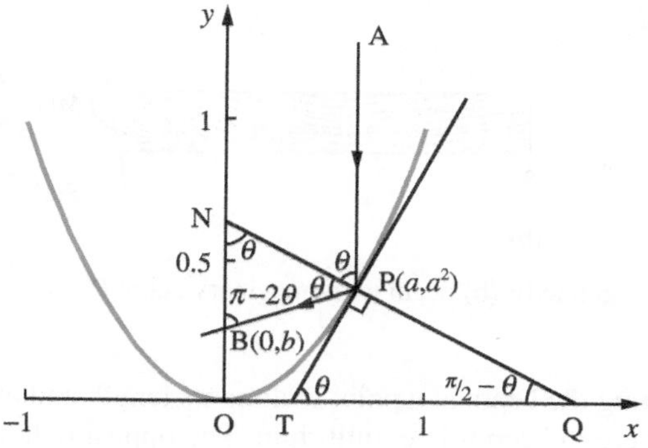

Figure 7.10 Section of paraboloid through axis of symmetry.

$$\tan \angle \text{NBP} = \frac{a}{a^2 - b}$$

Since $\angle\text{NBP} = \pi - 2\theta$, this implies $\tan 2\theta = \dfrac{a}{b - a^2}$. Also

$$\tan\theta = \left(\frac{\mathrm{d}y}{\mathrm{d}x}\right)_{x=a} = 2a$$

and since $\tan 2\theta = \dfrac{2\tan\theta}{1 - \tan^2\theta}$, identity (2.27e), we obtain

$$\frac{4a}{1 - 4a^2} = \frac{a}{b - a^2}$$

This gives $b = \frac{1}{4}$. Notice that the value of b is independent of a. Thus all the reflected rays pass through $(0, \frac{1}{4})$. As was indicated in Section 1.4.5, this property is important in many engineering design projects.

Example 7.7 Show that the shear force F acting in a beam is related to the bending moment M by

$$F = \frac{\mathrm{d}M}{\mathrm{d}x}$$

Solution This was briefly discussed in Section 7.9.2. We now explore the ideas more thoroughly. A beam is a horizontal structural member which carries loads. These induce forces and stresses inside the beam in transmitting the loads to the supports. For design safety two internal quantities are used, the shear force F and the bending moment M. At each point along the beam the forces are in equilibrium. These forces can be thought of as acting along the beam and (vertically) perpendicular to it. When a beam bends, its upper surface is compressed and its lower surface is stretched, so that forces on the upper and lower surfaces at any point along the beam are acting in opposite directions. There will, of course, be a line within the beam, which is neither stretched nor compressed. This is the neutral axis. The situation is illustrated in Figure 7.11(a). To analyse the situation

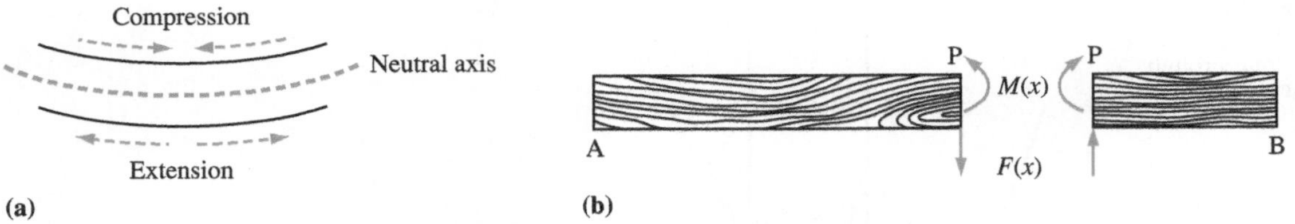

Figure 7.11 (a) The bending of a beam (exaggerated); (b) beam with imaginary cut at P.

we imagine cutting the beam at a point P along its length and examine the forces which are necessary there to keep it in equilibrium. The opposing horizontal forces at P, give a moment M about the neutral axis, as shown in Figure 7.11(b). This is called the **bending moment**. As the beam is in equilibrium there will be an equal and opposite bending moment on the other side of our imaginary cut. In the same way the vertical forces F balance at the cut. This vertical force is called the **shear force**. The shear force and bending moment are important in considering design safety.

We find the shear force F at a point distance x from the left-hand end of the beam by considering the vertical equilibrium of forces for the left-hand portion of the beam, and we find the bending moment M by looking at the balance of moments of force for that left-hand portion (see Figure 7.12(a)). The force F is the sum of the forces acting vertically on AP, and M is the sum of moments.

Consider the small element of the beam of length Δx between P and Q shown in Figure 7.12(b). Then examining the balance of moments about Q we see that

$$M(x+\Delta x) = M(x) + \Delta x F(x)$$

so that

$$M(x+\Delta x) - M(x) = \Delta x F(x)$$

giving

$$F(x) = \frac{M(x+\Delta x) - M(x)}{\Delta x}$$

Now letting $\Delta x \to 0$, we obtain

$$F(x) = \frac{\mathrm{d}M}{\mathrm{d}x}$$

as required.

Figure 7.12
(a) Horizontal beam.
(b) Element of the beam.

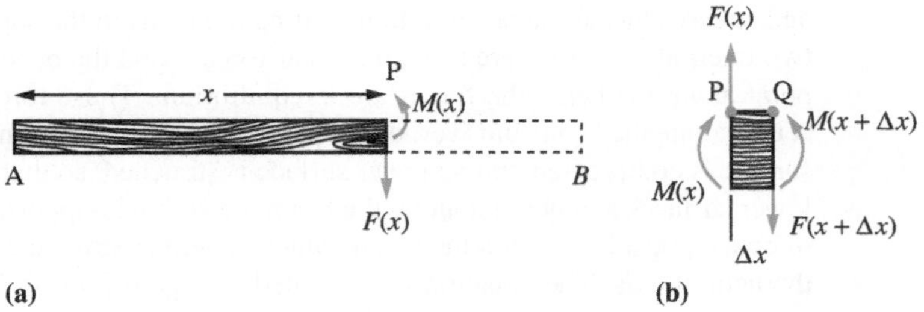

We saw in Section 7.9.2 that for a freely hinged beam with a point load W at $x = a$

$$M(x) = \begin{cases} W(l - a)x/l & 0 < x \leqslant a \\ W(l - x)a/l & a \leqslant x < l \end{cases}$$

$$F(x) = \begin{cases} W - Wa/l & 0 < x < a \\ -Wa/l & a \leqslant x < l \end{cases}$$

It is left to the reader to verify that these satisfy the equation relating $M(x)$ and $F(x)$.

Example 7.8

An open box, illustrated in Figure 7.13(a), is made from an A4 sheet of card using the folds shown in Figure 7.13(b). Find the dimensions of the tray which maximize its capacity.

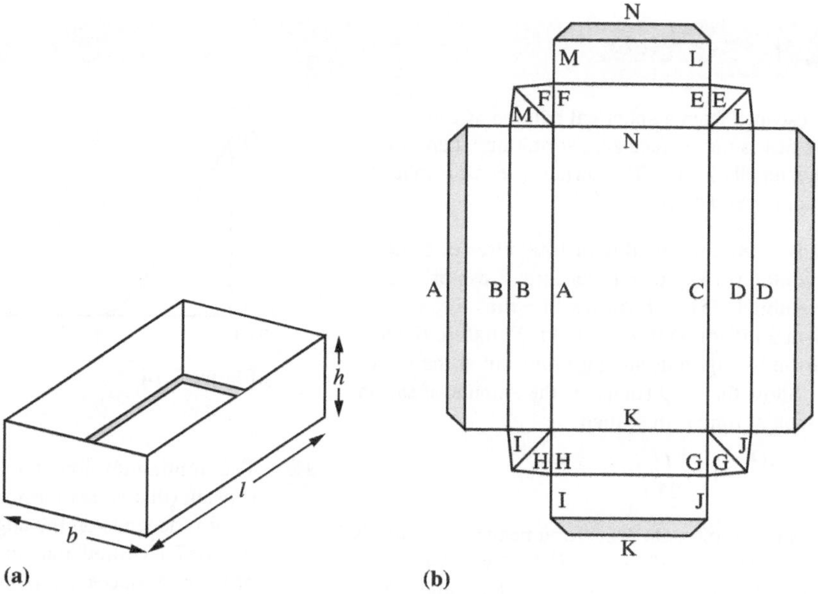

Figure 7.13
(a) The open box.
(b) The net of an open box used commercially.

Solution Boxes like these are used commercially for food sales. Packaging is expensive, so that manufacturers often try to design a container that has the biggest capacity for a standard size of cardboard. An A4 sheet has size 210 × 297 mm.

Allowing 10 mm flaps as stiffeners, shaded in the diagram, and denoting the length, breadth and height by l, b and h (in mm) respectively, we have

$$l + 4h + 20 = 297$$

$$b + 4h + 20 = 210$$

and the capacity C is $l \times b \times h\,\text{mm}^3$. Thus

$$C(h) = (277 - 4h)(190 - 4h)h = 52\,630h - 1868h^2 + 16h^3$$

The maximum capacity C^* occurs where $C'(h) = 0$.

It can be shown from first principles, see Question 5 of Exercises 7.2.6, that the general cubic function

$$f(x) = ax^3 + bx^2 + cx + d$$

has derivative

$$f'(x) = 3ax^2 + 2bx + c$$

In this example $a = 16$, $b = -1868$, $c = 52\,630$, $d = 0$ and $x = h$. Thus

$$C'(h) = 52\,630 - 3736h + 48h^2$$

so that the value h^* of h which yields the maximum capacity is $h^* = 18.47$ where $C'(h^*) = 0$. We can verify that it is a maximum by showing that

$$C'(18.4) > 0 \quad \text{and} \quad C'(18.5) < 0$$

7.2.8 Exercises

8 Gas escapes from a spherical balloon at $2\,\text{m}^3\,\text{min}^{-1}$. How fast is the surface area shrinking when the radius equals 12 m? (The surface area of a sphere of radius r is $4\pi r^2$.)

9 A tank is initially filled with 1000 litres of brine, containing 0.15 kg of salt per litre. Fresh brine containing 0.25 kg of salt per litre runs into the tank at a rate of 4 litres s^{-1}, and the mixture (kept uniform by vigorous stirring) runs out at the same rate. Show that if Q (in kg) is the amount of salt in the tank at time t (in s) then

$$\frac{dQ}{dt} = 1 - \frac{Q}{250}$$

10 The bending moment $M(x)$ for a beam of length l is given by $M(x) = W(2x - l)^3/8l^2$, $0 \leqslant x \leqslant l$. Find the formula for the shear force F. (See Example 7.7.)

11 A small weight is dragged across a horizontal plane by a string PQ of length a, the end P being attached to the weight while the end Q is made to move steadily along a fixed line perpendicular to the original position of PQ. Choosing the coordinate axes so that Oy is that fixed line and Ox passes through the initial position of P, as shown in Figure 7.14, show that the curve $y = y(x)$ described by P is such that

$$\frac{dy}{dx} = -\frac{\sqrt{(a^2 - x^2)}}{x}$$

The resulting curve is called a ***tractrix***.
This is investigated further in Exercises 7.8.14, Question 125.

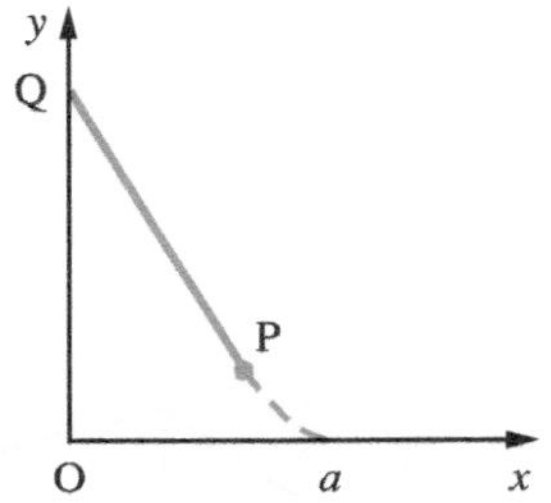

Figure 7.14

12 The limiting tension in a rope wound round a capstan (that is, the tension when the rope is about to slip) depends on the angle of wrap θ, as shown in Figure 7.15. Show that an increase $\Delta\theta$ in the angle of wrap produces a corresponding increase ΔT in the value of the limiting tension such that

$$\Delta T \approx \mu T \Delta\theta$$

where μ is the coefficient of friction. Deduce $dT/d\theta$.

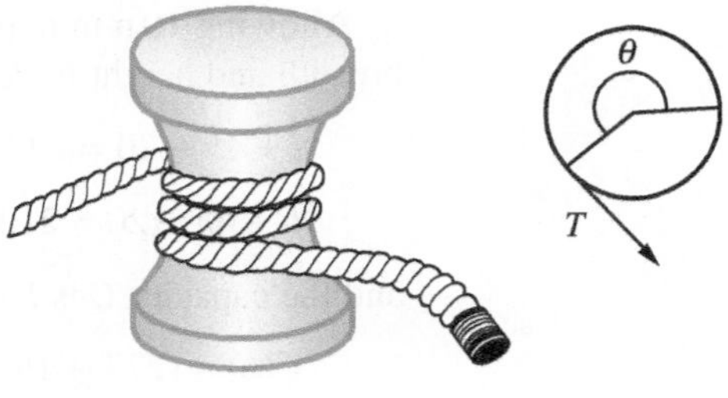

Figure 7.15

13 A chemical dissolves in water at a rate jointly proportional to the amount undissolved and to the difference between the concentration in the solution and that in the saturated solution. Initially none of the chemical is dissolved in the water. Show that the amount $x(t)$ of undissolved chemical satisfies the differential equation

$$\frac{dx}{dt} = kx(M - x_0 + x)$$

where k is a constant, M is the amount of the chemical in the saturated solution and $x_0 = x(0)$.

14 The rate at which a solute diffuses through a membrane is proportional to the area and to the concentration difference across the membrane. A solution of concentration C flows down a tube with constant velocity v. The solute diffuses through the wall of the tube into an ambient solution of the same solute of a lower fixed concentration C_0. If the tube has constant circular cross-section of radius r, show that at distance x along the tube the concentration $C(x)$ satisfies the differential equation

$$\frac{dC}{dx} = -\frac{2k}{rv}(C - C_0)$$

where k is a constant.

15 A lecture theatre having volume $1000\,m^3$ is designed to seat 200 people. The air is conditioned continuously by an inflow of fresh air at a constant rate V (in $m^3\,min^{-1}$). An average person generates $980\,cm^3$ of CO_2 per minute, while fresh air contains 0.04% of CO_2 by volume. Show that the percentage concentration x of CO_2 by volume in the lecture theatre at time t (in min) after the audience enters satisfies the differential equation

$$1000\frac{dx}{dt} = 19.6 + 0.04V - Vx(t)$$

If initially $x(0) = 0.04$, show that $x(t)$ is an increasing function of t for $t > 0$. Deduce that the maximum x^* of $x(t)$ is given by

$$x^* = (19.6 + 0.04V)/V$$

If the specification is that x does not exceed 0.06 (that is, 50% increase above fresh air), deduce that V must be chosen so that $V > 980$. Comment on this result.

16 Consider the chemical reaction

$$A + B \rightarrow X$$

Let x be the amount of product X, and a and b the initial amounts of A and B (with x, a and b in mol). The rate of reaction is proportional to the product of the uncombined amounts of A and B remaining. Express this relationship in terms of $\frac{dx}{dt}$, x, a and b.

17 A wire of length l metres is bent so as to form the boundary of a sector of a circle of radius r metres and angle θ radians. Show that

$$\theta = \frac{l - 2r}{r}$$

and prove that the area of the sector is greatest when the radius is $l/4$.

18 A manufacturer found that the sales figure for a certain item depended on the selling price. The market research department found that the maximum number of items that could be sold was 20 000 and that the number actually sold decreased by 100 for every 1p increase in price. The total cost of production of the items consisted of a set-up cost of £200 plus 50p per item manufactured. Show that the profit y pence as a function of the selling price x pence is

$$y = 25\,000x - 100x^2 - 1\,020\,000$$

What price should be adopted to maximize profits, and how many items are produced?

7.3 Techniques of differentiation

In this section we shall obtain the derivatives of some basic functions from 'first principles', that is, using the definition of a derivative given in (7.1), and will show how we obtain the derivatives of other functions using the basic results and some elementary rules. The rules themselves may be derived from the basic definition of the differentiation process. In practice, we make use of a very few basic facts, which, together with the rules, enable us to differentiate a wide variety of functions.

7.3.1 Basic rules of differentiation

To enable us to exploit the basic derivatives as we obtain them, we will first obtain the rules which make that exploitation possible. These rules you should know 'by heart'.

Rule 1 (constant multiplication rule)

If $y = f(x)$ and k is a constant then

$$\frac{\mathrm{d}}{\mathrm{d}x}(ky) = k\frac{\mathrm{d}y}{\mathrm{d}x} = kf'(x)$$

Rule 2 (sum rule)

If $u = f(x)$ and $v = g(x)$ then

$$\frac{\mathrm{d}}{\mathrm{d}x}(u + v) = \frac{\mathrm{d}u}{\mathrm{d}x} + \frac{\mathrm{d}v}{\mathrm{d}x} = f'(x) + g'(x)$$

Rule 3 (product rule)

If $u = f(x)$ and $v = g(x)$ then

$$\frac{\mathrm{d}}{\mathrm{d}x}(uv) = u\frac{\mathrm{d}v}{\mathrm{d}x} + v\frac{\mathrm{d}u}{\mathrm{d}x} = f(x)g'(x) + g(x)f'(x)$$

Rule 4 (quotient rule)

If $u = f(x)$ and $v = g(x)$ then

$$\frac{\mathrm{d}}{\mathrm{d}x}\left(\frac{u}{v}\right) = \frac{v(\mathrm{d}u/\mathrm{d}x) - u(\mathrm{d}v/\mathrm{d}x)}{v^2} = \frac{g(x)f'(x) - f(x)g'(x)}{[g(x)]^2}$$

Rule 5 (composite-function or chain rule)

If $z = g(x)$ and $y = f(z)$, then

$$\frac{\mathrm{d}y}{\mathrm{d}x} = \frac{\mathrm{d}y}{\mathrm{d}z}\frac{\mathrm{d}z}{\mathrm{d}x} = f'(z)g'(x)$$

Rule 6 (inverse-function rule)

If $y = f^{-1}(x)$, then $x = f(y)$ and

$$\frac{\mathrm{d}y}{\mathrm{d}x} = \frac{1}{\mathrm{d}x/\mathrm{d}y} = \frac{1}{f'(y)}$$

Rule 7 (parametric differentiation rule)

If $y = f(x)$ where $x = g(t)$ and $y = h(t)$ and t is a parameter, then

$$\frac{dy}{dx} = \frac{dy}{dt}\bigg/\frac{dx}{dt}$$

Verification of rules

Rule 1 follows directly from the definition given in (7.1), for if

$$g(x) = kf(x), \quad k \text{ constant}$$

$$g(x + \Delta x) = kf(x + \Delta x)$$

and

$$\Delta g = g(x + \Delta x) - g(x) = k[f(x + \Delta x) - f(x)]$$

so that

$$\frac{dg}{dx} = \lim_{\Delta x \to 0} \frac{\Delta g}{\Delta x} = \lim_{\Delta x \to 0} k\left[\frac{f(x + \Delta x) - f(x)}{\Delta x}\right] = kf'(x)$$

using the properties of limits given in Section 7.5.2.

Likewise, for *Rule 2*, if

$$h(x) = f(x) + g(x)$$

$$h(x + \Delta x) = f(x + \Delta x) + g(x + \Delta x)$$

and

$$\Delta h = h(x + \Delta x) - h(x) = [f(x + \Delta x) - f(x)] + [g(x + \Delta x) - g(x)]$$

so that

$$\frac{dh}{dx} = \lim_{\Delta x \to 0} \frac{\Delta h}{\Delta x} = \lim_{\Delta x \to 0}\left[\frac{f(x + \Delta x) - f(x)}{\Delta x}\right] + \lim_{\Delta x \to 0}\left[\frac{g(x + \Delta x) - g(x)}{\Delta x}\right]$$

using the properties of limits given in Section 7.5.2.

Thus

$$\frac{dh}{dx} = f'(x) + g'(x)$$

It also readily follows that if

$$y = f(x) - g(x)$$

then

$$\frac{dy}{dx} = f'(x) - g'(x)$$

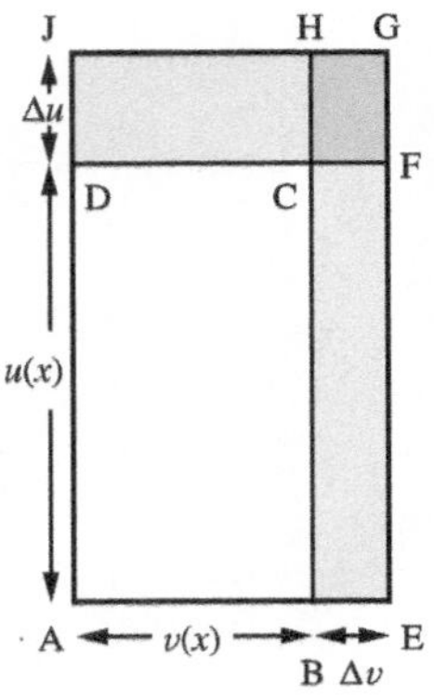

Figure 7.16

To verify *Rule 3* consider Figure 7.16. For any value of x, the area y of the rectangle ABCD is

$$y = u(x)v(x)$$

Increasing x by the increment Δx changes u and v by amounts Δu and Δv respectively, giving

$$u(x + \Delta x) = u(x) + \Delta u \quad \text{and} \quad v(x + \Delta x) = v(x) + \Delta v$$

From the diagram we see that the corresponding increment in y is given by

$$\begin{aligned}\Delta y &= \text{area EFCB} + \text{area CHJD} + \text{area CFGH} \\ &= u\,\Delta v + v\,\Delta u + \Delta u\,\Delta v\end{aligned}$$

so that

$$\frac{\mathrm{d}y}{\mathrm{d}x} = \lim_{\Delta x \to 0} \frac{\Delta y}{\Delta x} = \lim_{\Delta x \to 0} \left[u\frac{\Delta v}{\Delta x} + v\frac{\Delta u}{\Delta x} + \frac{\Delta u \Delta v}{\Delta x} \right]$$

leading to the result

$$\frac{\mathrm{d}y}{\mathrm{d}x} = u(x)v'(x) + u'(x)v(x)$$

since Δu and $\Delta v \to 0$ as $\Delta x \to 0$.

Rule 4 may then be deduced from Rule 3, for if

$$y = \frac{u}{v}$$

where $u = f(x)$ and $v = g(x)$, then $u = yv$ and Rule 3 gives

$$\begin{aligned}\frac{\mathrm{d}u}{\mathrm{d}x} &= y\frac{\mathrm{d}v}{\mathrm{d}x} + v\frac{\mathrm{d}y}{\mathrm{d}x} \\ &= \frac{u}{v}\frac{\mathrm{d}v}{\mathrm{d}x} + v\frac{\mathrm{d}y}{\mathrm{d}x} \quad \text{on substituting for } y\end{aligned}$$

Rearranging then gives the required result

$$\frac{\mathrm{d}y}{\mathrm{d}x} = \frac{v\dfrac{\mathrm{d}u}{\mathrm{d}x} - u\dfrac{\mathrm{d}v}{\mathrm{d}x}}{v^2}$$

Rule 5 will be verified in Section 7.3.6, *Rule 6* in Section 7.3.7 and *Rule 7* in Section 7.3.14.

7.3.2 Derivative of x^r

Using the definition of a derivative given in (7.1) and following the procedure of Example 7.1, we can proceed to obtain the derivative of the power function $f(x) = x^r$ when r is a real number.

Since $f(x) = x^r$ we have

$$f(x + \Delta x) = (x + \Delta x)^r$$

Using the binomial series (7.16) from Section 7.7.2 we have

$$(x + \Delta x)^r = x^r\left(1 + \frac{\Delta x}{x}\right)^r, \quad x \neq 0$$

$$= x^r\left[1 + r\frac{\Delta x}{x} + \frac{1}{2}r(r-1)\left(\frac{\Delta x}{x}\right)^2 + \dots\right]$$

$$= x^r + rx^{r-1}\Delta x + \frac{1}{2}r(r-1)x^{r-2}(\Delta x)^2 + \dots$$

so that

$$\frac{\Delta f}{\Delta x} = \frac{f(x + \Delta x) - f(x)}{\Delta x} = rx^{r-1} + \frac{1}{2}r(r-1)x^{r-2}(\Delta x) + \dots$$

Now letting $\Delta x \to 0$ we have that

$$\frac{\mathrm{d}f}{\mathrm{d}x} = \frac{\mathrm{d}(x^r)}{\mathrm{d}x} = \lim_{\Delta x \to 0}\frac{\Delta f}{\Delta x} = rx^{r-1}$$

leading to the general result

$$\frac{\mathrm{d}}{\mathrm{d}x}(x^r) = rx^{r-1}, \; r \in \mathbb{R} \tag{7.9}$$

Note that the solutions of Example 7.1 satisfy this general result.

Note also that (7.9) implies that if k is a constant then $\frac{\mathrm{d}k}{\mathrm{d}x} = 0$, which is as expected since the derivative measures the rate of change of the function.

Check that result (7.9), is determined by the following MATLAB commands:

```
syms h r x
df = limit(((x + h)^r - x^r)/h,h,0);
pretty(df)
```

Example 7.9 Using result (7.9), find $f'(x)$ when $f(x)$ is

(a) $\sqrt{x}$ (b) $\frac{1}{x^5}$ (c) $\frac{1}{\sqrt[3]{x}}$

Solution (a) Taking $r = \frac{1}{2}$ in (7.9) gives

$$\frac{\mathrm{d}}{\mathrm{d}x}(\sqrt{x}) = \frac{\mathrm{d}}{\mathrm{d}x}(x^{1/2}) = \tfrac{1}{2}x^{-1/2} = \frac{1}{2\sqrt{x}}$$

(b) Taking $r = -5$ in (7.9) gives

$$\frac{d}{dx}\left(\frac{1}{x^5}\right) = \frac{d}{dx}(x^{-5}) = -5x^{-6} = -\frac{5}{x^6}$$

(c) Taking $r = -\frac{1}{3}$ in (7.9) gives

$$\frac{d}{dx}\left(\frac{1}{\sqrt[3]{x}}\right) = \frac{d}{dx}(x^{-1/3}) = -\tfrac{1}{3}x^{-4/3} = -\frac{1}{3}\left(\frac{1}{\sqrt[3]{x^4}}\right)$$

Example 7.10 Using the result (7.9) and the rules of Section 7.3.1, find $f'(x)$ where $f(x)$ is

(a) $8x^4 - 4x^2$ (b) $(2x^2 + 5)(x^2 + 3x + 1)$ (c) $4x^7(x^2 - 3x)$

(d) $(x + 1)\sqrt{x}$ (e) $\dfrac{\sqrt{x}}{x + 1}$ (f) $\dfrac{x^3 + 2x + 1}{x^2 + 1}$

Solution (a) Using Rule 1 and result (7.9) with $r = 4$, we have

$$\frac{d}{dx}(8x^4) = 32x^3$$

Similarly

$$\frac{d}{dx}(4x^2) = 8x$$

Using Rule 2, we have

$$\frac{d}{dx}(8x^4 - 4x^2) = 32x^3 - 8x$$

(b) Using the result (7.9) with Rules 1 and 2, we obtain

$$\frac{d}{dx}(2x^2 + 5) = 4x \quad \text{and} \quad \frac{d}{dx}(x^2 + 3x + 1) = 2x + 3$$

Taking $u = 2x^2 + 5$ and $v = x^2 + 3x + 1$ in Rule 3, we obtain

$$\frac{d}{dx}[(2x^2 + 5)(x^2 + 3x + 1)] = 4x(x^2 + 3x + 1) + (2x^2 + 5)(2x + 3)$$

Multiplying out these terms we obtain

$$f'(x) = 8x^3 + 18x^2 + 14x + 15$$

(c) Using Rule 3 with $u(x) = 4x^7$ and $v(x) = (x^2 - 3x)$ we obtain

$$\begin{aligned} f'(x) &= (28x^6)(x^2 - 3x) + (4x^7)(2x - 3) \\ &= 36x^8 - 96x^7 \\ &= 12x^7(3x - 8) \end{aligned}$$

Alternatively, we could write $f(x) = 4x^9 - 12x^8$ giving $f'(x) = 36x^8 - 96x^7$ directly. It is important to look at expressions carefully before applying the rules. Sometimes there are quicker routes to the solution.

(d) Multiplying out we have

$$f(x) = x\sqrt{x} + \sqrt{x} = x^{3/2} + x^{1/2}$$

so that

$$f'(x) = \tfrac{3}{2}x^{1/2} + \tfrac{1}{2}x^{-1/2} = \frac{(3x + 1)}{2\sqrt{x}}$$

(e) Using Rule 4 with $u = \sqrt{x}$ and $v = x + 1$ so that $u'(x) = \tfrac{1}{2}x^{-1/2}$ and $v'(x) = 1$, we obtain

$$f'(x) = \frac{\tfrac{1}{2}x^{-1/2}(x + 1) - x^{1/2}(1)}{(x + 1)^2} = \frac{1 - x}{2(1 + x)^2\sqrt{x}}$$

(f) Using Rule 4 with $u = x^3 + 2x + 1$ and $v = x^2 + 1$, we obtain

$$f'(x) = \frac{(3x^2 + 2)(x^2 + 1) - (x^3 + 2x + 1)(2x)}{(x^2 + 1)^2}$$

$$= \frac{x^4 + x - 2x + 2}{(x^2 + 1)^2}$$

Symbolically in MATLAB, if $y = f(x)$ then its derivative, with respect to x, is determined using the `diff(y)` or `diff(y,x)` commands (either can be used as y is a function of only one variable). Thus the derivative is determined by the commands

```
syms x y
y = f(x); dy = diff(y)
```

The corresponding commands in MAPLE are

```
y:= f(x); dy:= diff(y,x);
```

In both cases the `simplify` command may be used to simplify the answer returned by the `diff` command. To illustrate, we consider Example 7.10(b), for which the commands

MATLAB	MAPLE
`syms x y`	
`y = (2*x^2 + 5)*(x^2 + 3*x + 1);`	`y:= (2*x^2 + 5)*` `(x^2 + 3*x + 1);`
`dy = diff(y)`	`dy:= diff(y,x);`

return

MATLAB	MAPLE
`dy = 4*x*(x^2 + 3*x + 1) + (2*x^2 + 5)*(2*x + 3)`	dy:= $4x(x^2 + 3x + 1) + (2x^2 + 5)(2x + 3)$

Using the *simplify* command, coupled with the *pretty* command for MATLAB, we have that the commands

```
dy = simplify(dy);                          dy:= simplify(dy);
pretty(dy)
```

return the derivative as

```
dy = 8x^3 + 18x^2 + 14x + 15
```

In practice we often anticipate the need to simplify and use the single command `simplify(diff(y))` in MATLAB and `simplify(diff(y,x));` in MAPLE. Considering Example 7.10(e), the MATLAB commands

```
syms x y
y = sqrt(x)/(x + 1); dy = simplify(diff(y));
pretty(dy)
```

return the derivative as

```
                x - 1
dy = -1/2 ---------------
          x^(1/2) (x + 1)^2
```

For practice check the answers to sections (a), (c), (d) and (f) of Example 7.10 using MATLAB or MAPLE.

7.3.3 Differentiation of polynomial functions

Using the result

$$\frac{\mathrm{d}}{\mathrm{d}x}(x^r) = rx^{r-1}$$

given in equation (7.9), together with the rules developed in Section 7.3.1, we proceed in this and following sections to find the derivatives of a range of algebraic functions. It is a simple matter to find the derivative of the polynomial function

$$f(x) = a_0 + a_1x + a_2x^2 + a_3x^3 + \dots + a_{n-1}x^{n-1} + a_nx^n = \sum_{r=0}^{n} a_rx^r \qquad \mathbf{(7.10)}$$

where n is a non-negative integer and the coefficients a_r, $r = 0, 1, \dots, n$, are real numbers.

Using the constant multiplication rule together with the sum rule we may differentiate term by term to give

$$f'(x) = a_1 + 2a_2x + 3a_3x^2 + \dots + (n-1)a_{n-1}x^{n-2} + na_nx^{n-1} = \sum_{r=1}^{n} ra_rx^{r-1}$$

Example 7.11 If $y = 2x^4 - 2x^3 - x^2 + 3x - 2$, find $\dfrac{dy}{dx}$.

Solution Differentiating term by term, using the sum rule, gives

$$\frac{dy}{dx} = \frac{d}{dx}(2x^4) - \frac{d}{dx}(2x^3) - \frac{d}{dx}(x^2) + \frac{d}{dx}(3x) - \frac{d}{dx}(2)$$

which on using the constant multiplication rule gives

$$\frac{dy}{dx} = 2\frac{d}{dx}(x^4) - 2\frac{d}{dx}(x^3) - \frac{d}{dx}(x^2) + 3\frac{d}{dx}(x) - \frac{d}{dx}(2)$$

$$= 2(4x^3) - 2(3x^2) - (2x) + 3(1) - 0$$

so that

$$\frac{dy}{dx} = 8x^3 - 6x^2 - 2x + 3$$

Example 7.12 The distance s metres moved by a body in t seconds is given by

$$s = 2t^3 - 1.5t^2 - 6t + 12$$

Determine the velocity and acceleration after 2 seconds.

Solution

$$s = 2t^3 - 1.5t^2 - 6t + 12$$

The velocity v (m s^{-1}) is given by $v = \dfrac{ds}{dt}$, so that

$$v = \frac{ds}{dt} = 2(3t^2) - 1.5(2t) - 6(1) = 6t^2 - 3t - 6$$

When $t = 2$ seconds

$$v = 6(4) - 3(2) - 6 = 12$$

so that the velocity after 2 seconds is 12 m s^{-1}.

The acceleration a (m s^{-2}) is given by $a = \dfrac{dv}{dt}$, so that

$$a = \frac{dv}{dt} = \frac{d}{dt}(6t^2 - 3t - 6) = 12t - 3$$

When $t = 2$ seconds

$$a = 12(2) - 3 = 21$$

so that the acceleration after 2 seconds is 21 m s^{-2}.

Sometimes polynomial functions are not expressed in the standard form of (7.10), $f(x) = (2x + 5)^3$ and $f(x) = (3x - 1)^2(x + 2)^3$ being such examples. Such cases will be considered in Section 7.3.6 where the differentiation of composite functions will be discussed.

The derivatives of polynomial functions can be evaluated numerically by a simple extension of the method of synthetic division (or nested multiplication) which is used for evaluating the function itself. We saw in Section 2.4.3 that

$$f(x) = a_n x^n + a_{n-1}x^{n-1} + \ldots + a_1 x + a_0$$

could be written as $f(x) = g(x)(x - c) + f(c)$ where

$$g(x) = b_{n-1}x^{n-1} + b_{n-2}x^{n-2} + \ldots + b_1 x + b_0$$

and where the coefficients $b_{n-1}, \ldots, b_0$ were generated in the process of nested multiplication. Differentiating $f(x)$ with respect to x using the product rule gives

$$f'(x) = g'(x)(x - c) + g(x)(1)$$

so that

$$f'(c) = g'(c)(0) + g(c)(1) = g(c)$$

Thus we can evaluate $f'(c)$ by applying the nested multiplication method again but this time to $g(x)$.

Example 7.13 Evaluate $f(2)$ and $f'(2)$ for the polynomial function

$$f(x) = 2x^4 - 2x^3 - x^2 + 3x - 2$$

Solution

$$\begin{array}{r|rrrrl} & 2 & -2 & -1 & 3 & -2 \\ \times 2 & 0 & 4 & 4 & 6 & 18 \\ \hline & 2 & 2 & 3 & 9 & 16 = f(2) \\ \times 2 & 0 & 4 & 12 & 30 & \\ \hline & 2 & 6 & 15 & 39 = f'(2) & \end{array}$$

This method of evaluating the function and its derivative is very efficient and is often used in computer packages which require finding the roots of polynomial equations.

7.3.4 Differentiation of rational functions

As we saw in Section 2.5, rational functions have the general form

$$f(x) = \frac{p(x)}{q(x)}$$

where $p(x)$ and $q(x)$ are polynomials. To obtain the derivatives of such functions we make use of the constant multiplication, sum and quotient rules, as illustrated in Example 7.14.

Example 7.14 Find the derivative of the following functions of x:

(a) $\dfrac{3x+2}{2x^2+1}$ (b) $\dfrac{2x+3}{x^2+x+1}$

(c) $x^3+2x^2-\dfrac{1}{x}+\dfrac{1}{x^2}+3,\quad x\neq 0$

Solution (a) Taking $u = 3x + 2$ and $v = 2x^2 + 1$ gives

$$\frac{du}{dx}=3 \quad\text{and}\quad \frac{dv}{dx}=4x$$

so, from the quotient rule,

$$\frac{d}{dx}\left[\frac{3x+2}{2x^2+1}\right]=\frac{v\left(\frac{du}{dx}\right)-u\left(\frac{dv}{dx}\right)}{v^2}$$

$$=\frac{(2x^2+1)3-(3x+2)4x}{(2x^2+1)^2}$$

$$=\frac{-(6x^2+8x-3)}{(2x^2+1)^2}$$

(b) Taking $u = 2x + 3$ and $v = x^2 + x + 1$

$$\frac{du}{dv}=2 \quad\text{and}\quad \frac{dv}{dx}=2x+1$$

so, from the quotient rule,

$$\frac{d}{dx}\left[\frac{2x+3}{x^2+x+1}\right]=\frac{(x^2+x+1)(2)-(2x+3)(2x+1)}{(x^2+x+1)^2}$$

$$=-\frac{(2x^2+6x+1)}{(x^2+x+1)^2}$$

(c) In this case we can express the function as

$$y=x^3+2x^2-x^{-1}+x^{-2}+3,\quad x\neq 0$$

and differentiate term by term to give

$$\frac{dy}{dx}=3x^2+2(2x)-(-x^{-2})+(-2x^{-3})+0=3x^2+4x+x^{-2}-2x^{-3}$$

$$=3x^2+4x+\frac{1}{x^2}-\frac{2}{x^3},\quad x\neq 0$$

7.3.5 Exercises

19 Differentiate the function f where $f(x)$ is

(a) x^9 (b) $\sqrt{(x^3)}$ (c) $-4x^2$

(d) $4x^4 + 2x^5$ (e) $4x^3 + x - 8$ (f) $1/(2x^2)$

(g) $x + \sqrt{x}$ (h) $2x^{7/2}$ (i) $1/(3x^3)$

20 Using the product rule, differentiate the function f where $f(x)$ is

(a) $(3x^4 - 1)(x^2 + 5x)$ (b) $(5x + 1)(x^3 + 3x - 6)$

(c) $(7x + 3)(\sqrt{x} + 1/\sqrt{x})$ (d) $(3 - 2x)(2x - 9/x)$

(e) $(\sqrt{x} - 1/\sqrt{x})(x - 1/x)$

(f) $(x^2 + x + 1)(2x^2 + x - 1)$

21 Using the quotient rule, differentiate the function f where $f(x)$ is

(a) $(3x^2 + x + 1)/(x^3 + 1)$ (b) $\sqrt{(2x)}/(x^2 + 4)$

(c) $(x + 1)/(x^2 + 1)$ (d) $x^{2/3}/(x^{1/3} + 1)$

(e) $(x^2 + 1)/(x + 1)$

(f) $(2x^2 - x + 1)/(x^2 - 2x + 2)$

22 Differentiate the function f where $f(x)$ is

(a) $(ax + b)(cx + d)$ (b) $(ax + b)/(cx + d)$

(c) $3ax^2 + 5bx + c$ (d) $ax^2/(bx + c)$

23 A fruit juice manufacturer wishes to design a carton that has a square face, as shown in Figure 7.17(a). The carton is to contain 1 litre of juice and is made from a rectangular sheet of waxed cardboard by folding it into a rectangular tube and sealing down the edge and then folding and sealing the top and bottom. To make the carton airtight and robust for handling, an overlap of at least 0.5 cm is needed. The net for the carton is shown in Figure 7.17(b).

Show that the amount $A(h)$ cm^2 of card used is given by

$$A(h) = \left[h + \frac{1000}{h^2} + 1\right]\left[2h + \frac{2000}{h^2} + 0.5\right]$$

Verify that

$$A(h) = 2\left[h + \frac{1000}{h^2} + \frac{5}{8}\right]^2 - \frac{9}{32}$$

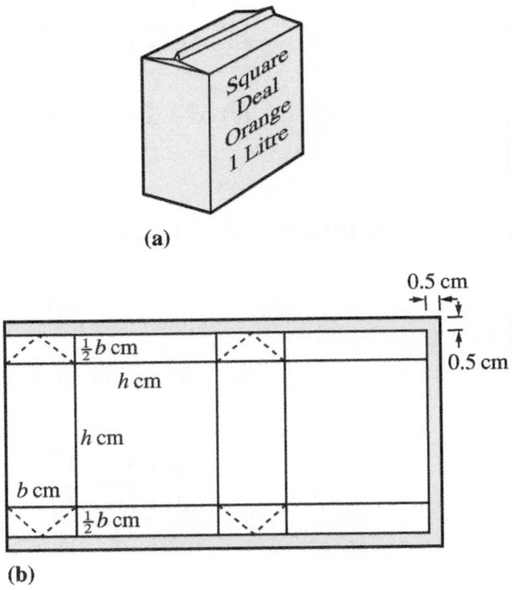

Figure 7.17 Carton of Question 23.

By finding the value x^* of x which minimizes $y = x + \dfrac{1000}{x^2}$, find the value h^* of h which minimizes $A(h)$.

24 Using the method of Example 7.13, evaluate $f(3)$, $f'(3)$, $f(-1)$ and $f'(-1)$ for the polynomal function

$$f(x) = 5x^4 - 3x^3 + x^2 - 2$$

25 Differentiate the function f where $f(x)$ is

(a) $5x^2 - 2x + 1$

(b) $4x^3 + x - 8$

(c) $x^{24} + 3$

(d) $(x^2 + x - 2)(3x^2 - 5x + 1)$

(e) $(x^4 - 3x + 1)(6x^2 + 5)$

(f) $(x - 3)/(x - 2)$

(g) $x/(x + 1)$

(h) $1/(x^2 - 4x + 1)$

(i) $x/(x^2 + 5x + 6)$

7.3.6 Differentiation of composite functions

As mentioned earlier, to differentiate many functions we need a further rule to deal with composite functions.

Rule 5 (composite-function or chain rule)

If $z = g(x)$ and $y = f(z)$ then

$$\frac{dy}{dx} = \frac{dy}{dz}\frac{dz}{dx} = f'(z)g'(x)$$

Verifying Rule 5 is a little more difficult than Rules 1–4. For an increment Δx in x, let Δz and Δy be the corresponding increments in z and y respectively. It then follows from definition (7.1) that

$$\Delta z = g'(x)\Delta x + \varepsilon_1 \Delta x \tag{7.11}$$

where $\varepsilon_1 \to 0$ as $\Delta x \to 0$. Likewise

$$\Delta y = f'(z)\Delta z + \varepsilon_2 \Delta z \tag{7.12}$$

where $\varepsilon_2 \to 0$ as $\Delta z \to 0$. Combining (7.11) and (7.12) then gives

$$\Delta y = [f'(z) + \varepsilon_2][g'(x) + \varepsilon_1]\Delta x$$

so that

$$\frac{\Delta y}{\Delta x} = f'(z)g'(x) + \varepsilon_2 g'(x) + \varepsilon_1 f'(z) + \varepsilon_1\varepsilon_2$$

As $\Delta x \to 0$ so does $\Delta z \to 0$, $\varepsilon_1 \to 0$ and $\varepsilon_2 \to 0$ and

$$\frac{dy}{dx} = \lim_{\Delta x \to 0} \frac{\Delta y}{\Delta x} = f'(z)g'(x)$$

as required.

Adapting Figure 2.12 (Section 2.2.4), the chain rule

$$\frac{dy}{dx} = \frac{dy}{dz} \cdot \frac{dz}{dx}$$

may be represented as in Figure 7.18.

Figure 7.18
The chain rule of differentiation.

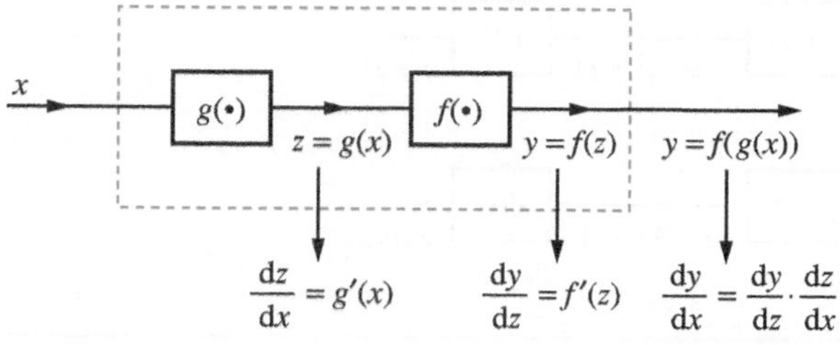

Example 7.15 Find $\frac{dy}{dx}$ when y is

(a) $(5x^2 + 11)^9$ (b) $\sqrt{(3x^2 + 1)}$

Solution (a) In this case we could expand out $(5x^2 + 11)^9$ and treat it as a polynomial of degree 18. However, it is advantageous to view it as a composite function, as represented in Figure 7.19(a). Thus, taking

$$y = z^9 \quad \text{and} \quad z = 5x^2 + 11$$

$$\frac{dy}{dz} = 9z^8 \quad \text{and} \quad \frac{dz}{dx} = 10x$$

so, by the chain rule,

$$\frac{dy}{dx} = \frac{dy}{dz}\frac{dz}{dx} = 9(5x^2 + 11)^8(10x) = 90x(5x^2 + 11)^8$$

(b) The composite function $y = \sqrt{(3x^2 + 1)}$ may be represented as in Figure 7.19(b). Thus, taking

$$y = \sqrt{z} = z^{1/2} \quad \text{and} \quad z = 3x^2 + 1$$

$$\frac{dy}{dz} = \tfrac{1}{2}z^{-1/2} = \frac{1}{2\sqrt{z}} \quad \text{and} \quad \frac{dz}{dx} = 6x$$

so, by the chain rule,

$$\frac{dy}{dx} = \frac{dy}{dz}\frac{dz}{dx} = \frac{1}{2\sqrt{(3x^2 + 1)}}6x = \frac{3x}{\sqrt{(3x^2 + 1)}}$$

It is usual to refer to z as the **intermediate** (or auxiliary) variable, and once the process has been understood the schematic representation, by a block diagram, stage is dispensed with. Note that when $z = g(z)$ is a linear function $z = ax + b$, then $\frac{dz}{dx} = a$ and $\frac{dy}{dx} = af'(ax + b)$.

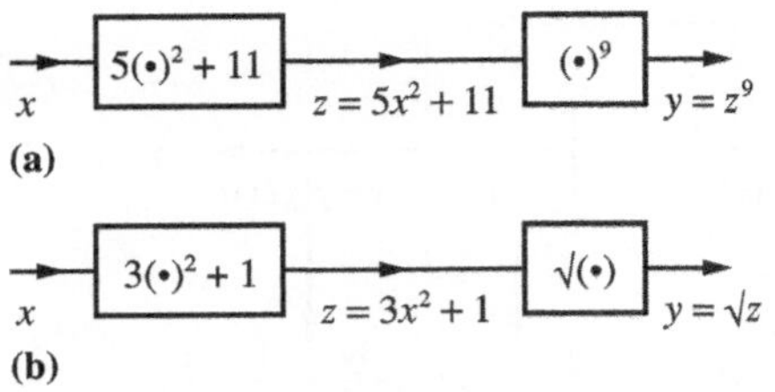

Figure 7.19 (a) Representation of $y = (5x^2 + 11)^9$. (b) Representation of $y = \sqrt{(3x^2 + 1)}$.

Example 7.16 Find $\dfrac{dy}{dx}$ when y is

(a) $(3x^3 - 2x^2 + 1)^5$ (b) $\dfrac{1}{(5x^2 - 2)^7}$

(c) $(x^2 + 1)^3\sqrt{(x - 1)}$ (d) $\dfrac{\sqrt{(2x + 1)}}{(x^2 + 1)^3}$

Solution (a) Introducing the intermediate variable $z = 3x^3 - 2x^2 + 1$ we have

$$y = z^5 \quad \text{and} \quad z = 3x^3 - 2x^2 + 1$$

$$\frac{dy}{dz} = 5z^4 \quad \text{and} \quad \frac{dz}{dx} = 9x^2 - 4x$$

so, by the chain rule,

$$\frac{dy}{dx} = \frac{dy}{dz}\frac{dz}{dx} = 5(3x^3 - 2x^2 + 1)^4(9x^2 - 4x)$$

$$= 5x(9x - 4)(3x^3 - 2x^2 + 1)^4$$

(b) Introducing the intermediate variable $z = 5x^2 - 2$ we have

$$y = \frac{1}{z^7} = z^{-7} \quad \text{and} \quad z = 5x^2 - 2$$

$$\frac{dy}{dz} = -7z^{-8} = -\frac{7}{z^8} \quad \text{and} \quad \frac{dz}{dx} = 10x$$

so, by the chain rule,

$$\frac{dy}{dx} = \frac{dy}{dz}\frac{dz}{dx} = -\frac{7}{(5x^2 - 2)^8}10x = -\frac{70x}{(5x^2 - 2)^8}$$

(c) In this case we are dealing with the product $y = uv$ where $u = (x^2 + 1)^3$ and $v = \sqrt{(x - 1)}$. Then by the product rule

$$\frac{dy}{dx} = u\frac{dv}{dx} + v\frac{du}{dx}$$

To find $\dfrac{du}{dx}$ we introduce the intermediate variable $z = x^2 + 1$ giving $u = z^3$ and so, by the chain rule,

$$\frac{du}{dx} = \frac{du}{dz}\frac{dz}{dx} = 3(x^2 + 1)^2 2x = 6x(x^2 + 1)^2$$

Likewise, to find $\dfrac{dv}{dx}$ we introduce the intermediate variable $w = x - 1$ giving $v = \sqrt{w} = w^{1/2}$ and $w = x - 1$, so by the chain rule

$$\frac{dv}{dx} = \frac{1}{2\sqrt{(x - 1)}}$$

It then follows from the product rule that

$$\begin{array}{cccc} u & \dfrac{dv}{dx} & v & \dfrac{du}{dx} \\ \downarrow & \downarrow & \downarrow & \downarrow \end{array}$$

$$\frac{dy}{dx} = (x^2+1)^3\frac{1}{2\sqrt{(x-1)}} + \sqrt{(x-1)}6x(x^2+1)^2$$

$$= \frac{(x^2+1)^2}{2\sqrt{(x-1)}}[(x^2+1) + 12x(x-1)]$$

$$= \frac{(x^2+1)^2(13x^2-12x+1)}{2\sqrt{(x-1)}}$$

(d) In this case we are dealing with the quotient

$$y = \frac{u}{v}$$

where $u = \sqrt{(2x+1)}$ and $v = (x^2+1)^3$. Then by the quotient rule

$$\frac{dy}{dx} = \frac{v\left(\dfrac{du}{dx}\right) - u\left(\dfrac{dv}{dx}\right)}{v^2}$$

To find $\dfrac{du}{dx}$ we introduce the intermediate variable $z = 2x + 1$, giving $u = z^{1/2}$ and $z = 2x + 1$, so by the chain rule

$$\frac{du}{dx} = \frac{du}{dz}\frac{dz}{dx} = \frac{1}{\sqrt{(2x+1)}}$$

To find $\dfrac{dv}{dx}$ we introduce the intermediate variable $w = x^2 + 1$, giving $v = w^3$ and $w = x^2 + 1$, so by the chain rule

$$\frac{dv}{dx} = \frac{dv}{dw}\frac{dw}{dx} = 3(x^2+1)^2 2x = 6x(x^2+1)^2$$

Then, by the quotient rule,

$$\begin{array}{ccccc} v & \dfrac{du}{dx} & u & \dfrac{dv}{dx} & v^2 \\ \downarrow & \downarrow & \downarrow & \downarrow & \end{array}$$

$$\frac{dy}{dx} = \frac{(x^2+1)^3\dfrac{1}{\sqrt{(2x+1)}} - \sqrt{(2x+1)}6x(x^2+1)^2}{(x^2+1)^6} = \frac{1-6x-11x^2}{(x^2+1)^4\sqrt{(2x+1)}}$$

Both MATLAB and MAPLE can handle the functions covered in previous sections. To illustrate, consider Examples 7.14(a), 7.15(b) and 7.16(c). For 7.14(a) the commands

MATLAB

```
syms x y
y = (3*x + 2)/(2*x^2 + 1);
dy = simplify(diff(y))
pretty(dy)
```

MAPLE

```
y:= (3*x + 2)/(2*x^2 + 1);
dy:= simplify(diff(y,x));
```

return the derivative as

$$dy = -\frac{6x^2 - 3 + 8x}{(2x^2 + 1)^2}$$

For Example 7.15(b) the commands

```
syms x y
y = sqrt(3*x^2 + 1);
dy = diff(y);
pretty(dy)
```

```
y:= sqrt(3*x^2 + 1);
dy:= diff(y,x);
```

return the derivative as

$$dy = 3\frac{x}{(3x^2 + 1)^{1/2}} \qquad dy = \frac{3x}{\sqrt{(3x^2 + 1)}}$$

For Example 7.16(c) the commands

```
syms x y
y = (x^2 + 1)^3*sqrt(x - 1);
dy = simplify(diff(y));
pretty(dy)
```

```
y:= (x^2 + 1)^3*sqrt(x - 1);
dy:= simplify(diff(y,x));
```

return the derivative as

$$dy = \frac{1}{2}\frac{(x^2 + 1)^2(13x^2 - 12x + 1)}{(x - 1)^{1/2}} \qquad dy = \frac{(x^2 + 1)^2(13x^2 - 12x + 1)}{2\sqrt{(x - 1)}}$$

For practice, check the answers to the remaining sections of Examples 7.14–7.16.

7.3.7 Differentiation of inverse functions

The algebraic and graphical properties of inverse functions were described in Section 2.2.3 earlier. It is often useful to be able to express the derivative of an inverse function in terms of the derivatives of the original function from which it came. To do this we use the following rule

Rule 6 (inverse-function rule)

If $y = f^{-1}(x)$ then $x = f(y)$ and

$$\frac{dy}{dx} = \frac{1}{dx/dy} = \frac{1}{f'(y)}$$

Rule 6 may be readily deduced from graphical considerations. Since the graph of $y = f^{-1}(x)$ is the mirror image of the graph of $y = f(x)$ in the line $y = x$ (see Figure 7.20) it follows that since $\tan\theta = \cot(\frac{1}{2}\pi - \theta)$, the gradient with respect to the x direction is

$$\frac{dy}{dx} = \frac{1}{\text{gradient with respect to the } y \text{ direction}} = \frac{1}{dx/dy}$$

We will be making use of this rule in following sections, but a simple example is to consider the function defined by $y = x^{1/3}$. Then $x = y^3$ and $\frac{dx}{dy} = 3y^2$. Using the inverse-function rule we obtain

$$\frac{dy}{dx} = 1\Big/\frac{dx}{dy} = \frac{1}{3y^2}, \qquad y \neq 0$$

Since $y = x^{1/3}$ we deduce that $\frac{dy}{dx} = \frac{1}{3}x^{-2/3}$, $x \neq 0$ (agreeing with the general result $\frac{d}{dx}(x^r) = rx^{r-1}$)

Figure 7.20 Derivative of inverse function.

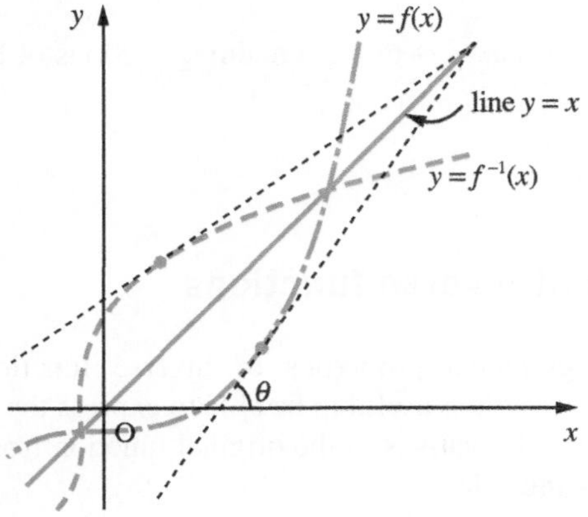

7.3.8 Exercises

Check your answers using MATLAB or MAPLE whenever possible.

26 Differentiate the function f where $f(x)$ is

(a) $(5x + 3)^9$ (b) $(4x - 2)^7$

(c) $(1 - 3x)^6$ (d) $(3x^2 - x + 1)^3$

(e) $(4x^3 - 2x + 1)^6$ (f) $(1 + x - x^4)^5$

27 Differentiate the function f where $f(x)$ is

(a) $(2x + 4)^7(3x - 2)^5$ (b) $(5x + 1)^3(3 - 2x)^4$

(c) $(\frac{1}{2}x + 2)^2(x + 3)^4$

(d) $(x^2 + x + 1)^2(x^3 + 2x^2 + 1)^4$

(e) $(x^5 + 2x + 1)^3(2x^2 + 3x - 1)^4$

(f) $(2x + 1)^3(7 - x)^5$ (g) $(x^2 + 4x + 1)(3x + 1)^5$

28 The algebraic function

$$y = \frac{\sqrt{(1 + x)} - 1}{\sqrt{(1 + x)} + 1}, \quad x > -1$$

is a root of the equation

$$xy^2 - 2(2 + x)y + x = 0$$

Show that $x = 4y/(y - 1)^2$ and hence that

$$\frac{dy}{dx} = -\frac{(y - 1)^3}{4(y + 1)}, \quad |y| < 1$$

29 An open water conduit is to be cut in the shape of an isosceles trapezium and lined with material which is available in a standard width of 1 metre, as shown in Figure 7.21.

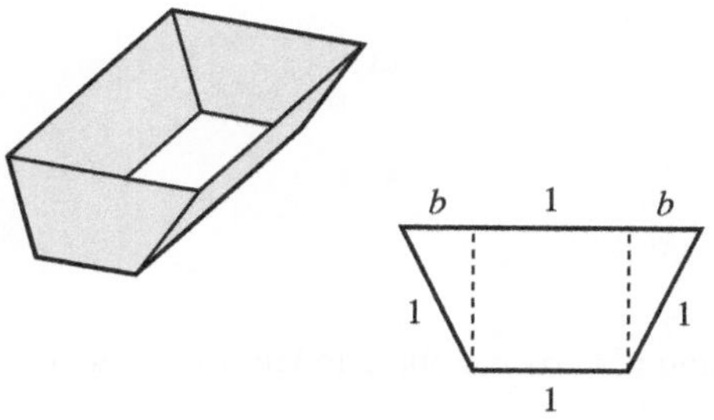

Figure 7.21 Water conduit of Question 29.

To achieve maximum potential capacity, the designer has to maximize the area of cross-section $A(b)$. Show that

$$A(b) = [(1 + b)^3(1 - b)]^{1/2}$$

and that this is maximized when $b = 0.5$.

30 A carton is made from a sheet of A4 card (210 mm × 297 mm) using the net shown in Figure 7.22. Find the dimensions that yield the largest capacity.

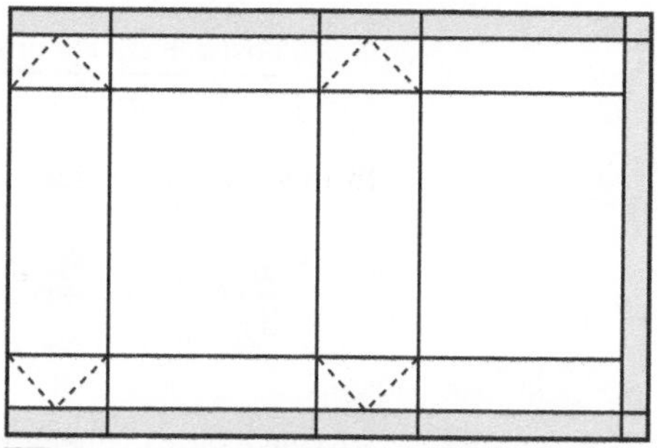

5 mm overlap for seal

Figure 7.22 Net used in Question 30.

31 Differentiate

(a) $\sqrt{(1 + 2x)}$ (b) $x\sqrt{(x + 2)}$ (c) $\sqrt{(x^2 + 2x)}$

32 Differentiate

(a) $x\sqrt{(4 + x^2)}$ (b) $x\sqrt{(9 - x^2)}$

(c) $(x + 1)\sqrt{(x^2 + 2x + 3)}$ (d) $x^{2/3} - x^{1/4}$

(e) $\sqrt[3]{(x^2 + 1)}$ (f) $x(2x - 1)^{1/3}$

33 Differentiate

(a) $1/(x + 3)^2$ (b) $\left(\sqrt{x} + \frac{1}{\sqrt{x}}\right)^2$

(c) $x/\sqrt{(x^2 - 1)}$ (d) $(2x + 1)^2/(3x^2 + 1)^3$

7.3.9 Differentiation of circular functions

Taking $f(x) = \sin x$ and using the sum identity (2.26b) gives from the formal definition (7.1)

$$f'(x) = \lim_{\Delta x \to 0} \frac{\sin(x + \Delta x) - \sin x}{\Delta x} = \lim_{\Delta x \to 0} \frac{\cos(x + \frac{1}{2}\Delta x)\sin(\frac{1}{2}\Delta x)}{\frac{1}{2}\Delta x}$$

Since, from Section 7.8.1, remembering that x is measured in radians here,

$$\lim_{\Delta x \to 0} \frac{\sin(\frac{1}{2}\Delta x)}{\frac{1}{2}\Delta x} = 1 \quad \text{and} \quad \lim_{\Delta x \to 0} \cos(x + \tfrac{1}{2}\Delta x) = \cos x$$

we have

$$f'(x) = \frac{\mathrm{d}}{\mathrm{d}x}(\sin x) = \cos x \tag{7.13}$$

Likewise, using the sum identity (2.25d), we have

$$\frac{\cos(x + \Delta x) - \cos x}{\Delta x} = \frac{-\sin(x + \frac{1}{2}\Delta x)\sin(\frac{1}{2}\Delta x)}{\frac{1}{2}\Delta x}$$

from which we deduce using (7.1) that

$$\frac{\mathrm{d}}{\mathrm{d}x}(\cos x) = -\sin x \tag{7.14}$$

As an exercise check results (7.13) and (7.14) using MATLAB or MAPLE.

Since $\tan x = \sin x/\cos x$, we take $u = \sin x$ and $v = \cos x$, giving

$$\frac{\mathrm{d}u}{\mathrm{d}x} = \cos x \quad \text{and} \quad \frac{\mathrm{d}v}{\mathrm{d}x} = -\sin x$$

Then, from the quotient rule,

$$\frac{\mathrm{d}}{\mathrm{d}x}(\tan x) = \frac{(\cos x)(\cos x) - (\sin x)(-\sin x)}{\cos^2 x}$$

$$= \frac{\cos^2 x + \sin^2 x}{\cos^2 x} = \frac{1}{\cos^2 x}$$

That is,

$$\frac{\mathrm{d}}{\mathrm{d}x}(\tan x) = \sec^2 x \tag{7.15}$$

Since $\sec x = 1/\cos x$, we take $u = 1$ and $v = \cos x$ in the quotient rule to give

$$\frac{\mathrm{d}}{\mathrm{d}x}(\sec x) = \frac{(\cos x)(0) - (1)(-\sin x)}{\cos^2 x} = \frac{1}{\cos x}\frac{\sin x}{\cos x}$$

That is,

$$\frac{d}{dx}(\sec x) = \sec x \tan x \tag{7.16}$$

Since cosec $x = 1/\sin x$, following the same procedure as above we obtain

$$\frac{d}{dx}(\text{cosec}\, x) = -\text{cosec}\, x \cot x \tag{7.17}$$

Since $\cot x = \cos x/\sin x$, taking $u = \cos x$ and $v = \sin x$ and using the quotient rule gives

$$\frac{d}{dx}(\cot x) = -\text{cosec}^2 x \tag{7.18}$$

Taking $y = \sin^{-1}x$, we have $x = \sin y$, so that

$$\frac{dx}{dy} = \cos y$$

Then, from the inverse-function rule,

$$\frac{dy}{dx} = \frac{1}{\cos y}$$

Using the identity $\cos^2 y = 1 - \sin^2 y$, this simplifies to

$$\frac{d}{dx}(\sin^{-1}x) = \frac{1}{\sqrt{(1 - x^2)}}, \quad |x| < 1 \tag{7.19}$$

(Note that we have taken the positive square root, since from Figure 2.70(b) the derivative must be positive.)

Taking $y = \cos^{-1}x$, we have $x = \cos y$, so that

$$\frac{dy}{dx} = \frac{1}{dx/dy} = -\frac{1}{\sin y}$$

which, using the identity $\sin^2 y = 1 - \cos^2 y$, reduces to

$$\frac{d}{dx}(\cos^{-1}x) = -\frac{1}{\sqrt{(1 - x^2)}}, \quad |x| < 1 \tag{7.20}$$

(Note from Figure 2.71 that the derivative is negative.)

Taking $y = \tan^{-1}x$, we have $x = \tan y$, so that

$$\frac{dy}{dx} = \frac{1}{dx/dy} = \frac{1}{\sec^2 y}$$

Using the identity $1 + \tan^2 y = \sec^2 y$, this reduces to

$$\frac{d}{dx}(\tan^{-1}x) = \frac{1}{1 + x^2} \tag{7.21}$$

Summary

$$\frac{d}{dx}(\sin x) = \cos x, \quad \frac{d}{dx}(\cos x) = -\sin x$$

$$\frac{d}{dx}(\tan x) = \sec^2 x, \quad \frac{d}{dx}(\sec x) = \sec x \tan x$$

$$\frac{d}{dx}(\text{cosec}\, x) = -\text{cosec}\, x \cot x, \quad \frac{d}{dx}(\cot x) = -\text{cosec}^2 x$$

$$\frac{d}{dx}(\sin^{-1} x) = \frac{1}{\sqrt{(1 - x^2)}}, \quad |x| < 1$$

$$\frac{d}{dx}(\cos^{-1} x) = \frac{-1}{\sqrt{(1 - x^2)}}, \quad |x| < 1$$

$$\frac{d}{dx}(\tan^{-1} x) = \frac{1}{1 + x^2}$$

Example 7.17 Find $\frac{dy}{dx}$ when y is given by

(a) $\sin(2x + 3)$ (b) $x^2 \cos x$ (c) $\frac{\sin 2x}{x^2 + 2}$

(d) $\sec 6x$ (e) $x \tan 2x$ (f) $\sin^{-1} 6x$

(g) $x^2 \cos^{-1} x$ (h) $\tan^{-1} \frac{2x}{1 + x^2}$

Solution (a) Introducing the intermediate variable $z = 2x + 3$, we have $y = \sin z$ and $z = 2x + 3$, so by the chain rule

$$\frac{dy}{dx} = \frac{dy}{dz}\frac{dz}{dx} = \cos(2x + 3)2 = 2\cos(2x + 3)$$

Note that this result could have been written using the particular linear case of the composite-function rule given in Section 7.3.6 after Example 7.15.

(b) Taking $u = x^2$ and $v = \cos x$ gives

$$\frac{du}{dx} = 2x \quad \text{and} \quad \frac{dv}{dx} = -\sin x$$

so by the product rule

$$\frac{dy}{dx} = -x^2 \sin x + 2x \cos x$$

(c) Taking $u = \sin 2x$ and $v = x^2 + 2$ gives

$$\frac{du}{dx} = 2\cos 2x \quad \text{and} \quad \frac{dv}{dx} = 2x$$

so by the quotient rule

$$\frac{dy}{dx} = \frac{2(x^2+2)\cos 2x - 2x\sin 2x}{(x^2+2)^2}$$

(d) Introducing the intermediate variable $z = 6x$ we have

$y = \sec z$ and $z = 6x$, so by the chain rule

$$\frac{dy}{dx} = \frac{dy}{dz}\frac{dz}{dx} = 6\sec 6x \tan 6x$$

(e) Taking $u = x$ and $v = \tan 2x$ gives

$$\frac{du}{dx} = 1 \quad \text{and} \quad \frac{dv}{dx} = 2\sec^2 2x$$

where the chain rule, with intermediate variable $z = 2x$, has been used to find $\frac{dv}{dx}$. Then by the product rule

$$\frac{dy}{dx} = 2x\sec^2 2x + \tan 2x$$

(f) Introducing the intermediate variable $z = 6x$ we have $y = \sin^{-1} z$ and $z = 6x$

$$\frac{dy}{dz} = \frac{1}{\sqrt{(1-z^2)}} \quad \text{and} \quad \frac{dz}{dx} = 6, \quad |z| < 1$$

so by the chain rule

$$\frac{dy}{dx} = \frac{dy}{dz}\frac{dz}{dx} = \frac{6}{\sqrt{(1-36x^2)}}, \quad |x| < \tfrac{1}{6}$$

(g) Taking $u = x^2$ and $v = \cos^{-1} x$ gives

$$\frac{du}{dx} = 2x \quad \text{and} \quad \frac{dv}{dx} = -\frac{1}{\sqrt{(1-x^2)}}$$

so by the product rule

$$\frac{dy}{dx} = -\frac{x^2}{\sqrt{(1-x^2)}} + 2x\cos^{-1} x$$

(h) Introducing the intermediate variable $z = \frac{2x}{1+x^2}$ we have

$$y = \tan^{-1} z \qquad \text{and} \qquad z = \frac{2x}{1+x^2}$$

$$\frac{dy}{dz} = \frac{1}{1+z^2} \quad \text{and} \quad \frac{dz}{dx} = \frac{(1+x^2)2 - 2x(2x)}{(1+x^2)^2} = \frac{2(1-x^2)}{(1+x^2)^2}$$

so from the chain rule

$$\frac{dy}{dx} = \frac{dy}{dz}\frac{dz}{dx} = \frac{1}{1 + \left(\frac{2x}{1 + x^2}\right)^2} \cdot \frac{2(1 - x^2)}{(1 + x^2)^2} = \frac{2(1 - x^2)}{(1 + x^2)^2 + (2x)^2}$$

$$= \frac{2(1 - x^2)}{x^4 + 6x^2 + 1}$$

7.3.10 Extended form of the chain rule

Sometimes there are more than two component functions involved in a composite function. For example, consider the composite function

$$y = f(w), \quad w = g(z), \quad z = h(x)$$

which may be represented schematically by the block diagram of Figure 7.23. To obtain the derivative $\frac{dy}{dx}$ we first consider y as a composite function of h and the 'dotted box', giving, on applying the chain rule,

$$\frac{dy}{dx} = \frac{dy}{dz}\frac{dz}{dx}$$

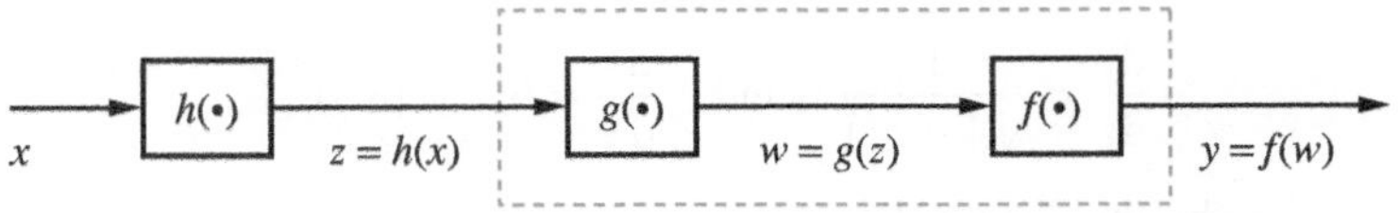

Figure 7.23 Composite function containing three component functions.

Reapplying the chain rule, this time with z as the domain variable, gives

$$\frac{dy}{dz} = \frac{dy}{dw}\frac{dw}{dz}$$

which on back substitution gives

$$\frac{dy}{dx} = \frac{dy}{dw}\frac{dw}{dz}\frac{dz}{dx}$$

as the extended form of the chain rule.

Example 7.18 Find $\frac{dy}{dx}$ when y is given by

(a) $\sin^2(x^2 + 1)$ (b) $\cos^{-1}\sqrt{(1 - x^2)}$

Solution (a) Introducing the intermediate variables $z = x^2 + 1$ and $w = \sin z$, then

$$y = w^2, \qquad w = \sin z, \qquad z = x^2 + 1$$

$$\frac{dy}{dw} = 2w, \qquad \frac{dw}{dz} = \cos z, \qquad \frac{dz}{dx} = 2x$$

so by the extended chain rule

$$\frac{dy}{dx} = \frac{dy}{dw}\frac{dw}{dz}\frac{dz}{dx} = (2w)(\cos z)(2x)$$

Since $z = x^2 + 1$ and $w = \sin z = \sin(x^2 + 1)$,

$$\frac{dy}{dx} = 4x \sin(x^2 + 1)\cos(x^2 + 1)$$

(b) Introducing the intermediate variables $z = 1 - x^2$ and $w = \sqrt{z}$, then

$$y = \cos^{-1}w, \qquad w = z^{1/2}, \qquad z = 1 - x^2$$

$$\frac{dy}{dw} = -\frac{1}{\sqrt{(1 - w^2)}}, \qquad \frac{dw}{dz} = \tfrac{1}{2}z^{-1/2}, \qquad \frac{dz}{dx} = -2x$$

Since $z = 1 - x^2$ and $w = \sqrt{(1 - x^2)}$ we have, by the extended chain rule,

$$\frac{dy}{dx} = \frac{dy}{dw}\frac{dw}{dz}\frac{dz}{dx} = \left(-\frac{1}{\sqrt{[1 - (1 - x^2)]}}\right)\left(\frac{1}{2\sqrt{(1 - x^2)}}\right)(-2x) = \frac{1}{\sqrt{(1 - x^2)}}$$

Here we have assumed $0 < x < 1$. If $-1 < x < 0$ the derivative is $-1/\sqrt{(1 - x^2)}$. The function has no derivative at $x = 0$. This is illustrated in Figure 7.24.

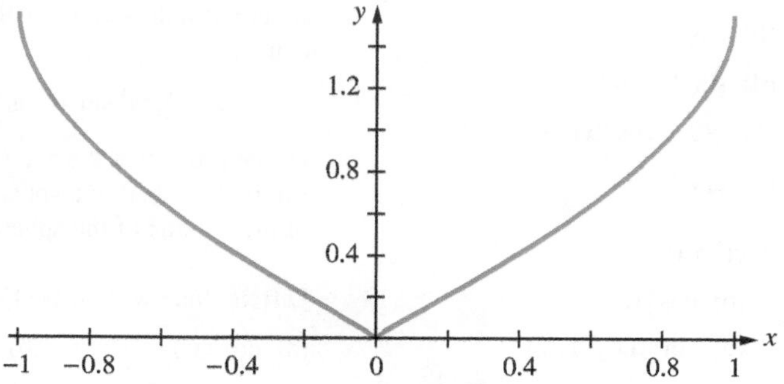

Figure 7.24 Graph of $y = \cos^{-1}(1 - x^2)$.

For practice, use MATLAB or MAPLE to check the answers to Examples 7.17 and 7.18. As illustrative examples we consider Examples 7.17(c and h) and Example 7.18(a). For Example 7.17(c) the MATLAB commands

```
syms x y
y = sin(2*x)/(x^2 + 2); dy = simplify(diff(y)); pretty(dy)
```

return the derivative as

```
            2 cos(2x)  + cos(2x)x^2  - sin(2x)x
dy  =  2 ------------------------------------
                      (2 + x^2)^2
```

For Example 7.17(h) the commands

MATLAB	MAPLE
`syms x y`	
`y = atan(2*x/(1 + x^2));`	`y:= arctan(2*x/(1 + x^2)):`
`dy = simplify(diff(y));`	`dy:= simplify(diff(y,x));`
`pretty(dy)`	

return the derivative as

$$dy = -2\frac{x^2 - 1}{x^4 + 6x^2 + 1}$$

For Example 7.18(a) the MATLAB commands

```
syms x y
y = (sin(x^2 + 1))^2; dy = diff(y); pretty(dy)
```

return the answer

$$4 \sin(x^2 + 1)\cos(x^2 + 1)x$$

7.3.11 Exercises

Check your answers using MATLAB or MAPLE whenever possible.

34 Differentiate with respect to x:

(a) $\sin(3x - 2)$ (b) $\cos^4 x$

(c) $\cos^2 3x$ (d) $\sin 2x \cos 3x$

(e) $x \sin x$ (f) $\sqrt{(2 + \cos 2x)}$

(g) $a \cos(x + \theta)$ (h) $\tan 4x$

35 Differentiate with respect to x:

(a) $\sin^{-1}(x/2)$ (b) $\cos^{-1}(5x)$

(c) $\sqrt{(1 + x^2)}\tan^{-1}x$ (d) $\sin^{-1}((x - 1)/2)$

(e) $\tan^{-1}3x$

(f) $\sqrt{(1 - x^2)}\sin^{-1}x$

36 A cone of semi-vertical angle θ is inscribed in a sphere of radius a. Show that the volume of the cone is

$$V = \tfrac{8}{3}\pi a^3 \sin^2\theta \cos^4\theta$$

Hence prove that the cone of maximum volume that can be inscribed in a sphere of given radius is $\frac{8}{27}$th of the volume of the sphere.

37 Differentiate with respect to x:

(a) $\cos^3(x^3)$ (b) $\tan^{-1}(\frac{1}{2}\tan\frac{1}{2}x)$

(c) $\sqrt{(1 + \sin^3 x)}$ (d) $\cos\sqrt{(x)}$

7.3.12 Differentiation of exponential and related functions

The formal definition (7.1) gives the derivative of e^x as

$$\frac{d}{dx}(e^x) = \lim_{\Delta x \to 0} \frac{e^{x+\Delta x} - e^x}{\Delta x} = \lim_{\Delta x \to 0} \frac{e^x(e^{\Delta x} - 1)}{\Delta x}$$

$$= e^x \lim_{\Delta x \to 0} \frac{1 + \Delta x + (\Delta x)^2/2! + (\Delta x)^3/3! + \ldots - 1}{\Delta x}$$

(using (7.16))

$$= e^x \lim_{\Delta x \to 0} [1 + \tfrac{1}{2}\Delta x + \tfrac{1}{6}(\Delta x)^2 + \dots]$$

so that

$$\frac{d}{dx}(e^x) = e^x \tag{7.22}$$

Thus the exponential function (to base e) has the special property that it is its own derivative. This was described in Section 2.7.1 earlier.

Taking $y = \ln x$, we have $x = e^y$ so that

$$\frac{dx}{dy} = e^y$$

Then, from the inverse-function rule,

$$\frac{dy}{dx} = \frac{1}{e^y} = \frac{1}{x}$$

That is

$$\frac{d}{dx}(\ln x) = \frac{1}{x}, \quad x > 0 \tag{7.23}$$

Example 7.19

Find $\frac{dy}{dx}$ when y is given by

(a) x^2e^x (b) $3e^{-2x}$ (c) $\frac{\ln x}{x^2}$

(d) $\ln(x^2 + 1)$ (e) $e^{-x}(\sin x + \cos x)$

Solution

(a) Taking $u = x^2$ and $v = e^x$

$$\frac{du}{dx} = 2x \quad \text{and} \quad \frac{dv}{dx} = e^x$$

Then by the product rule

$$\frac{dy}{dx} = x^2e^x + 2xe^x = x(x + 2)e^x$$

(b) Introducing the intermediate variable $z = -2x$ then

$$y = 3e^z \quad \text{and} \quad z = -2x$$

$$\frac{dy}{dz} = 3e^z \quad \text{and} \quad \frac{dz}{dx} = -2$$

so by the chain rule

$$\frac{dy}{dx} = \frac{dy}{dz}\frac{dz}{dx} = (3e^{-2x})(-2) = -6e^{-2x}$$

(c) Taking $u = \ln x$ and $v = x^2$ gives

$$\frac{du}{dx} = \frac{1}{x} \quad \text{and} \quad \frac{dv}{dx} = 2x \quad (x \neq 0)$$

so by the quotient rule

$$\frac{d}{dx}\left(\frac{\ln x}{x^2}\right) = \frac{(1/x)x^2 - (\ln x)(2x)}{x^4}$$

$$= \frac{1 - 2\ln x}{x^3}$$

(d) Introducing the intermediate variable $z = x^2 + 1$ then

$$y = \ln z \quad \text{and} \quad z = x^2 + 1$$

$$\frac{dy}{dz} = \frac{1}{z} \quad \text{and} \quad \frac{dz}{dx} = 2x$$

so by the chain rule

$$\frac{dy}{dx} = \frac{dy}{dz}\frac{dz}{dx} = \frac{1}{x^2+1}(2x) = \frac{2x}{x^2+1}$$

(e) Taking $u = e^{-x}$ and $v = \sin x + \cos x$

$$\frac{du}{dx} = -e^{-x} \quad \text{and} \quad \frac{dv}{dx} = \cos x - \sin x$$

Then by the product rule

$$\frac{dy}{dx} = e^{-x}(\cos x - \sin x) + (\sin x + \cos x)(-e^{-x})$$

$$= -2e^{-x}\sin x$$

The hyperbolic functions, introduced in Section 2.7.4, are closely related to the exponential function and their derivatives are readily deduced. From their definitions

$$\frac{d}{dx}(\sinh x) = \frac{d}{dx}\left[\frac{e^x - e^{-x}}{2}\right] = \tfrac{1}{2}(e^x + e^{-x}) = \cosh x \qquad \textbf{(7.24a)}$$

$$\frac{d}{dx}(\cosh x) = \frac{d}{dx}\left[\frac{e^x + e^{-x}}{2}\right] = \tfrac{1}{2}(e^x - e^{-x}) = \sinh x \qquad \textbf{(7.24b)}$$

$$\frac{d}{dx}(\tanh x) = \frac{d}{dx}\left[\frac{\sinh x}{\cosh x}\right] = \frac{(\cosh x)(\cosh x) - (\sinh x)(\sinh x)}{\cosh^2 x}$$

$$= \frac{1}{\cosh^2 x} = \text{sech}^2 x \qquad \textbf{(7.24c)}$$

$$\frac{d}{dx}(\text{sech}\, x) = \frac{d}{dx}\left[\frac{1}{\cosh x}\right] = \frac{-\sinh x}{\cosh^2 x} = -\text{sech}\, x \tanh x \quad \textbf{(7.24d)}$$

$$\frac{d}{dx}(\text{cosech}\, x) = \frac{d}{dx}\left[\frac{1}{\sinh x}\right] = -\text{cosech}\, x \coth x \quad \textbf{(7.24e)}$$

$$\frac{d}{dx}(\coth x) = \frac{d}{dx}\left[\frac{\cosh x}{\sinh x}\right] = -\text{cosech}^2 x \quad \textbf{(7.24f)}$$

Following the same procedure as for the inverse circular functions in Section 7.3.9 the following derivatives of the inverse hyperbolic functions are readily obtained.

$$\frac{d}{dx}(\sinh^{-1} x) = \frac{1}{\sqrt{(1 + x^2)}} \quad \textbf{(7.25a)}$$

$$\frac{d}{dx}(\cosh^{-1} x) = \frac{1}{\sqrt{(x^2 - 1)}}, \quad x > 1 \quad \textbf{(7.25b)}$$

$$\frac{d}{dx}(\tanh^{-1} x) = \frac{1}{1 - x^2}, \quad |x| < 1 \quad \textbf{(7.25c)}$$

Example 7.20

Find $\frac{dy}{dx}$ when y is given by

(a) $\tanh 2x$ (b) $\cosh^2 x$ (c) $e^{-3x} \sinh 3x$ (d) $\sinh^{-1}\left[\frac{3x}{4}\right]$

Solution (a) Introducing the intermediate variable $z = 2x$ gives

$$y = \tanh z \quad \text{and} \quad z = 2x$$

$$\frac{dy}{dz} = \text{sech}^2 z \quad \text{and} \quad \frac{dz}{dx} = 2$$

so by the chain rule

$$\frac{dy}{dx} = 2\,\text{sech}^2(2x)$$

(b) Introducing the intermediate variable $z = \cosh x$ gives

$$y = z^2 \quad \text{and} \quad z = \cosh x$$

$$\frac{dy}{dz} = 2z \quad \text{and} \quad \frac{dz}{dx} = \sinh x$$

so by the chain rule

$$\frac{dy}{dx} = 2\cosh x \sinh x = \sinh 2x$$

(c) Taking $u = e^{-3x}$ and $v = \sinh 3x$

gives using the chain rule

$$\frac{du}{dx} = -3e^{-3x} \quad \text{and} \quad \frac{dv}{dx} = 3\cosh 3x$$

so by the product rule

$$\frac{dy}{dx} = (e^{-3x})(3\cosh 3x) + (\sinh 3x)(-3e^{-3x}) = 3e^{-3x}(\cosh 3x - \sinh 3x)$$

$$= 3e^{-3x}(e^{-3x}) = 3e^{-6x}$$

(d) Introducing the intermediate variable $z = \frac{3}{4}x$ gives

$$y = \sinh^{-1} z \qquad \text{and} \quad z = \tfrac{3}{4}x$$

$$\frac{dy}{dz} = \frac{1}{\sqrt{(1+z^2)}} \quad \text{and} \quad \frac{dz}{dx} = \frac{3}{4}$$

so by the chain rule

$$\frac{dy}{dx} = \frac{3}{4} \cdot \frac{1}{\sqrt{(1+\frac{9}{16}x^2)}} = \frac{3}{\sqrt{(16+9x^2)}}$$

For practice, use MATLAB or MAPLE to check the answers to Examples 7.19 and 7.20. As illustrative examples we consider Examples 7.19(a) and 7.20(c). For Example 7.19(a) the MATLAB commands

```
syms x y
y = (x^2)*exp(x); dy = simplify(diff(y)); pretty(dy)
```

return the derivative as

```
dy = xexp(x)(2 + x)
```

For Example 7.20(c) the commands

MATLAB	MAPLE
`syms x y`	
`y = exp(-3*x)*sinh(3*x);`	`y:= exp(-3*x)*sinh(3*x):`
`dy = simplify(diff(y));`	`dy:= simplify(diff(y,x));`
`pretty(df)`	

return the derivative as

MATLAB	MAPLE
`dy = -3exp(-3x)sinh3x + 3 exp(3x)cosh3x`	`dy:= -3e^(-3x)(sinh(3x) - cosh(3x))`

In MAPLE the answer may be converted to exponential form and then simplified using the command `simplify(convert(%,exp));` to give the answer $3e^{(-6x)}$.

7.3.13 Exercises

Check your answers using MATLAB or MAPLE whenever possible.

38 Differentiate with respect to x:

(a) e^{2x} (b) $e^{-x/2}$

(c) $\exp(x^2 + x)$ (d) x^2e^{5x}

(e) $(3x + 2)e^{-x}$ (f) $e^x/(1 + e^x)$

(g) $\sqrt{(1 + e^x)}$ (h) e^{ax+b}

39 Differentiate with respect to x:

(a) $\ln(2x + 3)$ (b) $\ln(x^2 + 2x + 3)$

(c) $\ln[(x - 2)/(x - 3)]$ (d) $\dfrac{1}{x}\ln x$

(e) $\ln[(2x + 1)/(1 - 3x)]$ (f) $\ln[(x + 1)x]$

40 Differentiate with respect to x:

(a) $\sinh 3x$ (b) $\tanh 4x$ (c) $x^3\cosh 2x$

(d) $\ln(\cosh \frac{1}{2}x)$ (e) $\cos x \cosh x$ (f) $1/\cosh x$

41 Differentiate with respect to x:

(a) $\sinh^{-1}2x$ (b) $\cosh^{-1}(2x^2 - 1)$

(c) $\tanh^{-1}(1/x)$ (d) $\sqrt{(1 + x^2)}\sinh^{-1}x$

(e) $\sqrt{(4 - x^2)} - 2\cosh^{-1}(2/x)$

(f) $\tanh^{-1}x/(1 + x^2)$

42 Draw a careful sketch of $y = e^{-ax}\sin \omega x$ where a and ω are positive constants. What is the ratio of the heights of successive maxima of the function?

43 The line AB joins the points A(a, 0), B(0, b) on the x and y axes respectively and passes through the point (8, 27). Find the positions of A and B which minimize the length of AB.

44 Sketch the curve $y = e^{-x^2}$. Find the rectangle inscribed under the curve having one edge on the x axis, which has maximum area.

45 Show that $y = 9e^{-9t}/(10 - e^{-9t})$ satisfies the differential equation

$$\frac{dy}{dt} = -y(9 + y)$$

46 A sky diver's downward velocity $v(t)$ is given by

$$v(t) = u(1 - e^{-\alpha t})/(1 + e^{-\alpha t})$$

Where u and α are constants. What is the terminal velocity achieved? When does the sky diver achieve half that velocity and what is the acceleration then?

7.3.14 Parametric and implicit differentiation

The chain rule is used with the inverse-function rule to evaluate derivatives when a function is specified **parametrically**.

Rule 7 (parametric differentiation)

In general, if a function is defined by $y = f(x)$, where $x = g(t)$ and $y = h(t)$ and t is a parameter, then

$$\frac{dy}{dx} = \frac{dy}{dt}\Big/\frac{dx}{dt} \quad \text{or} \quad \frac{dy}{dx} = \frac{dy}{dt}\frac{dt}{dx} \tag{7.26}$$

Example 7.21 The function $y = f(x)$ is defined by $x = t^3$, $y = t^2$ ($t \in \mathbb{R}$). Find dy/dx.

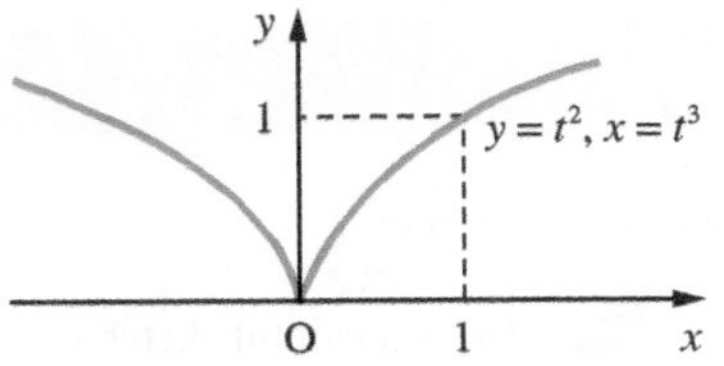

Figure 7.25
The graph of $\{(x, y): y = t^2, x = t^3, -\infty < t < \infty\}$.

Solution The graph of $f(x)$ is shown in Figure 7.25. There are many ways in which dy/dx may be evaluated. The simplest uses the result (7.26). In this case

$$\frac{dy}{dt} = 2t \quad \text{and} \quad \frac{dx}{dt} = 3t^2$$

so that

$$\frac{dy}{dx} = \frac{dy}{dt}\bigg/\frac{dx}{dt} = \frac{2}{3t} \qquad (t \neq 0)$$

This gives the result in terms of t. In terms of x, it may be written as

$$\frac{dy}{dx} = \tfrac{2}{3}x^{-1/3} \qquad (x \neq 0)$$

In terms of x and y, we have

$$\frac{dy}{dx} = \frac{2y}{3x} \qquad (x \neq 0)$$

Note from Figure 7.25 that the graph does not have a well-defined tangent at $x = 0$, so the derivative does not exist at this point; that is, the function is not differentiable at $x = 0$.

We can also obtain these results directly. Eliminating t between the defining equations for x and y, we have

$$y = x^{2/3}$$

Differentiating with respect to x gives

$$\frac{dy}{dx} = \tfrac{2}{3}x^{-1/3}$$

The chain rule may also be used to differentiate functions expressed in an implicit form (see Section 2.8.2). For example, the function of Example 7.21 may be expressed implicitly, by eliminating t, as

$$y^3 = x^2$$

To obtain the derivative dy/dx, we use the method known as **implicit differentiation**. In this method we treat y as an unknown function of x and differentiate both sides term by term with respect to x. This gives

$$\frac{d}{dx}(y^3) = \frac{d}{dx}(x^2)$$

Now y^3 is a composite function of x, with y being the intermediate variable, so the chain rule gives

$$\frac{d}{dx}(y^3) = \frac{d}{dy}(y^3)\frac{dy}{dx} = 3y^2\frac{dy}{dx}$$

Then, substituting back, we have

$$3y^2\frac{dy}{dx} = 2x$$

giving

$$\frac{dy}{dx} = \frac{2x}{3y^2} = \frac{2y}{3x} \quad \text{(on substituting for } y^3\text{)}$$

Parametric differentiation is achieved using the MATLAB commands (or comparable MAPLE commands)

```
syms x y t
x = x(t); y = y(t); dx = diff(x,t); dy = diff(y,t);
dydx = dy/dx
```

Example 7.22 Find $\frac{dy}{dx}$ when $x^2 + y^2 + xy = 1$.

Solution Differentiating both sides, term by term, gives

$$\frac{d}{dx}(x^2) + \frac{d}{dx}(y^2) + \frac{d}{dx}(xy) = \frac{d}{dx}(1)$$

Recognizing that y is a function of x and taking care over the product term xy, the chain rule gives

$$2x + \frac{d}{dy}(y^2)\frac{dy}{dx} + x\frac{dy}{dx} + y = 0$$

$$2x + 2y\frac{dy}{dx} + x\frac{dy}{dx} + y = 0$$

leading to

$$\frac{dy}{dx} = -\frac{(2x + y)}{(x + 2y)}$$

Implicit differentiation is useful in calculating the slopes of tangents and normals to curves specified implicitly, such as in Example 7.22. Having obtained the slope of the tangent at the point (x, y) as $\frac{dy}{dx}$, the slope of the normal to the curve at the corresponding point is $-1/(\text{slope of tangent})$ as inferred from Figure 7.5.

Example 7.23 Find the equations of the tangent and normal to the curve having equation $x^2 + y^2 - 3xy + 4 = 0$ at the point (2, 4).

Solution Differentiating the equation implicitly with respect to x

$$2x + 2y\frac{dy}{dx} - 3x\frac{dy}{dx} - 3y = 0$$

gives

$$\frac{dy}{dx} = \frac{3y - 2x}{2y - 3x}$$

This represents the slope of the tangent at the point (x, y) on the curve. Thus the slope of the tangent at the point (2, 4) is

$$\left[\frac{dy}{dx}\right]_{(2,4)} = \frac{12 - 4}{8 - 6} = 4$$

Remembering from equation (1.14) that the equation of a line passing through a point (x, y) and having slope m is $y - y_1 = m(x - x_1)$ we have that the equation of the tangent to the graph at (2, 4) is

$$(y - 4) = 4(x - 2) \quad \text{or} \quad y = 4x - 4$$

The slope of the normal at (2, 4) is $-\frac{1}{4}$, so it has equation

$$y - 4 = -\tfrac{1}{4}(x - 2) \quad \text{or} \quad 4y = 18 - x$$

Example 7.24 Find the slope of the tangents to the circle

$$x^2 + y^2 - 2x + 4y - 20 = 0$$

at the points A(1, 3), B(4, 2) and C(−2, −6).

Solution The circle defined by the equation is shown in Figure 7.26, together with the three points A, B and C. Clearly this equation does not define a function in general, but near specific points we can restrict it so that it behaves locally like a function. To compute the slopes of the tangents, we differentiate the equation defining the curve with respect

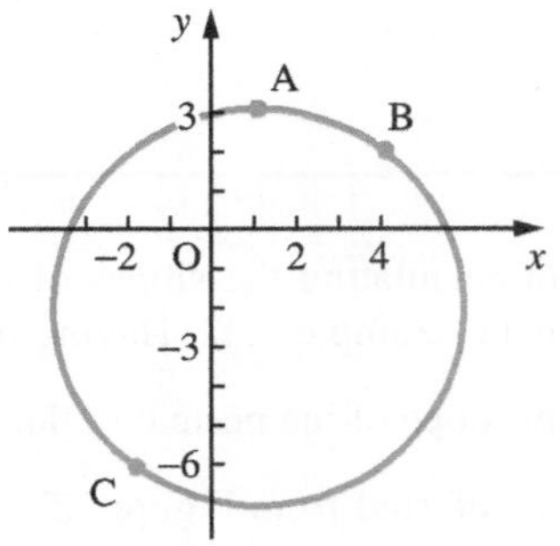

Figure 7.26 Graph of the circle $x^2 + y^2 - 2x + 4y - 20 = 0$.

to x implicitly, and then we insert the x and y coordinates of the points. Thus in this example we have

$$2x + 2y\frac{dy}{dx} - 2 + 4\frac{dy}{dx} = 0$$

giving

$$\frac{dy}{dx} = \frac{1 - x}{2 + y} \quad (y \neq -2)$$

Then at A the slope is zero, at B the slope is $-\frac{3}{4}$, and at C the slope is $-\frac{3}{4}$. Note that dy/dx is not defined at $y = -2$. There are two corresponding points: $(-4, -2)$ and $(6, -2)$. At these points the curve has a vertical tangent.

The implicit differentiation rule can be used in a double way to obtain derivatives of functions of the form $f(x)^{g(x)}$, as illustrated in Example 7.25.

Example 7.25 Find the derivative of the function

$$f(x) = (\sin x)^x \quad (x \in (0, \pi))$$

Solution The simplest way of dealing with this is first to take logarithms. Thus $y = (\sin x)^x$ gives

$$\ln y = x \ln \sin x$$

Then differentiating implicitly with respect to x, remembering that y is a function of x, gives

$$\frac{1}{y}\frac{dy}{dx} = \ln \sin x + x\frac{\cos x}{\sin x} = \ln \sin x + x \cot x$$

and so

$$\frac{dy}{dx} = (\ln \sin x + x \cot x)(\sin x)^x$$

Sometimes the technique used in Example 7.25 is described as **logarithmic differentiation**. It is useful for differentiating complicated functions.

Example 7.26 Differentiate with respect to x

$$y = \frac{(x - 2)^3(x + 3)^9}{\sqrt{(x^2 + 1)}}$$

Solution To simplify the process, we first take logarithms

$$\ln y = 3\ln(x - 2) + 9\ln(x + 3) - \tfrac{1}{2}\ln(x^2 + 1)$$

Then differentiating with respect to x gives

$$\frac{1}{y}\frac{dy}{dx} = \frac{3}{x-2} + \frac{9}{x+3} - \frac{1}{2}\frac{2x}{x^2+1}$$
$$= \frac{3(x+3)(x^2+1) + 9(x-2)(x^2+1) - x(x-2)(x+3)}{(x-2)(x+3)(x^2+1)}$$
$$= \frac{11x^3 - 10x^2 + 18x - 9}{(x-2)(x+3)(x^2+1)}$$

Hence

$$\frac{dy}{dx} = (11x^3 - 10x^2 + 18x - 9)(x-2)^2(x+3)^8/(x^2+1)^{3/2}$$

7.3.15 Exercises

Check your answers using MATLAB or MAPLE whenever possible.

47 The equations $x = t\sin t$, $y = t\cos t$ are the parametric equations for a spiral. Find $\frac{dy}{dx}$ in terms of t.

48 A curve is defined parametrically by the equations

$$x = 2\cos\theta + \cos 2\theta$$
$$y = 2\sin\theta - \sin 2\theta$$

Draw a sketch of the curve for $0 \leqslant \theta \leqslant 2\pi$. Find the equation of the tangent to the curve at the point where $\theta = \pi/4$.

49 Find $\frac{dy}{dx}$ when

(a) $x^2 + y^2 + 4x - 2y = 20$

(b) $xy = 2e^{x+y-3}$

50 Find the equations of the tangent and normal to the curve having equation

$$y^2 - 2y - 4x + 1 = 0$$

at the point (1, 3).

51 Find the equation of the tangent, at the point (0, 4), to the curve defined by

$$y^3x + y + 7x^4 = 4$$

52 Find the value of $\frac{dy}{dx}$ at the point (1, −1) on the curve given by the equation

$$x^3 - y^3 - xy - x = 0$$

53 Differentiate with respect to x:

(a) 10^x (b) 2^{-x} (c) $\dfrac{(x-1)^{7/2}(x+1)^{1/2}}{x^2+2}$

54 Use logarithmic differentiation to prove that

$$\frac{d}{dx}(y_1y_2 \dots y_n) = \sum_{k=1}^{n}(y_1y_2 \dots y_{k-1}y_{k+1} \dots y_n)y_k'$$

Hence differentiate $x^3e^{-2x}\sin\pi x$.

55 The equation of a curve is

$$xy^3 - 2x^2y^2 + x^4 - 1 = 0$$

Show that the tangent to the curve at the point (1, 2) has a slope of unity. Hence write down the equation of the tangent to the curve at this point. What are the coordinates of the points at which this tangent crosses the coordinate axes?

56 A **cycloid** is a curve traced out by a point p on the rim of a wheel as it rolls along the ground. Using

the coordinate system shown in Figure 7.27, show that the curve has the parametric representation

$$x = a(\theta - \sin\theta), \quad y = a(1 - \cos\theta)$$

where θ is the angle through which the wheel has turned.

Draw a sketch of the curve.

Find the gradient of the curve at a general point (x, y).

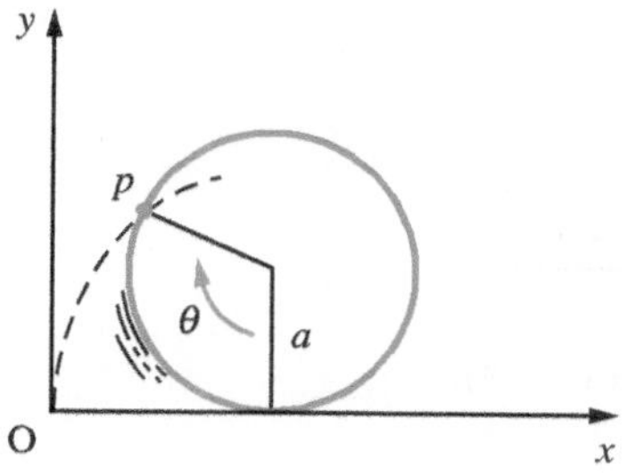

Figure 7.27

If the wheel rotates at a constant speed, with $\theta = \omega t$, where ω is constant and t is the time, show that the speed V of the point on the rim is given by

$$V(t) = 2a\omega|\sin\tfrac{1}{2}\omega t|$$

57 Find the slope of the tangent to the lemniscate

$$(x^2 + y^2)^2 = a^2(x^2 - y^2)$$

at the point (x, y). (See Review Exercises 2.11, Question 19.)

58 Use logarithmic differentiation to differentiate

(a) $(\ln x)^x$ (b) $x^{\ln x}$

(c) $(1 - x^2)^{1/2}(2x^2 + 3)^{-4/3}$

59 Using logarithmic differentiation, find the derivatives of

(a) $x^3e^{-2x}\ln x$ (b) $\dfrac{1}{x}e^x\sin 2x$

7.4 Higher derivatives

The derivative df/dx of function $f(x)$ is itself a function and may be differentiable. The derivative of a derivative is called the **second derivative**, and is written as

$$\frac{d^2f}{dx^2} \quad \text{or} \quad f''(x) \quad \text{or} \quad f^{(2)}(x)$$

This may in turn be differentiated, yielding **third derivatives** and so on. In general, the ***n*th derivative** is written as

$$\frac{d^nf}{dx^n} \quad \text{or} \quad f^{(n)}(x)$$

7.4.1 The second derivative

In mechanics the second derivative of the displacement of an object with respect to time is its acceleration and this is used in the mathematical modelling of problems in mechanics using the law:

mass × acceleration = applied force

Example 7.27 Find the second derivative of the functions given by

(a) $y = 3x^4 - 2x^2 + x - 1$ (b) $y = x/(x^2 + 1)$

(c) $y = e^{-x}\sin 2x$ (d) $y = \dfrac{\ln x}{x}$

Solution (a) Differentiating once gives

$$\frac{dy}{dx} = 12x^3 - 4x + 1$$

and differentiating a second time gives

$$\frac{d^2y}{dx^2} = 36x^2 - 4$$

(b) This simply requires two differentiations, as above,

$$\frac{dy}{dx} = \frac{1(x^2+1) - 2x(x)}{(x^2+1)^2} = \frac{1-x^2}{(x^2+1)^2}$$

Then $$\frac{d^2y}{d^2x} = \frac{(-2x)(x^2+1)^2 - 2(2x)(x^2+1)(1-x^2)}{(x^2+1)^4}$$

$$= \frac{(-2x)(x^2+1) - 4x(1-x^2)}{(x^2+1)^3} = \frac{2x(x^2-3)}{(x^2+1)^3}$$

(c) This simply requires two differentiations. Applying the product rule, we have

$$\frac{dy}{dx} = (e^{-x})(2\cos 2x) + (\sin 2x)(-e^{-x}) = e^{-x}(2\cos 2x - \sin 2x)$$

Applying the rule again we have

$$\frac{d^2y}{dx^2} = (e^{-x})(-4\sin 2x - 2\cos 2x) + (2\cos 2x - \sin 2x)(-e^{-x})$$

$$= -e^{-x}(3\sin 2x + 4\cos 2x)$$

(d) Again this simply requires two differentiations. Applying the quotient rule, we have

$$\frac{dy}{dx} = \frac{(1/x)x - \ln x}{x^2} = \frac{1-\ln x}{x^2}$$

Applying the rule again, we obtain

$$\frac{d^2y}{dx^2} = \frac{-(1/x)x^2 - (1-\ln x)(2x)}{x^4} = \frac{2\ln x - 3}{x^3} \quad (x \neq 0)$$

The second derivative is obtained using the commands

MATLAB	MAPLE
`d2y = diff(y,2)`	`d2y:= diff(y,x,x);`

and the third derivative by the commands

MATLAB	MAPLE
`d3y = diff(y,3)`	`d3y:= diff(y,x,x,x);` or `d3y:= diff(y,x$3);`

and so on for higher derivatives.

Considering Example 7.27(c) the commands

MATLAB	MAPLE
`syms x y`	
`y = exp(-x)*sin(2*x);`	`y:= exp(-x)*sin(2*x):`
`d2y = simplify(diff(y,2));`	`d2y:= diff(y,x,x);`
`pretty(d2y)`	

return the second derivative as

MATLAB	MAPLE
`d2y = -exp(-x)(3sin(2x) + 4cos(2x))`	`d2y:= -3e^(-x) sin(2x) - 4 e^(-x) cos(2x)`

Example 7.28 Show that

$$y = e^{-t}(A \cos t + B \sin t) + 2 \sin 2t - \cos 2t$$

satisfies the equation

$$\frac{d^2y}{d^2t} + 2\frac{dy}{dt} + 2y = 10 \cos 2t$$

Solution Differentiating y twice with respect to t gives

$$\frac{dy}{dt} = e^{-t}[(A - B)\cos t + (A + B)\sin t] + 4\cos 2t + 2\sin 2t$$

$$\frac{d^2y}{d^2t} = e^{-t}[-2B\cos t + 2A\sin t] - 8\sin 2t + 4\cos 2t$$

Thus

$$\frac{d^2y}{d^2t} + 2\frac{dy}{dt} + 2y = 10\cos 2t$$

When determining the second derivative using parametric or implicit differentiation care must be taken to ensure correct use of the chain rule. The approach is illustrated in Example 7.29.

Example 7.29 Find $\frac{d^2y}{dx^2}$ when y is given by

(a) $y = t^2$, $x = t^3$ (b) $x^2 + y^2 - 2x + 4y - 20 = 0$

Solution (a) Here $y = t^2$ and $x = t^3$ gives, as in Example 7.21,

$$\frac{dy}{dx} = \frac{2}{3}\frac{1}{t} \quad (t \neq 0)$$

Differentiating again, using the chain rule, gives

$$\frac{d^2y}{dx^2} = \frac{d}{dx}\left(\frac{dy}{dx}\right) = \frac{d}{dt}\left(\frac{dy}{dx}\right)\frac{dt}{dx} \quad \text{(this is an important step)}$$

$$= \frac{d}{dt}\left(\frac{dy}{dx}\right)\bigg/\frac{dx}{dt}$$

$$= \frac{\frac{2}{3}(-1/t^2)}{3t^2} = -\frac{2}{9}\frac{1}{t^4}$$

(b) Here x and y are related by the equation

$$x^2 + y^2 - 2x + 4y - 20 = 0$$

so that as in Example 7.24

$$2x + 2y\frac{dy}{dx} - 2 + 4\frac{dy}{dx} = 0$$

and

$$(y + 2)\frac{dy}{dx} + x - 1 = 0$$

Differentiating a second time gives

$$\left(\frac{dy}{dx}\right)\frac{dy}{dx} + (y + 2)\frac{d^2y}{dx^2} + 1 = 0$$

using the product rule and remembering that

$$\frac{d}{dx}\left(\frac{dy}{dx}\right) = \frac{d^2y}{dx^2}$$

After rearrangement, we have

$$\frac{d^2y}{dx^2} = -\frac{1 + (dy/dx)^2}{y + 2} \quad (y \neq -2)$$

and substituting

$$\frac{dy}{dx} = \frac{1 - x}{2 + y}$$

into the right-hand side gives eventually

$$\frac{d^2y}{dx^2} = -\frac{x^2 + y^2 - 2x + 4y + 5}{(2 + y)^3}$$

This may be further simplified, using the original equation, to give

$$\frac{d^2y}{dx^2} = -\frac{25}{(2 + y)^3} \quad (y \neq -2)$$

Further results for higher derivatives are developed in Exercises 7.4.2. These are on the whole straightforward extensions of previous work. One result that sometimes causes blunders is the extension of the inverse-function rule to higher derivatives.

We know that

$$\frac{dx}{dy} = 1\Big/\frac{dy}{dx}$$

To find the second derivative of x with respect to y needs a little care:

$$\frac{d^2x}{dy^2} = \frac{d}{dy}\left(\frac{dx}{dy}\right) = \frac{d}{dy}\left[\left(\frac{dy}{dx}\right)^{-1}\right]$$

$$= \frac{d}{dx}\left[\left(\frac{dy}{dx}\right)^{-1}\right]\frac{dx}{dy} \quad \text{(using the chain rule)}$$

$$= \left[-\frac{d}{dx}\left(\frac{dy}{dx}\right)\Big/\left(\frac{dy}{dx}\right)^2\right]\left(1\Big/\frac{dy}{dx}\right)$$

Thus

$$\frac{d^2x}{dy^2} = -\frac{d^2y}{dx^2}\Big/\left(\frac{dy}{dx}\right)^3$$

7.4.2 Exercises

Check your answers using MATLAB or MAPLE.

60 Find $\dfrac{d^2y}{dx^2}$ when y is given by

(a) $x^3\sqrt{(1 + x^2)}$

(b) $\ln(x^2 + x + 1)$

(c) $y^3x + y + 7x^4 = 4$

(d) $x^3 - y^3 - xy - x = 0$

61 Find $\dfrac{d^2y}{dx^2}$ when x and y are given by

(a) $x = t \sin t$ and $y = t \cos t$

(b) $x = 2 \cos t + \cos 2t$ and $y = 2 \sin t - \sin 2t$

62 If $y = 3e^{2x} \cos(2x - 3)$, verify that

$$\frac{d^2y}{dx^2} - 4\frac{dy}{dx} + 8y = 0$$

63 If $y = (\sin^{-1}x)^2$, prove that

$$(1 - x^2)\left(\frac{dy}{dx}\right)^2 = 4y$$

and deduce that

$$(1 - x^2)\frac{d^2y}{dx^2} - x\frac{dy}{dx} - 2 = 0$$

64 (a) If $y = x^2 + 1/x^2$, find dy/dx and d^2y/dx^2. Hence show that

$$x^2\frac{d^2y}{dx^2} + 4x\frac{dy}{dx} + 2y = 12x^2$$

(b) If $x = \tan t$ and $y = \cot t$, show that

$$\frac{d^2y}{dx^2} + 2y\frac{dy}{dx} = 0$$

65 If $x = a(\theta - \sin \theta)$ and $y = a(1 - \cos \theta)$, find dy/dx and d^2y/dx^2.

66 Find dy/dx in terms of t for the curve with parametric representation

$$x = \frac{1-t}{1+2t} \qquad y = \frac{1-2t}{1+t}$$

Show that

$$\frac{d^2y}{dx^2} = -\frac{2}{3}\left(\frac{1+2t}{1+t}\right)^3$$

and find a similar expression for d^2x/dy^2.

67 Confirm that the point (1, 1) lies on the curve with equation $x^3 - y^2 + xy - x^2 = 0$ and find the values of dy/dx and d^2y/dx^2 at that point.

68 Find $f^{(4)}(x)$ and $f^{(n)}(x)$ for the following functions $f(x)$:

(a) e^{3x} (b) $\ln(x+2)$

(c) $\dfrac{1}{1-x^2}$

69 Find the fourth derivative of $f(x) = \sin(ax + b)$ and verify that $f^{(n)}(x) = a^n \sin(ax + b + \frac{1}{2}n\pi)$.

70 Prove that

$$\frac{d^n}{dx^n}(e^{ax}\sin bx) = (a^2+b^2)^{n/2}e^{ax}\sin(bx+n\theta)$$

where $\cos\theta = a/\sqrt{(a^2+b^2)}$, $\sin\theta = b/\sqrt{(a^2+b^2)}$.

71 If $y = u(x)v(x)$, prove that

(a) $y^{(2)}(x) = u^{(2)}(x)v(x) + 2u^{(1)}(x)v^{(1)}(x) + u(x)v^{(2)}(x)$

(b) $y^{(3)}(x) = u^{(3)}(x)v(x) + 3u^{(2)}(x)v^{(1)}(x) + 3u^{(1)}(x)v^{(2)}(x) + u(x)v^{(3)}(x)$

Hence prove **Leibniz's theorem** for the nth derivative of a product:

$$y^{(n)}(x) = u^{(n)}(x)v(x) + \binom{n}{1}u^{(n-1)}(x)v^{(1)}(x) + \binom{n}{2}u^{(n-2)}(x)v^{(2)}(x) + \ldots + u(x)v^{(n)}(x)$$

72 Use Leibniz's theorem (Question 71) to find the following:

(a) $\dfrac{d^5}{dx^5}(x^2\sin x)$ (put $u = \sin x$, $v = x^2$)

(b) $\dfrac{d^4}{dx^4}(xe^{-x})$ (c) $\dfrac{d^3}{dx^3}[x^2(3x+1)^{12}]$

7.4.3 Curvature of plane curves

The second derivative d^2f/dx^2 represents the rate of change of df/dx as x increases; geometrically, this gives us information as to how the slope of the tangent to the graph of $y = f(x)$ is changing with increasing x.

- If $d^2f/dx^2 > 0$ then df/dx is increasing as x increases, and the tangent rotates in an anticlockwise direction as we move along the horizontal axis, as illustrated in Figure 7.28(a).
- If $d^2f/dx^2 < 0$ then df/dx is decreasing as x increases, and the tangent rotates in a clockwise direction as we move along the horizontal axis, as illustrated in Figure 7.28(b).

Also note that when $d^2f/dx^2 > 0$, the graph of $y = f(x)$ is 'concave up', and when $d^2f/dx^2 < 0$ the graph is 'concave down'. Thus the sign of d^2f/dx^2 relates to the concavity of the graph; we shall use this information in Section 7.5.1 to define a point of inflection.

The **curvature** κ of a plane curve, having equation $y = f(x)$, at any point is the rate at which the curve is bending or curving away from the tangent at that point. In other words, the curvature measures the rate at which the tangent to the curve changes as it moves along the curve. This implies that it will depend on d^2f/dx^2 in some way.

Take two points P and Q on the curve $y = f(x)$ and a distance Δs apart *measured along the curve*. Then, with the notation of Figure 7.29(a), the average curvature of the

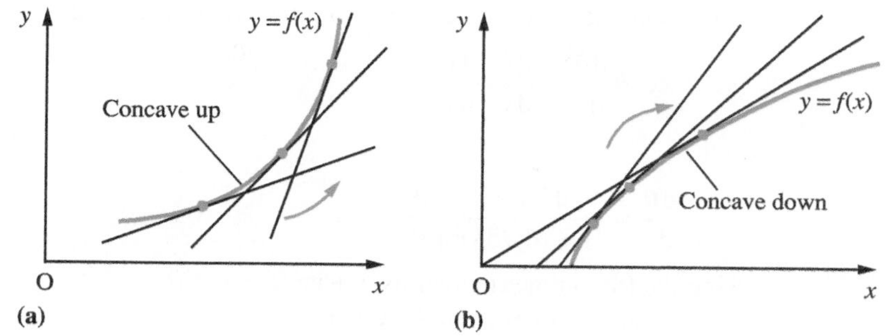

Figure 7.28 Rates of change of $\frac{dy}{dx}$ as x increases.

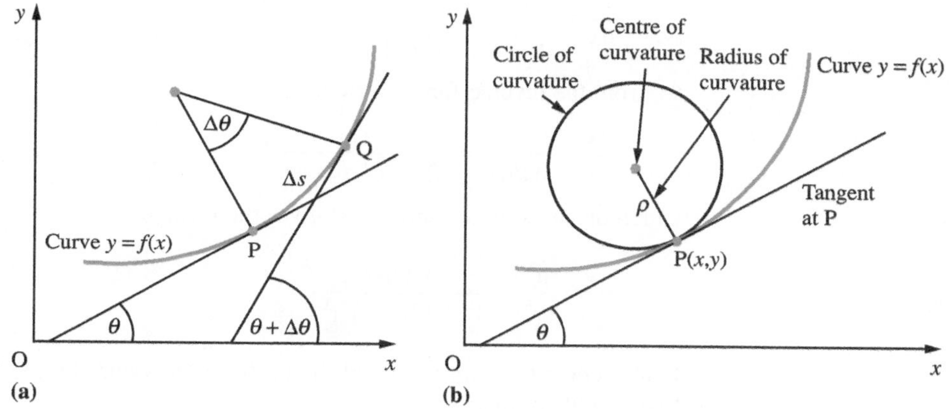

Figure 7.29 Curvature and radius of curvature.

curve PQ is $\Delta\theta/\Delta s$. We then define the curvature κ of the curve at the point P to be the absolute value of the average curvature as Q approaches P. That is,

$$\kappa = \left| \lim_{\Delta s \to 0} \frac{\Delta\theta}{\Delta s} \right| = \left| \frac{d\theta}{ds} \right| \qquad \textbf{(7.27)}$$

If we now construct a circle, as shown in Figure 7.29(b), so that it

- has the same tangent at P as $y = f(x)$,
- lies on the same side of the tangent as $y = f(x)$ and
- has the same curvature κ as $y = f(x)$ at P

then this is called the **circle of curvature** at P. Its radius ρ is called the **radius of curvature** at P and is given by

$$\rho = \text{radius of curvature} = \frac{1}{\kappa}$$

The centre of the circle is called the **centre of curvature** at P. Clearly the curvature is zero when the radius of curvature is infinite.

In order to obtain the curvature of a curve given by an equation of the form $y = f(x)$, we must obtain a more usable formula than (7.27). Since

$$\tan\theta = \text{slope of the tangent at P} = \frac{dy}{dx}$$

differentiating with respect to s, using the chain rule, gives

$$\sec^2\theta \frac{d\theta}{ds} = \frac{d^2y}{dx^2}\frac{dx}{ds}$$

so that

$$\frac{d\theta}{ds} = \frac{d^2y/dx^2}{[1 + (dy/dx)^2]}\frac{dx}{ds} \tag{7.28}$$

using the trigonometric identity $1 + \tan^2\theta = \sec^2\theta$.

We shall see in Section 7.9.6 that

$$\frac{ds}{dx} = \sqrt{\left[1 + \left(\frac{dy}{dx}\right)^2\right]}$$

so, from the inverse-function rule,

$$\frac{dx}{ds} = \frac{1}{ds/dx} = \frac{1}{\sqrt{[1 + (dy/dx)^2]}}$$

which on substituting into (7.28) gives the formula

$$\kappa = \left|\frac{d\theta}{ds}\right| = \frac{|d^2y/dx^2|}{[1 + (dy/dx)^2]^{3/2}} \tag{7.29}$$

If we denote the coordinates of the centre of curvature by (X, Y) then it follows from Figure 7.29(b) that

$$X = x - \rho \sin\theta, \quad Y = y + \rho\cos\theta$$

Since $\tan\theta = dy/dx$, it follows that

$$\sin\theta = \frac{dy/dx}{\sqrt{[1 + (dy/dx)^2]}}, \quad \cos\theta = \frac{1}{\sqrt{[1 + (dy/dx)^2]}}$$

Using these results together with $\rho = 1/\kappa$, with κ from (7.29), gives the coordinates of the centre of curvature as

$$X = x - \frac{dy}{dx}\left[1 + \left(\frac{dy}{dx}\right)^2\right]\Bigg/\frac{d^2y}{dx^2}, \quad Y = y + \left[1 + \left(\frac{dy}{dx}\right)^2\right]\Bigg/\frac{d^2y}{dx^2} \tag{7.30}$$

Although these results have been deduced for the curve of Figure 7.29(b), which at the point $P(x, y)$ has positive slope ($dy/dx > 0$) and is concave upwards ($d^2y/dx^2 > 0$), it can be shown that these are valid in all cases.

It is left as an exercise for the reader to show that if the curve $y = f(x)$ is given in parametric form

$$x = g(t), \quad y = h(t)$$

then the curvature κ is given by

$$\kappa = \left|\frac{dg}{dt}\frac{d^2h}{dt^2} - \frac{d^2g}{dt^2}\frac{dh}{dt}\right|\Bigg/\left[\left(\frac{dg}{dt}\right)^2 + \left(\frac{dh}{dt}\right)^2\right]^{3/2} \tag{7.31}$$

7.4.4 Exercises

73 Find the radius of curvature at the point (2, 8) on the curve $y = x^3$.

74 Show that the radius of curvature at the origin to the curve

$$x^3 + y^3 + 2x^2 - 4y + 3x = 0$$

is $\frac{125}{64}$.

75 Find the radius of curvature and the coordinates of the centre of curvature of the curve

$$y = (11 - 4x)/(3 - x)$$

at the point (2, 3).

76 Find the radius of curvature at the point where $\theta = \frac{1}{3}\pi$ on the curve defined parametrically by

$$x = 2\cos\theta, \quad y = \sin\theta$$

77 Find the radius of curvature at (x, y) of the curve

$$y = \tanh^{-1} x \quad (|x| < 1)$$

78 Find the radius of curvature at (1, 1) of the curve defined by

$$x = t^3, y = t^2 \quad (t \in R)$$

7.5 Applications to optimization problems

In many industrial situations the role of management is to make decisions that will lead to the most effective use of the resources available. These decisions seldom affect the whole operation in one sweeping decision, but are usually a chain of small decisions: organizing stock control, designing a product, pricing it, servicing equipment and so on. Effective management seeks to optimize the constituent parts of the whole operation. A wide variety of mathematical techniques are used to solve such optimization problems. Here, and later in Section 9.4.9, we consider methods based on the methods and concepts of calculus.

7.5.1 Optimal values

The basic idea is that the **optimal value** of a differentiable function $f(x)$ (that is, its **maximum** or **minimum value**) generally occurs where its derivative is zero; that is, where

$$f'(x) = 0$$

As can be seen from Figure 7.30, this is a necessary condition, since at a maximum or minimum value of the function its graph has a horizontal tangent. Figure 7.30 does, however, show that these extremal values are generally only local maximum or

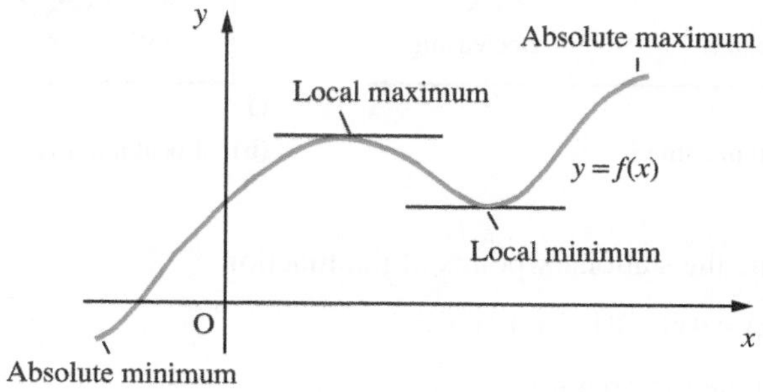

Figure 7.30 Maximum and minimum values.

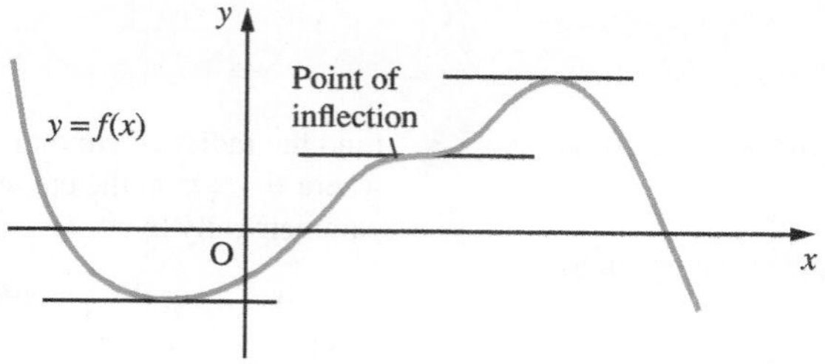

Figure 7.31
Graph with horizontal tangents.

minimum values, corresponding to turning points on the graph, so some care must be exercised in using the horizontal tangent as a test for an optimal value. In seeking the extremal values of a function it is also necessary to check the end points (if any) of the domain of the function.

Figure 7.31 gives another illustration of why care must be exercised: at some **points of inflection** – that is, points where the graph crosses its own tangent – the tangent may be horizontal.

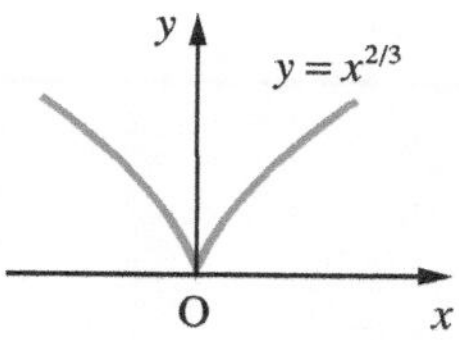

Figure 7.32
Graph of $f(x) = x^{2/3}$, with minimum at $x = 0$.

A third reason for caution is that a function may have an optimal value at a point where its derivative does not exist. A simple example of this is given by $f(x) = x^{2/3}$, whose graph is shown in Figure 7.32.

Having determined the **critical or stationary points** where $f'(x) = 0$, we need to be able to determine their character or nature; that is, whether they correspond to a local maximum, a local minimum or a point of inflection of the function $f(x)$. We can do this by examining values of $f'(x)$ close to and on either side of the critical point. From Figure 7.33 we see that

- if the value of $f'(x)$, the slope of the tangent, changes from positive to negative as we pass from left to right through a stationary point then the latter corresponds to a **local maximum**;
- if the value of $f'(x)$ changes from negative to positive as we pass from left to right through a stationary point then the latter corresponds to a **local minimum**;
- if $f'(x)$ does not change sign as we pass through a stationary point then the latter corresponds to a **point of inflection**.

Figure 7.33
Change in slope on passing through a turning point.

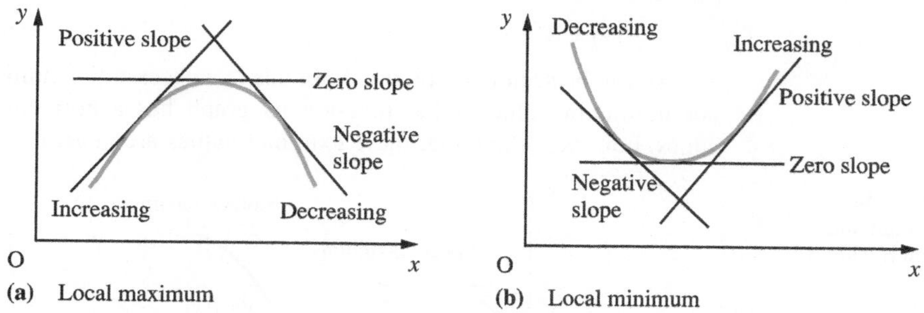

Example 7.30

Determine the stationary points of the function

$$f(x) = 4x^3 - 21x^2 + 18x + 6$$

and examine their nature.

Solution The derivative is

$$f'(x) = 12x^2 - 42x + 18 = 6(2x - 1)(x - 3)$$

Stationary points occur when $f'(x) = 0$; that is,

$$6(2x - 1)(x - 3) = 0$$

the solutions of which are $x = \frac{1}{2}$ and $x = 3$. The corresponding values of the function are

$$f(\tfrac{1}{2}) = 4(\tfrac{1}{8}) - 21(\tfrac{1}{4}) + 18(\tfrac{1}{2}) + 6 = \tfrac{41}{4}$$

and

$$f(3) = 4(27) - 21(9) + 18(3) + 6 = -21$$

so that the stationary points of $f(x)$ are

$$(\tfrac{1}{2}, \tfrac{41}{4}) \quad \text{and} \quad (3, -21)$$

In order to investigate their nature, we use the procedure outlined above.

(a) Considering the point $(\frac{1}{2}, \frac{41}{4})$: if x is a little less than $\frac{1}{2}$ then $2x - 1 < 0$ and $x - 3 < 0$, so that

$$f'(x) = 6(2x - 1)(x - 3) = (\text{negative})(\text{negative}) = (\text{positive})$$

while if x is a little greater than $\frac{1}{2}$ then $2x - 1 > 0$ and $x - 3 < 0$, so that

$$f'(x) = (\text{positive})(\text{negative}) = (\text{negative})$$

Thus $f'(x)$ changes from (positive) to (negative) as we pass through the point so that $(\frac{1}{2}, \frac{41}{4})$ is a local maximum.

(b) Considering the point $(3, -21)$: if x is a little less than 3 then $2x - 1 > 0$ and $x - 3 < 0$, so that

$$f'(x) = (\text{positive})(\text{negative}) = (\text{negative})$$

while if x is a little greater than 3 then $2x - 1 > 0$ and $x - 3 > 0$, so that

$$f'(x) = (\text{positive})(\text{positive}) = (\text{positive})$$

Thus $f'(x)$ changes from (negative) to (positive) as we pass through the point so that $(3, -21)$ is a local minimum.

This information may now be used to sketch a graph of $f(x)$, as illustrated in Figure 7.34.

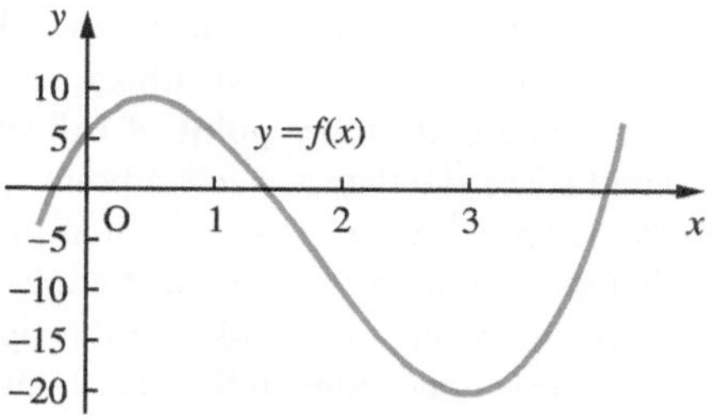

Figure 7.34
Graph of $f(x) = 4x^3 - 21x^2 + 18x + 6$.

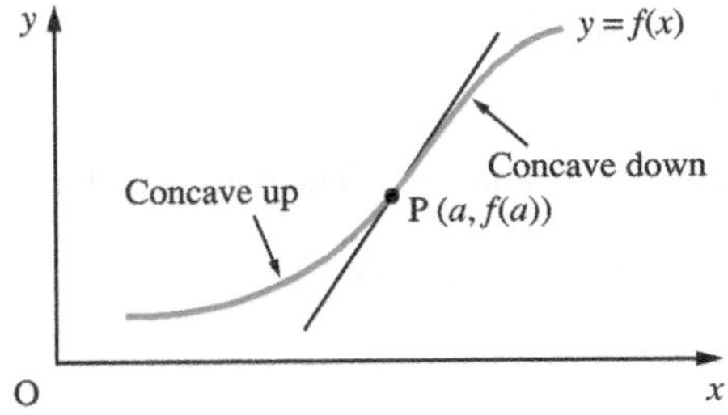

Figure 7.35 A point of inflection at $(a, f(a))$.

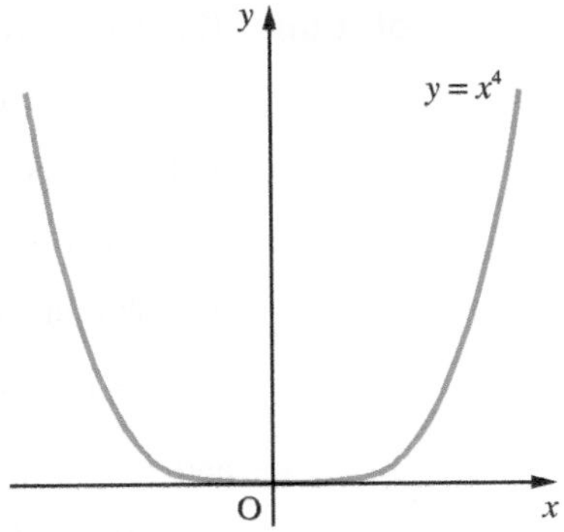

Figure 7.36 Graph of $f(x) = x^4$, illustrating the local minimum at $x = 0$.

An alternative approach to determining the nature of a stationary point is to calculate the value of the second derivative $f''(x)$ at the point. Recall from Section 7.4.1 that $f''(x)$ determines the rate of change of $f'(x)$. Suppose that $f(x)$ has a stationary point at $x = a$, so that $f'(a) = 0$. Then, provided $f''(a)$ is defined, either $f''(a) < 0$, $f''(a) = 0$ or $f''(a) > 0$.

If $f''(a) < 0$ then $f'(x)$ is decreasing at $x = a$; and since $f'(a) = 0$, it follows that $f'(x) > 0$ for values of x just less than a and $f'(x) < 0$ for values of x just greater than a. We therefore conclude that $x = a$ corresponds to a local maximum. Note that this concurs with our observation in Section 7.4.1 that the sign of $f''(x)$ determines the concavity of the graph of $f(x)$. Since the graph is concave down at a local maximum, $f''(a) \leqslant 0$. The equality case is discussed further in Section 9.4.9.

Similarly, we can argue that if $f''(a) > 0$ then the stationary point $x = a$ corresponds to a local minimum. Again this concurs with our observation that the graph is concave up at a local minimum.

Summarizing, we have

- the function $f(x)$ has a local maximum at $x = a$ provided $f'(a) = 0$ and $f''(a) < 0$;
- the function $f(x)$ has a local minimum at $x = a$ provided $f'(a) = 0$ and $f''(a) > 0$.

If $f''(a) = 0$, we cannot assume that $x = a$ corresponds to a point of inflection, and we must revert to considering the sign of $f'(x)$ on either side of the stationary point. As mentioned earlier, at a point of inflection the graph crosses its own tangent, or, in other words, the concavity of the graph changes. Since the concavity is determined by the sign of $f''(x)$, it follows that $f''(x) = 0$ at a point of inflection and that $f''(x)$ changes sign as we pass through the point. Note, as illustrated by the graph of Figure 7.35, that it is not necessary for $f'(x) = 0$ at a point of inflection. If, as illustrated in Figure 7.31, $f'(x) = 0$ at a point of inflection then it is a **stationary point of inflection**. It does not follow, however, that if $f'(a) = 0$ and $f''(a) = 0$ then $x = a$ is a point of inflection. An example of when this is not the case is $y = x^4$, which, as illustrated in Figure 7.36, has a local minimum at $x = 0$ even though both dy/dx and d^2y/dx^2 are zero at $x = 0$. It is for this reason that we must take care and revert to considering the sign of $f'(x)$ on either side. We shall return to reconsider these conditions in Section 9.4.9 following consideration of Taylor series.

Example 7.31 Using the second derivative, confirm the nature of the stationary points of the function

$$f(x) = 4x^3 - 21x^2 + 18x + 6$$

determined in Example 7.30.

Solution We have

$$f'(x) = 12x^2 - 42x + 18$$

so that

$$f''(x) = 24x - 42$$

At the stationary point $(\frac{1}{2}, \frac{41}{4})$

$$f''(\tfrac{1}{2}) = 12 - 42 = -30 < 0$$

confirming that it corresponds to a local maximum.

At the stationary point (3, –21)

$$f''(3) = 72 - 42 = 30 > 0$$

confirming that it corresponds to a local minimum.

Note also that $f''(x) = 0$ at $x = \frac{7}{4}$ and that $f''(x) < 0$ for $x < \frac{7}{4}$ and $f''(x) > 0$ for $x > \frac{7}{4}$. Thus $(\frac{7}{4}, -\frac{43}{8})$ is a point of inflection (but not a stationary point of inflection), which is clearly identifiable in the graph of Figure 7.34.

Considering the cubic of Examples 7.30 and 7.31 the stationary points may be investigated using the following MATLAB commands

```
syms x y
y = 4*x^3 - 21*x^2 + 18*x + 6; dy = diff(y); solve(dy)
```

The last command solves dy = 0 to obtain the x coordinates `3` and `1/2` of the stationary points, and the commands

```
y1 = subs(y,x,3)
y2 = subs(y,x,1/2)
```

determine the corresponding y coordinates `-21` and `10.25`; so that the stationary points are `(3,-21)` and `(1/2,10.25)`. The commands

```
d2y = diff(y,2);
subs(d2y,x,3)
subs(d2y,x,1/2)
```

return the value of the second derivative at each stationary point as `30` and `-30` respectively; thus confirming that `(3,-21)` is a local minimum and that

`(1/2,10.25)` is a local maximum. Finally, to illustrate the results the plot of the cubic is given by the command

```
ezplot(y,[-1,5]).
```

The corresponding commands in MAPLE are

```
y:= 4*x^3 - 21*x^2 + 18*x + 6; dy:= diff(y,x);
solve(dy = 0,x);
y1:= subs(x = 3,y); y2:= subs(x = 1/2,y);
d2y:= diff(y,x,x); subs(x = 3,d2y); subs(x = 1/2,d2y);
plot(y,x = -1..5);
```

Example 7.32 Determine the stationary values of the function

$$f(x) = x^2 - 6x + \frac{82}{x} + \frac{45}{x^2}, \quad x \neq 0$$

Solution The derivative is

$$f'(x) = 2x - 6 - \frac{82}{x^2} - \frac{90}{x^3}$$

and $f'(x) = 0$ when

$$2x^4 - 6x^3 - 82x - 90 = 0$$

Factorizing we have

$$2(x^2 - 4x - 5)(x^2 + x + 9) = 0$$

or

$$2(x + 1)(x - 5)(x^2 + x + 9) = 0$$

So the real roots are $x = 5$ and $x = -1$.

At $x = 5$, $f(5) = 66/5$. To decide whether this is a maximum or minimum we examine the value of $f''(x)$ at $x = 5$.

$$f''(x) = 2 + \frac{164}{x^3} + \frac{270}{x^4} \quad \text{and} \quad f''(5) > 0$$

Thus $f(5) = 66/5$ is a minimum value of the function.

At $x = -1$, $f(-1) = -30$ and $f''(-1) > 0$, so that $f(-1) = -30$ is also a minimum of the function.

Note that $f(x)$ has an asymptote $x = 0$ and behaves like $(x - 3)^2$ where $|x|$ is very large.

In many applications, we know for practical reasons that a particular problem has a minimum (or maximum) solution. If the equation $f'(x) = 0$ is satisfied by only one sensible value of x then that value must determine the unique minimum (or maximum) we are seeking. We will illustrate using three simple examples.

Example 7.33 A manufacturer has to supply N items per month at a uniform daily rate. Each time a production run is started it costs £c_1, the 'set-up' cost. In addition, each item costs £c_2 to manufacture. To avoid unnecessarily high production costs, the manufacturer decides to produce a large quantity q in one run and store it until the contract calls for delivery. The cost of storing each item is £c_3 per month. What is the optimal size of a production run?

Solution As the contract calls for a monthly supply of N items, we need to look for a production run size that will minimize the total monthly cost to the manufacturer.

The costs the manufacturer incurs are the production costs and the storage costs. The production cost for a production run of q items is

$$£(c_1 + c_2q)$$

This production run will satisfy the contract for q/N months, so the monthly production cost will be

$$£\frac{c_1 + c_2q}{q/N} = £\left(\frac{c_1}{q} + c_2\right)N$$

To this must be added the monthly storage cost, which will be £$\frac{1}{2}qc_3$, since the stock is depleted at a uniform rate and the average stock size is $\frac{1}{2}q$. Thus the total monthly cost £C is given by

$$C = \left(\frac{c_1}{q} + c_2\right)N + \tfrac{1}{2}qc_3$$

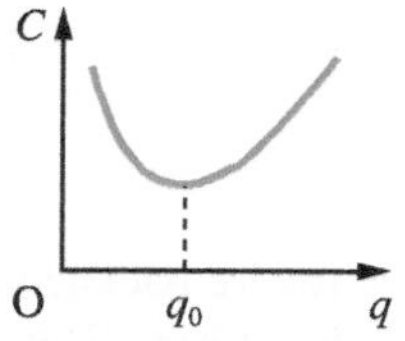

Figure 7.37
Monthly cost versus run size.

which has a graph similar to that shown in Figure 7.37.

To find the value q^* of q that minimizes C, we differentiate the expression for C with respect to q and set the derivative equal to zero:

$$\frac{dC}{dq} = \frac{-c_1N}{q^2} + \tfrac{1}{2}c_3$$

and

$$\frac{dC}{dq} = 0 \quad \text{implies} \quad \frac{-c_1N}{(q^*)^2} + \tfrac{1}{2}c_3 = 0$$

and hence

$$q^* = \sqrt{\left(\frac{2c_1N}{c_3}\right)}$$

This quantity is called the **economic lot size.**

Optimization plays an important role in design, and in Example 7.34 we illustrate this by applying it to the relatively easy problem of designing a milk carton.

Example 7.34 A milk retailer wishes to design a milk carton that has a square cross-section, as illustrated in Figure 7.38(a), and is to contain two pints of milk (2 pints ≡ 1.136 litres). The carton is to be made from a rectangular sheet of waxed cardboard, by folding into a square tube and sealing down the edge, and then folding and sealing the top and bottom. To make the resulting carton airtight and robust for handling, an overlap of at least 5 mm is needed. The procedure is illustrated in Figure 7.38(b). As the milk retailer will be using a large number of such cartons, there is a requirement to use the design that is least expensive to produce. In particular the retailer desires the design that minimizes the amount of waxed cardboard used.

Solution If, as illustrated in Figure 7.38(a), the final dimensions of the container are $h \times b \times b$ (all in mm) then the area of waxed cardboard required is

$$A = (4b + 5)(h + b + 10) \tag{7.32}$$

Since the capacity of the carton is fixed at two pints (1.136 litres), the values of h and b must be such that

$$\text{volume} = hb^2 = 1\,136\,000\,\text{mm}^3 \tag{7.33}$$

Substituting (7.33) back into (7.32) gives

$$A = (4b + 5)\left(\frac{1\,136\,000}{b^2} + b + 10\right)$$

To find the value of b that minimizes A, we differentiate A with respect to b to obtain $A'(b)$ and then set $A'(b) = 0$. Differentiating gives

$$A'(b) = 8b + 45 - \frac{4\,544\,000}{b^2} - \frac{11\,360\,000}{b^3}$$

so the required value of b is given by the root of the equation

$$8b^4 + 45b^3 - 4\,544\,000b - 11\,360\,000 = 0$$

A straightforward tabulation of this polynomial, or use of a suitable software package, yields a root at $b = 81.8$. From (7.33) the corresponding value of h is $h = 169.8$. Thus the optimal design of the milk carton will have dimensions 81.8 mm × 81.8 mm × 169.8 mm.

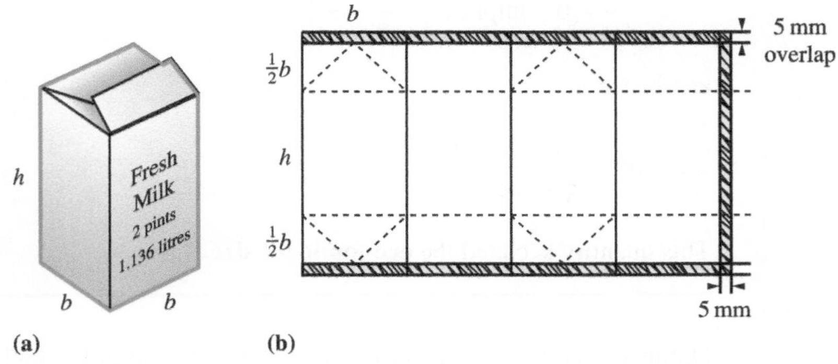

Figure 7.38 The construction of a milk carton.

Optimization problems also occur in programmes for replacing equipment and machinery in industry. We will illustrate this by a more commonplace decision: the best policy for replacing a car.

Example 7.35 For a particular model of car, bought for £14 750, the second-hand value after t years is given fairly accurately by the formula

$$\text{price} = £e^{9.55-0.11t}$$

The running costs of the car increase as the car gets older, so after t years the annual running cost is £$(917 + 163t)$. When should it be replaced?

Solution The accumulated running cost for the car over t years is

$$£\sum_{r=0}^{t-1}(917 + 163r) = £917t + £163[1 + 2 + 3 + \ldots + (t-1)]$$

$$= £917t + £\tfrac{163}{2}(t-1)t \qquad \left(\text{using } \sum_{r=1}^{n} r = \tfrac{1}{2}n(n+1)\right)$$

$$= £(835.5 + 81.5t)t$$

The total cost of the car clearly includes depreciation as well as running costs, so the average annual cost £C of the car is given by

$$C = \frac{14\,750 - e^{9.55-0.11t} + (835.5 + 81.5t)t}{t}$$

To find the optimal time for replacing the car, we find the value of t that minimizes C. Differentiating C with respect to t gives

$$C'(t) = -\frac{1}{t^2}(14\,750 - e^{9.55-0.11t}) + \frac{1}{t}(0.11e^{9.55-0.11t}) + 81.5$$

Setting $C'(t) = 0$ gives

$$e^{9.55-0.11t} = \frac{14\,750 - 81.5t^2}{1 + 0.11t}$$

Solving this numerically gives $t = 5.3$.

7.5.2 Exercises

Check your answers using MATLAB or MAPLE whenever possible.

79 Find the stationary values of the following functions and determine their nature. In each case also find the point of inflection and sketch a graph of the function.

(a) $f(x) = 2x^3 - 5x^2 + 4x - 1$

(b) $f(x) = x^3 + 6x^2 - 15x + 51$

(c) $f(x) = x^4 - 6x^2 + 8x + 2$

80 Find the stationary values of the following functions, distinguishing carefully between them. In each case sketch a graph of the function.

(a) $f(x) = \dfrac{3x}{(x-1)(x-4)}$

(b) $f(x) = 2e^{-x}(x-1)^3$

(c) $f(x) = x^2e^{-x}$

(d) $f(x) = \dfrac{1}{x^2} + \dfrac{8}{(1-x)^2}$

81 Consider the can shown in Figure 7.39, which has capacity 500 ml. The cost of manufacture is proportional to the amount of metal used, which in turn is proportional to the surface area of the can. Ignoring the overlaps necessary for the manufacture of the can, find the diameter and height of the can which minimizes its cost.

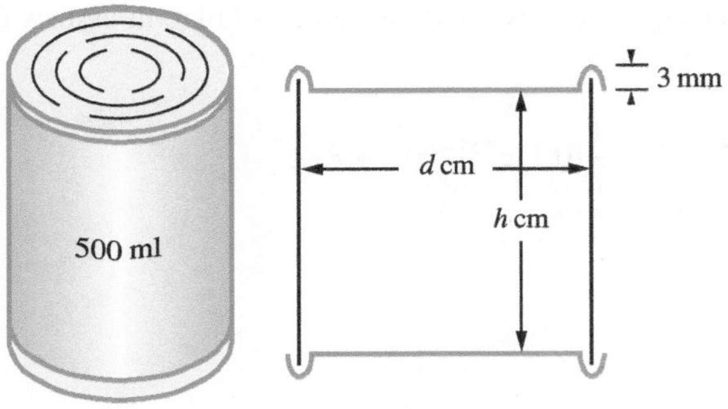

Figure 7.39 Can of Questions 81 and 82.

82 Consider again the can shown in Figure 7.39. Allowing for an overlap of 6 mm top and bottom surfaces to give a rim of 3 mm on the can, show that the area A mm² of metal used is given by

$$A(d) = \pi(d^2 + 3.6d + 1.44)/2 + 2000/d$$

where d cm is the diameter of the can.

Show that the value of d^* which minimizes the area of the can satisfies the equation

$$\pi d^2(d + 1.8) = 2000$$

Calculate d^* and the corresponding value of the height of the can.

83 In an underwater telephone cable the ratio of the radius of the core to the thickness of the protective sheath is denoted by x. The speed v at which a signal is transmitted is proportional to $x^2 \ln(1/x)$. Show that

$$\frac{dv}{dx} = Kx\left[2\ln\left(\frac{1}{x}\right) - 1\right]$$

where K is some constant, and hence deduce the stationary values of v. Distinguish between these stationary values and show that the speed is greatest when $x = 1/\sqrt{e}$.

84 A closed hollow vessel is in the form of a right-circular cone, together with its base, and is made of sheet metal of negligible thickness. Express the total surface area S in terms of the volume V and the semi-vertical angle θ of the cone. Show that for a given volume the total area of the surface is a minimum if $\sin\theta = \frac{1}{3}$. Find the value of S if $V = \frac{8}{3}\pi a^3$.

85 A numerical method which is more efficient than repeated subtabulation for obtaining the optimal solution is the following **bracketing method.** The initial tabulation locates an interval in which the solution occurs. The optimal solution is then estimated by optimizing a suitable quadratic approximation.

Consider again the milk carton problem, Example 7.34. Calculate $A(70)$, $A(80)$ and $A(90)$ and deduce that a minimum occurs in [70, 90]. Next find numbers p, q and r such that

$$C(b) = p(b - 80)^2 + q(b - 80) + r$$

satisfies $C(70) = A(70)$, $C(80) = A(80)$ and $C(90) = A(90)$. The minimum of C occurs at $80 - q/(2p)$. Show that this yields the estimate $b = 82.2$. Evaluate $A(82.2)$ and deduce that the solution lies in the interval [80, 90]. Next repeat the process using the values $A(80)$, $A(82.2)$ and $A(90)$ and show that the solution lies in the interval [80, 83.1]. Apply the method once more to obtain an improved estimate of the solution.

86 A pipeline is to be laid from a point A on one bank of a river of width 1 unit to a point B 2 units downstream on the opposite bank, as shown in Figure 7.40. Because it costs more to lay the pipe under water than on dry land, it is proposed to take it in a straight line across the river to a point C and then along the river bank to B. If it costs $\alpha\%$ more to lay a given length of pipe under the river than along the bank, write down a formula for the cost of the pipeline, specifying the domain of the function carefully. What recommendation would you make about the position of C when (a) $\alpha = 25$, (b) $\alpha = 10$?

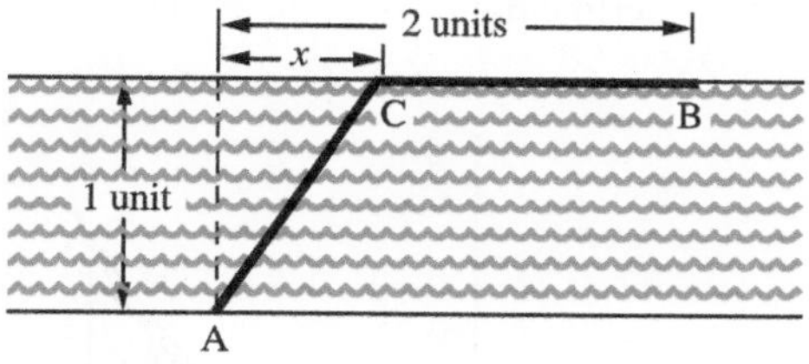

Figure 7.40

87 Cross-current extraction methods are used in many chemical processes. Solute is extracted from a stream of solvent by repeated washings with water. The solvent stream is passed consecutively through a sequence of extractors, in each of which a cross-current of wash water, flowing at a determined rate, carries out some of the solute. The aim is to choose the individual wash flowrates in such a way as to extract as much solute as possible by the end, the total flow of wash water being fixed.

Consider the three-state extractor process shown in Figure 7.41, where c, x, y and z are the solute concentrations in the main stream, and αx, αy and αz are the solute concentrations in the effluent wash-water streams, with α a constant. The solute balance equations for the extractors are

$$Q(c - x) = u\alpha x$$

$$Q(x - y) = v\alpha y$$

$$Q(y - z) = w\alpha z$$

The total wash-water flowrate is W, so that

$$u + v + w = W$$

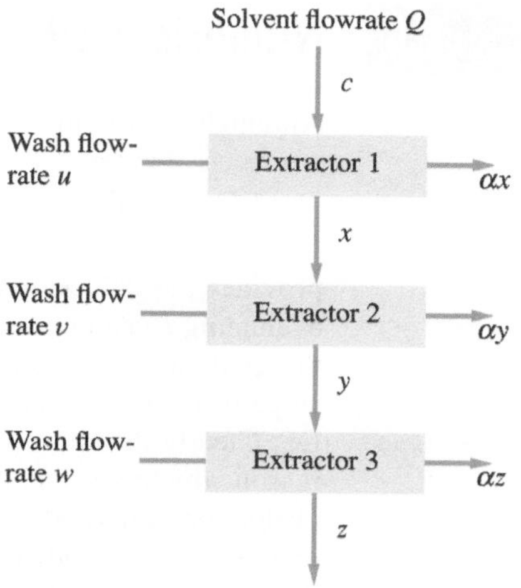

Figure 7.41

We wish to find u, v and w such that the outflow concentration z is minimized.

This is an example of **dynamic programming**. The key to its solution is the **Principle of Optimality**, which states that an optimal programme has the property that, whatever the initial state and decisions, the remaining decisions must constitute an optimal policy with respect to the state resulting from the initial decision. This means we solve the problem first for a one-extractor process, then for a two-extractor process, then for a three-extractor process, and so on.

For a one-stage process, x is minimized when $u = W$, giving $x^* = Qc/(Q + \alpha W)$.

For a two-stage process, $y = Qx/(Q + \alpha v)$, where $x = \frac{1}{2}W$ with $v = \frac{1}{2}W$, giving $y^* = Q^2c/(Q + \frac{1}{2}\alpha W)^2$.

For a three-stage process, $z = Q^2x/[Q + \frac{1}{2}\alpha(W - u)]^2$, where $x = Qc/(Q + \alpha u)$. Show that z is minimized when $u = \frac{1}{3}W$, with $v = w = \frac{1}{3}W$, giving $z^* = Q^3c/(Q + \frac{1}{3}\alpha W)^3$.

Generalize your answers to the case where n extractors are used.

88 The management of resources often requires a chain of decisions similar to that described in Question 87. Consider the harvesting policy for a large forest. The profit produced from the sale of felled timber is proportional to the square root of the volume sold, while the volume of standing timber increases in proportion to itself year on year. Use the technique outlined in Question 87 to produce a 10-year harvesting programme for a forest.

7.6 Numerical differentiation

Although the formula

$$f'(x) = \lim_{\Delta x \to 0} \frac{f(x + \Delta x) - f(x)}{\Delta x} = \lim_{\Delta x \to 0} \frac{\Delta f}{\Delta x}$$

provides the definition of the derivative of $f(x)$, it does not provide a good basis for evaluating $f'(x)$ numerically. This is because it provides a one-sided approximation of the gradient at x, as shown in Figure 7.42. When we set $\Delta x = h$ (> 0), we obtain the slope of the chord PR. When we set $\Delta x = -h$ (< 0), we obtain the slope of the chord QP. Clearly the chord QR offers a better approximation to the tangent at P. A second reason why the formal definition of a derivative yields a poor approximation is that the evaluation of derivatives involves the division of a small quantity Δf by a second small quantity Δx. This process magnifies the rounding errors involved in calculating Δf from the values of $f(x)$, a process that worsens as $\Delta x \to 0$. This phenomenon is called **ill-conditioning**. Generally speaking, numerical differentiation is a process in which accuracy is lost and the 'noise' caused by experimental error is magnified.

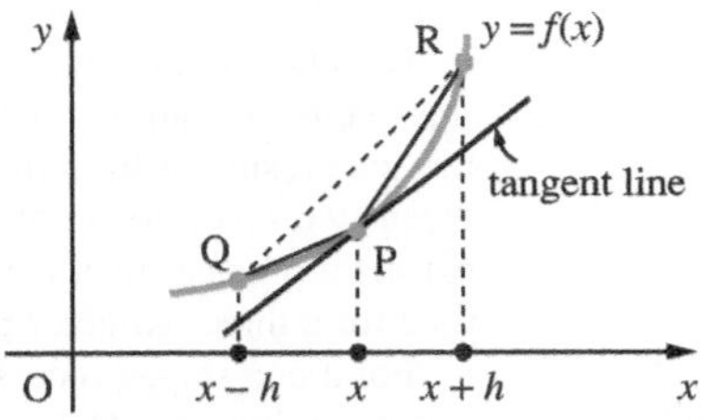

Figure 7.42 Approximations to the tangent at P.

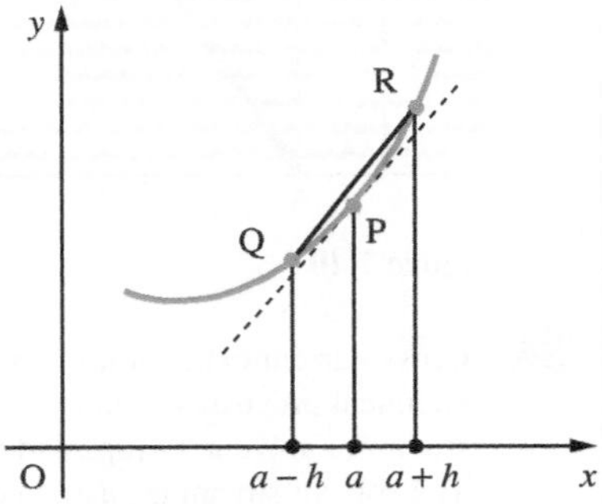

Figure 7.43 Chord approximation.

7.6.1 The chord approximation

This method uses the slope of a chord QR symmetrically disposed about x to approximate the slope of the tangent at x, as shown in Figure 7.43. Thus

$$f'(x) \approx \frac{f(x + h) - f(x - h)}{2h} = \phi(h)$$

Thus when the function is specified graphically, a value of h is chosen, and at a series of points along the curve the quotient $\phi(h)$ is calculated. When the function is given as a table of values, we do not have control of the value of h, but the same approximation is used using the tabular interval as h. Consequently, to estimate the value of the derivative $f'(a)$ at $x = a$ we use the approximation

$$\frac{f(a + h) - f(a - h)}{2h} = \phi(h)$$

as the basis for an extrapolation. For almost all functions commonly occurring in engineering applications

$$f'(a) = \phi(h) + \text{terms involving powers of } h \text{ greater than or equal to } h^2$$

For example, considering $f(x) = x^3$

$$\phi(h) = \frac{(a+h)^3 - (a-h)^3}{2h} = \frac{6a^2h + 2h^3}{2h} = 3a^2 + h^2$$

Similarly, for $f(x) = x^4$

$$\phi(h) = 4a^3 + 4ah^2$$

In general, we may write

$$f'(a) = \phi(h) + Ah^2 + \text{terms involving higher powers of } h$$

where A is independent of h. Interval-halving gives

$$f'(a) = \phi(\tfrac{1}{2}h) + \tfrac{1}{4}A'h^2 + \text{terms involving higher powers of } h$$

where $A' \approx A$. Hence we obtain a better estimate for $f'(a)$ by extrapolation, eliminating the terms involving h^2:

$$f'(a) \approx \tfrac{1}{3}[4\phi(\tfrac{1}{2}h) - \phi(h)] \qquad \textbf{(7.34)}$$

We illustrate this technique in Example 7.36.

Example 7.36 Estimate $f'(0.5)$, where $f(x)$ is given by the table

x	0.1	0.2	0.3	0.4	0.5	0.6	0.7	0.8	0.9
$f(x)$	0.0998	0.1987	0.2955	0.3894	0.4794	0.5646	0.6442	0.7174	0.7833

Solution Using the data provided, taking $h = 0.4$ and 0.2, we obtain

$$\phi(0.4) = \frac{0.7833 - 0.0998}{0.8} = 0.8544$$

and

$$\phi(0.2) = \frac{0.6442 - 0.2955}{0.4} = 0.8718$$

Hence, by extrapolation, we have, using (7.34),

$$f'(0.5) \approx (4 \times 0.8718 - 0.8544)/3 = 0.8776$$

The tabulated function is actually $\sin x$, so that in this illustrative example we can compare the estimate with the true value $\cos 0.5$, and we find that the answer is correct to 4dp.

In general, any numerical procedure is subject to two types of error. One is due to the accumulation of rounding errors within a calculation, while the other is due to the nature of the approximation formula (the truncation error). In this example the truncation error is of order h^2 for $\phi(h)$, but we do not have an estimate for the truncation error for the extrapolated estimate for $f'(a)$. This will be discussed in the next chapter following the introduction of the Taylor series (see Exercises 9.4.6, Question 23). The effect of the rounding errors on the answer can be assessed, however, and, using the methods of Chapter 1, we see that the maximum effect of the rounding errors on the answer in Example 7.36 is $\pm 2.5 \times 10^{-4}$.

7.6.2 Exercises

89 Use the chord approximation to obtain two estimates for $f'(1.2)$ using $h = 0.2$ and $h = 0.1$ where $f(x)$ is given in the table below.

x	1.0	1.1	1.2	1.3	1.4
$f(x)$	1.000	1.008	1.061	1.192	1.414

Use extrapolation to obtain an improved approximation.

90 Use your calculator (in radian mode) to calculate the quotient $\{f(x + h) - f(x - h)\}/(2h)$ for $f(x) = \sin x$, where $x = 0(0.1)1.0$ and $h = 0.001$. Compare your answers with $\cos x$.

91 Consider the function $f(x) = x\mathrm{e}^x$, tabulated below:

x	0.96	0.97	0.98	0.99	1.00
$f(x)$	2.5072	2.5588	2.6112	2.6643	2.7183

x	1.01	1.02	1.03	1.04
$f(x)$	2.7731	2.8287	2.8851	2.9424

(a) Find, *exactly*, $f'(1)$ and $f''(1)$.

(b) Use the tabulated values and the formula

$$f'(a) \simeq (f(a + h) - f(a - h))/2h$$

to estimate $f'(1)$, for various h. Compute the errors involved and comment on the results.

(c) Repeat (b) for $f''(1)$ using

$$f''(a) \simeq (f(a + h) - 2f(a) + f(a - h))/h^2$$

92 Use the following table of $f(x) = (\mathrm{e}^x - \mathrm{e}^{-x})/2$ to estimate $f'(1.0)$ by means of an extrapolation method.

x	0.2	0.6	0.8	1.2	1.4	1.8
$f(x)$	0.2013	0.6367	0.8881	1.5095	1.9043	2.9422

Compare your answer with $(\mathrm{e} + \mathrm{e}^{-1})/2 = 1.5431$ correct to 4dp.

93 Investigate the effect of using a smaller value for h in Example 7.36. Show that $\phi(0.1)$ gives a poorer estimate for $f'(0.5)$ and the error bound for the consequent extrapolation $[4\phi(0.1) - \phi(0.2)]/3$ is 7×10^{-4}.

7.7 Integration

In this section we shall introduce the concept of integration and illustrate its role in problem-solving and modelling situations.

7.7.1 Basic ideas and definitions

Consider an object moving along a line with constant velocity u (in m s^{-1}). The distance s (in m) travelled by the object between times t_1 and t_2 (in s) is given by

$$s = u(t_2 - t_1)$$

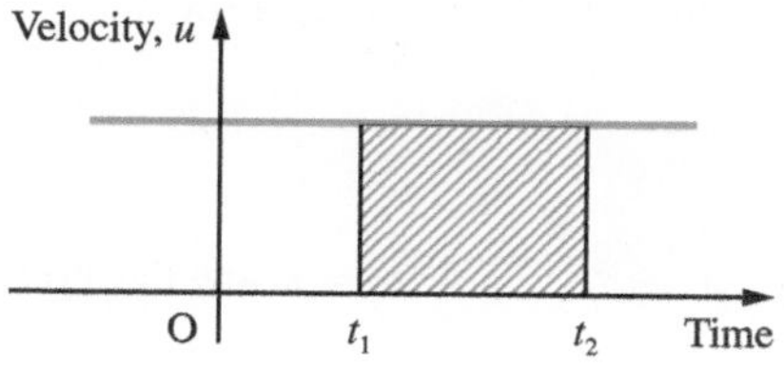

Figure 7.44 Velocity–time graph for an object moving with constant velocity u. The shaded area shows the distance travelled by the object between times t_1 and t_2.

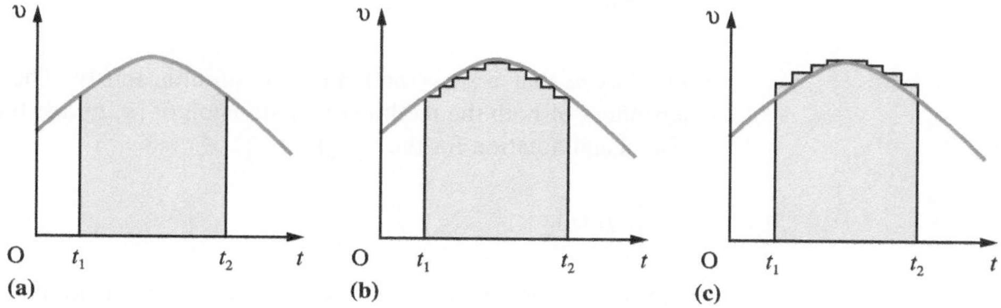

Figure 7.45 A velocity–time graph and two piecewise-constant approximations to it.

This is the area 'under' the graph of the velocity function between $t = t_1$ and $t = t_2$, as shown in Figure 7.44. This, of course, deals with the special case where the velocity is a constant function. However, even when the velocity varies with time, the area under the velocity graph still gives the distance travelled. Consider the velocity graph shown in Figure 7.45(a). We can approximate the velocity–time graph by a series of small horizontal lines that lie either entirely below the curve (as in Figure 7.45(b)) or entirely above it (Figure 7.45(c)). An object moving such that its velocity–time graph is (b) would always be slower at a particular time than an object with velocity–time graph (a), so that the distance it covers is less than that of the object with graph (a). Similarly, an object with velocity–time graph (c) will cover a greater distance than an object with graph (a). Thus

distance with graph (b) < distance with graph (a) < distance with graph (c)

In cases (b) and (c), because the velocities are piecewise-constant, the distances covered are represented by the areas under the graphs between $t = t_1$ and $t = t_2$. So we have

area under graph (b) < area under graph (a) < area under graph (c)

If the horizontal steps of graphs (b) and (c) are made very small, the difference between the areas for the approximating graphs (b) and (c) becomes very small. In other words, the distance for graph (a) is just the area under the graph between $t = t_1$ and $t = t_2$.

This is one of many practical problems that involve this process of area evaluation at some stage in their solution. This process is called **integration**: the summing together of all the parts that make up a given area. The area under the graph is called the **integral** of the function. For some functions it is possible to obtain formulae for their integrals; for others we have to be content with numerical approximations.

Formally, we define the integral of the function $f(x)$ between $x = a$ and $x = b$ to be

$$\lim_{\substack{n\to\infty \\ \Delta x\to 0}} \sum_{r=1}^{n} f(x_r^*)\Delta x_{r-1}$$

where $a = x_0 < x_1 < x_2 < \ldots < x_{n-1} < x_n = b$ are the points of subdivision of the interval $[a, b]$,

$$\Delta x_{r-1} = x_r - x_{r-1},\ \Delta x = \max(\Delta x_0, \Delta x_1, \ldots, \Delta x_{n-1}) \text{ and } x_{r-1} \leqslant x_r^* \leqslant x_r$$

Here we have used the special notation

$$\lim_{\substack{n\to\infty \\ \Delta x\to 0}}$$

to emphasize that $n \to \infty$ and $\Delta x \to 0$ simultaneously. The value of the integral is independent of both the method of subdivision of $[a, b]$ and the choices of x_r^*.

The usual notation for the integral is

$$\int_a^b f(x)\mathrm{d}x$$

where the integration symbol $\int$ is an elongated S, standing for 'summation'. The dx is called the **differential** of x, and a and b are called the **limits of integration**. The function $f(x)$ being integrated is the **integrand**.

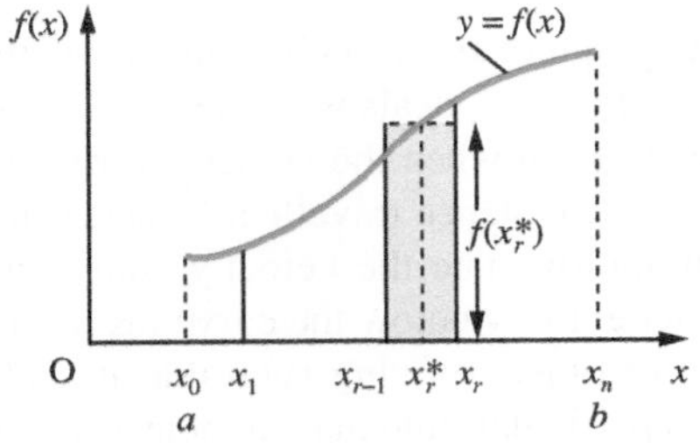

Figure 7.46
Strip about typical value $x = x_r^*$.

The process is illustrated in Figure 7.46, where the area under the graph of $f(x)$ for $x \in [a, b]$ has been subdivided into n vertical strips (by which we strictly mean that the area has been approximated by the n vertical strips). The area of a typical strip is given by

$$f(x_r^*)(x_r - x_{r-1}) = f(x_r^*)\Delta x_{r-1}$$

where $x_{r-1} \leqslant x_r^* \leqslant x_r$ and $\Delta x_{r-1} = x_r - x_{r-1}$. Thus the area under the graph can be approximated by

$$\sum_{r=1}^{n} f(x_r^*)\Delta x_{r-1}$$

This approximation becomes closer to the exact area as the number of strips is increased and their widths decreased. In the limiting case as $n \to \infty$ and $\Delta x \to 0$ this leads to the exact area being given by

$$A = \int_a^b f(x)\mathrm{d}x$$

so that

$$\int_a^b f(x)\mathrm{d}x = \lim_{\substack{n\to\infty \\ \Delta x\to 0}} \sum_{r=1}^{n} f(x_r^*)\Delta x_{r-1} \qquad (7.35)$$

In line with the definition of an integral, we note that if the graph of $f(x)$ is below the x axis then the summation involves products of negative ordinates with positive widths, so that areas below the x axis must be interpreted as being negative.

Example 7.37 By considering the area under the graph of $y = x + 3$, evaluate the integral $\int_{-5}^{5}(x + 3)\mathrm{d}x$.

Solution The area under the graph is shown hatched in Figure 7.47, with the area A_1 being negative, as explained immediately above, and the area A_2 positive. So we determine each area independently. In each case the areas are triangular, so that

$$A_1 = -\tfrac{1}{2} \times 2 \times 2 = -2$$

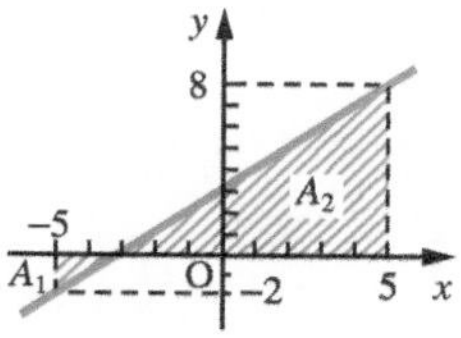

Figure 7.47

and

$$A_2 = \tfrac{1}{2} \times 8 \times 8 = 32$$

Thus

$$\int_{-5}^{5} (x + 3)\mathrm{d}x = A_1 + A_2 = -2 + 32 = 30$$

Example 7.38 Using the definition of an integral (7.35), show that

$$\int_a^b (x^2 - 1)\mathrm{d}x = \tfrac{1}{3}(b^3 - a^3) - (b - a)$$

Solution From the definition we have:

$$\int_a^b (x^2 - 1)\mathrm{d}x = \lim_{\substack{n\to\infty \\ \Delta x\to 0}} \left[\sum_{r=1}^{n}(x_r^{*2}\Delta x_{r-1} - 1\Delta x_{r-1})\right]$$

$$= \lim_{\substack{n\to\infty \\ \Delta x\to 0}} \sum_{r=1}^{n} x_r^{*2}\Delta x_{r-1} - \lim_{\substack{n\to\infty \\ \Delta x\to 0}} \sum_{r=1}^{n} \Delta x_{r-1}$$

The second term here is easy to evaluate since $\Delta x_{r-1} = x_r - x_{r-1}$ and $\sum_{r=1}^{n}(x_r - x_{r-1}) = (x_1 - x_0) + (x_2 - x_1) + \ldots + (x_n - x_{n-1})$, which simplifies to $\sum_{r=1}^{n}(x_r - x_{r-1}) = b - a$ since $x_0 = a$ and $x_n = b$.

There are several different methods for evaluating the first term. Here we shall illustrate one method; another method is set out in Question 98 of Exercises 7.7.3. We shall use three different choices for x_r^*:

$$x_r^* = x_{r-1},\ x_r,\ \sqrt{(x_{r-1}x_r)}$$

(Notice $x_{r-1} < \sqrt{(x_{r-1}x_r)} < x_r$.) Then we have

$$S_1 = \sum_{r=1}^{n} x_{r-1}^2 \Delta x_{r-1} = \sum_{r=1}^{n} x_{r-1}^2 (x_r - x_{r-1}) = \sum_{r=1}^{n} (x_{r-1}^2 x_r - x_{r-1}^3)$$

Similarly

$$S_2 = \sum_{r=1}^{n} x_r^2 \Delta x_{r-1} = \sum_{r=1}^{n} (x_r^3 - x_r^2 x_{r-1})$$

and

$$S_3 = \sum_{r=1}^{n} x_{r-1} x_r \Delta x_{r-1} = \sum_{r=1}^{n} (x_{r-1} x_r^2 - x_{r-1}^2 x_r)$$

Hence $S_1 + S_2 + S_3 = \sum_{r=1}^{n} (x_r^3 - x_{r-1}^3)$

$$= (x_1^3 - x_0^3) + (x_2^3 - x_1^3) + \ldots + (x_n^3 - x_{n-1}^3)$$

$$= x_n^3 - x_0^3$$

In the limit $n \to \infty$, S_1, S_2 and S_3 tend to the same limit, so

$$\sum_{r=1}^{n} x_r^{*} \Delta x_{r-1} \to \tfrac{1}{3}(S_1 + S_2 + S_3) = \tfrac{1}{3}(b^3 - a^3)$$

Hence $\int_a^b (x^2 - 1)\mathrm{d}x = \tfrac{1}{3}(b^3 - a^3) - (b - a)$

7.7.2 Mathematical modelling using integration

We have seen that the area under the graph $y = f(x)$ can be expressed as an integral, but integrals have a much wider application. Any quantity that can be expressed in the form of the limit of a sum as in (7.35) can be represented by an integral, and this occurs in many practical situations. Because areas can be expressed as integrals, it follows that we can always interpret an integral geometrically as an area under a graph.

Example 7.39 What is the volume of a pyramid with square base, of side 4 metres and height 6 metres?

Solution Imagine the pyramid of Figure 7.48(a) is cut into horizontal slices of thickness Δh, as shown in Figure 7.48(b), and then sum their volumes to give the volume of the pyramid.

From Figure 7.48(b) the volume of the slice is

$$\Delta V_k = \text{area of square flat face} \times \text{thickness} = 4d_k^2 \Delta h$$

where $2d_k$ is the length of one side of the square slice. The length of the side is related to the height h_k of the slice above the base, and using similar triangle relation (see Figure 7.48(c)) we have

Figure 7.48
Pyramid of Example 7.38.

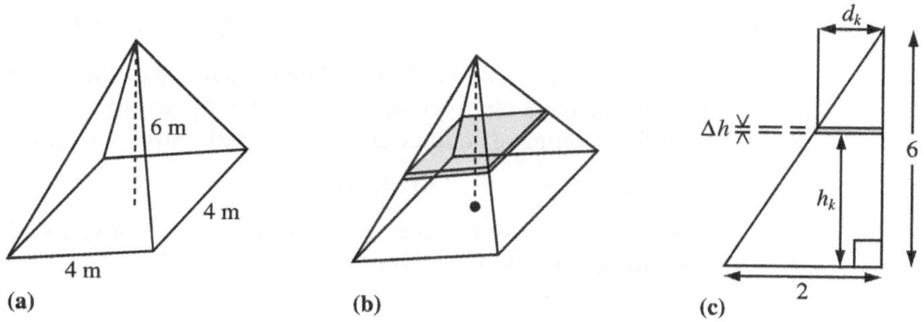

$$\frac{d_k}{2} = \frac{6 - h_k}{6}$$

Thus the slice has volume

$$\Delta V_k = \frac{4(6 - h_k)^2}{9}\Delta h$$

The volume of all slices is

$$\sum_{k=1}^{n} \Delta V_k = \sum_{k=1}^{n} \frac{4(6 - h_k)^2}{9}\Delta h$$

Proceeding to the limit ($n \to \infty$, $\Delta h \to 0$) as in (7.35) gives the volume of the pyramid as the integral

$$V = \int_0^6 \tfrac{4}{9}(6 - h)^2 dh$$

We will see later, in Example 7.42, that $V = 32$ and the volume is 32 m³.

Example 7.40

A reservoir is created by constructing a dam across a glacial valley. Its wet face is vertical and has approximately the shape of a parabola, as shown in Figure 7.49. The water pressure p (Pascals) varies with depth according to

$$p = p_0 - gy + 10g$$

where p_0 is the pressure at the surface, g is the acceleration due to gravity and y metres is the height from the bottom of the parabola, as shown in the figure. Calculate the total force acting on the wet face of the dam.

Figure 7.49
Schematic representation of dam showing strip of width Δy_k at height y_k.

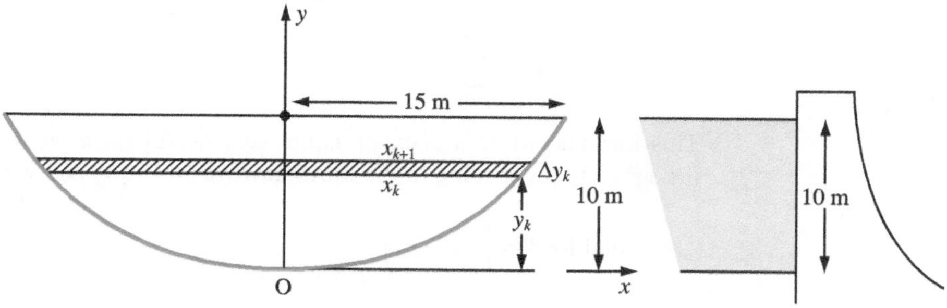

Solution From the dimensions given in Figure 7.49 the equation of the parabola is $y = \dfrac{2x^2}{45}$, where x m is the half width. Dividing the surface of the parabola into horizontal strips we can calculate the force acting on each strip and then sum these forces to obtain the total force acting. The force ΔF_k acting on the strip at height y_k is

$$\Delta F_k = (p_0 - g\bar{y}_k + 10g)(2\bar{x}_k \Delta y_k)$$

where $\bar{x}_k$ and $\bar{y}_k$ are the average values of x and y on $[y_k, y_{k+1}]$. Thus, using (7.35), the total force F newtons is given by

$$\begin{aligned} F &= \lim_{\substack{n\to\infty \\ \Delta y\to 0}} \sum_{k=1}^{n} \Delta F_k \\ &= \lim_{\substack{n\to\infty \\ \Delta y\to 0}} \sum_{k=1}^{n} (p_0 - g\bar{y}_k + 10g)(2\bar{x}_k \Delta y_k) \\ &= \int_0^{10} 2x(p_0 - gy + 10g)\mathrm{d}y \end{aligned}$$

Now $y = \dfrac{2x^2}{45}$, so that $2x = (90y)^{1/2}$ and we may rewrite the expression for F as

$$F = \int_0^{10} 3\sqrt{10}(p_0 + 10g - gy)\sqrt{(y)}\mathrm{d}y$$

Later in Example 7.45 we will show that $F = 200p_0 + 800g$.

Example 7.41 A beam of length l is freely hinged at both ends and carries a distributed load $w(x)$ where

$$w(x) = \begin{cases} 4Wx/l^2 & 0 \leq x \leq l/2 \\ 4W(l - x)/l^2 & l/2 \leq x \leq l \end{cases}$$

Show that the total load is W and find the shear force at a point on the beam.

Solution To find the total load on the beam we divide the interval $(0, l)$ into n subintervals of length Δx, so that $x_k = k\Delta x$ and $\Delta x = l/n$. Then the load on the subinterval (x_k, x_{k+1}) is $w(x_k^*)\Delta x$, where $w(x_k^*)$ is the average value of $w(x)$ in that subinterval. The total load on the beam is the sum of all such elementary loads, and we have

$$\text{total load} = \sum_{k=0}^{n-1} w(x_k^*)\Delta x$$

This formula, while it is exact, is not very useful since we do not know the values of the x_k^*'s. By proceeding to the limit, however, $x_k^* \to x_k$ and we obtain the formula

$$\text{total load} = \int_0^{l} w(x)\mathrm{d}x$$

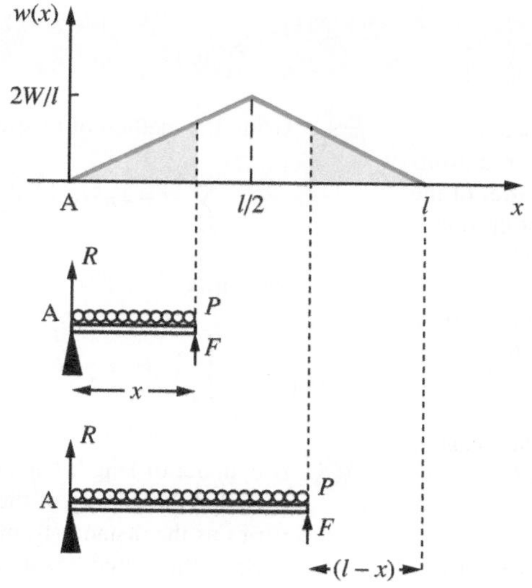

Figure 7.50 Non-uniform load on a beam.

Now the integral $\int_0^l w(x)\mathrm{d}x$ is the area under the curve $y = w(x)$ between $x = 0$ and $x = l$, and by considering the graph of $w(x)$ shown in Figure 7.50 we see that this is W.

From the symmetry of the loading and the end conditions we see that the reactions at the supports at both ends are equal (to R, say). Then the vertical forces must balance for equilibrium, giving

$$2R = W$$

for equilibrium. To find the shear force F we have to consider the vertical equilibrium of the portion of the beam to the left of P. Thus

$R + F =$ load between A and P which is represented by the area under the graph between A and P

Consideration of the areas under the graph of $y = w(x)$ for x shows that

$$R + F = \begin{cases} \frac{1}{2}x(4Wx/l^2) & 0 \leqslant x \leqslant l/2 \\ W - \frac{1}{2}(l - x)[4W(l - x)/l^2] & l/2 \leqslant x \leqslant l \end{cases}$$

This simplifies as

$$R + F = \begin{cases} 2Wx^2/l^2 & 0 \leqslant x \leqslant l/2 \\ W - 2W(l - x)^2/l^2 & l/2 \leqslant x \leqslant l \end{cases}$$

Thus

$$F = \begin{cases} 2Wx^2/l^2 - W/2 & 0 \leqslant x \leqslant l/2 \\ W/2 - 2W(l - x)^2/l^2 & l/2 \leqslant x \leqslant l \end{cases}$$

7.7.3 Exercises

94 Two hot-rodders, Alan and Brian, compete in a drag race. Each accelerates at a constant rate from a standing start. Alan covers the last quarter of the course in 3 s, while Brian covers the last third in 4 s. Who wins and by what time margin?

95 Show that the area under the graph of the constant function $f(x) = 1$ between $x = a$ and $x = b$ $(a < b)$ is given by $b - a$.

96 Show that the area under the graph of the linear function $f(x) = x$ between $x = a$ and $x = b$ $(a < b)$ is given by $\frac{1}{2}(b^2 - a^2)$.

97 Draw the graph of the function $f(x) = 2x - 1$ for $-3 < x < 3$. By considering the area under the graph, evaluate the integral $\int_{-3}^{3}(2x - 1)\mathrm{d}x$.

98 Using n strips of equal width, show that the area under the graph $y = x^2$ between $x = 0$ and $x = c$ satisfies the inequality

$$h^3 \sum_{r=1}^{n-1} r^2 < \text{area} < h^3 \sum_{r=1}^{n} r^2$$

and deduce

(a) $\displaystyle\int_0^c x^2\,\mathrm{d}x = \frac{1}{3}c^3$ (b) $\displaystyle\int_a^b x^2\,\mathrm{d}x = \frac{1}{3}(b^3 - a^3)$

(c) $\displaystyle\int_a^b x^{1/2}\,\mathrm{d}x = \frac{2}{3}(b^{3/2} - a^{3/2})$

(Recall that $\sum_{r=1}^{n} r^2 = \frac{1}{6}n(n+1)(2n+1)$ (see Example 7.10).)

99 Using the method of Question 98 and the fact that

$$\sum_{r=1}^{n} r^3 = \frac{1}{4}n^2(n+1)^2$$

show that

$$\int_a^b x^3\,\mathrm{d}x = \frac{1}{4}(b^4 - a^4)$$

100 A cylinder of length l and diameter D is constructed such that the density of the material comprising it varies as the distance from the base. Show that the mass of the cylinder is given by

$$\int_0^l \frac{1}{4}KD^2\pi x\,\mathrm{d}x$$

where K is a proportionality constant.

101 A beam of length l is freely hinged at both ends and carries a distributed load $w(x)$ where

$$w = \begin{cases} 4W/l & 0 \leqslant x \leqslant l/4 \\ 0 & l/4 < x \leqslant l \end{cases}$$

Find the shear force at a point on the beam.

102 A hemi-spherical vessel has internal radius 0.5 m. It is initially empty. Water flows in at a constant rate of 1 litre per second. Find an expression for the depth of the water after t seconds.

7.7.4 Definite and indefinite integrals

We have seen that the area under the graph $y = f(x)$ between $x = a$ and $x = b$ is given by the integral

$$\int_a^b f(x)\mathrm{d}x$$

Clearly, this area depends on the values of a and b as well as on the function $f(x)$. Thus the integral of a function $f(x)$ may be regarded as a function of a and b. If we replace the number b by the variable x, we obtain a function, F say, that is the area under the graph between a and x, as shown in Figure 7.51. This type of integral is called an

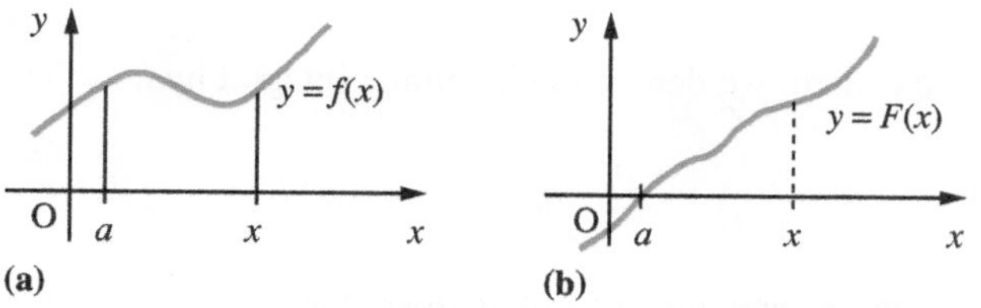

Figure 7.51 (a) Graph of $y = f(x)$. (b) Graph of $\int_a^x f(t)\mathrm{d}t$.

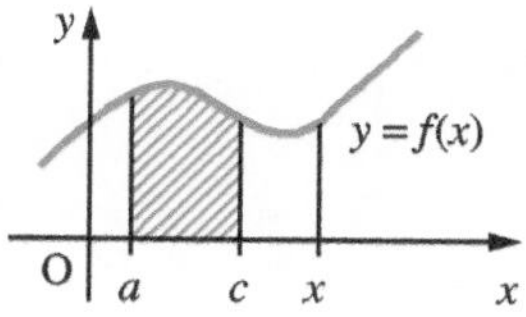

Figure 7.52

indefinite integral to distinguish it from integrals with fixed a and b, which are called **definite integrals**. We have defined F by the relation

$$F(x) = \int_a^x f(t)\mathrm{d}t$$

Notice here that the dummy variable t, used as the integrator, is chosen to be different from the variable x on which the function F depends.

If a different lower limit is chosen, a different function is obtained, say G:

$$G(x) = \int_c^x f(t)\mathrm{d}t$$

By interpreting an integral as the area under a curve, we see from Figure 7.52 that this new function differs from F only by a constant. This follows since

$$F(x) - G(x) = \int_a^x f(t)\mathrm{d}t - \int_c^x f(t)\mathrm{d}t = \int_a^c f(t)\mathrm{d}t$$

which is a definite integral having a constant value representing the area under the graph between a and c, shown shaded in Figure 7.52.

For example, using the definition of an integral, we know (see Example 7.38) that

$$\int_a^b (t^2 - 1)\mathrm{d}t = \tfrac{1}{3}(b^3 - a^3) - (b - a)$$

so that

$$\int_a^x (t^2 - 1)\mathrm{d}t = \tfrac{1}{3}(x^3 - a^3) - (x - a) = \tfrac{1}{3}x^3 - x + (a - \tfrac{1}{3}a^3)$$

Giving a the values 1 and 2 leads to the two functions

$$F(x) = \int_1^x (t^2 - 1)\mathrm{d}t = \tfrac{1}{3}x^3 - x + \tfrac{2}{3}$$

and

$$G(x) = \int_2^x (t^2 - 1)\mathrm{d}t = \tfrac{1}{3}x^3 - x - \tfrac{2}{3}$$

In fact, all indefinite integrals of $f(x) = x^2 - 1$ are of the general form

$\frac{1}{3}x^3 - x + \text{constant}$

When the lower limit is not specified, we denote the indefinite integral by

$$\int f(x)\mathrm{d}x \quad \text{or} \quad \int^x f(t)\mathrm{d}t$$

and include the constant as an arbitrary **constant of integration**. Thus

$$\int (x^2 - 1)\mathrm{d}x = \tfrac{1}{3}x^3 - x + c$$

where c is the arbitrary constant of integration.

It is important to recognize that an indefinite integral is itself a function, while a definite integral is a number.

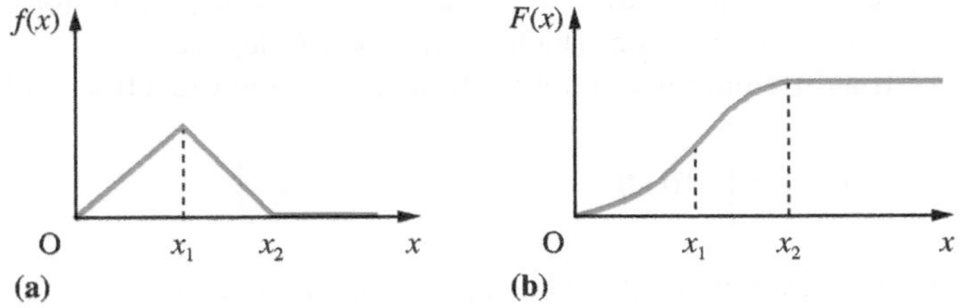

Figure 7.53
(a) Graph of $f(x)$.
(b) Graph of

$$F(x) = \int_0^x f(t)\mathrm{d}(t).$$

We noted in Section 7.2.4 that a function could only be differentiated at points where its graph had a unique tangent, and that, for example, the function represented by the graph of Figure 7.7(a), reproduced as Figure 7.53(a), is not differentiable at domain values $x = x_1$ and $x = x_2$. However, such functions are integrable, with the corresponding indefinite integrals being functions having 'smooth' graphs. For example, the graph of the indefinite integral $F(x)$ of the function $f(x)$ shown in Figure 7.53(a) has the form shown in Figure 7.53(b). For this reason, engineers often refer to integration as being a 'smoothing' process, and an integrator is frequently incorporated within a system design in order to ensure 'smoother' operation.

We can express definite integrals in terms of indefinite integrals. Thus

$$\int_a^b f(x)\mathrm{d}x = g(b) - g(a) \quad \text{where} \quad g(x) = \int f(x)\mathrm{d}x$$

This is often denoted by

$$\int_a^b f(x)\mathrm{d}x = [g(x)]_a^b$$

a notation introduced by Fourier. Thus, for example,

$$\int_1^5 (x^2 - 1)\mathrm{d}x = [\tfrac{1}{3}x^3 - x + c]_1^5 = [\tfrac{125}{3} - 5 + c] - [\tfrac{1}{3} - 1 + c] = 37\tfrac{1}{3}$$

When evaluating definite integrals, the constant of integration can be omitted, since it cancels out in the arithmetic.

7.7.5 The Fundamental Theorem of Calculus

From Questions 95, 96 and 98 (Exercises 7.7.3) we have

$$\int_a^b 1\,\mathrm{d}x = b - a, \qquad \text{giving} \qquad \int 1\,\mathrm{d}x = x + \text{constant}$$

$$\int_a^b x\,\mathrm{d}x = \tfrac{1}{2}(b^2 - a^2), \qquad \text{giving} \qquad \int x\,\mathrm{d}x = \tfrac{1}{2}x^2 + \text{constant}$$

$$\int_a^b x^2\,\mathrm{d}x = \tfrac{1}{3}(b^3 - a^3), \qquad \text{giving} \qquad \int x^2\,\mathrm{d}x = \tfrac{1}{3}x^3 + \text{constant}$$

The comparable results for differentiation are

$$\frac{\mathrm{d}}{\mathrm{d}x}(k) = 0, \quad k \text{ constant}$$

$$\frac{\mathrm{d}}{\mathrm{d}x}(x) = 1$$

$$\frac{\mathrm{d}}{\mathrm{d}x}(x^2) = 2x$$

Using the sum and constant multiplication rules for differentiation from Section 7.3.1,

$$\frac{\mathrm{d}}{\mathrm{d}x}[f(x) + k] = \frac{\mathrm{d}}{\mathrm{d}x}f(x) + \frac{\mathrm{d}}{\mathrm{d}x}(k) = \frac{\mathrm{d}}{\mathrm{d}x}f(x), \quad k \text{ constant}$$

$$\frac{\mathrm{d}}{\mathrm{d}x}[kf(x)] = k\frac{\mathrm{d}}{\mathrm{d}x}f(x)$$

the above results may be combined to give

$$\frac{\mathrm{d}}{\mathrm{d}x}\left(\int 1\,\mathrm{d}x\right) = \frac{\mathrm{d}}{\mathrm{d}x}(x + \text{constant}) = 1$$

$$\frac{\mathrm{d}}{\mathrm{d}x}\left(\int x\,\mathrm{d}x\right) = x$$

$$\frac{\mathrm{d}}{\mathrm{d}x}\left(\int x^2\,\mathrm{d}x\right) = x^2$$

These results suggest a more general result:

> The process of differentiation is the inverse of that of integration.

This conjecture is also supported by elementary applications of the processes. We obtained the distance travelled by an object by integrating its velocity function. We obtained the velocity of an object by differentiating its distance function. The general result is called the **Fundamental Theorem of Integral and Differential Calculus**, and may be stated in the form of the following theorem.

Theorem 7.1 The indefinite integral $F(x)$ of a continuous function $f(x)$ always possesses a derivative $F'(x)$, and, moreover, $F'(x) = f(x)$.

Proof The formula for $F(x)$ may be written as

$$F(x) = \int_a^x f(t)\mathrm{d}t, \quad \text{where } a \text{ is a constant}$$

The quotient

$$\frac{F(x+h) - F(x)}{h}$$

may be written in terms of $f(x)$ as

$$\frac{F(x+h) - F(x)}{h} = \frac{\int_a^{x+h} f(t)\mathrm{d}t - \int_a^x f(t)\mathrm{d}t}{h} = \frac{1}{h}\int_x^{x+h} f(t)\mathrm{d}t$$

Consider the case when h is positive. The function $f(x)$ is continuous, and so it is bounded on $[x, x + h]$. Suppose it attains its upper bound at x_1, as shown in Figure 7.54, and its lower bound at x_2. Then by considering the area under the graph, we see that

Figure 7.54

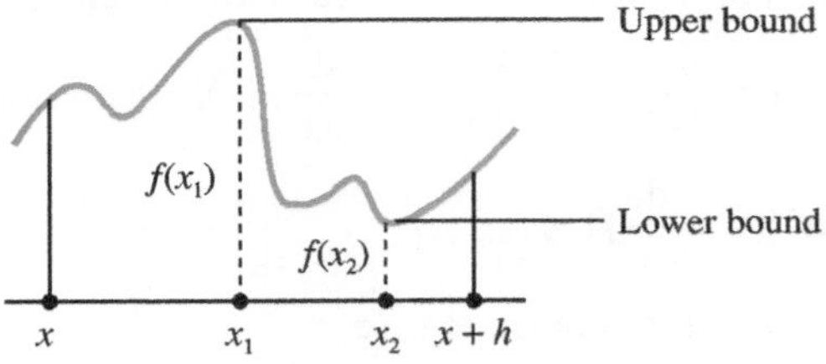

$$hf(x_2) \leqslant \int_x^{x+h} f(t)\mathrm{d}t \leqslant hf(x_1)$$

which implies that

$$f(x_2) \leqslant \frac{1}{h}\int_x^{x+h} f(t)\mathrm{d}t \leqslant f(x_1)$$

or equivalently

$$f(x_2) \leqslant \frac{F(x+h) - F(x)}{h} \leqslant f(x_1)$$

As $h \to 0$, $x_2 \to x$ and $x_1 \to x$, and we obtain the result

$$F'(x) = f(x)$$

(The proof when h is negative is similar.)

end of theorem

This theorem is of fundamental importance, and is used repeatedly in practical problem-solving using calculus.

7.7.6 Exercise

103 Using the Fundamental Theorem of Integral and Differential Calculus, evaluate the following integrals:

(a) $\int x^6\,dx$, noting that $\frac{d}{dx}x^7 = 7x^6$

(b) $\int e^{3x}\,dx$, noting that $\frac{d}{dx}e^{3x} = 3e^{3x}$

(c) $\int \sin 5x\,dx$, noting that $\frac{d}{dx}\cos 5x = -5\sin 5x$

(d) $\int (2x+1)^3\,dx$, noting that $\frac{d}{dx}(2x+1)^4 = 8(2x+1)^3$

(e) $\int \sec^2 3x\,dx$, noting that $\frac{d}{dx}(\tan 3x) = 3\sec^2 3x$

(f) $\int \frac{2}{x}\,dx$, noting that $\frac{d}{dx}\ln x = \frac{1}{x}$

(g) $\int \frac{3}{x^2}\,dx$, noting that $\frac{d}{dx}\left(\frac{1}{x}\right) = -\frac{1}{x^2}$

(h) $\int \cos 2x\,dx$, noting that $\frac{d}{dx}\sin 2x = 2\cos 2x$

(i) $\int \sec 4x \tan 4x\,dx$, noting that $\frac{d}{dx}\sec 4x = 4\sec 4x \tan 4x$

(j) $\int \sqrt{(4x-1)}\,dx$, noting that $\frac{d}{dx}(4x-1)^{3/2} = 6(4x-1)^{1/2}$

7.8 Techniques of integration

In this section we consider some of the methods available for determining the integrals of functions. Again we shall concentrate on developing techniques, leaving problem-solving applications for later in both this chapter and the rest of the book. The technical process of obtaining integrals is much more complicated than that of obtaining derivatives. In the following sections the techniques for finding integrals are discussed, but these techniques are often interconnected. It is strongly recommended that the student works through the examples, line by line, to gain experience in using these techniques. The integrals of many functions cannot be expressed in terms of elementary functions and sometimes these integrals themselves define new functions. An example of this is the error function erf(x) defined by

$$\operatorname{erf}(x) = \frac{2}{\sqrt{\pi}}\int_0^x e^{-t^2}\,dt$$

This occurs in the analysis of heat transfer. A related function also occurs in applied statistics (see Section 13.5.3).

Figure 7.55 Some standard integrals.

$f(x)$	$\int f(x)\mathrm{d}x$ *Here c is a constant of integration*
$x^n \quad (n \neq -1)$	$\dfrac{x^{n+1}}{n+1} + c$
$\dfrac{1}{x}$	$\left.\begin{array}{l}\ln x \quad + c \ (x > 0)\\ \ln(-x) + c \ (x < 0)\end{array}\right\} = \ln\lvert x\rvert + c$
$\sin x$	$-\cos x + c$
$\cos x$	$\sin x + c$
e^x	$e^x + c$
$\sec^2 x$	$\tan x + c$
$\dfrac{1}{\sqrt{(1-x^2)}}, \lvert x\rvert < 1$	$\sin^{-1} x + c$
$\dfrac{1}{1+x^2}$	$\tan^{-1} x + c$

7.8.1 Integration as antiderivative

Applying the Fundamental Theorem of Calculus to some of the standard derivatives deduced in Section 7.3, we deduce the integrals given in Figure 7.55. A more extensive list is given in the Appendices A1.3 and A1.4. Note that we have used the notation

$$\ln\lvert x\rvert = \begin{cases}\ln x, & x > 0\\ \ln(-x), & x < 0\end{cases}$$

To help extend the number of functions that can be integrated analytically, using the results of Figure 7.55, the following rules may be used.

Rule 1 (scalar-multiplication rule)
If k is a constant then

$$\int kf(x)\mathrm{d}x = k\int f(x)\mathrm{d}x$$

Rule 2 (sum rule)

$$\int [f(x) \pm g(x)]\mathrm{d}x = \int f(x)\mathrm{d}x \pm \int g(x)\mathrm{d}x$$

Rule 3 (linear composite rule)
If a and b are constants and $F'(x) = f(x)$ then

$$\int f(ax+b)\mathrm{d}x = \frac{1}{a}F(ax+b) + \text{constant}, \quad a \neq 0$$

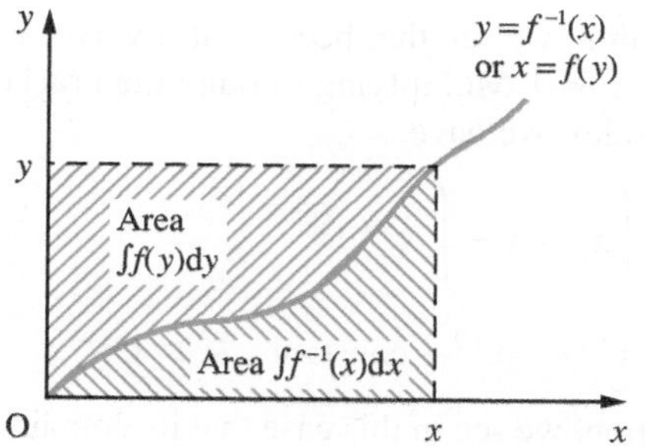

Figure 7.56 Illustration of $\int f^{-1}(x)\,\mathrm{d}x = xy - \int f(y)\,\mathrm{d}y$.

Rule 4 (inverse-function rule)

If $y = f^{-1}(x)$, so that $x = f(y)$, then

$$\int f^{-1}(x)\mathrm{d}x = xy - \int f(y)\mathrm{d}y$$

Rule 5 (integration by parts)

$$\int f(x)g'(x)\mathrm{d}x = f(x)g(x) - \int f'(x)g(x)\mathrm{d}x$$

Rule 6 (composite function rule)

$$\int f'(g(x))g'(x)\mathrm{d}x = f(g(x)) + \textbf{constant}$$

Rules 1–3 follow directly from the definition of an integral, while *Rule 4* may be demonstrated graphically, as illustrated in Figure 7.56. *Rules 5 and 6* are discussed in Sections 7.8.3 and 7.8.5.

Example 7.42

Find the indefinite integrals of

(a) $6x^4 + 4x - \dfrac{3}{x}$ (b) $(2 - x)\sqrt{x}$ (c) $\sqrt{(5x + 2)}$ (d) $\dfrac{x + 1}{x}$

Solution (a) Using the scalar-multiplication and sum rules,

$$\int\left(6x^4 + 4x - \frac{3}{x}\right)\mathrm{d}x = 6\int x^4\,\mathrm{d}x + 4\int x\,\mathrm{d}x - 3\int\frac{1}{x}\mathrm{d}x$$

$$= \tfrac{6}{5}x^5 + 2x^2 - 3\ln|x| + \text{constant}$$

using the standard integrals of Figure 7.53.

(b) Looking at the function, we see that because it involves a square root, its domain is restricted to values of $x \geqslant 0$. Multiplying through the brackets and using the scalar-multiplication and sum rules, we have

$$\int (2-x)\sqrt{x}\,dx = 2\int x^{1/2}\,dx - \int x^{3/2}\,dx$$

$$= \tfrac{4}{3}x^{3/2} - \tfrac{2}{5}x^{5/2} + \text{constant} \quad (x \geqslant 0)$$

(c) Examining the function, we see in this case that its domain is restricted to values of x greater than or equal to $-\frac{2}{5}$. We note that the formula is the square root of a linear function, and so we use the linear composite rule to obtain its integral. Thus, since

$$\int \sqrt{x}\,dx = \tfrac{2}{3}x^{3/2} + \text{constant}$$

we obtain

$$\int \sqrt{(5x+2)}\,dx = \tfrac{1}{5}[\tfrac{2}{3}(5x+2)^{3/2}] + \text{constant}$$

$$= \tfrac{2}{15}(5x+2)^{3/2} + \text{constant} \quad (x \geqslant -\tfrac{2}{5})$$

(d) In this case we see that the function is defined except at $x = 0$. Expressing $(x+1)/x$ as $1 + 1/x$ and using the sum rule, we obtain

$$\int \frac{x+1}{x}\,dx = \int \left(1 + \frac{1}{x}\right)dx = \int 1\,dx + \int \frac{1}{x}\,dx$$

$$= \begin{cases} x + \ln x + \text{constant} & (x > 0) \\ x + \ln(-x) + \text{constant} & (x < 0) \end{cases}$$

$$= x + \ln|x| + \text{constant}$$

Example 7.43 Evaluate the definite integrals

(a) $\displaystyle\int_1^2 (x^4 + 6x^2 - 4)\,dx$ (b) $\displaystyle\int_1^2 \frac{(x^2-1)^2}{x^2}\,dx$

(c) $\displaystyle\int_{-2}^4 4e^x\,dx$ (d) $\displaystyle\int_0^{\pi/6} (\cos 3x + 2\sin 3x)\,dx$

Solution (a) Integrating each term in the intgrand separately and then summing we have:

$$\int_1^2 (x^4 + 6x^2 - 4)\,dx = [\tfrac{1}{5}x^5 + 2x^3 - 4x]_1^2$$

$$= [\tfrac{32}{5} + 2.8 - 4.2] - [\tfrac{1}{5} + 2 - 4]$$

$$= 16\tfrac{1}{5}$$

(b) Expanding the integrand and then integrating term by term we obtain:

$$\int_1^2 \frac{(x^2-1)^2}{x^2}\,dx = \int_1^2 \frac{x^4-2x^2+1}{x^2}\,dx$$

$$= \int_1^2 \left(x^2 - 2 + \frac{1}{x^2}\right)dx$$

$$= \left[\tfrac{1}{3}x^3 - 2x - \frac{1}{x}\right]_1^2$$

$$= [\tfrac{8}{3} - 4 - \tfrac{1}{2}] - [\tfrac{1}{3} - 2 - 1] = \tfrac{5}{6}$$

(c) $$\int_{-2}^{4} 4e^x dx = [4e^x]_{-2}^{4} \quad \text{since} \quad \frac{d}{dx}(e^x) = e^x$$

$$= 4(e^4 - e^{-2})$$

(d) $$\int_0^{\pi/6} (\cos 3x + 2\sin 3x)dx = [\tfrac{1}{3}\sin 3x - \tfrac{2}{3}\cos 3x]_0^{\pi/6}$$

$$= [\tfrac{1}{3}\sin\tfrac{\pi}{2} - \tfrac{1}{3}\cos\tfrac{\pi}{2}] - [\tfrac{1}{3}\sin 0 - \tfrac{2}{3}\cos 0]$$

$$= \tfrac{1}{3} + \tfrac{2}{3} = 1$$

Example 7.44 Using the inverse-function rule, obtain the integrals of

(a) $\sin^{-1}x$ (b) $\ln x$

Solution (a) If $y = \sin^{-1}x$ then $x = \sin y$ and

$$\int \sin^{-1}x\,dx = xy - \int \sin y\,dy$$

$$= xy + \cos y + \text{constant}$$

which, on using the identity $\sin^2 y + \cos^2 y = 1$, gives

$$\int \sin^{-1}x\,dx = x\sin^{-1}x + \sqrt{(1-x^2)} + \text{constant}$$

since $\cos y \geqslant 0$ on the domain of $\sin^{-1}x$.

(b) If $y = \ln x$ then $x = e^y$, and

$$\int \ln x\,dx = xy - \int e^y dy = xy - e^y + \text{constant}$$

$$= x\ln x - x + \text{constant}$$

since $e^{\ln x} = x$.

MATLAB's Symbolic Math Toolbox and MAPLE can evaluate both indefinite and definite integrals. If $y = f(x)$ then the MATLAB command `int(y)` returns the indefinite integral of $f(x)$, provided it exists in closed form. (Symbolic integration is more difficult than symbolic differentiation and difficulties can arise in computing the integral.) Thus in MATLAB the indefinite integral of $y = f(x)$ is returned using the commands

```
syms x y
y = f(x); int(y)
```

To determine the definite integral of $y = f(x)$ from $x = a$ to $x = b$ the last command is replaced by

```
int(y,a,b)
```

The corresponding commands in MAPLE are

```
y:= f(x); int(y,x); int(y,x = a..b);
```

Note that MATLAB and MAPLE do not supply a constant of integration when evaluating indefinite integrals. To illustrate, we consider Examples 7.42(a) and (c). For Example 7.42(a) the commands

MATLAB

```
syms x y
y = 6*x^4 + 4*x - 3/x;
int(y);
pretty(ans)
```

MAPLE

```
y:= 6*x^4 + 4*x - 3/x;
int(y,x);
```

return the integral as

$$6/5x^5 + 2x^2 - 3\log(x)$$

For Example 7.42(c) the commands

MATLAB

```
syms x y
y = sqrt(5*x + 2);
int(y);
pretty(ans)
```

MAPLE

```
y:= sqrt(5*x + 2);
int(y,x);
```

return the integral as

MATLAB: $2/15(5x + 2)^{3/2}$ MAPLE: $\frac{2}{15}(5x + 2)^{(3/2)}$

For practice, check the answers to Examples 7.42(b) and (d) using MATLAB or MAPLE.

Example 7.45 Evaluate the following integrals encountered earlier in Section 7.7.2:

(a) $\displaystyle\int_0^6 \tfrac{4}{9}(6-h)^2 \mathrm{d}h$ (b) $\displaystyle\int_0^{10} 3\sqrt{10}(p_0 + 10g - gy)\sqrt{(y)}\mathrm{d}y$

Solution (a) Notice first of all that the label used for the integrating variable in a **definite** integral does not affect the value of the integral. It is a dummy variable. Thus

$$\int_0^6 \tfrac{4}{9}(6-h)^2\mathrm{d}h = \int_0^6 \tfrac{4}{9}(6-x)^2\mathrm{d}x$$

Expanding the integrand, we have

$$\int_0^6 \tfrac{4}{9}(6-x)^2\mathrm{d}x = \int_0^6 \tfrac{4}{9}(36-12x+x^2)\mathrm{d}x = \tfrac{4}{9}[36x-6x^2+\tfrac{1}{3}x^3]_0^6$$

$$= \tfrac{4}{9}[36\times 6 - 6\times 36 + \tfrac{1}{3}\times 216] - \tfrac{4}{9}[0]$$

$$= \tfrac{4}{9}[72] = 32$$

as predicted in Example 7.39.

(b) $$\int_0^{10} 3\sqrt{10}(p_0+10g-gy)\sqrt{(y)}\mathrm{d}y = 3\sqrt{10}\int_0^{10}[(p_0+10g)y^{1/2}-gy^{3/2}]\mathrm{d}y$$

$$= 3\sqrt{10}[\tfrac{2}{3}(p_0+10g)y^{3/2}-\tfrac{2}{5}gy^{5/2}]_0^{10}$$

$$= 3\sqrt{10}[\tfrac{2}{3}(p_0+10g)10^{3/2}-\tfrac{2}{5}g10^{5/2}]-0$$

$$= 200p_0 + 800g$$

as predicted in Example 7.40.

Example 7.46 (a) An object moves along a straight line. Its displacement from its initial position is $s(t)$. Show that its velocity $v(t)$ is given by $s'(t)$. The acceleration of the object is $a(t)$. Show that

$$v(t) = v(0) + \int_0^t a(t)\mathrm{d}t$$

and deduce that $a(t) = s''(t)$.

(b) A ball bearing travels along a track with velocity $v(t)$ ms^{-1} given by the function

$$v(t) = 8 - 0.5t^2$$

where t is the time in seconds. Calculate the exact distance travelled by the ball bearing over the time periods (0, 4) and (4, 5). Obtain also the formula for the acceleration of the ball bearing at time t.

Solution (a) Velocity is defined as the rate of change of displacement, so that in the time interval $(t, t+\Delta t)$, the rate of change is $\dfrac{s(t+\Delta t)-s(t)}{\Delta t}$. This is the average rate of change over the time interval. The instantaneous rate of change at time t, the velocity, is given by the limit $\Delta t \to 0$. That is:

$$v(t) = \lim_{\Delta t \to 0} \frac{s(t + \Delta t) - s(t)}{\Delta t} = s'(t)$$

from the definition of a derivative.

In the same way, the acceleration $a(t)$ at time t is given by the instantaneous rate of change of velocity $v(t)$

$$a(t) = \lim_{\Delta t \to 0} \frac{v(t + \Delta t) - v(t)}{\Delta t} = v'(t)$$

By the Fundamental Theorem of Calculus, we have

$$v(t) = v(0) + \int_0^t a(t)\mathrm{d}t$$

(b) The distance $s(t)$ m travelled by the ball bearing after t seconds satisfies the differential equation

$$\frac{\mathrm{d}s}{\mathrm{d}t} = v(t)$$

Thus the distance travelled over the time period (0, 4) is

$$\begin{aligned} s(4) - s(0) &= \int_0^4 (8 - \tfrac{1}{2}t^2)\mathrm{d}t = [8t - \tfrac{1}{6}t^3]_0^4 \\ &= 32 - \tfrac{1}{6}(64) = 21\tfrac{1}{3} \end{aligned}$$

so the distance travelled is $21\frac{1}{3}$ m.

The distance travelled over the time interval (4, 5) is given by

$$s(5) - s(4) = \int_4^5 (8 - \tfrac{1}{2}t^2)\mathrm{d}t = [8t - \tfrac{1}{6}t^3]_4^5 = -\tfrac{13}{6}$$

so the distance travelled is $2\frac{1}{6}$ m in the opposite direction.

Example 7.47 Find the definite integrals

(a) $\displaystyle\int_0^1 \frac{\mathrm{d}x}{\sqrt{(3 - x^2)}}$ (b) $\displaystyle\int_0^2 \frac{\mathrm{d}x}{\sqrt{(3 + 2x - x^2)}}$

(c) $\displaystyle\int_0^2 \frac{\mathrm{d}x}{4 + x^2}$ (d) $\displaystyle\int_{-5}^5 \frac{\mathrm{d}x}{x^2 + 10x + 50}$

Solution (a) Here we use the standard integral $\displaystyle\int \frac{\mathrm{d}x}{\sqrt{(1 - x^2)}} = \sin^{-1} x + c$.

Rewriting the integrand we have $\displaystyle\frac{1}{\sqrt{3}}\int \frac{\mathrm{d}x}{\sqrt{\left[1 - \left(\frac{x}{\sqrt{3}}\right)^2\right]}}$.

Then using the linear composite rule with $a = \frac{1}{\sqrt{3}}$ we deduce that

$$\int_0^1 \frac{\mathrm{d}x}{\sqrt{(3-x^2)}} = \left[\frac{1}{\sqrt{3}}\frac{\sqrt{3}}{1}\sin^{-1}\left(\frac{x}{\sqrt{3}}\right)\right]_0^1 = \sin^{-1}\left(\frac{1}{\sqrt{3}}\right) = \frac{\pi}{3}$$

(b) Rewriting the integrand and using the linear composite rule again:

$$\int_0^2 \frac{1}{\sqrt{(3+2x-x^2)}}\mathrm{d}x = \int_0^2 \frac{1}{\sqrt{[4-(x-1)^2]}}\mathrm{d}x$$

$$= \frac{1}{2}\int_0^2 \frac{1}{\sqrt{\left[1-\left(\frac{x-1}{2}\right)^2\right]}}\mathrm{d}x$$

$$= \left[\frac{1}{2}\times 2\sin^{-1}\left(\frac{x-1}{2}\right)\right]_0^2$$

$$= \sin^{-1}(\tfrac{1}{2}) - \sin^{-1}(-\tfrac{1}{2}) = \frac{\pi}{3}$$

(c) Here we recall $\int \frac{1}{1+x^2}\mathrm{d}x = \tan^{-1}x + c.$

Rewriting the integrand we have

$$\int_0^2 \frac{\mathrm{d}x}{4+x^2} = \frac{1}{4}\int_0^2 \frac{\mathrm{d}x}{1+\left(\frac{x}{2}\right)^2} = \frac{1}{4}\left[2\tan^{-1}\left(\frac{x}{2}\right)\right]_0^2$$

using the linear composite-function rule. Thus

$$\int_0^2 \frac{\mathrm{d}x}{4+x^2} = \frac{1}{2}\tan^{-1}1 = \frac{\pi}{8}$$

(d) Rewriting the integrand we have

$$\int_{-5}^5 \frac{1}{x^2+10x+50}\mathrm{d}x = \int_{-5}^5 \frac{1}{(x+5)^2+5^2}\mathrm{d}x$$

$$= \frac{1}{25}\int_{-5}^5 \frac{1}{1+(\frac{x}{5}+1)^2}\mathrm{d}x$$

$$= \tfrac{1}{25}[5\tan^{-1}(\tfrac{x}{5}+1)]_{-5}^5$$

$$= \tfrac{1}{5}[\tan^{-1}2 - \tan^{-1}0] = \tfrac{1}{5}\tan^{-1}2$$

Comment From these examples we can deduce two more standard integrals:

$$\int \frac{\mathrm{d}x}{\sqrt{(a^2-x^2)}} = \sin^{-1}\frac{x}{a} + c$$

$$\int \frac{\mathrm{d}x}{a^2+x^2} = \frac{1}{a}\tan^{-1}\frac{x}{a} + c$$

7.8.2 Integration of piecewise continuous functions

In addition to the rules given earlier, two further results follow immediately from the basic definition of an integral. These are

$$\int_a^b f(x)\mathrm{d}x = -\int_b^a f(x)\mathrm{d}x$$

and

$$\int_a^b f(x)\mathrm{d}x = \int_a^c f(x)\mathrm{d}x + \int_c^b f(x)\mathrm{d}x$$

(Thus we may break the interval $[a, b]$ into convenient subintervals if the function is defined piecewise, as illustrated in Example 7.48.)

Example 7.48 Evaluate

(a) $\int_{-1}^{2} |x|\mathrm{d}x$ (b) $\int_{0}^{10} H(x-5)\mathrm{d}x$

where H is the Heaviside step function given by (2.45).

Solution The areas involved are illustrated in Figure 7.57.

(a) Since

$$|x| = \begin{cases} -x & (x \leqslant 0) \\ x & (x \geqslant 0) \end{cases}$$

we split the integral at $x = 0$ and write

$$\int_{-1}^{2} |x|\mathrm{d}x = \int_{-1}^{0} -x\,\mathrm{d}x + \int_{0}^{2} x\,\mathrm{d}x = [-\tfrac{1}{2}x^2]_{-1}^{0} + [\tfrac{1}{2}x^2]_0^2 = \tfrac{5}{2}$$

(b) Since $H(x-5)$ has a discontinuity at $x = 5$, we write

$$\int_0^{10} H(x-5)\mathrm{d}x = \int_0^5 H(x-5)\mathrm{d}x + \int_5^{10} H(x-5)\mathrm{d}x = \int_0^5 0\,\mathrm{d}x + \int_5^{10} 1\,\mathrm{d}x = 5$$

These results can be readily confirmed by inspection of the relevant areas.

Figure 7.57

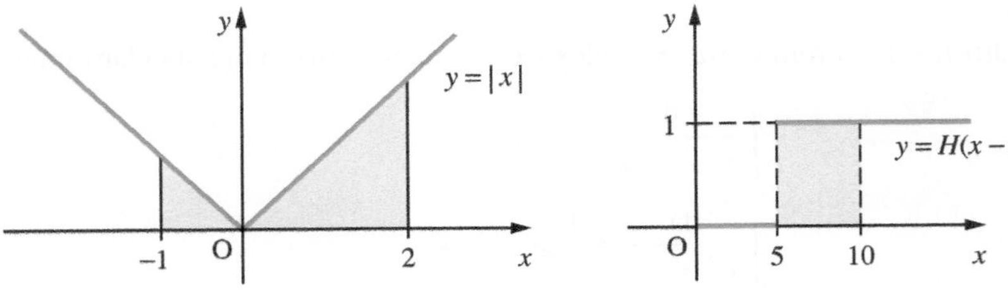

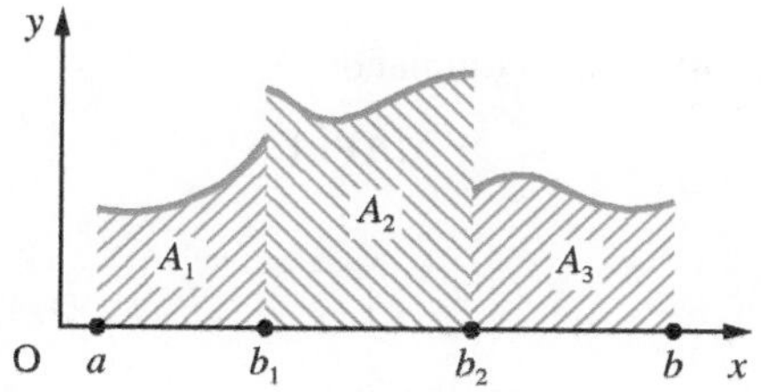

Figure 7.58 Piecewise-continuous function.

We see from this last example that it is sometimes possible to integrate functions even if they have discontinuities. This is possible provided that there are only a finite number of finite discontinuities within the domain of integration and that elsewhere the function is continuous and bounded. To illustrate this, consider the function $f(x)$ illustrated in Figure 7.58 where

$$y = f(x) = \begin{cases} f_1(x) & (a \leqslant x < b_1) \\ f_2(x) & (b_1 < x < b_2) \\ f_3(x) & (b_2 < x \leqslant b) \end{cases}$$

Such a function is called a **piecewise-continuous function**. Interpreting the integral as the area under the curve, we have

$$\int_a^b f(x)\mathrm{d}x = A_1 + A_2 + A_3$$

but in this case we interpret the individual areas as

$$\int_a^b f(x)\mathrm{d}x = \int_a^{b_1^-} f_1(x)\mathrm{d}x + \int_{b_1^+}^{b_2^-} f_2(x)\mathrm{d}x + \int_{b_2^+}^{b} f_3(x)\mathrm{d}x$$

where, as before, b_1^- signifies approaching b_1 from the left and b_1^+ signifies approaching b_1 from the right (see Section 7.8.1). It is in this sense that we evaluated $\int_0^{10} H(x-5)\mathrm{d}x$ in Example 7.48, and – strictly speaking – we should have written

$$\int_0^{10} H(x-5)\mathrm{d}x = \int_0^{5^-} H(x-5)\mathrm{d}x + \int_{5^+}^{10} H(x-5)\mathrm{d}x$$

and, since

$$H(x-5) = \begin{cases} 0 & (x < 5) \\ 1 & (x \geqslant 5) \end{cases}$$

$$\int_0^{10} H(x-5)\mathrm{d}x = \int_0^{5^-} 0\,\mathrm{d}x + \int_{5^+}^{10} 1\,\mathrm{d}x = 5$$

Considering Example 7.48(a) the commands

MATLAB	MAPLE
`syms x y`	
`y = abs(x);`	`y:= abs(x);`
`int(y,-1,2)`	`int(y,x = -1..2);`

return the answer `5/2`

and, for Example 7.48(b), the commands

MATLAB	MAPLE
`syms x y`	
`y = sym('Heaviside(x - 5)')`	
`int(y,0,10)`	`int(Heaviside(x - 5), x = 0..10);`

return the answer `5`

Example 7.49 As shown in Example 7.7, the bending moment M and shear force F acting in a beam satisfy the differential equation

$$F = \frac{dM}{dx}$$

In Example 7.41, we showed that for a continuously non-uniformly loaded beam which is freely hinged at both ends the shear force F is given by

$$F(x) = \begin{cases} 2Wx^2/l^2 - W/2 & 0 \leqslant x \leqslant l/2 \\ W/2 - 2W(l-x)^2/l^2 & l/2 \leqslant x \leqslant l \end{cases}$$

Given that $M = 0$ at $x = 0$, find an expression for $M(x)$ at a general point.

Solution Since $\frac{dM}{dx} = F(x)$ with $M(0) = 0$ we deduce by the Fundamental Theorem

$$M(x) = \int_0^x F(t)dt$$

In evaluating this integral we have to remember that $F(x)$ is defined separately on $(0, l/2)$ and $(l/2, l)$.

For $x < l/2$, we have

$$M(x) = \int_0^x (2Wt^2/l^2 - W/2)dt$$

For $x > l/2$, we have

$$M(x) = \int_0^{l/2} (2Wt^2/l^2 - W/2)dt + \int_{l/2}^x (W/2 - 2W(l-t)^2/l^2)dt$$

Thus

$$M(x) = \begin{cases} \dfrac{Wx}{6l^2}(4x^2 - 3l^2) & 0 \leqslant x \leqslant l/2 \\[2ex] \dfrac{W(l-x)}{6l^2}(4(l-x)^2 - 3l^2) & l/2 \leqslant x \leqslant l \end{cases}$$

7.8.3 Exercises

Check your answers using MATLAB or MAPLE whenever possible.

104 Find the indefinite integrals of

(a) $3x^{2/3}$ (b) $\sqrt{(2x)}$

(c) $2x^3 - 2x^2 + \dfrac{1}{x} - 2$ (d) $2e^x + 3\cos 2x$

(e) $x^2 + 3e^x - \dfrac{1}{x^2}$ (f) $(2x + 1)^3$

(g) $(1 - 2x)^{1/3}$ (h) $(2x^2 + 1)^3$

(i) $\cos(2x + 1)$ (j) 2^x (*Hint*: $2 = e^{\ln 2}$)

105 Evaluate the definite integrals

(a) $\displaystyle\int_2^3 \frac{x\,dx}{\sqrt{(x+1)}}$ (b) $\displaystyle\int_0^1 x(x-1)^{11}dx$

(c) $\displaystyle\int_1^2 \left(x^{3/2} - \frac{1}{x^2}\right)dx$ (d) $\displaystyle\int_0^{\pi/2} \sin x\,dx$

(e) $\displaystyle\int_0^2 \frac{dx}{\sqrt{(3 + 2x - x^2)}}$

(*Hint*: Replace the x in (a) by $(x + 1) - 1$ and in (b) by $(x - 1) + 1$.)

106 Find the indefinite integrals of

(a) x^{-2} (b) $(x + 1)^{-1/3}$

(c) $\dfrac{4x^3 - 7x^2 + 1}{x^2}$ (d) $\sin x + \cos x$

(e) $\dfrac{1}{9 - 16x^2}$ (f) $\dfrac{1}{\sqrt{(2x - x^2)}}$

(g) $\dfrac{1}{\sqrt{(1 - 9x^2)}}$ (h) $\dfrac{1}{\sqrt{(4 - x^2)}}$

(i) $\dfrac{1}{\sqrt{(1 - x - x^2)}}$ (j) $\dfrac{1}{\sqrt{[x(1 - x)]}}$

(k) $\dfrac{1}{\sqrt{(5 + 4x - x^3)}}$ (l) $\dfrac{1}{x^2 + 6x + 13}$

107 Evaluate

(a) $\displaystyle\int_0^3 |x - 2|\,dx$ (b) $\displaystyle\int_0^5 (x - 2)H(x - 2)dx$

(c) $\displaystyle\int_0^3 \lfloor x \rfloor dx$ (d) $\displaystyle\int_0^3 \text{FRACPT}(x)dx$

(e) $\displaystyle\int_0^3 x\lfloor x \rfloor dx$

108 The function $f(x)$ is periodic with period 1 and is defined on [0, 1] by

$$f(x) = 1 \qquad 0 \leqslant x < \tfrac{1}{2}$$
$$f(x) = -1 \qquad \tfrac{1}{2} \leqslant x < 1$$

Sketch its graph and obtain the graph of

$$g(x) = \int_0^x f(t)dt$$

for $-4 \leqslant x \leqslant 4$. Show that $g(x)$ is a periodic function of period 1.

109 Draw the graph of the function $f(x)$ defined by

$$f(x) = \int_0^x \sin^{-1}(\sin t)dt$$

for $-2\pi < x < 2\pi$ (see Example 2.51).

7.8.4 Integration by parts

The product rule for differentiation

$$\frac{\mathrm{d}}{\mathrm{d}x}(uv) = \frac{\mathrm{d}u}{\mathrm{d}x}v + u\frac{\mathrm{d}v}{\mathrm{d}x}$$

may also be used for integration after a little rearrangement. From the above we have

$$u\frac{\mathrm{d}v}{\mathrm{d}x} = \frac{\mathrm{d}}{\mathrm{d}x}(uv) - v\frac{\mathrm{d}u}{\mathrm{d}x}$$

and on integrating we have

$$\int u\frac{\mathrm{d}v}{\mathrm{d}x}\mathrm{d}x = uv - \int v\frac{\mathrm{d}u}{\mathrm{d}x}\mathrm{d}x$$

We may use this result to determine an integral when the integrand is the product of the two functions. The method is called **integration by parts**. The procedure is to choose one term of the product to be u and the other to be $\mathrm{d}v/\mathrm{d}x$. We then calculate $\mathrm{d}u/\mathrm{d}x$ and v, and the hope is that the resulting integral on the right-hand side is easier than the one we started with. We shall illustrate the method with a few examples.

Example 7.50 Find the indefinite integrals of

(a) $x \ln x$ (b) $x^2 \cos x$ (c) $\mathrm{e}^x \sin 2x$

Solution (a) With this integral, we set

$$u = \ln x \quad \text{and} \quad \frac{\mathrm{d}v}{\mathrm{d}x} = x$$

giving

$$\frac{\mathrm{d}u}{\mathrm{d}x} = \frac{1}{x} \quad \text{and} \quad v = \tfrac{1}{2}x^2$$

Note: There is no need to introduce a constant of integration when determining v. Substituting in the formula for integration by parts gives

$$\underset{\mathrm{d}v/\mathrm{d}x\ u}{\int x \ln x\,\mathrm{d}x} = \underset{v\quad u}{(\tfrac{1}{2}x^2)\ln x} - \underset{v\quad \mathrm{d}u/\mathrm{d}x}{\int (\tfrac{1}{2}x^2)\left(\frac{1}{x}\right)\mathrm{d}x} = \tfrac{1}{2}x^2 \ln x - \int \tfrac{1}{2}x\,\mathrm{d}x$$

$$= \tfrac{1}{2}x^2 \ln x - \tfrac{1}{4}x^2 + \text{constant}$$

(b) Since differentiation reduces the squared term to a linear one, leading to some simplification, we choose

$$u = x^2 \quad \text{and} \quad \frac{dv}{dx} = \cos x$$

so that

$$\frac{du}{dx} = 2x \quad \text{and} \quad v = \sin x$$

Integration by parts then gives

$$\underset{\substack{u\ \ \mathrm{d}v/\mathrm{d}x}}{\int x^2 \cos x \, dx} = \underset{u\ \ v}{x^2(\sin x)} - \underset{v\ \ \mathrm{d}u/\mathrm{d}x}{\int (\sin x)(2x) \, dx} = x^2 \sin x - 2\int x \sin x \, dx$$

We now apply the same technique to the last integral, taking

$$u = x \quad \text{and} \quad \frac{dv}{dx} = \sin x$$

to give

$$\int x \sin x \, dx = (x)(-\cos x) - \int (-\cos x)(1) \, dx = -x \cos x + \sin x + \text{constant}$$

Substituting back gives

$$\int x^2 \cos x \, dx = x^2 \sin x - 2(-x \cos x + \sin x) + \text{constant}$$

$$= x^2 \sin x - 2 \sin x + 2x \cos x + \text{constant}$$

(c) In this case it is not obvious that any choice of u and v will result in a simpler integral. Setting

$$u = \sin 2x \quad \text{and} \quad \frac{dv}{dx} = e^x$$

(only because integrating sin $2x$ will mean dividing by 2 and getting clumsy fractions!) gives

$$\frac{du}{dx} = 2 \cos 2x \quad \text{and} \quad v = e^x$$

Integration by parts then gives

$$\int e^x \sin 2x \, dx = e^x \sin 2x - \int e^x (2 \cos 2x) \, dx$$

$$= e^x \sin 2x - 2 \int e^x \cos 2x \, dx$$

which has produced no simplification at all. We repeat the process, however, on the last integral, taking care to integrate the part we integrated the first time and to differentiate the part we differentiated the first time. Thus we take

$$u = \cos 2x \quad \text{and} \quad \frac{dv}{dx} = e^x$$

giving

$$\int e^x \cos 2x \, dx = e^x \cos 2x - \int e^x (-2 \sin 2x) \, dx$$

$$= e^x \cos 2x + 2 \int e^x \sin 2x \, dx$$

Substituting in the previous expression, we obtain

$$\int e^x \sin 2x \, dx = e^x \sin 2x - 2\left(e^x \cos 2x + 2 \int e^x \sin 2x \, dx \right)$$

Hence

$$5 \int e^x \sin 2x \, dx = e^x (\sin 2x - 2 \cos 2x)$$

so

$$\int e^x \sin 2x \, dx = \tfrac{1}{5} e^x (\sin 2x - 2 \cos 2x) + \text{constant}$$

For Example 7.50(b) the MATLAB commands

```
syms x y
y = (x^2)*cos(x); int(y); pretty(ans)
```

return the integral as x^2`sin(x) - 2sin(x) + 2xcos(x)`, which checks with the given solution.

For practice, check the answers to Examples 7.48(a) and (c) using MATLAB or MAPLE.

7.8.5 Exercises

Check your answers using MATLAB or MAPLE whenever possible

110 Use integration by parts to find the indefinite integrals of

(a) $x \sin x$ (b) xe^{3x} (c) $x^3 \ln x$

(d) $e^{-2x} \sin 3x$ (e) $x \tan^{-1} x$ (f) $x \cos 2x$

111 Using integration by parts, evaluate the definite integrals

(a) $\int_0^{\pi/2} x^2 \sin x \, dx$

(b) $\int_1^3 x^2 \ln x \, dx$

(c) $\int_0^1 xe^{3x} \, dx$

7.8.6 Integration using the general composite rule

The composite-function rule for differentiation

$$\frac{d}{dx}[f(g(x))] = f'(g(x))g'(x)$$

can be used to evaluate some integrals. Reversing the differentiation process, we may write

$$\int f'(g(x))g'(x)dx = f(g(x)) + \text{constant}$$

The key step here is identifying the function $g(x)$. This will not be unique: different choices of $g(x)$ may differ by a constant. To make the process of manipulation easier to follow, it is usual to set $t = g(x)$, so that the integral becomes

$$\int f'(g(x))g'(x)dx = \int f'(t)\frac{dt}{dx}dx = \int f'(t)dt = f(t) + \text{constant}$$

$$= f(g(x)) + \text{constant} \quad \text{(on back substitution)}$$

which is the composite function rule for integration.

This technique for evaluating integrals is called the **substitution method**; we shall illustrate its use with a number of examples.

Example 7.51 Find the indefinite integrals

(a) $\int 2x\sqrt{(x^2 + 3)}dx$ (b) $\int \frac{x+1}{x^2 + 2x + 2}dx$

Solution (a) Comparison with the general form above suggests that we take

$$g(x) = x^2 + 3, \quad \text{with } g'(x) = 2x$$

Setting $t = x^2 + 3$ so that $\frac{dt}{dx} = 2x$, the integral becomes

$$\int 2x\sqrt{(x^2+3)}dx = \int \frac{dt}{dx}\sqrt{t}\,dx = \int t^{1/2}dt$$

$$= \tfrac{2}{3}t^{3/2} + \text{constant} = \tfrac{2}{3}(x^2+3)^{3/2} + \text{constant}$$

(b) Comparison with the general form suggests that we choose

$$g(x) = x^2 + 2x + 2, \quad \text{with } g'(x) = 2x + 2$$

This necessitates a slight modification of the integral giving

$$\int \frac{x+1}{x^2+2x+2}dx = \tfrac{1}{2}\int \frac{2x+2}{x^2+2x+2}dx = \tfrac{1}{2}\int \frac{1}{t}dt$$

where $t = x^2 + 2x + 2$ and $dt = (2x + 2)dx$. Thus

$$\int \frac{x+1}{x^2+2x+2}dx = \tfrac{1}{2}\ln t + \text{constant} = \tfrac{1}{2}\ln(x^2+2x+2) + \text{constant}$$

Comment This example is a special case of a commonly occurring form when the integrand can be written as

$$\frac{\text{derivative of denominator}}{\text{denominator}}$$

so that the integral is the logarithm of the denominator.

7.8.7 Exercises

112 Use the composite function rule to integrate the following functions:

(a) $x\sqrt{(1+x^2)}$ (b) $\cos x \sin^3 x$ (c) $\dfrac{x}{(1+x^2)^2}$

(d) $\dfrac{x}{\sqrt{(x^2-1)}}$ (e) $\dfrac{2x+3}{x^2+3x+2}$ (f) $\sin^3 x \cos^5 x$

(g) $\dfrac{x}{(1+x^2)^2}$ (h) $\dfrac{x}{\sqrt{(4-x^2)}}$

113 Find the values of the constants a and b such that

$$\frac{3x+2}{x^2+2x+5} = \frac{a(2x+2)}{x^2+2x+5} + \frac{b}{x^2+2x+5}$$

and hence find its integral. (Note that $(d/dx)(x^2 + 2x + 5) = 2x + 2$.)

114 Use the technique of Question 113 to integrate

(a) $\dfrac{x+1}{x^2+4x+5}$

(b) $\dfrac{2x+3}{\sqrt{(5+4x-x^2)}}$

(c) $\dfrac{\sin x}{\sin x+\cos x}$

115 Evaluate the following definite integral with the given substitution:

(a) $\displaystyle\int_{1/6}^{1/2}\frac{\mathrm{d}x}{(5+6x)^3}$, with $u = 5 + 6x$

(b) $\displaystyle\int_0^{\sqrt{3}}\frac{\tan^{-1}x}{1+x^2}\mathrm{d}x$, with $u = \tan^{-1}x$

(c) $\displaystyle\int_4^9\frac{\mathrm{d}x}{(\sqrt{x}-1)\sqrt{x}}$, with $u = \sqrt{x} - 1$

(d) $\displaystyle\int_1^4\frac{e^{\sqrt{x}}}{\sqrt{x}}\mathrm{d}x$, with $u = \sqrt{x}$

116 Show that

$$\int f(x)\mathrm{d}x = xf(x) - \int xf'(x)\mathrm{d}x$$

Use this result to integrate

(a) $\sin^{-1}x$ (b) $\ln x$ (c) $\cosh^{-1}x$ (d) $\tan^{-1}x$

7.8.8 Integration using partial fractions

In this section, we consider the use of partial fractions in evaluating integrals of rational functions. Partial fractions, discussed earlier in Section 2.5.1, are so frequently used to evaluate such integrals that one talks of the **partial fraction method of integration**.

Example 7.52 Using partial fractions, evaluate the integrals

(a) $\displaystyle\int\frac{6}{x^2-2x-8}\mathrm{d}x$ (b) $\displaystyle\int\frac{9}{(x-1)(x+2)^2}\mathrm{d}x$ (c) $\displaystyle\int_0^6\frac{1}{x^2+5x+6}\mathrm{d}x$

Solution (a) Factorizing the denominator as $x^2 - 2x - 8 = (x + 2)(x - 4)$, we can express the integrand in terms of its partial fractions:

$$\frac{6}{x^2-2x-8} = \frac{6}{(x+2)(x-4)} = \frac{-1}{x+2} + \frac{1}{x-4}$$

Thus

$$\int\frac{6}{x^2-2x-8}\mathrm{d}x = \int\frac{-1}{x+2}\mathrm{d}x + \int\frac{1}{x-4}\mathrm{d}x$$

$$= -\ln|x+2| + \ln|x-4| + \text{constant}$$

$$= \ln\left|\frac{x-4}{x+2}\right| + \text{constant}$$

(b) In partial fractions we have

$$\frac{9}{(x-1)(x+2)^2} = \frac{1}{x-1} + \frac{-1}{x+2} + \frac{-3}{(x+2)^2}$$

Then

$$\int \frac{9}{(x-1)(x+2)^2}\,\mathrm{d}x = \int \frac{1}{x-1}\,\mathrm{d}x - \int \frac{1}{x+2}\,\mathrm{d}x - \int \frac{3}{(x+2)^2}\,\mathrm{d}x$$

$$= \ln|x-1| - \ln|x+2| + 3(x+2)^{-1} + \text{constant}$$

$$= \ln\left|\frac{x-1}{x+2}\right| + \frac{3}{x+2} + \text{constant}$$

(c) In partial fractions we have

$$\frac{1}{x^2+5x+6} = \frac{1}{x+2} - \frac{1}{x+3}$$

so that

$$\int_0^6 \frac{1}{x^2+5x+6}\,\mathrm{d}x = \int_0^6 \left[\frac{1}{x+2} - \frac{1}{x+3}\right]\mathrm{d}x$$

$$= [\ln(x+2) - \ln(x+3)]_0^6$$

$$= \ln(\tfrac{8}{2}) - \ln(\tfrac{9}{3}) = \ln 4 - \ln 3 = \ln(\tfrac{4}{3})$$

When the rational function has an irreducible quadratic factor we make use of the integral

$$\int \frac{1}{a^2+x^2}\,\mathrm{d}x = \frac{1}{a}\tan^{-1}\left(\frac{x}{a}\right) + c$$

as illustrated in Example 7.53.

Example 7.53 Find the indefinite integrals of

(a) $\dfrac{1}{x^2-10x+50}$ (b) $\dfrac{1}{(x+1)(x^2+2x+2)}$ (c) $\dfrac{3x^2}{(x-1)(x+2)}$

Solution (a) The denominator here is an irreducible quadratic:

$$\int \frac{1}{x^2-10x+50}\,\mathrm{d}x = \int \frac{1}{(x-5)^2+5^2}\,\mathrm{d}x$$

Using the standard form above, we have

$$\int \frac{1}{x^2-10x+50}\,\mathrm{d}x = \frac{1}{5}\tan^{-1}\left(\frac{x-5}{5}\right) + c$$

(b) Expressing the integrand as partial fractions we have

$$\frac{1}{(x+1)(x^2+2x+2)} \equiv \frac{A}{x+1} + \frac{Bx+C}{x^2+2x+2}$$

or $\quad 1 \equiv A(x^2 + 2x + 2) + (x + 1)(Bx + C)$

Setting $x = -1$ gives $1 = A$

Setting $x = 0$ gives $1 = 2A + C$ giving $C = -1$

Setting $x = 1$ gives $1 = 5A + 2B + 2C$ giving $B = -1$

Thus

$$\int \frac{1}{(x+1)(x^2+2x+2)}\,\mathrm{d}x = \int \frac{1}{x+1} - \frac{x+1}{x^2+2x+2}\,\mathrm{d}x$$

$$= \ln(x+1) - \tfrac{1}{2}\ln(x^2+2x+2) + c$$

(c) Using the result of Example 2.35, we have

$$\frac{3x^2}{(x-1)(x+2)} = 3 + \frac{1}{x-1} - \frac{4}{x+2}$$

Thus

$$\int \frac{3x^2}{(x-1)(x+2)}\,\mathrm{d}x = 3x + \ln(x-1) - 4\ln(x+2) + c$$

Example 7.54 Evaluate $\displaystyle\int_0^1 \frac{2}{(1+x)^2(1+x^2)}\,\mathrm{d}x.$

Solution Expressing the integrand as partial fractions, we have

$$\frac{2}{(1+x)^2(1+x^2)} \equiv \frac{Ax+B}{(1+x)^2} + \frac{Cx+D}{1+x^2}$$

Thus $\quad 2 \equiv (Ax + B)(1 + x^2) + (Cx + D)(1 + 2x + x^2)$

Comparing coefficients of each power of x gives

$x^0 : B + D = 2$

$x^1 : A + C + 2D = 0$

$x^2 : B + D + 2C = 0$

$x^3 : A + C = 0$

from which we deduce $A = 1$, $B = 2$, $C = -1$ and $D = 0$. Thus

$$\int_0^1 \frac{2}{(1+x)^2(1+x^2)}\,\mathrm{d}x = \int_0^1 \left[\frac{x+2}{(1+x)^2} - \frac{1x}{1+x^2}\right]\mathrm{d}x$$

$$= \left[\ln(1+x) - \frac{1}{1+x} - \tfrac{1}{2}\ln(1+x^2)\right]_0^1$$

$$= \tfrac{1}{2} + \tfrac{1}{2}\ln 2$$

7.8.9 Exercises

117 Using partial fractions, integrate

(a) $\dfrac{x}{x^2-3x-4}$ (b) $\dfrac{x}{(x-2)^2}$

(c) $\dfrac{1}{x(x+1)}$ (d) $\dfrac{x}{x^2+2x+1}$

(e) $\dfrac{1}{x^2-1}$ (f) $\dfrac{1}{x^2(x-1)}$

(g) $\dfrac{1}{x(x-1)(x-2)}$ (h) $\dfrac{1}{1+x-2x^2}$

(i) $\dfrac{2x^3}{x^3-1}$ (j) $\dfrac{3x^3-3x^2+4x-2}{x(x-1)(x^2+1)}$

(k) $\dfrac{9}{(x-1)(x+2)^2}$ (l) $\dfrac{x^2-2x+3}{(x-1)(x^2-x-1)}$

118 Express $12/(x-3)(x+1)$ in partial fractions and hence show that

$$\int_4^6 \frac{12}{(x-3)(x+1)}\,dx = 3\ln\tfrac{15}{7}$$

7.8.10 Integration involving the circular and hyperbolic functions

We have seen in many examples earlier in the chapter how a carefully chosen rearrangement of the integrand makes it possible to evaluate non-standard integrals. This rearrangement method is widely used to find integrals of products of sines and cosines. This makes use of the trigonometric sum identities (Section 2.6.4) as well as the rules of integration. The same techniques are used with the hyperbolic sines and cosines.

Example 7.55 Find the indefinite integrals of

(a) $\cos^2 x$ (b) $\sin(5x+1)\cos(x+2)$

Solution (a) First we express $\cos^2 x$ in terms of $\cos 2x$ using the identity

$$\cos 2x = 2\cos^2 x - 1$$

So

$$\int \cos^2 x\,dx = \int \tfrac{1}{2}(\cos 2x + 1)dx$$

$$= \tfrac{1}{4}\sin 2x + \tfrac{1}{2}x + \text{constant}$$

(b) First we express the product as the sum of two sine terms

$$\sin(5x+1)\cos(x+2) = \tfrac{1}{2}[\sin(6x+3) + \sin(4x-1)]$$

Then we evaluate the integral using the rules of integration

$$\int \sin(5x+1)\cos(x+2)dx = -\tfrac{1}{12}\cos(6x+3) - \tfrac{1}{8}\cos(4x-1) + \text{constant}$$

In other examples we make use of the general composite function rule and of integration by parts.

Example 7.56 Find the indefinite integrals of

(a) $\sin^3 x \cos^2 x$ (b) $\tan x$

Solution (a) Here we can rewrite the product as

$$\sin x(1 - \cos^2 x)\cos^2 x$$

So we have the integral

$$\int \sin^3 x \cos^2 x \, dx = \int (\cos^2 x \sin x - \cos^4 x \sin x) dx$$

Now $\frac{d}{dx}(\cos x) = -\sin x$, so using the general composite rule we have

$$\int \sin^3 x \cos^2 x \, dx = -\tfrac{1}{3}\cos^3 x + \tfrac{1}{5}\cos^5 x + \text{constant}$$

(b) Here, again, we notice that $\frac{d}{dx}(\cos x) = -\sin x$, to obtain

$$\int \tan x \, dx = \int \frac{\sin x}{\cos x} dx = -\ln \cos x + \text{constant}$$

and since $\frac{1}{\cos x} = \sec x$, we may write this as

$$\int \tan x \, dx = \ln \sec x + \text{constant}$$

Sometimes using different methods to find an integral may give results that appear different but only differ by a constant.

Example 7.57 Find the indefinite integrals of

(a) $\sinh 5x \cosh 2x$ (b) $\operatorname{sech} x$

Solution (a) Here we rewrite the integrand as $\frac{1}{2}(\sinh 7x + \sinh 3x)$ to obtain

$$\int \sinh 5x \cosh 2x \, dx = \tfrac{1}{14}\cosh 7x + \tfrac{1}{6}\cosh 3x + \text{constant}$$

Alternatively we can express the integrand in terms of exponential functions

$$\int \sinh 5x \cosh 2x \, \mathrm{d}x = \tfrac{1}{4}\int (\mathrm{e}^{5x} - \mathrm{e}^{-5x})(\mathrm{e}^{2x} + \mathrm{e}^{-2x})\mathrm{d}x$$

$$= \tfrac{1}{4}\int (\mathrm{e}^{7x} - \mathrm{e}^{-7x} + \mathrm{e}^{3x} - \mathrm{e}^{-3x})\mathrm{d}x$$

$$= (\mathrm{e}^{7x} + \mathrm{e}^{-7x}) + \tfrac{1}{3}(\mathrm{e}^{3x} + \mathrm{e}^{-3x}) + \text{constant}$$

$$= \tfrac{1}{14}\cosh 7x + \tfrac{1}{6}\cosh 3x + \text{constant}$$

(b) $$\int \operatorname{sech} x \, \mathrm{d}x = \int \frac{1}{\tfrac{1}{2}(\mathrm{e}^{x} + \mathrm{e}^{-x})}\mathrm{d}x = \int \frac{2\mathrm{e}^{x}}{\mathrm{e}^{2x} + 1}\mathrm{d}x$$

$$= 2\tan^{-1}(\mathrm{e}^{x}) + \text{constant}$$

Alternatively we can write

$$\int \frac{1}{\cosh x}\mathrm{d}x = \int \frac{\cosh x}{\cosh^2 x}\mathrm{d}x = \int \frac{\cosh x}{1 + \sinh^2 x}\mathrm{d}x$$

$$= \tan^{-1}(\sinh x) + \text{constant}$$

since $\dfrac{\mathrm{d}}{\mathrm{d}x}(\sinh x) = \cosh x$.

It is left as an exercise for the reader to show (using the result of Question 68 of Exercises 2.6.9) that

$$2\tan^{-1}(\mathrm{e}^{x}) = \tan^{-1}(\sinh x) - \frac{\pi}{2}$$

7.8.11 Exercises

119 Find the indefinite integrals

(a) $\sin 3x \cos 5x$ (b) $\cos 7x \cos 5x$

(c) $\sin^2 x$ (d) $\cos^2 x$

(e) $\cosh^2 x$ (f) $\sinh(5x + 1)$

120 Evaluate the definite integrals

(a) $\displaystyle\int_0^{\pi} \sin 5x \sin 6x \, \mathrm{d}x$ (b) $\displaystyle\int_0^{\pi} \sin^2 5x \, \mathrm{d}x$

7.8.12 Integration by substitution

Sometimes it is possible to simplify an integral by means of a change of integrating variable. This uses the composite-function rule (Section 7.8.6) in a slightly different way. This is illustrated in Example 7.58.

Example 7.58 Find the indefinite integral

$$\int \frac{1}{2 + \sqrt{(1 - x)}} \mathrm{d}x$$

Solution The source of the difficulty with this integral is the square-root term in the denominator. We try to simplify the integral by the substitution $t = \sqrt{(1 - x)}$. Thus $x = 1 - t^2$ and $\mathrm{d}x/\mathrm{d}t = -2t$, giving

$$\int \frac{1}{2 + \sqrt{(1 - x)}} \mathrm{d}x = \int \frac{1}{2 + t} \frac{\mathrm{d}x}{\mathrm{d}t} \mathrm{d}t = \int \frac{1}{2 + t} (-2t) \mathrm{d}t$$

$$= \int \frac{-2t}{2 + t} \mathrm{d}t = 2 \int \left(\frac{2}{2 + t} - 1 \right) \mathrm{d}t$$

$$= 4 \ln(2 + t) - 2t + \text{constant}$$

$$= 4 \ln[2 + \sqrt{(1 - x)}] - 2\sqrt{(1 - x)} + \text{constant}$$

The choice of such substitutions is not always immediately obvious. We shall consider a further example and then give a list of substitutions commonly used to simplify integrals.

Example 7.59 Find the indefinite integral $\int \sqrt{(1 - x^2)} \mathrm{d}x$, $0 \leqslant x \leqslant 1$.

Solution Based on our experience with Example 7.51, we are tempted to try to remove the square-root term using the substitution

$$u = \sqrt{(1 - x^2)}$$

Then $u^2 = 1 - x^2$ and $2u = -2x \mathrm{d}x/\mathrm{d}u$, so that

$$\frac{\mathrm{d}x}{\mathrm{d}u} = -\frac{u}{x} = -\frac{u}{\sqrt{(1 - u^2)}}$$

giving

$$\int \sqrt{(1 - x^2)} \mathrm{d}x = -\int \frac{u^2 \mathrm{d}u}{\sqrt{(1 - u^2)}}$$

which leaves us with an integral more complicated than the one with which we started.

Thus in this case the simple substitution does not work, and we need to look for a more sophisticated substitution, bearing in mind that what we wish to do is to remove the awkward square-root term $\sqrt{(1 - x^2)}$. Noting that $\cos^2\theta = 1 - \sin^2\theta$ we try the substitution $x = \sin \theta$, so that $\dfrac{\mathrm{d}x}{\mathrm{d}\theta} = \cos \theta$, giving

$$\int \sqrt{(1-x^2)}\mathrm{d}x = \int \sqrt{(1-\sin^2\theta)}\frac{\mathrm{d}x}{\mathrm{d}\theta}\mathrm{d}\theta$$

$$= \int \cos\theta\cos\theta\mathrm{d}\theta$$

$$= \int \cos^2\theta\mathrm{d}\theta$$

which looks simpler than the original integral but is not immediately integrable.

Using the double-angle trigonometric identity (see 2.27c)

$$\cos 2\theta = 2\cos^2\theta - 1$$

we obtain

$$\int \sqrt{(1-x^2)}\mathrm{d}x = \int \tfrac{1}{2}(1+\cos 2\theta)\mathrm{d}\theta$$

$$= \tfrac{1}{2}\theta + \tfrac{1}{4}\sin 2\theta + \text{constant}$$

This gives the answer in terms of θ rather than the original variable x. Since $\theta = \sin^{-1}x$, back substitution gives

$$\int \sqrt{(1-x^2)}\mathrm{d}x = \tfrac{1}{2}\sin^{-1}x + \tfrac{1}{4}\sin(2\sin^{-1}x) + \text{constant}$$

or, since $\sin 2\theta = 2\sin\theta\cos\theta = 2\sin\theta\sqrt{(1-\sin^2\theta)}$, we may write this in the alternative form

$$\int \sqrt{(1-x^2)}\mathrm{d}x = \tfrac{1}{2}\sin^{-1}x + \tfrac{1}{2}x\sqrt{(1-x^2)} + \text{constant}$$

Figure 7.59 shows a number of substitutions that are often used in the evaluation of $\int f(x)\mathrm{d}x$. This list is not exhaustive. There are many special cases, some of which are given in Exercises 7.8.14.

When using substitution methods with definite integrals, it is usually best to change the limits of the integral when the integrating variable is changed. This saves returning to the original variable, which can sometimes be very tedious. In general, setting $x = g(t)$ gives

$$\int_a^b f(x)\mathrm{d}x = \int_{g^{-1}(a)}^{g^{-1}(b)} f(g(t))g'(t)\mathrm{d}t$$

$$= \int_{t_a}^{t_b} h(t)\mathrm{d}t, \quad \text{where } a = g(t_a),\ b = g(t_b) \text{ and } h(t) = f(g(t))g'(t)$$

Figure 7.59
Substitutions for evaluation of $\int f(x)\mathrm{d}x$.

If f(x) contains	***try***	
$\sqrt{(a^2 - x^2)}$	$x = a\sin\theta$,	$\dfrac{\mathrm{d}x}{\mathrm{d}\theta} = a\cos\theta$
	or $x = a\tanh u$,	$\dfrac{\mathrm{d}x}{\mathrm{d}u} = a\,\mathrm{sech}^2 u$
$\sqrt{(a^2 + x^2)}$	$x = a\sinh u$,	$\dfrac{\mathrm{d}x}{\mathrm{d}u} = a\cosh u$
	or $x = a\tan\theta$,	$\dfrac{\mathrm{d}x}{\mathrm{d}\theta} = a\sec^2\theta$
$\sqrt{(x^2 - a^2)}$	$x = a\cosh u$	$\dfrac{\mathrm{d}x}{\mathrm{d}u} = a\sinh u$
	or $x = a\sec\theta$	$\dfrac{\mathrm{d}x}{\mathrm{d}\theta} = a\sec\theta\tan\theta$
Circular functions	$s = \sin x$,	$\dfrac{\mathrm{d}s}{\mathrm{d}x} = \cos x$
	or $c = \cos x$,	$\dfrac{\mathrm{d}c}{\mathrm{d}x} = -\sin x$
	or $t = \tan\frac{1}{2}x$,	
	$\left(\sin x = \dfrac{2t}{1+t^2},\quad \cos x = \dfrac{1-t^2}{1+t^2},\quad \dfrac{\mathrm{d}x}{\mathrm{d}t} = \dfrac{2}{1+t^2}\right)$	
Hyperbolic functions	$u = \mathrm{e}^x$,	$\dfrac{\mathrm{d}u}{\mathrm{d}x} = \mathrm{e}^x$
	or $s = \sinh x$,	$\dfrac{\mathrm{d}s}{\mathrm{d}x} = \cosh x$
	or $c = \cosh x$,	$\dfrac{\mathrm{d}c}{\mathrm{d}x} = \sinh x$
	or $t = \tanh\frac{1}{2}x$,	$\dfrac{\mathrm{d}t}{\mathrm{d}x} = \frac{1}{2}\mathrm{sech}^2\frac{1}{2}x$

Example 7.60 Using the substitution $u = \sqrt{(x + 2)}$, evaluate the definite integral

$$\int_{-2}^{2} \frac{\sqrt{(x+2)}}{x+6}\,\mathrm{d}x$$

Solution Setting $u = \sqrt{(x + 2)}$, or $u^2 = x + 2$, gives $2u\,\mathrm{d}u = \mathrm{d}x$. Regarding limits, when $x = -2$, $u = 0$ and when $x = 2$, $u = \sqrt{4} = 2$.

Making the substitution gives

$$\int_{-2}^{2} \frac{\sqrt{(x+2)}}{x+6}\,dx = \int_{0}^{2} \frac{u}{u^2+4}\,2u\,du = \int_{0}^{2} \frac{2u^2}{u^2+4}\,du = \int_{0}^{2} 2 - \frac{8}{u^2+4}\,du$$

$$= \left[2u - 4\tan^{-1}\frac{u}{2}\right]_0^2 = 4 - \pi$$

For Example 7.58 the MATLAB commands

```
syms x y
y = 1/(2 + sqrt(1 - x)); int(y); pretty(ans)
```

return the integral as

```
2log(-x - 3) - 2(1 - x)^(1/2) - 2log(-2 + (1 - x)^(1/2))
+ 2log(2 + (1 - x)^(1/2))
```

Some algebraic manipulation is necessary to obtain the answer in the form given in the solution. Collecting the `log` terms gives

$$-2(1-x)^{1/2} + 2\log\frac{(-x-3)[2+(1-x)^{1/2}]}{[-2+(1-x)^{1/2}]}$$

Multiplying 'top and bottom' of the log term by $(2+(1-x)^{1/2})$ and subsequent cancelling of the $(-x-3)$ term gives the answer in the form given in the solution.

The corresponding MAPLE commands

```
y:= 1/(2 + sqrt(1 - x)); int(y,x);
```

return the integral as

$$2\ln(-x-3) - 2\sqrt{(1-x)} + 4\operatorname{arctanh}\left(\frac{1}{2}\sqrt{(1-x)}\right)$$

Using the command

```
convert(%, ln);
```

the answer is expressed in the logarithmic form

$$2\ln(-x-3) - 2\sqrt{(1-x)} + 2\ln(2+\sqrt{(1-x)}) - 2\ln(2-\sqrt{(1-x)})$$

This example clearly emphasizes the fact that integrals can be the same even if they look totally different.

7.8.13 Integration involving $\sqrt{(ax^2 + bx + c)}$

We have seen in many examples that the use of the linear composite rule combined with standard integrals enables us to evaluate many integrals, including ones involving terms like $\sqrt{(ax^2 + bx + c)}$. In this section we will deal with several integrals of that type.

Example 7.61 Find the indefinite integrals of the following functions

(a) $\sqrt{(x^2 + 6x - 7)}$ (b) $\dfrac{1}{\sqrt{(x^2 - 5x + 4)}}$ (c) $\dfrac{1}{\sqrt{(3x^2 - 6x + 7)}}$

(d) $\dfrac{2x + 3}{\sqrt{(x^2 + 4x + 9)}}$ (e) $x\sqrt{(x^2 + 4x - 3)}$ (f) $\sqrt{(3 + 2x - 2x^2)}$

Solution (a) First we complete the square of the term inside the square root

$$\int \sqrt{(x^2 + 6x - 7)}\,\mathrm{d}x = \int \sqrt{[(x + 3)^2 - 16]}\,\mathrm{d}x$$

Using the table (Figure 7.59), we select the substitution

$$(x + 3) = 4 \cosh u, \quad \text{so that } \frac{\mathrm{d}x}{\mathrm{d}u} = 4 \sinh u \text{ and}$$

$$\sqrt{(x^2 + 6x - 7)}\,\mathrm{d}x = \int \sqrt{[(16 \cosh^2 u - 16)]}\, 4 \sinh u\,\mathrm{d}u$$

Now $\cosh^2 u - 1 = \sinh^2 u$, and the integral becomes

$$16\int \sinh^2 u\,\mathrm{d}u = 16\int \tfrac{1}{2}(\cosh 2u - 1)\mathrm{d}u = 4 \sinh 2u - 8u + \text{constant}$$

Since $\cosh u = (x + 3)/4$ we deduce that $\sinh u = \sqrt{(\cosh^2 - 1)}$; that is, $\sinh u = \sqrt{\left[\left(\frac{x+3}{4}\right)^2 - 1\right]}$ and

$$\sinh 2u = 2\sinh u \cosh u = \frac{2(x + 3)}{4}\sqrt{\left[\left(\frac{x+3}{4}\right)^2 - 1\right]}$$

Also $u = \cosh^{-1}(\frac{x+3}{4})$ and hence

$$\int \sqrt{(x^2 + 6x - 7)}\,\mathrm{d}x = (x + 3)\sqrt{(x^2 + 6x - 7)} - 8 \cosh^{-1}\left(\frac{x+3}{4}\right) + \text{constant}$$

(b) Using the same approach, we have

$$\int \frac{\mathrm{d}x}{\sqrt{(x^2 - 5x + 4)}} = \int \frac{\mathrm{d}x}{\sqrt{[(x - \frac{5}{2})^2 - \frac{9}{4}]}}$$

Setting $x - \frac{5}{2} = \frac{3}{2}\cosh u$, so that $\frac{\mathrm{d}x}{\mathrm{d}u} = \frac{3}{2}\sinh u$, the integral becomes $\int \frac{\frac{3}{2}\sinh u}{\sqrt{(\frac{9}{4}\sinh^2 u)}}\mathrm{d}u$ since $\cosh^2 u - 1 = \sinh^2 u$. Thus

$$\int \frac{\mathrm{d}x}{\sqrt{(x^2 - 5x + 4)}} = \int 1\mathrm{d}u = u + c, \text{ where } \cosh u = \tfrac{2}{3}(x - \tfrac{3}{2})$$

Hence

$$\int \frac{\mathrm{d}x}{\sqrt{(x^2 - 5x + 4)}} = \cosh^{-1}\left(\frac{2x - 5}{3}\right) + \text{constant}$$

(c) Rewriting the integrand gives

$$\int \frac{dx}{\sqrt{(3x^2 - 6x + 7)}} = \int \frac{dx}{\sqrt{3}\sqrt{[(x-1)^2 + \frac{4}{3}]}}$$

Setting $x - 1 = \frac{2}{\sqrt{3}}\sinh u$, so that $\frac{dx}{du} = \frac{2}{\sqrt{3}}\cosh u$, the integral becomes $\frac{1}{\sqrt{3}}\int \frac{\frac{2}{\sqrt{3}}\cosh u}{\sqrt{(\frac{4}{3}\cosh^2 u)}}\,du$ since $\sinh^2 u + 1 = \cosh^2 u$. Thus

$$\int \frac{dx}{\sqrt{(3x^2 - 6x + 7)}} = \frac{1}{\sqrt{3}}\int 1\,du = \frac{1}{\sqrt{3}}u + c, \text{ where } \sinh u = \frac{\sqrt{[3(x-1)]}}{2}$$

Hence

$$\int \frac{dx}{\sqrt{(3x^2 - 6x + 7)}} = \frac{1}{\sqrt{3}}\sinh^{-1}\left[\frac{\sqrt{[3(x-1)]}}{2}\right] + \text{constant}$$

(d) Here we notice that

$$\frac{d}{dx}[\sqrt{(x^2 + 4x + 9)}] = \frac{\frac{1}{2}(2x + 4)}{\sqrt{(x^2 + 4x + 9)}}$$

so we first rewrite the integrand as $\frac{2x + 4 - 1}{\sqrt{(x^2 + 4x + 9)}}$ and the integral as

$$2\int \frac{\frac{1}{2}(2x + 4)}{\sqrt{(x^2 + 4x + 9)}}\,dx - \int \frac{dx}{\sqrt{(x^2 + 4x + 9)}}$$

The first term may be evaluated at once as $2\sqrt{(x^2 + 4x + 9)}$.

The second term is rewritten as $\int \frac{dx}{\sqrt{[(x+2)^2 + 5]}}$.

Using the substitution $x + 2 = \sqrt{5}\sinh u$, the reader should show that the value of this integral is $\sinh^{-1}(\frac{x+2}{\sqrt{5}})$. Hence

$$\int \frac{2x + 3}{\sqrt{(x^2 + 4x + 9)}}\,dx = 2\sqrt{(x^2 + 4x + 9)} - \sinh^{-1}\left(\frac{x+2}{\sqrt{5}}\right) + \text{constant}$$

(e) Here $x^2 + 4x - 3 = (x + 2)^2 - 7$, so we choose the substitution $x + 2 = \sqrt{7}\cosh u$. Hence

$$\int x\sqrt{(x^2 + 4x - 3)}\,dx = \int (\sqrt{7}\cosh u - 2)\,7\sinh^2 u\,du$$

$$= 7\sqrt{7}\int \cosh u \sinh^2 u\,du - 14\int \sinh^2 u\,du$$

$$= \frac{7\sqrt{7}}{3}\sinh^3 u - 14\int \frac{\cosh 2u - 1}{2}\,du$$

$$= \frac{7\sqrt{7}}{3}\sinh^3 u - \frac{7}{2}\sinh 2u + 7u + \text{constant}$$

Since $\cosh u = \dfrac{x+2}{\sqrt{7}}$, $\sinh u = \sqrt{\left[\left(\dfrac{x+2}{\sqrt{7}}\right)^2 - 1\right]}$ and we obtain

$$\int x\sqrt{(x^2+4x-3)}\mathrm{d}x = \tfrac{7\sqrt{7}}{3}\,\tfrac{1}{7\sqrt{7}}[(x+2)^2-7]^{3/2} - (x+2)[(x+2)^2-7]^{1/2}$$

$$+ 7\cosh^{-1}(\tfrac{x+2}{\sqrt{7}}) + \text{constant}$$

$$= \tfrac{1}{3}(x^2+4x-3)^{3/2} - (x+2)(x^2+4x-3)^{1/2} + 7\cosh^{-1}(\tfrac{x+2}{\sqrt{7}}) + \text{constant}$$

(f) Here $3 + 2x - 2x^2 = \frac{7}{2} - 2(x-\frac{1}{2})^2 = 2[\frac{7}{4} - (x-\frac{1}{2})^2]$, so we choose $x - \frac{1}{2} = \frac{\sqrt{7}}{2}\sin u$ and the integral becomes $\int\sqrt{(3+2x-2x^2)}\mathrm{d}x = \sqrt{2}\int\frac{7}{4}\cos^2 u\,\mathrm{d}u$ since $1 - \sin^2 u = \cos^2 u$.

Now $$\int \tfrac{7}{4}\cos^2 \mathrm{d}u = \int \tfrac{7}{8}(\cos 2u + 1)\mathrm{d}u = \tfrac{7}{16}\sin 2u + \tfrac{7}{8}u + \text{constant}$$

$$= \tfrac{7}{8}\sin u\cos u + \tfrac{7}{8}u + \text{constant}$$

Substituting back we obtain

$$\int\sqrt{(3+2x-2x^2)}\mathrm{d}x = \tfrac{7\sqrt{2}}{8}\sin^{-1}(\tfrac{2x-1}{\sqrt{7}}) + \tfrac{7\sqrt{2}}{8}\tfrac{2x-1}{\sqrt{7}}\sqrt{[1-(\tfrac{2x-1}{\sqrt{7}})^2]} + \text{constant}$$

$$= \tfrac{7\sqrt{2}}{8}\sin(\tfrac{2x-1}{\sqrt{7}}) + \tfrac{1}{4}(2x-1)\sqrt{(3+2x-2x^2)} + \text{constant}$$

Comment These examples illustrate the complexity of such integrals that provided the motivation for the development of computer packages like MAPLE.

7.8.14 Exercises

Check your answers using MATLAB or MAPLE whenever possible.

121 Use the given substitutions to integrate the following functions:

(a) $x^3\sqrt{(1+x^2)}$, with $t = \sqrt{(1+x^2)}$

(b) $\dfrac{3}{x\sqrt{(x^2+9)}}$, with $t = \dfrac{1}{x}$

(c) $\dfrac{1}{3+\sqrt{x}}$, with $t = \sqrt{x}$

122 Use an appropriate substitution to integrate the following functions:

(a) $\dfrac{1}{1+\sqrt{(1+x)}}$ (b) $\sin^2 x\cos^3 x$ (c) $\sin\sqrt{x}$

123 Show that $t = \tan\frac{1}{2}x$ implies

$$\sin x = \frac{2t}{1+t^2},$$

$$\cos x = \frac{1-t^2}{1+t^2}$$

and

$$\mathrm{d}x = \frac{2}{1+t^2}\mathrm{d}t$$

Hence integrate

(a) $\operatorname{cosec} x$ (b) $\sec x$

(c) $\dfrac{1}{3+4\sin x}$ (d) $\dfrac{1}{5\sin x + 12\cos x}$

124 Evaluate the following definite integral with the given substitution:

$$\int_{-2}^{2} \frac{x+6}{\sqrt{(x+2)}}\,dx, \qquad \text{with } u = \sqrt{(x+2)}$$

125 In Question 11 (Exercises 7.2.8) the equation of the path of P was found to be such that

$$\frac{dy}{dx} = \frac{\sqrt{(a^2 - x^2)}}{x}, \quad \text{with } y = 0 \text{ at } x = a$$

Use the substitution $x = a\,\text{sech}\,u$ to integrate this differential equation and show that

$$y = \ln\left[\frac{a + \sqrt{(a^2 - x^2)}}{x}\right] - \sqrt{(a^2 - x^2)}$$

This curve is called a **tractrix**.

126 Find the indefinite integrals

(a) $\int \sqrt{(3 + 2x - x^2)}dx$

(b) $\int \frac{dx}{\sqrt{(x^2 - 6x + 5)}} dx$

(c) $\int \frac{dx}{\sqrt{(x^2 - 4x + 8)}} dx$

(d) $\int \frac{x+3}{\sqrt{(x^2 + 4x + 13)}} dx$

(e) $\int x\sqrt{(3 + 2x - x^2)}dx$

7.9 Applications of integration

Integration is widely used in engineering applications. In this section we consider some situations in which integration is used.

7.9.1 Volume of a solid of revolution

Imagine rotating the plane area A under the graph of the function $f(x)$, $x \in [a, b]$, of Figure 7.60 through a complete revolution about the x axis. The result would be to generate a solid having the x axis as axis of symmetry, as shown in Figure 7.61(a): this is called a **solid of revolution**. If we wish to determine the volume of this solid, we proceed as in Section 7.7.1 and subdivide the rotating area into n vertical strips. When a typical strip within the subinterval $[x_{r-1}, x_r]$ is rotated through a revolution about the x axis, it will generate a thin disc of radius $f(x_r^*)$ (with $x_{r-1} < x_r^* < x_r$) and thickness Δx_{r-1}, as shown in Figure 7.61(b). The volume of the disc is given by

$$\Delta V_r = \pi[f(x_r^*)]^2 \Delta x_{r-1}$$

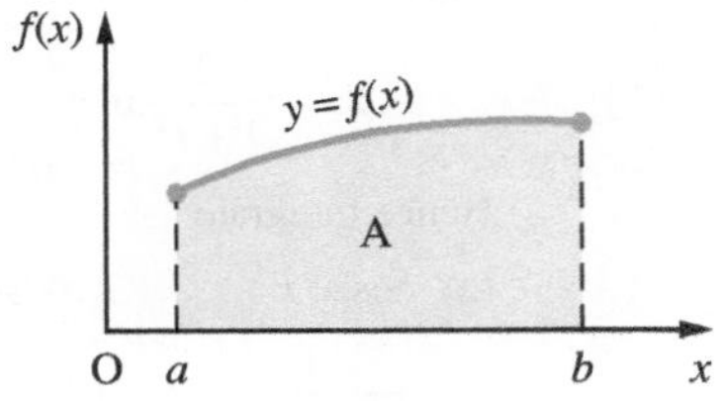

Figure 7.60
Plane area rotated.

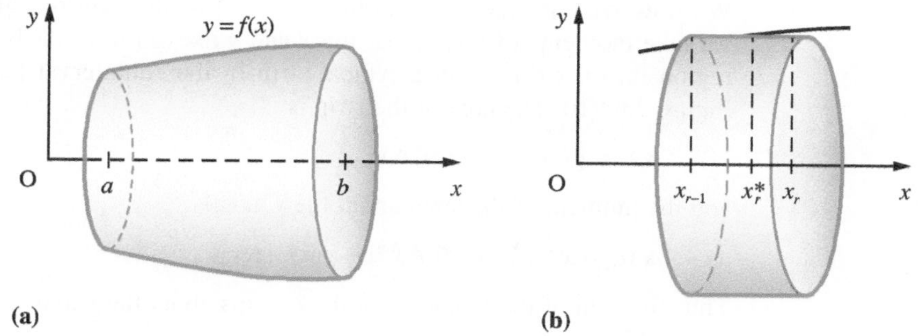

Figure 7.61
Solid of revolution.

Thus the volume of the solid can be approximated by

$$V \approx \sum_{r=1}^{n} \Delta V_r = \pi \sum_{r=1}^{n} [f(x_r^*)]^2 \Delta x_{r-1}$$

Again this approximation is closer to the exact volume as the number of strips is increased. Thus in the limiting case as $n \to \infty$ and $\Delta x \to 0$, $\Delta x = \max_r \Delta x_r$; it leads to the volume being given by

$$V = \lim_{\substack{n\to\infty \\ \Delta x\to 0}} \pi \sum_{r=1}^{n} [f(x_r^*)]^2 \Delta x_{r-1} = \pi \int_a^b [f(x)]^2 \mathrm{d}x \tag{7.36}$$

7.9.2 Centroid of a plane area

Consider the plane region of Figure 7.62(a) bounded between the graphs of the two continuous functions $f(x)$ and $g(x)$ on the interval $x \in [a, b]$, with $g(x) \leqslant f(x)$ on the interval. The area A of this region is clearly given by

$$A = \text{area under the graph of } f(x) - \text{area under the graph of } g(x)$$

$$= \int_a^b f(x)\mathrm{d}x - \int_a^b g(x)\mathrm{d}x$$

That is

$$A = \int_a^b [f(x) - g(x)]\mathrm{d}x \tag{7.37}$$

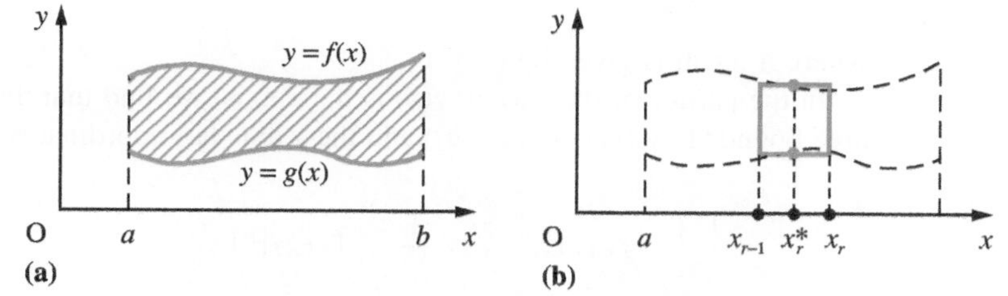

Figure 7.62

We now wish to find the coordinates $(\bar{x}, \bar{y})$ of the centroid of this area. To do this, we take moments of area about the x and y axes in turn. As before, we subdivide the region into n strips, with a typical strip in the subinterval $[x_{r-1}, x_r]$ being shown in Figure 7.62(b). The area of the strip is

$$\Delta A_r = [f(x_r^*) - g(x_r^*)]\Delta x_{r-1}$$

and the moment of this area about the y axis is

$$\Delta M_{y_r} = x_r^*\Delta A_r = x_r^*[f(x_r^*) - g(x_r^*)]\Delta x_{r-1}$$

Thus the sum of the moments of the n strips about the y axis is

$$\sum_{r=1}^{n}\Delta M_{y_r} = \sum_{r=1}^{n} x_r^*\Delta A_r = \sum_{r=1}^{n} x_r^*[f(x_r^*) - g(x_r^*)]\Delta x_{r-1}$$

Proceeding to the limit $n \to \infty$, $\Delta x \to 0$, $\Delta x = \max_r \Delta x_r$, we have the moment of the plane area about the y axis being given by

$$M_y = \lim_{\substack{n\to\infty \\ \Delta x\to 0}} \sum_{r=1}^{n} x_r^*[f(x_r^*) - g(x_r^*)]\Delta x_{r-1} = \int_a^b x[f(x) - g(x)]\,\mathrm{d}x$$

Because the 'x' in the integrand is raised to the power '1', this is termed the first moment of the area about the y axis. Since the x coordinate of the centroid of the plane area is $\bar{x}$, it follows that the moment of the area about the y axis is also given by

$$M_y = A\bar{x}$$

Equating, we have

$$\bar{x} = \frac{1}{A}\int_a^b x[f(x) - g(x)]\,\mathrm{d}x \qquad \textbf{(7.38)}$$

where the area A is given by (7.37).

Likewise, taking moments about the x axis,

$$M_x = A\bar{y} = \lim_{\substack{n\to\infty \\ \Delta x\to 0}}\left[\sum_{r=1}^{n} \tfrac{1}{2}f(x_r^*)f(x_r^*)\Delta x_{r-1} - \sum_{r=1}^{n} \tfrac{1}{2}g(x_r^*)g(x_r^*)\Delta x_{r-1}\right]$$

$$= \lim_{\substack{n\to\infty \\ \Delta x\to 0}} \tfrac{1}{2}\sum_{r=1}^{n}\{[f(x_r^*)]^2 - [g(x_r^*)]^2\}\Delta x_{r-1} = \tfrac{1}{2}\int_a^b \{[f(x)]^2 - [g(x)]^2\}\,\mathrm{d}x$$

giving

$$\bar{y} = \frac{1}{2A}\int_a^b \{[f(x)]^2 - [g(x)]^2\}\,\mathrm{d}x \qquad \textbf{(7.39)}$$

where A again is given by (7.37).

In the particular case when $g(x)$ is the x axis, we find that the centroid of the plane area bounded by $f(x)$ $(x \in [a, b])$ and the x axis has coordinates

$$\bar{x} = \frac{1}{A}\int_a^b xf(x)\,\mathrm{d}x, \quad \bar{y} = \frac{1}{2A}\int_a^b [f(x)]^2\,\mathrm{d}x \qquad \textbf{(7.40)}$$

7.9.3 Centre of gravity of a solid of revolution

Proceeding as in Section 7.9.2, we can obtain the coordinates $(\overline{X}, \overline{Y})$ of the centre of gravity of the solid of revolution generated by $f(x)$ $(x \in [a, b])$ and shown in Figure 7.58. By symmetry, it lies on the x axis, so that

$$\overline{Y} = 0$$

Taking moments about the y axis gives

$$V\overline{X} = \lim_{\substack{n\to\infty \\ \Delta x\to 0}} \pi \sum_{r=1}^{n} x_r^*[f(x_r^*)]^2 \Delta x_{r-1} = \pi \int_a^b x[f(x)]^2 \, dx \quad (7.41)$$

giving

$$\overline{X} = \frac{\pi}{V} \int_a^b x[f(x)]^2 \, dx \quad (7.42)$$

where the volume V is given by (7.36).

7.9.4 Mean values

In many engineering applications we need to know the mean value of a continuously varying quantity. When dealing with a sequence of values we can compute the mean value simply by adding the values together and then dividing by the number of values taken. When dealing with a continuously varying quantity, we cannot do that directly. Using integration, however, we are able to calculate the mean value.

Consider the function $f(x)$ on the interval $[a, b]$ and divide the interval into n equal strips of width h so that $nh = b - a$. Now evaluate the function at the midpoint of each strip. Formally, let $x_k = a + kh$ be the points of subdivision, so that the points of evaluation are $f(x_k^*)$ where $x_k^* = x_k + h/2$. Then the mean value (m.v.) of $f(x)$ on $[a, b]$ is approximately

$$\text{m.v.}(f(x)) \approx \frac{1}{n} \sum_{k=0}^{n-1} f(x_k^*) = \frac{1}{b-a} \sum_{k=0}^{n-1} f(x_k^*)h$$

Now allowing $n \to \infty$ (with $h \to 0$), the summation becomes an integral and the approximation becomes exactly true. Thus

$$\text{m.v.}(f(x)) = \frac{1}{b-a} \int_a^b f(x)\,dx \quad (7.43)$$

The graphical representation of this makes the situation quite clear. In Figure 7.63, the sum of the shaded areas above the line y = (mean value) is equal to the sum of the shaded areas below it, so that the area of the rectangle ABCD is the same as the area between the curve and the x axis.

7.9.5 Root mean square values

In some contexts the computation of the mean value of a function is not useful, for example the mean of an alternating current is zero but that does not imply it is not

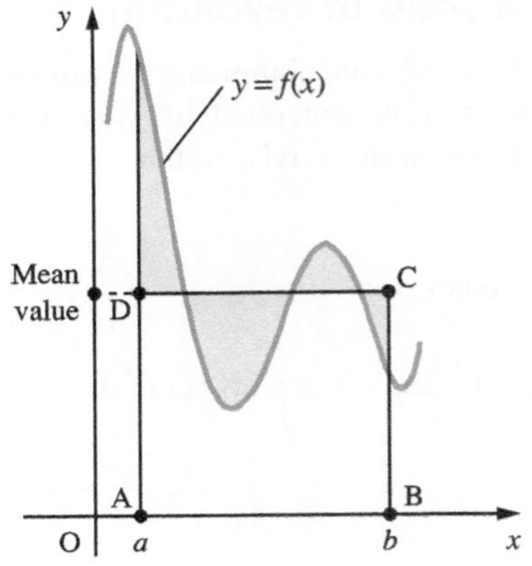

Figure 7.63
Mean value of a function $y = f(x), x \in [a, b]$.

dangerous! To deal with such situations we use the root mean square (r.m.s.) of the function $f(x)$. Literally this is the square root of the mean value of $[f(x)]^2$. Thus we can write

$$[\text{r.m.s.}(f(x))]^2 = \frac{1}{b-a}\int_a^b [f(x)]^2\,\mathrm{d}x \tag{7.44}$$

Although the obvious applications of root mean square values are in electrical engineering, they also occur in the application of statistics to engineering contexts (as standard deviations of continuously distributed random variables). They also occur in the design of gyroscopes and in mechanics, where the 'radius of gyration' is in effect the root mean of moments about an axis.

7.9.6 Arclength and surface area

In many practical problems we are required to work out the length of a curve or the surface area generated by rotating a curve. The formula for the length s of a curve with formula $y = f(x)$ between two points corresponding to $x = a$ and $x = b$ is obtained using the basic idea of integration. Let Δs_k be the element of arclength between $x = x_k$ and $x = x_{k+1}$. Then for a curve that is concave upwards, as in Figure 7.64, we deduce that

$$\Delta x_k \sec\theta_k \leqslant \Delta s_k \leqslant \Delta x_k \sec\theta_{k+1}$$

where θ_k and θ_{k+1} are the angles of slope made by the tangents to the curve at P_k and P_{k+1}. Thus the length s of the curve between $x = a$ and $x = b$ satisfies the inequality

$$\sum_{k=0}^{n-1} \Delta x_k \sec\theta_k \leqslant s = \sum_{k=0}^{n-1} \Delta s_k \leqslant \sum_{k=0}^{n-1} \Delta x_k \sec\theta_{k+1}$$

Letting $n \to \infty$ and $\max \Delta x_k \to 0$ yields the inequality

$$\int_a^b \sec\theta\,\mathrm{d}x \leqslant s \leqslant \int_a^b \sec\theta\,\mathrm{d}x$$

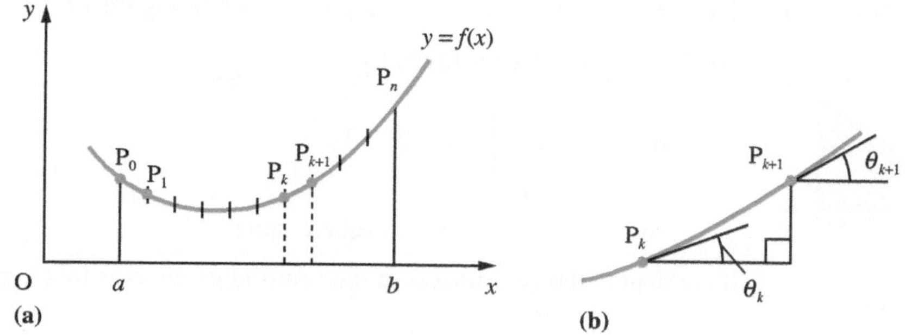

Figure 7.64
(a) Curve $y = f(x)$.
(b) Element of arclength.

from which we deduce that

$$s = \int_a^b \sec\theta \, dx$$

A similar analysis for curves that are concave downwards yields the same result.

We can express $\sec\theta$ in terms of dy/dx by means of the identity

$$\sec^2\theta = 1 + \tan^2\theta$$

Here $\tan\theta = dy/dx$, so, using the convention that s increases with x, we obtain

$$\sec\theta = \sqrt{\left[1 + \left(\frac{dy}{dx}\right)^2\right]}$$

so that the length of the curve is

$$s = \int_a^b \sqrt{\left[1 + \left(\frac{dy}{dx}\right)^2\right]} dx \tag{7.45}$$

The surface area S generated by s when it is rotated through 2π radians about the x axis is calculated in a similar way. The element of arc Δs_k generates an element of surface area ΔS_k, where

$$\Delta S_k = 2\pi \bar{y}_k \Delta s_k$$

where $\bar{y}_k$ is the average value of y between $y_k = f(x_k)$ and $y_{k+1} = f(x_{k+1})$. Thus the total surface area is given by

$$S = \int_a^b 2\pi y \sqrt{\left[1 + \left(\frac{dy}{dx}\right)^2\right]} dx \tag{7.46}$$

Example 7.62

The area enclosed between the curve $y = \sqrt{(x - 2)}$ and the ordinates $x = 2$ and $x = 5$ is rotated through 2π radians about the x axis. Calculate

(a) the rotating area and the coordinates of its centroid;

(b) the volume of the solid of revolution generated and the coordinates of its centre of gravity.

Solution The rotating area is the shaded region shown in Figure 7.65.

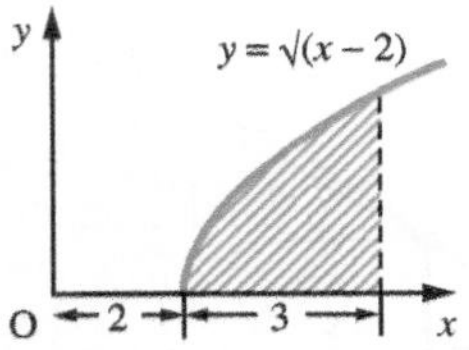

Figure 7.65
Rotating area.

(a) The rotating area is given by

$$A = \int_2^5 y\,dx = \int_2^5 (x-2)^{1/2}\,dx$$

$$= [\tfrac{2}{3}(x-2)^{3/2}]_2^5 = 2\sqrt{3} \text{ square units}$$

If we denote the coordinates of the centroid of the area by $(\bar{x}, \bar{y})$ then, from (7.37),

$$\bar{x} = \frac{1}{A}\int_2^5 xy\,dx = \frac{1}{A}\int_2^5 x(x-2)^{1/2}\,dx = \frac{1}{A}\int_2^5 [(x-2)^{3/2} + 2(x-2)^{1/2}]\,dx$$

$$= \frac{1}{A}\left[\frac{2}{5}(x-2)^{5/2} + \frac{4}{3}(x-2)^{3/2}\right]_2^5 = \frac{1}{A}\left[\frac{2}{5}(3)^{5/2} + \frac{4}{3}(3)^{3/2}\right] = \frac{1}{A}\frac{38}{5}\sqrt{3}$$

Inserting the value $A = 2\sqrt{3}$ obtained earlier gives $\bar{x} = \frac{19}{5}$.

Likewise, from (7.40),

$$\bar{y} = \frac{1}{A}\int_2^5 \tfrac{1}{2}y^2\,dx = \frac{1}{A}\int_2^5 \tfrac{1}{2}(x-2)\,dx$$

$$= \frac{1}{A}[\tfrac{1}{4}(x-2)^2]_2^5 = \frac{9}{4A}$$

Inserting $A = 2\sqrt{3}$ then gives $\bar{y} = \frac{3}{8}\sqrt{3}$ so that the coordinates of the centroid are $(\frac{19}{5}, \frac{3}{8}\sqrt{3})$.

(b) From (7.36) the volume V of the solid of revolution formed is

$$V = \pi\int_2^5 y^2\,dx = \pi\int_2^5 (x-2)\,dx$$

$$= \pi[\tfrac{1}{2}x^2 - 2x]_2^5 = \tfrac{9}{2}\pi \text{ cubic units}$$

If we denote the coordinates of the centre of gravity of the solid of revolution by $(\bar{X}, \bar{Y})$ then, from (7.41) and (7.42),

$$\bar{Y} = 0$$

and

$$\bar{X} = \frac{\pi}{V}\int_2^5 xy^2\,dx = \frac{\pi}{V}\int_2^5 x(x-2)\,dx$$

$$= \frac{\pi}{V}[\tfrac{1}{3}x^3 - x^2]_2^5 = \frac{\pi}{V}[(\tfrac{125}{3} - 25) - (\tfrac{8}{3} - 4)]$$

$$= \frac{18\pi}{V}$$

Inserting the value $V = \frac{9}{2}\pi$ obtained earlier gives $\bar{X} = 4$ so that the coordinates of the centre of gravity are (4, 0).

Example 7.63 Show that the volume of a cap of height h of a sphere of radius r is $\pi(3r - h)h^2/3$.

Solution As shown in Figure 7.66 the volume of the elementary disc of thickness Δx is

$$\pi y^2 \Delta x = \pi(r^2 - x^2)\Delta x$$

and hence the volume of the spherical cap is

$$\begin{aligned}\int_{r-h}^{r} \pi(r^2 - x^2)\mathrm{d}x &= \pi[r^2x - \tfrac{1}{3}x^3]_{r-h}^{r}\\ &= \pi[r^3 - \tfrac{1}{3}r^3 - r^2(r-h) + \tfrac{1}{3}(r-h)^3]\\ &= \pi(r^2h - r^2h + rh^2 - \tfrac{1}{3}h^3)\\ &= \pi(3r - h)h^2/3\end{aligned}$$

Figure 7.66
Spherical cap

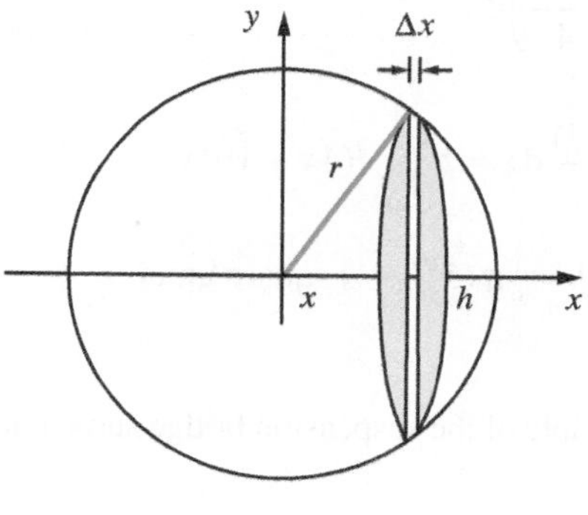

Example 7.64 An electric current i is given by the expression

$$i = I \sin \theta$$

where I is a constant. Find the root mean square value of the current over the interval $0 \leqslant \theta \leqslant 2\pi$.

Solution Using (7.44) the r.m.s. value of the given current is given by

$$\begin{aligned}(\text{r.m.s.}\, i)^2 &= \frac{1}{2\pi - 0}\int_0^{2\pi} I^2 \sin^2\theta \,\mathrm{d}\theta\\ &= \frac{I^2}{2\pi}\int_0^{2\pi} \tfrac{1}{2}(1 - \cos 2\theta)\mathrm{d}\theta\\ &= \frac{I^2}{4\pi}[\theta - \tfrac{1}{2}\sin 2\theta]_0^{2\pi} = \frac{I^2}{4\pi}2\pi = \tfrac{1}{2}I^2\end{aligned}$$

so that

$$\text{r.m.s. current} = \sqrt{(\tfrac{1}{2}I^2)} = I/\sqrt{2}$$

Example 7.65 A parabolic reflector is formed by rotating the part of the curve $y = \sqrt{x}$ between $x = 0$ and $x = 1$ about the x axis. What is the surface area of the reflector?

Solution The parabolic reflector is shown in Figure 7.67. Since $y = x^{1/2}$,

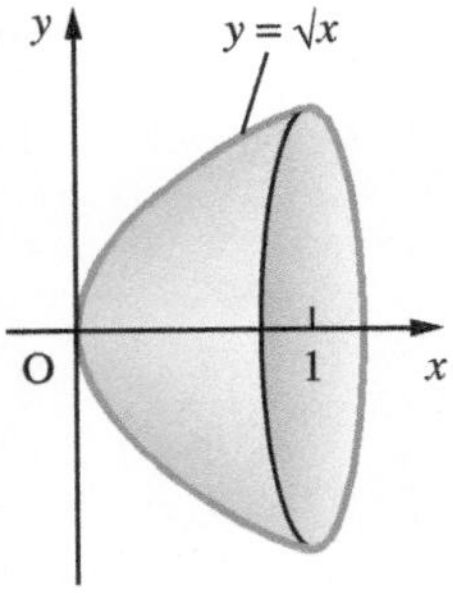

Figure 7.67
Parabolic reflector.

$$\frac{dy}{dx} = \frac{1}{2}x^{-1/2} = \frac{1}{2\sqrt{x}}$$

so that, using (7.46), the surface area S of the reflector is given by

$$S = 2\pi \int_0^1 y \sqrt{\left[1 + \left(\frac{dy}{dx}\right)^2\right]}\,dx$$

$$= 2\pi \int_0^1 \sqrt{x} \sqrt{\left(1 + \frac{1}{4x}\right)}\,dx$$

$$= 2\pi \int_0^1 \sqrt{x}\frac{\sqrt{(4x+1)}}{2\sqrt{x}}\,dx = \pi \int_0^1 \sqrt{(4x+1)}\,dx$$

$$= \pi\left[\tfrac{1}{4}\tfrac{2}{3}(4x+1)^{3/2}\right]_0^1 = \tfrac{1}{6}\pi(5^{3/2} - 1) \text{ square units}$$

Example 7.66 The curve described by the cable of the suspension bridge shown in Figure 7.68 is given by

$$y = \frac{hx^2}{l^2} - \frac{2h}{l}x + h$$

where x is the distance measured from one end of the bridge. What is the length of the cable? (see Example 7.5)

Solution Here the equation of the curve is

$$y = h\left(\frac{x}{l} - 1\right)^2 \quad \text{so that} \quad \frac{dy}{dx} = \frac{2h}{l}\left(\frac{x}{l} - 1\right)$$

Figure 7.68
Suspension bridge.

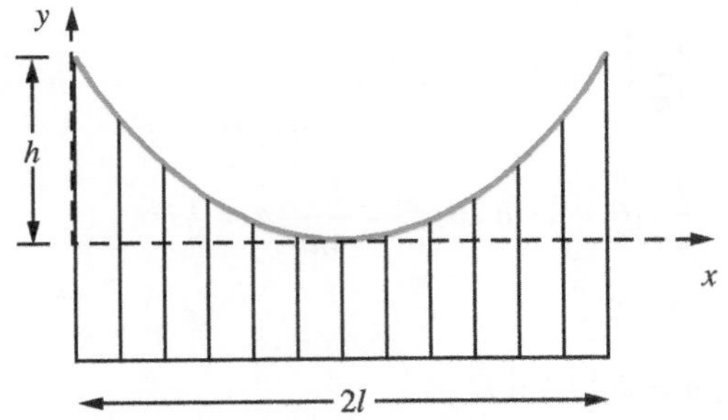

Using (7.45), the length s of the cable is

$$s = \int_0^{2l} \sqrt{\left[1 + \frac{4h^2}{l^2}\left(\frac{x}{l} - 1\right)^2\right]} dx$$

This integral can be simplified by putting

$$t = \frac{2h}{l}\left(\frac{x}{l} - 1\right)$$

Thus

$$s = \frac{l^2}{2h}\int_{-2h/l}^{2h/l} \sqrt{(1 + t^2)}dt = \frac{l^2}{h}\int_0^{2h/l} \sqrt{(1 + t^2)}dt \quad \text{(from symmetry)}$$

This can be further simplified by putting $t = \sinh u$, giving

$$s = \frac{l^2}{h}\int_0^{\sinh^{-1}(2h/l)} \cosh^2 u \, du = \frac{l^2}{2h}\int_0^{\sinh^{-1}(2h/l)} (\cosh 2u + 1) \, du$$

$$= \frac{l^2}{2h}\left[\tfrac{1}{2}\sinh 2u + u\right]_0^{\sinh^{-1}(2h/l)} = \frac{l^2}{2h}\left[\sinh u \cosh u + u\right]_0^{\sinh^{-1}(2h/l)}$$

$$= \frac{l^2}{2h}\left[\frac{2h}{l}\sqrt{\left(1 + \frac{4h^2}{l^2}\right)} + \sinh^{-1}\left(\frac{2h}{l}\right)\right]$$

That is,

$$s = \sqrt{(l^2 + 4h^2)} + \frac{l^2}{2h}\sinh^{-1}\left(\frac{2h}{l}\right)$$

Example 7.67 Find the equation of the curve described by a heavy cable hanging, without load, under gravity, from two equally high points.

Solution Consider the cable illustrated in Figure 7.69. Let T be the tension acting at a point P that is a horizontal distance x from the axis of symmetry, as shown, and let the tangent to the curve at P make an angle θ to the horizontal. If s is the length of the curve between A and P, and T_0 is the tension at A, then resolving the forces acting on the length of cable between A and P horizontally and vertically gives

$$T_0 = T\cos\theta \quad \text{and} \quad s\rho g = T\sin\theta$$

where ρ is the line density of the cable and g is the acceleration due to gravity. Dividing these equations, we obtain

$$\tan\theta = \frac{s}{c}$$

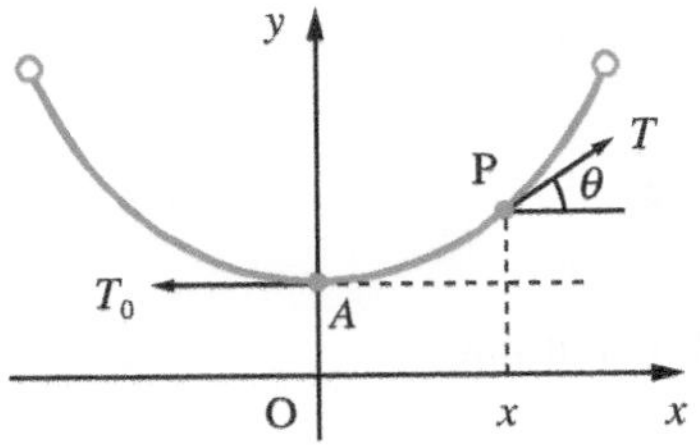

Figure 7.69
Heavy hanging cable.

This is known as the intrinsic equation of the curve, where $c = T_0/\rho g$. In terms of x and y, this equation, using (7.45), implies that the co-ordinates of P satisfy

$$y'(x) = \frac{1}{c}\int_0^x \sqrt{[1 + (y'(t))^2]}\,\mathrm{d}t$$

To solve this equation to obtain the equation of the curve, we first differentiate it with respect to x, giving

$$y''(x) = \frac{1}{c}\sqrt{[1 + (y'(x))^2]}$$

with $\mathrm{d}y/\mathrm{d}x = 0$ at $x = 0$. This may be rewritten as

$$\frac{\mathrm{d}^2y/\mathrm{d}x^2}{\sqrt{[1 + (\mathrm{d}y/\mathrm{d}x)^2]}} = \frac{1}{c}$$

and integrating with respect to x, using the substitution $\mathrm{d}y/\mathrm{d}x = \sinh u$, and remembering that $(\mathrm{d}/\mathrm{d}x)(\mathrm{d}y/\mathrm{d}x) = \mathrm{d}^2y/\mathrm{d}x^2$, gives

$$\sinh^{-1}\left(\frac{\mathrm{d}y}{\mathrm{d}x}\right) = \frac{x}{c} + A$$

Since $\mathrm{d}y/\mathrm{d}x = 0$ at $x = 0$, we deduce that $A = 0$ and

$$\frac{\mathrm{d}y}{\mathrm{d}x} = \sinh\frac{x}{c}$$

This is easy to integrate, giving

$$y = c\cosh\frac{x}{c} + B$$

The value of B is fixed by the value of y at $x = 0$. This may be chosen quite arbitrarily without changing the shape of the curve. Choosing $y(0) = c$ gives a neat answer (with $B = 0$):

$$y = c\cosh\frac{x}{c}$$

Note that this curve, called the **catenary**, is different from the shape of the cable of a suspension bridge, which is a parabola. The catenary has many applications, including the design of roofs and arches.

7.9.7 Moments of inertia

We have seen in Section 7.9.2 that moments of inertia occur in the design of structures involving beams. They also occur in the mechanics of rotating parts of machinery and in the design of ships. The formal definition of a moment of inertia of an object about an axis is its second moment of mass about that axis. The simplest case to consider is that of a plane rectangular area of sides a and b, with mass per unit area ρ, as shown in Figure 7.70(a).

The elementary strip PQ has mass $\rho b\Delta x$ and its second moment of mass about OY is $x^2\rho b\Delta x$. The moment of inertia I_{OY} of the rectangle about OY is the sum of all such second moments. Thus

$$I_{OY} = \int_0^a x^2\rho b\,dx = [\tfrac{1}{3}x^3 b\rho]_0^a$$

$$= \tfrac{1}{3}\rho a^3 b = \tfrac{1}{3}ma^2$$

where $m = \rho ab$ is the mass of the rectangle.

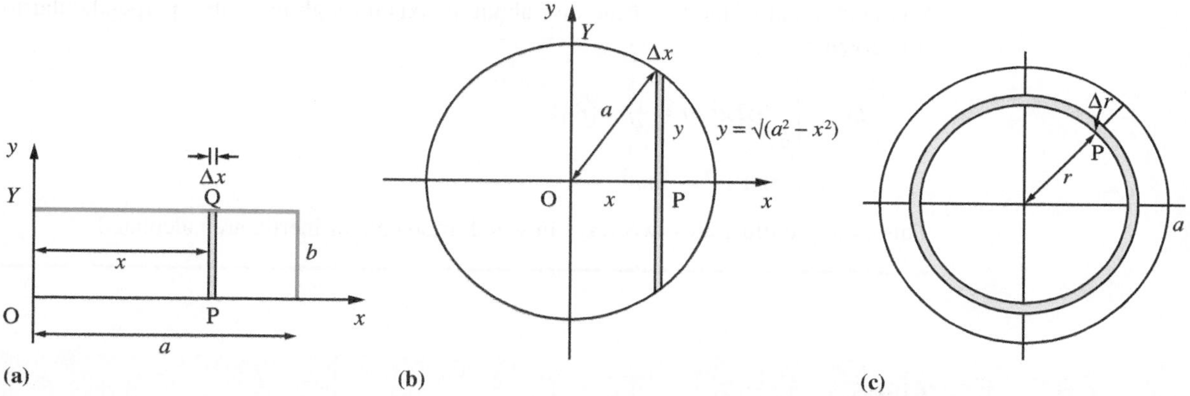

Figure 7.70 (a) Plane rectangular area. (b) Circular disc about diameter. (c) Circular disc about perpendicular axis.

Example 7.68 Find the moments of inertia of a circular disc of radius a about

(a) a diameter;
(b) an axis through its centre and perpendicular to it.

Assume uniform mass per unit area is ρ.

Solution (a) The second moment of the elementary strip at P about OY (see Figure 7.70(b)) is $2x^2\rho y\Delta x$. Thus the moment of inertia of the disc is

$$I_{OY} = \int_{-a}^{+a} 2x^2\rho\sqrt{(a^2 - x^2)}\,dx$$

$$= 4\rho\int_0^a x^2\sqrt{(a^2 - x^2)}\,dx$$

using symmetry properties of the integrand.

Putting $x = a \sin \theta$ gives

$$I_{OY} = 4\rho \int_0^{\pi/2} a^4 \sin^2\theta \cos^2\theta \, d\theta$$

$$= \rho a^4 \int_0^{\pi/2} \sin^2 2\theta \, d\theta$$

$$= \tfrac{1}{2}\rho a^4 \int_0^{\pi/2} (1 - \cos 4\theta) d\theta$$

$$= \tfrac{1}{2}\rho a^4 [\theta - \tfrac{1}{4} \sin 4\theta]_0^{\pi/2}$$

$$= \tfrac{1}{4}(\rho\pi a^2)a^2 = \tfrac{1}{4}ma^2$$

where m is the mass of the disc.

(b) The second moment of the elementary ring at P (see Figure 7.70(c)) is $r^2(\rho 2\pi r)\Delta r$. So the moment of inertia of the disc about an axis through its centre, perpendicular to it is given by

$$I_{OZ} = \int_0^a r^2 \rho 2\pi r \, dr = \tfrac{1}{2}\rho\pi \, [r^4]_0^a$$

$$= \tfrac{1}{2}(\rho\pi a^2)a^2 = \tfrac{1}{2}ma^2$$

This example illustrates two ways in which moments of inertia are calculated.

7.9.8 Exercises

Check your answers using MATLAB or MAPLE whenever possible.

127 Find the volume generated when the plane figure bounded by the curve $xy = x^3 + 3$, the x axis and the ordinates at $x = 1$ and $x = 2$ is rotated about the x axis through one complete revolution.

128 Express the length of the arc of the curve $y = \sin x$ from $x = 0$ to $x = \pi$ as an integral. Also find the volume of the solid generated by revolving the region bounded by the x axis and this arc about the x axis through 2π radians.

129 (a) Sketch the curve whose equation is

$$y = (x - 2)(x - 1)$$

Show that the volume generated when the finite area between the curve and the x axis is rotated through 2π radians about the x axis is $\pi/30$.

(b) Show that the curved surface generated by the revolution about the x axis of the portion of the curve $y^2 = 4ax$ included between the origin and the ordinate $x = 3a$ is $\frac{56}{3}\pi a^2$.

130 A curve is represented parametrically by

$$x(t) = 3t - t^3, \quad y(t) = 3t^2 \quad (0 \leqslant t \leqslant 1)$$

Find the volume and surface area of the solid of revolution generated when the curve is rotated about the x axis through 2π radians.

131 The electrical resistance R (in Ω) of a rheostat at a temperature θ (in °C) is given by $R = 38(1 + 0.004\theta)$. Find the average resistance of the rheostat as the temperature varies uniformly from 10°C to 40°C.

132 The area enclosed between the x axis, the curve $y = x(2 - x)$ and the ordinates $x = 1$ and $x = 2$ is rotated through 2π radians about the x axis. Calculate

(a) the rotating area and the coordinates of its centroid;

(b) the volume of the solid of revolution formed and the coordinates of its centre of gravity.

133 Show that the area enclosed between the x axis, the curve $4y = x^2 - 2\ln x$ and the coordinates $x = 1$ and $x = 3$ is $\frac{1}{6}(19 - 9\ln 3)$.

134 The speed V of a rocket at a time t after launch is given by

$$V = at^2 + b$$

where a and b are constants. The average speed over the first second was $10\,\text{m}\,\text{s}^{-1}$, and that over the next second was $50\,\text{m}\,\text{s}^{-1}$. Determine the values of a and b. What was the average speed over the third second?

135 Find the centroid of the area bounded by $y^2 = 4x$ and $y = 2x$ and also the centroid of the volume obtained by revolving this area about the x axis.

136 Show that the moment of inertia of an equilateral triangular lamina of side $2a$ about an altitude is $ma^2/6$, where m is the mass of the lamina.

7.10 Numerical evaluation of integrals

In many practical problems the functions that have to be integrated are often specified by a graph or by a table of values. Even when the function is given analytically, it often cannot be integrated to give an answer in terms of simple functions. Also, in many engineering and scientific problems it is often known in advance that the value of an integral is only required to a certain precision and the use of an approximate method can avoid considerable unwanted labour. In all these cases we have to evaluate the integrals numerically. There are many ways of doing this, varying from the simplest square-counting for working out the area under a graph to sophisticated computer procedures. In this section we shall develop a simple numerical method known as the trapezium rule, which is the basis of many computer algorithms, and a hand computation method known as Simpson's rule.

7.10.1 The trapezium rule

The simplest methods return to the initial ideas about integration introduced in Section 7.7.1. As indicated in Figure 7.71, they involve slicing up the area to be found into a number of strips of equal width, approximating the area of each strip in some way; the sum of these approximations then gives the final numerical result.

The points of subdivision of the domain of integration $[a, b]$ are labelled $x_0, x_1, \dots, x_n$, where $x_0 = a$, $x_n = b$, $x_r = x_0 + rh$ $(r = 0, 1, 2, \dots, n)$, and the width of each strip is $h = (b - a)/n$. The value of the integrand $f(x)$ at these points is, as usual, denoted by $f_r = f(x_r)$. A basic method for numerical integration approximates the area of each strip by the area of the trapezium formed when the upper end is replaced by the chord of the graph, as shown in Figure 7.72.

By the sum rule of integration

$$\int_a^b f(x)\mathrm{d}x = \int_{x_0}^{x_1} f(x)\mathrm{d}x + \int_{x_1}^{x_2} f(x)\mathrm{d}x + \dots + \int_{x_{n-1}}^{x_n} f(x)\mathrm{d}x = \sum_{r=0}^{n-1}\int_{x_r}^{x_{r+1}} f(x)\mathrm{d}x$$

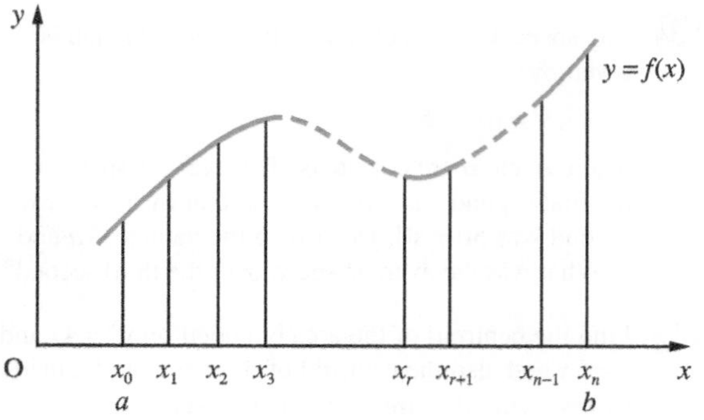

Figure 7.71 Slicing up an area into vertical strips of equal width.

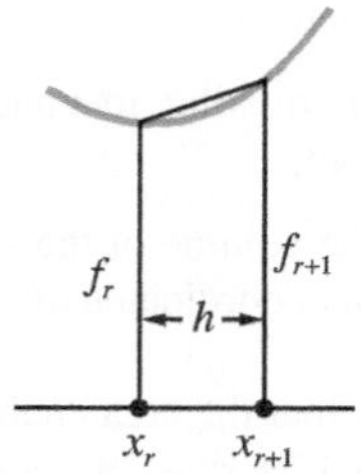

Figure 7.72 Trapezium approximation to area of strip.

From Figure 7.72 we can see that the approximate area of the rth strip is

$$\tfrac{1}{2}(f_r + f_{r+1})h$$

so that

$$\int_a^b f(x)\mathrm{d}x \approx \sum_{r=0}^{n-1} \tfrac{1}{2}(f_r + f_{r+1})h = \tfrac{1}{2}h\sum_{r=0}^{n-1}(f_r + f_{r+1})$$

$$= \tfrac{1}{2}h[(f_0 + f_1) + (f_1 + f_2) + \ldots + (f_{n-1} + f_n)]$$

That is,

$$\int_a^b f(x)\mathrm{d}x \approx h(\tfrac{1}{2}f_0 + f_1 + f_2 + \ldots + f_{n-1} + \tfrac{1}{2}f_n) \qquad \textbf{(7.47)}$$

This approximation method is called the **trapezium rule**. As we shall see below, the best method for using it is given in formula (7.48).

Example 7.69 Evaluate the integral $\int_1^2 (1/x)\mathrm{d}x$ to 5dp, using the trapezium rule.

Solution This integral is one of the standard integrals given in Figure 7.55, and so can be evaluated analytically. Its value is $\ln 2 = 0.693\,147$ to 6dp. This enables us, in this illustrative example, to check our methods. Usually, of course, the value of the integral is not known beforehand, and assessing the accuracy of the estimate obtained using the trapezium rule is an important aspect of the evaluation.

The first decision to be made in the numerical procedure is that of how many strips should be used; that is, what value n should have. A large number of strips may yield a good approximation to each strip, but will involve a lot of calculation, with the possibility of consequent rounding error accumulation. A small number of strips will obviously involve a large error in the approximation to the area of each strip. We shall investigate the situation.

First of all, we shall introduce the notation $T(h)$ to denote the approximation to the value of the integral given by the trapezium rule using strips of width h. Obviously, ignoring the possible effects of rounding errors, we expect

$$\lim_{h\to 0} T(h) = \int_1^2 \frac{1}{x}\,dx$$

Taking $n = 1$ gives $h = (2 - 1)/n = 1$, $x_0 = 1$ and $x_1 = 2$. This gives the estimate

$$\int_1^2 \frac{1}{x}\,dx = \tfrac{1}{2}(1)(f_0 + f_1) = T(1)$$

Here $f_0 = 1$ and $f_1 = 0.5$, so that $T(1) = 0.75$. This estimate for the value of the integral has an error of $0.75 - 0.693 = +0.057$.

Taking $n = 2$ gives $h = 0.5$, $x_0 = 1$, $x_2 = 2$ and $x_1 = 1.5$. Note that x_0 and x_2 are the two points used before, but now relabelled. This gives the estimate

$$T(0.5) = (0.5)[f_1 + \tfrac{1}{2}(f_0 + f_2)]$$

where $f_0 = 1$, $f_1 = 0.666\,667$ and $f_2 = 0.5$, so that $T(0.5) = 0.708\,333$. This estimate has an error of $+0.015$, so by doubling the number of strips, we have reduced the error by a factor of nearly four.

Taking $n = 4$ gives $h = 0.25$, $x_0 = 1$, $x_4 = 2$, $x_1 = 1.25$, $x_2 = 1.5$ and $x_3 = 1.75$. Note that three of these points were used in the previous calculation. This value of n gives the estimate

$$T(0.25) = (0.25)[f_1 + f_2 + f_3 + \tfrac{1}{2}(f_0 + f_4)]$$

where $f_0 = 1$, $f_1 = 0.8$, $f_2 = 0.666\,667$, $f_3 = 0.571\,429$ and $f_4 = 0.5$, so that $T(0.25) = 0.697\,024$. This estimate has an error of $+0.004$, so by doubling the number of strips, we have again reduced the error by a factor of four.

Continuing this process, with $n = 8$, we obtain the estimate $T(0.125) = 0.694\,122$, with an error of $+0.001$.

Based on these four calculations, we can estimate the values of n and h that will give an answer correct to 5dp; that is, with an absolute error less than 0.000 005. If we continue the process of doubling the number of strips, reducing the error by a factor of four each time, we shall obtain an answer with the required accuracy when $n = 128$. With this large number of strips, we clearly need to organize the calculation to do it as economically as possible. Looking back at the previous calculations, we see that at each new value of n we almost double the number of points at which the integrand has to be evaluated, but as can be seen from Figure 7.73, at half of these points it has been evaluated in previous calculations.

Taking into account the effect of interval-halving on h, we can reduce the amount of calculation to evaluate $T(h)$ by making use of the result obtained for $T(2h)$:

$$T(h) = h[f_1 + f_2 + f_3 + \ldots + f_{n-1} + \tfrac{1}{2}(f_0 + f_n)], \quad h = \frac{b-a}{n}$$

$$T(2h) = (2h)[f_2 + f_4 + \ldots + f_{n-2} + \tfrac{1}{2}(f_0 + f_n)]$$

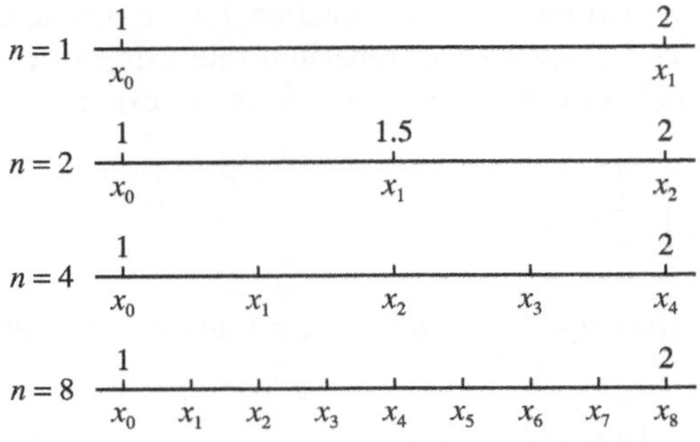

Figure 7.73 Points at which integrand is evaluated.

Here f_0, f_2, f_4, …, f_n were all calculated previously, in the evaluation of $T(2h)$. Rearranging, we have

$$T(h) = h(f_1 + f_3 + f_5 + \ldots + f_{n-1}) + \tfrac{1}{2}(2h)[f_2 + f_4 + \ldots + f_{n-2} + \tfrac{1}{2}(f_0 + f_n)]$$

Thus

$$T(h) = h(f_1 + f_3 + f_5 + \ldots + f_{n-1}) + \tfrac{1}{2}T(2h) \qquad \textbf{(7.48)}$$

(remembering that if h is the strip width for n intervals then $2h$ is the strip width for $\frac{1}{2}n$ intervals).

This formula enables us to perform the calculations economically, but we can exploit it in a more subtle way.

We have seen that halving the strip width reduces the error by a factor of approximately four. This means that the error is proportional to h^2. In fact, this behaviour is typical of the application of the trapezium rule to the evaluation of many kinds of integrals, and we can use it to obtain a more accurate estimate of the value of the integral. Since the error is proportional to h^2, we can write

$$T(h) - \int_1^2 \frac{1}{x}\,\mathrm{d}x = Ah^2$$

where $h = 1/n$ and A is some number that, in general, will depend upon n but will remain bounded as n becomes large. A similar formula holds for $T(2h)$:

$$T(2h) - \int_1^2 \frac{1}{x}\,\mathrm{d}x = 4A'h^2$$

where h has the same value as before and $A' \approx A$. These two formulae enable us to estimate the error in the approximation for the integral. Subtracting them gives

$$3Ah^2 \approx T(2h) - T(h)$$

so that the approximation $T(h)$ to the integral has an error estimate of $\frac{1}{3}[T(2h) - T(h)]$. Thus in the calculation above the estimated error for $T(0.125)$ is

$$\tfrac{1}{3}(0.697\,024 - 0.694\,122) = +0.000\,967$$

as we found before. This means that we can estimate the error in the usual situation of not knowing (unlike in this example) the true value of the integral. It also enables us to obtain a better approximation. Subtracting the estimated error from $T(h)$ gives the improved approximation (Richardson's extrapolation)

$$\int_1^2 \frac{1}{x}\,\mathrm{d}x \approx T(h) - \tfrac{1}{3}[T(2h) - T(h)]$$

Alternatively we may write

$$\int_1^2 \frac{1}{x}\,\mathrm{d}x \approx \tfrac{1}{3}[4T(h) - T(2h)]$$

Using the values for $T(0.25)$ and $T(0.125)$ obtained above, we have

$$\int_1^2 \frac{1}{x}\,\mathrm{d}x \approx 0.694\,122 - 0.000\,967 = 0.69315$$

which is correct to 5dp. In general, of course, we could not know how good an approximation this extrapolated value is, and the usual practice is to continue interval-halving until two successive extrapolated values agree to the accuracy required. Not all integrals will converge as quickly as in this example. For example, $\int_0^1 \sqrt{x}\,\mathrm{d}x$ requires a large number of evaluations to achieve reasonable accuracy. The reason for the slow convergence of the approximation to $\int_0^1 \sqrt{x}\,\mathrm{d}x$ compared with that of $\int_1^2 (1/x)\mathrm{d}x$ is readily seen from Figure 7.74.

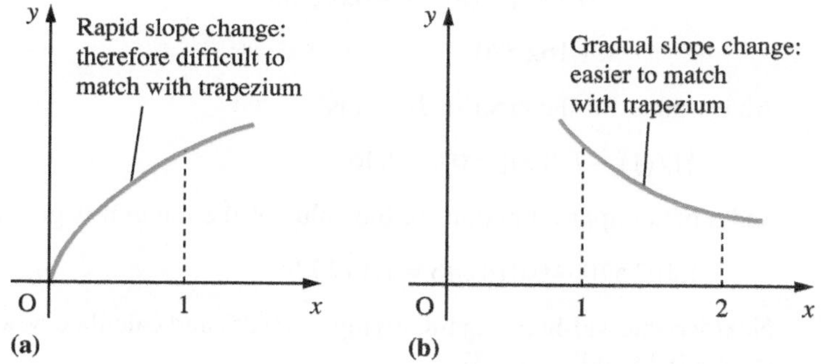

Figure 7.74
(a) Graph of $y = \sqrt{x}$.
(b) Graph of $y = 1/x$.

The trapezium rule as given in (7.47) is implemented in MATLAB using the commands

```
a = lower limit; b = upper limit; n = number of strips;
h = (b - a)/n; x = (a:h:b)'
```

(which outputs the x_i values as a column array)

```
y = f(x)
```

(which outputs the corresponding values of y as a column array)

```
h*trapz(y)
```

Considering the integral in Example 7.69 and taking 8 strips then the commands

```
a = 1; b = 2; n = 8; h = (b - a)/n; x = (a:h:b)';
y = 1./x;
```

(Note use of `./` as we are dealing with arrays.)

```
h*trapz(y)
```

return the answer `0.6941` to 4dp, which checks with the value of $T(0.125)$ in the given solution.

The corresponding commands in MAPLE are:

```
with(student):
y:= f(x): trapezoid(y, x = a..b, n): evalf (%);
```

Example 7.70 Evaluate the integral $\int_0^1 \sqrt{(1 + x^2)}\,dx$ to 5dp, using the trapezium rule and extrapolation.

Solution As before, we begin with just one strip, so that $h = 1$ and $T(1) = \frac{1}{2}(f_0 + f_1)$, where $f_0 = f(x_0) = f(0) = 1.000\,000$ and $f_1 = f(x_1) = f(1) = 1.414\,214$. Thus $T(1) = 1.207\,107$. Next we set $h = \frac{1}{2}$, and we calculate one new value of the integrand at $x = \frac{1}{2}$, giving a new $f_1 = \frac{1}{2}\sqrt{5} = 1.118\,034$ and

$$\begin{aligned} T(0.5) &= hf_1 + \tfrac{1}{2}T(1) \\ &= 0.5 \times 1.118\,034 + 0.603\,554 \\ &= 1.162\,570 \end{aligned}$$

An estimate for the error in $T(0.5)$ is

$$\tfrac{1}{3}[T(1) - T(0.5)] = 0.014\,846$$

and a better approximation for the value of the integral is given by

$$1.162\,570 - 0.014\,846 = 1.147\,724$$

Next we interval-halve again, giving $h = 0.25$, and calculate new values of the integrand (at $x = 0.25$ and $x = 0.75$):

$$f_1 = f(0.25) = 1.030\,776 \quad \text{and} \quad f_3 = f(0.75) = 1.25$$

Thus

$$T(0.25) = h(f_1 + f_3) + \tfrac{1}{2}T(0.5) = 1.151\,479$$

with an error estimate of $\frac{1}{3}[T(0.5) - T(0.25)] = 0.003\,697$ and an extrapolated value

$$1.151\,479 - 0.003\,697 = 1.147\,782$$

At this stage we can see that the value of the integral is 1.148 to 3dp. We continue interval-halving, giving: for $h = 0.125$, $T(0.125) = 1.148\,714$, with an error estimate of 0.000 922 and an extrapolated value 1.147 793; and for $h = 0.0625$, $T(0.0625) = 1.148\,714$, with an error estimate of 0.000 230 and an extrapolated value 1.147 793. Thus the extrapolated values agree to 6dp, so that we can write

$$\int_0^1 \sqrt{(1 + x^2)}\,dx = 1.147\,79$$

with confidence that the value is correct to the number of decimal places given.

7.10.2 Simpson's rule

The interval-halving algorithm developed in Section 7.10.1 is the appropriate algorithm to use for automatic computation. It is easy to program and is computationally efficient when used with extrapolation. It is, however, cumbersome for hand computation. For pencil and paper calculations a method that has been commonly used is equivalent to the extrapolated result obtained in Section 7.10.1 but does not give any estimate of error or permit easy interval-halving to check the accuracy of the result.

The trapezium rule approximation to $\int_a^b f(x)\mathrm{d}x$ using one strip is

$$T_1 = \tfrac{1}{2}(b - a)[f(a) + f(b)]$$

and that using two strips is

$$T_2 = \frac{b-a}{4}\left[f(a) + 2f\left(\frac{a+b}{2}\right) + f(b)\right]$$

The extrapolation based on these two estimates is

$$\begin{aligned} S &= [4T_2 - T_1]/3 \\ &= \frac{(b-a)}{6}\left[f(a) + 4f\left(\frac{a+b}{2}\right) + f(b)\right] \end{aligned}$$

The formula provides the basic approximation for the area under the curve between $x = a$ and $x = b$. It can be shown to be the area under the parabola which passes through the three points $(a, f(a))$, $((a + b)/2, f((a + b)/2))$ and $(b, f(b))$.

Now consider the interval $[a, b]$ divided into n equal strips of width h where n is an even number. Then we may write

$$\int_a^b f(x)\mathrm{d}x = \int_{x_0}^{x_2} f(x)\mathrm{d}x + \int_{x_2}^{x_4} f(x)\mathrm{d}x + \int_{x_4}^{x_6} f(x)\mathrm{d}x + \ldots + \int_{x_{n-2}}^{x_n} f(x)\mathrm{d}x$$

where $x_k = a + kh$.

Applying the basic formula to each of the integrals on the right-hand side yields the approximation

$$\int_a^b f(x)\mathrm{d}x \approx \frac{h}{3}[f_0 + 4f_1 + f_2] + \frac{h}{3}[f_2 + 4f_3 + f_4] + \frac{h}{3}[f_4 + 4f_5 + f_6] + \ldots + \frac{h}{3}[f_{n-2} + 4f_{n-1} + f_n]$$

$$\int_a^b f(x)\mathrm{d}x \approx \frac{h}{3}[f_0 + 4f_1 + 2f_2 + 4f_3 + 2f_4 + \ldots + 2f_{n-2} + 4f_{n-1} + f_n] \qquad \textbf{(7.49)}$$

or in words

> The integral is approximately one-third the step size times the sum of four times the odd ordinates plus twice the even ordinates plus first and last ordinates.

This is referred to as **Simpson's rule** and a pencil and paper calculation would be set out as shown in Example 7.71.

There is no command in MATLAB for implementing Simpson's rule (7.49), in which the number of strips is specified. Instead the package incorporates the command `quad(f,a,b)`, which tries to approximate the integral of the scalar-valued function `f = f(x)` from a to b to within an error of $1.e^{-6}$ using recursive adaptive Simpson quadrature. There is no need to specify the number of strips and the method is somewhat hidden from the user. It is an efficient approach to evaluate an integral numerically but is of limited value as a learning tool. When using the `quad` command the function $f(x)$ must be expressed as an `inline` function with the array operations `.*`, `./` and `.^` used in its specification, so that it can be evaluated with a vector argument. As an illustration we consider the integral of Example 7.69, for which the commands

```
f = inline('(1 + x.^2).^(1/2)'); quad(f, 0,1)
```

return the answer `1.1478`.

In MAPLE, Simpson's rule (7.49) is evaluated by the commands

```
with(student):
f:= x->f(x); simpson(f(x),x = a..b,n); evalf(%);
```

For the integral of Example (7.69) the commands

```
with(student):
f:= 1/x; simpson(f,x = 1..2,8); evalf(%);
```

return the answer `.6931545307`.

MAPLE also has the facility to produce a sequence of answers corresponding to an array of values for the number of strips; for example the commands

```
nn = [4,8,12];
seq(evalf(simpson(1/x,x = 1..2,n)),n = nn);
```

return the sequence of answers

```
.6932539681, .6931545307, .6931486622
```

This facility provides a valuable learning tool; it is also available for the trapezium rule using the command

```
seq(evalf(trapezoidal(1/x,x = 1..2,n)), n = nn);
```

Example 7.71 Figure 7.75 shows a longitudinal section PQ of rough ground through which a straight horizontal road is to be cut. The width of the road is to be 10 m, and the sides of the cutting and embankment slope at 2 horizontal to 1 vertical. Estimate the net volume of earth removed in making the road.

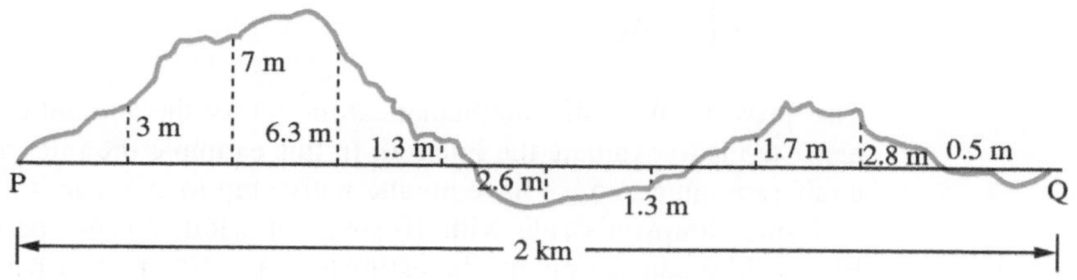

Figure 7.75 Cross-section with distances above or below datum at 200 m intervals (not to scale).

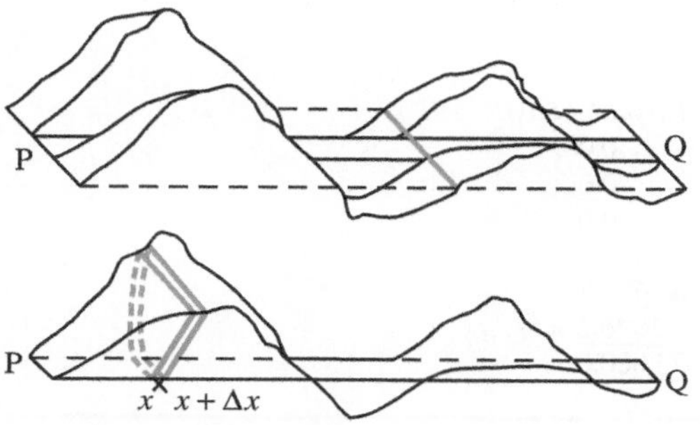

Figure 7.76 Volume of soil to be removed in road construction.

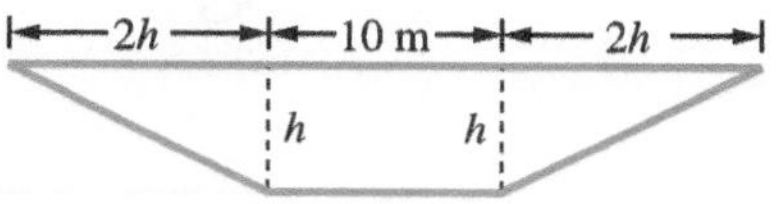

Figure 7.77 Cross-section of cutting with sides sloping at 1 in 2.

Solution In this case we are not dealing with a solid of revolution, and so cannot use (7.36) to find the volume. Instead, we slice the volume up, estimate the volume of each slice and then add all the individual volumes together, as illustrated in Section 7.7.1. The volume above the datum PQ is counted as positive and that below the datum as negative, so that infill on site is accounted for automatically.

Consider the 'slice' between the points at distances x and $x + \Delta x$ from P, as shown in Figure 7.76. The volume of this slice is $\bar{A}\Delta x$ where $\bar{A}$ is the average cross-sectional area between x and $x + \Delta x$. The cross-sectional area A depends on the height h of the soil above the datum line PQ. This relationship is given by

$$A = (2h + 10)h$$

as shown in Figure 7.77.

The height h depends on the distance x along the road, so that we can construct a table of values for A as a function of x, as shown in Figure 7.78.

Figure 7.78 Cross-sectional area versus distance.

x	0	200	400	600	800	1000	1200	1400	1600	1800	2000
h	0.0	3.0	7.0	6.3	1.3	−2.6	−1.3	1.7	2.8	−0.5	0.0
A	0.0	48.0	168.0	142.4	16.4	−39.5	−16.4	22.8	43.7	−5.5	0.0

The total volume V of soil removed from the site is the sum of the volumes of the individual slices:

$$V = \sum A(\bar{x})\Delta x$$

where $A(\bar{x})$ is given by

$$A(\bar{x}) = \bar{A} \quad (x \leqslant \bar{x} \leqslant x + \Delta x)$$

Letting the number of slices tend to infinity while making their thicknesses all tend to zero gives V in the form of an integral:

$$V = \int_0^{2000} A(x)\,\mathrm{d}x$$

This provides us with a mathematical model for the amount of soil to be removed: the next step is to evaluate the integral. In this example the integrand is known only from a table of values, so we have no alternative but to evaluate it numerically.

Using Simpson's rule with 10 strips of width 200 m, the calculation is shown in Figure 7.79 and we obtain the estimate $7.3 \times 10^4\,\mathrm{m}^3$. If a better estimate is required, more data will have to be collected.

Figure 7.79
Simpson's rule 'paper and pencil' calculation.

Odds	*Evens*	*First and Last*
48.0	168.0	0.0
142.4	16.4	0.0
−39.5	−16.4	0.0
22.8	43.7	423.4
−5.5	211.7 × 2	672.8
168.2 × 4		$1096.2 \times \frac{200}{3}$
		73 080.0

7.10.3 Exercises

Check your answers using MATLAB or MAPLE.

137 Use the trapezium rule to evaluate $\int_0^{0.8} \mathrm{e}^{-x^2}\mathrm{d}x$. Take the step size h equal to 0.8, 0.4, 0.2, 0.1 in turn and use extrapolation to improve the accuracy of your answer.

138 Use the trapezium rule, with interval-halving and extrapolation, to evaluate

$$\int_0^1 \log(\cosh x)\mathrm{d}x \quad \text{to 4dp}$$

139 An ellipse has parametric equations $x = \cos t$, $y = \frac{1}{2}\sqrt{3}\sin t$. Show that the length of its circumference is given by

$$2\int_0^{\pi/2} \sqrt{(3 + \sin^2 t)}\,\mathrm{d}t$$

This integral cannot be evaluated in terms of elementary functions. Use the trapezium rule with interval-halving to evaluate it to 6dp.

140 The capacity of a battery is measured by $\int i\,\mathrm{d}t$, where i is the current. Estimate, using Simpson's rule, the capacity of a battery whose current was measured over an 8 h period with the results shown below:

Time/h	0	1	2	3	4	5	6	7	8
Current/A	25.2	29.0	31.8	36.5	33.7	31.2	29.6	27.3	28.6

141 The speed $V(t)\,\mathrm{m\,s^{-1}}$ of a vehicle at time t s is given by the table below. Use Simpson's rule to estimate the distance travelled over the eight seconds.

t	0	1	2	3	4	5	6	7	8
$V(t)$	0	0.63	2.52	5.41	9.02	13.11	16.72	18.75	20.15

142 Use Simpson's rule with $h = 0.1$ to estimate

$$\int_0^1 \sqrt{(1 + x^3)}\,\mathrm{d}x$$

(Notice that by this method you have no way of knowing how accurate your estimate is.)

7.11 Engineering application: design of prismatic channels

The mean velocity V of flow in straight prismatic channels is proportional to $(A/p)^r$, where A is the cross-sectional area of the flow, p is the wetted perimeter and r is approximately a constant ($\frac{7}{12}$). Given the channel section for minimum flows (that is, A_0 and p_0), the objective is to design a channel such that V has the same value for all larger discharges.

Assume a symmetric channel cross-section as shown in Figure 7.80, where A_0 and p_0 are the minimum flow values of A and p. Let the shape of the channel be given by $x = f(y)$. (Note that in this application y, the height of the surface above the datum line, is the independent variable.) Then we want to find the function $f(y)$ such that the mean flow velocity is independent of y. This implies because it is proportional to $(A/p)^r$ that

Figure 7.80
Channel cross-section.

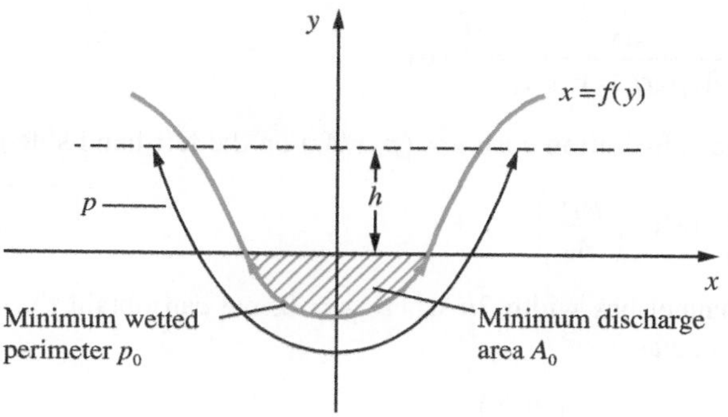

$$\frac{A}{p} = \frac{A_0}{p_0}$$

The area A is given by the integral of $f(y)$. Thus

$$A = A_0 + 2\int_0^h x\,\mathrm{d}y$$

where $x = f(y)$ and $h > 0$.

Using (7.45), the wetted perimeter p is given by

$$p = p_0 + 2\int_0^h \sqrt{\left[1 + \left(\frac{\mathrm{d}x}{\mathrm{d}y}\right)^2\right]}\mathrm{d}y \quad (h > 0)$$

Since $A/A_0 = p/p_0$, we deduce that

$$1 + \frac{2}{A_0}\int_0^h x\,\mathrm{d}y = 1 + \frac{2}{p_0}\int_0^h \sqrt{\left[1 + \left(\frac{\mathrm{d}x}{\mathrm{d}y}\right)^2\right]}\mathrm{d}y$$

Rearranging the integrals under a common integral sign gives

$$\int_0^h \left\{\frac{x}{A_0} - \frac{1}{p_0}\sqrt{\left[1 + \left(\frac{\mathrm{d}x}{\mathrm{d}y}\right)^2\right]}\right\}\mathrm{d}y = 0 \quad (h > 0)$$

Since this is true for all $h > 0$, it implies that the integrand must be identically zero. Thus $x = f(y)$ satisfies the differential equation

$$\frac{x}{A_0} = \frac{1}{p_0}\sqrt{\left[1 + \left(\frac{dx}{dy}\right)^2\right]}$$

which, assuming $\frac{dx}{dy} \geqslant 0$, implies

$$\frac{dx}{dy} = \sqrt{\left[\left(\frac{p_0 x}{A_0}\right)^2 - 1\right]} \tag{7.50}$$

Integrating with respect to y then gives

$$\int \frac{dx}{\sqrt{[(p_0 x/A_0)^2 - 1]}} = \int 1\,dy$$

Using the substitution $\cosh u = (p_0 x/A_0)$ on the left-hand side gives

$$\frac{A_0}{p_0}\cosh^{-1}\left(\frac{p_0 x}{A_0}\right) = y + c$$

If the channel has width $2b$ where $y = 0$, we can obtain the value of the constant of integration c as

$$c = \frac{A_0}{p_0}\cosh^{-1}\left(\frac{p_0 b}{A_0}\right)$$

and deduce the formula for a suitable channel shape as

$$y = \frac{A_0}{p_0}\left[\cosh^{-1}\left(\frac{p_0 x}{A_0}\right) - \cosh^{-1}\left(\frac{p_0 b}{A_0}\right)\right]$$

This solution, however, is not unique and we note that the differential equation (7.50) is also satisfied by

$$x = \frac{A_0}{p_0}$$

As an exercise, use this information to show that the general solution may take the form of either of the cross-sections shown in Figures 7.81(a) and (b). Notice that the line shape in Figure 7.81(b) does not have $\frac{dx}{dy} \geqslant 0$.

Figure 7.81

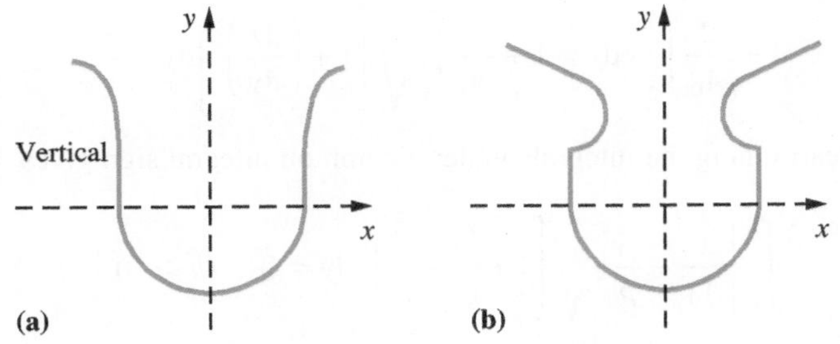

7.12 Engineering application: harmonic analysis of periodic functions

Periodic functions occur frequently in practical problems and in natural phenomena like tidal systems. Rotating parts of machinery produce vibrations, which may become dangerous when resonance occurs. Indeed such a resonance led to the failure of the Tacoma Road bridge (see Section 10.10.3). Periodic motions usually involve several frequencies of vibrations at the same time and the method of finding the amplitude of each frequency is called **harmonic analysis**.

Consider, for example, the crank and connecting rod mechanism discussed in Example 2.44. The displacement function of the slider is

$$y = r\cos x + \sqrt{(l^2 - r^2\sin^2 x)}$$

where r is the radius of the crank, l the length of the connecting rod and x (radians) is the angle turned through. The motion is periodic but is not a simple sinusoid. It involves many harmonics and we may write

$$y = a_0 + a_1\cos x + a_2\cos 2x + a_3\cos 3x + \dots$$

where the a's are constants and we choose a cosine series since y is an even function $y(-x) = y(x)$. To simplify the problem, we take a special case with $r = 1$ and $l = 3$. Then

$$y = \cos x + \sqrt{(8 + \cos^2 x)}$$

A graph of y is shown in Figure 7.82.

The displacement y has period 2π and its mean value $\bar{y}$ is given by

$$\bar{y} = \frac{1}{2\pi}\int_0^{2\pi} [\cos x + \sqrt{(8 + \cos^2 x)}]\,dx$$

The contribution of $\cos x$ to the value of the integral over a complete period is zero, so this simplifies to

$$\bar{y} = \frac{1}{2\pi}\int_0^{2\pi} \sqrt{(8 + \cos^2 x)}\,dx$$

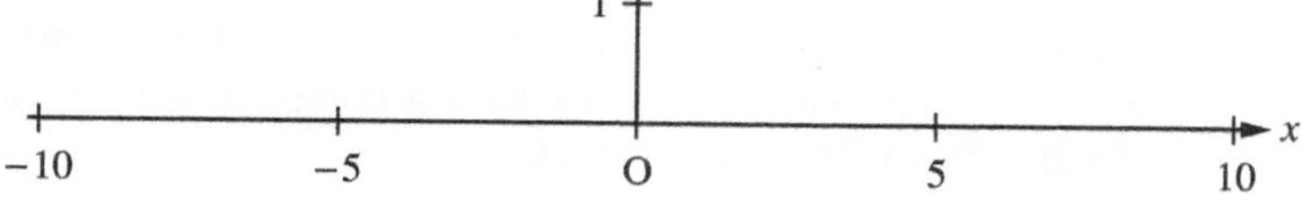

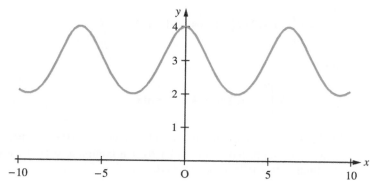

Figure 7.82 Graph of $y = \cos x + \sqrt{(8 + \cos^2 x)}$

This integral cannot be evaluated analytically. Using the trapezium rule with step sizes $\pi/2$, $\pi/4$ and $\pi/8$, together with Richardson's extrapolation, we obtain

$$\bar{y} = 2.9148$$

We now seek an approximation to $y(x)$ having the form

$$y(x) \simeq \bar{y} + \cos x + a \cos 2x$$

such that the integral of the squared error over a complete period is as small as possible. That is, a is chosen so that

$$\frac{\mathrm{d}}{\mathrm{d}a}\left\{\int_{-\pi}^{\pi} [\bar{y} + \cos x + a\cos 2x - y(x)]^2 \mathrm{d}x\right\} = 0$$

Expanding the integrand this gives

$$\frac{\mathrm{d}}{\mathrm{d}a}\left\{\int_{-\pi}^{\pi} [\bar{y}^2 + a^2\cos^2 2x + 8 + \cos^2 x + 2\bar{y}a\cos 2x\right.$$

$$\left. - 2\bar{y}\sqrt{(8 + \cos^2 x)} - 2a\cos 2x\sqrt{(8 + \cos^2 x)}]\mathrm{d}x\right\} = 0$$

This tidies up to

$$\frac{\mathrm{d}}{\mathrm{d}a}\left\{\int_{-\pi}^{\pi} [\bar{y}^2 + 8 + \cos^2 x - 2\bar{y}\sqrt{(8 + \cos^2 x)}]\mathrm{d}x + 2a\bar{y}\int_{-\pi}^{\pi} \cos 2x\,\mathrm{d}x\right.$$

$$\left. - 2a\int_{-\pi}^{\pi} \cos 2x\sqrt{(8 + \cos^2 x)}\,\mathrm{d}x + a^2\int_{-\pi}^{\pi} \cos^2 2x\,\mathrm{d}x\right\} = 0$$

The first integral inside the curly brackets is independent of a, and so differentiates to zero. The second integral is zero in value and the last integral has value π. Thus differentiating with respect to a gives

$$-2\int_{-\pi}^{\pi} \cos 2x\sqrt{(8 + \cos^2 x)}\,\mathrm{d}x + 2a\pi = 0$$

Hence

$$a = \frac{1}{\pi}\int_{-\pi}^{\pi} \cos 2x\sqrt{(8 + \cos^2 x)}\,\mathrm{d}x$$

Evaluating this integral numerically gives $a = 0.0858$. Investigating the difference between the approximation and y over a complete period shows that the size of the maximum error is less than 0.0007.

7.13 Review exercises (1–39)

Check your answers using MATLAB or MAPLE whenever possible.

1 Differentiate the following expressions, giving your answers as simply as possible:

(a) e^{x^2+x} (b) $\dfrac{x^3}{(3-x)^2}$

(c) $\sin(5x-1)$ (d) $(\tan x)^x$

(e) $\cos^{-1}\sqrt{(1-x^2)}$ (f) $\dfrac{1}{\sqrt{(x+1)}}$

(g) $\sin^{-1}\dfrac{1}{\sqrt{(1+x^2)}}$ (h) $\dfrac{1}{(x-1)(x+2)}$

(i) $\sin(3x+1)$ (j) $x^3 \ln x$

(k) $\dfrac{x^3}{(3-x^2)}$ (l) $\tan^{-1}(e^{-2x})$

(m) $\sqrt{(1+\cosh x)}$ (n) $(x^2+1)\sin 2x$

(o) $\dfrac{x-1}{(x+2)^2}$ (p) $e^{\sqrt{x}}$

(q) $\ln \tan x$ (r) $\dfrac{(2x-1)^{3/2}}{(x+1)^5}$

(s) $x \sin x$ (t) e^{x^2}

(u) 2^x (v) $\dfrac{\cos x}{1+\sin x}$

(w) $\sin^{-1}\left(\dfrac{1}{x}\right)$ (x) $x^3 \cos 2x$

(y) $\sqrt{(x^3+x+3)}$ (z) $\dfrac{e^{-x}}{1+x}$

2 Evaluate

(a) $\displaystyle\int x^{1/2}\ln x\,dx$ (b) $\displaystyle\int \frac{(2x+3)\,dx}{x^2+2x+2}$

(c) $\displaystyle\int_0^3 \frac{1}{x}\lfloor x\rfloor\,dx$ (d) $\displaystyle\int_{1/2}^1 \frac{x\sin^{-1}x\,dx}{\sqrt{(1-x^2)}}$ (set $x = \sin t$)

(e) $\displaystyle\int \frac{x\,dx}{(x-1)(x-2)}$ (f) $\displaystyle\int \tan^4 x\,dx$

(g) $\displaystyle\int_0^1 \sqrt{(4-3x^2)}\,dx$ (h) $\displaystyle\int \frac{dx}{\sqrt{(4-9x^2)}}$

(i) $\displaystyle\int \frac{x^2\,dx}{\sqrt{(x^3-1)}}$ (j) $\displaystyle\int \frac{(x^2+1)\,dx}{x+1}$

(k) $\displaystyle\int \frac{dx}{x^2+6x+13}$ (l) $\displaystyle\int \sqrt{x}\sin\sqrt{x}\,dx$

(m) $\displaystyle\int_0^2 \text{FRACPT}(x)\,dx$ (n) $\displaystyle\int_0^1 \sinh^2 x\,dx$

(o) $\displaystyle\int (1-3x)^9\,dx$ (p) $\displaystyle\int \sin 3x \sin 2x\,dx$

(q) $\displaystyle\int \ln 2x\,dx$ (r) $\displaystyle\int x e^{-x^2/2}\,dx$

(s) $\displaystyle\int \frac{dx}{\sqrt{(4x^2-9)}}$ (t) $\displaystyle\int_{-1}^4 \frac{(3x-1)\,dx}{\sqrt{(4+3x-x^2)}}$

(u) $\displaystyle\int_0^1 \frac{x\,dx}{(x+1)(x^2+1)}$ (v) $\displaystyle\int (4-3x)^4\,dx$

(w) $\displaystyle\int \cos 2x \cos 3x\,dx$ (x) $\displaystyle\int \sin^{-1}x\,dx$

(y) $\displaystyle\int x^2 e^{-x}\,dx$ (z) $\displaystyle\int \frac{dx}{1+x+x^2}$

3 Find the equation of the tangent and normal at the point (1, 4) to the curve whose equation is

$$y = 2x^4 - 3x^3 + 5x^2 + 3x - 3$$

4 Find the equation of the tangent to the curve $x^2 - 3xy + 2y^2 = 3$ at the point (1, 2) and the equation of the normal to the curve $y = x^3 - x^2$ at the point (1, 0). Find the distance of the point of intersection of these lines from the point (−1, 2).

5 With reference to Example 2.10, confirm that the function

$$E(x) = x^2(1-x), \qquad 0 \leqslant x \leqslant 1$$

has maximum value when $x = 2/3$.

6 Find the turning points on the curve

$$y = 2x^3 - 5x^2 + 4x - 1$$

and determine their nature. Find the point of inflection and sketch the graph of the curve.

7 The turning moment T on the crankshaft of an engine is given by

$$T = 6 + 2.5\sin 2\theta - 3.8\cos 2\theta$$

Find the maximum and minimum values of T for $0 \leqslant \theta \leqslant 2\pi$.

8 The deflection of a beam of length L is given by

$$y = wx^2\frac{(L-x)^2}{EI} \qquad (0 \leqslant x \leqslant L)$$

where w, E and I are constants. Determine

(a) the maximum deflection;

(b) the points along the beam at which points of inflection lie.

9 A running track is set out in the form of a rectangle, of length L and width W, with two semicircular areas, of radius $\frac{1}{2}W$, adjoined at each end of the rectangle. If the perimeter of the whole track is fixed at 400 m, determine the values of L and W that maximize the area of the rectangle.

10 Find the maximum and minimum values of y where

$$y = \frac{x^2}{(x-2)(x-6)}$$

justifying your answers. Sketch the curve, indicating the stationary points and any asymptotes.

11 Light sources are placed at two fixed points Q and R which are 1 metre apart. The source at R is twice as intense as that at Q. The total illumination at a point P on the line QR x metres distant from Q is $cf(x)$ where c is a positive constant and

$$f(x) = \frac{1}{x^2} + \frac{2}{(1-x)^2} \qquad 0 < x < 1$$

Evaluate $f(0.3)$, $f(0.4)$ and $f(0.5)$ and find the quadratic function

$$g(x) = A(x-0.4)^2 + B(x-0.4) + C$$

which passes through $(0.3, f(0.3))$, $(0.4, f(0.4))$ and $(0.5, f(0.5))$. Use this function to estimate the value of x at which the minimum of $f(x)$ occurs. Compare your result with that obtained by calculus methods.

12 Using partial fractions, show that

(a) $\displaystyle\int_2^4 \frac{2x+3}{x(x-1)(x+2)}\,dx = \frac{7}{2}\ln 3 - \frac{4}{3}\ln 2$

(b) $\displaystyle\int_1^2 \frac{6x^2\,dx}{(x+1)^2(2x-1)} = 3\ln 3 - \frac{8}{3}\ln 2 - \frac{1}{3}$

13 Working to 5dp, evaluate $\int_0^1(1+x^2)^{-1}dx$ using the trapezium rule with five ordinates. Evaluate the integral by direct integration and comment on the accuracy of the numerical method.

14 The parametric equations of a curve are

$$x = at^2, \quad y = 2at$$

If ρ is the radius of curvature and (h, k) is its centre of curvature, prove that

(a) $\dfrac{d^2y}{dx^2} = -\dfrac{1}{2at^3}$ (b) $\rho = 2a(1+t^2)^{3/2}$

(c) $h = a(2+3t^2)$, $k = -2at^3$

15 (a) Using the substitution $u = x + 1$, evaluate

$$\int_3^8 x\sqrt{(x+1)}\,dx$$

(b) Using the substitution $u = \sqrt{x} + 6$, evaluate

$$\int_0^1 \frac{dx}{2(x+6\sqrt{x})}$$

(c) The region R is bounded by the x axis, the line $x = \frac{9}{2}$ and the curve with parametric equations

$$x = a\cos t, \quad y = b\sin t \quad (0 \leqslant t \leqslant \tfrac{1}{3}\pi)$$

where a and b are positive coordinates. Let A, $\bar{x}$ and I_y denote respectively the area of R, the x coordinate of the centroid of R and the second moment of area of R about the y axis. Prove that

$$I_y = \tfrac{1}{4}a^2A + \tfrac{3}{8}a\bar{x}A$$

16 A curve has parametric equations

$$x = 2t + \sin 2t, \quad y = \cos 2t$$

Show that

$$\frac{dy}{dx} = -\tan t$$

Find d^2y/dx^2 and d^2x/dy^2 in terms of t, and demonstrate that

$$\frac{d^2y}{dx^2} \neq 1\bigg/\frac{d^2x}{dy^2}$$

17 Verify that the point (−1, 1) lies on the curve

$$y(y - 3x) = y^3 - 3x^3$$

and find the values of dy/dx and d^2y/dx^2 there. What is the radius of curvature at that point?

18 Sketch the curve whose equation is

$$y^2 = x(x - 1)^2$$

and find the area enclosed by the loop.

19 Sketch the curve whose parametric representation is

$$x = a\sin^3 t, \quad y = b\cos^3 t \quad (0 \leq t \leq 2\pi)$$

Find the area enclosed.

20 Sketch the curve whose polar equation is

$$r = 1 + \cos\theta$$

Show that the tangent to the curve at the point $r = \frac{3}{2}$, $\theta = \frac{1}{3}\pi$ is parallel to the line $\theta = 0$. Find the total area enclosed by the curve.

21 A curve is specified in polar coordinates (r, θ) in the form $r = f(\theta)$. Show that the sectorial area bounded by the line $\theta = \alpha$, $\theta = \beta$ and the curve $r = f(\theta)$ $(\alpha \leq \theta \leq \beta)$ is given by

$$\frac{1}{2}\int_{\alpha}^{\beta} [f(\theta)]^2 d\theta$$

Also show that the angle ϕ between the tangent to the curve at any point P and the polar line OP is given by

$$\cot\phi = \frac{1}{r}\frac{dr}{d\theta}$$

22 Find the length of the arc of the parabola $y = x^2$ that lies between (−1, 1) and (1, 1).

23 The parametric equations

$$x = t^2 - 1, \quad y = t^3 - t$$

describe a closed curve as t increases from −1 to 1. Sketch the curve and find the area enclosed.

24 (a) Find the area of the region bounded by the x axis and one arch of the cycloid

$$x = a(\theta - \sin\theta),$$
$$y = a(1 - \cos\theta) \quad (0 \leq \theta \leq 2\pi)$$

where a is a positive constant.

(b) Show that the radius of curvature of the cycloid defined in (a) at the point O is given by

$$\rho = 2\sqrt{2}a(1 - \cos\theta)^{1/2}$$

What is the maximum value of ρ?

(c) Discuss the nature of the radius of curvature when $\theta = 0$ or $\theta = 2\pi$.

(d) Determine the length of one arch of the cycloid.

25 Consider the integral

$$I_n = \int_0^{\pi/4} \tan^n x\, dx$$

where n is an integer. Using the trigonometric identity $1 + \tan^2 x = \sec^2 x$, show that

$$I_n + I_{n-2} = \int_0^{\pi/4} \tan^{n-2} x \sec^2 x\, dx$$

and hence obtain the recurrence relation

$$I_n = \frac{1}{n-1} - I_{n-2}$$

Use this to find

(a) $\int_0^{\pi/4} \tan^6 x\, dx$ (b) $\int_0^{\pi/4} \tan^7 x\, dx$

(Recurrence relations of this type are often called **reduction formulae**, since they provide a systematic way of reducing the value of the parameter n so that a difficult integral may be reduced to an easier one.)

26 Use integration by parts (writing the integrand as $\sin\theta \sin^{n-1}\theta$) to show that

$$I_n = \int_0^{\pi/2} \sin^n\theta\, d\theta$$

satisfies the reduction formula

$$nI_n = (n - 1)I_{n-2}$$

Hence prove that

$$I_{2k+1} = \frac{2k}{2k+1}\frac{2k-2}{2k-1}\cdots\frac{2}{3}$$

and

$$I_{2k} = \frac{2k-1}{2k}\frac{2k-3}{2k-2}\cdots\frac{1}{2}\frac{\pi}{2}$$

These results are known as **Wallis's formulae.**

Use them to show that

(a) $\displaystyle\int_0^{\pi/2} \sin^5 x\,\mathrm{d}x = \tfrac{8}{15}$ (b) $\displaystyle\int_0^{\pi/2} \cos^6 x\,\mathrm{d}x = \tfrac{5}{32}\pi$

27 Consider the integral

$$I_{m,n} = \int_0^{\pi/2} \cos^m x \sin^n x\,\mathrm{d}x$$

Show that $I_{m,n}$ satisfies the reduction formula

$$I_{m,n} = \frac{n-1}{m+n} I_{m,n-2}$$

28 Reduction formulae of the type discussed in Questions 24–26 are iteration formulae – and, like other iteration formulae, when they are used, attention must be paid to their numerical properties. This is illustrated by considering the integral

$$I_n = \int_0^1 x^n \mathrm{e}^{x-1}\,\mathrm{d}x$$

Prove that

$$I_n = 1 - nI_{n-1} \quad (n > 0)$$

with $I_0 = 1 - \mathrm{e}^{-1}$.

Evaluate I_0 on your calculator and use the reduction formula to calculate I_n, $n = 1, 2, \ldots, 10$.

Since

$$0 < x^{n+1}\mathrm{e}^{x-1} < x^n \mathrm{e}^{x-1} < x^n \quad (0 < x < 1)$$

we know that

$$0 < I_{n+1} < I_n < \frac{1}{n+1} \quad (n = 0, 1, 2, 3, \ldots)$$

Compare this with your results, and explain the discrepancy.

Since the iteration diverges when used for n increasing (that is, on setting $n = 1, 2, 3, \ldots$ in turn), it will converge when used for n decreasing (say $n = 50, 49, 48, \ldots$). Since $0 < I_{19} < \frac{1}{20}$, try using the iteration with $n = 19, 18, 17, \ldots$ to obtain I_{10}. Continue the iteration backwards to find, eventually, I_0.

29 The function $F(r)$ is defined by

$$F(r) = \int_0^{\pi/2} \sin^r x\,\mathrm{d}x \quad r > -1$$

By considering $\mathrm{d}(\cos x \sin^{r-1} x)/\mathrm{d}x$, or otherwise, show that

$$(r+1)\int \sin^r x\,\mathrm{d}x = \cos x \sin^{r+1} x + (r+2)\int \sin^{r+2} x\,\mathrm{d}x$$

and deduce that $(r+1)F(r) = (r+2)F(r+2)$.

Show that $F(-\frac{1}{2}) = \frac{21}{5}F(\frac{7}{2})$. Tabulate $f(x) = \sin^{7/2} x$ for $x = 0(\frac{1}{8}\pi)\frac{1}{2}\pi$ to 3dp and use the values to obtain three approximations to $F(3.5)$ using the trapezium rule with strips of width $\frac{1}{2}\pi$, $\frac{1}{4}\pi$ and $\frac{1}{8}\pi$ respectively. Hence obtain an approximation to $F(-0.5)$.

30 A solid of revolution is generated by rotating the area between the y axis, the line $y = 1$ and the parabola $y = x^2$ about the y axis. Find its volume and its surface area.

31 The numerical procedures developed in this chapter for evaluating integrals have all used strips of equal width. An alternative procedure is to specify the number of tabular points to be used but not their position. It is possible to find tabular points within the domain of integration for the most accurate evaluation of the integral for the given number of points. Consider the two-point formula

$$\int_{-h}^{h} f(x)\,\mathrm{d}x \approx h[af(\alpha h) + bf(\beta h)]$$

where a, b, α and β are constants to be found. Symmetry about $x = 0$ implies $\beta = -\alpha$. If the formula evaluates all quadratic functions exactly, prove that

$$2h = h(a+b)$$

$$0 = h(a\alpha h - b\alpha h)$$

$$\tfrac{2}{3}h^2 = h(a\alpha^2 h^2 + b\alpha^2 h^2)$$

Deduce that $a = b = 1$ and $\alpha = 1/\sqrt{3}$.

32 The symbols T_n and S_n are defined as the estimates of the integral

$$I = \int_0^1 (1+2x)^{-1}\,dx$$

using n intervals with the trapezium and Simpson's rules respectively. Calculate T_1, T_2, T_4, S_2 and S_4, working to 3dp only. Verify that your numerical results satisfy

$$S_{2n} = \tfrac{1}{3}(4T_{2n} - T_n)$$

for $n = 1$ and 2. Prove this result.

33 (a) A curve is represented parametrically by

$$x(t) = 3t - t^3, \quad y(t) = 3t^2 \quad (0 \leqslant t \leqslant 1)$$

Find the volume and the surface area of the solid of revolution generated when the curve is rotated about the x axis through 2π radians.

(b) Find the position of the centroid of the plane figure bounded by the curve $y = 5 \sin 2x$, $y = 0$ and $x = \frac{1}{6}\pi$.

34 When a homogeneous bar of constant cross-sectional area A (see Figure 7.83) is under uniformly distributed tensile stress, the elongation in the direction of the stress for a material obeying Hooke's law is given by

$$\text{stress} = E \times \text{strain}$$

where E is Young's modulus, the stress is the applied force per unit area and the strain is the ratio of the elongation to the unstretched length of the bar. That is,

$$E\frac{e}{L} = \frac{P}{A}$$

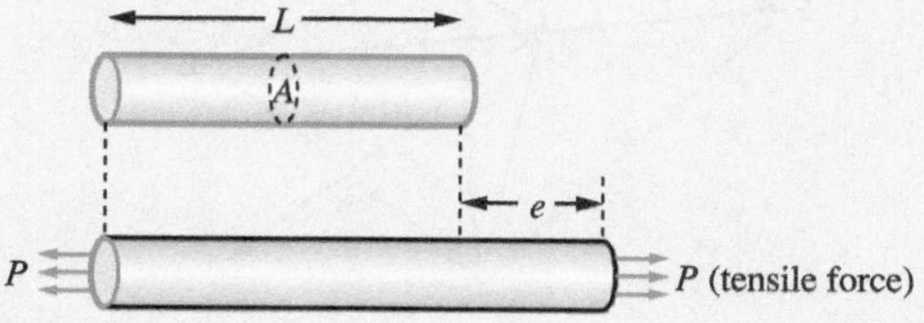

Figure 7.83

Consider a bar of circular cross-section whose diameter varies along its length as shown in Figure 7.84, so that

$$A = A_0 + kx^2, \quad k = \frac{A_1 - A_0}{L^2}$$

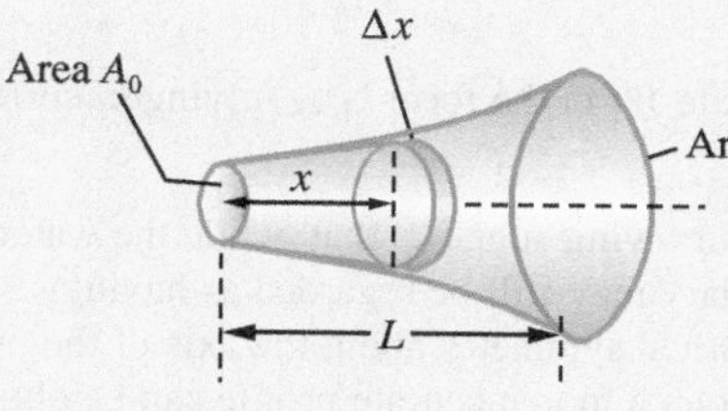

Figure 7.84

By considering the elongation of an element of thickness Δx of the bar, show that the total elongation of the bar under the tensile force P is

$$l = \int_0^L \frac{P\,dx}{E(A_0 + kx^2)}$$

Show that

$$l = \frac{4PL}{\pi d_0 d_2 E} \cos^{-1}\left(\frac{d_0}{d_1}\right)$$

where d_0 and d_1 are the end diameters of the bar, $d_0 < d_1$ and $d_2^2 = d_1^2 - d_0^2$.

35 Figure 7.85 shows an old cylindrical borehole that has been filled in part with silt and in part with water. Before the hole can be redrilled, the water has to be pumped to the surface. We wish to estimate the work required for this purpose.

(a) As a first approximation, assume that the silting has been uniform – as indicated in Figure 7.85 – and that the water thus forms a right-circular cone

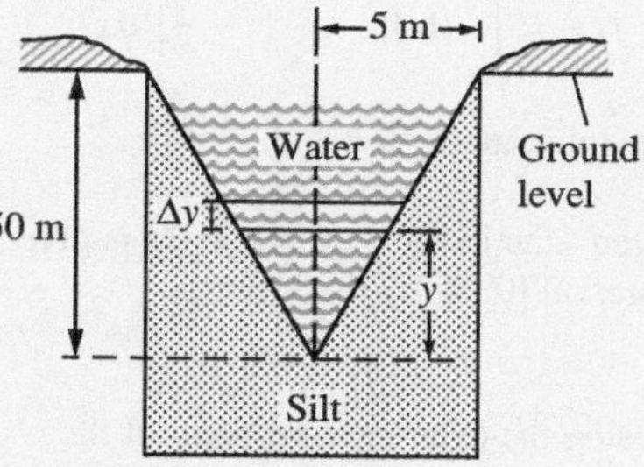

Figure 7.85

of base radius 5 m and height 50 m. Hence, by considering the small element of water shown, show that an estimate of the work (in J) required to raise the water to ground level is

$$W_1 = 10^3 \times \pi g \int_0^{50} \left(\frac{y}{10}\right)^2 (50 - y)\mathrm{d}y$$

Evaluate W_1 in the form $k_1\pi g$, giving k_1 correct to 3sf.

(b) Surveying suggests that, while the water–silt boundary may still be regarded as having cylindrical symmetry about the axis of the original borehole, a more accurate profile can be obtained from the data below.

Depth below ground level **(50 − y)/m**	***Radius of water/m***
0	5
5	4.7
10	4.3
15	4.1
20	3.9
25	3.3
30	2.8
35	2.0
40	1.2
45	0.3
50	0

Use this data, with Simpson's rule, to obtain a second approximation W_2 to the work required. Give your answer in the form $k_2\pi g$, with k_2 given to 3sf.

36 Draw the graph of the function $f(x)$ defined by

$$f(x) = \int_0^x \{\lfloor x \rfloor - \tfrac{1}{2} - \lfloor x - \tfrac{1}{2} \rfloor\}\mathrm{d}x$$

for the interval $-5 \leqslant x \leqslant 5$.

37 An even function $f(x)$ of period 2π is given on the interval $[0, \pi]$ by the formula

$$y = x/\pi$$

(a) Using the even-ness property of the function, draw the graph of the function for $-\pi \leqslant x \leqslant \pi$.

(b) Using the periodicity property of the function, draw the graph of the function for $-4\pi \leqslant x \leqslant 4\pi$.

(c) Draw also the graph of the function $g(x) = \frac{1}{2} - \frac{1}{2}\cos x$, for $-4\pi \leqslant x \leqslant 4\pi$.

The function $h(x) = \frac{1}{2} + a\cos x$ is used as an approximation to $f(x)$ by choosing the value for the constant a which makes the total squared error, $[h(x) - f(x)]^2$, over $[0, \pi]$ a minimum, that is the value of a which minimizes

$$\mathrm{E}(a) = \int_0^\pi [h(x) - f(x)]^2\,\mathrm{d}x$$

Show that

$$\mathrm{E}(a) = \frac{\pi}{2}\left[a^2 + \frac{8a}{\pi^2} + \frac{1}{6}\right]$$

and that E(a) is a minimum when $a = -4/\pi^2$. Draw a graph of the difference, $h(x) - f(x)$, between the approximation and the original function, for $0 \leqslant x \leqslant \pi$. What is its period?

38 A frame tent has a square of side 2 m and two semi-circular cross members, FBE and GBD, as shown in Figure 7.86.

(a) Show that the cross-section ABC has equation

$$2x^2 + z^2 = 2$$

(b) Show that the capacity of the tent is $8\sqrt{2/3}$ m^3.

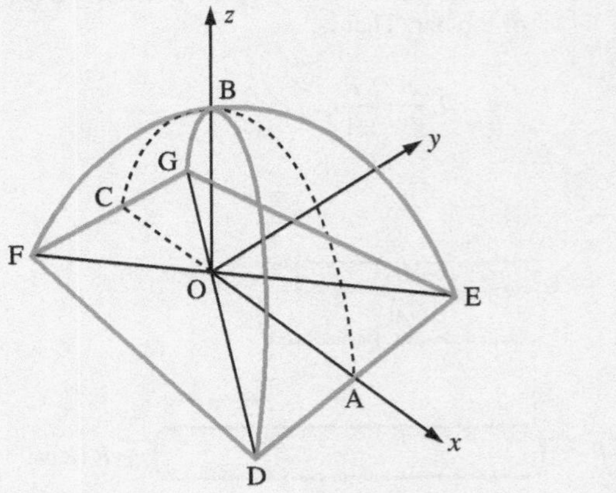

Figure 7.86 Frame tent of Question 38.

(c) Show that the surface area S m^2 of the tent is given by

$$S = 8\int_0^1 x\sqrt{\left(\frac{1+x^2}{1-x^2}\right)}\mathrm{d}x$$

Use the substitution $t = x^2$ to show that

$$S = 4\int_0^1 \frac{1+t}{\sqrt{(1-t^2)}}\mathrm{d}t$$

and deduce that $S = 2\pi + 4$.

(d) Show that the length s^* m of the arc length AB is given

$$s^* = \int_0^1 \sqrt{\left(\frac{1+x^2}{1-x^2}\right)}\mathrm{d}x$$

Use the substitution $x = \sin\theta$ to show that

$$s^* = \int_0^{\pi/2} \sqrt{(1+\sin^2\theta)}\,\mathrm{d}\theta$$

and evaluate (to 3dp) this integral using the trapezium rule.

(e) We wish to compute the shape of one of the panels, BDE, of the tent. Show that the semi-width y, at a distance s from B and illustrated in Figure 7.87, satisfies the differential equation

$$\frac{\mathrm{d}y}{\mathrm{d}s} = \sqrt{\left(\frac{1-y^2}{1+y^2}\right)} \qquad (7.51)$$

with $y = 0$ at $s = 0$.

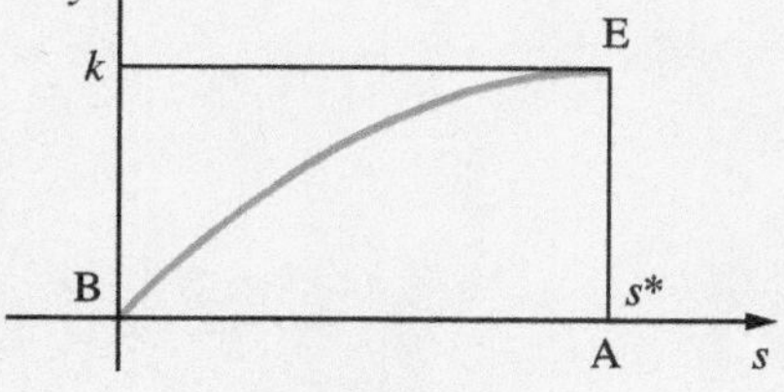

Figure 7.87 Semi-width y.

(f) A method, which constructs the solution of (7.51) graphically, is the following. Draw quarter circles of radius 1 and $\sqrt{2}$ in the first and fourth quadrants, as shown in Figure 7.88. Assuming that the solution curve OP has been drawn correctly as far as the point P(s, y), draw the line through P parallel to the s axis until it cuts the quarter circle at Q. Then draw the line through Q parallel to the y axis until it cuts the quarter circle at R. The line RT is drawn to pass through the origin O. The graphical solution is continued at P by drawing a small straight segment PP′ perpendicular to RT. The process is then repeated at P′ and so on, generating the line shape required.

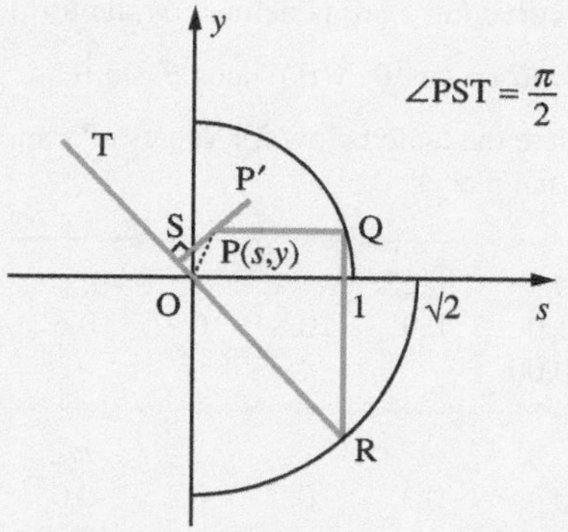

Figure 7.88 Quarter circles for Question 38.

(g) Show that the slope of the line OR is

$$-\sqrt{\left(\frac{1+y^2}{1-y^2}\right)}$$

and explain why the construction described in (f) generates an approximate solution to the differential equation.

(h) Use the method to obtain a graphical solution to the differential equation. (Use A4 graph paper with a step size PP′ of 2 cm.)

(i) To use Euler's method (see ahead, Section 10.6.1) to compute the solution, it is easiest to rescale the independent variable s by setting $s = s^*t$ where $0 \leqslant t \leqslant 1$. Show that the initial value problem becomes

$$\frac{\mathrm{d}y}{\mathrm{d}t} = s^*\sqrt{\left(\frac{1-y^2}{1+y^2}\right)},\ y(0) = 0$$

for $0 \leqslant t \leqslant 1$. Using $s^* = 1.91$ and step size of 0.1 for t, compute $y_k \simeq y(t_k)$ where $t_k = k/10$ and $k = 1, \ldots, 10$.

39 (a) A curve (an oval) is defined by the formulae

$$x(\theta) = \cos^4\theta,\ y(\theta) = \cos^3\theta \sin\theta$$

Complete the table below for values of x and y to 2 decimal places.

θ	0	0.23				0.57
x	1.0	0.9	0.8	0.7	0.6	0.5
y	0.00					0.32
θ					$\pi/2$	
x	0.4	0.3	0.2	0.1	0.0	
y					0.00	

Use these data to draw the oval on graph paper.

(b) Show that the volume of the body whose surface is generated by rotating the curve in part (a) about the x axis (an ovaloid) is $\pi/15$.

(c) Assuming that the ovaloid generated in part (b) has uniform density, show that its centre of mass is at the point (15/28, 0).

(d) Show that the tangent to the curve in part (a) at the point $(\cos^4\theta, \cos^3\theta \sin\theta)$ has the equation

$$y - \cos^3\theta \sin\theta$$
$$= (4\sin^2\theta - 1)(x - \cos^4\theta)/(4\sin\theta\cos\theta)$$

Deduce the turning points of the curve and show that the breadth (that is, distance between maximum and minimum values of y) of the oval is $3\sqrt{3}/4$.

(e) Show that the normal to the curve in part (a) at the point $(\cos^4\theta, \cos^3\theta \sin\theta)$ has the equation

$$y - \cos^3\theta \sin\theta$$
$$= 4\sin\theta\cos\theta\,(x - \cos^4\theta)/(4\cos^2\theta - 3)$$

(f) For what values of θ does the normal to the curve found in (e) pass through the centre of mass?

(g) Show that the distance from a point on the surface of the ovaloid to its centre of mass has stationary values where $\theta = 0$, $\cos^{-1}(\sqrt{(5/7)})$, $\pi/2$, $\cos^{-1}(-\sqrt{(5/7)})$, and π, and classify their nature.

(h) If the ovaloid is to rest in *stable* equilibrium on a horizontal plane, which points on the generating oval correspond to possible points of contact with the plane?

8 Further Calculus

Chapter 8 Contents

8.1 Introduction

In Chapter 7 we discussed the fundamental ideas and concepts of integral and differential calculus and applied them to various practical problems. We also developed techniques for solving problems using calculus. In this chapter we shall extend the techniques developed in Chapter 7 to deal with a wide range of problems and develop the theory to enable us to understand the numerical techniques widely used in practical problem-solving. We shall introduce multivariable calculus and use it to solve problems in optimization.

8.2 Improper integrals

When we considered the definite integral $\int_a^b f(x)\mathrm{d}x$ in Chapter 7 and showed its equivalence with an area under a curve, it was assumed that the integrand $f(x)$ was continuous, or at least piecewise-continuous, over the closed domain of integration $[a, b]$. To illustrate a possible consequence of this not being the case, consider the apparent definite integral $\int_{-1}^{1}(1/x^2)\mathrm{d}x$. If we proceed in a mechanistic way and follow the usual procedure, we should write

$$\int_{-1}^{1} \frac{1}{x^2}\mathrm{d}x = \left[\frac{-1}{x}\right]_{-1}^{1} = -2$$

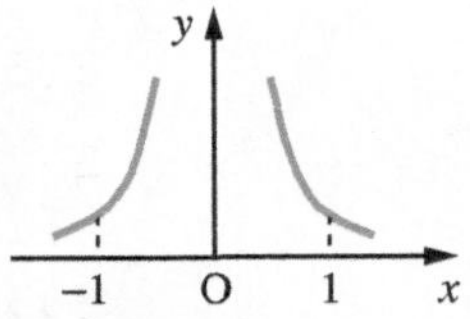

Figure 8.1
Graph of $f(x) = 1/x^2$.

However, if we plot the graph of $f(x) = 1/x^2$, as in Figure 8.1, it is clear that this is not correct, since it implies that the area under a curve that lies entirely above the x axis is negative. So where have we gone wrong? The answer lies in the fact that $f(x) = 1/x^2$ has an **infinite discontinuity** or **singularity** (that is, it is unbounded) at $x = 0$. As a consequence, the region under the curve over the domain of integration $[-1, 1]$ is unbounded, and our integration process was invalid.

In this section we consider the conditions under which the integral $\int_a^b f(x)\mathrm{d}x$ exists when either

(a) the integrand $f(x)$ becomes unbounded (that is, $f(x)$ has an infinite discontinuity) at some point within the domain of integration, or

(b) the domain of integration is infinite (that is, either a or b or both are infinite).

Such integrals are called **improper integrals**, and are encountered in many contexts in engineering. For example, the period of a simple pendulum of length l released from rest with angle α is given by

$$2\sqrt{\left(\frac{l}{g}\right)}\int_0^{\alpha} \frac{1}{\sqrt{(\sin^2\frac{\alpha}{2} - \sin^2\frac{\theta}{2})}}\mathrm{d}\theta$$

where g is the acceleration due to gravity. The integrand is infinite at $\theta = \alpha$; yet we know that the answer is meaningful from elementary physics.

8.2.1 Integrand with an infinite discontinuity

Suppose that the lower limit $x = a$ is the only point of infinite discontinuity of $f(x)$ in $[a, b]$. Then we define

$$\int_a^b f(x)\mathrm{d}x = \lim_{X\to a+}\int_X^b f(x)\mathrm{d}x \qquad \textbf{(8.1)}$$

provided that the one-sided limit exists (see Section 7.8.2). Otherwise $\int_a^b f(x)\mathrm{d}x$ has no meaning.

Similarly, if the upper limit $x = b$ is the only point of infinite discontinuity in $[a, b]$, we define

$$\int_a^b f(x)\mathrm{d}x = \lim_{X\to b-}\int_a^X f(x)\mathrm{d}x \qquad \textbf{(8.2)}$$

provided that the limit exists. Otherwise $\int_a^b f(x)\mathrm{d}x$ has no meaning.

Example 8.1 Evaluate the following, if they are defined:

(a) $\int_0^1 x^{-2/3}\mathrm{d}x$ (b) $\int_0^1 \frac{\mathrm{d}x}{\sqrt{(1-x^2)}}$ (c) $\int_0^1 \ln x\,\mathrm{d}x$ (d) $\int_0^1 \frac{\mathrm{d}x}{x^2}$

Solution (a) Here the integral has an infinite discontinuity at the lower limit $x = 0$, and we consider

$$\lim_{X\to 0+}\int_X^1 x^{-2/3}\mathrm{d}x = \lim_{X\to 0+}[3x^{1/3}]_X^1 = \lim_{X\to 0+}(3 - 3X^{1/3}) = 3$$

Since the limit exists, it follows from (8.1) that

$$\int_0^1 x^{-2/3}\mathrm{d}x = 3$$

(b) Here the discontinuity in the integrand occurs at the upper limit $x = 1$, and so we consider

$$\lim_{X\to 1-}\int_0^X \frac{\mathrm{d}x}{\sqrt{(1-x^2)}} = \lim_{X\to 1-}[\sin^{-1}x]_0^X = \lim_{X\to 1-}(\sin^{-1}X) = \tfrac{1}{2}\pi$$

Since the limit exists, it follows from (8.2) that

$$\int_0^1 \frac{\mathrm{d}x}{\sqrt{(1-x^2)}} = \tfrac{1}{2}\pi$$

(c) Again the integrand has an infinite discontinuity at the lower limit $x = 0$, and so we consider

$$\begin{aligned}\lim_{X\to 0+}\int_X^1 \ln x\,\mathrm{d}x &= \lim_{X\to 0+}[x\ln x - x]_X^1 \quad \text{(integrating by parts)}\\ &= \lim_{X\to 0+}(X - X\ln X - 1)\\ &= -1 \quad (\text{since } X\ln X \to 0 \text{ as } X \to 0+, \text{ Question 61, Section 7.8.3})\end{aligned}$$

Since the limit exists, it follows from (8.1) that

$$\int_0^1 \ln x\,\mathrm{d}x = -1$$

(d) In this case the integrand has an infinite discontinuity at the lower limit $x = 0$, and we consider the limit

$$\lim_{X\to 0+}\int_X^1 \frac{\mathrm{d}x}{x^2} = \lim_{X\to 0+}\left[\frac{-1}{x}\right]_X^1 = \lim_{X\to 0+}\left(\frac{1}{X} - 1\right)$$

This becomes infinite as $X \to 0$ and so the integral has no meaning.

If the integrand $f(x)$ has an infinite discontinuity at $x = c$, where $a < c < b$, then we define

$$\int_a^b f(x)\mathrm{d}x = \lim_{X\to 0+}\int_a^{c-X} f(x)\mathrm{d}x + \lim_{X\to 0+}\int_{c+X}^b f(x)\mathrm{d}x \qquad \textbf{(8.3)}$$

provided that both limits on the right-hand side exist. Otherwise $\int_a^b f(x)\mathrm{d}x$ is not defined.

Example 8.2 Confirm that $\int_{-1}^1 (1/x^2)\mathrm{d}x$ is not defined.

Solution This is the apparent integral considered in the introductory discussion, where we saw that following the usual integration techniques in a mechanistic sense led to a ridiculous answer. In this case the integrand has an infinite discontinuity at $x = 0$, so, following (8.3), we consider the two limits

$$\lim_{X\to 0+}\int_{-1}^{-X} \frac{\mathrm{d}x}{x^2} \quad \text{and} \quad \lim_{X\to 0+}\int_X^1 \frac{\mathrm{d}x}{x^2}$$

From the solution to Example 8.1(d) it is clear that both these tend to infinity, so that neither limit exists and the integral $\int_{-1}^1 (1/x^2)\mathrm{d}x$ is not defined.

Both MATLAB and MAPLE can evaluate such integrals. Considering Example 8.1

(a) The MATLAB commands

```
syms x y
y = x^(-2/3); int(y,0,1)
```

return the answer 3.

(b) The MAPLE commands

```
y:= 1/sqrt(1 - x^2); int(y,x = 0..1);
```

return the answer $\frac{1}{2}\pi$.

(c) The MATLAB commands

```
syms x
int(log(x),0,1)
```

return the answer -1.

(d) The MAPLE command

```
int(1/x^2,x = 0..1);
```

returns infinity.

As an exercise consider how MATLAB or MAPLE deals with Example 8.2.

The numerical evaluation of integrals whose integrands have infinite discontinuities will clearly cause numerical problems. Often such integrals can be evaluated by first changing the integrand by means of a substitution, as illustrated in the following example.

Example 8.3

Obtain the value of the integral

$$T(\alpha) = 2\sqrt{\left(\frac{l}{g}\right)}\int_0^{\alpha} \frac{\mathrm{d}\theta}{\sqrt{(\sin^2\frac{\alpha}{2} - \sin^2\frac{\theta}{2})}}$$

where $\alpha = \pi/3$. This is the period of oscillation of a simple pendulum released from rest from the angle α.

Solution

This integral has an integrand which is unbounded at $\theta = \alpha$. In this case we can 'remove' the difficulty by the substitution $\sin\dfrac{\theta}{2} = \sin\dfrac{\alpha}{2}\sin\phi$. Then

$$\tfrac{1}{2}\cos\frac{\theta}{2}\,\mathrm{d}\theta = \sin\frac{\alpha}{2}\cos\phi\,\mathrm{d}\phi$$

with $\theta = 0$ corresponding to $\phi = 0$ and $\theta = \alpha$ corresponding to $\phi = \pi/2$ and

$$T(\alpha) = 2\sqrt{\left(\frac{l}{g}\right)}\int_0^{\pi/2} \frac{1}{\sin\frac{1}{2}\alpha\sqrt{(1-\sin^2\phi)}}\cdot\frac{2\sin\frac{1}{2}\alpha\cos\phi}{\sqrt{(1-\sin^2\frac{1}{2}\alpha\sin^2\phi)}}\,\mathrm{d}\phi$$

$$= 4\sqrt{\left(\frac{l}{g}\right)}\int_0^{\pi/2} \frac{1}{\sqrt{(1-\sin^2\frac{1}{2}\alpha\sin^2\phi)}}\,\mathrm{d}\phi$$

When $\alpha = \pi/3$, we have

$$T\left(\frac{\pi}{3}\right) = 8\sqrt{\left(\frac{l}{g}\right)}\int_0^{\pi/2} \frac{1}{\sqrt{(4 - \sin^2\phi)}}\,\mathrm{d}\phi = 8\sqrt{\left(\frac{l}{g}\right)}\int_0^{\pi/2} \frac{1}{\sqrt{(3 + \cos^2\phi)}}\,\mathrm{d}\phi$$

This integral cannot be evaluated analytically. Applying the trapezium rule, Section 8.10.1, (with 4 intervals) gives $T\left(\frac{\pi}{3}\right) = 13.4864\sqrt{\left(\frac{l}{g}\right)}$.

8.2.2 Infinite integrals

The second case, where the domain of integration is infinite, is dealt with in a similar manner. We define

$$\int_a^{\infty} f(x)\mathrm{d}x = \lim_{X\to\infty}\int_a^{X} f(x)\mathrm{d}x \qquad \mathbf{(8.4)}$$

if that limit exists. Otherwise $\int_a^{\infty} f(x)\mathrm{d}x$ has no meaning.

Example 8.4 Evaluate the following:

(a) $\int_1^{\infty} x^{-3/2}\,\mathrm{d}x$ (b) $\int_0^{\infty} \frac{\mathrm{d}x}{1+x^2}$ (c) $\int_0^{\infty} \mathrm{e}^{-x}\sin x\,\mathrm{d}x$ (d) $\int_{-\infty}^{\infty} \mathrm{e}^{3x}\exp(-\mathrm{e}^x)\mathrm{d}x$

Solution (a) $\int_1^{\infty} x^{-3/2}\mathrm{d}x = \lim_{X\to\infty}\int_1^{X} x^{-3/2}\mathrm{d}x = \lim_{X\to\infty}[-2x^{-1/2}]_1^X = \lim_{X\to\infty}(2 - 2X^{-1/2}) = 2$

(b) $\int_0^{\infty} \frac{\mathrm{d}x}{1+x^2} = \lim_{X\to\infty}\int_0^{X} \frac{\mathrm{d}x}{1+x^2} = \lim_{X\to\infty}[\tan^{-1}x]_0^X = \lim_{X\to\infty}(\tan^{-1}X) = \tfrac{1}{2}\pi$

(c) $\int_0^{\infty} \mathrm{e}^{-x}\sin x\,\mathrm{d}x = \lim_{X\to\infty}\int_0^{X} \mathrm{e}^{-x}\sin x\,\mathrm{d}x$

$$= \lim_{X\to\infty}[-\tfrac{1}{2}\mathrm{e}^{-x}(\cos x + \sin x)]_0^X \quad \text{(integration by parts)}$$

$$= \lim_{X\to\infty}[\tfrac{1}{2} - \tfrac{1}{2}\mathrm{e}^{-X}(\cos X + \sin X)] = \tfrac{1}{2}$$

The indefinite integral is obtained using integration by parts, as in Example 8.50(c). It can be verified by direct differentiation.

(d) Here we simplify the integral by the substitution $t = \mathrm{e}^x$, so that $x \to -\infty$ gives $t = 0$, $x \to \infty$ gives $t \to \infty$ and $\mathrm{d}t = \mathrm{e}^x\mathrm{d}x$. The integral becomes

$$\int_{-\infty}^{\infty} \mathrm{e}^{3x}\exp(-\mathrm{e}^x)\,\mathrm{d}x = \int_0^{\infty} t^2\mathrm{e}^{-t}\,\mathrm{d}t = \left[-t^2\mathrm{e}^{-t} - 2t\mathrm{e}^{-t} - 2\mathrm{e}^{-t}\right]_0^{T\to\infty}$$

using integration by parts twice.

Hence

$$\int_{-\infty}^{\infty} e^{3x}\exp(-e^x)\,dx = 2$$

Again such integrals may be evaluated directly by MATLAB and MAPLE. To illustrate we consider Examples 8.4(b) and (d). For 8.4(b) the commands

MATLAB	MAPLE
`syms x y`	
`y = 1/(1 + x^2);`	`y:= 1/(1 + x^2);`
`int(y,0,inf)`	`int(y,x = 0..infinity);`

return the answer

`1/2*pi`	$\frac{1}{2}\pi$

and for 8.4(d) the commands

`syms x`	
`int(exp(3*x)*`	`int(exp(3*x)*`
`exp(-exp(x)),-inf,inf)`	`exp(-exp(x)),-infinity..infinity);`

return the answer 2

For practice, check the answers to Examples 8.4(a) and (c).

8.2.3 Exercise

Check your answer using MATLAB or MAPLE whenever possible.

1 Evaluate the following improper integrals:

(a) $\int_0^1 (-x\ln x)\,dx$

(b) $\int_0^{\infty} x\exp(-x^2)\,dx$

(c) $\int_0^{\infty} x^2e^{-2x}\,dx$

(d) $\int_{-\infty}^{\infty} e^x\exp(-e^x)\,dx$

(e) $\int_0^1 x^2(1 - x^3)^{-1/2}\,dx$

(f) $\int_0^1 (x - 1)/\sqrt{x}\,dx$

(g) $\int_0^{\frac{\pi}{2}} \frac{\sin x}{\sqrt{\cos x}}\,dx$

(h) $\int_0^{\frac{\pi}{2}} \cos x\sin^{-1/3}x\,dx$

(i) $\int_0^{\infty} \frac{x}{1 + x^4}\,dx$

8.3 Some theorems with applications to numerical methods

There are a number of theorems involving integration and differentiation that are useful in understanding why certain numerical methods are better than others and in devising new methods. They are also useful in the more mundane tasks of assessing the effect of data error when evaluating functions and probing the accuracy of analytical approximations to functions. We shall now briefly consider such theorems and indicate their potential uses. Deriving the results is not easy and the reader may prefer to omit the proofs. The results, however, have many practical implications and should be studied carefully.

8.3.1 Rolle's theorem and the first mean value theorems

The simplest result is the following

Theorem 8.1 Rolle's theorem

If the function $f(x)$ is continuous on the domain $[a, b]$ and differentiable on (a, b) with $f(a)=f(b)$ then there is at least one point $x=c$ in (a, b) such that $f'(c)=0$.

end of theorem

The validity of this theorem can be easily illustrated geometrically, as shown in Figure 8.2, since what the theorem tells us is that it is possible to find at least one point on the curve $y=f(x)$ between the values $x=a$ and $x=b$ where the tangent is parallel to the x axis; that is, there must exist at least one maximum or minimum between $x=a$ and $x=b$.

In Section 7.9.1 we discussed the properties of continuous functions. All continuous functions are integrable, and this fact enables us to calculate the mean value of a continuous function over a given domain, say $[a, b]$. The mean value is given by

$$\frac{1}{b-a}\int_a^b f(x)\mathrm{d}x$$

Figure 8.2
Four examples of Rolle's theorem.

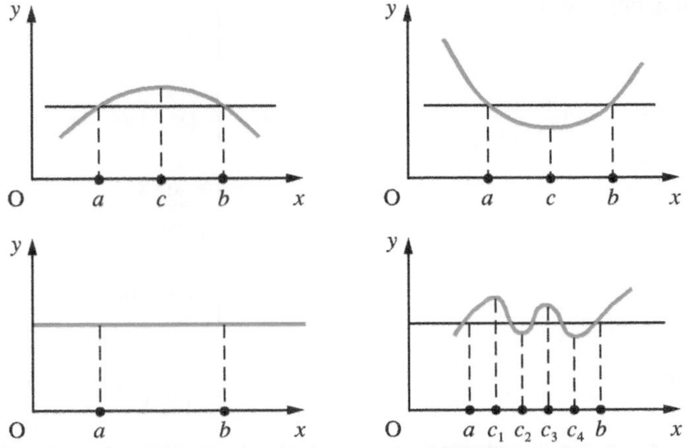

Clearly the mean value of $f(x)$ lies between its maximum and minimum values on the domain $[a, b]$ and, from the intermediate value theorem (Property (c), Section 7.9.1), we deduce that there is a point $x = c$ in the interval $[a, b]$ such that (see 8.43)

$$f(c) = \text{mean value of } f(x) = \frac{1}{b-a}\int_a^b f(x)\,\mathrm{d}x$$

This result is referred to as the first mean value theorem of integral calculus and may be stated as follows.

Theorem 8.2 **The first mean value theorem of integral calculus**

If the function $f(x)$ is continuous over the domain $[a, b]$ then there exists at least one point $x = c$, with $a < c < b$, such that

$$f(c) = \frac{1}{b-a}\int_a^b f(x)\,\mathrm{d}x$$

end of theorem

This theorem is illustrated geometrically in Figure 8.3(a).

If $f(x)$ is a differentiable function then

$$\int_a^b f'(x)\,\mathrm{d}x = f(b) - f(a)$$

Applying Theorem 8.2 to $f'(x)$ gives

$$\int_a^b f'(x)\,\mathrm{d}x = (b-a)f'(c), \quad \text{with } a < c < b$$

and hence, by equating the two values of $\int_a^b f'(x)\,\mathrm{d}x$,

$$\frac{f(b) - f(a)}{b-a} = f'(c)$$

This result is referred to as the first mean value theorem of differential calculus, and may be stated as follows.

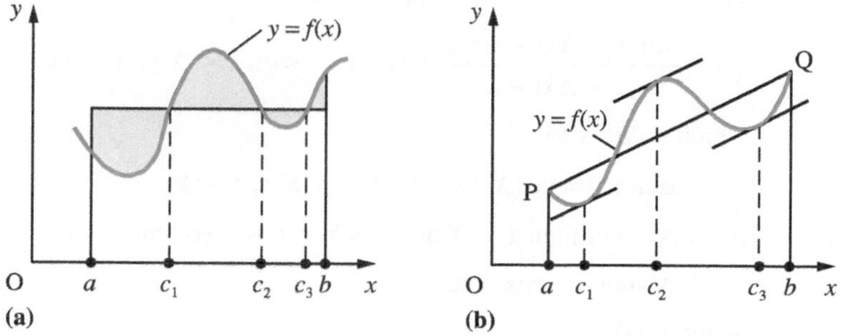

Figure 8.3
The first mean value theorems: (a) $f(c_i)$ is the mean value of $f(x)$ $(a \leq x \leq b)$; (b) the chord PQ is parallel to the tangents at $x = c_i$.

Theorem 8.3 **First mean value theorem of differential calculus**

If the function $f(x)$ is continuous on the domain $[a, b]$ and differentiable on (a, b) then there exists at least one point $x = c$, with $a < c < b$, such that

$$\frac{f(b) - f(a)}{b - a} = f'(c)$$

end of theorem

It is this theorem that is normally referred to as the first mean value theorem. Geometrically, it implies that at some point on the interval $[a, b]$ the slope of the tangent to the graph of $f(x)$ is parallel to the chord between the end points $x = a$ and $x = b$ of the graph, as shown in Figure 8.2(b).

An immediate application of Theorem 8.3 is in the estimation of the effect of rounding errors in the independent variable x on the calculated value of the dependent variable $y = f(x)$. If ε_x is the error bound for x then the error bound for y is ε_y, where

$$\varepsilon_y = \max_{x-\varepsilon_x<x^*<x+\varepsilon_x} |f(x^*) - f(x)|$$

Applying the first mean value theorem with $a = x$, $b = x^*$ gives

$$|f(x^*) - f(x)| = |x^* - x|\,|f'(c)|$$

with c lying between x and x^*. Since $x - \varepsilon_x < x^* < c, f'(c) \approx f'(x)$, we have

$$\varepsilon_y \approx \max_{x-\varepsilon_x<x^*<x+\varepsilon_x} |f'(x)(x^* - x)| = |f'(x)|\varepsilon_x \tag{8.5}$$

We illustrate this by Example 8.5.

Example 8.5 Show that

$$\Delta(\sin x) \approx \cos x\,\Delta x$$

and hence estimate an error bound for $\sin a$, where $a = 1.935$ (3dp). Compare the error interval obtained with [sin 1.9355, sin 1.9345]. Express $\sin a$ as a correctly rounded number with the maximum number of decimal places.

Solution The difference $\Delta(\sin x)$ is given by

$$\Delta(\sin x) = \sin(x + \Delta x) - \sin x$$

Since $(\mathrm{d}/\mathrm{d}x)\sin x = \cos x$, application of Theorem 8.3 gives

$$\frac{\sin(x + \Delta x) - \sin x}{(x + \Delta x) - x} = \cos X, \quad \text{with } x < X < x + \Delta x$$

which reduces to

$$\Delta(\sin x) = \cos X\,\Delta x, \quad \text{with } x < X < x + \Delta x$$

If Δx is small then $x \approx X$ and $\cos X \approx \cos x$, so that

$$\Delta(\sin x) \approx \cos x\,\Delta x$$

as required.

Setting $x = a$ gives $\Delta(\sin a) \approx \cos a\,\Delta a$, and hence, using (8.5), an error bound estimate for $\sin a$ is

$$\varepsilon_{\sin a} = |\cos a|\,\varepsilon_a$$

In this example $a = 1.935$ and $\varepsilon_a = 0.0005$, so that

$$\varepsilon_{\sin a} = |\cos 1.935|(0.0005) = |-0.3562|(0.0005) = 0.000\,18$$

Thus

$$\sin a = \sin 1.935 \pm 0.000\,18 = 0.934\,41 \pm 0.000\,18$$

which spans the interval [0.934 23, 0.934 59].

Now $\sin 1.9355 = 0.934\,23$ and $\sin 1.9345 = 0.934\,59$, so that in this example the estimate of the error interval and the error interval are the same to 5dp.

Thus

$$\sin a = 0.9344 \pm 0.0002$$

or

$$\sin a = 0.93$$

8.3.2 Convergence of iterative schemes

In Section 7.9.3 the solution of equations by iteration was discussed. We now consider the convergence of such iterative schemes. As before, suppose that an iteration for the root $x = \alpha$ of the equation $f(x) = 0$ is given by

$$x_{n+1} = g(x_n) \quad (n = 0, 1, 2, \dots)$$

where $\alpha = g(\alpha)$. When we use such an iteration we need a rule which tells us when to stop the process. The usual practice is to stop the iteration when the difference $|x_{n+1} - x_n|$ between two successive iterates is sufficiently small, that is, when it is less than half-a-unit of the least significant figure required in the answer.

There are two separate issues here: one concerns the convergence of the iteration formula to the root, and the other concerns the 'stopping' mechanism. In practical computation, the rule of stopping an iteration is important because it vitally affects the accuracy of the estimate of the root of the equation.

Convergence process

To examine the convergence of the iteration to the root α, we estimate $|x_{n+1} - \alpha|$ as $n \to \infty$. Now

$$x_{n+1} = g(x_n) \quad \text{and} \quad \alpha = g(\alpha)$$

so that

$$x_{n+1} - \alpha = g(x_n) - g(\alpha)$$

Using the mean value Theorem 8.3, this may be written as

$$x_{n+1} - \alpha = (x_n - \alpha)g'(X_n)$$

where X_n lies in the interval (x_n, α), assuming $x_n < \alpha$. Writing $\varepsilon_n = x_n - \alpha$, we obtain

$$|\varepsilon_{n+1}| \leqslant r|\varepsilon_n|$$

where $r = |g'(x)|_{\max}$ in the neighbourhood of $x = \alpha$. By comparison with the geometric sequence, we deduce that $\varepsilon_n \to 0$, as $n \to \infty$, if $0 < r < 1$ and that, provided we start near $x = \alpha$, the iteration converges if $|g'(x)| < 1$ near $x = \alpha$. Note that the more horizontal the graph of $g(x)$ near the root, the smaller r is and hence the more rapid is the convergence. We will discuss this further in Section 8.4.7.

Stopping process

The 'stopping' rule can be investigated similarly. The rule says that the iteration is stopped when $|x_{n+1} - x_n| < \varepsilon$, where ε is the maximum acceptable error. We therefore seek a relationship between $|x_{n+1} - \alpha|$ and $|x_{n+1} - x_n|$.

Now we can rewrite $x_{n+1} - \alpha$ as

$$x_{n+1} - \alpha = (x_{n+1} - x_{n+2}) + (x_{n+2} - x_{n+3}) + (x_{n+3} - x_{n+4}) + \ldots + (x_{n+k} - \alpha)$$

Since $x_n \to \alpha$ as $n \to \infty$, it follows that $x_{n+k} \to \alpha$ as $k \to \infty$, since all the previous terms on the right-hand side tend to zero. The terms on the right-hand side can be thought of as the corrections made to successive iterates in the process. We may therefore write

$$x_{n+1} - \alpha = \sum_{k=1}^{\infty} (x_{n+k} - x_{n+k+1}) \tag{8.6}$$

Using the first mean value Theorem 8.3, we have

$$\begin{aligned} x_{n+1} - x_{n+2} &= g(x_n) - g(x_{n+1}) \\ &= (x_n - x_{n+1})g'(X_n) \end{aligned}$$

where X_n lies in the interval (x_n, x_{n+1}), assuming $x_n < x_{n+1}$. By repeated application of this result, we have

$$x_{n+2} - x_{n+3} = (x_{n+1} - x_{n+2})g'(X_{n+1}) = (x_n - x_{n+1})g'(X_n)g'(X_{n+1})$$
$$\vdots$$

leading to

$$x_{n+k} - x_{n+k+1} = (x_n - x_{n+1})g'(X_n)g'(X_{n+1}) \ldots g'(X_{n+k-1}) \tag{8.7}$$

If, as before, $|g'(x)| < r < 1$ in the neighbourhood of $x = \alpha$ then we obtain from (8.6)

$$\begin{aligned} |x_{n+1} - \alpha| &\leqslant \sum_{k=1}^{\infty} |x_{n+k} - x_{n+k+1}| \\ &\leqslant \sum_{k=1}^{\infty} |x_n - x_{n+1}| r^k \qquad \text{(using (8.7) with } |g'(x)| < r) \\ &= |x_n - x_{n+1}| \sum_{k=1}^{\infty} r^k \\ &= \frac{r}{1-r} |x_n - x_{n+1}| \end{aligned}$$

using the expression for the sum of a geometric progression given in (7.14). Hence

$$|x_{n+1} - \alpha| < \frac{r\varepsilon}{1 - r}$$

Thus $|x_{n+1} - \alpha| < \varepsilon$ provided that $r < \frac{1}{2}$, and the 'stopping' rule is valid provided that $|g'(x)| < \frac{1}{2}$ near the root $x = \alpha$. In many practical problems it is necessary to estimate r by

$$|x_{n+1} - x_n|/|x_n - x_{n-1}| = |g(x_n) - g(x_{n-1})|/|x_n - x_{n-1}|$$

Clearly, the smaller the value of r, the more rapid is the convergence. Note, however, that this discussion has ignored the effects of rounding errors on the computation, so that the result above has been shown only for exact arithmetic.

Example 8.6 Show that the iteration

$$\theta_{n+1} = \tan^{-1}(\tanh \theta_n), \quad \text{with } \theta_0 = \tfrac{5}{4}\pi \approx 3.9$$

considered in Section 7.9.3 is convergent to the root near $\theta = 3.9$ of the equation $\tan \theta = \tanh \theta$ (see Figure 8.4).

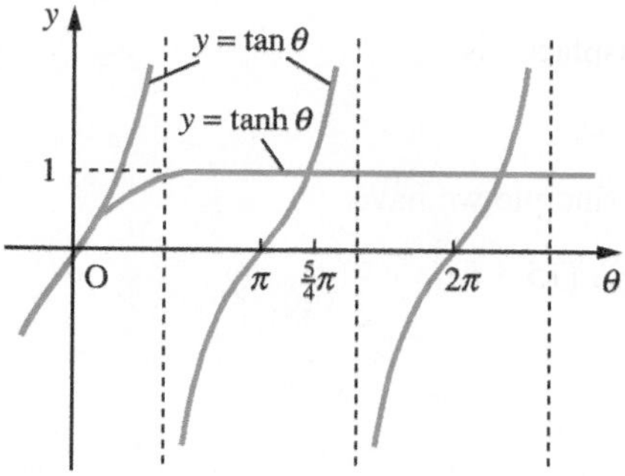

Figure 8.4 Roots of the equation $\tan \theta = \tanh \theta$.

Solution Here the iteration function has formula

$$g(\theta) = \tan^{-1}(\tanh \theta)$$

with derivative

$$g'(\theta) = \frac{1}{1 + \tanh^2\theta}\operatorname{sech}^2\theta$$

$$= \frac{1}{\cosh^2\theta + \sinh^2\theta} = \frac{1}{\cosh 2\theta}$$

Near $\theta = 3.9$, $\cosh 2\theta \approx 1220$, so $|g'(\theta)|$ is small (in fact $r < 0.004$) and the method converges.

Example 8.7 A spherical wooden ball floats in water, as illustrated in Figure 8.5. Its diameter is 10 cm and its density is 0.8 g cm^{-3}. Find the depth h cm to which it sinks.

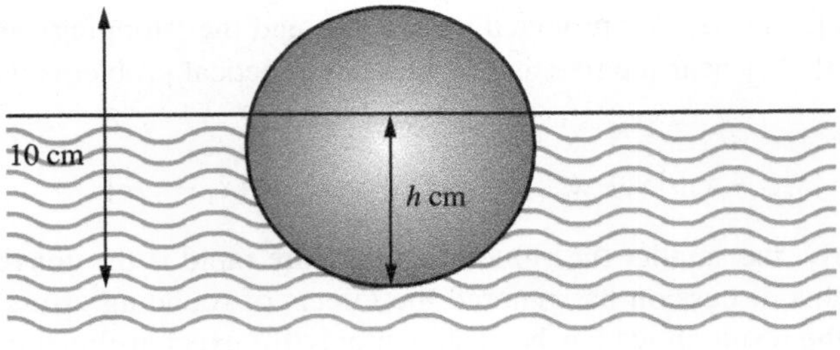

Figure 8.5 Floating ball of Example 8.7.

Solution Archimedes shouted 'ευρηκα!' when he realized that the weight of a floating body must balance the weight of water it displaces. In this case we have the weight of the ball is

$$\tfrac{4}{3}\pi(5)^3 \times 0.8\,\mathrm{g}$$

The volume of a zone depth h of a sphere of radius r is

$$\tfrac{1}{3}\pi h^2(3r - h) \text{ (see Example 8.63)}$$

so the weight of water displaced is

$$\tfrac{1}{3}\pi h^2(15 - h)\,\mathrm{g}$$

Hence by Archimedes' principle we have

$$\tfrac{4}{3}\pi \times 125 \times \tfrac{4}{5} = \tfrac{1}{3}\pi h^2(15 - h)$$

that is

$$400 = h^2(15 - h)$$

Graphing $y = (x - 15)x^2 + 400$ shows that there is a root near $x = 7$. To find the root more accurately we can construct an iteration. For example

$$h_{n+1} = [(h_n^3 + 400)/15]^{1/2}$$

Starting with $h_0 = 7.00$, we obtain the iterates given in the table below.

n	0	1	2	3	4	5	6	7	8	9	10
h_n	7.00	7.04	7.06	7.08	7.10	7.11	7.11	7.12	7.12	7.12	7.12

With this set of iterates we would be tempted to conclude that the root is 7.11 or 7.12. In fact the correct answer is 7.13. This example shows the importance of the size of the derivative of the iteration function. In this case it is 0.7 near the root and there is danger of premature termination of the process. Clearly it is not of vital importance here but the example illustrates the danger of using an iteration without due care.

8.3.3 Exercises

2 By means of sketches of the graphs $y = 1/x$ and $y = \tan x$, show that the equation $x \tan x = 1$ has a root between $x = 0$ and $x = \frac{1}{2}\pi$ and an infinity of roots near $x = k\pi$, where $k = 1, 2, 3, \ldots$. Deduce which of the two iterations

(a) $x_{n+1} = \cot x_n$ (b) $x_{n+1} = \tan^{-1}(1/x_n) + k\pi$

is convergent to the roots, and use it to locate the smallest positive root to 6dp.

3 If $\alpha = f(\alpha)$ but the iteration $x_{n+1} = f(x_n)$ fails to converge to the root α, under what condition on $f(x)$ will the iteration $x_{n+1} = f^{-1}(x_n)$ converge?

4 Show the cubic equation $x^3 - 2x - 1 = 0$ has a root near $x = 2$. Prove that the iteration

$$x_{n+1} = \tfrac{1}{2}(x_n^3 - 1)$$

fails to converge to that root. Devise a simple iteration formula for the root of the equation, and use it to find the root to 6dp.

5 The equation $f(x) = 0$ has a root at $x = \alpha$. Show that rewriting the equation as $x = x + \lambda f(x)$, where λ is a constant, yields a convergent iteration for α if $\lambda = -1/f'(x_0)$ and x_0 is sufficiently close to α.

Use this method to devise an iteration for the root near $x = 2$ of the equation $x^3 - 2x - 1 = 0$.

6 Consider the iteration defined by

$$x_{n+1} = \tfrac{1}{3}(x_n^3 + 2)$$

Show that

(a) if $0 < x_0 < 1$ then the iteration tends to a limit as $n \to \infty$;

(b) if $x_0 > 1$ then the iteration is divergent.

Explain this behaviour.

7 Consider the iteration

$$x_{n+1} = \frac{2 + 30x_n - x_n^2}{30}, \quad x_0 = 1.5$$

Working to 2dp, obtain the first three iterates. Then continue to obtain the following six iterates. From the numerical evidence what do you estimate as the limit of the sequence?

Assuming that the sequence has a limit near 1.5, obtain its value algebraically and then explain the phenomena observed above.

8.4 Taylor's theorem and related results

A question that frequently arises in both engineering and mathematical problem-solving is the behaviour of a solution when one (or more) of the parameters in the problem statement is changed. This occurs in sensitivity analysis when we examine solutions for their dependence on errors in the original data. It is also relevant to analysing the equilibrium of structures. One of the mathematical tools for such analyses is Taylor's theorem. In this section we shall develop the theorem and then use it to solve problems in design and numerical methods.

8.4.1 Taylor polynomials and Taylor's theorem

In Section 2.9.1 we discussed the use of interpolating functions to approximate functions specified by a table of values. The simplest case was linear interpolation. With this, we require a different formula between successive tabular points. Another approach to the problem of function approximation is to construct a polynomial that, together with its derivatives, takes the same values as those of the function and its derivatives at a particular point in the domain. That is, we seek a polynomial $p(x)$ such that

$$p(a) = f(a),\quad p'(a) = f'(a),\quad p''(a) = f''(a),\ \ldots$$

The idea is illustrated by Example 8.8.

Example 8.8 Find a polynomial approximation to the function $f(x)$ such that

$$f(0) = 3,\quad f'(0) = 4,\quad f''(0) = -10 \quad \text{and} \quad f'''(0) = 12$$

Solution In this example we have information about the value of the function and its first three derivatives at $x = 0$. This means that we can form an approximating polynomial of degree 3

$$p(x) = a + bx + cx^2 + dx^3$$

and determine the values of a, b, c and d from the information given.

Setting $p(0) = f(0)$ gives $a = 3$.

Differentiating gives

$$p'(x) = b + 2cx + 3dx^2$$

and on setting $p'(0) = f'(0) = 4$, we have $b = 4$.

Differentiating again gives

$$p''(x) = 2c + 6dx$$

and on setting $p''(0) = f''(0) = -10$, we have $c = -5$.

Differentiating again gives

$$p'''(x) = 6d$$

and on setting $p'''(0) = f'''(0) = 12$, we have $d = 2$.

Thus the approximating polynomial is

$$p(x) = 3 + 4x - 5x^2 + 2x^3$$

The technique used in Example 8.8 can be applied at points other than $x = 0$, as shown in Example 8.9.

Example 8.9 Find a polynomial approximation to $f(x)$ such that

$$f(1) = 4,\quad f'(1) = 0,\quad f''(1) = 2 \quad \text{and} \quad f'''(1) = 12$$

Solution Because the information concerns the value of the function and its derivatives at the point $x = 1$, we look for a polynomial in powers of $x - 1$. So in this case we are seeking an approximation in the form

$$p(x) = a + b(x - 1) + c(x - 1)^2 + d(x - 1)^3$$

Setting $x = 1$ in $p(x)$ and its derivatives gives, in turn,

$$p(1) = a = 4 \qquad p'(1) = b = 0$$
$$p''(1) = 2c = 2 \qquad p'''(1) = 6d = 12$$

Thus the required approximation is

$$p(x) = 4 + 0(x-1) + 1(x-1)^2 + 2(x-1)^3 = 4 + (x-1)^2 + 2(x-1)^3$$

Such polynomial approximations to functions are called **Taylor polynomials**. In general, we can write the nth-degree Taylor polynomial approximation to the function $f(x)$, given the value of the function and its derivatives at $x = a$, in the form

$$f(x) \approx p_n(x)$$

where

$$p_n(x) = f(a) + \frac{x-a}{1!}f'(a) + \frac{(x-a)^2}{2!}f''(a) + \frac{(x-a)^3}{3!}f'''(a) + \dots + \frac{(x-a)^n}{n!}f^{(n)}(a) \quad \textbf{(8.8)}$$

Clearly, $p_n(a) = f(a)$, and also the first n derivatives of $p_n(x)$ match the first n derivatives of $f(x)$ at $x = a$.

The approximation of $f(x)$ given in (8.8) can be made exact by writing

$$f(x) = p_n(x) + R_n(x) \quad \textbf{(8.9)}$$

where $R_n(x)$ is the **remainder**. The remainder term can be expressed in many different forms, with the simplest, known as **Lagrange's form**, being

$$R_n(x) = \frac{(x-a)^{n+1}}{(n+1)!}f^{(n+1)}(a + \theta h)$$

where $h = x - a$ and $0 < \theta < 1$.

The result (8.9) constitutes **Taylor's theorem**, which may be stated as follows.

Theorem 8.4 **Taylor's theorem**

If $f(x), f'(x), \dots, f^{(n)}(x)$ exist and are continuous on the closed domain $[a, x]$ and $f^{(n+1)}(x)$ exists on the open domain (a, x) then there exists a number θ, with $0 < \theta < 1$, such that

$$f(x) = f(a) + \frac{x-a}{1!}f'(a) + \frac{(x-a)^2}{2!}f''(a) + \dots + \frac{(x-a)^n}{n!}f^{(n)}(a) + \frac{(x-a)^{n+1}}{(n+1)!}f^{(n+1)}(a + \theta h) \quad \textbf{(8.10)}$$

where $h = x - a$.

end of theorem

Taylor's theorem is in fact a natural extension of the first mean value theorem (Theorem 8.3), and it is sometimes referred to as the ***n*th mean value theorem**. It may be proved by repeated use of Rolle's theorem (Theorem 8.1), but, since the proof does not add to our understanding of how to apply the result to the solution of engineering problems, it is not developed here.

8.4.2 Taylor and Maclaurin series

An alternative form of the Taylor polynomial (8.10) is obtained when we replace x in the expansion by $a + x$. Then we obtain a polynomial in x, rather than $x - a$, namely

$$f(x+a) = f(a) + \frac{x}{1!}f'(a) + \frac{x^2}{2!}f''(a) + \frac{x^3}{3!}f'''(a) + \ldots + \frac{x^n}{n!}f^{(n)}(a) + R_n(x) \quad \textbf{(8.11)}$$

where

$$R_n(x) = \frac{x^{n+1}}{(n+1)!}f^{(n+1)}(a+\theta x), \quad \text{with } 0 < \theta < 1$$

Equation (8.11) is called the **Taylor polynomial expansion of $f(x)$ about $x = a$.**

The remainder $R_n(x)$ represents the error involved in approximating $f(x)$ by the polynomial

$$f(a) + \frac{x}{1!}f'(a) + \frac{x^2}{2!}f''(a) + \ldots + \frac{x^n}{n!}f^{(n)}(a)$$

If $R_n(x) \to 0$ as $n \to \infty$ then we may represent $f(x)$ by the power series

$$f(x+a) = f(a) + \frac{x}{1!}f'(a) + \frac{x^2}{2!}f''(a) + \ldots = \sum_{n=0}^{\infty} \frac{x^n}{n!}f^{(n)}(a) \quad \textbf{(8.12)}$$

The power series (8.12) is called the **Taylor series expansion of $f(x)$ about $x = a$.** We saw in Section 7.7.1 that a power series may have a restricted domain of convergence. Similarly, $R_n(x)$ may tend to zero as $n \to \infty$ only for a restricted interval of values of x or not at all. In that case the power series given by (8.12) will only represent the function $f(x)$ in that interval of convergence.

Setting $a = 0$ in (8.13) leads to the special case

$$f(x) = f(0) + \frac{x}{1!}f'(0) + \frac{x^2}{2!}f''(0) + \ldots = \sum_{n=0}^{\infty} \frac{x^n}{n!}f^{(n)}(0) \quad \textbf{(8.13)}$$

which is known as the **Maclaurin series expansion of $f(x)$.**

Example 8.10 Find the Maclaurin series expansion of $e^x \sin x$.

Solution Since $f(x) = e^x \sin x$,

$$f'(x) = e^x(\sin x + \cos x)$$

This may be rewritten (see Section 2.6.5) as

$$f'(x) = \sqrt{2}e^x \sin(x + \tfrac{1}{4}\pi)$$

so the process of differentiation is equivalent to multiplying by $\sqrt{2}$ and adding $\frac{1}{4}\pi$ to the argument of the sine function. Thus we can write the second derivative directly as

$$f''(x) = (\sqrt{2})^2 e^x \sin(x + 2 \times \tfrac{1}{4}\pi) = 2e^x \cos x$$

and so on for higher derivatives, giving in general

$$f^{(k)}(x) = (\sqrt{2})^k e^x \sin(x + \tfrac{1}{4}k\pi)$$

Putting $x = 0$ gives $f(0) = 0, f^{(1)}(0) = 1, f^{(2)}(0) = 2, f^{(3)}(0) = 2, f^{(4)}(0) = 0, f^{(5)}(0) = -4, f^{(6)}(0) = -8, \ldots$, which, on substituting into (8.13), gives

$$e^x \sin x = 0 + x(1) + \frac{1}{2!}x^2(2) + \frac{1}{3!}x^3(2) + \frac{1}{4!}x^4(0) + \frac{1}{5!}x^5(-4) + \ldots$$

$$= x + x^2 + \tfrac{1}{3}x^3 - \tfrac{1}{30}x^5 + \ldots$$

It remains to show that $R_n(x) \to 0$ as $n \to \infty$. Since

$$R_n(x) = \frac{x^{n+1}}{(n+1)!}f^{(n+1)}(\theta x), \quad \text{with } 0 < \theta < 1$$

we have in this particular example

$$R_n(x) = \frac{x^{n+1}}{(n+1)!}(\sqrt{2})^{n+1}e^{\theta x}\sin[\theta x + \tfrac{1}{4}(n+1)\pi]$$

$$= \frac{(x\sqrt{2})^{n+1}}{(n+1)!}e^{\theta x}\sin[\theta x + \tfrac{1}{4}(n+1)\pi], \quad \text{with } 0 < \theta < 1$$

We recall that the series for e^x is convergent for all x, so that $x^n/n! \to 0$ as $n \to \infty$. Hence $(x\sqrt{2})^{n+1}/(n+1)! \to 0$ as $n \to \infty$, and $|\sin[\theta x + \frac{1}{4}(n+1)\pi]| \leq 1$, and so

$$R_n(x) \to 0 \quad \text{as } n \to \infty \quad \text{for all } x$$

Thus the Maclaurin expansion of $e^x \sin x$ is

$$e^x \sin x = x + x^2 + \tfrac{1}{3}x^3 - \tfrac{1}{30}x^5 + \ldots$$

In practice it is rarely the case that we obtain the Maclaurin series expansion of a function by direct calculation of the derivatives as in Example 8.10. More commonly, we obtain such series by the manipulation of known standard Maclaurin series as we did in Section 7.7.2. Most of the standard series were given in Figure 7.13. For convenience, we reproduce some of them in Figure 8.6.

(a) $(1+x)^r = 1 + rx + \frac{r(r-1)x^2}{2!} + \frac{r(r-1)(r-2)x^3}{3!} + \ldots + \frac{r(r-1)\ldots(r-n+1)}{n!}x^n + \ldots \quad (-1 < x < 1, r \in \mathbb{R})$

(b) $e^x = 1 + \frac{x}{1!} + \frac{x^2}{2!} + \frac{x^3}{3!} + \ldots + \frac{x^n}{n!} + \ldots \quad (\text{all } x)$

(c) $\sin x = x - \frac{x^3}{3!} + \frac{x^5}{5!} - \ldots + \frac{(-1)^n x^{2n+1}}{(2n+1)!} + \ldots \quad (\text{all } x)$

(d) $\cos x = 1 - \frac{x^2}{2!} + \frac{x^4}{4!} - \ldots + \frac{(-1)^n x^{2n}}{(2n)!} + \ldots \quad (\text{all } x)$

(e) $\ln(1+x) = x - \frac{x^2}{2} + \frac{x^3}{3} - \frac{x^4}{4} + \ldots + \frac{(-1)^n x^{n+1}}{n+1} + \ldots \quad (-1 < x \leqslant 1)$

(f) $\tan x = x + \frac{x^3}{3} + \frac{2x^5}{15} + \frac{17x^7}{315} + \ldots \quad (-\tfrac{1}{2}\pi < x < \tfrac{1}{2}\pi)$

(g) $\sinh x = x + \frac{x^3}{3!} + \frac{x^5}{5!} + \ldots + \frac{x^{2n+1}}{(2n+1)!} + \ldots \quad (\text{all } x)$

(h) $\cosh x = 1 + \frac{x^2}{2!} + \frac{x^4}{4!} + \ldots + \frac{x^{2n}}{(2n)!} + \ldots \quad (\text{all } x)$

Figure 8.6 Some standard Maclaurin series expansions.

In MATLAB the command `taylor(f,n,x,a)` returns $(n-1)$th order Taylor series expansion of $f(x)$ about $x=a$, while the command `taylor(f,n,x)` returns the Maclaurin series expansion of $f(x)$. The corresponding command in MAPLE is `taylor(f,x = a,n);` (Note that in this case we need to specify $x=0$ or $x=a$ or similar and if n is not specified then 6 is the default value). Considering Example 8.10 the commands

MATLAB	MAPLE
`syms x`	
`f = taylor(exp(x)*sin(x), 6,x);`	`taylor(exp(x)*sin(x), x = 0);`
`pretty(ans)`	

return the answers

$x + x^2 + 1/3x^3 - 1/30x^5$	$x + x^2 + \frac{1}{3}x^3 - \frac{1}{30}x^5 + O(x^6)$

which check with the answer given in the solution.

To obtain the first three terms of the corresponding series about $x=a$ the commands

`syms x a`	
`f = taylor(exp(x)*sin(x), 3,x,a);`	`taylor(exp(x)*sin(x), x = a,3);`

return the answer

$$e^a \sin(a) + (e^a \cos(a) + e^a \sin(a))(x - a) + e^a \cos(a)(x - a)^2 + O((x - a)^3)$$

with e^a expressed as `exp(a)` in the MATLAB response.

Example 8.11 Using the Maclaurin series expansions of e^x and $\sin x$, confirm the Maclaurin series expansion of $e^x \sin x$ obtained in Example 8.10.

Solution From entries (b) and (c) of Figure 8.6

$$e^x = 1 + \frac{x}{1!} + \frac{x^2}{2!} + \frac{x^3}{3!} + \dots \quad (\text{all } x)$$

$$\sin x = x - \frac{x^3}{3!} + \frac{x^5}{5!} - \dots \quad (\text{all } x)$$

As indicated in Section 7.7.2, we can multiply two power series within their common domain of convergence, giving in this case

$$\begin{aligned} e^x \sin x &= \left(1 + \frac{x}{1!} + \frac{x^2}{2!} + \frac{x^3}{3!} + \frac{x^4}{4!} + \dots\right)\left(x - \frac{x^3}{3!} + \frac{x^5}{5!} - \dots\right) \\ &= x + x^2 + x^3(\tfrac{1}{2} - \tfrac{1}{6}) + x^4(\tfrac{1}{6} - \tfrac{1}{6}) + x^5(\tfrac{1}{120} + \tfrac{1}{24} - \tfrac{1}{12}) + \dots \\ &= x + x^2 + \tfrac{1}{3}x^3 - \tfrac{1}{30}x^5 + \dots \quad (\text{all } x) \end{aligned}$$

which is the series obtained in Example 8.10.

Example 8.12 Obtain the binomial expansion of $(1 - x^2)^{-1/2}$ and deduce a power series expansion for $\sin^{-1}x$.

Solution From entry (a) of Figure 8.5.

$$(1 + x)^r = 1 + rx + \frac{r(r-1)x^2}{2!} + \frac{r(r-1)(r-2)x^3}{3!} + \dots \quad (|x| < 1)$$

To obtain the expansion of $(1 - x^2)^{-1/2}$, we need to set $r = -\frac{1}{2}$ and replace x by $-x^2$. We shall do this in two steps. First setting $r = -\frac{1}{2}$ gives

$$\begin{aligned} (1 + x)^{-1/2} &= 1 + \frac{-\frac{1}{2}}{1}x + \frac{(-\frac{1}{2})(-\frac{3}{2})}{1\cdot 2}x^2 + \frac{(-\frac{1}{2})(-\frac{3}{2})(-\frac{5}{2})}{1\cdot 2\cdot 3}x^3 + \frac{(-\frac{1}{2})(-\frac{3}{2})(-\frac{5}{2})(-\frac{7}{2})}{1\cdot 2\cdot 3\cdot 4}x^4 + \dots \\ &= 1 - \tfrac{1}{2}x + \frac{1\cdot 3}{2\cdot 4}x^2 - \frac{1\cdot 3\cdot 5}{2\cdot 4\cdot 6}x^3 + \frac{1\cdot 3\cdot 5\cdot 7}{2\cdot 4\cdot 6\cdot 8}x^4 + \dots \quad (|x| < 1) \end{aligned}$$

Then, replacing x by $-x^2$, we have

$$(1 - x^2)^{-1/2} = 1 - \tfrac{1}{2}(-x^2) + \frac{1\cdot 3}{2\cdot 4}(-x^2)^2 - \frac{1\cdot 3\cdot 5}{2\cdot 4\cdot 6}(-x^2)^3 + \frac{1\cdot 3\cdot 5\cdot 7}{2\cdot 4\cdot 6\cdot 8}(-x^2)^4 + \dots$$

giving the required binomial expansion

$$\begin{aligned} (1 - x^2)^{-1/2} &= 1 + \tfrac{1}{2}x^2 + \frac{1\cdot 3}{2\cdot 4}x^4 + \frac{1\cdot 3\cdot 5}{2\cdot 4\cdot 6}x^6 + \frac{1\cdot 3\cdot 5\cdot 7}{2\cdot 4\cdot 6\cdot 8}x^8 + \dots \\ &= 1 + \tfrac{1}{2}x^2 + \tfrac{3}{8}x^4 + \tfrac{5}{16}x^6 + \tfrac{35}{128}x^8 + \dots \quad (|x| < 1) \end{aligned} \quad \textbf{(8.14)}$$

Now

$$\int_0^x \frac{dt}{\sqrt{(1-t^2)}} = \sin^{-1}x$$

and so, integrating the series (8.14) term by term, we obtain

$$\sin^{-1}x = x + \tfrac{1}{6}x^3 + \tfrac{3}{40}x^5 + \tfrac{5}{112}x^7 + \ldots \quad (|x| < 1)$$

Notice that in Example 8.12 we have integrated a power series to obtain the expansion of another function. In general, we may integrate and differentiate power series within their domains of absolute convergence.

For Example 8.12 check that the commands

MATLAB

```
syms x
taylor((1 - x^2)^(-1/2),
9,x);
pretty(ans)
```

MAPLE

```
taylor((1 - x^2)^(-1/2),
x = 0,9);
```

both return the answer given in (8.12) and that the additional commands

MATLAB

```
int(ans);
pretty(ans)
```

MAPLE

```
int(%,x);
```

return the integrated series for $\sin^{-1}x$.

Note: In both cases the square root term could be entered as `1/sqrt(1 - x^2)` and this is often preferred.

Example 8.13 The continuous belt of Example 1.48 has length L given by

$$L = 2[l^2 - (R-r)^2]^{1/2} + \pi(R+r) + 2(R-r)\sin^{-1}\left(\frac{R-r}{l}\right)$$

Show that when $R - r \ll l$, a good approximation to L is given by

$$L \simeq 2l + \pi(R+r) + (R-r)^2/l$$

Solution Taking the first and last term of the formula for L separately we obtain

$$2[l^2 - (R-r)^2]^{1/2} = 2l\left[1 - \left(\frac{R-r}{l}\right)^2\right]^{1/2}$$

$$= 2l\left[1 - \tfrac{1}{2}\left(\frac{R-r}{l}\right)^2 + \frac{\tfrac{1}{2}(-\tfrac{1}{2})}{1\cdot 2}\left(\frac{R-r}{l}\right)^4 - \ldots\right]$$

and

$$2(R-r)\sin^{-1}\left(\frac{R-r}{l}\right)=2(R-r)\left[\left(\frac{R-r}{l}\right)+\tfrac{1}{6}\left(\frac{R-r}{l}\right)^3+\dots\right]$$

Hence

$$L=2l+\pi(R+r)+\frac{(R-r)^2}{l}+\tfrac{1}{12}\frac{(R-r)^4}{l^3}+\dots$$

Thus when $l \gg R-r$, we have

$$L \simeq 2l+\pi(R+r)+(R-r)^2/l$$

See Question 18 in Exercises 8.4.4 for an examination of the error.

8.4.3 L'Hôpital's rule

Sometimes we need to find limits of the form

$$\lim_{x\to a}\frac{f(x)}{g(x)}$$

where $f(a)=g(a)=0$. Even though such a limit may be defined, it cannot be found by substituting $x=a$, since this produces the indeterminate form 0/0. Using Taylor's theorem (Theorem 8.4), we can formulate a rule for obtaining such limits if they exist.

Using Taylor's series, we may write

$$\frac{f(x)}{g(x)}=\frac{f(a)+(x-a)f'(a)+\frac{1}{2}(x-a)^2f''(a)+\dots}{g(a)+(x-a)g'(a)+\frac{1}{2}(x-a)^2g''(a)+\dots}$$

$$=\frac{f'(a)+\frac{1}{2}(x-a)f''(a)+\dots}{g'(a)+\frac{1}{2}(x-a)g''(a)+\dots}\quad \text{since } f(a)=g(a)=0,\ x\neq a$$

Hence

$$\lim_{x\to a}\frac{f(x)}{g(x)}=\frac{f'(a)}{g'(a)}$$

provided $g'(a)\neq 0$. This is known as **L'Hôpital's rule**.

It may be that $f'(a)/g'(a)$ is also indeterminate. Consequently, when applying L'Hôpital's rule to obtain the limit

$$\lim_{x\to a}\frac{f(x)}{g(x)}$$

we must repeat the process of differentiating $f(x)$ and $g(x)$ each time we have the indeterminate form 0/0 at $x=c$. If, however, at any stage in the process, one or other of the derivatives is non-zero at $x=a$ then we must stop the process, since the rule will no longer apply. In such cases the limit is either zero or infinite or does not exist; for example, $\lim_{x\to 0}\frac{1}{x}$ does not exist.

Example 8.14 Using L'Hôpital's rule, obtain the limits

(a) $\lim_{x\to 0}\dfrac{\sin x - x}{x^3}$ (b) $\lim_{x\to 0}\dfrac{1-\cos x}{x+x^2}$

Solution (a) Since $(\sin x - x)/x^3$ takes the indeterminate form 0/0 at $x = 0$, we apply L'Hôpital's rule to give

$$\lim_{x\to 0}\frac{\sin x - x}{x^3} = \lim_{x\to 0}\frac{\cos x - 1}{3x^2} \quad \text{(again 0/0 at } x = 0)$$

$$= \lim_{x\to 0}\frac{-\sin x}{6x} \quad \text{(again 0/0 at } x = 0)$$

$$= \lim_{x\to 0}\frac{-\cos x}{6} = -\tfrac{1}{6}$$

so that

$$\lim_{x\to 0}\frac{\sin x - x}{x^3} = -\tfrac{1}{6}$$

(b) Since $(1 - \cos x)/(x + x^2)$ takes the form 0/0 at $x = 0$, we apply L'Hôpital's rule to give

$$\lim_{x\to 0}\frac{1-\cos x}{x+x^2} = \lim_{x\to 0}\frac{\sin x}{1+2x} = 0$$

Note that in this case the limit is zero since $(\sin x)/(1 + 2x)$ takes the form 0/1 at $x = 0$. If we mistakenly proceeded to apply the rule once again, we should obtain

$$\lim_{x\to 0}\frac{1-\cos x}{x+x^2} = \lim_{x\to 0}\frac{\sin x}{1+2x} = \lim_{x\to 0}\frac{\cos x}{2} = \frac{1}{2}$$

an incorrect answer, since the rule was not applicable. The reader may have noticed that both of these limits can be readily evaluated using Maclaurin series.

8.4.4 Exercises

8 Show that if $f(x) = e^{\cos x}$ then

$$f'(x) = -f(x)\sin x$$

and find $f(0)$ and $f'(0)$. Differentiating the expression for $f'(x)$, obtain $f''(x)$ in terms of $f(x)$ and $f'(x)$, and find $f''(0)$. Repeating the process, obtain $f^{(n)}(0)$ for $n = 3, 4, 5$ and 6, and hence obtain the Maclaurin polynomial of degree six for $f(x)$. Confirm your answer by obtaining the series using the Maclaurin expansions of e^x and $\cos x$.

9 A function $y = y(x)$ satisfies the equation

$$\frac{dy}{dx} = y - x + 1$$

with $y = 1$ when $x = 0$. By repeated differentiation, show that $y^{(n)}(0) = 1$ $(n \geqslant 2)$, and find the Maclaurin series for y.

10 An alternative approach to Question 9 uses the method of successive approximation, rewriting the equation as

$$y_{n+1}(x) = 1 + \int_0^x [y_n(t) - t + 1]\,dt,$$

with $y_0(x) = y(0) = 1$

Putting $y_0(x) = 1$ into the integral, show that

$$y_1(x) = 1 + 2x - \tfrac{1}{2}x^2$$
$$y_2(x) = 1 + 2x + \tfrac{1}{2}x^2 - \tfrac{1}{6}x^3$$

and find y_3 and y_4.

11 Show that the binomial expansion of $(1 + x)^{-1}$ is

$$(1 + x)^{-1} = 1 - x + x^2 - x^3 + \dots \quad (-1 < x < 1)$$

Hence find the Maclaurin series expansion of $\tan^{-1}x$.

12 Use the series for $\sin x$ and $\cos x$ to obtain the Maclaurin series for $\tan x$ as far as the term in x^7. Deduce the series for $\ln \cos x$.

13 Show that

$$\coth x = \frac{1}{x}(1 + \tfrac{1}{3}x^2 - \tfrac{1}{45}x^4 + \tfrac{2}{945}x^6 - \dots)$$

14 The field strength H of a magnet at a point on the axis at a distance x from its centre is given by

$$H = \frac{M}{2l}\left[\frac{1}{(x - l)^2} - \frac{1}{(x + l)^2}\right]$$

where $2l$ is the length of the magnet and M is its moment. Show that if l is very small compared with x then

$$H \approx \frac{2M}{x^3}$$

15 Using the Maclaurin series expansions of e^x and $\cos x$, show that

$$\lim_{x\to 0}\left(\frac{e^x + e^{-x} - 2}{2\cos 2x - 2}\right) = -\tfrac{1}{4}$$

16 Show that

$$\ln\left(\frac{\sin x}{x}\right) \approx -\tfrac{1}{6}x^2 - \tfrac{1}{180}x^4$$

if powers of x greater than x^5 are neglected.

17 By expanding e^{-x^2} as a Maclaurin series, show that

$$\int_0^{1/2} e^{-x^2}\,dx \approx 0.461$$

18 Considering the problem of Example 8.13, for what values of l does the approximation

$$L \approx 2l + \frac{(R - r)^2}{l} + 3.14(R + r)$$

have a percentage error of less than 0.05% when $R = 5$ and $r = 4$?

19 Using L'Hôpital's rule, find the following limits:

(a) $\lim_{x\to 2}\dfrac{x^3 - 3x - 2}{x^3 - 8}$ (b) $\lim_{x\to 0}\dfrac{1 - (1 - x)^{1/4}}{x}$

(c) $\lim_{x\to \pi}\dfrac{\sin 3x}{\sin 2x}$ (d) $\lim_{x\to 1}\left(\dfrac{3}{x^3 - 1} - \dfrac{1}{x - 1}\right)$

(e) $\lim_{x\to 0}\dfrac{x\cos x - \sin x}{x^3}$ (f) $\lim_{x\to \pi/2}\dfrac{1 - \sin x}{\ln \sin x}$

20 Consider again the design of the milk carton discussed in Example 8.34. Show that if the overlap used in its construction is x mm instead of 5 mm, the objective function that must be minimized is

$$f(b) = (4b + x)\left(\frac{1\,136\,000}{b^2} + b + 2x\right)$$

Show that when $x = 0$, the optimal value for b is $b_0^* = 10(568)^{1/3}$. The optimal value b^* depends on x. Obtain the Maclaurin series expansion for b^* as far as the term in x^2 and discuss the effect of the overlap size on the design of the carton. (*Hint*: Let $b^* \approx b_0 + b_1x + b_2x^2$.)

8.4.5 Interpolation revisited

In Section 2.9.1 we developed the idea of linear interpolation and showed that the approximation

$$f(x) \approx f_i + \frac{x - x_i}{x_{i+1} - x_i}(f_{i+1} - f_i)$$

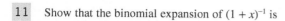

gave a value for $f(x)$ which was as accurate as the original data when $|\Delta^2 f_i|$ is less than 4 units of the least significant figure. In many applications, it is easier to express this condition in terms of the second derivative rather than the second difference.

Now

$$\Delta^2 f_i = f(x_i + h) - 2f(x_i) + f(x_i - h)$$

Replacing $f(x_i + h)$ and $f(x_i - h)$ by their Taylor expansions about $x = x_i$, we have (after some cancelling of terms)

$$\Delta^2 f_i = h^2 f''(x_i) + \frac{h^4}{12} f''''(x_i) + \ldots$$

The leading term provides a good estimate for $\Delta^2 f_i$ so that the condition for accurate linear interpolation becomes

$$h^2 |f''(x)| < 4 \text{ units of the least significant figure}$$

This enables us to choose an appropriate tabular interval, as is shown in Example 8.15.

Example 8.15 The function $f(x) = e^{-x}$ is to be tabulated to 4dp on the interval [0, 0.5]. Find the maximum tabular interval such that the resulting table is suitable for linear interpolation to 4dp, that is, to yield an interpolated value which is as accurate as the tabulated value.

Solution Here we require that

$$h^2 |f''(x)| < 4 \times 0.0001$$

Since $f(x) = e^{-x}$ we deduce that $f''(x) = e^{-x}$. On the interval [0, 0.5], the maximum value of e^{-x} occurs at $x = 0$, where $e^0 = 1$. Thus we need the largest value of h such that

$$h^2 < 4 \times 0.0001$$

Hence $h < 0.02$, so that the largest tabular interval is 0.02.

8.4.6 Exercises

21 A table for e^x is required for use with linear interpolation to 6dp. It is tabulated for values of x from $x = 0$ to $x = X$ at intervals of 0.001. What is the largest possible value of X?

22 A table for $\tan x$ is required for use with linear interpolation to 6dp. It is tabulated for values of x from $x = 0$ to $x = 1$ at intervals of h rad. What is the largest possible value of h?

23 In Section 8.6 we discussed the process of numerical differentiation using the approximation

$$\phi(h) = \frac{f(a+h) - f(a-h)}{2h}$$

Using the Taylor series for $f(a + h)$ and $f(a - h)$ about $x = a$, show that

$$f'(a) = \phi(h) - \frac{h^2}{3!} f^{(3)}(a) - \frac{h^4}{5!} f^{(5)}(a) - \ldots$$

and deduce that

$$f'(a) = \tfrac{1}{3}[4\phi(\tfrac{1}{2}h) - \phi(h)] + \tfrac{1}{4}\frac{h^4}{5!} f^{(5)}(a) + \ldots$$

Writing $\psi(h) = \frac{1}{3}[4\phi(\frac{1}{2}h) - \phi(h)]$, show that $\frac{1}{15}[16\psi(\frac{1}{2}h) - \psi(h)]$ yields an approximation to $f'(a)$ with truncation error $O(h^6)$. Apply this extrapolation procedure to find $f'(1)$ when $f(x) = \cosh x$, taking $h = 0.4$, 0.2 and 0.1, working to as many decimal places as your calculator will permit.

8.4.7 The convergence of iterations revisited

In Section 8.4.2 we analysed the convergence of an iteration $x_{n+1} = g(x_n)$ for the root α of an equation $f(x) = 0$. We can use the Taylor expansion to analyse the **rate of convergence** of such schemes. Setting $x_n = \alpha + \varepsilon_n$, so that ε_n is the error after n iterations, we have

$$\alpha + \varepsilon_{n+1} = g(\alpha + \varepsilon_n)$$

Expanding $g(\alpha + \varepsilon_n)$ about $x = \alpha$, using the Taylor series (8.12), gives

$$g(\alpha + \varepsilon_n) = \alpha + \varepsilon_{n+1} = g(\alpha) + \frac{\varepsilon_n}{1!}g'(\alpha) + \frac{\varepsilon_n^2}{2!}g''(\alpha) + \frac{\varepsilon_n^3}{3!}g'''(\alpha) + \ldots \quad \textbf{(8.15)}$$

Since α is a root of the equation $f(x) = 0$, we have $\alpha = g(\alpha)$ and (8.15) simplifies to

$$\varepsilon_{n+1} = \frac{\varepsilon_n}{1!}g'(\alpha) + \frac{\varepsilon_n^2}{2!}g''(\alpha) + \frac{\varepsilon_n^3}{3!}g'''(\alpha) + \ldots \quad \textbf{(8.16)}$$

If $g'(\alpha) \neq 0$ then ε_{n+1} is proportional to ε_n, and we have a first-order process. If $g'(\alpha) = 0$ and $g''(\alpha) \neq 0$ then ε_{n+1} is proportional to ε_n^2, and we have a second-order process, and so on.

Example 8.16

The equation $x \tan x = 4$ has an infinite number of roots. To find the root near $x = 1$, we may use the iteration

$$x_{n+1} = \tan^{-1}\left(\frac{4}{x_n}\right)$$

Show that this is a first-order process. Starting with $x_0 = 1$, find x_3 and assess its accuracy.

Solution

Here $g(x) = \tan^{-1}(4/x)$, so that

$$g'(x) = \frac{-4}{x^2 + 16}$$

which is non-zero for all x, i.e. $g'(\alpha) \neq 0$. Thus the iteration is a first-order process.

Starting with $x_0 = 1$, we obtain, working to 4dp, the following table.

n	x_n	$4/x_n$	$\tan^{-1}(4/x_n)$
0	1.0000	4.0000	1.3258
1	1.3258	3.0170	1.2507
2	1.2507	3.1982	1.2678
3	1.2678		

From (8.16) we can assess the accuracy of x_n using

$$\varepsilon_{n+1} = \varepsilon_n g'(\alpha) + \ldots$$

and approximating ε_n by $x_n - x_{n+1}$ and α by x_3. Thus in this case we have

$$\varepsilon_3 \approx g'(x_3)(x_2 - x_3) = \frac{-4}{16 + (1.2678)^2}(-0.0171) = 0.0039$$

so that the root is 1.26 to 3sf.

8.4.8 Newton–Raphson procedure

One of the most popular techniques used by engineers for solving non-linear equations is the **Newton–Raphson procedure**. The basic idea is that if x_0 is an approximation to the root $x = \alpha$ of the equation $f(x) = 0$ then a closer approximation will be given by the point $x = x_1$ where the tangent to the graph at $x = x_0$ cuts the x axis, as shown in Figure 8.7.

Figure 8.7
The Newton–Raphson root-finding method.

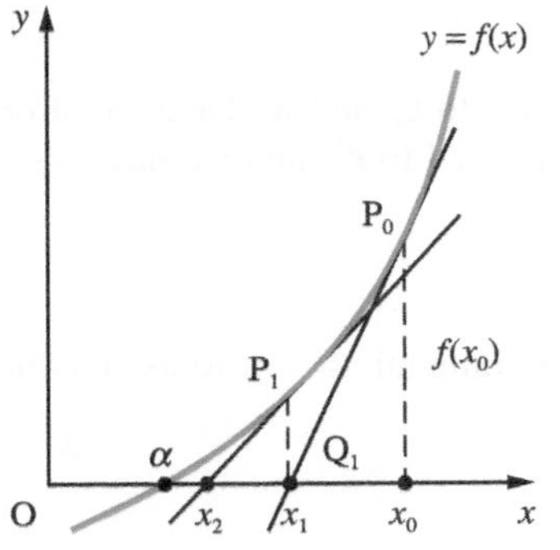

From the definition of the derivative

$$f'(x_0) = \text{slope of } P_0Q_1 = \frac{f(x_0)}{x_0 - x_1}$$

which can be rearranged to give

$$x_1 = x_0 - \frac{f(x_0)}{f'(x_0)}$$

Taking x_1 as the new approximation to the root $x = \alpha$ and repeating the procedure, as illustrated in Figure 8.7, we obtain the closer aproximation

$$x_2 = x_1 - \frac{f(x_1)}{f'(x_1)}$$

and so on. In general, we may write

$$x_{n+1} = x_n - \frac{f(x_n)}{f'(x_n)} \quad (n = 0, 1, 2, \ldots) \qquad \textbf{(8.17)}$$

Equation (8.7) is known as the Newton–Raphson iteration procedure for obtaining an approximation to the root of $f(x) = 0$. Note that if $f'(x_n) = 0$ then (8.7) cannot be used to obtain x_{n+1}. This is because the tangent to the graph of $y = f(x)$ at $x = x_n$ will be parallel to the horizontal x axis.

Comparing with the general iteration $x_{n+1} = g(x_n)$, we see that in the case of the Newton–Raphson procedure (8.19) the iteration function is

$$g(x) = x - \frac{f(x)}{f'(x)}$$

which, using the quotient rule, has derivative

$$g'(x) = 1 - \frac{[f'(x)]^2 - f(x)f''(x)}{[f'(x)]^2} = \frac{f(x)f''(x)}{[f'(x)]^2}$$

Since α is a root of $f(x) = 0$, we have $f(\alpha) = 0$, giving

$$g'(\alpha) = 0$$

so the procedure is not a first-order process. Differentiating again and substituting $x = \alpha$, we obtain

$$g''(\alpha) = \frac{f''(\alpha)}{f'(\alpha)}$$

and we have a second-order process provided that $f'(\alpha) \neq 0$. If $f''(\alpha) = 0, f'(\alpha) \neq 0$ then we have a third- or higher-order process. When $f(x) = 0$ has a repeated root at $x = \alpha$, $g'(\alpha)$ has the indeterminate form 0/0, and the analysis fails. Repeated roots cause numerical as well as theoretical problems.

Example 8.17 The equation $x \tan x = 4$ was considered earlier in Example 8.16. Apply the Newton–Raphson method to find the root near $x = 1$.

Solution First, we rewrite the equation in the more convenient (for differentiation) form

$$x \sin x - 4 \cos x = 0$$

Then taking $f(x) = x \sin x - 4 \cos x$ we have $f'(x) = x \cos x + 5 \sin x$. Using the iteration

$$x_{n+1} = x_n - f(x_n)/f'(x_n), \quad x_0 = 1$$

gives the values (to 9dp)

1.000 000 000
1.277 976 731
1.264 600 951
1.264 591 571
1.264 591 571

so that after four iterations we obtain an answer correct to 9dp.

Example 8.18 Find the root of

$$8.0000x^4 + 0.4500x^3 - 4.5440x - 0.1136 = 0$$

near $x = 0.8$ to 4sf.

Figure 8.8
Iteration for the root of the equation $8.0000x^4 + 0.4500x^3 - 4.5440x - 0.1136 = 0$.

n	x_n	$f(x_n)$	$f'(x_n)$	$-f_n/f'_n$
0	0.8000	−0.241 600	12.7040	0.019 018
1	0.8190	0.011 436	13.9408	−0.000 820
2	0.8182	0.000 340	13.8876	−0.000 022
3	0.8182			

Solution In this particular example

$$f(x) = 8.0000x^4 + 0.4500x^3 - 4.5440x - 0.1136$$

giving

$$f'(x) = 32.0000x^3 + 1.3500x^2 - 4.5440$$

When iterating for the root using the Newton–Raphson procedure (8.17), it is usual to present the calculations in tabular form, as shown in Figure 8.8 for this particular example. To 4sf the root is given by $x = 0.8182$. When using the Newton–Raphson method, it is recommended that the iteration formula is *not* tidied up into a single expression but is left in the 'approximation minus error' format. Tidying up may lead to ill-conditioning of the numerical procedure.

There are no built-in programs for Newton–Raphson in either MATLAB or MAPLE. The method is basically a numerical procedure, so MATLAB seems to be the obvious package to use. You will need to develop a little program, as illustrated below for Example 8.18.

```
% Set up initial data and put initial results into R
e = 0.0001; acc = 1; x = .8; f = 8*x^4 + .45*x^3 -
4.544*x - 0.1136; fd = 32*x^3 + 1.35*x^2 - 4.544;
R = [x;f;fd];
% Now iterate until acc is less than e and add results
to R
while acc>e xold = x;
x = x - f/fd; f = 8*x^4 + .45*x^3 - 4.544*x - 0.1136;
fd = 32*x^3 + 1.35*x^2 - 4.5440;
R = [R [x;f;fd]];
acc = abs(x - xold);
end
R
```

which returns

```
R =
     0.8000    0.8190    0.8182    0.8182
    -0.2416    0.0117    0.0000    0.0000
    12.7040   13.9420   13.8863   13.8861
```

Note: Small discrepancies with answers given in Figure 8.8 are due to the number of decimal places being retained during working.

8.4.9 Optimization revisited

In Section 8.5 we indicated that we would return to reconsider the conditions for determining the nature of stationary points following the introduction of the Taylor series.

If a minimum value of a differentiable function $f(x)$ occurs at $x = a$ then the difference $f(a + h) - f(a)$ will be positive for all small h. However, from the Taylor series (8.12)

$$f(a + h) - f(a) = hf'(a) + \frac{1}{2!}h^2 f''(a) + \frac{1}{3!}h^3 f'''(a) + \dots$$

and the sign of the expression on the right-hand side depends on the sign of h. It will change sign as h changes sign unless $f'(a) = 0$, in which case the sign depends on the sign of $f''(a)$. Thus a necessary condition for the minimum to occur at $x = a$ is that $f'(a) = 0$, and a necessary and sufficient condition for a minimum of $f(x)$ at $x = a$ is $f'(a) = 0$ and $f''(a) > 0$. Similarly, the maxima of differentiable functions occur when $f'(a) = 0$ and $f''(a) < 0$. If $f'(a) = 0$ and $f''(a) = 0$, we may have a maximum or minimum value or a point of inflection. If $f'(a) = f''(a) = 0$, a necessary condition for a minimum or maximum at $x = a$ is $f'''(a) = 0$, and so on. However, it is important to remember that a function may have an optimal value at a point where its derivative does not exist, as illustrated in Figure 8.9. A numerical scheme for locating the optimal point of a function using the Newton–Raphson procedure can be established. The resulting iteration

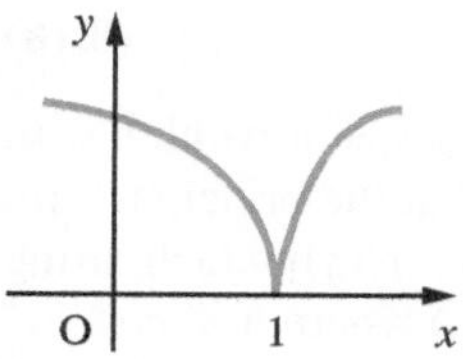

Figure 8.9
$y = (x - 1)^{2/3}$ has a minimum at $x = 1$ but it is not differentiable here.

$$x_{n+1} = x_n - \frac{f'(x_n)}{f''(x_n)}$$

is, however, rarely used in practice. Generally, bracketing methods are used similar to that described in Question 85 (Exercises 8.5.2).

8.4.10 Exercises

24 Given below are three methods for calculating $\sqrt{2}$ by iteration. Find the order of each process and discuss their numerical properties.

(a) $x_{n+1} = 1 + 1/(1 + x_n)$ (b) $x_{n+1} = \frac{1}{2}(x_n + 2/x_n)$

(c) $x_{n+1} = (3x_n^4 + 12x_n^2 - 4)/(8x_n^3)$

25 Use the Newton–Raphson iteration procedure to find the real root of $x^3 - 6x^2 + 9x + 1 = 0$ to 4dp.

26 Use the Newton–Raphson method to find the two positive roots of $x^4 - 4x^3 - 12x^2 + 32x + 28 = 0$.

27 The iteration $x_{n+1} = x_n(3 - 3ax_n + a^2x_n^2)$ may be used to calculate the reciprocal of a, that is, to solve $ax = 1$. Show that this is a third-order process with $\varepsilon_{n+1} = a^2\varepsilon_n^3$. Apply the iteration with $a = 1.735$, starting with $x_0 = 0.5$, and prove that x_2 is correct to 8dp.

8.4.11 Numerical integration

A remarkable mathematical result that follows from the Taylor series is known as the **Euler–Maclaurin formula**:

$$\int_a^b f(x)\mathrm{d}x = \frac{b-a}{2}[f(b) + f(a)] - \frac{(b-a)^2}{12}[f'(b) - f'(a)]$$
$$+ \frac{(b-a)^4}{720}[f^{(3)}(b) - f^{(3)}(a)] - \frac{(b-a)^6}{30\,240}[f^{(5)}(b) - f^{(5)}(a)] \dots$$

Subdividing the interval $[a, b]$ into n equal strips of width h, we have

$$\int_a^b f(x)\mathrm{d}x = \sum_{r=0}^{n-1}\int_{x_r}^{x_{r+1}} f(x)\mathrm{d}x, \quad x_r = a + rh$$

Applying the Euler–Maclaurin formula to each term in the summation, we obtain the trapezium rule together with a power series expansion of the truncation error in terms of h:

$$\int_a^b f(x)\mathrm{d}x = \tfrac{1}{2}h(f_0 + 2f_1 + 2f_2 + \ldots + 2f_{n-1} + f_n) - \tfrac{1}{12}h^2(f'_n - f'_0)$$

$$+ \tfrac{1}{720}h^4(f_n^{(3)} - f_0^{(3)}) - \tfrac{1}{30\,240}h^6(f_n^{(5)} - f_0^{(5)}) + \ldots$$

$$= T(h) + \alpha_1 h^2 + \alpha_2 h^4 + \alpha_3 h^6 + \ldots \qquad \textbf{(8.18)}$$

where $T(h)$ is the trapezium approximation to the integral using n strips of width h with $nh = b - a$, and the α's are independent of h. From this we see that the principal term of the **global truncation** error for the approximation is $\frac{1}{12}h^2[f'(b) - f'(a)]$ which, using the first mean value Theorem 8.3, may be written $\frac{1}{12}h^2(b - a)f''(c)$ where $a < c < b$.

This analysis makes no allowance for the effect of rounding errors in the values of f_i $(i = 0, 1, \ldots, n)$. A simple estimate of these is

$$h(\tfrac{1}{2} + \underbrace{1 + 1 + \ldots + 1}_{n-1 \text{ terms}} + \tfrac{1}{2}) \times (\tfrac{1}{2} \text{ unit of the least significant figure})$$

$$= nh(\tfrac{1}{2} \text{ unit of the least significant figure})$$

$$= (b - a)(\tfrac{1}{2} \text{ unit of the least significant figure})$$

This result assumes a fixed number of decimal places in the values of the integrand, and is suitable for calculator work. For computers, when h is small and n large, there is the problem of loss of significant digits when adding a large number of almost-equal numbers.

Example 8.19 In Example 8.68 the integral $\int_1^2(1/x)\mathrm{d}x$ was estimated using the trapezium rule with $h = \frac{1}{4}$ and tabulating the integrand to 6dp. Estimate an error bound for the answer obtained.

Solution Here $f(x) = 1/x$, $a = 1$ and $b = 2$. The global error is given by

$$\tfrac{1}{12}(b - a)h^2f''(X), \quad \text{with } a \leqslant X \leqslant b$$

so that in this example it is

$$\tfrac{1}{12}(1)(0.25)^2\frac{2}{X^3}, \quad \text{with } 1 \leqslant X \leqslant 2$$

The largest possible value this can take is when $X = 1$, so we obtain an estimate for the truncation error of 0.010. The rounding-error effect, 0.000 000 5, is negligible compared with this. The error bound we have now calculated safely overestimates the actual error 0.004 obtained in the calculation.

Returning to the full Euler–Maclaurin expansion (8.18), using $2n$ strips of width $\frac{1}{2}h$, we obtain

$$\int_a^b f(x)\mathrm{d}x = T(\tfrac{1}{2}h) + \tfrac{1}{4}\alpha_1 h^2 + \tfrac{1}{16}\alpha_2 h^4 + \tfrac{1}{64}\alpha_3 h^6 + \ldots \qquad \textbf{(8.19)}$$

Eliminating the α_1 terms from (8.18) and (8.19) (by subtracting the former from $4\times$ the latter, and dividing the result by 3) gives

$$\int_a^b f(x)\mathrm{d}x = \tfrac{1}{3}[4T(\tfrac{1}{2}h) - T(h)] - \tfrac{1}{4}\alpha_2 h^4 - \tfrac{5}{16}\alpha_3 h^6 - \ldots$$

Thus the estimate $\frac{1}{3}[4T(\frac{1}{2}h) - T(h)]$ is more accurate than either $T(\frac{1}{2}h)$ or $T(h)$ taken separately. This implies that the truncation error for Simpson's rule is proportional to h^4, which explains why it is a good method for hand computation (as opposed to automatic computation).

8.4.12 Exercises

28 Simpson's rule, Section 8.10.2, for the numerical evaluation of an integral is

$$\int_a^b f(x)\mathrm{d}x \approx \frac{b-a}{n}(f_0 + 4f_1 + 2f_2 + \ldots + 2f_{n-2} + 4f_{n-1} + f_n)$$

where n is an even number. The global truncation error is

$$\frac{(b-a)^5}{180n^4}f^{(4)}(c), \quad \text{with } a < c < b$$

If $f(x) = \ln\cosh x$ and $a = 0$, $b = 0.5$, show that $|f^{(4)}(x)| < 2$ for $0 \leqslant x \leqslant 0.5$ and deduce that the global truncation error will be less than $1/(2880n^4)$.

If $f(x)$ is tabulated to 4dp, show that the accumulated rounding error using the formula is less than 1/40 000, and find n such that, using the formula, the integral $\int_0^{0.5}\ln\cosh x\,\mathrm{d}x$ would be evaluated correctly to 4dp.

29 (a) Use the trapezium rule, Section 8.10.1, with $h = 0.25$ to evaluate $\int_0^1\sqrt{x}\,\mathrm{d}x$. Compare your answer with the exact value, $\frac{2}{3}$.

(b) Put $x = t^2$ in the integral and again evaluate it using the trapezium rule with four strips. Compare your answer with the exact value and with the answer found in (a).

(c) Examine the global truncation errors in both cases and draw some general conclusions.

30 The trapezium rule estimate for $\int_0^1 \mathrm{e}^{x^2}\mathrm{d}x$ with $h = 0.25$ is 1.490 68 to 5dp. Estimate the size of the global truncation error in this approximation and show that

$$1.40 \leqslant \int_0^1 \mathrm{e}^{x^2}\mathrm{d}x < 1.48$$

What value of h will give an answer correct to 4dp?

31 Show that the composite trapezium rule with step length h yields the approximation

$$\int_0^1 \mathrm{e}^x\,\mathrm{d}x \approx \tfrac{1}{2}h(\mathrm{e}-1)\coth\left(\frac{h}{2}\right)$$

Using the series expansion for $\coth x$

$$\coth x = \frac{1}{x}(1 + \tfrac{1}{3}x^2 - \tfrac{1}{45}x^4 + \tfrac{2}{945}x^6 - \ldots)$$

obtain the approximation

$$\int_0^1 \mathrm{e}^x\,\mathrm{d}x \approx (\mathrm{e}-1)(1 + \tfrac{1}{12}h^2 - \tfrac{1}{720}h^4 + \tfrac{1}{30240}h^6 - \ldots)$$

Compare this answer with the Euler–Maclaurin theorem.

8.5 Calculus of vectors

In mechanics the vectors describing a dynamic system are time-dependent. Such vectors may be integrated and differentiated in a natural extension of the same processes for scalar quantities. In this section we briefly introduce the relevant definitions.

8.5.1 Differentiation and integration of vectors

The formal definition gives the derivative of a vector $\boldsymbol{v}(t)$ as

$$\frac{\mathrm{d}\boldsymbol{v}}{\mathrm{d}t} = \lim_{\Delta t \to 0} \frac{\boldsymbol{v}(t + \Delta t) - \boldsymbol{v}(t)}{\Delta t}$$

so if $\boldsymbol{v} = (v_1(t), v_2(t), v_3(t))$ then

$$\frac{\mathrm{d}\boldsymbol{v}}{\mathrm{d}t} = \left(\frac{\mathrm{d}v_1}{\mathrm{d}t}, \frac{\mathrm{d}v_2}{\mathrm{d}t}, \frac{\mathrm{d}v_3}{\mathrm{d}t}\right)$$

For example, the position vector $\boldsymbol{r}(t) = (x(t), y(t), z(t))$ of a particle may be differentiated with respect to time t to give its velocity $\boldsymbol{v}(t)$ as

$$\boldsymbol{v}(t) = \frac{\mathrm{d}\boldsymbol{r}}{\mathrm{d}t} = \left(\frac{\mathrm{d}x}{\mathrm{d}t}, \frac{\mathrm{d}y}{\mathrm{d}t}, \frac{\mathrm{d}z}{\mathrm{d}t}\right)$$

Differentiating again gives the acceleration of the particle as

$$\boldsymbol{f}(t) = \frac{\mathrm{d}\boldsymbol{v}}{\mathrm{d}t} = \frac{\mathrm{d}^2\boldsymbol{r}}{\mathrm{d}t^2} = \left(\frac{\mathrm{d}^2x}{\mathrm{d}t^2}, \frac{\mathrm{d}^2y}{\mathrm{d}t^2}, \frac{\mathrm{d}^2z}{\mathrm{d}t^2}\right)$$

When differentiating a vector with respect to time, it is conventional to use a 'dot' notation and write

$$\frac{\mathrm{d}\boldsymbol{r}}{\mathrm{d}t} = \dot{\boldsymbol{r}} \quad \text{and} \quad \frac{\mathrm{d}^2\boldsymbol{r}}{\mathrm{d}t^2} = \ddot{\boldsymbol{r}}$$

The usual rules of differentiation may be deduced from this definition.

(a) $\dfrac{\mathrm{d}}{\mathrm{d}t}[\boldsymbol{u}(t) + \boldsymbol{v}(t)] = \dfrac{\mathrm{d}\boldsymbol{u}}{\mathrm{d}t} + \dfrac{\mathrm{d}\boldsymbol{v}}{\mathrm{d}t}$

(b) $\dfrac{\mathrm{d}}{\mathrm{d}t}[\lambda(t)\boldsymbol{v}(t)] = \dfrac{\mathrm{d}\lambda}{\mathrm{d}t}\boldsymbol{v}(t) + \lambda(t)\dfrac{\mathrm{d}\boldsymbol{v}}{\mathrm{d}t}$, where $\lambda(t)$ is a scalar function

(c) $\dfrac{\mathrm{d}}{\mathrm{d}t}[\boldsymbol{u}(t)\cdot \boldsymbol{v}(t)] = \dfrac{\mathrm{d}\boldsymbol{u}}{\mathrm{d}t}\cdot \boldsymbol{v}(t) + \boldsymbol{u}(t)\cdot\dfrac{\mathrm{d}\boldsymbol{v}}{\mathrm{d}t}$

(d) $\dfrac{\mathrm{d}}{\mathrm{d}t}[\boldsymbol{u}(t)\times \boldsymbol{v}(t)] = \dfrac{\mathrm{d}\boldsymbol{u}}{\mathrm{d}t}\times \boldsymbol{v}(t) + \boldsymbol{u}(t)\times\dfrac{\mathrm{d}\boldsymbol{v}}{\mathrm{d}t}$, note importance of order

Example 8.20 Sketch the curve

$$\boldsymbol{r} = \sin t\boldsymbol{i} + \cos t\boldsymbol{j}$$

Calculate

(a) $\dfrac{d\boldsymbol{r}}{dt}$ (b) $\dfrac{d^2\boldsymbol{r}}{dt^2}$ (c) $\left|\dfrac{d\boldsymbol{r}}{dt}\right|$ (d) $\dfrac{d}{dt}(|\boldsymbol{r}|)$

Solution A sketch of the curve is shown in Figure 8.10. It is a circle with centre at the origin and of unit radius.

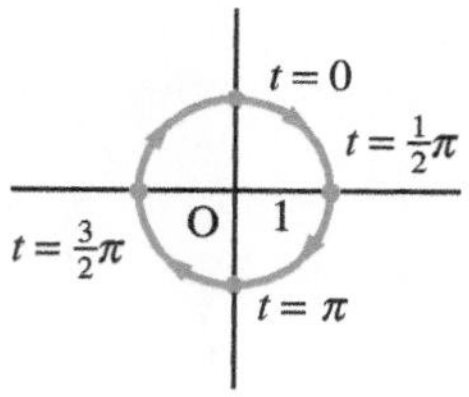

Figure 8.10

(a) $\dfrac{d\boldsymbol{r}}{dt} = \dfrac{d}{dt}(\sin t)\boldsymbol{i} + \dfrac{d}{dt}(\cos t)\boldsymbol{j} = \cos t\boldsymbol{i} - \sin t\boldsymbol{j}$

(b) $\dfrac{d^2\boldsymbol{r}}{dt^2} = \dfrac{d}{dt}(\cos t)\boldsymbol{i} - \dfrac{d}{dt}(\sin t)\boldsymbol{j} = -\sin t\boldsymbol{i} - \cos t\boldsymbol{j}$

(c) $\left|\dfrac{d\boldsymbol{r}}{dt}\right| = (\cos^2 t + \sin^2 t)^{1/2} = 1$

(d) $|\boldsymbol{r}| = (\sin^2 t + \cos^2 t)^{1/2} = 1$

so that

$$\frac{d}{dt}(|\boldsymbol{r}|) = \frac{d}{dt}(1) = 0$$

Note that

$$\frac{d}{dt}(|\boldsymbol{r}|) \neq \left|\frac{d\boldsymbol{r}}{dt}\right|$$

In the same way, the integration of a vector $\boldsymbol{v}(t)$ with respect to the variable t is usually performed in terms of its components:

$$\int \boldsymbol{v}(t)dt = \int (v_1(t), v_2(t), v_3(t))\,dt$$

$$= \left(\int v_1(t)\,dt, \int v_2(t)\,dt, \int v_3(t)\,dt\right)$$

Of course, the arbitrary constant of integration is now a vector constant $\boldsymbol{c} = (c_1, c_2, c_3)$.

Example 8.21 Given

$$\frac{d^2\boldsymbol{r}}{dt^2} = -g\boldsymbol{k} \quad \text{with} \quad \boldsymbol{r}(0) = 0 \quad \text{and} \quad \dot{\boldsymbol{r}}(0) = \boldsymbol{V}$$

find $\boldsymbol{r}(t)$. Obtain the locus of the point P, such that $\overrightarrow{OP} = \boldsymbol{r}$, in terms of x and z when $\boldsymbol{V} = (u, 0, v)$.

Solution This is the equation of motion of a projectile under gravity. Integrating the equation once gives

$$\frac{d\boldsymbol{r}}{dt} = -gt\boldsymbol{k} + \boldsymbol{c}$$

Since $\dot{\boldsymbol{r}}(0) = \boldsymbol{V}$, we have

$$\boldsymbol{c} = \boldsymbol{V} \quad \text{and} \quad \frac{d\boldsymbol{r}}{dt} = -gt\boldsymbol{k} + \boldsymbol{V}$$

Integrating a second time gives

$$\boldsymbol{r}(t) = \boldsymbol{V}t - \tfrac{1}{2}gt^2\boldsymbol{k} + \boldsymbol{a}$$

Since $\boldsymbol{r}(0) = 0$, we have $\boldsymbol{a} = 0$, giving

$$\boldsymbol{r} = \boldsymbol{V}t - \tfrac{1}{2}gt^2\boldsymbol{k}$$

Now $\boldsymbol{r} = (x, y, z)$, so that when $\boldsymbol{V} = (u, 0, v)$, we have

$$\begin{aligned}(x, y, z) &= (u, 0, v)t + (0, 0, -\tfrac{1}{2}gt^2)\\ &= (ut, 0, vt) + (0, 0, -\tfrac{1}{2}gt^2)\\ &= (ut, 0, vt - \tfrac{1}{2}gt^2)\end{aligned}$$

Thus

$$x = ut, \quad y = 0 \quad \text{and} \quad z = vt - \tfrac{1}{2}gt^2$$

Substituting $t = x/u$ into the equation for z gives, after some rearrangement,

$$z = \frac{1}{2}\frac{v^2}{g} - \frac{g}{2u^2}\left(x - \frac{uv}{g}\right)^2$$

This is a parabola with vertex at $(uv/g, 0, v^2/2g)$.

8.5.2 Exercises

32 If $\boldsymbol{r} = (t, t^2, t^3)$, find $\dot{\boldsymbol{r}}(t)$ and $\ddot{\boldsymbol{r}}(t)$.

33 Given the vector

$$\boldsymbol{r} = (1 + t)\boldsymbol{i} + t^2\boldsymbol{j} + \tfrac{2}{3}t^3\boldsymbol{k}$$

evaluate $d\boldsymbol{r}/dt$ and write it in the form

$$\frac{d\boldsymbol{r}}{dt} = f(t)\hat{\boldsymbol{T}}(t)$$

where $\hat{\boldsymbol{T}}$ is the unit tangent direction. Calculate $d\hat{\boldsymbol{T}}/dt$ in its simplest form and show that it is perpendicular to $\hat{\boldsymbol{T}}$.

34 In polar coordinates (r, θ), the unit vectors $\hat{\boldsymbol{r}}$ and $\hat{\boldsymbol{\theta}}$ are defined as in Figure 8.11. Show that

$$\begin{aligned}\hat{\boldsymbol{r}} &= \cos\theta\boldsymbol{i} + \sin\theta\boldsymbol{j}\\ \hat{\boldsymbol{\theta}} &= -\sin\theta\boldsymbol{i} + \cos\theta\boldsymbol{j}\end{aligned}$$

Hence from the definition $\boldsymbol{r} = r\hat{\boldsymbol{r}}$ show that

$$\frac{d\boldsymbol{r}}{dt} = \frac{dr}{dt}\hat{\boldsymbol{r}} + r\omega\hat{\boldsymbol{\theta}} \quad \text{where} \quad \omega = \frac{d\theta}{dt}$$

Deduce that

$$\frac{d\hat{\boldsymbol{r}}}{dt} = \omega\hat{\boldsymbol{\theta}} \quad \text{and} \quad \frac{d\hat{\boldsymbol{\theta}}}{dt} = -\omega\hat{\boldsymbol{r}}$$

and

$$\frac{d^2\boldsymbol{r}}{dt^2} = \left(\frac{d^2r}{dt^2} - r\omega^2\right)\hat{\boldsymbol{r}} + \left(2\omega\frac{dr}{dt} + r\frac{d\omega}{dt}\right)\hat{\boldsymbol{\theta}}$$

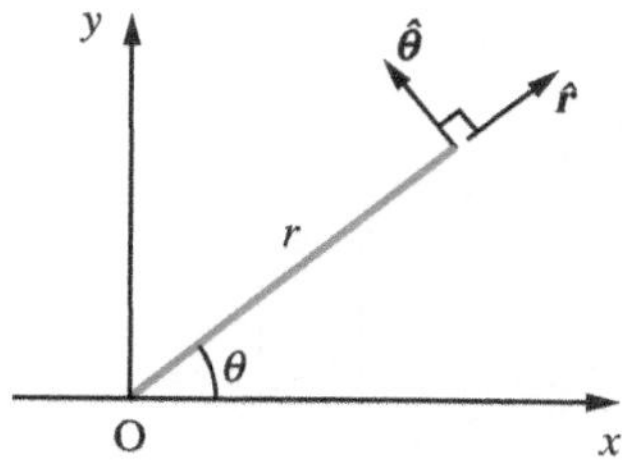

Figure 8.11

35 Show that if the vector $\boldsymbol{a}(t) = f(t)\boldsymbol{i} + g(t)\boldsymbol{j}$ has constant magnitude, then $\boldsymbol{a}$ and $\dfrac{\mathrm{d}\boldsymbol{a}}{\mathrm{d}t}$ are perpendicular.

36 A curve is given parametrically by $\boldsymbol{r}(t) = f(t)\boldsymbol{i} + g(t)\boldsymbol{j}$. Show that, if s is the length of an arc measured from a fixed point P_0 on the curve so that s increases as t increases, then

$$\left|\frac{\mathrm{d}\boldsymbol{r}}{\mathrm{d}t}\right| = \frac{\mathrm{d}s}{\mathrm{d}t}$$

Deduce that $\dfrac{\mathrm{d}\boldsymbol{r}}{\mathrm{d}s}$ is a unit tangent vector to the curve at $\boldsymbol{r}(t)$ and that (using the result of Question 38 in Exercises 8.6.4), $\dfrac{\mathrm{d}\boldsymbol{r}}{\mathrm{d}s}$ and $\dfrac{\mathrm{d}^2\boldsymbol{r}}{\mathrm{d}s^2}$ are perpendicular. Show that

$$\left|\frac{\mathrm{d}^2\boldsymbol{r}}{\mathrm{d}s^2}\right| = |\kappa|$$

where κ is the curvature of the curve at that point.

8.6 Functions of several variables

In many applications we use functions of several independent variables, for example, the velocity of a fluid at a point depends on its space coordinates, the temperature in a heat furnace depends upon its position and so on. The basic ideas of calculus apply to functions of several variables as well as to functions of one variable. Of course, because more variables are involved, the notation and technical detail are more complicated but the essential ideas are the same. In the remainder of this chapter we will explore the extension of the process and ideas of differentiation to functions of several independent variables. As we shall see below, the rate of change of the function with respect to its variables can be expressed in terms of the rates of change of the function with respect to each of the independent variables separately.

8.6.1 Representation of functions of two variables

For functions of two independent variables, we are able to extend the ideas of a function of one variable. We use three coordinate axes, conventionally setting x and y as the independent variables and $z = f(x, y)$ as the dependent variable. Instead of a function being represented by a curve in two dimensions, now a function is represented by a surface in three dimensions, as illustrated in Figure 8.12(a) for the function $f(x, y) = 3x - x^3 - y^2$. Often it is easier to understand the behaviour of a function by sketching its **contours** (or **level curves**), that is, the curves defined by $f(x, y) = c$ for various values of the constant c, as shown in Figure 8.12(b) for the same function. Such plots are readily produced using MATLAB or MAPLE.

Figure 8.12
(a) Surface
$f(x, y) = 3x - x^3 - y^2$.
(b) Contours
$3x - x^3 - y^2 = c$.

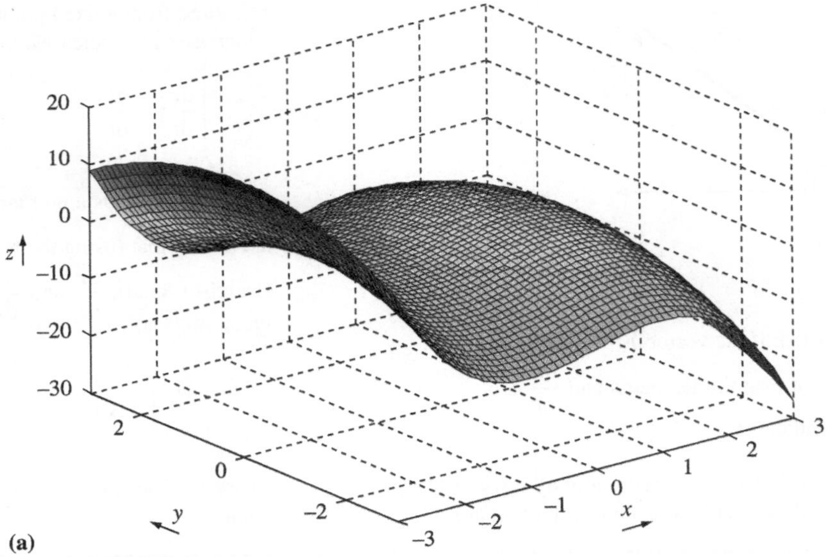

(a)

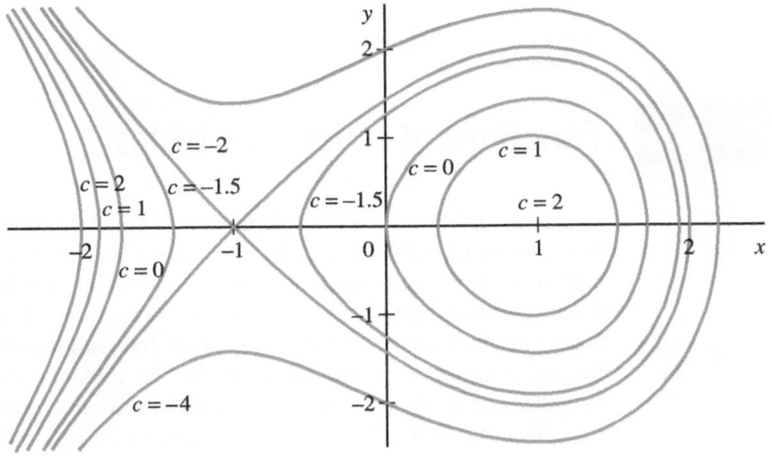

(b)

Using the Symbolic Math Toolbox in MATLAB the commands

```
syms x y
ezsurf(f(x,y))
```

where $f(x, y)$ is a symbolic expression expressed in terms of x and y, plot the surface $z = f(x, y)$ over the default domain $-2\pi < x < 2\pi$, $-2\pi < y < 2\pi$, with the computational grid being chosen according to the amount of variation that occurs. If we wish to specify the domain then we use the command

```
ezsurf (f(x,y),domain)
```

where the domain is specified as either the 4-array $[a, b, c, d]$, with $a \leqslant x \leqslant b$, $c \leqslant y \leqslant b$, or the 2-array $[a, b]$ with $a \leqslant x \leqslant b$, $a \leqslant y \leqslant b$.

In MAPLE the surface $f(x, y)$, $a \leqslant x \leqslant b$, $c \leqslant y \leqslant b$ is obtained using the command

```
plot3d(f(x,y), x = a..b, y = c..d);
```

where $f(x, y)$ is expressed in terms of x and y.

Likewise, in MATLAB the commands

```
syms x y
ezcontour(f(x,y))
```

plot the contour of $f(x, y)$ over the default domain $-2\pi < x < 2\pi$, $-2\pi < y < 2\pi$. The domain may be specified using the command

```
ezcontour(f(x,y), domain)
```

where the domain may be the 4-array or 2-array specified above for `ezsurf`. The corresponding commands in MAPLE are

```
with(plots):
contourplot(f(x,y), x = a..b, y = c..d);
```

8.6.2 Partial derivatives

Given a function of one variable, $f(x)$, we recall from Section 8.2.2 that the derivative was defined by

$$\frac{df}{dx} = \lim_{\Delta x \to 0} \frac{\Delta f}{\Delta x} = \lim_{\Delta x \to 0} \left[\frac{f(x + \Delta x) - f(x)}{\Delta x} \right]$$

and that this was a measure of the rate of change of the value of the function $f(x)$ with respect to its variable (or argument) x. For a function of several variables it is also useful to know how the function changes when one, some or all of the variables change. To achieve this we define the **partial derivatives** of a function.

First, we consider a function $f(x, y)$ of the two variables x and y. The partial derivative $\frac{\partial f}{\partial x}$, of $f(x, y)$ with respect to x is its derivative with respect to x treating the value of y as being constant. Thus

$$\frac{\partial f}{\partial x} = \left[\frac{df}{dx} \right]_{y=\text{const}} = \lim_{\Delta x \to 0} \left[\frac{f(x + \Delta x, y) - f(x, y)}{\Delta x} \right]$$

Likewise, the partial derivative, $\frac{\partial f}{\partial y}$, of $f(x, y)$ with respect to y is its derivative with respect to y treating the value of x as being constant, so that

$$\frac{\partial f}{\partial y} = \left[\frac{df}{dy} \right]_{x=\text{const}} = \lim_{\Delta y \to 0} \left[\frac{f(x, y + \Delta y) - f(x, y)}{\Delta y} \right]$$

The process of obtaining the partial derivatives is called **partial differentiation**. Note the use of 'curly dees', which is to distinguish between partial differentiation and ordinary differentiation. In writing, care must be taken to distinguish between $\frac{df}{dx}, \frac{\Delta f}{\Delta x}$ and $\frac{\partial f}{\partial x}$, all of which have different meanings.

A concise notation is sometimes used for partial derivatives; as an alternative to the 'curly dee', we write

$$f_x = \frac{\partial f}{\partial x} \quad \text{and} \quad f_y = \frac{\partial f}{\partial y}$$

It should be noted, however, that subscripts often have other connotations, so care should be taken in using them in this way.

If we write $z = f(x, y)$ then the partial derivatives may also be written as

$$\frac{\partial z}{\partial x}, \frac{\partial z}{\partial y} \quad \text{or} \quad z_x, z_y$$

Summary

The **partial derivatives** of the function $z = f(x, y)$ with respect to the variables x and y respectively are given by

$$\frac{\partial f}{\partial x} = f_x = \frac{\partial z}{\partial x} = z_x = \lim_{\Delta x \to 0}\left[\frac{f(x+\Delta x, y) - f(x, y)}{\Delta x}\right] \tag{8.20}$$

$$\frac{\partial f}{\partial y} = f_y = \frac{\partial z}{\partial y} = z_y = \lim_{\Delta y \to 0}\left[\frac{f(x, y+\Delta y) - f(x, y)}{\Delta y}\right] \tag{8.21}$$

Finding partial derivatives is no more difficult than finding derivatives of functions of one variable, with the constant multiplication, sum, product and quotient rules having counterparts for partial derivatives. Note, however, that, despite the notation, partial derivatives do not behave like fractions. For example, $\frac{\partial x}{\partial z} \neq 1\Big/\left(\frac{\partial z}{\partial x}\right)$.

Example 8.22 Find from first principles $\frac{\partial f}{\partial x}$ and $\frac{\partial f}{\partial y}$ at the point (1, 2) where $f(x, y) = x^3 + 3xy + y^2$.

Solution The partial derivative of $f(x, y)$ with respect to x at (1, 2) is given by

$$\begin{aligned}
\frac{\partial f}{\partial x} &= \lim_{\Delta x \to 0} \frac{f(1+\Delta x, 2) - f(1, 2)}{\Delta x} \\
&= \lim_{\Delta x \to 0} \frac{[(1+\Delta x)^3 + 3(1+\Delta x)2 + 4] - 11}{\Delta x} \\
&= \lim_{\Delta x \to 0} \frac{3\Delta x + 3\Delta x^2 + 3\Delta x^3 + 6\Delta x}{\Delta x} \\
&= \lim_{\Delta x \to 0} (9 + 3\Delta x + \Delta x^2) \\
&= 9
\end{aligned}$$

Similarly $\dfrac{\partial f}{\partial y}$ at (1, 2) is given by

$$\frac{\partial f}{\partial y} = \lim_{\Delta y \to 0} \frac{[1 + 3(2 + \Delta y) + (2 + \Delta y)^2] - 11}{\Delta y}$$

$$= \lim_{\Delta y \to 0} \frac{3\Delta y + 4\Delta y + \Delta y^2}{\Delta y} = 7$$

Example 8.23 Find from first principles the first partial derivatives of $f(x, y) = y \sin x$ at the general point (x, y).

Solution Since y is independent of x

$$\frac{\partial f}{\partial x} = \lim_{\Delta x \to 0} \frac{y \sin(x + \Delta x) - y \sin x}{\Delta x} = y \lim_{\Delta x \to 0} \frac{\sin(x + \Delta x) - \sin x}{\Delta x}$$

$$\frac{\sin(x + \Delta x) - \sin x}{\Delta x} = \frac{2\cos\frac{1}{2}(2x + \Delta x)\sin\frac{1}{2}\Delta x}{\Delta x} = \cos(x + \tfrac{1}{2}\Delta x)\frac{\sin\frac{1}{2}\Delta x}{\frac{1}{2}\Delta x}$$

As $\Delta x \to 0$, $\cos(x + \frac{1}{2}\Delta x) \to \cos x$ and $\dfrac{\sin\frac{1}{2}\Delta x}{\frac{1}{2}\Delta x} \to 1$

(see Section 7.8.1). Thus

$$\frac{\partial f}{\partial x} = y \cos x$$

Similarly $$\frac{\partial f}{\partial y} = \lim_{\Delta y \to 0} \frac{(y + \Delta y)\sin x - y \sin x}{\Delta y}$$

$$= \lim_{\Delta y \to 0} \frac{\Delta y \sin x}{\Delta y} = \sin x$$

Example 8.24 Find $\dfrac{\partial f}{\partial x}$ and $\dfrac{\partial f}{\partial y}$ where $f(x, y)$ is given by

(a) $3x^2 + 2xy + y^3$ (b) $(y^2 + x)\mathrm{e}^{-xy}$

Solution (a) $f(x, y) = 3x^2 + 2xy + y^3$

To find $\dfrac{\partial f}{\partial x}$, we differentiate $f(x, y)$ with respect to x regarding y as a constant. Thus we obtain

$$\frac{\partial f}{\partial x} = \frac{\partial}{\partial x}(3x^2) + \frac{\partial}{\partial x}(2xy) + \frac{\partial}{\partial x}(y^3)$$

$$= 3\frac{\mathrm{d}}{\mathrm{d}x}(x^2) + 2y\frac{\mathrm{d}}{\mathrm{d}x}(x) + 0 \quad \text{(Note: term in brackets involves } x \text{ only)}$$

$$= 6x + 2y$$

Similarly,

$$\frac{\partial f}{\partial y} = \frac{\partial}{\partial y}(3x^2) + \frac{\partial}{\partial y}(2xy) + \frac{\partial}{\partial y}(y^3)$$

$$= 0 + 2x\frac{\mathrm{d}}{\mathrm{d}y}(y) + \frac{\mathrm{d}}{\mathrm{d}y}(y^3) = 2x + 3y^2$$

(b) $f(x, y) = (y^2 + x)\,\mathrm{e}^{-xy}$

Using the product rule, differentiating with respect to x, regarding y as a constant, gives

$$\frac{\partial f}{\partial x} = (\mathrm{e}^{-xy})\frac{\partial}{\partial x}(y^2 + x) + (y^2 + x)\frac{\partial}{\partial x}(\mathrm{e}^{-xy})$$

$$= (\mathrm{e}^{-xy})(1) + (y^2 + x)(-y\mathrm{e}^{-xy})$$

$$= (1 - y^3 - xy)\,\mathrm{e}^{-xy}$$

Similarly,

$$\frac{\partial f}{\partial y} = (\mathrm{e}^{-xy})\frac{\partial}{\partial y}(y^2 + x) + (y^2 + x)\frac{\partial}{\partial y}(\mathrm{e}^{-xy})$$

$$= (\mathrm{e}^{-xy})(2y) + (y^2 + x)(-x\mathrm{e}^{-xy})$$

$$= (2y - xy^2 - x^2)\,\mathrm{e}^{-xy}$$

Example 8.25 Find $\partial f/\partial x$ and $\partial f/\partial y$ when $f(x, y)$ is

(a) $xy^2 + 3xy - x + 2$ (b) $\sin(x^2 - 3y)$

Solution (a) Taking $f(x, y) = xy^2 + 3xy - x + 2$ and differentiating with respect to x, keeping y fixed, gives

$$\frac{\partial f}{\partial x} = f_x = y^2 + 3y - 1$$

Differentiating with respect to y, keeping x fixed, gives

$$\frac{\partial f}{\partial y} = f_y = 2xy + 3x$$

(b) Taking $f(x, y) = \sin(x^2 - 3y)$ and applying the composite-function rule, we obtain

$$\frac{\partial f}{\partial x} = \cos(x^2 - 3y)\frac{\partial}{\partial x}(x^2 - 3y) = \cos(x^2 - 3y)\,2x$$

$$= 2x\cos(x^2 - 3y)$$

and

$$\frac{\partial f}{\partial y} = \cos(x^2 - 3y)\frac{\partial}{\partial y}(x^2 - 3y) = -3\cos(x^2 - 3y)$$

Although we have introduced partial derivatives in the context of functions of two variables, the concept may be readily extended to obtain the partial derivatives of a function of as many variables as we please. Thus for a function $f(x_1, x_2, \ldots, x_n)$ of n variables the partial derivative with respect to x_i is given by

$$f_{x_i} = \frac{\partial f}{\partial x_i} = \lim_{\Delta x_i \to 0} \frac{f(x_1, x_2, \ldots, x_{i-1}, x_i + \Delta x_i, x_{i+1}, \ldots, x_n) - f(x_1, x_2, \ldots x_i, x_n)}{\Delta x_i}$$

and is obtained by differentiating the function with respect to x_i with all the other $n - 1$ variables kept constant.

Example 8.26 Find the partial derivatives of

$$f(x, y, z) = xyz^2 + 3xy - z$$

with respect to x, y and z.

Solution Differentiating $f(x, y, z)$ with respect to x, keeping y and z fixed, gives

$$f_x = \frac{\partial f}{\partial x} = yz^2 + 3y$$

Differentiating $f(x, y, z)$ with respect to y, keeping x and z fixed, gives

$$f_y = \frac{\partial f}{\partial y} = xz^2 + 3x$$

Differentiating $f(x, y, z)$ with respect to z, keeping x and y fixed, gives

$$f_z = \frac{\partial f}{\partial z} = xy(2z) + 0 - 1 = 2xyz - 1$$

The partial derivatives f_x and f_y of the function $f(x, y)$, with respect to x and y respectively, are given by the commands

MATLAB	MAPLE
`syms x y`	
`f = f(x,y)`	`f:= f(x,y);`
`fx = diff(f,x)`	`fx:= diff(f,x);`
`fy = diff(f,y)`	`fy:= diff(f,y);`

Considering Example 8.24(b). The commands

MATLAB	MAPLE
`syms x y`	
`f = (y^2 + x)*exp(-x*y);`	`f:= (y^2 + x)*exp(-x*y);`
`fx = diff(f,x);`	`fx:= diff(f,x);`
`fx = simplify(fx);`	
`pretty (fx)`	

return the answer

```
-exp(-xy)(-1 + y^3 + xy)                    -e^(-xy) (-1 + y^3 + xy)
```

with the additional commands

```
fy = diff(f,y);                             fy:= diff(f,y);
fy = simplify(fy);
pretty(fy)
```

returning the answer

```
-exp(-xy)(-2y + xy^2 + x^2)                 -e^(-xy) (-2y + xy^2 + x^2)
```

The commands for partial derivatives can readily be extended to functions of more than two variables. For example, considering Example 8.26 the MATLAB commands

```
syms x y z
f = x*y*z^2 + 3*x*y - z;
fx = diff(f,x); pretty(fx)
```
return the answer $yz^2 + 3y$
```
fy = diff(f,y); pretty(fy)
```
return the answer $xz^2 + 3x$, and
```
fz = diff(fz); pretty(fz)
```
return the answer $2xyz - 1$

For practice, check the answers to Examples 8.24(a) and 8.25(a) and (b).

8.6.3 Directional derivatives

Consider a function of two variables $z = f(x, y)$. This may be represented as a surface in three dimensions, as shown in Figure 8.13.

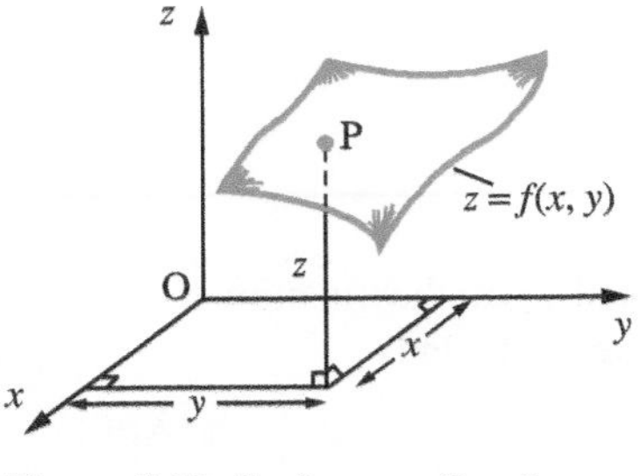

Figure 8.13 Surface $z = f(x, y)$.

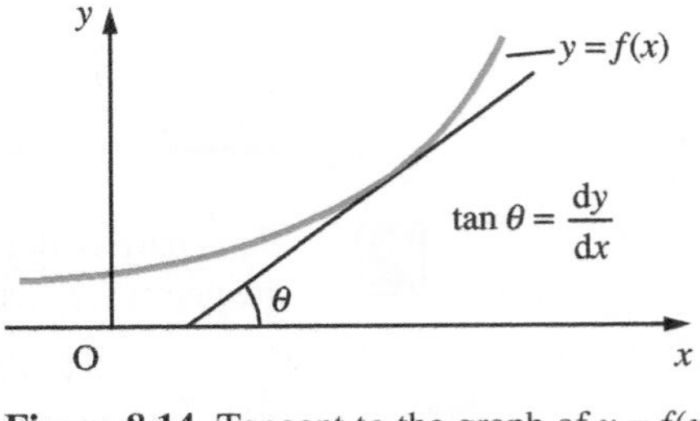

Figure 8.14 Tangent to the graph of $y = f(x)$.

We recall from Chapter 7 that the derivative of a function $f(x)$ of one variable measures the slope of the tangent to the graph of the function, as illustrated in Figure 8.14. In the case of a function of two variables, because $z = f(x, y)$ defines a surface in three dimensions, there is no unique meaning of 'slope' unless we specify the direction in which it is to be measured. In general, the slope will be different for different directions. Now consider two points P and Q on the surface $z = f(x, y)$, as shown in Figure 8.15 and let P′ and Q′ be their projections on the x–y plane. To simplify, set $P'Q' = l$; then the coordinates of P′ and Q′ are given by

$$(x, y, 0) \quad \text{and} \quad (x + l\cos\alpha, y + l\sin\alpha, 0)$$

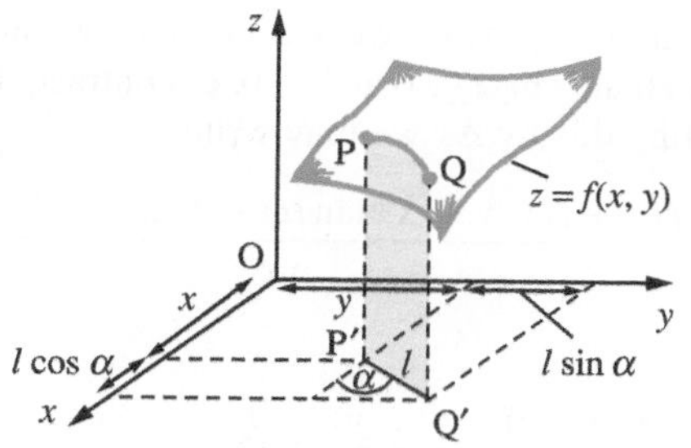

Figure 8.15
Directional derivative.

respectively, where α is the angle that P′Q′ makes with the positive x direction. The slope of the line PQ is then

$$\frac{f(x + l\cos\alpha,\ y + l\sin\alpha) - f(x, y)}{l}$$

and the slope of the surface at P in the direction of $\overrightarrow{PQ}$ is the limit of this quotient as $l \to 0$. Denoting this slope by $m_\alpha(x, y)$, we have

$$m_\alpha(x, y) = \lim_{l\to 0} \frac{f(x + l\cos\alpha,\ y + l\sin\alpha) - f(x, y)}{l}$$

Here the subscript α indicates the direction with respect to which the slope is measured, and the (x, y) shows the point at which it is evaluated. Essentially, we have reduced the problem of a function of two variables to a function of one variable by fixing the direction along which we allow x and y to vary. It would be very clumsy to have to perform the calculation this way every time we wish to work out the rate of change or slope of the function. To simplify the process, we shall show how to represent the slope m_α in terms of two standard slopes: one in the x direction and the other in the y direction.

To do this, we rearrange the numerator of the quotient as a sum of terms, one showing the change in $f(x, y)$ due to the change $l\cos\alpha$ in x, the other showing the change in $f(x, y)$ due to the change $l\sin\alpha$ in y. Thus

$$f(x + l\cos\alpha, y + l\sin\alpha) - f(x, y) = [f(x + l\cos\alpha, y + l\sin\alpha) - f(x, y + l\sin\alpha)] + [f(x, y + l\sin\alpha) - f(x,y)]$$

and $$m_\alpha(x, y) = \lim_{l\to 0} \frac{f(x + l\cos\alpha,\ y + l\sin\alpha) - f(x,\ y + l\sin\alpha)}{l\cos\alpha}\cos\alpha + \lim_{l\to 0} \frac{f(x,\ y + l\sin\alpha) - f(x, y)}{l\sin\alpha}\sin\alpha$$

$$= p(x, y)\cos\alpha + q(x, y)\sin\alpha$$

where $p(x, y)$ and $q(x, y)$ are the values of the respective limits

$$p(x, y) = \lim_{l\to 0} \frac{f(x + l\cos\alpha,\ y + l\sin\alpha) - f(x,\ y + l\sin\alpha)}{l\cos\alpha}$$

$$q(x, y) = \lim_{l\to 0} \frac{f(x,\ y + l\sin\alpha) - f(x, y)}{l\sin\alpha}$$

Examining the numerator of $p(x, y)$, we see that the 'y value' in both terms is the same, $y + l\sin\alpha$, and also that $l\sin\alpha \to 0$ as $l \to 0$. In contrast, the 'x value' in the terms differs by $l\cos\alpha$. Denoting this by Δx we may write

$$p(x, y) = \lim_{\Delta x \to 0} = \frac{f(x + \Delta x, y + \Delta x\tan\alpha) - f(x, y + \Delta x\tan\alpha)}{\Delta x}$$

which simpifies to

$$p(x, y) = \lim_{\Delta x \to 0} \frac{f(x + \Delta x, y) - f(x, y)}{\Delta x} = \frac{\partial f}{\partial x} \tag{8.22}$$

In the same way,

$$q(x, y) = \lim_{\Delta y \to 0} \frac{f(x, y + \Delta y) - f(x, y)}{\Delta y} = \frac{\partial f}{\partial y} \tag{8.23}$$

and we may then write the slope in the direction at an angle α to the x axis as

$$m_\alpha(x, y) = \frac{\partial f}{\partial x}\cos\alpha + \frac{\partial f}{\partial y}\sin\alpha \tag{8.24}$$

Example 8.27 Find the partial derivatives of $f(x, y) = x^2y^3 + 3y + x$ with respect to x and y, and the slope of the function in the direction at an angle α to the x axis.

Solution To find the partial derivative of $f(x, y)$ with respect to x, we differentiate $f(x, y)$ with respect to x, keeping y constant. Thus

$$\frac{\partial f}{\partial x} = 2xy^3 + 1$$

Similarly, we obtain the partial derivative with respect to y by differentiating $f(x, y)$ with respect to y, keeping x constant. Thus

$$\frac{\partial f}{\partial y} = 3x^2y^2 + 3$$

The general expression for the slope of the surface $z = f(x, y)$ in the direction at an angle α to the x axis is

$$m_\alpha(x, y) = \frac{\partial f}{\partial x}\cos\alpha + \frac{\partial f}{\partial y}\sin\alpha$$

So for this function we have

$$m_\alpha(x, y) = (2xy^3 + 1)\cos\alpha + (3x^2y^2 + 3)\sin\alpha$$

Since in evaluating $\partial f/\partial x$ we consider only the variation of $f(x, y)$ in the x direction, $\partial f/\partial x$ gives the slope of the surface $z = f(x, y)$ at the point (x, y) in the x direction ($\alpha = 0$ in (8.24)). Similarly, $\partial f/\partial y$ gives the slope in the y direction ($\alpha = \frac{1}{2}\pi$ in (8.24)). This is illustrated in Figure 8.16.

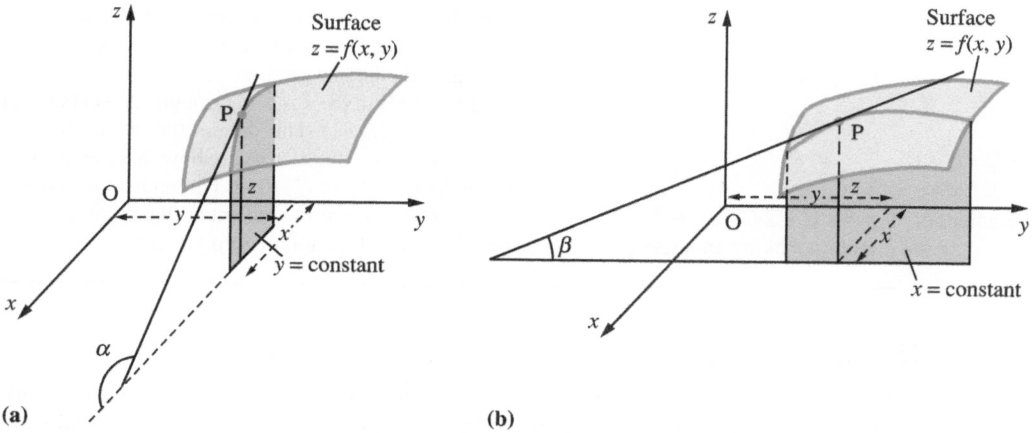

Figure 8.16 Geometrical illustration of partial derivatives (a) $\dfrac{\partial f}{\partial x} = \tan\alpha$ and (b) $\dfrac{\partial f}{\partial y} = \tan\beta$.

Thus if we know $\partial f/\partial x$ and $\partial f/\partial y$, we can calculate the slope $m_\alpha(x, y)$ of the function in any given direction using (8.24). This is called the **directional derivative** of $f(x, y)$, and may be regarded as the projection of the vector $(\partial f/\partial x, \partial f/\partial y)$ onto the direction represented by the unit vector $(\cos\alpha, \sin\alpha)$, so that $(\cos\alpha, \sin\alpha)$ is a unit vector in the direction of the required derivative. Thus we may express $m_\alpha(x, y)$ as the scalar product

$$m_\alpha(x, y) = \left(\frac{\partial f}{\partial x}, \frac{\partial f}{\partial y}\right)\cdot(\cos\alpha, \sin\alpha)$$

8.6.4 Exercises

Check your answers using MATLAB or MAPLE whenever possible.

37 Obtain from first principles the partial derivatives $\partial f/\partial x$ and $\partial f/\partial y$ of the function $f(x, y)$ at the point (1, 2), where

$$f(x, y) = 2x^2 - xy + y^2$$

38 Obtain from first principles the partial derivatives $\partial f/\partial x$ and $\partial f/\partial y$ of the function $f(x, y)$ at the general point (x, y) where

$$f(x, y) = x\cos y$$

39 Find $\partial f/\partial x$ and $\partial f/\partial y$ when $f(x, y)$ is

(a) $x^3y + 2x^2 + 9y^2 + xy + 10$

(b) $(x + y^2)^3$ (c) $(3x^2 + y^2 + 2xy)^{1/2}$

40 Find $\partial f/\partial x$ and $\partial f/\partial y$ when $f(x, y)$ is

(a) $e^{xy}\cos x$ (b) $\dfrac{x}{x^2 + y^2}$ (c) $\dfrac{x + y}{x^2 + 2y^2 + 6}$

41 Find $\partial z/\partial x$ and $\partial z/\partial y$ when $z(x, y)$ satisfies

(a) $x^2 + y^2 + z^2 = 10$

(b) $xyz = x - y + z$

42 Show that $z = x^2y^2/(x^2 + y^2)$ satisfies the differential equation

$$x\frac{\partial z}{\partial x} + y\frac{\partial z}{\partial y} = 2z$$

43 Find f_x, f_y and f_z when $f(x, y, z)$ is

(a) $x^2y + 3yxz - 2z^3x^2y$

(b) $e^{2z}\cos xy$

44 Show that

$$f(x, y, z) = (x^2 + y^2 + z^2)^{-1/2}$$

satisfies

$$xf_x + yf_y + zf_z = -f(x, y, z)$$

45 Show that

$$f(x, y, z) = x + \frac{x - y}{y - z}$$

satisfies

$$f_x + f_y + f_z = 1$$

46 Find the gradient of $f(x, y) = x^2 + 2y^2 - 3x + 2y$ at the point (x, y) in the direction making an angle α with the positive x direction. What is the value of the gradient at $(2, -1)$ when $\alpha = \frac{1}{6}\pi$? What values of α give the largest gradient at $(2, -1)$?

The level curve of $f(x, y)$ through $(2, -1)$ is given by $f(x, y) = f(2, -1)$. This defines the relationship between x and y on the curve. Show that the tangent to the level curve at $(2, -1)$ is perpendicular to the direction of maximum gradient at that point and parallel to the direction of zero gradient.

8.6.5 The chain rule

As can be seen from Examples 8.24–8.26, the rules and results of ordinary differentiation carry over to partial differentiation. In particular, the composite-function rule still holds, but in a modified form. Consider the two-variable case where $z = f(x, y)$ and x and y are themselves functions of two independent variables, s and t. Then z itself is also a function of s and t, say $F(s, t)$, and we can find its derivatives using a composite-function rule that gives the rates of change of z with respect to s and t in terms of the rates of change of z with respect to x and y and the rates of change of x and y with respect to s and t. Thus

$$\frac{\partial z}{\partial s} = \frac{\partial z}{\partial x}\frac{\partial x}{\partial s} + \frac{\partial z}{\partial y}\frac{\partial y}{\partial s} \quad \text{and} \quad \frac{\partial z}{\partial t} = \frac{\partial z}{\partial x}\frac{\partial x}{\partial t} + \frac{\partial z}{\partial y}\frac{\partial y}{\partial t} \tag{8.25}$$

or, in vector–matrix form,

$$\begin{bmatrix} \dfrac{\partial z}{\partial s} & \dfrac{\partial z}{\partial t} \end{bmatrix} = \begin{bmatrix} \dfrac{\partial z}{\partial x} & \dfrac{\partial z}{\partial y} \end{bmatrix} \begin{bmatrix} \dfrac{\partial x}{\partial s} & \dfrac{\partial x}{\partial t} \\ \dfrac{\partial y}{\partial s} & \dfrac{\partial y}{\partial t} \end{bmatrix}$$

This result is often called the **chain rule**. The proof is straightforward. Consider $\partial z/\partial s$, given by

$$\frac{\partial z}{\partial s} = \lim_{\Delta s \to 0} \frac{F(s + \Delta s, t) - F(s, t)}{\Delta s}$$

The point $(s + \Delta s, t)$ in the s–t plane will correspond to the point $(x + \Delta x, y + \Delta y)$ in the x–y plane, while (s, t) corresponds to (x, y). Thus

$$\begin{aligned} \frac{\partial z}{\partial s} &= \lim_{\Delta s \to 0} \frac{f(x + \Delta x, y + \Delta y) - f(x, y)}{\Delta s} \\ &= \lim_{\Delta s \to 0} \frac{f(x + \Delta x, y + \Delta y) - f(x, y + \Delta y)}{\Delta x} \frac{\Delta x}{\Delta s} \\ &\quad + \lim_{\Delta s \to 0} \frac{f(x, y + \Delta y) - f(x, y)}{\Delta y} \frac{\Delta y}{\Delta s} \\ &= \frac{\partial f}{\partial x}\frac{\partial x}{\partial s} + \frac{\partial f}{\partial y}\frac{\partial y}{\partial s} \end{aligned}$$

We can similarly prove the result for $\partial z/\partial t$.

It may happen, of course, that x and y are functions of one variable only or of three variables or more. In all these cases the chain rule still applies when the functions involved are differentiable.

Example 8.28 Find $\partial T/\partial r$ and $\partial T/\partial \theta$ when

$$T(x, y) = x^3 - xy + y^3$$

and

$$x = r\cos\theta \quad \text{and} \quad y = r\sin\theta$$

Solution By the chain rule (8.25),

$$\frac{\partial T}{\partial r} = \frac{\partial T}{\partial x}\frac{\partial x}{\partial r} + \frac{\partial T}{\partial y}\frac{\partial y}{\partial r}$$

In this example

$$\frac{\partial T}{\partial x} = 3x^2 - y \quad \text{and} \quad \frac{\partial T}{\partial y} = -x + 3y^2$$

and

$$\frac{\partial x}{\partial r} = \cos\theta \quad \text{and} \quad \frac{\partial y}{\partial r} = \sin\theta$$

so that

$$\frac{\partial T}{\partial r} = (3x^2 - y)\cos\theta + (-x + 3y^2)\sin\theta$$

Substituting for x and y in terms of r and θ gives

$$\frac{\partial T}{\partial r} = 3r^2(\cos^3\theta + \sin^3\theta) - 2r\cos\theta\sin\theta$$

Similarly,

$$\begin{aligned}\frac{\partial T}{\partial \theta} &= (3x^2 - y)(-r\sin\theta) + (-x + 3y^2)r\cos\theta \\ &= 3r^3(\sin\theta - \cos\theta)\cos\theta\sin\theta + r^2(\sin^2\theta - \cos^2\theta)\end{aligned}$$

Example 8.29 Find $\mathrm{d}H/\mathrm{d}t$ when

$$H(t) = \sin(3x - y)$$

and

$$x = 2t^2 - 3 \quad \text{and} \quad y = \tfrac{1}{2}t^2 - 5t + 1$$

Solution We note that x and y are functions of t only, so that the chain rule (8.5) becomes

$$\frac{dH}{dt} = \frac{\partial H}{\partial x}\frac{dx}{dt} + \frac{\partial H}{\partial y}\frac{dy}{dt}$$

Note the mixture of partial and ordinary derivatives. H is a function of the one variable t, but its dependence is expressed through the two variables x and y.

Substituting for the derivatives involved, we have

$$\frac{dH}{dt} = 3[\cos(3x - y)]4t - [\cos(3x - y)](t - 5)$$

$$= (11t + 5)\cos(3x - y)$$

$$= (11t + 5)\cos(\tfrac{11}{2}t^2 + 5t - 10)$$

Example 8.30 The base radius r cm of a right-circular cone increases at 2 cm s^{-1} and its height h cm at 3 cm s^{-1}. Find the rate of increase in its volume when $r = 5$ and $h = 15$.

Solution The volume V of a cone having base radius r and height h is

$$V = \tfrac{1}{3}\pi r^2 h$$

We wish to determine dV/dt given dr/dt and dh/dt. Applying the chain rule (8.25) gives

$$\frac{dV}{dt} = \frac{\partial V}{\partial r}\frac{dr}{dt} + \frac{\partial V}{\partial h}\frac{dh}{dt}$$

Now

$$\frac{\partial V}{\partial r} = \tfrac{2}{3}\pi rh, \quad \frac{\partial V}{\partial h} = \tfrac{1}{3}\pi r^2, \quad \frac{dr}{dt} = 2, \quad \frac{dh}{dt} = 3$$

so that

$$\frac{dV}{dt} = \tfrac{4}{3}\pi rh + \pi r^2$$

When $r = 5$ cm and $h = 15$ cm, the rate of increase in volume is

$$\frac{dV}{dt} = (\tfrac{4}{3}\pi \times 5 \times 15 + \pi \times 5^2)\,\text{cm}^3\,\text{s}^{-1}$$

$$= 125\pi\,\text{cm}^3\,\text{s}^{-1}$$

Example 8.31 Find $\dfrac{dz}{dt}$ when

(a) $z = e^{-x} \cos y$, where $x = 2t + t^2$ and $y = 4t$

(b) $z = x^3 + t^2$ and $x^2 + 2t^2 + 3xt = 0$.

Solution (a) $\dfrac{dz}{dt} = \dfrac{\partial z}{\partial x}\dfrac{dx}{dt} + \dfrac{\partial z}{\partial y}\dfrac{dy}{dt}$

$$= -e^{-x} \cos y(2 + 2t) - e^{-x} \sin y(4)$$

$$= -2e^{-x}[(1 + t) \cos y + 2 \sin y]$$

$$= -2e^{-2t-t^2} [(1 + t) \cos 4t + 2 \sin 4t]$$

The final step in the above may or may not be appropiate to the application in which the derivative is evaluated.

(b) $\dfrac{dz}{dt} = 3x^2\dfrac{dx}{dt} + 2t$

and differentiating implicitly we have

$$2x\frac{dx}{dt} + 4t + 3\frac{dx}{dt}t + 3x = 0$$

so that $\dfrac{dx}{dt} = -\dfrac{4t + 3x}{3t + 2x}$

Hence $\dfrac{dz}{dt} = -\dfrac{3x^2(4t + 3x)}{3t + 2x} + 2t$

$$= -\frac{6t^2 + 4xt - 12x^2t - 9x^3}{3t + 2x}$$

The chain rule can be readily handled in both MATLAB and MAPLE. Considering Example 8.28, in MATLAB the solution may be developed as follows:

The commands

```
syms x y r theta
T = x^3 - x*y + y^3; Tx = diff(T,x); Ty = diff(T,y);
x = r*cos(theta); y = r*sin(theta);
xr = diff(x,r), xtheta = diff(x,theta); yr = diff(y,r);
ytheta = diff(y,theta);
Tr = Tx*xr + Ty*yr
```

return

```
Tr = (3*x^2 - y)*cos(theta) + (-x + 3*y^2)*sin(theta)
```

To substitute for x and y in terms of r and *theta* we make use of the `eval` command, with

```
eval(Tr); pretty(ans)
```

returning the answer

```
(3r^2cos(theta)^2 - rsin(theta))cos(theta) + (-rcos(theta)
+ 3r^2sin(theta)^2)sin(theta)
```

which readily reduces to the answer given in the solution.
Similarly the commands

```
Ttheta = Tx*xtheta + Ty*ytheta;
eval(Ttheta); pretty(ans)
```

return the answer

```
(-3r^2cos(theta)^2 + rsin(theta))rsin(theta) + (-rcos(theta)
+ 3r^2sin(theta)^2)rcos(theta)
```

which also readily reduces to the answer given in the solution.
MAPLE solves this problem much more efficiently using the commands

```
T:= (x,y) -> x^3 - x*y + y^3;
diff(T(r*cos(theta), r*sin(theta)), r);
diff(T(r*cos(theta), r*sin(theta)), theta);
collect(%,r);
```

returning the final answer

```
(-3cos(θ)^2sin(θ) + 3sin(θ)^2cos(θ))r^3 + (sin(θ)^2 - cos(θ)^2)r^2
```

8.6.6 Exercises

Check your answers using MATLAB or MAPLE whenever possible.

47 Find $\dfrac{dA}{dt}$ where $A = r\tan^{-1}(r\tan\theta)$ and $r = 2t + 1$, $\theta = \pi t$.

48 Find $\partial f/\partial s$ and $\partial f/\partial t$ when $f(x, y) = e^x\cos y$, $x = s^2 - t^2$ and $y = 2st$.

49 Find dz/dt when

(a) $z^2 = x^2 + y^2$, $x = t^2 + 1$ and $y = t - 1$

(b) $z = x^2t^2$ and $x^2 + 3xt + 2t^2 = 1$

50 Show that if $u = x + y$, $v = xy$ and $z = f(u, v)$ then

(a) $x\dfrac{\partial z}{\partial x} - y\dfrac{\partial z}{\partial y} = (x - y)\dfrac{\partial z}{\partial u}$

(b) $\dfrac{\partial z}{\partial x} - \dfrac{\partial z}{\partial y} = (y - x)\dfrac{\partial z}{\partial v}$

51 Show that if $z = x^nf(u)$, where $u = y/x$, then

$$x\frac{\partial z}{\partial x} + y\frac{\partial z}{\partial y} = nz$$

Verify this result for $z = x^4 + 2y^4 + 3xy^3$.

52 Show that, if f is a function of the independent variables x and y, and the latter are changed to independent variables u and v where $u = e^{y/x}$ and $v = x^2 + y^2$, then

(a) $x\dfrac{\partial f}{\partial x} + y\dfrac{\partial f}{\partial y} = 2v\dfrac{\partial f}{\partial v}$

(b) $x^3\dfrac{\partial f}{\partial y} - x^2y\dfrac{\partial f}{\partial x} = uv\dfrac{\partial f}{\partial u}$

53 In a right-angled triangle a cm and b cm are the sides containing the right-angle. a is increasing at 2 cm s^{-1} and b is increasing at 3 cm s^{-1}. Calculate the rate of change of (a) the area and (b) the hypotenuse when $a = 5$ and $b = 3$.

54 Show that the total surface area S of a closed cone of base radius r cm and perpendicular height h cm is given by

$$S = \pi r^2 + \pi r\sqrt{(r^2 + h^2)}$$

If r and h are each increasing at the rate of 0.25 cm s^{-1}, find the rate at which S is increasing at the instant when $r = 3$ and $h = 4$.

55 (Continuing Question 32). A particle moves such that its position at time t is given by $\mathbf{r} = (t, t^2, t^3)$. Find the rate of change of the distance $|\mathbf{r}|$ of the particle from the origin.

56 Find $\partial f/\partial s$ and $\partial f/\partial t$ where

$$f(x, y) = x^2 + 2y^2$$

and $x = e^{-s} + e^{-t}$ and $y = e^{-s} - e^{-t}$.

8.6.7 Successive differentiation

Consider the function $f(x, y)$ with partial derivatives $\partial f/\partial x$ and $\partial f/\partial y$. In general, these partial derivatives will themselves be functions of x and y, and thus may themselves be differentiated to yield second derivatives. We write

$$\frac{\partial}{\partial x}\left(\frac{\partial f}{\partial x}\right) = \frac{\partial^2 f}{\partial x^2} = f_{xx}$$

$$\frac{\partial}{\partial y}\left(\frac{\partial f}{\partial x}\right) = \frac{\partial^2 f}{\partial y\partial x} = \frac{\partial}{\partial y}(f_x) = f_{xy}$$

$$\frac{\partial}{\partial x}\left(\frac{\partial f}{\partial y}\right) = \frac{\partial^2 f}{\partial x\partial y} = \frac{\partial}{\partial x}(f_y) = f_{yx}$$

and

$$\frac{\partial}{\partial y}\left(\frac{\partial f}{\partial y}\right) = \frac{\partial^2 f}{\partial y^2} = f_{yy}$$

There are some functions for which the mixed second derivatives are not equal, that is

$$\frac{\partial^2 f}{\partial x\partial y} \neq \frac{\partial^2 f}{\partial y\partial x}$$

and the order of differentiation is therefore important, but for most of the functions that occur in engineering problems, when the second derivatives are usually continuous functions, these mixed derivatives are the same in value. In a similar manner we can define higher-order partial derivatives

$$\frac{\partial^{m+n} f}{\partial x^m \partial y^n}$$

Example 8.32 Find the second partial derivatives of $f(x, y) = x^2y^3 + 3y + x$.

Solution We found in Example 8.27 that

$$\frac{\partial f}{\partial x} = 2xy^3 + 1 \quad \text{and} \quad \frac{\partial f}{\partial y} = 3x^2y^2 + 3$$

Differentiating again, we obtain

$$\frac{\partial}{\partial x}\left(\frac{\partial f}{\partial x}\right) = \frac{\partial^2 f}{\partial x^2} = 2y^3, \quad \frac{\partial}{\partial y}\left(\frac{\partial f}{\partial x}\right) = \frac{\partial^2 f}{\partial y \partial x} = 6xy^2$$

$$\frac{\partial}{\partial y}\left(\frac{\partial f}{\partial y}\right) = \frac{\partial^2 f}{\partial y^2} = 6x^2y, \quad \frac{\partial}{\partial x}\left(\frac{\partial f}{\partial y}\right) = \frac{\partial^2 f}{\partial x \partial y} = 6xy^2$$

Note that in this example

$$\frac{\partial^2 f}{\partial x \partial y} = \frac{\partial^2 f}{\partial y \partial x}$$

In MATLAB and MAPLE, second-order partial derivatives can be obtained by suitably differentiating the first-order partial derivatives already found. Thus in MATLAB the second-order partial derivatives of $f(x, y)$ are given by

```
fxx = diff(fx,x), fxy = diff(fx,y), fyy = diff(fy,y),
fyx = diff(fy,x)
```

Alternatively, the non-mixed derivatives can be obtained directly using the commands

```
fxx = diff(f,x,2), fyy = diff(f,y,2)
```

which can be extended to higher-order partial derivatives.

The corresponding commands in MAPLE are

```
fxx:= diff(f,x,x); fxy:= diff(f,x,y);
fyy:= diff(f,y,y);
```

Considering Example 8.32 the MATLAB commands

```
syms x y
f = x^2*y^3 + 3*y + x;
fx = diff(f,x); fy = diff(f,y); fxx = diff(fx,x) return
fxx = 2*y^3
fxy = diff(fx,y) returns fxy = 6*x*y^2
fyy = diff(fy,y) returns fyy = 6*x^2*y
fyx = diff(fy,x) returns fyx = 6*x*y^2
```

Example 8.33 Find the second partial derivatives of

$$f(x, y, z) = xyz^2 + 3xy - z$$

Solution In Example 8.26 we obtained the first partial derivatives as

$$f_x = \frac{\partial f}{\partial x} = yz^2 + 3y, \quad f_y = \frac{\partial f}{\partial y} = xz^2 + 3x, \quad f_z = \frac{\partial f}{\partial z} = 2xyz - 1$$

Differentiating again, we obtain

$$\frac{\partial}{\partial x}\left(\frac{\partial f}{\partial x}\right) = \frac{\partial^2 f}{\partial x^2} = f_{xx} = 0, \quad \frac{\partial}{\partial y}\left(\frac{\partial f}{\partial x}\right) = \frac{\partial^2 f}{\partial y \partial x} = f_{xy} = z^2 + 3$$

$$\frac{\partial}{\partial z}\left(\frac{\partial f}{\partial x}\right) = \frac{\partial^2 f}{\partial z \partial x} = f_{xz} = 2yz, \quad \frac{\partial}{\partial x}\left(\frac{\partial f}{\partial y}\right) = \frac{\partial^2 f}{\partial x \partial y} = f_{yx} = z^2 + 3$$

$$\frac{\partial}{\partial y}\left(\frac{\partial f}{\partial y}\right) = \frac{\partial^2 f}{\partial y^2} = f_{yy} = 0, \quad \frac{\partial}{\partial z}\left(\frac{\partial f}{\partial y}\right) = \frac{\partial^2 f}{\partial z \partial y} = f_{yz} = 2xz$$

$$\frac{\partial}{\partial x}\left(\frac{\partial f}{\partial z}\right) = \frac{\partial^2 f}{\partial x \partial z} = f_{zx} = 2yz, \quad \frac{\partial}{\partial y}\left(\frac{\partial f}{\partial z}\right) = \frac{\partial^2 f}{\partial y \partial z} = f_{zy} = 2xz$$

$$\frac{\partial}{\partial z}\left(\frac{\partial f}{\partial z}\right) = \frac{\partial^2 f}{\partial z^2} = f_{zz} = 2xy$$

Note that, as expected,

$$f_{xy} = f_{yx}, \quad f_{xz} = f_{zx} \quad \text{and} \quad f_{yz} = f_{zy}$$

Example 8.34 $f(x, y)$ is a function of two variables x and y that we wish to change to variables s and t, where

$$s = x^2 - y^2, \quad t = xy$$

Determine f_{xx} and f_{yy} in terms of s, t, f_s, f_t, f_{ss}, f_{tt} and f_{st}. Show that

$$f_{xx} + f_{yy} = \sqrt{(s^2 + 4t^2)}(4f_{ss} + f_{tt})$$

Solution Using the chain rule,

$$f_x = \frac{\partial f}{\partial x} = \frac{\partial f}{\partial s}\frac{\partial s}{\partial x} + \frac{\partial f}{\partial t}\frac{\partial t}{\partial x} = 2x\frac{\partial f}{\partial s} + y\frac{\partial f}{\partial t}$$

$$f_y = \frac{\partial f}{\partial y} = \frac{\partial f}{\partial s}\frac{\partial s}{\partial y} + \frac{\partial f}{\partial t}\frac{\partial t}{\partial y} = -2y\frac{\partial f}{\partial s} + x\frac{\partial f}{\partial t}$$

Differentiating f_x with respect to x gives

$$f_{xx} = \frac{\partial}{\partial x}\left(2x\frac{\partial f}{\partial s} + y\frac{\partial f}{\partial t}\right)$$

$$= 2\frac{\partial f}{\partial s} + 2x\frac{\partial}{\partial x}\left(\frac{\partial f}{\partial s}\right) + y\frac{\partial}{\partial x}\left(\frac{\partial f}{\partial t}\right) \quad \text{(using the product rule)}$$

Repeated use of the chain rule as indicated above leads to

$$f_{xx} = 2\frac{\partial f}{\partial s} + 2x\left[\frac{\partial}{\partial s}\left(\frac{\partial f}{\partial s}\right)\frac{\partial s}{\partial x} + \frac{\partial}{\partial t}\left(\frac{\partial f}{\partial s}\right)\frac{\partial t}{\partial x}\right] + y\left[\frac{\partial}{\partial s}\left(\frac{\partial f}{\partial t}\right)\frac{\partial s}{\partial x} + \frac{\partial}{\partial t}\left(\frac{\partial f}{\partial t}\right)\frac{\partial t}{\partial x}\right]$$

$$= 2f_s + 2x(2xf_{ss} + yf_{st}) + y(2xf_{ts} + yf_{tt})$$

which, on assuming $f_{st} = f_{ts}$, gives

$$f_{xx} = 2f_s + 4x^2f_{ss} + y^2f_{tt} + 4xyf_{st} \quad \textbf{(8.26)}$$

Following a similar procedure, we can determine f_{yy}. Differentiating f_y with respect to y gives

$$f_{yy} = \frac{\partial}{\partial y}(-2yf_s + xf_t)$$

$$= -2f_s - 2y\frac{\partial}{\partial y}(f_s) + x\frac{\partial}{\partial y}(f_t)$$

$$= -2f_s - 2y\left[\frac{\partial}{\partial s}(f_s)\frac{\partial s}{\partial y} + \frac{\partial}{\partial t}(f_s)\frac{\partial t}{\partial y}\right] + x\left[\frac{\partial}{\partial s}(f_t)\frac{\partial s}{\partial y} + \frac{\partial}{\partial t}(f_t)\frac{\partial t}{\partial y}\right]$$

$$= -2f_s - 2y(-2yf_{ss} + xf_{st}) + x(-2yf_{ts} + xf_{tt})$$

giving

$$f_{yy} = -2f_s + 4y^2f_{ss} + x^2f_{tt} - 4xyf_{st} \quad \textbf{(8.27)}$$

Adding (8.26) and (8.27), we obtain

$$f_{xx} + f_{yy} = 4(x^2 + y^2)f_{ss} + (x^2 + y^2)f_{tt}$$

$$= (x^2 + y^2)(4f_{ss} + f_{tt})$$

$$= \sqrt{[(x^2 - y^2)^2 + 4x^2y^2]}(4f_{ss} + f_{tt})$$

which leads to the required result

$$f_{xx} + f_{yy} = \sqrt{(s^2 + 4t^2)}(4f_{ss} + f_{tt})$$

8.6.8 Exercises

Check your answers using MATLAB or MAPLE whenever possible.

57 Find all the second partial derivatives of $f(x, y) = xe^{xy}$.

58 Find all the second partial derivatives of $f(x, y, z) = (x + 2y)\cos 3z$.

59 Verify that

$$f(x, y) = \frac{x}{x^2 + y^2}$$

satisfies the equation

$$\frac{\partial^2 f}{\partial x^2} + \frac{\partial^2 f}{\partial y^2} = 0$$

60 Find the value of the constant a if $V(x, y) = x^3 + axy^2$ satisfies

$$\frac{\partial^2 V}{\partial x^2} + \frac{\partial^2 V}{\partial y^2} = 0$$

61 Verify that

$$\frac{\partial^2 f}{\partial x \partial y} = \frac{\partial^2 f}{\partial y \partial x}$$

in the cases

(a) $f(x, y) = x^2 \cos y$ (b) $f(x, y) = \sinh x \cos y$

62 Show that

$$V(x, y, z) = \frac{1}{z} \exp\left(-\frac{x^2 + y^2}{4z}\right)$$

satisfies the differential equation

$$\frac{\partial^2 V}{\partial x^2} + \frac{\partial^2 V}{\partial y^2} = \frac{\partial V}{\partial z}$$

63 Prove that $z = xf(x + y) + yF(x + y)$, where f and F are arbitrary functions, satisfies the equation

$$z_{xx} + z_{yy} = 2z_{xy}$$

64 Show that, if $z = xe^{Kxy}$, where K is a constant, then

$$xz_x - yz_y = z \quad \text{and} \quad xz_{xx} - yz_{xy} = 0$$

65 If $u = ax + by$ and $v = bx - ay$, where a and b are constants, obtain $\partial u/\partial x$ and $\partial v/\partial y$. By expressing x and y in terms of u and v, obtain $\partial x/\partial u$ and $\partial y/\partial v$ and deduce that

$$\frac{\partial u}{\partial x}\frac{\partial x}{\partial u} = \frac{a^2}{a^2 + b^2}$$

$$\frac{\partial v}{\partial y}\frac{\partial y}{\partial v} = \frac{a^2 + b^2}{a^2}$$

Show also that

$$\frac{\partial^2 f}{\partial x \partial y} = ab\left(\frac{\partial^2 f}{\partial u^2} - \frac{\partial^2 f}{\partial v^2}\right) + (b^2 - a^2)\frac{\partial^2 f}{\partial u \partial v}$$

66 Find the values of the constants a and b such that $u = x + ay$, $v = x + by$ transforms

$$9\frac{\partial^2 f}{\partial x^2} - 9\frac{\partial^2 f}{\partial x \partial y} + 2\frac{\partial^2 f}{\partial y^2} = 0$$

into

$$\frac{\partial^2 f}{\partial u \partial v} = 0$$

67 Regarding u and v as functions of x and y and defined by the equations

$$x = e^u \cos v, \qquad y = e^u \sin v$$

show that

(a) $\dfrac{\partial u}{\partial x}\dfrac{\partial x}{\partial u} = \cos^2 v = \dfrac{\partial v}{\partial y}\dfrac{\partial y}{\partial v}$

(b) $\dfrac{\partial^2 z}{\partial x^2} + \dfrac{\partial^2 z}{\partial y^2} = e^{-2u}\left(\dfrac{\partial^2 z}{\partial u^2} - \dfrac{\partial^2 z}{\partial v^2}\right)$

where z is a twice-differentiable function of u and v.

8.6.9 The total differential and small errors

Consider a function $u = f(x, y)$ of two variables x and y. Let Δx and Δy be increments in the values of x and y. Then the corresponding increment in u is given by

$$\Delta u = f(x + \Delta x, y + \Delta y) - f(x, y)$$

We rewrite this as two terms: one showing the change in u due to the change in x, and the other showing the change in u due to the change in y. Thus

$$\Delta u = [f(x + \Delta x, y + \Delta y) - f(x, y + \Delta y)] + [f(x, y + \Delta y) - f(x, y)]$$

Dividing the first bracketed term by Δx and the second by Δy gives

$$\Delta u = \frac{f(x + \Delta x, y + \Delta y) - f(x, y + \Delta x)}{\Delta x}\Delta x + \frac{f(x, y + \Delta y) - f(x, y)}{\Delta y}\Delta y$$

From the definition of the partial derivative, we may approximate this expression by

$$\Delta u \approx \frac{\partial f}{\partial x}\Delta x + \frac{\partial f}{\partial y}\Delta y$$

We define the **differential** du by the equation

$$du = \frac{\partial f}{\partial x}\Delta x + \frac{\partial f}{\partial y}\Delta y \tag{8.28}$$

By setting $f(x, y) = f_1(x, y) = x$ and $f(x, y) = f_2(x, y) = y$ in turn in (8.28), we see that

$$dx = \frac{\partial f_1}{\partial x}\Delta x + \frac{\partial f_1}{\partial y}\Delta y = \Delta x \quad \text{and} \quad dy = \Delta y$$

so that for the independent variables, increments and differentials are equal. For the dependent variable we have

$$du = \frac{\partial f}{\partial x}dx + \frac{\partial f}{\partial y}dy \tag{8.29}$$

We see that the differential du is an approximation to the change Δu in $u = f(x, y)$ resulting from small changes Δx and Δy in the independent variables x and y; that is,

$$\Delta u \approx du = \frac{\partial f}{\partial x}dx + \frac{\partial f}{\partial y}dy = \frac{\partial f}{\partial x}\Delta x + \frac{\partial f}{\partial y}\Delta y \tag{8.30}$$

a result illustrated in Figure 8.17.

This extends to functions of as many variables as we please, provided that the partial derivatives exist. For example, for a function of three variables (x, y, z) defined by $u = f(x, y, z)$ we have

$$\begin{aligned}\Delta u \approx du &= \frac{\partial f}{\partial x}dx + \frac{\partial f}{\partial y}dy + \frac{\partial f}{\partial z}dz \\ &= \frac{\partial f}{\partial x}\Delta x + \frac{\partial f}{\partial y}\Delta y + \frac{\partial f}{\partial z}\Delta z\end{aligned}$$

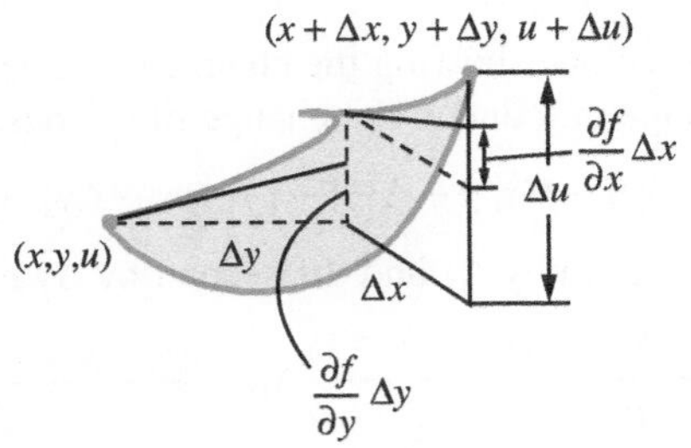

Figure 8.17
Total differential.

The differential of a function of several variables is often called a **total differential**, emphasizing that it shows the variation of the function with respect to small changes in *all* the independent variables.

Example 8.35 Find the total differential of $u(x, y) = x^2y^3$.

Solution Taking partial derivatives we have

$$\frac{\partial u}{\partial x} = 2xy^3 \quad \text{and} \quad \frac{\partial u}{\partial y} = 3x^2y^2$$

Hence, using (8.29)

$$du = 2xy^3\,dx + 3x^2y^2dy$$

All physical measurements are subject to error, and a calculated quantity usually depends on several measurements. It is very important to know the degree of accuracy that can be relied upon in a quantity that has been calculated. The total differential can be used to estimate error bounds for quantities calculated from experimental results or from data that is subject to errors. This is illustrated in Example 8.36.

Example 8.36 The volume $V\,\text{cm}^3$ of a circular cylinder of radius $r\,\text{cm}$ and height $h\,\text{cm}$ is given by $V = \pi r^2h$. If $r = 3 \pm 0.01$ and $h = 5 \pm 0.005$ find the greatest possible error in the calculation of V and compare it with the estimate obtained using the total differential.

Solution The total differential is

$$dV = \frac{\partial V}{\partial r}dr + \frac{\partial V}{\partial h}dh = 2\pi rh\,dr + \pi r^2\,dh$$

Then from (8.30)

$$\Delta V \approx dV = 2\pi rh\,dr + \pi r^2\,dh = \pi r(2h\,\Delta r + r\,\Delta h)$$

When $r = 3$ and $h = 5$, we are given that $\Delta r = \pm 0.01$ and $\Delta h = \pm 0.005$, so that

$$\Delta V \approx \pm 3\pi(10 \times 0.01 + 3 \times 0.005)$$

giving

$$\Delta V \approx \pm 0.345\pi$$

(It should be noted that Δr, Δh, ΔV represent maximum errors.) The calculated volume V is subject to a maximum positive error of

$$\{(3.01)^2(5.005) - 45\}\pi = 0.3458\pi$$

and a maximum negative error of

$$\{(2.99)^2(4.995) - 45\}\pi = -0.3442\pi$$

Thus the approximation gives a good guide to the accuracy of the result.

Example 8.37 Two variables, x and y, are related by $y = ae^{-bx}$, where a and b are constants. The values of a and b are determined from experimental data and have relative error bounds p and q respectively. What is the relative error bound for a value of y calculated using the formula with these values of a and b?

Solution Note that in this example it is assumed that the value of x is known exactly. We are given $y = ae^{-bx}$, where a and b are approximations with errors Δa and Δb, which are unknown but are such that

$$\left|\frac{\Delta a}{a}\right| \leqslant p \quad \text{and} \quad \left|\frac{\Delta b}{b}\right| \leqslant q$$

The formula for the total differential gives

$$\mathrm{d}y = \frac{\partial y}{\partial a}\mathrm{d}a + \frac{\partial y}{\partial b}\mathrm{d}b$$

For the independent variables a and b the increments and the differentials are the same quantity, so that $\mathrm{d}a = \Delta a$ and $\mathrm{d}b = \Delta b$. Also, from the given formula for y, we have

$$\frac{\partial y}{\partial a} = \mathrm{e}^{-bx} \quad \text{and} \quad \frac{\partial y}{\partial b} = -xa\mathrm{e}^{-bx}$$

Thus, from (8.28),

$$\mathrm{d}y = \mathrm{e}^{-bx}\Delta a - xa\mathrm{e}^{-bx}\Delta b$$

and division by y gives

$$\frac{\mathrm{d}y}{y} = \frac{\Delta a}{a} - bx\frac{\Delta b}{b}$$

Hence

$$\left|\frac{\mathrm{d}y}{y}\right| \leqslant \left|\frac{\Delta a}{a}\right| + |bx|\left|\frac{\Delta b}{b}\right| \leqslant p + |bx|q$$

Since $\Delta y \approx \mathrm{d}y$, we obtain an estimate for the relative error bound for y as $p + |bx|q$.

8.6.10 Exercises

68 The function z is defined by

$$z(x, y) = x^2y - 3y$$

Find Δz and $\mathrm{d}z$ when $x = 4$, $y = 3$, $\Delta x = -0.01$ and $\Delta y = 0.02$.

68 An open box has internal dimensions 2 m × 1.25 m × 0.75 m. It is made of sheet metal 4 mm thick. Find the actual volume of metal used and compare it with the approximate volume found using the differential of the capacity of the box.

70 The angle of elevation of the top of a tower is found to be 30° ± 0.5° from a point 300 ± 0.1 m on a horizontal line through the base of the tower. Estimate the height of the tower.

71 The equations

$$x + 2y + 3z + 4u = -3$$
$$x^2 + y^2 + z^2 + u^2 = 10$$
$$x^3 + y^3 + z^3 + u^3 = 0$$

define u as a function of y if x and z are eliminated. Find du/dy when $x = 1, y = -1, z = 2, u = -2$.

72 The acceleration f of a piston is given by

$$f = r\omega^2\left(\cos\theta + \frac{r}{L}\cos 2\theta\right)$$

When $\theta = \frac{1}{6}\pi$ radians and when $r/L = \frac{1}{2}$, calculate the approximate percentage error in the calculated value of f if the values of both r and ω are 1% too small.

73 The area of a triangle ABC is calculated using the formula

$$S = \tfrac{1}{2}bc\sin A$$

and it is known that b, c and A are measured correctly to within 1%. If the angle A is measured as 45°, prove that the percentage error in the calculated value of S is not more than about 2.8%.

74 The angular deflection θ of a beam of electrons in a cathode-ray tube due to a magnetic field is given by

$$\theta = K\frac{HL}{V^{1/2}}$$

where H is the intensity of the magnetic field, L is the length of the electron path, V is the accelerating voltage and K is a constant. If errors of up to ±0.2% are present in each of the measured H, L and V, what is the greatest possible percentage error in the calculated value of θ (assume that K is known accurately)?

75 In a coal processing plant the flow V of slurry along a pipe is given by

$$V = \frac{\pi p r^4}{8\eta l}$$

If r and l both increase by 5%, and p and η decrease by 10% and 30% respectively, find the approximate percentage change in V.

8.6.11 Exact differentials

Differentials sometimes arise naturally when modelling practical problems. An example in fluid dynamics is given in Section 8.9. When this occurs, it is often possible to analyse the problem further by testing to see if the expression in which the differentials occur is a total differential. Consider the equation

$$P(x, y)dx + Q(x, y)dy = 0$$

connecting x, y and their differentials. The left-hand side of this equation is said to be an **exact differential** if there is a function $f(x, y)$ such that

$$df = P(x, y)dx + Q(x, y)dy$$

Now we know that

$$df = \frac{\partial f}{\partial x}dx + \frac{\partial f}{\partial y}dy$$

so if $f(x, y)$ exists then

$$P(x, y) = \frac{\partial f}{\partial x} \quad \text{and} \quad Q(x, y) = \frac{\partial f}{\partial y}$$

For functions with continuous second derivatives we have

$$\frac{\partial^2 f}{\partial x \partial y} = \frac{\partial^2 f}{\partial y \partial x}$$

Thus if $f(x, y)$ exists then

$$\frac{\partial P}{\partial y} = \frac{\partial Q}{\partial x} \tag{8.31}$$

This gives us a test for the existence of $f(x, y)$, but does not tell us how to find it! The technique for finding $f(x, y)$ is shown in Example 8.38.

Example 8.38 Show that

$$(6x + 9y + 11)\mathrm{d}x + (9x - 4y + 3)\mathrm{d}y$$

is an exact differential and find the relationship between y and x given

$$\frac{\mathrm{d}y}{\mathrm{d}x} = -\frac{6x + 9y + 11}{9x - 4y + 3}$$

and the condition $y = 1$ when $x = 0$.

Solution In this example

$$P(x, y) = 6x + 9y + 11 \quad \text{and} \quad Q(x, y) = 9x - 4y + 3$$

First we test whether the expression is an exact differential. In this example

$$\frac{\partial P}{\partial y} = 9 \quad \text{and} \quad \frac{\partial Q}{\partial x} = 9$$

so from (8.31) we have an exact differential. Thus we know that there is a function $f(x, y)$ such that

$$\frac{\partial f}{\partial x} = 6x + 9y + 11, \quad \frac{\partial f}{\partial y} = 9x - 4y + 3 \qquad \textbf{(8.32), (8.33)}$$

Integrating (8.32) with respect to x, keeping y constant (that is, reversing the partial differentiation process), we have

$$f(x, y) = 3x^2 + 9xy + 11x + g(y) \tag{8.34}$$

Note that the 'constant' of integration is a function of y. You can check that this expression for $f(x, y)$ is correct by differentiating it partially with respect to x. But we also know from (8.33) the partial derivative of $f(x, y)$ with respect to y, and this enables us to find $g'(y)$. Differentiating (8.34) partially with respect to y and equating it to (8.33), we have

$$\frac{\partial f}{\partial y} = 9x + \frac{\mathrm{d}g}{\mathrm{d}y} = 9x - 4y + 3$$

(Note that since g is a function of y only we use $\mathrm{d}g/\mathrm{d}y$ rather than $\partial g/\partial y$.) Thus

$$\frac{\mathrm{d}g}{\mathrm{d}y} = -4y + 3$$

so, on integrating,

$$g(y) = -2y^2 + 3y + C$$

Substituting back into (8.34) gives

$$f(x, y) = 3x^2 + 9xy + 11x - 2y^2 + 3y + C$$

Now we are given that

$$\frac{dy}{dx} = -\frac{6x + 9y + 11}{9x - 4y + 3}$$

which implies that

$$(6x + 9y + 11)dx + (9x - 4y + 3)dy = 0$$

which in turn implies that

$$3x^2 + 9xy + 11x - 2y^2 + 3y + A = 0$$

The arbitrary constant A is fixed by applying the given condition $y = 1$ when $x = 0$, giving $A = -1$. Thus x and y satisfy the equation

$$3x^2 + 9xy + 11x - 2y^2 + 3y = 1$$

8.6.12 Exercises

76 Determine which of the following are exact differentials of a function, and find, where appropriate, the corresponding function.

(a) $(y^2 + 2xy + 1)dx + (2xy + x^2)dy$

(b) $(2xy^2 + 3y\cos 3x)dx + (2x^2y + \sin 3x)dy$

(c) $(6xy - y^2)dx + (2xe^y - x^2)dy$

(d) $(z^3 - 3y)dx + (12y^2 - 3x)dy + 3xz^2dz$

77 Find the value of the constant λ such that

$$(y\cos x + \lambda\cos y)dx + (x\sin y + \sin x + y)dy$$

is the exact differential of a function $f(x, y)$. Find the corresponding function $f(x, y)$ that also satisfies the condition $f(0, 1) = 0$.

78 Show that the differential

$$g(x, y) = (10x^2 + 6xy + 6y^2)dx + (9x^2 + 4xy + 15y^2)dy$$

is not exact, but that a constant m can be chosen so that

$$(2x + 3y)^m g(x, y)$$

is equal to dz, the exact differential of a function $z = f(x, y)$. Find $f(x, y)$.

8.7 Taylor's theorem for functions of two variables

In this section we extend Taylor's theorem for one variable (Theorem 8.4) to a function of two variables and apply it to unconstrained and constrained optimization problems.

8.7.1 Taylor's theorem

First we consider a function of two variables. Suppose $f(x, y)$ is a function all of whose nth-order partial derivatives exist and are continuous on some circular domain D with centre (a, b). Then, if $(a + h, b + k)$ lies in D, we have

$$f(a+h, b+k) = f(a, b) + \frac{1}{1!}\left(h\frac{\partial}{\partial x} + k\frac{\partial}{\partial y}\right)f(a, b) + \frac{1}{2!}\left(h\frac{\partial}{\partial x} + k\frac{\partial}{\partial y}\right)^2 f(a, b)$$

$$+ \ldots + \frac{1}{(n-1)!}\left(h\frac{\partial}{\partial x} + k\frac{\partial}{\partial y}\right)^{n-1} f(a, b)$$

$$+ \frac{1}{n!}\left(h\frac{\partial}{\partial x} + k\frac{\partial}{\partial y}\right)^{n} f(a+\theta h, b+\theta k) \tag{8.35}$$

where $0 < \theta < 1$. Here we have introduced the notation

$$\left(h\frac{\partial}{\partial x} + k\frac{\partial}{\partial y}\right)^{r} f(a, b)$$

to represent the value of the expression

$$h^r\frac{\partial^r f}{\partial x^r} + \binom{r}{1}h^{r-1}k\frac{\partial^r f}{\partial x^{r-1}\partial y} + \binom{r}{2}h^{r-2}k^2\frac{\partial^r f}{\partial x^{r-2}\partial y^2} + \ldots$$

$$+ \binom{r}{r-1}hk^{r-1}\frac{\partial^r f}{\partial x\partial y^{r-1}} + k^r\frac{\partial^r f}{\partial y^r}$$

at the point (a, b).

This result is obtained by repeated use of the chain rule. Setting $x = a + ht$ and $y = b + kt$, where $0 \leqslant t \leqslant 1$, we obtain

$$g(t) = f(a + ht, b + kt)$$

which is a function of one variable, so that, from Theorem 8.4, it has a Taylor expansion

$$g(t) = g(0) + \frac{t}{1!}g'(0) + \frac{t^2}{2!}g''(0) + \ldots + \frac{t^{n-1}}{(n-1)!}g^{(n-1)}(0) + \frac{t^n}{n!}g^{(n)}(\theta t)$$

where $0 \leqslant \theta \leqslant 1$. The derivatives of g are found using the chain rule:

$$g' = \frac{\mathrm{d}g}{\mathrm{d}t} = \frac{\mathrm{d}x}{\mathrm{d}t}\frac{\partial f}{\partial x} + \frac{\mathrm{d}y}{\mathrm{d}t}\frac{\partial f}{\partial y} = h\frac{\partial f}{\partial x} + k\frac{\partial f}{\partial y} = \left(h\frac{\partial}{\partial x} + k\frac{\partial}{\partial y}\right)f$$

$$g'' = \frac{\mathrm{d}^2 g}{\mathrm{d}t^2} = \frac{\mathrm{d}}{\mathrm{d}t}\left(h\frac{\partial}{\partial x} + k\frac{\partial}{\partial y}\right)f = \left(h\frac{\partial}{\partial x} + k\frac{\partial}{\partial y}\right)\left(h\frac{\partial}{\partial x} + k\frac{\partial}{\partial y}\right)f$$

$$= \left(h\frac{\partial}{\partial x} + k\frac{\partial}{\partial y}\right)^2 f$$

and, in general,

$$g^{(r)} = \frac{d^r g}{dt^r} = \left(h\frac{\partial}{\partial x} + k\frac{\partial}{\partial y}\right)^r f \quad (r = 0, 1, 2, \dots, n)$$

Putting $t = 1$ into the Taylor expansion of g gives the required result.

The same method can be used to extend the result to as many variables as we please. For the function $f(\boldsymbol{x})$, where $\boldsymbol{x} = (x_1, x_2, \dots, x_n)$, we have

$$f(\boldsymbol{a} + \boldsymbol{h}) = f(\boldsymbol{a}) + \sum_{i=1}^{n} h_i \frac{\partial f}{\partial x_i}(\boldsymbol{a}) + \frac{1}{2!}\left(\sum_{i=1}^{n} h_i \frac{\partial}{\partial x_i}\right)^2 f(\boldsymbol{a}) + \dots$$
$$+ \frac{1}{(m-1)!}\left(\sum_{i=1}^{n} h_i \frac{\partial}{\partial x_i}\right)^{m-1} f(\boldsymbol{a}) + \frac{1}{m!}\left(\sum_{i=1}^{n} h_i \frac{\partial}{\partial x_i}\right)^{m} f(\boldsymbol{a} + \theta\boldsymbol{h}) \qquad \textbf{(8.36)}$$

where $0 \leq \theta \leq 1$, provided that all the partial derivatives exist and are continuous.

By setting $h = x - a$ and $k = y - b$ in (8.35), we have the following alternative form of the Taylor expansion:

$$f(x, y) = f(a, b) + \frac{1}{1!}\left[(x - a)\frac{\partial}{\partial x} + (y - b)\frac{\partial}{\partial y}\right] f(a, b)$$
$$+ \frac{1}{2!}\left[(x - a)\frac{\partial}{\partial x} + (y - b)\frac{\partial}{\partial y}\right]^2 f(a, b)$$
$$+ \dots$$
$$+ \frac{1}{n!}\left[(x - a)\frac{\partial}{\partial x} + (y - b)\frac{\partial}{\partial y}\right]^n f(a + \theta(x - a), b + \theta(y - b))$$
$$\textbf{(8.37)}$$

which is referred to as the **Taylor expansion** of $f(x, y)$ about the point (a, b).

Example 8.39 Obtain the Taylor series of the function $f(x, y) = \sin xy$ about the point $(1, \frac{1}{3}\pi)$, neglecting terms of degree three and higher.

Solution From (8.37) the required series is

$$f(x, y) = f(1, \tfrac{1}{3}\pi) + \frac{1}{1!}\left[(x - 1)\frac{\partial}{\partial x} + (y - \tfrac{1}{3}\pi)\frac{\partial}{\partial y}\right] f(1, \tfrac{1}{3}\pi)$$
$$+ \frac{1}{2!}\left[(x - 1)\frac{\partial}{\partial x} + (y - \tfrac{1}{3}\pi)\frac{\partial}{\partial y}\right]^2 f(1, \tfrac{1}{3}\pi) \dots$$

Since $f(x, y) = \sin xy$, $f(1, \frac{1}{3}\pi) = \frac{\sqrt{3}}{2}$. Also,

$$\frac{\partial f}{\partial x} = y\cos xy \quad \text{giving} \quad \left(\frac{\partial f}{\partial x}\right)_{(1,\pi/3)} = \tfrac{1}{6}\pi$$

$$\frac{\partial f}{\partial y} = x\cos xy \quad \text{giving} \quad \left(\frac{\partial f}{\partial y}\right)_{(1,\pi/3)} = \tfrac{1}{2}$$

$$\frac{\partial^2 f}{\partial x^2} = -y^2\sin xy \quad \text{giving} \quad \left(\frac{\partial^2 f}{\partial x^2}\right)_{(1,\pi/3)} = -\tfrac{1}{18}\pi^2\sqrt{3}$$

$$\frac{\partial^2 f}{\partial x\,\partial y} = \cos xy - xy\sin xy \quad \text{giving} \quad \left(\frac{\partial^2 f}{\partial x\,\partial y}\right)_{(1,\pi/3)} = \tfrac{1}{2} - \tfrac{1}{6}\pi\sqrt{3}$$

$$\frac{\partial^2 f}{\partial y^2} = -x^2\sin xy \quad \text{giving} \quad \left(\frac{\partial^2 f}{\partial y^2}\right)_{(1,\pi/3)} = -\tfrac{1}{2}\sqrt{3}$$

Hence, neglecting terms of degree three and higher,

$$\sin xy \approx \frac{\sqrt{3}}{2} + \tfrac{1}{6}\pi(x-1) + \tfrac{1}{2}(y - \tfrac{1}{3}\pi) - \tfrac{1}{36}\pi^2\sqrt{3}(x-1)^2$$
$$+ (\tfrac{1}{2} - \tfrac{1}{6}\pi\sqrt{3})(x-1)(y - \tfrac{1}{3}\pi) - \tfrac{1}{4}\sqrt{3}(y - \tfrac{1}{3}\pi)^2$$

There appears to be no command in MATLAB for determining directly the Taylor series expansion of $f(x, y)$ about a point (a, b). In MAPLE the first n terms in such an expansion may be obtained using the multivariable Taylor command

```
readlib(mtaylor):
mtaylor(f(x,y), [x = a,y = b], n);
```

For example, considering Example 8.39, the MAPLE commands

```
readlib(mtaylor):
mtaylor(sin(x*y), [x = 1, y = Pi/3],3);
```

return the first three terms of the series as

$$\tfrac{1}{2}\sqrt{3} + \tfrac{1}{2}y - \tfrac{1}{6}\pi + \tfrac{1}{6}(x - 1)\pi - \tfrac{1}{36}\sqrt{(3)}\pi^2(x - 1)^2 +$$
$$(\tfrac{1}{2} - \tfrac{1}{6}\sqrt{3}\pi)(y - \tfrac{1}{3}\pi)(x - 1) - \tfrac{1}{4}\sqrt{3}(y - \tfrac{1}{3}\pi)^2$$

which checks with the answer given in the solution.

Using the `maple` command, such an expansion may be obtained in MATLAB using the command

```
maple('mtaylor(f(x,y),[x = a,y = b],n)')
```

Considering Example 8.39, check that the MATLAB commands

```
syms x y
f = sin(x*y);
s = maple('mtaylor(sin(x*y),[x = 1,y = pi/3],3)')
```

return the same answer as above.

8.7.2 Optimization of unconstrained functions

In Section 8.5 we considered the problem of determining the maximum and minimum values of a function $f(x)$ of one variable. We now turn our attention to obtaining the maximum and minimum values of a function $f(x, y)$ of two variables. Geometrically $z = f(x, y)$ represents a surface in three-dimensional space, with z being the height of the surface above the x–y plane. Suppose that $f(x, y)$ has a local maximum value at the point (a, b), as illustrated in Figure 8.18(a). Then for all possible (small) values of h and k

$$f(a, b) > f(a + h, b + k)$$

so that the difference (increment)

$$\Delta f = f(a + h, b + k) - f(a, b)$$

is negative. Then, provided that the partial derivatives exist and are continuous, using Taylor's theorem we can express Δf in terms of the partial derivatives of $f(x, y)$ evaluated at (a, b):

$$\Delta f = \left(h\frac{\partial f}{\partial x} + k\frac{\partial f}{\partial y}\right)_{(a,b)} + \frac{1}{2!}\left(h^2\frac{\partial^2 f}{\partial x^2} + 2hk\frac{\partial^2 f}{\partial x \partial y} + k^2\frac{\partial^2 f}{\partial y^2}\right)_{(a,b)} + \ldots$$

where h and k may be negative or positive numbers. Since h and k are small, the sign of Δf depends on the sign of

$$\left(h\frac{\partial f}{\partial x} + k\frac{\partial f}{\partial y}\right)_{(a,b)}$$

That is, the sign of Δf depends on the values of h and k. But for a maximum value of $f(x, y)$ at (a, b) the sign of Δf must be negative whatever the values of h and k. This implies that for a maximum to occur at (a, b), $\partial f/\partial x$ and $\partial f/\partial y$ must be zero there.

If $f(x, y)$ has a local minimum at (a, b), as illustrated in Figure 8.18(b), then

$$f(a, b) < f(a + h, b + k)$$

and, using the above argument, we find that for a local minimum to occur at (a, b), $\partial f/\partial x$ and $\partial f/\partial y$ must again be zero.

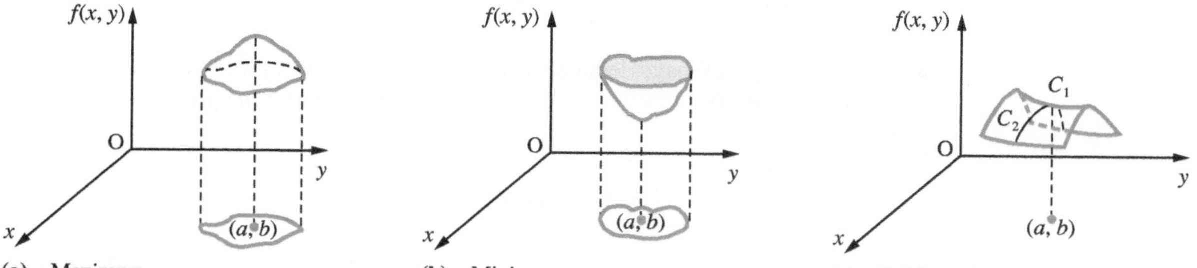

(a) Maximum **(b)** Minimum **(c)** Saddle point (maximum for curve C_2, minimum for curve C_1)

Figure 8.18

Thus a first necessary condition for a maximum or a minimum is

$$\frac{\partial f}{\partial x} = \frac{\partial f}{\partial y} = 0 \quad \text{at } (a, b)$$

In terms of differentials, this means that

$$\mathrm{d}f = 0 \quad \text{at } (a, b)$$

Points at which this occurs are called **stationary points** of the function and the values of the function at those points are called its **stationary values**. When this condition is satisfied, we have

$$\Delta f = \frac{1}{2!}\left(h^2\frac{\partial^2 f}{\partial x^2} + 2hk\frac{\partial^2 f}{\partial x \partial y} + k^2\frac{\partial^2 f}{\partial y^2}\right)_{(a,b)} + \ldots$$

Putting

$$R = \frac{\partial^2 f}{\partial x^2}, \quad S = \frac{\partial^2 f}{\partial x \partial y} \quad \text{and} \quad T = \frac{\partial^2 f}{\partial y^2}$$

we deduce that the sign of Δf depends on the sign of the second differential

$$\mathrm{d}^2 f = Rh^2 + 2Shk + Tk^2$$

Rearranging, we have, provided that $R \neq 0$,

$$\mathrm{d}^2 f = \frac{1}{R}(R^2h^2 + 2RShk + RTk^2) = \frac{1}{R}[(Rh + Sk)^2 + (RT - S^2)k^2]$$

If $RT - S^2 > 0$, the sign of $\mathrm{d}^2 f$ is independent of the values of h and k; while if $RT - S^2 < 0$, its sign depends on those values. Thus a second necessary condition for a maximum or minimum value to occur at (a, b) is that

$$\frac{\partial^2 f}{\partial x^2}\frac{\partial^2 f}{\partial y^2} - \left(\frac{\partial^2 f}{\partial x \partial y}\right)^2 = f_{xx}f_{yy} - f_{xy}^2 \geqslant 0 \quad \text{at } (a, b)$$

Note that $f_{xx}f_{yy} - f_{xy}^2 = \begin{vmatrix} f_{xx} & f_{xy} \\ f_{yx} & f_{yy} \end{vmatrix}$. If strict inequality is satisfied, the sign of Δf depends on $R = \partial^2 f/\partial x^2$. If $\partial^2 f/\partial x^2 > 0$, there is a minimum at (a, b). If $\partial^2 f/\partial x^2 < 0$, there is a maximum at (a, b).

By expressing $\mathrm{d}^2 f$ as

$$\mathrm{d}^2 f = \frac{1}{T}[(TK + Sh)^2 + (RT - S^2)h^2], \quad T \neq 0$$

we could equally well have deduced that there is a minimum at (a, b) if $\partial^2 f/\partial y^2 > 0$ and a maximum at (a, b) if $\partial^2 f/\partial y^2 < 0$, assuming the above strict inequality.

If

$$\frac{\partial^2 f}{\partial x^2}\frac{\partial^2 f}{\partial y^2} - \left(\frac{\partial^2 f}{\partial x \partial y}\right)^2 < 0 \quad \text{at } (a, b)$$

then the sign of Δf depends on the values of h and k, and along some paths through (a, b) the function has a maximum value while along other paths it has a minimum value. Such a point is called a **saddle point**, as illustrated in Figure 8.18(c).

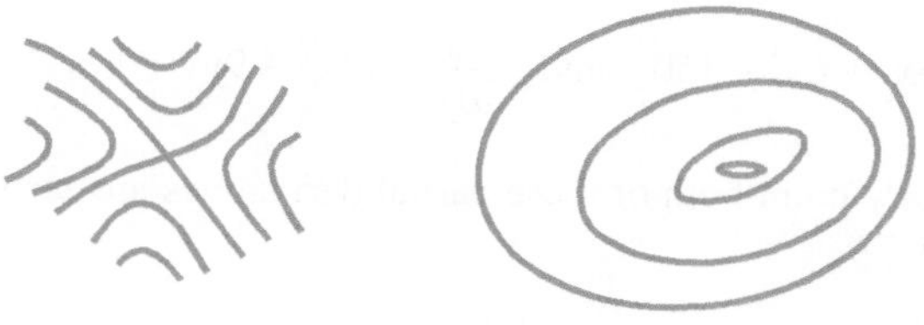

(a) (b)

Figure 8.19 Nature of stationary points: (a) saddle and (b) maximum or minimum.

The contours of a function often show clearly where maximum or minimum or saddle points occur, as illustrated in Figure 8.19.

Summary

(1) A necessary condition for the function $f(x, y)$ to have a stationary value at (a, b) is that

$$\frac{\partial f}{\partial x} = 0 \quad \text{and} \quad \frac{\partial f}{\partial y} = 0 \quad \text{at } (a, b)$$

(2) If $\dfrac{\partial^2 f}{\partial x^2}\dfrac{\partial^2 f}{\partial y^2} - \left(\dfrac{\partial^2 f}{\partial x \partial y}\right)^2 > 0$ and $\dfrac{\partial^2 f}{\partial x^2}$ or $\dfrac{\partial^2 f}{\partial y^2} < 0$ at (a, b)

then the stationary point is a local maximum.

(3) If $\dfrac{\partial^2 f}{\partial x^2}\dfrac{\partial^2 f}{\partial y^2} - \left(\dfrac{\partial^2 f}{\partial x \partial y}\right)^2 > 0$ and $\dfrac{\partial^2 f}{\partial x^2}$ or $\dfrac{\partial^2 f}{\partial y^2} > 0$ at (a, b)

then the stationary point is a local minimum.

(4) If $\dfrac{\partial^2 f}{\partial x^2}\dfrac{\partial^2 f}{\partial y^2} - \left(\dfrac{\partial^2 f}{\partial x \partial y}\right) < 0$ at (a, b)

then the stationary point is a saddle point.

(5) If $\dfrac{\partial^2 f}{\partial x^2}\dfrac{\partial^2 f}{\partial y^2} - \left(\dfrac{\partial^2 f}{\partial x \partial y}\right)^2 = 0$ at (a, b)

we cannot draw a conclusion, and the point may be a maximum, minimum or saddle point. Further investigation is required, and it may be necessary to consider the third-order terms in the Taylor series.

Example 8.40

Find the stationary points of the function

$$f(x, y) = 2x^3 + 6xy^2 - 3y^3 - 150x$$

and determine their nature.

Solution

$$\frac{\partial f}{\partial x} = 6x^2 + 6y^2 - 150 \quad \text{and} \quad \frac{\partial f}{\partial y} = 12xy - 9y^2$$

For a stationary point both of these partial derivatives are zero, which gives

$$x^2 + y^2 = 25$$

and

$$y(4x - 3y) = 0$$

From the second equation we see that either $y = 0$ or $4x = 3y$. Putting $y = 0$ in the first equation gives $x = \pm 5$, so that the points (5, 0) and (−5, 0) are solutions of the equations. Putting $x = \frac{3}{4}y$ into the first equation gives $y = \pm 4$, so that the points (3, 4) and (−3, −4) are also solutions of the equation. Thus the function has stationary points at (5, 0), (−5, 0), (3, 4) and (−3, −4).

Next we have to classify these points as maxima or minima or saddle points. Working out the second derivatives, we have

$$\frac{\partial^2 f}{\partial x^2} = 12x, \quad \frac{\partial^2 f}{\partial y^2} = 12x - 18y \quad \text{and} \quad \frac{\partial^2 f}{\partial x \partial y} = 12y$$

and we can complete the following table.

Point	$\frac{\partial^2 f}{\partial x^2}$	$\frac{\partial^2 f}{\partial y^2}$	$\frac{\partial^2 f}{\partial x \partial y}$	$\frac{\partial^2 f}{\partial x^2}\frac{\partial^2 f}{\partial y^2} - \left(\frac{\partial^2 f}{\partial x \partial y}\right)^2$	*Nature*	*Value*
(5, 0)	60	60	0	positive	minimum	−500
(−5, 0)	−60	−60	0	positive	maximum	500
(3, 4)	36	−36	48	negative	saddle point	−300
(−3, −4)	−36	36	−48	negative	saddle point	300

The situation is shown quite clearly on the contour plot (level curves) of the function shown in Figure 8.20. Looking at the figure, we see that the contours distinguish clearly between saddle points and other stationary points, as indicated in Figure 8.19.

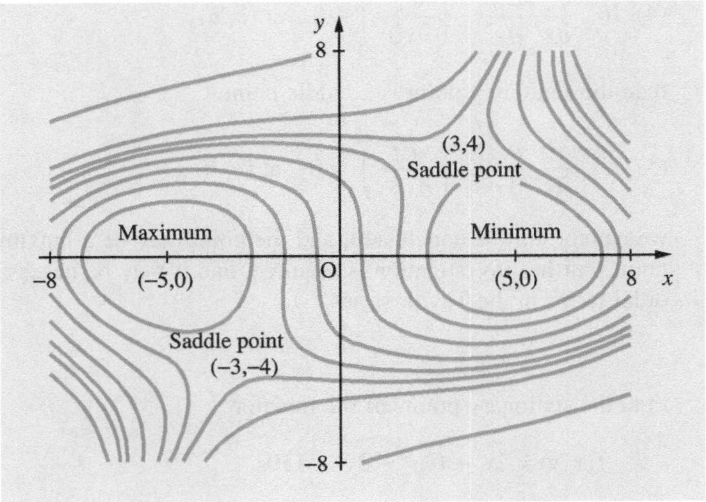

Figure 8.20
Contour plot of $f(x, y) = 2x^3 + 6xy^2 - 3y^3 - 150x$.

To illustrate the use of MATLAB for determining and classifying the stationary points of a function of two variables we consider the function of Example 8.40. The MATLAB commands

```
syms x y
f = 2*x^3 + 6*x*y^2 - 3*y^3 - 150*x;
fx = diff(f,x); fy = diff(f,y); [X,Y] = solve(fx,fy)
```

return the two column vectors `X` and `Y` giving the stationary points as `(5,0)`, `(-5,0)`, `(3,4)` and `(-3,-4)`. Next we determine the second partial derivatives and evaluate

$$\Delta = \frac{\partial^2 f}{\partial x^2}\frac{\partial^2 f}{\partial y^2} - \left(\frac{\partial^2 f}{\partial x \partial y}\right)^2$$

at each of the stationary points, using the commands

```
fxx = diff(f,x); fxy = diff(fx,y); fyy = diff(fy,y);
delta = fxx*fyy - fxy^2;
```

and substituting the coordinates of the four points

```
subs(delta,{x,y},{X(1),Y(1)}) giving ans = 3600
subs(delta,{x,y},{X(2),Y(2)}) giving ans = 3600
subs(delta,{x,y},{X(3),Y(3)}) giving ans = -3600
subs(delta,{x,y},{X(4),Y(4)}) giving ans = -3600
```

For the first two points `delta > 0` so we look at the sign of `fxx` or `fyy`

`subs(fxx,{x,y},{X(1),Y(1)})` giving `ans = 60` so `(5,0)` is a minimum point
`subs(fxx,{x,y},{X(2),Y(2)})` giving `ans = -60` so `(-5,0)` is a maximum point

For the last two points `delta < 0` so `(3,4)` and `(-3,4)` are both saddle points. The contour plot can be investigated using the command

```
ezcontour(f,[10,10])
```

The corresponding commands in MAPLE are:

```
f:= f(x,y); fx: = diff(f,x); fy:= diff(f,y);
stat:= solve({fx = 0,fy = 0},{x,y});
```

giving the four stationary points in form $\{a, b\}$

```
fxx:= diff(f,x,x); fxy:= diff(f,x,y); fyy:= diff(f,y,y);
delta:= fxx*fyy - fxy^2;
subs(stat[1],delta); subs(stat[2],delta);
subs(stat[3],delta); subs(stat[4],delta);
subs(stat[1],fxx); subs(stat[2],fxx);
```

The process indicated above can be extended to functions of as many variables as we please. At a stationary point the first differential df, is zero, so that all the first partial derivatives are zero there. If, at that stationary point, the second differential d^2f is negative for all small changes in the independent variables then we have a maximum. If it is positive, we have a minimum. If it is zero, further analysis is required. However, the general conditions for this to occur are extremely complicated both to write down and to apply.

8.7.3 Exercises

Check your answers using MATLAB or MAPLE whenever possible.

79 Find the stationary values (and their classification) of

(a) $x^3 - 15x^2 - 20y^2 + 5$

(b) $2 - x^2 - xy - y^2$

(c) $2x^2 + y^2 + 3xy - 3y - 5x + 2$

(d) $x^3 + y^2 - 3(x + y) + 1$

(e) $xy^2 - 2xy - 2x^2 - 3x$

(f) $x^3y^2(1 - x - y)$

(g) $x^2 + y^2 + \dfrac{2}{x} + \dfrac{2}{y}$

80 Prove that $(x + y)/(x^2 + 2y^2 + 6)$ has a maximum at (2, 1) and a minimum at (−2, −1).

81 Show that

$$f(x, y) = x^3 + y^3 - 2(x^2 + y^2) + 3xy$$

has stationary values at (0, 0) and $(\frac{1}{3}, \frac{1}{3})$ and investigate their nature.

82 A manufacturer produces an article in batches of N items. Each production run has a set-up cost of £100 and each item costs an additional £0.05 to produce. The weekly storage costs are a basic rental of £50 plus an additional £0.10 per item stored. Assuming that there is a steady sale of n items per week, so that the average number of items stored is $\frac{1}{2}N$, and that, when the store is exhausted, it is immediately replenished by a new production run, show that the weekly cost £K is given by

$$K = 50 + 0.05N + 0.05n + \frac{100n}{N}$$

The weekly demand n is a function of the selling price £p, and

$$n = 5000 - 10\,000p$$

Show that the weekly profit £P is

$$P = (5000 - 10\,000p)\left(p - 0.05 - \frac{100}{N}\right) - 0.05N - 50$$

If the manufacturer is able to decide both the batch size N and the price £p, show that a maximum weekly profit is realized where $p = 0.3$, and find the corresponding values of N, n and P.

83 The gravitational attraction at the point (x, y) in the x–y plane due to point masses in the plane is

$$G(x, y) = \frac{1}{x} + \frac{4}{y} + \frac{9}{4 - x - y}$$

Show that $G(x, y)$ has a stationary value of 9.

84 Find constants a and b such that

$$\int_0^{\pi} [\sin x - (ax^2 + bx)]^2\,dx$$

is a minimum.

85 A tank has the shape of a cuboid and is open at the top and has a volume of 4 m^3. If the base measurements (in m) are x by y, show that the surface area (in m^2) is given by

$$A = xy + \frac{8}{y} + \frac{8}{x}$$

and find the dimensions of the tank for A to be a minimum.

86 A flat circular metal plate has a shape defined by the region $x^2 + y^2 \leqslant 1$. The plate is heated so that the temperature T at any point (x, y) on it is given by

$$T = x^2 + 2y^2 - x$$

Find the temperatures at the hottest and coldest points on the plate and the points where they occur. (*Hint*: Consider the level curves of T.)

87 A metal channel is formed by turning up the sides of width x of a rectangular sheet of metal through an angle θ. If the sheet is 200 mm wide, determine the values of x and θ for which the cross-section of the channel will be a maximum.

8.7.4 Optimization of constrained functions

As we have seen in Exercises 8.7.3, Questions 82 and 85–87, there are frequent situations in engineering applications when we wish to obtain the stationary values of functions of more than one variable and for which the variables themselves are subject to one or more constraint conditions. The general theory for these applications is discussed in the companion text *Advanced Modern Engineering Mathematics.* Here we will show the technique for solving such problems.

Example 8.41 Obtain the extremum value of the function

$$f(x, y) = 2x^2 + 3y^2$$

subject to the constraint $2x + y = 1$.

Solution In this particular example it is easy to eliminate one of the two variables x and y. Eliminating y, we can write $f(x, y)$ as

$$f(x, y) = f(x) = 2x^2 + 3(1 - 2x)^2 = 14x^2 - 12x + 3$$

We can now apply the techniques used for functions of one variable to obtain the extremum value. Differentiating gives

$$f'(x) = 28x - 12 \quad \text{and} \quad f''(x) = 28$$

An extremal value occurs when $f'(x) = 0$; that is, $x = \frac{3}{7}$, and, since $f''(\frac{3}{7}) > 0$, this corresponds to a minimum value. Thus the extremum is a minimum $f_{\text{min}} = \frac{3}{7}$ at $x = \frac{3}{7}$, $y = \frac{1}{7}$.

In Example 8.41 we were fortunate in being able to use the constraint equation to eliminate one of the variables. In practice, however, it is often difficult, or even impossible, to do this, and we have to retain all the original variables. Let us consider the general problem of obtaining the stationary points of $f(x, y, z)$ subject to the constraint $g(x, y, z) = 0$. We shall refer to such points as **conditional stationary points**.

At stationary points of $f(x, y, z)$ we have

$$\mathrm{d}f = \frac{\partial f}{\partial x}\mathrm{d}x + \frac{\partial f}{\partial y}\mathrm{d}y + \frac{\partial f}{\partial z}\mathrm{d}z = 0 \tag{8.38}$$

This implies that the vector $(\partial f/\partial x, \partial f/\partial y, \partial f/\partial z)$ is perpendicular to the vector $(\mathrm{d}x, \mathrm{d}y, \mathrm{d}z)$. Since $g(x, y, z) = 0$

$$\mathrm{d}g = \frac{\partial g}{\partial x}\mathrm{d}x + \frac{\partial g}{\partial y}\mathrm{d}y + \frac{\partial g}{\partial z}\mathrm{d}z = 0 \tag{8.39}$$

Thus, the vector $(\partial g/\partial x, \partial g/\partial y, \partial g/\partial z)$ is also perpendicular to the vector $(\mathrm{d}x, \mathrm{d}y, \mathrm{d}z)$. This implies that the vector $(\partial f/\partial x, \partial f/\partial y, \partial f/\partial z)$ is parallel to the vector $(\partial g/\partial x, \partial g/\partial y, \partial g/\partial z)$ and that we can find a number λ such that

$$\left(\frac{\partial f}{\partial x}, \frac{\partial f}{\partial y}, \frac{\partial f}{\partial z}\right) - \lambda\left(\frac{\partial g}{\partial x}, \frac{\partial g}{\partial y}, \frac{\partial g}{\partial z}\right) = (0, 0, 0) \tag{8.40}$$

Geometrically this means that the level surface of the objective function $f(x, y, z)$ touches the constraint surface $g(x, y, z) = 0$ at the stationary point.

This can be neatly summarized by writing $\phi(x, y, z) = f(x, y, z) - \lambda g(x, y, z)$. Then $f(x, y, z)$ will have a stationary point subject to the constraint $g(x, y, z) = 0$ when

$$\frac{\partial \phi}{\partial x} = \frac{\partial \phi}{\partial y} = \frac{\partial \phi}{\partial z} = 0 \quad \text{and} \quad g(x, y, z) = 0 \tag{8.41}$$

This gives four equations to determine $(x, y, z; \lambda)$ for the stationary point. The scalar multiplier λ is called a **Lagrange multiplier** and the function $\phi(x, y, z)$ is called the **auxiliary function.**

Example 8.42 Rework Example 8.41 using the method of Lagrange multipliers.

Solution Here we need to obtain the extremum of the function

$$f(x, y) = 2x^2 + 3y^2$$

subject to the constraint

$$g(x, y) = 2x + y - 1 = 0$$

The auxiliary function is

$$\begin{aligned}\phi(x, y, z) &= f(x, y) - \lambda g(x, y)\\ &= 2x^2 + 3y^2 - \lambda(2x + y - 1)\end{aligned}$$

and we find that the conditional extrema of $f(x, y)$ are given by

$$\frac{\partial \phi}{\partial x} = \frac{\partial \phi}{\partial y} = 0, \quad g(x, y) = 0$$

that is

$$\frac{\partial \phi}{\partial x} = 4x - 2\lambda = 0 \tag{8.42}$$

$$\frac{\partial \phi}{\partial y} = 6y - \lambda = 0 \tag{8.43}$$

$$g(x, y) = 2x + y - 1 = 0 \tag{8.44}$$

Solving (8.42)–(8.44) gives

$$\lambda = \tfrac{6}{7}, \quad x = \tfrac{3}{7} \quad \text{and} \quad y = \tfrac{1}{7}$$

so that the conditional extremal value of $f(x, y)$ is $\frac{3}{7}$ and occurs at $x = \frac{3}{7}$, $y = \frac{1}{7}$.

It is clear from the level curves of $f(x, y)$, shown in Figure 8.21, that the function has a minimum at $(\frac{3}{7}, \frac{1}{7})$. In general, however, to determine the nature of the conditional stationary point, we have to resort to Taylor's theorem and consider the sign of the difference $f(x + h, y + k) - f(x, y)$. Taking a point near $(\frac{3}{7}, \frac{1}{7})$, say $(\frac{3}{7} + h, \frac{1}{7} + k)$,

Figure 8.21
Level curves of $f(x, y) = 2x^2 + 3y^2$.

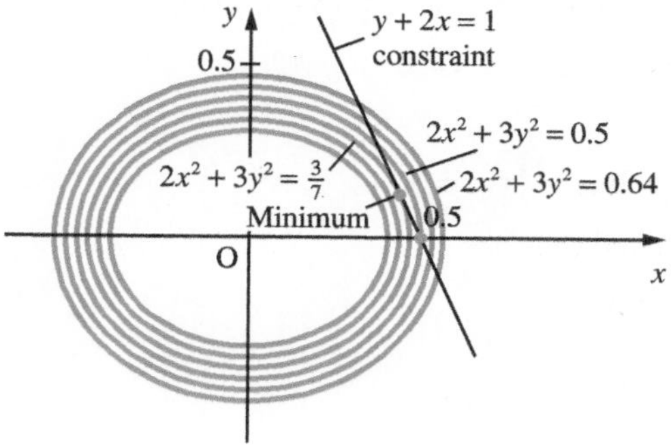

that still satisfies the constraint $2x + y - 1 = 0$, we have $2h + k = 0$, so that $k = -2h$. Hence a near point satisfying the constraint is $(\frac{3}{7} + h, \frac{1}{7} - 2h)$, and thus

$$f(\tfrac{3}{7} + h, \tfrac{1}{7} - 2h) - f(\tfrac{3}{7}, \tfrac{1}{7}) = 2(\tfrac{3}{7} + h)^2 + 3(\tfrac{1}{7} - 2h)^2 - [2(\tfrac{3}{7})^2 - 3(\tfrac{1}{7})^2]$$
$$= 14h^2 > 0$$

Since this is positive, it follows that the point is a minimum, confirming the result of Example 8.41.

In general, classifying conditional stationary points into maxima, minima or saddle points can be very difficult, but in the majority of engineering applications this can be done using physical reasoning.

Example 8.43 Find the dimensions of the cuboidal box, without a top, of maximum capacity whose surface area is 12 m^2.

Solution If the dimensions of the box are $x \times y \times z$ then we are required to maximize

$$f(x, y, z) = xyz$$

subject to the constraint

$$xy + 2xz + 2yz = 12 \tag{8.45}$$

The auxiliary function is

$$\phi(x, y, z) = xyz + \lambda(xy + 2xz + 2yz - 12)$$

and the equations we have to solve are

$$\frac{\partial \phi}{\partial x} = yz + \lambda(y + 2z) = 0 \tag{8.46}$$

$$\frac{\partial \phi}{\partial y} = xz + \lambda(x + 2z) = 0 \tag{8.47}$$

$$\frac{\partial \phi}{\partial z} = xy + \lambda(2x + 2y) = 0 \tag{8.48}$$

together with (8.45).

Taking $x \times (8.46) + y \times (8.47) + z \times (8.48)$ gives

$$3xyz + \lambda(2xy + 4xz + 4yz) = 0$$

or

$$\lambda(xy + 2xz + 2yz) + \tfrac{3}{2}xyz = 0 \qquad \textbf{(8.49)}$$

Then, from (8.49) and (8.45),

$$12\lambda + \tfrac{3}{2}xyz = 0$$

so that

$$\lambda = -\tfrac{1}{8}xyx$$

Substituting into (8.46)–(8.48) in succession and dividing throughout by common factors gives

$$1 - \tfrac{1}{8}x(y + 2z) = 0 \qquad \textbf{(8.50)}$$

$$1 - \tfrac{1}{8}y(x + 2z) = 0 \qquad \textbf{(8.51)}$$

$$1 - \tfrac{1}{8}z(2x + 2y) = 0 \qquad \textbf{(8.52)}$$

Subtracting (8.51) from (8.50) gives

$$\tfrac{1}{4}yz - \tfrac{1}{4}xz = 0 \quad \text{hence} \quad y = x \quad (\text{since clearly } z \neq 0)$$

Putting this into (8.52), we have

$$1 - \tfrac{1}{2}yz = 0, \quad \text{or} \quad yz = 2$$

Substituting this and $x = y$ into (8.50) gives

$$1 - \tfrac{1}{8}y^2 - \tfrac{1}{2} = 0$$

that is

$$y^2 = 4, \quad \text{or} \quad y = 2 \ (\text{since } y > 0)$$

It then follows that $x = 2$, $z = 1$. Thus the required dimensions are 2 m × 2 m × 1 m, and it follows from physical considerations that this corresponds to the maximum volume, since the minimum volume is zero (Figure 8.22).

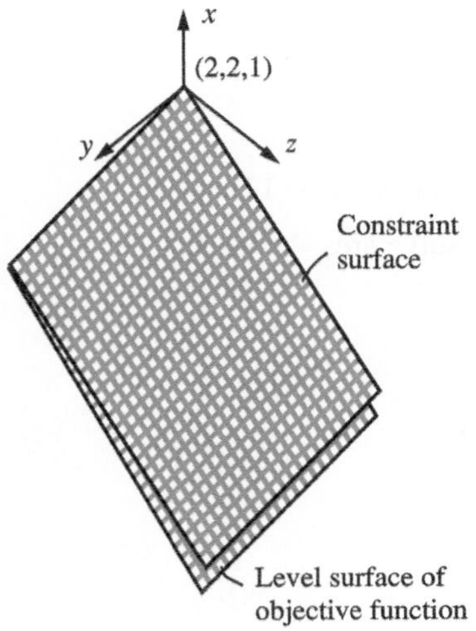

Figure 8.22 Level surface of objective function touches constraint surface at (2, 2, 1).

Denoting ϕ by `F` this example may be solved in MATLAB as follows:

```
syms x y z lam
F = x*y*z + lam*(x*y + 2*x*z + 2*y*z - 12);
Fx = diff(F,x) returning Fx = y*z + lam*(y + 2*z)
Fy = diff(F,y) returning Fy = x*z + lam*(x + 2*z)
Fz = diff(F,z) returning Fz = x*y + lam*(2*x + 2*y)
[lam,x,y,z] = solve('x*y + 2*x*z + 2*y*z = 12',
'y*z + lam*(y + 2*z) = 0','x*z + lam*(x + 2*z) = 0',
'x*y + lam*(2*x + 2*y) = 0')
```

returning

```
lam = -1/2     x =  2     y =  2     z =  1
       1/2         -2         -2         -1
```

Since x, y and z represent dimensions they must be positive, so the required dimensions are 2m × 2m × 1m. (Note that the variables in the solution array when using the `solve` command are given in alphabetical order.)

Example 8.44 Apply the method of Lagrange multipliers to solve the design problem of Section 2.10.

Solution Here the objective function $A(l, b, h, t)$ is subject to the constraint function $C(l, b, h)$ where

$$A(l, b, h, t) = (lb + 6bh + 2hl)t + (2l + 6b + 12h)t^2 + 12t^3$$

and $C(l, b, h) = lhb = K$

and t and K are constants.

The auxiliary function is

$$\phi(l, b, h, \lambda) = A(l, b, h, t) + \lambda[C(l, b, h) - K]$$

and we find the conditional extrema of A are given by

$$\frac{\partial\phi}{\partial l} = 0, \quad \frac{\partial\phi}{\partial b} = 0, \quad \frac{\partial\phi}{\partial h} = 0 \quad \text{and } C(l, b, h) = K$$

Thus

$$(b + 2h)t + 2t^2 + \lambda hb = 0 \qquad \textbf{(8.53)}$$

$$(l + 6h)t + 6t^2 + \lambda lh = 0 \qquad \textbf{(8.54)}$$

$$(6b + 2l)t + 12t^2 + \lambda lb = 0 \qquad \textbf{(8.55)}$$

Equation (8.54) – 3 × (8.53) gives

$$(l - 3b)t + \lambda(l - 3b)h = 0$$

which implies $l = 3b$. Equation (8.55) – 6 × (8.53) gives

$$(2l - 12h)t + \lambda(l - 6h)b = 0$$

which implies $l = 6h$.

So $b = 2h$, $l = 6h$ with $lbh = K$. Thus $12h^3 = K$ and $h = (K/12)^{1/3}$ as before.

The Lagrange multiplier method outlined above may be extended to a function of any number of variables. It also extends naturally to situations where there is more than one constraint equation by introducing the equivalent number of Lagrange multipliers. In general, if $f(x_1, x_2, \dots, x_n)$ is a function of n variables subject to m ($< n$) constraints

$$g_i(x_1, \dots, x_n) = 0 \quad (i = 1, 2, \dots, m)$$

then, to determine the constrained stationary values of $f(x_1, x_2, \dots, x_n)$, the procedure is to set up the auxiliary function

$$\phi(x_1, x_2, \dots, x_n) = f(x_1, x_2, \dots, x_n) + \lambda_1 g_1 + \dots + \lambda_m g_m$$

and solve the resulting $m + n$ equations

$$\frac{\partial \phi}{\partial x_j} = \frac{\partial f}{\partial x_j} + \sum_{i=1}^{m} \lambda_i \frac{\partial g_i}{\partial x_j} = 0 \quad (j = 1, 2, \dots, n)$$

$$\frac{\partial \phi}{\partial \lambda_i} = g_i = 0 \quad (i = 1, 2, \dots, m)$$

Often the algebraic equations involved in this method of solution are not amenable to algebraic solution and numerical methods are used. These are described in detail in the companion volume *Advanced Modern Engineering Mathematics.*

8.7.5 Exercises

Check your answers using MATLAB or MAPLE whenever possible.

88 Find the extremum of $x^2 - 2y^2 + 2xy + 4x$ subject to the constraint $2x = y$ and verify that it is a maximum value.

89 Find the extremum of $3x^2 + 2y^2 + 6z^2$ subject to the constraint $x + y + z = 1$ and verify that it is a minimum value.

90 The equation $5x^2 + 6xy + 5y^2 - 8 = 0$ represents an ellipse whose centre is at the origin. By considering the extrema of $x^2 + y^2$, obtain the lengths of the semi-axes.

91 Which point on the sphere $x^2 + y^2 + z^2 = 1$ is at the greatest distance from the point having coordinates (1, 2, 2)?

92 Find the maximum and minimum values of

$$f(x, y) = 4x + y + y^2$$

where (x, y) lies on the circle $x^2 + y^2 + 2x + y = 1$.

93 Obtain the stationary value of $2x + y + 2z + x^2 - 3z^2$ subject to the two constraints $x + y + z = 1$ and $2x - y + z = 2$.

8.8 Engineering application: deflection of a built-in column

In this section we consider an example in which the techniques developed in Section 8.4 may be used to solve an engineering problem.

The deflection $y(x)$ of a column buckling under its own weight satisfies the differential equation

$$EI\frac{d^3y}{dx^3} + wx\frac{dy}{dx} = 0 \tag{8.56}$$

where E is Young's modulus, I the second moment of area of the cross-section and w is the weight per unit run of the column. The deflection of the built-in column shown in Figure 8.23 also satisfies the conditions

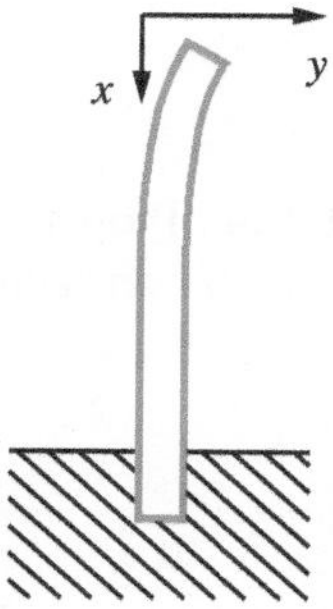

Figure 8.23 Deflection of a column.

$$\frac{d^2y}{dx^2} = 0 \quad \text{at } x = 0$$

and

$$y = 0 \quad \text{and} \quad \frac{dy}{dx} = 0 \quad \text{at } x = l$$

where l is the length of the column. We need to find the greatest height attainable for the column without collapse.

To make the algebraic manipulations easier, we first simplify the differential equation. Putting $x = ct$ gives

$$\frac{dy}{dx} = \frac{dy}{dt}\frac{dt}{dx} = \frac{1}{c}\frac{dy}{dt}$$

$$\frac{d^2y}{dx^2} = \frac{d}{dt}\left(\frac{1}{c}\frac{dy}{dt}\right)\frac{dt}{dx} = \frac{1}{c^2}\frac{d^2y}{dt^2}$$

and

$$\frac{d^3y}{dx^3} = \frac{d}{dt}\left(\frac{1}{c^2}\frac{d^2y}{dt^2}\right)\frac{dt}{dx} = \frac{1}{c^3}\frac{d^3y}{dt^3}$$

which on substituting into (8.56) transforms it to

$$\frac{EI}{c^3}\frac{d^3y}{dt^3} + wt\frac{dy}{dt} = 0$$

so that choosing $c^3 = EI/w$ and setting $f(t) = dy/dt$ simplifies the equation further to

$$\frac{d^2f}{dt^2} + tf = 0 \tag{8.57}$$

with the conditions

$$\frac{df}{dt} = 0 \quad \text{at } t = 0 \quad \text{and} \quad f(t) = 0 \quad \text{at } t = l(EI/w)^{-1/3} = T$$

Assuming that $f(t)$ has a Maclaurin series expansion, we may write it as

$$f(t) = a_0 + a_1 t + a_2 t^2 + a_3 t^3 + \ldots + a_n t^n + \ldots$$

Differentiating this, we have

$$f'(t) = a_1 + 2a_2 t + 3a_3 t^2 + \ldots + na_n t^{n-1} + (n+1)a_{n+1} t^n + \ldots$$

and

$$f''(t) = 2a_2 + 6a_3 t + 12a_4 t^2 + \ldots + n(n-1)a_n t^{n-2} + \ldots$$

Since $f'(0) = 0$, we deduce at once that $a_1 = 0$. Since $f(t)$ satisfies the differential equation (8.57), we deduce on substitution that

$$2a_2 + 6a_3 t + 12a_4 t^2 + \ldots + n(n-1)a_n t^{n-2} + \ldots$$
$$= -a_0 t - a_1 t^2 - a_2 t^3 - \ldots - a_n t^{n+1} - \ldots$$

This expression is true for all values of t, with $0 < t < T$, so we deduce from Property (i) of polynomials given in Section 2.4.1 that the coefficients of each power of t on each side of the equation are equal. That is,

$$2a_2 = 0 \qquad \text{(coefficient of } t^0)$$
$$6a_3 = -a_0 \qquad \text{(coefficient of } t^1)$$
$$12a_4 = -a_1 \qquad \text{(coefficient of } t^2)$$

and so on. In general, the coefficient of t^r (obtained by setting $n - 2 = r$ on the left-hand side and $n + 1 = r$ on the right-hand side) yields

$$(r+2)(r+1)a_{r+2} = -a_{r-1}$$

This recurrence relation enables us to calculate a_{r+3} in terms of a_r as

$$a_{r+3} = \frac{-a_r}{(r+3)(r+2)} \qquad (r = 0, 1, 2, \ldots) \tag{8.58}$$

Thus

$$a_3 = \frac{-a_0}{3\cdot 2} \quad (r = 0), \quad a_4 = \frac{-a_1}{4\cdot 3} \quad (r = 1)$$

$$a_5 = \frac{-a_2}{5\cdot 4} \quad (r = 2), \quad a_6 = \frac{-a_3}{6\cdot 5} \quad (r = 3)$$

$$a_7 = \frac{-a_4}{7\cdot 6} \quad (r = 4), \quad a_8 = \frac{-a_5}{8\cdot 7} \quad (r = 5)$$

and so on.

Since we deduced earlier, using the condition $f'(0) = 0$, that $a_1 = 0$, some terms can be eliminated immediately, and we have

$$a_4 = 0, \quad a_7 = 0, \quad a_{10} = 0, \quad a_{13} = 0, \quad \ldots$$

Since $a_2 = 0$ (from the coefficient of t^0), we have

$$a_5 = 0, \quad a_8 = 0, \quad \ldots$$

We are therefore left with

$$f(t) = a_0 + a_3t^3 + a_6t^6 + a_9t^9 + \ldots$$

Substituting for $a_3, a_6, a_9, \ldots$ in terms of a_0, using (8.58) gives

$$f(t) = a_0\left(1 - \frac{1}{3!}t^3 + \frac{1\cdot4}{6!}t^6 - \frac{1\cdot4\cdot7}{9!}t^9 + \frac{1\cdot4\cdot7\cdot10}{12!}t^{12} - \ldots\right)$$

So far we have only applied the condition at $t = 0$. Now we apply the condition at $t = T$, namely $f(T) = 0$. This gives

$$a_0\left(1 - \frac{1}{3!}T^3 + \frac{4}{6!}T^6 - \frac{4\cdot7}{9!}T^9 \ldots\right) = 0$$

so that either

$$a_0 = 0 \quad \text{or} \quad 1 - \frac{1}{3!}T^3 + \frac{4}{6!}T^6 - \frac{4\cdot7}{9!}T^9 + \ldots = 0$$

This means that there is no deflection ($a_0 = 0$) unless

$$1 - \frac{1}{3!}T^3 + \frac{4}{6!}T^6 - \frac{4\cdot7}{9!}T^9 + \ldots = 0$$

The smallest value of T that satisfies this equation gives the critical height of the column. At that height the value of a_0 becomes arbitrary (and non-zero), and the column buckles. A first approximation to the critical value of T can be found by solving the quadratic equation (in T^3)

$$1 - \frac{1}{3!}T^3 + \frac{4}{6!}T^6 = 1 - \tfrac{1}{6}T^3 + \tfrac{1}{180}(T^3)^2 = 0$$

giving $T^3 = 8.292$. This may be refined using the Newton–Raphson procedure (8.19), eventually giving the critical length L in terms of E, I and w:

$$L = 1.99(EI/w)^{1/3}$$

The detailed calculation is left as an exercise for the reader.

8.9 Engineering application: streamlines in fluid dynamics

As we mentioned in Section 8.6.10, differentials often occur in mathematical modelling of practical problems. An example occurs in fluid dynamics. Consider the case of steady-state incompressible fluid flow in two dimensions. Using rectangular cartesian coordinates (x, y) to describe a point in the fluid, let u and v be the velocities of the fluid in the x and y directions respectively. Then by considering the flow in and flow out of a small rectangle, as shown in Figure 8.24, per unit time, we obtain a differential

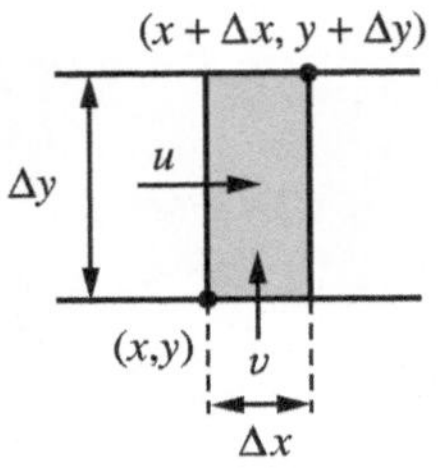

Figure 8.24
Flow through rectangular element.

relationship between $u(x, y)$ and $v(x, y)$ that models the fact that no fluid is lost or gained in the rectangle; that is, the fluid is conserved.

The velocity of the fluid $\boldsymbol{q}$ is a vector point function. The values of its components u and v depend on the spatial coordinates x and y. The flow into the small rectangle in unit time is

$$u(x, \bar{y})\Delta y + v(\bar{x}, y)\Delta x$$

where $\bar{x}$ lies between x and $x + \Delta x$, and $\bar{y}$ lies between y and $y + \Delta y$. Similarly, the flow out of the rectangle is

$$u(x + \Delta x, \tilde{y})\Delta y + v(\tilde{x}, y + \Delta y)\Delta x$$

where $\tilde{x}$ lies between x and $x + \Delta x$ and $\tilde{y}$ lies between y and $y + \Delta y$. Because no fluid is created or destroyed within the rectangle, we may equate these two expressions, giving

$$u(x, \bar{y})\Delta y + v(\bar{x}, y)\Delta x = u(x + \Delta x, \tilde{y})\Delta y + v(\tilde{x}, y + \Delta y)\Delta x$$

Rearranging, we have

$$\frac{u(x + \Delta x, \tilde{y}) - u(x, \bar{y})}{\Delta x} + \frac{v(\tilde{x}, y + \Delta y) - v(\bar{x}, y)}{\Delta y} = 0$$

Letting $\Delta x \to 0$ and $\Delta y \to 0$ gives the **continuity equation**

$$\frac{\partial u}{\partial x} + \frac{\partial v}{\partial y} = 0$$

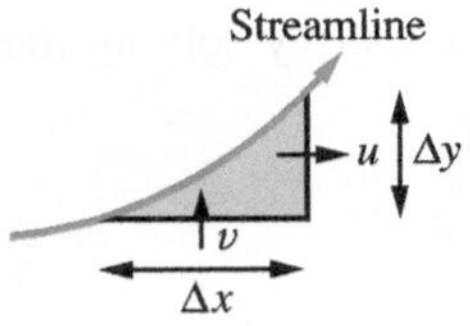

Figure 8.25
Streamline.

The fluid actually flows along paths called **streamlines**, so that there is no flow across a streamline. Thus from Figure 8.25 we deduce that

$$v\,\Delta x = u\,\Delta y$$

and hence

$$v\,\mathrm{d}x - u\,\mathrm{d}y = 0$$

The condition for this expression to be an exact differential is

$$\frac{\partial}{\partial y}(v) = \frac{\partial}{\partial x}(-u)$$

or

$$\frac{\partial u}{\partial x} + \frac{\partial v}{\partial y} = 0$$

This is satisfied for incompressible flow since it is just the continuity equation, so that we deduce that there is a function $\psi(x, y)$, called the **stream function**, such that

$$v = \frac{\partial \psi}{\partial x} \quad \text{and} \quad u = -\frac{\partial \psi}{\partial y}$$

It follows that if we are given u and v, as functions of x and y, that satisfy the continuity equation then we can find the equations of the streamlines given by $\psi(x, y) = \text{constant}$.

Example 8.45 Find the stream function $\psi(x, y)$ for the incompressible flow that is such that the velocity $\boldsymbol{q}$ at the point (x, y) is

$$(-y/(x^2 + y^2), x/(x^2 + y^2))$$

Solution From the definition of the stream function, we have

$$u(x, y) = -\frac{\partial \psi}{\partial y} \quad \text{and} \quad v(x, y) = \frac{\partial \psi}{\partial x}$$

provided that

$$\frac{\partial u}{\partial x} + \frac{\partial v}{\partial y} = 0$$

Here we have

$$u = \frac{-y}{x^2 + y^2} \quad \text{and} \quad v = \frac{x}{x^2 + y^2}$$

so that

$$\frac{\partial u}{\partial x} = \frac{2xy}{(x^2 + y^2)^2} \quad \text{and} \quad \frac{\partial v}{\partial y} = -\frac{2yx}{(x^2 + y^2)^2}$$

confirming that

$$\frac{\partial u}{\partial x} + \frac{\partial v}{\partial y} = 0$$

Integrating

$$\frac{\partial \psi}{\partial y} = -u(x, y) = \frac{y}{x^2 + y^2}$$

with respect to y, keeping x constant, gives

$$\psi(x, y) = \tfrac{1}{2}\ln(x^2 + y^2) + g(x)$$

Differentiating partially with respect to x gives

$$\frac{\partial \psi}{\partial x} = \frac{x}{x^2 + y^2} + \frac{\mathrm{d}g}{\mathrm{d}x}$$

Since it is known that

$$\frac{\partial \psi}{\partial x} = v(x, y) = \frac{x}{x^2 + y^2}$$

we have

$$\frac{\mathrm{d}g}{\mathrm{d}x} = 0$$

which on integrating gives

$$g(x) = C$$

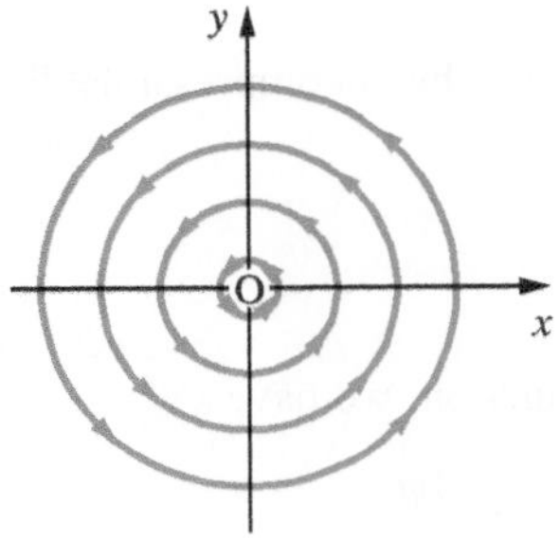

Figure 8.26
A vortex.

where C is a constant. Substituting back into the expression obtained for $\psi(x, y)$, we have

$$\psi(x, y) = \tfrac{1}{2}\ln(x^2 + y^2) + C$$

A streamline of the flow is given by the equation $\psi(x, y) = k$, where k is a constant. After a little manipulation this gives

$$x^2 + y^2 = a^2 \quad \text{and} \quad \ln a = k - C$$

and the corresponding streamlines are shown in Figure 8.26. This is an example of a **vortex**.

8.10 Review exercises (1–35)

Check your answers using MATLAB or MAPLE whenever possible.

1 Use the Newton–Raphson method to find the root of

$$e^x - x^2 + 3x - 2 = 0$$

in the interval $0 \leqslant x \leqslant 1$. Start with $x = 0.5$ and give the root correct to 4dp.

2 The deflection at the midpoint of a uniform beam of length l, flexural rigidity EI and weight per unit length w, subject to an axial force P, is

$$d = \frac{w}{m^2P}(\sec\tfrac{1}{2}ml - 1) - \frac{wl^2}{8P}$$

where $m^2 = P/EI$. On making the substitution $\theta = \tfrac{1}{2}ml$, show that

$$d = \frac{wl^4}{32EI}\,\frac{2\sec\theta - 2 - \theta^2}{\theta^4}$$

As the force P is relaxed, the deflection should reduce to that of a beam sagging under its own weight. By first representing $\sec\theta$ by its Maclaurin series expansion, show that

$$\lim_{\theta\to 0} d = \frac{5wl^4}{384EI}$$

3 Using the Maclaurin series expansion of e^x, determine the Maclaurin series expansion of $x/(e^x - 1)$ as far as the term in x^4, and hence obtain the approximation

$$\int_0^1 \frac{x}{e^x - 1}\,dx \approx \frac{311}{400}$$

4 Use L'Hôpital's rule to find

$$\lim_{x\to 1}\frac{\ln x}{x^2 - 1}$$

5 Determine

$$\lim_{x \to 2} \frac{2 \sin kx - x \sin 2k}{2(4 - x^2)}$$

where k is a constant.

6 Show that the equation

$$x^3 - 2x - 5 = 0$$

has a root in the neighbourhood of $x = 2$ and find it to three significant figures using the Newton–Raphson method.

7 (a) Obtain the Maclaurin series expansions of $\sinh x$ and $\cosh x$.

(b) A telegraph wire is stretched between two poles at the same height and a distance $2l$ apart. The sag at the midpoint is h. If the axes are taken as shown in Figure 8.27, it can be shown that the equation of the curve followed by the wire is

$$y = c \cosh \frac{x}{c}$$

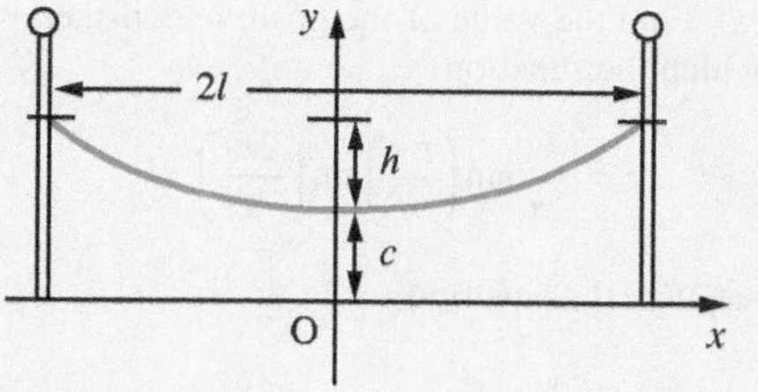

Figure 8.27 Telegraph wire of Question 7.

where c is an undetermined constant (see Example 8.66).

(i) Show that the length $2s$ of the wire is given by

$$2s = 2c \sinh \frac{l}{c}$$

(ii) If the wire is taut, so that h/c is small, it can be shown that l/c is also small. Ignoring powers of l/c higher than the second, show that

$$\frac{h^2}{l^2} \approx \frac{1}{4}\left(\frac{l}{c}\right)^2$$

Hence show that the length of the wire is approximately

$$2l\left[1 + \frac{2}{3}\left(\frac{h}{l}\right)^2\right]$$

8 Prove that

$$\int_0^{\infty} \operatorname{sech} x \, dx = \pi$$

and deduce $\int_0^1 \operatorname{sech}^{-1} x \, dx$.

9 Evaluate

(a) $\displaystyle\int_1^{\infty} \frac{1}{x^3} dx$ (b) $\displaystyle\int_0^{\infty} \frac{1}{x^2 + 2x + 2} dx$

(c) $\displaystyle\int_0^{\infty} x e^{-4x} dx$ (d) $\displaystyle\int_1^{\infty} \frac{\ln x}{x^3} dx$

(e) $\displaystyle\int_0^{\infty} e^{-2x} \cos x \, dx$ (f) $\displaystyle\int_0^{\infty} e^{-2x} \cosh x \, dx$

10 Evaluate

(a) $\displaystyle\int_0^{8} x^{-1/3} dx$ (b) $\displaystyle\int_{3/2}^{6} \frac{1}{\sqrt{(2x - 3)}} dx$

(c) $\displaystyle\int_0^{1} \ln x \, dx$

stating in each case the value of x for which the integrand becomes unbounded.

11 Use the Taylor series to show that the principal term of the truncation error of the approximation

$$f''(a) \approx [f(a + h) - 2f(a) + f(a - h)]/h^2$$

is $\frac{1}{12} h^2 f^{(4)}(a)$.

Consider the function $f(x) = xe^x$. Estimate $f''(1)$ using the approximation above with $h = 0.01$, and $h = 0.02$. Compare your answer with the true value.

12 A particle moves in three-dimensional space such that its position at time t (seconds) is given by the vector $(4 \cos t, 4 \sin t, 3)$ where distance is measured in metres. Find the magnitude of its velocity and acceleration.

13 The acceleration $\boldsymbol{a}$ (m s^{-2}) of a particle at time t (s) is given by $\boldsymbol{a} = (1 + t)\boldsymbol{i} + t^2\boldsymbol{j} + 2\boldsymbol{k}$. At $t = 0$ its displacement $\boldsymbol{r}$ is zero and its velocity $\boldsymbol{v}$ (m s^{-1}) is $\boldsymbol{i} - \boldsymbol{j}$. Find its displacement at time t.

14 The temperature gradient u at a point in a solid is

$$u(x, t) = t^{-1/2}e^{-x^2/4kt}$$

where k is a constant. Verify that

$$\frac{\partial^2 u}{\partial x^2} = \frac{1}{k}\frac{\partial u}{\partial t}$$

15 Show that the surfaces defined by

$$z^2 = \tfrac{1}{2}(x^2 + y^2) - 1$$

and

$$z = 1/xy$$

intersect, and that they do so orthogonally.

16 The height h of the top of a pylon is calculated by measuring its angle of elevation α at a point a distance s horizontally from the base of the pylon. Find the error in h due to small errors in s and α. If s and α are taken as 20 m and 30° respectively when the correct values are 19.8 m and 30.2°, find the error and the relative error in the calculated height.

17 The resistance of a length of wire is given by

$$R = \frac{k\rho L}{D^2}$$

where k is a constant. L is increasing at a rate of 0.4% min^{-1}, ρ is increasing at a rate of 0.01% min^{-1} and D is decreasing at a rate of 0.1% min^{-1}. At what percentage rate is the resistance R increasing?

18 The deflection H of a metal structure can be calculated using the formula

$$H = \sqrt{\left(\frac{I\rho^4 D^2 L^{3/2}}{20g}\right)}$$

where I, ρ, D and L are the moment of inertia, density, diameter and length respectively, and g is the acceleration due to gravity. If the value of H is to remain unaltered when I increases by 0.1%, ρ by 0.2% and D decreases by 0.3%, what percentage change in L is required?

19 In the calculation of the power in an a.c. circuit using the formula $W = EI\cos\phi$, errors of +1% in I, −0.7% in E and +2% in ϕ occur. Find the percentage error in the calculated value of W when $\phi = \frac{1}{3}\pi$ rad.

20 (a) Prove that $u = x^3 - 3xy^2$ satisfies

$$\frac{\partial^2 u}{\partial x^2} + \frac{\partial^2 u}{\partial y^2} = 0$$

(b) Given

$$u = x^2\tan^{-1}\left(\frac{y}{x}\right) - y^2\tan^{-1}\left(\frac{x}{y}\right)$$

evaluate

$$x\frac{\partial u}{\partial x} + y\frac{\partial u}{\partial y}$$

in terms of u.

21 Verify that $z = \ln\sqrt{(x^2 - y^2)}$ satisfies the equation

$$\left(\frac{\partial z}{\partial x}\right)^2 + \frac{\partial^2 z}{\partial y \partial x} + \left(\frac{\partial z}{\partial y}\right)^2 = \frac{1}{(x - y)^2}$$

22 (a) Find the value of the positive constant c for which the function

$$y = \frac{k}{2\pi}\sin\left(\frac{\pi x}{k}\right)\sin\left(\frac{2\pi t}{k}\right)$$

satisfies the equation

$$c^2\frac{\partial^2 y}{\partial x^2} = \frac{\partial^2 y}{\partial t^2}$$

(b) V is a function of the independent variables x and y. Given that $x = r\cos\theta$ and $y = r\sin\theta$, find $\partial V/\partial\theta$ and $\partial V/\partial r$ in terms of $\partial V/\partial x$ and $\partial V/\partial y$, and hence show that

$$\frac{\partial V}{\partial y} = \frac{1}{r}\left(r\sin\theta\frac{\partial V}{\partial r} + \cos\theta\frac{\partial V}{\partial\theta}\right)$$

and

$$\frac{\partial V}{\partial x} = \frac{1}{r}\left(r\cos\theta\frac{\partial V}{\partial r} - \sin\theta\frac{\partial V}{\partial\theta}\right)$$

23 A curve C in three dimensions is given parametrically by $(x(t), y(t), z(t))$, where t is a real parameter, with $a \leqslant t \leqslant b$. Show that the equation of the tangent line at a point P on this curve where $t = t_0$ is given by

$$\frac{x - x_0}{x_0'} = \frac{y - y_0}{y_0'} = \frac{z - z_0}{z_0'}$$

where $x_0 = x(t_0)$, $x_0' = x'(t_0)$, and so on.

Hence find the equation of the tangent line to the circular helix

$$x = a\cos t, \quad y = a\sin t, \quad z = at$$

at $t = \frac{1}{4}\pi$ and show that the length of the helix between $t = 0$ and $t = \frac{1}{2}\pi$ is $\pi a/\sqrt{2}$.

24 Show that $u = f(x + y) + g(x - y)$ satisfies the differential equation

$$\frac{\partial^2 u}{\partial x^2} - \frac{\partial^2 u}{\partial y^2} = 0$$

25 Show that if

$$\phi(x, t) = \frac{f(z)}{\sqrt{t}} \quad \text{and} \quad z = \frac{x}{2\sqrt{t}}$$

then

$$\frac{\partial \phi}{\partial t} = -\frac{zf'(z) + f(z)}{2t\sqrt{t}}$$

and find a similar expression for $\partial^2\phi/\partial x^2$.

Deduce that if

$$\frac{\partial^2 \phi}{\partial x^2} = \frac{1}{k}\frac{\partial \phi}{\partial t}$$

then

$$kf''(z) + 2zf'(z) + 2f(z) = 0$$

26 Water waves move in the direction of the x axis with speed c. Their height h at time t is given by

$$h(t) = a\sin(x - ct)$$

where a is a constant. A small cork floats on the water and is blown by the wind in the direction of the x axis with constant velocity U. Show that the vertical acceleration of the cork at time t is given by

$$\frac{d^2h}{dt^2} = -(U - c)^2 h$$

27 The components of velocity of an inviscid incompressible fluid in the x and y directions are u and v respectively, where

$$u = \frac{x^2 - y^2}{(x^2 + y^2)^2} \quad \text{and} \quad v = \frac{2xy}{(x^2 + y^2)^2}$$

Find the stream function $\psi(x, y)$ such that

$$d\psi = v\,dx - u\,dy$$

and verify that it satisfies Laplace's equation

$$\frac{\partial^2 \psi}{\partial x^2} + \frac{\partial^2 \psi}{\partial y^2} = 0$$

28 Show that the function

$$f(x, y) = x^2y^2 - 5x^2 - 8xy - 5y^2$$

has one maximum and four saddle points. Sketch the part of the surface $z = f(x, y)$ that lies in the first quadrant.

29 Determine the position and nature of the stationary points on the surface

$$z = e^{-(x+y)}(3x^2 + y^2)$$

30 A trough of capacity 1 m^3 is to be made from sheet metal in the shape shown in Figure 8.28. Calculate the dimensions that use the least amount of metal. (*Hint*: Set $y = xY$ and $z = xZ$ and show that the area of sheet metal needed is

$$\frac{2(1 + Y\cos\theta)Y\sin\theta + (2Y + 1)Z}{[(1 + Y\cos\theta)YZ\sin\theta]^{2/3}})$$

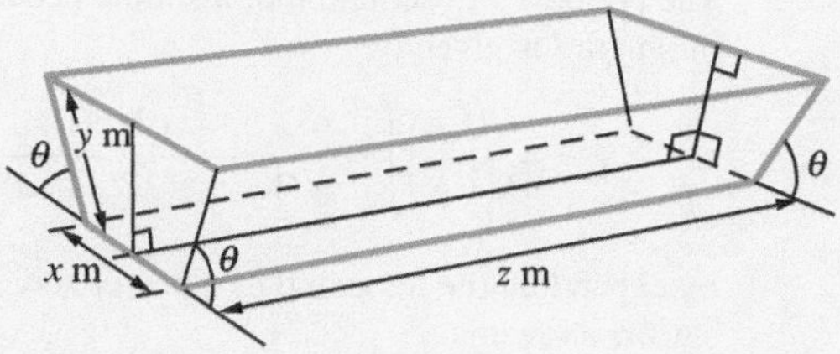

Figure 8.28 Trough of Question 30.

31 Find the critical points of the function

$$z = 12xy - 3xy^2 - x^3$$

and identify the character of each point.

32 Find the local maxima and minima of the function

$$f(x, y) = y^2 - 8x + 17$$

subject to the constraint

$$x^2 + y^2 = 9$$

33 A non-linear spring has a restoring force which is proportional to the cube of the displacement x.

The period T of oscillation from an initial displacement a is given by

$$T = 4\sqrt{2}\int_0^a \frac{1}{\sqrt{(a^4 - x^4)}}\,dx$$

Use the substitution $x^2 = a^2 \sin\theta$ to transform this integral to give

$$T = \frac{2\sqrt{2}}{a}\int_0^{\pi/2} \sin^{-1/2}\theta\, d\theta$$

Use the recurrence relation

$$(r+1)F(r) = (r+2)F(r+2)$$

where

$$F(r) = \int_0^{\pi/2} \sin^r x\, dx,\ r > -1$$

to show that

$$T = \frac{42\sqrt{2}}{5a}\int_0^{\pi/2} \sin^{7/2}\theta\, d\theta$$

and use the trapezium rule to evaluate this integral.

34 The period T of oscillation of a simple pendulum of length l is given by

$$T = 4\sqrt{\left(\frac{l}{g}\right)}\int_0^{\pi/2} \frac{1}{\sqrt{(1 - \sin^2\frac{1}{2}\alpha\sin^2\phi)}}\,d\phi$$

by expanding the integrand as a power series in $\sin^2\frac{1}{2}\alpha$ show that

$$T = 2\pi\sqrt{\left(\frac{l}{g}\right)}[1 + 4\sin^2\tfrac{1}{2}\alpha + \tfrac{9}{64}\sin^4\tfrac{1}{2}\alpha + \ldots$$

35 (a) An oil tanker runs aground on a reef and its tanks rupture. Assuming that the oil forms a layer of uniform thickness on the sea and that the rate of spill is constant, show that the rate at which the radius r of the outer boundary of the oil spill increases in still water is proportional to $1/r$.

(b) The spillage takes place in a current flowing north with constant speed V. Assuming that the velocity of the oil with the current is the vector sum of the velocity of the oil in still water and the velocity of the current, show that the velocity (u, v) of the oil at the point (x, y) relative to the stricken tanker is given by

$$u = \frac{kx}{x^2 + y^2},\quad v = V + \frac{ky}{x^2 + y^2}$$

where k is a constant of proportionality and the x and y axes are drawn in the easterly and northerly directions (see Figure 8.29).

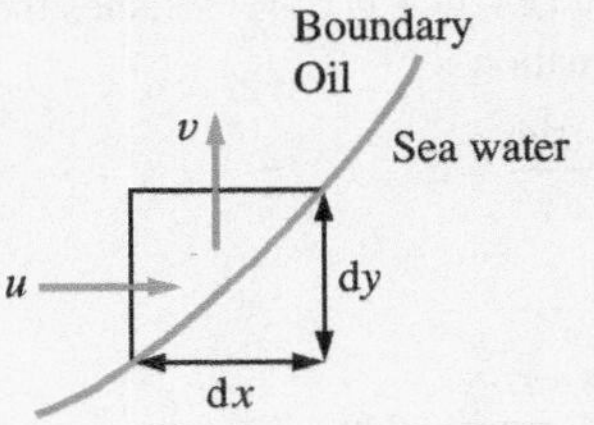

Figure 8.29

(c) Deduce that the most southerly point $(0, -c)$ reached by the oil slick is given by $c = k/V$.

(d) Show that, after a large interval of time, the oil slick occupies a region whose boundary $y = f(x)$ is the solution of the differential equation

$$\frac{dy}{dx} = \frac{x^2 + y^2 + cy}{cx}$$

that also satisfies the condition $y = -c$ at $x = 0$.

(e) Use the substitution $y = xz$ to transform the differential equation and initial conditions of part (d) to the differential equation

$$c\frac{dz}{dx} = 1 + z^2 \qquad \textbf{(8.59)}$$

where $z \to -\infty$ as $x \to 0+$.

(f) Show that the solution of (8.59) together with the boundary condition is $z = -\cot\frac{x}{c}$. Hence find y and sketch its graph.

9 Introduction to Ordinary Differential Equations

Chapter 9 Contents

9.1 Introduction

The essential role played by mathematical models in both engineering analysis and engineering design has been noted earlier in this book. It often happens that, in creating a mathematical model of a physical system, we need to express such relationships as 'the acceleration of A is directly proportional to B' or 'changes in D produce proportionate changes in E with constant of proportionality F'. Such statements naturally give rise to equations involving derivatives and integrals of the variables in the model as well as the variables themselves. Equations which introduce derivatives are called **differential equations**, those which introduce integrals are called **integral equations** and those which introduce both are called **integro-differential equations**. Generally speaking, integral and integro-differential equations are rather more difficult to solve than purely differential ones. This chapter starts with a discussion of the general characteristics of differential equations and then deals with ways of solving first-order differential equations. It is concluded by an examination of the solution of differential equations of second and higher orders.

Before we go any further in our study of differential equations we need to note that there are two main categories of differential equation. We met, in Chapter 7, the idea of differentiation of a function of a single variable, and then, in Chapter 8, the idea of partial differentiation of functions of more than one variable. Differential equations may involve either ordinary or partial derivatives; those which involve only ordinary differentials are called **ordinary differential equations** and those involving partial differentials are **partial differential equations**, commonly abbreviated to **ODE**s and **PDE**s.

For the remainder of this chapter we shall concentrate on learning the most common techniques for solving ordinary differential equations. This is not because partial differential equations are not important in engineering. On the contrary, partial differential equations have many applications, but the methods used to solve them are significantly different from the methods used for ordinary differential equations. The solution of partial differential equations is covered in the companion text *Advanced Modern Engineering Mathematics*.

9.2 Engineering examples

Firstly we shall give some examples of engineering problems which naturally give rise to differential equations. In due course we shall meet techniques which allow us to find solutions to these equations and hence to make predictions about the engineering systems modelled.

9.2.1 The take-off run of an aircraft

Aeronautical engineers need to be able to predict the length of runway that an aircraft will require to take off safely. To do this, a mathematical model of the forces acting on the aircraft during the take-off run is constructed, and the relationships holding between the forces are identified. Figure 9.1 shows an aircraft and the forces acting on it. If the mass of the aircraft is m, gravity causes a downward force mg. There is a ground reaction force through the wheels, denoted by G, and an aerodynamic lift force L. The engines provide a thrust T, which is opposed by an aerodynamic drag D and a rolling

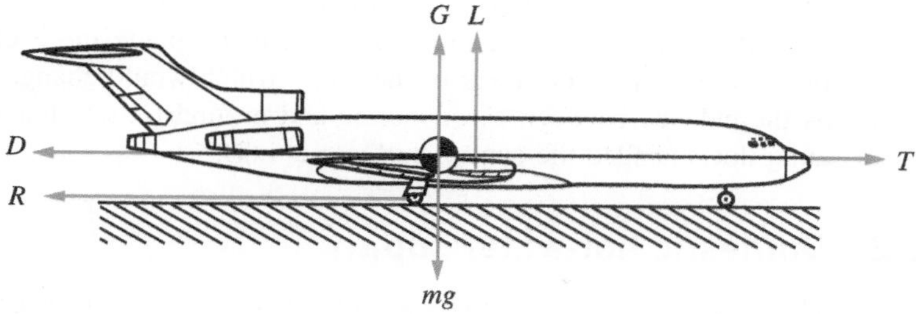

Figure 9.1 Forces on an aircraft during the take-off run.

resistance from contact with the ground R. Since the aircraft is rolling along the runway, it is not accelerating vertically, so the vertical forces are in balance and the vertical equation of motion yields

$$L + G = mg \tag{9.1}$$

On the other hand, the aircraft is accelerating along the runway, so the horizontal equation of motion is

$$T - D - R = m\frac{d^2s}{dt^2} \tag{9.2}$$

where s is the distance the aircraft has travelled along the runway.

We know from experimental evidence that both aerodynamic lift and aerodynamic drag forces on a body vary roughly as the square of the velocity of the airflow relative to the body. We shall therefore choose to model the lift and drag forces as proportional to velocity squared. The rolling resistance is also known to be roughly proportional to the reaction force between ground and aircraft. Thus we make the modelling assumptions

$$L = \alpha v^2, \quad D = \beta v^2 \quad \text{and} \quad R = \mu G$$

Substituting for L, D and R in (9.1) and (9.2) and eliminating G results in the equation

$$m\frac{d^2s}{dt^2} - (\mu\alpha - \beta)v^2 + \mu mg = T$$

or, replacing v by ds/dt,

$$m\frac{d^2s}{dt^2} - (\mu\alpha - \beta)\left(\frac{ds}{dt}\right)^2 = T - \mu mg \tag{9.3}$$

Thus our model of the aircraft travelling along the runway provides an equation relating the first and second time derivatives of the distance travelled by the aircraft, the thrust provided by the engines and various constants – the model is expressed as a differential equation for the distance s travelled along the runway. The model is not yet really complete, since we have not specified how the thrust varies. The thrust could, of course, vary with time (the pilot could open or close the throttles during the take-off run), and may also vary with the forward speed of the aircraft. On the other hand, we could just assume that thrust is constant. Also, the constants m, μ, α and β need to be determined. This information might be provided by measurements on the aircraft or on scale models of it, by other calculations or by engineers' estimates.

Once the model is complete it could be used, for instance, to predict the length of runway needed by the aircraft to attain flying speed. Flying speed is, of course, the speed at which the lift (αv^2) is equal to the weight (mg) of the aircraft. For a real aircraft our model would probably need to be made more elaborate, including, for instance, the angle of attack of the wing, which would change during the take-off run as the balance between aerodynamic and ground forces changed and as the pilot (or autopilot) changed the control surface settings.

9.2.2 Domestic hot-water supply

The second example involves modelling the heating of water in a hot-water storage tank. Figure 9.2 shows schematically an 'indirect' domestic hot-water tank. In this design of a hot-water system the central heating boiler, or other primary source of heat, supplies hot water to a calorifier (which takes the form of a coiled pipe) inside the hot-water storage tank. The main mass of water in the tank is then heated by the hot water passing through the calorifier coil. We wish to calculate how quickly the hot water in the tank will heat up.

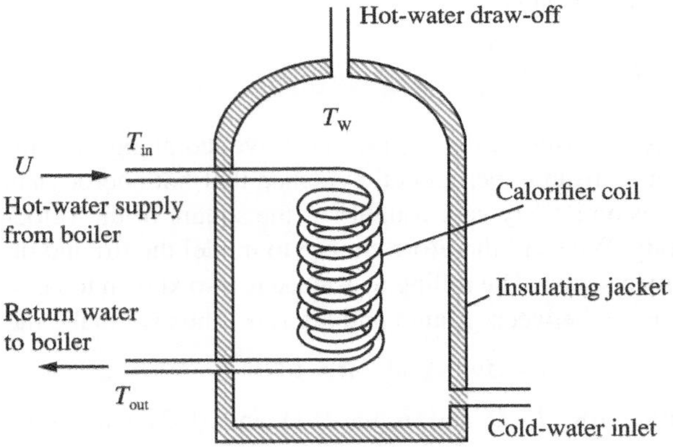

Figure 9.2 An 'indirect' hot-water tank.

We shall assume that, to a good approximation, during heating, convection ensures that the main mass of water in the tank is well mixed and at a uniform temperature T_w. The heating water flows into the calorifier at a speed U at a temperature T_{in}. The outflow from the calorifier is at temperature T_{out}. The cross-sectional area of the calorifier tube is A. The mass flowrate of heating water through the calorifier is therefore ρAU, where ρ is the density of water, and the rate of heat loss from the heating water is $\rho AU(T_{in} - T_{out})c$, where c is the specific heat of water. The heat capacity of the main mass of water in the tank is ρVc, where V is the volume of the tank, and so the rate of gain of heat in the main mass of water is given by

$$\rho Vc \frac{dT_w}{dt}$$

The tank is well insulated, so, to a first approximation, we shall assume that the heat loss from the external shell of the tank is negligible. The rate of heat gain of the main mass of water is therefore equal to the rate of heat loss from the heating water; that is,

$$AU(T_{in} - T_{out}) = V\frac{dT_w}{dt} \tag{9.4}$$

where it is assumed that no hot water is being drawn off.

We should also expect that the difference in temperature of the heating water flowing in and that flowing out of the calorifier will be greater the cooler the mass of water in the tank. If we assume direct proportionality of these two quantities, we may express this modelling assumption as

$$T_{\text{in}} - T_{\text{out}} = \alpha(T_{\text{in}} - T_{\text{w}}) \tag{9.5}$$

where α is a constant of proportionality. Eliminating T_{out} between (9.4) and (9.5) leads to the equation

$$V\frac{\mathrm{d}T_{\text{w}}}{\mathrm{d}t} + AU\alpha T_{\text{w}} = AU\alpha T_{\text{in}} \tag{9.6}$$

Thus we have a differential equation relating the temperature of the water in the tank and its derivative with respect to time to the temperature of the heating water supplied by the boiler. The equation also involves various constants determined by the characteristics of the system. We will see later, in Question 35, Exercises 9.5.11, how this equation can be solved to find T_{w} as a function of time.

9.2.3 Hydro-electric power generation

Our third example is drawn from the sphere of hydraulic engineering. Figure 9.3 shows a cross-section through a hydro-power generation plant. Water, retained behind a dam, is drawn off through a conduit and drives a generator. In order to control the power generated, there is also a control valve in series with the generator. The conduit from the dam to the generator is typically quite long and of considerable cross-section, so that it contains many tonnes of water. Hence, when the control valve is opened or closed, the power generated does not increase or decrease instantaneously. Because of the large mass of water in the conduit that must be accelerated or decelerated, the system may take several minutes or even tens of minutes to attain its new equilibrium flowrate and power generation level. We wish to predict the behaviour of the system when the control valve setting is changed.

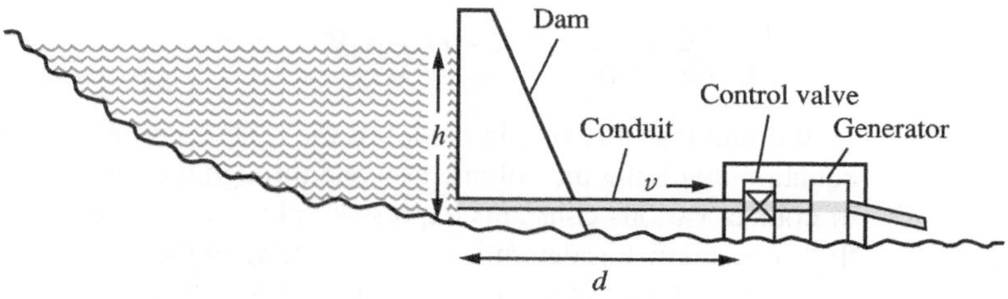

Figure 9.3 A hydro-electric generation plant.

The pressure at the entry to the conduit will be atmospheric plus ρgh, where ρ is the density of the water in the dam and h is the depth of the entry below the water surface. It is known that for flow in pipes, to a good approximation, the volume flowrate is proportional to the pressure differential between the ends of the pipe. We shall express this as

$$Q = \alpha\Delta p_1$$

where Q is the volume flowrate through the conduit, α is a constant and Δp_1 is the pressure difference between the two ends of the conduit. It is also known that the pressure loss across a turbine such as the generator in this case is proportional to the discharge (volume flow through the turbine), so we can write

$$\Delta p_2 = \beta Q$$

where Δp_2 is the pressure loss across the generator and β is a characteristic of the generator. The discharge of the turbine must, of course, be equal to the flowrate through the conduit feeding the turbine. In a similar way, the pressure differential across a control valve is also proportional to its discharge, so we have

$$\Delta p_3 = \gamma Q$$

where Δp_3 is the pressure loss across the valve and γ is a constant whose value will vary with the setting of the control valve. The total pressure differential between the entry to the conduit and the exit from the control valve is ρgh. Hence the pressure differential between the ends of the conduit is $\rho gh - \Delta p_2 - \Delta p_3$. If this exceeds Δp_1, the pressure differential needed to maintain the flow through the conduit at its current level, then the mass of water in the conduit will accelerate and the volume flowrate through the system will increase; if it is less than Δp_1 then the mass of water will decelerate and the volume flow will decrease. The net force on the mass of water in the conduit is the excess pressure differential multiplied by the cross-sectional area of the conduit, A, say. The mass of water is ρAd, where d is the length of the conduit, and Q, the volume flowrate, is vA, where v is the velocity of the water in the conduit. Thus we can write

$$(\rho gh - \Delta p_1 - \Delta p_2 - \Delta p_3)A = \rho dA\frac{\mathrm{d}v}{\mathrm{d}t}$$

Assuming that the cross-sectional area of the conduit is constant and substituting for Δp_1, Δp_2 and Δp_3, we can rewrite this as

$$\left(\rho gh - \frac{Q}{\alpha} - \beta Q - \gamma Q\right)A = \rho d\frac{\mathrm{d}Q}{\mathrm{d}t}$$

that is,

$$\frac{\rho d}{A}\frac{\mathrm{d}Q}{\mathrm{d}t} + \left(\frac{1}{\alpha} + \beta + \gamma\right)Q = \rho gh \tag{9.7}$$

We find that this simple model of the hydro-power generation system results in an equation involving the volume flowrate through the system and its time derivative and, of course, various constants expressing physical characteristics of the system. One of these constants, γ, is determined by the setting of the valve controlling the whole system. Again we will see later (Question 36, Exercises 9.5.11) how (9.7) can be solved to find the flowrate Q as a function of time.

9.2.4 Simple electrical circuits

The fourth example comes from electrical engineering. A resistor, an inductor and a capacitor are connected in a series circuit with a switch and battery, as shown in Figure 9.4. The switch is a spring-biased one that, when released, moves immediately on to contact B. While the switch is held against contact A, a current flows in the circuit. When it is released, the circuit must eventually become quiescent, with no current flowing. What is the manner of the decay to the quiescent state?

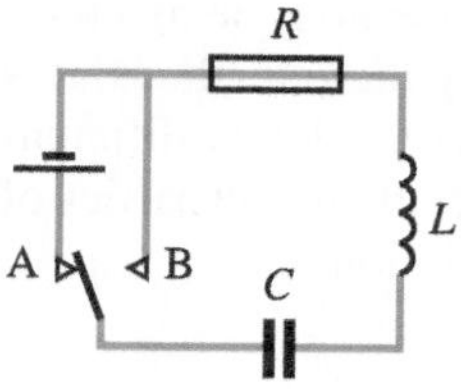

Figure 9.4
An inductor, capacitor, resistor (LCR) electrical circuit.

We know from experiment that the relation $V = iR$ holds between the potential difference across the resistor and the current flowing through a pure resistor of resistance R. In the same way, we know that for a pure capacitor of capacitance C we have $V = q/C$, where V is the potential difference across the capacitor and q is the charge on it, and that for a pure inductor of inductance L we have $V = L\,\mathrm{d}i/\mathrm{d}t$. If we assume that the circuit components are a pure resistor, inductor and capacitor respectively, and that the switch and the wires joining the components have negligible resistance, capacitance and inductance, then, when the switch is in contact with B, the total potential difference around the circuit must be zero and we have

$$L\frac{\mathrm{d}i}{\mathrm{d}t} + Ri + \frac{q}{C} = 0$$

This differential equation appears to relate two different quantities: the current i flowing in the circuit and the charge q on the capacitor. Of course, these two quantities are not independent. If the current is flowing then the charge on the capacitor must be increasing or decreasing (depending on the direction in which the current is flowing). The principle of conservation of charge tells us that the current is equal to the rate of change of charge; that is, we must have

$$i = \frac{\mathrm{d}q}{\mathrm{d}t} \tag{9.8}$$

We can use this in one of two ways: either to eliminate q, in which case we obtain the integro-differential equation

$$L\frac{\mathrm{d}i}{\mathrm{d}t} + Ri + \frac{1}{C}\int i\,\mathrm{d}t = 0$$

or to eliminate i, in which case we obtain the differential equation

$$L\frac{\mathrm{d}^2q}{\mathrm{d}t^2} + R\frac{\mathrm{d}q}{\mathrm{d}t} + \frac{1}{C}q = 0$$

Alternatively, differentiating either of these equations with respect to time, we obtain

$$L\frac{\mathrm{d}^2i}{\mathrm{d}t^2} + R\frac{\mathrm{d}i}{\mathrm{d}t} + \frac{1}{C}i = 0 \tag{9.9}$$

The equations are, of course, equivalent, but the final form is probably the most usual and most tractable of the three.

Thus we have found that a simple analysis of an LCR electrical circuit results in a differential equation for one of the variables: either the charge on the capacitor in the circuit or the current in the circuit. Once the equation has been solved to yield one of these, the other can be obtained from (9.8). Equation (9.9) is an example of a type of differential equation which occurs widely in engineering applications. A general method for solving such equations will be developed in Section 9.8.

9.3 The classification of ordinary differential equations

In Section 9.2 we created mathematical models of problems chosen from different areas of engineering science. Each gave rise to an ordinary differential equation. There are many techniques for solving differential equations – different methods being applicable to different kinds of equation – so, before we go on to study these methods, it is necessary to understand the various categories and classifications of ordinary differential equations. We shall then be in a position to recognize the overall characteristics of an equation and identify which techniques will be useful in its solution.

9.3.1 Independent and dependent variables

The first type of classification we must understand is that of the variables occurring in a differential equation. The variables with respect to which differentiation occurs are called **independent variables** while those that are differentiated are **dependent variables.** This terminology reflects the fact that what a differential equation actually expresses is the way in which the dependent variable (or variables) depends on the independent variable. A single ordinary differential equation has one independent variable and one dependent variable. In much the same way as algebraic equations may occur in sets that must be solved simultaneously, we can also have sets of coupled ordinary differential equations. In this case there will be a single independent variable but more than one dependent variable.

Example 9.1

In the ordinary differential equation

$$\frac{\mathrm{d}^2 f}{\mathrm{d}x^2} - 4x\frac{\mathrm{d}f}{\mathrm{d}x} = \cos 2x$$

the independent variable is x and the dependent variable is f. In the pair of coupled ordinary differential equations

$$4\frac{\mathrm{d}x}{\mathrm{d}t} + 3\frac{\mathrm{d}y}{\mathrm{d}t} - x + 2y = \cos t$$

$$6\frac{\mathrm{d}x}{\mathrm{d}t} - 2\frac{\mathrm{d}y}{\mathrm{d}t} - 2x + y = 2\sin t$$

the independent variable is t and the dependent variables are x and y.

9.3.2 The order of a differential equation

Another classification of differential equations is in terms of their order. The **order of a differential equation** is the degree of the highest derivative that occurs in the equation. The order of an equation is not affected by any power to which the derivatives may be raised.

Example 9.2

$$\frac{\mathrm{d}^2 f}{\mathrm{d}x^2} - 4x\frac{\mathrm{d}f}{\mathrm{d}x} = \cos 2x$$

is a second-order ordinary differential equation. The coupled ordinary differential equations

$$4\frac{\mathrm{d}x}{\mathrm{d}t} + 3\frac{\mathrm{d}y}{\mathrm{d}t} - x + 2y = \cos t$$

$$6\frac{\mathrm{d}x}{\mathrm{d}t} - 2\frac{\mathrm{d}y}{\mathrm{d}t} - 2x + y = 2\sin t$$

are both first-order equations as is the equation

$$\left(\frac{dx}{dt}\right)^2 + 4\frac{dx}{dt} = 0$$

despite the term in $(dx/dt)^2$.

9.3.3 Linear and nonlinear differential equations

Differential equations are also classified as linear or nonlinear. We may informally define **linear equations** as those in which the dependent variable or variables and their derivatives do not occur as products, raised to powers or in nonlinear functions. We shall meet a more formal definition of a linear differential equation in Section 9.8. **Nonlinear equations** are those that are not linear. Linear equations are an important category, since they have useful simplifying properties. Many of the nonlinear equations that occur in engineering science cannot be solved easily as they stand, but can be solved, for practical engineering purposes, by the process of replacing them with linear equations that are a close approximation – at least in some region of interest – and then studying the solution of the linear approximation. We shall see more of this later.

Example 9.3

$$\frac{d^2f}{dx^2} - 4x\frac{df}{dx} = \cos 2x$$

and the coupled differential equations

$$4\frac{dx}{dt} + 3\frac{dy}{dt} - x + 2y = \cos t$$

$$6\frac{dx}{dt} - 2\frac{dy}{dt} - 2x + y = 2\sin t$$

are linear ordinary differential equations.

$$\left(\frac{dx}{dt}\right)^2 + 4\frac{dx}{dt} = 0$$

$$\frac{d^2x}{dt^2} + x\frac{dx}{dt} = 4\sin t$$

$$4\frac{dx}{dt} + \sin x = 0$$

are all nonlinear differential equations, the first because the derivative dx/dt is squared, the second because of the product between the dependent variable x and its derivative, and the third because of the nonlinear function, $\sin x$, of the dependent variable.

9.3.4 Homogeneous and nonhomogeneous equations

There is a further classification that can be applied to linear equations: the distinction between homogeneous and nonhomogeneous equations. In all the examples we have presented so far the differential equations have been arranged so that all terms containing the dependent variable occur on the left-hand side of the equality sign, and those terms that involve only the independent variable and constant terms occur on the right-hand side. This is a standard way of arranging terms, and aids in the identification of equations. Specifically, when linear equations are arranged in this way, those in which the right-hand side is zero are called **homogeneous equations** and those in which it is non-zero are **nonhomogeneous equations**. Expressed another way, each term in a homogeneous equation involves the dependent variable or one of its derivatives. In a nonhomogeneous equation there is at least one term that does not contain the independent variable or any of its derivatives.

Example 9.4 The equations

$$\frac{\mathrm{d}x}{\mathrm{d}t} + 4x = 0$$

and

$$4\frac{\mathrm{d}x}{\mathrm{d}t} + (\sin t)x = 0$$

are both homogeneous ordinary differential equations, while

$$\frac{\mathrm{d}^2x}{\mathrm{d}t^2} + t\frac{\mathrm{d}x}{\mathrm{d}t} = 4\sin t$$

and

$$\frac{\mathrm{d}^2f}{\mathrm{d}x^2} - 4x\frac{\mathrm{d}f}{\mathrm{d}x} = \cos 2x$$

are both nonhomogeneous ordinary differential equations.

Example 9.5 Classify the equations (9.3), (9.6), (9.7) and (9.9) derived in the engineering examples of Section 9.2.

Solution (a) Equation (9.3) is a second-order nonlinear ordinary differential equation whose dependent variable is s and whose independent variable is t.

(b) Equation (9.6) is a first-order linear nonhomogeneous ordinary differential equation whose dependent variable is T_w and whose independent variable is t.

(c) Equation (9.7) is a first-order linear nonhomogeneous ordinary differential equation whose dependent variable is Q and whose independent variable is t.

(d) Equation (9.9) is a second-order linear homogeneous ordinary differential equation whose dependent variable is i and whose independent variable is t.

9.3.5 Exercises

1 State the order of each of the following differential equations and name the dependent and independent variables. Classify each equation as linear homogeneous, linear nonhomogeneous or nonlinear differential equations.

(a) $\frac{dx}{dt} + 2x = 0$

(b) $\frac{d^2x}{dt^2} + 2\frac{dx}{dt} + 3x = 0$

(c) $\left(\frac{dx}{dt}\right)^2 + x = 0$

(d) $\frac{dx}{dt} + 2x = t^2$

(e) $\frac{d^2x}{dt^2} + \frac{dx}{dt} - 4x = \cos t + e^t$

2 Classify the following differential equations as linear homogeneous, linear nonhomogeneous or nonlinear differential equations, state their order and name the dependent and independent variables.

(a) $\frac{d^2p}{dz^2}\frac{dp}{dz} + (\sin z)p = \ln z$

(b) $\frac{d^2s}{dt^2} + (\sin t)\frac{ds}{dt} + (t + \cos t)s = e^t$

(c) $\left(\frac{d^3p}{dy^3}\right)^{1/2} + 4\frac{d^2p}{dy^2} - 6\frac{dp}{dy} + 8p = 0$

(d) $\frac{dr}{dz} + z^2 = 0$

(e) $\frac{dx}{dt} = f(t)x$

(f) $\frac{dx}{dt} = f(t)x + g(t)$

(g) $\frac{d^3p}{dq^3} + \frac{d^2p}{dq^2}p + 4q^2 = 0$

(h) $\frac{d^2x}{dy^2} = \frac{y}{x^2 - 1}$

(i) $(\sin z)\frac{dy}{dz} + \frac{\cos z}{z}y = 0$

9.4 Solving differential equations

So far we have said that differential equations are equations which express relationships between a dependent variable and the derivatives of that variable with respect to the independent variable. We are now going to study some methods of solving differential equations. First, though, we should give some thought to exactly what form we expect that solution to take.

When we solve an algebraic equation we expect the solution to be a number (e.g. the solution of the equation $4x + 9 = 7$ is $x = -\frac{1}{2}$) or, perhaps, a set of numbers (e.g. the solution of a cubic polynomial equation like $x^3 - 5x^2 + 8x - 12 = 0$ is that x is one of a set of three real or complex numbers). Again, equations involving vectors and matrices have solutions that are constant vectors or one of a set of constant vectors. Differential equations, on the other hand, are equations involving not a simple scalar or vector variable but a function and its derivatives. The solution of a differential equation is, therefore, not a single value (or one from a set of values) but a function (or a family of functions). With this in mind let us proceed.

9.4.1 Solution by inspection

The solution to some differential equations can be obtained by recalling some results about differentiation.

Example 9.6

Faced with the differential equation

$$\frac{dx}{dt} = -4x \tag{9.10}$$

we might recall that if $x(t) = e^{-4t}$ then

$$\frac{dx}{dt} = -4e^{-4t} = -4x$$

In other words, the function $x(t) = e^{-4t}$ is a solution of the differential equation.

Example 9.7

The differential equation

$$\frac{d^2x}{dt^2} + \lambda^2 x = 0 \tag{9.11}$$

may be solved by recollecting that

$$\frac{d^2}{dt^2}(\sin \alpha t) = -\alpha^2 \sin \alpha t$$

Therefore, the function $x(t) = \sin \lambda t$ satisfies the differential equation.

Many differential equations can be solved by inspection in a similar manner to Examples 9.6 and 9.7. Solution by inspection requires the recognition of the equation and its connection to a familiar result in differentiation. It is therefore dependent upon experience and inspiration, and for this reason is only practical for solving the simplest differential equations.

MATLAB and MAPLE can both readily solve differential equations like these. In MATLAB, using the Symbolic Math Toolbox, analytic solutions of differential equations are computed using the `dsolve` command. The letter `D` denotes differentiation. The dependent variable is that preceded by `D`, whilst the default independent variable is `t`. Thus the general solution of the first-order differential equation

$$\frac{dx}{dt} = f(t, x)$$

is given by the commands

```
syms x
dsolve('equation')
```

In MAPLE the routine used is also called `dsolve` thus:

```
dsolve(equation)
```

So, to solve Example 9.6, we would use

```
dsolve('Dx = -4*x')
```

in MATLAB and

```
dsolve(diff(x(t),t) = -4*x(t));
```

in MAPLE. The answer returned by MATLAB is `C1*exp(-4*t)` and by MAPLE is `_C1*exp(-4*t)`. In each case `C1` (or `_C1`) indicates an arbitrary constant. The reason for this will become apparent in the next section. To solve Example 9.7 we could use

```
dsolve('D2x + lambda^2*x','t')
```

in MATLAB and

```
dsolve(diff(x(t),t,t) + lambda^2*x(t));
```

in MAPLE. Notice here that MATLAB requires a second argument to specify what is the independent variable (otherwise how does the package know that `lambda` is not the independent variable?) whereas MAPLE does not require this because it has effectively been specified in the expression `diff(x(t),t,t)` for $\dfrac{d^2x}{dt^2}$.

9.4.2 General and particular solutions

Examples 9.6 and 9.7 also illustrate a pitfall of solving equations in this way. The function $x(t) = e^{-4t}$ is certainly a solution of the equation in Example 9.6, but so is the function $x(t) = Ae^{-4t}$, where A is an arbitrary constant. The function $x(t) = \sin \lambda t$ is certainly a solution of the equation in Example 9.7, but so is the function $x(t) = A \sin \lambda t + B \cos \lambda t$, where A and B are arbitrary constants. Differential equations in general have this property – the most general function that will satisfy the differential equation contains one or more arbitrary constants. Such a function is known as the **general solution** of the differential equation. Giving particular numerical values to the constants in the general solution results in a **particular solution** of the equation. The general solution normally contains a number of arbitrary constants equal to the order of the differential equation.

Example 9.8 Find the general solution of the differential equation

$$\frac{d^2x}{dt^2} = t - 3e^{3t}$$

Solution This differential equation can be solved by twice integrating both sides, remembering that each time we integrate the right-hand side an unknown constant of integration is introduced. Thus integrating

$$\frac{d^2x}{dt^2} = t - 3e^{3t}$$

twice we have

$$\frac{dx}{dt} = \tfrac{1}{2}t^2 - e^{3t} + A$$

and

$$x(t) = \tfrac{1}{6}t^3 - \tfrac{1}{3}e^{3t} + At + B$$

This solution contains two arbitrary constants, A and B. The equation $\frac{d^2x}{dt^2} = t - 3e^{3t}$ is a second-order differential equation so, as a general rule, we would expect two constants.

When solving differential equations, we should, as a rule, seek the most general solution that is compatible with the constraints imposed by the problem. If we do not do this, we run the risk of neglecting some feature of the problem which may have serious implications for the performance, efficiency or even safety of the engineering equipment or system being analysed.

9.4.3 Boundary and initial conditions

The arbitrary constants in the general solution of a differential equation can often be determined by the application of other conditions.

Example 9.9 Find the function $x(t)$ that satisfies the differential equation

$$\frac{dx}{dt} = -4x$$

and that has the value 2.5 when $t = 0$.

Solution We noted in Section 9.4.2 that $x(t) = Ae^{-4t}$ is a solution of the differential equation

$$\frac{dx}{dt} = -4x$$

(This can be checked by differentiating $x(t)$ to find $\frac{dx}{dt}$ and substituting into the differential equation.) But the solution $x(t) = Ae^{-4t}$ does not have the value 2.5 at $t = 0$ as required by the example. We can impose the boundary condition by $x(0) = 2.5$ to give

$$Ae^{-4\times 0} = Ae^{-0} = A = 2.5$$

so the solution that satisfies the boundary condition is $x(t) = 2.5e^{-4t}$.

Additional conditions on the solution of a differential equation such as that in Example 9.9 are called **boundary conditions**. In the special case in which all the boundary conditions are given at the same value of the independent variable the boundary conditions are called **initial conditions**. In many circumstances it is convenient to consider a differential equation as incomplete until the boundary conditions have been specified. A differential equation together with its boundary conditions is referred to as a **boundary-value problem**, unless the boundary conditions satisfy the requirements for being initial conditions, in which case the differential equation together with its boundary conditions is referred to as an **initial-value problem**.

Example 9.10 Find the function $x(t)$ that satisfies the initial-value problem

$$\frac{d^2x}{dt^2} + \lambda^2 x = 0 \quad x(0) = 4, \quad \frac{dx}{dt}(0) = 3, \quad \lambda \neq 0$$

Solution We know from Section 9.4.2 that the general solution of this differential equation is

$$x(t) = A \sin \lambda t + B \cos \lambda t$$

We can confirm this by differentiating $x(t)$ twice and substituting into the differential equation to demonstrate that this $x(t)$ does satisfy the differential equation. With this $x(t)$ we have

$$\frac{dx}{dt} = \lambda A \cos \lambda t - \lambda B \sin \lambda t$$

Applying the initial conditions gives rise to the equations

$$0A + 1B = 4$$

$$\lambda A + 0B = 3$$

and hence to the solution

$$x(t) = \frac{3}{\lambda} \sin \lambda t + 4 \cos \lambda t$$

which is the particular solution of the initial value problem.

Example 9.11 Find the function $x(t)$ that satisfies the boundary-value problem

$$\frac{d^2x}{dt^2} + \lambda^2 x = 0 \quad x(0) = 4, \quad \frac{dx}{dt}\left(\frac{\pi}{\lambda}\right) = 3, \quad \lambda \neq 0$$

Solution As in the previous example, the general solution of the differential equation is

$$x(t) = A \sin \lambda t + B \cos \lambda t$$

and so

$$\frac{dx}{dt} = \lambda A \cos \lambda t - \lambda B \sin \lambda t$$

Applying the boundary conditions gives rise to the equations

$$0A + 1B = 4$$

$$-\lambda A + 0B = 3$$

and hence to the particular solution

$$x(t) = -\frac{3}{\lambda} \sin \lambda t + 4 \cos \lambda t$$

Obviously, since a first-order differential equation has only one arbitrary constant in its solution, only one boundary condition is needed to determine the constant, and so the boundary condition of a first-order equation can always be treated as an initial condition. For higher-order equations (and for sets of coupled first-order equations) the distinction between initial-value and boundary-value problems is an important one, not least because, generally speaking, initial-value problems are easier to solve than boundary-value problems.

MATLAB and MAPLE can both solve initial and boundary-value problems. In MAPLE the differential equation and its boundary conditions must be presented as a set (indicated by placing curly brackets round the list of equation and boundary conditions), thus for Example 9.11 the solution is given by the commands

```
ode:= diff(x(t),t,t) + lambda^2*x(t)
dsolve({ode,x(0) = 4,D(x)(Pi/lambda) = 3});
```

Notice that the derivative boundary condition uses `D(x)` to denote $\frac{dx}{dt}$. In MATLAB the boundary conditions are defined by a separate list of boundary conditions, thus for Example 9.10 we have

```
dsolve('D2x + lambda^2*x','x(0) = 4,Dx(Pi/lambda) = 3','t')
```

In MATLAB we define the derivative boundary condition using `Dx` to denote $\frac{dx}{dt}$. In both MAPLE and MATLAB an initial-value problem would be solved in exactly the same way; the difference would be that both boundary conditions would be defined at the same value of the independent variable.

9.4.4 Analytical and numerical solution

We have seen that some differential equations are so simple that they can be solved by inspection, given a reasonable knowledge of differentiation. There are many differential equations that are not amenable to solution in this way. For some of these we may be able, by the use of more complex mathematical techniques, to find a solution that expresses a functional relationship between the dependent and independent variables. We say that such equations have an **analytical solution**. In the case of other equations we may not be able to find a solution in such a form – either because no suitable mathematical technique for finding the solution exists or because there is no analytical solution. In these cases the only way of solving the equation is by the use of numerical techniques, leading to a **numerical solution**.

An analytical solution is almost always preferable to a numerical one. This is chiefly because an analytical solution is a mathematical function, and so the numerical value of the dependent variable can be computed for any value of the independent variable. In contrast with this, a numerical solution takes the form of a table giving the values of the dependent variable at a discrete set of values of the independent variable. The value of the dependent variable corresponding to any value of the independent variable not included in that discrete set can only be computed by interpolation from the table (or by repeating the whole numerical solution process, making sure the desired value of the independent variable is included in the solution set).

If the differential equation being solved contains parameters (such as the constant λ in Example 9.7) then an analytical solution of the equation will contain that parameter. The behaviour of the solution of the equation as the parameter value changes can be readily understood. For a numerical solution the parameter must be given a specific numerical value before the solution is computed. The numerical solution will then be valid only for that value of the parameter. If the behaviour of the solution as the parameter value is changed is of interest then the equation must be solved repeatedly using different parameter values.

When we obtain an analytical solution of a differential equation without its associated boundary conditions, the arbitrary constants in the solution are effectively parameters of the solution. A numerical solution to a differential equation cannot be obtained unless the boundary conditions are specified. This is one reason why it is sometimes convenient to refer to the whole problem (differential equation and boundary conditions) as a unit rather than consider the differential equation separately from its boundary conditions.

Another reason for preferring an analytical solution to a numerical one when such a solution is available is that the work required to obtain a numerical solution is generally much greater than that required to obtain an analytical one. On the other hand, most of this greater quantity of work can be delegated to a computer (and this may sometimes be considered to be an argument for numerical solutions being preferable to analytical ones).

Finally, it should be pointed out that this somewhat simplified overview of the contrast between analytical and numerical solutions of differential equations is becoming increasingly blurred by the availability of computerized symbolic manipulation systems (often known as computer algebra systems). We shall, in the remainder of this chapter, be studying methods for both the numerical and analytical solution of ordinary differential equations.

9.4.5 Exercises

3 Give the general solution of the following differential equations. In each case state how many arbitrary constants you expect to find in the general solution. Are your expectations confirmed in practice?

(a) $\dfrac{dx}{dt} = 4t^2$

(b) $\dfrac{d^2x}{dt^2} = t^3 - 2t$

(c) $\dfrac{d^2x}{dt^2} = e^{4t}$

(d) $\dfrac{dx}{dt} = -6x$

(e) $\dfrac{d^3x}{dt^3} = \dfrac{2}{t^3} + \sin 5t$

(f) $\dfrac{d^2x}{dt^2} = 8x$

4 For each of the following differential equation problems, state how many arbitrary constants you would expect to find in the most general solution satisfying the problem. Find the solution and check whether your expectation is confirmed.

(a) $\dfrac{d^2x}{dt^2} = 4t, \quad x(0) = 2$

(b) $\dfrac{d^2x}{dt^2} = \sin 2t, \quad x(\frac{1}{4}\pi) = 2, \quad x(\frac{3}{4}\pi) = 2$

(c) $\dfrac{dx}{dt} = 4$

(d) $\dfrac{dx}{dt} + 2t = 0, \quad x(1) = 1$

(e) $\dfrac{d^2x}{dt^2} = 2e^{-2t}, \quad x(0) = a$

(f) $\dfrac{dx}{dt} - 2\sin 2t = 0$

(g) $\dfrac{dx}{dt} = 2x, \quad x(0) = 1$

(h) $\dfrac{d^2x}{dt^2} - x = 0, \quad x(0) = 0, \quad x(1) = 1$

5 State which of the following problems are **under-determined** (that is, have insufficient boundary conditions to determine all the arbitrary constants in the general solution) and which are **fully determined**. In the case of fully determined problems state which are boundary-value problems and which are initial-value problems. (Do not attempt to solve the differential equations.)

(a) $4x\dfrac{d^2x}{dt^2} + \left(2t^2 - \dfrac{1}{x}\right)\dfrac{dx}{dt} - 4x^2t = 0, \quad x(0) = 4$

(b) $\left(\dfrac{d^3x}{dt^3}\right)^2 + t\dfrac{d^2x}{dt^2} - x\left(\dfrac{dx}{dt}\right)^2 = 0$

$x(0) = 0, \quad \dfrac{dx}{dt}(0) = 1, \quad x(2) = 0$

(c) $\left(\dfrac{dx}{dt}\right)^2 - x^2 = \sin t, \quad x(0) = a$

(d) $\dfrac{d^4x}{dt^4} + 4\dfrac{d^3x}{dt^3} - 2\dfrac{d^2x}{dt^2} + \dfrac{dx}{dt} - 4x = e^t$

$x(0) = 1, \quad x(2) = 0$

(e) $\dfrac{d^2x}{dt^2} - 2t\dfrac{dx}{dt} = t^2 - 4, \quad x(0) = 1, \quad x(2) = 0$

(f) $\dfrac{d^2x}{dt^2} + 2x\left(\dfrac{dx}{dt}\right)^2 - \dfrac{x}{t} = 0$

$x(1) = 0, \quad \dfrac{dx}{dt}(1) = 4$

(g) $\left(\dfrac{d^2x}{dt^2}\right)^2 + 2t = 0, \quad \dfrac{dx}{dt}(2) = 1$

(h) $\dfrac{d^3x}{dt^3}\dfrac{dx}{dt} + x\dfrac{d^2x}{dt^2} = 2t^2$

$x(0) = 0, \quad \dfrac{dx}{dt}(0) = 0$

(i) $\left(\dfrac{d^3x}{dt^3}\right)^{1/2} + t\dfrac{d^2x}{dt^2} + x\dfrac{dx}{dt} - \dfrac{x}{t} = 0$

$x(1) = 1, \quad \dfrac{dx}{dt}(1) = 0, \quad \dfrac{d^2x}{dt^2}(3) = 0$

(j) $\dfrac{dx}{dt} = (x - t)^2, \quad x(4) = 2$

(k) $\dfrac{d^2x}{dt^2} - 4\dfrac{dx}{dt} + 4x = \cos t, \quad x(1) = 0, \quad x(3) = 0$

(l) $\dfrac{1}{t}\dfrac{d^3x}{dt^3} - t^2\left(\dfrac{dx}{dt}\right)^2 + x\left(\dfrac{dx}{dt}\right)^{1/2} - (t^2 + 4)x = 0$

$x(0) = 0, \quad \dfrac{dx}{dt}(0) = U, \quad \dfrac{d^2x}{dt^2}(0) = 0$

6 A uniform horizontal beam OA, of length a and weight w per unit length, is clamped horizontally at O and freely supported at A. The transverse displacement y of the beam is governed by the differential equation

$$EI\frac{d^2y}{dx^2} = \tfrac{1}{2}w(a - x)^2 - R(a - x)$$

where x is the distance along the beam measured from O, R is the reaction at A, and E and I are physical constants. At O the boundary conditions are $y(0) = 0$ and $\dfrac{dy}{dx}(0) = 0$. Solve the differential equation. What is the boundary condition at A? Use this boundary condition to determine the reaction R. Hence find the maximum transverse displacement of the beam.

All of the differential equations in Questions 3, 4 and 6 of Exercises 9.4.5 could be solved using MATLAB or MAPLE. For example, using MAPLE, Questions 3(c) would be solved by

```
dsolve(diff(x(t),t,t) = exp(4*t));
```

Question 4(g) could be solved in MATLAB as

```
dsolve('Dx = 2*x','x(0) = 1','t')
```

and the first part of Question 6 would be solved by

```
ode:= E*I*diff(y(x),x,x) = 1/2*w*(a - x)^2 - R*(a - x);
dsolve({ode,y(0) = 0,D(y)(0) = 0});
```

or by

```
ode = 'E*I*D2y = 1/2*w*(a - x)^2 - R*(a - x)'
dsolve(ode,'y(0) = 0,Dy(0) = 0','x')
```

in MAPLE and MATLAB respectively. Now, for practice, use MAPLE or MATLAB to check your solutions to Questions 3, 4 and 6.

9.5 First-order ordinary differential equations

For the next three sections of this chapter we are going to concentrate our attention on the solution of first-order differential equations. This is not as restrictive as it might at first sight seem, since higher-order differential equations can, using a technique that we shall meet in Section 9.11.2, be expressed as sets of coupled first-order differential equations. Some of the methods used for the solution of first-order equations, particularly the numerical techniques, are also applicable to such sets of coupled first-order equations, and thus may be used to solve higher-order differential equations.

9.5.1 A geometrical perspective

Most first-order differential equations can be expressed in the form

$$\frac{\mathrm{d}x}{\mathrm{d}t} = f(t, x) \tag{9.12}$$

Expressing the equation in this form means that, for any point in the t–x plane for which $f(t, x)$ is defined, we can compute the value of $\mathrm{d}x/\mathrm{d}t$ at that point. If we then do this for a grid of points in the t–x plane, we can draw a picture such as Figure 9.5. At each point a short line segment with gradient $\mathrm{d}x/\mathrm{d}t$ is drawn. Such a diagram is called the **direction field** of the differential equation. Obviously, there is a gradient direction at every point of the t–x plane, but it is equally obviously only practical to draw in a finite number of them, as we have done in Figure 9.5. The equation whose direction field is drawn in Figure 9.5 is in fact

$$\frac{\mathrm{d}x}{\mathrm{d}t} = x(1 - x)t$$

but the same process could be carried out for any equation expressible in the form (9.12).

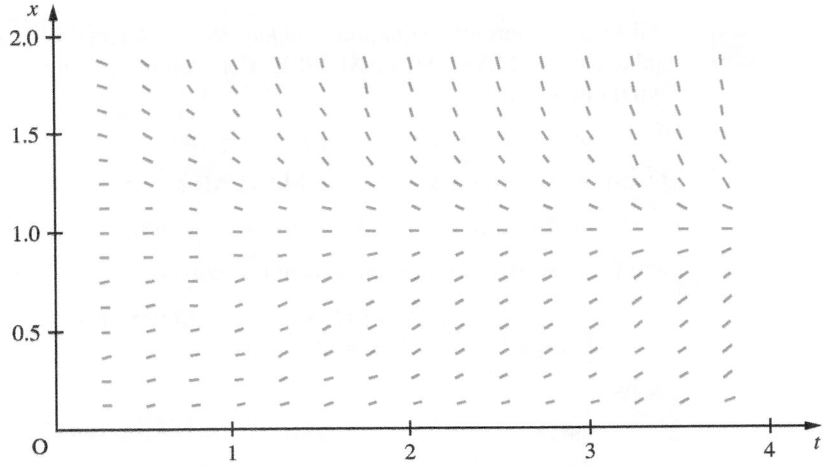

Figure 9.5 The direction field for the equation $\mathrm{d}x/\mathrm{d}t = x(1 - x)t$.

A solution of the differential equation is a function relating x and t (that is, a curve in the t–x plane) which satisfies the differential equation. Since the solution function satisfies the differential equation, the solution curve has the property that its gradient is the same as the direction of the direction field of the equation at every point on the curve; in other words, the direction field consists of line segments that are tangential to the solution curves. With this insight, it is then fairly easy to infer what the solution curves of the equation whose direction field is shown in Figure 9.5 must look like. Some typical solution curves are shown in Figure 9.6.

By continuing this process, we could cover the whole t–x plane with an infinite number of different solution curves. Each solution curve is a particular solution of the differential equation. Since we are considering first-order equations, we expect the general solution to contain one unknown constant. Giving a specific value to that constant derives, from the general solution, one or other of the particular solution curves. In other words, the general solution, with its unknown constant, represents a **family of solution curves**. The curves drawn in Figure 9.6 are particular members of that family.

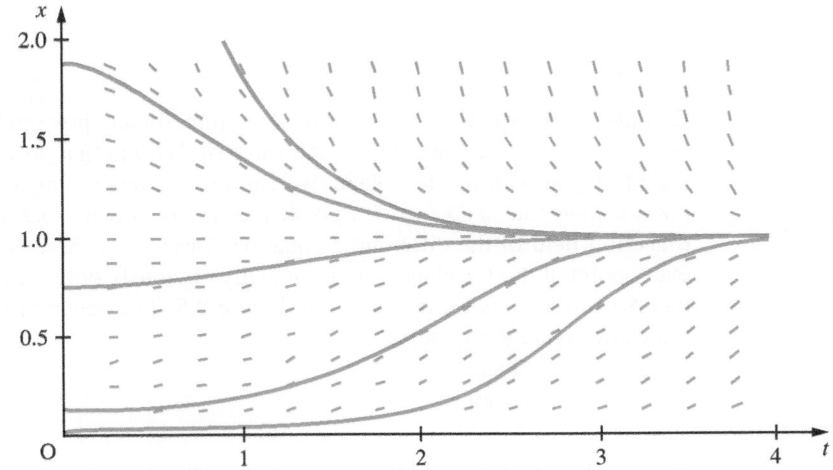

Figure 9.6 Solutions of $\mathrm{d}x/\mathrm{d}t = x(1 - x)t$ superimposed on its direction field.

Example 9.12 Sketch the direction field of the differential equation

$$\frac{dx}{dt} = -\tfrac{1}{2}x$$

Verify that $x(t) = Ce^{-t/2}$ is the general solution of the differential equation. Find the particular solution that satisfies $x(0) = 2$ and sketch it on the direction field. Do the same with the solution for which $x(3) = -1$.

Solution The direction field is shown in Figure 9.7. Substituting the function $x(t) = Ce^{-t/2}$ into the equation immediately verifies that it is a solution. The initial condition $x(0) = 2$ implies $C = 2$. The condition $x(3) = -1$ implies $C = -e^{3/2}$. Both of these curves are shown on Figure 9.7, and are readily seen to be in the direction of the direction field at every point.

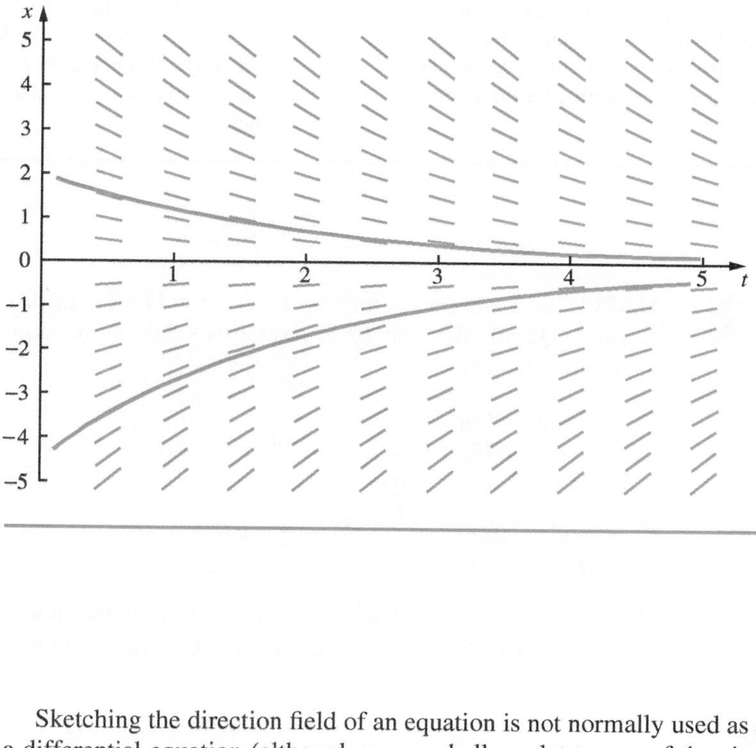

Figure 9.7 The direction field and some solution curves of $dx/dt = -x/2$.

Sketching the direction field of an equation is not normally used as a way of solving a differential equation (although, as we shall see later, one of the simplest techniques for the numerical solution of ordinary differential equations may be interpreted as following lines through a direction field). It is, however, a very valuable aid to understanding the nature of the equation and its solutions. The sketching of direction fields is made very much simpler by the use of computers and particularly computer graphics. In cases of difficulty or uncertainty about the solution of a differential equation, sketching the direction field often greatly illuminates the problem.

9.5.2 Exercises

7 Sketch the direction field of the differential equation

$$\frac{dx}{dt} = -2t$$

Find the solution of the equation. Sketch the particular solutions for which $x(0) = 2$, and for which $x(2) = -3$, and check that these are consistent with your direction field.

8 Sketch the direction field of the differential equation

$$\frac{dx}{dt} = t - x$$

Verify that $x = t - 1 + Ce^{-t}$ is the solution of the equation. Sketch the solution curve for which $x(0) = 2$, and that for which $x(4) = 0$, and check that these are consistent with your direction field.

9 Draw the direction field of the equation

$$\frac{dx}{dt} = -\frac{2x}{t-3}$$

Sketch some of the solution curves suggested by the direction field. Verify that the general solution of the equation is $x = C/(t-3)^2$ and check that the members of this family resemble the solution curves you have sketched on the direction field.

10 Draw the direction field of the equation

$$\frac{dx}{dt} = \frac{1-t}{t}x$$

Sketch some of the solution curves suggested by the direction field. Verify that the general solution of the equation is $x = Cte^{-t}$ and check that the members of this family resemble the solution curves you have sketched on the direction field.

MAPLE has tools for examining direction field plots of differential equations. For instance, Questions 9 and 10 of Exercises 9.5.2 can be completed with the following commands

```
with(DETools):
ode:= diff(x(t),t) = -2*x(t)/(t - 3);
dfieldplot(ode, x(t),t = -2..2,x = -3..3);

ode:= diff(x(t),t) = (1-t)*x(t)/t
dfieldplot(ode, x(t),t = -2..4,x = -3..3)
```

Notice that we must give MAPLE a range of both the independent variable and the dependent variable over which to construct the direction field.

9.5.3 Solution of separable differential equations

So far we have only solved differential equations such as (9.10) and (9.11) whose solution is immediately obvious. We are now going to introduce some techniques that allow us to solve somewhat more difficult equations. These techniques are basically ways of manipulating differential equations into forms in which their solutions become obvious. The first method applies to equations that take what is known as a separable form. If the function $f(t, x)$ in the first-order differential equation

$$\frac{dx}{dt} = f(t, x)$$

is such that the equation can be manipulated (by algebraic operations) into the form

$$g(x)\frac{dx}{dt} = h(t) \tag{9.13}$$

then the equation is called a **separable equation**. We may find an expression for the solution of such equations by the following argument.

Integrating both sides of (9.13) with respect to t we have

$$\int g(x)\frac{dx}{dt}\,dt = \int h(t)\,dt \tag{9.14}$$

Now let

$$G(x) = \int g(x)\,dx$$

Then

$$\frac{dG(x)}{dx} = g(x)$$

and

$$\frac{d}{dt}G(x) = \frac{dG(x)}{dx}\frac{dx}{dt} = g(x)\frac{dx}{dt}$$

Integrating both sides of this equation with respect to t we have

$$G(x) = \int g(x)\frac{dx}{dt}\,dt$$

Hence we have

$$\int g(x)\frac{dx}{dt}\,dt = G(x) = \int g(x)\,dx$$

Finally, substituting $\int g(x)\,dx$ for $\int g(x)\frac{dx}{dt}\,dt$ in (9.14) we have

$$\int g(x)\,dx = \int h(t)\,dt \tag{9.15}$$

so we have demonstrated that if a differential equation can be manipulated into the form of (9.13) then (9.15) holds. If the functions $g(x)$ and $h(t)$ are integrable then (9.15) leads to a solution of the differential equation.

Example 9.13 Solve the equation

$$\frac{dx}{dt} = 4xt, \quad x > 0$$

Solution This equation can be written as

$$\frac{1}{x}\frac{dx}{dt} = 4t$$

and so is a separable equation. The solution is given by

$$\int \frac{dx}{x} = \int 4t\, dt$$

That is,

$$\ln x = 2t^2 + C$$

or

$$x = e^{2t^2+C} = e^{2t^2}e^C$$
$$= C'e^{2t^2}, \quad \text{where } C' = e^C$$

Note: The cases $x < 0$ and $x = 0$ can be solved by allowing C' to be negative and zero respectively.

Note that a constant of integration has been introduced. We might expect such constants as a result of the integration of both left- and right-hand sides. However, if two constants had been introduced, they could then have been combined into one constant either on the left- or the right-hand side of the equation, so only one constant is actually necessary.

9.5.4 Exercises

MATLAB or MAPLE may be used to check your answers to the following questions.

11 Find the general solutions of the following differential equations:

(a) $\frac{dx}{dt} = kx$ (b) $\frac{dx}{dt} = 6xt^2$

(c) $\frac{dx}{dt} = \frac{bx}{t}$ (d) $\frac{dx}{dt} = \frac{a}{xt}$

12 Find the solutions of the following initial-value problems:

(a) $\frac{dx}{dt} = \frac{\sin t}{x^2}, \quad x(0) = 4$

(b) $t^2\frac{dx}{dt} = \frac{1}{x}, \quad x(4) = 9$

13 Find the general solutions of the following differential equations:

(a) $\sqrt{t}\frac{dx}{dt} = \sqrt{x}$ (b) $\frac{dx}{dt} = (1 + \sin t)\cot x$

(c) $\frac{dx}{dt} = xte^{t^2}$ (d) $x^2\frac{dx}{dt} = e^t$

(e) $\frac{dx}{dt} = ax(x-1)$ (f) $x\frac{dx}{dt} = \sin t$

14 Find the solutions of the following initial-value problems:

(a) $\frac{dx}{dt} = \frac{t^2+1}{x+2}, \quad x(0) = -2$

(b) $t(t-1)\dfrac{dx}{dt} = x(x+1), \quad x(2) = 2$

(c) $\dfrac{dx}{dt} = (x^2 - 1)\cos t, \quad x(0) = 2$

(d) $\dfrac{dx}{dt} = e^{x+t}, \quad x(0) = a$

(e) $\dfrac{dx}{dt} = \dfrac{4 \ln t}{x^2}, \quad x(1) = 0$

15 A chemical reaction is governed by the differential equation

$$\frac{dx}{dt} = K(5 - x)^2$$

where $x(t)$ is the concentration of the chemical at time t. The initial concentration is zero and the concentration at time 5 s is found to be 2. Determine the reaction rate constant K and find the concentration at time 10 s and 50 s. What is the ultimate value of the concentration?

16 A skydiver's vertical velocity is governed by the differential equation

$$m\frac{dv}{dt} = mg - Kv^2$$

where K is the skydiver's coefficient of drag. If the skydiver leaves her aeroplane at time $t = 0$ with zero vertical velocity, find at what time she reaches half her final velocity.

17 A chemical A is formed by an irreversible reaction from chemicals B and C. Assuming that the amounts of B and C are adequate to sustain the reaction, the amount of A formed at time t is governed by the differential equation

$$\frac{dA}{dt} = K(1 - \alpha A)^7$$

If no A is present at time $t = 0$, find an expression for the amount of A present at time t.

Either MAPLE or MATLAB can be used to solve any of the equations above. Sometimes the answers given may differ in exact form from those given in the 'Answers to Exercises' section at the end of this book. For instance, both MAPLE and MATLAB give three answers to Question 14(e). This is because the differential equation can be solved to show $x(t)^3 = 12[t(\ln(t) - 1) + 1]$. There are then, of course, three cube roots of a real quantity, one real and two complex conjugates. Sometimes, the physical origins of a problem will indicate that the real root is the one of interest. In the answers in this chapter, where multiple roots exist, only the principal root is usually given.

9.5.5 Solution of differential equations of $\dfrac{dx}{dt} = f\left(\dfrac{x}{t}\right)$ form

Some differential equations, while not being in separable form, can be transformed, by means of a substitution, into separable equations. The best-known example of this is a differential equation of the form

$$\frac{dx}{dt} = f\left(\frac{x}{t}\right) \tag{9.16}$$

Note: Equations of the form (9.16) are sometimes called 'homogeneous equations', but this use of the term homogeneous is different from the definition of homogeneous equations which we gave in Section 9.3.4.

If the substitution $y = x/t$ is made then, since $x = yt$ and therefore, by the rule for differentiation of a product,

$$\frac{dx}{dt} = t\frac{dy}{dt} + y$$

we obtain

$$t\frac{dy}{dt} + y = f(y)$$

That is,

$$\frac{1}{f(y) - y}\frac{dy}{dt} = \frac{1}{t}$$

which is an equation of separable form.

Example 9.14 Solve the equation

$$t^2\frac{dx}{dt} = x^2 + xt, \quad t > 0, x \neq 0$$

Solution Dividing both sides of the equation by t^2 results in

$$\frac{dx}{dt} = \frac{x^2}{t^2} + \frac{x}{t}$$

which is of the form (9.16). Making the substitution $y = x/t$ results in

$$t\frac{dy}{dt} + y = y^2 + y$$

that is,

$$\frac{1}{y^2}\frac{dy}{dt} = \frac{1}{t}$$

which is of separable form. The solution of this equation is given by

$$\int \frac{dy}{y^2} = \int \frac{dt}{t}$$

that is,

$$-\frac{1}{y} = \ln t + C \quad \text{or} \quad y = \frac{-1}{\ln t + C} = \frac{x}{t}$$

so

$$x = \frac{-t}{\ln t + C}$$

Note: The requirement that $t > 0$ and $x \neq 0$ means that it is valid to divide throughout by t, and later by y, in the solution process. Solutions can be obtained without these restrictions and this is left as an exercise for the reader.

9.5.6 Exercises

Again either MATLAB or MAPLE may be used to check your answers to all the following questions.

18 Find the general solutions of the following differential equations:

(a) $xt\frac{dx}{dt} = x^2 + t^2$ (b) $x^2\frac{dx}{dt} = \frac{t^3 + x^3}{t}$

(c) $t\frac{dx}{dt} = \frac{x^2 + xt}{t}$

19 Find the solution of the following initial-value problem:

$$x^3t\frac{dx}{dt} = t^4 + x^4, \quad x(1) = 4$$

20 Find the general solutions of the following differential equations:

(a) $2xt\frac{dx}{dt} = -x^2 - t^2$ (b) $t\frac{dx}{dt} = x + t\sin^2\left(\frac{x}{t}\right)$

(c) $t\frac{dx}{dt} = \frac{3t^2 - x^2}{t - 2x}$ (d) $t\frac{dx}{dt} = x + t\tan\left(\frac{x}{t}\right)$

(e) $\frac{dx}{dt} = \frac{x + t}{x - t}$ (f) $t\frac{dx}{dt} = x + te^{x/t}$

21 Find the solutions of the following initial-value problems:

(a) $\frac{dx}{dt} = \frac{x^3 - xt^2}{t^3}, \quad x(1) = 2$

(b) $xt\frac{dx}{dt} = 2(x^2 + t^2), \quad x(2) = -1$

(c) $t\frac{dx}{dt} = te^{-x/t} + x, \quad x(2) = 4$

(d) $xt\frac{dx}{dt} = t^2e^{-x^2/t^2} + x^2, \quad x(1) = 2$

(e) $t^2\frac{dx}{dt} = x^2 + 2xt, \quad x(1) = 4$

22 Show that, by making the substitution $y = at + bx + c$, equations of the form

$$\frac{dx}{dt} = f(at + bx + c)$$

can be reduced to separable form. Hence find the general solutions of the following differential equations:

(a) $\frac{dx}{dt} = \frac{t - x + 2}{t - x + 3}$ (b) $2\frac{dx}{dt} = -\frac{(t + 2x)}{t + 2x + 1}$

(c) $\frac{dx}{dt} = \frac{1 - 2x - t}{4x + 2t}$ (d) $\frac{dx}{dt} = \frac{x - t + 2}{x - t + 1}$

(e) $\frac{dx}{dt} = 2t + x + 2$ (f) $2\frac{dx}{dt} = 2x - t + 5$

(g) $\frac{dx}{dt} = 4t^2 + 4xt + x^2 - 2$

9.5.7 Solution of exact differential equations

Some first-order differential equations are of a form (or can be manipulated into a form) that is called **exact**. Since such equations can be solved readily, it would be useful to be able to recognize them or, better still, to have a test for them. In this section we shall see how exact equations are solved, and develop a test that allows us to recognize them.

The solution of exact equations depends on the following observation: if $h(t, x)$ is a function of the variables x and t, and the variable x is itself a function of t, then, by the chain rule of differentiation,

$$\frac{dh}{dt} = \frac{\partial h}{\partial x}\frac{dx}{dt} + \frac{\partial h}{\partial t}$$

Now if a first-order differential equation is of the form

$$p(t, x)\frac{dx}{dt} + q(t, x) = 0 \quad \textbf{(9.17)}$$

and a function $h(t, x)$ can be found such that

$$\frac{\partial h}{\partial x} = p(t, x) \quad \text{and} \quad \frac{\partial h}{\partial t} = q(t, x) \tag{9.18}$$

then (9.17) is equivalent to the equation

$$\frac{\mathrm{d}h}{\mathrm{d}t} = 0$$

and the solution must be

$$h(t, x) = C$$

Example 9.15 Solve the differential equation

$$2xt\frac{\mathrm{d}x}{\mathrm{d}t} + x^2 - 2t = 0$$

Solution If $h(t, x) = x^2 t - t^2$ then

$$\frac{\partial h}{\partial x} = 2xt \quad \text{and} \quad \frac{\partial h}{\partial t} = x^2 - 2t$$

so the differential equation takes the form

$$\frac{\mathrm{d}}{\mathrm{d}t}(x^2 t - t^2) = 0$$

and the solution is

$$x^2 t - t^2 = C$$

Assuming $t > 0$ and $C > 0$ the solution can be written as

$$x = \pm\sqrt{\left(t + \frac{C}{t}\right)}$$

Thus we can solve equations of the form (9.17) provided that we can guess a function $h(t, x)$ that satisfies the conditions (9.18). If such a function is not immediately obvious, there are two possibilities: first there is no such function, and, secondly, there is such a function but we don't see what it is. We shall now develop a test that enables us to answer the question of whether an appropriate function $h(t, x)$ exists and a procedure that enables us to find such a function if it does exist. If

$$\frac{\partial h}{\partial x} = p(t, x) \quad \text{and} \quad \frac{\partial h}{\partial t} = q(t, x)$$

then

$$\frac{\partial p}{\partial t} = \frac{\partial^2 h}{\partial x \partial t} = \frac{\partial q}{\partial x}$$

so, for a function $h(t, x)$ satisfying (9.18) to exist, the functions $p(t, x)$ and $q(t, x)$ must satisfy

$$\frac{\partial p}{\partial t} = \frac{\partial q}{\partial x} \tag{9.19}$$

If $p(t, x)$ and $q(t, x)$ do not satisfy this condition then there is no point in seeking a function $h(t, x)$ satisfying (9.18).

If $p(t, x)$ and $q(t, x)$ do satisfy (9.19), how do we find the function $h(t, x)$ that satisfies (9.18) and thus solve the equation (9.17)? It may be that, as in Example 9.14, the function is obvious. If not, it can be obtained by solving the two equations (9.18) independently and then comparing the answers, as in Example 9.15.

Example 9.16 Solve the differential equation

$$(\ln \sin t - 3x^2)\frac{dx}{dt} + x\cot t + 4t = 0$$

Solution First, since

$$\frac{\partial}{\partial t}(\ln \sin t - 3x^2) = \cot t = \frac{\partial}{\partial x}(x\cot t + 4t)$$

an appropriate function $h(t, x)$ may exist. Now

$$\frac{\partial h}{\partial x} = \ln \sin t - 3x^2 \quad \text{gives} \quad h = x\ln \sin t - x^3 + C_1(t)$$

and

$$\frac{\partial h}{\partial t} = x\cot t + 4t \quad \text{gives} \quad h = x\ln \sin t + 2t^2 + C_2(x)$$

where $C_1(t)$ and $C_2(x)$ are arbitrary functions of t and x respectively. Comparing the two results, we see that

$$h(t, x) = x\ln \sin t - x^3 + 2t^2$$

satisfies (9.18) and so the solution of the differential equation is

$$x\ln \sin t - x^3 + 2t^2 = C$$

Notice that the solution, in this case, is not an explicit expression for $x(t)$ in terms of t, but an implicit equation relating $x(t)$ and t, to be precise, a cubic polynomial in x with coefficients which are functions of t.

If an initial condition had been given, say $x(\frac{1}{2}\pi) = 3$, we would impose that initial condition on the implicit equation resulting in a value for the constant of integration C, thus

$$x(\tfrac{1}{2}\pi) = 3$$

giving

$$3 \ln \sin \tfrac{1}{2}\pi - 3^3 + 2 \times 0^2 = C \text{ or } 0 - 27 + 0 = C$$

so $\quad x^3 - x \ln \sin t - 2t^2 - 27 = 0$

Both MAPLE and MATLAB can solve differential equations of the exact differential type. One drawback of systems such as MAPLE and MATLAB is that they may seek an explicit solution and, in doing so, give an answer which is of a more complex form and correspondingly less easily comprehended than the solution which might be obtained by a human. For instance, we can use MAPLE or MATLAB to solve Example 9.16. In MAPLE we would use

```
ode:= (ln(sin(t)) - 3*x(t)^2)*diff(x(t),t) +
x(t)*cot(t) + 4*t;
dsolve(ode);
```

and an equivalent form in MATLAB. The solution given in Example 9.16 is an implicit one which takes the form of a cubic function of $x(t)$, $x(t)^3 - \ln[\sin(t)]x(t) - 2t^2 + C = 0$. There is a general method for solving cubic algebraic equations which the computer algebra packages use to derive an explicit form for $x(t)$. There are, of course, three roots of the cubic equation, all of which are much less immediately understandable than the implicit solution given above.

All of the questions in Exercises 9.5.8 may be tackled with MAPLE or MATLAB. Some of the solutions derived in that way will appear different from those given in the Answers section but, with some persistence, all can be shown equivalent. Use of the `simplify` command can often be helpful.

9.5.8 Exercises

Check your answers using MATLAB or MAPLE whenever possible.

23 For each of the following differential equations determine whether they are exact equations and, if so, find the general solutions:

(a) $x\dfrac{dx}{dt} + t = 0$

(b) $x\dfrac{dx}{dt} - t = 0$

(c) $(x + t)\dfrac{dx}{dt} + x - t = 0$

(d) $(x - t^2)\dfrac{dx}{dt} - 2xt = 0$

(e) $(x - t)\dfrac{dx}{dt} - x + t - 1 = 0$

(f) $(2x + t)\dfrac{dx}{dt} + x + 2t = 0$

24 Find the solution of the following initial-value problems:

(a) $(x - 1)\dfrac{dx}{dt} + t + 1 = 0, \quad x(0) = 2$

(b) $(2x + t)\dfrac{dx}{dt} + x - t = 0, \quad x(0) = -1$

(c) $(2 - xt^2)\dfrac{dx}{dt} - x^2t = 0, \quad x(1) = 2$

(d) $\cos t\dfrac{dx}{dt} - x\sin t + 1 = 0, \quad x(0) = 2$

25 For each of the following differential equations determine whether they are exact, and, if so, find the general solution:

(a) $(x + t)\dfrac{dx}{dt} - x + t = 0$

(b) $\sqrt{t}\dfrac{dx}{dt} - xt = 0$

(c) $[\sin(x+t) + x\cos(x+t)]\dfrac{dx}{dt} + x\cos(x+t) = 0$

(d) $\sin(xt)\dfrac{dx}{dt} + \cos xt = 0$

(e) $(1 + te^{xt})\dfrac{dx}{dt} + xe^{xt} = 0$

(f) $2(x + \sqrt{t})\dfrac{dx}{dt} + \dfrac{x}{\sqrt{t}} + 1 = 0$

(g) $te^{-xt}\dfrac{dx}{dt} - xe^{xt} = 0$

(h) $\dfrac{t}{x+t}\dfrac{dx}{dt} + \dfrac{t}{x+t} + \ln(x+t) = 0$

26 Find the solutions of the following initial-value problems:

(a) $\cos(x+t)\left(\dfrac{dx}{dt} + 1\right) + 1 = 0, \quad x(0) = \tfrac{1}{2}\pi$

(b) $3(x+2t)^{1/2}\dfrac{dx}{dt} + 6(x+2t)^{1/2} + 1 = 0,$

$x(-1) = 6$

(c) $x(x^2 - t^2)\dfrac{dx}{dt} - t(x^2 - t^2) + 1 = 0, \quad x(0) = -1$

(d) $\dfrac{1}{x+t}\dfrac{dx}{dt} + \dfrac{1}{x+t} - \dfrac{1}{t^2} = 0, \quad x(2) = 2$

27 What conditions on the constants a, b, e and f must be satisfied for the differential equation

$$(ax + bt)\frac{dx}{dt} + ex + ft = 0$$

to be exact, and what is the solution of the equation when they are satisfied?

28 What conditions on the functions $g(t)$ and $h(t)$ must be satisfied for the differential equation

$$g(t)\frac{dx}{dt} + h(t)x = 0$$

to be exact, and what is the solution of the equation when they are satisfied?

29 For what value of k is the function $(x + t)^k$ an integrating factor for the differential equation

$$[(x+t)\ln(x+t) + x]\frac{dx}{dt} + x = 0?$$

30 For what value of k is the function t^k an integrating factor for the differential equation

$$(t^2\cos xt)\frac{dx}{dt} + 3\sin xt + xt\cos xt = 0?$$

9.5.9 Solution of linear differential equations

In Section 9.3.3 we defined linear differential equations. The most general first-order linear differential equation must have the form

$$\frac{dx}{dt} + p(t)x = r(t) \tag{9.20}$$

where $p(t)$ and $r(t)$ are arbitrary functions of the independent variable t. We shall first see how to solve the slightly simpler equation

$$\frac{dx}{dt} + p(t)x = 0 \tag{9.21}$$

If we multiply this equation throughout by a function $g(t)$, the resulting equation

$$g(t)\frac{dx}{dt} + g(t)p(t)x = 0$$

will be exact if

$$\frac{\partial g}{\partial t} = \frac{\partial}{\partial x}(gpx)$$

Since g and p are functions of t only, this reduces to

$$\frac{\mathrm{d}g}{\mathrm{d}t} = gp$$

which is a separable equation with solution

$$\int \frac{\mathrm{d}g}{g} = \int p(t)\mathrm{d}t$$

That is,

$$\ln g = \int p(t)\mathrm{d}t$$

or

$$g(t) = \mathrm{e}^{k(t)}, \quad \text{where } k(t) = \int p(t)\mathrm{d}t$$

Hence, multiplying (9.21) throughout by $g(t)$, we obtain

$$\mathrm{e}^{k(t)}\frac{\mathrm{d}x}{\mathrm{d}t} + p(t)\mathrm{e}^{k(t)}x = 0$$

or

$$\frac{\mathrm{d}}{\mathrm{d}t}(\mathrm{e}^{k(t)}x) = 0, \quad \text{since} \quad \frac{\mathrm{d}}{\mathrm{d}t}(\mathrm{e}^{k(t)}) = \mathrm{e}^{k(t)}\frac{\mathrm{d}}{\mathrm{d}t}(k(t)) = p(t)\mathrm{e}^{k(t)}$$

Hence, integrating with respect to t, we have

$$\mathrm{e}^{k(t)}x = C$$

so the solution can be written as

$$x = C\mathrm{e}^{-k(t)}$$

The function $g(t)$ is called the **integrating factor** for the differential equation. This name expresses the property that, whilst

$$\frac{\mathrm{d}x}{\mathrm{d}t} + p(t)x$$

is not an exact integral, the expression

$$g(t)\frac{\mathrm{d}x}{\mathrm{d}t} + g(t)p(t)x$$

is an exact integral. In other words $g(t)$ is a factor which makes the expression integrable.

This technique can, in fact, be used on the full equation (9.20). In that case, multiplying by the integrating factor $g(t)$, we obtain

$$e^{k(t)}\frac{dx}{dt} + p(t)e^{k(t)}x = e^{k(t)}r(t)$$

or

$$\frac{d}{dt}(e^{k(t)}x) = e^{k(t)}r(t)$$

Then, integrating with respect to t, we have

$$e^{k(t)}x = \int e^{k(t)}r(t)dt + C$$

and the solution

$$x = e^{-k(t)}\left[\int e^{k(t)}r(t)dt + C\right] \qquad \textbf{(9.22)}$$

Thus (9.22) is an analytical solution of (9.20). The form of the solution can be simplified considerably if $\int p(t)dt$ has a simple analytical form, as in Examples 9.17 and 9.18.

Example 9.17 Solve the first-order linear differential equation

$$\frac{dx}{dt} + tx = t$$

Solution We have shown that the integrating factor for a linear differential equation is

$$g(t) = e^{k(t)} \quad \text{where} \quad k(t) = \int p(t)dt$$

In this case

$$p(t) = t \quad \text{so} \quad k(t) = \int t\,dt = \tfrac{1}{2}t^2 \quad \text{and} \quad g(t) = e^{\frac{1}{2}t^2}$$

Multiplying both sides of the differential equation by this integrating factor we have

$$e^{\frac{1}{2}t^2}\frac{dx}{dt} + te^{\frac{1}{2}t^2}x = te^{\frac{1}{2}t^2}$$

Now the left-hand side is a perfect differential (the form of the integrating factor is chosen to make this so), so the differential equation can be written

$$\frac{\mathrm{d}}{\mathrm{d}t}(\mathrm{e}^{\frac{1}{2}t^2}x) = t\mathrm{e}^{\frac{1}{2}t^2}$$

and integrating both sides of the equation with respect to t we have

$$\mathrm{e}^{\frac{1}{2}t^2}x = \int t\mathrm{e}^{\frac{1}{2}t^2}\mathrm{d}t = \mathrm{e}^{\frac{1}{2}t^2} + C$$

Finally, dividing both sides by $\mathrm{e}^{\frac{1}{2}t^2}$ we find

$$x(t) = 1 + C\mathrm{e}^{-\frac{1}{2}t^2}$$

Note: In evaluating $\int t\,\mathrm{d}t$ for the integrating factor we have taken the constant of integration to be zero. Any other value of the constant of integration would also produce a valid (but more complicated!) integrating factor.

Example 9.18 Solve the first-order linear initial-value problem

$$\frac{\mathrm{d}x}{\mathrm{d}t} + \frac{1}{t}x = t, \quad x(2) = \tfrac{1}{3}$$

Solution We have shown that the integrating factor for a linear differential equation is

$$g(t) = \mathrm{e}^{k(t)} \quad \text{where} \quad k(t) = \int p(t)\,dt$$

In this case

$$p(t) = \frac{1}{t} \quad \text{so} \quad k(t) = \int \frac{1}{t}d(t) = \ln t \quad \text{and} \quad g(t) = \mathrm{e}^{\ln t} = t$$

Multiplying both sides of the differential equation by this integrating factor we have

$$t\frac{\mathrm{d}x}{\mathrm{d}t} + x = t^2$$

Now the left-hand side is a perfect differential, so the differential equation can be written

$$\frac{\mathrm{d}}{\mathrm{d}t}(tx) = t^2$$

and integrating both sides of the equation with respect to t we have

$$tx = \int t^2\mathrm{d}t = \tfrac{1}{3}t^3 + C$$

Now, dividing both sides by t, we find

$$x(t) = \tfrac{1}{3}t^2 + \frac{C}{t}$$

The initial value $x(2) = \frac{1}{3}$ so we must have

$$\tfrac{1}{3} = \tfrac{1}{3}4 + \frac{C}{2} \quad \text{or} \quad C = -2$$

So, finally,

$$x(t) = \tfrac{1}{3}t^2 - \frac{2}{t}$$

Again both MAPLE and MATLAB can be used to solve first-order linear differential equations. The preceding examples and the exercises in the next section can all be tackled in this way. It is worth observing that this is not at all unexpected. Computer algebra packages derive their results by following standard mathematical methods, which have been programmed by the package designers. All of the analytical methods for solving differential equations described in this chapter are well known and certainly included in the spectrum of methods incorporated into the `dsolve` and related routines used by MAPLE and by MATLAB. MAPLE provides a facility to see 'inside' the workings of the dsolve routine. The commands

```
infolevel[dsolve]:= 3:
ode:= t*diff(x(t),t) + x(t) = t^2;
dsolve({ode,x(2) = 1/3});
```

cause MAPLE to give a commentary on the different methods it is trying out in order to solve the differential equation. In this case it almost immediately identifies the equation as '1st order linear' and solves it by that method.

9.5.10 Solution of the Bernoulli differential equations

Differential equations of the form

$$\frac{\mathrm{d}x}{\mathrm{d}t} + p(t)x = q(t)x^{\alpha}$$

are called Bernoulli differential equations. If the index α is 0 or 1 then the equation reduces to

$$\alpha = 0, \quad \frac{\mathrm{d}x}{\mathrm{d}t} + p(t)x = q(t)$$

$$\alpha = 1, \quad \frac{\mathrm{d}x}{\mathrm{d}t} + [p(t) - q(t)]x = 0$$

Both these forms are linear, first-order, differential equations which we can solve by the method of Section 9.5.9. But if α does not take either of these values then the equation is nonlinear. However, these equations can be reduced to a linear form by a substitution. Let

$$y(t) = x(t)^{1-\alpha}$$

then

$$\frac{dy}{dt} = (1-\alpha)x^{-\alpha}\frac{dx}{dt}$$

giving

$$\frac{dx}{dt} = \frac{x^{\alpha}}{1-\alpha}\frac{dy}{dt}$$

Substituting for $\frac{dx}{dt}$ in the original differential equation $\frac{dx}{dt} + p(t)x = q(t)x^{\alpha}$ we have

$$\frac{x^{\alpha}}{1-\alpha}\frac{dy}{dt} + p(t)x = q(t)x^{\alpha}$$

Now dividing throughout by x^{α} we have

$$\frac{1}{1-\alpha}\frac{dy}{dt} + p(t)x^{1-\alpha} = q(t)$$

But $y(t) = x(t)^{1-\alpha}$, so substituting for $x(t)^{1-\alpha}$ and multiplying throughout by $(1-\alpha)$ we obtain

$$\frac{dy}{dt} + (1-\alpha)p(t)y = (1-\alpha)q(t)$$

which is a linear differential equation for $y(t)$. Hence we can solve the equation for $y(t)$ using the method of Section 9.5.9.

Example 9.19 Solve the differential equation

$$t^2x - t^3\frac{dx}{dt} = x^4\cos t$$

Solution Firstly we rearrange the equation into canonical form

$$\frac{dx}{dt} - \frac{1}{t}x = \frac{\cos t}{t^3}x^4$$

We recognize this as a Bernoulli differential equation with index $\alpha = 4$, so we make the substitution

$$y(t) = x(t)^{1-4} = x(t)^{-3}$$

giving

$$\frac{dy}{dt} = -3x^{-4}\frac{dx}{dt} \quad \text{and} \quad \frac{dx}{dt} = -\frac{x^4}{3}\frac{dy}{dt}$$

Substituting into the equation we have

$$-\frac{x^4}{3}\frac{dy}{dt} - \frac{1}{t}x = -\frac{\cos t}{t^3}x^4 \quad \text{so that} \quad \frac{dy}{dt} + \frac{3}{t}x^{-3} = \frac{3\cos t}{t^3}$$

and substituting y for x^{-3} we have

$$\frac{dy}{dt} + \frac{3}{t}y = \frac{3\cos t}{t^3}$$

This is now seen to be a linear equation, so the integrating factor $g(t)$ is obtained by the standard method

$$p(t) = \frac{3}{t} \quad \text{giving} \quad k(t) = \int \frac{3}{t}\,dt = 3\ln t \quad \text{and} \quad g(t) = e^{3\ln t} = \left(e^{\ln t}\right)^3 = t^3$$

Multiplying both sides of the differential equation by this integrating factor we have

$$t^3\frac{dy}{dt} + 3t^2y = 3\cos t$$

Now the left-hand side is a perfect differential, so the differential equation can be written

$$\frac{d}{dt}(t^3y) = 3\cos t$$

and integrating both sides of the equation with respect to t we have

$$t^3y = \int 3\cos t\,dt = 3\sin t + C$$

Finally, substituting for $y(t)$ to obtain a solution for $x(t)$ we have

$$\frac{t^3}{x^3} = 3\sin t + C \quad \text{giving} \quad x(t)^3 = \frac{t^3}{3\sin t + C}$$

so that

$$x(t) = \sqrt[3]{\left(\frac{t^3}{3\sin t + C}\right)}$$

9.5.11 Exercises

Check your answers using MATLAB or MAPLE whenever possible.

31 Find the solution of the following differential equations:

(a) $\frac{dx}{dt} + 3x = 2$ (b) $\frac{dx}{dt} - 4x = t$

(c) $\frac{dx}{dt} + 2x = e^{-4t}$ (d) $\frac{dx}{dt} + tx = -2t$

32 Find the solution of the following initial-value problems:

(a) $\frac{dx}{dt} - 2x = 3, \quad x(0) = 2$

(b) $\frac{dx}{dt} + 3x = t, \quad x(0) = 1$

(c) $\dfrac{dx}{dt} - \dfrac{x}{t} = t^2 - 3, \quad x(1) = -1$

33 Find the solutions of the following differential equations:

(a) $\dfrac{dx}{dt} - x = t + 2t^2$ (b) $\dfrac{dx}{dt} - 4tx = t^3$

(c) $\dfrac{dx}{dt} + \dfrac{2x}{t} = \cos t$ (d) $t\dfrac{dx}{dt} + 4x = e^t$

(e) $\dfrac{dx}{dt} - (2\cot 2t)x = \cos t$

(f) $\dfrac{dx}{dt} + 6t^2x = t^2 + 2t^5$ (g) $\dfrac{dx}{dt} - \dfrac{x}{t^2} = \dfrac{4}{t^2}$

34 Find the solutions of the following initial-value problems:

(a) $\dfrac{dx}{dt} - 2t(2x - 1) = 0, \quad x(0) = 0$

(b) $\dfrac{dx}{dt} = -x \ln t, \quad x(1) = 2$

(c) $\dfrac{dx}{dt} + 5x - t = e^{-2t}, \quad x(-1) = 0$

(d) $t^2\dfrac{dx}{dt} - 1 + x = 0, \quad x(2) = 2$

(e) $\dfrac{dx}{dt} - \dfrac{1 - 2x}{t} = 4t + e^t, \quad x(1) = 0$

(f) $\dfrac{dx}{dt} + (x - U)\sin t = 0, \quad x(\pi) = 2U$

35 Solve (9.6), which arose from the model of the heating of the water in a domestic hot-water storage tank developed in Section 9.2.2. If the water in the tank is initially at 10°C and T_{in} is 80°C, what is the ratio of the times taken for the water in the tank to reach 60°C, 70°C and 75°C?

36 Solve (9.7), which arose from the model of a hydro-electric power station developed in Section 9.2.3. The setting of the control valve is represented in the model by the value of the parameter γ. Derive an expression for the discharge $Q(t)$ following a sudden increase in the valve opening such that the parameter γ changes from γ_0 to $\frac{1}{2}\gamma_0$.

37 Find the solutions of the following differential equations:

(a) $\dfrac{dx}{dt} + \dfrac{1}{t}x = \dfrac{1}{x^2}$

(b) $\dfrac{dx}{dt} + 2x = tx^2$

(c) $\dfrac{dx}{dt} - x = \dfrac{e^t}{x}$

(d) $\dfrac{dx}{dt} + \dfrac{2}{t}x = x^2$

38 Find the solutions of the following initial-value problems:

(a) $\dfrac{dx}{dt} + \dfrac{1}{t}x = t^2x^3, \quad x(1) = 1$

(b) $\dfrac{dx}{dt} + 3x = x^3, \quad x(0) = 6$

(c) $\dfrac{dx}{dt} + x = \sin t\, x^4, \quad x(0) = -1$

(d) $\dfrac{dx}{dt} - \dfrac{3}{t}x = \dfrac{1}{x^2}, \quad x(-1) = 1$

9.6 Numerical solution of first-order ordinary differential equations

Having met, in the last few sections, some techniques that may yield analytical solutions for first-order ordinary differential equations, we are now going to see how first-order ordinary differential equations can be solved numerically. In this chapter we shall only study the simplest such method, Euler's method. Many more sophisticated (but also more complex) methods exist which yield solutions more efficiently, but space precludes their inclusion in this introductory treatment.

9.6.1 A simple solution method: Euler's method

In Section 9.5.1 we met the concept of the direction field of a differential equation

$$\frac{dx}{dt} = f(t, x)$$

We noted that solutions of the differential equation are curves in the t–x plane to which the direction field lines are tangential at every point. This immediately suggests that a curve representing a solution can be obtained by sketching on the direction field a curve that is always tangential to the lines of the direction field. In Figure 9.8 a way of systematically constructing an approximation to such a curve is shown.

Starting at some point (t_0, x_0), a straight line with gradient equal to the value of the direction field at that point, $f(t_0, x_0)$, is drawn. This line is followed to a point with abscissa $t_0 + h$. The ordinate at this point is $x_0 + hf(t_0, x_0)$, which we shall call X_1. The value of the direction field at this new point is calculated, and another straight line from this point with the new gradient is drawn. This line is followed as far as the point with abscissa $t_0 + 2h$. The process can be repeated any number of times, and a curve in the t–x plane consisting of a number of short straight line segments is constructed. The curve is completely defined by the points at which the line segments join, and these can obviously be described by the equations

$$\begin{aligned}
t_1 &= t_0 + h, \qquad & X_1 &= x_0 + hf(t_0, x_0)\\
t_2 &= t_1 + h, \qquad & X_2 &= X_1 + hf(t_1, X_1)\\
t_3 &= t_2 + h, \qquad & X_3 &= X_2 + hf(t_2, X_2)\\
&\vdots & &\vdots\\
t_{n+1} &= t_n + h, \qquad & X_{n+1} &= X_n + hf(t_n, X_n)
\end{aligned}$$

These define, mathematically, the simplest method for integrating first-order differential equations. It is called **Euler's method**. Solutions are constructed step by step, starting from some given starting point (t_0, x_0). For a given t_0 each different x_0 will give rise to

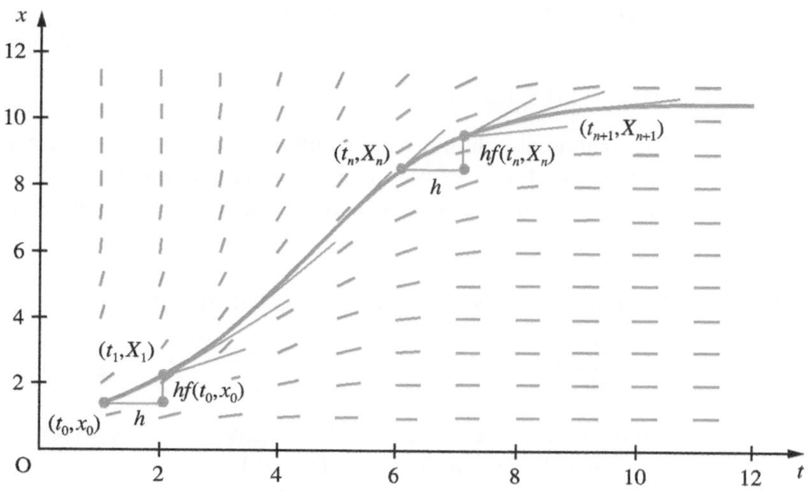

Figure 9.8 The construction of a numerical solution of the equation $dx/dt = f(t, x)$.

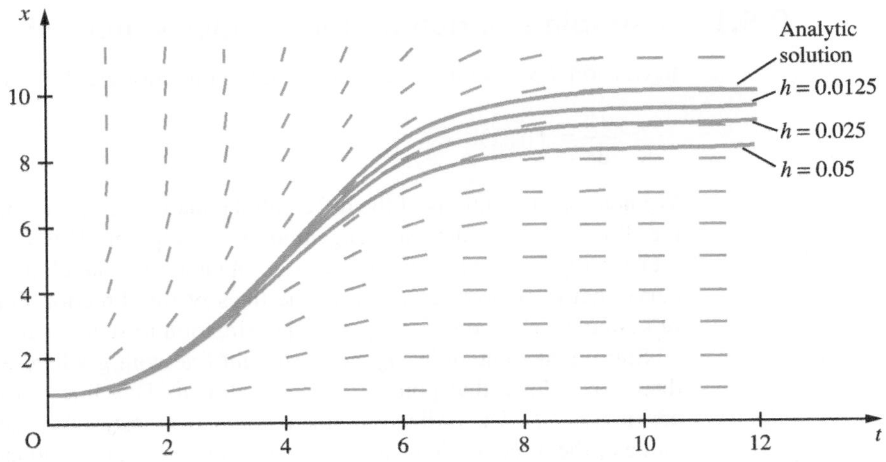

Figure 9.9 The Euler-method solutions of $dx/dt = x^2te^{-t}$ for $h = 0.05, 0.025$ and 0.0125.

a different solution curve. These curves are all solutions of the differential equation, but each corresponds to a different initial condition.

The solution curves constructed using this method are obviously not exact solutions but only approximations to solutions, because they are only tangential to the direction field at certain points. Between these points, the curves are only approximately tangential to the direction field. Intuitively, we expect that, as the distance for which we follow each straight line segment is reduced, the curve we are constructing will become a better and better approximation to the exact solution. The increment h in the independent variable t along each straight-line segment is called the **step size** used in the solution. In Figure 9.9 three approximate solutions of the initial-value problem

$$\frac{dx}{dt} = x^2te^{-t}, \quad x(0) = 0.91 \tag{9.23}$$

for step sizes $h = 0.05$, 0.025 and 0.0125 are shown. These steps are sufficiently small that the curves, despite being composed of a series of short straight lines, give the illusion of being smooth curves. The equation (9.23) actually has an analytical solution, which can be obtained by separation:

$$x = \frac{1}{(1+t)e^{-t} + C}$$

The analytical solution to the initial-value problem is also shown in Figure 9.9 for comparison. It can be seen that, as we expect intuitively, the smaller the step size the more closely the numerical solution approximates the analytical solution.

Example 9.20 The function $x(t)$ satisfies the differential equation

$$\frac{dx}{dt} = \frac{x+t}{xt}$$

and the initial condition $x(1) = 2$. Use Euler's method to obtain an approximation to the value of $x(2)$ using a step size of $h = 0.1$.

Solution The solution is obtained step by step as set out in Figure 9.10. The approximation $X(2) = 3.1162$ results.

Figure 9.10
Computational results for Example 9.21.

t	X	$X+t$	Xt	$h\frac{X+t}{Xt}$
1.0000	2.0000	3.0000	2.0000	0.1500
1.1000	2.1500	3.2500	2.3650	0.1374
1.2000	2.2874	3.4874	2.7449	0.1271
1.3000	2.4145	3.7145	3.1388	0.1183
1.4000	2.5328	3.9328	3.5459	0.1109
1.5000	2.6437	4.1437	3.9656	0.1045
1.6000	2.7482	4.3482	4.3971	0.0989
1.7000	2.8471	4.5471	4.8400	0.0939
1.8000	2.9410	4.7410	5.2939	0.0896
1.9000	3.0306	4.9306	5.7581	0.0856
2.0000	3.1162			

9.6.2 Analysing Euler's method

We have introduced Euler's method via an intuitive argument from a geometrical understanding of the problem. Euler's method can be seen in another light – as an application of Taylor series. The Taylor series given in Section 9.4.2 applied to a function $x(t)$ gives

$$x(t+h) = x(t) + h\frac{\mathrm{d}x}{\mathrm{d}t}(t) + \frac{h^2}{2!}\frac{\mathrm{d}^2x}{\mathrm{d}t^2}(t) + \frac{h^3}{3!}\frac{\mathrm{d}^3x}{\mathrm{d}t^3}(t) + \dots \tag{9.24}$$

Using this formula, we could, in theory, given the value of $x(t)$ and all the derivatives of x at t, compute the value of $x(t + h)$ for any given h. If we choose a small value for h then the Taylor series truncated after a finite number of terms will provide a good approximation to the value of $x(t + h)$. Euler's method can be interpreted as using the Taylor series truncated after the second term as an approximation to the value of $x(t + h)$.

In order to distinguish between the exact solution of a differential equation and a numerical approximation to the exact solution (and it should be appreciated that all numerical solutions, however accurate, are only approximations to the exact solution), we shall now make explicit the convention that we used in the last section. The exact solution of a differential equation will be denoted by a lower-case letter and a numerical approximation to the exact solution by the corresponding capital letter. Thus, truncating the Taylor series, we write

$$X(t+h) = x(t) + h\frac{\mathrm{d}x}{\mathrm{d}t}(t) = x(t) + hf(t, x) \tag{9.25}$$

Applying this truncated Taylor series, starting at the point (t_0, x_0) and denoting $t_0 + nh$ by t_n, we obtain

$$X(t_1) = X(t_0 + h) = x(t_0) + hf(t_0, x_0)$$

$$X(t_2) = X(t_1 + h) = X(t_1) + hf(t_1, X_1)$$

$$X(t_3) = X(t_2 + h) = X(t_2) + hf(t_2, X_2)$$

and so on

which is just the Euler-method formula obtained in Section 9.6.1. As an additional abbreviated notation, we shall adopt the convention that $x(t_0 + nh)$ is denoted by x_n, $X(t_0 + nh)$ by X_n, $f(t_n, x_n)$ by f_n, and $f(t_n, X_n)$ by F_n. Hence we may express Euler's method, in general terms, as the recursive rule

$$X_0 = x_0$$

$$X_{n+1} = X_n + hF_n \quad (n \geqslant 0)$$

The advantage of viewing Euler's method as an application of Taylor series in this way is that it gives us a clue to obtaining more accurate methods for the numerical solution of differential equations. It also enables us to analyse in more detail how accurate Euler's method may be expected to be. We can abbreviate (9.24) to

$$x(t + h) = x(t) + hf(t, x) + O(h^2)$$

where $O(h^2)$ covers all the terms involving powers of h greater than or equal to h^2. Combining this with (9.25), we see that

$$X(t + h) = x(t + h) + O(h^2) \tag{9.26}$$

(Note that in obtaining this result we have used the fact that signs are irrelevant in determining the order of terms; that is, $-O(h^p) = O(h^p)$.) Equation (9.26) expresses the fact that at each step of the Euler process the value of $X(t + h)$ obtained has an error of order h^2, or, to put it another way, the formula used is accurate as far as terms of order h. For this reason Euler's method is known as a **first-order method**. The exact size of the error is, as we intuitively expected, dependent on the size of h, and decreases as h decreases. Since the error is of order h^2, we expect that halving h, for instance, will reduce the error at each step by a factor of four.

This does not, unfortunately, mean that the error in the solution of the initial-value problem is reduced by a factor of four. To understand why this is so, we argue as follows. Starting from the point (t_0, x_0) and using Euler's method with a step size h to obtain a value of $X(t_0 + 4)$, say, requires $4/h$ steps. At each step an error of order h^2 is incurred. The total error in the value of $X(t_0 + 4)$ will be the sum of the errors incurred at each step, and so will be $4/h$ times the value of a typical step error. Hence the total error is of the order of $(4/h)O(h^2)$; that is, the total error is $O(h)$. From this argument we should expect that if we compare solutions of a differential equation obtained using Euler's method with different step sizes, halving the step size will halve the error in the solution. Examination of Figure 9.9 confirms that this expectation is roughly correct in the case of the solutions presented there.

Example 9.21 Let X_a denote the approximation to the solution of the initial-value problem

$$\frac{dx}{dt} = \frac{x^2}{t + 1}, \quad x(0) = 1$$

obtained using Euler's method with a step size $h = 0.1$, and X_b that obtained using a step size of $h = 0.05$. Compute the values of $X_a(t)$ and $X_b(t)$ for $t = 0.1, 0.2, \ldots, 1.0$. Compare these values with the values of $x(t)$, the exact solution of the problem. Compute the ratio of the errors in X_a and X_b.

Solution The exact solution, which may be obtained by separation, is

$$x = \frac{1}{1 - \ln(t + 1)}$$

The numerical solutions X_a and X_b and their errors are shown in Figure 9.11. Of course, in this figure the values of X_a are recorded at every step whereas those of X_b are only recorded at alternate steps.

Again, the final column of Figure 9.11 shows that our expectations about the effects of halving the step size when using Euler's method to solve a differential equation are confirmed. The ratio of the errors is not, of course, exactly one-half, because there are some higher-order terms in the errors, which we have ignored.

Figure 9.11
Computational results for Example 9.21.

t	X_a	X_b	$x(t)$	$\lvert x - X_a\rvert$	$\lvert x - X_b\rvert$	$\dfrac{\lvert x - X_b\rvert}{\lvert x - X_a\rvert}$
0.000 00	1.000 00	1.000 00	1.000 00			
0.100 00	1.100 00	1.102 50	1.105 35	0.005 35	0.002 85	0.53
0.200 00	1.210 00	1.216 03	1.222 97	0.012 97	0.006 95	0.54
0.300 00	1.332 01	1.342 94	1.355 68	0.023 67	0.012 75	0.54
0.400 00	1.468 49	1.486 17	1.507 10	0.038 61	0.020 92	0.54
0.500 00	1.622 52	1.649 52	1.681 99	0.059 47	0.032 47	0.55
0.600 00	1.798 03	1.837 91	1.886 81	0.088 78	0.048 90	0.55
0.700 00	2.000 08	2.057 92	2.130 51	0.130 42	0.072 59	0.56
0.800 00	2.235 40	2.318 57	2.425 93	0.190 53	0.107 36	0.56
0.900 00	2.513 01	2.632 51	2.792 16	0.279 15	0.159 65	0.57
1.000 00	2.845 39	3.018 05	3.258 89	0.413 50	0.240 84	0.58

Both MAPLE and MATLAB can be used to obtain numerical solutions of differential equations. Both encapsulate highly sophisticated numerical methods, which enable the production of very accurate numerical solutions. The Euler method described above is the simplest numerical method available and it might be considered somewhat perverse to use MAPLE or MATLAB to obtain an Euler method solution when much more accurate methods are available within the packages. Nonetheless, the numerical results in column X_a of Figure 9.11 could be obtained in MAPLE as follows.

```
odeprob:= {diff(x(t),t) = x(t)^2/(t + 1),x(0) = 1};
oseq:= array([seq(0.1*i,i = 0..10)]):
oput:= dsolve(odeprob,numeric,
          method = classical[foreuler],
          output = oseq,stepsize = 0.1);
evalm(oput[2,1]);
```

The results in column X_b of Figure 9.11 could be obtained by changing the stepsize argument in the `dsolve` routine to `stepsize=0.05`. A more extensive programming effort would be required to obtain the same numerical results through MATLAB.

9.6.3 Using numerical methods to solve engineering problems

In Example 9.21 the errors in the values of X_a and X_b are quite large (up to about 14% in the worst case). While carrying out computations with large errors such as these is quite useful for illustrating the mathematical properties of computational methods, in engineering computations we usually need to keep errors very much smaller. Exactly how small they must be is largely a matter of engineering judgement. The engineer must decide how accurately a result is needed for a given engineering purpose. It is then up to that engineer to use the mathematical techniques and knowledge available to carry out the computations to the desired accuracy. The engineering decision about the required accuracy will usually be based on the use that is to be made of the result. If, for instance, a preliminary design study is being carried out then a relatively approximate answer will often suffice, whereas for final design work much more accurate answers will normally be required. It must be appreciated that demanding greater accuracy than is actually needed for the engineering purpose in hand will usually carry a penalty in time, effort or cost.

Let us imagine that, for the problem posed in Example 9.21, we had decided we needed the value of $x(1)$ accurate to 1%. In the cases in which we should normally resort to numerical solution we should not have the analytical solution available, so we must ignore that solution. We shall suppose then that we had obtained the values of $X_a(1)$ and $X_b(1)$ and wanted to predict the step size we should need to use to obtain a better approximation to $x(1)$ accurate to 1%. Knowing that the error in $X_b(1)$ should be approximately one-half the error in $X_a(1)$ suggests that the error in $X_b(1)$ will be roughly the same as the difference between the errors in $X_a(1)$ and $X_b(1)$, which is the same as the difference between $X_a(1)$ and $X_b(1)$; that is, 0.172 66. One per cent of $X_b(1)$ is roughly 0.03, that is, roughly one-sixth of the error in $X_b(1)$. Hence we expect that a step size roughly one-sixth of that used to obtain X_b will suffice; that is, a step size $h = 0.008\,33$. In practice, of course, we shall round to a more convenient non-recurring decimal quantity such as $h = 0.008$. This procedure is closely related to the Aitken extrapolation procedure introduced in Section 7.5.3 for estimating limits of convergent sequences and series.

Example 9.22 Compute an approximation $X(1)$ to the value of $x(1)$ satisfying the initial-value problem

$$\frac{dx}{dt} = \frac{x^2}{t+1}, \quad x(0) = 1$$

by using Euler's method with a step size $h = 0.008$.

Solution It is worth commenting here that the calculations performed in Example 9.21 could reasonably be carried out on any hand-held calculator, but this new calculation requires 125 steps. To do this is on the boundaries of what might reasonably be done on a hand-held calculator, and is more suited to a computer. Repeating the calculation with a step size $h = 0.008$ produces the result $X(1) = 3.213\,91$.

We had estimated from the evidence available (that is, values of $X(1)$ obtained using step sizes $h = 0.1$ and 0.05) that the step size $h = 0.008$ should provide a value of $X(1)$ accurate to approximately 1%. Comparison of the value we have just computed with the exact solution shows that it is actually in error by approximately 1.4%. This does not quite meet the target of 1% that we set ourselves. This example therefore serves, first, to illustrate how, given two approximations to $x(1)$ derived using Euler's method with different step sizes, we can estimate the step size needed to compute an approximation within a desired accuracy, and, secondly, to emphasize that the estimate of the appropriate step size is only an *estimate*, and will not *guarantee* an approximate solution to the problem meeting the desired accuracy criterion. If we had been more conservative and rounded the estimated step size down to, say, 0.005, we should have obtained $X(1) = 3.230\,43$, which is in error by only 0.9% and would have met the required accuracy criterion.

Since we have mentioned in Example 9.22 the use of computers to undertake the repetitious calculations involved in the numerical solution of differential equations, it is also worth commenting briefly on the writing of computer programs to implement those numerical solution methods. While it is perfectly possible to write informal, unstructured programs to implement algorithms such as Euler's method, a little attention to planning and structuring a program well will usually be amply rewarded – particularly in terms of the reduced probability of introducing 'bugs'. Another reason for careful structuring is that, in this way, parts of programs can often be written in fairly general terms and can be re-used later for other problems. The two pseudocode algorithms in Figures 9.12 and 9.13 will both produce the table of results in Example 9.21. The pseudocode program of Figure 9.12 is very specific to the problem posed, whereas that of Figure 9.13 is more general, better structured, and more expressive of the structure of mathematical problems. It is generally better to aim at the style of Figure 9.13.

Both the MAPLE and MATLAB packages include a procedural programming language with all the basic structures of such languages. The pseudocode algorithms in Figures 9.12 and 9.13 can be implemented as programs in both MAPLE and MATLAB. But, again, it would be perverse to do so when very much more sophisticated numerical algorithms are packaged within the standard procedures of both languages. Nevertheless, either package could be used as a programming environment for implementing simple programs to complete Questions 43–45 in Exercises 9.6.4.

Figure 9.12
A poorly structured algorithm for Example 9.21.

```
x1←1
x2←1
write(printer,0,1,1,1)
for i is 1 to 10 do
   x1←x1 + 0.1*x1*x1/((i – 1)*0.1 + 1)
   x2←x2 + 0.05*x2*x2/((i – 1)*0.1 + 1)
   x2←x2 + 0.05*x2*x2/((i – 1)*0.1 + 1.05)
   x←1/(1 – ln(i*0.1 + 1))
   write(printer,0.1*i,x1,x2,x,x – x1,x – x2,(x – x2)/(x – x1))
endfor
```

Figure 9.13
A better structured algorithm for Example 9.21.

```
initial_time←0
final_time←1
initial_x←1
step←0.1
t←initial_time
x1←initial_x
x2←initial_x
h1←step
h2←step/2
write(printer,initial_time,x1,x2,initial_x)
repeat
   euler(t,x1,h1,1→x1)
   euler(t,x2,h2,2→x2)
   t←t + h
   x←exact_solution(t,initial_time,initial_x)
   write(printer,t,x1,x2,x,abs(x – x1),abs(x – x2),abs((x – x2)/(x– x1)))
until t ⩾ final_time

procedure euler(t_old,x_old,step,number→x_new)
   temp_x←x_old
   for i is 0 to number – 1 do
      temp_x←temp_x + step*derivative(t_old + step*i,temp_x)
   endfor
   x_new←temp_x
endprocedure

procedure derivative(t,x → derivative)
   derivative←x*x/(t+1)
endprocedure

procedure exact_solution(t,t0,x0→exact_solution)
   c←ln(t0 + 1) + 1/x0
   exact_solution←1/(c – ln(t + 1))
endprocedure
```

9.6.4 Exercises

39 Find the value of $X(0.3)$ for the initial-value problem

$$\frac{dx}{dt} = x - 2t, \quad x(0) = 1$$

using Euler's method with steps of $h = 0.1$.

40 Find the value of $X(0.25)$ for the initial-value problem

$$\frac{dx}{dt} = xt, \quad x(0) = 2$$

using Euler's method with steps of $h = 0.05$.

41 Find the value of $X(1)$ for the initial-value problem

$$\frac{dx}{dt} = \frac{x}{2\sqrt{(t + x)}}, \quad x(0.5) = 1$$

using Euler's method with step size $h = 0.1$.

42 Find the value of $X(0.5)$ for the initial-value problem

$$\frac{dx}{dt} = \frac{4 - t}{t + x}, \quad x(0) = 1$$

using Euler's method with step size $h = 0.05$.

43 Denote the Euler-method solution of the initial-value problem

$$\frac{dx}{dt} = \frac{xt}{t^2 + 2}, \quad x(1) = 2$$

using step size $h = 0.1$ by $X_a(t)$, and that using $h = 0.05$ by $X_b(t)$. Find the values of $X_a(2)$ and $X_b(2)$. Estimate the error in the value of $X_b(2)$, and suggest a value of step size that would provide a value of $X(2)$ accurate to 0.1%. Find the value of $X(2)$ using this step size. Find the exact solution of the initial-value problem, and determine the actual magnitude of the errors in $X_a(2)$, $X_b(2)$ and your final value of $X(2)$.

44 Denote the Euler-method solution of the initial-value problem

$$\frac{dx}{dt} = \frac{1}{xt}, \quad x(1) = 1$$

using step size $h = 0.1$ by $X_a(t)$, and that using $h = 0.05$ by $X_b(t)$. Find the values of $X_a(2)$ and $X_b(2)$. Estimate the error in the value of $X_b(2)$, and suggest a value of step size that would provide a value of $X(2)$ accurate to 0.2%. Find the value of $X(2)$ using this step size. Find the exact solution of the initial-value problem, and determine the actual magnitude of the errors in $X_a(2)$, $X_b(2)$ and your final value of $X(2)$.

45 Denote the Euler-method solution of the initial-value problem

$$\frac{dx}{dt} = \frac{1}{\ln x}, \quad x(1) = 1.2$$

using step size $h = 0.05$ by $X_a(t)$, and that using $h = 0.025$ by $X_b(t)$. Find the values of $X_a(1.5)$ and $X_b(1.5)$. Estimate the error in the value of $X_b(1.5)$, and suggest a value of step size that would provide a value of $X(1.5)$ accurate to 0.25%. Find the value of $X(1.5)$ using this step size. Find the exact solution of the initial-value problem, and determine the actual magnitude of the errors in $X_a(1.5)$, $X_b(1.5)$ and your final value of $X(1.5)$.

9.7 Engineering application: analysis of damper performance

In this section we shall carry out a modest engineering design exercise that will illustrate the modelling of an engineering problem using first-order differential equations and the solution of that problem using the techniques we have met so far in this chapter.

A small engineering company produces, among other artefacts, hydraulic dampers for specialized applications. One of the test rigs used by the company to check the quality and consistency of the operational characteristics of its output is illustrated in Figure 9.14. A carriage carrying a mass, which can be altered to suit the damper under test, is projected along a track of very low friction at a carefully controlled speed. At the end of the track the carriage impacts into a buffer which is connected to the damper under test. Immediately prior to impact the carriage passes through a pair of photocells whose output is used to measure the carriage speed accurately. The mass of

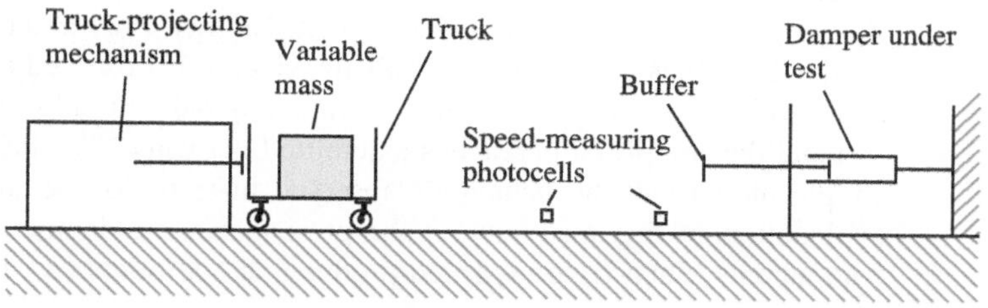

Figure 9.14 The damper test apparatus.

the buffer is very small compared with the mass of the carriage and test weight. The time/displacement history of the damper as it is compressed by the impact of the carriage is recorded digitally. The apparatus can produce time/displacement graphs and time/compression speed graphs for dampers on test.

In order to interpret the test results, the company needs to know how a damper should, in theory, behave under such a test. The simplest classical model of a damper assumes that the resistance of the damper is proportional to the velocity of compression. Since the mass of the buffer and damper components is small compared with the mass of the test apparatus carriage, it is reasonable to assume that, on impact, the moving components of the buffer and damper accelerate instantaneously to the velocity of the carriage, with negligible loss of speed on the part of the carriage. Since the track is of very low friction, it will be assumed that the only force decelerating the carriage is that provided by the damper (this also means assuming the carriage is not moving sufficiently fast for air resistance to have a significant effect). With these assumptions, the equation of motion of the carriage is

$$m\frac{\mathrm{d}v}{\mathrm{d}t} = -kv, \quad v(0) = U \tag{9.27}$$

where m is the mass of the carriage, $v(t)$ is its speed and k is the damper constant. Time is measured from the moment of impact and U is the impact speed of the carriage. The damper constant describes the force produced by the damper per unit speed of compression (and, for double-acting dampers, extension). The design engineer can adjust this constant by altering the internal design and dimensions of the damper. Equation (9.27) can be solved on sight, or by separation. The solution is

$$v = Ce^{-\lambda t}, \quad \text{with } \lambda = k/m$$

which, upon substituting in the initial conditions, becomes

$$v = Ue^{-\lambda t} \tag{9.28}$$

Writing $v = \mathrm{d}x/\mathrm{d}t$, where x is the compression of the damper and is taken as zero initially, this equation can be expressed as

$$\frac{\mathrm{d}x}{\mathrm{d}t} = Ue^{-\lambda t}, \quad x(0) = 0$$

This can be integrated directly, giving the solution, after substitution of the initial condition,

$$x = \frac{U}{\lambda}(1 - e^{-\lambda t}) \tag{9.29}$$

The velocity and displacement curves predicted by this model, (9.28) and (9.29), show that as $t \to \infty$, $v \to 0$ and $x \to U/\lambda$. Neither v nor x actually ever achieve these limits! This does not seem very realistic, since it is observed in tests that, after a finite and fairly short time (short at least when compared with infinity), the carriage comes to rest and the compression reaches a definite final value. The behaviour predicted by the simple model and the behaviour observed in tests do not quite agree. One possible explanation of this mismatch is the presence in the damper of friction between the components. Such friction would produce an additional resistance in the damper that does not vary with the speed of compression. The force resisting compression might therefore be better modelled as $kv + b$, where b is some constant force, rather than just kv. The compression of such a damper would be described by the equation

$$m\frac{dv}{dt} = -kv - b, \quad v(0) = U \tag{9.30}$$

Equation (9.30) is a linear first-order equation whose solution is

$$v = Ce^{-\lambda t} - \frac{b}{\lambda m}$$

or, substituting in the initial conditions,

$$v = Ue^{-\lambda t} - \frac{b}{\lambda m}(1 - e^{-\lambda t}) \tag{9.31}$$

This can be integrated again to provide displacement as a function of time:

$$x = \frac{1}{\lambda}\left(U + \frac{b}{\lambda m}\right)(1 - e^{-\lambda t}) - \frac{bt}{\lambda m} \tag{9.32}$$

Equation (9.31) predicts that the compression velocity of the damper will be zero when

$$t = \frac{1}{\lambda}\ln\left(\frac{b + \lambda Um}{b}\right) \tag{9.33}$$

at which time the compression of the damper will be

$$x = \frac{U}{\lambda} - \frac{b}{\lambda^2 m}\ln\left(\frac{b + \lambda Um}{b}\right) \tag{9.34}$$

This model therefore seems more realistic.

Figures 9.15 and 9.16 show the velocity and displacement curves represented by (9.28) and (9.29) and (9.31) and (9.32) for a test in which the carriage carries a mass of 2 kg and travels at $1.5\,\mathrm{m\,s^{-1}}$ at impact, the damper has a damping constant $25\,\mathrm{N\,s\,m^{-1}}$ and the constant frictional force in the damper amounts to 1.5 N.

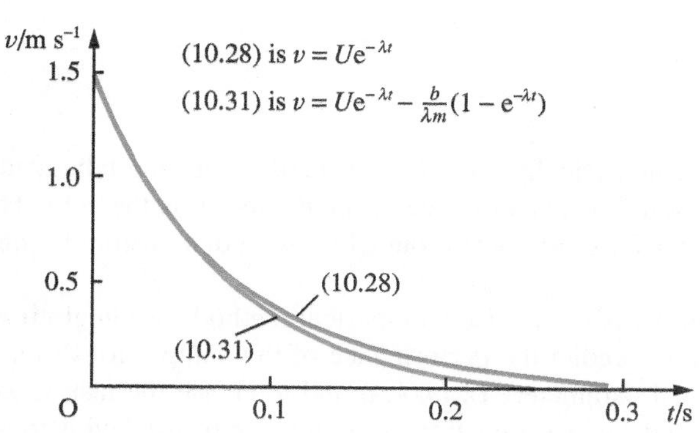

Figure 9.15 The predicted velocity–time curves for the damper test, both with and without the constant friction term.

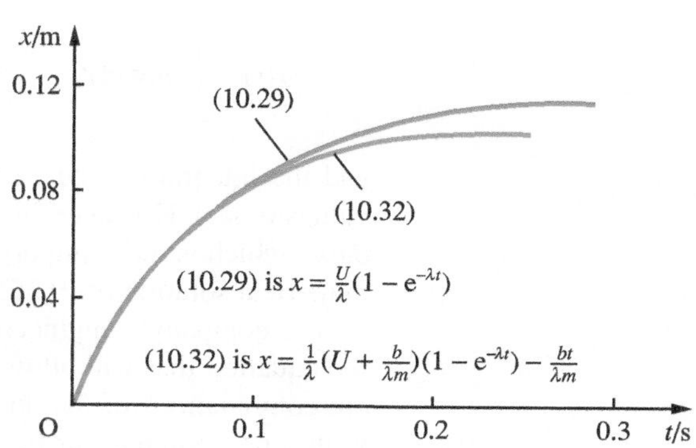

Figure 9.16 The predicted displacement–time curves for the damper test, both with and without the constant friction term.

The company perceives that one of the disadvantages of the classical hydraulic damper is, as may be inferred from Figure 9.15, that the largest force, and hence the largest deceleration of the damped object, is produced early in the history of the impact, when the velocity is largest. This means that the object, whatever it is, must be able to withstand this high deceleration. If a damper could be designed that produced a more even force over the deceleration process, the maximum deceleration experienced by an object being stopped from a given speed in a given distance would be reduced. The company's designers think they may have a solution to this problem – they have devised a new pattern of damper with a patent internal mechanism such that the damping constant increases as the damper operates. The effect of this mechanism is that, during any given operating cycle, the damping constant may be expressed as $k(1 + at)$, where t is the time elapsed in the operating cycle. The internal mechanism is such that in a short time after an operating cycle the effective damper constant returns to its initial state and the damper is ready for another operating cycle.

A model of this new design of damper is provided by the equation

$$m\frac{\mathrm{d}v}{\mathrm{d}t} = -k(1 + at)v - b, \quad v(0) = U \tag{9.35}$$

This is a linear first-order differential equation. Applying the appropriate solution method gives the solution as

$$v = -\frac{b}{m}\mathrm{e}^{-\lambda g(t)}\int \mathrm{e}^{\lambda g(t)}\,\mathrm{d}t, \quad \text{where } g(t) = t + \tfrac{1}{2}at^2$$

The integral in this solution does not result in a simple expression for $v(t)$, although it can be expressed in terms of a standard tabulated function called the error function. However, (9.35) can be solved numerically to produce $v(t)$ in tabulated form. Although we will not obtain $x(t)$ immediately using this method, we could readily derive $x(t)$ from the tabulated values of $v(t)$. Since

$$v = \frac{\mathrm{d}x}{\mathrm{d}t}$$

we can integrate both sides of this equation to obtain

$$x(t) = \int_0^t v(\tau)\,\mathrm{d}\tau$$

and the integral can be evaluated numerically (see Section 8.10) using the tabulated values of $v(t)$. However, in evaluating the performance of the damper it is the velocity curve which is more important, and we shall content ourselves with demonstrating the numerical solution of (9.35).

The company's engineers would wish to devise a numerical method for integrating the equation that will allow them to predict the performance of the damper for different combinations of the operational parameters U, m, k, a and b. Hence the task is to write a program that can be validated against some test cases and then be used with considerable confidence in other circumstances. If the value of a is taken to be 0 then the program to solve (9.35) should produce the same results as the analytical solution (9.31) of (9.30). This provides an appropriate test for the adequacy of the method and

Figure 9.17
Computational results for the damper design problem.

t	V_a	V_b	$V_a - V_b$	*(9.31)*
0.000	1.500 00	1.500 00		1.500 00
0.020	1.154 76	1.154 77	0.000 01	1.154 78
0.040	0.885 92	0.885 94	0.000 01	0.885 95
0.060	0.676 58	0.676 60	0.000 02	0.676 62
0.080	0.513 57	0.513 59	0.000 02	0.513 61
0.100	0.386 63	0.386 65	0.000 02	0.386 67
0.120	0.287 79	0.287 81	0.000 02	0.287 82
0.140	0.210 82	0.210 84	0.000 01	0.210 85
0.160	0.150 89	0.150 90	0.000 01	0.150 91
0.180	0.104 21	0.104 23	0.000 01	0.104 24
0.200	0.067 87	0.067 88	0.000 01	0.067 89
0.220	0.039 57	0.039 58	0.000 01	0.039 59
0.240	0.017 54	0.017 54	0.000 01	0.017 55
0.260	0.000 38	0.000 38	0.000 01	0.000 39
0.280	−0.012 98	−0.012 98	0.000 01	−0.012 97

step size chosen. A program written to integrate equation (9.35) by Euler's method produced the results in the table in Figure 9.17. Several test runs of the program were undertaken using different step sizes, and results using $h = 0.000\,01$ (V_a) and $h = 0.000\,005$ (V_b) together with analytical solution (9.31) are shown in the figure.

It can be seen that the results using a step size of $h = 0.000\,005$ are in agreement with the analytical solution to at least 4 decimal places, and the agreement between the two numerical solutions V_a and V_b is good to 4dp. This agreement suggests that the accuracy of the numerical solution is adequate.

It therefore seems that a step size of $h = 0.000\,005$ will produce results that are accurate to at least 4dp and probably more. Using this step size, the (v, t) traces shown in Figure 9.18 were produced. First, for comparison, the predicted result of a test on a standard damper described by (9.30) is shown. Secondly, the predicted result of a test with a new model of damper with a parameter $a = 4$ is shown. It can be seen that the modified damper stops the carriage in a shorter time than the original model. The

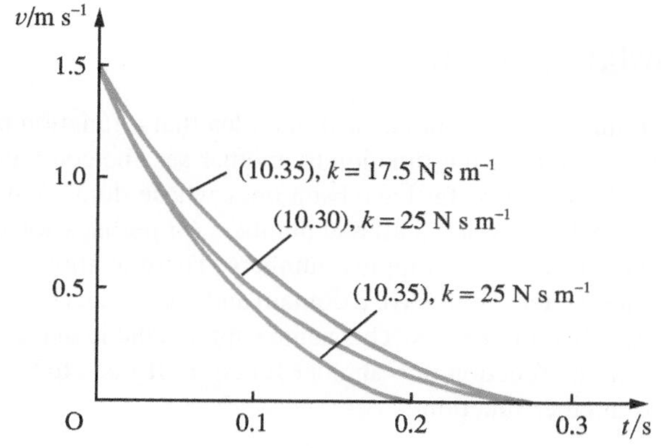

Figure 9.18
Comparison of velocity–time curves for the damper test.

velocity–time trace is also slightly straighter, indicating that the design objective of making the deceleration more nearly uniform has been, at least in part, achieved. The third trace shown is for a new model damper with the basic damper constant k reduced to 17.5 and the parameter a kept at 4. This damper is able to halt the carriage in the same time as the original unmodified damper, but, in so doing, the maximum deceleration is somewhat smaller. This is the advantage of the new design that the company hope to exploit in the market.

In this section we have seen how differential equations and numerical solution methods can be used to provide an analytical tool that the company can now use as a routine design tool for predicting the performance of a new model damper with any given combination of parameters. Such a tool is an invaluable aid to the designer, whose task will usually be to specify appropriate parameters to meet an operational requirement specified by a client, for instance something like 'to be capable of halting a mass M travelling at velocity U within a time T while subjecting it to a deceleration of no more than D'.

It should also be commented here that we have completed the numerical work in this example using Euler's method. In practice it would be far better to use a more sophisticated method, which would yield a solution of equivalent accuracy while using a much larger time step and therefore much less computing effort. Although the difference for a single computation would be very small (and, therefore, considerably outweighed by the additional programming effort of implementing a more complex method), if we were undertaking a large number of comparative runs or creating a design tool which would be used by many engineers over a long period of time then such issues would be important.

9.8 Linear differential equations

Having dealt, in the last three sections, with first-order differential equations we shall now turn our attention to differential equations of higher orders. To begin with we shall restrict our attention to linear differential equations.

In Section 9.3.3 we defined the concept of linearity and mentioned that the solutions of linear equations have important simplifying properties. In this section we are going to study these simplifying properties in more detail. Before we do so, however, it is helpful to define some new notation.

9.8.1 Differential operators

We are familiar from Section 2.2 with the idea that a function is a mapping from a set known as the domain of the function to another set, the codomain of the function. The functions we have met so far have been ones whose domain and codomain have been familiar sets, such as the set of all real numbers (or perhaps some subset of that set), the set of integers or the set of complex numbers. There is, though, no reason why a function should not be defined to have a domain and codomain consisting of functions. Such functions are called **operators**. This name captures the idea that operators are functions that transform one function into another function. If f is a function and ϕ is an operator then $\phi[f]$ is another function.

Example 9.23

Let the set A be the set of functions on the real numbers, that is, functions whose domain and codomain are both the real numbers. The operator ϕ has domain A and is defined by

$$\phi[f(t)] = f(t)^2$$

In other words, the effect of an operator ϕ on a function f is defined by specifying the function $\phi[f(t)]$. Thus for the ϕ defined here

$$\phi[3t^2 - 2t + 4] = 9t^4 - 12t^3 + 28t^2 - 16t + 16$$

and

$$\phi[\sin t - t] = \sin^2 t - 2t\sin t + t^2$$

Example 9.24

The operator ϕ is defined by

$$\phi[f(t)] = tf(t)^2 - 4f(t) + t^2$$

Then $tg(t)^4 - 4g(t)^2 + t^2$ may be expressed as $\phi[g(t)^2]$ and $te^{2t} - 4e^t + t^2$ may be expressed as $\phi[e^t]$.

Where no ambiguity is likely to result, it is permissible and conventionally acceptable to write $\phi[f(t)]$ as $\phi f(t)$, that is, to omit the square brackets.

We may view the operation of differentiation as transforming a differentiable function to another function, its derivative. When we are going to take this view, we often write the differentiation symbol separately from the function on which it will operate; for instance, we write

$$\frac{dx}{dt} \quad \text{as} \quad \frac{d}{dt}[x] \qquad \text{or} \qquad \frac{d^2x}{dt^2} \quad \text{as} \quad \frac{d^2}{dt^2}[x]$$

This notation is already familiar in those contexts in which we habitually write such expressions as

$$\frac{d}{dt}[f(t)g(t)] = \frac{df}{dt}g + f\frac{dg}{dt}$$

In such contexts we refer to the symbol d/dt as a **differential operator**.

Example 9.25

Let the operator ϕ be defined by

$$\phi[f(t)] = \frac{d}{dt}f(t)$$

Then we have

$$\phi[t^2] = 2t, \quad \phi[\sin t] = \cos t, \quad \phi[4t^3 - \tan t] = 12t^2 - \sec^2 t, \quad \text{and so on}$$

Using this notation, a differential equation may be expressed as an operator equation.

Example 9.26 Let the operator L be defined by

$$\mathrm{L}[f(t)] = \frac{\mathrm{d}^2 f}{\mathrm{d}t^2} - (\sin t)\frac{\mathrm{d}f}{\mathrm{d}t} + \mathrm{e}^t f$$

The differential equation

$$\frac{\mathrm{d}^2 f}{\mathrm{d}t^2} - (\sin t)\frac{\mathrm{d}f}{\mathrm{d}t} + \mathrm{e}^t f = t^4$$

may, using the operator notation, be written as

$$\mathrm{L}[f(t)] = t^4$$

In Section 9.3.4 we introduced the concept of homogeneous and nonhomogeneous linear differential equations and mentioned the convention whereby differential equations are usually written with the terms involving the dependent variable on the left-hand side and those not involving it on the right-hand side. When written in this way, a homogeneous equation can be characterized as an equation of the form

$$\mathrm{L}[x(t)] = 0$$

and a nonhomogeneous one as an equation of the form

$$\mathrm{L}[x(t)] = f(t)$$

where L is the differential operator of the equation.

9.8.2 Linear differential equations

Returning now to linear and nonlinear equations, we see that linear ones can be more precisely and compactly defined as those for which the operator satisfies

$$\mathrm{L}[ax_1 + bx_2] = a\mathrm{L}[x_1] + b\mathrm{L}[x_2] \qquad \textbf{(9.36)}$$

for all functions x_1 and x_2 and all constants a and b.

Example 9.27 The equation

$$\frac{\mathrm{d}^2 x}{\mathrm{d}t^2} + 4t\frac{\mathrm{d}x}{\mathrm{d}t} - (\sin t)x = \cos t$$

is a linear differential equation. Identify the operator of the equation and show that (9.36) holds for this operator.

Solution The operator is

$$\mathrm{L} \equiv \frac{\mathrm{d}^2}{\mathrm{d}t^2} + 4t\frac{\mathrm{d}}{\mathrm{d}t} - \sin t$$

Hence we have

$$\begin{aligned}
L[ax_1 + bx_2] &= \frac{d^2}{dt^2}[ax_1 + bx_2] + 4t\frac{d}{dt}[ax_1 + bx_2] - (\sin t)(ax_1 + bx_2) \\
&= a\frac{d^2x_1}{dt^2} + b\frac{d^2x_2}{dt^2} + 4t\left(a\frac{dx_1}{dt} + b\frac{dx_2}{dt}\right) - (a\sin t)x_1 - (b\sin t)x_2 \\
&= a\left[\frac{d^2x_1}{dt^2} + 4t\frac{dx_1}{dt} - (\sin t)x_1\right] + b\left[\frac{d^2x_2}{dt^2} + 4t\frac{dx_2}{dt} - (\sin t)x_2\right] \\
&= aL[x_1] + bL[x_2]
\end{aligned}$$

Equation (9.36) is the strict mathematical definition of linearity for any type of operator, and the definition we gave earlier in Section 9.3.3 is considerably less satisfactory mathematically. The formal definition of a linear differential equation is therefore any differential equation whose differential operator is linear in the sense of (9.36).

We said before that linear differential equations are an important subcategory of differential equations because they have particularly useful simplifying properties. The most important simplifying property can be summed up in the following principle:

Linearity principle: if x_1 and x_2 are both solutions of the homogeneous linear differential equation $L[x] = 0$ then so is $ax_1 + bx_2$, where a and b are arbitrary constants.

This result follows directly from the definition of a linear operator. Since x_1 and x_2 are solutions of the differential equation, we have

$$L[x_1] = 0 \quad \text{and} \quad L[x_2] = 0$$

Since the equation is linear, we have

$$L[ax_1 + bx_2] = aL[x_1] + bL[x_2] = 0$$

Therefore $ax_1 + bx_2$ is a solution of the equation $L[x] = 0$.

Example 9.28

We noted in Section 9.4.2 that the general solution of the equation

$$\frac{d^2x}{dt^2} + \lambda^2 x = 0$$

is

$$x = A\sin\lambda t + B\cos\lambda t$$

This solution can be interpreted in the light of the linearity principle. Let $x_1 = \sin\lambda t$ and $x_2 = \cos\lambda t$. Then x_1 and x_2 are solutions of the differential equation. The equation is linear, so we know that $Ax_1 + Bx_2$ is also a solution.

Example 9.29 Find the general solution of the equation

$$\frac{d^4x}{dt^4} - \lambda^4 x = 0$$

Solution We can check, by substitution into the equation, that $\sin \lambda t$, $\cos \lambda t$, $\sinh \lambda t$ and $\cosh \lambda t$ are all solutions of the equation. Therefore, since the equation is linear, the general solution is

$$x = A\sin \lambda t + B\cos \lambda t + C\sinh \lambda t + D\cosh \lambda t$$

MAPLE and MATLAB are able to solve higher-order differential equations much as they solve first-order differential equations. Thus, to find the solution of the differential equation in Example 9.29 the MAPLE commands are

```
ode:= diff(x(t),t$4) - lambda^4*x(t);
dsolve(ode);
```

and, for MATLAB, the commands are

```
ode = 'D4x - lambda^4*x'
dsolve(ode,'t')
```

In each case the general solution with 4 arbitrary constants is returned.

In Example 9.29 we have implicitly used our expectation, introduced in Section 9.4.2, that the general solution of a pth-order differential equation contains p arbitrary constants. Since the equation is a fourth-order one, once we have found four solutions, we assemble them with four arbitrary constants and we have the general solution. Is this always the case? Not quite – we need an additional constraint on the solutions, as is shown by Example 9.30.

Example 9.30 Find the general solution of the differential equation

$$\frac{d^3x}{dt^3} - 2\frac{d^2x}{dt^2} - \frac{dx}{dt} + 2x = 0$$

Solution We can show, by substituting into the equation, that e^t, e^{-t} and $\cosh(t)$ are all solutions of the differential equation. Because the equation is linear, the function

$$x = Ae^t + Be^{-t} + C\cosh(t)$$

is also a solution. Is it the general solution? The function $\cosh(t)$ can be written as

$$\cosh(t) = \tfrac{1}{2}(e^t + e^{-t})$$

so the solution proposed can be rewritten as

$$x = Ae^t + Be^{-t} + \tfrac{1}{2}C(e^t + e^{-t}) = (A + \tfrac{1}{2}C)e^t + (B + \tfrac{1}{2}C)e^{-t}$$

and replacing the constants $(A + \frac{1}{2}C)$ with D and $(B + \frac{1}{2}C)$ with E we see that

$$x = De^t + Ee^{-t}$$

The proposed solution only really has two arbitrary constants, not the three we would expect for the general solution. Of course if we notice that e^{2t} is also a solution of the differential equation we can apply the linearity principle to demonstrate that

$$x = Ae^t + Be^{-t} + Ce^{2t}$$

is a solution and, since it has the expected number of arbitrary constants and cannot be rewritten in a form with fewer constants, it is the general solution of the differential equation.

In order to resolve this problem, we need the idea of linear independence.

The functions $f_1(t), f_2(t), \ldots, f_p(t)$ are said to be **linearly dependent** if a set of numbers $k_1, k_2, \ldots, k_p$, which are not all zero, can be found such that

$$k_1f_1(t) + k_2f_2(t) + \ldots + k_pf_p(t) = 0$$

that is,

$$\sum_{j=1}^{p} k_jf_j(t) = 0$$

The functions are **linearly independent** if no such set of numbers exists.

Example 9.31 Which of the following sets of functions are linearly dependent and which are linearly independent?

(a) $\{1 + t, t, 1\}$
(b) $\{1 + t, 1 + t + t^2, 1 + t^2\}$
(c) $\{\sin(t), \cos(t)\}$
(d) $\{e^t, e^{2t}, e^{3t}\}$

Solution (a) Writing $f_1 = 1 + t, f_2 = t, f_3 = 1$, we seek a relationship of the form

$$a_1f_1 + a_2f_2 + a_2f_2 + a_3f_3 + \ldots + a_nf_n = 0$$

where the coefficients $a_1, a_2, \ldots, a_n$ are not all zero. It is easily seen that

$$(1 + t) - t - 1 = 0$$

so we have the required relationship with $a_1 = 1, a_2 = -1, a_3 = -1$. Hence $\{1 + t, t, 1\}$ is a linearly dependent set of functions.

(b) Writing $f_1 = 1 + t, f_2 = 1 + t + t^2, f_3 = 1 + t^2$, we seek a relationship of the form

$$a_1f_1 + a_2f_2 + a_2f_2 + a_3f_3 + \ldots + a_nf_n = 0$$

where the coefficients $a_1, a_2, \ldots, a_n$ are not all zero. That is, we seek $\{a_1, a_2, a_3\}$ such that

$$a_1(1+t) + a_2(1+t+t^2) + a_3(1+t^2) = 0$$

Taking coefficients of 1, t and t^2 on both sides of the equation, we require

$$a_1 + a_2 + a_3 = 0$$
$$a_1 + a_2 = 0$$
$$a_2 + a_3 = 0$$

that is $\begin{bmatrix} 1 & 1 & 1 \\ 1 & 1 & 0 \\ 0 & 1 & 1 \end{bmatrix} \begin{bmatrix} a_1 \\ a_2 \\ a_3 \end{bmatrix} = 0$

This is a homogeneous linear equation and we know that such equations only have a non-zero solution if the determinant of the matrix is zero. In this case

$$\begin{vmatrix} 1 & 1 & 1 \\ 1 & 1 & 0 \\ 0 & 1 & 1 \end{vmatrix} = 1$$

so the only solution is $\begin{bmatrix} a_1 \\ a_2 \\ a_3 \end{bmatrix} = 0$, that is $a_1 = a_2 = a_3 = 0$. Hence the functions $\{1+t, 1+t+t^2, 1+t^2\}$ are linearly independent.

(c) We shall demonstrate that $\{\sin(t), \cos(t)\}$ are linearly independent. We shall do this by seeking a relationship of the form

$$a_1 f_1 + a_2 f_2 + a_2 f_2 + a_3 f_3 + \ldots + a_n f_n = 0$$

We shall demonstrate that the coefficients $a_1, a_2, \ldots, a_n$ must be all zero and therefore conclude that the functions are not linearly dependent (and so are linearly independent).

In this case the relationship reduces to

$$a_1 \cos(t) + a_2 \sin(t) = 0$$

This must hold for all t in the domain of the functions. So we can choose particular values of t and say the relation must hold for those. Hence we have

$$t = 0 \Rightarrow a_1 1 + a_2 0 = 0 \Rightarrow a_1 = 0$$
$$t = \pi/2 \Rightarrow a_1 0 + a_2 1 = 0 \Rightarrow a_2 = 0$$

Hence the coefficients must be all zero and the functions are linearly independent.

(d) This set of functions can be investigated in an analogous manner to part (c). So we seek a relationship of the form

$$a_1 f_1 + a_2 f_2 + a_2 f_2 + a_3 f_3 + \ldots + a_n f_n = 0$$

and will demonstrate that the coefficients $a_1, a_2, \ldots, a_n$ must be all zero and therefore conclude that the functions are not linearly dependent (and so are linearly independent).

In this case the relationship reduces to

$$a_1 e^t + a_2 e^{2t} + a_3 e^{3t} = 0$$

This must hold for all t in the domain of the functions, so we can choose particular values of t and say the relation must hold for those. Hence we have

$$t = 0 \Rightarrow a_1 e^0 + a_2 e^0 + a_3 e^0 = 0 \Rightarrow a_1 + a_2 + a_3 = 0$$

$$t = 1 \Rightarrow a_1 e + a_2 e^2 + a_3 e^3 = 0$$

$$t = 2 \Rightarrow a_1 e^2 + a_2 e^4 + a_3 e^6 = 0$$

that is $\begin{bmatrix} 1 & 1 & 1 \\ e & e^2 & e^3 \\ e^2 & e^4 & e^6 \end{bmatrix} \begin{bmatrix} a_1 \\ a_2 \\ a_3 \end{bmatrix} = 0$

This is a homogeneous linear equation and we know that such equations only have a non-zero solution if the determinant of the matrix is zero. In this case

$$\begin{vmatrix} 1 & 1 & 1 \\ e & e^2 & e^3 \\ e^2 & e^4 & e^6 \end{vmatrix} = e^8 - e^7 - e^7 + e^5 + e^5 - e^4 = (e^4 - 2e^3 + 2e - 1)e^4 \approx 1029.9$$

so the only solution is $\begin{bmatrix} a_1 \\ a_2 \\ a_3 \end{bmatrix} = 0$, that is $a_1 = a_2 = a_3 = 0$. The coefficients are all zero, hence the functions $\{e^t, e^{2t}, e^{3t}\}$ are linearly independent.

The essential difference between a set of linearly dependent functions and a set of linearly independent ones is that for a linearly dependent set there are functions in the set that can be written as linear combinations of some or all of the remaining functions. For a linearly independent set this is not possible. We can see that the three solutions that we first used in Example 9.30 are linearly dependent solutions. In effect this means that one of them is just a disguised form of the other two, and so we don't really have three solutions at all, only two. The additional constraint that we mentioned immediately after Example 9.29 is just that the solutions must be linearly independent. This gives us the following principle:

General solution of a linear homogeneous equation: Let L be a pth order linear differential operator, that is

$$L[x] = a_p \frac{d^p x}{dt^p} + a_{p-1} \frac{d^{p-1} x}{dt^{p-1}} + \ldots + a_2 \frac{d^2 x}{dt^2} + a_1 \frac{dx}{dt} + a_0 x$$

Then if $x_1, x_2, \ldots, x_p$ are all solutions of the pth-order homogeneous linear differential equation

$$L[x] = 0$$

and $x_1, x_2, \ldots, x_p$ are also linearly independent then the general solution of the differential equation is

$$x = A_1 x_1 + A_2 x_2 + \ldots + A_p x_p$$

A formal proof of this result is not straightforward, and is not given here. We may, however, argue for its plausibility in the following way. Since the equation is linear, repeated application of the linearity principle shows that $A_1x_1 + A_2x_2 + \ldots + A_px_p$ is a solution of $\mathrm{L}[x] = 0$. The expression $A_1x_1 + A_2x_2 + \ldots + A_px_p$ has p arbitrary constants and, since $x_1, x_2, \ldots, x_p$ are linearly independent, there is no way of rewriting the expression to reduce the number of arbitrary constants. Hence $A_1x_1 + A_2x_2 + \ldots + A_px_p$ has the characteristics of the general solution of the differential equation.

The relatively simple structure of the general solution of a homogeneous linear differential equation has now been exposed. The general solution of a nonhomogeneous equation is only slightly more complex. It is given by the following result:

General solution of a linear nonhomogeneous equation: let

$$\mathrm{L}[x] = f(t)$$

be a nonhomogeneous linear differential equation. If x^* is *any* solution of this equation and x_c is a solution of the equivalent homogeneous equation

$$\mathrm{L}[x] = 0$$

then $x^* + x_c$ is also a solution of the nonhomogeneous equation.

This result is relatively straightforward to prove. By definition of x^* and x_c, we have

$$\mathrm{L}[x^*] = f(t) \quad \text{and} \quad \mathrm{L}[x_c] = 0$$

Since L is a linear operator, we have

$$\mathrm{L}[x^* + x_c] = \mathrm{L}[x^*] + \mathrm{L}[x_c] = f(t) + 0 = f(t)$$

Hence $x^* + x_c$ is a solution of $\mathrm{L}[x] = f(t)$.

It follows from this that finding the general solution of a nonhomogeneous linear differential equation can be reduced to the problem of finding any solution of the nonhomogeneous equation and adding to it the general solution of the equivalent homogeneous equation. The resulting expression is a solution of the nonhomogeneous equation containing the appropriate number of arbitrary constants, and so is the general solution. The first part of the solution (the 'any solution' of the nonhomogeneous equation, x^*) is known as a **particular integral** and the second part of the solution (the general solution of the equivalent homogeneous equation, x_c) is called the **complementary function**. The reader should note the similarity in structure with the general solution of linear recurrence relations developed in Section 7.4.

Example 9.32 Find the general solution of the differential equation

$$\frac{d^2x}{dt^2} + \lambda^2 x = 4t^3, \quad \lambda > 0$$

Solution A particular integral of the equation is

$$x = \frac{4}{\lambda^2}t^3 - \frac{24}{\lambda^4}t$$

which you can check by direct substitution.

The complementary function is the general solution of the equation

$$\frac{d^2x}{dt^2} + \lambda^2 x = 0$$

that is,

$$x = A\sin\lambda t + B\cos\lambda t$$

Hence the general solution of

$$\frac{d^2x}{dt^2} + \lambda^2 x = 4t^3$$

is

$$x = \frac{4}{\lambda^2}t^3 - \frac{24}{\lambda^4}t + A\sin\lambda t + B\cos\lambda t$$

Example 9.33 Find the general solution of the boundary-value problem

$$\frac{d^2x}{dt^2} - k^2 x = \sin 2t, \quad k > 0, \quad x(0) = 0,\ x\left(\frac{\pi}{4}\right) = 0$$

Solution A particular integral of the equation is

$$x = -\frac{\sin 2t}{4 + k^2}$$

which again can be checked by direct substitution. The complementary function is the general solution of the equation

$$\frac{d^2x}{dt^2} - k^2 x = 0$$

that is

$$x = Ae^{kt} + Be^{-kt}$$

Hence the general solution of

$$\frac{d^2x}{dt^2} - k^2 x = \sin 2t$$

is

$$x = -\frac{\sin 2t}{4 + k^2} + Ae^{kt} + Be^{-kt}$$

Now, imposing the boundary conditions gives two equations from which we obtain values for the two arbitrary constants in the general solution.

$$x(0) = 0 \quad \text{implies} \quad -\frac{\sin 0}{4 + k^2} + Ae^0 + Be^0 = 0$$

$$x\left(\frac{\pi}{4}\right) = 0 \quad \text{implies} \quad -\frac{\sin(\frac{1}{2}\pi)}{4 + k^2} + Ae^{k\pi/4} + Be^{-k\pi/4} = 0$$

which gives

$$A + B = 0$$

$$Ae^{k\pi/4} + Be^{-k\pi/4} = \frac{1}{4 + k^2}$$

Solving these equations for A and B yields

$$A = \frac{1}{2(4 + k^2)\sinh(\frac{1}{4}k\pi)}, \qquad B = -\frac{1}{2(4 + k^2)\sinh(\frac{1}{4}k\pi)}$$

so finally

$$x(t) = \frac{1}{4 + k^2}\left(\frac{\sinh kt}{\sinh(\frac{1}{4}k\pi)} - \sin 2t\right)$$

Linear nonhomogeneous differential equations present no problem to MAPLE and MATLAB. To find the solution of the differential equation in Example 9.33 the MAPLE and MATLAB commands are

```
ode:= diff(x(t),t$2) - k^2*x(t) = sin(2*t);
dsolve(ode);
```

and

```
ode = 'D2x - k^2*x = sin(2*t)'
dsolve(ode,'t')
```

respectively. It is quite instructive to precede the MAPLE commands with

```
infolevel[dsolve]:= 3:
```

to obtain a commentary from MAPLE on the sequence of methods explored to solve this equation.

9.8.3 Exercises

46 For each of the following differential equations write down the differential operator L that would enable the equation to be expressed to $L[x(t)] = 0$:

(a) $\frac{dx}{dt} + t^2 x = 0$ (b) $\frac{dx}{dt} = 6xt^2$

(c) $\frac{dx}{dt} - kx = 0$

47 Which of the following two sets are linearly dependent and which are linearly independent?

(a) $\{1, t, t^2, t^3, t^4, t^5, t^6\}$

(b) $\{1 + t, t^2, t^2 - t, 1 - t^2\}$

48 For each of the following sets of linearly dependent functions find $k_1, k_2, \ldots$ such that $k_1 f_1 + k_2 f_2 + \ldots = 0$.

(a) $\{t + 1, t, 2\}$ (b) $\{t^2 - 1, t^2 + 1, t - 1, t + 1\}$

49 For each of the following differential equations write down the differential operator L that would enable the equation to be expressed as $L[x(t)] = 0$:

(a) $\frac{dx}{dt} = f(t)x$

(b) $\frac{d^3x}{dt^3} + (\sin t)\frac{d^2x}{dt^2} + 4t^2 x = 0$

(c) $\dfrac{d^2x}{dt^2} + (\sin t)\dfrac{dx}{dt} = (t + \cos t)x$

(d) $(\sin t)\dfrac{dx}{dt} = \dfrac{\cos t}{t}x$

(e) $\dfrac{dx}{dt} = \dfrac{bx}{t}$ (f) $\dfrac{dx}{dt} = xte^{t^2}$

(g) $\dfrac{d}{dt}\left(t^2\dfrac{dx}{dt}\right) = t\dfrac{d}{dt}(xt)$

(h) $\dfrac{d}{dt}\left[\dfrac{1}{t}\dfrac{d}{dt}(t^2x)\right] = xt$

50 Which of the following sets of functions are linearly dependent and which are linearly independent?

(a) $\{\sin t + 2\cos t, \sin t - 2\cos t, 2\sin t + \cos t, 2\sin t - \cos t\}$

(b) $\{\sin t, \cos t, \sin 2t, \cos 2t, \sin 3t, \cos 3t\}$

(c) $\{1 + 2t, 2t - 3t^2, 3t^2 + 4t^3, 4t^3 - 5t^4\}$

(d) $\{1 + 2t, 2t - 3t^2, 3t^2 + 4t^3, 4t^3\}$

(e) $\{1, 1 + 2t, 2t - 3t^2, 3t^2 + 4t^3, 4t^3\}$

(f) $\{\ln a, \ln b, \ln ab\}$

(g) $\{e^s, e^t, e^{s+t}\}$

(h) $\{e^t, e^{2t} - e^t, e^{3t} - e^{2t}, e^{2t}\}$

(i) $\{f(t), f(t) - g(t), f(t) + g(t)\}$

(j) $\{1 - 2t^2, t - 3t^3, 2t^2 - 4t^4, 3t^3 - 5t^5\}$

(k) $\{1, 1 + t, 1 + t + t^2, 1 + t + t^2 + t^3\}$

51 For each of the following sets of linearly dependent functions find $k_1, k_2, \ldots$ such that $k_1f_1 + k_2f_2 + \ldots = 0$:

(a) $\{\sin t, \cos t + \sin t, \cos 2t - \sin t, \cos t - \cos 2t\}$

(b) $\{t + t^3, t - t^2, t^2 + 2t^3, t^2 - t^3\}$

(c) $\{\ln t, \ln 2t, \ln 4t^2\}$

(d) $\{f(t) + g(t), f(t)(1 + f(t)), g(t) - f(t), f(t)^2 - g(t)\}$

(e) $\{1 + t + 2t^2, t - 2t^2 + 3t^3, 1 + t - 2t^2, t - 2t^2 - 3t^3, t^3\}$

52 Determine which members of the given sets are solutions of the following differential equations. Hence, in each case, write down the general solution of the differential equation.

(a) $\dfrac{d^4x}{dt^4} = 0$ $\{1, t, t^2, t^3, t^4, t^5, t^6\}$

(b) $\dfrac{d^2x}{dt^2} - p^2x = 0$ $\{e^{pt}, e^{-pt}, \cos pt, \sin pt\}$

(c) $\dfrac{d^4x}{dt^4} - p^4x = 0$

$\{e^{pt}, e^{-pt}, \cos pt, \sin pt, \cosh pt, \sinh pt\}$

(d) $\dfrac{d^2x}{dt^2} + 2\dfrac{dx}{dt} = 0$

$\{\cos 2t, \sin 2t, e^{-2t}, e^{2t}, t^2, t, 1\}$

(e) $\dfrac{d^3x}{dt^3} + 4\dfrac{dx}{dt} = 0$

$\{\cos 2t, \sin 2t, e^{-2t}, e^{2t}, t^2, t, 1\}$

(f) $\dfrac{d^2x}{dt^2} + 2\dfrac{dx}{dt} + x = 0$

$\{e^t, e^{-t}, e^{2t}, e^{-2t}, te^t, te^{-t}, te^{2t}, te^{-2t}\}$

(g) $\dfrac{d^3x}{dt^3} - \dfrac{d^2x}{dt^2} - \dfrac{dx}{dt} + x = 0$

$\{e^t, e^{-t}, e^{2t}, e^{-2t}, te^t, te^{-t}, te^{2t}, te^{-2t}\}$

53 The operators L and M are defined by

$$L = \frac{d^2}{dt^2} - 4t\frac{d}{dt} + 6t^2$$

and

$$M = \frac{1}{t}\frac{d}{dt} - e^t$$

Find L[M[$x(t)$]]. Hence write down the operator LM. Find M[L[$x(t)$]]. Is LM = ML?

54 The operators L and M are defined by

$$L = f_1(t)\frac{d}{dt} + g_1(t)$$

and

$$M = f_2(t)\frac{d}{dt} + g_2(t)$$

Find expressions for the operators LM and ML. Under what conditions on f_1, g_1, f_2 and g_2 is LM = ML? What conditions do you think linear differential operators must satisfy in order to be commutative?

9.9 Linear constant-coefficient differential equations

9.9.1 Linear homogeneous constant-coefficient equations

One class of linear equation that arises relatively frequently in engineering practice is the linear constant-coefficient equation. These are linear equations in which the coefficients of the dependent variable and its derivatives do not depend on the independent variable but are constants. In view of the frequency with which such equations arise, and the fundamental importance of the problems that give rise to such equations, it is perhaps fortunate that they are relatively easy to solve.

We shall demonstrate the method of solution of such equations by considering, first of all, the second-order linear homogeneous constant-coefficient equation. The most general form this can take is

$$a\frac{d^2x}{dt^2} + b\frac{dx}{dt} + cx = 0, \quad a \neq 0 \tag{9.37}$$

Now the solution of the first-order linear homogeneous constant-coefficient equation

$$a\frac{dx}{dt} + bx = 0, \quad a \neq 0$$

is

$$x = Ae^{mt}, \quad \text{where } am + b = 0$$

Let us, by analogy, try the function $x(t) = e^{mt}$ as a solution of the second-order equation (9.37). Then direct substitution gives

$$am^2e^{mt} + bme^{mt} + ce^{mt} = 0$$

That is,

$$(am^2 + bm + c)e^{mt} = 0$$

Thus e^{mt} is a solution of the equation provided that

$$am^2 + bm + c = 0 \tag{9.38}$$

Suppose the roots of this quadratic equation are m_1 and m_2. Then e^{m_1t} and e^{m_2t} are solutions of the differential equation. Since it is a linear homogeneous equation, the general solution must be

$$x(t) = Ae^{m_1t} + Be^{m_2t} \tag{9.39}$$

provided that $m_1 \neq m_2$.

The form of the solution to (9.37) is deceptively simple. We know that the roots of a quadratic equation will take one of three forms:

(a) two different real numbers;
(b) a pair of complex-conjugate numbers;
(c) a repeated root (which must be real).

In the first case the solution is expressed as in (9.39). In the second case the roots may be written as

$$m_1 = \phi + j\psi \quad \text{and} \quad m_2 = \phi - j\psi$$

where ϕ and ψ are real, so that the solution is

$$\begin{aligned} x(t) &= Ae^{(\phi+j\psi)t} + Be^{(\phi-j\psi)t} \\ &= e^{\phi t}(Ae^{j\psi t} + Be^{-j\psi t}) \\ &= e^{\phi t}[A(\cos \psi t + j\sin \psi t) + B(\cos \psi t - j\sin \psi t)] \\ &= e^{\phi t}[(A+B)\cos \psi t + j(A-B)\sin \psi t] \end{aligned}$$

using Euler's formula (3.9). Writing $A + B = C$ and $j(A - B) = D$, we have

$$x(t) = e^{\phi t}(C\cos \psi t + D\sin \psi t)$$

In the third case the two roots m_1 and m_2 are equal, say, to k; therefore the solution (9.39) reduces to

$$x(t) = Ae^{kt} + Be^{kt} = Ce^{kt}$$

In this case the two solutions are not linearly independent, so we do not yet have the complete solution of (9.37). The complete solution, in this case, can be obtained by using the trial solution $x(t) = t^p e^{mt}$. In order for (9.38) to have a repeated root $m = k$, the constants in (9.37) must be such that (9.37) is of the form

$$a\frac{d^2x}{dt^2} - 2ak\frac{dx}{dt} + ak^2x = 0$$

Substituting the trial solution into this equation gives

$$a[p(p-1)t^{p-2}e^{mt} + 2mpt^{p-1}e^{mt} + m^2t^pe^{mt}] - 2ak(pt^{p-1}e^{mt} + mt^pe^{mt}) + ak^2t^pe^{mt} = 0$$

That is,

$$p(p-1) + 2mpt + m^2t^2 - 2k(pt + mt^2) + k^2t^2 = 0$$

or

$$p(p-1) + 2(m-k)pt + (m-k)^2t^2 = 0$$

This equation is satisfied, for all values of t, if $m = k$ and $p = 1$ or $p = 0$. Hence te^{kt} and e^{kt} are two solutions of the differential equation. These are linearly independent functions, so the general solution in the case of two equal roots is

$$x(t) = Ate^{kt} + Be^{kt} = (At + B)e^{kt}$$

Evidently the solutions of (9.38) that arise from substituting the trial solution into the differential (9.37) determine the form of the solution to the latter. Equation (9.38) is an important adjunct to the original equation, and is known as the **characteristic equation** of the differential (9.37). It is sometimes referred to as the **auxiliary equation**.

Summary

To solve the second-order, linear, homogeneous, constant-coefficient differential equation

$$a\frac{d^2x}{dt^2} + b\frac{dx}{dt} + cx = 0, \quad a \neq 0$$

first form the characteristic equation

$$am^2 + bm + c = 0$$

and find its roots, m_1 and m_2. Then if the two roots are

- real and distinct then the corresponding solution is

$$x(t) = Ae^{m_1 t} + Be^{m_2 t}$$

- both equal to k then the corresponding solution is

$$x(t) = (At + B)e^{kt}$$

- complex conjugates $\phi \pm j\psi$ then the corresponding solution is

$$x(t) = e^{\phi t}(C\cos \psi t + D\sin \psi t)$$

Example 9.34 Find the general solution of the equation

$$\frac{d^2x}{dt^2} - 9\frac{dx}{dt} + 6x = 0$$

Solution The characteristic equation is

$$m^2 - 9m + 6 = 0$$

The roots of this equation are $m = 4.5 \pm \frac{1}{2}\sqrt{57}$, or, to 2dp, $m_1 = 8.27$ and $m_2 = 0.73$. Thus the solution is

$$x(t) = Ae^{8.27t} + Be^{0.73t}$$

Example 9.35 Find the general solution of the equation

$$2\frac{d^2x}{dt^2} - 3\frac{dx}{dt} + 5x = 0$$

Solution The characteristic equation is

$$2m^2 - 3m + 5 = 0$$

The roots of this equation are $m = \frac{1}{4}(3 \pm j\sqrt{31})$, or, to 2dp, $m_1 = 0.75 + j1.39$ and $m_2 = 0.75 - j1.39$. Thus the solution is

$$x(t) = e^{0.75t}(A\cos 1.39t + B\sin 1.39t)$$

Example 9.36 Find the solution of the initial-value problem

$$\frac{d^2x}{dt^2} + 6\frac{dx}{dt} + 9x = 0, \quad x(0) = 1, \quad \frac{dx}{dt}(0) = 2$$

Solution The characteristic equation is

$$m^2 + 6m + 9 = (m + 3)^2 = 0$$

This equation has a repeated root $m = -3$. Thus the solution is

$$x(t) = (At + B)e^{-3t}$$

Now substituting in the initial conditions gives

$$B = 1, \quad -3B + A = 2$$

Hence $x(t) = (5t + 1)e^{-3t}$.

Notice, in Example 9.36, that the two initial conditions allow us to determine the values of the two arbitrary constants in the general solution of the second-order differential equation.

We have thus far demonstrated a technique that will solve any second-order linear homogeneous constant-coefficient equation. The technique extends quite satisfactorily to higher-order homogeneous constant-coefficient equations. When the same trial solution e^{mt} is substituted into a pth-order equation,

$$a_p\frac{d^px}{dt^p} + a_{p-1}\frac{d^{p-1}x}{dt^{p-1}} + \ldots + a_2\frac{d^2x}{dt^2} + a_1\frac{dx}{dt} + a_0x = 0$$

it gives rise to a characteristic equation that is a polynomial equation of degree p in m,

$$a_pm^p + a_{p-1}m^{p-1} + a_{p-2}m^{p-2} + \ldots + a_1m + a_0 = 0$$

We know from the theory of polynomial equations (see Section 3.1) that such an equation has p roots. These may be real or complex, with the complex ones occurring in conjugate pairs. The roots may also be simple or repeated. These various possibilities are dealt with just as for a second-order equation. The only additional complexity over and above the solution of the second-order equation lies in the possibility of roots being repeated more than twice. In the case of a root $m = k$ of multiplicity n, the technique employed above can be used to show that the corresponding solutions are $e^{kt}, te^{kt}, t^2e^{kt}, \ldots, t^{n-1}e^{kt}$.

Example 9.37 Find the general solution of the equation

$$\frac{d^3x}{dt^3} - 2\frac{d^2x}{dt^2} - 5\frac{dx}{dt} + 6x = 0$$

Solution The characteristic equation is

$$m^3 - 2m^2 - 5m + 6 = (m - 1)(m + 2)(m - 3) = 0$$

This equation has roots $m = 1, -2, 3$. Thus the solution is

$$x(t) = Ae^t + Be^{-2t} + Ce^{3t}$$

Example 9.38 Find the general solution of the equation

$$2\frac{d^4x}{dt^4} + 3\frac{d^3x}{dt^3} - 22\frac{d^2x}{dt^2} - 73\frac{dx}{dt} - 60x = 0$$

Solution The characteristic equation is

$$2m^4 + 3m^3 - 22m^2 - 73m - 60 = 0$$

that is,

$$(m - 4)(2m + 3)(m^2 + 4m + 5) = 0$$

The roots are therefore $m = 4, -3/2, -2 \pm j$. Thus the solution is

$$x(t) = Ae^{4t} + Be^{-3t/2} + e^{-2t}(C\cos t + D\sin t)$$

Example 9.39 Find the general solution of the equation

$$\frac{d^4x}{dt^4} + \frac{d^3x}{dt^3} - 3\frac{d^2x}{dt^2} - 5\frac{dx}{dt} - 2x = 0$$

Solution The characteristic equation is

$$m^4 + m^3 - 3m^2 - 5m - 2 = 0$$

that is,

$$(m - 2)(m^3 + 3m^2 + 3m + 1) = (m - 2)(m + 1)^3 = 0$$

The roots are therefore $m = 2$ and $m = -1$ repeated three times. Thus the solution is

$$x(t) = Ae^{2t} + (Bt^2 + Ct + D)e^{-t}$$

MAPLE implements the general method which we have just developed for linear, constant coefficient, differential equations of arbitrary order (and so, by extension, this method is also available via MATLAB). Any of the Examples 9.34–9.39 can be solved using either package. For instance, Example 9.37 would be solved in MAPLE and MATLAB respectively by the commands

```
ode:= diff(x(t),t$3) - 2*diff(x(t),t$2)
      -5*diff(x(t),t) + 6*x(t);
dsolve(ode);
```

and

```
ode = 'D3x - 2*D2x - 5*Dx + 6*x'
dsolve(ode,'t')
```

The solutions of all the questions in Exercises 9.9.2 can be readily checked using either package. For instance, Question 59(f) would be solved by

```
ode:= diff(x(t),t$3) + 6*diff(x(t),t$2)
    + 12*diff(x(t),t) + 8*x(t);
dsolve({ode,(D@@2)(x)(1) = 0,D(x)(1) = 1,x(1) = 1});
```

in MAPLE and, in MATLAB, by

```
ode = 'D3x + 6*D2x + 12*Dx + 8*x'
dsolve(ode,'x(1) = 1,Dx(1) = 1,D2x(1) = 0','t');
```

Notice the notation used in MAPLE to denote a higher-order initial condition. The condition $\frac{d^2x}{dt^2}(1) = 0$ is expressed either as `(D@@2)(x)(1) = 0` or as `D(D(x))(1) = 0`.

9.9.2 Exercises

Check your answers using MATLAB or MAPLE whenever possible.

55 Find the general solution of the following differential equations:

(a) $2\frac{d^2x}{dt^2} - 5\frac{dx}{dt} + 3x = 0$

(b) $\frac{d^2x}{dt^2} + 2\frac{dx}{dt} + 5x = 0$

(c) $\frac{d^2x}{dt^2} + 3\frac{dx}{dt} - 4x = 0$

(d) $\frac{d^2x}{dt^2} - 4\frac{dx}{dt} + 13x = 0$

56 Solve the following initial-value problems:

(a) $5\frac{d^2x}{dt^2} - 3\frac{dx}{dt} - 2x = 0,\ x(0) = -1,\ \frac{dx}{dt}(0) = 1$

(b) $\frac{d^2x}{dt^2} - 6\frac{dx}{dt} + 10x = 0,\ x(0) = 2,\ \frac{dx}{dt}(0) = 0$

(c) $\frac{d^2x}{dt^2} - 4\frac{dx}{dt} + 3x = 0,\ x(0) = 0,\ \frac{dx}{dt}(0) = 1$

57 Find the general solutions of the following differential equations:

(a) $4\frac{d^2x}{dt^2} - 2\frac{dx}{dt} + 7x = 0$

(b) $\frac{d^2x}{dt^2} + 6\frac{dx}{dt} - 4x = 0$

(c) $3\frac{d^2x}{dt^2} + 3\frac{dx}{dt} + 3x = 0$

(d) $\frac{d^2x}{dt^2} - 8\frac{dx}{dt} + 16x = 0$

(e) $9\frac{d^3x}{dt^3} - 9\frac{d^2x}{dt^2} - 4\frac{dx}{dt} + 4x = 0$

(f) $\frac{d^3x}{dt^3} - \frac{d^2x}{dt^2} + 7\frac{dx}{dt} + 9x = 0$

(g) $\frac{d^3x}{dt^3} - 2\frac{d^2x}{dt^2} + 3\frac{dx}{dt} = 0$

58 Show that the characteristic equation of the differential equation

$$\frac{d^4x}{dt^4} - 4\frac{d^3x}{dt^3} + 11\frac{d^2x}{dt^2} - 14\frac{dx}{dt} + 10x = 0$$

is

$$(m^2 - 2m + 2)(m^2 - 2m + 5) = 0$$

and hence find the general solution of the equation.

59 Solve the following initial-value problems:

(a) $2\frac{d^2x}{dt^2} - 2\frac{dx}{dt} + 3x = 0,\ x(0) = 1,\ \frac{dx}{dt}(0) = 0$

(b) $\frac{d^2x}{dt^2} - 4\frac{dx}{dt} + 4x = 0,\ x(1) = 0,\ \frac{dx}{dt}(1) = 2$

(c) $\frac{d^2x}{dt^2} + 5\frac{dx}{dt} + 8x = 0,\ x(0) = 1,\ \frac{dx}{dt}(0) = -2$

(d) $9\frac{d^2x}{dt^2} + 6\frac{dx}{dt} + x = 0,\ x(-3) = 2,\ \frac{dx}{dt}(-3) = \frac{1}{2}$

(e) $\frac{d^3x}{dt^3} - 6\frac{d^2x}{dt^2} + 11\frac{dx}{dt} - 6x = 0,$

$x(0) = 1,\ \frac{dx}{dt}(0) = 0,\ \frac{d^2x}{dt^2}(0) = 1$

(f) $\frac{d^3x}{dt^3} + 6\frac{d^2x}{dt^2} + 12\frac{dx}{dt} + 8x = 0,$

$$x(1) = 1, \quad \frac{dx}{dt}(1) = 1, \quad \frac{d^2x}{dt^2}(1) = 0$$

60 Show that the characteristic equation of the differential equation

$$\frac{d^4x}{dt^4} - 2\frac{d^3x}{dt^3} + 3\frac{d^2x}{dt^2} - 2\frac{dx}{dt} + x = 0$$

is

$$(m^2 - m + 1)^2 = 0$$

and hence find the general solution of the equation.

61 Show that the characteristic equation of the differential equation

$$\frac{d^4x}{dt^4} - \frac{d^3x}{dt^3} - 9\frac{d^2x}{dt^2} - 11\frac{dx}{dt} - 4x = 0$$

is

$$(m^3 + 3m^2 + 3m + 1)(m - 4) = 0$$

and hence find the general solution of the equation.

9.9.3 Linear nonhomogeneous constant-coefficient equations

Having dealt with linear homogeneous constant-coefficient differential equations, much of the groundwork for linear nonhomogeneous constant-coefficient differential equations is already covered. The general form of such an equation of pth order is

$$\mathrm{L}[x] = a_p\frac{d^px}{dt^p} + a_{p-1}\frac{d^{p-1}x}{dt^{p-1}} + \dots \dots + a_1\frac{dx}{dt} + a_0 = f(t)$$

where L is a pth-order linear differential operator. We have seen in Section 9.8.2 that the general solution of this equation takes the form of the sum of a particular integral and the complemetary function. The complementary function is the general solution of the equation

$$\mathrm{L}[x] = 0$$

Hence the complementary function may be found by the methods of the last section, and, in order to complete the treatment of the nonhomogeneous equation, we need only to discuss the finding of the particular integral.

There is no general mathematical theory that will guarantee to produce a particular integral by routine manipulation – rather, finding a particular integral relies on recall of empirical rules or on intellectual inspiration. We shall proceed by first giving some examples.

Example 9.40 Find the general solution of the equation

$$\frac{d^2x}{dt^2} + 5\frac{dx}{dt} - 9x = t^2$$

Solution First we shall seek a particular integral. Try the polynomial

$$x(t) = Pt^2 + Qt + R$$

Then direct substitution gives

$$2P + 5(2Pt + Q) - 9(Pt^2 + Qt + R) = t^2$$

that is,

$$-9Pt^2 + (10P - 9Q)t + 2P + 5Q - 9R = t^2$$

Equating coefficients of the various powers of t on the left- and right-hand sides of this equation leads to a set of three linear equations for the unknown parameters P, Q and R:

$$\begin{aligned} -9P \qquad\qquad &= 1 \\ 10P - 9Q \qquad &= 0 \\ 2P + 5Q - 9R &= 0 \end{aligned}$$

This set of equations has solution

$$P = -\tfrac{1}{9}, \quad Q = -\tfrac{10}{81}, \quad R = -\tfrac{68}{729}$$

so the particular integral is

$$x(t) = -\tfrac{1}{9}t^2 - \tfrac{10}{81}t - \tfrac{68}{729}$$

The method of Section 9.9.1 provides the complementary function, which is

$$Ae^{-(5-\sqrt{61})t/2} + Be^{-(5+\sqrt{61})t/2}$$

so the general solution of the equation is

$$x(t) = -\tfrac{1}{9}t^2 - \tfrac{10}{81}t - \tfrac{68}{729} + Ae^{-(5-\sqrt{61})t/2} + Be^{-(5+\sqrt{61})t/2}$$

Example 9.41 Find the general solution of the equation

$$\frac{d^2x}{dt^2} + 5\frac{dx}{dt} - 9x = \cos 2t$$

Solution As in Example 9.40, we first seek a particular integral. In this case the right-hand-side function is $\cos 2t$. If we considered as a trial function $x(t) = P\cos 2t$, we should find that the left-hand side produced $\cos 2t$ and $\sin 2t$ terms. This suggests that the trial function should be

$$x(t) = P\cos 2t + Q\sin 2t$$

Then direct substitution gives

$$\begin{aligned} &-4P\cos 2t - 4Q\sin 2t + 5(-2P\sin 2t + 2Q\cos 2t) - 9(P\cos 2t + Q\sin 2t) \\ &= \cos 2t \end{aligned}$$

that is,

$$(-13P + 10Q)\cos 2t - (10P + 13Q)\sin 2t = \cos 2t$$

Equating coefficients of $\cos 2t$ and $\sin 2t$ on the left- and right-hand sides of this equation leads to two linear equations for the unknown parameters P and Q:

$$\begin{aligned} -13P + 10Q &= 1 \\ 10P + 13Q &= 0 \end{aligned}$$

so

$$P = -\tfrac{13}{269} \quad \text{and} \quad Q = \tfrac{10}{269}$$

and the particular integral is

$$x(t) = \tfrac{1}{269}(10\sin 2t - 13\cos 2t)$$

The complementary function is the same as for Example 9.40,

$$Ae^{-(5-\sqrt{61})t/2} + Be^{-(5+\sqrt{61})t/2}$$

so the general solution of the equation is

$$x(t) = \tfrac{1}{269}(10\sin 2t - 13\cos 2t) + Ae^{-(5-\sqrt{61})t/2} + Be^{-(5+\sqrt{61})t/2}$$

Example 9.42 Find the general solution of the equation

$$\frac{d^2x}{dt^2} + 5\frac{dx}{dt} - 9x = e^{4t}$$

Solution Again we first seek a particular integral. In this case the right-hand-side function is e^{4t}. Since all derivatives of e^{4t} are multiples of e^{4t}, the trial function Pe^{4t} seems suitable. Then direct substitution gives

$$16Pe^{4t} + 20Pe^{4t} - 9Pe^{4t} = e^{4t}$$

Equating coefficients of e^{4t} on the left- and right-hand sides of this equation yields

$$27P = 1$$

so the particular integral is

$$x(t) = \tfrac{1}{27}e^{4t}$$

The complementary function is the same as for Example 9.40,

$$Ae^{-(5-\sqrt{61})t/2} + Be^{-(5+\sqrt{61})t/2}$$

so the general solution of the equation is

$$x(t) = \tfrac{1}{27}e^{4t} + Ae^{-(5-\sqrt{61})t/2} + Be^{-(5+\sqrt{61})t/2}$$

Examples 9.40–9.42 show how to deal with the most common right-hand-side functions. In each case a trial solution function is chosen to match the right-hand-side function. The trial solution function contains unknown parameters, which are determined by substituting the trial solution into the differential equation and matching the left- and right-hand sides of the equation. Figure 9.19 summarizes the standard trial functions which are used.

Although the examples that we have shown above all involve the solution of second-order equations, the trial solutions used to find particular integrals that are given in Figure 9.19 apply to linear nonhomogeneous constant-coefficient differential equations of any order.

If the right-hand side is a linear sum of more than one of these functions then the appropriate trial function is the sum of the trial functions for the terms making up the

Figure 9.19
Trial functions for particular integrals.

Right-hand-side function	***Trial function***	***Unknown parameters***
Polynomial in t of degree p, for example $6t^3 + 4t^2 - 2t + 5$	Polynomial in t of degree p, for example $Pt^3 + Qt^2 + Rt + S$	Coefficients of the polynomial, for example P, Q, R and S
Exponential function of t, for example e^{-3t}	Exponential function of t with the same exponent, for example Pe^{-3t}	Coefficient of the exponential function, for example P
Sine or cosine of a multiple of t, for example $\sin 5t$	Linear combination of sine and cosine of the same multiple of t, for example $P\sin 5t + Q\cos 5t$	Coefficients of sine and cosine terms, for example P and Q

right-hand side. This can be seen from the properties of linear equations expressed in the following principle:

> If L is a linear differential operator and x_1 is a solution of the equation
>
> $$L[x(t)] = f_1(t)$$
>
> and x_2 is a solution of the equation
>
> $$L[x(t)] = f_2(t)$$
>
> then $x_1 + x_2$ is a solution of the equation
>
> $$L[x(t)] = f_1(t) + f_2(t)$$

This result can readily be proved as follows. Since L is a linear operator

$$\begin{aligned} L[x_1 + x_2] &= L[x_1] + L[x_2] \\ &= f_1(t) + f_2(t) \end{aligned}$$

Hence $x_1 + x_2$ is a solution of $L[x] = f_1(t) + f_2(t)$.

Example 9.43 Find the general solution of the equation

$$\frac{d^2x}{dt^2} + 5\frac{dx}{dt} - 9x = e^{-2t} + 2 - t$$

Solution First we find the particular integral. Since the right-hand side is the sum of an exponential and a polynomial of degree one, the trial function for this equation is

$$Pe^{-2t} + Q + Rt$$

So, by direct substitution

$$4Pe^{-2t} + 5(-2Pe^{-2t} + R) - 9(Pe^{-2t} + Q + Rt) = e^{-2t} + 2 - t$$

Equating coefficients of e^{-2t}, 1 and t on the left- and right-hand sides of this equation yields

$$\begin{aligned} -15P \quad &= 1 \\ -9Q + 5R &= 2 \\ -9R &= -1 \end{aligned}$$

so the particular integral is

$$x(t) = -\tfrac{1}{15}e^{-2t} - \tfrac{13}{81} + \tfrac{1}{9}t$$

The complementary function is the same as for Example 9.40,

$$Ae^{-(5-\sqrt{61})t/2} + Be^{-(5+\sqrt{61})t/2}$$

so the general solution of the equation is

$$x(t) = -\tfrac{1}{15}e^{-2t} - \tfrac{13}{81} + \tfrac{1}{9}t + Ae^{-(5-\sqrt{61})t/2} + Be^{-(5+\sqrt{61})t/2}$$

The solution of linear nonhomogeneous constant-coefficient differential equations of order higher than two follows directly from the method for second-order equations. Finding a particular integral is the same whatever the degree of the equation. The principle that the solution is constructed from a particular integral added to the complementary function requires that the differential operator be linear, but is valid for an operator of any degree. Hence completing the solution of the higher-order nonhomogeneous equation only requires that the derived homogeneous equation can be solved – and we learnt how to do that in Section 9.9.1.

There is one complication that we have not yet mentioned. This is illustrated in Example 9.44.

Example 9.44 Find the general solution of the equation

$$\frac{d^2x}{dt^2} + \frac{dx}{dt} - 2x = e^{-2t}$$

Solution Substituting in the appropriate trial solution Pe^{-2t} produces the result

$$4Pe^{-2t} - 2Pe^{-2t} - 2Pe^{-2t} = e^{-2t}$$

This equation has no solution for P.

The problem in Example 9.44 lies in the fact that the right-hand side of the equation consists of a function that is also a solution of the equivalent homogeneous equation. In such cases we must multiply the appropriate trial function for the particular integral by t.

So, to find the particular integral for Example 9.44, the appropriate trial solution is Pte^{-2t}. Substituting this into the equation we have

$$(-2Pe^{-2t} + 4Pte^{-2t} - 2Pe^{-2t}) + (-2Pte^{-2t} + Pe^{-2t}) - 2Pte^{-2t} = e^{-2t}$$

so, gathering terms, we have

$$-3Pe^{-2t} = e^{-2t} \quad \text{giving} \quad P = -\tfrac{1}{3}$$

and the general solution to Example 9.43 is

$$x(t) = -\tfrac{1}{3}te^{-2t} + Ae^{-2t} + Be^{t}$$

If the right-hand-side function corresponds to a function that is a repeated root of the characteristic equation then the trial function must be multiplied by t^n, where n is the multiplicity of the root of the characteristic equation.

Example 9.45 Find the general solution of the equation

$$\frac{d^4x}{dt^4} - 2\frac{d^3x}{dt^3} + 5\frac{d^2x}{dt^2} - 8\frac{dx}{dt} + 4x = e^t$$

Solution Substituting in the appropriate trial solution Pe^t produces the result

$$Pe^t - 2Pe^t + 5Pe^t - 8Pe^t + 4Pe^t = e^t$$

for which, as in Example 9.44, there is no solution for P. The characteristic equation for the homogeneous equation is

$$m^4 - 2m^3 + 5m^2 - 8m + 4 = 0$$

that is,

$$(m-1)^2(m^2+4) = 0$$

so the general solution of the homogeneous equation is

$$x(t) = (At + B)e^t + C\cos 2t + D\sin 2t$$

The right-hand side of the equation, e^t, is the function corresponding to the double root $m = 1$, so the standard trial function for this right-hand side, Pe^t, must be multiplied by t^2. Substituting this trial function, we obtain

$$P(t^2e^t + 8te^t + 12e^t) - 2P(t^2e^t + 6te^t + 6e^t)$$

$$+ 5P(t^2e^t + 4te^t + 2e^t) - 8P(t^2e^t + 2te^t) + 4Pt^2e^t = e^t$$

that is,

$$10Pe^t = e^t$$

Hence the solution of the differential equation is

$$x(t) = \tfrac{1}{10}t^2e^t + (At + B)e^t + C\cos 2t + D\sin 2t$$

Examples 9.40–9.45 have all found general solutions to problems with no boundary conditions given. Obviously values could be determined for the constants to fit the general solution to given boundary or initial conditions. Each boundary condition allows the value of one constant to be fixed. Hence, in general, the number of boundary conditions needed to completely determine the solution is equal to the order of the differential equation.

Again MAPLE implements the method which we have just developed for non-homogeneous, linear, constant coefficient, differential equations of arbitrary order (and, of course, this method is therefore also available in the MATLAB Symbolic Math Toolbox). Any of the Examples 9.40–9.45 can be solved using either package. For instance, Example 9.45 would be solved by

```
ode:= diff(x(t),t$4) - 2*diff(x(t),t$3) +
5*diff(x(t),t$2) - 8*diff(x(t),t) + 4*x(t) = exp(t);
sol:= dsolve(ode);
```

or, using MATLAB, by

```
ode = 'D4x - 2*D3x + 5*D2x - 8*Dx + 4*x = exp(t)'
dsolve(ode,'t')
```

Solutions of any of the questions in Exercises 9.9.4 may readily be checked using either package.

9.9.4 Exercises

Check your answers using MATLAB or MAPLE whenever possible.

62 Find the general solution of the following differential equations:

(a) $\dfrac{d^2x}{dt^2} - 2\dfrac{dx}{dt} - 3x = t$

(b) $\dfrac{d^2x}{dt^2} - 2\dfrac{dx}{dt} - 5x = t^2 - 2t$

(c) $\dfrac{d^2x}{dt^2} - \dfrac{dx}{dt} - x = 5e^t$

63 Find the general solutions of the following differential equations:

(a) $\dfrac{d^2x}{dt^2} - 3\dfrac{dx}{dt} + 4x = \cos 4t - 2\sin 4t$

(b) $9\dfrac{d^2x}{dt^2} - 12\dfrac{dx}{dt} + 4x = e^{-3t}$

(c) $2\dfrac{d^2x}{dt^2} + 4\dfrac{dx}{dt} - 7x = 7\cos 2t$

(d) $\dfrac{d^2x}{dt^2} + \dfrac{dx}{dt} + 4x = 5t - 7$

(e) $16\dfrac{d^2x}{dt^2} + 8\dfrac{dx}{dt} + x = t + 6$

(f) $\dfrac{d^2x}{dt^2} - 8\dfrac{dx}{dt} + 16x = -3\sin 3t$

(g) $\dfrac{d^2x}{dt^2} - 4\dfrac{dx}{dt} + 7x = e^{-5t}$

(h) $3\dfrac{d^2x}{dt^2} + 3\dfrac{dx}{dt} - x = t^2 + e^{-2t}$

(i) $\dfrac{d^2x}{dt^2} + 2\dfrac{dx}{dt} - 3x = 5e^{-3t} + \sin 2t$

(j) $\dfrac{d^2x}{dt^2} + 16x = 1 + 2\sin 4t$

(k) $\dfrac{d^2x}{dt^2} - 4\dfrac{dx}{dt} = 7 - 3e^{4t}$

64 Show that the characteristic equation of the differential equation

$$\frac{d^4x}{dt^4} - 3\frac{d^3x}{dt^3} - 5\frac{d^2x}{dt^2} + 9\frac{dx}{dt} - 2x = 0$$

is

$$(m^2 + m - 2)(m^2 - 4m + 1) = 0$$

and hence find the general solutions of the equations

(a) $\dfrac{d^4x}{dt^4} - 3\dfrac{d^3x}{dt^3} - 5\dfrac{d^2x}{dt^2} + 9\dfrac{dx}{dt} - 2x = \cos 2t$

(b) $\dfrac{d^4x}{dt^4} - 3\dfrac{d^3x}{dt^3} - 5\dfrac{d^2x}{dt^2} + 9\dfrac{dx}{dt} - 2x = e^{2t} + e^{-2t}$

(c) $\dfrac{d^4x}{dt^4} - 3\dfrac{d^3x}{dt^3} - 5\dfrac{d^2x}{dt^2} + 9\dfrac{dx}{dt} - 2x = t^2 - 1 + e^{-t}$

65 Show that the characteristic equation of the differential equation

$$\frac{d^3x}{dt^3} - 9\frac{d^2x}{dt^2} + 27\frac{dx}{dt} - 27x = 0$$

is

$$(m-3)^3 = 0$$

and hence find the general solutions of the equations

(a) $\dfrac{d^3x}{dt^3} - 9\dfrac{d^2x}{dt^2} + 27\dfrac{dx}{dt} - 27x = \cos t - \sin t + t$

(b) $\dfrac{d^3x}{dt^3} - 9\dfrac{d^2x}{dt^2} + 27\dfrac{dx}{dt} - 27x = e^t$

(c) $\dfrac{d^3x}{dt^3} - 9\dfrac{d^2x}{dt^2} + 27\dfrac{dx}{dt} - 27x = e^{3t} + t$

9.10 Engineering application: second-order linear constant-coefficient differential equations

In this section we are going to show how simple mathematical models of a variety of engineering systems give rise to second-order linear constant-coefficient differential equations. We shall also investigate the major features of the solutions of such models.

9.10.1 Free oscillations of elastic systems

If a wooden plank or a metal beam is attached firmly to a rigid foundation at one end with its other end projecting and unsupported, as shown in Figure 9.20 then the imposition of a force on the free end, or equivalently the placing of a heavy object on it, will cause the plank or beam to bend under the load. The greater the force or load, the greater will be the deflection. If the load is moderate then the plank or beam will spring back to its original position when the load is removed. If the load is great enough, the plank will eventually break. The metal beam, on the other hand, may either deform permanently (so that it does not return to its original position when the load is removed) or fracture, depending on the type of metal. Experiments on planks or beams such as described here have revealed that for beams made of a wide variety of materials there is commonly a

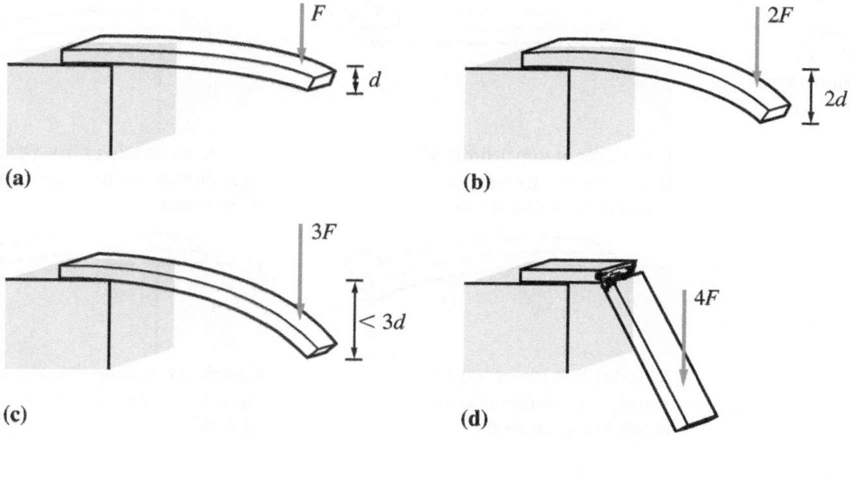

Figure 9.20
The deflection of a cantilever by a load.

range of loads for which the deflection of the beam is roughly proportional to the load applied (Figures 9.20(a), (b)). When the load becomes large enough, however, there is usually a region in which the deflection increases either less rapidly or more rapidly than the load (Figure 9.20(c)), and finally a load beyond which the beam either breaks or is permanently deformed (Figure 9.20(d)).

A beam that is fixed rigidly at one end and designed to support a load of some sort on the other end is called a cantilever. There are many common everyday and engineering applications of cantilevers. One with which most readers will be familiar is a diving springboard. Engineering applications include such things as warehouse hoists, the wings of aircraft and some types of bridges. For most of these applications the cantilever is designed to operate with small deflections; that is, the size and material of construction of the cantilever will be chosen by the designer so that, under the greatest anticipated load, the deflection of the cantilever will be small. Within this regime, the deflection of the tip of the cantilever will be proportional to the load applied. In the notation of Figure 9.20, we can write

$$d = \frac{1}{k}F \tag{9.40}$$

where d is the deflection of the cantilever, F is the load applied and k is a constant. Equation (9.40) essentially expresses a mathematical model of the cantilever, albeit a very simple one. The model is valid for applied loads such that the deflection of the cantilever remains within the linear range (where the deflection is proportional to load), and would not be valid for larger loads leading to nonlinear deflections, permanent distortions and breakages.

Equation (9.40) can also be used to investigate the dynamic behaviour of cantilevers. So far, we have assumed that the cantilever is in equilibrium under the applied load. Such situations, in which the cantilever is not moving, are called **static**. The term **dynamic** is conventionally used to describe situations and analyses in which the deflection of the cantilever is not constant in time. When the deflection of a cantilever is either greater than or less than the static deflection under the same load, the cantilever exerts a net force accelerating the mass back towards its equilibrium position. As a result, the deflection of the cantilever oscillates about the static equilibrium position. The situation is illustrated in Figure 9.21.

Figure 9.21 The dynamic behaviour of a loaded cantilever.

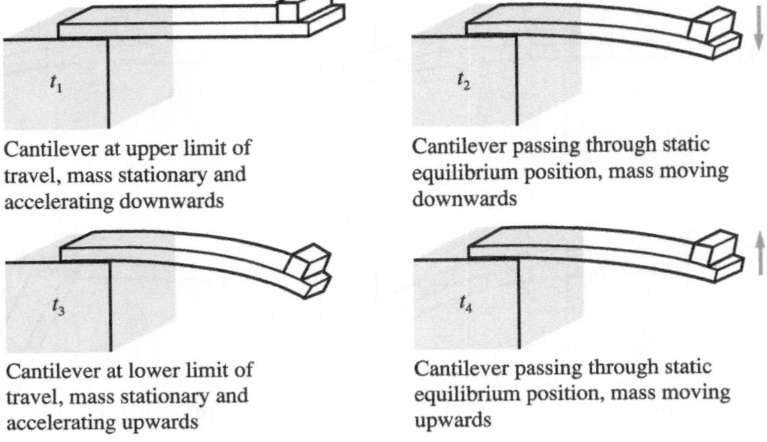
t_1
Cantilever at upper limit of travel, mass stationary and accelerating downwards
t_2
Cantilever passing through static equilibrium position, mass moving downwards
t_3
Cantilever at lower limit of travel, mass stationary and accelerating upwards
t_4
Cantilever passing through static equilibrium position, mass moving upwards

Such oscillations can be analysed fairly readily. If the mass supported on the end of the cantilever is large compared with the mass of the cantilever itself, the effect of the cantilever is merely to apply a force to the mass. The vertical equation of motion of the mass is then

$$m\frac{d^2x}{dt^2} = mg - F$$

where x is the instantaneous deflection of the tip of the cantilever below the horizontal, m is the mass and F is the upward force exerted on the mass by the cantilever due to its bending. But the restoring force, provided the deflection of the cantilever remains small enough at all times during the motion, is given by (9.40). Thus the motion is governed by the equation

$$m\frac{d^2x}{dt^2} = mg - kx$$

This equation, rearranged in the form

$$\frac{d^2x}{dt^2} + \frac{kx}{m} = g \tag{9.41}$$

is recognizable as a second-order linear nonhomogeneous constant-coefficient equation. In the static case, when the load is not moving, the solution of this equation is $x = mg/k$. This is, of course, also a particular integral for (9.41). The complementary function for (9.41) is

$$x = A\cos\omega t + B\sin\omega t, \quad \text{where } \omega^2 = k/m$$

The complete solution of (9.41) is therefore

$$x = \frac{mg}{k} + A\cos\omega t + B\sin\omega t \tag{9.42}$$

The constants A and B could of course be determined if suitable initial conditions were provided. What is at least as important – if not more so for the engineer – is to understand the physical meaning of the solution (9.42). This is more easily done if (9.42) is slightly rearranged. Taking $C = (A^2 + B^2)^{1/2}$ and $\tan\delta = B/A$, so that

$$A = C\cos\delta \quad \text{and} \quad B = C\sin\delta$$

(9.42) becomes

$$x = \frac{mg}{k} + C\cos(\omega t - \delta) \tag{9.43}$$

In physical terms this equation implies that the deflection of the cantilever takes the form of periodic oscillations of angular frequency ω and constant amplitude C about the position of static equilibrium of the cantilever (the position at which $kx = mg$).

The interested reader can check the accuracy of this description by constructing a cantilever from a flexible wooden or plastic ruler (the flexible plastic type is the most effective). The ruler should be held firmly by one end so that it projects over the edge of a desk or table, and the free end loaded with a sufficient mass of plasticine or other suitable material. The static equilibrium position is easily found. If the end of the ruler is displaced from this position and released, the plasticine-loaded end will be found to vibrate up and down around the equilibrium position. If the mass of plasticine is increased, the frequency of the vibration will be found to decrease as predicted by the relation $\omega^2 = k/m$.

A cantilever is not the only engineering system that gives rise to linear constant-coefficient equations. The pendulum shown in Figure 9.22 can be analysed thus. It is of length l and carries a mass m at its free end. If the mass of the pendulum arm is very small compared with m then, resolving forces at right-angles to the pendulum arm, the equation of motion of the mass is

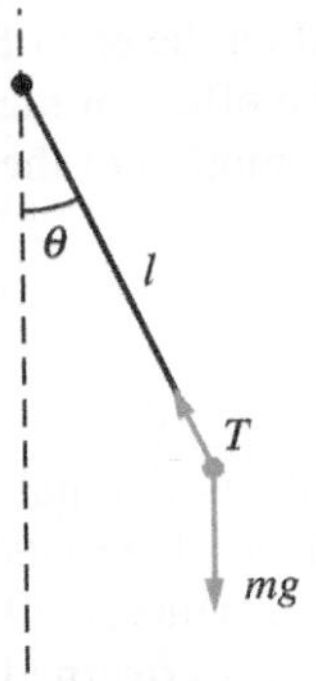

Figure 9.22
A pendulum.

$$ml\frac{d^2\theta}{dt^2} = -mg\sin\theta$$

This is a second-order nonlinear differential equation, but if the displacement from the equilibrium position (in which the pendulum hangs stationary and vertically below the pivot) is small then $\sin\theta \approx \theta$ and the equation becomes

$$\frac{d^2\theta}{dt^2} + \frac{g}{l}\theta = 0 \tag{9.44}$$

The solution of this equation is

$$\theta = A\cos\omega t + B\sin\omega t, \quad \text{with } \omega^2 = g/l \tag{9.45}$$

In other words, the pendulum's displacement from its equilibrium position oscillates sinusoidally with a frequency that decreases as the pendulum increases in length but is independent of the mass of the pendulum bob.

The buoy (or floating oil drum or similar) shown in Figure 9.23 also gives rise to a second-order linear constant-coefficient equation. Suppose the immersed depth of the buoy is z. Its mass (which is concentrated near the bottom of the buoy in order that it should float upright and not tip over) is m. We know, by Archimedes' principle, that the water in which the buoy floats exerts an upthrust on the buoy equal to the weight of the water displaced by the latter. If the cross-sectional area of the buoy is A and the density of the water is ρ, the upthrust will be ρAzg. Hence the equation of motion is

$$m\frac{d^2z}{dt^2} = mg - \rho Azg$$

that is,

$$\frac{d^2z}{dt^2} + \frac{\rho Ag}{m}z = g \tag{9.46}$$

Equation (9.46) has particular integral $z = m/\rho A$ and complementary function

$$z = A\cos\omega t + B\sin\omega t, \quad \text{with } \omega^2 = \rho Ag/m$$

Figure 9.23
A floating buoy.

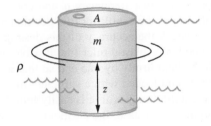

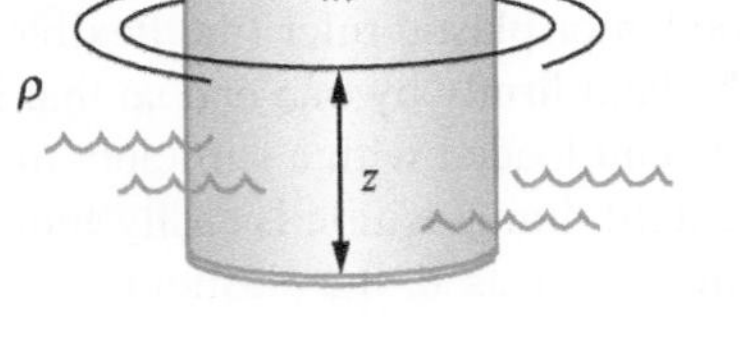

so the complete solution is

$$z = \frac{m}{\rho A} + A\cos\omega t + B\sin\omega t, \quad \text{with } \omega^2 = \frac{\rho A g}{m} \tag{9.47}$$

As in the case of the cantilever, the particular integral of the equation corresponds to the static equilibrium solution (when the buoy is floating just sufficiently immersed that the upthrust exerted by the water equals the weight of the buoy), and the complementary function describes oscillations of the buoy about this position. In this case the buoy oscillates with constant amplitude and a frequency that decreases as the mass of the buoy increases and increases as the density of the water and/or the cross-sectional area of the buoy increases.

9.10.2 Free oscillations of damped elastic systems

Equations (9.42), (9.45) and (9.47) all describe oscillations of constant amplitude. In reality, in all the situations described, a vibrating cantilever, an oscillating pendulum and a bobbing buoy, experience leads us to expect that the oscillations or vibrations are of decreasing amplitude, so that the motion eventually decays away and the system finally comes to rest in its static equilibrium position. This suggests that the mathematical models of the situation that we constructed in Section 9.10.1, and which are represented by (9.41), (9.44) and (9.46), are inadequate in some way.

What has been ignored in each case is the effect of dissipation of energy. Suppose, in the case of the pendulum, the motion of the pendulum were opposed by air resistance. The work which the pendulum does against the air resistance represents a continuous loss of energy, as a result of which the amplitude of oscillation of the pendulum decreases until it finally comes to rest. The situation is illustrated in Figure 9.24. The forces acting on the pendulum mass are gravity, air resistance (which opposes motion) and the tension in the pendulum arm. Resolving these forces perpendicular to the pendulum arm results in the equation of motion.

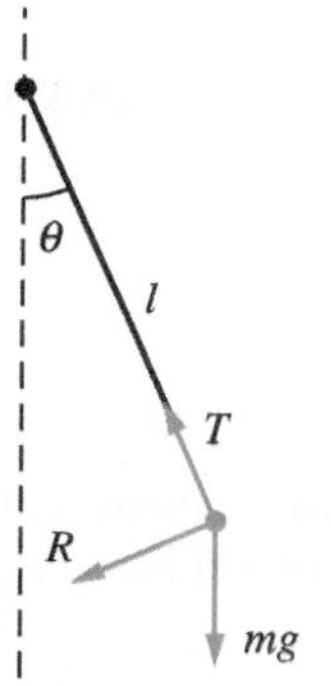

Figure 9.24
A pendulum with air resistance.

$$ml\frac{d^2\theta}{dt^2} = -R - mg\sin\theta$$

If the air resistance is assumed to be proportional to the speed of the pendulum mass then, since the speed of the mass is $l(d\theta/dt)$, we have

$$R = kl\frac{d\theta}{dt}$$

Hence

$$ml\frac{d^2\theta}{dt^2} = -kl\frac{d\theta}{dt} - mg\sin\theta$$

or, assuming θ is small so that $\sin\theta \approx \theta$ and rearranging the terms,

$$\frac{d^2\theta}{dt^2} + \frac{k}{m}\frac{d\theta}{dt} + \frac{g}{l}\theta = 0 \tag{9.48}$$

This is a second-order linear constant-coefficient differential equation. It should be noted that the assumption that air resistance is proportional to speed is not the only possible assumption. For very slow-moving objects air resistance may well be more nearly constant, while for very fast-moving objects air resistance is usually taken to be proportional to the square of speed, which is a much better description of reality for fast-moving objects. For objects moving at modest speeds, however, the assumption that air resistance is proportional to speed is commonly adopted.

In the case of the cantilever and the buoy, also, we might assume that there is a resistance to motion that is proportional to the speed of motion. Again these are not the only possible assumptions, but they are ones that, under appropriate circumstances, are reasonable. The guiding principle when modelling physical systems such as these is to identify the physical source of the resistance and try to describe its behaviour. This is not a problem of mathematics but rather one of mathematical modelling, in which engineers must use their knowledge of physics and engineering as well as of mathematics in order to arrive at an appropriate mathematical description of reality.

Constructing models of a whole host of other engineering situations also leads to equations similar to (9.48). Basically, any situation in which the motion of some mass is caused by the sum of a force opposing displacement that is proportional to the displacement from some fixed position and a force that resists motion and is proportional to the speed of motion gives rise to an equation of the form

$$m\frac{\mathrm{d}^2x}{\mathrm{d}t^2} = -\mu\frac{\mathrm{d}x}{\mathrm{d}t} - \lambda x$$

that is,

$$\frac{\mathrm{d}^2x}{\mathrm{d}t^2} + p\frac{\mathrm{d}x}{\mathrm{d}t} + qx = 0 \qquad \textbf{(9.49)}$$

where

$$p = \frac{\mu}{m} \quad \text{and} \quad q = \frac{\lambda}{m}$$

We must have $p > 0$ and $q > 0$, because the two forces oppose displacement and motion respectively. We know from Section 9.10.1 that the solution of (9.49) is

$$x(t) = A\mathrm{e}^{m_1 t} + B\mathrm{e}^{m_2 t}$$

where m_1 and m_2 are the roots of the characteristic equation

$$m^2 + pm + q = 0$$

For reasons that will become apparent, it is convenient to put (9.49) into the standard form

$$\frac{\mathrm{d}^2x}{\mathrm{d}t^2} + 2\zeta\omega\frac{\mathrm{d}x}{\mathrm{d}t} + \omega^2 x = 0 \qquad \textbf{(9.50)}$$

where, because $p, q > 0$, so are ζ and ω. The characteristic equation is then $m^2 + 2\zeta\omega m + \omega^2 = 0$, whose roots are

$$m = \begin{cases} -\zeta\omega \pm (\zeta^2 - 1)^{1/2}\omega & (\zeta > 1) \\ -\omega \text{ (twice)} & (\zeta = 1) \\ -\zeta\omega \pm \mathrm{j}(1 - \zeta^2)^{1/2}\omega & (0 < \zeta < 1) \end{cases}$$

and the solution of (9.50) is therefore

$$x = A\exp\{-[\zeta - (\zeta^2 - 1)^{1/2}]\omega t\} + B\exp\{-[\zeta + (\zeta^2 - 1)^{1/2}]\omega t\} \quad (\zeta > 1) \qquad \textbf{(9.51a)}$$

$$x = e^{-\omega t}(At + B) \quad (\zeta = 1) \qquad \textbf{(9.51b)}$$

$$x = e^{-\zeta\omega t}\{A\cos[(1 - \zeta^2)^{1/2}\omega t] + B\sin[(1 - \zeta^2)^{1/2}\omega t]\} \quad (0 < \zeta < 1) \qquad \textbf{(9.51c)}$$

The first point to note about these solutions is that, since $\zeta > 0$ and $\omega > 0$, we have $x \to 0$ as $t \to \infty$ in all cases. Figure 9.25 shows the typical form of the solution (9.51) for various values of ζ. Variation of ω will only change the scale along the horizontal axis. For $0 < \zeta < 1$ the solution takes an oscillatory form with decaying amplitude. For $\zeta > 1$ the solution has the form of an exponential decay. The larger ζ, the slower is the final decay, since the exponential coefficient $\zeta - (\zeta^2 - 1)^{1/2} \to 0$ as $\zeta \to \infty$. In Figure 9.25 the envelopes of the oscillatory solutions are shown as broken lines. If the envelope of the oscillatory decay is compared with the solutions for $\zeta > 1$ it is quickly apparent that the most rapid decay is when $\zeta = 1$. It is now apparent why we chose to take (9.50) as the standard form for the description of second-order damped systems. The parameter ω is the **natural frequency** of the system, that is, the frequency with which it would oscillate in the absence of damping, and the parameter ζ is the **damping parameter** of the system. When $\zeta = 1$, the decay of the motion of the system to its equilibrium state is as fast as is possible. For this reason, $\zeta = 1$ is referred to as **critical damping**. When $\zeta < 1$, the motion described by the equation decays to its equilibrium

Figure 9.25
The motion of damped second-order systems.

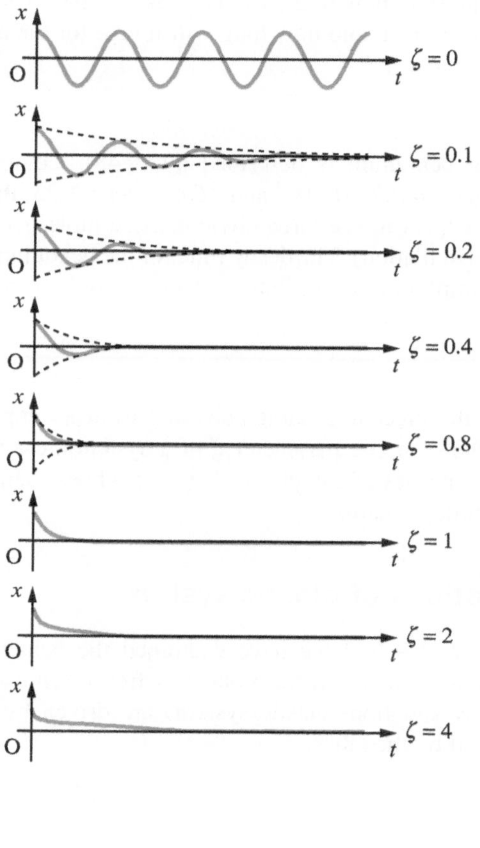

state in an oscillatory manner, passing through the equilibrium position on a number of occasions before coming to rest. For this reason, the motion is described as **under-damped**. When $\zeta > 1$, the motion described by the equation decays to the equilibrium position in a direct manner, but less rapidly than for a critically damped system. In this case the motion is described as **over-damped**.

For the under-damped case an engineering rule of thumb that is commonly used is that when $\zeta = 0.3$ the system shows three *discernible* overshoots before settling down. That is not to say that there are only three overshoots – on the contrary, there are an infinite number – but by the fourth and subsequent overshoots the amplitude of the oscillations has decayed to less than 2% of the initial amplitude. When $\zeta = 0.5$, there are two discernible overshoots (the third and subsequent ones have amplitude less than $\frac{1}{2}$% of initial); and when $\zeta = 0.7$, there is only one significant overshoot.

Another rule of thumb relates to the envelope containing the response. The response is contained within an envelope defined by the function $e^{-\zeta\omega t}$. Now $e^{-3} = 0.0498$ and $e^{-4.5} = 0.0111$; so when $\zeta\omega t = 3$, the amplitude of the response will have fallen to approximately 5% of its original amplitude; and when $\zeta\omega t = 4.5$, it will have fallen to roughly 1% of its original amplitude. For this reason, $t = 1/\zeta\omega$ is called the **decay time** of the system, and engineers use the rule of thumb that response falls to 5% in three decay times and 1% in four and a half decay times.

Example 9.46 A pendulum of mass 4 kg, length 2 m and an air resistance coefficient of $5\ \mathrm{N\,s\,m^{-1}}$ is released from an initial position in which it makes an angle of 20° with the vertical. Assuming that this angle is small enough for the small-angle approximation to be made in the equation of motion, how many oscillations will be obviously observable before the pendulum comes to rest, and how long will it take for the amplitude of the motion to have fallen to less than 1°?

Solution The motion of the pendulum is described by (9.48). Comparing this with (9.50), we see that $\omega = (g/l)^{1/2} = 2.215\ \mathrm{rad\,s^{-1}}$ and $2\zeta\omega = k/m = 1.25$; that is, $\zeta = 0.282$. Hence, since $\zeta \approx 0.3$, we expect to see three obvious discernible overshoots (one and a half complete cycles of oscillation). The decay time for the pendulum is $1/\zeta\omega = 2m/k = 1.6$ s, so we expect the amplitude of oscillation of the pendulum to fall to 5% of its initial amplitude in 4.8 s.

It is evident from the preceding paragraphs and from Example 9.46 that the natural frequency ω and the damping parameter ζ of a system are a very convenient way of summarizing the properties of any physical system whose oscillations are described by a damped second-order equation.

9.10.3 Forced oscillations of elastic systems

In Sections 9.10.1 and 9.10.2 we have examined the behaviour of elastic systems undergoing oscillations in which the system is free to choose its own frequency of oscillation. In many situations elastic systems are driven by some external force at a frequency imposed by the latter.

A familiar example of such a situation is the vibration of lamp posts in strong winds. The lightweight tubular metal lamp posts that have frequently been installed by highway authorities since the 1960s are a form of cantilever. The vertical post is rigidly mounted in the ground, and carries at its top a lamp apparatus. The lamp is effectively a concentrated mass, though it would probably not be sufficiently massive to allow the assumption, which we made for the cantilevers treated in Sections 9.10.1 and 9.10.2, that the mass of the post is small compared with the mass of the lamp. Nonetheless, if the top of the lamp post were to be pulled to one side and released, the post would certainly vibrate. The frequency of that vibration would be a function of the stiffness (restoring force per unit lateral tip displacement) of the lamp post and the mass of both the post and the lamp apparatus carried at the top. The stiffer the lamp post, the higher would be the frequency of vibration. The more massive the post and the lamp apparatus, the lower the frequency.

When the wind blows past the lamp post, aerodynamic effects (known as vortex shedding) result in an oscillating side-force on the lamp post. The frequency of this side-force is a function of the wind speed and the diameter of the lamp post. There is no reason why the frequency of oscillation of the wind-induced side-force should coincide with the frequency of the oscillations that result if the top of the lamp post is displaced sideways and released to vibrate freely. Under the influence of the oscillating side-force, such lamp posts commonly vibrate from side to side in time with the oscillating side-force. As the wind speed changes, so the frequency of the side-force and therefore of the lamp post's vibrations changes. Other types of lamp post, notably the reinforced concrete type and the older cast-iron lamp posts, do not seem to exhibit this behaviour. This can be explained in terms of their greater stiffness, as we shall see later.

Oscillations of elastic systems in which the system is free to adopt its own natural frequency of vibration are called **free vibrations**, while those caused by oscillating external forces (and in which the system must vibrate at the frequency of the external forcing) are called **forced vibrations**.

Other large structures can also be forced to oscillate by the wind blowing past them, just like lamp posts. Large modern factory chimneys made of steel or aluminium sections bolted together and stayed by wires exhibit this type of vibration, as do the suspension cables and hangers of suspension bridges and the overhead power transmission lines of electricity grid systems. The legs of offshore oil rigs can be forced to vibrate by ocean currents and waves. The wings of an aircraft (which, being mounted rigidly in the fuselage of the aircraft, are also a form of cantilever) may vibrate under aerodynamic loads, particularly from atmospheric turbulence. Large pieces of static industrial machinery are usually bolted down to the ground. If such fastening is subjected to a large load, it will usually give a little, so the attachment of the machinery to the floor must be considered as elastic. If the machinery, when in operation, produces an internal side-load (such as an out-of-balance rotor would produce) then the machinery is seen to rock from side to side on its mountings at the frequency of the internally generated side-loading. This effect can often be observed in the rocking vibrations of a car engine when it is idling in a stationary car. It is well known that bodies of men or women marching are ordered to break step when passing over bridges. If they did not, the regular footfalls of the whole group would create a periodic force on the bridge. The dangers of such regular forces will become apparent in our analysis. All these situations are similar in nature to the forced vibrations of the lamp post under the influence of the wind. In most of them the oscillations induced by the side-force are potentially

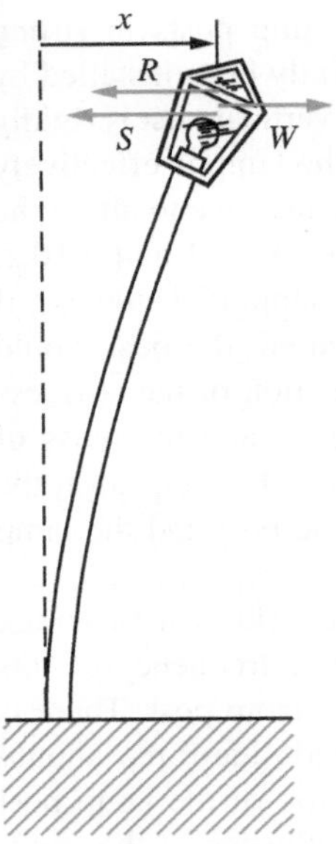

Figure 9.26
The forces acting on a vibrating lamp post.

disastrous, and must be understood by the engineer so that engineering artefacts may be designed to avoid the destructive effects of forced vibrations.

A simple model of the vibrations of a lamp post can be constructed as shown in Figure 9.26. The lamp apparatus, of mass m, is displaced from its equilibrium position by a distance x. The structure of the cantilever results in a restoring force S and air resistance in a restoring force R. The wind load (which, remember, is not a force in the direction of the wind but rather an oscillatory side-force) is W. If the displacement x is small and the displacement velocity is not too great then we may reasonably assume

$$S = kx \quad \text{and} \quad R = \lambda \frac{dx}{dt}$$

Making the somewhat unrealistic assumption that the mass of the lamp post itself is small compared with the mass of the lamp apparatus, the equation of motion of the lamp is seen to be

$$m\frac{d^2x}{dt^2} = -\lambda \frac{dx}{dt} - kx + W$$

The wind-induced force W is oscillatory, so we shall assume that it is of the form

$$W = W_0 \cos \Omega t$$

Hence the equation of motion becomes

$$m\frac{d^2x}{dt^2} + \lambda \frac{dx}{dt} + kx = W_0 \cos \Omega t \tag{9.52}$$

which is a second-order linear nonhomogeneous constant-coefficient differential equation. In order to facilitate the interpretation of the result, we shall replace (9.52) with the equivalent equation

$$\frac{d^2x}{dt^2} + 2\zeta\omega \frac{dx}{dt} + \omega^2 x = F \cos \Omega t \tag{9.53}$$

The particular integral for (9.53) is obtained by assuming the form $A \cos \Omega t + B \sin \Omega t$, and is found to be

$$\frac{(\omega^2 - \Omega^2)F \cos \Omega t + 2\zeta\omega\Omega F \sin \Omega t}{(\omega^2 - \Omega^2)^2 + 4\zeta^2\omega^2\Omega^2} \tag{9.54a}$$

or equivalently

$$\frac{F}{[(\omega^2 - \Omega^2)^2 + 4\zeta^2\omega^2\Omega^2]^{1/2}} \cos (\Omega t - \delta) \tag{9.54b}$$

where

$$\delta = \tan^{-1}\left(\frac{2\zeta\omega\Omega}{\omega^2 - \Omega^2}\right)$$

The complementary function is of course the solution of the homogeneous equivalent of (9.52), which is just (9.50). The complementary function is therefore given by (9.51). The motion of a damped second-order system in response to forcing by a force

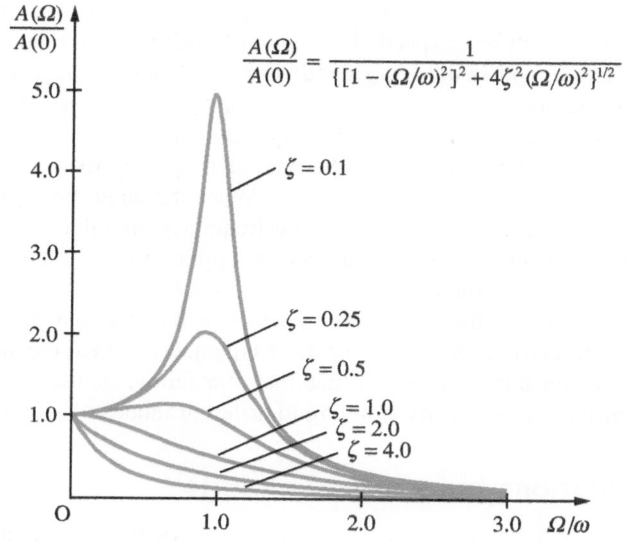

Figure 9.27
The response of damped second-order systems to sinusoidal forcing.

$F\cos\Omega t$ is therefore the sum of (9.51) and (9.54a) or (9.54b). In Section 9.10.2 we saw that (9.51) is, for positive ζ, always a decaying function of time. The complementary function for (9.53) therefore represents a motion that decays to nothing with time, and is therefore called a **transient solution**. The particular integral, on the other hand, does not decay, but continues at a steady amplitude for as long as the forcing remains. The long-term response of a damped second-order system to forcing by a force $F\cos\Omega t$ is therefore to oscillate at the forcing frequency Ω with amplitude

$$A(\Omega) = \frac{1}{[(\omega^2 - \Omega^2)^2 + 4\zeta^2\omega^2\Omega^2]^{1/2}} \quad \textbf{(9.55)}$$

times the amplitude of the forcing term. This is called the **steady-state response** of the system. Evidently, the amplitude of the steady-state response changes as the frequency Ω of the forcing changes. In Figure 9.27 the form of the response amplitude $A(\Omega)$ as a function of Ω is shown for a range of values of ζ. Obviously, the characteristics of the response of a damped second-order system to forcing depend crucially on the damping. For lightly damped systems (ζ near to 0) the response has a definite maximum near to ω, the natural frequency of the system. For more heavily damped systems the peak response is smaller, and for large enough ζ the peak disappears altogether.

The significance of this is that systems subjected to an oscillatory external force at a frequency near to the natural frequency of the system will, unless they are sufficiently heavily damped, respond with large-amplitude motion. This phenomenon is known as **resonance**. Resonance can cause catastrophic failure of the structure of a system. The history of engineering endeavour contains many examples of structures that have failed because they have been subjected to some external exciting force with a frequency near to one of the natural frequencies of vibration of the structure. Perhaps the most famous example of such a failure is the collapse in 1941 of the suspension bridge at Tacoma Narrows in the USA. This failure, due to wind-induced oscillations, was recorded on film and provides a salutary lesson for all engineers. Similar forces have destroyed factory chimneys, power transmission lines and aircraft.

It should now be obvious why the amplitude of oscillation of the tubular metal lamp post varies with wind speed. The natural frequency of the lamp post is determined by its structure, and is therefore fixed. The frequency of the vortex shedding, and so of the oscillatory side-force, is directly proportional to the wind speed. Hence, as the wind speed increases, so does the frequency of external forcing of the lamp post. As the forcing frequency approaches the natural frequency of the lamp post, the amplitude of the lamp post's vibrations increases. When the wind speed increases sufficiently, the forcing frequency exceeds the natural frequency, and the amplitude of the oscillations decreases again. The same explanation applies to the Tacoma Narrows bridge. The bridge, once constructed, stood for some months without serious difficulty. The failure was the result of the first storm in which wind speeds rose sufficiently to excite the bridge structure at one of its natural frequencies. (Since the structure of a suspension bridge is much more complex than that of a simple cantilever, such a bridge has many natural frequencies, corresponding to different modes of vibration.)

9.10.4 Oscillations in electrical circuits

In Section 9.2.4 we analysed a simple electrical circuit composed of a resistor, a capacitor and an inductor. In that case we considered what happened when a switch was thrown in a circuit containing a d.c. voltage source. If an alternating voltage signal is applied to a similar circuit the equation governing the resulting oscillations also turns out to be a second-order linear differential equation.

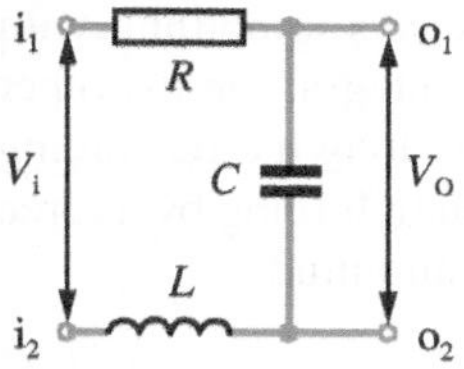

Figure 9.28
An *LCR* electrical circuit.

Consider the circuit shown in Figure 9.28. Suppose a voltage V_i is applied across the input terminals i_1 and i_2. The voltage drop across the inductor is $L(di/dt)$, that across the capacitor is $\int(i/C)dt$ and that across the resistor is Ri. Kirchhoff's laws (or the principle of conservation of charge) tell us that the current in each component must be the same. The voltage across the output terminals o_1 and o_2 is $\int(i/C)dt = V_o$. Hence we have

$$L\frac{di}{dt} + Ri + \frac{1}{C}\int i\,dt = V_i$$

with

$$V_o = \frac{1}{C}\int i\,dt$$

That is,

$$LC\frac{d^2V_o}{dt^2} + RC\frac{dV_o}{dt} + V_o = V_i$$

or

$$\frac{d^2V_o}{dt^2} + \frac{R}{L}\frac{dV_o}{dt} + \frac{V_o}{LC} = \frac{V_i}{LC} \tag{9.56}$$

This is a second-order linear nonhomogeneous constant-coefficient differential equation. If the signal V_i is of the form $V\cos\Omega t$ then we essentially have forced oscillations of a second-order system again. If we write

$$\omega^2 = \frac{1}{LC}, \quad 2\zeta\omega = \frac{R}{L} \quad \text{and} \quad F = \frac{V}{LC}$$

then (9.56) takes the standard form of (9.53), and we can infer that the voltage V_0 will be sinusoidal with amplitude

$$\frac{A(\Omega)}{LC}V$$

where

$$A(\Omega) = \frac{1}{[(\omega^2 - \Omega^2)^2 + 4\zeta^2\omega^2\Omega^2]^{1/2}}$$

Thus when a sinusoidal voltage waveform is applied to the input terminals of the circuit, the voltage appearing at the output terminals is also a sinusoidal waveform, but one whose amplitude, relative to the input waveform amplitude, depends on the frequency of the input. A circuit that has this property is of course called a **filter**.

The form of $A(\Omega)$ will depend on ω and ζ, which in turn are determined by the values of L, R and C. The latter could be chosen so that ζ is small. In that case the circuit provides a large output when the input frequency Ω is near some frequency ω (which is determined by the choice of L and C) and a smaller output otherwise. This is a **tuned circuit** or a **bandpass filter**. If L, R and C are chosen so that ζ is larger (say near unity) then the circuit provides a larger output for small Ω and a smaller output for larger Ω. Such a circuit is a **low-pass filter**.

In this section, we have seen how problems in two very different areas of engineering – one mechanical and the other electrical – both give rise to very similar equations. Our knowledge of the form of the solutions of the equation is applicable to either area. This is a good example of the unifying properties of mathematics in engineering science. There are many other applications of the theory of the solution of second-order linear constant-coefficient differential equations in engineering.

It is also worth commenting here that filters of the type that we have described in this section are called **passive filters** since they use only inductors, resistors and capacitors – components that are referred to as **passive components**. Modern practice in electrical engineering involves the use of **active components** such as operational amplifiers in filter design, such filters being known as **active filters**. The analysis of the operation of active filters is more complex than that of passive filters. While, for many applications, active filters have displaced passive filters in modern practice, there are also many applications in which passive filters remain the norm.

9.10.5 Exercises

66 Find the damping parameters and natural frequencies of the systems governed by the following second-order linear constant-coefficient differential equations:

(a) $\dfrac{d^2x}{dt^2} + 6\dfrac{dx}{dt} + 9x = 0$

(b) $\dfrac{d^2x}{dt^2} + 4\dfrac{dx}{dt} + 7x = 0$

67 Determine the values of the appropriate parameters needed to give the systems governed by the following second-order linear constant-coefficient differential equations the damping parameters and natural frequencies stated:

(a) $\dfrac{d^2x}{dt^2} + 2a\dfrac{dx}{dt} + bx = 0,\quad \zeta = 0.5,\quad \omega = 2$

(b) $\dfrac{d^2x}{dt^2} + p\dfrac{dx}{dt} + qx = 0,\quad \zeta = 1.4,\quad \omega = 0.5$

(c) $\dfrac{d^2x}{dt^2} + \beta\dfrac{dx}{dt} + \gamma x = 0,\quad \zeta = 1,\quad \omega = 1.1$

68 Find the damping parameters and natural frequencies of the systems governed by the following second-order linear constant-coefficient differential equations:

(a) $\dfrac{d^2x}{dt^2} + 2a\dfrac{dx}{dt} + 16p^2x = 0$

(b) $2\dfrac{d^2x}{dt^2} + 14\dfrac{dx}{dt} + \dfrac{1}{\alpha}x = 0$

(c) $2.41\dfrac{d^2x}{dt^2} + 1.02\dfrac{dx}{dt} + 7.63x = 0$

(d) $\dfrac{1}{\eta}\dfrac{d^2x}{dt^2} + 40\dfrac{dx}{dt} + 25\eta x = 0$

(e) $1.88\dfrac{d^2x}{dt^2} + 4.71\dfrac{dx}{dt} + 0.48x = 0$

69 Determine the values of the appropriate parameters needed to give the systems governed by the following second-order linear constant-coefficient differential equations the damping parameters and natural frequencies stated:

(a) $\dfrac{d^2x}{dt^2} + \alpha\dfrac{dx}{dt} + \beta x = 0, \quad \zeta = 0.5, \quad \omega = \pi$

(b) $\dfrac{d^2x}{dt^2} + a\dfrac{dx}{dt} + bx = 0, \quad \zeta = 0.1, \quad \omega = 2\pi$

(c) $4\dfrac{d^2x}{dt^2} + q\dfrac{dx}{dt} + rx = 0, \quad \zeta = 1, \quad \omega = 1$

(d) $a\dfrac{d^2x}{dt^2} + b\dfrac{dx}{dt} + 14x = 0, \quad \zeta = 2, \quad \omega = 2\pi$

70 The function $A(\Omega)$ is as given by (9.55) and shown in Figure 9.27. Show that $A(\Omega)$ has a simple maximum point when $\zeta < \sqrt{\tfrac{1}{2}}$. Let the value of Ω for which this maximum occurs be Ω_{max}. Find Ω_{max} as a function of ζ and ω, and also find $A(\Omega_{max})$.

For $\zeta > \sqrt{\tfrac{1}{2}}$, $A(\Omega)$ has no maximum, but does have a single point of inflection. Show, by consideration of Figure 9.27, that $|dA/d\Omega|$ is a maximum at the point of inflection. Let Ω_c be the value of Ω for which the point of inflection occurs. Show that Ω_c satisfies the equation

$$3\Omega^6 + 5\beta\omega^2\Omega^4 + (4\beta^2 - 3)\omega^4\Omega^2 - \beta\omega^6 = 0$$

where $\beta = 2\zeta^2 - 1$. Hence show that for $\zeta = \sqrt{\tfrac{1}{2}}$ the greatest value of $|dA/d\Omega|$ occurs when $\Omega = \omega$ and is $1/(\sqrt{2}\omega^3)$. Also find the greatest values of $|dA/d\Omega|$ when $\zeta = \sqrt{(\tfrac{1}{2} + \tfrac{1}{6}\sqrt{3})}$ and when $\zeta = 1$.

Show that $|d^2A(0)/d\Omega^2|$ is minimized when $\zeta = \sqrt{\tfrac{1}{2}}$. The two values of ζ that minimize the maxima of $|dA/d\Omega|$ and $|d^2A(0)/d\Omega^2|$ respectively are important, particularly in control theory, since, in different senses, they maximize the flatness of the response function $A(\Omega)$.

71 An underwater sensor is mounted below the keel of the fast patrol boat shown in Figure 9.29. The supporting bracket is of cylindrical cross-section (diameter 0.04 m), and so is subject to an oscillating side-force due to vortex shedding. The bracket is of negligible mass compared with the sensor itself, which has a mass of 4 kg. The bracket has a tip displacement stiffness of 25 000 N m^{-1}. The frequency of the oscillating side-force is SU/d, where U is the speed of the vessel through the water, d is the diameter of the supporting bracket and S is the Strouhal number for vortex shedding from a circular cylinder. S has the value 0.20 approximately. At what speed will the frequency of the side-force coincide with the natural frequency of the sensor and mounting?

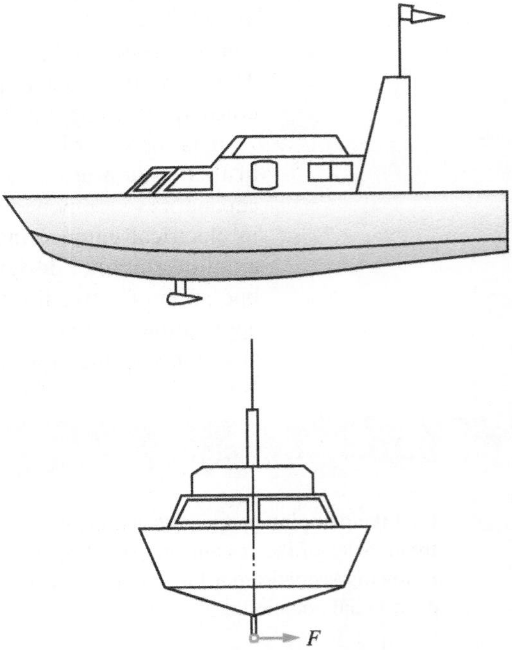

Figure 9.29 An underwater sensor mounting.

72 The piece of machinery shown in Figure 9.30 is mounted on a solid foundation in such a way that the mounting may be characterized as a rigid pivot and two stiff springs as shown. A damper is

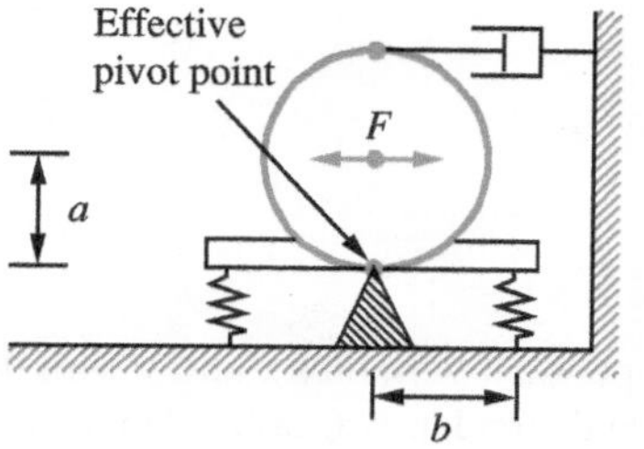

Figure 9.30 A compliantly mounted piece of machinery.

connected between the machine and an adjacent strong point. The mass of the machine is 500 kg, the length $a = 1$ m, the length $b = 1.2$ m and the spring stiffness is $8000\,\text{N m}^{-1}$. The moment of inertia of the machine about the pivot point is $2ma^2$. The machine generates internally a side-force F that may be approximated as $F_0 \cos 2\pi ft$. As the machine runs up to speed, the frequency f increases from 0 to 6 Hz. What is the minimum damper coefficient that will prevent the machine from vibrating with any amplitude greater than twice its zero-frequency amplitude $A(0)$ during a run-up?

73 Figure 9.31 shows a radio tuner circuit. Show that the natural frequency and damping parameters of the circuit are $1/\sqrt{(LC)}$ and

$$\frac{1}{2}\left(\frac{L}{C}\right)^{1/2}\left(\frac{1}{R_1}+\frac{1}{R_2}\right)$$

respectively. If $R_1 = 300\,\Omega$ and $R_2 = 50\,\Omega$ what value should L have, and over what range should C be adjustable in order that the circuit have a damping factor of $\zeta = 0.1$ and can be tuned to the medium waveband (505–1605 kHz)?

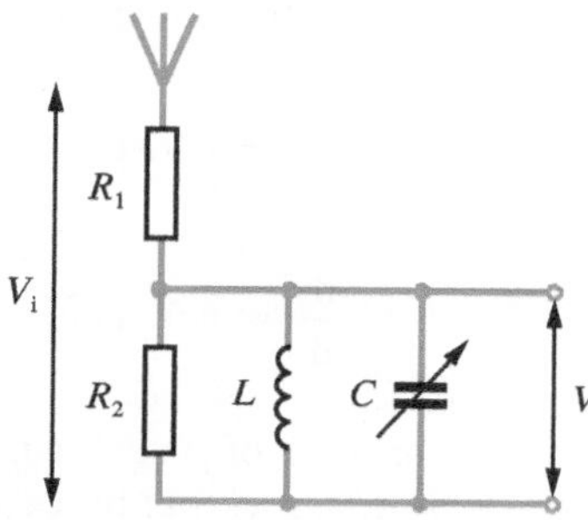

Figure 9.31 A radio tuner circuit.

9.11 Numerical solution of second- and higher-order differential equations

Obviously, the classes of second- and higher-order differential equations that can be solved analytically, while representing an important subset of the totality of such equations, are relatively restricted. Just as for first-order equations, those for which no analytical solution exists can still be solved by numerical means. The numerical solution of second- and higher-order equations does not, in fact, need any significant new mathematical theory or technique.

9.11.1 Numerical solution of coupled first-order equations

In Section 9.6 we met Euler's method for the numerical solution of equations of the form

$$\frac{\mathrm{d}x}{\mathrm{d}t} = f(t, x)$$

that is, first-order differential equations involving a single dependent variable and a single independent variable. In Section 9.3 we noted that it was possible to have sets of coupled first-order equations, each involving the same independent variable but with more than one dependent variable. An example of this type of equation set is

$$\frac{dx}{dt} = x - y^2 + xt \quad \textbf{(9.57a)}$$

$$\frac{dy}{dt} = 2x^2 + xy - t \quad \textbf{(9.57b)}$$

This is a pair of differential equations in the dependent variables x and y with the independent variable t. The derivative of each of the dependent variables depends not only on itself and on the independent variable t, but also on the other dependent variable. Neither of the equations can be solved in isolation or independently of the other – both must be solved simultaneously, or side by side. A pair of coupled differential equations such as (9.57) may be characterized as

$$\frac{dx}{dt} = f_1(t, x, y) \quad \textbf{(9.58a)}$$

$$\frac{dy}{dt} = f_2(t, x, y) \quad \textbf{(9.58b)}$$

For a set of p such equations it is convenient to denote the dependent variables not by $x, y, z, \ldots$ but by $x_1, x_2, x_3, \ldots, x_p$ and to denote the set of equations by

$$\frac{dx_i}{dt} = f_i(t, x_1, x_2, \ldots, x_p) \quad (i = 1, 2, \ldots, p)$$

or equivalently, using vector notation,

$$\frac{d}{dt}[\mathbf{x}] = \boldsymbol{f}(t, \mathbf{x})$$

where $\mathbf{x}(t)$ is a vector function of t given by

$$\mathbf{x}(t) = [x_1(t) \quad x_2(t) \quad \ldots \quad x_p(t)]^T$$

$\boldsymbol{f}(t, \mathbf{x})$ is a vector-valued function of the scalar variable t and the vector variable $\mathbf{x}$.

Euler's method for the solution of a single differential equation takes the form

$$X_{n+1} = X_n + hf(t_n, X_n)$$

If we were to try to apply this method to (9.58a), we should obtain

$$X_{n+1} = X_n + hf_1(t_n, X_n, Y_n)$$

In other words, the value of X_{n+1} depends not only on t_n and X_n but also on Y_n. In the same way, we would obtain

$$Y_{n+1} = Y_n + hf_2(t_n, X_n, Y_n)$$

for Y_{n+1}. In practice, this means that to solve two coupled differential equations, we must advance the solution of both equations simultaneously in the manner shown in Example 9.47.

Example 9.47 Find the value of $X(1.4)$ satisfying the following initial-value problem:

$$\frac{dx}{dt} = x - y^2 + xt, \quad x(1) = 0.5$$

$$\frac{dy}{dt} = 2x^2 + xy - t, \quad y(1) = 1.2$$

using Euler's method with time step $h = 0.1$.

Solution The right-hand sides of the two equations will be denoted by $f_1(t, x, y)$ and $f_2(t, x, y)$ respectively, so

$$f_1(t, x, y) = x - y^2 + xt \quad \text{and} \quad f_2(t, x, y) = 2x^2 + xy - t$$

The initial condition is imposed at $t = 1$, so t_n will denote $1 + nh$, X_n will denote $X(1 + nh)$, and Y_n will denote $Y(1 + nh)$. Then we have

$$\begin{aligned} X_1 &= x_0 + hf_1(t_0, x_0, y_0) & Y_1 &= y_0 + hf_2(t_0, x_0, y_0) \\ &= 0.5 + 0.1f_1(1, 0.5, 1.2) & &= 1.2 + 0.1f_2(1, 0.5, 1.2) \\ &= 0.4560 & &= 1.2100 \end{aligned}$$

for the first step. The next step is therefore

$$\begin{aligned} X_2 &= X_1 + hf_1(t_1, X_1, Y_1) & Y_2 &= Y_1 + hf_2(t_1, X_1, Y_1) \\ &= 0.4560 & &= 1.2100 \\ &\quad + 0.1f_1(1.1, 0.4560, 1.2100) & &\quad + 0.1f_2(1.1, 0.4560, 1.2100) \\ &= 0.4054 & &= 1.1968 \end{aligned}$$

and the third step is

$$\begin{aligned} X_3 &= 0.4054 & Y_3 &= 1.1968 \\ &\quad + 0.1f_1(1.2, 0.4054, 1.1968) & &\quad + 0.1f_2(1.2, 0.4054, 1.1968) \\ &= 0.3513 & &= 1.1581 \end{aligned}$$

Finally, we obtain

$$\begin{aligned} X_4 &= 0.3513 + 0.1f_1(1.3, 0.3513, 1.1581) \\ &= 0.2980 \end{aligned}$$

Hence we have $X(1.4) = 0.2980$.

It should be obvious from Example 9.47 that the main drawback of extending Euler's method to sets of differential equations is the additional labour and tedium of the computations. Intrinsically, the computations are no more difficult, merely much more laborious – a prime example of a problem ripe for computerization.

9.11.2 State-space representation of higher-order systems

The solution of differential equation initial-value problems of order greater than one can be reduced to the solution of a set of first-order differential equations. This is achieved by a simple transformation, illustrated by Example 9.48.

Example 9.48 The initial-value problem

$$\frac{d^2x}{dt^2} + x^2t\frac{dx}{dt} - xt^2 = \tfrac{1}{2}t^2, \quad x(0) = 1.2, \quad \frac{dx}{dt}(0) = 0.8$$

can be transformed into two coupled first-order differential equations by introducing an additional variable

$$y = \frac{dx}{dt}$$

With this definition, we have

$$\frac{d^2x}{dt^2} = \frac{dy}{dt}$$

and so the differential equation becomes

$$\frac{dy}{dt} + x^2ty - xt^2 = \tfrac{1}{2}t^2$$

Thus the original differential equation can be replaced by a pair of coupled first-order differential equations, together with initial conditions:

$$\frac{dx}{dt} = y, \quad x(0) = 1.2$$

$$\frac{dy}{dt} = -x^2ty + xt^2 + \tfrac{1}{2}t^2, \quad y(0) = 0.8$$

This process can be extended to transform a pth-order initial-value problem into a set of p first-order equations, each with an initial condition. Once the original equation has been transformed in this way, its solution by numerical methods is just the same as if it had been a set of coupled equations in the first place.

Example 9.49 Find the value of $X(0.2)$ satisfying the initial-value problem

$$\frac{d^3x}{dt^3} + xt\frac{d^2x}{dt^2} + t\frac{dx}{dt} - t^2x = 0, \quad x(0) = 1, \quad \frac{dx}{dt}(0) = 0.5, \quad \frac{d^2x}{dt^2}(0) = -0.2$$

using Euler's method with step size $h = 0.05$.

Solution Since this is a third-order equation, we need to introduce two new variables:

$$y = \frac{dx}{dt} \quad \text{and} \quad z = \frac{dy}{dt} = \frac{d^2x}{dt^2}$$

Then the equation is transformed into a set of three first-order differential equations

$$\frac{dx}{dt} = y \qquad x(0) = 1$$

$$\frac{dy}{dt} = z \qquad y(0) = 0.5$$

$$\frac{dz}{dt} = -xtz - ty + t^2x \quad z(0) = -0.2$$

Applied to the set of differential equations

$$\frac{dx}{dt} = f_1(t, x, y, z)$$

$$\frac{dy}{dt} = f_2(t, x, y, z)$$

$$\frac{dz}{dt} = f_3(t, x, y, z)$$

the Euler scheme is of the form

$$X_{n+1} = X_n + hf_1(t_n, X_n, Y_n, Z_n)$$

$$Y_{n+1} = Y_n + hf_2(t_n, X_n, Y_n, Z_n)$$

$$Z_{n+1} = Z_n + hf_3(t_n, X_n, Y_n, Z_n)$$

In this case, therefore, we have

$$X_0 = x_0 = 1$$

$$Y_0 = y_0 = 0.5$$

$$Z_0 = z_0 = -0.2$$

$$f_1(t_0, X_0, Y_0, Z_0) = Y_0 = 0.5000$$

$$f_2(t_0, X_0, Y_0, Z_0) = Z_0 = -0.2000$$

$$\begin{aligned} f_3(t_0, X_0, Y_0, Z_0) &= -X_0t_0Z_0 - t_0Y_0 + t_0^2X_0 \\ &= -1.0000 \times 0 \times (-0.2000) - 0 \times 0.5000 + 0^2 \times 1.0000 \\ &= 0.0000 \end{aligned}$$

$$X_1 = 1.0000 + 0.05 \times 0.5000 = 1.0250$$

$$Y_1 = 0.5000 + 0.05 \times (-0.2000) = 0.4900$$

$$Z_1 = -0.2000 + 0.05 \times 0.0000 = -0.2000$$

$$f_1(t_1, X_1, Y_1, Z_1) = Y_1 = 0.4900$$

$$f_2(t_1, X_1, Y_1, Z_1) = Z_1 = -0.2000$$

$$f_3(t_1, X_1, Y_1, Z_1) = -X_1 t_1 Z_1 - t_1 Y_1 + t_1^2 X_1$$

$$= -1.0250 \times 0.05 \times (-0.2000) - 0.05 \times 0.4900$$

$$+ 0.05^2 \times 1.0250 = -0.0117$$

$$X_2 = 1.0250 + 0.05 \times 0.4900 = 1.0495$$

$$Y_2 = 0.4900 + 0.05 \times (-0.2000) = 0.4800$$

$$Z_2 = -0.2000 + 0.05 \times (-0.0117) = -0.2005$$

Proceeding similarly we have

$$X_3 = 1.0495 + 0.05 \times 0.4800 = 1.0735$$

$$Y_3 = 0.4800 + 0.05 \times (-0.2005) = 0.4700$$

$$Z_3 = -0.2005 + 0.05 \times (-0.0165) = -0.2013$$

$$X_4 = 1.0735 + 0.05 \times 0.4700 = 1.0970$$

$$Y_4 = 0.4700 + 0.05 \times (-0.2013) = 0.4599$$

$$Z_4 = -0.2013 + 0.05 \times (-0.0139) = -0.2018$$

Hence $X(0.2) = X_4 = 1.0970$. It should be obvious by now that computations like these are sufficiently tedious to justify the effort of writing a computer program to carry out the actual arithmetic. The essential point for the reader to grasp is not the mechanics but the principle whereby methods for the solution of first-order differential equations (and this includes the more sophisticated methods as well as Euler's method) can be extended to the solution of sets of equations and hence to higher-order equations.

We noted earlier that both MAPLE and MATLAB can be used to obtain numerical solutions of differential equations and commented that they both implement very accurate methods of solution which are much more sophisticated than the Euler method illustrated here. But MAPLE could be used to obtain an Euler method solution of the third-order differential equation in Example 9.49, as follows:

```
ode:= diff(x(t),t$3) + x(t)*t*diff(x(t),t$2) +
      t*diff(x(t),t) - x(t)*t^2 = 0:
odeprob:= {ode,x(0) = 1,D(x)(0) = 0.5,D(D(x))(0) =
      -0.2};
oseq:= array([seq(0.05*i,i = 0..4)]);
oput:= dsolve(odeprob,numeric,
      method = classical[foreuler],
      output = oseq,stepsize = 0.05):
evalm(oput[2,1]);
```

MAPLE is equally able to solve the same equation presented in state space form, thus

```
odel:= diff(x(t),t) = y(t):
ode2:= diff(y(t),t) = z(t):
ode3:= diff(z(t),t) = -x(t)*t*z(t) - t*y(t) + x(t)*t^2:
odeprob:= {odel,ode2,ode3,x(0) = 1,y(0) = 0.5,z(0) =
        -0.2};
oseq:= array([seq(0.05*i,i = 0..4)]);
oput:= dsolve(odeprob,numeric,
        method = classical[foreuler],
        output = oseq,stepsize = 0.05):
evalm(oput[2,1]);
```

In fact, if we set the `infolevel` system variable thus

```
infolevel[dsolve]:= 3:
```

before calling `dsolve` to integrate the differential equation in the third-order form above, we discover that MAPLE first translates it into state space form just as we have done in Example 9.49!

9.11.3 Exercises

74 Transform the following initial-value problems into sets of first-order differential equations with appropriate initial conditions:

(a) $\dfrac{d^2x}{dt^2} + 6(x^2 - t)\dfrac{dx}{dt} - 4xt = 0,$

$x(0) = 1, \quad \dfrac{dx}{dt}(0) = 2$

(b) $\dfrac{d^2x}{dt^2} - \sin\left(\dfrac{dx}{dt}\right) + 4x = 0,$

$x(0) = 0, \quad \dfrac{dx}{dt}(0) = 0$

75 Find the value of $X(0.3)$ for the initial-value problem

$$\frac{d^2x}{dt^2} + x^2\frac{dx}{dt} + x = \sin t,$$

$$x(0) = 0, \quad \frac{dx}{dt}(0) = 1$$

using Euler's method with step size $h = 0.1$.

76 Transform the following initial-value problems into sets of first-order differential equations with appropriate initial conditions:

(a) $\dfrac{d^2x}{dt^2} + 4(x^2 - t^2)^{1/2} = 0,$

$x(1) = 2, \quad \dfrac{dx}{dt}(1) = 0.5$

(b) $\dfrac{d^3x}{dt^3} + t\dfrac{d^2x}{dt^2} + 6e^t\dfrac{dx}{dt} - x^2t = e^{2t},$

$x(0) = 1, \quad \dfrac{dx}{dt}(0) = 2, \quad \dfrac{d^2x}{dt^2}(0) = 0$

(c) $\dfrac{d^3x}{dt^3} + t\dfrac{d^2x}{dt^2} + x^2 = \sin t,$

$x(1) = 1, \quad \dfrac{dx}{dt}(1) = 0, \quad \dfrac{d^2x}{dt^2}(1) = -2$

(d) $\left(\dfrac{d^3x}{dt^3}\right)^{1/2} + t\dfrac{d^2x}{dt^2} + x^2t^2 = 0,$

$x(2) = 0, \quad \dfrac{dx}{dt}(2) = 0, \quad \dfrac{d^2x}{dt^2}(2) = 2$

(e) $\dfrac{d^4x}{dt^4} + x\dfrac{d^2x}{dt^2} + x^2 = \ln t, \quad x(0) = 0,$

$\dfrac{dx}{dt}(0) = 0, \quad \dfrac{d^2x}{dt^2}(0) = 4, \quad \dfrac{d^3x}{dt^3}(0) = -3$

(f) $\dfrac{d^4x}{dt^4} + \left(\dfrac{dx}{dt} - 1\right)\dfrac{d^3x}{dt^3} + \dfrac{dx}{dt} - (xt)^{1/2}$

$= t^2 + 4t - 5,$

$x(0) = a, \dfrac{dx}{dt}(0) = 0, \dfrac{d^2x}{dt^2}(0) = b, \dfrac{d^3x}{dt^3}(0) = 0$

77 Use Euler's method to compute an approximation $X(0.65)$ to the solution $x(0.65)$ of the initial-value problem

$$\frac{d^3x}{dt^3} + \frac{d^2x}{dt^2}(x - t) + \left(\frac{dx}{dt}\right)^2 - x^2 = 0,$$

$$x(0.5) = -1, \quad \frac{dx}{dt}(0.5) = 1, \quad \frac{d^2x}{dt^2}(0.5) = 2$$

using a step size of $h = 0.05$.

78 Write a computer program to solve the initial-value problem

$$\frac{d^2x}{dt^2} + x^2\frac{dx}{dt} + x = \sin t,$$

$$x(0) = 0, \quad \frac{dx}{dt}(0) = 1$$

using Euler's method. Use your program to find the value of $X(0.4)$ using steps of $h = 0.01$ and $h = 0.005$. Hence estimate the accuracy of your value of $X(0.4)$ and estimate the step size that would be necessary to obtain a value of $X(0.4)$ accurate to 4dp.

79 A water treatment plant deals with a constant influx Q of polluted water with pollutant concentration s_0. The treatment tank contains bacteria which consume the pollutant and protozoa which feed on the bacteria, thus keeping the bacteria from increasing too rapidly and overwhelming the system. If the concentration of the bacteria and the protozoa are denoted by b and p the system is governed by the differential equations

$$\frac{ds}{dt} = r(s_0 - s) - \alpha m\frac{bs}{1+s}$$

$$\frac{db}{dt} = -rb + m\frac{bs}{1+s} - \beta n\frac{bp}{1+p}$$

$$\frac{dp}{dt} = -rp + n\frac{bp}{1+p}$$

Write a program to solve these equations numerically.

Measurements have determined that the (biological) parameters α, m, β and n have the values 0.5, 1.0, 0.8 and 0.1 respectively. The parameter r is a measure of the inflow rate of polluted water and s_0 is the level of pollutant. Using the initial conditions $s(0) = 0$, $b(0) = 0.2$ and $p(0) = 0.05$ determine the final steady level of pollutant if $r = 0.05$ and $s_0 = 0.4$. What effect does doubling the inflow rate (r) have?

The solution of Questions 77, 78 and 79 could be accomplished using MAPLE. Taking Question 78 as an example

```
ode:= diff(x(t),t$2) + x(t)^2*diff(x(t),t) +
        x(t) = sin(t):
odeprob:= {ode,x(0) = 0,D(x)(0) = 1};
oseq:= array([seq(0.1*i,i = 0..4)]);
oput1:= dsolve(odeprob,numeric,
        method = classical[foreuler],
        output = oseq,stepsize = 0.01);
oput2:= dsolve(odeprob,numeric,
        method = classical[foreuler],
        output = oseq,stepsize = 0.005);
```

The values of `x(0.4)` using step sizes of 0.01 and 0.005 are found to be `0.398022` and `0.397919` to 6sf respectively. This enables us to predict, using Richardson extrapolation, that a step size of approximately $h = 0.0024$ or smaller would be required to obtain the specified accuracy. In fact, as we have already noted, the MAPLE `dsolve/numeric` procedure can integrate differential equations numerically using much more sophisticated methods and providing answers to a specified accuracy. The `dsolve/numeric` procedure uses methods similar to the Richardson extrapolation method to achieve this.

9.12 Qualitative analysis of second-order differential equations

Sometimes it is easier or more convenient to discover the qualitative properties of the solutions of a differential equation than to solve it completely. In some cases this qualitative knowledge is just as useful as a complete solution. In other cases the qualitative knowledge is more illuminating than a quantitative solution, particularly if the only quantitative solutions that can be derived are numerical ones. One technique that is very useful in this context is the **phase-plane plot**.

9.12.1 Phase-plane plots

The second-order nonlinear differential equation

$$\frac{d^2x}{dt^2} + \mu(x^2 - 1)\frac{dx}{dt} + \lambda x = 0$$

is known as the Van der Pol oscillator. It has properties that are typical of many nonlinear oscillators. The equation has no simple analytical solution, so, if we wish to investigate its properties, we must resort to a numerical computation. The equation can readily be recast in state-space form as described in Section 9.11.2 and solved by Euler's method described in Section 9.6.

Figure 9.32 shows displacement and velocity plots for a Van der Pol oscillator with $\lambda = 40$ and $\mu = 3$. The initial conditions used were $x(0) = 0.05$ and $(dx/dt)(0) = 0$. It can be seen that initially the amplitude of the displacement oscillations grows quite rapidly, but after about three cycles this rapid growth stops and the displacement curve appears to settle into a periodically repeating pattern. Similar comments could be made about the velocity curve. Is the Van der Pol oscillator tending towards some fixed cyclical pattern?

This question can be answered much more easily if the displacement and velocity curves are plotted in a different way. Instead of plotting each individually against time, we plot velocity against displacement, as in Figure 9.33. Such a plot is called a phase-plane plot. Figure 9.33(a) shows the same data as plotted in Figure 9.32. Time increases in the direction shown by the arrows, the plot starting at the point (0.05, 0) and spiralling outwards. From this plot it is easy to see that the fourth and fifth cycles of the oscillations are nearly indistinguishable. Continuing the computations for a larger number of cycles would confirm that, after an initial period, the oscillations settle down into a cyclical pattern. The pattern is called a **limit cycle**. The Van der Pol oscillator has the property that the limit cycle is independent of the initial conditions chosen (but

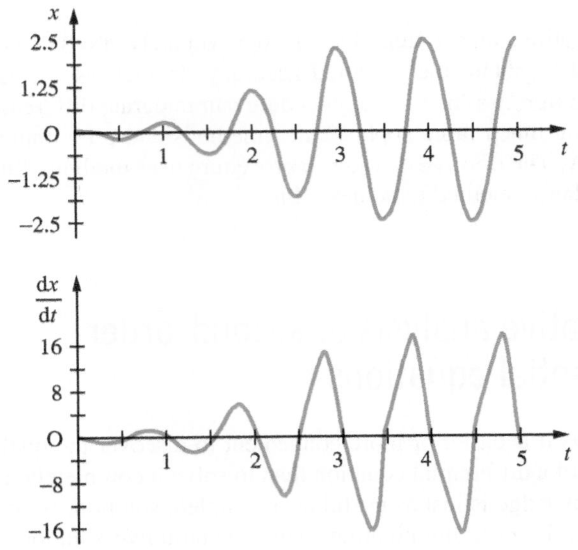

Figure 9.32 Displacement and velocity traces for a Van der Pol oscillator.

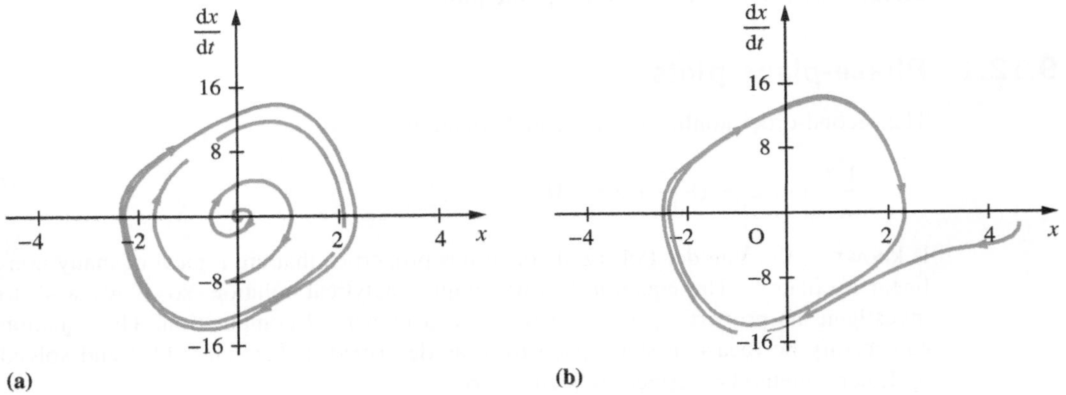

Figure 9.33 Phase-plane plots for Van der Pol oscillators – two different initial conditions.

depends on the parameters μ and λ). Figure 9.33(b) shows a phase-plane plot of the oscillations of the Van der Pol oscillator, starting from the initial condition (4.5, 0). The interested reader may wish to explore the Van der Pol oscillator further – perhaps by writing a computer program to solve the equation and plotting solution paths in the phase plane for a number of other initial conditions. Exploration of this type will confirm that the limit cycle is independent of initial conditions, and exploration of other values of μ and λ will show how the limit cycle varies as these parameters change.

Other equations will of course produce different solution paths in the phase plane. The second-order linear constant-coefficient equation

$$\frac{d^2x}{dt^2} + \mu\frac{dx}{dt} + \lambda x = 0$$

yields a phase-plane plot like that shown in Figure 9.34(a). In that particular case the parameters have the values $\mu = 1.5$ and $\lambda = 40$. Other values of μ and λ that result

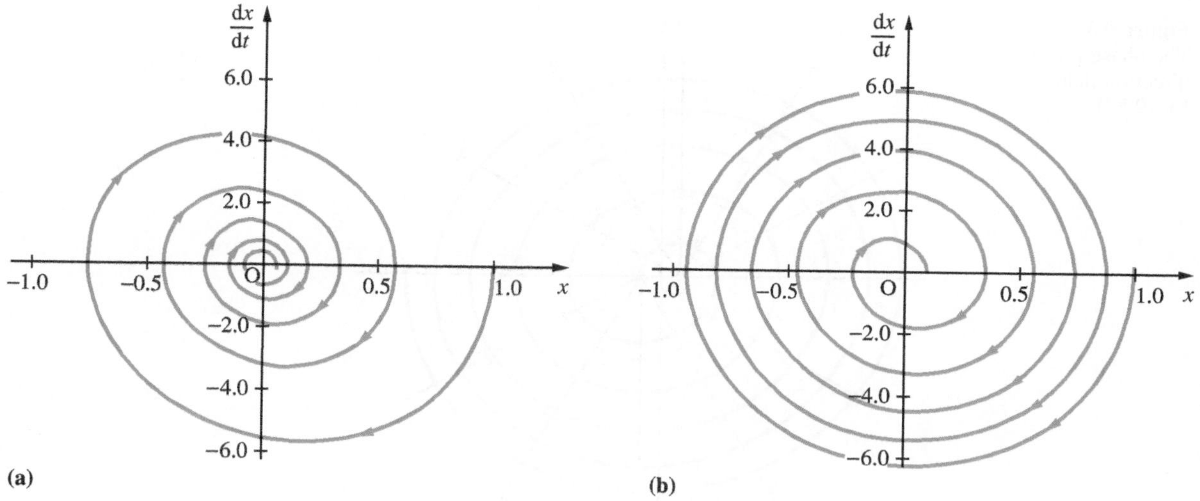

Figure 9.34 Phase-plane plots for some second-order oscillators.

in decaying oscillatory solutions of the equation yield similar spiral phase-plane plots tending towards the origin as $t \to \infty$. Such a plot is typical of any system whose behaviour is oscillatory and decaying. For instance, Figure 9.34(b) shows the phase-plane plot of the nonlinear second-order equation

$$\frac{d^2x}{dt^2} + \mu \operatorname{sgn}\left(\frac{dx}{dt}\right) + \lambda x = 0 \tag{9.59}$$

with $\mu = 3$ and $\lambda = 40$ (recall that the function sgn(x) takes the value 1 if $x \geqslant 0$ and -1 if $x < 0$). The general characters of Figures 9.34(a), (b) are similar. The difference between the two equations is manifest in the difference between the pattern of changing spacing of successive turns of the spirals.

The utility of phase-plane plotting is not restricted to enhancing the understanding of numerical solutions of differential equations. Second-order differential equations which can be expressed in the form

$$\frac{d^2x}{dt^2} = f\left(x, \frac{dx}{dt}\right)$$

arise in mathematical models of many engineering systems. An equation of this form can be expressed as

$$\frac{dv}{dx} = \frac{f(x, v)}{v}, \quad \text{where } v = \frac{dx}{dt}$$

The derivative dv/dx is of course just the gradient of the solution path in the phase plane. Hence we can sketch the path in the phase plane of the solutions of a second-order differential equation of this type without actually obtaining the solution. This provides a useful qualitative insight into the form of solution that might be expected.

As an example, consider (9.59). This may be expressed as

$$\frac{dv}{dx} = -\frac{\mu \operatorname{sgn}(v) + \lambda x}{v}$$

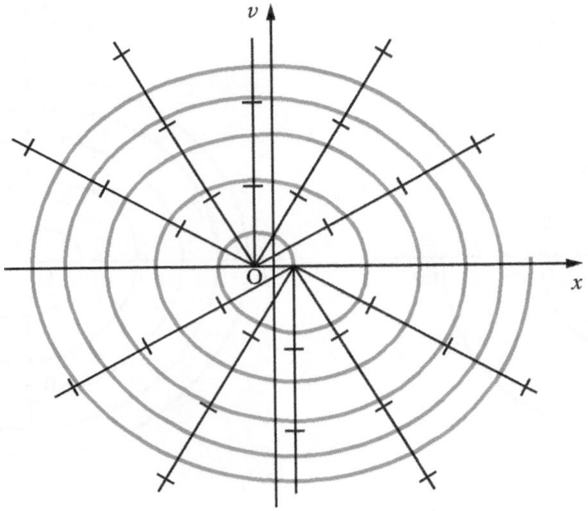

Figure 9.35 The phase-plane direction field for (9.59).

Thus the gradient of the solution path in the phase plane is equal to k for all points on the curve

$$v = -\frac{\lambda}{k}x - \frac{\mu\,\mathrm{sgn}(v)}{k}, \quad k \neq 0$$

These curves are of course a family of straight lines. Hence we can construct a diagram similar to the direction-field diagrams described in Section 9.5.1. The phase-plane direction-field diagram is shown, with the solution path from Figure 9.34(b) superimposed upon it, in Figure 9.35.

This technique can also be used for equations for which the lines of constant gradient in the phase plane are not straight. Example 9.50 illustrates this.

MAPLE provides tools to assist in the construction of phase-plane plots. One such tool is the `phaseportrait` procedure. The following MAPLE commands produce a diagram similar to Figure 9.33(a) but with a direction field shown in addition to the solution curve.

```
with(DEtools):
vdp2:= {diff(x(t),t) = v(t),
        diff(v(t),t) = -3*(x(t)^2 - 1)*v(t) - 40*x(t)};
phaseportrait(vdp2,{x(t),v(t)},t = 0..10,
        [[x(0) = 0.05,v(0) = 0]],x = -2..2,stepsize = 0.01);
```

Notice that it is necessary to load the `DEtools` package in order to access the `phaseportrait` procedure. Also the second-order differential equation is converted into a state space form for use in `phaseportrait`.

The `phaseportrait` procedure can be used to produce a diagram similar to Figure 9.36 for Example 9.50, and also to check your solutions to all parts of Question 78.

Example 9.50 Draw a phase-plane direction field for the equation

$$\frac{d^2x}{dt^2} + 1.5\left(\frac{dx}{dt}\right)^3 + 40x = 0 \qquad \textbf{(9.60)}$$

Hence sketch the solution path of the equation that starts from the initial conditions $x = 1$, $dx/dt = 0$.

Solution Equation (9.60) can be expressed as

$$v\frac{dv}{dx} = -1.5v^3 - 40x$$

so the curve on which the solution-path gradient is equal to k is given by

$$x = -\tfrac{1}{40}(kv + 1.5v^3)$$

Thus, as shown in Figure 9.36, the curves of constant solution-path gradient are in this case cubic functions of v. The solution path of the equation starting from the point (1, 0) is sketched.

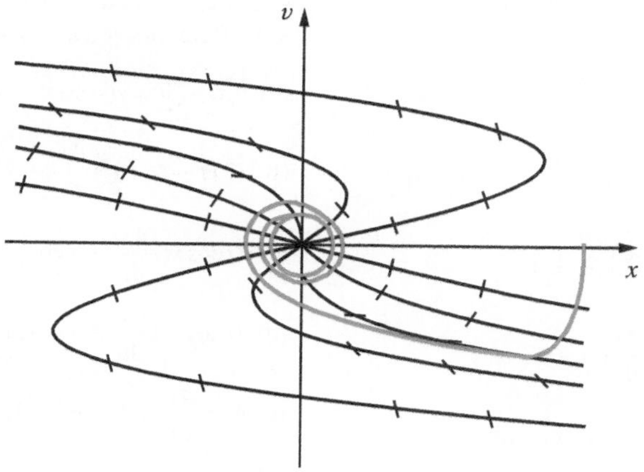

Figure 9.36 The phase-plane direction field for (9.60).

9.12.2 Exercises

80 Draw phase-plane direction fields for the following equations and sketch the form you would expect the solution paths to take, starting from the points $(x, v) = (1, 0), (0, 1), (-1, 0)$ and $(0, -1)$ in each case:

(a) $\dfrac{d^2x}{dt^2} + \dfrac{dx}{dt} + x^3 = 0$

(b) $\dfrac{d^2x}{dt^2} + \dfrac{dx}{dt} + \text{sgn}(x) = 0$

(c) $\dfrac{d^2x}{dt^2} + \dfrac{dx}{dt} + x^2\,\text{sgn}(x) = 0$

(d) $\dfrac{d^2x}{dt^2} + \text{sgn}\left(\dfrac{dx}{dt}\right) + 2\,\text{sgn}(x) = 0$

81 For each of the problems in Question 78 solve the differential equation numerically and check that the solutions you obtain are similar to your sketch solutions.

9.13 Review exercises (1–35)

Whenever possible check your answers using MATLAB or MAPLE.

1 Classify each of the following as ordinary and as linear homogeneous, linear nonhomogeneous or nonlinear differential equations, state the order of the equations and name the dependent and independent variables:

(a) $\dfrac{d^2x}{dt^2} + x\dfrac{dx}{dt} + x^2 = 0$

(b) $\dfrac{dz}{dx} + 4z^2 = \sin x$

(c) $\dfrac{d^3p}{ds^3} + 4s\dfrac{d^2p}{ds^2} + s^2 = \cos as$

(c) $\dfrac{dx}{dt} = xt^2, \quad x(2) = 1$

(d) $t\dfrac{dx}{dt} = \dfrac{t}{\sin(x/t)} + x, \quad x(1) = 1$

(e) $\dfrac{dx}{dt} = \dfrac{8t - x}{2x + t}, \quad x(0) = 2$

(f) $t\dfrac{dx}{dt} + x\ln t = x(\ln x + 1), \quad x(1) = 2$

(g) $t\dfrac{dx}{dt} = x - t, \quad x(1) = 3$

(h) $\dfrac{dx}{dt} = \dfrac{x - 7t}{x - t}, \quad x(0) = 2$

2 Classify the following differential equation problems as under-determined, fully determined or over-determined, and solve them where possible:

(a) $\dfrac{d^2x}{dt^2} = t, \quad x(0) = 1$

(b) $\dfrac{d^3x}{dt^3} - t = 0, \quad x(0) = 0, \quad x(1) = 0, \quad x(2) = 0$

(c) $\dfrac{dx}{dt} = \sin t, \quad x(0) = 0, \quad \dfrac{dx}{dt}(0) = 1$

(d) $\dfrac{d^2x}{dt^2} = e^{4t}, \quad x(0) = 0, \quad \dfrac{dx}{dt}(1) = 0$

3 Sketch the direction field of the differential equation

$$\frac{dx}{dt} = ax(1 - x^2)$$

and sketch the form of solution suggested by the direction field. Solve the equation and confirm that the solution supports the inferences you made from the direction field.

4 Solve the following differential equation problems:

(a) $\dfrac{dx}{dt} + \dfrac{\cos t}{\sin x} = 0, \quad x(0) = -\pi$

(b) $t\dfrac{dx}{dt} - e^{-x} = 0, \quad x(1) = 2$

5 For each of the following problems, determine which are exact differentials, and hence solve the differential equations where possible:

(a) $2xt^2\dfrac{dx}{dt} = a - 2x^2t, \quad x(1) = 2$

(b) $(2xt + 2t + t^2)\dfrac{dx}{dt} + x^2 + 2tx = 0, \quad x(2) = 2$

(c) $(t\cos xt)\dfrac{dx}{dt} + x\cos xt + 1 = 0, \quad x(\pi) = 0$

(d) $(t\cos xt)\dfrac{dx}{dt} - x\cos xt = 0, \quad x(\pi) = 0$

(e) $te^{xt}\dfrac{dx}{dt} + 1 + xe^{xt} = 0, \quad x(2) = 4$

6 Solve the following differential equation problems:

(a) $\dfrac{dx}{dt} - 2x = t, \quad x(0) = 2$

(b) $\dfrac{dx}{dt} + 2tx = (t - \tfrac{1}{2})e^{-t}, \quad x(0) = 1$

(c) $\dfrac{dx}{dt} + 3x = e^{2t}, \quad x(0) = 2$

(d) $\dfrac{dx}{dt} + x\sin t = \sin t, \quad x(\pi) = e$

7 Solve the differential equation

$$\frac{dx}{dt} = \left(\frac{xt}{x^2 + t^2}\right)^{1/2}, \quad x(0) = 1$$

to find the value of $X(0.4)$ using Euler's method with step size 0.1 and 0.05. By comparing these two estimates of $x(0.4)$, estimate the accuracy of the better of the two values that you have obtained and also the step size you would need to use in order to calculate an estimate of $x(0.4)$ accurate to 2dp.

8 Solve the differential equation

$$\frac{dx}{dt} = \sin t^2, \quad x(0) = 2$$

to find the value of $X(0.25)$ using Euler's method with steps of size 0.05 and 0.025. By comparing these two estimates of $x(0.25)$, estimate the accuracy of the better of the two values that you have obtained and also the step size you would need to use in order to calculate an estimate of $x(0.25)$ accurate to 3dp.

9 Solve the differential equation

$$\frac{dx}{dt} + \frac{3x}{20 - t} = 2$$

obtained in Example 8.4 to determine the amount $x(t)$ of salt in the tank at time t minutes. Initially the tank contains pure water.

10 An open vessel is in the shape of a right circular cone of semi-vertical angle 45° with axis vertical and apex downwards. At time $t = 0$ the vessel is empty. Water is pumped in at a constant rate $p\,\text{m}^3\,\text{s}^{-1}$ and escapes through a small hole at the vertex at a rate $ky\,\text{m}^3\,\text{s}^{-1}$, where k is a positive constant and y is the depth of water in the cone.

Given that the volume of a circular cone is $\pi r^2 h/3$, where r is the radius of the base and h its vertical height, show that

$$\pi y^2 \frac{dy}{dt} = p - ky$$

Deduce that the water level reaches the value $y = p/(2k)$ at time

$$t = \frac{\pi p^2}{k^3}\left(\ln 2 - \frac{5}{8}\right)$$

11 Stefan's law states that the rate of change of temperature of a body due to radiation of heat is

$$\frac{dT}{dt} = -k(T^4 - T_0^4)$$

where T is the temperature of the body, T_0 is the temperature of the surrounding medium (both measured in K) and k is a constant. Show that the solution of this differential equation is

$$2\tan\left(\frac{T}{T_0}\right) + \ln\left(\frac{T + T_0}{T - T_0}\right) = 4T_0^3(kt + C)$$

Show that, when the temperature difference between the body and its surroundings is small, Stefan's law can be approximated by Newton's law of cooling

$$\frac{dT}{dt} = -\alpha(T - T_0)$$

and find α in terms of k and T_0.

12 A motor under load generates heat internally at a constant rate H and radiates heat, in accordance with Newton's law of cooling, at a rate $k\theta$, where k is a constant and θ is the temperature difference of the motor over its surroundings. With suitable non-dimensionalization of time the temperature of the motor is given by the differential equation

$$\frac{d\theta}{dt} = H - k\theta$$

Given that $\theta = 0$ and $d\theta/dt = 10$ when $t = 0$ and $\theta = 60$ when $t = 10$ show that

(a) the ultimate rise in temperature is $\theta = 10/k$;

(b) k is a solution of the equation $e^{-10k} = 1 - 6k$;

(c) $t = 10 + \dfrac{1}{k}\ln\left(\dfrac{10 - 60k}{10 - k\theta}\right)$.

13 A linear cam is to be made whose rate of rise (as it moves in the negative x direction) at the point (x, y) on the profile is equal to one half of the gradient of the line joining (x, y) to a fixed point on the cam (x_0, y_0). Show that the cam profile is a solution of the differential equation

$$\frac{dy}{dx} = \frac{y - y_0}{2(x - x_0)}$$

and hence find its equation. Sketch the cam profile.

14 Radioactive elements decay at a constant rate per unit mass of the element. Show that such decays obey equations of the form

$$\frac{dm}{dt} = -km$$

where k is the decay rate of the element and m is the mass of the element present. The half life of an element is the time taken for one half of any given mass of the element to decay. Find the relationship between the decay constant k and the half life of an element.

15 In Section 9.2.4 we showed that the equation governing the current flowing in a series LRC electrical circuit is (equation 9.9)

$$L\frac{\mathrm{d}^2i}{\mathrm{d}t^2} + R\frac{\mathrm{d}i}{\mathrm{d}t} + \frac{1}{C}i = 0$$

Show, by a similar method, that the equation governing the current flowing in a series LR circuit containing a voltage source E is

$$L\frac{\mathrm{d}i}{\mathrm{d}t} + Ri = E$$

At time $t = 0$ a switch is closed applying a d.c. potential of V to an initially quiescent series LR circuit consisting of an inductor L and a resistor R. Show that the current flowing in the circuit is

$$i(t) = \frac{V}{R}(1 - \mathrm{e}^{-Rt/L})$$

and hence find the time needed for the current to reach 95% of its final value.

16 The tread of a car tyre wears more rapidly as it becomes thinner. The tread-wear rate, measured in mm per 10000 miles, may be modelled as

$$a + b(d - t)^2$$

where d is the initial tread depth, t is the current tread depth and a and b are constants. A tyre company takes measurements on a new design of tyre whose initial tread depth is 8 mm. When the tyre is new its wear rate is found to be 1.03 mm per 10000 miles run and when the tread depth is reduced to 4 mm the wear rate is 3.43 mm per 10000 miles. Assuming that a tyre is discarded when the tread depth has been reduced to 2 mm what is its estimated life?

17 Express each of the following differential equations in the form

$$\mathrm{L}[x(t)] = f(t)$$

(a) $\dfrac{\mathrm{d}^2x}{\mathrm{d}t^2} + (\sin t)\dfrac{\mathrm{d}x}{\mathrm{d}t} - 9x + \cos t = 0$

(b) $\dfrac{\mathrm{d}^3x}{\mathrm{d}t^3} + t\dfrac{\mathrm{d}^2x}{\mathrm{d}t^2} + t^2\dfrac{\mathrm{d}x}{\mathrm{d}t} - 4t\dfrac{\mathrm{d}x}{\mathrm{d}t} + \mathrm{e}^t + x = 0$

(c) $\dfrac{\mathrm{d}x}{\mathrm{d}t} = \mathrm{e}^t + \mathrm{e}^{-t}x$

(d) $\dfrac{\mathrm{d}^2x}{\mathrm{d}t^2} = \cos \Omega t - 4x$

(e) $t^2\dfrac{\mathrm{d}^3x}{\mathrm{d}t^3} + \ln(t^2 + 4) = \dfrac{1}{t^2 + 2t + 4}\dfrac{\mathrm{d}x}{\mathrm{d}t}$

18 For each of the following pairs of operators calculate the operator LM – ML; hence state which of the pairs are commutative (that is, satisfy LM$x(t)$ = ML$x(t)$):

(a) $\mathrm{L} = \dfrac{\mathrm{d}}{\mathrm{d}t} + \sin t, \quad \mathrm{M} = \dfrac{\mathrm{d}}{\mathrm{d}t} - \cos t$

(b) $\mathrm{L} = \dfrac{\mathrm{d}}{\mathrm{d}t} + 4, \quad \mathrm{M} = \dfrac{\mathrm{d}}{\mathrm{d}t} + 9$

(c) $\mathrm{L} = \dfrac{\mathrm{d}}{\mathrm{d}t} + \sin t + 2, \quad \mathrm{M} = \dfrac{\mathrm{d}}{\mathrm{d}t} + \sin t - 2$

(d) $\mathrm{L} = \dfrac{\mathrm{d}^2}{\mathrm{d}t^2} + 2t^2 - 9, \quad \mathrm{M} = \dfrac{\mathrm{d}^2}{\mathrm{d}t^2} + 2t^2 + t$

19 What conditions must the functions $f(t)$ and $g(t)$ satisfy in order for the following operator pairs to be commutative?

(a) $\mathrm{L} = \dfrac{\mathrm{d}}{\mathrm{d}t} + f(t), \quad \mathrm{M} = \dfrac{\mathrm{d}}{\mathrm{d}t} + g(t)$

(b) $\mathrm{L} = \dfrac{\mathrm{d}^2}{\mathrm{d}t^2} + f(t), \quad \mathrm{M} = \dfrac{\mathrm{d}^2}{\mathrm{d}t^2} + g(t)$

20 Find the general solution of the following differential equations:

(a) $\dfrac{\mathrm{d}^2x}{\mathrm{d}t^2} - 3\dfrac{\mathrm{d}x}{\mathrm{d}t} + 2x = \sin t$

(b) $\dfrac{\mathrm{d}^3x}{\mathrm{d}t^3} - 7\dfrac{\mathrm{d}x}{\mathrm{d}t} + 6x = t$

(c) $\dfrac{\mathrm{d}^3x}{\mathrm{d}t^3} - 7\dfrac{\mathrm{d}x}{\mathrm{d}t} + 6x = \mathrm{e}^{2t}$

(d) $\dfrac{\mathrm{d}x}{\mathrm{d}t} - 4x = \mathrm{e}^{4t}$

(e) $\dfrac{\mathrm{d}^2x}{\mathrm{d}t^2} + 3\dfrac{\mathrm{d}x}{\mathrm{d}t} + \frac{13}{4}x = t^2$

(f) $\dfrac{d^2x}{dt^2} + 3\dfrac{dx}{dt} + \frac{13}{4}x = \sin t$

(g) $\dfrac{d^3x}{dt^3} - 5\dfrac{d^2x}{dt^2} + 2\dfrac{dx}{dt} + 8x = t^2 - t$

(h) $\dfrac{d^2x}{dt^2} - 2\dfrac{dx}{dt} + 5x = e^{-t}$

(i) $\dfrac{d^3x}{dt^3} - 5\dfrac{d^2x}{dt^2} + 2\dfrac{dx}{dt} + 8x = e^{2t} + e^t$

(j) $\dfrac{d^2x}{dt^2} - 2\dfrac{dx}{dt} + 5x = t + e^t \cos 2t$

21 Solve the following initial-value problems:

(a) $\dfrac{d^2x}{dt^2} + 2\dfrac{dx}{dt} + 5x = 1,\ x(0) = 0,\ \dfrac{dx}{dt}(0) = 0$

(b) $3\dfrac{d^2x}{dt^2} - 2\dfrac{dx}{dt} - x = 2t - 1,$

$x(0) = 7,\ \dfrac{dx}{dt}(0) = 2$

(c) $\dfrac{d^2x}{dt^2} + 2\dfrac{dx}{dt} + x = 4\cos 2t,$

$x(0) = 0,\ \dfrac{dx}{dt}(0) = 2$

(d) $\dfrac{d^2x}{dt^2} - \dfrac{dx}{dt} = -2e^{2t},\ x(0) = 0,\ \dfrac{dx}{dt}(0) = 1$

(e) $\dfrac{d^2x}{dt^2} - 3\dfrac{dx}{dt} + 2x = 2e^{-4t},$

$x(0) = 0,\ \dfrac{dx}{dt}(0) = 1$

(f) $\dfrac{d^3x}{dt^3} + 5\dfrac{d^2x}{dt^2} + 17\dfrac{dx}{dt} + 13x = 1,$

$x(0) = 1,\ \dfrac{dx}{dt}(0) = 1,\ \dfrac{d^2x}{dt^2}(0) = 0$

22 Find the damping parameters and natural frequencies of the systems governed by the following second-order linear constant-coefficient differential equations:

(a) $\dfrac{d^2x}{dt^2} + 7\dfrac{dx}{dt} + 2x = 0$

(b) $\dfrac{d^2x}{dt^2} + p\dfrac{dx}{dt} + p^{1/2}x = 0$

(c) $\dfrac{d^2x}{dt^2} + 2aq\dfrac{dx}{dt} + \frac{1}{2}qx = 0$

(d) $\dfrac{d^2x}{dt^2} + 14\dfrac{dx}{dt} + 2\alpha x = 0$

23 Determine the values of the appropriate parameters needed to give the systems governed by the following second-order linear constant-coefficient differential equations the damping parameters and natural frequencies stated:

(a) $\dfrac{d^2x}{dt^2} + \dfrac{a}{2}\dfrac{dx}{dt} + bx = 0,\quad \zeta = 0.25,\quad \omega = 2$

(b) $\dfrac{d^2x}{dt^2} + a\dfrac{dx}{dt} + bx = 0,\quad \zeta = 2,\quad \omega = \pi$

(c) $a\dfrac{d^2x}{dt^2} + 4\dfrac{dx}{dt} + cx = 0,\quad \zeta = 0.5,\quad \omega = 2$

(d) $p\dfrac{d^2x}{dt^2} + q^2\dfrac{dx}{dt} + 6x = 0,\quad \zeta = 1.2,\quad \omega = 0.2$

24 Show that by making the substitution

$$v = \frac{dx}{dt}$$

the equation

$$\frac{d^2x}{dt^2} + \frac{dx}{dt} = 1$$

may be expressed as

$$\frac{dv}{dt} + v = 1$$

Show that the solution of this equation is $v = 1 + Ce^{-t}$ and hence find $x(t)$.

This technique is a standard method for solving second-order differential equations in which the dependent variable itself does not appear explicitly. Apply the same method to obtain the solutions of the differential equations

(a) $\dfrac{d^2x}{dt^2} = 4\dfrac{dx}{dt} + e^{-2t}$

(b) $\dfrac{d^2x}{dt^2} - \left(\dfrac{dx}{dt}\right)^2 = 1$

(c) $t\dfrac{d^2x}{dt^2} = 2\dfrac{dx}{dt}$

25 Using the method introduced in Question 24, find the solutions of the following initial-value problems:

(a) $\dfrac{d^2x}{dt^2} + k\dfrac{dx}{dt} = t^2, \quad x(0) = 0, \quad \dfrac{dx}{dt}(0) = 1$

(b) $\dfrac{d^2x}{dt^2} = \left(\dfrac{dx}{dt}\right)^2 e^{-kt}, \quad x(0) = 0, \quad \dfrac{dx}{dt}(0) = U$

(c) $(t^2 + 4)\dfrac{d^2x}{dt^2} = 2t\dfrac{dx}{dt}, \quad x(1) = 0, \quad \dfrac{dx}{dt}(1) = 2$

(d) $\dfrac{d^2x}{dt^2} + 4\dfrac{dx}{dt} = \sin t, \quad x(\pi) = 0, \quad \dfrac{dx}{dt}(\pi) = 1$

26 Show that by making the substitution

$$v = \frac{dx}{dt}$$

and noting that

$$\frac{d^2x}{dt^2} = \frac{dv}{dt} = \frac{dv}{dx}\frac{dx}{dt} = v\frac{dv}{dx}$$

the equation

$$\frac{d^2x}{dt^2} = x\frac{dx}{dt}$$

may be expressed as

$$v\frac{dv}{dx} = xv$$

Show that the solution of this equation is $v = \frac{1}{2}x^2 + C$ and hence find $x(t)$.

This technique is a standard method for solving second-order differential equations in which the independent variable does not appear explicitly. Apply the same method to obtain the solutions of the differential equations

(a) $\dfrac{d^2x}{dt^2} = p\dfrac{dx}{dt}$

(b) $\dfrac{d^2x}{dt^2} = \left(\dfrac{dx}{dt}\right)^2$

(c) $\dfrac{d^2x}{dt^2} = \left(\dfrac{dx}{dt}\right)^2\left(2x - \dfrac{1}{x}\right)$

27 Using the method introduced in Question 26, find the solutions of the following initial-value problems:

(a) $x\dfrac{d^2x}{dt^2} = p\left(\dfrac{dx}{dt}\right)^2, \quad x(0) = 4, \quad \dfrac{dx}{dt}(0) = 1$

(b) $\dfrac{d^2x}{dt^2} = \dfrac{dx}{dt}e^x, \quad x(1) = 1, \quad \dfrac{dx}{dt}(1) = 0$

(c) $\dfrac{d^2x}{dt^2} = x^2\dfrac{dx}{dt}, \quad x(0) = 2, \quad \dfrac{dx}{dt}(0) = \dfrac{8}{3}$

(d) $\dfrac{d^2x}{dt^2} + \dfrac{1}{2}\left(\dfrac{dx}{dt}\right)^2 = x, \quad x(0) = 1, \quad \dfrac{dx}{dt}(0) = 0$

28 Equation (9.3), arising from the model of the take-off run of an aircraft developed in Section 9.2.1, can be solved by the techniques introduced in Exercises 24 and 26. Assuming that the thrust is constant find the speed of the aircraft both as a function of time and of distance run along the ground. The take-off speed of the aircraft is denoted by V_2. Find expressions for the length of runway required and the time taken by the aircraft to become airborne in terms of take-off speed.

29 Find the values of $X(t)$ for t up to 2, where $X(t)$ is the solution of the differential equation problem

$$\frac{d^3x}{dt^3} + \left(\frac{d^2x}{dt^2}\right)^2 + 4\left(\frac{dx}{dt}\right)^2 - xt = \sin t,$$

$$x(1) = 0.2, \quad \frac{dx}{dt}(1) = 1, \quad \frac{d^2x}{dt^2}(1) = 0$$

using Euler's method with step size $h = 0.025$. Repeat the computation with $h = 0.0125$. Hence estimate the accuracy of the value of $X(2)$ given by your solution.

30 The end of a chain, coiled near the edge of a horizontal surface, falls over the edge. If the friction between the chain and the horizontal surface is negligible and the chain is inextensible then, when a length x of chain has fallen, the equation of motion is

$$\frac{d}{dt}(mxv) = mgx$$

where m is the mass per unit length of the chain, g is gravitational acceleration and v is the velocity of the falling length of the chain. If the mass per unit length of the chain is constant show that this equation can be expressed as

$$xv\frac{dv}{dx} + v^2 = gx$$

and, by putting $y = v^2$, show that $v = \sqrt{(2gx/3)}$.

31 A simple mass spring system, subject to light damping, is vibrating under the action of a periodic force $F\cos pt$. The equation of motion is

$$\frac{d^2x}{dt^2} + 2\frac{dx}{dt} + 4x = F\cos pt$$

where F and p are constants.

Solve the differential equation for the displacement $x(t)$. Show that one part of the solution tends to zero as $t \to \infty$ and show that the amplitude of the steady-state solution is

$$F[(4 - p^2)^2 + 4p^2]^{-1/2}.$$

Hence show that resonance occurs when $p = \sqrt{2}$.

32 An alternating emf of $E\sin\omega t$ volt is supplied to a circuit containing an inductor of L henry, a resistor of R ohm and a capacitor of C farad in series. The differential equation satisfied by the current i amp and the charge q coulomb on the capacitor is

$$L\frac{di}{dt} + Ri + \frac{q}{C} = E\sin\omega t$$

Using $i = dq/dt$ obtain a second-order differential equation satisfied by i. Find the resistance if it is just large enough to prevent natural oscillations. For this value of R and $\omega = (LC)^{-1/2}$ prove that

$$i = \frac{E}{2K}(\sin\omega t - \omega t e^{-\omega t})$$

where $K^2 = L/C$, when the current and charge on the capacitor are both zero at time $t = 0$.

The following three questions are intended to be open-ended – there is no single 'correct' answer. They should be approached in an enquiring frame of mind, with the objective of discovering, by use of mathematical knowledge and technique, something more about how the physical world functions. The questions are designed to use primarily mathematical knowledge introduced in this chapter.

33 A truck of mass m moves along a horizontal test track subject only to a force resisting motion that is proportional to its speed. At time $t = 0$ the truck passes a reference point moving with speed U. Find the velocity of the truck both as a function of time and as a function of displacement from the reference point. Find the displacement of the truck from the reference point as a function of time.

Repeat these calculations for similar trucks subject to resistance forces proportional to

(a) square root of speed;

(b) square of speed;

(c) cube of speed.

How long does the truck take to come to rest in each case? Draw plots of velocity against displacement in each case. Explain, in qualitative terms, the behaviour of the truck under each type of resistance.

How would you model mathematically a truck that is subject to a small constant resistance plus a resistance proportional to its speed? How far would such a truck travel before coming to rest, and how long would it take to do so? Can you repeat these calculations for trucks subject to a small constant resistance plus a resistance proportional to speed squared or speed cubed?

What general conclusions can you draw about the type of terms that it is sensible to use in mathematical models of engineering systems to describe resistance to motion?

34 Figure 9.37 shows a system that serves as a simplified model of the phenomenon of 'tool chatter'. The mass A rests on a moving belt and is connected to a rigid support by a spring. The coefficient of sliding friction between the belt and the mass is less than the coefficient of static friction. When the spring is uncompressed, the mass moves to the right with the belt. As it does so, the spring is compressed until the force exerted by the spring exceeds the maximum static frictional force available. The mass then starts to slide. The spring force slows the mass, brings it

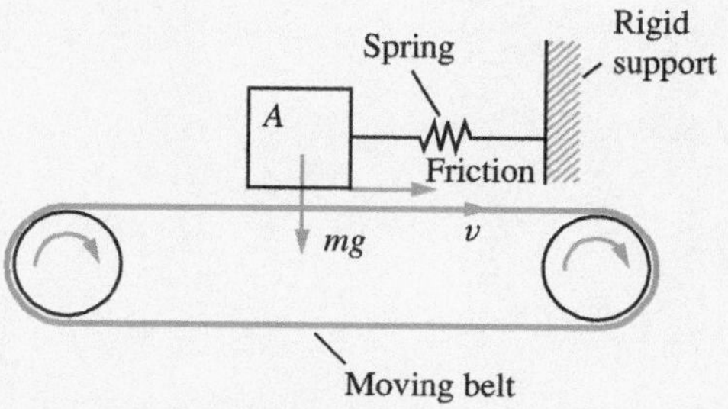

Figure 9.37 Diagram of a model of the 'tool chatter' phenomenon.

to rest, and then accelerates it back along the belt so that it moves leftwards. As it does so, the compression in the spring is reduced, the force of sliding friction slows the mass to rest, and then accelerates it so that its velocity is directed to the right. When its velocity matches that of the belt, sliding ceases and static friction takes over again.

Thus the mass undergoes a cyclic process of being pushed forwards by static friction until the spring is sufficiently compressed and then being flung backwards by the stored energy in the spring until the energy is dissipated. Analyse the model, determining such quantities as how the amplitude and frequency of motion of the mass depend on the coefficients and static friction and the other physical parameters.

35 The second-order linear nonhomogeneous constant-coefficient differential equation

$$\frac{\mathrm{d}^2x}{\mathrm{d}t^2} + 2\zeta\omega\frac{\mathrm{d}x}{\mathrm{d}t} + \omega^2 x = F\cos\Omega t$$

(often referred to as a **forced harmonic oscillator**) has a response $A(\Omega)F\cos(\Omega t - \delta)$, where $A(\Omega)$ is often called the **frequency response** (strictly it is the *amplitude response* or *gain spectrum*) and is given by (9.55) and shown in Figure 9.27. How does the frequency response of the second-order nonlinear nonhomogeneous constant-coefficient differential equation

$$\frac{\mathrm{d}^2x}{\mathrm{d}t^2} + 2\zeta\omega\left|\frac{\mathrm{d}x}{\mathrm{d}t}\right|\frac{\mathrm{d}x}{\mathrm{d}t} + \omega^2 x = F\cos\Omega t$$

differ from that of the linear one?

SUPPLEMENTARY CHAPTERS

6 PROBABILITY

Scientists, engineers and social scientists often conduct experiments or surveys where what is being measured has a **random** or **stochastic** element. The **statistical** analysis of the results has various objectives, such as:

- to extract the most reliable numerical measure;
- to judge the significance of the observations.

To achieve both of these requires a measure of how likely each outcome of the experiment is, i.e., a measurement of its **probability**.

In addition to its use in statistics, probability underpins some fundamental topics in science, such as quantum theory and statistical mechanics, the latter including the kinetic theory of gases.

6.1 Sets

Although we shall start by assessing how to assign a probability measure to 'elementary' events, such as obtaining *Heads* when a coin is tossed, we soon encounter 'compound' events, such as obtaining *Heads* on the first toss and no *Heads* on the following two. These events are handled by a notation and set of rules borrowed from *Set Theory*. Indeed, at a deep level, Set Theory is involved in the theoretical definition of probability itself, although we shall adopt a more practical approach.

A **set** of **elements** is just a collection of well-defined objects, with no ordering in the collection, unlike a **list**. We are interested in the interplay between different sets, for which a useful device is a pictorial representation known as a **Venn Diagram**.

Example 6.1 Consider a class of students.

U = **universe**,
F = set of all males,
M = set of all females
$= \overline{F}$, the **complement** of F.

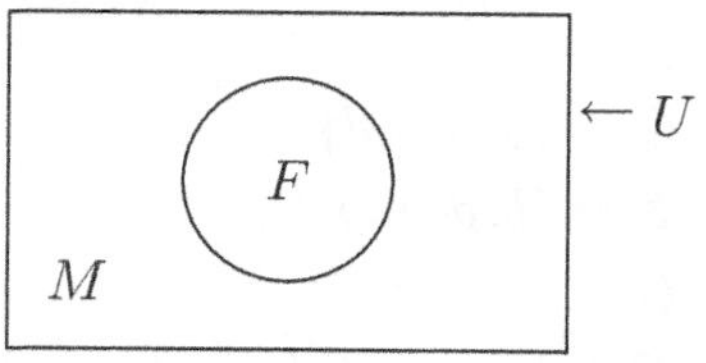

The terms **universe** and **complement** are general ones.

The complement of A represents all elements in U, but **not** in A. It is written $\overline{A}$, $C(A)$, A' or $\mathfrak{C}(A)$, although we shall prefer the first version. Note that $\overline{\overline{A}} = A$.

The universe is the set of all elements under investigation. The complement of the universe is the **empty set**, written $\emptyset$, which contains no elements: $\emptyset = \overline{U}$.

There are two key ways to combine sets:

union (OR): $A \cup B$ = set of elements in A **or** B **or** both, (6.1)

intersection (AND): $A \cap B$ = set of elements in both A **and** B. (6.2)

Think about it like this

$\cup$ is sometimes pronounced as 'cup' and $\cap$ as 'cap', but it may be found more helpful to use 'or' and 'and', since they indicate the meaning. That said, great care must be taken since everyday English can be imprecise: "This class consists of male and female students" should be interpreted as $M \cup F$ (M **or** F) rather than $M \cap F$, assuming no student is both male and female!

The following Venn Diagram shows their representation.

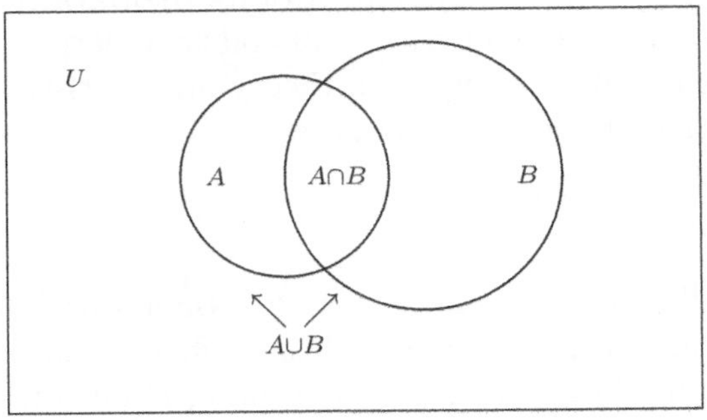

It is often the case, in probability calculations, that it is easier to calculate the *opposite* of what we wish, i.e., to work with the *complement*. The following rules, which can be verified by interpreting each side using the diagram above, are helpful:

$$\overline{A \cup B} = \overline{A} \cap \overline{B}, \qquad \overline{A \cap B} = \overline{A} \cup \overline{B}. \tag{6.3}$$

Example 6.2 Members of a class of 10 Mathematics students also study Chemistry (C), Engineering (E) and Geology (G):

$$\begin{aligned} C &= \{a, b, c, d\}, \\ E &= \{b, d, f, g, h\}, \\ G &= \{a, c, e, i\} \\ C \cup E &= \{a, b, c, d, f, g, h\}, \\ C \cap E &= \{b, d\}, \qquad E \cap G = \emptyset. \end{aligned}$$

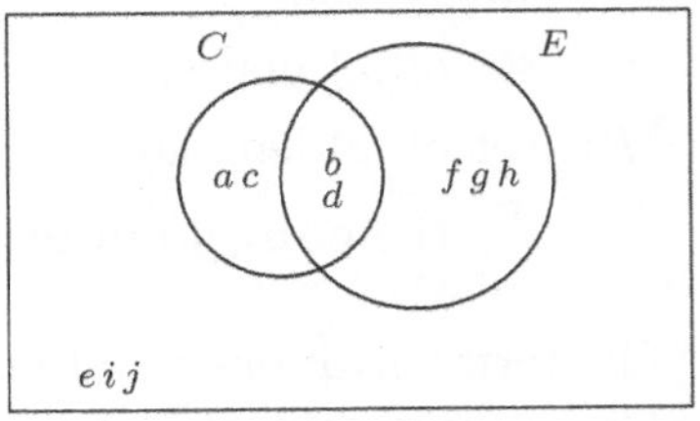

We also have $C \cup E \cup G = \{a, b, c, d, e, f, g, h, i\}$, so that $\overline{C \cup E \cup G} = \{j\}$, which identifies the only student in the class not taking one of these three subjects.

The first of the rules in (6.3) is illustrated by $A = C,\ B = E$:

$$\begin{aligned} &\overline{C \cup E} = \{e, i, j\}, \\ &\overline{C} \cap \overline{E} = \{e, f, g, h, i, j\} \cap \{a, c, e, i, j\} = \{e, i, j\}. \end{aligned}$$

■

6.2 Assignment of Probability

Suppose we conduct an 'experiment' whose outcome cannot be predicted, in the sense that a repetition may produce a different outcome; it is **random** or **stochastic**. We wish to measure the likelihood of each possible outcome: its **probability**.

The set U of all possible outcomes is the **sample space**. (Its contents are what we might find if we "sample" the experiment.)

An **event** is a subset A of U, to which we seek to allocate a **probability**, written $P(A)$ or $\Pr(A)$ or $\mathbb{P}(A)$.

Informally, $P(A)$ should be proportional to the 'size' of A. To achieve a standard that allows us to compare probabilities in different contexts, the chosen measure is the size of A *relative to* U. This idea leads to the following desirable properties for our measure.

Frame 6.1 Properties of $P(A)$

$$0 \leqslant P(A) \leqslant 1 \tag{6.4}$$

$$P(U) = 1, \qquad P(\emptyset) = 0 \tag{6.5}$$

$$P(\overline{A}) = 1 - P(A) \tag{6.6}$$

$$A \text{ subset of } B \quad \Rightarrow \quad P(A) \leqslant P(B) \tag{6.7}$$

Notation

There is no necessity for $P(A)$ to be defined as a number in $[0, 1]$, but this is the universal convention. For convenience, however, it is sometimes the case that a value will be quoted as $100P(A)\%$.

There are three principal ways in which to assign probabilities to events.

1. **Experimental**

   Suppose that N trials produce M instances of the event A. Then an estimate of the probability is $P(A) = \frac{M}{N}$.

   Example 6.3 A coin is tossed 100 times, producing 55 'Heads' (H) and 45 'Tails' (T).

   We may decide to use $P(H) = 0.55$, $P(T) = 0.45$ in our subsequent calculations. But this is not reliable: a second experiment could produce quite different results. ■

2. **Model-based**

   We identify all of the simplest – **elementary** – events and assume they obey simple rules. The most common such rule is that they are all equally likely and hence have equal probability.

Example 6.4 We may assume our coin in the previous example is unbiased; it is often called **fair**. The only elementary events are H and T. They must have equal probability and, between them, they account for all the probability. Hence $P(H) = P(T) = 0.5$. ■

3. **Personal**

   We make a guess based on our own intuitions or past experience, e.g., as a gambler does when deciding appropriate odds at which to bet on a horse. We shall not pursue this; it is not very different from the experimental measure.

Our approach will be to concentrate on **models**, eventually using **experiments** to test their validity.

Example 6.5 If a coin is fair, how likely is it to get 55 or more H in an experiment (as in Example 6.3).

The answer – using a method considered later – is that the probability of 55 or more H is 0.184. This is low, but not unreasonably so. It is not, on its own, sufficient evidence to disprove the fairness of the coin. ■

There are several **standard models**, used to mimic real situations.

- **Coin**: as above.
- **Die**: a six-sided (unbiased) die has $P(1) = P(2) = P(3) = P(4) = P(5) = P(6) = 1/6$.
- **Bag of balls**: usually a mixture, e.g., of colours.

  Example 6.6 A bag contains 4 black (B) and 6 white (W) balls; one is drawn at random. Then $P(B) = 0.4,\ P(W) = 0.6$. ■

- **Cards**: such as a standard pack of 52, without Jokers.

  Example 6.7 A card is selected at random: $P(\heartsuit) = 1/4,\ P(\text{A}) = 1/13$, where A represents an 'Ace'. ■

The preferred term for such 'experiments' is **sampling**, the idea being that there is a set of all possible outcomes, which we *sample* to obtain the result. For the **bag** and the **card** models, there are two fundamentally different types:

sampling **with** *and* **without** *replacement.*

Example 6.8 Returning to Example 6.6, if a ball is **replaced** after each sample, $P(B) = 0.4$ in every case.

Otherwise, repeated sampling leads to variable probabilities. Suppose we label the sample number by $\#n$ for the nth selection:

$$\text{if } \#1 = B \text{ then } P(\#2 = B) = 3/9,$$
$$\text{if } \#1 = W \text{ then } P(\#2 = B) = 4/9.$$

Note the use of $P(X = x)$ to denote the probability of a sampling labelled X resulting in the value x, a notation to be developed in §7.1. ■

The **coin** and **die** models are always *with replacement*, since coins and dice have no memory of what has previously occurred.

These basic models can be compounded in various ways to build more elaborate ones.

Example 6.9 A fair coin is tossed twice (or two coins are tossed together). What are the outcomes and their probabilities?

The order of tossing is important, as is the distinction between the two coins, if that model is preferred. In either case there are four outcomes: HH, HT, TH, TT, which should be equally likely, so each has probability $1/4$. ■

A useful tool in analysing multiple sampling from *non-replacement* models is the **binomial coefficient** $\binom{n}{r}$. This counts the number of ways in which r objects can be selected from n, without replacement and with the order unimportant. If these are all equally likely, each has probability $1/\binom{n}{r}$.

Example 6.10 The number of possible outcomes in the UK *National Lottery* is

$$\binom{49}{6} = 13,983,816,$$

since it is not allowed to choose the same number twice and the order of choice is irrelevant. Hence the probability of winning the jackpot is about 7×10^{-8}, or 1 in 14 million.

To find the probability (p) of winning the lowest prize, by getting three correct numbers from the six chosen, we first count how many draws (N), out of all possible draws (above), produce this. We must choose 3 of the 6 winning numbers and 3 of the 43 non-winning numbers:

$$N = \binom{6}{3}\binom{43}{3}, \qquad p = N\Big/\binom{49}{6} \simeq 0.0177.$$

■

Example 6.11 Suppose we deal a hand of two cards from a shuffled pack. There are $\binom{52}{2}$ different possible hands.

$$P(\text{AK}) = \binom{4}{1} \times \binom{4}{1}\Big/\binom{52}{2}.$$

(There are $4 \times 4 = 16$ different AK combinations.)

Similarly, for a hand of three cards,

$$P(3 \text{ Aces}) = \binom{4}{3}\Big/\binom{52}{3}.$$

(There are $\binom{4}{3} = 4$ different sets of three aces.) ■

Ex 6.1 Four numbers are chosen at random from the set $\{1, 2, 3, \ldots, 10\}$, allowing repetition. What is the probability that they are all different?

Ex 6.2 A college has a class of 100 students and it is known that:

60 read French, 40 German, 10 Italian; 4 read French and Italian, 6 German and Italian, 4 French and German; 2 read all three languages.

A student is selected from the class at random. What are the probabilities that the student reads (a) precisely two languages, (b) at least one language?

Ex 6.3 Construct the entire sample space, i.e., a list of all possible outcomes, when two fair dice are thrown, recording their readings separately, e.g., as $(1, 1)$.

Hence find the probabilities for the events:

a 1 or a 6 is included; there is no double; the sum of the throws is 9;

the sum is more than 9; the readings differ by 4;

the maximum reading is 4 or 5.

Ex 6.4

(a) **Betting odds** are a different way to specify probabilities. The odds 'a to b on' or, equivalently, 'b to a against' means the event is rated to have probability $\dfrac{a}{a+b}$. Thus '10 to 1' on has probability $10/11$, while '7 to 1' against has probability $1/8$.

Calculate the probabilities for 'evens' (1 to 1), 2 to 1 on, 5 to 2 against, 100 to 8 against.

(b) Calculate the odds for probabilities $3/4$ and $1/5$.

(c) To calculate the odds for a 'treble', i.e., three horses winning in separate races, the odds are converted to probabilities, multiplied and converted back to odds. Find the odds for the treble: 2 to 1, 7 to 2, 100 to 30 (all 'against').

6.3 The Addition Rule

Constructing compound models by listing elementary outcomes, as done in Example 6.9, is time-consuming and it is better to seek *rules* that allow the probabilities to be calculated from the simpler models.

Suppose the areas in the Venn Diagram are scaled versions of the associated probabilities. Then we can perform calculations using those areas. An immediate result is a rule for combining probabilities.

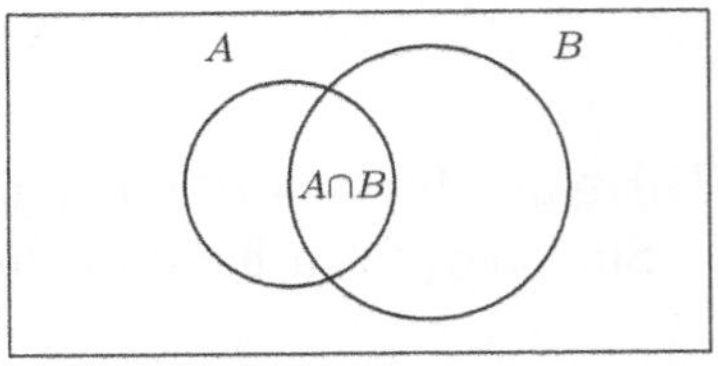

The total area covering A and B can be found by summing the separate areas for A and B, provided we subtract the common area representing $A \cap B$, since it would otherwise be counted twice. This leads to the **addition rule**.

> *Frame 6.2* The addition rule for probability
>
> $$P(A \cup B) = P(A) + P(B) - P(A \cap B) \tag{6.8}$$

There is a very useful special case, when $A \cap B = \emptyset$. This means that A and B cannot both occur and the term for such a situation is that the events are **mutually exclusive**.

> *Frame 6.3* The addition rule for mutually exclusive events
>
> $$P(A \cup B) = P(A) + P(B) \quad \text{if } A \cap B = \emptyset \tag{6.9}$$

Example 6.12 Suppose that 90% of a group of people can ride a bicycle, while 80% can drive a car. Then, writing these properties as B and C, we have, for an individual in the group, $P(B) = 0.9$, $P(C) = 0.8$. What is the probability that this person can either ride a bike or drive a car?

The simple-minded approach, using (6.9),

$$P(B \text{ or } C) = P(B \cup C) = P(B) + P(C) = 1.7,$$

clearly fails: no probability can exceed 1. The problem here is that the properties are not mutually exclusive: there are people who can do both. We cannot answer this question without knowing how many. Suppose it is 75%: $P(B \cap C) = 0.75$. Then (6.8) gives

$$P(B \cup C) = 0.9 + 0.8 - 0.75 = 0.95.$$

■

Note the shorthand notation here, choosing a letter that represents a property to stand for "x has the property X".

Example 6.13 In a group of 100 students, 60 speak F(rench), 30 speak G(erman) and 10 speak both.

$$P(F \cup G) = 0.6 + 0.3 - 0.1 = 0.8.$$

It is possible to analyse the given data and deduce that 20 speak N(either) language. This follows much more simply from the rules of probability:

$$P(N) = 1 - P(\overline{N}) = 1 - P(F \cup G) = 1 - 0.8 = 0.2.$$

It is very common in this subject to calculate the probability of the exact opposite of what is asked, then subtract from 1. ■

For the remainder of this section we concentrate on **mutual exclusivity** and use (6.9).

Example 6.14 A fair die is thrown. $P(5 \text{ or } 6) = 1/6 + 1/6 = 1/3$, since the events of throwing a 5 and a 6 clearly cannot occur simultaneously. ■

This special case can be easily extended to many events. (The general case can also be extended, but the resulting formula is very complicated.)

$$P(A_1 \cup A_2 \cup \cdots \cup A_n) = P(A_1) + P(A_2) + \cdots + P(A_n), \qquad (6.10)$$

if $A_i \cap A_j = \emptyset$ for all i and j, $i \neq j$.

Example 6.15 Find the probability of obtaining a 'Flush' in poker: five cards of the same suit.

There are $\binom{52}{5}$ different hands that can be dealt. Of these, there are $\binom{13}{5}$ different sets of 5 Hearts, for example. Hence

$$p = P(5 \times \heartsuit) = \binom{13}{5} \Big/ \binom{52}{5}.$$

The probabilities for ♣, $\diamondsuit$ and ♠ are the same, by symmetry. These events are mutually exclusive, so

$$P(\text{Flush}) = p + p + p + p \simeq 0.02.$$

■

A consequence of (6.10) is that if the full set of outcomes is divided into mutually exclusive sets then their probabilities sum to 1.

Example 6.16 On a given day, there is a 40% chance of precipitation, with rain three times as likely as snow, the latter including hail and sleet. Then, with obvious notation,

$$P(R) + P(S) = 0.4, \quad P(R) = 3P(S),$$

which can be solved to find

$$P(S) = 0.1, \; P(R) = 0.3, \; P(\text{Dry}) = 0.6.$$

■

This division into mutually exclusive sets of outcomes underpins the very useful method of **tree diagrams**, where a 'branch' of the tree is used for each outcome. We draw the tree, identify branches delivering our desired property, then calculate the probability using (6.10), relying on mutual exclusivity.

Example 6.17 A bag contains 3 B(lack), 2 W(hite) and 5 B/W striped balls. One ball is chosen at random. What is the probability that it contains Black? The simplest approach is to use the reverse: $1 - P(W) = 1 - 2/10 = 0.8$, but we pursue a direct approach here.

The required probability is the sum of the probabilities for the two relevant branches:

$$0.3 + 0.5 = 0.8,$$

indicated by ✓ on the **leaf**, as such an end-point is often known.

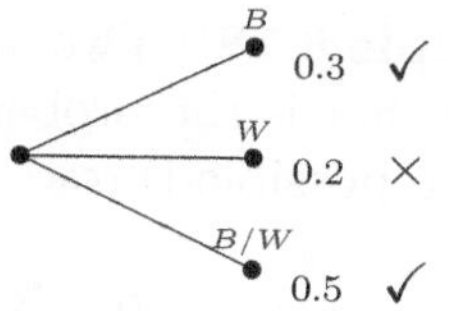

■

The real power of tree diagrams, as we see later, is when there are several components in the model. To incorporate this element requires us to derive a further rule.

Ex 6.5 A coin is weighted so that 'Heads' is twice as likely as 'Tails'. Find $P(\text{Heads})$ and $P(\text{Tails})$.

Ex 6.6

(a) Suppose $P(A \cup B) = 2/3$ and $P(A) = 1/4$. Find $P(B)$ when i. A and B are mutually exclusive, ii. $P(A \cap B) = 1/12$.

(b) **Mutually exclusive** events A and B have probabilities $P(A) = 1/6$ and $P(B) = 1/2$. Compute $P(\overline{A})$, $P(A \cup B)$, $P(A \cap \overline{B})$, $P(\overline{A \cup B})$.

6.4 Conditional Probability

A key value that the previous section required, but had no way to provide, is $P(A \cap B)$, i.e., the probability that the events A and B both occur. The difficulty with this quantity is that one event may depend on the other. This can range from A guaranteeing B, to A prohibiting B, as well as A making B more or less likely. For example, let A be the event that, in a game of cards, Player 1 holds four Aces and B that Player 2 holds one Ace. Clearly, if A occurs, B cannot occur, so $P(A \cap B) = 0$.

More realistic examples are:

- the chance of finding oil in one sector increases if it is found in an adjacent sector;
- an insurance company alters its judgement of an individual based on sex, smoking habits, family medical history, etc.;
- a person is more likely to get the flu if their partner has the flu.

This possible dependency is encapsulated in the idea of **conditional** probability, which we define and notate as follows.

> *Frame 6.4* *Definition of conditional probability*
>
> $P(B|A) =$ the probability that B occurs, given that A occurs

In general, $P(B|A) \neq P(B)$.

Example 6.18 Two dice are thrown and the values are added, with a result of 8. What is the probability that one die shows a six?

The possible throws are, with the dice in order:

$$\mathbf{6+2}, \quad 5+3, \quad 4+4, \quad 3+5, \quad \mathbf{2+6},$$

where the emboldened ones are those showing a six. These are all equally likely, so

$$P(\text{one shows six}|\text{sum is 8}) = {}^2\!/\!_5.$$

Without knowing the sum of the faces, the probability is, using (6.8),

$$\begin{aligned} P(\text{one shows six}) &= P(\text{1st is six}) + P(\text{2nd is six}) - P(\text{both are six}) \\ &= {}^1\!/\!_6 + {}^1\!/\!_6 - {}^1\!/\!_{36} = {}^{11}\!/\!_{36}, \end{aligned}$$

which is different. ■

This concept is particularly relevant for *selection without replacement*, since later selections depend on earlier ones.

Example 6.19 A bag contains 2 White and 3 Black balls. For sampling with replacement, $P(B) = {}^3\!/\!_5$ for every selection. Otherwise, for a second draw:

$$P(B|W \text{ drawn first}) = {}^3\!/\!_4, \qquad P(B|B \text{ drawn first}) = {}^1\!/\!_2.$$

■

Ex 6.7 Two fair dice are thrown, generating probabilities as in Exercise 6.3. Given that the sum of the numbers is 8, find the probability that both are even.

The experiment is repeated until as sum of either 6 or 7 is recorded. What is the probability that this stops with a total of 7?

6.5 The Product Rule

The most useful rule for calculating $P(A \cap B)$ – the **product rule** – depends on conditional probability.

Frame 6.5 *The product rule for probability*

$$P(A \cap B) = P(A)P(B|A) = P(B)P(A|B) \tag{6.11}$$

This rule can be used to calculate *any* of these three quantities, given the value of the other two. Its most common uses are to calculate $P(A \cap B)$, and to calculate one of the conditional probabilities from the value of the other.

Before looking at examples of conditional probability, there is one important special simple case, which applies when the events A and B are

independent. By this we mean that B's probability does not depend on A, and *vice versa*. Thus $P(B|A) = P(B)$ and (6.11) becomes

$$P(A \cap B) = P(A)P(B). \tag{6.12}$$

This is often taken as the definition of **independence**.

Frame 6.6 Definition of independent events
$P(A \cap B) = P(A)P(B)$ *or* $P(B|A) = P(B)$ *or* $P(A|B) = P(A)$

The more usual procedure in practice is to argue, *on physical grounds*, that A and B must be independent, then to use (6.12). Typical of such arguments are that dice cannot influence each other so throws of two dice or repeated throws of one die are independent, and that atoms in a radioactive specimen decay independently of each other.

Events must never be assumed to be independent without good evidence; the alluringly simple (6.12) will otherwise give false results.

Example 6.20 A bag contains 5 Black balls and 5 White balls and two are drawn. What is the probability that both are Black?

Replacement: The draws are independent, so (6.12) gives $P(BB) = \frac{1}{2} \times \frac{1}{2} = \frac{1}{4}$.

Non-replacement: After drawing one Black, we are left with $5W$, $4B$, so the probability for the next to be Black is $\frac{4}{9}$. Hence

$$P(BB) = P(1\text{st } B)P(2\text{nd } B|1\text{st } B) = \tfrac{1}{2} \times \tfrac{4}{9} = \tfrac{2}{9},$$

which is less than $\frac{1}{4}$. ■

Think about it like this

The following outlines the justification for (6.11). Suppose we know that A occurs. Then the probability for B must be conditional. When we use the Venn diagram in §6.1, we have to exclude all parts that do not occur inside A, which means two things. The sets for all other events must have their non-A parts removed, which we can do using an intersection: the relevant part of B is $A \cap B$. Also, all the individual (mutually exclusive) probabilities add up to $P(A)$, not 1, so we need to *rescale* them by dividing by that sum, $P(A)$. Hence

$$P(B|A) = \frac{P(A \cap B)}{P(A)},$$

which rearranges to give (6.11).

Example 6.21 In Example 6.18, suppose A represents the sum of 8. Only 5 of the 36 elementary events are in A, their probabilities adding up to $P(A) = \frac{5}{36}$. When we consider getting a six, B say, only 2 of the 11 such events overlap with A, so $P(A \cap B) = \frac{2}{36}$. Dividing by $P(A)$, to rescale this probability, gives $\frac{2}{5}$ as before. ■

We shall now concentrate on cases where **independence** can be assumed, returning to the more general case when we develop tree diagrams further.

Example 6.22 A coin is tossed twice. Then $P(HH) = 1/2 \times 1/2 = 1/4$, which we could have calculated by allocating the probability evenly across the four elementary events: $HH,\ HT,\ TH,\ TT$. ■

Example 6.23 A gambler bets on three horses, with probabilities of winning – as judged by the bookmaker – $1/2,\ 2/3,\ 1/10$.

We can reasonably assume the races are independent of each other, so the probability of winning a *treble*, through all three horses winning, is

$$P(\text{Treble}) = 1/2 \times 2/3 \times 1/10 = 1/30,$$

so a stake of £1 should result in £30 being paid back. ■

The product rule is particularly useful for calculating

$$P(\text{all events occur}) \quad \text{and} \quad P(\text{no event occurs}).$$

The first of these is a straightforward generalisation of (6.12):

$$P(A_1 \cap A_2 \cap \cdots \cap A_n) = P(A_1)P(A_2)\cdots P(A_n) \quad \text{(independent events)}.$$

The second is the same, but using $\overline{A_k}$: no event occurs if all events fail to occur.

It is a short step to a very useful formula:

$$P(\text{at least one event occurs}) = 1 - P(\text{no event occurs}), \qquad (6.13)$$

a value that is usually very time-consuming to calculate directly, as the next example shows.

Example 6.24 [*The first significant probability calculation, due to Fermat.*] A professional gambler discovered that betting on throwing at least one six in four throws of a die wins in the long-term, but betting on throwing at least one double-six in 24 throws of two dice loses. Why?

For the first case, $P(\text{non-6}) = 5/6$, so $P(\text{all non-6}) = (5/6)^4$. Hence

$$P(\text{at least one six}) = 1 - (5/6)^4 \simeq 0.518.$$

We analyse the second case similarly, with $P(66) = 1/36$, $P(\text{non-66}) = 35/36$:

$$P(\text{at least one double-six}) = 1 - (35/36)^{24} \simeq 0.491.$$

■

We finish with application of the product rule to the important practical problem of **Reliability** of a device constructed by connecting individual components. In the simplest model we wish to connect two components A and B to form the device D. Let

$$P(A) = \text{ probability of } A \textbf{ failing}, \text{ etc.}$$

and we assume that such failures are **independent** of each other, i.e., one component failing does not affect the other's performance. We note that

$$\text{probability that } A \text{ does not fail } = P(\overline{A}) = 1 - P(A).$$

There are two ways to connect A and B.

Series

$$\begin{aligned} P(D) &= P(\text{one fails}) = 1 - P(A \text{ works } \textbf{and } B \text{ works}) \\ &= 1 - [1 - P(A)]\,[1 - P(B)] \\ P(D) &= P(A) + P(B) - P(A)P(B). \end{aligned} \tag{6.14}$$

Note that the product rule was used in the middle step, reflecting the "and" (as well as independence).

Parallel

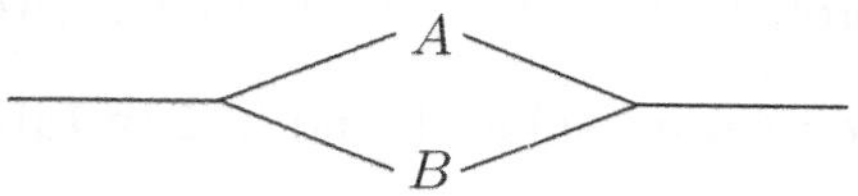

$$P(D) = P(\text{both fail}) = P(A)P(B). \tag{6.15}$$

Note that again independence was relied upon.

Example 6.25 Suppose A is 90% reliable and B is 80% reliable. Then $P(A) = 0.1$, $P(B) = 0.2$ and

$$\begin{aligned} &\text{series:} && P(D) = 0.1 + 0.2 - 0.1 \times 0.2 = 0.28, \\ &\text{parallel:} && P(D) = 0.1 \times 0.2 = 0.02. \end{aligned}$$

We see that the parallel device is much safer. That ought to be clear from commonsense, but we now have a measure to show how much safer it is. ■

Ex 6.8 Suppose that $P(A) = 0.4$, $P(B) = 0.6$ and $P(B|A) = 0.8$. Find:

$$P(A \cap B), \quad P(A \cup B), \quad P(A|B), \quad P(B|\overline{A}), \quad P(\overline{A}|\overline{B}).$$

Ex 6.9 Two cards are drawn at random from 10 cards numbered 1 to 10. Find the probability that the sum is odd if (a) the two cards are drawn together, (b) the first is replaced before the second is drawn.

Ex 6.10 A circuit consists of three components A, B, C in series. A is itself built from two components A_1 and A_2 in parallel, C is built from C_1, C_2 and C_3 in parallel, while B is a single component. Find the probability of overall failure, given the individual probabilities of failure and assuming *independence*:

$$P(A_1) = 0.2, \; P(A_2) = 0.1; \quad P(B) = 0.05;$$

$$P(C_1) = 0.2, \; P(C_2) = 0.25, \; P(C_3) = 0.2.$$

6.6 Tree Diagrams

We can extend the simple tree diagram, introduced in §6.3, to deal with multiple events, which we can think of as sequences of 'simple' events.

At the end of each branch for the first event, we draw new branches to cover **all** possibilities in the second, *assuming that the indicated outcome of the first event has taken place.* This last statement is key to the calculations: the method relies on **mutually exclusivity** of the branches and **conditional probabilities** assigned to each. It is summed up as follows.

Frame 6.7 *Method of tree diagrams*

1. Assign probabilities to all parts of each branch: these will be **conditional** probabilities.
2. Multiply probabilities along each branch (**product rule**).
3. Add up the relevant values found in 2 (**addition rule**).

Example 6.26 A box contains 9 bulbs, of which 3 are defective (D). Select 2 bulbs, *without replacement*, and test them.

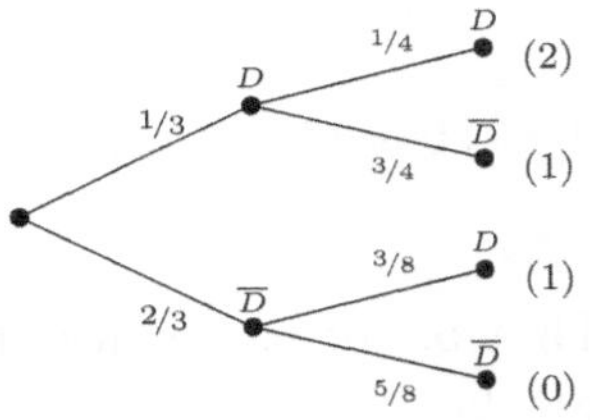

For the top two branches, the second draw has 2 defective bulbs out of 8, while for the bottom two, it is 3 out of 8. The probabilities differ on account of that. The number of defectives is written at the end of each 'leaf' and informs the calculation of the probabilities.

$$P(0D) = \tfrac{2}{3} \cdot \tfrac{5}{8} = \tfrac{5}{12},$$
$$P(1D) = \tfrac{1}{3} \cdot \tfrac{3}{4} + \tfrac{2}{3} \cdot \tfrac{3}{8} = \tfrac{6}{12},$$
$$P(2D) = \tfrac{1}{3} \cdot \tfrac{1}{4} = \tfrac{1}{12}.$$

Note that these add to 1, as we would expect. ■

In some situations, e.g., sampling until an event occurs, the sampling and the tree can go on for ever. Summing the probabilities then needs infinite series.

Example 6.27 A and B play a game: a coin is tossed repeatedly until two consecutive tosses are the same. If this occurs on an **even**-numbered throw, A wins; if on an **odd**-numbered throw, B wins.

The first part of the tree diagram is shown below, with leaves labelled by the winner. It goes on forever, but we now have enough data to set up the probability sums. Note the symmetry between the top and bottom, which allows us to use just one half, and double the result.

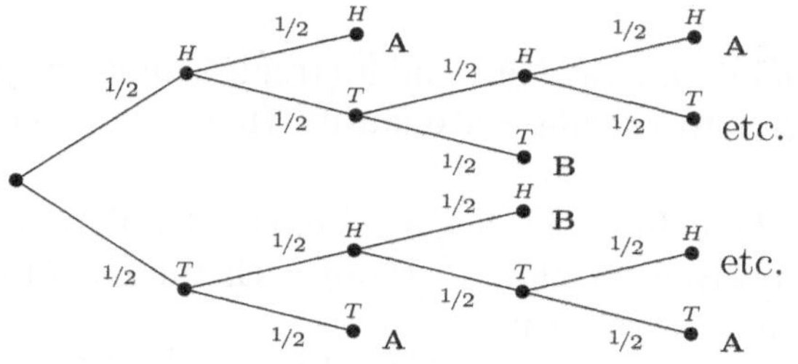

We find geometric series in the results:

$$P(A \text{ wins}) = 2\left[\frac{1}{4} + \frac{1}{16} + \frac{1}{64} + \cdots\right] = 2\,\frac{1/4}{1 - 1/4} = \frac{2}{3},$$
$$P(B \text{ wins}) = 2\left[\frac{1}{8} + \frac{1}{32} + \frac{1}{128} + \cdots\right] = 2\,\frac{1/8}{1 - 1/4} = \frac{1}{3}.$$

■

One of the most useful applications of the general product rule comes from the fact that there are two expressions for $P(A \cap B)$ in Frame 6.5:

$$P(A \cap B) = P(A)P(B|A) = P(B)(P(A|B)$$

can be rearranged to give

$$P(B|A) = \frac{P(A|B)P(B)}{P(A)}, \tag{6.16}$$

i.e., we can *reverse* conditional probabilities.

Think about it like this

It is often the case that we can measure one conditional probability but require the other. Equations such as (6.16) provide the necessary formulae. This is known as **Bayesian analysis** and we shall use tree diagrams to illustrate it.

Example 6.28 A box contains three coins: two are fair and the other is double-headed. A coin is chosen at random and tossed. If it shows *Heads*, what is the probability it is double-headed?

Let F = fair and D = double-headed. The crux of the problem is that we know $P(H|D)$, which must be 1, but wish to know $P(D|H)$.

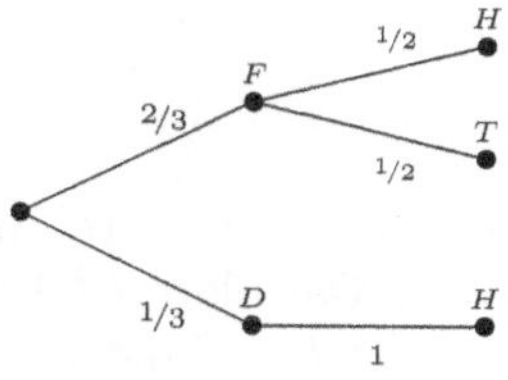

Sum the first and third branches to find $P(H)$, while $P(D)$ can be read off the tree:

$$P(H) = 2/3 \cdot 1/2 + 1/3 \cdot 1 = 2/3,$$
$$P(D) = 1/3.$$

Then (6.16) gives $P(D|H) = \dfrac{1 \times {}^1\!/_3}{{}^2\!/_3} = {}^1\!/_2.$

■

The next example is a more practical one and its result is quite surprising. It illustrates well the ability to calculate a quantity that cannot be easily measured.

Example 6.29 A medical condition C affects 2% of the population. There is a test T, which shows positive for 90% of those with the condition and falsely positive for 1% of those without it.

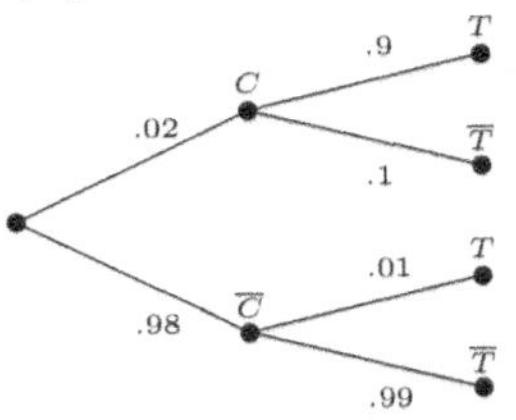

Sum the first and third branches to find the probability of a positive result:

$$P(T) = .02 \times .9 + .98 \times .01 = 0.0278,$$

while the first branch gives

$$P(C \cap T) = .02 \times .9 = 0.018.$$

Then the probability that a positive test shows the person has the condition is

$$P(C|T) = \frac{P(C \cap T)}{P(T)} = \frac{.018}{.0278} = \frac{180}{278} \simeq 0.65.$$

Then $P(\overline{C}|T) \simeq 0.35$ and we find that about one-third of those who test positively do *not* have the condition. ■

Ex 6.11 A coin is thrown twice. What is the probability that two 'Heads' appear, given that the first throw is a 'Head'? What is the probability that two 'Heads' appear, given that at least one throw is a 'Head'?

Ex 6.12 Heather produces 30% of a bank's economic forecasts and Trevor produces the rest. Heather's forecasts are correct 75% of the time and Trevor's are correct 60% of the time. If a forecast, chosen at random, is correct, what is the probability that it was produced by Heather?

Ex 6.13 A company owns drilling rights in the North Sea. From geological records they know that high quality oil deposits are found 20% of the time, low quality deposits 30% of the time and no oil 50% of the time. Pre-drilling seismic tests give positive results on 70% of high quality sites, 35% of low quality sites and 10% on sites with no oil.

(a) Find the overall probability of a positive result in the seismic test.

(b) If the result is positive, what is the probability of finding oil at the site, based on that information?

6.7 Revision Exercises

Ex 6.14 A die is thrown twice. Let A denote "the number of spots on the first throw" and B denote "the total score of both throws". Calculate $P(A = 2)$, $P(B = 6)$ and $P(B = 7)$. Is either the event $B = 6$ or the event $B = 7$ independent of the event $A = 2$?

Ex 6.15 A bag contains 3 **red** balls, 4 **green** balls and 1 **black** ball. Balls are drawn at random, one after the other **without replacement**, until either two of the balls that have been drawn are of the same colour, or the black ball is drawn. Calculate:

(a) the probability that the process stops without the black ball having been drawn;

(b) the probability that there are precisely two draws made;

(c) the probability that the black ball has been drawn, given that precisely two draws were required.

Ex 6.16 A bag contains 2 **red** balls, 3 **blue** balls and 4 **green** balls. Two balls are drawn at random, one after the other **without replacing the first**. Calculate:

(a) the probability that both balls are the same colour;

(b) the probability that the second ball is green;

(c) the probability that the first ball is red, given that the second is known to be green.

7 DISCRETE DISTRIBUTIONS

The isolated probability calculations carried out in the previous chapter are valuable for some contexts, but in most cases we wish to view the whole picture, i.e., to have a complete set of probabilities encompassing all events, preferably bundled into mutually exclusive sets, as used in tree diagrams.

One particularly useful way to control this is to allocate a *number* to each outcome. Once we have such a number, we can marry it to the probabilities to calculate informative information, such as an *average* value. These numbers are thought of as values of a **random variable**. A specification of *all* possible values of the random variable, and their associated probabilities, is a **probability distribution**: a statement of how the available probability has been "distributed" among the outcomes.

7.1 Random Variables

Statistically-based experiments, or **trials**, often measure a number, thought of as one of the possible values of a variable, X say. This can be an artificial code or a natural part of the model. The following examples illustrate the wide range of possibilities:

1. the number on the face of a die (**natural**);
2. coin toss: $X = 1$ for *Heads*, $X = 0$ for *Tails* (**encoded**);
3. sum of the throws of two dice (not an *elementary* event, so this simplifies the structure by having fewer cases to deal with);
4. number of defectives in a sample (as in Example 6.26);
5. the net win at roulette (can be negative);
6. the lifetime of a light bulb;
7. the time between arrivals at a checkout.

The variables involved here are called **random variables**, since the values for any given trial cannot be predicted. They are almost always notated by capital letters, including Greek letters.

There is a fundamental distinction between the cases 1–5 and 6–7. The values for the former cases are isolated, like the natural numbers $\mathbb{N}$: the random variable is **discrete**.

The values for the latter can take any value in an **interval** in $\mathbb{R}$: the random variable is **continuous**. We shall defer consideration of these until the next chapter.

Whatever the context, the events for different values of the random variable must be **mutually exclusive**, else many of the calculations that follow are invalid. This is similar to the restriction on ordinary variables for functions, where one input value can produce only one output value. Here, one outcome can produce only one value of the variable.

7.2 Probability Distributions

Once we identify all possible values of a random variable X, and the probability that each occurs, we have defined a **(probability) distribution**. Associated with this is a key function – where "function" is used in its normal sense – called the **probability function**. Some people insert the word "**density**" but we shall reserve this for continuous distributions.

Frame 7.1 *The probability function and its properties*

$$f(x) = P(X = x) \tag{7.1}$$

$$0 \leqslant f(x) \leqslant 1 \tag{7.2}$$

$$\sum_{\text{all } k} f(x_k) = 1 \tag{7.3}$$

(7.1) defines $f(x)$ to be the probability of obtaining that value of X and (7.2) is a consequence of $f(x)$ being a probability. (7.3), which relies on mutual exclusivity, shows that we have covered all possibilities.

The probability function can sometimes be specified by a formula (see §§7.4–7) but meanwhile we look at examples using tables and graphs.

Example 7.1 In Example 6.26 we found the probabilities for all possible draws of two bulbs from a box. The random variable was a natural one: the number of defectives.

The probabilities to be plotted are those in following table, using values referred to above:

x	0	1	2
$f(x)$	$5/12$	$6/12$	$1/12$

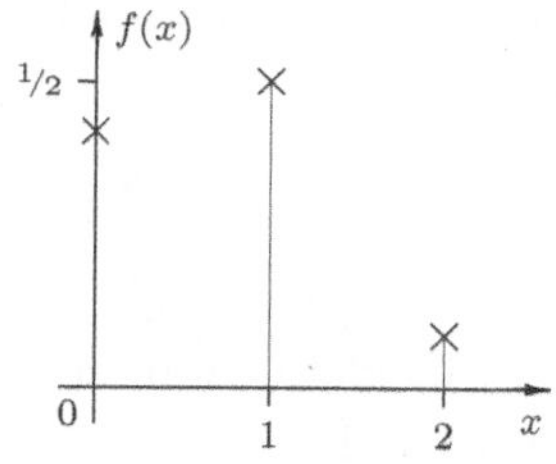

■

Example 7.2 Three fair coins are tossed and the number of *Heads* defines the random variable X. There are eight possibilities, listed as follows, with the number of *Heads* shown:

$HHH\,(3)$, $HHT\,(2)$, $HTH\,(2)$, $HTT\,(1)$, $THH\,(2)$, $THT\,(1)$, $TTH\,(1)$, $TTT\,(0)$.

Since each of these outcomes is equally-likely, we can calculate probabilities as follows:

x	0	1	2	3
$f(x)$	$1/8$	$3/8$	$3/8$	$1/8$

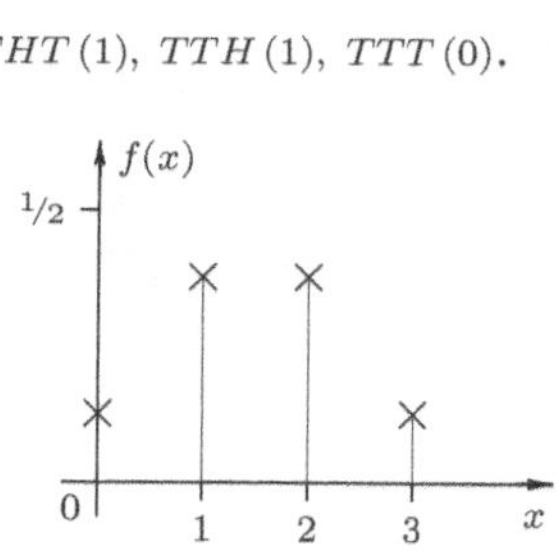

■

Example 7.3 Two four-sided dice are thrown and the numbers on the faces are added. There are 16 elementary events, each with probability $^1/_{16}$. The table on the left shows how the totals are distributed, which feeds into the table on the right, defining the probability function.

	1	2	3	4
1	2	3	4	5
2	3	4	5	6
3	4	5	6	7
4	5	6	7	8

x	2	3	4	5	6	7	8
$f(x)$	$^1/_{16}$	$^2/_{16}$	$^3/_{16}$	$^4/_{16}$	$^3/_{16}$	$^2/_{16}$	$^1/_{16}$

Note that the probabilities sum to 1. ■

There is a further useful function associated with all distributions: the **(cumulative) distribution function**. The bracketed word is a helpful reminder of its definition, but the function is so frequently used that it is often omitted.

Its definition and principal property are given in the following frame.

Frame 7.2 *The cumulative distribution function*

$$F(x) = P(X \leqslant x) = \sum_{y \leqslant x} f(y) \tag{7.4}$$

$$P(a < X \leqslant b) = F(b) - F(a) \tag{7.5}$$

The mutual exclusivity gives the summation formula and the obvious formula

$$\sum_{y \leqslant a} f(y) + \sum_{a<y\leqslant b} f(y) = \sum_{y \leqslant b} f(y)$$

rearranges to give (7.5).

From its definition we see that $F(x)$ never decreases, while $F(-\infty) = 0$ and $F(\infty) = 1$.

Example 7.4 Draw the graph of $F(x)$ for the distribution in Example 7.2.

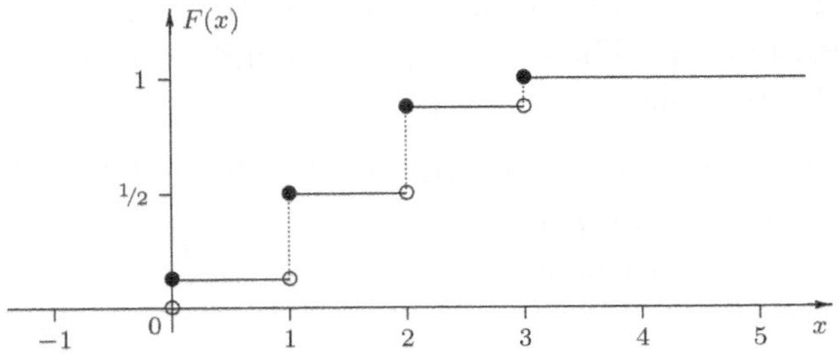

■

Think about it like this

The graph in this example shows a serious drawback to $F(x)$: it is defined piecewise and is discontinuous. Its key role is in **continuous** distributions. For those, it is the counterpart to $f(x)$ that proves difficult to use, while the distribution function has much simpler properties and is generally a continuous function.

Ex 7.1 Two fair dice are thrown. Let N be the larger of the two numbers. Find $P(N = k)$ for $k = 1, 2, \ldots, 6$.

Ex 7.2 A die has faces numbered from 1 to 6 and is weighted so that the probability of throwing n in a single throw is proportional to n, i.e., it is λn for some constant λ. Find λ.

7.3 Distribution Parameters

The numerical values of a random variable allow us to define and calculate certain 'summary' values, called **parameters**, which give an overall picture of the distribution. In *Statistics*, we carry out practical trials to measure certain values, which are direct counterparts of these parameters. These measures are, in fact, called **statistics**. As we shall see much later, using just two of these statistics can often allow us to draw conclusions from statistical trials irrespective of the details of the underlying distribution.

7.3.1 Mode

The **mode** for a distribution is the most probable value of X, i.e., the value x for which $f(x)$ is a maximum.

Example 7.5 For the four-sided dice in Example 7.3, the mode is 5, with probability $^4/_{16}$.

For the three coins in Example 7.2, there are two modes: 1 and 2, with equal probabilities $^3/_8$. ■

The mode is mostly used in 'descriptive', rather than computational, statistical work.

7.3.2 Median

The median is the 'middle' value in the sense that the probability of lying on each side is exactly $^1/_2$. Thus $F(m) = {}^1/_2$.

Frame 7.3 *The definition of the median*

$$m = F^{-1}(0.5) \tag{7.6}$$

This definition relies on the **inverse function** for $F(x)$, which may not exist. As we see in the following examples, this means that the median may not be defined or may have an infinite number of values.

Example 7.6 Consider a single coin toss.

Define

$$X = \begin{cases} 0 & \text{for } \textit{Tails}, \\ 1 & \text{for } \textit{Heads}, \end{cases}$$

each value having probability $1/2$.

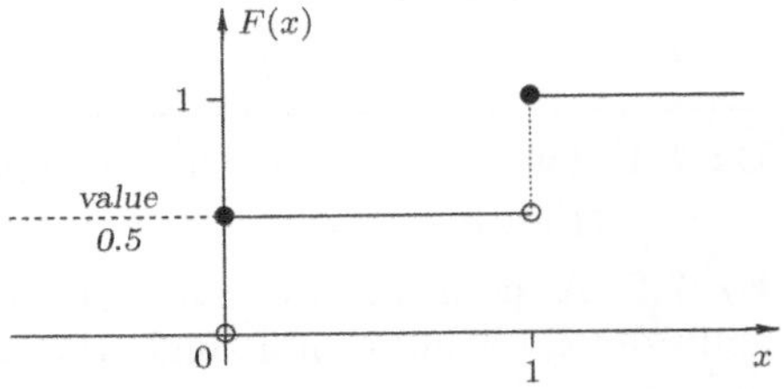

The distribution function's graph shows that $F(x) = 0.5$ for $0 \leqslant x < 1$, so there are an infinite number of 'medians'. A commonsense choice is the mid-point $1/2$, although this is not a possible value of X. ■

Example 7.7 Consider the choice of one card from a set of three.

We have $X = 1, 2, 3$, each with probability $1/3$. There is no x for which $F(x) = 0.5$, although $x = 2$ is an obvious commonsense choice, as the graph suggests.

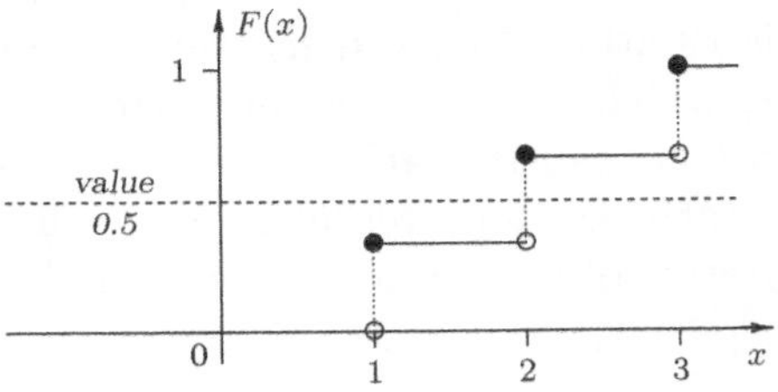

■

Nevertheless, the definition in Frame 7.3 is useful for *continuous* distributions, where we rarely encounter problems in defining the inverse function.

7.3.3 Expected Value (Mean)

For computational, rather than descriptive, purposes, a better measure of the centre of the distribution is the **expected value** or **mean**, defined and notated as follows.

Frame 7.4 Expected value or mean of a distribution

$$E(X) = \mu_X = \sum_k x_k P(X = x_k) = \sum_k x_k f(x_k) \tag{7.7}$$

The rationale for this definition is as follows. Suppose we take a sample of N values, where each x_k appears with a **frequency** f_k times. Then the **average** of the sample (in the everyday sense of the word) is

$$\frac{f_1 x_1 + f_2 x_2 + \cdots + f_n x_n}{N} = \frac{f_1}{N} x_1 + \frac{f_2}{N} x_2 + \cdots + \frac{f_n}{N} x_n \simeq \mu_X,$$

since $\frac{f_k}{N} \simeq f(x_k)$ when the sample is a representative one. Thus the mean and the average are approximately the same. Indeed, 'mean' is another word for 'average'.

Example 7.8 Consider a six-sided die, where the probabilities are all $^1/_6$. The mean score is

$$\mu_X = 1 \times {}^1/_6 + 2 \times {}^2/_6 + \cdots + 6 \times {}^1/_6 = 21 \times {}^1/_6 = 3.5.$$

■

Example 7.9 Consider the tossing of three coins, as in Example 7.2. The mean number of *Heads* is

$$\mu_X = 0 \times {}^1/_8 + 1 \times {}^3/_8 + 2 \times {}^3/_8 + 3 \times {}^1/_8 = {}^{12}/_8 = 1.5.$$

■

Example 7.10 Consider the number of defective bulbs in Example 6.26. The mean number of defectives is

$$\mu_X = 0 \times {}^5/_{12} + 1 \times {}^6/_{12} + 2 \times {}^1/_{12} = {}^8/_{12} = {}^2/_3.$$

■

The mean in all of these examples is a value that cannot be achieved by the random variable X. This is not unusual and is not a problem, since the mean is related to repeated sampling, not to a single sample. A typical application is to the situation when there are N samples and the outcomes are added, e.g., a gambler playing a game with mean winnings μ_X will "expect" to win an approximate amount $N\mu_X$ in N games. This helps explain the name **expected value**.

7.3.4 Variance

There is one further type of measure required for a distribution; once we have it we can make great advances in statistical calculations. We need to measure **dispersion**, i.e., how spread out a distribution is (about its mean). We would expect the result of throwing a die to have a larger spread than the result of tossing three coins, since the latter has the probabilities near the mean larger than the other values.

There are two such quantities; the easier to investigate is the **variance**. There are two equivalent formulae: the first is the theoretically justified one and the second is the computational one.

Frame 7.5 Variance of a distribution

$$\text{Var}(X) = \sum_k (x_k - \mu_X)^2 P(X = x_k) = \sum_k (x_k - \mu_X)^2 f(x_k) \quad (7.8)$$

$$\text{Var}(X) = \sum_k x_k^2 f(x_k) - \mu_X^2 = E(X^2) - [E(X)]^2 \quad (7.9)$$

Think about it like this

The idea for the variance is that we wish a representative value of the difference of the values of X from the mean μ, i.e., $X - \mu$. We cannot simply average these because the positive and negative values would cancel each other out. But if we *square* the values first, we banish negative values and get a true measure of the spread: $E\left[(X-\mu)^2\right]$, an 'average' value of $(X-\mu)^2$.

For convenience, we often suppress the subscript in μ_X when there is no ambiguity.

Example 7.11 Consider the tossing of three coins, as in Example 7.2. The mean, from Example 7.9, is $\mu = 3/2$. Aiming to use (7.8), we construct the table:

x_k	0	1	2	3
$(x_k-\mu)^2$	$9/4$	$1/4$	$1/4$	$9/4$
$f(x_k)$	$1/8$	$3/8$	$3/8$	$1/8$

Then multiply and add the last two rows:

$$\mathrm{Var}(X) = \tfrac{9}{32} + \tfrac{3}{32} + \tfrac{3}{32} + \tfrac{9}{32} = 3/4.$$

The formula (7.9) finds:

$$\mathrm{Var}(X) = 0^2 \times 1/8 + 1^2 \times 3/8 + 2^2 \times 3/8 + 3^2 \times 1/8 - (3/2)^2 = 3/4.$$

Note that this answer can be interpreted as $3 \times 1/2 \times 1/2 = n \times P(H) \times P(\overline{H})$, where n is the number of coins. We see in §7.6 that this is no accident. ■

Before looking at further examples, it is informative to see why the two versions are the same. From (7.8),

$$\begin{aligned}\mathrm{Var}(X) &= \sum_k \left[x_k^2 - 2\mu x_k + \mu^2\right] f(x_k)\\ &= \sum_k x_k^2 f(x_k) - 2\mu \sum_k x_k f(x_k) + \mu^2 \sum_k f(x_k)\\ &= E(X^2) - 2\mu\mu + \mu^2 \times 1\\ &= E(X^2) - \mu^2,\end{aligned}$$

using (7.7) and the fact that the probabilities add to 1.

Example 7.12 Consider a six-sided die, whose mean was found in Example 7.8 to be 3.5.

$$\mathrm{Var}(X) = 1^2 \times 1/6 + 2^2 \times 1/6 + \cdots + 6^2 \times 1/6 - (7/2)^2 = \tfrac{91}{6} - \tfrac{49}{4} = \tfrac{35}{12}.$$

We see that this is indeed larger than the variance for three coins ($3/4$). ■

Example 7.13 Consider the defective bulbs in Example 6.26, whose mean was found in Example 7.10 to be $2/3$.

$$\mathrm{Var}(X) = 0^2 \times 5/12 + 1^2 \times 6/12 + 2^2 \times 1/12 - (2/3)^2 = 10/12 - 4/9 = 7/18.$$

■

7.3.5 Standard Deviation

The variance Var(X) has one drawback for practical statistical work: its measurement unit (if there is one) is the square of that for X. This is easily remedied, by using the **standard deviation**.

Frame 7.6 Standard deviation of a distribution

$$\sigma_X = \sqrt{\text{Var}(X)} \tag{7.10}$$

Think about it like this

This does not make the variance redundant, since the algebraic difficulties involved with the square root means the necessary theoretical work associated with the standard deviation has to be done for the variance, before using the square root.

Notation

The subscript X is sometimes omitted, when the context is clear. Some authors use σ_X^2 to notate Var(X).

Example 7.14 For the three coins in Example 7.2 the standard deviation is $\sigma_X = \sqrt{3/4} = \sqrt{3}/2$. ■

Example 7.15 Consider the four-sided dice in Example 7.3.

This symmetric distribution has 5 as both its mode and median. The other parameters are

$$\begin{aligned}
E(X) &= \frac{1}{16}[2\times 1 + 3\times 2 + 4\times 3 + 5\times 4 + 6\times 3 + 7\times 2 + 8\times 1] \\
&= \frac{1}{16}[2 + 6 + 12 + 20 + 18 + 14 + 8] = 5, \\
\text{Var}(X) &= \frac{1}{16}\left[2^2\times 1 + 3^2\times 2 + \cdots + 8^2\times 1\right] - 5^2 \\
&= 27.5 - 25 = 2.5, \\
\sigma_X &= \sqrt{2.5}.
\end{aligned}$$

■

Ex 7.3 A fair 4-sided die has the numbers 1, 2, 3 and 4 inscribed on its faces, those being the values of a random variable X. Find the probability distribution for X, its mean and variance.

Ex 7.4 A bag contains 4 red and 2 blue counters. One counter at a time is removed from the bag but not replaced, until a blue counter appears. What is the expected number of counters drawn from the bag?

Ex 7.5 In a set of 5 objects, one is special. One object is selected at random and inspected to see if it is the special one. If so, the process stops. Otherwise the experiment is repeated, with the selected object **not replaced**. Let X be the number of selections required to obtain the special one, so X is from 1 to 5.

Find the probability distribution for X, graph the probability function and the distribution function. Calculate $P(X \leqslant 2)$, $P(X > 3)$ and $E(X)$. Suggest a value for the median.

Ex 7.6

(a) Calculate the mode and mean for the random variable N in Exercise 7.1.

(b) Calculate the mean, variance and standard deviation of the score obtained when the die in Exercise 7.2 is thrown.

7.4 Uniform Distribution

We now examine four key distributions that appear frequently in practice. It makes good sense to find the properties of the general forms of these, rather than have to undertake the work every time one appears.

Two are *finite*, in the sense of having a random variable taking values from 0 or 1 to n, while the other two are *infinite*, since the variables range from 0 or 1 to ∞.

The first is the **uniform** distribution, in which the values from 1 to n occur with equal probability:

$$P(X = k) = \frac{1}{n} \quad (1 \leqslant k \leqslant n).$$

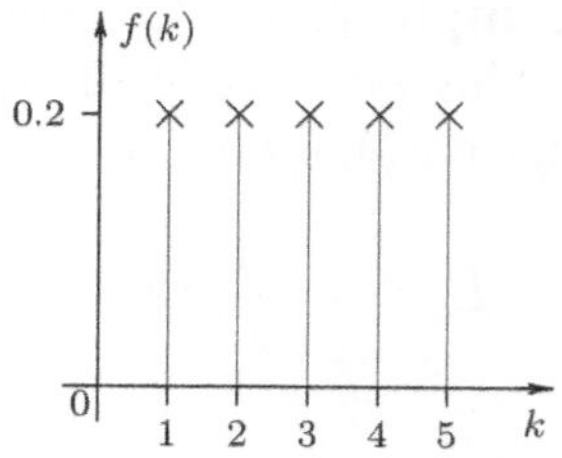

The graph shows the probability function for $n = 5$.

We can find the mean and variance using standard summation formulae:

$$E(X) = [1 + 2 + \cdots + n]\,\frac{1}{n} = \frac{n(n+1)}{2}\,\frac{1}{n} = \frac{n+1}{2},$$

$$\begin{aligned}\mathrm{Var}(X) &= \left[1^2 + 2^2 + \cdots + n^2\right]\frac{1}{n} - \left(\frac{n+1}{2}\right)^2\\ &= \frac{n(n+1)(2n+1)}{6}\,\frac{1}{n} - \frac{(n+1)^2}{4}\\ &= \frac{n+1}{12}\left[4n + 2 - 3n - 3\right] = \frac{n^2-1}{12}.\end{aligned}$$

We have already encountered the uniform distribution: a fair coin ($n = 2$), a fair die ($n = 6$), a pack of cards ($n = 52$).

To sum up, for the general case:

Frame 7.7 *Uniform distribution on {1,2,...,n}*

$$f(k) = \frac{1}{n} \quad (1 \leqslant k \leqslant n) \tag{7.11}$$

$$E(X) = \frac{n+1}{2} \tag{7.12}$$

$$\mathrm{Var}(X) = \frac{n^2-1}{12} \tag{7.13}$$

Example 7.16 For a coin with $P(\mathit{Tails}) = 1$, $P(\mathit{Heads}) = 2$,

$$E(X) = 3/2, \qquad \mathrm{Var}(X) = \frac{4-2}{12} = 1/4.$$

This is similar to Example 7.6, where we used values 0 and 1. There the mean is $1/2$; here it is $1/2 + 1$. As we would expect, adding one to the values adds one to the mean. The variance, however, is unchanged. It measures the *spread* about the mean and so is unaffected when all values (and hence the mean) are moved by the same amount. ■

Example 7.17 Consider $n = 10$. Then $E(X) = 5.5$ and $\mathrm{Var}(X) = \frac{99}{12} = \frac{33}{4}$.
More useful is the set of values $\{0, 1, \ldots, 9\}$, i.e., $Y = X - 1$. Then

$$E(Y) = 5.5 - 1 = 4.5, \qquad \mathrm{Var}(Y) = 33/4.$$

■

This example illustrates an important use of the uniform distribution. It controls streams of **random numbers**, i.e., sequences of numbers that are all of equal probability and occur at random, as if sampled from a uniform distribution. They are used in *simulation* programs. Those for a uniform random variable are fundamental, in the sense that a stream fitting a different distribution is usually derived from a uniform stream.

Example 7.18 To get a set of numbers uniformly distributed on $[0, 1]$ we could generate ones from 0 to 10,000, then divide by 10^4. ■

Ex 7.7 Find the probability distribution, mean and variance for the result of throwing a fair die. Verify that these results agree with the uniform distribution on $\{1, 2, 3, 4, 5, 6\}$.

7.5 Geometric Distribution

We first define a simple random process that underpins the key distributions in this section and the next.

A process with a probability p of *success* and probability q of *failure*, with $p + q = 1$, is a **Bernoulli trial**. We shall now use repeated (identical) Bernoulli trials, with an important assumption: *they are independent.* (This allows use of the simple form of the product rule.)

Suppose that X measures the number of trials needed to achieve a first success. Then, the product rule gives

$$X = k \quad \Rightarrow \quad k-1 \text{ failures, then success} \quad \Rightarrow \quad f(k) = P(X=k) = q^{k-1}p.$$

Note that

$$\sum_k f(k) = p + qp + q^2p + q^3p + \cdots$$
$$= p\left[1 + q + q^2 + \cdots\right] = p\frac{1}{1-q} = 1,$$

since $p + q = 1$. The sum involved is the geometric series, revealing the underlying sequence of probabilities to be a geometric progression; hence this is known as a **geometric distribution**. It has applications in *quality control.*

The expected value is

$$\begin{aligned} E(X) &= p + 2qp + 3q^2p + 4q^3p + \cdots \\ &= p\frac{d}{dq}\left[1 + q + q^2 + q^3 + \cdots\right] \\ &= p\frac{d}{dq}\left[\frac{1}{1-q}\right] \\ &= p(1-q)^{-2} = p\frac{1}{p^2} = \frac{1}{p}. \end{aligned}$$

Alternatively, one can argue that in N trials we expect Np successes, which are spaced out by $\frac{N}{Np} = \frac{1}{p}$, on average.

The variance can be found similarly. The key data are given in the following Frame.

Frame 7.8 *Geometric distribution with parameter p*

$$f(k) = q^{k-1}p \quad (k \geqslant 1) \tag{7.14}$$

$$E(X) = \frac{1}{p} \tag{7.15}$$

$$\mathrm{Var}(X) = \frac{q}{p^2} \tag{7.16}$$

Example 7.19 Consider the case $p = q = 1/2$.

$$P(X=k) = (1/2)^{k-1}\,1/2 = 2^{-k},$$

$$E(X) = \frac{1}{1/2} = 2,$$

$$\mathrm{Var}(X) = \frac{1/2}{(1/2)^2} = 2.$$

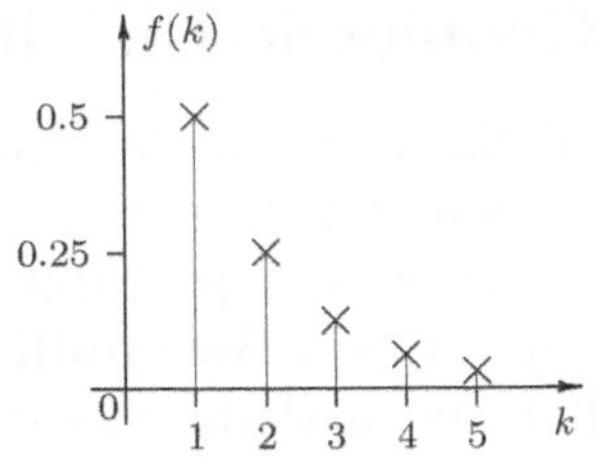

■

Example 7.20 One in every 100 cans of fizz has a special ring pull. What is the maximum number I may have to buy to ensure I have a 50–50 chance of finding one? We assume the stock of cans in infinite, so we are effectively "sampling with replacement", to ensure the trials are **independent**.

We seek N such that

$$P(X=1)+P(X=2)+\cdots+P(X=N)\simeq 0.5.$$

Let $p=0.01,\ q=0.99$. Then

$$p+qp+q^2p+\cdots+q^{N-1}p=p\left[\frac{1-q^N}{1-q}\right]=1-q^N,$$

which we could have found more easily by

$$P(X\leqslant N)=1-P(X>N)=1-P(N\text{ failures})=1-q^N.$$

We therefore require

$$1-0.99^N\simeq 0.5\quad\Rightarrow\quad 0.99^N\simeq 0.5\quad\Rightarrow\quad N\simeq\frac{\ln 0.5}{\ln 0.99}\simeq 69.$$

■

Ex 7.8 Two fair coins are tossed together. How many times, on average, does this have to be done to obtain: (a) two heads and (b) one head and one tail?

Ex 7.9 An event has a probability p of occurring (and $q=1-p$ of not occurring). A series of independent trials is carried out. Find the probabilities that the first occurrence is (a) at an even-numbered trial, (b) at an odd-numbered trial. Verify they add to one.

Ex 7.10 A gambler plays a game with probability $1/2$ of winning, when he receives back the original stake doubled. He adopts the following scheme: he gambles 1 unit on the first game. If he wins, he banks the winnings and starts again. If he loses, he doubles the stake on the next game, and so on until he wins.

Suppose that, in a 'losing' sequence, he requires X games to get a win. Show that $P(X=n)=1/2^n$. Show that the net win in any sequence is 1 unit.

In spite of this, the strategy is known as **Gambler's Ruin**. Why?

7.6 Binomial Distribution

The most important of all discrete distributions – the **binomial distribution** – is also based on *Bernoulli trials*, but this time a fixed number of trials, n. X counts the number of successes; we seek $P(X=k)$ for all possible k.

This value can be deduced in many ways, e.g., by analysing a tree diagram. In this case we have a **binary** tree: from each point there are **two** branches, success (S) and failure (F).

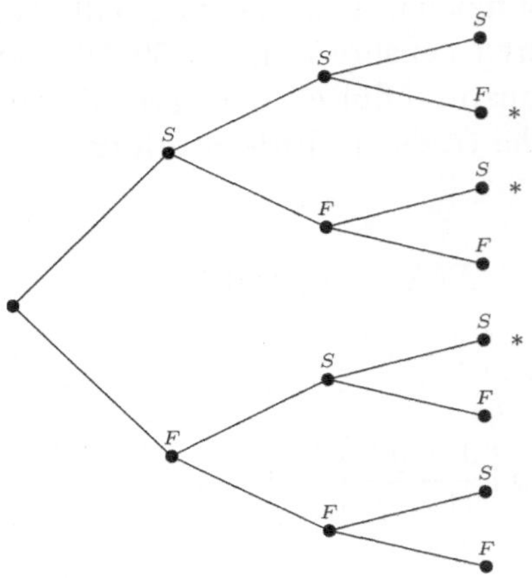

In general there are 2^n branches, since each of the n decisions doubles the number; in the case illustrated to the left, there are $8 = 2^3$.

We seek to identify all branches with $k\,S$ and $(n-k)\,F$. There are precisely $\binom{n}{k}$ ways in which to select k of the n segments in a branch, to label them as S.

For the example on the left, there are $\binom{3}{2}$ asterisked branches, each with $2\,S$ and $1\,F$.

Now, using the product rule and relying on *independence*, each branch has probability $p^k q^{n-k}$. Hence, using the addition rule, as usual for a tree diagram:

$$P(X = k) = \binom{n}{k} p^k q^{n-k}.$$

These are the probabilities for the distribution, often notated as $\text{Bin}(n, p)$.

Note again that independence is essential: the sampling must be "with replacement".

Example 7.21 For the three coins considered in Example 7.2, we have $\text{Bin}\,(3, {}^1\!/_2)$. Then $q = {}^1\!/_2$ also and

$$P(X = 0) = \binom{3}{0} ({}^1\!/_2)^0 ({}^1\!/_2)^3 = {}^1\!/_8,$$

$$P(X = 1) = \binom{3}{1} ({}^1\!/_2)^1 ({}^1\!/_2)^2 = {}^3\!/_8,$$

$$P(X = 2) = \binom{3}{2} ({}^1\!/_2)^2 ({}^1\!/_2)^1 = {}^3\!/_8,$$

$$P(X = 3) = \binom{3}{3} ({}^1\!/_2)^3 ({}^1\!/_2)^0 = {}^1\!/_8.$$

These are exactly the values found earlier by listing all cases, but now delivered by a formula. ■

The probabilities in this example added to 1, as they must. We can easily confirm this is true in general:

$$\sum_k P(X = k) = \sum_{k=0}^{n} \binom{n}{k} p^k q^{n-k} = (q + p)^n = 1^n = 1,$$

using the **Binomial Theorem**.

Further algebra of a binomial type gives simple formulae for the mean and variance.

Frame 7.9 Binomial distribution Bin(n,p)

$$f(k) = \binom{n}{k} p^k q^{n-k} \quad (0 \leqslant k \leqslant n) \tag{7.17}$$

$$E(X) = np \tag{7.18}$$

$$\text{Var}(X) = npq \tag{7.19}$$

The mean value is a natural one: for large n we 'expect' np successes.

Example 7.22 For tossing three coins, where $n = 3$, $p = 1/2$, we found in Examples 7.9 and 7.11:

$$E(X) = 3/2 = 3 \times 1/2, \qquad \text{Var}(X) = 3/4 = 3 \times 1/2 \times (1 - 1/2)\,.$$

■

The probabilities calculated in Example 7.21 are symmetrical, which is true whenever $p = 1/2$. The graph on the right is Bin $(5, 1/2)$.

The distribution can be very asymmetrical for p near 0 or 1, as the next example shows.

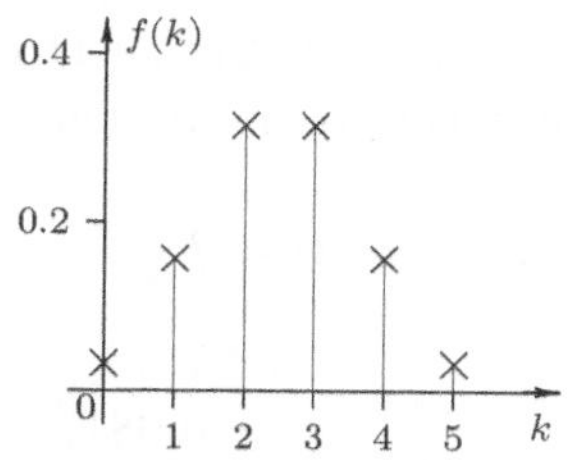

Example 7.23 Suppose we throw three fair dice and count the number of sixes. The distribution here is Bin $(3, 1/6)$.

Using binomial coefficients 1, 3, 3, 1, we find:

$$P(X = 0) = (1/6)^0\,(5/6)^3 = 125/216,$$
$$P(X = 1) = 3\,(1/6)^1\,(5/6)^2 = 75/216,$$
$$P(X = 2) = 3\,(1/6)^2\,(5/6)^1 = 15/216,$$
$$P(X = 3) = (1/6)^3\,(5/6)^0 = 1/216.$$

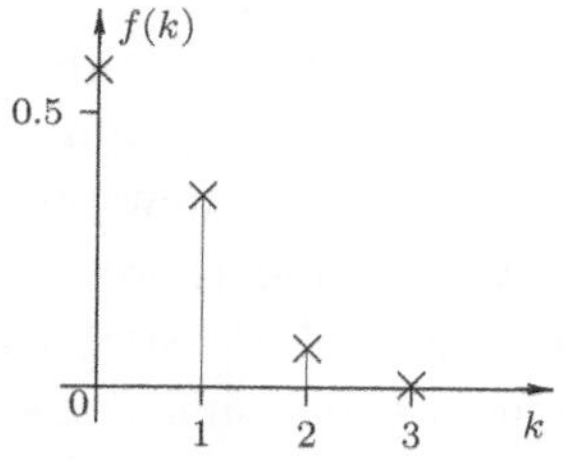

The formulae in Frame 7.9 give $E(X) = 3 \times 1/6 = 1/2$ and $\text{Var}(X) = 3 \times 1/6 \times 5/6 = 5/12$. We can verify these directly, e.g.,

$$E(X) = \frac{1}{216}\left[0 \times 125 + 1 \times 75 + 2 \times 15 + 3 \times 1\right] = \frac{108}{216} = \frac{1}{2}.$$

■

The binomial distribution is fundamental for statistical models where a *binary* test is made: working/faulty, yes/no, agree/disagree, win/lose, etc. We end this section with some realistic calculations, which will reveal a serious computational problem with the binomial distribution, one we shall tackle later.

Example 7.24 A piece of equipment whose reliability is critical is designed to work if at least **two** of its **eight** components function. The probability of a failure of any one, in a given period, is 0.1 *and* failure events are **independent**.

Let X be the number failing in the period. Then X is distributed as $\mathrm{Bin}(8, 0.1)$. We require to find

$$\begin{aligned} P(\text{total fail}) &= P(X = 8) + P(X = 7) \\ &= 0.1^8 + \binom{8}{1} 0.1^7(1 - 0.1) = 0.000\,000\,73. \end{aligned}$$

■

Example 7.25 A die is thrown 40 times and a *six* appears three times. Is the die biased?

Assume it is *not* biased and let X be the number of sixes that appear. X is distributed as $\mathrm{Bin}\,(40, 1/6)$. To judge the performance, we calculate the probability of getting **three or fewer** sixes. If this is small, our assumption – that the die is unbiased – is suspect.

$$\begin{aligned} P(X \leqslant 3) &= P(X = 0) + P(X = 1) + P(X = 2) + P(X = 3) \\ &= \left(\tfrac{5}{6}\right)^{40} + \binom{40}{1}\left(\tfrac{5}{6}\right)^{39}\left(\tfrac{1}{6}\right) + \binom{40}{2}\left(\tfrac{5}{6}\right)^{38}\left(\tfrac{1}{6}\right)^{2} + \binom{40}{3}\left(\tfrac{5}{6}\right)^{37}\left(\tfrac{1}{6}\right)^{3} \\ &\simeq 0.081, \end{aligned}$$

so we should not place much faith in this die. ■

Example 7.26 [*A sampling technique called a 'triangular test'*]

We wished to test the performance of a change to a production process. We gave 20 people three samples – two from the old process, one from the new – and asked them to identify the "odd" one; 10 did so correctly. Does this suggest the new process has produced a noticeably different product?

We assume there is no discernible difference, so people were in effect guessing. The distribution is $\mathrm{Bin}\,(20, 1/3)$, since each person has a 1-in-3 chance of guessing correctly. We now calculate the probability of guessing correctly 10 or more times.

$$\begin{aligned} P(X = k) &= \binom{20}{k}\left(1/3\right)^k \left(2/3\right)^{20-k}, \\ P(X \geqslant 10) &= \binom{20}{10}\frac{2^{10}}{3^{20}} + \binom{20}{11}\frac{2^{11}}{3^{20}} + \cdots . \end{aligned}$$

The arithmetic is dreadful, although the terms do decrease quickly in size and soon become negligible. The first term is 0.054 and the total is 0.092, to 3 dp. Such a low probability of achieving this many correct answers by guesswork suggests that the participants were *not* guessing and that there is a discernible difference, at least to some. ■

Example 7.27 An insurance company accepts applications from 2100 men, of the same age and health. The probability that each will still be alive 30 years later is 0.7. Find the probability that at least 1450 are still alive.

The model is Bin(2100, 0.7) and we require

$$\sum_{k=1450}^{2100} \binom{2100}{k} 0.7^k\, 0.3^{2100-k} \simeq 0.8356,$$

where the calculation has required use of a computer. ■

These last three examples have demonstrated, with increasing force, the potential computational difficulties in using the binomial distribution. We shall later find a much simpler method, using the renowned *Normal distribution*, to calculate an *approximation* to binomial probabilities. That method gives 0.8355 for the result of Example 7.27.

Ex 7.11

(a) For a **binomial** distributed variable X, with parameters $n = 6$ and $p = 0.2$, find

i. $P(X = 1)$ ii. $P(X = 4)$ iii. $P(X < 2)$

(b) A trial produces a success with probability $1/2$. What is the probability of exactly **four** successes in **eight** independent trials?

Ex 7.12

(a) In a ten question true/false examination, what is the probability of scoring 70% or better by guesswork?

(b) A component has a probability 0.98 of working throughout a 24 hour period. What is the probability that, out of **six** independent components, **at least five** are still working after 24 hours?

Ex 7.13

(a) A company guarantees to repair, free of charge, any car that has certain defects within one year of purchase. It is found that 15% of cars have such defects.

i. Find the probabilities that, in a random sample of 12 cars, none will need repaired, 3 or more will need repaired.

ii. The company sells 2500 such cars and the average cost of each repair is £400. What is the company's expected cost of repairs? You can answer this only by ignoring a flaw in the information supplied: what is it?

(b) As part of product testing of a new formulation of a household cleaner, each of a panel of 15 cleaners was given samples of the new and old formulations without being told which was which. Of these, 12 preferred the new formulation and 3 the old one. Suppose that there is no real difference between their effectiveness: what is the probability of 12 or more choosing the new one by chance?

7.7 Poisson Distribution

The approximation method just mentioned works only for values of p in $\mathrm{Bin}(n, p)$ that are not near 0 or 1. In these cases there is an alternative approximation, using the **Poisson distribution**. This applies to cases where p is near 0. (If p is near 1, we simply reword the problem in terms of $1-p = q$.)

The Poisson distribution is defined as follows.

Frame 7.10 Poisson distribution with parameter μ

$$f(k) = e^{-\mu}\frac{\mu^k}{k!} \quad (0 \leqslant k < \infty) \tag{7.20}$$

$$E(X) = \mu \tag{7.21}$$

$$\mathrm{Var}(X) = \mu \tag{7.22}$$

Before illustrating its use, we should verify that it is indeed a valid distribution. Clearly $f(k) \geqslant 0$, as required. Also

$$\sum_{k=0}^{\infty} f(k) = e^{-\mu}\sum_{k=0}^{\infty}\frac{\mu^k}{k!} = e^{-\mu}e^{\mu} = 1.$$

The mean can be verified by

$$\begin{aligned}\mu_X &= \sum_{k=0}^{\infty} k e^{-\mu}\frac{\mu^k}{k!} = \mu e^{-\mu}\sum_{k=1}^{\infty}\frac{\mu^{k-1}}{(k-1)!}\\ &= \mu e^{-\mu}e^{\mu} = \mu,\end{aligned}$$

where the series has had its first term removed since it has a factor $k = 0$. The variance can be verified similarly, although we shall indicate later that its value is suggested by the link to the binomial.

The Poisson distribution is the correct model for counting **independent** events that occur **entirely at random**. Such events have their occurrence controlled by a **rate of occurrence**: $R =$ so many events per unit (whatever). Examples are:

- decay of a radioactive substance: $R =$ number of detections per unit time;
- flaws in a length of material or artefact, such as a pipe: $R =$ flaws per unit distance;
- arrivals at a checkout; $R =$ number of arrivals per unit time.

To calculate the required probabilities, we first of all choose an appropriate time or space interval, T say. Then the expected number of occurrences in any such interval is

$$\mu = RT, \tag{7.23}$$

which provides the key parameter we need.

Example 7.28 A radioactive source decays at the rate of 1 detection per 20 minutes. What is the probability of **more than two** in one hour?

We have $R = \frac{1}{20}$ detection per minute and $T = 60$ minutes, so $\mu = \frac{1}{20} \times 60 = 3$. We require

$$\begin{aligned} P(X > 2) &= 1 - \big[P(X = 0)+ \\ &\qquad P(X = 1) + P(X = 2)\big] \\ &= 1 - e^{-3}\left[1 + \frac{3}{1!} + \frac{3^2}{2!}\right] \\ &= 0.577. \end{aligned}$$

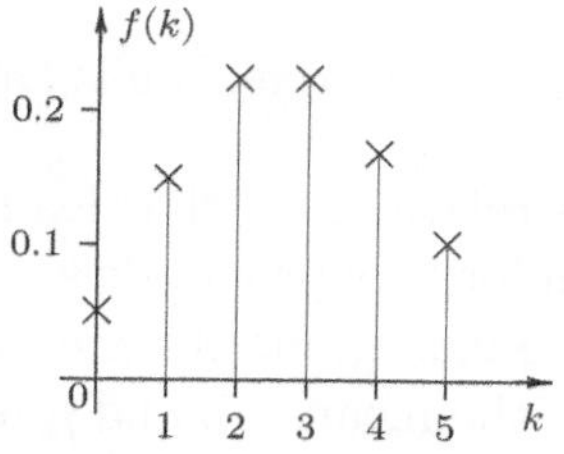

See the graph on the right. ■

Example 7.29 A steel sheet has an average of one flaw per 5 metres. Find the probabilities of (a) exactly one flaw in a 5 metre length, (b) at least two flaws in a 10 metre length.

(a) We have $R = \frac{1}{5}$ flaw per metre and $T = 5$ metres, so $\mu = \frac{1}{5} \times 5 = 1$. We require

$$P(X = 1) = e^{-1}\left[\tfrac{1}{1}\right] = 0.368.$$

(b) We now have $T = 10$ metres, so $\mu = \frac{1}{5} \times 10 = 2$. We require

$$\begin{aligned} P(X \geqslant 2) &= 1 - [P(X = 0) + P(X = 1)] \\ &= 1 - e^{-2}\left[1 + \frac{2}{1}\right] = 0.594. \end{aligned}$$

■

Although the calculations are generally easier than those for the binomial distribution – at least there are no binomial coefficients to find – the arithmetic can still be heavy, as the next example shows.

Example 7.30 Customers arrive at a checkout entirely at random, at a rate of 50 per hour. Find the probabilities of (a) no arrivals in one minute, (b) more than 10 arrivals in 6 minutes.

(a) We have $R = 50$ arrivals per hour and $T = \frac{1}{60}$ hour, so $\mu = 50 \times \frac{1}{60} = 5/6$. We require

$$P(X = 0) = e^{-5/6} = 0.435.$$

(b) We now have $T = \frac{1}{10}$ hour, so $\mu = 50 \times \frac{1}{10} = 5$. We require

$$\begin{aligned} P(X > 10) &= 1 - [P(X = 0) + P(X = 1) + \cdots + P(X = 10)] \\ &= 1 - e^{-5}\left[1 + \frac{5}{1!} + \frac{5^2}{2!} + \cdots + \frac{5^{10}}{10!}\right] = 0.014, \end{aligned}$$

on using a computer.

■

These examples treat the Poisson distribution in its natural form. Its other principal use is as an approximation for the binomial distribution. The link is that, in some sense, the Poisson distribution is the binomial distribution with an infinite number of trials and a zero probability, more precisely it is the limit of $\text{Bin}(n, p)$ as $n \to \infty$, $p \to 0$, $np = \mu$ (constant). Hence it should be a good approximation when:

$$n \text{ is large}, \quad p \text{ is small}, \quad \mu = np \text{ is moderate in size.}$$

It is this relationship that leads to recommendations to use the Poisson distribution for 'low probability events', although this is only an approximation.

Before examining its effectiveness, note that we take the natural step of equating the means np and μ for the two distributions. Pushing this further, for the Poisson distribution:

$$\text{Var}(X) \simeq npq = \mu q \simeq \mu,$$

since $q = 1 - p \simeq 1$. As we see in (7.22), this is in fact exact.

Example 7.31 Consider $\text{Bin}(100, 0.01)$, so $\mu = 100 \times 0.01 = 1$. The probabilities $P(X = k)$ are as follows:

r	Binomial	Poisson
0	0.366	0.368
1	0.370	0.368
2	0.185	0.184

■

Example 7.32 Consider the three dice problem in Example 7.23. The number of sixes is given by $\text{Bin}(3, 1/6)$. Suppose we try to use Poisson with $\mu = 3 \times 1/6 = 0.5$:

$$\begin{aligned}
P(X = 0) &= e^{-0.5} = 0.607, && \text{binomial: } 0.579,\\
P(X = 1) &= e^{-0.5}\,1/2 = 0.303, && \text{binomial: } 0.347,\\
P(X = 2) &= e^{-0.5}\,1/8 = 0.076, && \text{binomial: } 0.069,\\
P(X = 3) &= e^{-0.5}\,1/48 = 0.013, && \text{binomial: } 0.005.
\end{aligned}$$

The probabilities are not that dissimilar, in spite of n being small. But this example makes obvious a discrepancy between the distributions that underlines the fact that it is an approximation: we can readily calculate $P(X = 4) = 0.002$ for Poisson, although this is an impossible outcome. ■

The final example is much more realistic.

Example 7.33 Suppose that 5% of air passengers on a certain route order vegetarian meals. What is the probability that **at least four** require such a meal from a flight with 120 passengers?

The correct model is Bin(120, 0.05), which leads to a difficult calculation:

$$\begin{aligned}P(X \geqslant 4) &= 1 - P(X < 4)\\ &= 1 - \left[\binom{120}{0}0.95^{120} + \binom{120}{1}0.95^{119}0.05\right.\\ &\quad \left. + \binom{120}{2}0.95^{118}0.05^2 + \binom{120}{3}0.95^{117}0.05^3\right]\\ &= 0.8556.\end{aligned}$$

To approximate this by a Poisson calculation, we use $\mu = 120 \times 0.05 = 6$:

$$\begin{aligned}P(X \geqslant 4) &= 1 - P(X < 4)\\ &= 1 - e^{-6}\left[1 + 6 + \frac{6^2}{2} + \frac{6^3}{6}\right]\\ &= 1 - 61e^{-6} = 0.8488.\end{aligned}$$

■

Ex 7.14 Calls coming into a telephone exchange follow a Poisson distribution. A survey, held over a long period, suggests that the average is stable at 120 per hour. Find the probabilities that:

(a) there are no calls during a one-minute period;

(b) there are less than 3 calls in a two-minute period.

Ex 7.15 A bowler has a strike rate of taking a wicket every 96 balls. Calculate the probabilities of taking one wicket and two wickets in a spell of 72 balls, using (a) Poisson with mean: $\frac{72}{96} = \frac{3}{4}$, (b) Binomial: $n = 72$, $p = \frac{1}{96}$. Which is theoretically more appropriate?

Ex 7.16 Suppose that *Sciences United* scores, on average, 1 goal every 45 minutes. Similarly, *Arts FC* scores, on average, 1 goal every 60 minutes. Assuming these are modelled by independent Poisson distributions, calculate to 3 dp the probability of a draw when they play each other in a 90 minute match.

7.8 Revision Exercises

Ex 7.17 A coin with probability of '*Heads*' of $1/3$ is tossed until one '*Heads*' has appeared. What is the probability that k throws are required, for $k \geqslant 1$?

A and B bet on this experiment: A pays B £1 if 1 or 2 tosses are required. B pays A £n otherwise. What value should n have to ensure neither A nor B has an advantage?

Ex 7.18 A game is played between persons A and B. A throws a fair die and B pays out (in some currency):

0 for a throw of an odd number; 1 for a throw of 2;
2 for a throw of 4; 3 for a throw of 6.

Find A's expected winnings. Find the variance for A's winnings.

Ex 7.19 A study of pumps in a nuclear power station shows that the probability of failure of an individual pump is 0.16 in a given time period. A system uses **eight** pumps. Assuming that failure of each pump is independent of all others, what is the appropriate distribution to model the number of pumps that fail?

Calculate, to 4 dp, the probability that **at least two pumps fail** during the period.

Ex 7.20 A person attempts a newspaper crossword every weekday (Monday to Saturday) with probability 0.6 of solving any one correctly, independent of the others. Calculate the probabilities of the following:

(a) solving all six puzzles correctly;

(b) solving exactly half correctly;

(c) solving more than half correctly.

Ex 7.21 A speed camera is activated on average three times in an hour. Assuming the **Poisson distribution** is a good model, calculate to 3 dp:

(a) The probability that no cars are photographed in an hour.

(b) The probability that more than three cars are photographed in an hour.

Ex 7.22 A proportion 0.001 of certain cells are infected. Assuming the **Poisson distribution** is a good model, calculate to 3 dp:

(a) The probability that at least one cell is infected in a sample of 2000.

(b) The probability that more than three cells are infected in a sample of 10,000.

8 CONTINUOUS DISTRIBUTIONS

We now turn attention to **continuous** random variables, where the possible values are not 'discrete' or 'isolated', but cover all of an **interval** in the real line, possibly even the entire line itself. There is an immediate complication, which must be addressed and overcome since the most important distribution of all, one that underpins most elementary statistical calculation, is a continuous one: the *Normal distribution.*

The problem is that there are so many points in an interval that it is impossible to allocate a non-zero probability to any of them and still achieve all probabilities summing to 1. (It is possible to define hybrid distributions that are discrete in parts and continuous elsewhere, but they are not natural and still throw up the same problem.) Thus, for a continuous random variable:

$$P(X = \alpha) = 0 \quad (\text{all } \alpha \text{ in } \mathbb{R}).$$

The answer to this conundrum is to group the values for X in *intervals* and to measure $P(a \leqslant X \leqslant b)$, for any chosen interval $[a, b]$. Computationally, the mathematics must change from **summation** to **integration.** Some compensation for this change is that we no longer need take care to distinguish the above probability from $P(a < X < b)$, since they have the same value: integrals are unaffected by values at isolated points, such as a and b here.

8.1 Density and Distribution Functions

There is no point in defining a probability function, like $f(x)$ in the previous chapter, since it would be zero everywhere. The replacement is suggested in the following example.

Example 8.1 Suppose that every value in $[0, 1]$ is equally likely. Then the probability of X being in any interval of width Δ is the same and must, by proportion, be Δ.

For the graph on the right, the total area enclosed between $x = 0$ and $x = 1$ is 1. Also, it is reasonable to argue that

$$P\left(1/2 \leqslant X \leqslant 2/3\right) = 2/3 - 1/2 = 1/6,$$

the area between $x = 1/2$ and $2/3$. This is also $\int_{1/2}^{2/3} 1\, dx$.

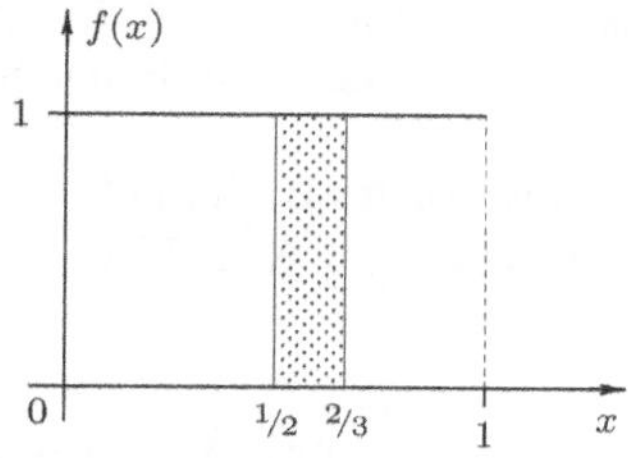

■

The function $f(x)$ used and graphed in this example is the key. It is called the **probability density function** for the distribution. Once it is defined we can use it to evaluate any of the probabilities we need, by calculating areas under its graph.

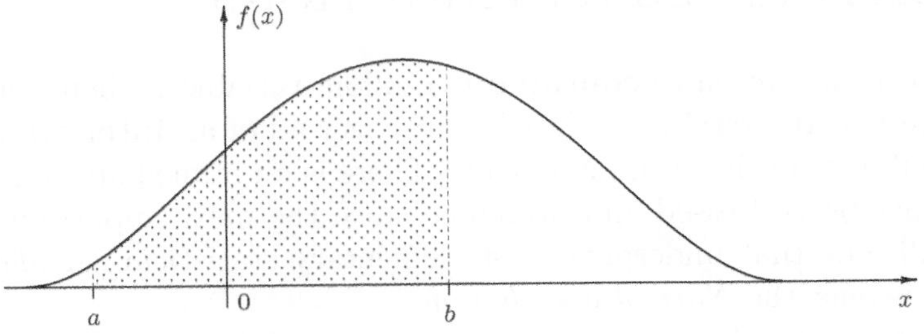

Frame 8.1 Probability calculation for a continuous distribution

$$P(a \leqslant X \leqslant b) = \int_a^b f(x)\,dx \tag{8.1}$$

Note that, following a comment made earlier, this is also $P(a < X \leqslant b)$, $P(a \leqslant X < b)$ and $P(a < X < b)$.

There is no concern about signs, in making the link between area and integration, since $f(x) \geqslant 0$ everywhere, due to its connection with probability. Also

$$\int_{-\infty}^{\infty} f(x)\,dx = 1, \tag{8.2}$$

since all probability must be captured by this integral. (The infinite limits make this an *improper* integral but in all cases we encounter we can either replace them by finite numbers, or the integrations are known to be 'safe'.)

Think about it like this

The difference between discrete and continuous distributions is analogous to the difference between the physics of point masses and rigid bodies. For point masses, various formulae, such as those for momentum and torque, require the summation of their individual contributions, whereas for rigid bodies it is necessary to use integration.

The use of the word **density** in the definition of $f(x)$ is therefore no accident. The mass of a segment of a rod of uniform cross-section is calculated by integrating the function defining the density, between appropriate limits, just as we integrate in Frame 8.1.

The mass of a small section of width Δx of a body with density $\rho(x)$ is approximately $\rho(x)\,\Delta x$. This translates to perhaps the most direct interpretation of $f(x)$:

$$P(x \leqslant X \leqslant x + \Delta x) \simeq f(x)\,\Delta x \quad [\Delta x \text{ small}]. \tag{8.3}$$

The larger $f(x)$ is, the more likely is the outcome of a statistical trial to be near x, as the probability measure in (8.3) confirms.

Example 8.2 Consider the graph shown below.

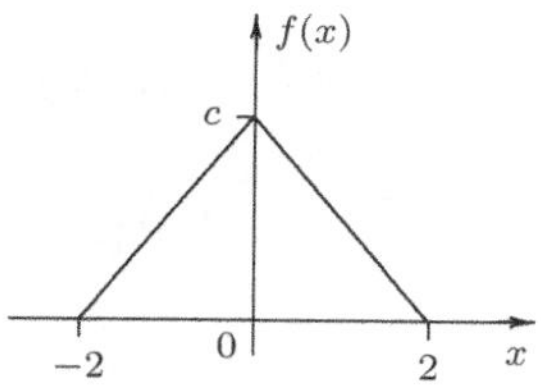

The function satisfies $f(x) \geqslant 0$ for all x, so the only requirement for it to be a probability density function is that it satisfies (8.2). It is easier to use areas:

$$\tfrac{1}{2} \times 2 \times c + \tfrac{1}{2} \times 2 \times c = 1,$$

which immediately shows $c = 1/2$. ■

It is in this context that the **(cumulative) distribution function** comes into its own. It has none of the discontinuity problems we found in the discrete case and avoids the approximation in (8.3). It is defined and used as in the discrete case.

Frame 8.2 *The distribution function for a continuous distribution*

$$F(x) = P(X \leqslant x) = \int_{-\infty}^{x} f(t)\,dt \tag{8.4}$$

$$P(a \leqslant X \leqslant b) = F(b) - F(a) \tag{8.5}$$

Again, because $P(X = x) = 0$, we can use either $\leqslant$ or $<$ in (8.4) and (8.5).

Example 8.3 For the distribution in Example 8.1, we have the following distribution function.

$$F(x) = \begin{cases} 0 & \text{if } x < 0, \\ x & \text{if } 0 \leqslant x \leqslant 1, \\ 1 & \text{if } x > 1. \end{cases}$$

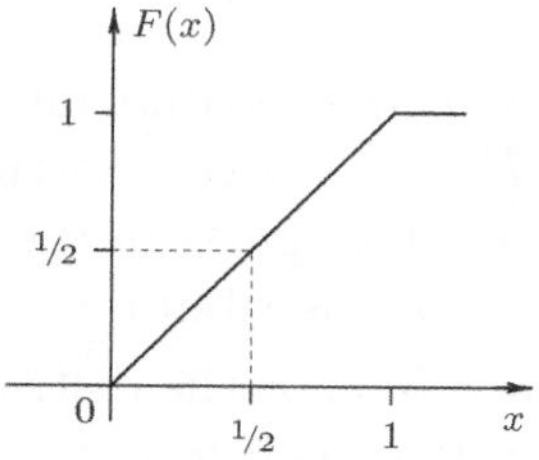

Then, as before,

$$P\left(1/2 \leqslant X \leqslant 2/3\right) = F\left(2/3\right) - F\left(1/2\right)$$
$$= 2/3 - 1/2 = 1/6.$$ ■

8.2 Distribution Parameters

The various parameters defined in §7.3 have direct counterparts for continuous distributions. Indeed, the **mean** and **variance** (and hence **standard deviation**) are defined in exactly the same way as in that section, provided we replace the sums by integrals. (Again there are two versions for the variance: a theoretical and a computational one.)

Frame 8.3 Mean, variance and standard deviation for a continuous distribution

$$E(X) = \mu_X = \int_{-\infty}^{\infty} x f(x)\,dx \tag{8.6}$$

$$\mathrm{Var}(X) = \int_{-\infty}^{\infty} (x - \mu_X)^2 f(x)\,dx \tag{8.7}$$

$$= \int_{-\infty}^{\infty} x^2 f(x)\,dx - \mu_X^2 \tag{8.8}$$

$$\sigma_X = \sqrt{\mathrm{Var}(X)} \tag{8.9}$$

Think about it like this

If $f(x)$ represents the density of a rod of uniform cross-section, then μ_X is the coordinate of the *centre of mass*, which is a natural analogue of the mean.

Example 8.4 Find the mean and variance for the distribution in Example 8.1.

The density function is zero outside $[0, 1]$, so all integrals have 0 and 1 as their limits, rather than $\pm\infty$.

$$\mu_X = \int_0^1 x \times 1\,dx = \left[\tfrac{1}{2}x^2\right]_0^1 = 1/2,$$

$$\mathrm{Var}(X) = \int_0^1 x^2 \times 1\,dx - (1/2)^2 = \left[\tfrac{1}{3}x^3\right]_0^1 - 1/4 = 1/12.$$

■

The **median** is defined precisely as in Frame 7.3:

$$F(m) = 0.5 \quad \Rightarrow \quad m = F^{-1}(0.5),$$

where now there is no difficulty, for 'well-behaved' distributions. (The inverse function $F^{-1}(x)$ for the distribution function is defined for all x in $(0, 1)$ if there are no 'flat' parts in the graph of $y = F(x)$ for $0 < y < 1$, which is the case for all the distributions we shall consider.)

Example 8.5 For the distribution in Example 8.1, $F(x) = x$ $(0 \leqslant x \leqslant 1)$, so $F(m) = 0.5$ when $m = 1/2$, the median. ■

Calculation of the median is only one of the uses of the inverse distribution function. Much statistical work is concerned with activity near the ends of distributions, where events are unlikely to occur by chance. In such cases it is important to answer questions like the following.

- For what value of α is $P(X < \alpha) = 0.01$?

  Answer: solve $F(\alpha) = 0.01$, i.e., $\alpha = F^{-1}(0.01)$.

- For what value of β is $P(X > \beta) = 0.01$?

  Answer: solve $1 - F(\beta) = 0.01$, i.e., $\beta = F^{-1}(0.99)$.

Example 8.6 Suppose the density function for a distribution is

$$f(x) = \frac{k}{x^3} \quad (x \text{ in } [1, 2]),$$

and is zero elsewhere. Then a limit $-\infty$ in any integral can be replaced by 1, and a limit ∞ by 2.

We find k using (8.2):

$$\int_1^2 \frac{k}{x^3}\, dx = k\left[-\frac{1}{2x^2}\right]_1^2 = \frac{3k}{8},$$

which is 1 if $k = 8/3$.

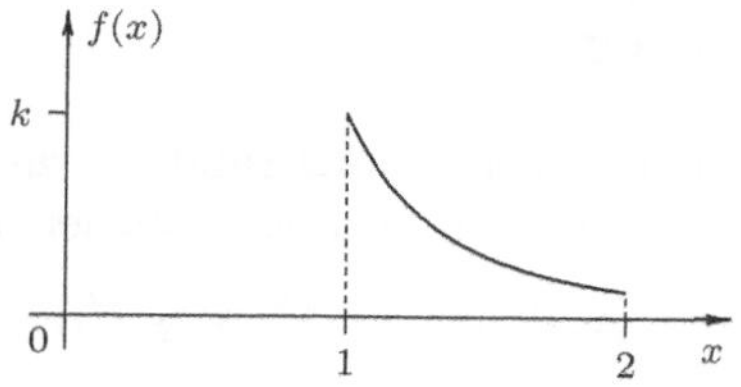

The **distribution function** is

$$F(x) = \int_1^x \frac{8}{3t^3}\, dt = \left[-\frac{4}{3t^2}\right]_1^x = \frac{4}{3}\left(1 - \frac{1}{x^2}\right).$$

Using this we can easily evaluate probabilities, for example:

$$P(4/3 \leqslant X \leqslant 5/3) = F(5/3) - F(4/3) = 0.27.$$

The **median** satisfies $F(m) = 0.5$, i.e.,

$$\frac{4}{3}\left(1 - \frac{1}{m^2}\right) = \frac{1}{2} \quad \Rightarrow \quad \frac{1}{m^2} = \frac{5}{8}$$

$$\Rightarrow \quad m = \sqrt{1.6} \simeq 1.26.$$

To illustrate calculations near the ends of the distribution, we find β such that $P(X > \beta) = 0.01$:

$$1 - F(\beta) = 0.01 \quad \Rightarrow \quad 1 - \frac{4}{3}\left(1 - \frac{1}{\beta^2}\right) = 0.01$$

$$\Rightarrow \quad \frac{1}{\beta^2} = 1 - 0.99 \times 0.75$$

$$\Rightarrow \quad \beta \simeq 1.97.$$

Finally, the other key parameters are:

$$\mu_X = \int_1^2 x \times \frac{8}{3x^3}\, dx = \int_1^2 \frac{8}{3x^2}\, dx$$

$$= \left[-\frac{8}{3x}\right]_1^2 = -8/6 + 8/3 = 4/3,$$

$$\text{Var}(X) = \int_1^2 x^2 \times \frac{8}{3x^3}\, dx - (4/3)^2 = \int_1^2 \frac{8}{3x}\, dx - 16/9$$

$$= \left[8/3 \ln x\right]_1^2 - 16/9 = 8/3 \ln 2 - 16/9 \simeq 0.071,$$

$$\sigma_X = \sqrt{\text{Var}(X)} \simeq 0.266.$$

■

Further examples will be presented in the following sections, where we consider three important practical distributions.

Ex 8.1 A random variable has density function $f(x) = 1 - \dfrac{x}{2}$ on $[0,2]$ (and zero elsewhere). Calculate $P(0 < X < 1)$, the α where $P(X < \alpha) = 0.19$, and the median.

Ex 8.2

(a) A continuous random variable has density function $f(x) = \alpha x(2-x)$ on $[0,1]$ (and zero elsewhere), where α is a constant. Find the value of α.

Calculate: $P(X \leqslant 1/4)$, $P(X \geqslant 1/2)$, $P(1/4 \leqslant X \leqslant 1/2)$.

(b) A continuous random variable has **distribution function** $F(x) = \frac{1}{8}x^{3/2}$ on an interval $[a,b]$, 0 for $x < a$, 1 for $x > b$. What are the values of a and b? What is the density function?

Ex 8.3 A random variable X has **density** function $f(x) = \dfrac{\alpha}{x^4}$ for $x \geqslant 1$ (and zero elsewhere). Calculate the following:

$$\alpha, \quad F(x), \quad P(2 < X < 3), \quad \mu_X, \quad \sigma_X, \quad \text{the median,}$$

where $F(x)$ is the (cumulative) distribution function.

8.3 Uniform Distribution

Like its discrete counterpart, the **uniform** distribution has all outcomes equally-likely, within some interval $[a,b]$. This means that the probability of X taking a value in any subinterval of width Δ is the same.

The density function is therefore a constant and to ensure the area under the graph is 1, that constant value must be $1/(b-a)$. Formally:

$$\int_a^b \frac{1}{b-a}\,dx = \frac{1}{b-a}\Big[x\Big]_a^b = 1.$$

The density and distribution functions are graphed below:

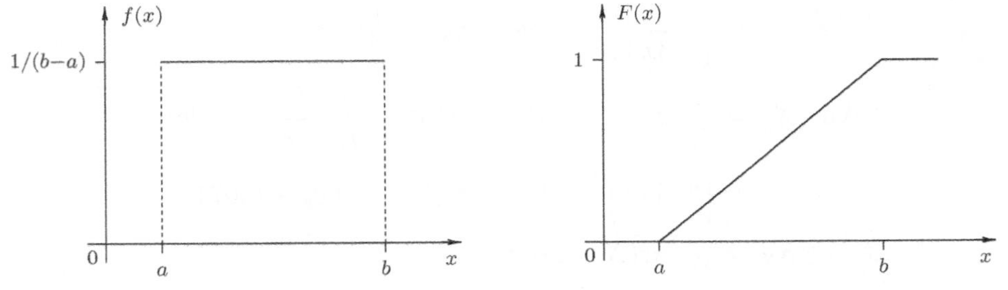

The key parameters are:

$$\mu_X = \int_a^b \frac{x}{b-a}\,dx = \frac{1}{b-a}\left[\frac{x^2}{2}\right]_a^b$$
$$= \frac{1}{2(b-a)}(b^2-a^2) = \frac{1}{2}(a+b),$$
$$\operatorname{Var}(X) = \int_a^b \frac{x^2}{b-a}\,dx - \mu_X^2 = \frac{1}{12}(b-a)^2,$$

after a similar calculation.

We can sum this up in the following Frame.

Frame 8.4 *Uniform distribution on* $[a,b]$

$$f(x) = \begin{cases} 0 & \text{if } x < a, \\ \frac{1}{b-a} & \text{if } a \leqslant x \leqslant b, \\ 0 & \text{if } x > b \end{cases} \tag{8.10}$$

$$\mu_X = \frac{1}{2}(a+b) \tag{8.11}$$

$$\operatorname{Var}(x) = \frac{1}{12}(b-a)^2 \tag{8.12}$$

Example 8.7 Example 8.1 is a uniform distribution with $a = 0$, $b = 1$:

$$\mu_X = \tfrac{1}{2}(0+1) = {}^1\!/_2, \quad \operatorname{Var}(X) = \tfrac{1}{12}(1-0)^2 = {}^1\!/_{12},$$

as before. ■

The uniform distribution is a good model for errors in individual measurements and rounding errors in individual calculations. If we know a number has been rounded to 2 dp, its error is somewhere in $[-0.005, 0.005]$ with equal likelihood.

Ex 8.4 Find the distribution function for the uniform distribution over $[1, 6]$. Hence calculate $P(2 < X < 5)$, the α where $P(X > \alpha) = 0.1$, and the median.

Ex 8.5 A bus service leaves every 30 minutes. A person, unaware of the timetable, arrives at random. What is the distribution for the waiting time, its mean and variance?

8.4 Exponential Distribution

The **exponential** distribution has data given as follows; the mean quoted here will be verified later.

Frame 8.5 *Exponential distribution with parameter λ*

$$f(x) = \begin{cases} 0 & \text{if } x < 0, \\ \lambda e^{-\lambda x} & \text{if } x \geqslant 0 \end{cases} \tag{8.13}$$

$$\mu_X = \sigma_X = \frac{1}{\lambda} \tag{8.14}$$

It models the intervals (in time or space) between the occurrence of purely random events, such as radioactive decay or the occurrence of flaws in a pipeline. *More generally, X models the interval between events counted by the Poisson distribution.*

We can check that it is a genuine distribution: $f(x) \geqslant 0$ everywhere and

$$\int_0^{\infty} \lambda e^{-\lambda x}\, dx = \left[-e^{-\lambda x}\right]_0^{\infty} = -0 + 1 = 1.$$

The **distribution function** is

$$F(x) = \int_0^{x} \lambda e^{-\lambda t}\, dt = \left[-e^{-\lambda t}\right]_0^{x} = 1 - e^{-\lambda x}. \tag{8.15}$$

The density and distribution functions are illustrated by the following graphs, where $\lambda = 1$.

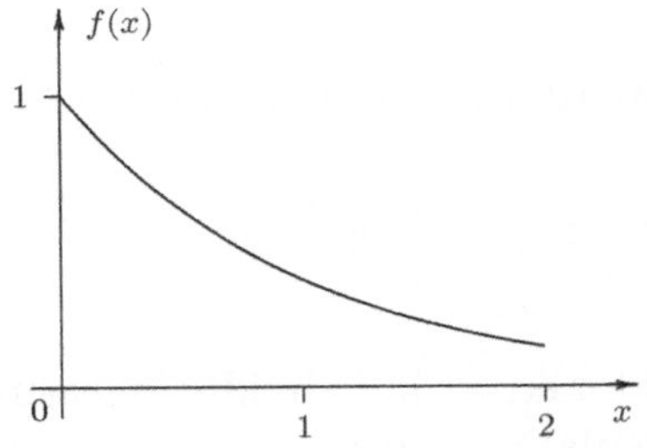

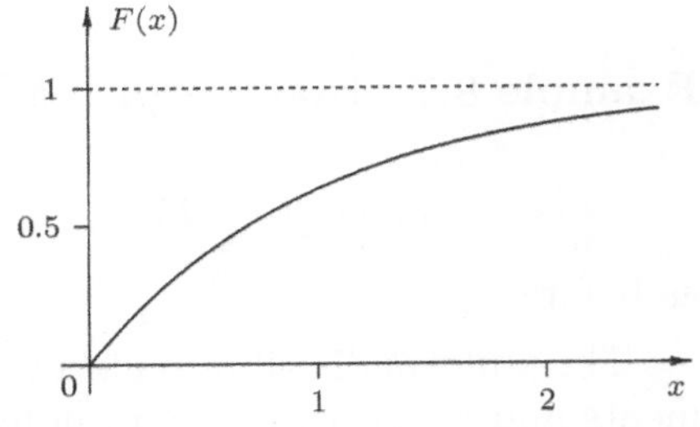

The **median** can be calculated by

$$1 - e^{-\lambda m} = 1/2 \quad \Rightarrow \quad e^{\lambda m} = 2 \quad \Rightarrow \quad \lambda m = \ln 2$$
$$\Rightarrow \quad m = \frac{1}{\lambda} \ln 2,$$

which, not surprisingly, is the **half-life** for an exponential process, with rate constant λ.

The **mean** requires *integration by parts*:

$$\begin{aligned} \mu_X &= \int_0^{\infty} \lambda x e^{-\lambda x}\, dx \\ &= \left[-x e^{-\lambda x} - \frac{1}{\lambda} e^{-\lambda x}\right]_0^{\infty} = \frac{1}{\lambda}. \end{aligned}$$

This gives an interpretation for λ and hence a way to estimate it: $1/\lambda$ is the **mean inter-event** measure.

Example 8.8 Suppose that a TV tube has its lifetime distributed exponentially with $\lambda = 1/8$.

Hence the mean lifetime is 8 years. The median is $8 \ln 2 \simeq 5.545$ years. What proportion is likely to lead to claims under a one-year warranty?

$$P(X \leqslant 1) = F(1) = 1 - e^{-0.125} \simeq 0.1175,$$

so 11.75% are likely to lead to such a claim.

At what time will just 10% of a batch of tubes still be working?

$$\begin{aligned} P(X > \alpha) = 0.1 \quad &\Rightarrow \quad F(\alpha) = P(X \leqslant \alpha) = 1 - 0.1 = 0.9 \\ &\Rightarrow \quad 1 - e^{-\alpha/8} = 0.9 \quad \Rightarrow \quad e^{-\alpha/8} = 0.1 \\ &\Rightarrow \quad \alpha = -8 \ln 0.1 \simeq 18.4 \text{ years.} \end{aligned}$$

■

The model used in this example is convenient but somewhat dubious, since TV tubes are likely to deteriorate with use, so the probabilities of survival decrease in time. This clashes with a striking property of the exponential distribution. It is fairly easy to prove (using integration) that

$$P(X \geqslant x + y | X \geqslant y) = P(X \geqslant x), \tag{8.16}$$

which means that the probabilities for future events do not depend on the past; the fact that an event has not occurred for some time makes it no more likely to occur in the near future. This is sometimes summed up by: *the exponential distribution has no memory.* For example, if a component has survived for $y = 20$ days, it is just as likely to survive another $x = 10$ days – and hence $x + y = 30$ days in total – as it would be to survive $x = 10$ days from new.

Ex 8.6 The time interval until a component fails has an exponential distribution with mean 50 days. Find the probability that the current component does not survive 30 days. By which time are we 90% certain to have had to replace it?

Ex 8.7 My hi-fi contains an amplifier, a CD player and a tape deck. The time between failures for these is given by exponential distributions, with means 8 years, 6 years and 4 years, respectively. I purchase a three-year guarantee. Find the probability that I do not need to make a claim under that guarantee.

8.5 Standard Normal Distribution

This final distribution is the most important of all. Like the exponential distribution it has different versions depending on parameters, in this case two: the **mean**, usually written μ, and the **variance**, usually written σ^2.

We start, however, with a very special (and important) case, where $\mu = 0$ and $\sigma^2 = 1$; the **standard normal** distribution, $N(0, 1)$, with random variable Z.

Frame 8.6 The standard normal distribution: Z is $N(0,1)$

$$f(z) = \frac{1}{\sqrt{2\pi}} e^{-z^2/2} \qquad (8.17)$$

$$\mu = 0, \quad \sigma^2 = 1 \qquad (8.18)$$

In this case the density function is not helpful, since it is impossible to integrate in terms of simple functions. Hence we have no formula for the distribution function and must use computer approximations or tables. The standard normal's distribution function is, however, the key to calculations using *all* normal distributions and even has a special notation: we write it as $\Phi(z)$ [*capital phi*]:

$$\Phi(z) = P(Z \leqslant z) = \int_{-\infty}^{z} f(t)\, dt. \qquad (8.19)$$

The graphs of $f(z)$ and $\Phi(z)$ are shown below. The shape of the former explains its common name: the **bell curve**.

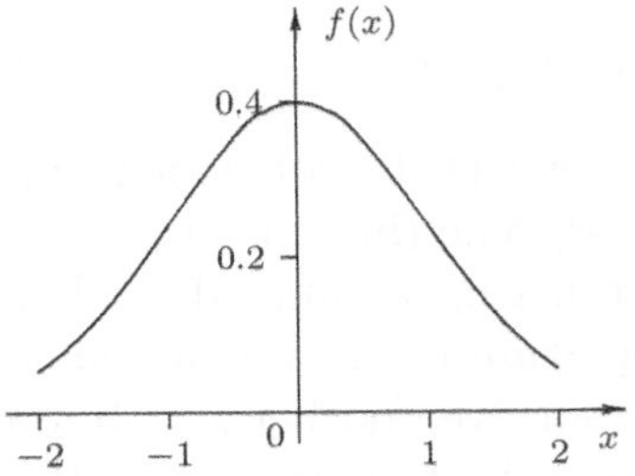

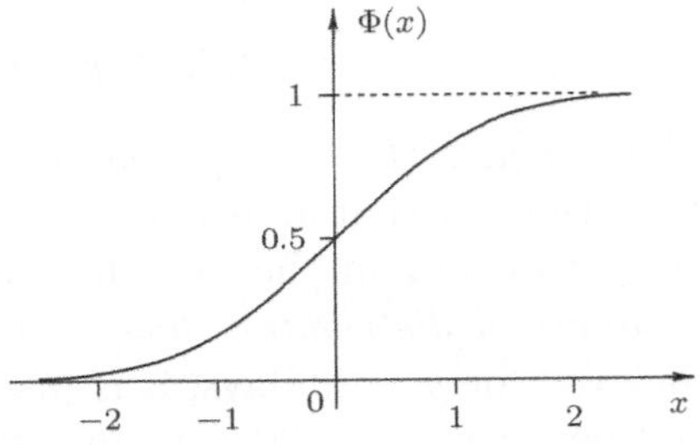

Before investigating how to use $\Phi(z)$ to deal with more general normal distributions, we must address how to extract values from a typical table, such as that presented in the *Appendix* that follows this part. A complication is that the distribution is clearly *symmetric*, which allows us to set out all the information needed in only half the space. There are various ways to do this, but the simplest is to tabulate $\Phi(z)$ only for $0 \leqslant z < \infty$.

Using the symmetry in the graph, we have

$$\Phi(-z) = P(Z \leqslant -z) = P(Z \geqslant z) = 1 - \Phi(z).$$

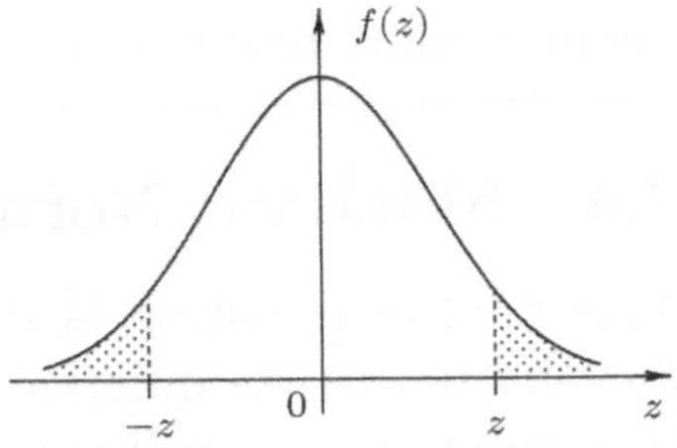

It is often good policy to draw a rough sketch of this type, as a guide.

From this, we find for all z, but primarily used for $z < 0$,

$$\Phi(z) = 1 - \Phi(-z). \qquad (8.20)$$

This, together with the table, allows us to calculate $\Phi(z)$ for any value of z. (There are two further frequent cases whose formulae we shall uncover after the following example.)

Example 8.9 Consider the following probabilities related to the standard normal. We use (8.5) and (8.19); remember that there is no difference between '$<$' and '$\leqslant$' in this context. (8.20) is also heavily used.

$$\begin{aligned}
&P(0.2 < Z \leqslant 1.1) = \Phi(1.1) - \Phi(0.2) = 0.8643 - 0.5793 = 0.2850,\\
&P(Z > 0.5) = 1 - P(Z < 0.5) = 1 - \Phi(0.5) = 1 - 0.6915 = 0.3085,\\
&P(Z < -1) = \Phi(-1) = 1 - \Phi(1) = 1 - 0.8413 = 0.1587,\\
&P(Z > -0.1) = 1 - P(Z < -0.1) = 1 - \Phi(-0.1)\\
&\quad = 1 - [1 - \Phi(0.1)] = \Phi(0.1) = 0.5398,\\
&P(-0.7 < Z < 0.9) = \Phi(0.9) - \Phi(-0.7)\\
&\quad = \Phi(0.9) - [1 - \Phi(0.7)] = 0.8159 + 0.7580 - 1 = 0.5739,\\
&P(|Z| > 2) = 1 - P(|Z| < 2) = 1 - P(-2 < Z < 2) = 1 - [\Phi(2) - \Phi(-2)]\\
&\quad = 1 - [\Phi(2) - (1 - \Phi(2))] = 2 - 2\Phi(2) = 2 - 2 \times 0.9772 = 0.0456.
\end{aligned}$$

■

This last calculation, and its companion $P(|Z| < 2)$, are very common: we work at points symmetrically disposed about the mean ($\mu = 0$). It is worth noting the general formulae:

$$P(|Z| > z) = 2 - 2\Phi(z), \tag{8.21}$$

$$P(|Z| < z) = 2\Phi(z) - 1, \tag{8.22}$$

which are easily found using the diagram above.

It is common for certain key values of z to be separately tabulated, e.g.,

$$\begin{aligned}
z = 1.645: &\quad P(Z < z) = 0.95\ (95\%), &\quad P(|Z| < z) = 0.90\ (90\%);\\
z = 1.960: &\quad P(Z < z) = 0.975\ (97.5\%), &\quad P(|Z| < z) = 0.95\ (95\%);\\
z = 2.576: &\quad P(Z < z) = 0.995\ (99.5\%), &\quad P(|Z| < z) = 0.99\ (99\%).
\end{aligned}$$

We shall exemplify the use of these in the next section. These values also deliver z such that $P(Z > z)$ is 5% or $P(|Z| > z)$ is 1%, etc.

One further property of these tables – which we shall encounter later – is that they are designed for the use of **linear interpolation**, to fill in between tabulated entries. By this we mean that the error in using linear interpolation is no worse than the error in rounding to 4 dp.

Ex 8.8 Calculate the following for a standard normal variate Z:
$P(Z < 0.5)$, $P(0.5 < Z \leqslant 0.6)$, $P(-0.1 < Z < 0.2)$, $P(Z = 0.5)$, $P(|Z| > 1)$.

8.6 General Normal Distribution

We can have a normal distribution – with a similarly shaped bell curve – for any given mean μ and variance σ^2. The random variable, often called a **normal variate**, has distribution notated by $N(\mu, \sigma^2)$, consistent with $N(0,1)$ for the standard normal distribution. We can write down a formula for its density function, but it is not particularly informative and suffers from the same integration problem as that for the standard normal.

They key to all calculations is to use the following simple and natural formulae to convert any calculation to a standard normal, and hence to $\Phi(z)$.

Frame 8.7 *Conversion to standard normal*

If X is $N(\mu, \sigma^2)$ then Z is $N(0,1)$:

$$Z = \frac{X - \mu}{\sigma} \tag{8.23}$$

$$X = \sigma Z + \mu \tag{8.24}$$

Think about it like this

It is worth looking at the structure of (8.23). Subtracting μ effectively moves the mean to $\mu - \mu = 0$, while dividing by σ effectively rescales the measurement, to change the variance to $\sigma^2/\sigma^2 = 1$.

Example 8.10 Suppose X has distribution $N(50, 25)$, i.e., $\mu = 50,\ \sigma = 5$. We use $Z = (X - 50)/5$.

$$P(40 < X \leqslant 57) = P\left(\frac{40-50}{5} < Z \leqslant \frac{57-50}{5}\right) = P(-2 < Z \leqslant 1.4)$$

$$= \Phi(1.4) - \Phi(-2) = \Phi(1.4) - [1 - \Phi(2)] = 0.8964,$$

$$P(X > 62) = 1 - P(X \leqslant 62) = 1 - P\left(Z \leqslant \frac{62-50}{5}\right)$$

$$= 1 - \Phi(2.4) = 0.0082,$$

$$P(|X - 50| < 8) = P\left(|Z| < \frac{8}{5}\right) = 2\Phi(1.6) - 1 = 0.8904.$$

This last calculation is worthy of note. The final part has used (8.22). Also, the fact that 50 is the mean allowed us a shortcut; otherwise we would have had to rewrite $|X - 50| < 8$ as $42 < X < 58$. It is very common to make measurements centred at the mean, in this way. ■

In the next example we examine the use of the special values at the 'tails' of the distribution, i.e., at large $|z|$, where little probability is located.

Example 8.11 Suppose X is distributed as $N(1,4)$, so $\mu = 1,\ \sigma = 2$. This time we effectively use the $X \leftrightarrow Z$ conversion in reverse:

$$Z = \frac{X-1}{2} \quad \Rightarrow \quad X = 2Z + 1.$$

If we seek α such that $P(X > \alpha) = 0.10$, then we read off, from the second last line of the table,

$$\begin{aligned} P(Z < 1.282) = 0.90 \quad &\Rightarrow \quad P(Z > 1.282) = 0.10 \\ &\Rightarrow \quad \alpha = 2 \times 1.282 + 1 = 3.564. \end{aligned}$$

If we seek β such that $P(|X - 1| > \beta) = 0.01$, then we read off, from the last line of the table,

$$\begin{aligned} P(|Z| < 2.576) = 0.99 \quad &\Rightarrow \quad P(|Z| > 2.576) = 0.01 \\ &\Rightarrow \quad \beta = 2 \times 2.576 = 5.152. \end{aligned}$$

There is no "+1" used here, since it is implicit in $|X - 1|$, 1 being the mean for X, corresponding to 0 for Z. ■

The normal distribution is often assumed – sometimes with no justification other than convenience – to model real data. We finish with two such cases.

Example 8.12 A production line fills 1 kg bags of sugar with an amount X, distributed as $N(1.05, 0.04^2)$. What proportion of a large batch of bags are underfilled?

Here we have

$$\mu = 1.05, \quad \sigma = 0.04, \quad Z = \frac{X - 1.05}{0.04},$$

and we seek $P(X < 1.00)$, since 1 kg is the advertised content.

$$\begin{aligned} P(X < 1.00) &= P\left(Z < \frac{1 - 1.05}{0.04}\right) = P(Z < -1.25) \\ &= \Phi(-1.25) = 1 - \Phi(1.25) = 0.1056, \end{aligned}$$

so approximately 11% are underfilled.

Suppose that we are able to adjust the mean, leaving the standard deviation unchanged. To what value should we set the mean to ensure only 1% are underfilled?

We require $P(X < 1.00) = 0.01$. From the foot of the table, we see

$$P(Z < 2.326) = 0.99 \quad \Rightarrow \quad P(Z < -2.326) = P(Z > 2.326) = 0.01,$$

Hence we set the mean to μ where

$$\frac{1 - \mu}{0.04} = -2.326 \quad \Rightarrow \quad \mu = 1.093,$$

which is the value we seek. ■

In the next example, we are faced with a similar unsatisfactory situation, but this time it makes no sense to alter the mean; the standard deviation is the only usable parameter available.

Example 8.13 A manufacturer produces $100\,\Omega$ [*capital omega*] resistors with a stated tolerance of 5%. The actual values produced are X, distributed as $N(100, 16)$. What proportion fail to meet the tolerance?

Here we have

$$\mu = 100, \quad \sigma = 4, \quad Z = \frac{X - 100}{4},$$

and we seek $P(|X - 100| > 5)$, since 5% of 100 is 5, which is the 'absolute' tolerance. Use (8.21):

$$P(|X - 100| > 5) = P\left(|Z| > \frac{5}{4}\right) = 2\,[1 - \Phi(1.25)] = 0.2112,$$

so approximately 21% fail.

This is unacceptable. To what value must we reduce the standard deviation to ensure only 10% fail?

We require $P(|X - 100| > 5) = 0.10$. From the foot of the table, we see

$$P(|Z| < 1.645) = 0.90 \quad \Rightarrow \quad P(|Z| > 1.645) = 0.10,$$

Hence we set the standard deviation to σ where

$$\frac{5}{\sigma} = 1.645 \quad \Rightarrow \quad \sigma = 3.04,$$

which is the value we seek. ■

Provided the normal model is reasonably accurate, the ability to use the table and these standard formulae for the normal distribution is convenient. But this distribution has a far more significant role in practical statistical work, to which we now turn.

Ex 8.9 For a general normal variate X, what is the probability that X takes a value within one standard deviation of its mean? What is the probability that it is larger than its mean by at least one standard deviation?

Ex 8.10

(a) A **normal variate** X has mean 8.5 and standard deviation 0.2. Calculate:

$$P(X > 8.8), \quad P(|X - 8.5| \leqslant 0.12), \quad P(8.4 < X \leqslant 8.7), \quad P(|X - 8.5| > 0.25).$$

Find values of x such that:

$$P(X > x) = 0.1, \quad P(X \leqslant x) = 0.05, \quad P(|X - 8.5| < x) = 0.99.$$

(b) Suppose that X is distributed as $N(\mu, \sigma^2)$ and that $P(X < 7.3) = 0.05$ and $P(X > 12.2) = 0.05)$. Calculate μ and σ.

Ex 8.11 The volume of beer delivered to a can on a filling line is normally distributed with mean 442 ml and standard deviation 2.5 ml. What is the probability that a randomly selected can contains less than 439 ml? What volume is exceeded by 90% of cans?

Ex 8.12 The length of a component is a normal variate with mean 5 mm and standard deviation 0.02 mm. If the length tolerance is $\pm 1\%$, find the proportion of components that are out of tolerance.

8.7 Revision Exercises

Ex 8.13 The **exponential distribution** models the inter-arrival times between people arriving at random. It has density function:

$$f(t) = \lambda e^{-\lambda t} \quad (t \geqslant 0), \qquad = 0 \quad (t < 0),$$

and mean $1/\lambda$.

Find its **cumulative distribution function.**

People arrive to use a computer at random, with mean inter-arrival time 40 minutes. One user arrives to find the computer free, then uses it for a period of 20 minutes. Find, to 3 dp, the probability that another user will arrive before the session is completed.

Calculate the **median** inter-arrival time, to 2 dp.

Ex 8.14 The **exponential** distribution has **density** function $f(t) = \lambda e^{-\lambda t}$ and **cumulative distribution** function $F(t) = 1 - e^{-\lambda t}$, where $t \geqslant 0$ and $1/\lambda$ is the **mean**.

A series of events, whose inter-event time is thought to be exponentially distributed, is observed until 100 events have occurred, i.e., there have been 100 inter-event periods, counting from the initial time. This took 854 minutes.

(a) What value is the best estimate of λ?

(b) Using that value, what is the probability that the interval between successive events exceeds 10 minutes?

(c) How many events happen in one hour, on average?

(d) An employee takes on average 20 minutes to process an event. What is the least number of employees needed to ensure the events can be coped with in the long run?

Ex 8.15

(a) Find the probability that for Z, modelled by a **standard normal distribution**, $|Z|$ is less than 1.5.

(b) Find α such that for Z, modelled by a **standard normal distribution**, $P(Z > \alpha) = 0.2$.

(c) X is modelled by a **normal distribution** with mean 75 and variance 4. Find the probability that X lies between 74 and 76.5.

Ex 8.16

(a) Find the probability that X, modelled by a **standard normal distribution**, lies between -0.3 and 0.7.

(b) Y is modelled by a **normal distribution** with mean 2 and variance 9. Find the value of α such that $P(Y > \alpha) = 0.1$.

(c) A rod has mean diameter 3.3 cm with variance 0.04 cm^2 obeying a normal distribution. What is the probability that a rod selected at random will fit a hole of width 3.6 cm?

9 STATISTICS

Statistics can be thought of as the practical companion to *Probability*. It has four main objectives:

- The representation of sampled data, in tabular and/or graphical form, to help the reader appreciate the salient features. See §§9.1–9.3.
- The calculation, from such a sample, of key (summary) *statistics*, sometimes with an estimate of their reliability or *error*. This is useful for results calculated following a practical experiment. The *Method of Least Squares* in §2.12 is often referred to by its statistical name **regression**; in that section we stopped short of estimating the error. See §§9.4–9.9.
- The judgement of the *significance* of a particular observation or set of observations. A *statistic* is calculated and the probability of obtaining such a value is considered. We shall not pursue this application, although it was illustrated in Examples 6.5, 7.25 and 7.26.
- The design of appropriate statistical experiments. This is the domain of the professional statistician and we shall not explore it here.

9.1 Discrete Data

We consider *real data*, i.e., a **sample** found by measuring outcomes from a random process. We shall suppose that there are n values and that they have *already* been ordered:

$$x_1 \leqslant x_2 \leqslant x_3 \leqslant \cdots \leqslant x_{n-1} \leqslant x_n.$$

We seek ways to *summarise* this data. The first method is to draw up a table for the data, **grouping** it in some way to reduce the number of displayed items.

It is necessary to distinguish *discrete* and *continuous* data, just as we had to distinguish between the two types of probability distribution.

In the **discrete** case the x_k take values from only a finite set of possibilities: $v_1, \ldots, v_m$, say. Suppose our data contains f_k copies of v_k, so

$$n = f_1 + f_2 + \cdots + f_m.$$

Then f_k is the **frequency** of v_k and

$$r_k = \frac{f_k}{n} \tag{9.1}$$

is the **relative frequency**. We can construct a **line chart** to summarise the data, drawing a vertical line at $x = v_k$ of height f_k or r_k. The relative frequency case is analogous in concept to the graph of the probability function $f(k)$. For a representative sample with large n, r_k and $P(X = v_k)$ should be similar in value and therefore the line chart and the graph of the **probability function** would be similar in shape.

We can also calculate the **cumulative** relative frequency:

$$c_k = r_1 + r_2 + \cdots + r_k, \tag{9.2}$$

giving the proportion of the sample **less than or equal to** v_k. Its graph, sometimes called an **ogive**, is analogous to that of the **distribution function**, although it is more usual to draw it as a type of line chart (without the lines) rather than the 'staircase' type of graph used for $F(x)$. The name 'ogive' is that of an architectural structure whose shape is similar to the graph of some typical cumulative frequencies.

Example 9.1 Asbestos-type fibres in air samples

The concentration of asbestos-type fibres in a workshop, which had been used for making brake linings containing asbestos, was investigated by collecting 143 one-litre samples of air. The numbers of fibres with length greater than 5 μm, width less than 3 μm and length-to-width ratio greater than 3 were automatically detected in each sample. These numbers were all equal to 0, 1, 2, 3, 4 or 5. They are summarised in the **frequency table** and the **line chart** shown below.

v_k	f_k	r_k	c_k
0	34	0.238	0.238
1	46	0.322	0.560
2	38	0.266	0.826
3	19	0.133	0.959
4	4	0.028	0.987
5	2	0.014	1.000
6 or more	0	0.000	1.000
Total	143	1.000	—

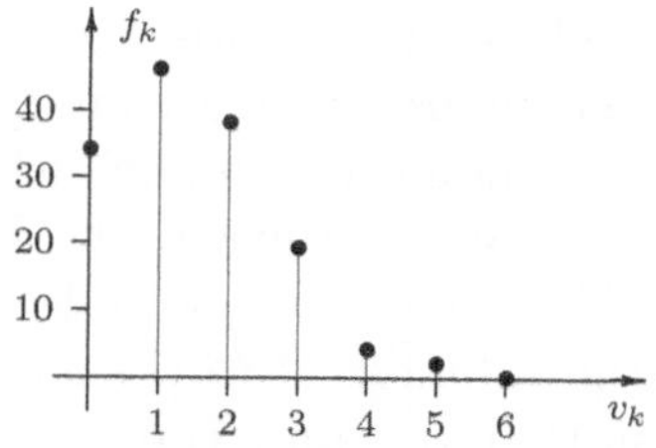

The relative frequency line chart is identical, except that the vertical scale is different.

The relative frequencies add up to 1.001. This is due to accidents of rounding and the small discrepancy is ignored.

The cumulative frequency graph (an ogive) is shown on the right; for discrete data the points are not joined up.

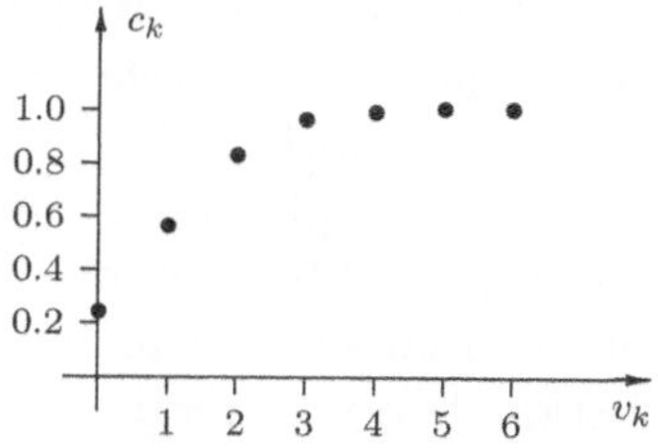

■

Ex 9.1 A data sample consists of 40 items with (values, frequencies):

$$(0, 2), \ (1, 12), \ (2, 14), \ (3, 8), \ (4, 4).$$

Calculate the relative frequencies and display them using a line chart. Plot the cumulative frequencies.

Ex 9.2 Two 4-sided dice are thrown 100 times and their sum recorded:

$$(\text{sum, frequency}): \quad (2, 5), \ (3, 10), \ (4, 17), \ (5, 24), \ (6, 20), \ (7, 15), \ (8, 9).$$

Plot the relative frequencies using a line chart. Superimpose the probability function, assuming the dice are fair. Comment on the results.

9.2 Continuous Data

Suppose now that the data are measurements of a quantity that can take a value anywhere on the real line (or an interval in the real line), i.e., from an infinite set of possibilities. The likelihood is that the sample could consist of entirely different numbers, so all frequencies would be one. Thus, more aggressive grouping is required, collecting the x_k into different **subintervals** from the whole range of values.

Think about it like this

In most practical cases, the natural restriction on the measurement device would mean that only a finite number of values are actually possible, but that number is likely to be so large that it can be regarded as effectively infinite.

Hence, given a range of possible values, we split it up into subintervals:

$$[t_0 = a, t_1], \quad [t_1, t_2], \quad \ldots, \quad [t_{k-1}, t_k], \quad \ldots, \quad [t_{m-1}, t_m = b],$$

where we can have $a = -\infty$ and/or $b = \infty$. In most cases, the subintervals have equal width, except possibly for the two end ones, which often 'mop up stragglers' at the ends.

There are two decisions to make here. The first one is: how many subintervals should we use, i.e., what is m? One 'rule' is to choose $m \simeq \sqrt{n}$, where n is the size of the sample. We shall not insist on this in our examples.

The other is what to do when $x_j = t_k$ for some j, k: is it to be counted in the subinterval to the left or the right? There is no definitive rule, other than to decide on a consistent policy for the example in hand and stick to it: use either $(t_{k-1}, t_k]$ or $[t_{k-1}, t_k)$ for all k (except for one of the end intervals). We shall choose the second option, so our x_j above would lie in $[t_k, t_{k+1})$ and the extreme right hand interval will have to be a fully closed one.

We can now count the frequencies inside each subinterval and compose a table of frequencies f_k, relative frequencies r_k and cumulative relative frequencies c_k, as in §9.1.

We can also graph these, but now we use a **histogram**, where the lines in §9.1 are replaced by 'boxes', to make it clear that all values in each subinterval are contenders for inclusion in the sample. The **area** of each box is proportional to the frequency, although when all subintervals have equal width this is the same as using the **height** to reflect the frequencies. But the mention of area makes it clear that the histogram for relative frequencies should be an approximation to the **probability density function**.

Again, we can graph the cumulative relative frequency data, which should resemble the **distribution function**. But this time there is some sense in joining the points with straight lines, although any intermediate readings are only indicative. Care is needed in the definition, since using intervals $[t_{k-1}, t_k)$ means c_k gives the measure **less than** t_k, while using $(t_{k-1}, t_k]$ relates to **less than or equal to** t_k.

Example 9.2 The following values are the crushing strengths of 25 concrete specimens (in MPa), after being ordered:

27.6	30.3	32.4	34.5	35.2	36.5	37.2	37.2	37.9	37.9
38.6	38.6	38.6	39.3	39.3	39.3	40.0	40.0	40.7	40.7
41.4	42.7	44.1	46.2	49.0					

The grouped table and histogram, are given below. The distribution of the crushing strengths looks roughly symmetric with a single mode at around 39 MPa. Another choice of intervals, such as 27.50–32.49, ..., 47.50–52.49, would give a slightly different histogram.

$[t_{k-1}, t_k)$	f_k	r_k	c_k
$[25.0, 30.0)$	1	.04	.04
$[30.0, 35.0)$	3	.12	.16
$[35.0, 40.0)$	12	.48	.64
$[40.0, 45.0)$	7	.28	.92
$[45.0, 50.0]$	2	.08	1.00
Total	25	1.00	—

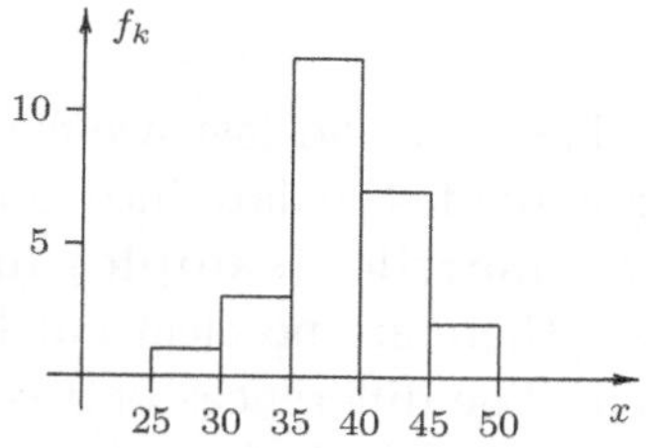

The cumulative frequency graph (an ogive) is shown on the right; this time the points are joined up. For the convention we have chosen, c_k represents the cumulative frequency up to **but not including** t_k.

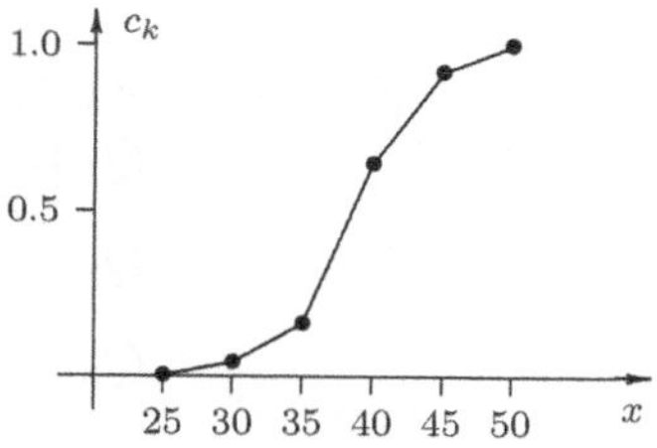

■

Ex 9.3 The response times by an engineer to repair a machine were as follows, in hours:

2.8	1.3	0.5	2.1	3.0	0.8	1.4	1.5	2.5	0.7	1.1	0.8	3.3
1.6	1.0	4.9	2.1	2.5	4.5	2.2	2.5	0.9	5.1	2.2	1.1	

(a) Draw a histogram with equal ranges 0–0.9, 1–1.9, and so on.

(b) Make up a table showing cumulative percentages for the response times and draw a cumulative percentage plot for the data.

9.3 Five-Figure Summary and Boxplot

Often we want to compare two or more data samples corresponding, for example, to different experimental conditions, product suppliers or times of day. Line charts and histograms are not convenient for this. They tend to provide 'information overload'; a better approach is to simplify each sample by computing *summary statistics*. These can then be graphed, with each sample plotted side by side (or one above the other) on a common scale.

One commonly used plot is a **boxplot**, which is based on a so-called **five-figure summary** of each data sample.

We start again with our sample:

$$x_1 \leqslant x_2 \leqslant x_3 \leqslant \cdots \leqslant x_{n-1} \leqslant x_n,$$

assumed to be ordered as shown. The five-figure summary consists of numbers, or **statistics** derived from the data:

$$[x_1,\ Q_1,\ Q_2,\ Q_3,\ x_n]. \tag{9.3}$$

The first and last are clearly the **minimum** and **maximum**. The other three divide the data into four parts and are called, respectively, the **lower** or **first quartile**, **(sample) median** and **upper** or **third quartile.** In most cases there are no clear-cut locations for the Q_i and various conventions are used. The differences between them are usually minor. The following is one of the more logical versions.

Frame 9.1 *The five-figure summary*

$$x_1 = \textbf{minimum} \tag{9.4}$$
$$Q_1 = x_{\left(\frac{n+2}{4}\right)} \tag{9.5}$$
$$Q_2 = x_{\left(\frac{2n+2}{4}\right)} = x_{\left(\frac{n+1}{2}\right)} \tag{9.6}$$
$$Q_3 = x_{\left(\frac{3n+2}{4}\right)} \tag{9.7}$$
$$x_n = \textbf{maximum} \tag{9.8}$$

The subscripts in the Q_i are often fractions and hence do not lead to x_i values in the sequence. They depend on the following conventions, which use a *weighted average* of the values on either side of where the quartile or median falls:

$$x_{m+1/4} = \tfrac{1}{4}\left(3x_m + x_{m+1}\right), \tag{9.9}$$
$$x_{m+1/2} = \tfrac{1}{2}\left(x_m + x_{m+1}\right), \tag{9.10}$$
$$x_{m+3/4} = \tfrac{1}{4}\left(x_m + 3x_{m+1}\right). \tag{9.11}$$

Note that for the median, which should be the middle value, there are two possibilities. If n is odd, there is a clearly defined middle value and $\frac{n+1}{2}$ is a whole number, corresponding to that value. If n is even, there are two values in the middle, and (9.6) delivers their average.

The logic involved in Frame 9.1 is that each internal number x_k has to cover the patch of values from halfway towards the value on its left, to halfway towards the value on its right. We can introduce notation $x_{k-1/2}$ and $x_{k+1/2}$ to describe this and illustrate it below. (The end-points have been dealt with arbitrarily, but this is of no consequence.)

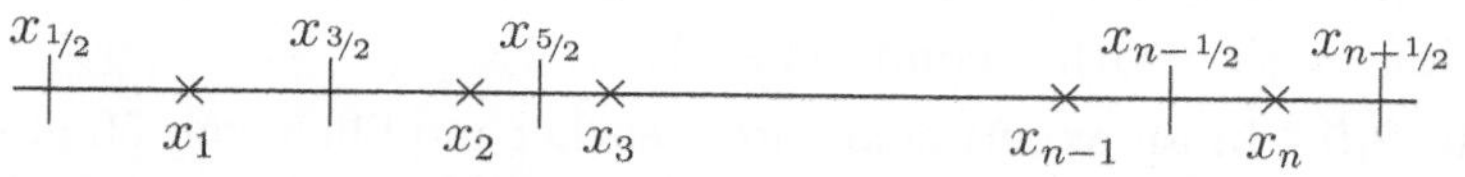

The set of values now spans from $x_{1/2}$ to $x_{n+1/2}$, a 'distance' of n. This is split into four equal distances of $n/4$, which must be added to the $1/2$ at the left, to find the quartile subscripts:

$$\tfrac{1}{2} + \tfrac{n}{4} = \tfrac{n+2}{4}, \qquad \tfrac{1}{2} + \tfrac{2n}{4} = \tfrac{n+1}{2}, \qquad \tfrac{1}{2} + \tfrac{3n}{4} = \tfrac{3n+2}{4},$$

which are precisely those in Frame 9.1.

Example 9.3 A set of $n = 7$ values is $\{17, 24, 32, 41, 55, 67, 73\}$.

The **minimum** and maximum are

$$x_1 = 17, \qquad x_7 = 73.$$

The **median** is

$$Q_2 = x_{\frac{7+1}{2}} = x_4 = 41.$$

The **lower quartile** is

$$Q_1 = x_{\frac{7+2}{4}} = x_{2^1/_4} = \tfrac{1}{4}(3x_2 + x_3) = \tfrac{1}{4}(3 \times 24 + 32) = 26.$$

The **upper quartile** is

$$Q_3 = x_{\frac{21+2}{4}} = x_{5^3/_4} = \tfrac{1}{4}(x_5 + 3x_6) = \tfrac{1}{4}(55 + 3 \times 67) = 64.$$

The five-figure summary is therefore: [17, 26, 41, 64, 73]. ■

These summary values are used pictorially in a **boxplot** or **box-and-whisker plot**. A rectangular 'box' is drawn from the lower quartile to the upper quartile, and the median is shown within this box; in the simplest form of the plot, 'whiskers' are drawn from the box to the minimum and maximum. The width of the box is not important, only its length.

Boxplots may be drawn vertically or, as below, horizontally:

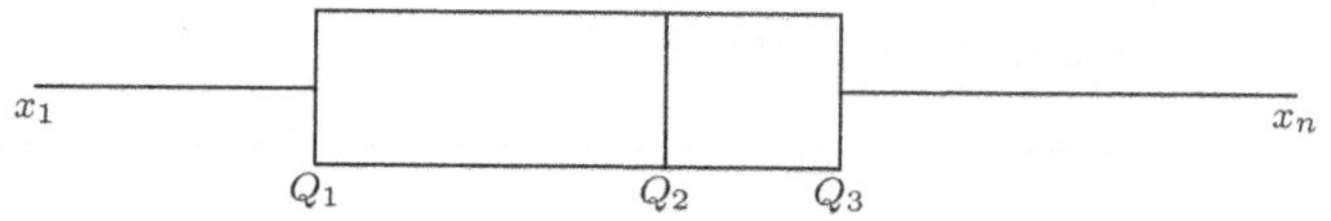

Example 9.4 For the data in Example 9.3, the boxplot is

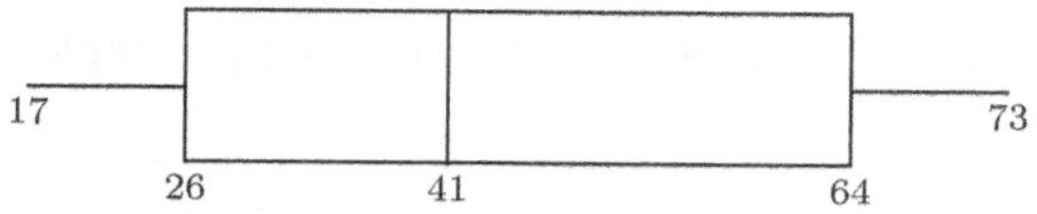

■

Think about it like this

Some statisticians restrict the length of the 'whiskers', e.g., allowing them to be no longer than $1.5(Q_3 - Q_1)$, showing any data points outside that range by dots. This is done in the example that follows, where vertical boxplots are used.

To compare several data sets, the (vertical) boxplots for the different sets are put side by side with a common scale.

Example 9.5 In an experiment into weather modification, 50 clouds were identified as suitable for seeding with silver iodide crystals, and 25 of them were chosen at random to be seeded. The following values are the summary statistics for the amounts of rainfall (in acre-feet) from the seeded and unseeded clouds, respectively.

$$[4.1,\ 79.45,\ 200.7,\ 358.075,\ 2745.6], \qquad [1.0, 23.725,\ 41.1,\ 183.325,\ 1202.6].$$

It is clear that the seeded clouds tend to produce more rainfall.

The corresponding boxplots are shown on the left below. Both distributions show that the small values are much closer together than the larger ones. As a result, the lower whiskers in the boxplot are shorter than the upper ones, and the comparison is obscured by the boxes being squashed to the bottom of the plot.

A boxplot of the (natural) logarithms of the amounts of rainfall (on the right) makes the comparison easier, showing more symmetrical distributions. (No restriction has been placed on the length of the 'whiskers' for that plot.)

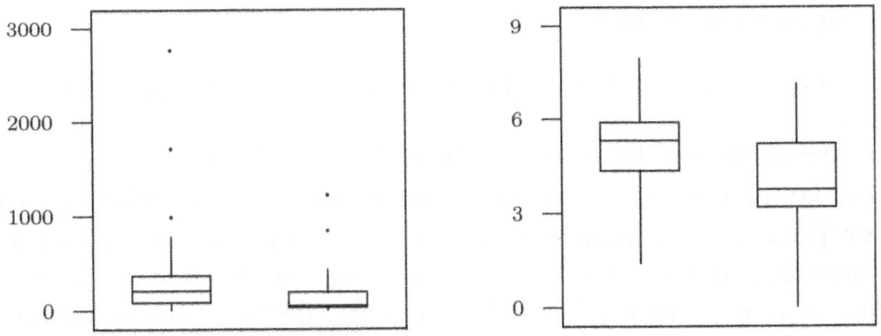

It is quite common in statistics, as in most data analysis, to try analysing or plotting the **logarithm** of the data values. This often reveals that an exponential type phenomenon is involved. ■

Ex 9.4

(a) Find the median and quartiles for the sample in Exercise 9.1.

(b) Find the median and quartiles for the following sample and use them to draw a boxplot:

$$[4.8,\ 5.7,\ 6.1,\ 6.3,\ 6.6,\ 7.1,\ 7.8,\ 8.6,\ 9.8].$$

Ex 9.5 The table below shows the number of entries (in millions) in the UK National Lottery for each of the first 10 games in which nobody won the jackpot and the prize was 'rolled-over' to the next game. (Double 'rollovers' have been excluded.)

Game no.	3	8	19	23	27	29	33	39	43	58
Entries	48.3	57.5	62.2	63.3	62.3	64.8	63.3	63.5	64.6	67.9
Game no.	4	9	20	24	28	30	34	40	44	59
Entries	61.5	69.8	76.2	74.4	74.8	72.2	73.4	74.6	76.7	78.4

Find the five-figure summaries for each set. *Note that the data values are not in numerical order.* Draw boxplots on the same diagram and hence comment on the data. Are there any features that are not apparent from the boxplots?

9.4 Sample Statistics

If we seek a single number to summarise our data sample $\{x_1, \ldots, x_n\}$, the **median** is a possibility. There is, however, an alternative: the **(sample) mean**, which is the more familiarly called the **average**.

Frame 9.2 *The (sample) mean for a data set*

$$\overline{x} = \frac{x_1 + x_2 + \cdots + x_n}{n} = \frac{1}{n}\sum_{k=1}^{n} x_k \tag{9.12}$$

Example 9.6 For the data in Example 9.3,

$$\overline{x} = \frac{1}{7}(17 + 24 + 32 + 41 + 55 + 67 + 73) = 44.14.$$

■

The mean in this example is quite near the median (41). But the mean is much more sensitive to **outliers**, i.e., data values that are so different from the others that they are potentially unreliable.

Example 9.7 Find the median and mean for $\{1, 2, 3, 4, 100\}$.

We have $\overline{x} = 22$, $Q_2 = 3$. ■

Think about it like this

In spite of this sensitivity, the sample mean lies at the heart of most statistical calculation, since it has much more elaborate theoretical support. As we shall see in later sections a great deal is known about the probabilities of the various possible values that $\overline{x}$ can take; the median has no similar support. When faced with possible outliers, the best solution is to exclude them, provided we are sure they really are unreliable.

One of the things we can achieve for the mean is an estimate of its reliability, a measure of its **error**, in a statistical sense. The key to this is the **variance**, which we often have to calculate from the sample itself. Calculators offer the facility to do this, but there is an apparent complication: they implement two different formulae.

The explanation lies in the nature of the 'sample' $\{x_1, \ldots, x_n\}$ itself: is it a *full* sample or a *representative* one, i.e., do these x_k constitute *all* the outcomes for the random event or just a *sample*, in the usual sense of the word?

Consider first the full sample, so that each x_k has the same probability $1/n$. Then Frame 7.4 gives

$$\mu_X = \frac{1}{n}(x_1 + x_2 + \cdots + x_n) = \overline{x},$$

the (sample) mean. Frame 7.5 gives

$$\mathrm{Var}(X) = \frac{1}{n}(x_1^2 + x_2^2 + \cdot + x_n^2) - \mu_X^2,$$

which rearranges to the following computational formulae.

Frame 9.3 Variance for a 'full' sample

$$\mathrm{Var}(X) = \frac{1}{n}(x_1^2 + x_2^2 + \cdots + x_n^2 - n\overline{x}^2) \quad (9.13)$$

$$= \frac{1}{n}\left[\sum x_k^2 - \frac{1}{n}\left(\sum x_k\right)^2\right] \quad (9.14)$$

The first version is suitable for hand calculation, while the second is often used in pre-programmed calculation.

Example 9.8 Five children in a family have heights (cm): 90, 115, 130, 145, 175.

$$\mu_X = \overline{x} = \frac{1}{5} \times 655 = 131,$$

$$\mathrm{Var}(X) = \frac{1}{5}\left(89875 - 5 \times 131^2\right) = 814,$$

$$\sigma_X = \sqrt{814} = 28.53.$$

The units for μ and σ are cm, while those for $\mathrm{Var}(X)$ are cm^2. ■

In this example it was clear that *all* the 'events' were covered in the data set. But in most cases we can sample only a small part, e.g., an opinion poll, a blood sample, a quality control sample.

The formulae above remain true except for two points. We must change the notation to make it clear that this is only "part of the story". Frame 9.2 holds true, but when analysing the variance we *must* use $\overline{x}$ rather than μ_X and should refer to the *sample* mean.

We also change notation from $\mathrm{Var}(X)$ to s^2 (and hence from σ_X to s), where s^2 is the **sample variance**, and s the **sample standard deviation**. Finally, we need to make a small change in the formulae in Frame 9.3.

> *Frame 9.4* Sample variance
>
> $$s^2 = \frac{1}{n-1}(x_1^2 + x_2^2 + \cdots + x_n^2 - n\overline{x}^2) \qquad (9.15)$$
>
> $$= \frac{1}{n-1}\left[\sum x_k^2 - \frac{1}{n}\left(\sum x_k\right)^2\right] \qquad (9.16)$$

The change from n to $n-1$ at the final division recognises that the formula is not accurate since it uses $\overline{x}$, which is only an estimate of the true mean μ_X. A deep mathematical analysis shows that this small change is an appropriate adjustment to take account of this.

Calculators providing for statistical calculation usually offer both (9.14) and (9.16), on keys typically labelled σ_n and σ_{n-1}, respectively.

Example 9.9 Suppose that the five heights in Example 9.8 are those of a sample from a school. Then $\overline{x} = 131$ as before. But now

$$s^2 = \frac{1}{4}\left(89875 - 5 \times 131^2\right) = 1017.5,$$
$$s = \sqrt{1017.5} = 31.90.$$

These are larger than before, as we might expect: s is computed using an untrustworthy value and so we ought to err "on the safe side". ■

Example 9.10 1000 whole numbers between 1 and 100 are sampled using a random number generator. They give values:

$$\sum x_k = 50045, \qquad \sum x_k^2 = 3.38336 \times 10^6.$$

We then calculate

$$\overline{x} = \frac{50045}{10000} = 50.045,$$
$$s^2 = \frac{1}{999}\left[3.38336 \times 10^6 - 1000 \times 50.045^2\right] = 879.74.$$

By way of comparison, the exact mean and variance for this distribution are given in Frame 7.7 as:

$$\mu_X = \frac{101}{2} = 50.5, \qquad \mathrm{Var}(X) = \frac{100^2 - 1}{12} = 833.25.$$

■

Ex 9.6

(a) A sample of 1000 data values x_k gives: $\sum x_k = 6434$, $\sum x_k^2 = 75128$. Calculate the sample mean, sample variance and sample standard deviation.

(b) A coin is tossed 10 times, the results recorded (Heads = 1, Tails = 0) and added. This experiment is carried out 100 times and the data gives $\sum x_k = 542$, $\sum x_k^2 = 3180$. Show that the sample mean is 5.42 and calculate the sample variance. Is it consistent with a binomial distribution, mean 5.42?

Ex 9.7 Suppose that the time to failure of an item of equipment follows an exponential distribution with parameter λ. This parameter can be estimated from the results of a test in which items are tested to failure, by equating $1/\lambda$ to the observed mean. Estimate λ from the following table of data for 10 components:

Day of installation	0	9	11	21	40	50	50	51	52	60
Day of failure	2	128	62	98	73	77	64	75	66	97

Also, calculate the sample standard deviation. For a true exponential distribution the standard deviation and mean are equal. Comment.

9.5 Distribution of the Sample Mean

A second sample as in Example 9.10 might give $\overline{x} = 49.048$, $s^2 = 848.73$. What this suggests is that these are sample values for two **random variables**. In principle we ought to be able to assign probabilities to the various possible values or ranges of values of $\overline{x}$ and s^2. This is clearly very difficult, but we can make progress, particularly for the sample mean.

We write $\overline{X}$ as the random variable for which $\overline{x}$ is a possible value. Then key questions are

- What is $E(\overline{X})$?
- What is $\text{Var}(\overline{X})$?
- What is the distribution for $\overline{X}$, e.g., what is its probability or density function?

The first two are quite straightforward to answer, provided the individual items are sampled **independently**. The third seems intractable, but we shall be able to provide an *approximate* answer in §9.6, an answer good enough to underpin a large amount of statistical calculation.

The first two answers are simple to state and their derivation is sufficiently informative to justify a small diversion.

First, consider two random variables X and Z, where $Z = \alpha X$, with α a constant. Then the definitions of mean and variance show that

$$E(Z) = \alpha E(X), \qquad \text{Var}(Z) = \alpha^2 \text{Var}(X). \tag{9.17}$$

Indeed, there is hardly any reason to go through the calculations: Z is simply a rescaled version of X, so the mean and variance are also rescaled; recall that the unit for the mean is that of the random variable, while the unit for the variance is its square.

Second, consider a random variable Y that is the sum of n other random variables, $X_1, \ldots, X_n$. Then the definition of the mean gives

$$E(Y) = E(X_1) + \cdots + E(X_n). \tag{9.18}$$

This time the variance calculation is quite complicated, although there is a simple result *in a special but important circumstance*:

$$\operatorname{Var}(Y) = \operatorname{Var}(X_1) + \cdots + \operatorname{Var}(X_n), \tag{9.19}$$

provided the probabilities for any pair are **independent**.

Example 9.11 Confirm the parameters for the binomial distribution X in Frame 7.9, which is the sum of n **independent** Bernoulli trials X_k, each with mean p and variance pq.

$$\begin{aligned} E(X) &= p + p + \cdots + p = np, \\ \operatorname{Var}(X) &= pq + pq + \cdots + pq = npq. \end{aligned}$$

■

We are now able to tackle $\overline{X}$. Suppose that each x_k in the calculation for $\overline{x}$ is a value of a random variable X_k, where all the X_k have the same distribution (and hence the same mean μ and variance σ^2):

$$\overline{X} = \frac{1}{n}\left(X_1 + X_2 + \cdots + X_n\right). \tag{9.20}$$

Using (9.17) with $\alpha = \frac{1}{n}$ and (9.18), we have:

$$\begin{aligned} E(\overline{X}) &= \frac{1}{n}\left(\mu + \mu + \cdots + \mu\right) = \mu, \\ \operatorname{Var}(\overline{X}) &= \frac{1}{n^2}\left(\sigma^2 + \sigma^2 + \cdots + \sigma^2\right) = \frac{\sigma^2}{n}, \end{aligned}$$

results that are certainly worthy of being summed up in a frame.

Frame 9.5 Mean, variance and standard error for $\overline{X}$

$$E(\overline{X}) = \mu \tag{9.21}$$

$$\operatorname{Var}(\overline{X}) = \frac{\sigma^2}{n} \tag{9.22}$$

$$\sigma_{\overline{X}} = \frac{\sigma}{\sqrt{n}} \quad \textbf{[standard error]} \tag{9.23}$$

Think about it like this

These results back up our decision to use the mean – the results should be scattered round the 'true' value – and explains the commonsense judgement of the average – the larger the sample size (n), the better the answer, since the sample means are less widely scattered.

Example 9.12 A four-sided die is thrown 100 times and the results are averaged.

The base distribution is a uniform one over {1, 2, 3, 4}. We know (from Frame 7.7, with $n = 4$) that

$$E(X) = \frac{1+4}{2} = {}^5\!/_2, \qquad \text{Var}(X) = \frac{4^2-1}{12} = {}^5\!/_4,$$

and hence

$$E(\overline{X}) = {}^5\!/_2, \qquad \text{Var}(\overline{X}) = \frac{1}{100}\frac{5}{4} = {}^1\!/_{80}.$$

■

The name **standard error** is used for both $\sigma/\sqrt{n}$ and $s/\sqrt{n}$, without the use of the word "sample" for the latter.

Example 9.13 For the sample of five children from a school, in Example 9.9, the standard error is

$$\frac{31.90}{\sqrt{5}} = 14.27.$$

■

Think about it like this

The standard error is not only an important quantity in calculations, but a measure of how statistical calculations perform. The 'errors' are inversely proportional to the square root of the sample size, so that to *halve* the error requires us to *quadruple* the sample size. This is a poor performance compared with what can be achieved in non-statistical calculations. Nevertheless, there are situations where the simplification offered by a statistical approach more than outweighs this. For example, the probability-based *Monte-Carlo method* is heavily used in practical calculations in Physics.

Ex 9.8

(a) The following sample is found using a die 10 times: 4, 2, 6, 1, 4, 5, 5, 2, 1, 3.

Calculate the sample mean and variance and compare them with the corresponding values for a fair die: see Exercise 7.6. What is the standard error?

(b) Three probability experiments are held together and the results are added: a fair coin is tossed ($H = 1$, $T = 2$); a fair die is thrown; a card is selected from a deck numbered 1 to 9. Calculate the mean and variance of the sum.

Ex 9.9 If X_1 is $N\left(\mu_1, \sigma_1^2\right)$ and X_2 is $N\left(\mu_2, \sigma_2^2\right)$, with X_1 and X_2 independent, then it is known that $X_1 - X_2$ is $N\left(\mu_1 - \mu_2, \sigma_1^2 + \sigma_2^2\right)$.

Circular rods have diameters $N(1, 0.003^2)$. Washers have holes with diameters $N(1.005, 0.004^2)$. (The units are consistent.) If rods and washers are paired randomly, what proportion do not fit?

9.6 The Central Limit Theorem

Returning to the random variable $Y = X_1 + \cdots + X_n$, where the X_k have the same distribution, that of X, we know that $\mu_Y = \mu_X$ and $\mathrm{Var}(Y) = n\,\mathrm{Var}(X)$ (assuming independence). But what about the *distribution* of Y, without which we cannot calculate probabilities?

The answer is the most remarkable fact in *Statistics*: the **Central Limit Theorem** tells us that the distribution is approximately that of a **normal distribution**, $N\left(n\mu_X, n\,\mathrm{Var}(X)\right)$, irrespective of the distribution of X. We can therefore calculate all the probabilities we wish, or at least approximations to them.

There are several versions of this Theorem. The following version gives a formal statement and also sets out an immediately useful formula.

Frame 9.6 *The Central Limit Theorem when X has mean μ, variance σ^2*

$$P(X_1 + \cdots + X_n \leqslant x) \to \Phi\left(\frac{x - n\mu}{\sqrt{n}\sigma}\right) \quad \text{as } n \to \infty \qquad (9.24)$$

Here, $\Phi(z)$ is the distribution function for the standard normal $N(0, 1)$, for which we have a table of values.

There are several comments to make about the practical interpretation of this result.

- It explains why the **normal distribution** is fundamental to much of Statistics.
- It also explains why it was so important to find the mean and variance for every distribution.
- **Independence** is essential.
- In the limit, the shape of the distribution for X is irrelevant.
- *But*, if X is already nearly normal, a small n will produce a very accurate approximation; if X is itself normal, then no limit is necessary: Y is exactly normal for all n.
- If X is far from normal, a large n may be needed to give even rudimentary accuracy; in particular, a lack of symmetry in the density function for X may necessitate a large n.
- The result holds for both **discrete** and **continuous** X distributions, although there is a small obstacle to overcome for the former; this is illustrated in the next section.

Example 9.14 Suppose X is the **uniform** distribution on $[-1,1]$. The graphs below show the density functions for the sums of two X_1+X_2 $[f_2(x)]$ and three $X_1+X_2+X_3$ $[f_3(x)]$ such random variables.

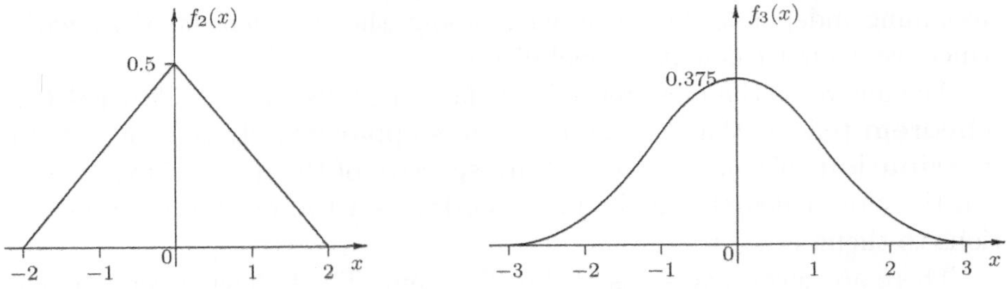

The shape is already similar to a normal density function. Although the density for X is very non-normal, it is symmetric, which speeds up the convergence. ■

Ex 9.10 A computer, in adding numbers, rounds each off to the nearest integer. Suppose that all rounding errors are independent and uniformly distributed over the interval $(-0.5, 0.5)$. If 1500 numbers are added, what is the probability that the size (absolute value) of the total error exceeds 15?

9.7 Approximating the Binomial Distribution

Some of the examples of using the **binomial** distribution in §7.6 led to calculations that were so time-consuming that a computer was required. Some simplification was possible for p near 0 or 1, through approximating with the **Poisson** distribution. We are now able to deal with other p, and 'reasonably large' n, using the **normal** distribution, backed up by the *Central Limit Theorem.*

In Example 9.11, we noted that the binomial was the sum of n *independent* Bernoulli trials, so the Central Limit Theorem applies. We match the mean and variance and claim the following.

Frame 9.7 *Normal approximation to binomial*

$$\mathrm{Bin}(n,p) \simeq N(np, npq) \tag{9.25}$$

This would appear to settle the issue: we merely calculate probabilities using $N(np, npq)$. But there is a fundamental problem. The binomial distribution is *discrete*, so we can talk of $P(X=k)$, while the normal is *continuous*, so we can talk only of $P(a \leqslant X \leqslant b)$. The solution is to use a simple adjustment, called the **continuity correction**.

We need to ensure that the isolated k values cover all the area under the curve, as in the graph on the right. We do this by 'smearing out' $X = k$:

$$X_B = k \;\Leftrightarrow\; X_N \text{ in } [k - 1/2, k + 1/2].$$

Care is needed since $<$ and $\leqslant$ give different answers using X_B, but the same values using X_N.

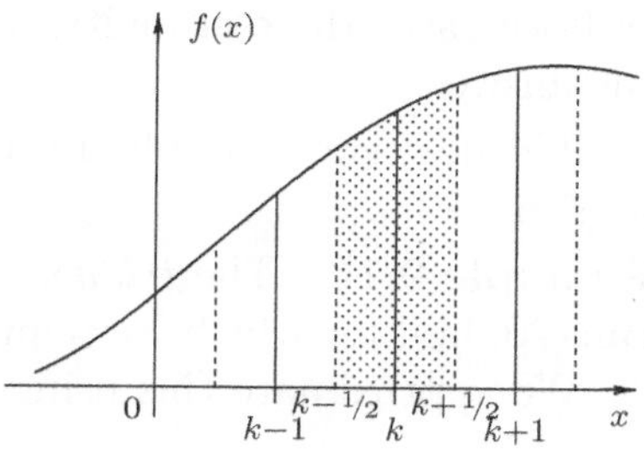

Frame 9.8 *The continuity correction*

$$X_B < k \;\Leftrightarrow\; X_N < k - 1/2, \qquad X_B \leqslant k \;\Leftrightarrow\; X_N < k + 1/2 \qquad (9.26)$$

$$X_B > k \;\Leftrightarrow\; X_N > k + 1/2, \qquad X_B \geqslant k \;\Leftrightarrow\; X_N > k - 1/2 \qquad (9.27)$$

Example 9.15 The following show the ease of calculation, but also the level of inaccuracy that may be involved: in the first case n is small, while in the second p is not near $1/2$, so the distribution is not very symmetric.

(a) Let X_B be distributed as $\text{Bin}(4, 0.5)$, and estimate $P(X_B \leqslant 1)$, which is exactly 0.3125.

The distribution is approximated by $N(4 \times 0.5, 4 \times 0.5 \times 0.5)$, i.e., $N(2, 1)$. Hence use

$$P(X_N < 1 + 1/2) = P\left(Z < \frac{1.5 - 2}{1}\right) = \Phi(-0.5) = 0.3085,$$

while the result ignoring the continuity correction would be

$$\Phi\left(\frac{1-2}{1}\right) = \Phi(-1) = 0.1587.$$

(b) Let X_B be distributed as $\text{Bin}(20, 0.8)$, and estimate $P(X_B \geqslant 16)$, which is exactly 0.6296.

The distribution is approximated by $N(20 \times 0.8, 20 \times 0.8 \times 0.2)$, i.e., $N(16, 3.2)$. Hence use

$$P(X_N > 16 - 1/2) = P\left(Z > \frac{15.5 - 16}{\sqrt{3.2}}\right) = 1 - \Phi(-0.28) = 0.6103,$$

while the result ignoring the continuity correction would be

$$1 - \Phi\left(\frac{16 - 16}{\sqrt{3.2}}\right) = 1 - \Phi(0) = 0.5.$$

In both cases the continuity correction significantly improved the quality of the answer. ■

The next two examples return to those that were computationally difficult in §7.6.

Example 9.16 The *triangular test* in Example 7.26 led to the distribution Bin (20, 1/3), for which we required $P(X_B \geqslant 10) = 0.092$.

We approximate this using $N\,(20/3, 40/9)$, calculating

$$\begin{aligned} P(X_N > 9.5) &= P\left(Z > \frac{9.5 - 20/3}{\sqrt{40/9}}\right) = P(Z > 1.344) \\ &= 1 - \Phi(1.344) = 1 - 0.9105 = 0.0895. \end{aligned}$$

(Linear interpolation was used in the table of $\Phi(z)$, between the entries for $z = 1.34$ and $z = 1.35$.) ■

Example 9.17 The insurance company's problem in Example 7.27 led to the distribution Bin(2100, 0.7), for which we required $P(X_B \geqslant 1450) = 0.8356$.

We approximate this using $N(1470, 441)$ (since $np = 2100 \times 0.7 = 1470$ and $npq = 2100 \times 0.7 \times 0.3 = 441$), calculating

$$\begin{aligned} P(X_N > 1449.5) &= P\left(Z > \frac{1449.5 - 1470}{\sqrt{441}}\right) \\ &= P(Z > -0.976) = \Phi(0.976) = 0.8355. \end{aligned}$$

(Again linear interpolation was used in the table.) ■

Ex 9.11 15% of women have Rhesus negative blood and need special treatment during pregnancy. Use the normal approximation to the binomial distribution to find the probability that more than 27 of the 140 women attending a clinic have Rhesus negative blood.

Ex 9.12 A brewery wished to investigate whether there would be a detectable difference in aroma or taste if production were transferred from Manchester to Edinburgh. They used a *triangular test* in which 45 subjects were given three samples of the beer in random order and told (correctly) that two of the samples came from one brewery and the third from the other. The odd beer was identified correctly by 24 of the 45.

The correct model here is Bin$(45, p)$. Use the normal approximation to estimate to 4 dp the probability of achieving *at least* 24 correct selections if there were no detectable difference, so each selection is made at random with $p = 1/3$. What conclusion would you make?

9.8 Confidence Intervals

In §9.5, we showed that $\overline{X}$ has mean μ and standard deviation $\sigma/\sqrt{n}$. The Central Limit Theorem now tells us that, approximately, the distribution is *normal*, which allows us to calculate probabilities associated with the mean.

Frame 9.9 *Distribution of $\overline{X}$*

$$\overline{X} \text{ is approximately distributed as } N\left(\mu, \frac{\sigma^2}{n}\right) \tag{9.28}$$

$$Z = \frac{\sqrt{n}(\overline{X} - \mu)}{\sigma} \text{ is approximately } N(0,1) \tag{9.29}$$

This result opens up a great many applications, but we shall concentrate on one. When attempting to measure a quantity, μ say, we obtain a sample of estimates, which we assume to be values of a random variable with mean μ. Then $\overline{x}$ is a good estimate of μ, but just how good is it?

Because the experiment is statistically based we cannot quote a definite error bound, as we can do when truncating a power series, for example. It is possible (with low probability, of course) for samples to be very poor.

A particularly successful approach, based on Frame 9.9, is as follows. From the table of $\Phi(z)$ we have

$$\begin{aligned} 0.95 &= P(|Z| \leqslant 1.960) \\ &= P\left(\frac{\sqrt{n}|\overline{X} - \mu|}{\sigma} \leqslant 1.960\right) \\ &= P\left(|\overline{X} - \mu| \leqslant \frac{1.960\sigma}{\sqrt{n}}\right). \end{aligned}$$

Hence, $\overline{x}$ should lie within $\dfrac{1.960\sigma}{\sqrt{n}}$ of the true mean, with 95% probability.

Reversing this statement:

> The true mean μ is within $\dfrac{1.960\sigma}{\sqrt{n}}$ of the sample mean $\overline{x}$, with 95% probability.

The range of values spanned by this statement is known as a **confidence interval** and the extremes are the **confidence limits**.

Frame 9.10 *Confidence intervals and limits*

$\left[\overline{x} - \dfrac{1.960\sigma}{\sqrt{n}}, \overline{x} + \dfrac{1.960\sigma}{\sqrt{n}}\right]$ is the 95% confidence interval for μ

$\overline{x} \pm \dfrac{1.960\sigma}{\sqrt{n}}$ are the 95% confidence limits for μ

Use 1.645 for 90% confidence and 2.576 for 99% confidence

Example 9.18 Suppose X is known to have distribution $N(\mu, (0.02)^2)$. A sample of 5 values is $\{3.12, 3.05, 2.83, 2.94, 3.21\}$. Find where μ may lie, with 95% confidence.

We have $\overline{x} = 3.03$. Also, noting that $\sigma = 0.02$ and $n = 5$, we have

$$\frac{1.960\sigma}{\sqrt{n}} = \frac{1.96 \times 0.02}{\sqrt{5}} \simeq 0.018,$$

so μ lies in $[3.012, 3.048]$ with 95% probability. ■

This example presupposed that we knew σ, which is often not the case. There are two approaches to this. One is to assume that historical evidence about the measurement process is extensive and has pointed to a stable value of σ. The other is to use the **sample** standard deviation, s, instead. This is safe provided n is not small. (There is a method, based on the so-called t-distribution, that compensates for small n.)

Example 9.19 A sample of 100 gives $\overline{x} = 1.72$ and $s = 0.32$. The 95% confidence limits are

$$1.72 \pm \frac{1.96 \times 0.32}{\sqrt{100}}, \quad \text{i.e., } 1.72 \pm 0.063.$$

Suppose that we require a precision 0.01 with 99% confidence. Then

$$\frac{2.576 \times 0.32}{\sqrt{n}} \leqslant 0.01 \quad \Rightarrow \quad n \geqslant \left(\frac{2.576 \times 0.32}{0.01}\right)^2 \simeq 7000.$$

This seems unrealistic, so it may be necessary to improve the process, e.g., by investing in new equipment, to reduce the standard deviation instead.

If the sample size remains at 100, we would require

$$\frac{2.576\sigma}{\sqrt{100}} \leqslant 0.01 \quad \Rightarrow \quad \sigma \leqslant \frac{0.01 \times 10}{2.576} \simeq 0.04.$$

■

Ex 9.13 Nails of specified length 2 cm have lengths distributed with mean 2.0 and standard deviation 0.08. Find the probability that the mean of a batch of 400 will lie between 1.99 and 2.01 cm.

Ex 9.14

(a) A sample of 100 items from a population with standard deviation $\sigma = 0.32$ has sample mean $\overline{x} = 1.72$. Find a 95% confidence interval for the true mean.

(b) A large group of animals have a known standard deviation of 2.2 kg. A sample of 80 are chosen and weighed, giving an average of 8.3 kg. Construct a 90% confidence interval for the (true) mean.

9.9 Experimental Errors

The context in the previous section is similar to standard practice for quoting values determined by experimental methods. Such values are conventionally reported as

$$\text{mean} \pm \text{standard error.}$$

Since the standard error is the standard deviation for the mean, this is equivalent to using $1 \times \sigma/\sqrt{n}$ in Frame 9.10, i.e., to

$$P(|Z| \leqslant 1) = \Phi(1) - [1 - \Phi(1)] = 0.6826,$$

so quoting $\overline{x} \pm \epsilon$ is equivalent to quoting a 68% confidence interval.

This convention opens up the possibility of using the Central Limit Theorem when adding or subtracting experimental values.

Example 9.20 A quantity Q_1, determined using 50 measurements, delivers a sample mean $\overline{x}_1 = 32.7$ and sample standard deviation $s_1 = 1.4$, which we assume is a reasonable approximation to σ, since n is fairly large.

The **standard error** in $\overline{Q}_1$ is $\frac{1.4}{\sqrt{50}} \simeq 0.2$, so we quote

$$Q_1 = 32.7 \pm 0.2 \quad (68\% \text{ confidence}).$$

Suppose that a second quantity is measured *independently* from the first:

$$Q_2 = -17.3 \pm 0.15.$$

What should we quote for the sum $Q_1 + Q_2$? Clearly the only sensible value to quote is 15.4, but we need to find an error estimate.

Because of independence, we have

$$\text{Var}(\overline{Q}_1 + \overline{Q}_2) = \text{Var}(\overline{Q}_1) + \text{Var}(\overline{Q}_2) = 0.2^2 + 0.15^2 = 0.0625,$$

giving a standard error in the sum: $\sqrt{0.0625} = 0.25$. Hence, we give the final result as

$$Q_1 + Q_2 = 15.4 \pm 0.25.$$

Note that the *relative* errors have increased, from 0.6% and 0.9% to 1.6%. This is typical of the danger of error inflation inherent in subtraction. ■

Ex 9.15 Experiment produces $x = 7.42 \pm 0.04$ and $y = 4.13 \pm 0.02$, with the '±' indicating one standard deviation. Find an equivalent expression for $2x + 3y$.

9.10 Revision Exercises

Ex 9.16 The following values are the distances (in miles) travelled by 20 armoured personnel carriers before they failed in service:

162	200	271	320	392	508	539	629	706	778
884	1008	1081	1101	1182	1464	1603	1984	2355	2880

(a) Calculate the median and the lower and upper quartiles of these values. $\left(Q_1 = x_{\frac{n+2}{4}},\ Q_3 = x_{\frac{3n+2}{4}}.\right)$

(b) Draw an accurate boxplot for the data set.

Ex 9.17 The following values are the distribution of ages of the workforce of 19 for a small company:

19	22	22	23	25	27	31	31	34	39
41	47	48	51	55	59	61	64	65	

Note: $\sum x_k = 764$.

Calculate the mean, median, and the lower and upper quartiles of these values.

Ex 9.18 Measurements of the density of dust particles in a gas were recorded on 180 occasions:

Number of particles seen	0	1	2	3	4	5	6 or more
Number of occasions	43	59	47	23	6	2	0

Show that the mean number per occasion is 1.422 and find the probabilities for a Poisson distribution with $\mu = 1.422$, for values $0, 1, 2, 3, 4, 5, \geqslant 6$. Multiply these by 180, convert to whole numbers and compare with the values above.

Ex 9.19 The diameter of refill leads of a mechanical pencil are supposed to be 0.5 mm. Refills whose diameter are less than 0.485 mm do not stay in the pencil while those whose diameter is greater than 0.520 mm do not fit in the pencil at all. A firm makes refills with mean diameter 0.50 mm with standard deviation 0.01 mm. Find the percentage of the production that fail to fit a pencil.

Ex 9.20 A sample of 64 items produces a mean $\overline{x} = 56.8$ and sample variance $s^2 = 3.24$. Find a 95% confidence interval for the mean of the distribution from which the sample was chosen.

(You may assume that the sample size is sufficiently large for s to be an acceptable approximation for σ.)

Ex 9.21 A machine producing an item with a stipulated measurement is thought to be unreliable, although the standard deviation could be assumed to be the historically known value 0.8. A sample is to be chosen to estimate the mean measurement within 0.1. What size should this be to deliver 90% confidence in the result?

The standard normal cumulative distribution function $\Phi(z)$

$P(Z < z) = \Phi(z)$, $P(|Z| < z) = 2\Phi(z) - 1$, $\Phi(-z) = 1 - \Phi(z)$

z	.00	.01	.02	.03	.04	.05	.06	.07	.08	.09
0.0	.5000	.5040	.5080	.5120	.5160	.5199	.5239	.5279	.5319	.5359
0.1	.5398	.5438	.5478	.5517	.5557	.5596	.5636	.5675	.5714	.5753
0.2	.5793	.5832	.5871	.5910	.5948	.5987	.6026	.6064	.6103	.6141
0.3	.6179	.6217	.6255	.6293	.6331	.6368	.6406	.6443	.6480	.6517
0.4	.6554	.6591	.6628	.6664	.6700	.6736	.6772	.6808	.6844	.6879
0.5	.6915	.6950	.6985	.7019	.7054	.7088	.7123	.7157	.7190	.7224
0.6	.7257	.7291	.7324	.7357	.7389	.7422	.7454	.7486	.7517	.7549
0.7	.7580	.7611	.7642	.7673	.7704	.7734	.7764	.7794	.7823	.7852
0.8	.7881	.7910	.7939	.7967	.7995	.8023	.8051	.8078	.8106	.8133
0.9	.8159	.8186	.8212	.8238	.8264	.8289	.8315	.8340	.8365	.8389
1.0	.8413	.8438	.8461	.8485	.8508	.8531	.8554	.8577	.8599	.8621
1.1	.8643	.8665	.8686	.8708	.8729	.8749	.8770	.8790	.8810	.8830
1.2	.8849	.8869	.8888	.8907	.8925	.8944	.8962	.8980	.8997	.9015
1.3	.9032	.9049	.9066	.9082	.9099	.9115	.9131	.9147	.9162	.9177
1.4	.9192	.9207	.9222	.9236	.9251	.9265	.9279	.9292	.9306	.9319
1.5	.9332	.9345	.9357	.9370	.9382	.9394	.9406	.9418	.9429	.9441
1.6	.9452	.9463	.9474	.9484	.9495	.9505	.9515	.9525	.9535	.9545
1.7	.9554	.9564	.9573	.9582	.9591	.9599	.9608	.9616	.9625	.9633
1.8	.9641	.9649	.9656	.9664	.9671	.9678	.9686	.9693	.9699	.9706
1.9	.9713	.9719	.9726	.9732	.9738	.9744	.9750	.9756	.9761	.9767
2.0	.9772	.9778	.9783	.9788	.9793	.9798	.9803	.9808	.9812	.9817
2.1	.9821	.9826	.9830	.9834	.9838	.9842	.9846	.9850	.9854	.9857
2.2	.9861	.9864	.9868	.9871	.9875	.9878	.9881	.9884	.9887	.9890
2.3	.9893	.9896	.9898	.9901	.9904	.9906	.9909	.9911	.9913	.9916
2.4	.9918	.9920	.9922	.9925	.9927	.9929	.9931	.9932	.9934	.9936
2.5	.9938	.9940	.9941	.9943	.9945	.9946	.9948	.9949	.9951	.9952
2.6	.9953	.9955	.9956	.9957	.9959	.9960	.9961	.9962	.9963	.9964
2.7	.9965	.9966	.9967	.9968	.9969	.9970	.9971	.9972	.9973	.9974
2.8	.9974	.9975	.9976	.9977	.9977	.9978	.9979	.9979	.9980	.9981
2.9	.9981	.9982	.9982	.9983	.9984	.9984	.9985	.9985	.9986	.9986
3.0	.9987	.9987	.9987	.9988	.9988	.9989	.9989	.9989	.9990	.9990
3.1	.9990	.9991	.9991	.9991	.9992	.9992	.9992	.9992	.9993	.9993
3.2	.9993	.9993	.9994	.9994	.9994	.9994	.9994	.9995	.9995	.9995
3.3	.9995	.9995	.9995	.9996	.9996	.9996	.9996	.9996	.9996	.9997
3.4	.9997	.9997	.9997	.9997	.9997	.9997	.9997	.9997	.9997	.9998

z	1.282	1.645	1.960	2.326	2.576	3.090	3.291	3.891
$P(Z < z)$	**0.90**	**0.95**	**0.975**	**0.99**	**0.995**	**0.999**	**0.999 5**	**0.999 95**
$P(\|Z\| < z)$	*0.80*	*0.90*	*0.95*	*0.98*	*0.99*	*0.998*	*0.999*	*0.999 9*

Answers to Exercises

6.1 0.504

6.2 (a) 0.08, (b) 0.98

6.3 $5/9$, $5/6$, $1/9$, $1/6$, $1/9$, $4/9$

6.4 (a) $1/2$, $2/3$, $2/7$, $2/27$, (b) 3 to 1 on, 4 to 1 against, (c) 115 to 2 against

6.5 $2/3$, $1/3$

6.6 (a) i. $5/12$, ii. $1/2$, (b) $5/6$, $2/3$, $1/6$, $1/3$

6.7 $3/5$, $6/11$

6.8 0.32, 0.68, 0.5333, 0.4667, 0.8

6.9 (a) $5/9$, (b) $1/2$

6.10 0.07831

6.11 $1/2$, $1/3$

6.12 $\frac{15}{43} = 0.3488$

6.13 (a) 0.295, (b) $\frac{49}{59} = 0.8305$

6.14 $1/6$, $5/36$, $6/36$, no, yes

6.15 (a) $\frac{19}{28}$, (b) $\frac{25}{56}$, (c) $\frac{7}{25}$

6.16 (a) $\frac{5}{18}$, (b) $\frac{4}{9}$, (c) $\frac{1}{4}$

7.1 $P(N = k) = (2k - 1)/36$

7.2 $\lambda = 1/21$

7.3 $P(X = x_k) = 1/4$, $\mu_X = 2.5$, $\text{Var}(X) = 1.25$

7.4 $P(X = 1) = 1/3$,
$P(X = 2) = 4/15$,
$P(X = 3) = 1/5$,
$P(X = 4) = 2/15$,
$P(X = 5) = 1/15$, $E(X) = 7/3$

7.5 $P(X = k) = 1/5$, $P(X \leqslant 2) = 2/5$, $P(X > 3) = 2/5$, $E(X) = 3$, median $= 3$

7.6 (a) mode is 6, $E(N) = \frac{161}{36}$, (b) $E(X) = 13/3$, $\text{Var}(X) = 20/9$, $\sigma_X = 2\sqrt{5}/3$

7.7 $E(X) = 7/2$, $\text{Var}(X) = 35/12$

7.8 (a) 4, (b) 2

7.9 (a) $q/(1 + q)$, (b) $1/(1 + q)$

7.11 (a) i. 0.3932, ii. 0.0154, iii. 0.6554, (b) $\frac{35}{128}$

7.12 (a) $\frac{11}{64} = 0.172$, (b) 0.9943

7.13 (a) i. 0.142, 0.264, ii. £150 000 (assuming only one breakdown for a car), (b) 0.0176

7.14 (a) 0.135, (b) 0.238

7.15 (a) 0.3543, 0.1329, (b) 0.3566, 0.1333, Binomial

7.16 0.216

7.17 $\left(\frac{2}{3}\right)^{k-1}\frac{1}{3}$, £1.25

7.18 1, $4/3$

7.19 Binomial, 0.3744

7.20 (a) 0.0467, (b) 0.2765, (c) 0.5443

7.21 (a) 0.050, (b) 0.353

7.22 (a) 0.865, (b) 0.990

8.1 $3/4$, 0.2, $2 - \sqrt{2}$

8.2 (a) $\frac{3}{2}$, $\frac{11}{128}$, $\frac{11}{16}$, $\frac{29}{128}$, (b) $[0, 4]$, $\frac{3}{16}\sqrt{x}$ $(0 \leqslant x \leqslant 4)$

8.3 3, $1 - x^{-3}$, 0.0880, $3/2$, $\sqrt{3}/2$, $\sqrt[3]{2}$

8.4 $\frac{1}{5}(x-1)$ (x in $[1,6]$), 0.6, 5.5, 3.5

8.5 Uniform, 15 min, 75 min^2

8.6 0.451, 115.13 days

8.7 0.197

8.8 0.6915, 0.0342, 0.1191, 0, 0.3174

8.9 0.6826, 0.1587

8.10 (a) 0.0668, 0.4514, 0.5328, 0.2112, 8.7564, 8.171, 0.5152, (b) 9.75, 1.489

8.11 0.1151, 438.8 ml

8.12 1.24%

8.13 $1 - e^{-\lambda x}$, 0.393, 27.73

8.14 (a) 0.117, (b) 0.3104, (c) 7, (d) 3

8.15 (a) 0.8664, (b) 0.842, (c) 0.4649

8.16 (a) 0.3759, (b) 5.846, (c) 0.9332

9.4 (a) $Q_1 = 1$, $Q_2 = 2$, $Q_3 = 3$, (b) $Q_1 = 6.0$, $Q_2 = 6.6$, $Q_3 = 8.0$

9.5 [48.3, 62.2, 63.3, 64.6, 67.9], [61.5, 72.2, 74.5, 76.2, 78.4]

9.6 (a) $\overline{x} = 6.434$, $s^2 = 33.8$, $s = 5.81$, (b) 2.45, yes

9.7 Mean is 39.8, λ is 0.025, variance is 34.98

9.8 (a) 3.3, 3.12, 0.56, (b) 10, $59/6$

9.9 15.87%

9.10 0.1796

9.11 0.0618

9.12 0.0036

9.13 0.9876

9.14 (a) [1.657, 1.783], (b) [7.9, 8.7]

9.15 27.23 ± 0.10

9.16 (a) 831, 450, 1323

9.17 40.21, 39, 25.5, 54

9.18 43, 62, 44, 21, 7, 2, 1

9.19 9%

9.20 [56.36, 57.24]

9.21 174